ArtScroll Tanach Series®

A traditional commentary on the Books of the Bible

Rabbi Nosson Scherman/Rabbi Meir Zlotowitz
General Editors

divrei hayamim II

I CHRONICLES / A NEW TRANSLATION WITH A COMMENTARY ANTHOLOGIZED FROM TALMUDIC, MIDRASHIC AND RABBINIC SOURCES.

Published by

Mesorah Publications, ltd

A PROJECT OF THE

Mesorah Heritage Foundation

ספר
דברי הימים ב

Translation and Commentary by

Rabbi Moshe Eisemann

FIRST EDITION
First Impression . . . May, 1992

Published and Distributed by
MESORAH PUBLICATIONS, Ltd.
Brooklyn, New York 11232

Distributed in Israel by
MESORAH MAFITZIM / J. GROSSMAN
Rechov Harav Uziel 117
Jerusalem, Israel

Distributed in Europe by
J. LEHMANN HEBREW BOOKSELLERS
20 Cambridge Terrace
Gateshead, Tyne and Wear
England NE8 1RP

Distributed in Australia & New Zealand by
GOLD'S BOOK & GIFT CO.
36 William Street
Balaclava 3183, Vic., Australia

Distributed in South Africa by
KOLLEL BOOKSHOP
22 Muller Street
Yeoville 2198
Johannesburg, South Africa

THE ARTSCROLL TANACH SERIES
DIVREI HAYAMIM / II CHRONICLES

ISBN
0-89906-093-5 (hard cover)
0-89906-094-3 (paperback)

Typography by CompuScribe at ArtScroll Studios, Ltd.
4401 Second Avenue / Brooklyn, N.Y. 11232 / (718) 921-9000

Printed in the United States of America by Moriah Offset
Bound by Sefercraft Quality Bookbinders, Ltd., Brooklyn, NY

לעילוי נשמת

רבקה בת ר׳ אברהם ע״ה

נפטרה בשם טוב

י״ט שבט תש״נ

תנצב״ה

Table of Contents

The Decline of the Kingdom of Judah

Section Two — *Analyses and Expositions*

Author's Preface

The publication of the second volume of *Divrei HaYamim* affords me the opportunity once more to acknowledge the many wonderful people at Mesorah Publications who made it all possible.

Not the least benefit of publishing with Mesorah lies in the fact that co-workers very quickly turn into good friends, and it is as friends that I want to thank them now. For various technical reasons there were special difficulties in preparing this particular volume for print, and the aplomb and goodwill that carried everybody through even the most trying times deserves mention and appreciation.

First and foremost I wish to express my profound gratitude to R' Eli Kroen. Both in this work and in his design of my *Haggadah*, which he produced while in the thick of his *Divrei HaYamim* activities, he has shown himself to be a master designer, producing works works of taste and beauty. I look forward with delight to future collaborations.

R' Eli was ably supported by the conscientious reading and editing of R' Yosef Gesser, Mrs. Ethel Gottlieb, and Mrs. Faygie Weinbaum. This book is huge, the corrections which were needed were many, and it must have taken a particular kind of devotion to plod through it all so many times and so carefully. The same holds true for Mrs. Yaffa Danziger, who so carefully typed all the corrections.

Special thanks to my good friends, Rabbis Meir Zlotowitz and Nosson Scherman, for making it all possible. Authors, by their nature, must be a particularly prickly and difficult breed with which to deal. Both R' Meir and R' Nosson have been the very souls of tact and kindness, and my long association with ArtScroll has been for me one of undiluted pleasure and satisfaction.

I would also like to thank my friend R' Sheah Brander, whose wonderful design of the first volume of this work set the standard for the second volume.

There is one person whom I have never thanked in any of my books, believing, as I still do, that any kind of verbalizing could only devalue the profundity of my feelings. On this occasion, too, I will trust the eloquence of silence to convey that which should be conveyed.

Moshe Eisemann
Baltimore, Md.
2 Iyar, 5752

DIVREI HAYAMIM II

א וַיִּתְחַזֵּק שְׁלֹמֹה בֶן־דָּוִיד עַל־מַלְכוּתוֹ וַיהוָה אֱלֹהָיו עִמּוֹ
ב וַיְגַדְּלֵהוּ לְמָעְלָה: וַיֹּאמֶר שְׁלֹמֹה לְכָל־יִשְׂרָאֵל לְשָׂרֵי
הָאֲלָפִים וְהַמֵּאוֹת וְלַשֹּׁפְטִים וּלְכֹל נָשִׂיא לְכָל־יִשְׂרָאֵל
ג רָאשֵׁי הָאָבוֹת: וַיֵּלְכוּ שְׁלֹמֹה וְכָל־הַקָּהָל עִמּוֹ לַבָּמָה
אֲשֶׁר בְּגִבְעוֹן כִּי־שָׁם הָיָה אֹהֶל מוֹעֵד הָאֱלֹהִים אֲשֶׁר
ד עָשָׂה מֹשֶׁה עֶבֶד־יהוה בַּמִּדְבָּר: אֲבָל אֲרוֹן הָאֱלֹהִים
הֶעֱלָה דָוִיד מִקִּרְיַת יְעָרִים בַּהֵכִין לוֹ דָּוִיד כִּי נָטָה־לוֹ
ה אֹהֶל בִּירוּשָׁלִָם: וּמִזְבַּח הַנְּחֹשֶׁת אֲשֶׁר עָשָׂה בְּצַלְאֵל
בֶּן־אוּרִי בֶן־חוּר שָׂם לִפְנֵי מִשְׁכַּן יהוה וַיִּדְרְשֵׁהוּ שְׁלֹמֹה
ו וְהַקָּהָל: וַיַּעַל שְׁלֹמֹה שָׁם עַל־מִזְבַּח הַנְּחֹשֶׁת לִפְנֵי יהוה

I

◆§ Solomon Consolidates His Rule

1. וַיִּתְחַזֵּק שְׁלֹמֹה בֶן־דָּוִיד עַל־מַלְכוּתוֹ — *Solomon the son of David then strengthened his hold over his kingdom.* A consolidation of power was required because, although Solomon's kingship had already been firmly established (*I Chronicles* 29:23-24), not everyone was willing to accept him as king. Thus Adoniyahu (*I Kings* 1:5 ff, 2:13 ff.), Evyasar and Yoav (there 2:26-34) and Shimei son of Geira (there 2:36-46) — each of whom, in one way or another sought to undermine the throne — had to be eliminated or neutralized. Solomon's actions against these men are detailed in the first two chapters of *I Kings*. This verse is a very concise summing up of those two chapters (*Ralbag*).

Malbim, however, thinks that our verse should be viewed as confirmation of the fulfillment of *I Kings* 2:2, where David, as he felt death approaching, had called Solomon and exhorted him, *You shall be strong so that you will become an independent person.* This verse does not so much describe how Solomon consolidated his kingship as it pinpoints the moment at which a tyro, formerly dependent upon his father's strengths and guidance, turned into an independent and self-confident monarch.

וַה׳ אֱלֹהָיו עִמּוֹ — *HASHEM his God was with him. Rashi* reads, *Because* HASHEM *was with him*; i.e., God's help made him able to consolidate his rule.

◆§ The Vision at Giveon

2. וַיֹּאמֶר שְׁלֹמֹה לְכָל־יִשְׂרָאֵל — *Solomon spoke to all Israel.* We are not told what Solomon said. We must assume that he issued an invitation to the various groups mentioned in this verse to accompany him to Giveon (*Mefaresh* and *Metzudos*).

In the parallel passage in *I Kings* 3:4, no mention is made of this invitation. The story there centers around Solomon alone. See comm. at *I Chronicles* 13:1-4.

לְשָׂרֵי הָאֲלָפִים — *To the officers of the thousands.* This part of the verse is in apposition to the earlier phrase. Solomon spoke to all Israel, namely, to the officers of the thousands, etc.

3. וַיֵּלְכוּ שְׁלֹמֹה וְכָל־הַקָּהָל עִמּוֹ — *Then Solomon together with the whole congregation went.* We may assume that this pilgrimage took place at the beginning of Solomon's reign. This seems borne out by the verse which ends the account: . . . *and [now] began to rule over Israel.*

I Kings describes the steps which Solomon took to consolidate his kingship before its account of the pilgrimage (ch. 3). This would seem to indicate that he dealt with these problems before he went to Giveon. However, there is the possibility that the account in *Kings* does not follow the chronological order of events (*Rashi* to v.3, there.)

If, indeed, the pilgrimage was first, then v. 1 of our chapter is to be understood as a sweeping introduction to the beginning of Solomon's reign, encompassing events which happened long after the pilgrimage to Giveon. V. 2 then takes up the sequential account.

לַבָּמָה אֲשֶׁר בְּגִבְעוֹן — *To the bamah at Giveon.* Although the Tabernacle which Moses had built stood at Giveon, as the next part of our verse relates, and therefore, Giveon was the location at which all communal sacrificial

Solomon the son of David then strengthened his hold over his
kingdom. Hashem *his God was with him and made him*
exceedingly great. 2 *Solomon spoke to all Israel, to the officers of*
the thousands and the hundreds, to the judges and to every
prince in all Israel, the heads of the families. 3 *Then Solomon*
together with the whole congregation went to the bamah at
Giveon, because the Tent of Meeting which Moses the servant of
Hashem *had made in the desert was there.* 4 *But David had*
brought up the Ark of God from Kiriath-Yearim to [the place]
which David had set aside for it, for he had spread a tent for it at
Jerusalem. 5 *Now the copper altar which Betzalel the son of Uri*
the son of Hur had made [was] there before the tabernacle of
Hashem. *Therefore, Solomon and the congregation sought it out.*
6 *Solomon made an offering there upon the copper altar — before*

services took place, it is still referred to as a *bamah* rather than as the Tabernacle since the Holy Ark was not there but in the tent which David had erected in Jerusalem (*Doros HaRishonim*). For a detailed discussion see commentary to *I Chronicles* 6:16-17.

It was fitting that for this festive occasion, as indeed for any communal service, the *bamah* in Giveon rather than a private one in Jerusalem would be used. See *I Chronicles* 21:29-30.

See further in Section II, *Solomon and Moses*.

עֶבֶד־ה׳ — *The servant of* Hashem. See Section II, *Solomon and Moses*, for a discussion.

4. אֲבָל אֲרוֹן הָאֱלֹהִים — *But . . . the Ark of God.* The meaning of this verse is clear enough: Although the Tabernacle which Moses had made was in Giveon, the Ark was not. From the time that it had been taken by the Philistines in the days of Eli, it had never been reunited with the Tabernacle and was now in the tent which David had erected in Jerusalem. [For details and discussion, see prefatory remarks to *I Chronicles* Ch. 13.]

It is not clear why it was necessary to point this out here. It might have been appropriate to mention this in the *Kings* account since mention is made there that after the pilgrimage to Giveon, Solomon brought sacrifices in front of the Ark in Jerusalem (V. 15 there). But *Chronicles* makes no mention of these sacrifices. Why then, is the fact that the Ark was in Jerusalem significant?

Perhaps the sentence has to be taken as a parenthetical one. Its purpose is simply to explain the use of the word *bamah* in the previous verse. The reader, at the time that *Chronicles* was written, would have wondered why the Tabernacle which Moses had made, is referred to as a *bamah* — an expression which connotes less sanctity than *Mishkan*. Our verse explains: In the absence of the Ark, Giveon could have no more than *bamah* status (*Doros HaRishonim*).

5. וּמִזְבַּח הַנְּחֹשֶׁת — *Now the copper altar . . .* This verse appears to follow directly upon the thought contained in the previous one. Although the Ark was not at Giveon, the copper altar was, and for that reason Solomon and the congregation sought it out while they were there.

וַיִּדְרְשֵׁהוּ שְׁלֹמֹה וְהַקָּהָל — *Therefore, Solomon and the congregation sought it out.* They *sought out* the altar by bringing sacrifices upon it (see next verse) (*Metzudos*).

The expression, *they sought it out*, is particularly appropriate. According to tradition (*Zevachim* 61b), the copper altar was not actually used for the bringing of sacrifices. For this there was a stone altar attached to the ground. The copper altar functioned only as repository of the heavenly fire which had burned there since the time of Moses. Solomon made a conscious decision to ignore this regular altar and to sacrifice upon the venerable copper one (*Mikra UMassores*).

6. וַיַּעַל שְׁלֹמֹה שָׁם — *Solomon made an offering there.* Throughout Scripture the *hiphil*, causative form, is used transitively. Since the verse contains no object, we must conclude that the structure of the verse is as *Metzudos* sees it: The sentence begins, intending to conclude with a description of what Solomon offered there, and this is indeed given at the

ז אֲשֶׁר לְאֹהֶל מוֹעֵד וַיַּעַל עָלָיו עֹלוֹת אָלֶף: בַּלַּיְלָה
הַהוּא נִרְאָה אֱלֹהִים לִשְׁלֹמֹה וַיֹּאמֶר לוֹ שְׁאַל
ח מָה אֶתֶּן־לָךְ: וַיֹּאמֶר שְׁלֹמֹה לֵאלֹהִים אַתָּה עָשִׂיתָ
ט עִם־דָּוִיד אָבִי חֶסֶד גָּדוֹל וְהִמְלַכְתַּנִי תַּחְתָּיו: עַתָּה יְהוָה
אֱלֹהִים יֵאָמֵן דְּבָרְךָ עִם דָּוִיד אָבִי כִּי אַתָּה הִמְלַכְתַּנִי
י עַל־עַם רַב כַּעֲפַר הָאָרֶץ: עַתָּה חָכְמָה וּמַדָּע תֶּן־לִי
וְאֵצְאָה לִפְנֵי הָעָם־הַזֶּה וְאָבוֹאָה כִּי־מִי יִשְׁפֹּט אֶת־עַמְּךָ
יא הַזֶּה הַגָּדוֹל: וַיֹּאמֶר אֱלֹהִים ׀ לִשְׁלֹמֹה יַעַן אֲשֶׁר הָיְתָה
זֹאת עִם־לְבָבֶךָ וְלֹא־שָׁאַלְתָּ עֹשֶׁר נְכָסִים וְכָבוֹד וְאֵת
נֶפֶשׁ שֹׂנְאֶיךָ וְגַם־יָמִים רַבִּים לֹא שָׁאָלְתָּ וַתִּשְׁאַל־לְךָ

end of the verse. However, the relatively long description of the altar which follows creates too great a gap between predicate and object, and thus makes it necessary to be repeated.

Targum, however, renders: *Solomon went up upon the copper altar ...*

מִזְבַּח הַנְּחֹשֶׁת לִפְנֵי ה׳ אֲשֶׁר לְאֹהֶל מוֹעֵד — *The copper altar — before HASHEM, for it was part of the Tent of Meeting ...* The syntax is unusual. Perhaps the meaning is as follows: Usually, the term *before HASHEM* implies: *in front of the Ark* (see *Rashi* to *Exodus* 16:33). Accordingly, since there was no Ark at Giveon, the copper altar should not have had the halachic status — *before HASHEM* (see *Rashi* to *Leviticus* 1:3). Nevertheless, the verse points out that in this situation, in which the altar stood at the actual Tabernacle which Moses had made, a sacrifice brought there would be considered *before HASHEM*, although the Holy Ark was at Jerusalem.

This detailed description does not appear in the *Kings* account. That it is used here can be explained upon the basis of the thesis which we have suggested in Section II, *Solomon and Moses*.

7. בַּלַּיְלָה הַהוּא נִרְאָה אֱלֹהִים לִשְׁלֹמֹה — *That night, God appeared to Solomon.* On the very night of his arrival, his craving for the Divine found an immediate response. See further in Section II, *The Vision at Giveon*.

שְׁאַל מָה אֶתֶּן־לָךְ — *Make a request! What shall I give you?* God's offer is unique in Scripture. None of the other many great men in Israel were ever told by God that whatever they wished was to be theirs.

Why was just Solomon given this choice and why at such a tender age, before he was even able to prove himself?

God's special love for Solomon found an even earlier expression. When Solomon was born, God sent His prophet to inform David that the child was to be given the name Yedidyah, *Beloved of God*, in addition to the name Solomon, which his father had given him (*II Samuel* 12:24-25). Why would God have such love for an untried infant?

For an explanation, we must go to a truth which we have recognized before and which we have discussed at length in Section II to *I Chronicles*, Ch.17. We wrote there: David lived a life of utmost purity and fought himself relentlessly for every second of that life. He never knew the sweetness of peace and repose until the very end of his life when, at last, final victory was his. It fell to Solomon to savor the fruits of his father's valiant efforts... The reigns of David and Solomon are thus one long continuum, the parts of which relate to one another as do labor and rest, effort and fruition. David finally wrested peace and harmony from the rigors of battle and Solomon was the expression of that victory.

David had managed to eradicate the יֵצֶר הָרָע, the *evil impulse*, from within himself completely, but it was in Solomon that his victory was manifest. Solomon was born completely pure; there were no barriers between himself and God, no base instincts which could drag him down into an abyss of physicality. He was, indeed, beloved by God — יְדִידְיָה. And as the prototype of perfect man, the world, as it were, lay at his feet. God called out to him, *Make a request! What shall I give you?* Nothing will be withheld — for all creation exists only so that man — perfect man — can enjoy its fruits.

8. חֶסֶד גָּדוֹל וְהִמְלַכְתַּנִי — *... Great kindness ... made me king ...* Since You made me [who

HASHEM, for it was part of the Tent of Meeting; he made an offering upon it of a thousand burnt offerings. 7 *That night, God appeared to Solomon and said to him, 'Make a request! What shall I give you?'* 8 *Solomon said to God, 'You have shown David my father great kindness in that You have made me king in his stead.'* 9 *Now O HASHEM, God, may Your words with my father David be fulfilled. [I ask this] for You have made me king over a people as numerous as the dust of the earth.* 10 *Now grant me wisdom and knowledge, that I may go out before this people, and come in, for who could [otherwise] provide leadership for this people of Yours that is so great?'* 11 *God said to Solomon, 'Because you had this in your heart and did not request wealth,*

am a son of Bathsheva] king rather than any of David's other sons, You showed that he had not sinned [irrevocably] in the matter of Bath-sheva, and that is indeed a great kindness (*Metzudos*). [See above at I *Chronicles* 28:5.]

9. יֵאָמֵן דְּבָרְךָ — *May Your words ... be fulfilled.* The translation follows *Metzudos*. God had promised David that the kingship would be firmly established through Solomon. [See also at *I Chronicles* 17:23-24]. Solomon felt that the stewardship of such a vast nation [*as numerous as the dust of the earth*] would require more than ordinary human wisdom.

History proved him correct. As a direct result of an unwise decision by Solomon's son, Rechav'am, the Davidic kingship was soon to be severely truncated by the establishment of a northern kingdom under Ephraimitic rule — never to be restored until Messianic times.[1]

10. חָכְמָה וּמַדָּע — *Wisdom and knowledge.* Although חָכְמָה and מַדָּע seem often to be used interchangeably, *Malbim* finds a difference in meaning. *Wisdom* is the faculty we use when making value judgments: It answers the question, 'Good or bad?' rather than, 'Correct or incorrect?' *Knowledge* comes into play when information must be absorbed, or axiomatic truths perceived.

For further discussion about the use of *wisdom and knowledge* here when *Kings* speaks of a *listening heart*, see Section II, *The Vision at Giveon*.

וְאֵצְאָה לִפְנֵי הָעָם־הַזֶּה וְאָבוֹאָה — *That I may go out before this people, and come in.* For an analysis of this concept, see Section II, ibid.

מִי יִשְׁפֹּט אֶת־עַמְּךָ הַזֶּה — *For who could [otherwise] provide leadership for this people of Yours* . . . *Genesis* 19:9 and *Hosea* 7:7 and 13:1 show clearly that the root שפט can be used in the sense of *to govern*. In Section II, ibid., we present the reasons for the choice of *to provide leadership* for this phrase.

11. יַעַן אֲשֶׁר הָיְתָה זֹאת עִם־לְבָבְךָ — *Because you had this in your heart.* It is likely that לֵבָב in this phrase has the meaning of *the mind* rather than the heart, a frequent occurrence in Scripture. Nevertheless, we have chosen to translate *heart* so as not to lose the nuance which the *Mefaresh* detects in our verse: Surely, no one would have asked as you have asked if his heart was not filled with a deep and abiding fear of God.

1. We may surmise another reason why Solomon would feel that he required more than ordinary wisdom.

Solomon's rule was the only period in history in which the full gamut of institutions by which the Torah defines ideal national existence were in place. Only in the circumstances of that particular generation could the entire range of Torah laws be fulfilled. For such a complete fulfillment, the following conditions are required: Prophecy in all its gradations; Divinely inspired *Kohanim*, the indispensable requirement for the consultation of the *Urim VeTumim*; a *Sanhedrin* functioning within the entire range of its prerogatives; the entire religious structure centered about the Temple service; the monarchy in all its manifestations; every man 'beneath his vine and beneath his fig tree' in the Land of Israel, being inhabited by [at least] a majority of the people of Israel. The only period in Jewish history in which all these conditions, in all their majestic splendor, were fulfilled was the reign of King Solomon (*Pachad Yitzchak, Shaar Chodesh HaAviv* 68:5).

Thus, Solomon's stewardship had to be one which lived up to the absolute and undiluted ideal of kingship as God wanted it. This was the one moment in history when the full grandeur of a society grounded absolutely in the values and categories of the Torah could be actualized. Another king in other circumstances may be permitted occasionally to falter. Solomon knew himself to be different, Divinely summoned for absolute perfection. In this he begged for God's help.

א חָכְמָה וּמַדָּע אֲשֶׁר תִּשְׁפּוֹט אֶת־עַמִּי אֲשֶׁר הִמְלַכְתִּיךָ
יב־יד יב עָלָיו: הַחָכְמָה וְהַמַּדָּע נָתוּן לָךְ וְעֹשֶׁר וּנְכָסִים וְכָבוֹד
אֶתֶּן־לָךְ אֲשֶׁר ׀ לֹא־הָיָה כֵן לַמְּלָכִים אֲשֶׁר לְפָנֶיךָ
יג וְאַחֲרֶיךָ לֹא יִהְיֶה־כֵּן: וַיָּבֹא שְׁלֹמֹה לַבָּמָה אֲשֶׁר־בְּגִבְעוֹן
יְרוּשָׁלַם מִלִּפְנֵי אֹהֶל מוֹעֵד וַיִּמְלֹךְ עַל־
יד יִשְׂרָאֵל: וַיֶּאֱסֹף שְׁלֹמֹה רֶכֶב וּפָרָשִׁים וַיְהִי־לוֹ

אֲשֶׁר תִּשְׁפּוֹט אֶת־עַמִּי — *So that you might provide leadership for My people.* See comm. to verse above.

12. נָתוּן לָךְ ... אֶתֶּן־לָךְ — *Have been given to you ... I shall grant you.* The change from the past tense [נָתוּן] in the case of wisdom to the future [אֶתֶּן] in the case of the wealth is logical. Solomon was granted wisdom right away — the Sages teach that immediately upon awakening he was able to understand the communication of the birds and beasts around him — but the acquisition of wealth and power still lay in the future. *Kings* uses the past tense in connection with the wealth also [נָתַתִּי], but only in the sense of establishing the absolute certainty that it would be granted. 'You can be absolutely certain that you will get this wealth; it is as though you already possessed it.'

13. וַיָּבֹא שְׁלֹמֹה ... — *Then Solomon came ...* This verse is extremely difficult to translate. Literally it reads: *And Solomon came to the bamah which is in Giveon-Jerusalem from before the Tent of Meeting ....*

But what is meant by saying that he came to the *bamah* when he was already there? Again, what is *Giveon-Jerusalem*? The *bamah* referred to in v. 3 was in Giveon, not in Jerusalem. The altar before the Ark upon which, as *I Kings* 3:15 teaches, he sacrificed upon his return was in Jerusalem and not in Giveon.

The Sages (*Yomah* 53a) address this problem. They reason as follows: Either it should have said, *From Jerusalem* [if our verse goes back to the beginning of the story and tells of Solomon's arrival at Giveon] or *From the bamah* [if the verse deals with his return to Jerusalem]. (See *Rashi* here, based on *Yerushalmi*.) Their solution is a homiletical one. The verse teaches us that a person who leaves the Temple or a student who leaves his teacher is to walk backwards, facing the source of his inspiration and is not to turn his back upon it. Our verse, by juxtaposing Giveon to Jerusalem, teaches us that his going to Jerusalem was similar to his coming to Giveon. Just as when he came to Giveon, he was facing the *bamah* there, so too, even as he was returning to Jerusalem, he did so while facing the *bamah*.

The verse is to be read as follows: Solomon came [originally] to the *bamah* in Giveon; [in precisely the same way he also came to] Jerusalem (*Rashi* there).

Metzudos reads the verse as follows: And David came [from the road which leads] to the *bamah* in Giveon, [to] Jerusalem, from before the Tent of Meeting. Thus, he takes the word לַבָּמָה which would normally translate *to the bamah* as though it meant *from the bamah* (that is, he has the prefix ל, *lamed*, mean the precise opposite of its usual connotation). *Ibn Janach* in *Sefer HaRikmah*, *Shaar* 6, under ל, makes the same assumption and adduces numerous examples where the prefix ל is used in the sense of *from*. See, for example, *Numbers* 31:21.

Radak rejects the idea that the prefix ל should be able to stand for two opposites. He renders: *Solomon, who had previously gone to the bamah at Giveon ... now came to Jerusalem ...*

וַיִּמְלֹךְ עַל־יִשְׂרָאֵל — *And [now] began to rule over Israel.* From now on, because of the great wisdom that he had been granted, his kingship was happily accepted by the people (*Metzudos*).

◆§ Solomon's Wealth

14-17. This passage is essentially the same as the one in I *Kings* 10:26-29. However, the very similarity between the two passages highlights a major difference between them: the position which it occupies in the respective accounts. In *Kings*, the description of Solomon's fabulous wealth comes at the end of the passage which tells of the visit of the Queen of Sheba where, in the context of that episode which in one way or another revolves around the ostentatious consumption of Solomon's court, it is entirely appropriate. [See 9:25-28 where there is a similar passage in that same position in the narrative.]

Our passage, however, comes immediately

1
12-14

possessions and honor, nor the life of your enemies, nor also did you ask for long life, but asked for wisdom and knowledge so that you might provide leadership for My people over whom I have made you king.' [12] *'Wisdom and knowledge have been given to you, and [moreover] I shall grant you riches, possessions and honor such as no king before you possessed and [also] after you it shall never be [again].'* [13] *Then Solomon came from the Giveonic bamah to Jerusalem, from before the Tent of Meeting, and [now] began to rule over Israel.* [14] *Solomon amassed chariots and horsemen; he*

after the account of the dream at Giveon, and in this position sounds a jarring note. Solomon had just been granted a Divine gift of wisdom and knowledge. The abrupt switch to a discussion of the size of his stables and the profligacy of his spending immediately focuses the mind upon an unspoken question: Is this the tangible expression of the wisdom and knowledge of Solomon which set him apart from any person who ever lived?

The stark, antithetical nature of this juxtaposition stands in sharp contrast to the treatment of the same subject matter in *Kings*. There, the story of the dream is followed by the judgment rendered in the case of the two women — a graphic example of the *listening heart* which Solomon had been granted. After that, the officers of Solomon's household are listed. This, in turn, is followed by a statement concerning the benign effects of Solomon's rule over all Israel — *Judah and Israel were multitudinous, many as the sand of the sea, eating, drinking and rejoicing* (4:20). Then, we have a statement concerning the dimensions of Solomon's realm (5:1). Only after all this is the sumptuous household and the size of his stables described (5:2-6), and even this account is interrupted with a description of the peace and tranquility enjoyed by Solomon's subjects (5:5). At the end comes a detailed and lyric description of Solomon's wisdom (5:9-14). In short, Solomon's wealth is only one aspect of a graphic picture of his benign rule and as such, it is put into a reasonable and non-jarring perspective. How different in *Chronicles* where the size of the stables and the abundance of silver is the only thing that is mentioned after the vision at Giveon before the story of the building of the Temple is picked up!

Moreover, a careful reading of *Chronicles'* treatment of Solomon's reign yields that Solomon's wisdom is never mentioned except as seen through the eyes of gentiles — see 2:11, 9:3 and [possibly] 9:22 and 23. There is no parallel to the story of the judgment of the two women and no statement anywhere asserting Solomon's wisdom as an objective fact such as at *Kings* 5:9- 13.

In short, the *Chronicles* account seems not only to downplay Solomon's wisdom by not mentioning it at all, but, by the subtle nuance of selectivity and positioning of its description of Solomon's reign, seems to be rendering a historical judgment upon the occurrence at Giveon. Solomon was indeed granted wisdom and knowledge, the wealth that he had been promised came to him only incidentally — but in practice it was the wealth which left its mark. In the perspective of eternity which is the hallmark of *Chronicles'* presentation of the events, Solomon's wisdom is overwhelmed by the profligacy of his consumption.

The explanation may be that from the perspective of the long-range history of Israel, Solomon's wisdom was misused and was the cause of untold tragedy. As *Shemos Rabbah* 6:1 teaches, Solomon himself bitterly regretted the use to which he had put his wisdom: Solomon said, ['That in my old age my wives *turned aside my heart* (*I Kings* 11:4) was my own fault. It came about] because I felt myself wiser then the Torah [מַה שֶׁהָיִיתִי מַרְאֶה לְעַצְמִי]. The *wisdom* and that *understanding* [which I had been given turned out to be] light-headedness and folly.'

As taught in *Kings* 11:11 ff. it was the questionable influence exercised by Solomon's wives which was the direct cause of the division of Israel into two kingdoms. In the course of Jewish history, this division ultimately proved to be catastrophic (See *Isaiah* 7:17), and from that perspective Solomon's wisdom may well have been regarded as a curse rather than a blessing.[1]

14. וַיֶּאֱסֹף שְׁלֹמֹה — *Solomon amassed ... Kings*

1. Our analysis centers only on the account of Solomon's reign and does not touch on the three books, *Songs of Songs, Ecclesiastes* and *Proverbs,* which are Solomon's eternal legacy, since these are not mentioned in either *Kings* or in *Chronicles*.

א
טו־יז

אֶ֫לֶף וְאַרְבַּע־מֵאוֹת֙ רֶ֔כֶב וּשְׁנֵים־עָשָׂ֥ר אֶ֖לֶף פָּֽרָשִׁ֑ים
טו וַיַּנִּיחֵם֙ בְּעָרֵ֣י הָרֶ֔כֶב וְעִם־הַמֶּ֖לֶךְ בִּירוּשָׁלָֽ͏ִם׃ וַיִּתֵּ֨ן
הַמֶּ֜לֶךְ אֶת־הַכֶּ֧סֶף וְאֶת־הַזָּהָ֛ב בִּירוּשָׁלַ֖͏ִם כָּאֲבָנִ֑ים וְאֵ֣ת
טז הָאֲרָזִ֗ים נָתַ֛ן כַּשִּׁקְמִ֥ים אֲשֶׁר־בַּשְּׁפֵלָ֖ה לָרֹֽב׃ וּמוֹצָ֥א
הַסּוּסִ֛ים אֲשֶׁ֥ר לִשְׁלֹמֹ֖ה מִמִּצְרָ֑יִם וּמִקְוֵ֕א סֹחֲרֵ֣י הַמֶּ֔לֶךְ
יז מִקְוֵ֥א יִקְח֖וּ בִּמְחִֽיר׃ וַֽ֠יַּעֲלוּ וַיּוֹצִ֨יאוּ מִמִּצְרַ֜יִם מֶרְכָּבָ֗ה

has two passages which describe Solomon's wealth. The first at 5:6, shortly after the description of the vision at Giveon, in approximately the same position as the one here. The other one is at 10:26-28 after the description of the visit of the Queen of Sheba. *Chronicles* too, at 9:25, has another description in that same position:

Chronicles	*Kings*
1. 1:14-15. וַיֶּאֱסֹף שְׁלֹמֹה רֶכֶב וּפָרָשִׁים וַיְהִי־לוֹ אֶלֶף וְאַרְבַּע־מֵאוֹת רֶכֶב וּשְׁנֵים־עָשָׂר אֶלֶף פָּרָשִׁים וַיַּנִּיחֵם בְּעָרֵי הָרֶכֶב וְעִם־הַמֶּלֶךְ בִּירוּשָׁלָם. וַיִּתֵּן הַמֶּלֶךְ אֶת־הַכֶּסֶף וְאֶת־הַזָּהָב בִּירוּשָׁלַם כָּאֲבָנִים וְאֵת־הָאֲרָזִים נָתַן כַּשִּׁקְמִים אֲשֶׁר־בַּשְּׁפֵלָה לָרֹב. — *Solomon amassed chariots and horsemen; he had fourteen hundred chariots and twelve thousand horsemen, and kept them in the chariot cities and at the king's [disposal] at Jerusalem. The king made silver and gold [as plentiful] as stones in Jerusalem, and cedars as plentiful as the sycamores in the Shephelah.*	1. 5:6. וַיְהִי לִשְׁלֹמֹה אַרְבָּעִים אֶלֶף אֻרְוֺת סוּסִים לְמֶרְכָּבוֹ וּשְׁנֵים־עָשָׂר אֶלֶף פָּרָשִׁים. — *Solomon had forty thousand horse mangers for his chariots, and twelve thousand riders.*
2. 9:25. וַיְהִי לִשְׁלֹמֹה אַרְבַּעַת אֲלָפִים אֻרְיוֹת סוּסִים וּמַרְכָּבוֹת וּשְׁנֵים־עָשָׂר אֶלֶף פָּרָשִׁים וַיַּנִּיחֵם בְּעָרֵי הָרֶכֶב וְעִם־הַמֶּלֶךְ בִּירוּשָׁלָם. — *Solomon had four thousand horse mangers, and chariots, and twelve thousand riders. He left them in the chariot cities and at the king's [disposal] in Jerusalem.*	2. 10:26-28. וַיֶּאֱסֹף שְׁלֹמֹה רֶכֶב וּפָרָשִׁים וַיְהִי־לוֹ אֶלֶף וְאַרְבַּע־מֵאוֹת רֶכֶב וּשְׁנֵים־עָשָׂר אֶלֶף פָּרָשִׁים וַיַּנְחֵם בְּעָרֵי הָרֶכֶב וְעִם־הַמֶּלֶךְ בִּירוּשָׁלָם. וַיִּתֵּן הַמֶּלֶךְ אֶת־הַכֶּסֶף בִּירוּשָׁלַם כָּאֲבָנִים וְאֵת הָאֲרָזִים נָתַן כַּשִּׁקְמִים אֲשֶׁר־בַּשְּׁפֵלָה לָרֹב. — *Solomon amassed chariots and riders. He had fourteen hundred chariots and twelve thousand riders, and he placed them in the chariot cities, and at the king's [disposal] in Jerusalem. The king made silver in Jerusalem [as little significant] as stones, and cedars as plentiful as the sycamores in the Shephelah.*

Clearly, the earlier passage in *Chronicles* is taken from the latter description in *Kings*, while the one which follows the visit of the Queen of Sheba is taken from the earlier one.

But why was this done; why were the two passages from *Kings* reversed in *Chronicles*?

Perhaps this bears out the ideas we developed above. *Chronicles* wants to create a sharp and shocking contrast between the profligacy of Solomon's court and the expectations which we would have had from the *wisdom* and *knowledge* which he had been granted at Giveon. This purpose is served better by the more detailed description which comes from a later period in Solomon's life and which, therefore, contrasts the ostentation at the peak period of Solomon's rule with these auspicious beginnings at which time his wealth is not

had fourteen hundred chariots and twelve thousand horsemen,
and kept them in the chariot cities and at the king's disposal at
Jerusalem. 15 *The king made silver and gold [as plentiful] as stones*
in Jerusalem, and cedars as plentiful as the sycamores in the She-
phelah. 16 *Solomon's horses were imported from Egypt [through a]*
cartel of the king's traders, and [as] a cartel they bought the horses
at their value. 17 *Thus, a chariot for export from Egypt would run*

viewed as necessarily evil. See further.

בְּעָרֵי הָרֶכֶב — *In the chariot cities*. In these cities, the king's horsemen made their homes. For this reason they were called *chariot cities*. (*Mefaresh*)

15. וַיִּתֵּן הַמֶּלֶךְ אֶת־הַכֶּסֶף וְאֶת־הַזָּהָב בִּירוּשָׁלִַם כָּאֲבָנִים — *The king made silver and gold [as plentiful] as stones in Jerusalem.* The tone of this statement is neutral; no judgment is implied as to whether this prolific wealth is to be regarded as a blessing or an abomination. In *Sanhedrin* 21b, there is the implication that the abundance of silver, in itself, was not bad. The Talmud contrasts our verse, which ascribes at least some small value to silver (*as stones*), with *I Kings* 10:21 where silver is described as being so plentiful as to be entirely worthless. The answer given is that before Solomon erred in marrying Pharaoh's daughter, silver was more abundant — and therefore less valuable — than it was afterwards. The implication is that before he married the Egyptian princess he was blameless and was blessed with the abundance of wealth described in the *Kings* account.

On the other hand, from *Seder Olam* 15 and from *Shir HaShirim Rabbah* 1:10 it appears that the abundance of silver is seen as a transgression of the Torah's law that a king is not to have too much silver and gold (*Deuteronomy* 17:17) [see *Gra* to *Seder Olam* there], and as such is to be regarded as an abomination.

It is perhaps significant that *Seder Olam*, in criticizing Solomon, quotes our verse — which as *Sanhedrin* 21b teaches — deals with the period after he married Pharaoh's daughter, rather than the one at *I Kings* 10:21 which describes the period before that event. It may be legitimate to conclude that only after Solomon's spiritual decline set in was the prolific wealth judged as wrong. Earlier, when Solomon was still at the peak of his closeness to God his inordinate riches did not offend.[1]

16. וּמוֹצָא הַסּוּסִים אֲשֶׁר לִשְׁלֹמֹה מִמִּצְרָיִם — *Solomon's horses were imported from Egypt*. מוֹצָא derives from יצא, *to go out*; thus, the place from which the horses came out, i.e., their *source*.

וּמִקְוֵא סֹחֲרֵי הַמֶּלֶךְ — *[Through a] cartel of the king's traders*. We follow *Rashi* in this difficult phrase. In *Kings*, מִקְוֶה is spelled with a ה, deriving from קוה, *to gather*; hence, a gathering, or *cartel* of horse traders. *Rashi* explains that the king's traders formed a cartel and arranged that no one would be allowed to export horses from Egypt except through their agency.

The next phrase must then be rendered: *and [as] a cartel they bought [the horses] at their value*.

Targum does not translate מִקְוֵא and *Metzudos* deduces from this that he takes the word as a proper noun. It is the name of a district in Egypt from which horses were exported. The *mem* in מִקְוֵא is the prefix *from*; thus, *from Kvei*. The sense of the entire verse is that while horses bought from the rest of Egypt were bought at a fixed price, the ones which came from Kvei were priced according to their individual value [מְחִיר].

1. This might be explained as follows: *Rabbeinu Bachya* in *Kad HaKemach* under עוֹשֶׁר quotes midrashic sources which teach that gold [and, by implication,] silver too, are a gift which God made to this world only so that they might be used for the building of the Temple. *Rabbeinu Bachya* explains Solomon's great wealth on the basis of these midrashim. God poured out the full abundance of His largesse upon Solomon because he, by building the Temple, was the one person in history who provided the justification for these Divine gifts. The wealth, as it were, flowed to Solomon from the Temple. It was not he who amassed gold and silver, thereby contravening the Torah's laws, but God who showered it upon him.

However, once Solomon married Pharaoh's daughter, the Sages detected a shift in his attitude. The Temple was no longer the exclusive focus in his life. His prolific wealth began to work the insidious harm which the Torah had feared and because of which it had forbidden a king to accumulate too many riches.

א בְּשֵׁשׁ מֵאוֹת כֶּסֶף וְסוּס בַּחֲמִשִּׁים וּמֵאָה וְכֵן לְכָל־מַלְכֵי
יח יח הַחִתִּים וּמַלְכֵי אֲרָם בְּיָדָם יוֹצִיאוּ: וַיֹּאמֶר שְׁלֹמֹה לִבְנוֹת
א בַּיִת לְשֵׁם יהוה וּבַיִת לְמַלְכוּתוֹ: וַיִּסְפֹּר שְׁלֹמֹה שִׁבְעִים
ב אֶלֶף אִישׁ סַבָּל וּשְׁמוֹנִים אֶלֶף אִישׁ חֹצֵב בָּהָר וּמְנַצְּחִים
א־ה עֲלֵיהֶם שְׁלֹשֶׁת אֲלָפִים וְשֵׁשׁ מֵאוֹת:
ב וַיִּשְׁלַח שְׁלֹמֹה אֶל־חוּרָם מֶלֶךְ־צֹר לֵאמֹר כַּאֲשֶׁר עָשִׂיתָ
עִם־דָּוִיד אָבִי וַתִּשְׁלַח־לוֹ אֲרָזִים לִבְנוֹת־לוֹ בַיִת לָשֶׁבֶת
ג בּוֹ: הִנֵּה אֲנִי בוֹנֶה־בַּיִת לְשֵׁם ׀ יהוה אֱלֹהָי לְהַקְדִּישׁ לוֹ
לְהַקְטִיר לְפָנָיו קְטֹרֶת־סַמִּים וּמַעֲרֶכֶת תָּמִיד וְעֹלוֹת
לַבֹּקֶר וְלָעֶרֶב לַשַּׁבָּתוֹת וְלֶחֳדָשִׁים וּלְמוֹעֲדֵי יהוה
ד אֱלֹהֵינוּ לְעוֹלָם זֹאת עַל־יִשְׂרָאֵל: וְהַבַּיִת אֲשֶׁר־אֲנִי בוֹנֶה
ה גָּדוֹל כִּי־גָדוֹל אֱלֹהֵינוּ מִכָּל־הָאֱלֹהִים: וּמִי יַעֲצָר־כֹּחַ
לִבְנוֹת־לוֹ בַיִת כִּי הַשָּׁמַיִם וּשְׁמֵי הַשָּׁמַיִם לֹא יְכַלְכְּלֻהוּ
וּמִי אֲנִי אֲשֶׁר אֶבְנֶה־לוֹ בַּיִת כִּי אִם־לְהַקְטִיר לְפָנָיו:

17. מֶרְכָּבָה בְּשֵׁשׁ מֵאוֹת כֶּסֶף — *A chariot ... six hundred silver [coins].* Since each horse cost one hundred and fifty silver coins, as stated in the next part of the verse, the price of four horses would be six hundred silver coins. Accordingly, the commentators assume that *chariot* in our verse does not refer to the vehicle itself but to the four horses needed to pull it. Thus, *a chariot* means, *[the span of four horses required to pull] a chariot.*

וְכֵן לְכָל־מַלְכֵי הַחִתִּים ... בְּיָדָם יוֹצִיאוּ — *So too did they export to all the Hittite kings.* Even foreign kings had to buy their horses through the cartel made up of Solomon's traders at the exorbitant prices mentioned in the earlier part of the verse. This, too, contributed to the wealth of Solomon's court (*Malbim*).

Metzudos, who according to his explanation of מִקְוֵא in the earlier verse knows nothing of a cartel, renders our verse: [This price] held good also for the Hittite kings [who might have been expected to pay less since they were forced to] take out the horses by themselves [rather than have them delivered as did Solomon].

The detailed account of Solomon's horse trade contained in these two verses seems to have the purpose of underlining his error in having so many horses. Since the best horses were raised in Egypt, this inexorably pulled Solomon and his people back to that country. The Torah had forbidden a king to have too many horses for just this reason: *[The king] however must not accumulate many horses so as not to bring the people back to Egypt to get more horses.* HASHEM *has told you that you must never again return on that path* (*Deuteronomy* 17:17) [see *Shir HaShirim Rabbah* 1:10].

18. וַיֹּאמֶר שְׁלֹמֹה לִבְנוֹת בַּיִת לְשֵׁם ה׳ וּבַיִת לְמַלְכוּתוֹ — *Solomon planned to build a House to* HASHEM *and a royal palace.* The initiative for building the Temple is ascribed to Solomon, without any prompting from Churam. See Section II to ch. 2, *Solomon and Churam.*

II

⁂ Solomon Solicits Churam's Help

This chapter deals with the request for help which Solomon addressed to Churam, king of Tyre, and that king's very generous response. *I Kings* 5:16 ff. describes a similar exchange of messages. We analyze the difference between the two accounts in Section II, *Solomon and Churam.*

1. וַיִּסְפֹּר שְׁלֹמֹה — *Solomon counted off ...* The information contained in this verse is repeated at the end of the chapter in vs. 16 and 17. In the *Kings* account it is given only after the description of the communications between Solomon and Churam. See Section II, ibid., for

1
18

six hundred silver [coins], and a horse, one hundred and fifteen [sil-
ver coins]. So too did they export to all the Hittite and Aramite
kings. [18] *Solomon planned to build a House to* HASHEM *and a royal*
palace.

2
1-5

Solomon counted off seventy thousand porters, eighty thou-
sand quarrymen and thirty-six hundred foremen over them.
[2] *Solomon sent to Churam king of Tyre saying, 'As you did for my*
father David when you sent him cedars to build a house for himself
in which to dwell — [3] *See! I am building a House to the Name of*
HASHEM *my God, setting it aside for Him that incense may be burn-*
ed before Him, that there may be a constant ordering [of bread],
that burnt offerings be brought in the morning, and in the evening,
on the Sabbaths, at the time of the new moons and on the festivals
of HASHEM *our God. Israel will always require this.* [4] *The Temple*
which I am building must be imposing, for our God is greater than
any power. [5] *Yet, who can bring himself to build a House for Him*
when heaven and the highest heavens cannot contain Him? Who
am I that I should build a House for Him — except to offer up before

a discussion of why it was placed here at the beginning of the narrative.

שִׁבְעִים אֶלֶף... וּשְׁמוֹנִים אֶלֶף... שְׁלֹשֶׁת אֲלָפִים וְשֵׁשׁ מֵאוֹת — *Seventy thousand ... eighty thousand ... and thirty-six hundred* ... The first two numbers are identical with those given in *Kings*. However, for the foremen *Kings* has only three thousand three hundred to our three thousand six hundred. *Rashi* suggests that the extra three hundred listed here were particularly high officials who were in charge of the other three thousand three hundred (see further at 8:10).

אִישׁ סַבָּל — *Porters.* סַבָּל from סבל, *to bear. Kings* has נֹשֵׂא סַבָּל, literally *bearers of burdens.*

וּמְנַצְּחִים עֲלֵיהֶם — *And ... foremen over them.* This expression parallels *Kings,...* שָׂרֵי הַנִּצָּבִים הָרֹדִים בָּעָם, *attendant officers ... who wielded authority over the people...*

2. כַּאֲשֶׁר עָשִׂיתָ עִם־דָּוִיד אָבִי — *As you did for my father David* ... Churam's help to David had demonstrated an awareness of the cosmic significance of the Davidic enterprise [see Section II to *I Chronicles* ch.14, p.424, *Ascendancy over Tyre*]. Solomon is now challenging Churam: Are you willing to take the next step? Are you willing to throw in your lot with me as I build a Temple to God?

See Section II, ibid., for a discussion of this idea and an analysis of the difference in the wording of the various messages as it is reported in *Kings* and *Chronicles*.

3. בַּיִת לְשֵׁם ה׳ אֱלֹהָי לְהַקְדִּישׁ לוֹ — *A House to the Name of* HASHEM *my God, setting it aside for Him* ... This description of the purpose for which the Temple is to be built is missing from *Kings*. There, Solomon simply speaks of a Temple for God. Section II, *Solomon and Churam*, helps to explain the difference. *Kings* describes a correspondence between two kings concerning technical cooperation. The details of the Divine service as practiced in Israel is of no interest to Churam. By contrast, in *Chronicles*, Solomon is attempting to inspire Churam to take part in the consecration of the world to the Divine, in bringing God to dwell among man. Churam is to know the entire range of implications which are a part of this idea.

לְעוֹלָם זֹאת עַל־יִשְׂרָאֵל — *Israel will always require this.* It is important that the house which I plan to erect be firmly built. It is to stand for a very long time (*Mefaresh* and *Metzudos*).

4. כִּי־גָדוֹל אֱלֹהֵינוּ מִכָּל־הָאֱלֹהִים — *For our God is greater than any power.* I cannot avoid asking you for help, for nothing less than a really magnificent structure will do justice to God's greatness (*Mefaresh*). [See comm. to *I Chronicles* 22:5, and also at 29:1, there.]

Nothing of all this is said in *Kings*. The comm. to v. 3 can explain this difference, too.

5. וּמִי יַעֲצָר־כֹּחַ לִבְנוֹת־לוֹ בַיִת ... כִּי אִם־לְהַקְטִיר לְפָנָיו — *Yet, who can bring himself to build a*

ו וְעַתָּה שְׁלַח־לִי אִישׁ־חָכָם לַעֲשׂוֹת בַּזָּהָב וּבַכֶּסֶף וּבַנְּחֹשֶׁת
וּבַבַּרְזֶל וּבָאַרְגְּוָן וְכַרְמִיל וּתְכֵלֶת וְיֹדֵעַ לְפַתֵּחַ פִּתּוּחִים
עִם־הַחֲכָמִים אֲשֶׁר עִמִּי בִּיהוּדָה וּבִירוּשָׁלַם אֲשֶׁר הֵכִין
ז דָּוִיד אָבִי: וּשְׁלַח־לִי עֲצֵי אֲרָזִים בְּרוֹשִׁים וְאַלְגּוּמִּים
מֵהַלְּבָנוֹן כִּי אֲנִי יָדַעְתִּי אֲשֶׁר עֲבָדֶיךָ יוֹדְעִים לִכְרוֹת עֲצֵי
ח לְבָנוֹן וְהִנֵּה עֲבָדַי עִם־עֲבָדֶיךָ: וּלְהָכִין לִי עֵצִים לָרֹב כִּי
ט הַבַּיִת אֲשֶׁר־אֲנִי בוֹנֶה גָּדוֹל וְהַפְלֵא: וְהִנֵּה לַחֹטְבִים
לְכֹרְתֵי | הָעֵצִים נָתַתִּי חִטִּים | מַכּוֹת לַעֲבָדֶיךָ כֹּרִים
עֶשְׂרִים אֶלֶף וּשְׂעֹרִים כֹּרִים עֶשְׂרִים אָלֶף וְיַיִן בַּתִּים
עֶשְׂרִים אֶלֶף וְשֶׁמֶן בַּתִּים עֶשְׂרִים אָלֶף:
י וַיֹּאמֶר חוּרָם מֶלֶךְ־צֹר בִּכְתָב וַיִּשְׁלַח אֶל־שְׁלֹמֹה בְּאַהֲבַת

House for Him ... — except to offer up before Him? Do not think that the purpose for the Temple is to contain God within it. This could never be done. Its purpose is only to serve as a place in which He might be served (*Metzudos*).

Solomon carefully seeks to dispel any distorted ideas concerning the function of a Temple which Churam might carry over from his idolatrous past. Later, in his inaugural prayer (6:18), Solomon himself will grapple with the philosophical problem involved in building a physical abode for an infinite God — see comm. there. He apparently feels no need to pass on the conclusions, which he reaches there, to the heathen king. For him, it is sufficient to point to the Temple's function as a place where sacrifices to God could be brought.

כִּי הַשָּׁמַיִם וּשְׁמֵי הַשָּׁמַיִם — *When heaven and the highest heavens.* שְׁמֵי הַשָּׁמַיִם, literally, *the heavens of the heavens*. These are the upper spheres above and beyond the visible sky (*Metzudos*).

One way in which the superlative can be expressed in Hebrew is by using the noun in the construct, before the plural of the same word. This is the same form as for example קֹדֶשׁ הַקֳּדָשִׁים, *the most holy place*.

לֹא יְכַלְכְּלֻהוּ — *Cannot contain Him.* He is the *Place* of the world; the world is not His *place* (*Metzudos*). God is ground of all existence which is finite. He alone is infinite.

וּמִי אֲנִי אֲשֶׁר אֶבְנֶה־לּוֹ בַיִת כִּי אִם־לְהַקְטִיר לְפָנָיו — *Who am I that I should build a House for Him — except to offer up before Him.* Even though I am king, I am as nothing at all in relation to God (*Metzudos*).

כִּי אִם־לְהַקְטִיר לְפָנָיו — *Except to offer up before Him*. Literally, *to burn* [incense or sacrifices] *before Him*.

6. וְעַתָּה שְׁלַח־לִי אִישׁ־חָכָם — *So now send me an artisan ...* The request that Churam send an artisan skilled in the work of precious metals is missing in *Kings*. A careful reading of the text yields that whereas in the matter of wood-cutting, Solomon admits the superiority of Churam's men (v. 7), there is no such admission in the case of the metal workers. It seems that Solomon's workers could have done just as well on their own. [Note that it is the artisan who is to *join* the trained men who are already in Judah and Jerusalem, while in the case of the woodcutters Solomon's workers are to work *with* those of Churam.]

The implication is clear. Churam's artisan was not really needed. For this reason he does not appear in the request as told in *Kings*. But in *Chronicles* where it is Solomon's aim to involve Churam in the building of the Temple, he offers him a part in everything.

וּבָאַרְגְּוָן — *Purple.* This expression for אַרְגָּמָן, *purple*, is unique in Scripture.

וְכַרְמִיל — *Crimson*. This is also a shade of red (*Radak*) the same as the תּוֹלַעַת שָׁנִי of *Exodus* 25:4 (*Metzudos*).

לְפַתֵּחַ פִּתּוּחִים — *Capable of cutting engravings.* פתח means *to engrave*. It occurs frequently in the *Exodus* description of the work done on the priestly vestments.

7. וּשְׁלַח־לִי — *Send me also* ... In *Kings*, Solomon asks only for cedar wood and does not mention the other kinds. Again, we may surmise that only the cedars were absolutely necessary. The different varieties would be an

Him? [6] *So now send me an artisan, with the skill to work in gold, silver, copper, iron, purple, crimson and sky-blue wool; capable of cutting engravings. Let him join the trained men who are with me in Judah and Jerusalem, whom David my father has provided.* [7] *Send me also cedar, cypress and algum wood from Lebanon, for I realize that your servants know well how to harvest lumber in the Lebanon. See, my servants will work with your servants.* [8] *To furnish me with lumber in abundance because the House which I am building is to be spectacularly imposing.* [9] *Now for the lumbermen, the ones who cut the wood: I shall give ground wheat to your servants — twenty thousand kor; twenty thousand kor of barley; twenty thousand bat of wine, and twenty thousand bat of oil.'* [10] *Churam king of Tyre said in a written reply — and this he*

attractive addition calculated to arouse Churam's enthusiasm.

8. גָּדוֹל וְהַפְלֵא — *Spectacularly imposing.* פלא is *a wonder*. The sheer size of the building will strike wonder into the heart of the beholder. Because of its size, the building will require huge quantities of wood.

9. וְהִנֵּה לַחֹטְבִים לְכֹרְתֵי הָעֵצִים — *Now for the lumbermen, the ones who cut the wood*. In Solomon's communication as reported in *Kings* 5:20, no amounts are specified. He offers to pay whatever Churam would demand. In v. 23, there, Churam specifies that he would like Solomon to supply *bread for my household*.

The two accounts appear to be dealing with two different payments. *Kings* (v. 20) talks of *the payment for your servants*, and this may well mean the fee which Solomon is prepared to pay Churam for the use of Tyrian labor. By contrast, *Chronicles* deals with the workers' salary.

We can readily understand the two approaches. *Kings* deals with a contract between two monarchs. A payment to Churam is in place from Solomon, who makes an offer but, quite properly, does not specify any particular amount. It is up to Churam to determine what he wants, and he asks food for his household. It is self-understood that Solomon would feed the forest workers. The amounts that he would give them are not a subject for negotiations between the two kings.

In *Chronicles*, a payment to Churam would have been completely out of place. Solomon wishes to involve Churam the man in the cause of sanctity. Such a step is not taken in consideration of payment. The fee to Churam is, accordingly, not mentioned. On the other hand, an assumption on Solomon's part, of a humanitarianism which would be concerned with the welfare of his workers, would set exactly that tone which would be appropriate if Churam was to make the kind of personal commitment which Solomon hoped he would make. (See Section II, *Solomon and Churam.*)

לַחֹטְבִים לְכֹרְתֵי הָעֵצִים — *To the lumbermen, the ones who cut the wood.* Why the double expression?

We may perhaps surmise that כֹּרְתֵי עֵצִים is not a professional definition, that it is not used as a synonym for חֹטְבִים, but rather as a statement of what these חֹטְבִים do. Solomon feels a sense of obligation to the חֹטְבִים for supplying the wood.

חִטִּים מַכּוֹת — *Ground wheat*. The word is obscure and commentators offer varying explanations. *Radak* quotes *Ibn Janach* who translates as we have done. Alternatively, he and *Metzudos* suggest that the root might be נכת, the Aramaic for *to chew*. Thus, *wheat for chewing* or *eating*.

כֹּרִים עֶשְׂרִים אֶלֶף — *Twenty thousand kor*. *Kor* is a measure of volume containing thirty *se'ah* (*Metzudos*)

בַּתִּים עֶשְׂרִים — *Twenty thousand bat*. *Bat* is a liquid measure containing three *se'ah* (*Metzudos*).

Churam's Reply

10-15. Churam's answer to Solomon's request is recorded differently in *Chronicles* than it is in *Kings*. See Section II, *Churam's Reply*, for a detailed analysis.

10. וַיֹּאמֶר חוּרָם מֶלֶךְ־צֹר בִּכְתָב — *Churam king of Tyre said in a written reply*. The combination וַיֹּאמֶר... בִּכְתָב is unique. Moreover, it is difficult

יא יהוה אֶת־עַמּוֹ נְתָנְךָ עֲלֵיהֶם מֶלֶךְ: וַיֹּאמֶר חוּרָם בָּרוּךְ
יהוה אֱלֹהֵי יִשְׂרָאֵל אֲשֶׁר עָשָׂה אֶת־הַשָּׁמַיִם וְאֶת־הָאָרֶץ
אֲשֶׁר נָתַן לְדָוִיד הַמֶּלֶךְ בֵּן חָכָם יוֹדֵעַ שֵׂכֶל וּבִינָה אֲשֶׁר
יב יִבְנֶה־בַּיִת לַיהוה וּבַיִת לְמַלְכוּתוֹ: וְעַתָּה שָׁלַחְתִּי אִישׁ־
יג חָכָם יוֹדֵעַ בִּינָה לְחוּרָם אָבִי: בֶּן־אִשָּׁה מִן־בְּנוֹת דָּן וְאָבִיו
אִישׁ־צֹרִי יוֹדֵעַ לַעֲשׂוֹת בַּזָּהָב־וּבַכֶּסֶף בַּנְּחֹשֶׁת בַּבַּרְזֶל
בָּאֲבָנִים וּבָעֵצִים בָּאַרְגָּמָן בַּתְּכֵלֶת וּבַבּוּץ וּבַכַּרְמִיל
וּלְפַתֵּחַ כָּל־פִּתּוּחַ וְלַחְשֹׁב כָּל־מַחֲשָׁבֶת אֲשֶׁר יִנָּתֶן־לוֹ
יד עִם־חֲכָמֶיךָ וְחַכְמֵי אֲדֹנִי דָּוִיד אָבִיךָ: וְעַתָּה הַחִטִּים
וְהַשְּׂעֹרִים הַשֶּׁמֶן וְהַיַּיִן אֲשֶׁר אָמַר אֲדֹנִי יִשְׁלַח לַעֲבָדָיו:
טו וַאֲנַחְנוּ נִכְרֹת עֵצִים מִן־הַלְּבָנוֹן כְּכָל־צָרְכֶּךָ וּנְבִיאֵם
לְךָ רַפְסֹדוֹת עַל־יָם יָפוֹ וְאַתָּה תַּעֲלֶה אֹתָם
טז יְרוּשָׁלָםִ: וַיִּסְפֹּר שְׁלֹמֹה כָּל־הָאֲנָשִׁים הַגֵּיוֹרִים

to see why it would be important to stress that this communication was made in writing. However, if Churam wished to augment his formal reply with a private message, we have a ready explanation. (See Section II, ibid.) Churam's formal answer which begins in v. 11 was probably announced orally, perhaps in the presence of Solomon's whole court. Witness the fact that the *Kings* account says nothing about any writing. If, in addition to his formal answer, Churam would have wanted to send a private message we could well imagine that he would do this in writing.

Metzudos understands the matter differently. He explains that Churam's entire message to Solomon was in writing. It begins in v. 10 and continues in v. 12. V. 11 was said orally to Churam's household [hence the second וַיֹּאמֶר חוּרָם]. As Churam was writing his message it occurred to him what a wise person Solomon was and he was moved to exclaim this in the middle of his letter.

11. ה׳ אֱלֹהֵי יִשְׂרָאֵל אֲשֶׁר עָשָׂה אֶת־הַשָּׁמַיִם וְאֶת־הָאָרֶץ — *HASHEM, God of Israel, Who has made heaven and earth.* We have noted the dichotomy between the particularization implied in *God of Israel* and the universality implied in ... *Who made heaven and earth* in Section II, ibid.

בֵּן חָכָם יוֹדֵעַ שֵׂכֶל וּבִינָה — *A wise son endowed with wisdom and understanding.* The combination שֵׂכֶל וּבִינָה occurs only once more in Scripture and that is in David's blessing to Solomon at *I Chronicles* 22:12. It is evident from Churam's assessment that David's blessing was fulfilled.

אֲשֶׁר יִבְנֶה־בַּיִת לַה׳ וּבַיִת לְמַלְכוּתוֹ — *Who ... will build a House for HASHEM and a palace for the exercise of his kingship.* If a man of such wisdom builds the Temple and the royal palace, it is quite certain that they will be erected in the very best possible way (*Metzudos*).

12. וְעַתָּה שָׁלַחְתִּי — *Now I have sent ...* This verse and the next are in answer to Solomon's request recorded in v. 6.

לְחוּרָם אָבִי — *One from my father Churam.* Churam's father had borne the same name as he. The artisan whom he was sending had already worked for Churam's father (*Mefaresh*).

Based on *I Kings* 7:13 which implies that the artisan's name happened to be Churam, *Metzudos* suggests that the prefix ל, *lamed*, in לְחוּרָם may have the meaning which is usually expressed by אֶת, that is, the accusative. The word אָבִי need not be understood as *my father* but rather as an expression of awe at the artisan's skill. He was, as it were, *father* to all skilled workers. Thus: I have sent you Churam, the master-craftsman.

13. בֶּן־אִשָּׁה מִן־בְּנוֹת דָּן וְאָבִיו אִישׁ־צֹרִי — *A son of a woman from among the daughters of Dan, but his father, a Tyrian.* In *I Kings* 7:13-14, mention is made of Solomon sending to Tyre for a certain Churam who is described as ... *the son of a widow from the tribe of Naphtali whose father was a man of Tyre.* The Sages

sent to Solomon — 'Because HASHEM loves this people He has
made you king over them.' 11 *Churam said, 'Praised be HASHEM,*
God of Israel, Who has made heaven and earth and Who has given
David a wise son endowed with wisdom and understanding who
will build a House for HASHEM and a palace for the exercise of his
kingship. 12 *Now I have sent an artisan, one from my father*
Churam, endowed with good judgment. 13 *A son of a woman from*
among the daughters of Dan, but his father, a Tyrian. He is skilled
in crafting from gold, silver, copper, iron, stone and wood, from
purple, sky-blue wool, linen and crimson [materials]. Also, he can
engrave any patterns and do any weaving that he may be asked
to do, together with your artisans and the artisans of your fa-
ther, David. 14 *And now, the wheat and the barley, the oil and the*
wine which my lord has promised — send all this to his servants.
15 *And we will cut all the timber you need from the Lebanon and*
ship it by floats on the sea of Jaffa. And, you take it up to
Jerusalem.' 16 *Then Solomon counted all the foreigners in the Land*

assume the two to have been one and the same man. His father came from the tribe of Naphtali, his mother from the tribe of Dan. The description of the father in both places as a *man of Tyre* means only that he lived in Tyre, not that he was a gentile.

The midrashim (cf. *Tanchuma, Ki Sisa* 14) make much of the fact that a descendant of the tribe of Dan was involved in the building of the Temple. The tribe of Dan was considered the *lowest* of the twelve tribes [פָּחוּת מִבַּשְׁבָטִים] and in spite of this, the Temple could not be raised by Solomon, scion of the great tribe of Judah, without the help of Dan. So it was when Moses had Betzalel build the Tabernacle in the wilderness. Betzalel's helper was Ahaliav, son of Achisamach from the tribe of Dan (*Exodus* 31:6). In the presence of the Divine, the most exalted and the least important are equal.

וּבַכַּרְמִיל — *And crimson.* See comm. to v. 6.

וּלְפַתֵּחַ כָּל־פִּתּוּחַ — *Also, he can engrave any patterns.* See comm. to v. 6.

וְלַחְשֹׁב כָּל־מַחֲשָׁבֶת — *And do any weaving.* We have translated this term as does *Rashi* at *Exodus* 31:4. *Rashi's* interpretation is based on *Exodus* 26:1 where מַעֲשֵׂה חֹשֵׁב is a form of weaving.

Metzudos here takes the word חֹשֵׁב in its more usual meaning, that is, *to think* or *consider*, and understands the phrase as describing any particularly exact and delicate art work which requires the artist's thought and imagination.

עִם־חֲכָמֶיךָ — *Together with your artisans...* The phrase reflects Solomon's formulation in v. 6. See comm. there.

14. וְעַתָּה הַחִטִּים וְהַשְּׂעֹרִים — *And now, the wheat and the barley ...* This part of Churam's response reacts to Solomon's offer in v. 9.

לַעֲבָדָיו — *To his servants.* Churam apparently wishes to honor Solomon by referring to the workers of Tyre as *his*, that is, Solomon's servants.

15. וַאֲנַחְנוּ נִכְרֹת עֵצִים — *And we will cut the timber.* This part of Churam's response reacts to Solomon's request in v. 7.

Churam uses the general term עֵצִים, *trees*, which incorporates all the various varieties of wood which Solomon mentioned in his request.

רַפְסֹדוֹת — *Floats.* This word replaces דֹּבְרוֹת which is used in *Kings*. *Rashi* there explains that the two terms describe a kind of raft which is formed by lashing together the logs which are to be transported and which is then floated on the water like a boat.

עַל־יָם יָפוֹ — *On the sea of Jaffa.* Apparently Jaffa was the closest port to the Lebanon (*Metzudos*).

וְאַתָּה תַּעֲלֶה אֹתָם יְרוּשָׁלָםִ — *Then, you take it up to Jerusalem.* See discussion on why Jerusalem is mentioned here and not in *Kings* in Section II, *Churam's Reply*.

16. וַיִּסְפֹּר שְׁלֹמֹה כָּל־הָאֲנָשִׁים הַגֵּירִים — *Then Solomon counted all the foreigners ...* V. 17

ב אֲשֶׁר בְּאֶרֶץ יִשְׂרָאֵל אַחֲרֵי הַסְּפָר אֲשֶׁר סְפָרָם דָּוִיד אָבִיו
יז וַיִּמָּצְאוּ מֵאָה וַחֲמִשִּׁים אֶלֶף וּשְׁלֹשֶׁת אֲלָפִים וְשֵׁשׁ
יז מֵאוֹת: וַיַּעַשׂ מֵהֶם שִׁבְעִים אֶלֶף סַבָּל וּשְׁמֹנִים אֶלֶף חֹצֵב
בָּהָר וּשְׁלֹשֶׁת אֲלָפִים וְשֵׁשׁ מֵאוֹת מְנַצְּחִים לְהַעֲבִיד
א אֶת־הָעָם: וַיָּחֶל שְׁלֹמֹה לִבְנוֹת אֶת־בֵּית־יהוה בִּירוּשָׁלַםִ
בְּהַר הַמּוֹרִיָּה אֲשֶׁר נִרְאָה לְדָוִיד אָבִיהוּ אֲשֶׁר הֵכִין
ב בִּמְקוֹם דָּוִיד בְּגֹרֶן אָרְנָן הַיְבוּסִי: וַיָּחֶל לִבְנוֹת בַּחֹדֶשׁ
ג ג הַשֵּׁנִי בַּשֵּׁנִי בִּשְׁנַת אַרְבַּע לְמַלְכוּתוֹ: וְאֵלֶּה הוּסַד שְׁלֹמֹה
א־ג לִבְנוֹת אֶת־בֵּית הָאֱלֹהִים הָאֹרֶךְ אַמּוֹת בַּמִּדָּה הָרִאשׁוֹנָה

tells how Solomon disposed of the 153,600 people whom he counted.

Our verse relates that Solomon counted these strangers a second time although David, as part of his preparations for building the Temple, had already counted them (see *I Chronicles* 22:2 and comm. there). Presumably their number must have increased since the time of David's census (*Radak*).

Who were these strangers? *Rashi* to *I Kings* 5:29 suggests that they were gentiles who had integrated themselves into Jewish life [גֵּרִים גְּרוּרִים, *self-made converts*, who had not been formally accepted] under the pull of the glory of Solomon's reign. They would not be true converts since these were not accepted into Judaism during the reign of David and Solomon. The situation of the Jews during those times was so favorable that the sincerity of any potential convert was suspect — see *Avodah Zarah* 3b.

Radak thinks that they may have been descendants of the seven Canaanite nations, who were not wiped out because they had accepted upon themselves not to serve idols.

Yevamos 79a had a different tradition. As recounted in *II Samuel* ch. 21, David wreaked a terrible vengeance on the house of Saul at the behest of the Giveonites who had felt themselves wronged at Saul's hands. Without regard to the lowly standing of the Giveonites and the exalted position of Saul's family in Israel, David, with uncompromising justice, redressed that wrong. This firm act of justice made such an overwhelming impression upon the surrounding gentile world that hundreds of thousands of them decided to throw in their lot with the Jewish people. It is these strangers who made up Solomon's work force.

17. וַיַּעַשׂ — *He made* ... See comm. to v. 1.

III

◆§ Solomon Builds the Temple

The following two chapters describe the Temple which Solomon built. In many ways they parallel *I Kings* chs. 6 and 7 which are devoted to the same topic. We cannot know what prompted *Chronicles* to repeat so much of the technical information readily available in the earlier book. The minor additions or elucidations which we will be able to pinpoint from time to time seem insufficient to justify the long, detailed descriptions which add nothing and appear to be redundant.

We may perhaps surmise that *Chronicles* took its lead from the Torah. There, the description of the Tabernacle is repeated no less than five times, not all of them strictly necessary. *Ramban* (*Exodus* 36:8) believes that this duplication is a mark of love. God, as it were, returns to the subject again and again because it is so dear to Him. We too, *Ramban* adds, earn merit by repeatedly delving into its intricacies.

When *Chronicles* was written, the glory of Solomon's Temple was already the stuff of history. We can imagine the writer, with longing in his heart, lovingly rehearsing the well-known details, not willing to tear himself away too soon from the sweet picture which tradition had passed down to him.

2 *of Israel, just as David his father had taken a census of them,*
17 *and they turned out to be one hundred and fifty-three thou-*
sand six hundred. 17 *He made seventy-thousand of them por-*
ters, eighty thousand of them quarrymen in the mountains and
three thousand six hundred of them foremen to keep the people at
work.

3 *So Solomon initiated the building of the House of* HASHEM *in*
Jerusalem on Mount Moriah, where his father David had had
1-3 *a vision. He set it about at the spot which David had located — the*
threshing floor of Ornan the Yevusite. 2 *He initiated the building*
in the second month on the second [day] in the fourth year of his
rule. 3 *Now this is the base which Solomon laid to build the House*
of God. The length — with cubits of the original size — sixty

1. וַיָּחֶל שְׁלֹמֹה לִבְנוֹת אֶת־בֵּית־ה׳ — *So Solomon initiated the building of the House of* HASHEM ... There are two significant differences between the account in *Kings* and the one given here. *Kings* points out that the building of the Temple began in the four hundred and eightieth year from the Exodus (6:1), while *Chronicles* makes no mentions of this. In addition, *Chronicles* records only the day on which the building was begun (v. 2), but says nothing about when it was finished, while *Kings* marks the dates of both the beginning and the end (6:1 and 38).

It seems clear that *Chronicles* has a different agenda than *Kings*. *Kings* is concerned with the facts: This is when it happened, this is how long it lasted. By contrast, *Chronicles* deals with the essence of this seminal event. With the building of the Temple, a new era in the relationship between God and man is about to begin. It provides the date upon which Solomon began to build only in order to inform us of the significance of that day.

It is in order to convey this nuance that we have rendered וַיָּחֶל as *initiated* [as in *Genesis* 9:20 and elsewhere] rather than the more common *began*. Solomon began much more than a building project, he established a new reality.

בִּירוּשָׁלַםִ בְּהַר הַמּוֹרִיָּה — *In Jerusalem on Mount Moriah.* We note that this description is not given in *Kings*. This appears consistent with *Samuel's* treatment of the story of the census [*II Samuel* ch. 24 paralleling *I Chronicles* ch. 21]. Whereas *Chronicles* relates that incident as a prelude to the discovery of the site for the future Temple, thus underlining the significance of the geographic location, *Samuel* does not mention this at all. See Section II to *I Chronicles*, p. 459, *The Census and Its Aftermath*.

אֲשֶׁר נִרְאָה לְדָוִיד אָבִיהוּ — *Where his father David had had a vision.*

For the details of this vision, see *I Chronicles* 21:18 ff.

אֲשֶׁר הֵכִין בִּמְקוֹם דָּוִיד — *He set it about at the spot which David had located.* The translation follows *Metzudos* who makes Solomon the subject of this phrase. *Malbim* makes David the subject: *At the place which David had located and prepared* ... David had prepared the ground by excavating for the foundations of the building and preparing all the subterranean structures which were required. [See comm. to *I Chronicles* 28:2, and fn., there, p. 340.]

2. בַּחֹדֶשׁ הַשֵּׁנִי בַּשֵּׁנִי — *In the second month on the second [day].* The translation follows *Targum*: The building was begun on the second day of *Iyar*.

Rosh HaShanah 3a would render: *In the second month, the second month in the fourth year of his rule.* The sense of the phrase is that the second chronological month [*Iyar*] is also the second month of the fourth year of Solomon's reign. This is so because the years of a Jewish king's reign are always dated from the first of *Nissan*. [See ArtScroll Mishnayos, *Rosh HaShanah* p. 3, for details.]

3. וְאֵלֶּה הוּסַד שְׁלֹמֹה לִבְנוֹת אֶת־בֵּית הָאֱלֹהִים — *Now this is the base which Solomon laid to build the House of God* ... The translation follows *Metzudos*. הוּסַד is from יסד, *to establish* or *found*; thus, *a base*.

Radak takes הוּסַד as deriving from סוד, to

ד אַמּוֹת שִׁשִּׁים וְרֹחַב אַמּוֹת עֶשְׂרִים׃ וְהָאוּלָם אֲשֶׁר
עַל־פְּנֵי הָאֹרֶךְ עַל־פְּנֵי רֹחַב־הַבַּיִת אַמּוֹת עֶשְׂרִים וְהַגֹּבַהּ
ה מֵאָה וְעֶשְׂרִים וַיְצַפֵּהוּ מִפְּנִימָה זָהָב טָהוֹר׃ וְאֵת ׀ הַבַּיִת
הַגָּדוֹל חִפָּה עֵץ בְּרוֹשִׁים וַיְחַפֵּהוּ זָהָב טוֹב וַיַּעַל עָלָיו
ו תִּמֹרִים וְשַׁרְשְׁרֹת׃ וַיְצַף אֶת־הַבַּיִת אֶבֶן יְקָרָה לְתִפְאָרֶת
ז וְהַזָּהָב זְהַב פַּרְוָיִם׃ וַיְחַף אֶת־הַבַּיִת הַקֹּרוֹת הַסִּפִּים
וְקִירוֹתָיו וְדַלְתוֹתָיו זָהָב וּפִתַּח כְּרוּבִים עַל־
ח הַקִּירוֹת׃ וַיַּעַשׂ אֶת־בֵּית־קֹדֶשׁ הַקֳּדָשִׁים אָרְכּוֹ
עַל־פְּנֵי רֹחַב־הַבַּיִת אַמּוֹת עֶשְׂרִים וְרָחְבּוֹ אַמּוֹת עֶשְׂרִים

converse or *take counsel*; thus, a plan reached on the basis of consultation. The phrase has the meaning: *Now these are the dimensions and configurations which derived from Solomon's [and David's] planning...* The sense derives from *I Chronicles* 28:11 ff. where David handed Solomon the blueprint for the future Temple.

הָאֹרֶךְ ... אַמּוֹת שִׁשִּׁים — *The length ... sixty cubits.* The Temple building had three main components. Running from west to east, they are: the *Holy of Holies*; the *Sanctuary*; and the *Hall* (See *Rambam, Bais HaBechirah* 1:5). The length of sixty cubits given here is for the Holy of Holies [twenty cubits] together with the Sanctuary [forty cubits] (see *I Kings* 6:16-17). The dimensions of the Hall are given in the next verse (see diagram).

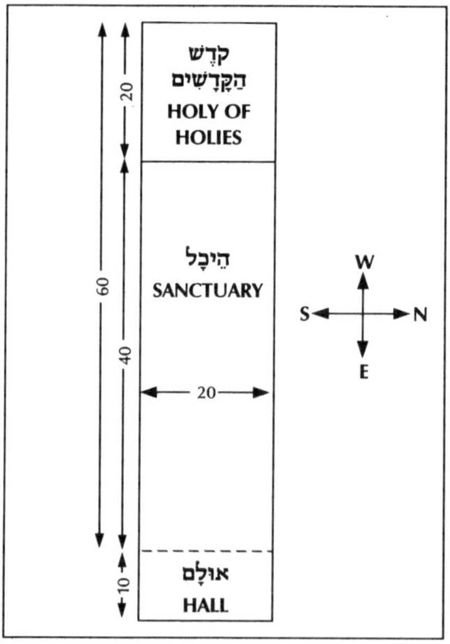

אַמּוֹת בַּמִּדָּה הָרִאשׁוֹנָה — *With cubits of the original size.*

At the time *Chronicles* was written, the standard cubit was five handbreadths. This can be shown from *Ezekiel* 40:5 where a cubit of six handbreadths is described as *a cubit and a handreadth* (*Malbim*). But the buildings of Solomon's Temple were to be measured by cubits of six hand-breadths and these are, here in this parenthetical phrase, described as having the dimension which the cubit had in Moses' day [six handbreadths] (*Metzudos*).

4. וְהָאוּלָם — *Now the Hall ...* To the east of the Sanctuary lay an entrance hall, the width of which was equal to the width of the Sanctuary. It extended outward ten cubits (*I Kings* 6:3). See diagram.

אֲשֶׁר עַל־פְּנֵי הָאֹרֶךְ — *The longer side of which* ... אֹרֶךְ always describes that side of any unit which is longer than the other. Thus, the אֹרֶךְ of the Hall is the רֹחַב of the Sanctuary (*Mefaresh.*)

The syntax is not smooth. But see *Appendix II* to *I Chronicles*, p. 480, which discusses the obscure language which Scripture invariably uses in its architectural descriptions.

וְהַגֹּבַהּ מֵאָה וְעֶשְׂרִים — *And its height was one hundred and twenty. I Kings* 6:2 gives the Temple height as thirty cubits. This seems to stand in contradiction to the one hundred and twenty cubits given here.

Mefaresh and *Radak* in one explanation point to *I Chronicles* 28:11 which tells of the Temple having upper chambers. Thus, the thirty cubits mentioned in *Kings* might be the height, from floor to ceiling, of the various components which were at ground level, while the one hundred and twenty cubits in the description given here could be the height of the entire structure, including the chambers on the upper floor.

cubits and a width of twenty cubits. [4] *Now the Hall, the longer*
side of which lay along the width of the Sanctuary, was twenty
cubits, and its height was one hundred and twenty. He overlaid
the inside with pure gold [5] *He paneled the large chamber with*
cypress wood and overlaid it with fine gold, and he decorated it
with palm and chain designs. [6] *He overlaid the chamber with*
precious stones to lend it majesty. The gold was Parvaim gold.
[7] *He covered the house, the rafters, the doorposts, its walls and its*
doors with gold. He engraved cheruvim upon the walls. [8] *He made*
the Holy of Holies, its length along the width of the house, twenty

In another explanation, *Radak* thinks that the one-hundred-and-twenty-cubit height was true only for the Hall. The attics were part of the Hall structure and it alone reached this fantastic height. The Sanctuary and Holy of Holies reached a height of only thirty cubits.

Malbim suggests that the entire structure may have been one-hundred-and-twenty cubits high. However, the Sanctuary and Holy of Holies had ceilings at the thirty-cubit mark which the Hall did not have. Thus, someone standing in the Hall was able to see the entire one-hundred-and-twenty-cubit height above himself.

וַיְצַפֵּהוּ מִפְּנִימָה — *He overlaid the inside . . .* This golden overlay was applied to the Sanctuary as described in the next few verses. It was not applied to the Hall (*Mefaresh*).

5. וְאֵת הַבַּיִת הַגָּדוֹל — *The large chamber.* This refers to the Sanctuary (*Metzudos*).

חִפָּה עֵץ בְּרוֹשִׁים — *He paneled . . . with cypress wood.* חפה, *to cover*, is used in the *pi'el* form to mean *to overlay*.

From *Kings* 6:15 and 16, it appears that the Temple walls were covered with cedar wood, and only the floors with cypress wood.

Because of this, *Metzudos* believes that, in this passage, the floor of the Temple, and not the walls, is being described.

וַיַּעַל עָלָיו תִּמֹרִים וְשַׁרְשְׁרֹת — *And he decorated it with palm and chain designs.* תָּמָר is a *date tree* and שַׁרְשֶׁרֶת is a *chain*.

These designs were either beaten into the gold (*Metzudos*) or carved into the wood so that when the gold overlay was attached to it the designs stood out in the gold. (*Mefaresh*).

I Kings 6:18 speaks of apparently different designs composed of orbs and flowered ropes (see *Rashi* there). *Ralbag* suggests either that all these designs were used but that neither *Kings* nor *Chronicles* gives a complete list; or that the designs mentioned in *Kings* were for the walls, while our verse deals only with the decoration of the floor. This would agree with *Metzudos*, quoted above, that our passage deals with the floor rather than the walls.

6. וַיְצַף אֶת־הַבַּיִת אֶבֶן יְקָרָה לְתִפְאָרֶת — *He overlaid the chamber with precious stones to lend it majesty.* He sank precious stones into settings (*Metzudos*) embedded into the gold overlay of the walls (*Mefaresh* and *Metzudos*) or the floor (*Ralbag* in one interpretation), in order to lend majesty to the building.

וְהַזָּהָב זְהַב פַּרְוָיִם — *The gold was Parvaim gold.* Parvaim is a place name (*Mefaresh* and *Radak*). Both commentators also bring the homiletical interpretation of the Sages who read the word as a contraction of the two words דַם פָּרִים, *the blood of oxen*. The gold was so called because of its deep crimson glow.

7. הַקֹּרוֹת — *The rafters.* קוֹרָה is a *beam* and is used here to describe those beams which supported the ceiling (*Metzudos*).

הַסִּפִּים — *The doorposts.* The translation follows *Metzudos*. *Rashi* to *Isaiah* 6:4 could be understood to mean that סַף is the entire threshold rather than the individual doorpost.

וּפִתַּח כְּרוּבִים עַל־הַקִּירוֹת — *He engraved cheruvim upon the walls.* The engraved *cheruvim* are mentioned in *I Kings* 6:29 together with various other decorations on the walls. See comm. to v. 5.

8. אָרְכּוֹ עַל־פְּנֵי רֹחַב־הַבַּיִת — *Its length along the width of the house.* See comm. to v. 4 for the use of these expressions. Both *Mefaresh* and *Metzudos* point out that in the case of the Holy of Holies, which was a square of twenty by twenty cubits, it is not really appropriate to talk of a *length* as opposed to a *width*. Nonetheless, since this formulation was used in the case of the Hall, it is repeated here. See Fig. I for the relationship of the Holy of Holies to the Sanctuary.

ט וַיְחַפֵּהוּ זָהָב טוֹב לְכִכָּרִים שֵׁשׁ מֵאוֹת׃ וּמִשְׁקָל לְמִסְמְרוֹת
י לִשְׁקָלִים חֲמִשִּׁים זָהָב וְהָעֲלִיּוֹת חִפָּה זָהָב׃ וַיַּעַשׂ
בְּבֵית־קֹדֶשׁ הַקֳּדָשִׁים כְּרוּבִים שְׁנַיִם מַעֲשֵׂה צַעֲצֻעִים
יא וַיְצַפּוּ אֹתָם זָהָב׃ וְכַנְפֵי הַכְּרוּבִים אָרְכָּם אַמּוֹת עֶשְׂרִים
כְּנַף הָאֶחָד לְאַמּוֹת חָמֵשׁ מַגַּעַת לְקִיר הַבַּיִת וְהַכָּנָף
יב הָאַחֶרֶת אַמּוֹת חָמֵשׁ מַגִּיעַ לִכְנַף הַכְּרוּב הָאַחֵר׃ וּכְנַף
הַכְּרוּב הָאֶחָד אַמּוֹת חָמֵשׁ מַגִּיעַ לְקִיר הַבָּיִת וְהַכָּנָף
יג הָאַחֶרֶת אַמּוֹת חָמֵשׁ דְּבֵקָה לִכְנַף הַכְּרוּב הָאַחֵר׃ כַּנְפֵי
הַכְּרוּבִים הָאֵלֶּה פֹּרְשִׂים אַמּוֹת עֶשְׂרִים וְהֵם עֹמְדִים
יד עַל־רַגְלֵיהֶם וּפְנֵיהֶם לַבָּיִת׃ וַיַּעַשׂ אֶת־הַפָּרֹכֶת

וַיְחַפֵּהוּ זָהָב טוֹב — *He overlaid it with fine gold.* There is no mention here of any wood paneling being applied to the walls of the Holy of Holies for anchoring the gold. Perhaps this is self-understood from v.5.

9. וּמִשְׁקָל לְמִסְמְרוֹת — *The weight of the nails ...* These were the nails with which he fixed the gold overlay to the wooden base (*Mefaresh* and *Metzudos*).

וְהָעֲלִיּוֹת חִפָּה זָהָב — *He overlaid the upper rooms with gold.* This refers to walls of the upper rooms (*Metzudos*). See comm. to v. 4 for these upper rooms.

10-13. These verses describe two golden, child-like figures (*Rashi* to *Exodus* 25:18) which Solomon erected in the Holy of Holies. These *cheruvim* are not the same as those which were a part of the lid of the Ark as described in *Exodus* 25:18, but were in addition to them (*Mefaresh*).

The description of these *cheruvim* is also given in *I Kings* 6:23-28.

10. וַיַּעַשׂ בְּבֵית־קֹדֶשׁ הַקֳּדָשִׁים — *He made ... in the Holy of Holies.* In v. 13, we learn that the *cheruvim* faced the Sanctuary. Thus, we have them standing with their backs to the west facing east. Their wings spanned the entire space of the Holy of Holies from north to south.

כְּרוּבִים שְׁנַיִם — *Two ... cheruvim. Malbim* notes that *Kings* has שְׁנֵי כְּרוּבִים. In his comm. to *Leviticus* 16:5, *Malbim* demonstrates that when the number is given in the construct form, i.e., שְׁנֵי, it denotes a perfectly matched pair, while שְׁנַיִם is used when there is a difference between the two. He notes that according to *Bava Basra* 99a the two *cheruvim* [which were made as male and female to denote *source* and *recipient* of Divine favor respectively — see *Malbim* there] miraculously portrayed God's relationship to Israel. They would face one another [that is, constitute one unit] when that relationship was as it should be, but disregard one another, each facing forward [and thus retaining their separate identity of *male* and *female*] when there was a barrier between God and Israel.

Thus, our passage in *Chronicles* which describes the *cheruvim* in their separate [and therefore different] identities uses שְׁנַיִם instead of שְׁנֵי.

מַעֲשֵׂה צַעֲצֻעִים — *Child-like.* Most commentators (*Mefaresh, Radak, Metzudos*) believe the *ayin* to be in place of an *aleph* and that the meaning is the same as that of צֶאֱצָא [from יצא, *to issue forth*], which means *child* or *offspring*; thus, *child-like*.

וַיְצַפּוּ אֹתָם זָהָב — *They overlaid them with gold. I Kings* 6:23 tells that the *cheruvim* were made from olive wood. The *Chronicles'* account assumes our knowledge of this and tells us only of the golden overlay.

11. אָרְכָּם אַמּוֹת עֶשְׂרִים — *A spread of twenty cubits.* This cumulative dimension is not given in *Kings*. *Malbim* thinks that it is mentioned here in order to make it clear that the *cheruvim* stood next to each other, their wings precisely spanning the entire twenty-cubit length of the Holy of Holies, rather than that they were facing one another. It is particularly important to stress this in view of the teaching of the Sages (*Bava Basra* 99a) that the bodies of the *cheruvim*, miraculously, did not take up any room in the Holy of Holies. [The Sages assume that the wings grew out of the sides of the bodies as do human arms, rather than sprouting out from the same spot in the center

3
9-14

cubits and its width, twenty cubits. He overlaid it with fine gold weighing six hundred talents. 9 *The weight of the nails was fifty gold shekels. He overlaid the upper rooms with gold.* 10 *He made two child-like cheruvim in the Holy of Holies. They overlaid them with gold.* 11 *The wings of the cheruvim had a spread of twenty cubits; one five-cubit wing touched the wall of the House and the other five-cubit wing reached the wing of the other cheruv.* 12 *And the wing of the other cheruv was five cubits, reaching the wall of the House, and the other five-cubit wing cleaved to the wing of the other cheruv.* 13 *The wings of these cheruvim were spread over twenty cubits. They stood on their feet with their faces toward the House.* 14 *He made the curtain of*

of the back. Given this assumption, the entire available space was taken up by the wings, leaving no room at all for the bodies.]

לְאַמּוֹת חָמֵשׁ — *Five-cubit*. The *lamed* seems to serve no discernible purpose and does not appear in the otherwise identical phrase in the later part of the verse. *Ibn Janach* in his *Sefer HaRikmah* demonstrates the existence of what he calls an *intrusive lamed*, that is, one which intrudes into a word without any purpose. For one example, see *Ezra* 9:4.

כְּנַף הָאֶחָד — *One . . . wing*. See comm. to v. 10 for the positioning of the *cheruvim*.

מַגִּיעַ — *Reached*. We have translated *reached* rather than *touched*, which would also be a legitimate translation of the root נגע, because of the expression דְּבֵקָה, *clove*, in the next verse. This expression is also used in *I Kings* 6:27. The root דבק has a stronger meaning than נגע, and to describe the same condition with both expressions seems inconsistent. Rather we assume that our verse, which deals with the first *cheruv* before the second one was erected, describes the extent to which the wing *reached*. It extended to the point which the other *cheruv*'s wing reached when it was up. V. 12 describes how they touched, which in the narrow space available is described with דבק.

12. דְּבֵקָה — *Cleaved*. See comm. to previous verse for the use of this expression.

13. פֹּרְשִׂים אַמּוֹת עֶשְׂרִים — *Were spread over twenty cubits*. Their wingspread covered the entire twenty-cubit space in the Holy of Holies. They were positioned to the north and south of the holy ark, and, thus, their wings covered part of the ark and its poles (*Rashi*).

וְהֵם עֹמְדִים עַל־רַגְלֵיהֶם — *They stood on their feet*. *I Kings* 6:23 teaches that each one of the *cheruvim* had a height of ten cubits. Our verse indicates that both stood at their full height. *Malbim* points out that it was necessary to stress this in order to reinforce the tradition of the Sages that a miracle was required to accommodate both of the *cheruvim* in the Holy of Holies (see comm. to v. 11). Without the information given in our verse, we might have supposed that one of the *cheruvim* was in a crouching position so that the wings would not have been in each other's way.

וּפְנֵיהֶם לַבָּיִת — *With their faces toward the house*. בַּיִת has been used throughout this chapter to describe the Sanctuary and this could well be the meaning of this phrase. The *cheruvim* were to stand facing east so that they looked towards the Sanctuary (*Ralbag* and perhaps *Rashbam* to *Bava Basra* 99a).

However, *Targum* renders, *inward* and this is also how *Mefaresh* takes the phrase. The meaning is that the heads of the *cheruvim* were not made in such a way that they would be looking outward, but that they were inclined so that they looked inward towards one another.

Both these opinions are represented in *Bava Basra* 99a.[1]

14. וַיַּעַשׂ אֶת־הַפָּרֹכֶת — *He made the curtain*. In the Tabernacle which Moses built, the Holy of Holies was separated from the Sanctuary by a curtain (*Exodus* 20:31 ff.). In Solomon's Temple, this dividing curtain was replaced by a

1. However, the opinion which holds that the *cheruvim* faced east believes that this was only so when Israel was not living according to God's will. When they acted as they should, the *cheruvim* looked toward one another.

ג תְּכֵלֶת וְאַרְגָּמָן וְכַרְמִיל וּבוּץ וַיַּעַל עָלָיו
טו־יז טו כְּרוּבִים׃ וַיַּעַשׂ לִפְנֵי הַבַּיִת עַמּוּדִים שְׁנַיִם
אַמּוֹת שְׁלֹשִׁים וְחָמֵשׁ אֹרֶךְ וְהַצֶּפֶת אֲשֶׁר־עַל־רֹאשׁוֹ אַמּוֹת
טז חָמֵשׁ׃ וַיַּעַשׂ שַׁרְשְׁרוֹת בַּדְּבִיר וַיִּתֵּן עַל־רֹאשׁ
יז הָעַמֻּדִים וַיַּעַשׂ רִמּוֹנִים מֵאָה וַיִּתֵּן בַּשַּׁרְשְׁרוֹת׃ וַיָּקֶם
אֶת־הָעַמּוּדִים עַל־פְּנֵי הַהֵיכָל אֶחָד מִיָּמִין וְאֶחָד
°הַיְמָנִי ק׳ מֵהַשְּׂמֹאול וַיִּקְרָא שֵׁם־°הימיני יָכִין וְשֵׁם הַשְּׂמָאלִי
ד א בֹּעַז׃ וַיַּעַשׂ מִזְבַּח נְחֹשֶׁת עֶשְׂרִים אַמָּה אָרְכּוֹ
א־ב ב וְעֶשְׂרִים אַמָּה רָחְבּוֹ וְעֶשֶׂר אַמּוֹת קוֹמָתוֹ׃ וַיַּעַשׂ
אֶת־הַיָּם מוּצָק עֶשֶׂר בָּאַמָּה מִשְּׂפָתוֹ אֶל־שְׂפָתוֹ עָגוֹל ׀
סָבִיב וְחָמֵשׁ בָּאַמָּה קוֹמָתוֹ וְקָו שְׁלֹשִׁים בָּאַמָּה יָסֹב אֹתוֹ

wall one cubit thick, which stood between the two areas (see *Yomah* 51b). This wall [but not its dimensions] is mentioned in *I Kings* 6:16 (*Rashi* there).

The curtain described here is not mentioned in *Kings*. We must assume that it was a decorative curtain and hung in front of the dividing wall.

וְכַרְמִיל — *And crimson*. See comm. to 2:6.

15-17. These verses give a short description of two pillars which were to stand in the Hall. A much more detailed description of these pillars and the intricate decorative designs which were part of them is given in *I Kings* 7:15-22.

15. לִפְנֵי הַבַּיִת — *In front of the chamber.* In front of the Sanctuary, that is in the Hall (*Metzudos*).

אַמּוֹת שְׁלֹשִׁים וְחָמֵשׁ אֹרֶךְ — *A length of thirty-five cubits.* In *Kings* (v. 15) the height of each pillar is given as eighteen cubits. *Malbim* explains that the two copper pillars (v. 15 there) were originally manufactured together as one long piece, measuring thirty-five cubits. This is the measurement given here.

This piece was then cut into two pieces, each section with a length of seventeen and one-half cubits. The ends of each pillar were then beaten into the shape of a rose (v. 22 there) and this process elongated each pillar by a one-half cubit so that in the end each one measured a total height of eighteen cubits.

וְהַצֶּפֶת — *The capping. Kings* (v. 16 and elsewhere) speaks of כֹּתָרוֹת, *crowning [pieces]*, with a height of 5 cubits which were placed on top of each pillar. Commentators explain that our צֶפֶת is identical with the כֹּתֶרֶת of *Kings*.

16. וַיַּעַשׂ שַׁרְשְׁרוֹת בַּדְּבִיר — *He made chains for the D'vir* ... The verse is to be understood as follows: He made chains which [as described in *I Kings* 6:21] were used for the decoration of the *D'vir*, and, in addition, he placed other chains around the cappings of the two pillars described in this passage (*Radak*).

[We have left *D'vir* untranslated. Commentators to the *King's* passage point out that it is used interchangeably for both the Holy of Holies (thus *Targum*, here) and for the wall which separated that area from the Sanctuary. See *Metzudos* to *I Kings* 6:5, *Tosefta* to *Yoma* ch.2, and *Rashi* to *Yoma* 52a s.v. דביר.]

וַיַּעַשׂ רִמּוֹנִים מֵאָה — *He made one hundred pomegranates.* These pomegranates were threaded onto the chains which, in turn, were twisted around the cappings (*Rashi*). *Kings* (v. 20) talks of two hundred pomegranates. *Malbim* suggests that there were two chains each with one hundred pomegranates threaded into them.

17. עַל־פְּנֵי הַהֵיכָל — *In front of the Sanctuary*. The pillars stood in the Hall on either side of the entrance to the Sanctuary (*Mefaresh*).

מִיָּמִין ... מֵהַשְּׂמֹאול — *To the right ... to the left.* To the right and to the left of the entrance into the Sanctuary (*Mefaresh*).

יָכִין ... בֹּעַז — *Yachin ... Boaz.* Yachin is from כון, *to be established*, and Boaz is a contraction of two words בּוֹ עֹז, *strength is within it*. As one entered the Temple he was to be greeted by these two pillars. Together, by means of their names, they were to imply a prayerful wish for the permanent establishment of the Temple (*Radak*).

3 15-17 *sky-blue wool, purple and crimson [materials] and of linen. He worked a cheruv [design] upon it.* 15 *He made two pillars in front of the chamber — a length of thirty-five cubits. The capping on its top was five cubits.* 16 *He made chains for the D'vir and placed them over the top of the pillars. He made one hundred pomegranates and threaded them onto the chains.* 17. *He put the pillars up in front of the Sanctuary, one to the right and one to the left. He called the right one Yachin and the left one Boaz.*

4 1-2 *He made a copper altar. Its length was twenty cubits and its width was twenty cubits and its height was ten cubits.* 2 *He made the cast-metal basin ten cubits from rim to rim, circular, with a height which was five cubits; a line of thirty cubits ran round*

IV

◆§ The Copper Altar

1. וַיַּעַשׂ מִזְבַּח נְחֹשֶׁת — *He made a copper altar.* In the tradition of the Sages, the altar which Solomon built was not made out of copper but out of stone in conformance with the Torah law at *Exodus* 20:21 and 22 (see *Rav* to *Midos* 3:1 for details). It is called a *copper altar* [here and elsewhere] only because it replaced the copper altar which Betzalel had built. See Section II, *The Copper Altar*.

עֶשְׂרִים אַמָּה אָרְכּוֹ וְעֶשְׂרִים אַמָּה רָחְבּוֹ — *Its length was twenty cubits and its width was twenty cubits.* *Malbim* points out that from *Midos* 3:1 it is clear that in the tradition of the Sages, Solomon's altar was actually twenty-eight by twenty-eight cubits. The twenty-by-twenty cubit measurement refers only to the מְקוֹם הַמַּעֲרָכָה, *the area upon which the woodpile was arranged,* at the center of the altar, where the sacrifices were burned.[1]

See Section II, *The Copper Altar*.

◆§ The Copper Basin

2-5. This section describes a huge copper basin [יָם, lit. *sea*] which Solomon built for the Temple courtyard. It was to serve as a ritual bath [מִקְוֶה] for the *Kohanim* (v. 6). A much more detailed description is given in *I Kings* 7:23-37. There are minor differences between the two accounts, and these will be addressed in the comm.

2. וַיַּעַשׂ אֶת־הַיָּם מוּצָק — *He made the cast-metal basin*. He achieved the hollowing out of the metal through the process of casting, rather than through beating it with a hammer (*Metzudos*)

עֶשֶׂר בָּאַמָּה מִשְּׂפָתוֹ אֶל־שְׂפָתוֹ — *Ten cubits from rim to rim*. The lower part of the basin was a cube of ten by ten by three cubits but the upper two cubits were round — see below. The diameter of the round section was ten cubits.[2]

עָגוֹל סָבִיב — *Circular*. *Eruvin* 14a quotes a tradition that the basin was large enough to contain an amount of water equal to that contained in one hundred and fifty *mikvaos* — see comment below at v. 5. If the basin had been a cylinder of ten by ten by five cubits, the volume would have been too small for such a large amount of water. Consequently, the Talmud postulates that the lower three cubits of the height were cube-shaped and only the upper two cubits were actually round.

וְקָו שְׁלֹשִׁים בָּאַמָּה — *A line of thirty cubits* ... The Talmud, assuming a value of 3 for *pi*,

1. The twenty-eight by twenty-eight measurement becomes twenty by twenty as follows: The base of the altar was twenty-eight by twenty-eight, but at two levels of its height there were indentations of one cubit around the whole perimeter, each indentation subtracting two cubits from the width of the altar, so that the top level of the altar was now only twenty-four by twenty-four cubits. On this top level there were *horns* protruding at each corner, each with a width of one cubit leaving a twenty-two by twenty-two-cubit space within these horns. A path of one cubit around the top of the altar was assigned as a walkway for the *Kohanim*. This left twenty by twenty cubits for the woodpile.

2. The basin was supported by twelve ox-like statues — three on each of the four sides.

ג סָבִיב: וּדְמוּת בְּקָרִים תַּחַת לוֹ סָבִיב | סָבִיב סוֹבְבִים אֹתוֹ
עֶשֶׂר בָּאַמָּה מַקִּיפִים אֶת־הַיָּם סָבִיב שְׁנַיִם טוּרִים הַבָּקָר
ד יְצוּקִים בְּמֻצַקְתּוֹ: עוֹמֵד עַל־שְׁנֵים עָשָׂר בָּקָר שְׁלֹשָׁה פֹנִים
| צָפוֹנָה וּשְׁלוֹשָׁה פֹּנִים | יָמָּה וּשְׁלֹשָׁה | פֹּנִים נֶגְבָּה
וּשְׁלֹשָׁה פֹּנִים מִזְרָחָה וְהַיָּם עֲלֵיהֶם מִלְמָעְלָה וְכָל־
ה אֲחֹרֵיהֶם בָּיְתָה: וְעָבְיוֹ טֶפַח וּשְׂפָתוֹ כְּמַעֲשֵׂה שְׂפַת־
כּוֹס פֶּרַח שׁוֹשַׁנָּה מַחֲזִיק בַּתִּים שְׁלֹשֶׁת אֲלָפִים
ו יָכִיל: וַיַּעַשׂ כִּיּוֹרִים עֲשָׂרָה וַיִּתֵּן חֲמִשָּׁה מִיָּמִין
וַחֲמִשָּׁה מִשְּׂמֹאול לְרָחְצָה בָהֶם אֶת־מַעֲשֵׂה הָעוֹלָה
ז יָדִיחוּ בָם וְהַיָּם לְרָחְצָה לַכֹּהֲנִים בּוֹ: וַיַּעַשׂ
אֶת־מְנֹרוֹת הַזָּהָב עֶשֶׂר כְּמִשְׁפָּטָם וַיִּתֵּן בַּהֵיכָל חָמֵשׁ
ח מִיָּמִין וְחָמֵשׁ מִשְּׂמֹאול: וַיַּעַשׂ שֻׁלְחָנוֹת עֲשָׂרָה

explains that this describes the inner circumference of the basin. At the outside, taking into account the thickness of the wall, the circumference would have been larger.

3. וּדְמוּת בְּקָרִים — *The likeness of cattle. I Kings* 7:24 has פְּקָעִים instead of בְּקָרִים. *Rashi*, based on *Targum*, thinks that פְּקָאִים are egg-shaped protrusions. We might render the word *knobs*. We assume that these knobs had faces of cattle etched upon them (*Metzudos*).

תַּחַת לוֹ — *In the lower section*. The lower, cubed section measured ten cubits on each side, making a perimeter of forty cubits. The entire perimeter was decorated with cattle-like knobs (*Metzudos*).

שְׁנַיִם טוּרִים — *Two rows*. The knobs, described earlier, ran in two rows around the basin (*Metzudos*).

יְצוּקִים בְּמֻצַקְתּוֹ — *Cast into a solid piece with it*. The knobs were not made separately and then attached, but were cast as one piece together with the basin (*Metzudos*).

4. וְכָל־אֲחֹרֵיהֶם בָּיְתָה — *And the haunches of all of them were turned inward*. The twelve oxen all faced outward so that their haunches came underneath the basin which rested upon them. The haunches of the oxen facing northward were opposite the haunches of the oxen facing south (*Metzudos*).

5. וְעָבְיוֹ טֶפַח וּשְׂפָתוֹ — *Its thickness was a handbreadth but its rim* ... The floor of the basin and its sides were a handbreadth thick but towards its rim it was hammered thin like the edge of a cup (*Rashi, Metzudos*).

פֶּרַח שׁוֹשַׁנָּה — *Lily blossoms*. This is to be taken as a description of the cup. It is a cup decorated with lily blossoms (*Rashi, Metzudos*).

שְׁלֹשֶׁת אֲלָפִים יָכִיל — *Its capacity enabled it to hold three thousand bat*. The basin was big enough to hold 3,000 *bat. I Kings* 7:26 has 2,000. *Eruvin* 14b explains that *Kings* gives the amount of liquid which the basin was able to contain, while *Chronicles* gives the capacity for solids. Since the latter can be heaped, there is a larger capacity.

A *bat* contains three *seah* and therefore 2,000 *bat* is the equivalent of 6,000 *seah* or the amount of water required for 150 *mikvaos* — see comm. to v. 2.

◈ Other Temple Utensils

6. וַיַּעַשׂ כִּיּוֹרִים עֲשָׂרָה — *He made ten bowls*. In *Exodus* 30:17 ff. we learn that there was a copper bowl in the Tabernacle courtyard from which the *Kohanim* were to wash their hands and feet before engaging in the sacred service. Solomon made an additional ten bowls and placed five to the right and five to the left of the one which Moses had made (*Mefaresh*)

וַיִּתֵּן חֲמִשָּׁה מִיָּמִין וַחֲמִשָּׁה מִשְּׂמֹאול — *Positioning them five to the right and five to the left*. Right and left in this phrase refers to the bowl which Moses had made and which Solomon also had incorporated into his Temple (*Mefaresh, Metzudos*)

I Kings 7:38, which describes these bowls in greater detail, gives their position relative to the Temple building: Five to the right of the Temple [that is the southern side for one

about it. [3] *The likeness of cattle in the lower section — which was ten cubits on each side — went the whole way around it, surrounding the basin on all sides. Two rows of cattle cast into a solid piece with it.* [4] *It stood upon twelve oxen, three turned toward the north and three turned toward the west. Three turned toward the south and three turned toward the east. The basin was on top of them and the haunches of all of them were turned inward.* [5] *Its thickness was a handbreadth but its rim was like the rim of a cup decorated by lily blossoms. Its capacity enabled it to hold three thousand bat.* [6] *He made ten bowls, positioning them five to the right and five to the left, so that ablutions might be made from them, [and] to rinse parts of the burnt offering in them. The basin served the Kohanim for immersion.* [7] *He made the ten golden candelabra according to their pattern and placed them in the Sanctuary; five to the right and five to the left.* [8] *He made ten tables*

facing east] and five to the left [which is the north].

לְרָחְצָה בָּהֶם – *So that ablutions might be made from them.* The *Kohanim* made the required ablutions – the washing of hands and feet prior to the Divine service – from these bowls. This was done through a system of faucets which were placed on the sides of the bowls (*Mefaresh*).

אֶת־מַעֲשֵׂה הָעוֹלָה יָדִיחוּ בָם – *[And] to rinse parts of the burnt offering in them.* The inner organs of the burnt offerings had to be rinsed before they were brought on the altar. We have inserted the word *and* in order to accommodate *Mefaresh's* rendering of the verse. See previous comment above on לְרָחְצָה בָּהֶם.

וְהַיָּם לְרָחְצָה לַכֹּהֲנִים בּוֹ – *The basin served the Kohanim for immersion.* The basin was used as a *mikveh* by the *Kohanim* (*Mefaresh*). The basin would surely not have been used under circumstances in which the *Kohanim* had to immerse their whole body; for this there were other *mikvaos* within the Temple complex. However, there are situations in which only the hands require immersion [see *Zevachim* 20b], and it was for that purpose that the basin was used (*Mikra UMassores*).

Normally, a vessel cannot be used as a *mikveh*. Two conditions were made in order that the basin should not be disqualified. Holes were punched into the feet of the supporting oxen, and the water in the basin was connected to the free-flowing waters of the Stream of Eithan (*Yerushalmi Yoma* 3:8).

7. וַיַּעַשׂ אֶת־מְנֹרוֹת הַזָּהָב עֶשֶׂר — *He made the ten golden candelabra.* See *I Chronicles* 28:15 and comm. there.

כְּמִשְׁפָּטָם — *According to their pattern.* This word is used in the same sense as it is used in *Exodus* 26:30. Solomon's ten candelabra were made in the precise pattern that Moses' had been made (*Radak*).

חָמֵשׁ מִיָּמִין וְחָמֵשׁ מִשְּׂמֹאול — *Five to the right and five to the left. Menachos* 98b and 99a work out the precise arrangement. The verse cannot mean that the candelabra were to be placed on the right and left sides of the Sanctuary since Torah law requires that the candelabra be on the southern side and the tables on the northern side of the building. It follows that *right* and *left* means that they were ranged on either side of the candelabrum which Moses had made.

The Talmud discusses the exact disposition of the tables (see next verse) and we assume that the candelabra were arranged in the same way. The basis for the Talmud's discussion is that both tables and candelabra were limited to the inner half of the forty-cubit length of the Sanctuary and, as we saw before, to the northern and southern quarters respectively. Given a length of two cubits and a width of one cubit for each table (*Exodus* 25:23), it is obvious that the tables had to be arranged in two rows.

Figures 1 and 2 on the following page illustrate two arrangements, as suggested in the discussion in the Talmud.

8. וַיַּעַשׂ שֻׁלְחָנוֹת עֲשָׂרָה — *He made ten tables.* See *I Chronicles* 28:16 and comm. there.

וַיַּנַּח בַּהֵיכָל חֲמִשָּׁה מִיָּמִין וַחֲמִשָּׁה מִשְּׂמֹאול וַיַּעַשׂ מִזְרְקֵי
ט זָהָב מֵאָה׃ וַיַּעַשׂ חֲצַר הַכֹּהֲנִים וְהָעֲזָרָה הַגְּדוֹלָה
י וּדְלָתוֹת לָעֲזָרָה וְדַלְתוֹתֵיהֶם צִפָּה נְחֹשֶׁת׃ וְאֶת־הַיָּם נָתַן
יא מִכֶּתֶף הַיְמָנִית קֵדְמָה מִמּוּל נֶגְבָּה׃ וַיַּעַשׂ

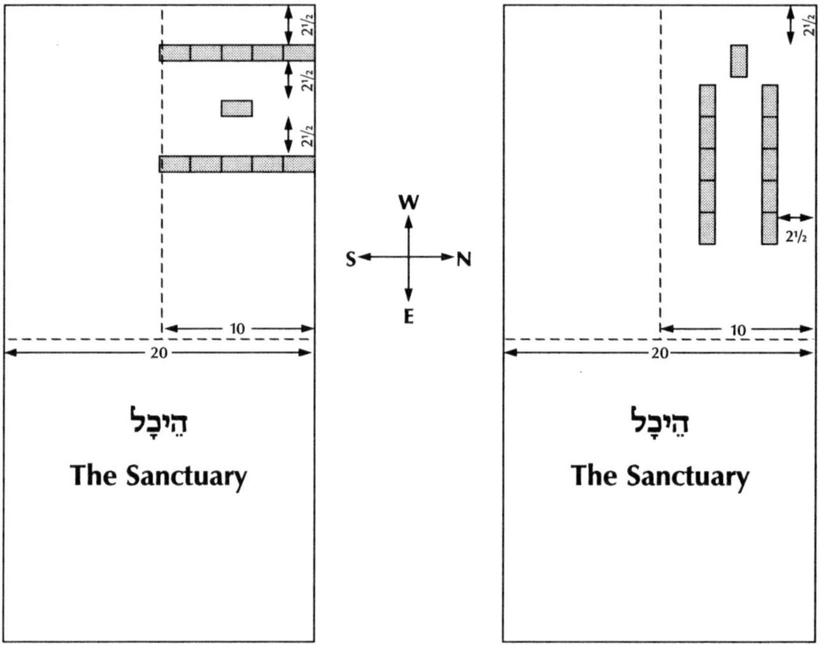

figure 1 **figure 2**

Figure 1: Two rows of tables, running north to south. Each table is two cubits long and one cubit wide. The two rows each protrude slightly into the southern quarter because it is impossible to contain ten cubits within a space of exactly ten cubits. Moses' table is centered between the two rows. The terms right and left are for one facing Moses' table from the southern quarter. Moses's table is removed 2½ cubits from northern wall.

Figure 2: The rows of tables are from east to west. There is a two and one half cubit passageway between the tables and the wall. Moses' table is all the way in the west. The descriptions, left and right are for one entering the sanctuary.

In contrast to the ten candelabra mentioned in the previous verse, these ten tables are not mentioned in *Kings*. There (7:48) it says only that *Solomon made ... the golden table upon which was the panim-bread. Radak* suggests that the singular *table* in *Kings* could be used to denote many tables, just as שׁוֹר and חֲמוֹר are used in *Genesis* 32:5 to denote many oxen and asses.

However, *Menachos* 99a takes the word literally to be a regular singular form, and derives from it that although Solomon made ten tables in addition to that of Moses, the *panim-bread* was placed only on that one.

[It is clear that although the Talmud refers to it as the table of Moses it does not mean the actual table which Moses had made — since the verse specifically says that Solomon made it. Rather the meaning must be that it replaced the table which Moses had made, and stood in its stead.]

An alternative suggestion could be as fol-

and placed [them] in the Sanctuary; five to the right and five to the left. He made one hundred golden tossing-bowls. [9] *He made the Court of the Kohanim and the great Azarah with doors for the Azarah. He covered their doors with copper.* [10] *He placed the basin on the right shoulder; eastward on the southern side.*

lows: It is clear from the Talmud that the ten candelabra and tables which Solomon made were in addition to the single ones which had always stood in the Tabernacle so that altogether, there were eleven of each. Now both in *Kings* and in *Chronicles* we hear of only ten candelabra being made. From this it seems clear that the original candelabrum was still in existence and thus Solomon had to make only the additional ten. However, the verse which says that Solomon made *the table* makes it clear that even the original table needed to be replaced, and it is the replacement of that table which is described in *Kings*.

In deference to the special sanctity of that one table — it was to replace the one that Moses had made — *Kings* makes no mention of the other ten. *Chronicles* fills in that gap in its account.

חֲמִשָּׁה מִיָּמִין וַחֲמִשָּׁה מִשְּׂמֹאול — *Five to the right and five to the left.* This does not mean to the right and left of the Sanctuary since the Torah requires that the table stand only in the north. Rather it means to the right and left of Moses' table (*Menachos* 98b). See elaboration and diagram in comm. to previous verse.

וַיַּעַשׂ מִזְרְקֵי זָהָב מֵאָה — *He made one hundred golden tossing-bowls*. זרק, *to throw* or *toss*, is used to describe the splattering of the sacrificial blood upon the altar (see *Exodus* 24:6). A מִזְרָק is a dish used in this process.

The manufacture of these dishes is mentioned in our verse in order that all vessels made out of gold might be mentioned together (*Radak*).

9. וַיַּעַשׂ חֲצַר הַכֹּהֲנִים — *He made the Court of the Kohanim.* The Temple building stood within an area which, in the Second Temple period, had a length of 137 cubits from east to west (*Midos* 2:6). The first 22 cubits to the east were divided into two sections, each with a width of 11 cubits. The more eastern of these was called the *Court of the Israelites*, the other, the *Court of the Kohanim*. This verse refers to the latter (*Mefaresh*).)[1]

וְהָעֲזָרָה הַגְּדוֹלָה — *And the great Azarah.* This is the *Court of the Israelites* (*Mefaresh, Radak, Metzudos, Malbim*).[2]

Why is this court — only eleven cubits in width — called the *Great Azarah*?[3]

Perhaps *great* does not refer to size, but is used as a qualitative description. [An analogy would be *Men of the Great Assembly*, or the *Great River*, used for the Euphrates because of its proximity to the Land of Israel.] The Temple Court was *great* because it was there that the highest levels of sanctity lay within each visitor's grasp (*R' Yitzchak Finkel*).

10. וְאֶת הַיָּם — *The basin*. See vs. 2-5 above.

מִכֶּתֶף הַיְמָנִית קֵדְמָה מִמּוּל נֶגְבָּה — *On the right shoulder; eastward on the southern side.* The prefix מ can denote position — see, for example, *Genesis* 1:7, and *Numbers* 21:1. From

1. We cannot know for certain whether the dimensions of the various courts were the same in Solomon's Temple as they were in the Second Temple, for which we have records in *Midos*. Thus, there is the possibility that the *Court of the Kohanim* which Solomon made was much larger than eleven cubits.

Certainly it seems justified to assume that this verse does not refer to only eleven cubits out of the huge area within which the Temple building stood. Why would the rest of the area not have been mentioned?

We may postulate that *Court of the Kohanim* in this verse means the entire area inward from the eastern beginning of the *Kohanite* Court.

2. In mishnaic Hebrew, *Azarah* is the common term for *Court*. We have left the word untranslated in order to retain the flavor of its original meaning, derived from עזר, *to help*: A place in which anyone may expect to find Divine *help* in answer to his prayers (*Radak* here and in *Sefer HaShorashim*).

3. According to *Midos* 2:5, there was a *Women's Court* measuring one hundred and thirty-five cubits by one hundred and thirty-five cubits to the east of the *Court of the Israelites.*

Such a huge area might well have been described as *great*.

Neither *Kings* nor *Chronicles* ever mentions such a court. However, there is at least a hint that it might have existed from *I Kings* 6:36 where there is a reference to an *Inner Court* — with the clear inference that there was another one toward the outside (see *Rashi* and *Gra* there).

Yet, the commentators make no suggestion that the *Great Court* in this verse might refer to the *Women's Court*.

ד
יב־יט

חוּרָם אֶת־הַסִּירוֹת וְאֶת־הַיָּעִים וְאֶת־הַמִּזְרָקוֹת וַיְכַל
°חִירָם לַעֲשׂוֹת אֶת־הַמְּלָאכָה אֲשֶׁר עָשָׂה לַמֶּלֶךְ שְׁלֹמֹה °חוּרָם ק׳
יב בְּבֵית הָאֱלֹהִים: עַמּוּדִים שְׁנַיִם וְהַגֻּלּוֹת וְהַכֹּתָרוֹת
עַל־רֹאשׁ הָעַמּוּדִים שְׁתָּיִם וְהַשְּׂבָכוֹת שְׁתַּיִם לְכַסּוֹת
אֶת־שְׁתֵּי גֻּלּוֹת הַכֹּתָרוֹת אֲשֶׁר עַל־רֹאשׁ הָעַמּוּדִים:
יג וְאֶת־הָרִמּוֹנִים אַרְבַּע מֵאוֹת לִשְׁתֵּי הַשְּׂבָכוֹת שְׁנַיִם טוּרִים
רִמּוֹנִים לַשְּׂבָכָה הָאֶחָת לְכַסּוֹת אֶת־שְׁתֵּי גֻּלּוֹת הַכֹּתָרוֹת
יד אֲשֶׁר עַל־פְּנֵי הָעַמּוּדִים: וְאֶת־הַמְּכֹנוֹת עָשָׂה וְאֶת־
טו הַכִּיֹּרוֹת עָשָׂה עַל־הַמְּכֹנוֹת: אֶת־הַיָּם אֶחָד וְאֶת־הַבָּקָר
טז שְׁנֵים־עָשָׂר תַּחְתָּיו: וְאֶת־הַסִּירוֹת וְאֶת־הַיָּעִים וְאֶת־
הַמִּזְלָגוֹת וְאֶת־כָּל־כְּלֵיהֶם עָשָׂה חוּרָם אָבִיו לַמֶּלֶךְ
יז שְׁלֹמֹה לְבֵית יְהוָה נְחֹשֶׁת מָרוּק: בְּכִכַּר הַיַּרְדֵּן יְצָקָם
יח הַמֶּלֶךְ בַּעֲבִי הָאֲדָמָה בֵּין סֻכּוֹת וּבֵין צְרֵדָתָה: וַיַּעַשׂ
שְׁלֹמֹה כָּל־הַכֵּלִים הָאֵלֶּה לָרֹב מְאֹד כִּי לֹא נֶחְקַר מִשְׁקַל
יט הַנְּחֹשֶׁת: וַיַּעַשׂ שְׁלֹמֹה אֵת כָּל־הַכֵּלִים אֲשֶׁר
בֵּית הָאֱלֹהִים וְאֵת מִזְבַּח הַזָּהָב וְאֶת־הַשֻּׁלְחָנוֹת וַעֲלֵיהֶם

an eastern orientation, the *right* shoulder would be south. The basin was placed in the southern half of the *Court of the Kohanim*, somewhat toward the east (*Metzudos*).

11. וַיַּעַשׂ חוּרָם — *Churam made* ... See comm. to 2:12-13.

אֶת־הַסִּירוֹת — *The receptacles. Kings* (7:40) has כִּירוֹת. *Rashi* writes that the two words have the same meaning and refer to the receptacles into which the ashes from the altar were swept by means of the *shovels*.

וְאֶת־הַיָּעִים — *The shovels*. The word occurs in *Exodus* 27:3 where *Targum* renders with גרף, *to sweep*. Thus the shovels were the means by which the ashes were swept off the altar (*Rashi* there).

וְאֶת־הַמִּזְרָקוֹת — *And the tossing-bowls*. See comm. to v. 8.

12. עַמּוּדִים שְׁנַיִם — *Two pillars*. See 3:15-17.

וְהַגֻּלּוֹת וְהַכֹּתָרוֹת — *The bowls of the cappings* ... The parallel verse in *I Kings* 7:41 has וְגֻלֹּת הַכֹּתָרֹת, which accords with the expression used at the end of our verse and wherever else it occurs. The translation of that phrase is as we have given it here — *the bowls of the cappings*, that is, the bowls which formed part of the cappings or crowning pieces. The crowning pieces of the pillars were formed from two bowls.

Given this, the ה, *hei*, in וְהַגֻּלּוֹת and the ו, *vav*, in וְהַכֹּתָרוֹת seem redundant. See *Ibn Janach's Sefer HaRikmah* 6 under ה and ו which states that both these letters occasionally occur without a discernible function [דְּחוּקָה in *Ibn Janach's* language].

וְהַשְּׂבָכוֹת — *Latticeworks*. The bowls which constituted the cappings of the two pillars were decorated with latticework. See v. 13.

13. וְאֶת־הָרִמּוֹנִים — *And the pomegranates*. The latticework which covered the cappings of the two pillars had decorative pomegranates worked into them.

עַל־פְּנֵי הָעַמּוּדִים — *Atop the pillars*. The translation follows *Metzudos*. פָּנִים describes the highest point of the pillars, just as the face is the highest point of the body.

14. וְאֶת־הַמְּכֹנוֹת עָשָׂה — *He made the stands*. In v. 6 we learned that Solomon made ten bowls. In accordance with *Exodus* 30:28 from which we see that the bowl in the Tabernacle was placed upon a stand, our verse teaches that each of those ten bowls had their own stand.

15. אֶת־הַיָּם אֶחָד — *The one basin*. See vs. 2-5 above.

4
11-19

[11] Churam made the receptacles, the shovels and the tossing-
bowls. Thus Churam brought the work which he had done for
Solomon in God's House to a conclusion: [12] Two pillars; the bowls
of the cappings for the top of the pillars — two; two latticeworks
to cover the two bowls of the cappings which were atop the
pillars. [13] And the pomegranates, four hundred for the two
latticeworks; two rows of pomegranates for one latticework to
cover the two bowls of the cappings which were atop the pillars.
[14] He made the stands; and he made the bowls upon the stands.
[15] The one basin and the twelve oxen beneath it. [16] The
receptacles, the shovels and the forks and all their utensils,
Churam, skilled as his father, made for the king for use in the
House of HASHEM, from polished copper. [17] The king cast them in
the Jordan Valley in the thickness of the earth between Succoth
and Tzereidasah. [18] Solomon made all these utensils in very great
quantities, for they had not ascertained the weight of the copper.
[19] Solomon made all the utensils which were for use in God's
Temple, and the golden altar and the tables, and upon them — the

16. וְאֶת־הַסִּירוֹת — *The receptacles ...* The receptacles and shovels had already been mentioned in v. 11; they are repeated here to let us know that they were made from polished copper (*Mefaresh, Metzudos*).

וְאֶת־הַמִּזְלָגוֹת — *And the forks.* The parallel verse in *I Kings* 7:45 has מִזְרָקוֹת, *tossing bowls*, as has our v. 11.

וְאֶת־כָּל־כְּלֵיהֶם — *And all their utensils. Their* refers to the Temple courts, meaning all the utensils required in the various parts of the Temple (*Metzudos*).

עָשָׂה חוּרָם אָבִיו — *Churam, skilled as his father, made. Metzudos* reads the phrase as though a כּ, *caf*, were placed before אָבִיו. *I Kings* 7:13 reports that the artisan's father had also been famous for his great skill.

נְחֹשֶׁת מָרוּק — *Polished copper. I Kings* 7:45 has נְחֹשֶׁת מְמֹרָט; the root מרט means *to smooth*. For example, it is used in *Isaiah* 50:6 to describe the act of pulling out hairs from the cheek — *smoothing* the cheek. Thus, we extend it also to the idea of polishing metal.

Our root מרק is used in 6:21 in the sense of a utensil being well-scoured. In our context, it would also carry the meaning of *polished*.

17. בְּכִכַּר הַיַּרְדֵּן — *In the Jordan Valley.* See *Genesis* 13:10-11. *Targum* renders כִּכַּר as מִישׁוֹר [from ישר, *straight*], *a plain*.

Malbim explains that the highly polished effect which was required for these utensils (v. 16) needed the particular soil of the Jordan Valley for the casting process. The other copper utensils were made in Jerusalem.

בַּעֲבִי הָאֲדָמָה — *In the thickness of the earth. Metzudos* thinks that the casting process took place in the ground. The molds for the various utensils were dug into the ground and the molten copper was poured into them. *Radak* understands *Targum* to say that a particularly high-quality red clay was used to fashion the moldings for the casting.

18. וַיַּעַשׂ שְׁלֹמֹה כָּל־הַכֵּלִים הָאֵלֶּה לָרֹב מְאֹד — *Solomon made all these utensils in very great quantities. I Kings* 7:47 has וַיַּנַּח שְׁלֹמֹה אֶת־כָּל־הַכֵּלִים מֵרֹב מְאֹד מְאֹד which means that *because* [מֵרֹב] of their great multitude, Solomon allowed the utensils to lie — either without weighing them [as per the end of the verse לֹא נֶחְקַר מִשְׁקַל הַנְּחֹשֶׁת] (*Rashi*), or in storage for future use (*Malbim*).

Perhaps our verse refers back to *I Chronicles* 22:3 where we learn that David amassed such vast quantities of copper that they were beyond weighing. The sense of our verse would be that because these vast amounts of copper were available, Solomon made many more utensils than were really required.

19. וְאֶת־הַשֻּׁלְחָנוֹת — *And the tables. I Kings* 7:48 has שֻׁלְחָן, in the singular, consistent with the fact that *Kings* does not make any mention

ד
כ־כב

כ לֶחֶם הַפָּנִים׃ וְאֶת־הַמְּנֹרוֹת וְנֵרֹתֵיהֶם לְבַעֲרָם כַּמִּשְׁפָּט
כא לִפְנֵי הַדְּבִיר זָהָב סָגוּר׃ וְהַפֶּרַח וְהַנֵּרוֹת וְהַמֶּלְקָחַיִם זָהָב
כב הוּא מִכְלוֹת זָהָב׃ וְהַמְזַמְּרוֹת וְהַמִּזְרָקוֹת וְהַכַּפּוֹת
וְהַמַּחְתּוֹת זָהָב סָגוּר וּפֶתַח הַבַּיִת דַּלְתוֹתָיו הַפְּנִימִיּוֹת
לְקֹדֶשׁ הַקֳּדָשִׁים וְדַלְתֵי הַבַּיִת לְהֵיכָל זָהָב׃

ה
א

א וַתִּשְׁלַם כָּל־הַמְּלָאכָה אֲשֶׁר־עָשָׂה שְׁלֹמֹה לְבֵית יְהוָה
וַיָּבֵא שְׁלֹמֹה אֶת־קָדְשֵׁי ׀ דָּוִיד אָבִיו וְאֶת־הַכֶּסֶף וְאֶת־הַזָּהָב

of the ten tables which Solomon made — see comm. to v. 8 above.

וַעֲלֵיהֶם לֶחֶם הַפָּנִים — *And upon them — the panim-bread*. In v. 8, we noted that although Solomon made ten additional tables, the *panim-bread* lay only upon that table which stood in the stead of the one Moses had made. Thus, our verse must be understood to mean only that the tables were available for the ordering of the bread — not that it was actually placed upon them.

20. וְאֶת־הַמְּנֹרוֹת — *And the candelabra*. See v. 7 and commentary there.

וְנֵרֹתֵיהֶם — *And their lamps.*
Menachos 98b discusses whether the lamps were beaten out of the same piece of gold as was the whole candelabrum or whether they were made separately, and then attached. *Mefaresh* points out that the separate mention of the lamps in our verse indicates that they were made separately. *Malbim* concurs and writes that he is unable to explain our verse according to the other opinion.

לִפְנֵי הַדְּבִיר — *Before the D'vir*. See comm. to 3:14 and 16 for the meaning of דְּבִיר as the Holy of Holies.

זָהָב סָגוּר — *Pure gold*. The meaning of סגר is *to close*. סָגוּר means *enclosed* and describes the enclosing of the gold in the furnace during the purifying process (*Metzudos*).
Yoma 29a explains differently. The gold used was of such high quality that when it appeared on the market, all the gold dealers whose merchandise was of lesser quality would close [סגר] their stores.

21. וְהַפֶּרַח — *And the flower*. The candelabrum of Moses was decorated by a flower motif (see *Exodus* 25:31-36) and these flowers are referred to here (*Metzudos*). *Mefaresh* explains that reference is to a single flower pattern which is not mentioned in *Exodus* but occurs in *Numbers* 8:4 as decorating the foot of the candelabrum.

Either way it is difficult to see the point of mentioning this flower pattern in this context. It was certainly made of the same piece of gold as the rest of the candelabrum and its separate mention seems redundant. *Malbim* suggests that it was mentioned as being representative of all the decoration of the candelabrum, none of which were required when it was made of material other than gold. It is mentioned to underscore the fact that Solomon's candelabrum was indeed made out of gold.

וְהַנֵּרוֹת — *And the lamps*. The lamps were already mentioned in the previous verse. Commentators do not explain why it was necessary to mention them again.

הוּא מִכְלוֹת זָהָב — *It was gold to perfection*. The word מִכְלוֹת is the construct form of מִכְלָה, deriving from כלה, *to be complete*, and not used anywhere else. Thus, it was a veritable perfection of gold — gold at its most pure (*Mefaresh*).
The singular הוּא argues for the fact that this is a descriptive phrase, having as its subject the *gold* mentioned in the previous verses rather than the candelabra which were made from it. However, explanations are offered which define it as describing the candelabra. Thus *Metzudos* explains: It [they] was [were] totally of gold. There was not the slightest impurity in the gold and thus every single portion of each candelabrum was made of gold.
The Sages in *Menachos* 29a also understand the phrase to describe all the candelabra. They *consumed totally* the gold which was available to Solomon. Each one was formed from a piece of gold weighing one thousand talents. This huge piece was fired one thousand times until it had been reduced to one talent. Only then were the candelabra formed from it.

22. וְהַמְזַמְּרוֹת — *The musical instruments*. *Rashi* and the commentators derive the word

4
20-22
panim-bread. [20] *And the candelabra, and their lamps to burn them as the law requires before the D'vir — pure gold.* [21] *And the flower and the lamps and the tongues — gold. It was gold to perfection.* [22] *The musical instruments and the tossing-bowls, the spoons and the fire-holders — pure gold. The entrance to the House, its inner doors to the Holy of Holies and the doors of the building which housed the Sanctuary — gold.*

5
1
All the work that Solomon had done for the House of HASHEM *was completed. Then Solomon brought all that David his father had consecrated, the silver and the gold*

from זמר, *to make music.*

וְהַמִּזְרָקוֹת — *And the tossing-bowls.* See comm. to v. 8.

וְהַמַּחְתּוֹת — *And the fire-holders.* The root חתה means *to snatch up [fire].*

זָהָב סָגוּר — *Pure gold.* See comm. to v. 20.

דַּלְתוֹתָיו הַפְּנִימִיּוֹת לְקֹדֶשׁ הַקֳּדָשִׁים וְדַלְתֵי הַבַּיִת לַהֵיכָל זָהָב — *Its inner doors to the Holy of Holies and the doors of the building which housed the Sanctuary — gold. Radak* points out that according to *I Kings* 6:32 and 34 these doors were made from wood. Our verse must mean that these wooden doors were *covered* with gold.

V

◆§ The Inauguration Begins

The next three chapters describe the inauguration of the Temple and parallels *I Kings* chs. 8 and 9. There are significant differences between the two accounts. The key to understanding the unique *Chronicles'* perspective is at 6:41-42 where Solomon concludes his inaugural prayer by invoking the merit of his father, David. This invocation is missing from the *Kings'* account.

Thus we may say that the spirit of David is a significant presence at the inauguration as presented by *Chronicles,* while the *Kings* account sees only Solomon. The comm. will note a number of instances in which *Chronicles* appears to intentionally excise Solomon's name from its account. More than as a king in his own right, he functions as David's son — and as David's vindicator.

The differences in emphasis between the two accounts are consistent with those which we traced at *I Chronicles* ch. 17. There, David had been refused permission to build the Temple, but had been told that his son Solomon would be granted that privilege. *Kings* had approached the matter from the perspective of the obligations of the monarchy, while *Chronicles* had dealt with the spiritual readiness of David, the man.

Each of the two books gives the account of the inauguration which follows naturally from the difference in perspective. In *Kings,* King Solomon celebrates the most significant accomplishment of his reign — the Temple has been built and the Divine Presence has come to rest among man. In *Chronicles,* Solomon son of David understands that his hands have wrought only that which David's heart had conceived. The building is Solomon's, but its soul is David's. [See further at Section II to *I Chronicles* ch. 17, p. 436, *Analysis . . .*]

1. וַתִּשְׁלַם כָּל־הַמְּלָאכָה אֲשֶׁר־עָשָׂה שְׁלֹמֹה — *All the work that Solomon had done ... was completed. Solomon* is the subject here, and not *King Solomon,* as in *I Kings* (7:51). The story is told from the perspective of the man, rather than as an account of the monarchy. See above.

וַיָּבֵא שְׁלֹמֹה אֶת־קָדְשֵׁי דָּוִיד אָבִיו — *Then Solomon brought all that David his father had consecrated.* In *I Chronicles* 22:14 and 29:2 ff. we learned of the vast amounts of material which David had prepared, for the day that the Temple would be built. Even after Solomon had used all that he needed, there was still much material left and this he now deposited in the Temple treasury (*Rashi*).

However, the Sages had a different tradition. All the material which David had amassed was deposited. Solomon used none of it. Two reasons are given for this opinion:

David's material had been won in war

ה
ב־ז

ב וְאֶת־כָּל־הַכֵּלִים נָתַן בְּאֹצְרוֹת בֵּית הָאֱלֹהִים׃ אָז
יַקְהִיל שְׁלֹמֹה אֶת־זִקְנֵי יִשְׂרָאֵל וְאֶת־כָּל־רָאשֵׁי הַמַּטּוֹת
נְשִׂיאֵי הָאָבוֹת לִבְנֵי יִשְׂרָאֵל אֶל־יְרוּשָׁלִָם לְהַעֲלוֹת
ג אֶת־אֲרוֹן בְּרִית־יהוָה מֵעִיר דָּוִיד הִיא צִיּוֹן׃ וַיִּקָּהֲלוּ
אֶל־הַמֶּלֶךְ כָּל־אִישׁ יִשְׂרָאֵל בֶּחָג הוּא הַחֹדֶשׁ הַשְּׁבִעִי׃
ד־ה וַיָּבֹאוּ כֹּל זִקְנֵי יִשְׂרָאֵל וַיִּשְׂאוּ הַלְוִיִּם אֶת־הָאָרוֹן׃ וַיַּעֲלוּ
אֶת־הָאָרוֹן וְאֶת־אֹהֶל מוֹעֵד וְאֶת־כָּל־כְּלֵי הַקֹּדֶשׁ אֲשֶׁר
ו בָּאֹהֶל הֶעֱלוּ אֹתָם הַכֹּהֲנִים הַלְוִיִּם׃ וְהַמֶּלֶךְ שְׁלֹמֹה
וְכָל־עֲדַת יִשְׂרָאֵל הַנּוֹעָדִים עָלָיו לִפְנֵי הָאָרוֹן מְזַבְּחִים
ז צֹאן וּבָקָר אֲשֶׁר לֹא־יִסָּפְרוּ וְלֹא יִמָּנוּ מֵרֹב׃ וַיָּבִיאוּ
הַכֹּהֲנִים אֶת־אֲרוֹן בְּרִית־יהוָה אֶל־מְקוֹמוֹ אֶל־דְּבִיר
הַבַּיִת אֶל־קֹדֶשׁ הַקֳּדָשִׁים אֶל־תַּחַת כַּנְפֵי הַכְּרוּבִים׃

against the idolatrous nations. Solomon knew that one day his Temple would be destroyed and was afraid that in gentile eyes this would be seen as a vindication of their idols. They would be perceived as avenging David's plunder by destroying the Temple that was built with its fruits.

Alternatively, it is suggested that Solomon thought David's treasures to be tainted. Three dreadful years of famine marked the end of David's reign (see *II Samuel* ch. 21). Solomon felt that when so many people were going hungry, it was morally wrong to keep such wealth from the poor. It should have been made available to those who needed it. Under the circumstances he did not want to use this wealth for the Temple.

וְאֶת־הַכֶּסֶף . . . — *The silver* . . . This phrase is appositional to . . . *that David his father had consecrated*. The ו, *vav*, is therefore redundant and is to be eliminated from the translation (*Metzudos*).

2. אֶת־זִקְנֵי יִשְׂרָאֵל — *The elders of Israel*. These are the judges — the *Sanhedrin* (*Metzudos*). The presence of the Sanhedrin is a halachic requirement at the inauguration of the Temple (*Shavuos* 15a).

וְאֶת־כָּל־רָאשֵׁי הַמַּטּוֹת נְשִׂיאֵי הָאָבוֹת — *And all the heads of the tribes, the princes of the fathers' [houses]*. These came as a mark of respect to the king and the Ark.

אֶל־יְרוּשָׁלָםִ — *To Jerusalem*. *Kings* has . . . *to King Solomon in Jerusalem*. The omission of Solomon's name here is a mark of *Chronicles'* perspective of the story. See prefatory remarks to this chapter.

לְהַעֲלוֹת אֶת־אֲרוֹן בְּרִית־ה׳ — *To bring up the Ark of the Covenant of* HASHEM . . . At the beginning of his reign, David had brought the Ark from the home of Oved Edom and housed it in a tent in the *City of David* (*I Chronicles* 15:25-16:1). Now that the Temple was completed it could be brought to its final resting place.

3. וַיִּקָּהֲלוּ אֶל־הַמֶּלֶךְ — . . . *Assembled before the king*. The *Kings'* account has *King Solomon*. Once more *Chronicles* omits Solomon's name. See comm. to previous verse and pref. remarks.

בֶּחָג — *On the festival*. This is the festival of Succos (*Mefaresh*). Actually, the inauguration took place a full seven days before Succos (see 7:9) and the phrase *on the festival* must be taken as an approximation.

הוּא הַחֹדֶשׁ הַשְּׁבִעִי — *That is the seventh month*. In the context of our verse this phrase is difficult. In the *Kings'* account the entire phrase reads: . . . *in the month of Eithanim, on the festival, that is the seventh month*. The phrase *that is the seventh month* is an explanation of *the month of Eithanim*. The usage is analogous with בְּחֹדֶשׁ זִו הוּא הַחֹדֶשׁ הַשֵּׁנִי, *in the month of Ziv, that is the second month* (*I Kings* 6:1), and with בְּיֶרַח בּוּל הוּא הַחֹדֶשׁ הַשְּׁמִינִי, *the month of Bul, that is the eighth month* (*I Kings* 6:38). In the *Chronicles'* version in which . . . *in the month of Eithanim* does not appear, the phrase *that is the seventh month* has nothing to describe.

4. וַיִּשְׂאוּ הַלְוִיִּם אֶת־הָאָרוֹן — *Then the Levites lifted up the Ark*. *Kings* has *the Kohanim*.

5
2-7

and all the utensils. He placed them in treasuries of God's
House. 2 *Then Solomon assembled the elders of Israel and all the*
heads of the tribes, the princes of the fathers' [houses] of the
Children of Israel, to Jerusalem; to bring up the Ark of the
Covenant of HASHEM *from the City of David, that is Zion.* 3 *All*
the men of Israel assembled before the king on the festival, that
is the seventh month. 4 *All the elders of Israel came. Then the*
Levites lifted up the Ark. 5 *They brought up the Ark and the*
Tabernacle and all the sacred utensils which were in the tent.
The Kohanim, the Levites brought them up. 6 *King Solomon and*
all the congregation of Israel who had specially joined him
in front of the Ark sacrificed sheep and cattle, too abundant
to be counted or numbered. 7 *The Kohanim brought the Ark*
of the Covenant of HASHEM *to its place; to the D'vir of the*
Temple to the Holy of Holies, beneath the wings of the cheruvim.

This is one of the twenty-four places in which *Kohanim* are called Levites (*Radak*).

Malbim suggests that the two versions could be reconciled differently. Our v. 7 says clearly that it was the *Kohanim* who brought the Ark *to its place*. This would be the Holy of Holies. Thus, it is possible that the Levites carried the Ark from the City of David up to the Temple. This is the subject of the *Chronicles'* version. The transfer to the Holy of Holies, however, required *Kohanim* since no Levites were permitted there. This is what is meant in the *Kings'* account.

See also comm. to *I Chronicles* 15:2.

5. וַיַּעֲלוּ אֶת־הָאָרוֹן וְאֶת־אֹהֶל מוֹעֵד — *They brought up the Ark and the Tabernacle...* The Ark was brought up from the City of David to be lodged in the Holy of Holies; the Tabernacle was brought from Giveon to be stored in the Temple vaults (*Radak* and *Metzudos*).

וְאֶת־כָּל־כְּלֵי הַקֹּדֶשׁ אֲשֶׁר בָּאֹהֶל — *And all the sacred utensils which were in the tent.* The identification of the holy utensils depends on which tent is meant. *Rashi* in *Kings* and *Mefaresh* here think that it is the tent which David had erected to house the Ark (*I Chronicles* 16:1). Since no service is associated with the Ark, it is not clear which utensils these were. Perhaps they were used in connection with sacrifices brought upon the *bamah* which was located there (see 1:13).

Malbim and *R' Yitzchak Isaac HaLevi* in *Tekufas HaMikra* assume that *tent* refers to the Tabernacle, and the utensils are those which had been used in the daily service at Giveon.

הַכֹּהֲנִים הַלְוִיִּם — *The Kohanim, the Levites. Mefaresh* sees this formulation as confirmation that the *Levites* of the previous verse were really *Kohanim*. However, *Radak* points out that the *Kings* version has *the Kohanim and the Levites*. Accordingly, he thinks that two separate groups are meant. The *Kohanim* carried the Ark and the Levites, the Tabernacle.

6. לִפְנֵי הָאָרוֹן — *In front of the Ark.* The meaning is, '[to walk] *in front of the Ark'* (*Metzudos*). The congregation of Israel came to accompany the Ark to its place.

Kings inserts the words *with him*, thus creating a slightly different division of the words: *All the congregation of Israel who had specially joined him were with him in front of the Ark*. This, in contrast to the verse here which has just the phrase: ... *who had specially joined him in front of the Ark*.

In the *Kings'* version, Solomon is central to the proceedings. The people who had come were now *with him*. The celebration is really his, they are subsidiary to him. The *Chronicles'* version, entirely consistent with what we have seen in the previous verses, deemphasizes this centrality; Solomon blends into the crowd.

7. וַיָּבִיאוּ הַכֹּהֲנִים — *The Kohanim brought*. See comm. to v. 4 for *Malbim's* remarks.

אֶל־תַּחַת כַּנְפֵי הַכְּרוּבִים — *Beneath the wings of the cheruvim*. See comm. to 3:11 for the positioning of the *cheruvim*. The Ark was placed beneath the wings which met in the center of the Holy of Holies.

ח וַיִּהְיוּ הַכְּרוּבִים פֹּרְשִׂים כְּנָפַיִם עַל־מְקוֹם הָאָרוֹן וַיְכַסּוּ
ט הַכְּרוּבִים עַל־הָאָרוֹן וְעַל־בַּדָּיו מִלְמָעְלָה: וַיַּאֲרִיכוּ
הַבַּדִּים וַיֵּרָאוּ רָאשֵׁי הַבַּדִּים מִן־הָאָרוֹן עַל־פְּנֵי הַדְּבִיר
י וְלֹא יֵרָאוּ הַחוּצָה וַיְהִי־שָׁם עַד הַיּוֹם הַזֶּה: אֵין בָּאָרוֹן
רַק שְׁנֵי הַלֻּחוֹת אֲשֶׁר־נָתַן מֹשֶׁה בְּחֹרֵב אֲשֶׁר כָּרַת יהוה
יא עִם־בְּנֵי יִשְׂרָאֵל בְּצֵאתָם מִמִּצְרָיִם: וַיְהִי בְּצֵאת
הַכֹּהֲנִים מִן־הַקֹּדֶשׁ כִּי כָּל־הַכֹּהֲנִים הַנִּמְצְאִים הִתְקַדָּשׁוּ
יב אֵין לִשְׁמוֹר לְמַחְלְקוֹת: וְהַלְוִיִּם הַמְשֹׁרְרִים לְכֻלָּם לְאָסָף

8. וַיִּהְיוּ ... וַיְכַסּוּ הַכְּרוּבִים — *... thus ... [the cheruvim] provided a canopy ...* The translation follows *Mefaresh* who introduces, *thus ...* into his rendering.

וְעַל־בַּדָּיו — *And over its poles.* Since the poles extended far beyond the Ark, all the way to the eastern extremity of the Holy of Holies, the wings cannot have covered the entire length of the poles. Our phrase means that they covered part of the poles (*Rashi*). *Radak* thinks that perhaps the wings of the *cheruvim* were broad enough to cover the entire length of the poles.

9. וַיַּאֲרִיכוּ הַבַּדִּים — *The poles were elongated.* As the end of the verse explains, the poles extended eastward so that they pushed against the curtain (3:14) and were thus visible in the Sanctuary as two protrusions in the curtain. The commentators ask how this is possible. The Holy of Holies in the Tabernacle was only ten by ten cubits. If the poles had fitted snugly into that space, then why in Solomon's Temple in which the Holy of Holies was twenty by twenty, would they have extended so far?

Three possibilities are suggested: New, longer poles may have been specially made for Solomon's Temple (*Radak* and *Ralbag*); the original poles were purposefully lengthened in order to reflect the new dimensions (*Mefaresh*); or, the poles which, in the Tabernacle had protruded both to the east and to the west, were now moved forward so that their entire length protruded to the east (*Radak*).

וַיֵּרָאוּ רָאשֵׁי הַבַּדִּים ... וְלֹא יֵרָאוּ — *So that the front of [the Ark's] poles were visible ... but they could not be seen [from the outside].* In the center of the wall dividing the Sanctuary from the Holy of Holies, there was an entrance which was covered by a curtain. The poles pushed against this curtain and thus caused it to protrude outward *like a woman's breasts*.[1] However, no holes were made in the curtain to actually allow the poles to run through, and therefore, they themselves could not be seen from outside (*Radak* and *Metzudos*).

עַד הַיּוֹם הַזֶּה — *Until this day.* This was in effect until the Ark was hidden during the reign of King Yoshiahu (*Metzudos*).

10. אֵין בָּאָרוֹן רַק שְׁנֵי הַלֻּחוֹת — *There was nothing in the Ark besides the two tablets...* In the view of the Sages, the use of the double negative [אֵין ... רַק] implies a positive. In fact, there was something in the Ark besides the tablets. This was either the *Sefer Torah* which Moses had written or, if that lay at the side of the Ark but not in it as implied by *Deuteronomy* 31:26, it was the shards of the first set of tablets which Moses had broken when Israel served the Golden Calf (*Bava Basra* 14a). *Berachos* 8b assumes that the shards did, in fact, lie in the Ark and *Targum*, both here and in the parallel verse in *Kings*, reads that reference into our verse. See fn. below.

אֲשֶׁר־נָתַן מֹשֶׁה בְּחֹרֵב — *Which Moses had placed there at Chorev.* The word *there* is to be inserted (*Targum*). This brings our verse in line with the *Kings* reading.

אֲשֶׁר כָּרַת ה׳ עִם־בְּנֵי יִשְׂרָאֵל ... — *Which* HASHEM *made with the Children of Israel ...* Clearly, reference is to the covenant which God had made with Israel at Sinai. See fn. for a discussion of why this is implied rather than stated.[2]

1. The Torah which resides in the Ark provides spiritual sustenance to the people, just as the mother's breasts provide for the infant's physical needs (*Malbim*).

2. In the absence of a specific mention of the covenant, the sentence lacks inner logic. The phrase *which* HASHEM *made* has no object. Furthermore, the inclusion of the entire sentence at this point in the narrative

5
8-12

[8] *The cheruvim spread their wings over the Ark's position, thus the cheruvim provided a canopy over the Ark and over its poles from above.* [9] *The poles were elongated so that the front of the Ark's poles were visible upon the face of the D'vir, but they could not be seen from outside. There it remains until this day.* [10] *There was nothing in the Ark besides the two tablets which Moses had placed there at Chorev, which* HASHEM *had made with the Children of Israel when they went out of Egypt.* [11] *When the Kohanim left the Sanctuary, all the Kohanim who were there had consecrated themselves; the duties were not performed by division.* [12] *The Levites, all of whom were choristers; Asaph, Heman and*

11. וַיְהִי בְּצֵאת הַכֹּהֲנִים מִן־הַקֹּדֶשׁ — *When the Kohanim left the Sanctuary* ... From *I Kings* 8:10, it is clear that the *Kohanim* left the Sanctuary because of the *anan*, cloud, which filled it when the Ark entered. In *Chronicles* this is told at v. 13.

כִּי כָּל־הַכֹּהֲנִים הַנִּמְצְאִים הִתְקַדָּשׁוּ — *All the Kohanim who were there had consecrated themselves.* The *Kohanim* had been divided into twenty-four divisions, each to serve in their own particular week (see *I Chronicles*, ch. 24). However, on the occasion of the dedication of the Temple, so many sacrifices were brought that the division which was formally on duty at that time could not have handled them. Consequently, all the *Kohanim* who were in Jerusalem at the time joined in the Divine service and purified themselves for that purpose (*Radak* and *Metzudos*)

Kings omits this information, there being no parallel therein for *I Chronicles* ch. 24, which teaches about the division into *Kohanite* groupings. This will also explain the omission of the next two verses from *Kings*. They deal with the Levite musicians identified in *I Chronicles* ch. 23.

הִתְקַדָּשׁוּ — *Consecrated themselves*. They made sure that they were ritually clean (*Metzudos*).

אֵין לִשְׁמוֹר לְמַחְלְקוֹת — *The duties were not performed by division*. The meaning is as explained above. Because of the overwhelming number of sacrifices, the formal breakdown into divisions was not operative. All the *Kohanim* served.

requires explanation. Why is a statement concerning the contents of the Ark, which were surely known, appropriate here?

We may surmise as follows:

We learned in the comm. to the beginning of this verse that the double negative was used to teach that, in fact, the Ark contained the shards of the original tablets which had been broken. That this lesson is taught by means of a double negative rather than by a more direct reference is significant. An implication of *inclusion* produced by a double term of *exclusion* implies a degree of hesitancy and inappropriateness (see *Pachad Yitzchak, Shavuos* 41:10). It is a suggestion that the included object really ought not to be there. It is to be included not because it truly belongs, but in spite of the fact that it really does not belong.

The fact that the shards were retained and not discarded is infinitely significant. Israel is reminded of a glorious past which is a harbinger of an attainable future, a potential which Israel will ultimately be capable of.

Perhaps that is why this verse is part of the narrative. It is not because of the tablets which were in it — a fact which was known — but because of the shards of which we only learn within this context. The moment at which the Ark is brought to its final resting place is an appropriate time to tell of a matter of underlying importance within it. Solomon's reign, and most certainly the establishment of the Temple which was the most significant accomplishment of that reign, was to be a precursor of a future in which the immeasurably greater sanctity of the original tablets would once more be in place.

It is perhaps for this reason that there is no specific mention of the covenant in our verse in spite of, or perhaps because of, the syntactical which this poses.

God's covenant had originally been made in connection with the first tablets. This covenant had been abrogated when Israel served the Golden Calf and the tablets were destroyed. Subsequently, a new covenant was made for the second tablets (see *Ramban, Leviticus* 25:1). If our verse had explicated *covenant* it would surely have had to be read as referring to that second, less exalted covenant. Left out, and only indicated, it can surely hint at that still greater covenant, the re-establishment of that which still lies in the future.

ה / יג־יד

לְהֵימָ֣ן לִֽידֻתוּן֮ וְלִבְנֵיהֶ֣ם וְלַאֲחֵיהֶם֒ מְלֻבָּשִׁ֣ים בּ֗וּץ
בִּמְצִלְתַּ֜יִם וּבִנְבָלִ֣ים וְכִנֹּר֔וֹת עֹמְדִ֖ים מִזְרָ֣ח לַמִּזְבֵּ֑חַ
וְעִמָּהֶ֤ם כֹּֽהֲנִים֙ לְמֵאָ֣ה וְעֶשְׂרִ֔ים °מחצררים בַּחֲצֹצְרֽוֹת׃ °מַחְצְרִ֥ים ק׳
יג וַיְהִ֣י כְאֶחָ֡ד °למחצצרים וְלַֽמְשֹׁרְרִ֜ים לְהַשְׁמִ֨יעַ קוֹל־ °לַמְחַצְּרִ֣ים ק׳
אֶחָ֗ד לְהַלֵּ֣ל וּלְהֹדוֹת֮ לַיהוָה֒ וּכְהָרִ֣ים ק֡וֹל בַּחֲצֹצְר֣וֹת
וּבִמְצִלְתַּ֩יִם֩ וּבִכְלֵ֨י הַשִּׁ֜יר וּבְהַלֵּ֤ל לַֽיהוָה֙ כִּ֣י ט֔וֹב כִּ֥י
יד לְעוֹלָ֖ם חַסְדּ֑וֹ וְהַבַּ֛יִת מָלֵ֥א עָנָ֖ן בֵּ֥ית יְהוָֽה׃ וְלֹא־יָכְל֧וּ
הַכֹּהֲנִ֛ים לַעֲמ֥וֹד לְשָׁרֵ֖ת מִפְּנֵ֣י הֶעָנָ֑ן כִּֽי־מָלֵ֥א כְבוֹד־
א יְהוָ֖ה אֶת־בֵּ֥ית הָאֱלֹהִֽים׃ אָ֖ז אָמַ֣ר שְׁלֹמֹ֑ה

ו / א־ג

ב יְהוָה֙ אָמַ֔ר לִשְׁכּ֖וֹן בָּעֲרָפֶֽל׃ וַאֲנִ֛י בָּנִ֥יתִי בֵית־זְבֻ֖ל לָ֑ךְ
ג וּמָכ֥וֹן לְשִׁבְתְּךָ֖ עוֹלָמִֽים׃ וַיַּסֵּ֤ב הַמֶּ֙לֶךְ֙ אֶת־פָּנָ֔יו וַיְבָ֕רֶךְ
אֵ֖ת כָּל־קְהַ֣ל יִשְׂרָאֵ֑ל וְכָל־קְהַ֥ל יִשְׂרָאֵ֖ל עוֹמֵֽד׃

12. לְכֻלָּם לְאָסָף לְהֵימָן לִידֻתוּן — *All of whom were choristers; Asaph, Heman and Yeduthun*. These Levite choristers had previously served at different locations [see *I Chronicles* 16:37 ff.]. For the inauguration they all served together.

For similar use of the prefix *lamed*, see *I Chronicles* 22:16 and *Ezra* 1:11.

13. וַיְהִי כְאֶחָד — *There was unison*. All made music together so that the various voices and the instrumental music were heard as a single sound (*Metzudos*), in perfect harmony with one another (*Ralbag*).

לְהַשְׁמִיעַ קוֹל־אֶחָד — *Producing music as with one voice* . . . This phrase is in apposition to the וַיְהִי כְאֶחָד at the beginning of the verse. They were in perfect unison and that unison expressed itself in that they sang God's praises as with one voice (*Mefaresh*).

וּבְהַלֵּל לַה׳ כִּי טוֹב כִּי לְעוֹלָם חַסְדּוֹ — *And as* HASHEM *was extolled, '. . . for He is good, His kindness endures forever'*. The translation follows *Metzudos*. The phrase . . . *for He is good, His kindness endures forever* is a quote from *Psalms* 136 known as הַלֵּל הַגָּדוֹל, *the Great Hallel*.

וְהַבַּיִת מָלֵא — *Then the House was full*. When the *Kohanim* left the Holy of Holies and the singing began, the *anan*, cloud, filled the Temple (*Metzudos*).

עָנָן בֵּית ה׳ — *The anan of the abode of* HASHEM. עָנָן is a *cloud*. We have chosen not to translate the word as a more reverent way of dealing with a mystery of the Divine Presence of which we cannot really have any meaningful idea. See below to 6:1.

Metzudos treats this phrase as a composite noun. It is the *anan* known to us to be associated with the Temple of HASHEM. Presumably, reference is to the *anan* — mark of HASHEM's presence — mentioned in *Exodus* 40:34 ff. (see comm. to 6:1).

Targum adds the word אֲמִטְתָא, that is, *the dark anan of the House of* HASHEM.

14. וְלֹא־יָכְלוּ הַכֹּהֲנִים — *The Kohanim were not able* . . . The thought is reminiscent of *Exodus* 40:35 where Moses was not able to enter the Tabernacle because of the cloud that rested upon it.

מִפְּנֵי הֶעָנָן — *Because of the anan*. This was because of the darkness of the cloud (*Metzudos*).

כְּבוֹד־ה׳ — *The glory of* HASHEM.

That is the same as the *anan* mentioned above (*Metzudos*).

VI

☙ The Inaugural Prayer

This chapter, which contains Solomon's inaugural prayer, parallels *I Kings* 8:12 ff. There are some differences, and these will be noted in the comm.

1. אָז — *Then*. At the time when the *anan* filled the Temple, and Solomon saw that all he had hoped for had come to pass.

ה׳ אָמַר לִשְׁכּוֹן בָּעֲרָפֶל — *It is* HASHEM*'s desire . . . to come to rest within the araphel*. We have left *araphel*, which implies *darkness*, untrans-

5
13-14

Yeduthun, their sons and their brothers, clothed in linen, equipped with mitzaltayim, nevalim and kinoros, stood east of the altar. With them were one hundred and twenty Kohanim blowing chatzotzros. [13] *There was unison among the trumpeters and the musicians; producing music as with one voice, extolling and praising HASHEM. As the sound of the trumpets and the mitzaltayim and the musical instruments grew, and as HASHEM was extolled,...'for He is good, His kindness endures forever', then the House was full of the anan of the abode of HASHEM.* [14] *The Kohanim were not able to stand and to serve, because of the anan; for the glory of HASHEM filled the House of God.*

6
1-3

Then Solomon said, 'It is HASHEM's desire to come to rest within the araphel. [2] *As for me, I have built a habitation for You, a firmly grounded home wherein You may dwell for all eternity'.* [3] *The king turned his face and blessed the whole congregation of Israel. The whole congregation of Israel was standing.*

lated. See comm. to 5:13. From the context, we would judge that this *araphel* is identical with the *anan* of the previous chapter. This *araphel* is also known to us from *Exodus* 20:18 where it appears as the darkness which Moses could approach but not penetrate at Sinai. This same *araphel* seems now to be residing within the Temple (*Shemos Rabbah* 33:4).

The implication from this is that the presence of God, manifest in some form of deep darkness, was within the Holy of Holies. To *Hirsch's* objection that *Exodus* 40:34-35 implies that the *anan* was over, not within, the Tabernacle, *R' Dovid Tzvi Hoffman* replies that both may well have been true. There was a lesser darkness over the Tabernacle as an indication of the Divine Presence within. At the locus of the *Shechinah*, in the Holy of Holies, there was a much denser darkness — the *araphel* mentioned here.

2. וַאֲנִי בָּנִיתִי — *As for me, I have built ...* The emphasis implied in the phrase *As for me* is missing in *Kings*, where the opening words are simply *I have built ...*

The different wording reflects the perspectives of the two books. From the *Samuel-Kings'* perspective, there is no particular significance in the fact that it was Solomon who finally built the Temple. It is incidental that in his reign the halachic requirements were fulfilled. This is not the case in the *Chronicles'* account. Solomon is overwhelmed by the implications of the fact that he — David's son — has been chosen. At last his father has been vindicated. See prefatory remarks to ch. 5.

בֵּית־זְבֻל — *A habitation.* R' Dovid Tzvi Hoffman notes that זְבֻל is used only to describe either God's dwelling in the heavens, or the Temple. Accordingly, it is no ordinary abode, but a habitation of a particularly exalted nature.

וּמָכוֹן לְשִׁבְתְּךָ עוֹלָמִים — *A firmly grounded home wherein You may dwell for all eternity.* מָכוֹן stems from כון and implies *the creation of a means toward a given end*; hence, a home wherein one might find welcome (*Hirsch* to *Exodus* 15:17).

Now that the Temple was built it would be God's eternal resting place. No other site would ever be chosen for the Temple and henceforth *bamos*, the *private altars* which had been permitted until now, would be forbidden (*Mefaresh* and commentators).

3. וַיַּסֵּב הַמֶּלֶךְ אֶת־פָּנָיו — *The king turned his face.* He turned towards the people (*Metzudos*).

וַיְבָרֶךְ אֵת כָּל־קְהַל יִשְׂרָאֵל — *And blessed the whole congregation of Israel.* The text of this blessing is not given.

Metzudos suggests that the blessing recorded in *I Kings* 8:55 ff. at the end of Solomon's long prayer quoted here, is meant; although that blessing is not recorded in *Chronicles*. See fn. to Section II, *The Temple or the People*.

וְכָל־קְהַל יִשְׂרָאֵל עוֹמֵד — *The whole congregation of Israel was standing.* Only kings from the Davidic line were allowed to sit in the

ו
ד־יא

ד וַיֹּאמֶר בָּרוּךְ יהוה אֱלֹהֵי יִשְׂרָאֵל אֲשֶׁר דִּבֶּר בְּפִיו אֵת
ה דָּוִיד אָבִי וּבְיָדָיו מִלֵּא לֵאמֹר: מִן־הַיּוֹם אֲשֶׁר הוֹצֵאתִי
אֶת־עַמִּי מֵאֶרֶץ מִצְרַיִם לֹא־בָחַרְתִּי בְעִיר מִכֹּל שִׁבְטֵי
יִשְׂרָאֵל לִבְנוֹת בַּיִת לִהְיוֹת שְׁמִי שָׁם וְלֹא־בָחַרְתִּי בְאִישׁ
ו לִהְיוֹת נָגִיד עַל־עַמִּי יִשְׂרָאֵל: וָאֶבְחַר בִּירוּשָׁלַםִ לִהְיוֹת
ז שְׁמִי שָׁם וָאֶבְחַר בְּדָוִיד לִהְיוֹת עַל־עַמִּי יִשְׂרָאֵל: וַיְהִי
עִם־לְבַב דָּוִיד אָבִי לִבְנוֹת בַּיִת לְשֵׁם יהוה אֱלֹהֵי
ח יִשְׂרָאֵל: וַיֹּאמֶר יהוה אֶל־דָּוִיד אָבִי יַעַן אֲשֶׁר הָיָה
עִם־לְבָבְךָ לִבְנוֹת בַּיִת לִשְׁמִי הֱטִיבוֹתָ כִּי הָיָה עִם־לְבָבֶךָ:
ט רַק אַתָּה לֹא תִבְנֶה הַבָּיִת כִּי בִנְךָ הַיּוֹצֵא מֵחֲלָצֶיךָ
י הוּא־יִבְנֶה הַבַּיִת לִשְׁמִי: וַיָּקֶם יהוה אֶת־דְּבָרוֹ אֲשֶׁר דִּבֵּר
וָאָקוּם תַּחַת דָּוִיד אָבִי וָאֵשֵׁב ׀ עַל־כִּסֵּא יִשְׂרָאֵל כַּאֲשֶׁר
דִּבֶּר יהוה וָאֶבְנֶה הַבַּיִת לְשֵׁם יהוה אֱלֹהֵי יִשְׂרָאֵל:
יא וָאָשִׂים שָׁם אֶת־הָאָרוֹן אֲשֶׁר־שָׁם בְּרִית יהוה אֲשֶׁר כָּרַת

Temple courtyard (*Metzudos*).

4. בָּרוּךְ ה׳ — *Praised be HASHEM*. בָּרוּךְ, when used in relation to God, is to be rendered *praised* (*Radak, Sefer HaShorashim*).

אֲשֶׁר דִּבֶּר בְּפִיו — *Who spoke directly*. This is probably the meaning of the anthropomorphism, *His mouth*. It would be analogous with *Numbers* 12:8 or with *Genesis* 45:12.

וּבְיָדָיו מִלֵּא — *And graciously* ... Again, an anthropomorphism. *Ibn Janach* (*Sefer HaShorashim*), based on *Nehemiah* 2:8, assigns *grace* as one of many meanings. We have chosen this meaning here because it fits well into the context.

5. לֹא־בָחַרְתִּי בְעִיר — *I chose no city*. *Deuteronomy* 12:5 speaks of a place which God will *choose* from among Israel's tribes so that His Presence might rest there. That choice eventually fell upon Jerusalem and was conveyed to David at Aravnah's threshing floor (*I Chronicles* 21:28 - 22:1). The previous locations at which the Tabernacle stood — Shiloh, Nov and Giveon — had not been chosen by God (*Radak*).

וְלֹא־בָחַרְתִּי בְאִישׁ — *Nor chose a man*. *I Chronicles* 28:4 describes David's designation as king as being part of the *choice* by which God had set aside the tribe of Judah as the tribe from which the monarchy would spring. Saul, from Benjamin, was not *chosen*, and his kingship was only a temporary one (see *Ramban* to *Genesis* 49:10).

נָגִיד — *Prince*. See *I Chronicles* 11:2 for a discussion of this term.

7. וַיְהִי עִם־לְבַב דָּוִיד אָבִי — *My father David intended*. This expression is used in *I Chronicles* 22:7 to describe David's intention.

8. יַעַן אֲשֶׁר הָיָה עִם־לְבָבְךָ — *Because you intended ... Because* ... does not flow smoothly into the second phrase, ... *you did well*.

Perhaps the two parts of the sentence are not to be taken together. The first phrase would be analogous to *Genesis* 4:15, *Therefore whoever kills Cain...*, where the threat is left hanging and no punishment is explicated. Here too, the reward for David's good intention is, as it were, left to the imagination. Perhaps such a formulation is used to convey the idea of limitless punishment or reward. It is too great to lend itself to description. The second phrase is then independent of the first.

הֱטִיבוֹתָ כִּי הָיָה עִם־לְבָבֶךָ — *You did well in that which you intended*. Your inspiration made it possible for you to make the vast preparations for the Temple's construction and administration, which are recounted at the end of *I Chronicles* (*Metzudos*).

9. כִּי בִנְךָ הַיּוֹצֵא מֵחֲלָצֶיךָ — *But your son who comes out from your loins*. This wording combines the expression used in *I Chronicles* 17:11, אֲשֶׁר יִהְיֶה מִבָּנֶיךָ, *who shall be from among your sons*, with that used in the parallel verse in *II Samuel* 7:12, אֲשֶׁר יֵצֵא מִמֵּעֶיךָ, *which comes*

[4] *He said, Praised be HASHEM God of Israel, who spoke directly to
my father David, and graciously fulfilled His promise, saying,*
[5] *From the day that I brought out My people from the land of
Egypt I chose no city from among all the tribes of Israel, where a
Temple might be built, so that My Presence could be there; nor
chose a man to be prince over My people Israel.* [6] *But I chose
Jerusalem that My Presence could be there and I chose David to
be over My people Israel.* [7] *My father David intended to build a
House to the Name of HASHEM, God of Israel.* [8] *HASHEM said to
David my father, Because you intended to build a House to My
Name ... you did well in that which you intended.* [9] *However, you
will not build the House. But your son who comes out from your
loins, he will build the House for My Presence.* [10] *HASHEM fulfilled
the promise which He had spoken. I succeeded my father David
and sat upon the throne of Israel as HASHEM had spoken and I built
the House for the name of HASHEM, God of Israel.* [11] *I placed the
Ark in which was the covenant of HASHEM, which He had made*

out of your womb. See Section II, *Analysis ...* to *I Chronicles* ch. 17, p. 445.

10. וָאֵשֵׁב עַל־כִּסֵּא יִשְׂרָאֵל — *And sat upon the throne of Israel.* The term *throne of Israel* occurs frequently in Scripture to describe the Davidic throne. However, when *I Chronicles* 28:5 talks of Solomon being chosen to succeed his father as scion to the kingly tribe of Judah, it uses *the throne of HASHEM's kingship over Israel* — a terminology which is evocative of a stewardship representing God's rulership on earth. (See Section II to *I Chronicles* ch. 17, p. 443, *Analysis ...*, as it relates to 17:14.) In the moment of his greatest triumph we would perhaps have expected Solomon to use that term or one that carries a similar connotation. Perhaps it was a mark of his modesty that he did not do so.[1]

11. וָאָשִׂים שָׁם אֶת־הָאָרוֹן — *I placed the Ark ... there.* The parallel in *Kings* (v.21) has: *[Within the Temple] I created a place in which to put the Ark* instead of *[I built the Temple and] I placed the Ark [in it].* In *Kings*, Solomon stresses the fact that he had created a home for the Ark. In *Chronicles*, his interest centers upon the transfer of the Ark into the Temple. *HaLevi* in *Doros HaRishonim, Tekufas HaMikra*, ch. 42, notes the appropriateness of the *Kings* formulation. David's request to build the Temple as reported in *II Samuel* ch. 7 and *I Chronicles* ch. 17 was couched entirely in terms of the need to build a permanent home for the Ark. God answered him that this was not of immediate importance; the Ark had been in temporary quarters since the Exodus.

It is entirely appropriate that when Solomon offers up his prayer of thanksgiving upon completion of the Temple, he should mention that he had done that which his father had wished to do, i.e., he had created a permanent resting place for the Ark. Nevertheless, from its own perspective, *Chronicles* has every reason to change this formulation. Its interest is David's vindication and that vindication took place when the recalcitrant Sanctuary gates opened to admit the Ark, only after Solomon had invoked David's merit.[See Section II to *I Chronicles* ch.17, *Analysis ...* p.436, and prefatory remarks to ch. 5.]

בְּרִית ה׳ — *The covenant of HASHEM.* This

1. The theory that modesty is involved may be borne out by the formulation which David used in *I Chronicles* 28:4 and 5. In v. 4 when he talks about himself he uses ... *to be king over Israel*, while in v. 5 when he talks about Solomon he uses ... *the throne of HASHEM's kingship.*

It is also possible that the description, ... *the throne of HASHEM's kingship*, is only appropriate after the Temple has been built and the Divine rulership is manifest in its most complete form. Thus it cannot describe David's kingship but only Solomon's once the Temple is built. Here, since Solomon is tracing the history of his reign as it was up to the point when he built the Temple [וָאֶבְנֶה], he correctly uses only such a term as would also describe David's kingship — *the throne of Israel.*

יב עִם־בְּנֵי יִשְׂרָאֵל: וַיַּעֲמֹד לִפְנֵי מִזְבַּח יְהוָה נֶגֶד כָּל־קְהַל
יג יִשְׂרָאֵל וַיִּפְרֹשׂ כַּפָּיו: כִּי־עָשָׂה שְׁלֹמֹה כִּיּוֹר נְחֹשֶׁת
וַיִּתְּנֵהוּ בְּתוֹךְ הָעֲזָרָה חָמֵשׁ אַמּוֹת אָרְכּוֹ וְחָמֵשׁ אַמּוֹת
רָחְבּוֹ וְאַמּוֹת שָׁלוֹשׁ קוֹמָתוֹ וַיַּעֲמֹד עָלָיו וַיִּבְרַךְ עַל־
בִּרְכָּיו נֶגֶד כָּל־קְהַל יִשְׂרָאֵל וַיִּפְרֹשׂ כַּפָּיו הַשָּׁמָיְמָה:
יד וַיֹּאמַר יְהוָה אֱלֹהֵי יִשְׂרָאֵל אֵין־כָּמוֹךָ אֱלֹהִים בַּשָּׁמַיִם
וּבָאָרֶץ שֹׁמֵר הַבְּרִית וְהַחֶסֶד לַעֲבָדֶיךָ הַהֹלְכִים לְפָנֶיךָ
טו בְּכָל־לִבָּם: אֲשֶׁר שָׁמַרְתָּ לְעַבְדְּךָ דָּוִיד אָבִי אֵת אֲשֶׁר־
טז דִּבַּרְתָּ לוֹ וַתְּדַבֵּר בְּפִיךָ וּבְיָדְךָ מִלֵּאתָ כַּיּוֹם הַזֶּה: וְעַתָּה
יְהוָה ׀ אֱלֹהֵי יִשְׂרָאֵל שְׁמֹר לְעַבְדְּךָ דָוִיד אָבִי אֵת אֲשֶׁר
דִּבַּרְתָּ לּוֹ לֵאמֹר לֹא־יִכָּרֵת לְךָ אִישׁ מִלְּפָנַי יוֹשֵׁב
עַל־כִּסֵּא יִשְׂרָאֵל רַק אִם־יִשְׁמְרוּ בָנֶיךָ אֶת־דַּרְכָּם לָלֶכֶת
יז בְּתוֹרָתִי כַּאֲשֶׁר הָלַכְתָּ לְפָנָי: וְעַתָּה יְהוָה אֱלֹהֵי יִשְׂרָאֵל
יח יֵאָמֵן דְּבָרְךָ אֲשֶׁר דִּבַּרְתָּ לְעַבְדְּךָ לְדָוִיד: כִּי הַאֻמְנָם יֵשֵׁב
אֱלֹהִים אֶת־הָאָדָם עַל־הָאָרֶץ הִנֵּה שָׁמַיִם וּשְׁמֵי הַשָּׁמַיִם

refers to the tablets of the covenant of HASHEM (*Metzudos*).

12. נֶגֶד כָּל־קְהַל יִשְׂרָאֵל — *Facing the whole congregation of Israel.* He was visible to the whole congregation. See v. 13.

וַיִּפְרֹשׂ כַּפָּיו — *And spread out his hands. Targum* adds: *in prayer.*

13. כִּי־עָשָׂה שְׁלֹמֹה כִּיּוֹר נְחֹשֶׁת — *For Solomon had made a copper kior.* We have left כִּיּוֹר untranslated.

Throughout Scripture, including 4:6 above, the word כִּיּוֹר means a bowl within which, or from which, it is possible to wash. However, it seems entirely incongruous that amid all the untold wealth and expenditure which surrounded the building and inauguration of the Temple, Solomon should make do and climb atop a bowl — not designed as a platform — and address the people from there. Such an act would seem to jar the tone of the inauguration and not add to the dignity of the king. Moreover, none of the bowls described at 4:6 stood before the altar.

Rather, it seems likely that *kior* here denotes a platform — possibly one with a shape reminiscent of the bowls.[1]

However, since none of the commentators raise this point and *Targum* renders the word in precisely the same way as he renders the כִּיּוֹרִים of ch. 4, it is impossible to ascribe the meaning *platform* with any certainty.

14. שֹׁמֵר הַבְּרִית וְהַחֶסֶד — *Who bears in mind covenant and loving concern.*

For שֹׁמֵר, *HaKesav VeHaKabalah* to *Deuteronomy* 7:9 suggests *to bear in mind*, a similar usage at *Genesis* 37:11. *Radak* (*Kings*), on the other hand, explains that the *covenant* meant here is the one between God and the Patriarchs. Thus, he reads this verse as an introduction of general praise to God rather than as a specific reference to promises made to David (see below).

When חֶסֶד is combined with בְּרִית [as is quite frequent — see *Deuteronomy* 7:9 and elsewhere], it seems to connote a close parallel to the concept of covenant. Thus, for example, *Isaiah* 54:10 seems to equate the חֶסֶד which defines the relationship between husband and wife with a בְּרִית שָׁלוֹם, *a covenant of peace* or *harmony*. Hence our rendering, *loving concern.*

1. There is another possibility.

Both *Radak* and *Ibn Janach* assert that the root, כיר, from which כִּיּוֹר is formed is also that of כִּירַיִם, (*Leviticus* 11:35) which is a kind of oven. *Ibn Janach* writes that this word can be used to describe any arrangement of stones or bricks upon which a dish might be placed. The use of the word כִּיּוֹר to describe a platform might derive from this meaning.

with the Children of Israel, there. 12 *He stood before the altar*
of HASHEM, *facing the whole congregation of Israel and spread*
out his hands. 13 *For Solomon had made a copper kior and placed*
it in the courtyard; its length was five cubits and five cubits was
its width and three cubits its height. He stood upon it and knelt
down upon his knees facing the whole congregation of Israel and
spread out his hands towards heaven. 14 *He said:* HASHEM, *God*
of Israel, there is none like You, O God, in heaven or on earth,
Who bears in mind covenant and loving concern for Your
servants, those who walk before You with all their heart. 15 *For*
You have kept trust to David Your servant, my father, that
which You had spoken to him. You spoke directly, and graciously
fulfilled Your promise, as can be seen this day. 16 *And now,*
HASHEM, *God of Israel, keep trust to Your servant David, my*
father, concerning that which You spoke to him saying: No
descendant of yours will be removed from before Me and be
prevented from occupying the throne of Israel, provided your
sons take heed of the path which they will follow, to walk in the
ways of My Torah, as you have walked before Me. 17 *And now, O*
HASHEM, *God of Israel, may Your word which You spoke to Your*
servant David be realized. 18 *For can it be true that God would*
dwell with man upon earth? Behold the heavens and the highest

הַהֹלְכִים לְפָנֶיךָ בְּכָל־לִבָּם — *Who walk before You with all their heart*. That do as David had done (*Mefaresh*). Perhaps *Mefaresh*, unlike *Radak* quoted above, thinks that *covenant* and *loving concern* refer to promises made to David, rather than to those made to the Patriarchs.

Sifrey to *Vezos HaBerachah* teaches that all prayer must be preceded and followed by a section detailing God's praises. The structure of our daily *Shemoneh Esrei* is based on that ruling. *Sifrey* derives this requirement from a number of prayers quoted in *Tanach*, among them Solomon's inaugural prayer. This verse is said to be the introductory praise of God and the concluding passage begins at v. 41.

15. אֲשֶׁר שָׁמַרְתָּ — *For You have kept trust* — All can see that You have kept the promises which You made to David — that I would be the one to build the Temple (*Metzudos*).

כַּיּוֹם הַזֶּה — *As can be seen this day*. Translation follows *Metzudos*.

16. רַק אִם־יִשְׁמְרוּ בָנֶיךָ אֶת־דַּרְכָּם — *Provided your sons take heed of the path which they will follow*. See comm. to *I Chronicles* 28:7.

17. יֵאָמֵן דְּבָרְךָ — *May Your word ... be realized*. See comm. to *I Chronicles* 17:23 and 24.

The relationship between this verse and the previous one is as follows: God's promise to David had contained two elements: that David's son would follow him in the kingship; and that, between God and that son, there would be a close relationship. (See *I Chronicles* 17:13 — *I shall be a father to him and he shall be a son to Me*.) The earlier promise was the subject of v. 16. In this verse, Solomon invokes the promise of love as a prelude to the entreaties contained in the rest of the prayer. He begs that God's love become manifest as He answers the supplication which will rise up to Him from the newly inaugurated Temple (*Abarbanel*).

The fact that the thoughts contained in the next verse flow from this one can be seen from כִּי, *for*, with which v. 18 begins.

18. כִּי הַאֻמְנָם יֵשֵׁב אֱלֹהִים אֶת־הָאָדָם עַל־הָאָרֶץ — *For can it be true that God would dwell with man upon the earth*? Here Solomon launches into a discussion of the issue of an infinite, incorporeal God, unfettered by limitations of time or space, *dwelling* in a Temple built for Him by man. The thought is couched in the form of a rhetorical question. Inevitably, we are called upon to conclude that the idea is

יט לֹא יְכַלְכְּלוּךָ אַף כִּי־הַבַּיִת הַזֶּה אֲשֶׁר בָּנִיתִי: וּפָנִיתָ
אֶל־תְּפִלַּת עַבְדְּךָ וְאֶל־תְּחִנָּתוֹ יהוה אֱלֹהָי לִשְׁמֹעַ
אֶל־הָרִנָּה וְאֶל־הַתְּפִלָּה אֲשֶׁר עַבְדְּךָ מִתְפַּלֵּל לְפָנֶיךָ:
כ לִהְיוֹת עֵינֶיךָ פְתֻחוֹת אֶל־הַבַּיִת הַזֶּה יוֹמָם וָלַיְלָה
אֶל־הַמָּקוֹם אֲשֶׁר אָמַרְתָּ לָשׂוּם שִׁמְךָ שָׁם לִשְׁמוֹעַ
אֶל־הַתְּפִלָּה אֲשֶׁר יִתְפַּלֵּל עַבְדְּךָ אֶל־הַמָּקוֹם הַזֶּה:
כא וְשָׁמַעְתָּ אֶל־תַּחֲנוּנֵי עַבְדְּךָ וְעַמְּךָ יִשְׂרָאֵל אֲשֶׁר יִתְפַּלְלוּ
אֶל־הַמָּקוֹם הַזֶּה וְאַתָּה תִּשְׁמַע מִמְּקוֹם שִׁבְתְּךָ מִן־
כב הַשָּׁמַיִם וְשָׁמַעְתָּ וְסָלָחְתָּ: אִם־יֶחֱטָא אִישׁ לְרֵעֵהוּ וְנָשָׁא־
בוֹ אָלָה לְהַאֲלֹתוֹ וּבָא אָלָה לִפְנֵי מִזְבַּחֲךָ בַּבַּיִת הַזֶּה:
כג וְאַתָּה | תִּשְׁמַע מִן־הַשָּׁמַיִם וְעָשִׂיתָ וְשָׁפַטְתָּ אֶת־עֲבָדֶיךָ
לְהָשִׁב לְרָשָׁע לָתֵת דַּרְכּוֹ בְּרֹאשׁוֹ וּלְהַצְדִּיק צַדִּיק לָתֶת
כד לוֹ כְּצִדְקָתוֹ: וְאִם־יִנָּגֵף עַמְּךָ יִשְׂרָאֵל לִפְנֵי

patently ridiculous. If the highest heavens cannot contain God, then He cannot be said to dwell in Solomon's Temple.

But, then, what is the purpose of the Temple?

It is to be no more than a locus through which Israel's prayers might flow. It is true that any man from anywhere can turn to God in prayer. Nonetheless, there is to be something special about prayers directed to God through this, His earthly abode (*Radak*). See Section II, *The Temple as a Dwelling for God*, for a discussion.

אַף כִּי — *How much more* ... אַף denotes *addition*. Together with כִּי it is to be rendered as we have done.

19-21. Superficially there seems to be some redundancy in these verses. However, a careful reading can accommodate every phrase. We shall first synopsize the three verses and then explain each one individually.

V. 19. Solomon asks that God accept his supplication.

V. 20. Its essence is that God should protect the Temple, so that it would always provide the means by which He might be approached.

V. 21. With the Temple safeguarded, God would then hear the prayers directed to Him through it. These would then, so to speak, rise up to heaven, eliciting God's merciful concern. He would then forgive the transgression of the supplicants.

19. וּפָנִיתָ — *Thus You will turn* ... We have rendered the verse in such a way that it follows the previous one as implied in the prefix ו. As we have interpreted the previous verse [Section II, *The Temple as a Dwelling for God*,] the thought could be expressed thus: Since Your real abode is in the heavens, making it possible for You to view even imperfections with mercy, I trust that You will hear my prayer.

תְּפִלָּה . . . תְּחִנָּה . . . רִנָּה — *Prayer . . . entreaty . . . cry*. *Malbim* defines the three expressions for prayer used here:.

תְּפִלָּה from פלל, which *Malbim* interprets as *to long for* or *to crave* (see *Genesis* 48:11), is: The longing of the soul for its roots in God, the craving for closeness to the Divine.

תְּחִנָּה from חנן, *to be gracious*, is an act of supplication. The supplicant seeks to elicit God's goodwill and grace.

רִנָּה from רנן, *to cry out* (cf. *I Kings* 22:36), is the proclamation of God's praises.

20. לִהְיוֹת עֵינֶיךָ פְתֻחוֹת — *That You might look upon* ... Lit., *That Your eyes might be open*. This is the beginning of Solomon's prayer (*Metzudos*).

To *look upon* has the meaning of *to protect* (*Targum*). You must protect this Temple if You are to be able to hear the prayers which will be recited there.

עַבְדְּךָ — *Your servant*. *Abarbanel* suggests that, in contrast to the servant mentioned in the previous verse which refers to Solomon himself, this word might describe any God-fearing person who wishes to pray in the Temple.

אֶל־הַמָּקוֹם הַזֶּה — *In this place*. *Radak* adduces a number of instances in which אֶל has the

heavens cannot contain You, how much more this House which I
have built. 19 *Thus You will turn to the prayer of Your servant and*
to his entreaty, O HASHEM *my God, listening to the cry and to the*
prayer which Your servant prays before You. 20 *That You might*
look upon this House day and night — the place at which You
determined to establish Your Presence — so that You may hear the
prayer which Your servant will recite in this place. 21 *You will*
accept the entreaties of Your servant and of Your people Israel
which they will pray in this place, and You will hear from where
You dwell — from heaven. You will hear and forgive. 22 *If a man*
sin to his fellow, and this one has a claim of an oath against him,
so that he can make him swear, and he takes the oath before Your
altar in this House. 23 *Then You shall hear from the heavens and*
act, rendering justice to Your servants, requiting the guilty one,
visiting his guilt upon him, and declaring the winner of the case
to be in the right, and rewarding him in accordance with the
justice of his course. 24 *Now if Your people Israel should be smitten*

same connotation as the prefix ב, meaning *in* rather than *toward*.

21. וְשָׁמַעְתָּ . . . אֶל הַמָּקוֹם הַזֶּה . . . וְאַתָּה תִּשְׁמַע . . . מִן הַשָּׁמַיִם — *You will accept . . . in this place . . . and you will hear . . . from heaven.* See Section II, *The Temple as a Dwelling for God*.

22-23. Solomon recognizes that the opportunity which the Temple provides for meaningful prayer may be abused by an unscrupulous person. Such a one is to be shown no mercy.

22. וְנָשָׁא־בוֹ אָלָה לְהַאֲלֹתוֹ — *And this one has a claim of an oath against him so that he can make him swear.* We have translated in accordance with *Rashi* who holds that נשא here has the same meaning as נשה, *to be a creditor* or *to have a claim*, Thus the claimant is the subject of the phrase.

וּבָא אָלָה — *And he takes the oath* . . . Lit., *And the oath comes*. Apparently *oath* is short for *he who has the obligation to make the oath*.

לִפְנֵי מִזְבַּחֲךָ — *Before Your altar*. He comes or is brought before the altar in order to give greater solemnity to his oath. Whoever is at fault, whether it be the claimant who imposes an unjustifiable oath or the defendant who commits perjury, is culpable. The sanctity of the Temple and the aura which it lends to the proceedings are not to be taken lightly (*Mefaresh*).

Because there is no halachic basis for a regular oath to be made in the Temple such as one made during normal litigation, the Sages interpret our passage as dealing with the specific claim and counter-claim involved in the case of a *sotah*, a woman suspected of adultery. According to *Numbers* ch. 5, such a woman has to take an oath asserting her innocence in the Temple.

23. לְהָשִׁב לְרָשָׁע — *Requiting the guilty one.* לְהָשִׁב replaces לְהַרְשִׁיעַ, *to declare guilty*, in *Kings*. The word seems to be a shortened form of לְהָשִׁיב גְּמוּל, *to deal with someone in the way in which he deserves*. *Targum*, in fact, inserts the word גּוּמְלָא in his rendition.

לְרָשָׁע . . . צַדִּיק — *The guilty one .. . the winner of the case*. The verse does not explicate who is guilty and who is righteous. If the litigant who took the oath told the truth, then the claimant is guilty of instigating a needless use of God's name. If he swore falsely, then he is, of course, the guilty party (*Commentators*).

24-31. Many situations arise in which a person would want to turn to God. Solomon entreats God that He be ever receptive to all the prayers which will be offered up to Him in the Temple.

24. וְאִם־יִנָּגֵף עַמְּךָ יִשְׂרָאֵל — *Now if Your people Israel should be smitten. Kings* has *when they shall be smitten*. There is an absolute assumption that Israel's sins will be followed by defeat at the hands of their enemies. Our verse talks in terms of such a possibility, not of a certainty.

We may suggest the following explanation. The Torah does indeed imply that whether or not Israel is victorious in battle or suffers

אוֹיֵב כִּי יֶחֶטְאוּ־לָךְ וְשָׁבוּ וְהוֹדוּ אֶת־שְׁמֶךָ וְהִתְפַּלְלוּ
כה וְהִתְחַנְּנוּ לְפָנֶיךָ בַּבַּיִת הַזֶּה׃ וְאַתָּה תִּשְׁמַע מִן־הַשָּׁמַיִם
וְסָלַחְתָּ לְחַטַּאת עַמְּךָ יִשְׂרָאֵל וַהֲשֵׁיבוֹתָם אֶל־הָאֲדָמָה
כו אֲשֶׁר־נָתַתָּה לָהֶם וְלַאֲבֹתֵיהֶם׃ בְּהֵעָצֵר
הַשָּׁמַיִם וְלֹא־יִהְיֶה מָטָר כִּי יֶחֶטְאוּ־לָךְ וְהִתְפַּלְלוּ אֶל־
הַמָּקוֹם הַזֶּה וְהוֹדוּ אֶת־שְׁמֶךָ מֵחַטָּאתָם יְשׁוּבוּן כִּי
כז תַעֲנֵם׃ וְאַתָּה ׀ תִּשְׁמַע הַשָּׁמַיִם וְסָלַחְתָּ לְחַטַּאת עֲבָדֶיךָ
וְעַמְּךָ יִשְׂרָאֵל כִּי תוֹרֵם אֶל־הַדֶּרֶךְ הַטּוֹבָה אֲשֶׁר יֵלְכוּ־
בָהּ וְנָתַתָּה מָטָר עַל־אַרְצְךָ אֲשֶׁר־נָתַתָּה לְעַמְּךָ
כח לְנַחֲלָה׃ רָעָב כִּי־יִהְיֶה בָאָרֶץ דֶּבֶר כִּי־יִהְיֶה
שִׁדָּפוֹן וְיֵרָקוֹן אַרְבֶּה וְחָסִיל כִּי יִהְיֶה כִּי יָצַר־לוֹ אֹיְבָיו
כט בְּאֶרֶץ שְׁעָרָיו כָּל־נֶגַע וְכָל־מַחֲלָה׃ כָּל־תְּפִלָּה כָל־תְּחִנָּה
אֲשֶׁר יִהְיֶה לְכָל־הָאָדָם וּלְכֹל עַמְּךָ יִשְׂרָאֵל אֲשֶׁר יֵדְעוּ
ל אִישׁ נִגְעוֹ וּמַכְאֹבוֹ וּפָרַשׂ כַּפָּיו אֶל־הַבַּיִת הַזֶּה׃ וְאַתָּה
תִּשְׁמַע מִן־הַשָּׁמַיִם מְכוֹן שִׁבְתֶּךָ וְסָלַחְתָּ וְנָתַתָּה לָאִישׁ
כְּכָל־דְּרָכָיו אֲשֶׁר תֵּדַע אֶת־לְבָבוֹ כִּי־אַתָּה לְבַדְּךָ יָדַעְתָּ
לא אֶת־לְבַב בְּנֵי הָאָדָם׃ לְמַעַן יִירָאוּךָ לָלֶכֶת בִּדְרָכֶיךָ

ignominious defeat is determined by the degree of its adherence to God's will. Israel's enemies flee in confusion when Israel walks loyally in God's statutes. When Israel sins they are no match for even the weakest foe. [See *Leviticus* 22:3 ff.]

However, this need not always hold true. When warranted, God's infinite mercies can be granted even when they are in no way deserved.

Yarov'am, son of Yoash, the thirteenth of the kings of the Northern Kingdom, is judged as wicked at *II Kings* 14:24 ff. By adherence to the dynamics of history, as laid down in *Leviticus*, he should have been humiliated on the field of battle. Nevertheless, it was just during his reign that Israel regained vast territories which it had lost in earlier years.

This apparent anomaly is addressed by *Kings*: . . . *For HASHEM saw Israel's affliction — so very bitter with no protector or helper, with no one to support them. HASHEM refused to countenance Israel's destruction from beneath heaven, so He saved them by the hands of Yarov'am son of Yoash* (*II Kings* 14:26-27).

Thus, by the time that Ezra wrote *Chronicles*, history had taught that sin need not inevitably be followed by military disaster. This is reflected in the change of expression.

כִּי יֶחֶטְאוּ־לָךְ — *When they sin against You*. Their defeat will not be because You are not strong enough to protect them; it will only be due to their sins (*Mefaresh*).

וְהוֹדוּ אֶת־שְׁמֶךָ — *And confess before Your Presence*. The translation follows *Mefaresh*.

וְהִתְפַּלְלוּ וְהִתְחַנְּנוּ — *And they pray and utter entreaties*. The first part of the verse implies that they had already been defeated by the enemy. The prayers mentioned here must be directed to the future that such a tragedy not happen again.

בַּבַּיִת הַזֶּה — *In this House*. The soldiers are still away (v. 25). The people who remained at home offer up these prayers (*Radak*). In a later section (v. 34 ff.), Solomon talks of prayers which soldiers, away from home, might direct to the Temple.

25. וַהֲשֵׁיבוֹתָם אֶל־הָאֲדָמָה — *And bring them back to the land*. This refers to the smitten army (*Malbim*) or to the prisoners of war whom the enemy may have taken (*Radak*).

26. כִּי תַעֲנֵם — *So that You should answer them*. The translation is *Rashi's* who follows *Targum*. *Ralbag* and *Malbim* derive the word from ענה, *to afflict*, and render: *when You afflict them*.

*by an enemy when they sin against You, but they repent
and confess before Your Presence, and they pray and utter
entreaties before You in this House.*
25 *Then You should hear from
heaven and forgive the sins of Your people and bring them
back to the land which You gave to them and to their fathers.*
26 *When the heavens are blocked and there is no rain, for they
sin against You, then, when they pray in this place, confessing before Your Presence, turning from their sin so that You
should answer them.*
27 *Then You should hear in heaven and
forgive the sin of Your servants and of Your people Israel,
thus guiding them towards the good path which they should
follow, and send rain upon Your land which You gave to
Your people as an inheritance.*
28 *If there should be a famine in the
land, if there be a plague, searing and blight, if there be arbeh or
chassil, if their enemies afflict them in the land, in their cities;
whatever plague or whatever sickness.*
29 *Every prayer and every
entreaty which might be [made] by any individual or by the whole
of Your people Israel as each man shall know his own affliction
and pain, and he spreads out his hands in this House.*
30 *Then You
should listen from heaven, Your firmly grounded home, and
forgive, and render unto every man according to all his ways, for
it is You Who knows his heart, for You alone know the hearts of
man.*
31 *That they may fear You to go in Your ways all the days*

27. וְאַתָּה תִּשְׁמַע... כִּי תוֹרֵם — *Then You should hear ... thus guiding them.* Their repentance had not come from love of God but because of the starvation caused by the drought. Nevertheless, Solomon begs God to accept these less-than-perfect prayers so that when they perceive the abundance of God's mercy, they would be encouraged in the future to pray with purer motives (*Metzudos*).

Mefaresh would render ... *and guide them.* Let the people know which of their sins brought about this disaster so that they may know what to correct.

28. רָעָב כִּי־יִהְיֶה — *If there should be a famine.* The earlier famine was drought induced. This one has different causes (*Radak*).

שִׁדָּפוֹן וְיֵרָקוֹן — *Searing and blight. Rashi* to *Deuteronomy* 28:22 explains שִׁדָּפוֹן as the east wind which sears crops with the heat in its blast, and יֵרָקוֹן as a drying-out and yellowing of the stalks of grain.

כִּי יָצַר־לוֹ אֹיְבָיו בְּאֶרֶץ שְׁעָרָיו — *If their enemies afflict them in the land, in their cities.* The phrase recalls *Deuteronomy* 28:52 which predicts a time when an enemy will *oppress you in all your cities, in all your land* (*Radak*).

שַׁעַר, lit. *gate*, is used throughout Scripture as a synonym for city.

29. לְכָל־הָאָדָם וּלְכֹל עַמְּךָ יִשְׂרָאֵל — *By any individual or by the whole of Your people Israel.* The Temple is to be available for both individual and communal prayers (*Radak* and *Metzudos*).

אֲשֶׁר יֵדְעוּ אִישׁ נִגְעוֹ וּמַכְאֹבוֹ — *As each man shall know his own affliction and pain.* Individuals will come to beg for relief from those personal pains of which only they can know (*Radak*).

אֶל־הַבַּיִת הַזֶּה — *In this House.* See comm. to v. 20.

30. וְנָתַתָּה לָאִישׁ כְּכָל־דְּרָכָיו אֲשֶׁר תֵּדַע אֶת־לְבָבוֹ — *And render unto every man according to all his ways, for it is You Who knows his heart.* Each man is to be given his just desserts. The righteous are to be rewarded by granting their requests, but the wicked are to be punished. This is because should the wicked go unpunished, this would call God's justice into question (*Mefaresh.*) If, however, punishment is meted out to the wicked, people will learn to fear God, and stand in awe of Him. This idea connects

כָּל־הַיָּמִים אֲשֶׁר־הֵם חַיִּים עַל־פְּנֵי הָאֲדָמָה אֲשֶׁר נָתַתָּה
לב לַאֲבֹתֵינוּ׃ וְגַם אֶל־הַנָּכְרִי אֲשֶׁר לֹא־מֵעַמְּךָ
יִשְׂרָאֵל הוּא וּבָא ׀ מֵאֶרֶץ רְחוֹקָה לְמַעַן שִׁמְךָ הַגָּדוֹל וְיָדְךָ
הַחֲזָקָה וּזְרוֹעֲךָ הַנְּטוּיָה וּבָאוּ וְהִתְפַּלְלוּ אֶל־הַבַּיִת הַזֶּה׃
לג וְאַתָּה תִּשְׁמַע מִן־הַשָּׁמַיִם מִמְּכוֹן שִׁבְתֶּךָ וְעָשִׂיתָ כְּכֹל
אֲשֶׁר־יִקְרָא אֵלֶיךָ הַנָּכְרִי לְמַעַן יֵדְעוּ כָל־עַמֵּי הָאָרֶץ אֶת־
שְׁמֶךָ וּלְיִרְאָה אֹתְךָ כְּעַמְּךָ יִשְׂרָאֵל וְלָדַעַת כִּי־שִׁמְךָ נִקְרָא
לד עַל־הַבַּיִת הַזֶּה אֲשֶׁר בָּנִיתִי׃ כִּי־יֵצֵא עַמְּךָ לַמִּלְחָמָה
עַל־אֹיְבָיו בַּדֶּרֶךְ אֲשֶׁר תִּשְׁלָחֵם וְהִתְפַּלְלוּ אֵלֶיךָ דֶּרֶךְ
הָעִיר הַזֹּאת אֲשֶׁר בָּחַרְתָּ בָּהּ וְהַבַּיִת אֲשֶׁר־בָּנִיתִי לִשְׁמֶךָ׃
לה וְשָׁמַעְתָּ מִן־הַשָּׁמַיִם אֶת־תְּפִלָּתָם וְאֶת־תְּחִנָּתָם וְעָשִׂיתָ
לו מִשְׁפָּטָם׃ כִּי יֶחֶטְאוּ־לָךְ כִּי אֵין אָדָם אֲשֶׁר לֹא־יֶחֱטָא

this verse to the next.[1]

31. לְמַעַן יִירָאוּךָ — *That they may fear You.* When punishment is meted out to the wicked [previous verse] all will learn to fear God (*Mefaresh*).

When people realize that their prayers are answered only when they are sincerely penitent, they will come to see that their troubles came because of their sins, and will make sure not to stray again (*Radak*).

32. לְמַעַן שִׁמְךָ הַגָּדוֹל וְיָדְךָ הַחֲזָקָה — *For the sake of Your great Name, Your strong hand ...* The parallel passage in *Kings* words this passage differently:

II Chronicles ch. 6	*I Kings* ch. 8
32. ... וּבָא מֵאֶרֶץ רְחוֹקָה לְמַעַן שִׁמְךָ הַגָּדוֹל וְיָדְךָ הַחֲזָקָה וּזְרוֹעֲךָ הַנְּטוּיָה וּבָאוּ וְהִתְפַּלְלוּ .... *when he comes from a far land for the sake of Your great Name, Your strong hand and Your outstretched arm; when they come and pray ...*	41. ... וּבָא מֵאֶרֶץ רְחוֹקָה לְמַעַן שְׁמֶךָ *When he comes from a far land for the sake of Your Name.*
	42. כִּי יִשְׁמְעוּן אֶת־שִׁמְךָ הַגָּדוֹל וְאֶת־יָדְךָ הַחֲזָקָה וּזְרֹעֲךָ הַנְּטוּיָה וּבָא וְהִתְפַּלֵּל ... *For they will hear about Your great Name, Your strong hand and Your outstretched arm and he shall come and pray.*

In *Kings*, the stranger hears about God's might (v. 42) as expressed in His *strong hand* and *outstretched arm*, and is impressed enough to want to come and to pray ... *for the sake of Your Name*. God's power is only a means of spreading His fame — it is not, in itself, the means of attraction.

By contrast, in the *Chronicles'* wording, we know nothing of what the stranger heard. We know only that he is attracted, not only by

1. The Sages have a different perception of the meaning of this verse (see *Rashi* to *Genesis* 27:28). They note that in Isaac's blessing to Jacob he used the term *Elokim* which describes God in terms of His attribute of justice. Jacob is to receive the fruits of Isaac's blessing only if, in the eyes of God the Judge, it is appropriate and beneficial that he should get them.

By contrast, Esau's blessing was given unconditionally.

The difference, as the Sages teach, lies in a divergence of attitude. Jacob will lovingly accept from God whichever measure He metes out to him. Esau, if he does not get his way, will resent the denial of his request and turn against God.

The Sages find this same idea expressed in Solomon's prayer. When he talks of God's answering the prayers which Israel pours out to Him, he asks only that God grant it ... *according to all his ways*, that is, if indeed it is best that his request be granted. By contrast, Solomon asks that the stranger's prayer be answered, ... *in accordance with all that he shall call to You* (v. 33). Yet, even this is ultimately so that *they will fear You ... and know that Your Name is called upon this House.*

which they live upon the earth which You have given to our
fathers. 32 *Also to the stranger who is not from Your people Israel,*
when he comes from a far land for the sake of Your great Name,
Your strong hand and Your outstretched arm; when they come
and pray in this house. 33 *Then do You listen from heaven, Your*
firmly grounded home, and do all that for which the stranger
prays, so that all the people of the world will know Your Name
and fear You, as does Your people Israel, and know that Your
Name is associated with this House which I have built. 34 *Should*
Your people go out to war against their enemies on the way that
You send them and they pray to You by way of this city which
You have chosen and by way of this House which I have built to
Your Name. 35 *And You shall hear their prayers and their*
entreaties from heaven, and champion their cause. 36 *Should they*
sin against You — for there is no man who will not sin — and You

God's Name, but also by His power.

The *Chronicles'* version appears to put Solomon's prayer into Messianic terms. Before the world is filled with the knowledge of God, the unsophisticated gentile stranger does not understand the exquisite mercy which underlies God's justice. He is attracted by power, but cannot wish its exercise upon himself. In the long-term perspective of *Chronicles*, that too will eventually come. God's might, as expression of God's love, will itself be the magnetic force which draws the stranger to Jerusalem.

33. כְּכֹל אֲשֶׁר־יִקְרָא אֵלֶיךָ הַנָּכְרִי — *All that for which the stranger prays*. As regards a Jew I ask only that You do *according to all his ways* (v. 30), but for a non-Jew, *Do . . . all that for which the stranger prays.* Because the Israelite knows God and knows that He is all-able, if his prayer is not answered he will blame himself and examine his deeds. But the stranger, disgruntled because of the wasted effort in dragging himself to Jerusalem, will simply conclude that the worship of God offers no advantage over that of any idol. Therefore You do whatever he asks of you (*Mefaresh*). See also fn. to v. 30, and Section II, *The Temple as a House of Prayer*.

34-39. Twice before (vs. 24 and 28), Solomon had asked that God accept the prayers of Israel when they turn to Him in times of war. But in both those instances those prayers were said in the Temple. Here, Solomon asks that God be receptive even to such prayers as are said away from Jerusalem, and even in distant lands. Let it suffice that Your people incline their hearts towards Jerusalem and the Temple (*Malbim*).[1]

34. בַּדֶּרֶךְ אֲשֶׁר תִּשְׁלָחֵם — *On the way that You send them*. They would not go to war without first asking God's guidance (*Metzudos*).

וְהִתְפַּלְלוּ אֵלֶיךָ דֶּרֶךְ הָעִיר הַזֹּאת — *And they pray to You by way of this city*. From wherever they are, they will face Jerusalem (*Mefaresh*). From the distance, this is all that they can do. Their sincere intention must substitute for their actual being there (*Metzudos*).

35. וְעָשִׂיתָ מִשְׁפָּטָם — *And champion their cause*. You will wreak vengeance upon their enemies (*Rashi* based on *Targum*).

36. כִּי יֶחֶטְאוּ־לָךְ — *Should they sin against*

1. There may be another difference between the war described here and the earlier ones. V.35 asks that, in this confrontation, God should exercise מִשְׁפָּט for this people. Now it is possible that the meaning of מִשְׁפָּט in this context is *vengeance*, and it is so taken by a number of commentators. But there is also the possibility that it should be understood in its more usual denotation, *the rendering of a judgment*.

In most of Israel's wars, the gentile enemies are unjustified aggressors. But, there is also a possibility that a war might be waged by an enemy who, in the framework of God's justice, could have a legitimate grievance against Israel. In such a case, the decision as to who should be granted victory would have the nature of a *judgment* between two parties.

In this section, Solomon is asking that, even when the enemy might have a legitimate grievance, God should favor His children when they incline their hearts toward Him by way of the Temple.

This thesis could explain why this section comes after the one which deals with the prayers of the strangers. In that section, Solomon had made it abundantly clear that Israel's relationship with God is very special. This gives him the courage to ask even such favoritism from God.

וְאָנַפְתָּ בָם וּנְתַתָּם לִפְנֵי אוֹיֵב וְשָׁבוּם שׁוֹבֵיהֶם אֶל־אֶרֶץ
לז רְחוֹקָה אוֹ קְרוֹבָה׃ וְהֵשִׁיבוּ אֶל־לְבָבָם בָּאָרֶץ אֲשֶׁר נִשְׁבּוּ־
שָׁם וְשָׁבוּ ׀ וְהִתְחַנְּנוּ אֵלֶיךָ בְּאֶרֶץ שִׁבְיָם לֵאמֹר חָטָאנוּ
לח הֶעֱוִינוּ וְרָשָׁעְנוּ׃ וְשָׁבוּ אֵלֶיךָ בְּכָל־לִבָּם וּבְכָל־נַפְשָׁם
בְּאֶרֶץ שִׁבְיָם אֲשֶׁר־שָׁבוּ אֹתָם וְהִתְפַּלְלוּ דֶּרֶךְ אַרְצָם אֲשֶׁר
נָתַתָּה לַאֲבוֹתָם וְהָעִיר אֲשֶׁר בָּחַרְתָּ וְלַבַּיִת אֲשֶׁר־בָּנִיתִי
לט לִשְׁמֶךָ׃ וְשָׁמַעְתָּ מִן־הַשָּׁמַיִם מִמְּכוֹן שִׁבְתְּךָ אֶת־תְּפִלָּתָם
וְאֶת־תְּחִנֹּתֵיהֶם וְעָשִׂיתָ מִשְׁפָּטָם וְסָלַחְתָּ לְעַמְּךָ אֲשֶׁר
מ חָטְאוּ־לָךְ׃ עַתָּה אֱלֹהַי יִהְיוּ־נָא עֵינֶיךָ פְּתֻחוֹת וְאָזְנֶיךָ
מא קַשֻּׁבוֹת לִתְפִלַּת הַמָּקוֹם הַזֶּה׃ וְעַתָּה
קוּמָה יהוה אֱלֹהִים לְנוּחֶךָ אַתָּה וַאֲרוֹן עֻזֶּךָ כֹּהֲנֶיךָ
יהוה אֱלֹהִים יִלְבְּשׁוּ תְשׁוּעָה וַחֲסִידֶיךָ יִשְׂמְחוּ בַטּוֹב׃
מב יהוה אֱלֹהִים אַל־תָּשֵׁב פְּנֵי מְשִׁיחֶךָ זָכְרָה לְחַסְדֵי דָּוִיד

You. The translation follows *Radak*. The previous verse has assumed that God would champion their cause because they are righteous. Our verse now deals with the eventuality that, in fact, they will be sinners and will indeed merit defeat.

37. וְהֵשִׁיבוּ אֶל־לְבָבָם — *Now, if they should consider well*. [Lit. *Now, if they should take the matter to heart*.] The expression comes from *Deuteronomy* 4:39.

. . . חָטָאנוּ הֶעֱוִינוּ — *We have sinned, transgressed . . .* חטא means *to miss a mark*. It is used to describe an inadvertent sin.

עוה means *to distort* that which is straight, and generally describes a sin committed intentionally, see *Yoma* 36b.

38. דֶּרֶךְ אַרְצָם . . . וְהָעִיר . . . וְלַבַּיִת — *By way of their land . . . the city . . . and towards the House*. The captives are in a foreign land and cannot come to the Temple to pray. However, from the land of their captivity they incline their heart towards their land, city and Temple.

Berachos 31a derives the correct stance of one who prays from this verse: If he stands outside the Land, let him incline his heart towards the Land of Israel. . . if he was standing in the Land of Israel let him incline his heart towards Jerusalem . If he was standing in Jerusalem let him incline his heart towards the Temple.

39. וְעָשִׂיתָ מִשְׁפָּטָם — *Champion their cause*. Punish their captors who had no pity on them (*Radak*).

וְסָלַחְתָּ לְעַמְּךָ אֲשֶׁר חָטְאוּ־לָךְ — *And forgive Your people concerning that which they sinned against You*. God is to answer the people's prayer in two ways. He is to champion their cause and He is to forgive their sins. The parallel passage in *Kings* is substantively different. See Section II, *The Temple or the People?*

40. לִתְפִלַּת הַמָּקוֹם הַזֶּה — *To the prayers of this place*. This phrase is in sharp contrast to the parallel phrase in *Kings*: . . .*that You may listen to them whenever they might call You*. See Section II, ibid.

41-42. As noted in pref. remarks to ch. 5, these two verses do not occur in *Kings*. See there for a possible explanation.

41. קוּמָה — *Arise*. God is exhorted to leave His heavenly abode, and to allow His Presence to come to rest in the Holy of Holies (*Metzudos*).

Or, reference is to the temporary locations which had housed the Ark up to that point. God is to *rise up* from those places, so that He might take up permanent residence in the Temple (*Radak*).

לְנוּחֶךָ — *Your resting place*. נוח is generally an infinitive and the phrase could be rendered *Your state of resting*. However, since it parallels מְנוּחָתֶךָ in *Psalms* 132:8, the commentators assume it to be a rare form of that noun.

. . . אַתָּה וַאֲרוֹן — *You and the Ark* . . . The Holy of Holies is to be both a permanent abode for Your Divine Presence and also for the Ark upon which it is manifest.

וַאֲרוֹן עֻזֶּךָ — *The Ark, symbol of Your might*. This means to say the Ark is the means by which You demonstrated Your might when You wrought havoc among the Philistines

are angry with them. Should You then give them over to their
enemy and their captors carry them off to a far or a close land.
37 *Now, if they should consider well in the land to which they*
were taken captive, and repent, and beg Your grace in the land of
their captivity, saying: 'We have sinned, transgressed and dealt
wickedly.' 38 *And they turn back to You with all their heart and*
all their soul in the land of their captivity where they carried
them captive and they pray to You by way of their land which
You gave to their fathers and by way of the city which You chose
and towards the House which I have built to Your Name. 39 *Now,*
do You, from heaven, Your firmly grounded home, listen to their
prayers and their entreaties. Champion their cause, and forgive
Your people concerning that which they sinned against You.
40 *Now, my God, may Your eyes be open and Your ears be*
attentive to the prayers of this place. 41 *And now arise,* HASHEM,
God, to Your resting place, You and the Ark, symbol of Your
might. May Your Kohanim HASHEM, *God be clothed in salvation*
and Your pious ones rejoice in beneficence. 42 HASHEM, *God, turn*
not away the face of Your anointed one. Remember the pieties of
Your servant David.

when they captured it (*Mefaresh, Metzudos*).

It is appropriate that the Ark should, just in this context, be described as the symbol of God's might. As it is brought to its permanent resting place, Solomon prays that it should never again be called upon to prove God's power in similar circumstances. I..e, never again should it be moved.

כֹּהֲנֶיךָ ... יִלְבְּשׁוּ תְשׁוּעָה — *Your Kohanim ... be clothed in salvation.* Your salvation will surround them as protectively as would a garment (*Metzudos*).

וַחֲסִידֶיךָ — *And Your pious ones.* This might refer to anyone who comes to the Temple to learn of God's ways (*Radak*), or to the Levites (*Mefaresh, Radak, Ibn Ezra*).

יִשְׂמְחוּ בַטּוֹב — *Rejoice in beneficence.* They will be gladdened by the abundance of goodness which God pours out upon His world (*Metzudos*, consonant with *Radak's* explanation of *the pious ones* in the previous verse).

Mefaresh sees the phrase in a narrower sense. The Levites are to rejoice in the tithes which are given them to reward them for their conscientious guarding of the Ark and for the *shir*, the choral music which was their part of the Divine service.

42. אַל־תָּשֵׁב פְּנֵי מְשִׁיחֶךָ — *Turn not away the face of Your anointed one.* Solomon is God's anointed one (see *I Kings* 1:3 and *I Chronicles* 29:22). He asks that his prayers be accepted (*Radak* and *Metzudos*).

Mefaresh writes: Do not desist from doing good to me; if not for my own sake, then for Your's, Whose anointed one I am.

Rashi in *Kings* brings *Shabbos* 30a: This is Solomon's entreaty that God permit the Ark to enter into the Holy of Holies.

זָכְרָה לְחַסְדֵי דָּוִיד — *Remember the pieties of ... David.* The same expression occurs in *Isaiah* 55:3 where *Radak* and *Metzudos* explain that it refers to the kindnesses which God did for David. In that sense our phrase would mean: Remember all the kindnesses which You have done for David in the past [and therefore, continue to do them].

Here, however, *Metzudos* explains the phrase to mean the meritorious deeds which David had performed [see also *Rashi* to *Isaiah* 55:3] and that is certainly how the Sages take it in *Shabbos* 30a.

We translate *pieties* rather than the more usual *kindnesses* because the latter word occurs frequently in Scripture with what appears to be the wider connotation. Cf. *Isaiah* 40:6; 57:1 and *Hosea* 6:4.

For an examination of the sages understanding of why Solomon invokes the memory of David's pieties here, see Section II to *I Chronicles* ch.17, p.436.

ז
א־ו

א עַבְדֶּךָ: וּכְכַלּוֹת שְׁלֹמֹה לְהִתְפַּלֵּל וְהָאֵשׁ יָרְדָה
מֵהַשָּׁמַיִם וַתֹּאכַל הָעֹלָה וְהַזְּבָחִים וּכְבוֹד יהוה מָלֵא
ב אֶת־הַבָּיִת: וְלֹא יָכְלוּ הַכֹּהֲנִים לָבוֹא אֶל־בֵּית יהוה
ג כִּי־מָלֵא כְבוֹד־יהוה אֶת־בֵּית יהוה: וְכֹל | בְּנֵי יִשְׂרָאֵל
רֹאִים בְּרֶדֶת הָאֵשׁ וּכְבוֹד יהוה עַל־הַבָּיִת וַיִּכְרְעוּ אַפַּיִם
אַרְצָה עַל־הָרִצְפָה וַיִּשְׁתַּחֲווּ וְהוֹדוֹת לַיהוה כִּי טוֹב
ד כִּי לְעוֹלָם חַסְדּוֹ: וְהַמֶּלֶךְ וְכָל־הָעָם זֹבְחִים זֶבַח לִפְנֵי
ה יהוה: וַיִּזְבַּח הַמֶּלֶךְ שְׁלֹמֹה אֶת־זֶבַח הַבָּקָר עֶשְׂרִים
וּשְׁנַיִם אֶלֶף וְצֹאן מֵאָה וְעֶשְׂרִים אָלֶף וַיַּחְנְכוּ אֶת־בֵּית
ו הָאֱלֹהִים הַמֶּלֶךְ וְכָל־הָעָם: וְהַכֹּהֲנִים עַל־מִשְׁמְרוֹתָם
עֹמְדִים וְהַלְוִיִּם בִּכְלֵי־שִׁיר יהוה אֲשֶׁר עָשָׂה דָּוִיד הַמֶּלֶךְ
לְהֹדוֹת לַיהוה כִּי־לְעוֹלָם חַסְדּוֹ בְּהַלֵּל דָּוִיד בְּיָדָם

VII

◆§ The Inauguration Ceremonies

1-3. *Kings* leaves out this section but has the text of Solomon's blessing, which *Chronicles* does not have.

For the omission in *Kings* of this section, see Section II, *The Heavenly Fire*. For the omission in *Chronicles* of the text of Solomon's blessing, see fn. to Section II, *The Temple or the People*.

1. וּכְכַלּוֹת שְׁלֹמֹה לְהִתְפַּלֵּל — *Now as Solomon finished praying* ... *Kings* has: *And it was when Solomon* ..., indicating a fresh beginning. This, because *Kings*, which omits the description of the descending fire, now turns to the new subject of Solomon's blessing. By contrast, *Chronicles* has not yet finished its account of Solomon's prayer.

וּכְבוֹד ה׳ מָלֵא אֶת־הַבָּיִת — *And the glory of* HASHEM *filled the Temple*. This and the following verse appear to be a repetition of 5:13 and 14. It was necessary to stress that the *anan* remained even after the heavenly fire descended and consumed the inaugural sacrifices. Unlike the *anan* at Sinai, this one was permanently ensconced in the Holy of Holies.

2. וְלֹא יָכְלוּ הַכֹּהֲנִים — *The Kohanim were not able* ... 5:14 had said that the *Kohanim* were not able to stand and to serve because of the presence of the *anan*. This verse appears to be an escalation of that fact. Here we see that they were not even able to enter.

3. וַיִּכְרְעוּ אַפַּיִם אַרְצָה — *They knelt down and prostrated themselves — their faces to the ground*. כרע implies a form of obeisance connected with the knees (*I Kings* 8:54 and elsewhere); thus, *to kneel down*.

עַל־הָרִצְפָה — *Upon the pavement*. The root רצף conveys the idea of gathering and joining things together (*Ibn Janach, Sefer HaShorashim*). A pavement or floor is called a רִצְפָּה because it is laid together from various stones — in the case of the Temple court these were made from marble (*Radak*).

The text points out that the people knelt down on the Temple floor — where they had been standing — in contrast to Solomon who had made his obeisance from his place on the platform (6:13) (*Radak*).

וְהוֹדוֹת לַה׳ — *And praised* HASHEM. They recited *Psalm* 136 which describes God's beneficence (*Metzudos*).

4. וְהַמֶּלֶךְ וְכָל־הָעָם — *And the king and all the people... Kings* has ... *and all Israel with him*. The omission here of *with him* seems consistent with the *Chronicles'* treatment of 5:6 — see comm. there.

5. וַיַּחְנְכוּ אֶת־בֵּית הָאֱלֹהִים — *Thereby ... inaugurated the House of God*. *Ramban* (*Numbers* 7:13) thinks that the appropriateness of an inaugural ceremony for the Temple was established when God told Moses to accept the gifts which the tribal princes had brought when the building of the Tabernacle was completed (*Numbers*, ch. 7).

V. 9 refers to these ceremonies as the

7
1-6

Now as Solomon finished praying, the fire came down from heaven and consumed the burnt offerings and the sacrifices and the glory of HASHEM *filled the Temple.* [2] *The Kohanim were not able to come into the House of* HASHEM, *because the glory of* HASHEM *filled the House of* HASHEM. [3] *All the Children of Israel could see as the fire descended. The glory of* HASHEM *was upon the Temple. They knelt down and prostrated themselves — their faces to the ground — upon the pavement, and praised* HASHEM: *'For He is good and His kindness is everlasting.'* [4] *And the king and all the people slaughtered sacrifices before* HASHEM.
[5] *King Solomon slaughtered the cattle sacrifice — twenty-two thousand, and sheep — one hundred and twenty thousand. Thereby the king and all the people inaugurated the House of God.*
[6] *The Kohanim stood according to their divisions and the Levites — controlling David's songs of jubilation by their hand — with the musical instruments of* HASHEM *which King David had made to praise* HASHEM, *'. . . for His kindness is everlasting.'*

inauguration of the *altar*. To the extent that the Temple is a *location at which sacrifices are to be brought* (see v. 12), *Temple* and *altar* are synonymous.[1]

6. וְהַכֹּהֲנִים עַל־מִשְׁמְרוֹתָם עוֹמְדִים — *The Kohanim stood according to their divisions*. In *I Chronicles*, ch. 24, we learned that, for the Temple service, the *Kohanim* were divided into twenty-four divisions which rotated weekly. In 5:11 we learned that for the inauguration all the divisions were represented since the work load would have been too heavy for one group. Here we learn that each division stood together (*Mefaresh*) in its own place (*Metzudos*). See further comm. to 8:13.

This verse is not recorded in *Kings* just as there is no parallel there for 5:11. This, because the division of the *Kohanim* into groupings is nowhere taught in *Kings*.

בִּכְלֵי־שִׁיר ה׳ אֲשֶׁר עָשָׂה דָּוִיד הַמֶּלֶךְ — *With the musical instruments of* HASHEM *which King David had made*. The translation follows the *trop* which combines *the musical instruments* with *HASHEM*. The expression is thus similar to, *. . . the instruments of God*, at *I Chronicles* 16:42. There we saw that the meaning is either: instruments made to be played in the Temple or, instruments with a particularly beautiful sound.

לְהֹדוֹת לַה׳ — *To praise* HASHEM. They used the musical instruments to aid them in singing God's praises (*Mefaresh*).

בְּהַלֵּל דָּוִיד בְּיָדָם — *Controlling David's songs of jubilation by their hand*. This rendering follows *Radak's* second interpretation. We have moved the phrase up in the translation in order to conform with English syntax.[2]

1. *Ramban*, quoted in the comm., bears out the synonymy of the two terms.

The ceremony in the wilderness was called, *the inauguration of the altar* (*Numbers* 7:10 and 84). Nevertheless, *Ramban* writes: It is conceivable that [God's acceptance of the sacrifices brought by the tribal princes] is to serve as a precedent that *Temple and altar are to be inaugurated*. For this reason Solomon engaged in an inauguration ceremony . .

Thus, *Ramban* finds a precedent for inaugurating the *Temple* in a ceremony which is specifically described as an inauguration of the *altar*.

2. We may consider another possibility for our phrase.

When *II Samuel* 23:1 describes David as the נְעִים זְמִירוֹת יִשְׂרָאֵל, *Israel's sweet singer of songs*, the meaning may well be much deeper than that David composed the songs and psalms which Israel was destined to sing.

Rather it may be an expression of the profound truth that: דָּוִד מֶלֶךְ יִשְׂרָאֵל חַי וְקַיָּם, *David King of Israel lives and endures!* Such an unqualified statement of fact which seems so manifestly contradicted by the evidence of our eyes can only be interpreted as does *Biberfeld* in his *David King of Israel*: The personality of the greatest king of Israel lives on. He has become so closely interwoven with the Jewish people as to be almost inseparable from it. The life of King David and the life of Israel's nation are fused into one. As long as Israel lives, King

ז
ז־יא

°מַחְצְרִים ק׳

ז וְהַכֹּהֲנִים °מחצצרים נֶגְדָּם וְכָל־יִשְׂרָאֵל עֹמְדִים׃ וַיְקַדֵּשׁ
שְׁלֹמֹה אֶת־תּוֹךְ הֶחָצֵר אֲשֶׁר לִפְנֵי בֵית־יהוה כִּי־
עָשָׂה שָׁם הָעֹלוֹת וְאֵת חֶלְבֵי הַשְּׁלָמִים כִּי־מִזְבַּח הַנְּחֹשֶׁת
אֲשֶׁר עָשָׂה שְׁלֹמֹה לֹא יָכוֹל לְהָכִיל אֶת־הָעֹלָה
ח וְאֶת־הַמִּנְחָה וְאֶת־הַחֲלָבִים׃ וַיַּעַשׂ שְׁלֹמֹה אֶת־הֶחָג בָּעֵת
הַהִיא שִׁבְעַת יָמִים וְכָל־יִשְׂרָאֵל עִמּוֹ קָהָל גָּדוֹל מְאֹד
ט מִלְּבוֹא חֲמָת עַד־נַחַל מִצְרָיִם׃ וַיַּעֲשׂוּ בַּיּוֹם הַשְּׁמִינִי
עֲצֶרֶת כִּי ׀ חֲנֻכַּת הַמִּזְבֵּחַ עָשׂוּ שִׁבְעַת יָמִים וְהֶחָג שִׁבְעַת
י יָמִים׃ וּבְיוֹם עֶשְׂרִים וּשְׁלֹשָׁה לַחֹדֶשׁ הַשְּׁבִיעִי שִׁלַּח
אֶת־הָעָם לְאָהֳלֵיהֶם שְׂמֵחִים וְטוֹבֵי לֵב עַל־הַטּוֹבָה אֲשֶׁר
יא עָשָׂה יהוה לְדָוִיד וְלִשְׁלֹמֹה וּלְיִשְׂרָאֵל עַמּוֹ׃ וַיְכַל שְׁלֹמֹה
אֶת־בֵּית יְהוָה וְאֶת־בֵּית הַמֶּלֶךְ וְאֵת כָּל־
הַבָּא עַל־לֵב שְׁלֹמֹה לַעֲשׂוֹת בְּבֵית־יְהוָה וּבְבֵיתוֹ

וְהַכֹּהֲנִים מַחְצְרִים נֶגְדָּם — *The Kohanim sounded trumpets over against them.* They stood over against the Levites (*Metzudos*), the Levites standing on their platform towards the east and the *Kohanim* further to the west (*Malbim*).

וְכָל־יִשְׂרָאֵל עֹמְדִים — *And all of Israel was standing.* They stood out of respect for the Divine service that was taking place.

7. וַיְקַדֵּשׁ שְׁלֹמֹה אֶת־תּוֹךְ הֶחָצֵר — *Solomon sanctified the inside of the courtyard.* As taught in the end of our verse, the copper [stone] altar which Solomon had built (see 4:1 and comm. there) proved inadequate for the great number of sacrifices brought on the day of the inauguration. Because of this, Solomon sanctified the pavement of the Temple court, in effect converting it into an extension of the altar. The overflow of sacrificial parts which could not be handled on the altar could now be burnt there (*Metzudos*).

This interpretation accords with the opinion of R' Yehudah as taught in *Zevachim* 59a ff.

R' Yosey's opinion is that no sacrifices were ever burned upon the pavement. The sanctification mentioned in our verse was not made in order to convert the floor into an extension of the altar but in order to ready it for the building of a new altar — the one mentioned at 4:1. It had become necessary to build this new altar because Moses' altar which had done service up to that time was now to be withdrawn.

Details of this Tannaic disagreement and of the complex issues involved in it can be found in *Zevachim* 59a ff.

◆§ The People Leave

8-10. There are significant differences between this passage and its parallel in *Kings*.

8. וַיַּעַשׂ שְׁלֹמֹה אֶת־הֶחָג — *Solomon celebrated the festival...* From the context it is clear that this is Succos.[1] See at 5:3.

מִלְּבוֹא חֲמָת עַד־נַחַל מִצְרָיִם — *From Lebo Chamas*

David lives in its midst; and as the Jewish commonwealth is immortal, its ruler is also immortal.

And further on: Thus, once the idea [of God] had become the very being of David, now the being of David became the idea of the Jewish people. As David was sent to prove and proclaim in word and deed the omnipresence of the Divine on earth, thus Israel was sent into the world a herald of the Kingdom of God. David's message was taken over by the Jewish nation. His wondrous deeds and inspired songs which expressed his inner essential person became the vital reality, the distinctive feature of the Jewish people.

Thus it is that David lives and endures in Israel and thus it is he who animates Israel's song. Every time the Levites, in the course of the Temple service, raised their voices and strummed their instruments in God's praise, it is Israel's sweet singer of songs who is the soul of their music.

In this sense our phrase may well be rendered: David, praising [God], animating their hands. Their hands are David's hands even as their music and the longings which it expresses are David's sweet songs.

1. This in contrast to the same phrase in the *Kings* account, which, as we see in Section II, *The Inauguration and Succos*, refers to the inauguration festivities.

The insight that these otherwise similar phrases have different meanings can help us understand the next

The Kohanim sounded trumpets over against them, and all
of Israel was standing. 7 *Solomon sanctified the inside of*
the courtyard which lay in front of the House of HASHEM*,*
for there he brought the burnt offerings and the fats of
the peace offerings. This, because the copper altar which
Solomon had made was unable to accommodate the burnt
offering, the meal offering and the fats. 8 *Solomon celebrated the*
festival at that time for seven days, and all Israel was with him
— a very great congregation, from Lebo Chamas up to the river of
Egypt. 9 *On the eighth day they made Atzeres, for they celebrated*
the inauguration of the altar for seven days, and the festival — for
seven days. 10 *On the twenty-third day of the seventh month he*
sent the people to their tents happy and of good heart because of
the good which HASHEM *had done to David, Solomon and Israel*
His people. 11 *And Solomon finished* HASHEM*'s House and the*
king's house and all that had occurred to Solomon to bring about
in HASHEM*'s Temple and in his house, he brought to a successful*

up to the river of Egypt. For precise identification of these places, see ArtScroll *Joshua* 13:5 and 15:4.

9. בַּיּוֹם הַשְּׁמִינִי — *On the eighth day*. This is *Shmini Atzeres*. See Section II, *The Inauguration and Succos*.

עָשׂוּ שִׁבְעַת יָמִים ... שִׁבְעַת יָמִים ... — *For they celebrated ... for seven days, and the festival — for seven days*. The celebration of *Shmini Atzeres* was in no way compromised by the inauguration festivities. These took place before Succos.

חֲנֻכַּת הַמִּזְבֵּחַ — ... *the inauguration of the altar* ... See comm. to v. 5.

10. שִׁלַּח אֶת־הָעָם — *He sent the people* ... This was the day after *Shmini Atzeres*. In *Kings* [see Section II, *The Inauguration and Succos*, [g]] we learn that he had already sent them on *Shmini Atzeres*. However, because of Yom Tov they were not able to make their way home on that day. Accordingly they came to Solomon once more on the next day, to repeat their farewells.

Moed Katan 9a derives a halachah from this. A student who bade his master goodbye on a given day and then stayed overnight must not leave without once more bidding farewell.

שְׂמֵחִים וְטוֹבֵי לֵב — *Happy and of good heart*. *Happy* because they had experienced the Divine Presence, and *of good heart* because their wives conceived and bore male children. (*Moed Katan* 9a).

עַל־הַטּוֹבָה אֲשֶׁר עָשָׂה ה׳ — *Because of the good which* HASHEM *had done*. A heavenly voice came forth and announced: 'All of you are destined for the world to come' (*Moed Katan* 9a).

לְדָוִיד וְלִשְׁלֹמֹה וּלְיִשְׂרָאֵל עַמּוֹ — *To David, Solomon and Israel His people*. David was finally vindicated, and the people were not punished for having eaten on Yom Kippur (*Moed Katan* 9a).

Solomon is not mentioned in the *Kings'* account. This is readily explained. In *Kings* he had stood at the center of the activities. There was no need to mention him once more at this point. But in *Chronicles* where his participation had been de-emphasized, it is appropriate to note how greatly the people rejoiced in the great accomplishment which he had wrought.

11. וַיְכַל שְׁלֹמֹה אֶת־בֵּית ה׳ וְאֶת־בֵּית הַמֶּלֶךְ — *Solomon finished* HASHEM*'s House and the king's house*. We learned of Solomon's intention to build himself a palace at 1:18 and 2:11. However, the account of the building which

part of our verse. There we learn that *all Israel was with him*. Now, in pref. remarks to ch. 5 and in v. 2 there, we saw that *Chronicles* tends to leave out such phrases from the inauguration narrative, even where they appear in *Kings*.

Since our verse refers to Succos rather than to the inauguration, there is no irregularity here.

ז
יב־יז

יב הִצְלִיחַ׃ וַיֵּרָא יְהוָה אֶל־שְׁלֹמֹה בַּלָּיְלָה וַיֹּאמֶר לוֹ
שָׁמַעְתִּי אֶת־תְּפִלָּתֶךָ וּבָחַרְתִּי בַּמָּקוֹם הַזֶּה לִי לְבֵית זָבַח׃
יג הֵן אֶעְצֹר הַשָּׁמַיִם וְלֹא־יִהְיֶה מָטָר וְהֵן־אֲצַוֶּה עַל־חָגָב
יד לֶאֱכוֹל הָאָרֶץ וְאִם־אֲשַׁלַּח דֶּבֶר בְּעַמִּי׃ וְיִכָּנְעוּ עַמִּי אֲשֶׁר
נִקְרָא־שְׁמִי עֲלֵיהֶם וְיִתְפַּלְלוּ וִיבַקְשׁוּ פָנַי וְיָשֻׁבוּ
מִדַּרְכֵיהֶם הָרָעִים וַאֲנִי אֶשְׁמַע מִן־הַשָּׁמַיִם וְאֶסְלַח
טו לְחַטָּאתָם וְאֶרְפָּא אֶת־אַרְצָם׃ עַתָּה עֵינַי יִהְיוּ פְתֻחוֹת
טז וְאָזְנַי קַשֻּׁבוֹת לִתְפִלַּת הַמָּקוֹם הַזֶּה׃ וְעַתָּה בָּחַרְתִּי
וְהִקְדַּשְׁתִּי אֶת־הַבַּיִת הַזֶּה לִהְיוֹת־שְׁמִי שָׁם עַד־עוֹלָם
יז וְהָיוּ עֵינַי וְלִבִּי שָׁם כָּל־הַיָּמִים׃ וְאַתָּה אִם־תֵּלֵךְ לְפָנַי

appears at *Kings* 7:1 has no parallel in *Chronicles*. See Section II, *Solomon's House*.

☙ God Appears To Solomon

12. לְבֵית זָבַח — *As the location at which sacrifices are to be brought*. This was not part of Solomon's prayer. He asked only that prayers directed to the Temple be accepted.

We must understand the sentence as follows: *I have heard your prayer*, and will listen to the entreaties which will be directed toward this Temple — as explicated in the following verses.

Moreover, over and beyond that which you have asked, I have also *designated this place as the location at which sacrifices are to be brought*. This, in accordance with the language used at *Deuteronomy* 12:14: *But at the location which God will designate, there you shall bring your burnt offerings ...*

The term does not occur in the *Kings'* narrative; indeed, there is not even a parallel phrase. If it is to be part of God's answer to Solomon it belongs more properly to *Chronicles* than to *Kings*. This, because in *Chronicles* there is at least passing reference to an inauguration of the altar — the fire descending from heaven at v. 1, and the mention of the inauguration of the altar at v. 9. Neither of these appear in *Kings*.

13-15. These verses are in direct answer to Solomon's entreaties. They do not appear in the *Kings* account. See fn. in Section II, *The Temple or the People?* to ch. 6.

13. הֵן אֶעְצֹר הַשָּׁמַיִם וְלֹא־יִהְיֶה מָטָר — *Should I shut up the heavens that there be no rain*. The eventuality of God shutting up the heavens so that there should be no rain is raised in 6:26 as an occasion when Israel would turn to God in prayer.

The commentators do not explain why in His answer, God addresses Himself to that particular eventuality and the others mentioned in this verse, and does not mention the catastrophe described earlier at 6:24 which talks of Israel being defeated in war.

וְהֵן־אֲצַוֶּה עַל־חָגָב לֶאֱכוֹל הָאָרֶץ — *Or should I command the chagav to devour the land*. *Chagav* is a type of locust. This eventuality is mentioned at 6:28 although there, *arbeh* and *chasil* are given as examples rather than *chagav*.

וְאִם־אֲשַׁלַּח דֶּבֶר בְּעַמִּי — *Or if I send plague against My people*. The possibility of the plague is also mentioned at 6:28.

14. וְיִכָּנְעוּ עַמִּי — *If My people ... will humble themselves*. This is meant as a prelude to the penitence mentioned in the second part of our verse.

וְאֶרְפָּא אֶת־אַרְצָם — *And will heal their land*. The root רפא with אֶרֶץ as object does not occur elsewhere. It is appropriate when applied to the conditions described in v. 13.

15. לִתְפִלַּת הַמָּקוֹם הַזֶּה — *To the prayers of this place*. See fn. to Section II, *The Temple or the People?* to ch. 6 for the difference between this wording and that of the parallel passage in *Kings*.

16. לִהְיוֹת־שְׁמִי שָׁם — *That My Name be there*. *Targum* renders: *To make My Presence remain there*; see comm. on *I Chronicles* 13:6, for similar usage.

עַד־עוֹלָם — *Forever*. I will never allow My Divine Presence to rest in any other place

7
12-17

conclusion. [12] HASHEM appeared to Solomon in the night and said to him: I have heard your prayer and I have designated this place, that it serve Me as the location at which sacrifices are to be brought. [13] Should I shut up the heavens that there be no rain, or should I command the chagav to devour the land, or if I send plague against My people. [14] If My people upon whom My Name is called will humble themselves before Me, and if they pray and beg from before Me and repent their evil ways, then I will listen from the heaven and forgive their sins and will heal their land. [15] Now My eyes will be open and My ears will listen carefully to the prayers of this place. [16] And now I have chosen and sanctified this House that My Name be there forever and My eyes and My heart will be there for all days. [17] As for you, if you will walk

(*Metzudos*). [See *Rambam, Bais HaBechirah* 1:3.]

וְהָיוּ עֵינַי וְלִבִּי שָׁם — *And My eyes and My heart will be there*. It will be the seat of My Providence (*Metzudos*).

17-22. In these verses, God exhorts Solomon to remain true to the paths of goodness and obedience which David had followed. If he does so, his throne will be firmly established and Israel's kingship will remain eternally his. The alternative is the utter destruction of Temple and land, and Israel's disgrace among the nations. The passage ends with a description of this dire eventuality. The last words — those which would surely have continued to ring in Solomon's ears — are, ... *for this reason He brought upon them all this evil*.

When we recall the proclivity of Jewish custom and halachah never to end anything on a sad or negative note, it strikes us as incongruous that precisely on the day of Solomon's delight (*Shir HaShirim* 3:11 and see *Taanis* 26b), that day upon which he achieved the very peak of closeness to God in prayer and sacrifice, God should have found such a somber and threatening ending to be appropriate.

The Sages have a tradition which would explain the tone of the passage perfectly.

R' Yudan taught: During the seven years that Solomon spent in building the Temple he did not drink any wine, but when he finished building and married Bisyah the daughter of Pharaoh, on that night he drank wine. There were two celebrations going on [at the same time] — the inauguration festivities and the wedding. So God was in a quandary. Which of the two should He consider? At that moment God wished to destroy Jerusalem ...

R' Huna taught: Pharaoh's daughter [amused Solomon with] eighty different kinds of dance during that night and [consequently] Solomon overslept the next morning. He had the Temple keys under his pillow, and delayed the bringing of the morning sacrifices ... (*Vayikra Rabbah* 12:5).

The tradition that Solomon married Pharaoh's daughter on the very day of the Temple inauguration is repeated in many different midrashim and is firmly entrenched in the aggadic tradition.

Solomon's decision to marry the Egyptian princess on the very day of the Temple inauguration indicates the thrust of his thinking. With the *Shechinah*, God's Presence, ensconced in the Temple, Israel was ready to take the first step in its Messianic destiny — the drawing of the entire human race, even the most depraved, into the orbit of sanctity. From David's task of fighting evil, the emphasis had now shifted to sublimating it. The foreign women whom Solomon married were to be the first trickle in the avalanche of humanity who would one day unite to go up to Jerusalem, to drink there, at the fount of Torah (*R' Tzadok HaKohen, Tzidkas HaTzadik* 244).

But, as the midrash's description of the debacle of the first night indicates, Solomon had miscalculated. The time for sublimation had not yet come. Solomon's marriage had catastrophic results for himself (see *I Kings* ch. 11), but even more so for the rest of Israel. When Solomon married Pharaoh's daughter, Gabriel descended [from heaven] and planted a rod in the sea around which a land mass coalesced and upon this the great city of Rome was built (*Shabbos* 56b). Far from ushering in

כַּאֲשֶׁר הָלַךְ דָּוִיד אָבִיךָ וְלַעֲשׂוֹת כְּכֹל אֲשֶׁר צִוִּיתִיךָ וְחֻקַּי
יח וּמִשְׁפָּטַי תִּשְׁמוֹר׃ וַהֲקִימוֹתִי אֵת כִּסֵּא מַלְכוּתֶךָ כַּאֲשֶׁר
כָּרַתִּי לְדָוִיד אָבִיךָ לֵאמֹר לֹא־יִכָּרֵת לְךָ אִישׁ מוֹשֵׁל
יט בְּיִשְׂרָאֵל׃ וְאִם־תְּשׁוּבוּן אַתֶּם וַעֲזַבְתֶּם חֻקּוֹתַי וּמִצְוֺתַי
אֲשֶׁר נָתַתִּי לִפְנֵיכֶם וַהֲלַכְתֶּם וַעֲבַדְתֶּם אֱלֹהִים אֲחֵרִים
כ וְהִשְׁתַּחֲוִיתֶם לָהֶם׃ וּנְתַשְׁתִּים מֵעַל אַדְמָתִי אֲשֶׁר־נָתַתִּי
לָהֶם וְאֶת־הַבַּיִת הַזֶּה אֲשֶׁר הִקְדַּשְׁתִּי לִשְׁמִי אַשְׁלִיךְ מֵעַל
כא פָּנָי וְאֶתְּנֶנּוּ לְמָשָׁל וְלִשְׁנִינָה בְּכָל־הָעַמִּים׃ וְהַבַּיִת הַזֶּה
אֲשֶׁר־הָיָה עֶלְיוֹן לְכָל־עֹבֵר עָלָיו יִשֹּׁם וְאָמַר בַּמֶּה עָשָׂה
כב יהוה כָּכָה לָאָרֶץ הַזֹּאת וְלַבַּיִת הַזֶּה׃ וְאָמְרוּ עַל אֲשֶׁר
עָזְבוּ אֶת־יהוה ׀ אֱלֹהֵי אֲבֹתֵיהֶם אֲשֶׁר הוֹצִיאָם מֵאֶרֶץ
מִצְרַיִם וַיַּחֲזִיקוּ בֵּאלֹהִים אֲחֵרִים וַיִּשְׁתַּחֲווּ לָהֶם וַיַּעַבְדוּם
עַל־כֵּן הֵבִיא עֲלֵיהֶם אֵת כָּל־הָרָעָה הַזֹּאת׃

a Messianic era, Solomon's marriage on the day of the inauguration injected a cancer into the very establishment of the Temple, which was meant to be the cause of all the rejoicing.

Small wonder, then, that God's answer to Solomon's prayer was muted. It was heavy with the intimation of the tragedies which, at that point, still lay far into the future, but which would now — without a superhuman repentance and change of course — inevitably come. Ultimately, God's grave exhortations did not sway Solomon and history took its course.

17. כַּאֲשֶׁר הָלַךְ דָּוִיד אָבִיךָ — *As David your father walked.* The wording appears to confirm the ideas worked out in prefatory remarks 17-22. The time is not yet ripe for a deviation from David's path of conquest.

18. וַהֲקִימוֹתִי — *Then I will establish* ... I will give it to you permanently through your children (*Metzudos*).

19. וְאִם־תְּשׁוּבוּן אַתֶּם — *But if you backslide.* שוב, *to return*, is used in this sense at *II Kings* 24:1 and *Jeremiah* 34:11 and 16.

20. וּנְתַשְׁתִּים מֵעַל אַדְמָתִי — *Then I will uproot them from My land. Kings* has וְהִכְרַתִּי אֶת־יִשְׂרָאֵל מֵעַל פְּנֵי הָאֲדָמָה, *and I will cut off Israel from upon the land.* Thus, *Chronicles* substitutes נתש for כרת and *My land* for *the land.*

נתש, when used in connection with trees (cf. *Michah* 5:13), means *to uproot* [*Targum* there renders עקר] and is thus a stronger term than כרת, *to cut down.* A tree which is cut down could conceivably grow again but one which is uprooted is lost forever. It is possible that *Chronicles* used the stronger term with the hindsight of history. If Ezra or the Men of the Great Assembly wrote the *Chronicles'* account after the return from Babylon, it must already have been painfully obvious that the majority of the people were opting to remain in exile and not to brave the rigors of their desolate homeland. The exile had been shown to be a permanent condition which would leave an indelible mark upon Jewish history. It was a true *uprooting* and not just a *cutting off.*

In that context, the change to *My land* is readily understandable. Only because it is God's own land, — that corner of the globe over which He exercises His direct Providence (see *Ramban, Leviticus* 18:25 and 26:16) — is it so unforgiving. Such a land demands that the evildoers be uprooted.

וְאֶת־הַבַּיִת הַזֶּה . . . אַשְׁלִיךְ . . . וְאֶתְּנֶנּוּ לְמָשָׁל וְלִשְׁנִינָה — *And this House ... I will cast out ... and I will make it a proverb and a byword.* In the *Kings'* account it is not the Temple but Israel which will become a *proverb* and *byword.*

The explanation may lie in the wording which appears in *Chronicles* and *Kings* respectively in the following verses:

before Me as David your father walked, doing all that I commanded you, guarding My statues and My laws. [18] *Then I will establish the throne of your kingship as I covenanted David your father saying, 'No descendant of yours will be prevented from occupying the throne of Israel.'* [19] *But if you backslide and forsake My statutes and My commandments which I placed before you and go and serve other gods and prostrate yourselves to them.* [20] *Then I will uproot them from My land which I have given to them, and this House which I have sanctified for My name I will cast out from before Me and I will make it a proverb and a byword among all the nations.* [21] *As for this House which was once exalted, every passer-by will be astonished and will say, 'Why has HASHEM done thus to this land and to this House?'* [22] *And they will answer, 'Because they forsook HASHEM, the God of their fathers, who took them out of the land of Egypt and they took hold of other gods and prostrated themselves to them and served them. For this reason He brought upon them all this evil.'*

Chronicles	Kings (ch. 9)
21. וְהַבַּיִת הַזֶּה אֲשֶׁר הָיָה עֶלְיוֹן . . . *As for this Temple which was once exalted . . .*	9. וְהַבַּיִת הַזֶּה יִהְיֶה עֶלְיוֹן . . . *As for this Temple, it shall be exalted . . .*

The *Chronicles'* version seems more logical. It speaks of the exaltedness of the destroyed Temple in the past tense. How are we to understand the future tense which *Kings* uses?

Meshech Chochmah (*Haftarah, Pekudei*) explains: In truth the *Shechinah*, the Divine Presence, never moved away from the Temple grounds even after the building had been destroyed. The sanctity of the location remained unimpaired. It existed in a hidden and concealed manner rather than an open and revealed one.

This hidden *Shechinah* was perceived by the prophetic writer of *Kings*, but not by the author of *Chronicles* who, while he was Divinely inspired, was no prophet. Consequently, for *Chronicles*, the Temple's glory was indeed a matter of the past, while the prophet of *Kings* saw it as ongoing.

Kings, with its perception of the continuing sanctity of the Temple site, could not or would not associate the gentile's calumny with it and had it refer to Israel. In the *Chronicles'* account, no such inhibition existed.

לְמָשָׁל וְלִשְׁנִינָה — *A proverb and a byword*. The expression occurs in *Deuteronomy* 28:37. There *Rashi* explains: מָשָׁל is a standard for comparison. If a catastrophe occurs, people will say: This is comparable to that other terrible event.

The root of שְׁנִינָה is שנן, *to sharpen* or *whet*. Its meaning was extended to describe modes of talk, as for example, וְשִׁנַּנְתָּם לְבָנֶיךָ, which we would render, *you shall teach incisively*.

In our context, it would convey the idea of a subject concerning which people speak sharply and derisively. They whet their tongues when they mention it.

21. אֲשֶׁר־הָיָה עֶלְיוֹן — *Which was once exalted*. See comm. to previous verse.

יִשֹּׁם — *Will be astonished*. The translation follows *Metzudos*. The enormity of the destruction will shock all the passersby.

בַּמֶּה עָשָׂה ה׳ כָּכָה — *Why has HASHEM done thus . . .* The formulation of this and the next verse is similar to *Deuteronomy* 29:23-27.

22. וְאָמְרוּ — *And they will answer*. Those who set themselves to the task of answering those who voice the question of the past verse (*Metzudos*).

ח
א־ג

א וַיְהִי מִקֵּץ ׀ עֶשְׂרִים שָׁנָה אֲשֶׁר בָּנָה שְׁלֹמֹה אֶת־בֵּית יְהֹוָה
ב וְאֶת־בֵּיתוֹ׃ וְהֶעָרִים אֲשֶׁר נָתַן חוּרָם לִשְׁלֹמֹה בָּנָה
ג שְׁלֹמֹה אֹתָם וַיּוֹשֶׁב שָׁם אֶת־בְּנֵי יִשְׂרָאֵל׃ וַיֵּלֶךְ שְׁלֹמֹה

VIII

Following is a list of topics dealt with in this chapter:

1. Solomon's far-flung building projects.
2. The conquest of Chamas Tzovah.
3. Description of the work force employed in the building programs.
4. Arrangements for the living quarters of Pharaoh's daughter.
5. Solomon's practices and dispositions concerning the Temple service.
6. Solomon fits out a navy and imports gold from Ophir.

This list parallels, with some additions and omissions, the list of topics dealt with in *Kings* immediately following upon the account of the inauguration.

However, while these descriptions seem appropriate for *Kings*, they appear out of place in *Chronicles*. The basic intent in *Kings* is clearly to give an extensive overview of Solomon's reign. While the building of the Temple plays a central role, it is by no means the only one of Solomon's many activities which is described. Before the building and inauguration of the Temple is broached, there is an abundance of information concerning Solomon's court, his wisdom, his relationship to his subjects and many other matters, all of which contribute to a broad picture of his reign. The topics listed above all have a legitimate place in such a context. It is entirely apt that the account of the building and inauguration of the Temple be followed by them.

By contrast, *Chronicles* told us nothing at all concerning the details of Solomon's rule. From the vision at Giveon it moved straight to the Temple narrative [with only a small digression to describe the ostentatious consumption of Solomon's court, see below]. *Chronicles*, then, is not interested in a description of Solomon's reign but only in those of his activities which loom large on the stage of history.

Why, in that case, are the six matters discussed in our chapter of greater significance than all those other details of Solomon's reign which do not appear in this book?

At 1:14-17, we discussed the purpose of the short description of Solomon's extreme wealth at that point. We thought that by having it follow immediately upon the vision at Giveon, *Chronicles* was making the point that, in the long view of history, Solomon misused the gift of wisdom which he had been granted on that occasion. The wealth — which, in God's promise, had been less important, — left a disproportionately significant mark.

Much the same purpose may underlie the choice of topics here. In 7:17-22, we noted the judgment of the Sages that the ultimate destruction of the Temple had its roots in Solomon's marriage to Pharaoh's daughter on the very day of the Temple inauguration. Perhaps that misjudgment moved Solomon's thinking, away from his people's spiritual well-being, into more worldly pursuits. We could have expected that the inauguration of the Temple would set in motion an enormous spiritual regeneration of the people. Solomon's activities did not reflect this. They were of a worldly nature, and did nothing to reinforce the spiritual impact which, otherwise, the Temple inauguration might have had.

◆§ Solomon's Building Projects

1. וַיְהִי מִקֵּץ עֶשְׂרִים שָׁנָה — *Now, it was after the twenty years.* The building of the Temple took seven years, and that of Solomon's palace thirteen years (*I Kings* 6:37-38, and 7:1) (*Mefaresh*).

2. וְהֶעָרִים אֲשֶׁר נָתַן חוּרָם לִשְׁלֹמֹה — *The cities which Churam had given Solomon.* All the commentators note that *Kings* speaks not of cities which Churam gave Solomon, but rather of cities which Solomon gave Churam.

The passage reads: *Churam king of Tyre supported Solomon with cedarwood and beroshim wood and with gold to his full desire. Then Solomon gave Churam twenty cities in the land of the Galil. Churam went out from Tyre to see the cities which Solomon had given him but they did not please him. He said, 'What are these cities which you have given me, my brother?' So he called it ' a muddy tract' up to this very day.*

8
1-3

Now, it was after the twenty years which it had taken Solomon to build HASHEM's House and his palace.
2 That Solomon built up the cities which Churam had given
Solomon, and settled the Children of Israel there. 3 Solomon went

Radak and *Metzudos* both write that the two accounts tell of two separate gifts. Each of the two men made a gift of some cities to the other. *Kings* reports the one transaction and *Chronicles* tells of the other. *Ralbag* supports this view on the basis that Solomon would not have given cities to Churam if this would have meant making the Land of Israel smaller. He did so only because he received equivalent cities in return.

Abarbanel and *Malbim* think it unlikely that two separate transactions should have taken place, each reported in one book with no reference to the other. Furthermore, it is unthinkable that Solomon would have given cities in Israel to Churam in direct contravention of the Torah's prohibition against giving land to a gentile (see *Rambam, Hilchos Avodah Zarah* 10:3).

They explain that Solomon never meant to make an outright gift of the cities to Churam. Rather, he gave them so that their produce could yield the wheat, barley, wine and oil which he had contracted to pay the workers (2:9). Title to the cities would remain in Jewish hands. This would explain Churam's dissatisfaction with the cities. It was not that he spurned the gift — it is inconceivable that the good relations which continued between them could have outlasted such an insult had this been the case. Rather, it was an assessment that factually the area was not fertile enough to yield the required amounts. Since the cities could not fill the purpose for which they were given, Churam returned them to Solomon. This is the subject of our passage. Thus there were not two separate transactions but only one. The two books deal with two different aspects of the same occurrence.

Daas Sofrim has a different explanation for the fact that Churam returned the cities. The Tyreans were a mercantile people not interested in agriculture. Solomon had offered them fertile lands which from the point of view of a farming people would have been worthy gifts. Churam returned them because they were not suited to his particular ventures.

None of these explanations help us to understand why *Kings* and *Chronicles* each chose different aspects of the incident to record. Yet, based on what we have learned in previous chapters, we can perhaps explain why *Chronicles* did not want to include that aspect of the story which concerned *Kings*.

In comm. to 2:1, we saw that the *Chronicles'* perspective on Solomon's relationship with Churam differed from that of *Kings*. The latter takes the relationship as between two neighboring and friendly monarchs who reach a mutually attractive and profitable agreement. By contrast, *Chronicles* saw Solomon's approach to Churam in spiritual terms. It was an attempt to draw the heathen king into the orbit of sanctity by allowing him a part in the building of the Temple.

Now the *Kings'* account ties the gift of the cities to the fact that Churam had conscientiously fulfilled his part of the contract by sending the lumber and the gold which he had promised. Apparently, in appreciation for this prompt compliance with the terms of the contract, Solomon felt moved to make an additional gift.

However, this is only appropriate in the *Kings'* account. From the point of view of Churam's legal obligations, he had indeed done all that could have been expected. But it is quite possible that from *Chronicles'* point of view, Solomon's hopes were never realized. Churam did not make the major inner commitment which Solomon had attempted to elicit. Thus, from within that context, there was no reason for Solomon to make the gift. Consequently *Chronicles* does not mention it.

What of the gift mentioned here? Why is it not reported in *Kings*?

Although both *Kings* chapter 9 and *Chronicles* here describe Solomon's extensive building program, they do so from different perspectives.

Kings reports the building program in the context of the work levy which Solomon organized. It may well be that from an historical perspective, it is this aspect which was most significant. It was these heavy levies which precipitated the rebellion against Rechav'am (ch. 10), ultimately causing the division of the kingdoms. In this context the cities which Churam returned were of no interest.

Chronicles has no parallel to v. 15 of *Kings*. It speaks of the levy in v. 8, but in a self-contained passage beginning with v. 7. *Chronicles* was interested in Solomon's build-

ד חֲמָת צוֹבָה וַיֶּחֱזַק עָלֶיהָ: וַיִּבֶן אֶת־תַּדְמֹר בַּמִּדְבָּר וְאֵת
ה כָּל־עָרֵי הַמִּסְכְּנוֹת אֲשֶׁר בָּנָה בַּחֲמָת: וַיִּבֶן אֶת־בֵּית חוֹרוֹן
הָעֶלְיוֹן וְאֶת־בֵּית חוֹרוֹן הַתַּחְתּוֹן עָרֵי מָצוֹר חוֹמוֹת
ו דְּלָתַיִם וּבְרִיחַ: וְאֶת־בַּעֲלָת וְאֵת כָּל־עָרֵי הַמִּסְכְּנוֹת
אֲשֶׁר־הָיוּ לִשְׁלֹמֹה וְאֵת כָּל־עָרֵי הָרֶכֶב וְאֵת עָרֵי
הַפָּרָשִׁים וְאֵת | כָּל־חֵשֶׁק שְׁלֹמֹה אֲשֶׁר חָשַׁק לִבְנוֹת
ז בִּירוּשָׁלַםִ וּבַלְּבָנוֹן וּבְכֹל אֶרֶץ מֶמְשַׁלְתּוֹ: כָּל־הָעָם הַנּוֹתָר
מִן־הַחִתִּי וְהָאֱמֹרִי וְהַפְּרִזִּי וְהַחִוִּי וְהַיְבוּסִי אֲשֶׁר לֹא
ח מִיִּשְׂרָאֵל הֵמָּה: מִן־בְּנֵיהֶם אֲשֶׁר נוֹתְרוּ אַחֲרֵיהֶם בָּאָרֶץ
אֲשֶׁר לֹא־כִלּוּם בְּנֵי יִשְׂרָאֵל וַיַּעֲלֵם שְׁלֹמֹה לְמַס עַד הַיּוֹם
ט הַזֶּה: וּמִן־בְּנֵי יִשְׂרָאֵל אֲשֶׁר לֹא־נָתַן שְׁלֹמֹה לַעֲבָדִים

Chronicles	*Kings*
	15. וְזֶה דְבַר־הַמַּס אֲשֶׁר־הֶעֱלָה הַמֶּלֶךְ שְׁלֹמֹה לִבְנוֹת אֶת־בֵּית ה׳ וְאֶת־בֵּיתוֹ וְאֶת־הַמִּלּוֹא — *The levy which Solomon the King imposed was for this purpose, to build* HASHEM*'s House and his palace and the plaza . . .*
4. וַיִּבֶן אֶת־תַּדְמֹר — *He built Tadmur . . .*	
5. וַיִּבֶן אֶת־בֵּית חוֹרוֹן — *He built Beis Choron*	17. וַיִּבֶן שְׁלֹמֹה אֶת־גָּזֶר וְאֶת־בֵּית חֹרֹן תַּחְתּוֹן — *Solomon built Gazer and the lower Beis Choron . . .*
7. כָּל־הָעָם הַנּוֹתָר מִן־הַחִתִּי — *All the people who remained from the Hittites*	20. כָּל־הָעָם הַנּוֹתָר מִן־הָאֱמֹרִי — *All the people who remained remained from the Emorites . . .*
8. מִן־בְּנֵיהֶם אֲשֶׁר נוֹתְרוּ אַחֲרֵיהֶם וַיַּעֲלֵם שְׁלֹמֹה לְמַס —*From among their sons who remained after them . . . Solomon drafted them into a levy*	21. בְּנֵיהֶם אֲשֶׁר נֹתְרוּ אַחֲרֵיהֶם . . . וַיַּעֲלֵם שְׁלֹמֹה לְמַס־עֹבֵד — *And their sons who remained after them . . . Solomon drafted them into a work levy . . .*

ing activities in their own right, which may have been because of the reasons suggested in the prefatory remarks to this chapter. In this context, Churam's gift of cities was significant. They were a part of the huge expansion which took place during Solomon's reign.

3. וַיֶּחֱזַק עָלֶיהָ — *And prevailed against it.* This is the only hint of any military activities on the part of Solomon, who had been described as a man whose life would be characterized by peace and tranquility (*I Chronicles* 22:9).

The verse has no parallel in *Kings* and there is no extant tradition of the Sages concerning the significance of this campaign.

Perhaps the root חזק does not imply an active military campaign as much as a bloodless occupation (see *Rambam, Bais HaBechirah* 6:16). However, *Targum,* who renders וְאַתְקֵיף, the standard translation for the root חזק, inserts the word צִיָרָא, which is the term used in *targumim* for *siege*, thus implying an active military campaign.

4-6. These verses contain a list of cities which Solomon either built or fortified. It approximates but does not precisely parallel a similar list in *Kings*. *Metzudos* points out that Solomon waited with these projects until he

8
4-9

to Chamas Tzovah and prevailed against it. 4 He built Tadmur
in the desert and all the storage cities which he had built
in Chamath. 5 He built Upper Beth Choron and Lower Beth
Choron, fortified cities; walls, gates and bolts. 6 Baalath and all the
storage cities which belonged to Solomon and all the cities
of the chariots and the cities of the riders and all that Solomon
desired to build in Jerusalem and in the Lebanon and through-
out the land of his rule. 7 All the people who remained from the
Hittites, the Emorites, the Prizites, the Hivites and the Jebusites,
who were not from Israel. 8 From among their sons who remained
after them in the land whom the Children of Israel did not destroy
— Solomon drafted them into a levy — up to this day. 9 But that
Solomon did not subordinate any of the Children of Israel to his

had completed the building of the Temple and of his palace.

4. וַיִּבֶן ... וְאֵת כָּל־עָרֵי הַמִּסְכְּנוֹת אֲשֶׁר בָּנָה בַּחֲמָת — *He built ... and all the storage cities which he built in Chamath.* He 'built' *the cities which he had built* can only mean that he fortified or improved them. The Chamath of this verse may refer to the one mentioned in the previous one (*Malbim*).

5. אֶת־בֵּית חוֹרוֹן הָעֶלְיוֹן — *Upper Beth Choron. Kings* mentions only the Lower Beth Choron.

6. וְאֵת כָּל־חֵשֶׁק שְׁלֹמֹה אֲשֶׁר חָשַׁק לִבְנוֹת — *And all that Solomon desired to build ...* In Section II, to ch. 7 *Solomon's House*, we noted that *Chronicles* had eliminated the phrase חֵשֶׁק שְׁלֹמֹה, which appeared in the parallel passage in *Kings*, and substituted another. We suggested that the expression in *Kings* hinted at Solomon's spiritual longings. By prematurely marrying Pharaoh's daughter on the very night of the inauguration, Solomon had cast a pall over these. His cravings had become narrowed and cramped and now seem directed towards fulfillment in the successful completion of the Temple and palace. The change of expression from the source in *Kings* clearly expressed this disappointment.

Perhaps by using this very phrase in the context of this verse, *Chronicles* is lending emphasis to this judgment. Indeed, Solomon *craved* — but these desires centered upon building projects in Jerusalem and the Lebanon.

7. כָּל־הָעָם הַנּוֹתָר מִן־הַחִתִּי — *All the people who remained from the Hittites...* This verse and the next describe the work levies which Solomon mustered for his building projects.

The levy drew upon descendants (v. 8) of the Canaanite nations which had occupied the land at the time of Joshua's conquest.

Ramban (*Deuteronomy* 20:10) explains that these people did not fall under the Torah's requirement that the seven Canaanite nations be totally destroyed, because they willingly renounced idol worship and accepted conditions of servitude. They had the status of the *Ger Toshav*, the former idol worshiper who had agreed to be bound by the seven Noachide laws.

8. אֲשֶׁר לֹא־כִלּוּם בְּנֵי יִשְׂרָאֵל — *Whom the Children of Israel did not destroy ...* The parallel passage in *Kings* has ... *whom the Children of Israel were not able to destroy. Ramban* explains that prior to Solomon's reign, the Israelites lacked military might. After Solomon came to power, this changed, but, in the meantime, the need had gone. At that time, they agreed to abide by the Noachide laws.

עַד הַיּוֹם הַזֶּה — *Up to this day.* Up to the time when all the building was completed (*Metzudos*).

9. וּמִן־בְּנֵי יִשְׂרָאֵל אֲשֶׁר לֹא־נָתַן שְׁלֹמֹה לַעֲבָדִים — *But that Solomon did not subordinate any of the Children of Israel to his work ...* The translation follows *Ralbag*. It is required in order to accommodate the word אֲשֶׁר, which does not appear in the parallel passage in *Kings*. There, the text reads simply: *Solomon did not make servants of the Children of Israel, because they were soldiers ...*[1]

1. There is a slight but significant change in nuance.
The *Kings'* version appears to speak of the high standing of the Israelites. They qualified for more

ח
י־יד

°הַנִּצָּבִים ק׳

לִמְלַאכְתּוֹ כִּי־הֵמָּה אַנְשֵׁי מִלְחָמָה וְשָׂרֵי שָׁלִישָׁיו וְשָׂרֵי
י רִכְבּוֹ וּפָרָשָׁיו: וְאֵלֶּה שָׂרֵי °הנציבים אֲשֶׁר־לַמֶּלֶךְ
יא שְׁלֹמֹה חֲמִשִּׁים וּמָאתָיִם הָרֹדִים בָּעָם: וְאֶת־בַּת־פַּרְעֹה
הֶעֱלָה שְׁלֹמֹה מֵעִיר דָּוִיד לַבַּיִת אֲשֶׁר בָּנָה־לָהּ כִּי אָמַר
לֹא־תֵשֵׁב אִשָּׁה לִי בְּבֵית דָּוִיד מֶלֶךְ־יִשְׂרָאֵל כִּי־קֹדֶשׁ
הֵמָּה אֲשֶׁר־בָּאָה אֲלֵיהֶם אֲרוֹן יהוה:
יב אָז הֶעֱלָה שְׁלֹמֹה עֹלוֹת לַיהוה עַל מִזְבַּח יהוה אֲשֶׁר
יג בָּנָה לִפְנֵי הָאוּלָם: וּבִדְבַר־יוֹם בְּיוֹם לְהַעֲלוֹת כְּמִצְוַת
מֹשֶׁה לַשַּׁבָּתוֹת וְלֶחֳדָשִׁים וְלַמּוֹעֲדוֹת שָׁלוֹשׁ פְּעָמִים
בַּשָּׁנָה בְּחַג הַמַּצּוֹת וּבְחַג הַשָּׁבֻעוֹת וּבְחַג הַסֻּכּוֹת:
יד וַיַּעֲמֵד כְּמִשְׁפַּט דָּוִיד־אָבִיו אֶת־מַחְלְקוֹת הַכֹּהֲנִים עַל־
עֲבֹדָתָם וְהַלְוִיִּם עַל־מִשְׁמְרוֹתָם לְהַלֵּל וּלְשָׁרֵת נֶגֶד

I Kings 5:27 does speak of levies made from among the Jews. However, the work that they were required to do cannot be described as *servitude*, because they were only on duty for one month out of every three (*Malbim*).

10. וְאֵלֶּה שָׂרֵי הַנִּצָּבִים — *Now these are the overseers of King Solomon's appointees*. With this opening, we would have expected a listing of the names of the overseers. Neither *Kings* nor *Chronicles* seems to have considered this necessary.

הַנִּצָּבִים — *Appointees*. The translation follows *Metzudos*.

חֲמִשִּׁים וּמָאתָיִם — *Two hundred and fifty*. In the *Kings'* account, the number is five hundred and fifty.

The discrepancy can be accounted for on the basis of 2:17 where *Chronicles* listed three hundred more overseers than did *Kings* — see comm. there for the explanation. *Kings* figures those three hundred into its total (*Rashi*).

☙ Pharaoh's Daughter Moves From the City of David

11. וְאֶת־בַּת־פַּרְעֹה הֶעֱלָה שְׁלֹמֹה מֵעִיר דָּוִיד — *Solomon brought up Pharaoh's daughter from the City of David... I Kings* 3:1 teaches that Solomon, when he married Pharaoh's daughter, installed her in the City of David (*I Chronicles* 11:5 and 7).

לֹא־תֵשֵׁב אִשָּׁה לִי — *No woman shall dwell for me ...* It was not the presence of a woman as such which was offensive, but that she dwells *for me*; that is, for the purpose of conjugal relations (*Metzudos*).

בְּבֵית דָּוִיד מֶלֶךְ־יִשְׂרָאֵל — *In the house of David, king of Israel*. In any of the houses within the City of David (*Radak* and *Metzudos*). Or, as *Daas Soferim* suggests, reference could be to the palace which Churam had built for David. It was there that Solomon had housed her.

כִּי־קֹדֶשׁ הֵמָּה — *For they are holy*. The whole City of David and all the houses in it — hence the plural *they* (*Mefaresh*).

אֲשֶׁר־בָּאָה אֲלֵיהֶם אֲרוֹן ה׳ — *Inasmuch as the Ark of HASHEM had been brought there*. The whole area was considered sacred, even though the Ark had not rested in the particular house in which she had taken residence (*Metzudos*).

See Section II, *Solomon and Pharaoh's Daughter*, for an analysis of this passage.

אֲשֶׁר־בָּאָה אֲלֵיהֶם אֲרוֹן ה׳ — *Inasmuch as the Ark of HASHEM had been brought there.*

respectable positions in the military, and were therefore not impressed into the work details.

In *Chronicles*, Solomon is concerned with his convenience. He could well have required even the Jews to work as laborers — that privilege is granted to a king (*Ralbag*) — but refrained from doing so, because the time they would have had to spend at the building sites [note: לַעֲבָדִים לִמְלַאכְתּוֹ, *servants to his work*] would cut into their duties as military men.

This formulation bespeaks a cavalier attitude toward the common people. It may have been the cause of the dissatisfaction which was voiced during the rebellion against Solomon's son, Rechav'am (10:4).

8
10-14

work, was because they were soldiers and chiefs of his captains, and overseers of his chariots and riders. [10] *Now these are the overseers of King Solomon's appointees, two hundred and fifty that exercise authority over the people.* [11] *Solomon brought up Pharaoh's daughter from the City of David to the house which he had built for her, for he said, 'No woman shall dwell for me in the house of David, king of Israel, for they are holy inasmuch as the Ark of HASHEM had been brought there.'* [12] *Then Solomon brought burnt offerings to HASHEM on the altar of HASHEM which he had built before the Entrance Hall.* [13] *Also the daily obligations, which were offered up in accordance with Moses' command; those for the Sabbaths, the New Moons and the appointed seasons, three times a year — on the Feast of Matzos, the Feast of Shavuos and the Feast of Succos.* [14] *And he established — according to the practice of his father, David — the divisions of the Kohanim for their service and the Levites according to their duties — to praise and to serve, corresponding*

Mefaresh and *Radak* point out that the use of the feminine form בָּאָה [instead of בָּא] is irregular with *Ark*, but not unique. *I Samuel* 4:17 has וַאֲרוֹן הָאֱלֹהִים נִלְקָחָה.[1]

The Temple Service Is Established

12. אָז — *Then*. From the time that the Temple was completed (*Metzudos*).

It is possible that, *Then*, refers to the time that the Egyptian princess moved out of the City of David. Only now did Solomon truly feel at ease with the Temple service. Once she was gone, the final obstacle to the Divine service in its ideal form had been removed.

עֹלוֹת — *Burnt offerings*. These burnt offerings need not refer to any specific sacrifices. Once the Temple was built, private altars were interdicted and all burnt offerings were brought only upon the altar in the Temple (*Metzudos*).

Perhaps a specific series of sacrifices is meant. Once the daughter of Pharaoh had been removed from close proximity to the Temple, Solomon brought offerings upon the altar to celebrate its now uncompromised state.

13. From Solomon's voluntary sacrifices, the account now moves to his establishment of the Temple service and organization.

וּבִדְבַר־יוֹם בְּיוֹם — *Also the daily obligations*. All those sacrifices which had to be brought every day (*Metzudos*).

This is descriptive of the regular components of the daily Temple service. These are described in tractate *Tamid* and in *Rambam, Temidim UMusafim*.

לְהַעֲלוֹת כְּמִצְוַת מֹשֶׁה — *Which were offered up in accordance with Moses' command*. See fn. to *I Chronicles* 6:34.

לַשַּׁבָּתוֹת — *Those for the Sabbaths*... These would be the *musafim*, the additional communal sacrifices, which were offered up on the special days listed in this verse.

14. כְּמִשְׁפַּט דָּוִיד־אָבִיו — *According to the practice of his father, David*. For מִשְׁפָּט, as *practice* or *habit*, see *I Samuel* 27:11.

אֶת־מַחְלְקוֹת הַכֹּהֲנִים — *The divisions of the Kohanim*. These divisions are described in *I Chronicles* ch. 24. At 7:6, the word מִשְׁמְרוֹתָם is used.

וְהַלְוִיִּם עַל־מִשְׁמְרוֹתָם — *And the Levites accord-*

1. In the example in *Samuel*, the use of the feminine form is particularly apt. The Ark was, as it were, too weak to have prevented its capture by the Philistines.

In our case, the explanation is less obvious. Perhaps it is used to show that it was not the physical presence of the Ark which made the proximity of the princess offensive, but the fact that the Divine Presence [*Shechinah* is feminine] rested upon it.

ח הַכֹּהֲנִים לִדְבַר־יוֹם בְּיוֹמוֹ וְהַשּׁוֹעֲרִים בְּמַחְלְקוֹתָם לְשַׁעַר
טו־יח טו וָשָׁעַר כִּי כֵן מִצְוַת דָּוִיד אִישׁ־הָאֱלֹהִים: וְלֹא סָרוּ
מִצְוַת הַמֶּלֶךְ עַל־הַכֹּהֲנִים וְהַלְוִיִּם לְכָל־דָּבָר וְלָאֹצָרוֹת:
טז וַתִּכֹּן כָּל־מְלֶאכֶת שְׁלֹמֹה עַד־הַיּוֹם מוּסַד בֵּית־יְהוָה
יז וְעַד־כְּלֹתוֹ שָׁלֵם בֵּית יְהוָה: אָז הָלַךְ
שְׁלֹמֹה לְעֶצְיוֹן־גֶּבֶר וְאֶל־אֵילוֹת עַל־שְׂפַת הַיָּם בְּאֶרֶץ
°אֳנִיּוֹת ק׳ יח אֱדוֹם: וַיִּשְׁלַח־לוֹ חוּרָם בְּיַד־עֲבָדָיו °אוניות וַעֲבָדִים
יוֹדְעֵי יָם וַיָּבֹאוּ עִם־עַבְדֵי שְׁלֹמֹה אוֹפִירָה וַיִּקְחוּ מִשָּׁם
ט אַרְבַּע־מֵאוֹת וַחֲמִשִּׁים כִּכַּר זָהָב וַיָּבִיאוּ אֶל־הַמֶּלֶךְ
א א שְׁלֹמֹה: וּמַלְכַּת־שְׁבָא שָׁמְעָה אֶת־שֵׁמַע שְׁלֹמֹה

ing to their duties. In *I Chronicles* 23:32, we find this word used with a number of different connotations: guarding; having charge; and serving. Any of these meanings could be assigned here. At 7:6, the word is used to describe the divisions of the *Kohanim* and the Levites — see above.

נֶגֶד הַכֹּהֲנִים — *Corresponding to the Kohanim*. The twenty-four Levite divisions served in conjunction with those of the *Kohanim* (*I Chronicles* 25:8).

וְהַשּׁוֹעֲרִים בְּמַחְלְקוֹתָם — *Also the gatekeepers according to their divisions*. See *I Chronicles* 9:18 ff.

15. וְלֹא סָרוּ מִצְוַת הַמֶּלֶךְ ... — *They did not deviate from the king's orders*. *Radak* and *Metzudos* point out that we must read the phrase as though a prefixed *mem* were inserted — מִמִּצְוַת הַמֶּלֶךְ.

וְלָאֹצָרוֹת — *And concerning the treasure houses*. See *I Chronicles* 26:22 and 24.

16. וַתִּכֹּן — ... *was firmly established*. The root כון has the general meaning of *to be firm* and is used frequently in the sense of *to establish* or *set in order*.

The entire project, from beginning to end, went without hindrance (*Metzudos*).

מוּסַד בֵּית־ה׳ — *From the day that the foundation of* HASHEM*'s House had been laid*. *Radak* points out that here too we must render as though the word was written with a prefixed *mem*: מִמּוּסָד.

יְסוֹד is a *foundation*; מוּסָד, the *laying of the foundation*.

שָׁלֵם בֵּית ה׳ — *The House of* HASHEM *was complete*. Because of Solomon's careful preparations, both the physical plant and the activities carried out within it worked smoothly (*Malbim*).

◆§ Other Activities

17. אָז הָלַךְ שְׁלֹמֹה — *Then Solomon went...* Solomon conquered these two cities, and was thus able to build the fleet at Etzion Gever, as is recorded in the *Kings'* account (*Radak*).

18. וַיִּקְחוּ ... זָהָב — *And took ... gold*. This passage seeks to explain how Solomon financed his vast building projects. There is no indication that he taxed the people in any way except for the work levies. Since, as noted above (5:1), he did not touch the treasures which David had collected but put them into the Temple storage houses, we would wonder from what source he drew the vast financial resources which would be required. We learn here that he imported great quantities of gold from Ophir (*Abarbanel*).

אַרְבַּע־מֵאוֹת וַחֲמִשִּׁים כִּכַּר זָהָב — *Four hundred and fifty talents of gold*. *Kings* talks of four hundred and twenty talents. *Radak* explains that the other thirty talents were used to defray the cost of the trip.

IX

◆§ The Visit of the Queen of Sheba

The *Chronicles'* account of the Queen of Sheba's visit parallels *I Kings*, 10:1-10. In almost every phrase, there are substantive differences. These reflect the perspective which each book

8
15-18

to the Kohanim — day by day. Also the gatekeepers according to
their divisions, over the various gates, for such was the command
of David the man of God. 15 *They did not deviate from the king's*
orders concerning the Kohanim and the Levites, relative to all
matters, and concerning the treasure houses. 16 *All that Solomon*
had wrought, from the day that the foundation of HASHEM's
House had been laid until it was finished, was firmly established.
The House of HASHEM was complete. 17 *Then Solomon went to*
Etzion Gever and to Eilath on the shore of the sea in the land of
Edom. 18 *Churam, by his servants, sent him ships and expert*
boatmen. They accompanied Solomon's servants to Ophir and
took from there four hundred and fifty talents of gold. They
brought them to King Solomon.

9
1

The Queen of Sheba heard the fame of Solomon and

brings to bear upon this event.

In Section II, *The Queen of Sheba*, we learn that the coming of the queen was meant to presage mighty events of Messianic significance. This potential was not fulfilled, and the visit ended instead in tragedy.

The comm. will show that *Kings* describes the story in the context of the original hopes which were attached to it, while *Chronicles* takes the realistic and bitter perspective of historical hindsight.

1. וּמַלְכַּת־שְׁבָא שָׁמְעָה אֶת־שֵׁמַע שְׁלֹמֹה — *The Queen of Sheba heard the fame of Solomon.* A comparison of this verse to the first two verses in the *Kings'* account yields the following:

Chronicles	*Kings*
(a) 1. וּמַלְכַּת־שְׁבָא שָׁמְעָה אֶת־שֵׁמַע שְׁלֹמֹה, — *The Queen of Sheba heard the fame of Solomon*	(a) 1. וּמַלְכַּת־שְׁבָא שֹׁמַעַת אֶת־שֵׁמַע שְׁלֹמֹה, — *The Queen of Sheba hears the fame of Solomon*
(b)	(b) לְשֵׁם ה׳ — *devoted to God*
(c) וַתָּבוֹא לְנַסּוֹת אֶת־שְׁלֹמֹה בְחִידוֹת, — *and came to test Solomon with riddles*	(c) וַתָּבֹא לְנַסֹּתוֹ בְּחִידוֹת. — *and came to test him with riddles.*
(d) בִּירוּשָׁלִַם — *in Jerusalem*	(d) וַתָּבֹא יְרוּשָׁלַיְמָה — *She came to Jerusalem*
(e) בְּחַיִל כָּבֵד מְאֹד, — *with an extremely large retinue ...*	(e) ... בְּחַיִל כָּבֵד מְאֹד — *with an extremely large retinue ...*

Significant differences are as follows:

1. In (a), *Chronicles* uses the perfect while *Kings* uses the imperfect tense.

2. *Chronicles* has no parallel to the (b) phrase in *Kings*.

3. The coming of the Queen of Sheba to Jerusalem is given in a separate statement in *Kings*, (d), but is not mentioned in *Chronicles* at all. There, Jerusalem appears only as the location at which the testing took place (d).

Each book uses language appropriate to its perspective.

The use of the perfect tense generally implies that the speaker wishes to see a particular action as completed, while the imperfect is used in cases where, even if the particular action referred to was done in the past, it is to be viewed as part of a continuing process. Thus, *Kings* introduces the story in the imperfect — the Queen of Sheba's *hearing* is only the beginning of an anticipated process. Many more will hear and follow her example. This, of course, did not transpire, and from the historical perspective of *Chronicles* it was a one-time occurrence —

ט
ב־ה

וַתָּבוֹא לְנַסּוֹת אֶת־שְׁלֹמֹה בְחִידוֹת בִּירוּשָׁלִַם בְּחַיִל כָּבֵד
מְאֹד וּגְמַלִּים נֹשְׂאִים בְּשָׂמִים וְזָהָב לָרֹב וְאֶבֶן יְקָרָה
וַתָּבוֹא אֶל־שְׁלֹמֹה וַתְּדַבֵּר עִמּוֹ אֵת כָּל־אֲשֶׁר הָיָה
ב עִם־לְבָבָהּ׃ וַיַּגֶּד־לָהּ שְׁלֹמֹה אֶת־כָּל־דְּבָרֶיהָ וְלֹא־נֶעְלַם
ג דָּבָר מִשְּׁלֹמֹה אֲשֶׁר לֹא הִגִּיד לָהּ׃ וַתֵּרֶא מַלְכַּת־שְׁבָא
ד אֵת חָכְמַת שְׁלֹמֹה וְהַבַּיִת אֲשֶׁר בָּנָה׃ וּמַאֲכַל שֻׁלְחָנוֹ
וּמוֹשַׁב עֲבָדָיו וּמַעֲמַד מְשָׁרְתָיו וּמַלְבּוּשֵׁיהֶם וּמַשְׁקָיו
וּמַלְבּוּשֵׁיהֶם וַעֲלִיָּתוֹ אֲשֶׁר יַעֲלֶה בֵּית יהוה וְלֹא־הָיָה
ה עוֹד בָּהּ רוּחַ׃ וַתֹּאמֶר אֶל־הַמֶּלֶךְ אֱמֶת הַדָּבָר אֲשֶׁר

expressed by the use of the perfect tense.

In *Kings*, the fact that the Queen of Sheba apprehended the Divine source of Solomon's wisdom (b) plays the central role. It is that which infuses the entire narrative with meaning. By leaving out the phrase, *Chronicles* reveals its assessment of the incident.

Finally, in *Kings*, the fact that she heard of Solomon's fame is presented as only a means towards an end. The theme of the story is that she *came to Jerusalem* (d) — locus of the Divine on earth. In *Chronicles*, it is just the place in which Solomon happened to be.

שֵׁמַע — *Fame*. From שמע, *to hear*. Fame is that which may be heard concerning him who has it.

לְנַסּוֹת אֶת־שְׁלֹמֹה בְחִידוֹת —*To test Solomon with riddles*. In Section II, *The Queen of Sheba*, we point out the seeming incongruity of attaching significance to the puerile riddles with which a heathen queen might want to test Israel's great king.

Both לְנַסּוֹת and חִידוֹת can have more than one meaning.

נסה is used not only to test whether a given answer is correct, but also, in a broader sense, to describe a careful probing of whether or not one would be well advised to subordinate oneself to another (*Ramban, Deuteronomy* 6:16).

חִידָה is not only a riddle but also a perplexing moral dilemma (cf. *Psalms* 49:5).

Thus, the Queen of Sheba may well have wished to seek solutions for her deepest moral perplexities from Solomon. She would have hoped that she could be persuaded to subordinate her and her people's spiritual fate to his wisdom.

This — with the tone set by the (b) phrase — would be the meaning in *Kings*. If she first 'tested the waters' with the sort of riddle suggested by *Midrash Mishlei* [see fn. to Section II], these would be very far indeed from her real intentions. In the *Chronicles'* perspective, however, these exalted hopes were seen to have been misplaced, as illustrated by the absence of the (b) phrase, and nothing was left but the childish conundrum.

בְּחַיִל כָּבֵד מְאֹד — *With an extremely large retinue*. כָּבֵד, whose basic meaning is *heavy* or *weighty*, is also used in the sense of *numerous*. Cf. *Exodus* 10:14 or 12:38.

אֵת כָּל־אֲשֶׁר הָיָה עִם־לְבָבָהּ — *All that was in her heart*. She had kept these riddles secret from everybody so that Solomon would not hear them before she had a chance to test him (*Metzudos*).

Solomon's Divine wisdom enabled him to hear not only the words of the riddle which she articulated with her mouth, but also the solution which she kept in her heart. By telling him the riddle, she was really communicating the solution to him (*Malbim*).

This, from the *Chronicles* perspective. But that which is *in one's heart* can also describe deeply cherished convictions, matters well understood (cf. *Deuteronomy* 8:5). The phrase could just as well be rendered: *She told him of her innermost concerns*. This would be the meaning in *Kings*.

A subtle change in language bears this out. Where *Kings* has וַתְּדַבֵּר אֵלָיו, *and spoke to him*, *Chronicles* has וַתְּדַבֵּר עִמּוֹ, *and spoke with him*. The difference in nuance is clear. When one speaks *to a person*, a distance is maintained. Speaking *with* a person places the two parties on an equal footing. In the *Kings'* perspective, which deals with the innermost thoughts of the Queen's heart, עִמּוֹ would have been inappropriate. No one can reveal everything that goes on in his heart — one can only selectively convey certain aspects. However,

came to test Solomon with riddles in Jerusalem with an extremely large retinue, camels carrying spices and gold in abundance and precious stones. She came to Solomon and spoke with him all that was in her heart.
2 *Solomon told her all her solutions; there was nothing hidden from Solomon that he did not tell her.*
3 *The Queen of Sheba observed Solomon's wisdom and the palace which he had built.*
4 *The food of his table, the seating of his servants, the office of his ministrants and their apparel, his cupbearers and their apparel and his ascent by which he ascended to the House of HASHEM, so that there was no more spirit left in her.*
5 *She said to the king, 'The things which I heard in my*

when a riddle is posed which does not touch on the inner nature of the person who asks it, the two parties in the conversation are equal.

2. וַיַּגֶּד־לָהּ שְׁלֹמֹה אֶת־כָּל־דְּבָרֶיהָ — *Solomon told her all her solutions*. The root נגד whose basic meaning seems to be, *to be conspicuous* is often used in the sense, *to tell*, and particularly, to make known something which up to that point had not been known or understood. Cf. *Genesis* 3:11, 12:18, 41:25.

דָּבָר is versatile and has many different shadings. Here *Malbim* interprets it as referring to the hidden words that lie behind the spoken word; that is, the solution to the riddles. In *Kings* it would mean, the concerns of her heart, as for example in *Deuteronomy* 15:9.

וְלֹא־נֶעְלַם דָּבָר — *There was nothing hidden*. The emphasis is different than in *Kings* which reads לֹא־הָיָה דָּבָר נֶעְלָם, *there was no matter which was hidden.*

The difference in emphasis reflects the two perspectives. In *Chronicles*, the subject is a series of riddles which the queen posed. Solomon knew the solutions and so nothing — no part of the problem — was hidden from him.

In *Kings*, where the queen bares her innermost heart to Solomon, the meaning is: there was no matter of concern to her which she did not reveal to the king.

3. אֶת חָכְמַת שְׁלֹמֹה — *Solomon's wisdom*. *Kings* has: אֵת כָּל חָכְמַת־שְׁלֹמֹה, *all of Solomon's wisdom.*

The omission of *all* here is entirely apt. The *Kings'* account deals with the entire range of the queen's innermost concerns. Solomon, in order to satisfy her needs, would have had to call on the full range of his profound understanding. In *Chronicles*, the issue is no more than the solution to specific riddles. These touched only those aspects of Solomon's wisdom to which they were addressed.

וְהַבַּיִת אֲשֶׁר בָּנָה — *And the palace which he had built*. Evidently, the design of the palace also revealed great wisdom (*Ralbag*).

4. וּמַאֲכַל שֻׁלְחָנוֹ — *The food of his table*. Even the food which was served at Solomon's table reflected his wisdom. It was correctly balanced so as to supply the needs of nutrition and health (*Ralbag*).

וּמוֹשַׁב עֲבָדָיו — *The seating of his servants*. Each one of Solomon's servants sat precisely where his station and function entitled him to sit (*Metzudos*).

וּמַעֲמַד מְשָׁרְתָיו — *The office of his ministrants*. See *Isaiah* 22:19 concerning the office or function to which a person is appointed. Each ministrant had his particular function and never changed it (*Mefaresh*).

וּמַלְבּוּשֵׁיהֶם — *And their apparel*. Clothes which they wore one day they would not wear again the next day (*Mefaresh*). *Metzudos* thinks that each one of Solomon's ministrants wore a livery suitable to his particular task.

וּמַשְׁקָיו — *His cupbearers*. From שקה, *to cause to drink*.

וַעֲלִיָּתוֹ — *And his ascent*. This was the ramp by which he went from his house to the Temple (*Rashi*). This ramp must have been made by a particularly complex architectural design, thus demonstrating Solomon's wisdom (*Ralbag*).

וְלֹא־הָיָה עוֹד בָּהּ רוּחַ — *So that there was no more spirit left in her*. She was so overwhelmed by all the wisdom that it was as though her spirit had left her (*Metzudos*).

She had thought that the sages of her country were wiser than those of any other.

ו שָׁמַעְתִּי בְּאַרְצִי עַל־דְּבָרֶיךָ וְעַל־חָכְמָתֶךָ: וְלֹא־הֶאֱמַנְתִּי
לְדִבְרֵיהֶם עַד אֲשֶׁר־בָּאתִי וַתִּרְאֶינָה עֵינַי וְהִנֵּה לֹא
הֻגַּד־לִי חֲצִי מַרְבִּית חָכְמָתֶךָ יָסַפְתָּ עַל־הַשְּׁמוּעָה אֲשֶׁר
ז שָׁמָעְתִּי: אַשְׁרֵי אֲנָשֶׁיךָ וְאַשְׁרֵי עֲבָדֶיךָ אֵלֶּה הָעֹמְדִים
ח לְפָנֶיךָ תָּמִיד וְשֹׁמְעִים אֶת־חָכְמָתֶךָ: יְהִי יְהוָה אֱלֹהֶיךָ
בָּרוּךְ אֲשֶׁר חָפֵץ בְּךָ לְתִתְּךָ עַל־כִּסְאוֹ לְמֶלֶךְ לַיהוָה
אֱלֹהֶיךָ בְּאַהֲבַת אֱלֹהֶיךָ אֶת־יִשְׂרָאֵל לְהַעֲמִידוֹ לְעוֹלָם
ט וַיִּתֶּנְךָ עֲלֵיהֶם לְמֶלֶךְ לַעֲשׂוֹת מִשְׁפָּט וּצְדָקָה: וַתִּתֵּן
לַמֶּלֶךְ מֵאָה וְעֶשְׂרִים | כִּכַּר זָהָב וּבְשָׂמִים לָרֹב מְאֹד וְאֶבֶן
יְקָרָה וְלֹא הָיָה כַּבֹּשֶׂם הַהוּא אֲשֶׁר־נָתְנָה מַלְכַּת־שְׁבָא
י לַמֶּלֶךְ שְׁלֹמֹה: וְגַם־עַבְדֵי °חירם וְעַבְדֵי שְׁלֹמֹה אֲשֶׁר־ °חוּרָם ק׳
הֵבִיאוּ זָהָב מֵאוֹפִיר הֵבִיאוּ עֲצֵי אַלְגּוּמִּים וְאֶבֶן יְקָרָה:
יא וַיַּעַשׂ הַמֶּלֶךְ אֶת־עֲצֵי הָאַלְגּוּמִּים מְסִלּוֹת לְבֵית־יהוה
וּלְבֵית הַמֶּלֶךְ וְכִנֹּרוֹת וּנְבָלִים לַשָּׁרִים וְלֹא־נִרְאוּ כָהֵם
יב לְפָנִים בְּאֶרֶץ יְהוּדָה: וְהַמֶּלֶךְ שְׁלֹמֹה נָתַן לְמַלְכַּת־שְׁבָא
אֶת־כָּל־חֶפְצָהּ אֲשֶׁר שָׁאָלָה מִלְּבַד אֲשֶׁר־הֵבִיאָה אֶל־

When she met Solomon she realized that he was much greater (*Mefaresh*).

5. עַל־דְּבָרֶיךָ וְעַל־חָכְמָתֶךָ — *Concerning your style of living and your wisdom.* Our translation follows *Malbim*. Normally, we would expect someone deeply involved with matters of the intellect to be less adept regarding the niceties of physical organization. Solomon excelled in both areas.

6. חֲצִי מַרְבִּית חָכְמָתֶךָ — *Half of your great wisdom. Kings* adds that, besides the great wisdom which Solomon showed, he also displayed an abundance of טוֹב, *goodness.* Whereas *Chronicles* deals only with the riddles which Solomon solved — thus demonstrating his wisdom — *Kings* deals with a much more profound contact with the queen. In that relationship, Solomon's goodness may well have come to the fore.

7. וְשֹׁמְעִים אֶת־חָכְמָתֶךָ — *And hear your wisdom. Kings* has *...those who hear your wisdom*. In *Chronicles*, the queen sees nothing special in the people themselves. They may be ordinary, but are still lucky to be constantly in the presence of such wisdom. In *Kings*, she realizes that men who are constantly exposed to Solomon's depth of understanding must be special indeed.

8. לְתִתְּךָ עַל־כִּסְאוֹ — *To place you upon His throne. Kings* has *upon Israel's throne*. In addition, it does not have *as king to* HASHEM *your God*. In this, *Chronicles* is consistent with its earlier language — cf. *I Chronicles* 28:5 and 29:23 — where the Davidic throne is described as God's throne. See Section II, *Analysis* ... to *I Chronicles*, ch. 17, p. 443, for a discussion.

לְהַעֲמִידוֹ לְעוֹלָם — *To establish them forever.* יִשְׂרָאֵל is treated in the singular as it is countless times throughout Scripture.

9. וְלֹא הָיָה כַּבֹּשֶׂם הַהוּא — *There had never been such spice. Kings* adds עוֹד לָרֹב, *in such multitude*, indicating that the uniqueness refers to the great quantity of the spices.

11. וַיַּעַשׂ הַמֶּלֶךְ. . . מְסִלּוֹת לְבֵית־ה׳ — *And the king made ... pathways to the House of* HASHEM. *Radak*, in *Sefer HaShorashim* under סלל, *to raise up*, suggests the meaning of *ceilings* or *stairways*, or perhaps, *supporting pillars*.

Abarbanel explains that this is mentioned here in order to explain the boundless wonder which the queen had displayed at the ramp which Solomon had built between his palace and the Temple (v. 4). Our verse explains that this walkway was made entirely from *Algumim wood* — an extremely rare and precious commodity — and this elicited her admiration.

land concerning your style of living and your wisdom are true.
6 *I had not believed their words until I came and my eyes saw.*
Behold, not half of your great wisdom was told to me. You
exceeded the fame which I heard. 7 *Happy are your men and*
happy are these, your servants, who stand continually before you
and hear your wisdom. 8 *Blessed be* H*ASHEM* *your God who*
found sufficient pleasure in you to place you upon His throne as
king for H*ASHEM* *your God. Because your God loved Israel to*
establish them forever, He made you king over them so that you
would practice justice and charity.' 9 *She gave the king a*
hundred and twenty talents of gold and spices in great
abundance, and precious stones. There had never been such spice
as the Queen of Sheba gave to King Solomon. 10 *Also the servants*
of Churam and the servants of Solomon, that brought gold from
Ophir, brought Algumim wood and precious stones. 11 *And the*
king made — from the Algumim wood — pathways to the House
of H*ASHEM* *and to the palace of the king, and kinoros and nebalim*
for the singers. There were none such seen before in the land of
Judah. 12 *King Solomon gave the Queen of Sheba all her desires*
for which she asked besides that which she had brought to the

12. וְהַמֶּלֶךְ שְׁלֹמֹה נָתַן לְמַלְכַּת־שְׁבָא אֶת־כָּל־חֶפְצָהּ — *King Solomon gave the Queen of Sheba all her desires.* He taught her the wisdom which she craved (*Rashi*).

The verse in *Kings* goes on: *Besides that which he gave [with the generosity to be expected] by the hand of King Solomon*. These are gifts and luxurious items which were available in the Land of Israel but not in Sheba (*Rashi*).

Apparently, then he showered her with both spiritual and monetary gifts.

In *Chronicles*, the structure of the verse is less simple. Instead of *Besides that which he gave . . .,* our phrase reads *Besides that which she brought to the king*, thereby apparently destroying the inner logic of the sentence. How do the two parts, *King Solomon gave to the Queen of Sheba all that she desired, besides that which she brought to the king* connect?

Targum's solution, adopted by many commentators, is to interpret the second phrase: *Besides that [which Solomon gave her* (as explicated in *Kings*) *in exchange for that] which she brought to the king*. *Mefaresh* adds that, by underlining the fact that she brought gifts, without mentioning that which Solomon gave in exchange, his prestige is enhanced. The queen brought more than she took away with her.

The question still remains why such an obscure sentence structure should have been substituted for the apparently clear wording in *Kings*.

Shalsheles HaKaballah (under *Mekor HaLeshonos*) brings a midrash [which seems not to be extant], which is interpolated into the printed versions of *Rashi* to *I Kings* 10:13. The phrase *all her desires* means that Solomon was intimate with the Queen of Sheba, and that she bore him a daughter from whom Nevuchadnezzar, the destroyer of the Temple, was descended.

The similarity between this midrash and the tradition of the Sages (see 7:17-22), that when Solomon married the daughter of Pharaoh, Gabriel descended from heaven and planted a rod in the sea around which a land mass coalesced and upon which the city of Rome was built, is obvious. Just as Solomon's marriage to Pharaoh's daughter, undertaken with the most exalted motivation, is nevertheless construed as having been misconceived and consequently at the root of the Temple's ultimate destruction; so too, his relationship with the Queen of Sheba is perceived as having been ill-advised and — in its long-range effect — tragic.

We need not necessarily take the midrash's

יג הַמֶּלֶךְ וַתַּהֲפֹךְ וַתֵּלֶךְ לְאַרְצָהּ הִיא וַעֲבָדֶיהָ׃ וַיְהִי
מִשְׁקַל הַזָּהָב אֲשֶׁר־בָּא לִשְׁלֹמֹה בְּשָׁנָה אֶחָת שֵׁשׁ
יד מֵאוֹת וְשִׁשִּׁים וָשֵׁשׁ כִּכְּרֵי זָהָב׃ לְבַד מֵאַנְשֵׁי הַתָּרִים
וְהַסֹּחֲרִים מְבִיאִים וְכָל־מַלְכֵי עֲרַב וּפַחוֹת הָאָרֶץ
טו מְבִיאִים זָהָב וָכֶסֶף לִשְׁלֹמֹה׃ וַיַּעַשׂ הַמֶּלֶךְ שְׁלֹמֹה
מָאתַיִם צִנָּה זָהָב שָׁחוּט שֵׁשׁ מֵאוֹת זָהָב שָׁחוּט יַעֲלֶה
טז עַל־הַצִּנָּה הָאֶחָת׃ וּשְׁלֹשׁ־מֵאוֹת מָגִנִּים זָהָב שָׁחוּט שְׁלֹשׁ
מֵאוֹת זָהָב יַעֲלֶה עַל־הַמָּגֵן הָאֶחָת וַיִּתְּנֵם הַמֶּלֶךְ בְּבֵית
יז יַעַר הַלְּבָנוֹן׃ וַיַּעַשׂ הַמֶּלֶךְ כִּסֵּא־שֵׁן גָּדוֹל וַיְצַפֵּהוּ

assertion literally. It would be well within the norm of legitimate agaddic interpretation to suppose that the Sages used the idea of intimate relations as a metaphor for the most pronounced expression for that subordination which we discussed in Section II, and which originally took the form of her coming to Jerusalem laden with gifts for the king from whom she anticipated the fulfillment of her spiritual cravings.

Our verse can be seen as the source of the midrash's insight — its structure would tend to yield it. Solomon gave the queen *all that she desired*; he permitted her to subjugate herself entirely to his overwhelming spirituality — this act of ultimate subordination taking place besides her original gesture, in coming to him laden with gifts.

That *Chronicles* changed the expression in the final phrase of our verse now takes on new significance — see below.

וַתַּהֲפֹךְ וַתֵּלֶךְ לְאַרְצָהּ — *But she turned around and returned to her land. Kings* has וַתֵּפֶן וַתֵּלֶךְ לְאַרְצָהּ, *She turned and returned to her land.* The change from וַתֵּפֶן to וַתַּהֲפֹךְ is particularly striking. The combination of פנה, *turned*, with another verb such as הלך occurs frequently in Scripture. It implies a readying of oneself to action. By contrast, הפך, *turn around*, never occurs with הלך.

Why would the *Chronicles* have changed a perfectly normal expression into one which is, at the very least, irregular?

The implication is clear. The phrase is meant to convey the idea of a changed attitude. In spite of Solomon's willingness to give her all that she asked for, she had a change of heart and decided to return — unregenerated — to her land. Potential friendship turned instead into an antagonism from which, in the end, Nevuchadnezzar, and all that he stands for, came about.

Thus our perception of *Chronicles'* perspective of the story of the Queen of Sheba derives from this verse.

We are left without guidance from the Sages as to what went wrong. Why, with all her good intentions, did the queen not succeed in maintaining her quest? We cannot know for sure. We must assume that the time for, תִּקּוּן עוֹלָם בְּמַלְכוּת שַׁדַּי, *the final sublimation of the world*, had not yet come.

◆§ Solomon's Wealth

13-28. This section describes the vast wealth which flowed, in one way or another, into Solomon's coffers, and the profligacy with which he disposed of it. See Section II, *Solomon's Wealth*, for a discussion.

13. בְּשָׁנָה אֶחָת — *In one year. Rashi* thinks that a specific year is meant. The 666 talents are made up of the 120 given by Churam (*I Kings* 9:14, but not mentioned in *Chronicles*); the 120 given by the Queen of Sheba (*I Kings* 10:10 and *Chronicles* v. 9), and the 420 imported from Ophir (*I Kings* 9:28). *Rashi* confesses ignorance concerning the source of the additional six talents.

Ralbag interprets the verse as describing an annual income brought about by the many gifts given Solomon by the neighboring kings.

14. לְבַד מֵאַנְשֵׁי הַתָּרִים וְהַסֹּחֲרִים מְבִיאִים — *Besides that which the traffickers and the merchants brought.* תָּרִים from תור, *to seek out, spy out or explore*. These are the small business people who need to travel to many places to buy and sell, because they do not have a wide choice of wares. סֹחֲרִים are the big merchants (*Radak* and *Metzudos*).

These people, through their business activities, also enriched Solomon's coffers.

Mefaresh thinks that מְבִיאִים, *brought*, implies that they did not come in the normal

king but she turned around and returned to her land, she and
her servants. 13 *The weight of the gold which came to Solomon*
in one year was six hundred and sixty six talents of gold.
14 *Besides that which the traffickers and the merchants brought.*
And all the kings of Arabia and the governor of the land brought
gold and silver to Solomon. 15 *King Solomon made two hundred*
body shields from drawn gold. Six hundred gold [pieces]
of drawn gold went into one body shield. 16 *And three hundred*
shields of drawn gold; three hundred gold pieces went into
one shield. The king put them in the Forest of Lebanon
palace. 17 *Solomon made a great throne of ivory and overlaid it*

course of their travels. They made a special point of bringing their wares so that they would be exposed to Solomon's wisdom.

וּפַחוֹת הָאָרֶץ — *And the governor of the land. Radak* (*Sefer HaShorashim*) says that the word has the same meaning as נָגִיד, *prince*. It occurs mainly but not exclusively in the later Scriptural books.

15. מָאתַיִם צִנָּה — *Two hundred body shields. Metzudos* writes that the צִנָּה surrounds the entire body. However, it cannot be a suit of armor since 14:7 talks of soldiers carrying the צִנָּה. Thus, we translate *body shield* to differentiate it from the smaller shields of the next verse.

זָהָב שָׁחוּט — *Drawn gold*. The softer the gold, the better its quality. The gold from which these body shields were made could be drawn out like wax (*Metzudos*).

שֵׁשׁ מֵאוֹת זָהָב — *Six hundred gold [pieces]*. Six hundred *dinarim* which are the equivalent of six *manah* (*Rashi*).

16. בְּבֵית יַעַר הַלְּבָנוֹן — *In the Forest of Lebanon palace. I Kings* 7:2 tells of a *Forest of Lebanon palace* constructed by Solomon. *Metzudos* explains the name, either because it was reminiscent of a forest because of the vast number of cedar logs used in its construction, or because it was situated in the Lebanon.

Solomon used the golden shields to decorate his palace.

◆§ Solomon's Throne

17-19. These verses contain a description of Solomon's throne. It seems to belong in this part of the narrative because the throne, which was made of ivory, was overlaid with gold. Thus it is another example of the profligate use of gold in Solomon's Jerusalem.

There is a vast body of aggadic literature which pictures a fantastic structure with many intricate features not explicated in the text. Deep allegorical significance is attached to all the throne's components, and the Sages (*Zohar* 1 p. 243) teach that it was meant to be a representation of God's heavenly throne.

There is a significant difference between the *Kings'* and the *Chronicles'* descriptions. After telling of the six steps leading up to the throne, *Kings* reports a *capping piece* to the rear of the throne. *Chronicles* does not mention this component, but substitutes a *golden ramp* leading up to the throne which, in turn, is not mentioned in *Kings*.

What can be the significance of this change?

R' Acha (quoted in *Pesikta d'R' Kahana*) taught that the *capping stone* was meant to give Solomon's throne the appearance of the *cathedra*[1] of Moses. [See *Shemos Rabbah* 43, that God set a *cathedra* for Moses at Sinai.]

Clearly, this midrash stands within the tradition which teaches that Solomon craved to be like Moses [see Section II to ch.1, *Solomon and Moses*]. He might well have expressed that craving by having his throne made just like the one ascribed to Moses at Sinai. The capping piece would have been, as it were, the crowning glory of the chair, acting as a reminder of Solomon's aspirations.

This being so, the omission of the phrase from *Chronicles* and the substitution of a phrase describing a ramp leading up to the throne become highly significant.

It is as though *Chronicles* wanted to move our attention away from the peak which represented Solomon's aspirations, to the ramp

1. The *cathedra* is a throne-like chair used by people of leisure, who can afford to sit in comfort (*Kesubos* 5:5), or by high officials — as, for example, the seventy-one elders of whom the *Sanhedrin* was comprised (*Succah* 51b).

יח זָהָב טָהוֹר׃ וְשֵׁשׁ מַעֲלוֹת לַכִּסֵּא וְכֶבֶשׁ בַּזָּהָב לַכִּסֵּא
מָאֳחָזִים וְיָדוֹת מִזֶּה וּמִזֶּה עַל־מְקוֹם הַשָּׁבֶת וּשְׁנַיִם
יט אֲרָיוֹת עֹמְדִים אֵצֶל הַיָּדוֹת׃ וּשְׁנֵים עָשָׂר אֲרָיוֹת עֹמְדִים
שָׁם עַל־שֵׁשׁ הַמַּעֲלוֹת מִזֶּה וּמִזֶּה לֹא־נַעֲשָׂה כֵן לְכָל־
כ מַמְלָכָה׃ וְכֹל כְּלֵי מַשְׁקֵה הַמֶּלֶךְ שְׁלֹמֹה זָהָב וְכֹל כְּלֵי
בֵּית־יַעַר הַלְּבָנוֹן זָהָב סָגוּר אֵין כֶּסֶף נֶחְשָׁב בִּימֵי שְׁלֹמֹה
כא לִמְאוּמָה׃ כִּי־אֳנִיּוֹת לַמֶּלֶךְ הֹלְכוֹת תַּרְשִׁישׁ עִם עַבְדֵי
חוּרָם אַחַת לְשָׁלוֹשׁ שָׁנִים תָּבוֹאנָה ׀ אֳנִיּוֹת תַּרְשִׁישׁ
כב נֹשְׂאוֹת זָהָב וָכֶסֶף שֶׁנְהַבִּים וְקוֹפִים וְתוּכִּיִּים׃ וַיִּגְדַּל
כג הַמֶּלֶךְ שְׁלֹמֹה מִכֹּל מַלְכֵי הָאָרֶץ לְעֹשֶׁר וְחָכְמָה׃ וְכֹל
מַלְכֵי הָאָרֶץ מְבַקְשִׁים אֶת־פְּנֵי שְׁלֹמֹה לִשְׁמֹעַ אֶת־
כד חָכְמָתוֹ אֲשֶׁר־נָתַן הָאֱלֹהִים בְּלִבּוֹ׃ וְהֵם מְבִיאִים אִישׁ
מִנְחָתוֹ כְּלֵי כֶסֶף וּכְלֵי זָהָב וּשְׂלָמוֹת נֶשֶׁק וּבְשָׂמִים סוּסִים
כה וּפְרָדִים דְּבַר־שָׁנָה בְּשָׁנָה׃ וַיְהִי לִשְׁלֹמֹה
אַרְבַּעַת אֲלָפִים אֻרְיוֹת סוּסִים וּמַרְכָּבוֹת וּשְׁנֵים־עָשָׂר
אֶלֶף פָּרָשִׁים וַיַּנִּיחֵם בְּעָרֵי הָרֶכֶב וְעִם־הַמֶּלֶךְ בִּירוּשָׁלִָם׃
כו וַיְהִי מוֹשֵׁל בְּכָל־הַמְּלָכִים מִן־הַנָּהָר וְעַד־אֶרֶץ פְּלִשְׁתִּים

which had to be mounted before one ever got onto the chair. In the long-range view of history, the one had replaced the other in significance. Solomon did not attain his goal, and, indeed, fell short of even his own potential.

18. וְכֶבֶשׁ בַּזָּהָב לַכִּסֵּא — *And a ramp [worked] in gold for the throne*. We have translated כֶּבֶשׁ as *ramp* in accordance with *Radak* and *Metzudos*. This is how the word is used in Mishnaic Hebrew where it describes the ramp leading up to the altar.

In Scripture, the word does not recur and its meaning must be judged from the context. A case can be made that it might be rendered *footstool*, since *Targum* uses כבש to translate הֲדֹם in *Isaiah* 67:1 and *Psalms* 110:1. הֲדֹם is always used together with רֶגֶל, e.g. הֲדֹם רַגְלָיו in *Isaiah*, and is obviously a *footstool*. The use in Aramaic of כבש for *footstool* could argue for that meaning in Scripture.

מָאֳחָזִים — *Attached*. The word goes back to the six stairs. They were fastened to the throne (*Metzudos*).

◆§ Solomon's Wealth and His Standing Among the Kings

20. זָהָב סָגוּר — *Refined gold*. Gold that had been enclosed [from סגר, *to close*] in a crucible to be refined (*Metzudos*).

אֵין כֶּסֶף נֶחְשָׁב בִּימֵי שְׁלֹמֹה לִמְאוּמָה — *Silver was not accounted for anything in Solomon's days*. None of the vessels were made from silver because it was so abundant that it had lost all real value (*Rashi*).

The Sages (*Sanhedrin* 21b) contrast this verse, which implies that silver had absolutely no value at all, with v. 27 where some small value seems to be assumed. They answer that the two verses describe two different periods in Solomon's life. Before he married Pharaoh's daughter, silver was so plentiful that it was worth nothing at all. Afterwards, a decline set in. There was still an abundance of silver, but there was not quite as much as there had been earlier.

21. שֶׁנְהַבִּים וְקוֹפִים וְתוּכִּיִּים — *Ivory, apes and peacocks*. The translation follow *Metzudos*.

22. וַיִּגְדַּל הַמֶּלֶךְ שְׁלֹמֹה — *King Solomon exceeded* ... This was in fulfillment of God's promise that even such honor as he had not requested would be granted him (*Mefaresh*).

23. וְכֹל מַלְכֵי הָאָרֶץ — *All the kings of the land* ... This was in fulfillment of God's promise

with pure gold. [18] The throne had six stairs attached, and a ramp
[worked] in gold for the throne; handrests on either side by the
the seat, and two lions standing next to the handrests. [19] Twelve
lions stood there on the six stairs on either side. There was not the
like made for any [other] kingdom. [20] All the king's drinking
vessels were gold and all the vessels of the Forest of Lebanon
palace were of refined gold. Silver was not accounted for
anything in Solomon's days. [21] For the king's ships go to Tarshish
with Churam's servants. Once in three years the ships of
Tarshish would arrive, carrying gold, silver, ivory, apes and
peacocks. [22] King Solomon exceeded all the kings of the earth for
wealth and wisdom. [23] All the kings of the land constantly sought
out the presence of Solomon to hear his wisdom, that with which
God had imbued his heart. [24] Each of them would bring his gift:
vessels of silver and vessels of gold; clothes, arms and spices,
horses' and mules — year by year. [25] Solomon had four thousand
horses' mangers and chariots, and twelve thousand riders. He left
them in the chariot cities and with the king in Jerusalem. [26] He
exercised dominion over all the kings; from the river to Philistia

that Solomon would be granted unparalleled wisdom (*Mefaresh*).

מְבַקְשִׁים אֶת־פְּנֵי שְׁלֹמֹה — *Constantly sought out the presence of Solomon.* בקש with פָּנִים connotes more than just a visit. It is more in the nature of attempting to elicit some positive response.

24. וְהֵם מְבִיאִים אִישׁ מִנְחָתוֹ — *Each of them would bring his gift.* All this was in order to give them an excuse to come and hear Solomon's wisdom. It would be inappropriate to come empty-handed (*Mefaresh*).

דְּבַר־שָׁנָה בְּשָׁנָה — *Year by year.* It was the custom to come once a year and on each such occasion they would bring gifts (*Metzudos*).

25. אֻרְיוֹת סוּסִים — *Horses' mangers. Metzudos* renders אֻרְיָה as *manger* and bases his translation on *Targum* to *Isaiah* 1:3.

In *I Kings* 5:6, Solomon is reported as owning forty thousand rather than four thousand mangers. *Sanhedrin* 21b notes the apparent discrepancy and solves it by assuming that one of the two verses deals with the stable in which the mangers were situated. There were either forty thousand stables each containing four thousand mangers, or four thousand stables each with forty thousand mangers.

There appear to have been vastly more horses than riders. The number for these is given as twelve thousand. Clearly, the remaining horses were not required for actual use, and this would indicate that Solomon transgressed against the Torah's prohibition against having too many horses. In the view of the Sages, this interdicts the possession of horses which are not needed for any purpose other than for show (*Radak*).

בְּעָרֵי הָרֶכֶב וְעִם־הַמֶּלֶךְ בִּירוּשָׁלָם — *In the chariot cities and with the king in Jerusalem.*

The cantillation marks a stop after הָרֶכֶב. The verse has the approximate meaning that Solomon had so-and-so-many horses which he legitimately kept in the chariot cities. However, he also kept horses in Jerusalem. These must have been just for show — and so, were forbidden.

This verse is parenthetical to vs. 24 and 26. V. 24 had mentioned the horses which Solomon's royal visitors were accustomed to bring as gifts. Accordingly, the information concerning the dispositions of the kings' horses is given.

V. 26 then continues with the narrative which v. 24 had begun.

26. ... וַיְהִי מוֹשֵׁל בְּכָל־הַמְּלָכִים — *He exercised dominion over all the kings ...* The fact that the verse talks of *kings* makes it evident that Solomon did not *rule* over these lands. They had their own kings. These, however, were subservient to Solomon and apparently acknowledged his ascendancy by sending him

ט
כז־לא

כז וְעַד גְּבוּל מִצְרָיִם׃ וַיִּתֵּן הַמֶּלֶךְ אֶת־הַכֶּסֶף בִּירוּשָׁלַםִ
כָּאֲבָנִים וְאֵת הָאֲרָזִים נָתַן כַּשִּׁקְמִים אֲשֶׁר־בַּשְּׁפֵלָה לָרֹב׃
כח וּמוֹצִיאִים סוּסִים מִמִּצְרַיִם לִשְׁלֹמֹה וּמִכָּל־הָאֲרָצוֹת׃
כט וּשְׁאָר דִּבְרֵי שְׁלֹמֹה הָרִאשֹׁנִים וְהָאַחֲרוֹנִים הֲלֹא־הֵם
כְּתוּבִים עַל־דִּבְרֵי נָתָן הַנָּבִיא וְעַל־נְבוּאַת אֲחִיָּה
ל הַשִּׁילוֹנִי וּבַחֲזוֹת °יעדי הַחֹזֶה עַל־יָרָבְעָם בֶּן־נְבָט׃ וַיִּמְלֹךְ — °יֶעְדּוֹ ק׳
לא שְׁלֹמֹה בִירוּשָׁלַםִ עַל־כָּל־יִשְׂרָאֵל אַרְבָּעִים שָׁנָה׃ וַיִּשְׁכַּב
שְׁלֹמֹה עִם־אֲבֹתָיו וַיִּקְבְּרֻהוּ בְּעִיר דָּוִיד אָבִיו וַיִּמְלֹךְ

י
א־ב

א רְחַבְעָם בְּנוֹ תַּחְתָּיו׃ וַיֵּלֶךְ רְחַבְעָם שְׁכֶמָה כִּי שְׁכֶם
ב בָּאוּ כָל־יִשְׂרָאֵל לְהַמְלִיךְ אֹתוֹ׃ וַיְהִי כִּשְׁמֹעַ יָרָבְעָם

the gifts mentioned in v. 24.

This verse has no parallel in the *Kings'* version of this passage. It does, however, occur earlier in *Kings*, at 5:1, as part of a passage which is not given in *Chronicles*.

It is significant that *Chronicles* chooses to quote this one verse from that much larger passage. There, a detailed picture is painted of Solomon's reign. It emerges that he was an extremely powerful monarch, to whom all the neighboring kings were vassals; from these foreign relationships, untold wealth poured into his coffers, and this wealth was used for a fabulously luxurious royal establishment. Internally, his reign was benign, and his own people lived in tranquility and happiness [4:20 and 5:5]. The context makes it clear that the two are connected. The people's well-being was, at least partly, the result of the king's riches.

Of this internal bliss nothing is said here, nor, indeed, anywhere else in *Chronicles*. The information that wealth poured into Solomon's coffers from the neighboring kings (vs. 24 and 26) is thus presented without the softening touch that, in the end, it was used to benefit the people.

Again, we have a muted criticism. With the hindsight of history it appears that Solomon's wealth was not used to the best purpose.

מִן־הַנָּהָר — *From the river ... The river* is always the Euphrates. Accordingly, the directions are east, south and west (*Malbim*).

27. כָּאֲבָנִים — *As stones.*

Metzudos reflects Midrashic interpretation by taking this phrase literally rather than as hyperbole. Silver actually lay in the streets but was not stolen because it was shaped into huge blocks which made it too heavy to pick up casually.

אֲשֶׁר־בַּשְּׁפֵלָה — *Which are in the lowlands.* Where sycamores grow in great profusion (*Metzudos*).

28. וּמוֹצִיאִים סוּסִים מִמִּצְרָיִם — *They would export horses . . .from Egypt*. The subject is the men of Egypt (*Metzudos*). See 1:16.

◆§ The End of the Reign

29. וּשְׁאָר דִּבְרֵי שְׁלֹמֹה — *What remains of Solomon's affairs.* See Section II, *Solomon Does Not Lose His Portion in the World to Come*, for a discussion of the contrast between *Chronicles* and *Kings* as they both end their accounts of Solomon's reign.

Kings has וְיֶתֶר דִּבְרֵי שְׁלֹמֹה. In *Malbim's* view שאר is used for things which should have had a natural place in the narrative but were, for one reason or another, omitted, while יתר describes matters which were not of sufficient significance to be included. Thus the *Kings'* account, which was complete in the sense that everything of Scriptural significance was recorded, left out only such matters as were deemed insignificant. *Chronicles*, however, for reasons of its own — see above in comm. to v. 26. — omitted even highly important incidents.

עַל־דִּבְרֵי נָתָן הַנָּבִיא — *In the words of Nathan the prophet* ... *Metzudos* thinks that each of the three men mentioned — Nathan the prophet — Achiah the Shilonite, and Yehdi the seer [whom we do not know from any other place] — wrote books which are no longer extant.

The *Mefaresh* thinks that the words of Nathan the prophet are those recorded at *II Samuel* 12:25, when he apprised David of God's wish that his newborn son be called Yedidyah. The prophecy of Achiah the Shilonite is the promise of kingship which he communicated to Yarov'am, as recorded in *I Kings* 11:29 ff.

9 27-31

up to the boundary of Egypt. [27] *And the king caused silver to be*
in Jerusalem as stones and he caused cedars to be like sycamores
which are in the lowlands for abundance. [28] *They would export*
horses for Solomon from Egypt and from all the lands. [29] *What*
remains of Solomon's affairs, the earlier and the latter, is
recorded in the words of Nathan the prophet and in the prophecy
of Achiah the Shilonite and in the vision of Yehdi the seer
concerning Yarov'am son of Nevat. [30] *Solomon ruled in Jerusalem*
over all Israel for forty years. [31] *Solomon lay with his fathers and*
they buried him in the city of his father David. His son
Rechav'am reigned in his stead.

10 1-2

Rechav'am went to Shechem, for all Israel came to Shechem to
crown him. [2] *When Yarov'am the son of Nevat heard, he*

30. עַל־כָּל־יִשְׂרָאֵל — *Over all Israel*. This is in contrast to David who, although he also reigned for forty years, was king over all Israel for only thirty-three of these. For the first seven years, he was king of only Judah in Hebron (*Mefaresh* and *Metzudos*).

X

Rechav'am's reign was to witness two seminal events. The division of the people into two kingdoms; and Judah's ignominious defeat at the hands of Egypt's King Shishak.

The stark tragedy of the first may be judged by the fact that it appears to have become the standard by which subsequent catastrophes were to be judged. When Isaiah warned Achaz of the imminent Assyrian attack which was to bring the entire Jewish presence in the land to the brink of destruction, he could think of no harsher description of the impending horror than that it would rival the terrible day on which *Ephraim departed from Judah* (*Isaiah* 7:17).

Shishak's successful campaign and his capture of the treasures of both the Temple and the royal palace (12:9) are, as we shall see in the comm., interpreted by the Sages as a turning point in Israel's standing as God's chosen people.

Given the profound significance of these two events, it becomes vital to understand how Scripture portrays this tragic king. We shall see in the comm. that in many obvious as well as more subtle ways, *Chronicles* projects perspectives which are not apparent from the *Kings'* narrative.

◈ The Confrontation

1. כִּי שְׁכֶם בָּאוּ כָל־יִשְׂרָאֵל לְהַמְלִיךְ אֹתוֹ — *For all Israel came to Shechem to crown him*. Strictly speaking, Rechav'am needed no formal investiture. He was Solomon's son and undisputed heir, and the succession should have followed automatically — see *Rambam, Melachim* 1:12. Nevertheless, the people insisted on a formal coronation. They wished to put the young king on notice that he could not automatically count on their loyalty. He would have to prove himself.

For the same reason, they chose Shechem rather than Jerusalem for the ceremony. In Jerusalem, Rechav'am could have counted upon the moral support of his tribe Judah. By contrast, Shechem lay in Ephraim, the tribe of his rival, Yarov'am (*Malbim*).

In all this, *Chronicles* is clearly assuming that the background to these developments is known from *Kings*. It is there that we learned of Yarov'am's confrontation with Solomon (*I Kings* 11:26), and there too, that Achiah the Shilonite prophesied that Yarov'am was to become king over the Ten Tribes (there, 11:29 ff.).

שְׁכֶמָה — *To Shechem*. R' Yose taught: Shechem is a location at which terrible things happened: There Dinah was violated; there the brothers sold Joseph and there the kingdom was divided (*Sanhedrin* 102a).

י
ג־ט

בֶּן־נְבָט וְהוּא בְמִצְרַיִם אֲשֶׁר בָּרַח מִפְּנֵי שְׁלֹמֹה הַמֶּלֶךְ
ג וַיָּשָׁב יָרָבְעָם מִמִּצְרָיִם: וַיִּשְׁלְחוּ וַיִּקְרְאוּ־לוֹ וַיָּבֹא יָרָבְעָם
ד וְכָל־יִשְׂרָאֵל וַיְדַבְּרוּ אֶל־רְחַבְעָם לֵאמֹר: אָבִיךָ הִקְשָׁה
אֶת־עֻלֵּנוּ וְעַתָּה הָקֵל מֵעֲבוֹדַת אָבִיךָ הַקָּשָׁה וּמֵעֻלּוֹ
ה הַכָּבֵד אֲשֶׁר־נָתַן עָלֵינוּ וְנַעַבְדֶךָּ: וַיֹּאמֶר אֲלֵהֶם עוֹד
ו שְׁלֹשֶׁת יָמִים וְשׁוּבוּ אֵלָי וַיֵּלֶךְ הָעָם: וַיִּוָּעַץ
הַמֶּלֶךְ רְחַבְעָם אֶת־הַזְּקֵנִים אֲשֶׁר־הָיוּ עֹמְדִים לִפְנֵי
שְׁלֹמֹה אָבִיו בִּהְיֹתוֹ חַי לֵאמֹר אֵיךְ אַתֶּם נוֹעָצִים לְהָשִׁיב
ז לָעָם־הַזֶּה דָּבָר: וַיְדַבְּרוּ אֵלָיו לֵאמֹר אִם־תִּהְיֶה לְטוֹב
לְהָעָם הַזֶּה וּרְצִיתָם וְדִבַּרְתָּ אֲלֵהֶם דְּבָרִים טוֹבִים וְהָיוּ
ח לְךָ עֲבָדִים כָּל־הַיָּמִים: וַיַּעֲזֹב אֶת־עֲצַת הַזְּקֵנִים אֲשֶׁר
יְעָצֻהוּ וַיִּוָּעַץ אֶת־הַיְלָדִים אֲשֶׁר גָּדְלוּ אִתּוֹ הָעֹמְדִים
ט לְפָנָיו: וַיֹּאמֶר אֲלֵהֶם מָה אַתֶּם נוֹעָצִים וְנָשִׁיב דָּבָר
אֶת־הָעָם הַזֶּה אֲשֶׁר דִּבְּרוּ אֵלַי לֵאמֹר הָקֵל מִן־הָעֹל

2. וְהוּא בְמִצְרַיִם אֲשֶׁר בָּרַח מִפְּנֵי שְׁלֹמֹה הַמֶּלֶךְ — *He being in Egypt having fled from King Solomon*. The background to this verse is as follows:

I Kings 11:26-28 tells how Yarov'am, son of Nevat, reprimanded the king publicly for encroaching upon the public plaza in order to build a palace for Pharaoh's daughter. After that (vs. 29-39) Achiah the Shilonite meets with Yarov'am and promises him kingship over ten tribes. In v. 40 we learn that Solomon attempted to kill Yarov'am, and that he fled to Egypt where he stayed under the protection of Shishak until Solomon's death.

וַיָּשָׁב יָרָבְעָם מִמִּצְרָיִם — *Then Yarov'am returned from Egypt*. In *Kings*, we have as follows: *Yarov'am remained in Egypt. They sent to summon him, and so they came, Yarov'am and all the community of Israel* ... The implication is that Yarov'am returned only after he was summoned by the people. Here, we have Yarov'am returning from Egypt seemingly on his own initiative, and only then being called by the people (v.3).

Malbim explains that the two accounts augment one another. First, Yarov'am returned from Egypt on his own initiative [*Chronicles*]. After he came back, the people sent for him so that he might join them at the coronation [*Kings*]. See Section II, *Yarov'am's Return* .

3. וַיִּשְׁלְחוּ וַיִּקְרְאוּ־לוֹ וַיָּבֹא יָרָבְעָם — *They sent to summon him, and so, Yarov'am ... came.* Yarov'am had no intention of rebelling against Rechav'am. He came with every intention of crowning him king. But God willed otherwise. Without planning so, Yarov'am found himself going to his own investiture (*Mefaresh*).

4. אָבִיךָ הִקְשָׁה אֶת עֻלֵּנוּ — *Your father made our yoke difficult to bear*. See Section II, *The Confrontation*, for an examination of the rights and wrongs in this argument.

The complaint seems to center upon the heavy work-levies which Solomon imposed upon the people (ch. 2). *R' Yonasan of Lunel* (*Sanhedrin* 21b) asserts that Solomon also levied unreasonably large monetary taxes. There is, however, no Scriptural evidence for this.

וְעַתָּה הָקֵל ... — *Now lighten* ... Your fame is less widespread than that of your father. Fewer people come to seek you out, and there is no need for you to have as elaborate a household (*Metzudos*).

Radak feels that the complaints were unjustified. The people should have weighed their admittedly considerable obligations against the peace and tranquility with which the land was blessed during Solomon's reign. Nonetheless, they complained because God placed dissatisfaction into their hearts, so that they would wish to throw off Rechav'am's rule and make Yarov'am king.

5. עוֹד שְׁלֹשֶׁת יָמִים וְשׁוּבוּ אֵלָי — *Return to me in*

being in Egypt having fled from King Solomon, then Yarov'am
returned from Egypt. 3 *They sent to summon him, and so,*
Yarov'am and all Israel came and spoke to Rechav'am, saying:
4 *'Your father made our yoke difficult to bear. Now lighten the*
heavy work load of your father, and the irksome yoke which he
placed upon us — and then we will serve you.' 5 *He said to them,*
'Return to me in three days.' So the people went. 6 *King*
Rechav'am sought counsel from the elders who, while he was yet
alive, had stood before his father Solomon, saying, 'How do you
advise that this people be given an answer?' 7 *They spoke to him,*
saying, 'If you will be of benefit to this people and find
satisfaction in them and speak good words to them, then they
shall be servants to you for all time. 8 *He forsook the advice*
which the elders had given him, and sought advice from the
young men who had grown up with him — who stood before him.
9 *He said to them, 'What do you advise that we answer this*
people who spoke to me, saying, "Lighten the yoke which your

three days. Malbim believes that this was an ill-advised and untimely tactic. A strong and confident ruler would not have procrastinated. The people did not miss this indication of weakness.

6. אֵיךְ אַתֶּם נוֹעָצִים — *How do you advise ... Malbim* notes the difference between the אֵיךְ, *how* of our verse and the מָה, *what,* which Rechav'am used when he consulted with his youthful peers. At this point he seems to have had no doubts about the correctness of his position. He would surely not accede to the people's request. His problem was only how best to formulate his response.

The elders planted doubts in his mind. Perhaps, after all, it would be wiser to give in? It was with this weighty question that he turned to his peers.

7. אִם־תִּהְיֶה לְטוֹב לְהָעָם הַזֶּה וּרְצִיתָם — *If you will be of benefit to this people and find satisfaction in them ...* טוֹב as a noun denotes *benefit, welfare* or *prosperity.* Cf. *Deuteronomy* 26:11.

רצה in the *kal, simple form* means *to be pleased with, favorable to.* See *S'forno* to *Genesis* 33:10.

Our rendering follows *Targum.* The elders are suggesting an ideal relationship between king and subjects. They do not address the immediate issue of how to respond to the people.

Metzudos renders: *If you will be a kindly person to them, thereby eliciting their goodwill ...,* i.e., placing the advice of the elders in the immediate context of formulating a suitable response. See Section II, *The Response of the Elders.*

וְהָיוּ לְךָ עֲבָדִים כָּל־הַיָּמִים — *Then they shall be servants to you for all time.* Then you will be able to give your kingship whatever form you wish (*Metzudos*).

Metzudos is interpreting this phrase consistently with his rendering of the first part of the verse (see above). As we understood the earlier part of the verse, the meaning would simply be that they will, throughout your reign, remain your loyal subjects.

8. וַיַּעֲזֹב אֶת־עֲצַת הַזְּקֵנִים — *He forsook the advice which the elders ...* He rejected the advice of the elders without bothering to present it to his peers for evaluation. He turned to the young men not for their sage advice — for that, a complete presentation of the options would have been necessary — but because he felt an affinity with them. They would understand his thinking (*Abarbanel*).

9. אֶת־הָעָם הַזֶּה אֲשֶׁר דִּבְּרוּ אֵלַי לֵאמֹר — *This people who spoke to me, saying.* When Rechav'am consulted the elders, he did not quote what the people had said. Perhaps, a verbatim quote would have stressed the enormity of their presumption. 'What shall I tell the people who had the temerity to make such a request?' To the elders he expressed a balanced question without allowing his feelings to intrude. Now he was letting his peers know what he wanted to hear from them.

י
י־טז

י אֲשֶׁר־נָתַן אָבִיךָ עָלֵינוּ: וַיְדַבְּרוּ אִתּוֹ הַיְלָדִים אֲשֶׁר גָּדְלוּ
אִתּוֹ לֵאמֹר כֹּה תֹאמַר לָעָם אֲשֶׁר־דִּבְּרוּ אֵלֶיךָ לֵאמֹר
אָבִיךָ הִכְבִּיד אֶת־עֻלֵּנוּ וְאַתָּה הָקֵל מֵעָלֵינוּ כֹּה תֹאמַר
יא אֲלֵהֶם קָטָנִּי עָבָה מִמָּתְנֵי אָבִי: וְעַתָּה אָבִי הֶעְמִיס עֲלֵיכֶם
עֹל כָּבֵד וַאֲנִי אֹסִיף עַל־עֻלְּכֶם אָבִי יִסַּר אֶתְכֶם בַּשּׁוֹטִים
יב וַאֲנִי בָּעֲקְרַבִּים: וַיָּבֹא יָרָבְעָם וְכָל־הָעָם אֶל־
רְחַבְעָם בַּיּוֹם הַשְּׁלִשִׁי כַּאֲשֶׁר דִּבֶּר הַמֶּלֶךְ לֵאמֹר שׁוּבוּ אֵלַי
יג בַּיּוֹם הַשְּׁלִשִׁי: וַיַּעֲנֵם הַמֶּלֶךְ קָשָׁה וַיַּעֲזֹב הַמֶּלֶךְ רְחַבְעָם
יד אֵת עֲצַת הַזְּקֵנִים: וַיְדַבֵּר אֲלֵהֶם כַּעֲצַת הַיְלָדִים לֵאמֹר
אַכְבִּיד אֶת־עֻלְּכֶם וַאֲנִי אֹסִיף עָלָיו אָבִי יִסַּר אֶתְכֶם
טו בַּשּׁוֹטִים וַאֲנִי בָּעֲקְרַבִּים: וְלֹא־שָׁמַע הַמֶּלֶךְ אֶל־הָעָם
כִּי־הָיְתָה נְסִבָּה מֵעִם הָאֱלֹהִים לְמַעַן הָקִים יְהוָה
אֶת־דְּבָרוֹ אֲשֶׁר דִּבֶּר בְּיַד אֲחִיָּהוּ הַשִּׁלוֹנִי אֶל־יָרָבְעָם
טז בֶּן־נְבָט: וְכָל־יִשְׂרָאֵל כִּי לֹא־שָׁמַע הַמֶּלֶךְ לָהֶם וַיָּשִׁיבוּ
הָעָם | אֶת־הַמֶּלֶךְ | לֵאמֹר מַה־לָּנוּ חֵלֶק בְּדָוִיד וְלֹא־נַחֲלָה

10. וַיְדַבְּרוּ אִתּוֹ — *. . . Spoke with him.* Here אִתּוֹ, *with him*, is used, in contrast to v. 7 where the elders spoke, אֵלָיו, *to him*. The change is eminently appropriate. It underlines the sense of community he felt with his peers, as opposed to the distance between him and the elders. See comm. to 9:1.

אֲשֶׁר־דִּבְּרוּ אֵלֶיךָ לֵאמֹר אָבִיךָ הִכְבִּיד אֶת־עֻלֵּנוּ — *Who spoke to you, saying, "Your father made our yoke heavy . . ."* Rechav'am had not quoted this part of the people's speech. We may surmise one of two reasons why the young men included it in their speech. They may have wanted to stir up Rechav'am's anger at the slur which the people had cast upon his father, or it may be meant to serve as an introduction to their suggested response — *My little finger is thicker than my father's loins.* To underline this thought, they introduced the thought that Solomon had placed a heavy yoke upon the people. Rechav'am was to respond that this yoke was as nothing compared with the one which he would impose.

קָטָנִּי עָבָה מִמָּתְנֵי אָבִי — *My little finger is thicker than my father's loins.* You suggested that my court might well be less elaborate than that of my father (see comm. to v. 4). The opposite is true. I shall be more powerful than he (*Metzudos*).

Abarbanel points out how inappropriate this answer was. It is in very poor taste for a son to boast of his ascendancy over his father — even if it were true. This form of address would certainly be calculated to antagonize the people.

The young men advised their king badly.

11. אָבִי הֶעְמִיס עֲלֵיכֶם עֹל כָּבֵד — *My father weighed you down with a heavy yoke . . .* Once more *Abarbanel* points out how poorly Rechav'am was served by his youthful counselors. Instead of explaining to the people how beneficial Solomon's reign had been for them, he agrees that his father had overstepped the bounds of that which is reasonable.

שׁוֹטִים . . . עַקְרַבִּים — *Whips . . . scorpions.* Again, the choice of words could not have been more unfortunate. Both שׁוֹט, *whip*, and עַקְרָב, lit. *scorpion*, but used for a lash with metal thongs, are implements used on animals. By talking of whips and scorpions, Rechav'am was denying the people human standing (*Abarbanel*).

12. וַיָּבֹא יָרָבְעָם וְכָל־הָעָם — *Yarov'am and all the people came.* Perhaps the singular וַיָּבֹא is used in order to indicate that Yarov'am and the people were of one mind. They were already planning to depose Rechav'am.

14. אַכְבִּיד אֶת־עֻלְּכֶם וַאֲנִי אֹסִיף עָלָיו — *I will make your yoke heavy but will go even further than him. Kings reads, My father made your yoke heavy, and I will add to your yoke.*

father placed upon us' " 10 The young men who grew up with him
spoke with him, saying, 'Thus should you speak to the people who
spoke to you, saying, "Your father made our yoke heavy and do
you make it lighter for us.' Thus shall you say to them, "My little
finger is thicker than my father's loins! 11 And now my father
weighed you down with a heavy yoke and I will add to your yoke;
my father chastised you with whips and I with scorpions." '
12 Yarov'am and all the people came to Rechav'am on the third
day as the king had said, 'Return to me on the third day.' 13 The
king answered them harshly. The king Rechav'am forsook the
counsel of the elders. 14 He spoke to them according to the counsel
of the young men saying, 'I will make your yoke heavy but will go
even further than him. My father chastised you with whips and
— I with scorpions'. 15 The king did not listen to the people for it
was brought about by God in order that Hashem might bring
about His word which He had spoken by the hand of Achiah the
Shilonite to Yarov'am son of Nevat. 16 All Israel saw that the king
did not listen to them so they answered the king saying, 'What
will be our portion through David, we will have no inheritance

Some printed versions have this same reading here, but we follow *Minchas Shai*. We have translated the verse as does *Radak*: *I will make your yoke heavy [as did my father] but will go ...*

Rather, than simply blustering, as he does in the *Kings'* version, Rechav'am invokes his father's memory in order to confirm his own perception of the kingship. 'I am confident that I am acting correctly, because I am doing as he did. I will continue in his path, and even go beyond what he did.'

15. וְלֹא־שָׁמַע הַמֶּלֶךְ אֶל־הָעָם — *The king did not listen to the people*. After the king had given them his harsh answer, the people tried to reason with him — perhaps to reach a compromise, but he was not willing to listen to them (*Abarbanel*).

כִּי־הָיְתָה נְסִבָּה מֵעִם הָאֱלֹהִים — *For it was brought about by God*. נְסִבָּה or סִבָּה, as it is used in *Kings*, derives from סבב, *turn about* or *go around*. Thus, a particular *turn of events* (*Radak*, *Sefer HaShorashim* and *Metzudos*).

God caused that he be not willing even to discuss the matter with the people — a monumental folly (*Abarbanel*).

Alternatively, the phrase is meant to explain Rechav'am's attitude to the whole matter. The advice of the elders was so obviously better than that of the youths that there can be no natural explanation for his obtuseness in ignoring their counsel.

God's interference in Rechav'am's decision was not a contradiction to the doctrine of free will. An individual who acts in his own affairs will never be subject to any Divine coercion. But a king whose decisions influence the entire people will not always be allowed total freedom: *A king's heart is like a divided river in the hands of* H*ASHEM*, *He directs it in whichever way He wishes* (*Proverbs* 21:1). See *Abarbanel* to *parashas Vayigash*.

לְמַעַן הָקִים ה׳ אֶת־דְּבָרוֹ — *In order that* H*ASHEM might bring about His word ... Chronicles* assumes our knowledge of the incident recorded in *I Kings* 11:29 ff.

Because of his grievous sins, Solomon had forfeited his right to the kingship. However, God's promise to David that the royal line would be permanently carried on through his children would assure that he would not lose everything. Only ten tribes would be taken from him. Even these would be taken, not during his own life, but only when his son became king.

Yarov'am, while walking outside Jerusalem, was accosted by Achiah the Shilonite and informed that he had been chosen by God to rule over Israel. The prophet's words were now about to be fulfilled.

16. מַה־לָּנוּ חֵלֶק בְּדָוִיד וְלֹא־נַחֲלָה בְּבֶן־יִשַׁי — *What will be our portion through David, we will have*

י בְּבֶן־יִשַׁי אִישׁ לְאֹהָלֶיךָ יִשְׂרָאֵל עַתָּה רְאֵה בֵיתְךָ דָּוִיד וַיֵּלֶךְ
יז־יט יז כָּל־יִשְׂרָאֵל לְאֹהָלָיו: וּבְנֵי יִשְׂרָאֵל הַיֹּשְׁבִים
יח בְּעָרֵי יְהוּדָה וַיִּמְלֹךְ עֲלֵיהֶם רְחַבְעָם: וַיִּשְׁלַח הַמֶּלֶךְ
רְחַבְעָם אֶת־הֲדֹרָם אֲשֶׁר עַל־הַמַּס וַיִּרְגְּמוּ־בוֹ בְנֵי־יִשְׂרָאֵל
אֶבֶן וַיָּמֹת וְהַמֶּלֶךְ רְחַבְעָם הִתְאַמֵּץ לַעֲלוֹת בַּמֶּרְכָּבָה לָנוּס
יט יְרוּשָׁלִָם: וַיִּפְשְׁעוּ יִשְׂרָאֵל בְּבֵית דָּוִיד עַד הַיּוֹם
יא א הַזֶּה: וַיָּבֹא רְחַבְעָם יְרוּשָׁלִַם וַיַּקְהֵל אֶת־
א בֵּית יְהוּדָה וּבִנְיָמִן מֵאָה וּשְׁמוֹנִים אֶלֶף בָּחוּר עֹשֵׂה
מִלְחָמָה לְהִלָּחֵם עִם־יִשְׂרָאֵל לְהָשִׁיב אֶת־הַמַּמְלָכָה

no inheritance through the son of Yishai. Metzudos takes חֵלֶק and נַחֲלָה as actual property and renders the phrase as we have done. We will gain nothing tangible through loyalty to the Davidic line.

However, both חֵלֶק and נַחֲלָה occur in Scripture with meanings other than physical possessions. Thus we find חֵלֶק as a *chosen form of life* (*Psalms* 50:18). The phrase could mean: Why should we chose to throw in our lot with David?

Again, נַחֲלָה means many things besides an inheritance. Thus, Israel is described as God's נַחֲלָה (*I Samuel* 10:1); hence, a *treasured possession* in a non-physical sense. The phrase would mean: We have no reason to regard Yishai's house as having a meaningful relationship to us.

This is how *Radak* takes these two words.

אִישׁ לְאֹהָלֶיךָ יִשְׂרָאֵל — *Every man to your tents O Israel*. Go to your homes and do not crown Rechav'am king (*Metzudos*).

See Section II, *The Confrontation*, for the tradition that Israel was not only repudiating Rechav'am the man, but also the Kingship of Heaven; the Davidic line, and the Temple service. Our phrase is seen as the rejection of the Kingdom of Heaven — Do not read לְאֹהָלֶיךָ, *to your tents*, but לֵאלֹהֶיךָ, *to your idols*.[1]

רְאֵה בֵיתְךָ דָּוִיד — *See to your own house, David*. Now you, Rechav'am, who are a descendant of David, concentrate on the needs of your own household. You have no more business with the kingship (*Metzudos*).

17. הַיֹּשְׁבִים בְּעָרֵי יְהוּדָה — *Who dwelt in the cities of Judah*. This is only because they dwelt in the cities of Judah; that is, in close proximity to the seat of royalty. Otherwise even they, Rechav'am's own tribe, would have rejected him (*Abarbanel*).

This verse is to be seen as parenthetical to the story, which is picked up once more in the next verse.

18. וַיִּשְׁלַח הַמֶּלֶךְ רְחַבְעָם אֶת־הֲדֹרָם — *King Rechav'am sent Hadoram ... Mefaresh* thinks that Rechav'am was not aware of the seriousness of the rebellion and sent Hadoram in the normal exercise of his duties to collect taxes.

Radak and *Abarbanel* think that the king sent him in order to persuade the people to give up their rebellion and to return to his rule. They did not listen to Rechav'am even as he had refused to listen to them.

הִתְאַמֵּץ לַעֲלוֹת בַּמֶּרְכָּבָה — *Made haste to get up upon the chariot*. אמץ is to be *strong, bold* or *alert*. Thus, in the reflexive, *to energize oneself* or *to make haste*.

לָנוּס יְרוּשָׁלָם — *To flee to Jerusalem*. The confrontation had taken place in Shechem, the home ground of Yarov'am. Certainly Rechav'am would have felt safer once he returned to Jerusalem.

19. עַד הַיּוֹם הַזֶּה — *Until this day*. The split was not healed at the time when *Chronicles* was written. The reconciliation between the two entities is to be left to Messianic times. See *ArtScroll Ezekiel*, prefatory remarks to 37:15-22.

1. There is some midrashic evidence that the reading in our *Chronicles'* passage was actually אֱלֹהֶיךָ, *to your idols*, while *Kings* has אֹהָלֶיךָ, *to your tents*. [See *Midrash Tanchuma* 16 to *Beshalach*. See *Minchas Shai*.

That there should have been a reading in *Chronicles'* which makes explicit that which is only hinted at in *Kings*, confirms the thesis which we suggested in Section II, *The Confrontation*. The people are more blatantly wicked, and consequently, Rechav'am appears in a better light in *Chronicles* than in *Kings*.

10 17-19 *through the son of Yishai, every man to your tents O Israel. Now,*
see to your own house, David.' So Israel went to its tents. 17 *But the*
Children of Israel who dwelt in the cities of Judah — Rechav'am
ruled over them. 18 *King Rechav'am sent Hadoram the tax*
collector but the Children of Israel pelted him with stones so that
he died. So King Rechav'am made haste to get up upon the chariot
to flee to Jerusalem. 19 *So Israel rebelled against the House of*
David until this day.

11 1 *Rechav'am came to Jerusalem and gathered the house of Judah and Benjamin, one hundred and eighty thousand chosen soldiers, to fight against Israel so that the kingship be returned to*

XI

◈§ Rechav'am Consolidates His Kingship

Rechav'am marshals his forces in order to prevent the secession of the Ten Tribes but abandons his plans when God's prophet Shemaiahu dissuades him.

The same passage occurs in *Kings* where it is preceded by a verse which is left out here:

When all Israel heard that Yarov'am had returned, the entire congregation sent and called to him, and crowned him king over all Israel. None but the tribe of Judah alone remained under David.

Why does *Chronicles* omit this most seminal of verses? Does the establishment of the Northern Kingdom not merit mention?

Perhaps, by its silence, *Chronicles* seeks to delegitimize the establishment of the Northern Kingdom. It was a time-based necessity which, in the long-range view of Jewish history which *Chronicles* adopts throughout, must be looked upon as an aberration [see further at 16:1]. The crowning of Yarov'am had no significance because it had no real validity.

This idea is clearly expressed — and therefore our thesis is reinforced — by Aviah's speech to the forces of the Northern Kingdom (13:4-12). In that speech he makes unambiguous claims to being the sole legitimate king of Israel. God's promise to David had been unqualified and none but a scion of the Davidic line can lay claim to the monarchy in Israel.

Aviah's speech does not appear in *Kings*.[1]

If Rechav'am shared his son Aviah's opinion of the nature of the Northern Kingdom, this might help explain his sudden regression into evil ways (12:1) after the auspicious start of his kingship reported at 11:17. Perhaps Rechav'am had the expectation that Yarov'am's secession was an aberration which would not last and that, if he acted as God would wish him to act, the kingship over all the Ten Tribes would be returned to him. When he saw that this was not so and that, on the contrary, the Northern Kingdom showed every sign of permanence, he threw off the yoke of Heaven.

1. אֶת־בֵּית יְהוּדָה וּבִנְיָמִן — *The house of Judah and Benjamin.* Although only the tribe of Judah was mentioned as having remained loyal to Rechav'am (*I Kings* 12:20), Benjamin — the tribe whose territory bordered on Judah's — also did not join in the revolt. He was not mentioned as a separate entity because Judah was by far the more important tribe, and Benjamin was subsidiary to it (*Metzudos*).

That there would be such a tribe — one who still accepted the Davidic kingship but did not merit mention as a separate entity — is implied in Achiah the Shilonite's original prophecy to Yarov'am (*I Kings* 11:35 ff.). There, Yarov'am is given Ten Tribes, but only one is promised to Rechav'am (v. 36). Clearly, the twelfth tribe, Benjamin, is subsumed under that one tribe — Judah.

עִם־יִשְׂרָאֵל — *Against Israel.* When Achiah

1. There seems to be disagreement between *Rambam* and *Ramban* concerning the halachic status of a king from a tribe other than Judah who was anointed to the monarchy by a prophet — for which case Yarov'am's anointment through the Shilonite is the paradigm. See *Rambam* (*Melachim* 1:8), and *Ramban* to *Genesis* 49:10.

ב לִרְחַבְעָם: וַיְהִי דְּבַר־יְהוָה אֶל־שְׁמַעְיָהוּ אִישׁ־
ג הָאֱלֹהִים לֵאמֹר: אֱמֹר אֶל־רְחַבְעָם בֶּן־שְׁלֹמֹה מֶלֶךְ
ד יְהוּדָה וְאֶל כָּל־יִשְׂרָאֵל בִּיהוּדָה וּבִנְיָמִן לֵאמֹר: כֹּה אָמַר
יְהוָה לֹא־תַעֲלוּ וְלֹא־תִלָּחֲמוּ עִם־אֲחֵיכֶם שׁוּבוּ אִישׁ
לְבֵיתוֹ כִּי מֵאִתִּי נִהְיָה הַדָּבָר הַזֶּה וַיִּשְׁמְעוּ אֶת־דִּבְרֵי
ה יְהוָה וַיָּשֻׁבוּ מִלֶּכֶת אֶל־יָרָבְעָם: וַיֵּשֶׁב רְחַבְעָם
ו בִּירוּשָׁלָםִ וַיִּבֶן עָרִים לְמָצוֹר בִּיהוּדָה: וַיִּבֶן אֶת־בֵּית־
ז לֶחֶם וְאֶת־עֵיטָם וְאֶת־תְּקוֹעַ: וְאֶת־בֵּית־צוּר וְאֶת־שׂוֹכוֹ
ח־ט וְאֶת־עֲדֻלָּם: וְאֶת־גַּת וְאֶת־מָרֵשָׁה וְאֶת־זִיף: וְאֶת־
י אֲדוֹרַיִם וְאֶת־לָכִישׁ וְאֶת־עֲזֵקָה: וְאֶת־צָרְעָה וְאֶת־אַיָּלוֹן
יא וְאֶת־חֶבְרוֹן אֲשֶׁר בִּיהוּדָה וּבְבִנְיָמִן עָרֵי מְצֻרוֹת: וַיְחַזֵּק
אֶת־הַמְּצוּרוֹת וַיִּתֵּן בָּהֶם נְגִידִים וְאֹצְרוֹת מַאֲכָל וְשֶׁמֶן

promised the kingship over the Ten Tribes to Yarov'am, he used expressions such as *So you shall be king over Israel* (*I Kings* 11:37) and *I shall give you Israel* (v. 38). Thus, the Northern Kingdom came to be known as Israel.

3. מֶלֶךְ יְהוּדָה — *King of Judah*. Here, in God's own words, the division is confirmed. Rechav'am is now king, only of Judah.

וְאֶל כָּל־יִשְׂרָאֵל בִּיהוּדָה וּבִנְיָמִין — *And to all Israel in Judah and Benjamin*. Taken by itself, we would interpret this phrase to refer to the people belonging to the tribes of Judah and Benjamin.

However, the parallel verse in *Kings* reads: . . . *to the house of Judah and Benjamin and the rest of the people* . . . . Now, *house of Judah and Benjamin* obviously refers to the people of those tribes. Thus *the rest of the people* must mean people from other tribes who were living in Judahite and Benjaminite territory.

If our phrase is to have the same meaning, we must interpret as follows: The people of Judah and Benjamin are subsumed under *Rechav'am son of Solomon king of Judah*, and *all Israel which are in Judah and Benjamin* would refer to the members of the other tribes.

4. עִם־אֲחֵיכֶם — *Against your brothers*. They are, after all, your brothers. You are children of one father (*Mefaresh*).

כִּי מֵאִתִּי נִהְיָה הַדָּבָר הַזֶּה — *For this thing came about through Me*. Even if, in the long run, there is no room for a split in the unity of Israel, for the moment it is God's wish that the Northern Kingdom be established.[1]

וַיִּשְׁמְעוּ אֶת־דִּבְרֵי ה׳ — *They listened to the words of* HASHEM. The plural form of וַיִּשְׁמְעוּ leaves open the question of whether Rechav'am willingly subjected himself to the Divine command — which would tend to confirm his righteousness at this point — or whether he, in fact, would have wanted to go to battle but his army deserted him.

1. We cannot know precisely what would have happened if the kings of the Northern Kingdom would have been righteous and would not have sinned as, in fact, they all did. From *I Kings* 11:37-38, it appears that their kingship would have extended beyond Yarov'am and turned into a legitimate royal dynasty: *You I will take and you shall rule over all that you desire and you will be king over Israel. Now if you will listen to all that I command you and go in My ways and do what is correct in My eyes to adhere to My laws and My commandments as did My servant, David, then I shall be with you and build you an enduring house as I built for David, and I shall give you Israel*.

But, see at 16:1 where we learn from *Seder Olam* that the division had been meant to last only thirty-six years.

Perhaps, if he had remained righteous, Yarov'am would have retained a kingship which would have had validity, but would have been subservient to the Davidic line. See *Ramban* to *Genesis* 49:10 on the question of what would have happened to Saul's kingship if he had not forfeited it as a result of his shortcomings.

See also *Yerushalmi, Horios* 3:2: Kings of Israel and of Judah are equal, the kings of one are not greater than the kings of the other . . . R' Yose taught in the Yeshivah of R. Bun: But only till [the descendants of] Yehu (see *Pnei Moshe* there) . . . from then on [the kingship] was taken by robbery.

Rechav'am. 2 *The word of* HASHEM *came to Shemaiahu, the man
of God, saying.* 3 *'Say to Rechav'am the son of Solomon, king of
Judah, and to all Israel in Judah and Benjamin, saying.* 4 *Thus
says* HASHEM, *"Do not go up and do not make war against your
brothers. Let every man return to his house. For this thing came
about through Me" '. They listened to the words of* HASHEM *and
turned back from going against Yarov'am.* 5 *So Rechav'am dwelt
in Jerusalem. He built cities for defense in Judah.* 6 *He built
Bethlehem, Eitam and Tekoa.* 7 *Beth Tzur, Socho and Adulam.*
8 *Gath, Moreishah and Ziph.* 9 *Adoraim, Lachish and Azeikah.*
10 *Tzera'ah, Ayalon and Hebron which were in Judah and
Benjamin: Entrenched cities.* 11 *He strengthened the fortified
cities and appointed captains in them and stores of food, oil and*

At 12:15 we learn that the war between Rechav'am and Yarov'am continued throughout Rechav'am's reign.

וַיָּשֻׁבוּ — *And turned back*. For שוב in the sense of *to turn back* or *change one's mind*, see *Jeremiah* 4:28 and elsewhere.

5-16. There is no parallel in *Kings* for this description of Rechav'am's building projects. In Section II to ch. 10, *The Confrontation*, we thought that its inclusion in the *Chronicles'* account would tend to justify Rechav'am's determination to impose heavier work levies than had been mustered by Solomon.

Altogether fifteen cities are mentioned, the great majority of them can be shown to have been in Judah's territory. Since v. 10 states that the cities were *in Judah and Benjamin*, we must assume that the few which cannot be identified were located in the territory of Benjamin.

We shall give one reference for each city — where possible from *Chronicles*.

5. עָרִים לְמָצוֹר — *Cities for defense*. צור is *to confine, bind* or *besiege*. Thus *to encircle*. *Cities for defense* would then be an entrenched city with ramparts built around it.

6. וַיִּבֶן אֶת־בֵּית־לֶחֶם וְאֶת־עֵיטָם וְאֶת־תְּקוֹעַ — *He built Bethlehem, Eitam and Tekoa*. All three cities were in Judah. For Bethlehem, see *I Chronicles* 2:51; for Eitan, there, 4:3; for Tekoa, there, 2:24.

7. וְאֶת־בֵּית־צוּר וְאֶת־שׂוֹכוֹ וְאֶת־עֲדֻלָּם — *Beth Tzur, Socho and Adulam*. All three cities were in Judah. For Beis Tzur see *I Chronicles* 2:45; for Socho, there, 4:18; for Adulam, see *Joshua* 15:35.

8. וְאֶת־גַּת וְאֶת־מָרֵשָׁה וְאֶת־זִיף — *Gath, Moreishah and Ziph.* Gath is a Philistine city. See ArtScroll *Joshua* 11:22 that *Kaftor V'Ferach* identifies it with the city of Remaleh which was in Dan's territory — see map on p. 391 there.

Moreishah and Ziph are both in Judah. See *I Chronicles* 2:42.

9. וְאֶת־אֲדוֹרַיִם וְאֶת־לָכִישׁ וְאֶת־עֲזֵקָה — *Adoraim, Lachish and Azeikah.* Adoraim is not mentioned again in Scripture. Perhaps this is a city which lay in Benjamin's portion. Lachish and Azeikah were both in Judah — see *Joshua* 15:35 and 39.

10. וְאֶת־צָרְעָה וְאֶת־אַיָּלוֹן וְאֶת־חֶבְרוֹן אֲשֶׁר בִּיהוּדָה וּבְבִנְיָמִן — *Tzera'ah, Ayalon and Hebron which were in Judah and Benjamin.* Tzera'ah and Hebron were both in Judah. See *Joshua* 15:33 and 54. Ayalon is given in *Joshua* 19:42 as belonging to Dan. ArtScroll *Joshua* there locates it at about twelve miles northwest of Jerusalem. It is, of course, possible that the boundaries between the Northern and Southern Kingdoms were not drawn exactly and a city twelve miles north of Jerusalem may well have been under Rechav'am's control.

עָרֵי מְצֻרוֹת — *Entrenched cities*. See comm. above to v. 5.

11. נְגִידִים — *Captains*. See comm. to *I Chronicles* 11:2.

וְאֹצְרוֹת מַאֲכָל וְשֶׁמֶן וָיָיִן — *And stores of food, oil and wine*. This was in case the people would ever have to sustain a siege within these fortified cities (*Mefaresh*).

יב וָיָיִן׃ וּבְכָל־עִיר וָעִיר צִנּוֹת וּרְמָחִים וַיְחַזְּקֵם לְהַרְבֵּה מְאֹד
יג וַיְהִי־לוֹ יְהוּדָה וּבִנְיָמִן׃ וְהַכֹּהֲנִים וְהַלְוִיִּם אֲשֶׁר
יד בְּכָל־יִשְׂרָאֵל הִתְיַצְּבוּ עָלָיו מִכָּל־גְּבוּלָם׃ כִּי־עָזְבוּ הַלְוִיִּם
אֶת־מִגְרְשֵׁיהֶם וַאֲחֻזָּתָם וַיֵּלְכוּ לִיהוּדָה וְלִירוּשָׁלִָם כִּי־
טו הִזְנִיחָם יָרָבְעָם וּבָנָיו מִכַּהֵן לַיהוָה׃ וַיַּעֲמֶד־לוֹ כֹּהֲנִים
טז לַבָּמוֹת וְלַשְּׂעִירִים וְלָעֲגָלִים אֲשֶׁר עָשָׂה׃ וְאַחֲרֵיהֶם מִכֹּל
שִׁבְטֵי יִשְׂרָאֵל הַנֹּתְנִים אֶת־לְבָבָם לְבַקֵּשׁ אֶת־יְהוָה אֱלֹהֵי
יִשְׂרָאֵל בָּאוּ יְרוּשָׁלִַם לִזְבּוֹחַ לַיהוָה אֱלֹהֵי אֲבוֹתֵיהֶם׃
יז וַיְחַזְּקוּ אֶת־מַלְכוּת יְהוּדָה וַיְאַמְּצוּ אֶת־רְחַבְעָם בֶּן־
שְׁלֹמֹה לְשָׁנִים שָׁלוֹשׁ כִּי הָלְכוּ בְּדֶרֶךְ דָּוִיד וּשְׁלֹמֹה
יח לְשָׁנִים שָׁלוֹשׁ׃ וַיִּקַּח־לוֹ רְחַבְעָם אִשָּׁה
°בֶּן ק׳ אֶת־מָחֲלַת °בת־יְרִימוֹת בֶּן־דָּוִיד אֲבִיהַיִל בַּת־אֱלִיאָב
יט בֶּן־יִשָׁי׃ וַתֵּלֶד לוֹ בָּנִים אֶת־יְעוּשׁ וְאֶת־שְׁמַרְיָה וְאֶת־
כ זָהַם׃ וְאַחֲרֶיהָ לָקַח אֶת־מַעֲכָה בַּת־אַבְשָׁלוֹם וַתֵּלֶד

12. וַיְחַזְּקֵם לְהַרְבֵּה מְאֹד — *Making them exceedingly strong.* It was done with all manner of fortification (*Metzudos*).

וַיְהִי־לוֹ יְהוּדָה וּבִנְיָמִן — *Thus Judah and Benjamin remained his.* The vast building projects which Rechav'am undertook, gave him the power-base which enabled him to hold on to Judah and Benjamin. Without them, he surely would have lost them to Yarov'am (*Metzudos*).

13-16. These verses also do not appear in *Kings*. In line with the rest of the *Chronicles'* account, they tend to throw a positive light on Rechav'am's reign. Both Levites and other people who sought to serve God according to the ways of the Torah found a haven in the Southern Kingdom.

13. הִתְיַצְּבוּ עָלָיו — *Presented themselves to him.* They came from all the Levite settlements which were scattered throughout the Land to stay in Judah under his rulership (*Metzudos*).

14. אֶת־מִגְרְשֵׁיהֶם וַאֲחֻזָּתָם — *Their cities, their possessions.* מִגְרְשֵׁיהֶם is to be taken as a shortened form of עָרֵי מִגְרְשֵׁיהֶם, a term which occurs frequently, and is to be rendered *their cities.* If so, אֲחֻזָּתָם would be an appositional phrase, meant to underline the enormity of the loss which the Levites sustained by leaving their homes in order to come to Jerusalem. These cities were their only patrimony since, as Levites, they were denied a portion in the Land. By leaving their cities they left their only anchorage in the Land.

הִזְנִיחָם — *Cast them off. Radak* (*I Kings* 12:31) interprets this as follows: When Yarov'am erected the calves at Dan and Bethel the Levites in accordance with their ancient tradition of loyalty to God and their abhorrence of any kind of idol worship — refused to serve before them. Because of this, Yarov'am was forced to create a new priesthood. In retaliation, Yarov'am refused to allow the *Kohanim* and Levites to receive the tithes to which the halachah entitled them. With the source of their livelihood cut off, they were forced to move to the south.

For הִזְנִיחַ in the sense of *casting off,* see *I Chronicles* 28:9.

יָרָבְעָם וּבָנָיו — *Yarov'am and his sons.* The *Kohanim* and Levites obviously did not all make their trek to Jerusalem at the same time. It was not only during Yarov'am's reign, but also during that of the subsequent kings of Israel, that they continued to travel south.

מִכַּהֵן לַה׳ — *From ministering to* HASHEM. Although כהן mostly means to serve as a *Kohen*, here, where the Levites are included it must have a broader meaning.

15. *I Kings* 12:26 ff. tells of the golden calves which Yarov'am erected at Bethel and Dan in an effort to discourage the people of the Northern Kingdom from going to the Temple in Jerusalem. He feared that once the people would be in Jerusalem, their loyalty would

wine. 12 *And in every city, shields and spears, making them*
exceedingly strong; thus Judah and Benjamin remained his.
13 *The Kohanim and the Levites who were throughout Israel*
presented themselves to him from all their areas. 14 *For the Levites*
left their cities, their possessions, to go to Judah and Jerusalem, for
Yarov'am and his sons cast them off from ministering to HASHEM.
15 *So he established priests for himself, for the bamos and the*
demons and the calves which he had made. 16 *And after them, out*
of all the tribes of Israel, those who set their heart to seek HASHEM
the God of Israel, came to Jerusalem to sacrifice to HASHEM *the*
God of their fathers. 17 *So they strengthened the kingdom of Ju-*
dah and fortified Rechav'am the son of Solomon for three years,
for they walked in the way of David and Solomon for three years.
18 *Rechav'am took for himself a wife — Machlath, daughter of*
Yerimoth, son of David; and Avihayil, daughter of Eliav, son of
Jesse. 19 *She bore him sons: Yeush, Shemariah and Zaham.*
20 *After her he took Maachah, daughter of Absalom; and she bore*

quickly shift back to Rechav'am.

Chronicles had not mentioned anything of these calves but here assumes knowledge of the whole matter from *Kings*.

לְבָמוֹת וְלַשְּׂעִירִים וְלָעֲגָלִים — *For the bamos and the demons and the calves* ... For the calves to serve as a creditable alternative to the Temple in Jerusalem, a form of sacrificial service had to be maintained there. Hence, the *bamos*.

But, *demons* is problematic. Nowhere is there any indication that the worship which took place there touched upon the occult.

We must assume that, as the people were gradually weaned away from the authentic Temple service by the calves, the superstitions which were never far removed from the surface of their consciousness gained renewed currency. In the long run, the entire moral fabric of the society disintegrated to a point at which the people turned to magic rites to replace what had so traumatically been removed from their lives. Yarov'am must have recognized this trend, and established a priesthood to service it.

16. וְאַחֲרֵיהֶם — *And after them*. Following the footsteps of the *Kohanim* and the Levites who came to find their spiritual fulfillment in the Southern Kingdom, came those people of the other tribes who refused to abandon God's Temple.

17. וַיְחַזְּקוּ ... וַיְאַמְּצוּ — *So they strengthened . . and fortified...* The influx of so many God-fearing people lent spiritual strength to the fledgling — and initially righteous — reign of Rechav'am (*Ralbag*).

כִּי הָלְכוּ בְּדֶרֶךְ דָּוִיד וּשְׁלֹמֹה לְשָׁנִים שָׁלוֹשׁ — *For they walked in the way of David and Solomon for three years*. This refers to Rechav'am and his subjects (*Ralbag*), or the people who trekked south to join him (*Metzudos*). If this latter rendering is true, there is no clear indication from our verse that Rechav'am himself was righteous.

Seder Olam Rabbah, ch. 16 confirms *Ralbag's* understanding: Now the days that Solomon ruled over Israel were forty years; Rechav'am his son, seventeen years as it is written, *Rechav'am was forty-one years when he became king and reigned for seventeen years in Jerusalem*. It turns out that David saw him for one year. He and his sons kept the Torah for three years ...

See further in ch. 12.

18. יְרִימוֹת בֶּן־דָּוִיד — ... *Yerimoth, son of David*. For a listing of David's sons, see *I Chronicles* 3:5. Yerimoth is never mentioned among them. It is possible that he also went under another name (*Metzudos*).

אֱלִיאָב בֶּן־יִשָׁי — *Eliav, son of Jesse*. Eliav was the eldest son of Jesse, the one whom Samuel initially deemed most suitable to assume the kingship (*I Samuel* 16:6).

20. מַעֲכָה בַּת־אַבְשָׁלוֹם — *Maachah, daughter of Absalom*. Absalom, David's rebel son (*II Samuel* ch. 15 ff.) was Rechav'am's uncle. Each of Rechav'am's three wives, who are

יא
כא־כג

כא לוֹ אֶת־אֲבִיָּה וְאֶת־עַתַּי וְאֶת־זִיזָא וְאֶת־שְׁלֹמִית׃ וַיֶּאֱהַב
רְחַבְעָם אֶת־מַעֲכָה בַת־אַבְשָׁלוֹם מִכָּל־נָשָׁיו וּפִילַגְשָׁיו כִּי
נָשִׁים שְׁמוֹנֶה־עֶשְׂרֵה נָשָׂא וּפִילַגְשִׁים שִׁשִּׁים וַיּוֹלֶד
כב עֶשְׂרִים וּשְׁמוֹנָה בָּנִים וְשִׁשִּׁים בָּנוֹת׃ וַיַּעֲמֵד לָרֹאשׁ
רְחַבְעָם אֶת־אֲבִיָּה בֶן־מַעֲכָה לְנָגִיד בְּאֶחָיו כִּי לְהַמְלִיכוֹ׃
כג וַיָּבֶן וַיִּפְרֹץ מִכָּל־בָּנָיו לְכָל־אַרְצוֹת יְהוּדָה וּבִנְיָמִן לְכֹל
עָרֵי הַמְּצֻרוֹת וַיִּתֵּן לָהֶם הַמָּזוֹן לָרֹב וַיִּשְׁאַל הֲמוֹן נָשִׁים׃
א וַיְהִי כְּהָכִין מַלְכוּת רְחַבְעָם וּכְחֶזְקָתוֹ עָזַב אֶת־תּוֹרַת
ב יְהוָה וְכָל־יִשְׂרָאֵל עִמּוֹ׃ וַיְהִי בַּשָּׁנָה הַחֲמִישִׁית
לַמֶּלֶךְ רְחַבְעָם עָלָה שִׁישַׁק מֶלֶךְ־מִצְרַיִם עַל־יְרוּשָׁלִָם כִּי
ג מָעֲלוּ בַּיהוָה׃ בְּאֶלֶף וּמָאתַיִם רֶכֶב וּבְשִׁשִּׁים אֶלֶף פָּרָשִׁים
וְאֵין מִסְפָּר לָעָם אֲשֶׁר־בָּאוּ עִמּוֹ מִמִּצְרַיִם לוּבִים סֻכִּיִּים

יב
א־ג

mentioned by name, came from his own noble family (*Ralbag*).

Perhaps the fact that Rechav'am married within his own family is mentioned to demonstrate his initial righteousness. Maachah, however, appears to have carried on her father's evil traits — see further at 13:2 and 15:16.

21-22. וַיֶּאֱהַב ... אֶת־מַעֲכָה ... וַיַּעֲמֵד לָרֹאשׁ ... אֶת־אֲבִיָּה ... לְהַמְלִיכוֹ — *[Rechav'am] loved Maachah ... and appointed Aviah as leader ... in order to make him king*. Since, apparently, Aviah was not Rechav'am's oldest son, he did wrong in allowing his love for Maachah to interfere with the normal line of succession (*Ralbag*).

כִּי נָשִׁים שְׁמוֹנֶה־עֶשְׂרֵה נָשָׂא — *For he married eighteen wives*. This information may also have been given as an indication of Rechav'am's initial righteousness. He did not go beyond the number of wives permitted him by halachah. (See *Sanhedrin* 21a).

23. וַיָּבֶן — *He had insight*. Rechav'am had the insight to see that promoting the younger Aviah to be leader during his own lifetime in order, ultimately, to make him king might call forth a rebellion on the part of the older sons who would feel themselves defrauded. With this in mind, he scattered them throughout the kingdom, gave them power, wealth and many wives, hoping thereby to defuse any incipient civil war (*Malbim*).

Alternatively, the subject of וַיָּבֶן could be Aviah. He understood his father's intentions and promptly and energetically seized the reigns of power. He sent his brothers out to the far-flung reaches of the kingdom so that he would be able to consolidate his own ascendancy (*Ralbag, Malbim*).

Radak and *Metzudos* think that the subject is Rechav'am and that he feared rebellion from his subjects. Accordingly, he dispersed his sons among the populace so that they should be of help in strengthening his rule.

וַיָּבֶן from בין, *to understand*.

וַיִּתֵּן לָהֶם הַמָּזוֹן לָרֹב. — *Gave them food in abundance*. This was in order that they would be independent of the populace (*Radak, Metzudos*) or in order that they would be busy with the administration of their own affairs and have no wish to conspire (*Malbim*).

וַיִּשְׁאַל הֲמוֹן נָשִׁים — *And sought out many wives*. He sought out these wives for his sons so that he would have a large family (*Radak*), or so that he would gain the support of the wives' families for the strengthening of his rule (*Metzudos*).

If the subject is Aviah, he married many women so that his large family would confirm him as leader among his brothers (*Ralbag*), or, in anticipation of becoming king (*Malbim*).

XII

◆§ The Egyptian Campaign

1. וַיְהִי כְּהָכִין מַלְכוּת רְחַבְעָם וּכְחֶזְקָתוֹ — *Now it was, once the kingdom of Rechav'am was firmly in place, and when he felt himself strong*. In prefatory remarks to ch. 11, we

11
21-23

him Aviah, Attai, Ziza and Shelomith. [21] *Rechav'am loved Maachah daughter of Absalom above all his wives and concubines — for he married eighteen wives and sixty concubines, and fathered twenty-eight sons and sixty daughters.* [22] *Rechav'am appointed Aviah, son of Maachah, to be leader among his brothers in order to make him king.* [23] *He had insight and dispersed some of his sons among all the lands of Judah and Benjamin, to all the entrenched cities, gave them food in abundance and sought out many wives.*

12
1-3

Now it was, once the kingdom of Rechav'am was firmly in place, and when he felt himself strong, that he forsook the Torah of HASHEM, and all Israel with him. [2] *It was in the fifth year of King Rechav'am, that Shishak the king of Egypt came up against Jerusalem for they had dealt treacherously with HASHEM.* [3] *With twelve hundred chariots and sixty thousand horsemen; and no number to the people that came with him from Egypt; the Luvim, the Sukkim and the*

suggested that Rechav'am's regression might have been precipitated by the realization that the Northern Kingdom was here to stay. He had been a righteous and effective king, had had every expectation that his exemplary bearing would be enough to undo the split — which, as he saw it, was essentially an aberration. His kingdom was *firmly in place and he felt himself strong* because he had been good. When he felt himself rejected in spite of his efforts — he turned against God.

The expression הָכִין מַלְכוּת does not recur in the *Chronicles'* description of any of the other reigns. The unique usage of כון in this context calls for an explanation. See comm. to v. 14.

עָזַב אֶת־תּוֹרַת ה׳ וְכָל־יִשְׂרָאֵל עִמּוֹ — *That he forsook the Torah of HASHEM, and all Israel with him. I Kings* (14:22 ff.) has: *And Judah did evil in the eyes of HASHEM and angered Him more than their fathers had done, in their transgression which they transgressed. They too built high places, altars and groves for themselves on every high hill and under every blooming tree. There was also promiscuity in the land; they did as all the abominations of the nations whom HASHEM had driven out from before the Children of Israel.*

The expansiveness of the *Kings'* account is in striking contrast to this sparse statement. For a discussion see Section II, *Rechav'am Fails as King.*

2. וַיְהִי בַּשָּׁנָה הַחֲמִישִׁית לַמֶּלֶךְ רְחַבְעָם — *It was in the fifth year of King Rechav'am.* In 11:17 we learned that during the first three years of Rechav'am's reign, king and people walked in the spirit of David and Solomon. Thus, the backsliding reported in v. 1 took place in the fourth year. Shishak's attack which came because *they had dealt treacherously with HASHEM*, then came in the fifth year.

עָלָה שִׁישַׁק מֶלֶךְ־מִצְרַיִם עַל־יְרוּשָׁלָם — *That Shishak the king of Egypt came up against Jerusalem. Rashi* to *Kings* notes from *Midrash Shir HaShirim* that this king was really known as Pharaoh as were all Egyptian kings. It was he whose daughter Solomon had married. He had always coveted the ivory throne which his son-in-law Solomon possessed, and now he set out to take it. For this reason he is called שִׁישַׁק, from חשק, *to crave*. See Section II, *Shishak's Campaign*, for a discussion of the significance of Shishak's attack.

כִּי מָעֲלוּ בַּה׳ — *For they had dealt treacherously with HASHEM. Chronicles* assumes the reader's knowledge of the earlier books. The treacherous dealings are those described in *Kings*.

Chronicles makes the connection between the two events directly. Shishak came *because they dealt treacherously*. His coming was a direct result of their sin (*Metzudos*). *Kings*, after the account of the sins which Judah had committed, simply notes the fact that Shishak came, but does not make an express connec-

ד וְכוּשִׁים: וַיִּלְכֹּד אֶת־עָרֵי הַמְּצֻרוֹת אֲשֶׁר לִיהוּדָה וַיָּבֹא
ה עַד־יְרוּשָׁלִָם: וּשְׁמַעְיָה הַנָּבִיא בָּא אֶל־רְחַבְעָם
וְשָׂרֵי יְהוּדָה אֲשֶׁר־נֶאֶסְפוּ עַל־יְרוּשָׁלִָם מִפְּנֵי שִׁישָׁק
וַיֹּאמֶר לָהֶם כֹּה־אָמַר יהוה אַתֶּם עֲזַבְתֶּם אֹתִי וְאַף־אֲנִי
ו עָזַבְתִּי אֶתְכֶם בְּיַד־שִׁישָׁק: וַיִּכָּנְעוּ שָׂרֵי־יִשְׂרָאֵל וְהַמֶּלֶךְ
ז וַיֹּאמְרוּ צַדִּיק ׀ יהוה: וּבִרְאוֹת יהוה כִּי נִכְנָעוּ הָיָה
דְבַר־יהוה אֶל־שְׁמַעְיָה ׀ לֵאמֹר נִכְנְעוּ לֹא אַשְׁחִיתֵם
וְנָתַתִּי לָהֶם כִּמְעַט לִפְלֵיטָה וְלֹא־תִתַּךְ חֲמָתִי בִּירוּשָׁלִָם
ח בְּיַד־שִׁישָׁק: כִּי יִהְיוּ־לוֹ לַעֲבָדִים וְיֵדְעוּ עֲבוֹדָתִי וַעֲבוֹדַת
ט מַמְלְכוֹת הָאֲרָצוֹת: וַיַּעַל שִׁישַׁק מֶלֶךְ־מִצְרַיִם
עַל־יְרוּשָׁלִַם וַיִּקַּח אֶת־אֹצְרוֹת בֵּית־יהוה וְאֶת־אֹצְרוֹת
בֵּית הַמֶּלֶךְ אֶת־הַכֹּל לָקָח וַיִּקַּח אֶת־מָגִנֵּי הַזָּהָב אֲשֶׁר
י עָשָׂה שְׁלֹמֹה: וַיַּעַשׂ הַמֶּלֶךְ רְחַבְעָם תַּחְתֵּיהֶם מָגִנֵּי נְחֹשֶׁת

tion. Perhaps such a connection is self-understood in the thought world of prophecy, but needed to be explicated in *Chronicles*.

4. וַיִּלְכֹּד אֶת־עָרֵי הַמְּצֻרוֹת אֲשֶׁר לִיהוּדָה וַיָּבֹא . . . — *He captured Judah's fortified cities and came* . . . The construction and fortification of these cities was described in several detailed verses at 11:5-12. By contrast, the terse statement that Shishak captured these cities and came to Jerusalem conveys their utter ineffectiveness. God had willed that Jerusalem fall. The fortifications helped not at all!

5. וּשְׁמַעְיָה הַנָּבִיא . . . — *Now Shemaiah the prophet* . . . Shemaiah was mentioned above at 11:2.

אַתֶּם עֲזַבְתֶּם אֹתִי וְאַף־אֲנִי עָזַבְתִּי — *You have forsaken Me, I too will abandon.* The language obviously takes up the word עזב, which described Rechav'am's backsliding in v. 1.

The implication of our verse seems clear. The punishment fits the crime. Rechav'am had *forsaken* God's Torah and everything else had — as described in Section II, *Rechav'am Fails as King* — followed from that fact. God does the same thing. He *abandons* them. Without His active intervention, Shishak will, by dint of his military prowess, overwhelm them.

6. שָׂרֵי־יִשְׂרָאֵל וְהַמֶּלֶךְ — *The princes of Israel and the king.* When the backsliding had been described in v. 1, it was the king who forsook God's Torah, and the rest of Israel *with him*. The repentance, on the other hand, seems to have been initiated by the princes, with the king following along.

This would tend to confirm the thesis proposed in Section II, *Rechav'am Fails as King*. The king had committed no palpable sin, had failed only to provide energetic and forceful leadership. Not so, the people. They had sunk into overt idol worship. To them, the need for repentance was clear. Rechav'am was not ready for serious *teshuvah* until, from their tragedy, he saw just how devastating his lethargy had been.

צַדִּיק ה׳ — *HASHEM is correct.* צַדִּיק can mean, *right, just, in one's cause.* Compare *Exodus* 23:7-8.

7. וּבִרְאוֹת ה׳ כִּי נִכְנָעוּ — *When HASHEM saw that they humbled themselves.* Who is the subject of נִכְנָעוּ? From a syntactic viewpoint it could be, equally well, either *the princes of Israel and the king*, or only *the princes of Israel*.

Since v. 12 implies that Rechav'am's humbling came later — see there — we assume that only the princes are the subject here.

This would tend to bear out that the princes were the real initiating force in the penitence described in v. 6 — see comm. there.

Targum renders נִכְנָעוּ in our verse as: אתכנעו; while for וּבְהִכָּנְעוֹ in v. 12, he has: וכד תבר לביה, *When his heart was broken.*

נִכְנְעוּ לֹא אַשְׁחִיתֵם — *They have humbled themselves. I will not destroy them.* Here *Targum* inserts אתכנעו עמי, *My people have humbled themselves*. . . The subject is neither of the two alternatives discussed above, but, *My people*. In this, *Targum* is just as consistent

Kushim. [4] *He captured Judah's fortified cities and came*
to Jerusalem. [5] *Now Shemaiah the prophet came to Recha-*
v'am and to the princes of Judah, who had gathered to Jeru-
salem because of Shishak, and said to them, 'Thus says
HASHEM, You have forsaken Me, I too will abandon you in the
hands of Shishak'. [6] *The princes of Israel and the king humbled*
themselves and they said, 'HASHEM is correct.' [7] *When HASHEM*
saw that they humbled themselves, the word of HASHEM came to
Shemaiah, saying, 'They have humbled themselves. I will not
destroy them and will give them a small part as a remnant and
My wrath shall not be poured out upon Jerusalem by the hand of
Shishak. [8] *But they will be slaves to him so that they should*
appreciate My service and the slavery of the kingdoms of the
lands'. [9] *So Shishak king of Egypt came up against Jerusalem and*
took away the treasures of the House of HASHEM and the
treasures of the palace of the king; he took everything away; he
took away also the shields of gold which Solomon had made.
[10] *And King Rechav'am made in their stead shields of copper*

as in v. 12 where only the king had been mentioned; he nevertheless renders the phrase: וְלֹא לְהַשְׁחִית לְכָלָה as ולא אמר לחבלא ולשיצאה לכל עמא.

Targum's reasoning may be that it is inconceivable that God should have even considered the annihilation of the Davidic line. This would have contravened the oath that He had made to David. Witness 21:7 where, concerning the wicked Yehoram, we are told, *HASHEM did not want to destroy the house of David because of the covenant which he had made with David*. Clearly, then, the threat was to the people as a whole. The Davidic line would have been preserved for a rebuilding which would take place in the future.

כִּמְעַט לִפְלֵיטָה — *A small part as a remnant.* The כ in כִּמְעַט is a pleonasm and the word is to be understood as though it were written without it. Compare *Isaiah* 1:9.

וְלֹא־תִתַּךְ חֲמָתִי — *My wrath shall not be poured out.* From נתך, *to pour out*; this form is often used metaphorically for God's anger. Compare 34:25.

8. כִּי יִהְיוּ־לוֹ לַעֲבָדִים וְיֵדְעוּ — *But they will be slaves to him so that they should appreciate* ... This verse yields the profound insight which the Sages had into the Shishak episode. [See Section II, *Shishak's Campaign*.] The Exodus had taken place so that from being Pharaoh's servants, Israel became servants of God: *For the Israelites are My servants. They are My slaves because I brought them out from the land of Egypt ...,* (*Leviticus* 25:35). Now, the process was to reverse itself. They were about to become slaves to Egypt once more! Some of the freedom which the Exodus had bestowed upon them was about to be forfeited.

They would learn to distinguish the beauty of servitude to God from the horrors of an Egyptian enslavement.

9. אֶת־הַכֹּל לָקָח — *He took everything away.* Egypt's treasure is now brought back to its rightful place. See Section II, *Shishak's Campaign*.

אֶת־מָגִנֵּי הַזָּהָב — *The shields of gold*. We learn of these shields at 9:16. Commentators do not explain their purpose, but we may assume that they symbolized God's role as Israel's protector [see *Genesis* 15:1, *I am your shield*]. If so, the fact that they were captured by Shishak adds poignancy to the defeat which Rechav'am suffered. The very shields behind which he and the people felt themselves secure in God's hands were taken by the enemy.

10. וַיַּעַשׂ הַמֶּלֶךְ רְחַבְעָם תַּחְתֵּיהֶם מָגִנֵּי נְחֹשֶׁת — *And King Rechav'am made in their stead shields of copper.* In v. 11 we learn that these shields always accompanied the king as he went to the Temple. It seems unlikely that the original, golden shields were used thus. Rather, it appears that Rechav'am looked

וְהִפְקִיד עַל־יַד שָׂרֵי הָרָצִים הַשֹּׁמְרִים פֶּתַח בֵּית הַמֶּלֶךְ׃
יא וַיְהִי מִדֵּי־בוֹא הַמֶּלֶךְ בֵּית יְהוָה בָּאוּ הָרָצִים וּנְשָׂאוּם
יב וֶהֱשִׁבוּם אֶל־תָּא הָרָצִים׃ וּבְהִכָּנְעוֹ שָׁב מִמֶּנּוּ אַף־יְהוָה
וְלֹא לְהַשְׁחִית לְכָלָה וְגַם בִּיהוּדָה הָיָה דְּבָרִים
יג טוֹבִים׃ וַיִּתְחַזֵּק הַמֶּלֶךְ רְחַבְעָם בִּירוּשָׁלַ͏ִם וַיִּמְלֹךְ
כִּי בֶן־אַרְבָּעִים וְאַחַת שָׁנָה רְחַבְעָם בְּמָלְכוֹ וּשְׁבַע עֶשְׂרֵה
שָׁנָה ׀ מָלַךְ בִּירוּשָׁלַ͏ִם הָעִיר אֲשֶׁר־בָּחַר יְהוָה לָשׂוּם
אֶת־שְׁמוֹ שָׁם מִכֹּל שִׁבְטֵי יִשְׂרָאֵל וְשֵׁם אִמּוֹ נַעֲמָה
יד הָעַמֹּנִית׃ וַיַּעַשׂ הָרָע כִּי לֹא הֵכִין לִבּוֹ לִדְרוֹשׁ אֶת־
טו יְהוָה׃ וְדִבְרֵי רְחַבְעָם הָרִאשֹׁנִים וְהָאַחֲרוֹנִים הֲלֹא־הֵם
כְּתוּבִים בְּדִבְרֵי שְׁמַעְיָה הַנָּבִיא וְעִדּוֹ הַחֹזֶה לְהִתְיַחֵשׂ
טז וּמִלְחֲמוֹת רְחַבְעָם וְיָרָבְעָם כָּל־הַיָּמִים׃ וַיִּשְׁכַּב רְחַבְעָם

upon these reduced artifacts as symbol of his folly. To mark his contrition (v. 12), he determined that he would, as much as possible, keep them before his eyes. He would not allow himself to forget the disastrous results of his weakness.

שָׂרֵי הָרָצִים — *The officers of the escort.* רָצִים, from רוץ, *to run*; hence, *runners*. From the context it would seem that they were outriders who escorted the king when he left the palace.

הַשֹּׁמְרִים — *Who were the sentry detail.* We have followed the cantillation. *At the entrance of the king's palace* would then describe where the shields were kept, rather than the location at which these officers of the escort stood guard.

11. וַיְהִי מִדֵּי־בוֹא הַמֶּלֶךְ — *Now, whenever the king would go.* See comm. to v. 10.

תָּא הָרָצִים — *The guard chamber.* תָּא is used throughout Scripture to denote a room or chamber. See *Ezekiel* 40:7.

12. וּבְהִכָּנְעוֹ — *And when he humbled himself.* See comm. to v. 7. Clearly Rechav'am, who had committed no overt sin, had not thought that the prophet's message had really been addressed to him. Because of this, his penitence, stimulated by that of the princes, had been less than enthusiastic. Now, that Shishak had actually come, the truth had hit home. He became truly contrite.

וְגַם בִּיהוּדָה הָיָה דְּבָרִים טוֹבִים — *And, moreover, there were admirable qualities in Judah.* We have translated according to *Metzudos*. God recognized that there was much that was positive in Judah. Once king and people had become penitent, there was every reason to halt the destruction.

However, the singular הָיָה is irregular. With דְּבָרִים טוֹבִים, we would have expected הָיוּ.

Perhaps for this reason *Targum* renders: *And moreover, He intended* (אמר לאיתאה) *to make good things happen to Judah.*

13. וַיִּתְחַזֵּק הַמֶּלֶךְ רְחַבְעָם בִּירוּשָׁלַ͏ִם — *King Rechav'am strengthened his hold in Jerusalem.* In recognition of Rechav'am's sincere contrition, God granted that he was able to reconstruct Jerusalem so thoroughly that Shishak's depredations were forgotten (*Malbim*).

כִּי בֶן־אַרְבָּעִים וְאַחַת שָׁנָה רְחַבְעָם בְּמָלְכוֹ — *For Rechav'am was forty-one years old when he became king.* He was able to summon the strength to rule firmly and effectively because he was already a mature man by the time he became king.

מִכֹּל שִׁבְטֵי יִשְׂרָאֵל — *From among all the tribes of Israel.* The phrase must be understood: *From among all* [the cities of] *the tribes of Israel.* (*Metzudos*).

14. וַיַּעַשׂ הָרָע — *But he did evil.* The contrast to the previous verse is all too clear. Rechav'am made every effort to be a powerful and effective ruler, but — for his own spiritual welfare he did not expend the same energy. He was a strong king but in the end, an evil one. See comm. to next phrase.

כִּי לֹא הֵכִין לִבּוֹ — *For he did not set his heart.* At v. 1 we noted the unique joining of מַלְכוּת to כון — כְּהָכִין מַלְכוּת. We may well surmise that a contrast with our verse was intended.

and deposited them with the officers of the escort who were the
sentry detail, at the entrance of the king's palace. 11 *Now,*
whenever the king would go to the House of HASHEM, *the escort*
would come and bear them, and [then] return them to the guard
chamber. 12 *And when he humbled himself the anger of* HASHEM
turned from him, so that there would not be total destruction; and,
moreover, there were admirable qualities in Judah. 13 *King Re-*
chav'am strengthened his hold in Jerusalem, for he was forty-
one years old when he became king and he ruled seventeen years
in Jerusalem, the city in which HASHEM *had chosen to put His name*
from among all the tribes of Israel. The name of his mother was Na-
amah the Amonitess. 14 *But he did evil, for he did not set his heart*
to seek out HASHEM. 15 *Now the earlier and later affairs of*
Rechav'am are recorded in the words of Shemaiah the prophet and
Ido the Seer in the genealogical record [of the Davidic line] and
the continual war between Rechav'am and Yarov'am. 16 *And*

Rechav'am's kingdom was firmly in place — his heart was not.

The only other combination between כון and לֵב in *Chronicles* is at 30:19, where, according to some commentators, Hezekiah is described as setting his whole heart to search out God. Clearly, an assessment which faults Rechav'am for not living up to the standards of the saintly Hezekiah cannot be seen as a judgment that he indulged in actual evil. Rather, we must assume that his evil lay in passivity. He failed to guide his people, failed to inspire them to lift themselves above the smallnesses which drove them ultimately to idol-worship. See Section II, *Rechav'am Fails as King.*

15. הָרִאשֹׁנִים וְהָאַחֲרוֹנִים — *The earlier and later.* *Earlier* refers to his rule before he sinned; *later* to the period after he sinned (*Malbim*).

Since this formula is constantly used to sum up the reigns of the various kings in *Chronicles*, but never occurs in *Kings* at all, it must have a meaning which makes it appropriate only in the *Chronicles'* context.

We have noted often that the perspective with which *Samuel* and *Kings*, the *earlier* books, describe the reigns of the various kings is different to that employed by *Chronicles*. Accordingly, we may surmise that *earlier* and *later* refer to these two perspectives. The meaning of this phrase would be that both perspectives, that taken by the earlier books and that taken by *Chronicles*, can be found in this or that source.

בְּדִבְרֵי שְׁמַעְיָה הַנָּבִיא וְעִדּוֹ הַחֹזֶה — *In the words of Shemayah the prophet and Ido the seer.* In *Kings* 1:11:41 we have, *And the rest of the details* [concerning the reign] *of Rechav'am and all that he did are written in the Chronicles of the Kings of Judah*. See chart next page.

The fact that a different source is given in *Chronicles* than in *Kings* where a source is given at all it is invariably סֵפֶר דִּבְרֵי הַיָּמִים לְמַלְכֵי יְהוּדָה, would seem to confirm our perception of the two books: Each is written from a different perspective with different spheres of interest. *Kings* describes Rechav'am's rule from a contemporary vantage point. Those aspects of his reign which, for one reason or another, were not recorded in *Kings*, nevertheless found their place in the book of records which chronicled the accomplishments of the royal house. By contrast, *Chronicles* views the events from the point of view of eternity. It delves into the nature and essence of events, sees the Davidic line not as contemporary kings, but as precursors to the Messiah. Its ideas find their place in other books.

לְהִתְיַחֵשׂ — *In the genealogical record [of the Davidic line].* We have translated this difficult word according to *Targum*. Ido the Seer wrote a book tracing the genealogies of the royal house and also recording the ongoing wars between Rechav'am and Yarov'am.

Although the Judean armies disbanded when Shemayah told them that God had willed that the Northern Kingdom be founded (11:4), there was no permanent peace. Subsequently, wars did break out between the two kingdoms and continued throughout Rechav'am's and Aviyah's reign (13:2) (*Metzudos*).

יג עִם־אֲבֹתָיו וַיִּקָּבֵר בְּעִיר דָּוִיד וַיִּמְלֹךְ אֲבִיָּה בְנוֹ תַּחְתָּיו:
א־ב א בִּשְׁנַת שְׁמוֹנֶה עֶשְׂרֵה לַמֶּלֶךְ יָרָבְעָם וַיִּמְלֹךְ אֲבִיָּה עַל־
ב יְהוּדָה: שָׁלוֹשׁ שָׁנִים מָלַךְ בִּירוּשָׁלַםִ וְשֵׁם אִמּוֹ מִיכָיָהוּ בַת־
אוּרִיאֵל מִן־גִּבְעָה וּמִלְחָמָה הָיְתָה בֵּין אֲבִיָּה וּבֵין יָרָבְעָם:

ROYAL RECORDS	
DAVID (1:29:29)	וְעַל־דִּבְרֵי נָתָן הַנָּבִיא וְעַל־דִּבְרֵי גָּד הַחֹזֶה — *in the records of Samuel the seer, Nathan the prophet, and Gad the seer.*
SOLOMON (2:9:29)	עַל־דִּבְרֵי נָתָן הַנָּבִיא וְעַל־נְבוּאַת אֲחִיָּה הַשִּׁילוֹנִי וּבַחֲזוֹת יֶעְדוֹ הַחֹזֶה עַל־יָרָבְעָם בֶּן־נְבָט — *in the words of Nathan the prophet, and the prophecy of Achiah the Shilonite, and in the visions of Yehdo the Seer concerning Yarov'am son of Nevat.*
RECHAV'AM (2:12:15)	בְּדִבְרֵי שְׁמַעְיָה הַנָּבִיא וְעִדּוֹ הַחֹזֶה — *in the words of Shemaiah the prophet and Ido the seer.*
AVIAH (2:13:22)	בְּמִדְרַשׁ הַנָּבִיא עִדּוֹ — *In the midrash of the prophet Ido.*
ASA (2:16:11)	עַל־סֵפֶר הַמְּלָכִים לִיהוּדָה וְיִשְׂרָאֵל — *In the Book of Kings of Judah and Israel.*
YEHOSHAPHAT (2:20:34)	בְּדִבְרֵי יֵהוּא בֶן־חֲנָנִי אֲשֶׁר הֹעֲלָה עַל־סֵפֶר מַלְכֵי יִשְׂרָאֵל — *In the words of Yehu son of Chanani which he recorded in the Book of Israel's kings.*
YOASH (2:24:27)	עַל־מִדְרַשׁ סֵפֶר הַמְּלָכִים — *In the midrash of the Book of Kings.*
AMATZIAH (2:25:26)	עַל סֵפֶר מַלְכֵי יְהוּדָה וְיִשְׂרָאֵל — *In the Book of the Kings of Judah and Israel.*
UZZIAH (2:26:22)	כָּתַב יְשַׁעְיָהוּ בֶן־אָמוֹץ הַנָּבִיא — *Isaiah son of Amotz the prophet wrote*
YOTHAM (2:27:7)	עַל־סֵפֶר מַלְכֵי יִשְׂרָאֵל וִיהוּדָה — *In the Book of the Kings of Israel and Judah.*
ACHAZ (2:28:26)	עַל־סֵפֶר מַלְכֵי יְהוּדָה וְיִשְׂרָאֵל — *In the Book of the Kings of Judah and Israel.*
CHIZKIAHU (2:32:32)	עַל סֵפֶר מַלְכֵי יְהוּדָה וְיִשְׂרָאֵל — *In the Book of the Kings of Judah and Israel.*
MENASHEH (2:33:18)	עַל־דִּבְרֵי מַלְכֵי יִשְׂרָאֵל — *In the matters of the Kings of Israel.*
YOSHIAHU (2:35:26)	עַל־סֵפֶר מַלְכֵי־יִשְׂרָאֵל וִיהוּדָה — *In the Book of the Kings of Judah and Israel.*
YEHOYAKIM (2:36:8)	עַל־סֵפֶר מַלְכֵי יִשְׂרָאֵל וִיהוּדָה — *In the Book of the Kings of Israel and Judah.*

XIII

◈ Internecine War

1. אֲבִיָּה — *Aviah.* For an examination of the significance of Aviah's reign, see Section II, *Analysis of Aviah's Reign.*

In the *Kings* account, the name is given as אבים. *Malbim* suggests that the real name may have been Aviah but that the *mem* ending was introduced in order to differentiate him from Yarov'am's son of the same name.

2. וְשֵׁם אִמּוֹ מִיכָיָהוּ בַת־אוּרִיאֵל מִן־גִּבְעָה — *His mother's name was Michayahu daughter of Uriel from Givah.* From 11:21-22 and *I Kings* 15:2, it appears that Aviah's mother was Maachah the daughter of Avshalom or Avishalom. This is one example among many in which Scripture introduces the same person by a different name (*Radak* and *Metzudos*).[1]

וּמִלְחָמָה הָיְתָה — *There was war ... The*

1. These two commentators offer no reason why *Kings* should introduce this woman by the one name and *Chronicles* by another.
In the light of the thesis suggested in Section II, *Analysis of Aviah's Reign*, the change is readily understood.

13
1-2

Rechav'am lay with his fathers and was buried in the City of David. Aviah his son ruled after him.

It was in the eighteenth year of King Yarov'am that Aviah ruled over Judah. [2] He ruled for three years in Jerusalem and his mother's name was Michayahu daughter of Uriel from Givah. There was war between Aviah and Yarov'am.

account of the war is central here but seems to have been intentionally eliminated in *Kings*. Moreover, the short line devoted to it is relegated to a subsidiary position at the very end of the narrative.[1] See Section II, *Analysis of Aviah's Reign*.

Kings and *Chronicles* view Aviah from differing perspectives. To bring this home, they each ascribe a different name. *Kings* tells of Aviah's kingship and in that context calls him son of Maa- chah daughter of Avshalom. Thus, also *Chronicles* when it discusses his choice as Rechav'am's successor in 11:21-22. But in our section where Aviah is projected as an individual rather than as king, a different name is ascribed.

1. The comm. states that mention of Aviah's war with Yarov'am seems to have been intentionally eliminated from the *Kings'* account, and that the mention of any war is relegated to a subsidiary context.

Herewith, the proofs:

The *King's* account can be broken down as follows:

v. 1: Aviah begins his rule.
v. 2: Duration of reign and mother's name.
v. 3: Condemnatory judgment.
v. 4-5: He owes his rule only to God's promise to David.
v. 6: Now there was war between Rechav'am and Yarov'am all his life.
v. 7: The details of Aviah's reign, including the fact that there was war between him and the Northern Kingdom throughout his reign, are recorded elsewhere.
v. 8: Aviah dies.

V. 6 is jarring. Why mention the wars between Rechav'am and Yarov'am in a passage devoted to Aviah's reign? Even if we grant that the verse can be interpreted legitimately — *Abarbanel* suggests that its purpose is to explain Aviah's military prowess; he had been hardened in his father's wars — we are still left with the fact that the *King's* passage tells us nothing which would indicate that Aviah was a particularly good soldier.

We cannot avoid the impression that there is an intentional shifting of the significance of these wars from Aviah to Rechav'am. Aviah's wars are portrayed as a continuation of those of his father's.

When we say that war is relegated to an apparently subsidiary context — v. 7 — we mean as follows:

Throughout *Kings* and *Chronicles* the accounts of the various kings are generally wound up by a statement that other details not mentioned here, are recorded in different sources. Frequently, such a statement is followed by some more information concerning the reign which has only now been described. V. 7 is an example: *The rest of the details of Aviah's reign and all that he wrought are recorded in the Chronicles of the kings of Judah; and there was war between Aviah and Yarov'am.*

By placing the information that there was war between the two kings after the closing statement, the writer seems to downplay its significance. Else why not report it together with all the other facts of the reign?

This is not an isolated case.

In the absence of guidance from the classical commentators the explanation may be as follows: *Kings* belongs to the *Prophets'* section of Scripture, and according to *Bava Basra* 15a it was written by the prophet Jeremiah — that is, by prophetic inspiration. We therefore know that the selection of what was to be included and what excluded was not the result of happenstance, but was determined by the suitability of the material to the prophet's purpose — whatever that may have been.

Given this, it seems possible that the material which actually belongs to the prophetic account comes to an end with the phrase, *And the rest* . . . When after that phrase some more information is given, then that is not part of the prophetically determined account, but rather a significant fact gleaned from the source book which is identified. It is sufficiently important to be recorded, but does not bear the stamp of prophetic inspiration.

An example which may indicate the correctness of this analysis can be taken from the account of Rechav'am's reign (ch. 14 in *Kings*). There, after v. 29 had stated that the remainder of the details of Rechav'am's reign are to be found in the Chronicles of the Kings of Judah, v. 30 goes on to say that there was constant war between Rechav'am and Yarov'am. But *Chronicles* (12:15) quotes this information from the writings of Ido the seer. This would tend to indicate that information given after the concluding sentence may be assumed to come from a different source than the rest of the prophetic account, and be separate from it.

Thus the wars between Aviah and Yarov'am are denied the status of the other details of the reign which were recorded by prophetic inspiration.

ג וַיֶּאְסֹר אֲבִיָּה אֶת־הַמִּלְחָמָה בְּחַיִל גִּבּוֹרֵי מִלְחָמָה
אַרְבַּע־מֵאוֹת אֶלֶף אִישׁ בָּחוּר וְיָרָבְעָם
עָרַךְ עִמּוֹ מִלְחָמָה בִּשְׁמוֹנֶה מֵאוֹת אֶלֶף אִישׁ בָּחוּר גִּבּוֹר
ד חָיִל: וַיָּקָם אֲבִיָּה מֵעַל לְהַר צְמָרַיִם אֲשֶׁר
ה בְּהַר אֶפְרָיִם וַיֹּאמֶר שְׁמָעוּנִי יָרָבְעָם וְכָל־יִשְׂרָאֵל: הֲלֹא
לָכֶם לָדַעַת כִּי יהוה ׀ אֱלֹהֵי יִשְׂרָאֵל נָתַן מַמְלָכָה
ו לְדָוִיד עַל־יִשְׂרָאֵל לְעוֹלָם לוֹ וּלְבָנָיו בְּרִית מֶלַח: וַיָּקָם
יָרָבְעָם בֶּן־נְבָט עֶבֶד שְׁלֹמֹה בֶן־דָּוִיד וַיִּמְרֹד עַל־אֲדֹנָיו:
ז וַיִּקָּבְצוּ עָלָיו אֲנָשִׁים רֵקִים בְּנֵי בְלִיַּעַל וַיִּתְאַמְּצוּ
עַל־רְחַבְעָם בֶּן־שְׁלֹמֹה וּרְחַבְעָם הָיָה נַעַר וְרַךְ־לֵבָב וְלֹא
ח הִתְחַזַּק לִפְנֵיהֶם: וְעַתָּה ׀ אַתֶּם אֹמְרִים לְהִתְחַזֵּק לִפְנֵי
מַמְלֶכֶת יהוה בְּיַד בְּנֵי דָוִיד וְאַתֶּם הָמוֹן רָב וְעִמָּכֶם
ט עֶגְלֵי זָהָב אֲשֶׁר עָשָׂה לָכֶם יָרָבְעָם לֵאלֹהִים: הֲלֹא

3. וַיֶּאְסֹר אֲבִיָּה אֶת־הַמִּלְחָמָה — *Aviah deployed for war.* The root אסר means *to tie* or *bind.* Its use with *war* as an object is rare, and the meaning obscure. *Targum* and *Radak* take it to refer to the harnessing of the horses in readiness for battle. The act is associated with the king because he would be the first to prepare his steed (*Radak*).

Metzudos associates the use with the related meaning of קשר which means, *to place an obligation* upon someone, i.e., to *bind* him by taking away his free choice. Thus the general is one who *binds* in the sense that he gives orders which must be followed.

We have translated *deploy* because *Rashi* at *I Kings* 20:14 uses עֲרַךְ לְצַוּוֹת אוֹתָהּ, to explain the term. עֲרַךְ means *to arrange* or *set up*; thus *to deploy*, and לְצַוּוֹת means *'to issue commands'* concerning the battle. Perhaps his understanding of the term is similar to that of *Metzudos.*

אַרְבַּע־מֵאוֹת אֶלֶף אִישׁ בָּחוּר — *Four hundred thousand chosen men.* Aviah's forces were only half as numerous as those of Yarov'am and moreover they are not, as are Yarov'am's, described as mighty warriors. Nevertheless, this smaller, weaker force was victorious because God had willed that it should be so (*Ralbag*).

Ralbag does not say so specifically but we may surmise that Aviah's forces deserved to win this war because they were motivated by the sentiments expressed in his speech — see below.

4. לְהַר צְמָרַיִם — *Of Mount Tzemoraim.* Our verse places Mount Tzemoraim in the hills of Ephraim. Since the territory of Ephraim lies directly to the north of that of Benjamin [see map in ArtScroll *Joshua*, p. 294], it would be safe to assume that this mountain stood on the boundary and was thus accessible to Aviah. However, ArtScroll *Joshua*, p. 370 locates it four miles north of Jericho which itself lies on the border (see *Joshua* 16:7). This would imply that when he made the speech, Aviah had already penetrated to some extent into the territory of the Northern Kingdom (*Mefaresh*). However, *Joshua* 18:22 identifies Tzemoraim as one of Benjamin's cities. Apparently it lay in Ephraimite territory but nevertheless belonged to Benjamin.

5. בְּרִית מֶלַח — *A covenant of salt.* A covenant as eternal and unchanging as the *promise* made to salt that it would never spoil (*Rashi* to *Numbers* 18:19).

Targum: Just like it is impossible ever to sweeten the [salty] sea water, so it is unthinkable that kingship would ever be lost from the Davidic dynasty.

6. עֶבֶד שְׁלֹמֹה בֶן־דָּוִיד — *The servant of Solomon son of David.* Yarov'am can have no real or legal pretension to the throne since he is no more than a rebellious slave (*Malbim*).

7. וַיִּקָּבְצוּ עָלָיו אֲנָשִׁים רֵקִים בְּנֵי בְלִיַּעַל — *And there were gathered to him hollow men of reckless nature.* One school of thought in *Yerushalmi, Yevamos* 16:3 ascribes Aviah's death in this war (see v. 20) to the thoughtlessness of this remark. One of Yarov'am's loyal followers was Achiah the Shilonite, the prophet who had first

3 *Aviah deployed for war with an army of warriors of four hun-
dred thousand chosen men and Yarov'am set up for battle against
him with eight hundred thousand chosen men — mighty warriors.*
4 *Aviah stood up on the heights of Mount Tzemoraim which is in
the hills of Ephraim and said, 'Hear me, Yarov'am and all Israel.*
5 *Surely you should know that HASHEM, God of Israel, gave the
kingdom over Israel to David forever; to him and to his sons, a
covenant of salt.'* 6 *Yet Yarov'am the son of Nevat, the servant of
Solomon son of David, rose up and rebelled against his master.*
7 *And there were gathered to him hollow men of reckless nature
that ranged themselves resolutely against Rechav'am the son of
Solomon, and Rechav'am was a youth and faint hearted and could
not summon determination against them.* 8 *And now you presume
to range yourselves resolutely against the kingdom of HASHEM in
the hands of David's descendants. Though you are a great
multitude, you have with you the golden calves which Yarov'am
made for you as representations of the Divine.* 9 *Have you not*

apprised Yarov'am of his destiny (*I Kings* ch. 11). The use of this phrase to describe a group of which this great man was a part, is unconscionable and deserving of death.

אֲנָשִׁים רֵקִים בְּנֵי בְלִיַּעַל — *Hollow men of reckless nature.* רֵק is *empty,* thus bereft of any redeeming quality (*Metzudos*).

בְלִיַּעַל is obviously a composite word with the prefix בלי, *without*. It can, however, be divided in two ways. בְּלִי/על, in which case על would be like עול, *yoke;* thus, *without a yoke.* These were men who did not feel the yoke of Heaven upon them (*Sanhedrin* 11b and *Rashi* to *Deuteronomy* 13:14).

It can also be divided בל/יעל, the root יעל meaning *'having use, purpose* or *profit.'* Thus, *utterly worthless people* (*Radak, Sharashim*).

וּרְחַבְעָם הָיָה נַעַר – *And Rechav'am was a youth.* Rechav'am was forty-one when the revolt took place (16:13) — hardly a youth! *Metzudos* explains that the meaning is that he was as weak and inexperienced as a youth.

וְלֹא הִתְחַזַּק לִפְנֵיהֶם — *And could not summon determination against them.* חזק, *to be strong;* הִתְחַזֵּק, *to strengthen oneself* or *to find strength or courage within oneself.*

8. לְהִתְחַזֵּק לִפְנֵי מַמְלֶכֶת ה׳ בְּיַד בְּנֵי דָוִיד — *To range yourselves resolutely against the kingdom of HASHEM in the hands of David's descendants.* Aviah sees his forces not as an ordinary army, but as the inexorable force of God's kingship, pressing forward to recover its recalcitrant sons into its orbit. The Northern Kingdom's determination to fight is seen as the means whereby God's kingship is to be resisted.

וְאַתֶּם הָמוֹן רָב וְעִמָּכֶם עֶגְלֵי זָהָב — *Though you are a great multitude, you have with you the golden calves.* We follow *Metzudos'* translation. Even if your army is much larger than ours, your advantage is outweighed by the fact that you are burdened by the sin of the calves which Yarov'am erected.

אֲשֶׁר עָשָׂה לָכֶם יָרָבְעָם לֵאלֹהִים — *Which Yarov'am made for you as representations of the Divine.* Our translation reflects the truth — initially stated by *Radak, I Kings* 12:28, and attested to and discussed in detail by *HaLevi* in *Tekufas HaMikra* ch. 5 — that Yarov'am's calves were not idols in the usual sense of that word. While they violated the Torah's prohibition against making images (*Exodus* 20:19), they were not worshiped as gods.

The term אֱלֹהִים is frequently used to describe beings who, while not Divine in themselves, project a divine image through their spirituality [angles] or their exalted standing and majestic bearing [judges].

According to one opinion in *Yerushalmi Yevamos* 16:3, we have here the sin for which Aviah met an early death. Even though Yarov'am had sinned and misled an entire people, Aviah should have respected his kingship and not rebuked him in public. *Sefer Chasidim* 54 equates shaming someone in public with bloodless murder, and cites Aviah's thoughtlessness and his subsequent punishment as a source.

יג
י־טו

הִדַּחְתֶּם אֶת־כֹּהֲנֵי יהוה אֶת־בְּנֵי אַהֲרֹן וְהַלְוִיִּם וַתַּעֲשׂוּ
לָכֶם כֹּהֲנִים כְּעַמֵּי הָאֲרָצוֹת כָּל־הַבָּא לְמַלֵּא יָדוֹ בְּפַר
י בֶּן־בָּקָר וְאֵילִם שִׁבְעָה וְהָיָה כֹהֵן לְלֹא אֱלֹהִים: וַאֲנַחְנוּ
יהוה אֱלֹהֵינוּ וְלֹא עֲזַבְנֻהוּ וְכֹהֲנִים מְשָׁרְתִים לַיהוה בְּנֵי
יא אַהֲרֹן וְהַלְוִיִּם בַּמְלָאכֶת: וּמַקְטִרִים לַיהוה עֹלוֹת בַּבֹּקֶר־
בַּבֹּקֶר וּבָעֶרֶב־בָּעֶרֶב וּקְטֹרֶת־סַמִּים וּמַעֲרֶכֶת לֶחֶם עַל־
הַשֻּׁלְחָן הַטָּהוֹר וּמְנוֹרַת הַזָּהָב וְנֵרֹתֶיהָ לְבָעֵר בָּעֶרֶב
בָּעֶרֶב כִּי־שֹׁמְרִים אֲנַחְנוּ אֶת־מִשְׁמֶרֶת יהוה אֱלֹהֵינוּ
יב וְאַתֶּם עֲזַבְתֶּם אֹתוֹ: וְהִנֵּה עִמָּנוּ בָרֹאשׁ הָאֱלֹהִים ׀
וְכֹהֲנָיו וַחֲצֹצְרוֹת הַתְּרוּעָה לְהָרִיעַ עֲלֵיכֶם בְּנֵי יִשְׂרָאֵל
אַל־תִּלָּחֲמוּ עִם־יהוה אֱלֹהֵי־אֲבֹתֵיכֶם כִּי־לֹא תַצְלִיחוּ:
יג וְיָרָבְעָם הֵסֵב אֶת־הַמַּאֲרָב לָבוֹא מֵאַחֲרֵיהֶם וַיִּהְיוּ לִפְנֵי
יד יְהוּדָה וְהַמַּאֲרָב מֵאַחֲרֵיהֶם: וַיִּפְנוּ יְהוּדָה וְהִנֵּה לָהֶם
הַמִּלְחָמָה פָּנִים וְאָחוֹר וַיִּצְעֲקוּ לַיהוה וְהַכֹּהֲנִים
טו °מחצצרים בַּחֲצֹצְרוֹת: וַיָּרִיעוּ אִישׁ יְהוּדָה וַיְהִי בְּהָרִיעַ

°מַחְצְרִים ק׳

9. הֲלֹא הִדַּחְתֶּם אֶת־כֹּהֲנֵי ה׳ — *Have you not driven out the Kohanim of* HASHEM*?* The *Kohanim* and Levites left the Northern Kingdom and came to settle in Judah when they saw that Yarov'am would not permit them to function as ministrants in HASHEM's Temple in Jerusalem (11:4-5).

וַתַּעֲשׂוּ לָכֶם כֹּהֲנִים כְּעַמֵּי הָאֲרָצוֹת — *And have made priests for yourselves in the manner of the people of other lands.* The fact that Yarov'am is criticized for appointing priests who were not *Kohanim* (see also at *I Kings* 12:31), confirms that the calves were not idols in the usual sense of the word. It would have been a travesty to have used real *Kohanim* for idol worship (*HaLevi*).

כָּל־הַבָּא — *Whoever comes ...* Anyone who wanted could qualify as a priest, by simply bringing the specified sacrifices (*Metzudos*).

לְמַלֵּא יָדוֹ — *To assume office.* Literally, *to fill his hand.*

לְלֹא אֱלֹהִים — *Without God.* They became priests without being legitimized by God (*Targum*).

10. וַאֲנַחְנוּ ה׳ אֱלֹהֵינוּ — *As for us,* HASHEM *is our God.* The word, הוּא is to be inserted: ה׳ [הוּא] אֱלֹהֵינוּ (*Metzudos*). You have only Yarov'am's icons to represent the divine. We have God in our midst.

בְּנֵי אַהֲרֹן — *Sons of Aaron.* In our Temple, the *Kohanim* who serve are authentic; they are descendants of Aaron (*Metzudos*).

וְהַלְוִיִּם בַּמְלָאכֶת — *And the Levites at their service.* An unusual usage of מְלָאכָה, *work.* Reference is to tasks such as acting as chorister or as gate-keepers, which the Levites performed in the Temple (*Mefaresh*).

11. וּמַקְטִרִים — *And they burn ...* The functions described in this verse are the constituents of the daily Temple service. *'They'* are the *Kohanim* of the previous verse; not the Levites (*Metzudos*).

עַל־הַשֻּׁלְחָן הַטָּהוֹר — *On the pure table.* The table which was made of pure gold (*Rashi* to *Leviticus* 24:6 where the same expression is used).

וּמְנוֹרַת הַזָּהָב — *And the golden candelabrum ...* Furthermore, the *Kohanim* conscientiously serviced the candelabrum ... (*Metzudos*).

12. וְהִנֵּה עִמָּנוּ בָרֹאשׁ — *And see, with us as Leader.* Hashem is accompanying us, as it were, at the head of our army (*Metzudos*).

וַחֲצֹצְרוֹת הַתְּרוּעָה — *With trumpets.* Lit. *trumpets upon which a staccato sound is to be blown.*

Numbers 10:9 reads: *When you go to war against an enemy who attacked you in your*

driven out the Kohanim of HASHEM *the sons of Aaron and the*
Levites and have made priests for yourselves in the manner of
the people of other lands so that whoever comes to assume
office with a young bullock and seven rams can become
priest without God. 10 *As for us,* HASHEM *is our God and we*
have not forsaken Him. Kohanim minister to HASHEM, *who*
are sons of Aaron, and the Levites at their service. 11 *And*
they burn burnt offerings every morning and every evening
to HASHEM, *and burned incense and an arrangement of bread*
upon the pure table and the golden candelabrum with its lamps
to burn every evening. For we are loyal to the charge of
HASHEM *our God, while you have forsaken Him.* 12 *And see,*
with us as Leader is God. There are His Kohanim with trum-
pets to sound against you. Children of Israel! Do not make
war against HASHEM *the God of your fathers for you will*
not succeed.' 13 *Yarov'am moved the ambushing party around*
so that it would come behind them. So they were in front of
Judah and the ambushing party was behind them. 14 *Ju-*
dah turned, and behold the battle was before them and be-
hind them. So they cried out to HASHEM *and the Kohanim sound-*
ed the trumpets. 15 *The men of Judah shouted and it was when*

land, you shall sound a staccato on the trumpets. You will then be remembered before HASHEM *your God and will be delivered from your enemies.*

In accordance with this command, Aviah's forces were preceded by *Kohanim* blowing the trumpets (*Metzudos*).

עֲלֵיכֶם — *Against you.* If the trumpets cause us to be *remembered before Hashem*, then they are instrumental in the destruction of the enemy.

אַל־תִּלָּחֲמוּ עִם־ה' — *Do not make war against* HASHEM. An escalation from v. 8. There the war is depicted against the *kingdom of* HASHEM; here against HASHEM Himself.

Perhaps the stress that HASHEM is the *God of your fathers* is designed to awaken a sense of solidarity with their brothers to the south. When God was recognized as the God of our fathers, we were all one people.

For an analysis of the sentiments expressed in this speech, see Section II, *Aviah's Speech.*

13. Yarov'am ignores Aviah's plea and readies himself for battle.

וְיָרָבְעָם הֵסֵב אֶת־הַמַּאֲרָב לָבוֹא מֵאַחֲרֵיהֶם — *Yarov'am moved the ambushing party around, so that it would come behind them.* ארב means *to lie in wait*, so מַאֲרָב is an *ambush* or *a group of people lying in ambush.* Evidently it was Yarov'am's purpose to put Aviah's forces to flight with the superior forces which he had facing them, and that the ambushing party would then attack the fleeing army.

וַיִּהְיוּ לִפְנֵי יְהוּדָה — *So they were in front of Judah.* This refers to the rest of the army, not the ones that lay in ambush.

14. וַיִּפְנוּ — *[Judah] turned.* פנה, *to turn*, can also carry the meaning of *to turn and look* around. See, for example, *Exodus* 2:12.

הַמִּלְחָמָה — *The battle. Metzudos* renders *the soldiers.*

15. וַיָּרִיעוּ אִישׁ יְהוּדָה — *The men of Judah shouted.* The root רוע can mean *to shout*, in either triumph, joy, or applause. It is sometimes used as synonym for prayer, and sometimes for *blowing* the *teruah*, the staccato sound made with a *shofar* or trumpet.

Two points could argue in favor of the latter explanation. The word was used with that meaning in v. 12, and the Torah commands that in time of war the *teruah* be sounded on the trumpets (*Numbers* 10:9). However, if that were the case it should not have been the *men of Judah* who blew, but the *Kohanim.* For this

אִישׁ יְהוּדָה וְהָאֱלֹהִים נָגַף אֶת־יָרָבְעָם וְכָל־יִשְׂרָאֵל לִפְנֵי
טז אֲבִיָּה וִיהוּדָה׃ וַיָּנוּסוּ בְנֵי־יִשְׂרָאֵל מִפְּנֵי יְהוּדָה וַיִּתְּנֵם
יז אֱלֹהִים בְּיָדָם׃ וַיַּכּוּ בָהֶם אֲבִיָּה וְעַמּוֹ מַכָּה רַבָּה וַיִּפְּלוּ
יח חֲלָלִים מִיִּשְׂרָאֵל חֲמֵשׁ־מֵאוֹת אֶלֶף אִישׁ בָּחוּר׃ וַיִּכָּנְעוּ
בְנֵי־יִשְׂרָאֵל בָּעֵת הַהִיא וַיֶּאֶמְצוּ בְּנֵי יְהוּדָה כִּי נִשְׁעֲנוּ
יט עַל־יהוה אֱלֹהֵי אֲבוֹתֵיהֶם׃ וַיִּרְדֹּף אֲבִיָּה אַחֲרֵי יָרָבְעָם
וַיִּלְכֹּד מִמֶּנּוּ עָרִים אֶת־בֵּית־אֵל וְאֶת־בְּנוֹתֶיהָ וְאֶת־יְשָׁנָה
כ וְאֶת־בְּנוֹתֶיהָ וְאֶת־°עפרון וּבְנֹתֶיהָ׃ וְלֹא־עָצַר כֹּחַ־יָרָבְעָם °עֶפְרַיִן ק׳
כא עוֹד בִּימֵי אֲבִיָּהוּ וַיִּגְּפֵהוּ יהוה וַיָּמֹת׃ וַיִּתְחַזֵּק אֲבִיָּהוּ
וַיִּשָּׂא־לוֹ נָשִׁים אַרְבַּע עֶשְׂרֵה וַיּוֹלֶד עֶשְׂרִים וּשְׁנַיִם בָּנִים
כב וְשֵׁשׁ עֶשְׂרֵה בָּנוֹת׃ וְיֶתֶר דִּבְרֵי אֲבִיָּה וּדְרָכָיו וּדְבָרָיו
כג כְּתוּבִים בְּמִדְרַשׁ הַנָּבִיא עִדּוֹ׃ וַיִּשְׁכַּב אֲבִיָּה עִם־אֲבֹתָיו

reason we have opted to translate as we have done.

Metzudos writes that this was a *teruah* of triumph. Their trust in God was so complete that even before victory was theirs, they already rejoiced in their success.

וַיְהִי בְּהָרִיעַ אִישׁ יְהוּדָה וְהָאֱלֹהִים נָגַף — *And it was when the men of Judah shouted that God smote* ... The defeat of the northern army is portrayed as completely miraculous. They are smitten by God rather than by Aviah's army. These appear active only in the pursuit described in the next verse.[1]

17. מַכָּה רַבָּה — *Mightily*. Lit. *a great smiting*.

Yerushalmi Yevamos 16:3, based on the redundancy of this phrase, sees an act of senseless cruelty here. Aviah not only killed these people but mutilated their bodies beyond recognition. This would make identification impossible, and would assure that the wives of the slain soldiers would not be able to remarry.

Because of this act of unnecessary cruelty, Aviah was to be killed in battle (v. 20).

חֲמֵשׁ־מֵאוֹת אֶלֶף — *Five hundred thousand*. This was from a total of 800,000 men (v. 3)! This is in spite of the fact that Aviah mustered only four hundred thousand soldiers.

18. כִּי נִשְׁעֲנוּ — *Because they relied*. This unequivocal statement of approval reinforces the sense of ambiguity which the description of Aviah's reign projects — see Section II, *Aviah's Speech*. The Sages criticized much of what Aviah did and said in the course of this confrontation — and yet, the bearing of his army appears to have been beyond reproach.

19. בֵּית־אֵל — *Bethel*. Again, *Yerushalmi Yevamos* 16:3 interprets negatively. One of the

1. *Eichah Rabbasi* (*Pesichta* 30) analyzes the divergent attitudes of four kings to their wars. In a descending progression each one demanded a greater involvement on the part of God in their battles. David had said, *'I will pursue my enemies and overtake them ...'*; Asa said, *'I have no strength to kill, I will only pursue'* [based on 14:12]; Yehoshaphat said, *'I have no strength to pursue, I will just pray to HASHEM'* [based on 20:22]; and Hezekiah said, *'I cannot even pray ... I will sleep on my bed'* [based on *II Kings* 19:35].

Commentators explain that although superficially there seems to be a progression here — each king seems to trust God more — there is really a regression. Each king trusts himself less. David was able to recognize that victory came from God even if he was totally involved in the fighting. The later kings knew that the more they were involved, the less they would see God's hand in the process.

On the scale of the midrash, Aviah's victory seems to fall into the same category as that of Yehoshaphat. He is uninvolved in the fighting.

But this would undermine the smooth progression posited by the midrash. Yehoshaphat's attitude — as reflected through Aviah — predates Asa.

Perhaps Aviah's victory does not, in fact, fit into the categories with which the midrash deals. That his victory came solely as a result of God's intervention may have been for a different reason. Aviah's war with Yarov'am centered directly and exclusively upon the legitimacy of the Davidic kingship, which is identical with that of God (v. 12). More than in the battles which Israel fought against outside enemies, God Himself was a party in this internecine struggle.

the men of Judah shouted that God smote Yarov'am and all Israel
before Aviah and Judah. 16 *The Children of Israel*
fled from before Judah, and God gave them into their hands.
17 *Aviah and his people smote them mightily. Five hun-*
dred thousand chosen men fell slain from Israel. 18 *Thus*
the Children of Israel were subdued at that time, and the chil-
dren of Judah prevailed because they relied on HASHEM, the God
of their fathers. 19 *Aviah pursued Yarov'am and captured*
cities from him: Bethel and its dependencies; Yeshanah and
its dependencies; Ephran and its dependencies. 20 *Yarov'am*
no longer retained any strength in the days of Aviah, and
HASHEM smote him and he died. 21 *Aviah established him-*
self and married fourteen women and fathered twenty-two
sons and sixteen daughters. 22 *The rest of Aviah's affairs,*
his ways and that which concerned him, are written in the
midrash of the prophet Ido. 23 *Then Aviah lay with his fathers*

golden calves which Yarov'am had erected stood at Bethel (*I Kings* 12:29). Once Aviah had captured that city it was surely in his power to destroy this icon which he had so roundly condemned in his speech (v. 8). That he did not do so, squandering the one great opportunity of eliminating this travesty, was considered a grave-enough sin to warrant his early death (v. 20).

20. וַיִּגְּפֵהוּ ה׳ וַיָּמֹת — *And HASHEM smote him and he died.* The syntax seems to demand that the object of וַיִּגְּפֵהוּ is Yarov'am; that is, that he was killed in this war by Aviah's forces.

This, however, cannot be true, since according to *I Kings* 14:20 Yarov'am reigned twenty-two years. If we subtract the seventeen years of Rechav'am's reign and the three years which Aviah ruled, this has him outlast Aviah by two years. Indeed, *I Kings* 15:25 reports that Yarov'am's son Nadav became king in the second year of Asa, who was Aviah's son and heir.

Radak suggests that Yarov'am did not die immediately. Rather, as a result of his defeat at Aviah's hands and the erosion of his strength which this brought about, he fell in one of the wars which he waged some years later.

The Sages in *Yerushalmi Yevamos* 16:3 teach that it is Aviah who died. He was killed in this war because of one of the four sins which he committed in the course of this confrontation. See vs. 7, 8, 17 and 19.[1]

21. וַיִּתְחַזֵּק אֲבִיָּהוּ וַיִּשָּׂא־לוֹ נָשִׁים — *Aviah established himself and married* . . . The phrase is to be understood as follows: Once Aviah had established himself on his throne he married . . . (*Metzudos*).

22. וּדְרָכָיו וּדְבָרָיו — *His ways and that which concerned him.* For this usage, particularly in relation to Aviah — see comm. to 28:26.

בְּמִדְרַשׁ הַנָּבִיא עִדּוֹ — *In the midrash of the prophet Ido.* In mishnaic Hebrew, the root דרש has the meaning of *to engage in exegesis,* usually of Scriptural texts. This no doubt, is because דרש in its original sense is *to seek out;* hence, to search after the less obvious meaning of the text. From this, the term מִדְרָשׁ developed to describe the lessons derived from this exegetical activity, and ultimately, to describe a collection of such interpretations.

However, in Scriptural Hebrew the root is never used to denote exegesis of a text,[2] but rather in the sense: *to investigate* (*Deuteronomy* 13:15); *to interest oneself in another's welfare* (*Jeremiah* 30:14); *to seek guidance* (*I*

1. As the Sages interpret our verse, the treatment of Aviah by *Chronicles* is entirely consistent. As noted many times, the *Chronicles'* account of his reign seems to be one of restrained approval. There were sins — even very serious ones — but these are derived from hints in the text — never explicated. Apparently, there was an inner malaise, not immediately visible to the eye.

Consistent with this, the report of his death — which came in punishment for these sins — is also veiled. We must delve beneath the surface of syntactical implication to learn of it.

2. The possible exception is *Ezra* 7:10. But this interpretation is by no means certain.

וַיִּקְבְּרוּ אֹתוֹ בְּעִיר דָּוִיד וַיִּמְלֹךְ אָסָא בְנוֹ תַּחְתָּיו בְּיָמָיו
א שָׁקְטָה הָאָרֶץ עֶשֶׂר שָׁנִים: וַיַּעַשׂ אָסָא הַטּוֹב
ב וְהַיָּשָׁר בְּעֵינֵי יהוה אֱלֹהָיו: וַיָּסַר אֶת־מִזְבְּחוֹת הַנֵּכָר
וְהַבָּמוֹת וַיְשַׁבֵּר אֶת־הַמַּצֵּבוֹת וַיְגַדַּע אֶת־הָאֲשֵׁרִים:

Kings 22:5); and, as frequently in the past several chapters, *to earnestly and energetically seek to discover and follow God's will.*

What, then, is the meaning of מִדְרַשׁ in our context?

Ibn Janah, under דרש, finds another meaning for that root: *to make something clear*. Hence, the *Midrash of the Prophet Ido* is the book in which he offers his explanations of the events which happened, just as in the *Midrash of the Book of Kings* (24:27) the customs of the various kings are examined and explained.

Radak interprets the word in the sense of *searching out* and thinks that the *Midrash of the Prophet Ido* was a book which was constantly sought out and consulted by people — presumably because of the depth of its insights. An analogy would be *Isaiah* 34:16 where דרש is used for the act of consulting the written record.

In the context of what we have learned about Aviah, we can readily understand why a book devoted to the analysis of his reign would be called a *Midrash*. Much that the sacred books write about him remains ambiguous and shrouded in mystery. We have seen that his wickedness was not as flagrant as some of the texts would seem to yield nor were his righteous acts untainted by hidden streaks of evil. We can see why an insightful record of his person and rule would require a searching, analytical mind which could catch the nuances of behavior not readily evident to the less perceptive observer. Such a record would surely be sought out and consulted by people who felt their own faculties inadequate to the true understanding of this complex king. Thus, in fact, many of the nuances of the word are applicable here, and also *Ibn Janah's* understanding is appropriate since the difficulties involved would indeed require a detailed exposition to clarify them.

23. בְּיָמָיו שָׁקְטָה הָאָרֶץ עֶשֶׂר שָׁנִים — *In his days the land was at peace for ten years.* These would be the first ten years of Asa's reign. If peace lasted for only ten years, we need to know what hostilities broke out after these had passed. The first war mentioned for Asa is that with Zerach the Kushite (14:8). But 15:10-11 seem to indicate that this war took place in Asa's fifteenth year — and that is how *Seder Olam* ch. 16 apparently records it. *Malbim* feels that this is also borne out by 15:19; see comm. there. If that is so, the hostilities hinted at in this verse must refer to some other unspecified battles.

However, on the strength of our verse, *Gra* emends *Seder Olam* to read that the war with Zerach the Kushite took place in Asa's eleventh year. *Gra* reinterprets such verses as seeming to indicate otherwise.

The fact that this verse appears in *Chronicles* but not in *Kings* may argue in favor of *Gra's* opinion. If it is meant to date the battle with Zerach the Kushite we would not expect it to be mentioned in *Kings*, since that book does not record that episode at all. If, however, it teaches that after the first ten years of Asa's reign there were other minor battles, we would know no reason why this should not be recorded in *Kings*.

XIV

◆§ The Kushite War

1. וַיַּעַשׂ אָסָא הַטּוֹב וְהַיָּשָׁר — *Asa did that which was good and right*. *Good* in matters between man and God, *right* in human relationships (*Malbim*).

Asa is one of those kings concerning whom *Chronicles* and *Kings* appear to be in absolute agreement. In both, the assessment offered is positive. See chart in *Section II to* ch. 12, p. 366.

However, a closer analysis reveals significant differences: *Kings* has *right* but not *good; Chronicles* omits the phrase, . . . *like his father David.*[1]

1. In this deviation Asa is unique. In other cases in which the comparison to David is made, it appears in both *Kings* and *Chronicles*. The instances are: Chizkiahu (2:18:3 and 2:29:2) and Yoshiyahu (2:22:2 and 2:34:2).

None of the other righteous kings is compared to David. But, Amatziah is contrasted to him.

That contrast may yield the precise meaning of a comparison to David.

II Kings 14:3 has: . . .*He did that which was right in the eyes of* HASHEM, *but not as David his father [had*

and they buried him in the City of David. Asa, his son, ruled instead of him; in his days the land was at peace for ten years.

Asa did that which was good and right in the eyes of HASHEM his God. [2] *He eradicated the altars of the alien gods, and the bamos, he smashed the sacred pillars and felled the asheirah-trees.*

Chronicles presents a very positive picture of Asa's reign, and there is no apparent reason why it should omit the judgment that Asa acted *like his father David.*

Perhaps, the phrase here has a more limited function than its parallel in *Kings*. Rather than being meant as an assessment of the whole reign, it introduces the topics which follow immediately upon it — the elimination of the idolatrous artifacts and the prosecution of the Kushite war. In both those instances, Asa's actions were *good* and *right*, but a comparison to David would have been inappropriate.

2. וַיָּסַר אֶת־מִזְבְּחוֹת הַנֵּכָר — *He eradicated the altars of the alien gods.* This passage clearly assumes knowledge of the *Kings'* account of Rechav'am's reign, where the proliferation of idol worship was mentioned. *Chronicles* has, up to this point, said nothing of an idolatrous cult.

But, *Kings* mentions that Asa also cleaned the land of prostitutes. Why should this not be recorded in *Chronicles*?

Moreover, *Chronicles* seems consistent in ignoring this aspect of Asa's reforms. One of the merits ascribed to Asa's son Yehoshaphat at *Kings* 22:47 is that he eliminated even those final vestiges of prostitution which had escaped Asa's efforts. Here, too, *Chronicles* is silent.

The explanation may be as follows:

We shall see that the prosecution of the Kushite war is central to the *Chronicles'* perception of Asa's reign. It is possible that *Chronicles* is interested in Asa's reforms only insofar as these explain his victory over Zerach. Now, the significance of that war has its locus at the very essence of Jewish peoplehood. Israel as a nation was judged to be once more worthy of disposing over *Egypt's treasure* — see below. Accordingly, the elimination of idol worship — a national malaise — is significant to that account. Prostitution, for all its pernicious horror, is a problem of the individual. It has no place in the *Chronicles'* perspective. [For *Kings'* silence concerning the Kushite war, see Section II to ch. 12, *Shishak's Campaign*.]

מִזְבְּחוֹת הַנֵּכָר — *The altars of the alien gods.* The translation can accommodate *Metzudos*: *The altars [which had been erected] to strange gods*, or that of *Targum*: *The altars of alien people*.

An alternative would be: *The strange altars*; that is, altars which are foreign to Israelite usage.

An *altar* is used for regular community worship while a *bamah* is for an individual, and used only as the occasion requires (*Malbim*).

וְהַבָּמוֹת — *And the bamos.* To avoid redundancy, *Metzudos* explains that here, this term refers not to the altars themselves but to the idolatrous temples in which these were housed.

At 15:17 we learn that in spite of Asa's righteousness, the *bamos* were not removed from Israel. But there is no contradiction. Those *bamos* are not to be confused with the ones mentioned here.

The base-meaning of *bamah* is a *high place*, specifically, an *altar*. Some of these *bamos* were used for idol worship[1] — and these Asa eliminated completely.

But many were used by the people to bring sacrifices to God. There were periods in history during which this form of private worship was permitted. However, with the building of Solomon's Temple, they became permanently interdicted [see *Zevachim* 14:4-8].

For reasons which we can only guess, the people found it extremely difficult to wean themselves away from these private *bamos*. Their continued proliferation bedeviled the reigns of some of even the most righteous kings.

It is these *bamos*, used for Divine worship, which are meant at 15:17 (*Rashi* and *Metzudos*).

הַמַּצֵּבוֹת — *The sacred pillars.* From נצב, *to stand*. These pillars were used for oil libations (*Malbim*).

done]. The parallel sentence at 2:25:2 reads: *He did that which was right in the eyes of HASHEM, but not with a complete heart.* Apparently, ... *as David [had done]* equals, ... *with a complete heart.*

1. This meaning must also be ascribed at *II Kings* 17:9-11. Perhaps also for those *bamos* mentioned in connection with Achaz (28:4) and Menasheh (33:3).

ג וַיֹּאמֶר לִיהוּדָה לִדְרוֹשׁ אֶת־יְהֹוָה אֱלֹהֵי אֲבוֹתֵיהֶם
ד וְלַעֲשׂוֹת הַתּוֹרָה וְהַמִּצְוָה: וַיָּסַר מִכָּל־עָרֵי יְהוּדָה אֶת־
ה הַבָּמוֹת וְאֶת־הַחַמָּנִים וַתִּשְׁקֹט הַמַּמְלָכָה לְפָנָיו: וַיִּבֶן עָרֵי
מְצוּרָה בִּיהוּדָה כִּי־שָׁקְטָה הָאָרֶץ וְאֵין־עִמּוֹ מִלְחָמָה
ו בַּשָּׁנִים הָאֵלֶּה כִּי־הֵנִיחַ יְהֹוָה לוֹ: וַיֹּאמֶר לִיהוּדָה נִבְנֶה ׀
אֶת־הֶעָרִים הָאֵלֶּה וְנָסֵב חוֹמָה וּמִגְדָּלִים דְּלָתַיִם וּבְרִיחִים
עוֹדֶנּוּ הָאָרֶץ לְפָנֵינוּ כִּי דָרַשְׁנוּ אֶת־יְהֹוָה אֱלֹהֵינוּ דָּרַשְׁנוּ
ז וַיָּנַח לָנוּ מִסָּבִיב וַיִּבְנוּ וַיַּצְלִיחוּ: וַיְהִי לְאָסָא
חַיִל נֹשֵׂא צִנָּה וָרֹמַח מִיהוּדָה שְׁלֹשׁ מֵאוֹת אֶלֶף וּמִבִּנְיָמִן
נֹשְׂאֵי מָגֵן וְדֹרְכֵי קֶשֶׁת מָאתַיִם וּשְׁמוֹנִים אֶלֶף כָּל־אֵלֶּה

3. וַיֹּאמֶר לִיהוּדָה לִדְרוֹשׁ אֶת־ה׳ — *He exhorted Judah to seek out* HASHEM. If we compare the *Chronicles'* and the *Kings'* accounts of Asa's reign, it is clear that the section which begins with this verse and ends at 15:15 is an insertion. In *Kings*, the information given in our 15:16 follows directly upon the parallel to our v. 2. There is no reference at all to the Kushite war — to which *Chronicles* devotes a full twenty-two verses.

Chronicles		*Kings*	
14:1	וַיַּעַשׂ אָסָא הַטּוֹב וְהַיָּשָׁר בְּעֵינֵי ה׳. — *Asa did that which was good and right in the eyes of* HASHEM *his God.*	15:11	וַיַּעַשׂ אָסָא הַיָּשָׁר בְּעֵינֵי ה׳ כְּדָוִד אָבִיו. — *Asa did that which was right in the eyes of God, just like his father David.*
14:2	וַיָּסַר אֶת־מִזְבְּחוֹת הַנֵּכָר וְהַבָּמוֹת וַיְשַׁבֵּר אֶת־הַמַּצֵּבוֹת וַיְגַדַּע אֶת־הָאֲשֵׁרִים. — *He eradicated the altars of the alien gods and the bamos, he smashed the sacred pillars and felled the asheirah trees.*	15:12	וַיַּעֲבֵר הַקְּדֵשִׁים מִן־הָאָרֶץ וַיָּסַר אֶת־כָּל־הַגִּלֻּלִים אֲשֶׁר עָשׂוּ אֲבֹתָיו. — *He eradicated the prostitutes from the land, and removed all of the idols which his fathers had made.*
14:3	וַיֹּאמֶר לִיהוּדָה לִדְרוֹשׁ אֶת־ה׳ ... — *He exhorted Judah to seek out* HASHEM ...		
15:15	וַיִּשְׂמְחוּ כָל־יְהוּדָה ... — *All Judah rejoiced ...*		
15:16	וְגַם־מַעֲכָה אֵם ... הַמֶּלֶךְ הֱסִירָהּ מִגְּבִירָה ... — *Also he deposed Maachah the king's mother from the position of queen...*	15:13	וְגַם אֶת־מַעֲכָה אִמּוֹ וַיְסִרֶהָ מִגְּבִירָה ... — *Also his mother Maachah, and deposed her from the position of queen ...*

The syntax of v. 13 in *Kings* is awkward. Clearly the first phrase must be read with the previous verse: *He removed the idols ... and also his mother*. The second part of the sentence then explains that he removed her from the position of queen (*Radak*).

V. 13 is a composite between the ending of v. 12 and a new thought.

It is this verse, which structurally so clearly belongs together with the previous one, which *Chronicles* moves to the middle of ch. 15, adjusting the syntax to the new requirements.

If the two verses so obviously belong together, why did *Chronicles* divide them from one another by the insertion of the description of the Kushite wars?

We may suggest the following solution. The victory over the Kushites is presented as a direct result of the national reforms instituted by Asa. Because of this, the description of the war follows hard upon the account of those reforms. While the eradication of idol worship

14
3-7

[3] *He exhorted Judah to seek out* HASHEM, *the God of their fathers,*
and to observe the Torah and the commandments. [4] *Thus he re-*
moved from all the cities of Judah the bamos and the sun images.
The kingdom was tranquil before him. [5] *He built cities for defense*
in Judah, for the land was quiet, and in those years there was no
war with him because HASHEM *had given him rest.* [6] *He said to*
Judah, 'Let us build up these cities and surround them with wall,
towers, gates and bolts. The land is yet before us, for we have
sought out HASHEM *our God; we have sought Him out and He has*
given us rest on every side'. So they built and they prospered.
[7] *Asa had an army that bore bucklers and spears, from Judah*
three hundred thousand and from Benjamin that bore shields and
drew bows two hundred and eighty thousand. All of these were

falls into the category of such national reforms, the deposing of the queen-mother clearly does not. That act affected only the king's household. Because it had no bearing upon the victory over the Kushites it is relegated to the next section.

לִדְרוֹשׁ אֶת־ה׳ אֱלֹהֵי אֲבוֹתֵיהֶם וְלַעֲשׂוֹת הַתּוֹרָה וְהַמִּצְוָה — *To seek out* HASHEM, *the God of their fathers, and to observe the Torah and the commandment*s. This verse serves as an introduction to the Kushite wars. As noted in Section II to ch. 12, *Shishak's Campaign*, this war was to undo the tragedy of Rechav'am's defeat at Shishak's hands. The *Treasure of Egypt*, which Israel had lost at that time, was to be returned to them. Under Asa they had earned another chance.

But, they could only succeed where the previous generation had failed if they would not fall prey to the same shortcomings. Those had been the result of excessive passivity on the part of the king. It is appropriate that before Asa's victory is described, we learn that he did that which his father had failed to do. He inspired the people to actively seek out a life devoted to Torah and *mitzvos*.

4. וַיָּסַר מִכָּל־עָרֵי יְהוּדָה — *Thus he removed from all the cities of Judah.* We have translated in accordance with *Malbim*. Asa's exhortations bore fruit. The people set about cleansing the land from those idolatrous altars which Asa's efforts described in v. 2 had not been able to touch.

הַחַמָּנִים — *The sun images.* חמה, from חמם *to be warm*, is the sun, and חַמָּן is an image set up for the worship of the sun (*Metzudos*).

וַתִּשְׁקֹט הַמַּמְלָכָה לְפָנָיו — *The kingdom was tranquil before him.* This tranquility is the inner calm and sense of spiritual well-being which resulted from the eradication of idol worship. At 13:23 the meaning had been that in the first ten years of Asa's reign, the nation was not at war.

5. עָרֵי מְצוּרָה — *Cities for defense*. See comm. to 11:5.

כִּי־שָׁקְטָה הָאָרֶץ — *Because the land was quiet.* With no battles to be waged, the building program flourished.

6. עוֹדֶנּוּ הָאָרֶץ לְפָנֵינוּ — *The land is yet before us*. Let us fortify our cities as long as we have the chance. Before long, an enemy may come against us (*Metzudos*).

Asa realized that the tranquility which the land was enjoying did not derive from military or political considerations but only from God's direct intervention as a reward for their constant [expressed in the repetition of דָרַשְׁנוּ] seeking out of HASHEM. Inasmuch as it was conditioned by their spiritual standing, the possibility always existed that times may come when they would no longer merit such providence. He urged the people to fortify their cities against such a time and not to rely on miracles (*Malbim*).

דָרַשְׁנוּ אֶת־ה׳ אֱלֹהֵינוּ — *For we have sought out* HASHEM *our God*. The cantillation joins this phrase to the earlier one and separates the next דָרַשְׁנוּ from it. Thus: *The land is yet before us for we have sought out* HASHEM *our God; we have sought Him out and He has given us rest on every side*.

7. וְדֹרְכֵי קֶשֶׁת — *And drew bows*. Bowmen tread down on their bows in order to steady them for accurate shooting. Therefore, they are described as those who *tread* [from דרך, *to*

ח גִּבּוֹרֵי חָיִל: וַיֵּצֵא אֲלֵיהֶם זֶרַח הַכּוּשִׁי בְּחַיִל אֶלֶף אֲלָפִים
ט וּמַרְכָּבוֹת שְׁלֹשׁ מֵאוֹת וַיָּבֹא עַד־מָרֵשָׁה: וַיֵּצֵא אָסָא לְפָנָיו
י וַיַּעַרְכוּ מִלְחָמָה בְּגֵיא צְפַתָה לְמָרֵשָׁה: וַיִּקְרָא אָסָא
אֶל־יהוה אֱלֹהָיו וַיֹּאמַר יהוה אֵין־עִמְּךָ לַעְזוֹר בֵּין רַב לְאֵין
כֹּחַ עָזְרֵנוּ יהוה אֱלֹהֵינוּ כִּי־עָלֶיךָ נִשְׁעַנּוּ וּבְשִׁמְךָ בָאנוּ
עַל־הֶהָמוֹן הַזֶּה יהוה אֱלֹהֵינוּ אַתָּה אַל־יַעְצֹר עִמְּךָ
יא אֱנוֹשׁ: וַיִּגֹּף יהוה אֶת־הַכּוּשִׁים לִפְנֵי אָסָא וְלִפְנֵי
יב יְהוּדָה וַיָּנֻסוּ הַכֻּשִׁים: וַיִּרְדְּפֵם אָסָא וְהָעָם אֲשֶׁר־עִמּוֹ
עַד־לִגְרָר וַיִּפֹּל מִכּוּשִׁים לְאֵין־לָהֶם מִחְיָה כִּי־נִשְׁבְּרוּ
יג לִפְנֵי־יהוה וְלִפְנֵי מַחֲנֵהוּ וַיִּשְׂאוּ שָׁלָל הַרְבֵּה מְאֹד: וַיַּכּוּ
אֵת כָּל־הֶעָרִים סְבִיבוֹת גְּרָר כִּי־הָיָה פַחַד־יהוה עֲלֵיהֶם
יד וַיָּבֹזּוּ אֶת־כָּל־הֶעָרִים כִּי־בִזָּה רַבָּה הָיְתָה בָהֶם: וְגַם־
אָהֳלֵי מִקְנֶה הִכּוּ וַיִּשְׁבּוּ צֹאן לָרֹב וּגְמַלִּים וַיָּשֻׁבוּ

step upon] on their bows (*Metzudos*).

8. Zerach the Kushite had wrested the *treasure of Egypt* from Shishak, who had taken it from Rechav'am (*Pesachim* 119a and see Section II to ch. 12 *Shishak's campaign*). He now comes to do battle with Asa, carrying it with him.[1]

Asa's carrying in this battle is beyond reproach, and his benign and righteous rule had lifted his people to a level at which God was once more willing to trust them with the temporal power implicit in the *treasure of Egypt*.

עַד־מָרֵשָׁה — *To Mareishah*. Mareishah is given in *Joshua* 15:44 as a city of Judah. If the location assigned in ArtScroll *Joshua* to that verse and in map on p. 317 there is accurate, then Zerach penetrated deeply into Judean territory by the time the two armies clashed.

9. צְפַתָה לְמָרֵשָׁה — *In full view of Moreishah*. We have followed *Metzudos* who thinks that צְפַתָה derives from צפה, *to look out*.

10. אֵין־עִמְּךָ — *There is none besides You*. The translation follows *Targum*. The use of עם as *besides* is attested to in *Deuteronomy* 32:39.

אַל־יַעְצֹר עִמְּךָ אֱנוֹשׁ — *Let no man prevail against You*. עצר means *to restrain*. *Radak*, based on *Judges* 18:7, believes the word to carry the connotation of kingship [see *Radak* there. Perhaps because the king controls or restrains his people]. Thus, Let no man arrogate to himself the idea that he might set himself up as king over You.

The use of אֱנוֹשׁ [from אנש, *to be weak*] is particularly appropriate. It describes man in his most puny state. Accordingly, any ideas — that he could master God — are the more preposterous (*Metzudos*).

11. וַיִּגֹּף ה׳ אֶת־הַכּוּשִׁים — *HASHEM smote the Kushites*. See fn. to 13:15 for the assessment which the Sages make concerning Asa's attitude to this battle.

12. לְאֵין־לָהֶם מִחְיָה — *So that they lost all vitality*. Their losses left them without hope; all life was drained from them (*Metzudos*).

וְלִפְנֵי מַחֲנֵהוּ — *And before His army*.

Asa's army is God's army. This could be either in the sense that the royal house of Judah represents God's kingship on earth (see above to 13:8), or because in destroying the Kushites they were doing God's work or bidding in much the same way that the locusts whom God sent are called *His army* in *Joel* 2:11.

וַיִּשְׂאוּ שָׁלָל הַרְבֵּה מְאֹד — *And they carried away very much booty*. This is apparently the *treasure of Egypt* which, as we saw above, Israel recovered during this war.

Malbim finds a difference between שָׁלָל and בִּזָּה in the next verse. The former describes

3. It was customary to carry the national treasure into battle so that awareness of what they stood to loose might spur the fighters to greater efforts (*Rashi* and *Rashbam* to *Pesachim*).

mighty warriors. 8 *Zerach the Kushite came out against them*
with an army of a thousand times a thousand and three hundred
chariots. He come to Mareishah. 9 *Asa came out before him and*
they waged battle in the valley which lay in full view of
Mareishah. 10 *Asa called to HASHEM his God and said, 'HASHEM,*
there is none besides You to help in the struggle between the
mighty and him that has no strength. Help us, HASHEM our God,
for we depend upon You and in Your Name we come against this
multitude. You are HASHEM our God; let no man prevail against
You'. 11 *HASHEM smote the Kushites before Asa and before Judah,*
and the Kushites fled. 12 *Asa and the people that were with him*
pursued them till Gerar. Men from the Kushite army fell, so that
they lost all vitality; for they were shattered before HASHEM and
before His army. And they carried away very much booty.
13 *They smote all the cities which were round about Gerar, for the*
fear of HASHEM was upon them, and they took spoils from all the
cities, for there was much spoil within them. 14 *They also smote*
Oholey Mikneh and carried away sheep in abundance and
camels. Then they returned to Jerusalem.

booty which was abandoned by the owners and is simply lying there for the taking; the latter requires effort to obtain. See next verse.

13. סְבִיבוֹת גְּרָר — *Round about Gerar*. From *Genesis* 26:1 we can see that Gerar was the capital city of Philistia. How then does it figure in the Kushite war?

Perhaps in Asa's times the city did in fact belong to Zerach. If he could field an army of a million men he must have been a major military power and may well have annexed parts of Philistia into his territory.

It may also be that the attack on the surroundings of Gerar was, in no way, part of the Kushite war but that, once in the vicinity because of their pursuit of Zerach's forces, the Israelites decided to extend their campaign to include the Philistines. We cannot know the conditions which would have made such an aggressive war appropriate or permissible, but the fact that we are told that *the fear of HASHEM* was upon the inhabitants of these cities indicates that the operation was Divinely sanctioned.

This later, is *Malbim's* view. Since this was not part of the Kushite war, these cities were not smitten by God as had been the Kushites (v. 11) but were conquered by natural means. For this reason the spoil is called בִּזָּה rather than שָׁלָל — see comm. to previous verse.

14. אָהֳלֵי מִקְנֶה — *Oholei Mikneh. Metzudos* seems to take this as a proper noun: He inserts: *the men of Oholei Mikneh*. However, *Targum* translates the words, which he would not have done if he had thought them to be a proper noun. Apparently, these were tents in which a pastoral people had their homes. Asa's forces destroyed them and took their herds.

XV

Azariahu's Exhortation

As Asa returns triumphantly to Jerusalem, he is accosted by Azariahu ben Oded who finds himself Divinely inspired to spell out the meaning and implications of his victory.

Here was a chance for Asa to re-establish the grandeur which had been Judah's during Solomon's reign, and which had been eroded progressively, first by the secession of the Ten Tribes, and then by Rechav'am's defeat at Shishak's hands.

It had been God's plan that, under Asa, the unity of the nation was to be re-established. The split had been meant to last no more than thirty-six years [see comm. at 16:1]. If Asa would but choose correctly, the aberration of a divided house of Israel could once and for all be laid to rest.

טו
א־ח

א יְרוּשָׁלָֽם׃ וַעֲזַרְיָהוּ בֶּן־עוֹדֵד הָיְתָה עָלָיו רוּחַ
ב אֱלֹהִֽים׃ וַיֵּצֵא לִפְנֵי אָסָא וַיֹּאמֶר לוֹ שְׁמָעוּנִי אָסָא וְכָל־
יְהוּדָה וּבִנְיָמִן יהוה עִמָּכֶם בִּהְיוֹתְכֶם עִמּוֹ וְאִם־תִּדְרְשֻׁהוּ
ג יִמָּצֵא לָכֶם וְאִם־תַּעַזְבֻהוּ יַעֲזֹב אֶתְכֶֽם׃ וְיָמִים
רַבִּים לְיִשְׂרָאֵל לְלֹא ׀ אֱלֹהֵי אֱמֶת וּלְלֹא כֹּהֵן מוֹרֶה וּלְלֹא
ד תוֹרָֽה׃ וַיָּשָׁב בַּצַּר־לוֹ עַל־יהוה אֱלֹהֵי יִשְׂרָאֵל וַיְבַקְשֻׁהוּ
ה וַיִּמָּצֵא לָהֶֽם׃ וּבָעִתִּים הָהֵם אֵין שָׁלוֹם לַיּוֹצֵא וְלַבָּא כִּי
ו מְהוּמֹת רַבּוֹת עַל כָּל־יוֹשְׁבֵי הָאֲרָצֽוֹת׃ וְכֻתְּתוּ גוֹי־בְּגוֹי
ז וְעִיר בְּעִיר כִּי־אֱלֹהִים הֲמָמָם בְּכָל־צָרָֽה׃ וְאַתֶּם חִזְקוּ וְאַל־
ח יִרְפּוּ יְדֵיכֶם כִּי יֵשׁ שָׂכָר לִפְעֻלַּתְכֶֽם׃ וְכִשְׁמֹעַ

This was to be his challenge, and at this point of the story there was every reason to hope that he would rise to it.

Azariahu would have to spell out the questions — and the answers. Would Israel be able to handle the challenges which independent, powerful nationhood would thrust upon them? Would they be able to infuse the temporal with the intimation of eternity; the apparently mundane with the soul of the Divine? Could Asa and his people handle the *treasure of Egypt*; could they be politically and militarily dominant, and use that dominance wisely — have it be God's more than theirs?

Everything hung in the balance. If Asa was to fail, mankind would have to wait till messianic times for Israel to flower into that beauty which it can attain only as a unified whole. Azariahu felt called upon to utter a stern warning of what failure would mean.

In actuality, as we shall see, Asa did not rise to the challenge of the moment; the terrible and unnatural division of Israel into two truncated parts was to remain the tragedy of the Jewish people. Reconciliation must await the Davidic kingship of the Messiah.

1. רוּחַ אֱלֹהִים — *The spirit of God.* This describes a level of Divine inspiration which falls short of actual prophecy (*Rambam, Moreh HaNevuchim* 2:45).

No prophecy was needed here. The events themselves were of such shattering import that a sensitive man would, as it were, from within himself, be driven to prophecy. As *Amos* 3:8 says: *HASHEM, God has spoken; who is it that would not prophesy?*

2. וַיֵּצֵא לִפְנֵי אָסָא — *He went out to confront Asa.* Azariahu left his home in order to meet up with Asa as he returned from the front (*Metzudos*).

ה׳ עִמָּכֶם בִּהְיוֹתְכֶם עִמּוֹ — *HASHEM is with you as long as you are with Him.* The concept of being עִם ה׳, *with HASHEM*, can cover an infinite range of meaning — from Boaz' greeting to his reapers, *'May HASHEM be with you!'* (*Ruth* 2:4), to the Torah's description of Moses' stay on Sinai, *'He was there with HASHEM'* (*Exodus* 34:28).

Certainly, in this context, Azariahu would be thinking of a unison of purpose which would make the newly united Israel that *holy nation*, of which God had spoken at Sinai.

וְאִם־תִּדְרְשֻׁהוּ . . . וְאִם־תַּעַזְבֻהוּ — *If you seek Him out . . . but forsake Him . . .* If our analysis of the import of Azariahu's words is correct, his choice of expression is extremely apt. Rechav'am had lost the *treasure of Egypt* to Shishak when he had *forsaken the Torah of HASHEM* (12:1) and not *sought Him out* (12:14). Asa, newly in possession of that wealth, must take care not to fall into the same trap.

3. וְיָמִים רַבִּים לְיִשְׂרָאֵל — *Many days will pass for Israel. Mefaresh* and *Malbim* read this and the next three verses as a description of the past — *There have been many days in Israel's past* .... Experience is summoned to prove how hollow and sad life can be when God is forsaken.

We have translated in accordance with *Radak*, *Metzudos* and *Gra*. They read these four verses as a description of what will happen if Azariahu's message is ignored.

לְלֹא אֱלֹהֵי אֱמֶת — *Without a true God.* This is a description of the exile years which will inevitably follow a rejection of God (*Radak*). Life among idol worshipers is tantamount to a

The spirit of God came upon Azariahu the son of Oded. [2] *He*
went out to confront Asa and said to him, 'Listen to me,
Asa and all Judah and Benjamin! HASHEM *is with you as long*
as you are with Him. If you seek Him out, He will make Him-
self accessible to you, but forsake Him, and He will forsake
you. [3] *Many days will pass for Israel without a true God, with-*
out a Kohen to instruct and without Torah. [4] *But as they*
find themselves in straits, they will turn back to HASHEM *the*
God of Israel; they will seek Him out and He will make Him-
self accessible to them. [5] *In those times there will be no*
peace, neither for him who goes out nor for him who comes in,
for there will be great discomfiture for all the dwellers of
the lands. [6] *One nation will be shattered against another, and one*
city against another, for God has discomfited them with all
manner of troubles. [7] *But as for you, be strong and do not let your*
hands be slack, for your efforts will be rewarded'. [8] *When*

life without God.

וְלֹא כֹּהֵן מוֹרֶה — *Without a Kohen to instruct. Deuteronomy* 33:10 depicts the *Kohanim* as the religious instructors of the people. Times would come when the people would not address their questions to the *Kohanim*, but to soothsayers and idolatrous priests (*Metzudos*).

וְלֹא תוֹרָה — *And without Torah*. People would no longer be interested in what God's Torah had to say, and would instead seek inspiration from alien sources (*Metzudos*).

Gra has each of these three expressions refer to one of the three exiles predicted in *Daniel* and described in countless Rabbinic sources: *Without a true God* describes the Babylonian exile; *Without a Kohen to instruct*, that of Persia and Media; *Without Torah*, that of Greece. The fourth and final exile, that of Rome, is hinted at in the next verse, *And when in distress, they will turn back ....*

It is particularly appropriate that Azariahu should hint at these four world powers. *Pesachim* 119a teaches that these were destined to be the last four in the long roster of nations who were to be entrusted with the *treasure of Egypt*. Azariahu's exhortation was motivated by the fact that the *treasure of Egypt* had now reverted to Israel. Asa needed to hear the dreadful future that awaited his people if he failed to live up to the challenge which possession imposed.

4. וַיָּשָׁב בַּצַּר־לוֹ — *But as they find themselves in straits, they will turn back*. The fourth exile will culminate in repentance — and return. The *treasure of Egypt* and all that it implies is not lost forever.

5-6. וּבָעִתִּים הָהֵם ... וְכֻתְּתוּ גוֹי־בְּגוֹי ... — *In those times ... One nation will be shattered against another ...* The subject of these verses is the constant hating and warring among the nations that will be the hallmark of history during the long centuries covered by the four exiles, stretching to our own days (*Gra*). The implication of the prophecy is that as long as the *treasure of Egypt* is in alien hands, as long as world dominion follows military and political supremacy instead of subjugation to God's will — so long will peace and tranquility elude mankind's grasp.

כתת is *to crush something by beating* (see, for example, *Isaiah* 2:4), hence also *to break* (*Metzudos*) and, figuratively, the disintegration of an army in defeat.

כִּי מְהוּמוֹת רַבּוֹת ... כִּי־אֱלֹהִים הֲמָמָם — *For there will be great discomfiture ... for God has discomfited them*. Although *Radak* (*Sefer HaShorashim*) and *Metzudos* render המם or הים, *to break*, we have followed *Targum*. He renders שגושתא and שגשינון from שגש, which he also uses to translate נרגן in *Proverbs* 18:8. This word derives from רגן, which means *to complain, backbite* or *slander* someone. Hence, in our context, *to discomfit* him.

7. וְאַתֶּם חִזְקוּ ... כִּי יֵשׁ שָׂכָר לִפְעֻלַּתְכֶם — *But as for you, be strong ... for your efforts will be rewarded.*

The phrase *for your efforts will be rewarded* duplicates *Jeremiah* 31:15. There, as *Radak* explains it, it promises vindication for the loyalty which the Israelites will have shown to

אָסָא הַדְּבָרִים הָאֵלֶּה וְהַנְּבוּאָה עֹדֵד הַנָּבִיא הִתְחַזַּק
וַיַּעֲבֵר הַשִּׁקּוּצִים מִכָּל־אֶרֶץ יְהוּדָה וּבִנְיָמִן וּמִן־הֶעָרִים
אֲשֶׁר לָכַד מֵהַר אֶפְרָיִם וַיְחַדֵּשׁ אֶת־מִזְבַּח יהוה אֲשֶׁר לִפְנֵי
ט אוּלָם יהוה׃ וַיִּקְבֹּץ אֶת־כָּל־יְהוּדָה וּבִנְיָמִן וְהַגָּרִים עִמָּהֶם
מֵאֶפְרַיִם וּמְנַשֶּׁה וּמִשִּׁמְעוֹן כִּי־נָפְלוּ עָלָיו מִיִּשְׂרָאֵל לָרֹב
י בִּרְאֹתָם כִּי־יהוה אֱלֹהָיו עִמּוֹ׃ וַיִּקָּבְצוּ יְרוּשָׁלַםִ
בַּחֹדֶשׁ הַשְּׁלִישִׁי לִשְׁנַת חֲמֵשׁ־עֶשְׂרֵה לְמַלְכוּת אָסָא׃
יא וַיִּזְבְּחוּ לַיהוה בַּיּוֹם הַהוּא מִן־הַשָּׁלָל הֵבִיאוּ בָּקָר שְׁבַע
יב מֵאוֹת וְצֹאן שִׁבְעַת אֲלָפִים׃ וַיָּבֹאוּ בַבְּרִית לִדְרוֹשׁ
יג אֶת־יהוה אֱלֹהֵי אֲבוֹתֵיהֶם בְּכָל־לְבָבָם וּבְכָל־נַפְשָׁם׃ וְכֹל
אֲשֶׁר לֹא־יִדְרֹשׁ לַיהוה אֱלֹהֵי־יִשְׂרָאֵל יוּמָת לְמִן־קָטֹן
יד וְעַד־גָּדוֹל לְמֵאִישׁ וְעַד־אִשָּׁה׃ וַיִּשָּׁבְעוּ לַיהוה בְּקוֹל גָּדוֹל
טו וּבִתְרוּעָה וּבַחֲצֹצְרוֹת וּבְשׁוֹפָרוֹת׃ וַיִּשְׂמְחוּ כָל־יְהוּדָה
עַל־הַשְּׁבוּעָה כִּי בְכָל־לְבָבָם נִשְׁבָּעוּ וּבְכָל־רְצוֹנָם בִּקְשֻׁהוּ

God throughout the long exile to which they were to be subjected. Their stubborn adherence to their covenant with God would not go unrecognized.

In the same sense Azariahu encourages Asa to hold fast to his course. This would surely avert the horrors foretold in the previous verses.

פְּעוּלָּה describes the effort expended, in contrast to מַעֲשֶׂה which describes the accomplishment (*Malbim*). Asa is to try his hardest. His efforts will be more significant than his accomplishments.

◆§ Reforms and a Covenant

8. וְהַנְּבוּאָה עֹדֵד הַנָּבִיא — *The prophecy of Oded the prophet*. Oded is to be taken as *the son of Oded*. It is Azariahu, not his father Oded, who prophesied (*Radak*).

The phrase is appositional and must be read as though a ל were inserted: ... לְעֹדֵד הַנָּבִיא (*Radak*).

וּמִן־הֶעָרִים — *And from the cities*. There is no mention beside this that Asa had conquered any cities.

וַיְחַדֵּשׁ אֶת־מִזְבַּח ה׳ — *He renewed the altar of* HASHEM. He repaired and rebuilt the altar (*Metzudos*).

Gra thinks that Asa used the materials from the idolatrous altars which he had removed, to make plates with which he covered the Temple altar. This is reminiscent of Moses' actions during Korach's rebellion (*Numbers* 17:1).

9. וְהַגָּרִים עִמָּהֶם מֵאֶפְרַיִם וּמְנַשֶּׁה וּמִשִּׁמְעוֹן — *And those that dwelt with them from Ephraim, Menasheh and from Shimeon*. This verse recalls 11:16 where we learn how in Rechav'am's reign the Southern Kingdom served as a refuge for those among the Ten Tribes who refused to allow themselves to be weaned away from God's service. Apparently Yarov'am's deviations did not strike a deep chord in the hearts of his people and it needed only a strong religious leadership in the south to attract large numbers of people who were willing to leave their patrimony in order to be close to God.

נָפְלוּ עָלָיו — *Joined*. נפל with the preposition על to denote *joining with someone* is rare, but does occur sometimes. See, for example, *I Chronicles* 12:19 and comm. there.

10. לִשְׁנַת חֲמֵשׁ־עֶשְׂרֵה — *The fifteenth year*. The people gathered in order to take part in the covenantal assembly described in the next few verses.

In v. 11 we learn that the animals that were sacrificed on this occasion came from the spoils taken during the Kushite war. This surely creates the assumption that this war was fought during the fifteenth year of Asa's reign. See above at 13:23.

As mentioned there, *Gra* disagrees and dates

Asa heard these words, the prophecy of the prophet Oded, he took courage and removed the detestable things from the whole land of Judah and from Benjamin and from the cities which he had captured from the hill-country of Ephraim. He renewed the altar of HASHEM which stood before the Hall of HASHEM. 9 *He gathered all of Judah and Benjamin and those that dwelt with them from Ephraim, Menasheh and from Shimeon; for a great many of Israel joined him when they saw that HASHEM his God was with him.* 10 *They gathered to Jerusalem in the third month of the fifteenth year of Asa's reign.* 11 *On that day they sacrificed to HASHEM seven hundred cattle and seven thousand sheep from the booty which they had brought.* 12 *They entered a covenant to seek out HASHEM, the God of their fathers, with all their heart and all their soul.* 13 *Whoever would not search out HASHEM, God of Israel, would be killed, whether small or great, man or woman.* 14 *They swore to HASHEM with a great voice, accompanied by staccato blasts, and by trumpets and horns.* 15 *The whole population of Judah was happy on account of the oath, because they had undertaken it wholeheartedly; they had sought Him*

the Kushite war in Asa's eleventh year. He sees no difficulty in the fact that the covenantal assembly was delayed till the fifteenth year. It is possible that the cleansing of the land described in v. 8 took that long. Animals taken during that war may well have still been alive a few years later.

11. מִן־הַשָּׁלָל הֵבִיאוּ — *From the booty which they had brought*. The phrase must be read as though אֲשֶׁר were inserted: מִן הַשָּׁלָל אֲשֶׁר הֵבִיאוּ (*Metzudos*).

12. וַיָּבֹאוּ בַבְּרִית — *They entered a covenant*. A covenant is always between two parties. Here the text uses none of the usual prepositions [את, עם, ל, לפני] which could help indicate who these parties were. If the covenant had been between Israel and God, this should have been indicated. Rather, it appears that the contracting parties were the people among themselves.

Why did their commitment to *seek out HASHEM* have to express itself in the form of a covenant?

Clearly, the death penalty for him who refuses to seek God, of which v. 13 speaks, is not a punishment imposed by the halachah. One who does not seek God is not legally subject to capital punishment. Rather, the people accepted this stringent sanction upon themselves — and it was in order to make this binding that the convocation was required (*Malbim*).

See *Ramban* to *Leviticus* 27:29 for the halachic possibility of creating such capital sanctions.

13. לְמִן־קָטֹן וְעַד־גָּדוֹל — *Whether small or great*. This is an idiom that occurs frequently in Scripture. *Small* does not mean one who is a minor — it would be inconceivable that a minor would be liable to the death penalty[1] — but someone insignificant in contrast to *great*. For a similar usage see *I Kings* 22:31.

14. וַיִּשָּׁבְעוּ לַה׳ — *They swore to HASHEM*. The death penalty would be enough to discourage public transgressions. The oath was needed so that the high standards set by the covenant would not be forgotten even when there were no witnesses present (*Malbim*).

15. וַיִּשְׂמְחוּ כָל־יְהוּדָה — *The whole population of Judah was happy* . . . The people entered the covenant and bound themselves by oath, not because they were forced by the king — that would have been no occasion for joy — but because they themselves felt inspired to do so (*Metzudos*).

1. Inasmuch as the death penalty here is not incurred through a halachic transgression but through covenantal agreement [see comm. to v. 12], it would be legally possible that minors were included. However, it seems unlikely that the people would have extended their sanctions so far.

טו
טז-יט

טז וַיִּמָּצֵא לָהֶם וַיָּנַח יהוה לָהֶם מִסָּבִיב: וְגַם־מַעֲכָה אֵם ׀
אָסָא הַמֶּלֶךְ הֱסִירָהּ מִגְּבִירָה אֲשֶׁר־עָשְׂתָה לַאֲשֵׁרָה
מִפְלָצֶת וַיִּכְרֹת אָסָא אֶת־מִפְלַצְתָּהּ וַיָּדֶק וַיִּשְׂרֹף בְּנַחַל
יז קִדְרוֹן: וְהַבָּמוֹת לֹא־סָרוּ מִיִּשְׂרָאֵל רַק לְבַב־אָסָא הָיָה
יח שָׁלֵם כָּל־יָמָיו: וַיָּבֵא אֶת־קָדְשֵׁי אָבִיו וְקָדָשָׁיו בֵּית
יט הָאֱלֹהִים כֶּסֶף וְזָהָב וְכֵלִים: וּמִלְחָמָה לֹא הָיָתָה עַד

טז
א

א שְׁנַת־שְׁלֹשִׁים וְחָמֵשׁ לְמַלְכוּת אָסָא: בִּשְׁנַת
שְׁלֹשִׁים וָשֵׁשׁ לְמַלְכוּת אָסָא עָלָה בַּעְשָׁא מֶלֶךְ־יִשְׂרָאֵל

וַיָּנַח ה׳ לָהֶם מִסָּבִיב — *So* HASHEM *granted them rest from their surrounding foes.* The translation follows the cantillation which separates this phrase from the previous one. *Metzudos* reads the two together: *He made Himself accessible to them and granted them rest . . .*

16. וְגַם־מַעֲכָה אֵם אָסָא הַמֶּלֶךְ — *Also . . . Maachah, the mother of King Asa.* See comm. to 14:3 for the position of this verse and its place in the narrative.

Based on 11:21-22 and *I Kings* 15:2, both *Radak* and *Metzudos* assume that *mother* here really means grandmother.

הֱסִירָהּ מִגְּבִירָה — *He deposed . . . from the position of queen.* גְּבִירָה from גבר, *to be strong* or *mighty*. Hence, a position of power.

מִפְלָצֶת — *An abomination.* פלץ means *to shudder*; thus, an object which would cause a person who sees it to shudder in horror (*Metzudos*). The Sages teach that this icon had obscene contours which Maachah used to satisfy her carnal cravings.

וַיִּשְׂרֹף בְּנַחַל קִדְרוֹן — *And burned it in the wadi of Kidron.* He burned it and threw the ashes into the wadi (*Metzudos*).

17. וְהַבָּמוֹת לֹא־סָרוּ . . . — *But the bamos were not eliminated . . .* See comm. to 14:2 that the *bamos* mentioned here were not idolatrous altars, but such as were used for private sacrifice to God. These had been permitted up to the time that the Temple was built, but were now forbidden. Their use carried the penalty of *kares* (*Rashi*).

Neither *Kings*, which has this same wording, nor *Chronicles* say that the people sacrificed on these *bamos*. We learn only that they were not eliminated.

If we are correct in assuming that these *bamos* were not actually used for illicit sacrifice, then the meaning of our phrase and its connection to the end of the verse would be as follows:

Asa, in the first great reform that a king of Judah undertook, eliminated all vestiges of idol worship from the land. However, although the use of *bamos* was now interdicted, there was certainly no obligation to destroy these altars which, when they were built, had been legitimate. Asa had every right to assume that with disuse they would eventually disappear on their own.

Because he was not derelict in permitting the *bamos* to remain, it may correctly be said that Asa's heart was *whole all his days*.

In fact, history proved that Asa miscalculated. Far from disappearing on their own, the *bamos* became a pernicious presence in the land, gradually seducing the people back to the private worship which had become detestable to God. See further at 20:33.

רַק לְבַב־אָסָא הָיָה שָׁלֵם כָּל־יָמָיו — *Nevertheless, the heart of Asa was whole all his days.* The fact that Asa did not remove the *bamos* did not reflect badly on him — see above.

Malbim assumes that when the verse says that the *bamos* were not removed, this means that the people still actively sacrificed upon them. Our phrase draws attention to the contrast between the righteous Asa and the less-than-perfect people. These continued thoughtlessly with a mode of service which had been forbidden; his behavior was above reproach, as witness the fact that he brought the hallowed objects to the Temple — see below.

18. וַיָּבֵא אֶת־קָדְשֵׁי אָבִיו — *He brought the things that his father had hallowed. Metzudos* surmises that Aviah may have consecrated certain objects which he then presumably deposited in the Temple treasury. He may at some later date have had a change of heart and removed them from the Temple. Asa now returned them.

15
16-19

out with total enthusiasm — and He had made Himself accessible
to them. So HASHEM granted them rest from their surrounding foes.
16 *Also he deposed Maachah, the mother of King Asa, from the*
position of queen, for she had dedicated an abomination to the
asheirah-tree. Asa cut down her abomination, ground it down, and
burned it in the wadi of Kidron.
17 *But the bamos were not*
eliminated from Israel; nevertheless, the heart of Asa was whole
all his days.
18 *He brought the things that his father had hallowed*
and those which he had hallowed into the House of God — gold,
silver and utensils.
19 *There was no war until the thirty-fifth year*
of Asa's reign.

16
1 *In the thirty-sixth year of Asa's reign, Basha king of Israel went*

See comm. to v. 17 for *Malbim's* perception of this verse's place in the narrative.

וְקָדָשָׁיו — *And those which he had hallowed.* Asa dedicated gifts to the Temple treasury independently of those which his father had given. We may surmise that he donated part of the spoils which he took during the Kushite war. This would explain why these donations are mentioned here.

19. עַד שְׁנַת־שְׁלֹשִׁים וְחָמֵשׁ לְמַלְכוּת אָסָא — *Until the thirty-fifth year of Asa's reign.* This verse must be studied together with the first one of the next chapter which dates the war with Basha in the thirty-sixth year of Asa's reign.

This dating cannot be taken literally. According to the dates given in *Kings*, Basha died long before Asa's thirty-sixth year. For computation, see at 16:1.

Seder Olam's solution is to interpret the thirty-six years mentioned in the next verse as being reckoned, not from the beginning of Asa's reign, but from the moment at which the two kingdoms were split in the first year of Rechav'am's reign. We shall discuss the ramifications of this interpretation in the comm. to the first verse of the next chapter.

Accordingly, the thirty-five years of our verse are also to be reckoned from the beginning of Rechav'am's reign. This brings them to the fifteenth year of Asa's reign. [We compute: seventeen for Rechav'am; three for Aviah and fifteen for Asa make thirty-five.] *Malbim* points out that in this way our verse confirms the implication of v. 10 — that the Kushite war took place in the fifteenth year of Asa's reign. Our verse tells us that up to the fifteenth year there was no war at all; in the fifteenth (thirty-fifth) year the Kushite war took place, and the next verse tells us that in the very next year — the sixteenth (thirty-sixth) of Asa's reign — came the confrontation with Basha.

However, as we saw above, *Gra* believes that the Kushite war took place in the eleventh year of Asa's reign; consequently he cannot, as does *Malbim*, read our verse as saying that it took place in the thirty-fifth (fifteenth) year. How then, does *Gra* interpret our verse? He does not say and we can only conjecture.

We begin by noting that our verse not only has no parallel in *Kings* but seems almost to be contradicted by the verse which replaces it there. In place of our verse *Kings* has: *There was war between Asa and Basha the king of Israel all their days.*

To avoid contradiction we must say that *Kings* means that throughout the reign there were minor skirmishes, while our verse means that the first major war was in the fifteenth year (*Malbim*).

But why does *Chronicles* ignore the earlier Kushite war?

It is clear that *Chronicles* considers the war with Basha to have been of the utmost importance — the opportunity for the reunification of the two kingdoms. Given the seminal nature of this war in the *Chronicles'* purview, we may interpret our verse as meaning: Up to and including the thirty-fifth year of Asa's reign, there was no war to rank in importance with the one which took place in the thirty-sixth year — the all-important war with Bashah.[1]

1. In this context we assume an unusual but legitimate interpretation for the word עַד. It is true that the word is usually to be understood as *until*. However, in rare instances, it is also used to mean *while, during, up to and including*. For some examples, see *II Kings* 9:22, *Jonah* 4:2, *Judges* 3:26.

טז
ב־ו

עַל־יְהוּדָה וַיִּבֶן אֶת־הָרָמָה לְבִלְתִּי תֵּת יוֹצֵא וָבָא לְאָסָא
ב מֶלֶךְ יְהוּדָה: וַיֹּצֵא אָסָא כֶּסֶף וְזָהָב מֵאֹצְרוֹת בֵּית יְהוָה
וּבֵית הַמֶּלֶךְ וַיִּשְׁלַח אֶל־בֶּן־הֲדַד מֶלֶךְ אֲרָם הַיּוֹשֵׁב
ג בְּדַרְמֶשֶׂק לֵאמֹר: בְּרִית בֵּינִי וּבֵינֶךָ וּבֵין אָבִי וּבֵין אָבִיךָ
הִנֵּה שָׁלַחְתִּי לְךָ כֶּסֶף וְזָהָב לֵךְ הָפֵר בְּרִיתְךָ אֶת־בַּעְשָׁא
ד מֶלֶךְ יִשְׂרָאֵל וְיַעֲלֶה מֵעָלָי: וַיִּשְׁמַע בֶּן־הֲדַד אֶל־הַמֶּלֶךְ
אָסָא וַיִּשְׁלַח אֶת־שָׂרֵי הַחֲיָלִים אֲשֶׁר־לוֹ אֶל־עָרֵי יִשְׂרָאֵל
וַיַּכּוּ אֶת־עִיּוֹן וְאֶת־דָּן וְאֵת אָבֵל מָיִם וְאֵת כָּל־מִסְכְּנוֹת
ה עָרֵי נַפְתָּלִי: וַיְהִי כִּשְׁמֹעַ בַּעְשָׁא וַיֶּחְדַּל מִבְּנוֹת אֶת־הָרָמָה
ו וַיַּשְׁבֵּת אֶת־מְלַאכְתּוֹ: וְאָסָא הַמֶּלֶךְ לָקַח אֶת־כָּל־

XVI

◆§ War With Basha

1. בִּשְׁנַת שְׁלֹשִׁים וָשֵׁשׁ לְמַלְכוּת אָסָא — *In the thirty-sixth year of Asa's reign. Seder Olam* (ch. 16) writes: *In the thirty-sixth year of Asa's reign, Basha the king of Israel came up against Judah.* Is this possible? Did not Asa bury Basha in the twenty-eighth year of his (Asa's) reign?[1] What then does it mean ... *of Asa's reign.* These are the thirty-six years that Solomon was married to Pharaoh's daughter,[2] and these are the thirty-six years that it was decreed that David's kingship be divided — but that it would eventually be reunited.

Thus, *Seder Olam* teaches that the words of our verse are not to be taken literally. The thirty-six years are reckoned not from the moment that Asa assumed the throne, but from the moment when, during Rechav'am's first year, the kingdoms were divided.

With the passing of these thirty-six years, the decree that Israel be split into two nations was to come to an end. It had been imposed because Solomon had married foreign wives — of whom the Egyptian princess was the most significant. The split need have lasted no longer than the duration of that tragic marriage.

Had Asa handled the war with Basha as he should have done, then he would have been victorious over both Ben Haddad and Basha, and could then have reunited the kingdom. As it is, he failed. Not only did he allow this unique opportunity to pass, but he also dissipated the *treasure of Egypt* in the vain bribe which he sent to Ben Haddad.

The Sages evidently found no difficulty in interpreting a dating which purports to describe the duration of *Asa's reign* as referring to the cumulative reigns of Asa and his two predecessors. In the light of the assumptions which they make, this can be readily understood. If Asa was indeed destined to reunite the two kingdoms under his rule, then in the long view of history, the intervening years have no independent status at all. They are simply stepping-stones toward the establishment of the kingdom as it should be. All that went before is an aberration and is to be subsumed under his reign.

These dates which reveal the inner dynamics of the events which marked the reigns of these Judean kings are not given in *Kings*. As we have noted many times, the earlier books are concerned with matters as they happened. The undercurrents of destiny which lay beneath the surface is not their purview. It is to *Chronicles* which paints Israel's history on the canvas of eternity that these revelations are left. See further in comm. to v. 13.

1. The duration which *Kings* assigns to the first three kings of the Northern Kingdom are : Twenty-two for Yarov'am; two for Nadav and twenty-four for Basha. Thus, Basha died in the forty-eighth year after the establishment of the Northern Kingdom.

In Judah, Rechav'am is assigned seventeen years; Aviah three years and Asa forty-one years. The forty-eighth year from the establishment of the two kingdoms — the year of Basha's death — coincides with the twenty-eighth year of Asa's reign.

2. Solomon married her in the fourth year of his reign and ruled for forty years.

up against Judah and built up the tower so as to deny Asa king of
Judah egress or access. 2 *Asa took out silver and gold from the*
treasuries of the House of HASHEM *and the king's palace, and sent*
to Ben Haddad the king of Aram who dwelt in Darmesek, saying.
3 *'There is a treaty between me and you and between my father*
and your father. See, I have sent you silver and gold. Go, break your
treaty with Basha king of Israel that he may withdraw from me.'
4 *Ben Haddad listened to King Asa and sent his army officers to*
the cities of Israel and they smote Iyon and Dan and Avel-maim
and all the storage cities of Naphtali. 5 *When Basha heard, he left*
off building the tower and brought his work to a close. 6 *King Asa*

וַיִּבֶן אֶת־הָרָמָה — *And built up the tower.* He built a tower outside the gates of Jerusalem in order to prevent people from entering or leaving the city (*Metzudos*).

There is also the possibility that *HaRamah* is a city by that name (see *Joshua* 18:25) in which Basha placed a garrison. See below on v. 6.

2. וַיֹּצֵא אָסָא כֶּסֶף וְזָהָב מֵאֹצְרוֹת בֵּית ה׳ — *Asa took out silver and gold from the treasuries of the House of* HASHEM. *Kings* has: *Asa took all the silver and gold which was left in the Temple treasury and in the palace treasury ...* These treasuries had been depleted by Shishak's plunder (12:9) and thus he was able to offer Ben Haddad only the remnants of the treasure (*Radak* there). This, in *Kings*, where there is no mention of Asa's Kushite wars, and where consequently we never learn how the resources of the treasuries were replenished by the huge spoils which he took on that occasion (14:12-14). In *Chronicles*, where we know of the vast riches which fell to Asa as a result of the Kushite war, the implication is the opposite. He took out silver and gold *from* the treasuries; the treasuries were full and retained much of value even after the tribute had been sent to Ben Haddad.

3. בְּרִית בֵּינִי וּבֵינֶךָ — *There is a treaty between me and you.* From the latter part of our verse it is apparent that Ben Haddad had concluded a treaty with Basha on the strength of which Basha launched his attack against Judah. Asa now argues that a pact which Ben Haddad had previously concluded with Asa's father superseded his commitment to Basha (*Malbim*).

הִנֵּה שָׁלַחְתִּי לְךָ כֶּסֶף וְזָהָב — *See, I have sent you silver and gold.* Not only does the agreement between us pre-empt your commitment to Basha, but I can also match any financial gain you may have received from him (*Malbim*).

הָפֵר בְּרִיתְךָ אֶת־בַּעְשָׁא ... וְיַעֲלֶה מֵעָלָי — *Break your treaty with Basha ... that he may withdraw from me.* Asa did not ask Ben Haddad to attack Basha; only that he should not assist him. Left alone, the crucial edge of Basha's strength would be eroded and he would, of himself, give up the fight. That Ben Haddad did, in fact, make war on Basha (v. 4) was on his own initiative, taken once he felt himself released from his pact (*Malbim*).

From Chanani the seer's castigations (v. 7 ff), we see that Asa's politic with Ben Haddad was deemed a sin. The uncompromising trust which Asa had placed in God during the Kushite wars had been replaced by a fear which sought assurance through an alliance with a heathen king. The very *treasure* which God had once more returned to Israel, when it had seemed as though Asa could be the king through whom the high destiny of the Davidic dynasty might be realized, was now dissipated in an act of desperation entirely unfitting for the exalted stature of which Asa had shown himself capable.

4. וַיִּשְׁלַח אֶת־שָׂרֵי הַחֲיָלִים אֲשֶׁר־לוֹ — *And sent his army officers.* His soldiers were already in Israel, poised to strike against Judah under the command of Basha's officers. Now that Ben Haddad decided to attack Basha, he had only to send his own officers (*Malbim*).

אָבֵל מָיִם — *Avel-maim.* This is identical with the Avel-beis-Maacha mentioned in *Kings* (*Metzudos*).

5. וַיַּשְׁבֵּת אֶת־מְלַאכְתּוֹ — *And brought his work to a close.* שבת, *to rest*, in the *hiphil* is causative, i.e., *to bring to a stop.*

יְהוּדָה וַיִּשְׂאוּ אֶת־אַבְנֵי הָרָמָה וְאֶת־עֵצֶיהָ אֲשֶׁר בָּנָה
ז בַּעְשָׁא וַיִּבֶן בָּהֶם אֶת־גֶּבַע וְאֶת־הַמִּצְפָּה: וּבָעֵת
הַהִיא בָּא חֲנָנִי הָרֹאֶה אֶל־אָסָא מֶלֶךְ יְהוּדָה וַיֹּאמֶר אֵלָיו
בְּהִשָּׁעֶנְךָ עַל־מֶלֶךְ אֲרָם וְלֹא נִשְׁעַנְתָּ עַל־יְהוָה אֱלֹהֶיךָ
ח עַל־כֵּן נִמְלַט חֵיל מֶלֶךְ־אֲרָם מִיָּדֶךָ: הֲלֹא הַכּוּשִׁים
וְהַלּוּבִים הָיוּ לְחַיִל ׀ לָרֹב לְרֶכֶב וּלְפָרָשִׁים לְהַרְבֵּה מְאֹד
ט וּבְהִשָּׁעֶנְךָ עַל־יְהוָה נְתָנָם בְּיָדֶךָ: כִּי יְהוָה עֵינָיו מְשֹׁטְטוֹת
בְּכָל־הָאָרֶץ לְהִתְחַזֵּק עִם־לְבָבָם שָׁלֵם אֵלָיו נִסְכַּלְתָּ
י עַל־זֹאת כִּי מֵעַתָּה יֵשׁ עִמְּךָ מִלְחָמוֹת: וַיִּכְעַס אָסָא
אֶל־הָרֹאֶה וַיִּתְּנֵהוּ בֵּית הַמַּהְפֶּכֶת כִּי־בְזַעַף עִמּוֹ עַל־זֹאת
יא וַיְרַצֵּץ אָסָא מִן־הָעָם בָּעֵת הַהִיא: וְהִנֵּה דִּבְרֵי אָסָא
הָרִאשׁוֹנִים וְהָאַחֲרוֹנִים הִנָּם כְּתוּבִים עַל־סֵפֶר הַמְּלָכִים
יב לִיהוּדָה וְיִשְׂרָאֵל: וַיֶּחֱלֶא אָסָא בִּשְׁנַת שְׁלוֹשִׁים וָתֵשַׁע
לְמַלְכוּתוֹ בְּרַגְלָיו עַד־לְמַעְלָה חָלְיוֹ וְגַם־בְּחָלְיוֹ לֹא־דָרַשׁ
יג אֶת־יְהוָה כִּי בָּרֹפְאִים: וַיִּשְׁכַּב אָסָא עִם־אֲבֹתָיו וַיָּמָת

6. גֶּבַע — *Geva.* From *Judges* 19:13, it appears that Geva was close to Ramah — perhaps the *HaRamah* mentioned in v. 1 (*Malbim*). See comm. there.

7. בְּהִשָּׁעֶנְךָ עַל־מֶלֶךְ אֲרָם ... עַל־כֵּן נִמְלַט — *Because you placed your trust in the king of Aram ... therefore ... escaped.* God had put it in Ben Haddad's heart to make a pact with Basha, so that you would be able to conquer both of them together. Had you put your trust in God, you could have won this great victory. Now, not only has he escaped your hands, but you have once more forfeited the *treasure of Egypt* in your vain attempt to curry his favor (*Mefaresh* and *Malbim*).

8. וְהַלּוּבִים — *And the Libyans.* No Libyans had been mentioned before; nevertheless, our verse makes clear that they were part of the Kushite forces (*Metzudos*). See comm. to 14:13 above.

לְרֶכֶב וּלְפָרָשִׁים לְהַרְבֵּה מְאֹד — *With multitudes of chariots and horsemen.* The translation follows *Metzudos*. The meaning of the verse is that the combined Kushite and Libyan forces added up to a great army with numerous chariots and horsemen.

9. כִּי — *For ...* This seems to continue the argument begun in the previous verse. It is not surprising that your trust in God was repaid. God actively seeks out those who are loyal to Him so that He can reinforce them in their endeavors.

מְשֹׁטְטוֹת — *Roam.* This comes from שטט, *to go* or *roam about*; usually with the object of finding something, as in *Numbers* 11:8 and *Jeremiah* 5:1.

לְהִתְחַזֵּק עִם־לְבָבָם שָׁלֵם אֵלָיו — *To lend encouragement to those who are loyal to Him.* The *hispael* voice of חזק, *to be strong*, usually means *to find strength within oneself* or *to assert oneself* (see 1:1 and elsewhere). It is rarely used with עם. When this occurs, it carries the connotation, *to reinforce* — see *I Chronicles* 11:10.

Perhaps such usage implies that the helper himself finds strength or courage in the act of aiding the one whom he is reinforcing. If so, the implications of the expression in our verse are profound. God, Himself, as it were, finds *strength* in the steadfast belief and trust of the righteous man [see *Ramban* to *Exodus* 29:46].

מֵעַתָּה יֵשׁ עִמְּךָ מִלְחָמוֹת — *From now on you will be dogged by war.* The expression contrasts precisely with the phrase וְאֵין־עִמּוֹ מִלְחָמָה in 14:5. Clearly, the association is intended. You may no longer expect the benign conditions which made all your constructive work possible.

10. הָרֹאֶה — *The seer.* The חוֶֹה is a seer who does not project himself into his message at all,

16
7-13

*took the whole population of Judah, and they carried off
the stones and the wood of the tower which Basha had built.
With them he built Geva and Mitzpah.* 7 *At that time
Chanani the seer came to Asa, king of Judah, and said to
him, 'Because you placed your trust in the king of Aram and
did not place your trust in* HASHEM *your God — therefore, the
army of the king of Aram has escaped from your hands.* 8 *Was is
not that the Kushites and the Libyans add up to a great army, with
multitudes of chariots and horsemen? Still, when you put your
trust in* HASHEM, *He gave them into your hands.* 9 *For* HASHEM'*s
eyes roam through the whole land to lend encouragement to those
who are loyal to Him. You have done foolishly in this, for from
now on you will be dogged by war.* 10 *Asa was angry with the seer
and placed him in the prison house, for he was furious with him
because of all this. Asa oppressed some of the people at that
time.* 11 *Now behold! The earlier and the later matters of Asa
are recorded in the Book of the Kings of Judah and Israel.* 12 *Asa
became ailing in his legs in the thirty-ninth year of his reign,
his sickness spreading upwards. Also, in his sickness he did not
seek out* HASHEM, *but doctors.* 13 *Asa lay with his fathers and died*

while the רֹאֶה, albeit Divinely inspired, proclaims ideas which had germinated in his own mind (*Malbim*).

Hence Asa's anger at Chanani. He believes that the latter is not passing on a message from God, but rather expressing his own assessment of what had happened.

בֵּית הַמַּהְפֶּכֶת — *The prison house. Rashi* to *Jeremiah* 29:26 renders כיפה which is often used to denote a cell or dungeon, perhaps from כפף, *to bend down*, because of the cramped position which the prisoner is forced to assume. Perhaps מהפכת from הפך, *to turn* or *overturn*, carries the same connotation.

Targum simply renders *prison*.

וַיְרַצֵּץ אָסָא — *Asa oppressed* ... From רצץ, *to crush*, which in the intensive *piel* voice becomes *to oppress grievously*. *Targum* renders ושעבד, *to subject*.

Not satisfied with placing the seer in prison, Asa also vented some of his frustrations upon the people (*Metzudos*).

Asa Dies

11. הָרִאשׁוֹנִים וְהָאַחֲרוֹנִים — *The earlier and the later*. See 9:29.

לִיהוּדָה וְיִשְׂרָאֵל — ... *Of Judah and Israel*. In *Kings*, only the chronicles of the kings of Judah, not those of the kings of Israel, are mentioned (*Metzudos*). The explanation may be that Asa warranted mention in the Israelite records only because of the potential for reunification which was rife during his reign. In the *Kings'* account, nothing is hinted of this potential. Therefore, Asa has no place in the Israelite chronicles.

12. וַיֶּחֱלֶא אָסָא ... בְּרַגְלָיו — *Asa became ailing in his legs*. When Asa sent the tribute to Ben Haddad, he demonstrated his inability to go out to battle on his own. It is as though his own feet would not carry him. The appropriate punishment was a sickness of the feet (*Ralbag*).

Asa's sickness is also mentioned in *Kings*, but neither the severity of the illness nor the criticism of Asa for putting his trust in doctors is mentioned there. See Section II, *Asa's Illness*, for a discussion.

עַד־לְמַעְלָה חָלְיוֹ — *His sickness spreading upwards*. The infection which began in his feet spread upwards through his body until it reached his head (*Mefaresh, Metzudos, Malbim*).

לְמַעְלָה can also be used as an idiom meaning *greatly* or *exceedingly* (cf. 26:8). Accordingly, the phrase would also lend itself to a rendering: *His sickness was exceedingly [grave]*.

לֹא־דָרַשׁ אֶת־ה׳ כִּי בָּרֹפְאִים — *He did not seek out* HASHEM *but doctors*. The phrase parallels

טז יד — יד בִּשְׁנַ֥ת אַרְבָּעִ֖ים וְאַחַ֥ת לְמָלְכֽוֹ׃ וַיִּקְבְּרֻ֨הוּ בְקִבְרֹתָ֜יו אֲשֶׁ֣ר
כָּֽרָה־לוֹ֮ בְּעִ֣יר דָּוִיד֒ וַיַּשְׁכִּיבֻ֗הוּ בַּמִּשְׁכָּב֙ אֲשֶׁ֣ר מִלֵּא֙
בְּשָׂמִ֔ים וּזְנִ֕ים מְרֻקָּחִ֖ים בְּמִרְקַ֣חַת מַעֲשֶׂ֑ה וַיִּשְׂרְפוּ־ל֛וֹ
א שְׂרֵפָ֥ה גְדוֹלָ֖ה עַד־לִמְאֹֽד׃ וַיִּמְלֹ֛ךְ יְהוֹשָׁפָ֥ט בְּנ֖וֹ
יז א־ב — ב תַּחְתָּ֑יו וַיִּתְחַזֵּ֖ק עַל־יִשְׂרָאֵֽל׃ וַיִּתֶּן־חַ֕יִל בְּכָל־עָרֵ֥י יְהוּדָ֖ה
הַבְּצֻר֑וֹת וַיִּתֵּ֣ן נְצִיבִ֗ים בְּאֶ֙רֶץ֙ יְהוּדָ֔ה וּבְעָרֵי֙ אֶפְרַ֔יִם אֲשֶׁ֥ר

Chanani's stricture in v. 7: *Because you placed your trust in the king of Aram and did not place your trust in HASHEM your God*. In his personal life Asa now displayed the same failing as he had previously shown in the execution of his kingship. [This is expressed in the word וְגַם, *and also*.]

Asa is criticized on two counts: He did not turn to God, and turned instead to doctors. Such reliance on human intervention is castigated. Sickness is a message from God that there is an inner malaise eating away at the spirit. The only truly legitimate reaction is repentance — a cauterizing of the pernicious cause, rather than a palliative for the outer manifestation (*Ramban, Leviticus* 26:11).[1]

13. וַיָּמָת בִּשְׁנַת אַרְבָּעִים וְאַחַת לְמָלְכוֹ — *And died in the forty-first year after the assumption of his kingship*. The verse begins with the phrase *Asa lay with his fathers*, which is the precise wording used to describe the death of almost every one of Judah's and Israel's kings. In this there is no irregularity. However, in every single case besides our own, this phrase is followed directly by the statement that the particular king who *lay with his fathers* was buried in such and such a way in this or that place — which, here, is said in v. 14.

Thus it is clear that the phrase *and died in the forty-first year after the assumption of his kingship* is an insertion which breaks the continuity of an otherwise standard formula. It is a fact that in no other instance is the phrase *'lay with his fathers'* followed by the word וַיָּמָת.

Why then was this phrase inserted here, and what are the implications of this insertion?

The *Chronicles'* account of Asa's reign is unique in another noteworthy way. In no other instance is the length of a reign given in the context of the king's death account as it is here. Invariably, it appears on the first occasion that the king is mentioned, or if not then, at the beginning of a section dealing with an overview of the events of that king's reign.

Indeed, in the *Kings'* account of Asa's reign, the statement that he reigned for forty-one years appears at 15:10, the point at which Asa is first introduced. In the *Chronicles'* account, this information is conspicuously absent at that position. Instead, it is introduced here, in what, as we have shown above, is obviously an artificial insertion into an otherwise standard formula.

The explanation may be as follows: At v. 1 we saw that in the *Chronicles'* perspective, the מַלְכוּת of Asa includes the reigns of the two previous kings, Rechav'am and Aviah. These are subsumed under his — for reasons given there.

In such a context, the statement at the beginning of the account, that Asa ruled for forty-one years, would have been inappropriate. In a sense, he 'ruled' for a much longer period in the persons of the two kings who preceded him. Consequently, nothing is said there concerning the duration of his reign. Instead, the information — needed for the correct dating of the subsequent kings — that Asa's actual rule extended for forty-one years is given here. It is presented as the dating of his death, not as a description of his actual reign.

The unusual wording used in our phrase is consistent with our perception. In contrast to *Kings* 15:19 and v. 1 of our chapter, which give the years according to the מַלְכוּת אָסָא, *the reign of Asa*, which as we have seen includes the reigns of Rechav'am and Aviah, our phrase uses לְמָלְכוֹ, *his assumption of the kingship*. This makes it abundantly clear that the dating is not meant to describe his reign — in the *Chronicles'* perspective that was of much longer duration — but to give the time from

1. It is probable that *Ramban* means to apply his stringent standards only to the very great — those to whom Divine Providence is such palpable reality that they can be expected to eschew any form of help, except that which is consonant with absolute truth.

Rambam (*Mishnah Commentary, Pesachim* ch. 4) disagrees with this attitude: To seek medical advice and to take prudent steps for the preservation of health is akin to eating when hungry. No possible stigma can attach to one who consults doctors in his sickness.

16
14
in the forty-first year after the assumption of his kingship. [14] *They buried him in the sepulchers which he had hewn out for himself in the City of David and laid him down in a resting place which he had filled with spices and all manner of products manufactured by the perfumer's art. They lighted a pyre for him that was exceedingly great.*

17
1-2
Yehoshaphat his son reigned in his stead and established himself over Israel. [2] *He stationed soldiery in the fortified cities of Judah and established governors in the land of Judah and in the Ephraimite cities which his father Asa*

the moment that he actually assumed the royal mantle.

14. בַּמִּשְׁכָּב אֲשֶׁר מִלֵּא . . . — *In a resting place which he had filled* ... The description of the elaborate funeral arrangements is not given in *Kings*. Perhaps the explanation is as follows. In the thought world of the *aggadah*, burial is a mark of respect to man's physical aspect — his body (See *Gur Aryeh* to *Genesis* 9:23). In Section II, *Asa's Illness* we noted that Asa's sickness in his legs was seen by *Chronicles* as indicating his failure to bridge the gap between the spiritual and physical parts of his being. He had not been able to plant his spiritual attainments firmly into the here and now. That Scripture found it important to stress the great honor done him at his burial indicates that at his death he was once more deserving — he had apparently overcome the earlier shortcoming.

וּזְנִים — *And all manner.* זן is the equivalent of מִין, *kind* (*Metzudos*).

מְרֻקָּחִים בְּמִרְקַחַת מַעֲשֶׂה — *Manufactured by the perfumer's art.* רקח means *to mix* or *compound*. Hence, רקח is the *perfumer* who mixes the oils and fragrances to produce the מִרְקַחַת, *the mixture, ointment*, or *perfume*.

שְׂרֵפָה גְּדוֹלָה עַד־לִמְאֹד — *A pyre ... that was exceedingly great.* It was customary to burn the king's bed and linens at his funeral (*Avodah Zarah* 11a, *Metzudos*).

XVII

☙ Yehoshaphat Consolidates His Reign

While the description of Yehoshaphat's reign occupies only a scant and terse eleven verses in *I Kings* (22:41-51), *Chronicles* devotes four chapters with a total of one hundred and one verses to it. Clearly, the two books are interested in different aspects of the reign. See discussion in Section II, *Yehoshaphat in Kings and Chronicles*.

1. וַיִּתְחַזֵּק עַל־יִשְׂרָאֵל — *And established himself over Israel.* Yehoshaphat established himself over *Israel* rather than over only Judah. This may be because his influence was not restricted to the boundaries of the Southern Kingdom. Thus, for example, in v. 2 we find him establishing governors in Ephraimite cities which Asa had conquered [see 15:8].

This influence appears to have increased with the death of Ahab, the king who ruled Israel when Yehoshaphat ascended the throne. Ahab was succeeded in turn by two of his sons, Achaziah and Yehoram, and these appear to have looked upon Yehoshaphat as an elder statesman from whom they sought advice and guidance.[1]

2. וַיִּתֶּן־חַיִל — *He stationed soldiery* ... This appears to be an elaboration of v. 1. He *established* his kingship by making sure that he would be able to exert his will over his far-flung lands.

וּבְעָרֵי אֶפְרַיִם — *And in the Ephraimite cities.*

1. This observation is made by both *Ralbag* and *Malbim* who base it on an extremely cryptic verse at *II Kings* 8:16, where there is a strong indication that Yehoshaphat was looked upon as a ruler over the Northern Kingdom.

Yehoshaphat came to the throne seventeen years before Ahab died, and was moreover related to the Israelite royal house by marriage. Thus, both age and family connections made him an ideal advisor to the young and inexperienced northern monarchs.

יז ג־ח

ג לְבַד אָסָא אָבִיו: וַיְהִי יהוה עִם־יְהוֹשָׁפָט כִּי הָלַךְ
ד בְּדַרְכֵי דָּוִיד אָבִיו הָרִאשֹׁנִים וְלֹא דָרַשׁ לַבְּעָלִים: כִּי
לֵאלֹהֵי אָבִיו דָּרָשׁ וּבְמִצְוֹתָיו הָלָךְ וְלֹא כְּמַעֲשֵׂה
ה יִשְׂרָאֵל: וַיָּכֶן יהוה אֶת־הַמַּמְלָכָה בְּיָדוֹ וַיִּתְּנוּ כָל־יְהוּדָה
ו מִנְחָה לִיהוֹשָׁפָט וַיְהִי־לוֹ עֹשֶׁר־וְכָבוֹד לָרֹב: וַיִּגְבַּהּ לִבּוֹ
בְּדַרְכֵי יהוה וְעוֹד הֵסִיר אֶת־הַבָּמוֹת וְאֶת־הָאֲשֵׁרִים
ז מִיהוּדָה: וּבִשְׁנַת שָׁלוֹשׁ לְמָלְכוֹ שָׁלַח לְשָׂרָיו
לְבֶן־חַיִל וּלְעֹבַדְיָה וְלִזְכַרְיָה וְלִנְתַנְאֵל וּלְמִיכָיָהוּ לְלַמֵּד
ח בְּעָרֵי יְהוּדָה: וְעִמָּהֶם הַלְוִיִּם שְׁמַעְיָהוּ וּנְתַנְיָהוּ וּזְבַדְיָהוּ

See 15:8 and comm. to previous verse.

These governors would be the civil administration who presumably worked in tandem with the military garrison.

3. כִּי הָלַךְ בְּדַרְכֵי דָּוִיד אָבִיו הָרִאשֹׁנִים — *For he walked in the earlier paths of his father David.* Three explanations are offered:

1. He acted as David had done in the earlier part of his life. In his later years David too had not been perfect in that he married Bathsheva and counted Israel (*Mefaresh, Radak, Metzudos*).

2. ראשנים means *original*. David, the first king, was also the one who came closest to the Torah ideal of kingship. This *original* form of the monarchy reflected God's vision of what it should be. None of the subsequent kings, except only Yehoshaphat, was able to live up to that exalted model. His was the *original*, pristine kingship (*Mefaresh, Radak*).

3. Acceptable standards vary with the spiritual level of each generation. As standards declined, it was relatively easy for a king to be admired. As long as he did not actively serve idols, he could be said to be walking in the paths of David. Not so Yehoshaphat. He emulated David, as that term had been understood in the earlier, finer days (*Malbim*).

See further in Section II, *Yehoshaphat Is Compared to David*.

וְלֹא דָרַשׁ לַבְּעָלִים — *And did not seek out the Baalim*. Baal worship was widespread in Canaan. It is first mentioned in *Judges* 2:11 and subsequently many times throughout Scripture.

4. כִּי לֵאלֹהֵי אָבִיו דָּרָשׁ — *For it was to the God of his father that his striving was directed.* See comm. to 14:3 for the use of the term דָּרַשׁ there. The same explanation holds good here too. In ch. 20 [and see particularly v. 3 there] we shall see that Yehoshaphat recaptured the *treasure of Egypt* for his people. It is important to stress that he, in contrast to Rechav'am who had originally lost it, was intent upon seeking out God.

וְלֹא כְּמַעֲשֵׂה יִשְׂרָאֵל — *And not as the Israelites did.* See Section II, *Yehoshaphat is Compared to David*.

5. וַיָּכֶן ה׳ אֶת־הַמַּמְלָכָה בְּיָדוֹ — *HASHEM gave him firm control over the kingdom.* כון means *to establish firmly*. יד is frequently used to denote *possession* or *control*.

Vs. 3, 4 and 5 provide a stronger endorsement for Yehoshaphat than is given to any other king. Some special circumstance, which calls forth God's special consideration, appears to be at play.

Indeed, the supreme self-confidence described in the next verse, creates the unmistakable impression of a man rising to an occasion, with self-assurance and pride.

We understand Yehoshaphat's unique position in the Davidic saga as follows:

At 16:1 we saw that the split between the two kingdoms was to have come to an end during Asa's reign. He was the man of the moment, the king who would lead an undivided and indivisible people along the road of destiny. Asa failed in his historic task. Tragically, the Northern Kingdom would sink deeper and deeper into the morass of its dissolution ultimately to be carried into oblivion by the Assyrians.

If there was to be a future to the messianic dream, if eternal Israel was indeed to be eternal, then tiny Judah would have to carry the burden of choseness. Yehoshaphat, untainted by his father's weakness, could be the man to nurture it along the path of greatness; the king entrusted with the sadly diminished, but still glorious remnant.

His reign, more than any other, would have to be firmly established so that he might have every help in his gargantuan task.

At the beginning, all signs pointed to success.

had taken. 3 *HASHEM was with Yehoshaphat, for he walked in the*
earlier paths of his father David and did not seek out the Baalim.
4 *For it was to the God of his father that his striving was directed,*
and he went in the ways of His commandments, and not as the
Israelites did. 5 *HASHEM gave him firm control over the kingdom.*
All Judah brought gifts to Yehoshaphat, so that he had abundant
wealth and honor. 6 *He was filled with exuberant self-assurance*
as he went in the paths of HASHEM; and, moreover, he eliminated
the bamos and the asheirah-trees from Judah. 7 *In the third year*
of his reign he sent his officers, Ben Chail, Ovadiah, Zechariah,
Nethanel and Michaiahu, to instruct in the cities of Judah.
8 *With them the Levites, Shemaiahu, Nethaniahu, Zevadiahu,*

In the end, Yehoshaphat too, fell short of the stature which had been expected of him.

וַיִּתְּנוּ כָל־יְהוּדָה מִנְחָה . . . וַיְהִי־לוֹ עֹשֶׁר־וְכָבוֹד לָרֹב — *All Judah brought gifts ... so that he had abundant wealth and honor. Tanchuma* to *Shoftim* (1) asserts that when Yehoshaphat became king he did not concern himself with consolidating his rule or with the acquisition of wealth and honor. His only interest was with the spiritual welfare of the people. Our verse tends to confirm this: Wealth and honor flowed to him without any effort on his part.

6. וַיִּגְבַּהּ לִבּוֹ בְּדַרְכֵי ה׳ — *He was filled with exuberant self-assurance as he went in the paths of HASHEM.* In Scripture, the term גבה לב always carries a negative connotation. It describes unwarranted arrogance and conceit (cf. *Ezekiel* 28:2, *Psalms* 131:1). *Tanchuma* (*Shoftim* 1) is therefore troubled by its use in combination with בְּדַרְכֵי ה׳, in obvious approbation. The midrash suggests that the phrase does not describe Yehoshaphat's feelings about himself, but rather that he made use of his exalted position to make reforms in the judicial system. *He asserted himself so that the ways of HASHEM might be followed.* The judges whom he appointed would guide the people in these paths.

However, commentators seem to see no problem in the positive use of the term: Even though he possessed wealth and honor, his pride derived not from those, but only from the fact that he walked *in the ways of HASHEM* (*Metzudos*).[1]

The phrase appears particularly appropriate in the context of what we saw above to be Yehoshaphat's challenge. He approached the task of molding tiny Judah into the bearers of Israel's destiny with supreme self-confidence. He knew himself to be treading the *paths of HASHEM*, and had no doubts that he could and would succeed.

וְעוֹד הֵסִיר אֶת־הַבָּמוֹת וְאֶת־הָאֲשֵׁרִים . . . — *Moreover, he eliminated the bamos and the asheirah-trees.* At 20:33 we learn that the *bamos* were not eliminated by Yehoshaphat. See 14:2 for a similar contradiction — and the solution — in the description of Asa's reign.

The use of וְעוֹד in our phrase is appropriate in the context of our understanding of the challenge which Yehoshaphat faced. Although Asa had already removed all vestiges of idolatry from the land (14:2,4; 15:8,16), Yehoshaphat was not satisfied. No reform can be absolute, and even after Asa's cleansing there must have been some remnants which had escaped his scrutiny. These would have been so small in number that within the framework of Asa's activities they could be tolerated. Not so for Yehoshaphat. Aware of the new destiny which had devolved upon his kingdom he went beyond [וְעוֹד] what his father had done. He vigorously pursued that which in other circumstances might well have been left alone.

7. שָׁלַח לְשָׂרָיו לְבֶן־חַיִל . . . — *He sent his officers, Ben Chail ...* The *lamed* in these names is to be taken as equivalent to the accusative את. Accordingly, *Ben Chail* is a proper noun, not a description of the valor of the men he sent (*Mefaresh*).

Yehoshaphat did not satisfy himself with the elimination of all vestiges of idol worship. He took positive steps to spread Torah among the people.

8. וְעִמָּהֶם הַלְוִיִּם . . . וְעִמָּהֶם . . . הַכֹּהֲנִים — *With*

1. Apparently, a degree of pride and a feeling of well-being concerning one's spiritual accomplishments can be legitimized. See *Gra* to *Proverbs* 31:30 and *Chovas HaLevavos, Shaar HaKeniah* 9.

יז °וּשְׁמִירָמוֹת ק׳

ט־יט

וַעֲשָׂהאֵל °ושמרימות וִיהוֹנָתָן וַאֲדֹנִיָּהוּ וְטוֹבִיָּהוּ וְטוֹב
אֲדוֹנִיָּה הַלְוִיִּם וְעִמָּהֶם אֱלִישָׁמָע וִיהוֹרָם הַכֹּהֲנִים׃
ט וַיְלַמְּדוּ בִּיהוּדָה וְעִמָּהֶם סֵפֶר תּוֹרַת יְהוָה וַיָּסֹבּוּ בְּכָל־עָרֵי
י יְהוּדָה וַיְלַמְּדוּ בָּעָם׃ וַיְהִי ׀ פַּחַד יְהוָה עַל כָּל־מַמְלְכוֹת
הָאֲרָצוֹת אֲשֶׁר סְבִיבוֹת יְהוּדָה וְלֹא נִלְחֲמוּ עִם־יְהוֹשָׁפָט׃
יא וּמִן־פְּלִשְׁתִּים מְבִיאִים לִיהוֹשָׁפָט מִנְחָה וְכֶסֶף מַשָּׂא גַּם
הָעַרְבִיאִים מְבִיאִים לוֹ צֹאן אֵילִים שִׁבְעַת אֲלָפִים וּשְׁבַע
יב מֵאוֹת וּתְיָשִׁים שִׁבְעַת אֲלָפִים וּשְׁבַע מֵאוֹת׃ וַיְהִי
יְהוֹשָׁפָט הֹלֵךְ וְגָדֵל עַד־לְמָעְלָה וַיִּבֶן בִּיהוּדָה בִּירָנִיּוֹת
יג וְעָרֵי מִסְכְּנוֹת׃ וּמְלָאכָה רַבָּה הָיָה לוֹ בְּעָרֵי יְהוּדָה וְאַנְשֵׁי
יד מִלְחָמָה גִּבּוֹרֵי חַיִל בִּירוּשָׁלִָם׃ וְאֵלֶּה פְקֻדָּתָם
לְבֵית אֲבוֹתֵיהֶם לִיהוּדָה שָׂרֵי אֲלָפִים עַדְנָה הַשָּׂר וְעִמּוֹ
טו גִּבֹּרֵי חַיִל שְׁלֹשׁ מֵאוֹת אָלֶף׃ וְעַל־יָדוֹ יְהוֹחָנָן
טז הַשָּׂר וְעִמּוֹ מָאתַיִם וּשְׁמוֹנִים אָלֶף׃ וְעַל־יָדוֹ
עֲמַסְיָה בֶן־זִכְרִי הַמִּתְנַדֵּב לַיהוָה וְעִמּוֹ מָאתַיִם אֶלֶף גִּבּוֹר
יז חָיִל׃ וּמִן־בִּנְיָמִן גִּבּוֹר חַיִל אֶלְיָדָע וְעִמּוֹ נֹשְׁקֵי־
יח קֶשֶׁת וּמָגֵן מָאתַיִם אָלֶף׃ וְעַל־יָדוֹ יְהוֹזָבָד וְעִמּוֹ
יט מֵאָה־וּשְׁמוֹנִים אֶלֶף חֲלוּצֵי צָבָא׃ אֵלֶּה הַמְשָׁרְתִים
אֶת־הַמֶּלֶךְ מִלְּבַד אֲשֶׁר־נָתַן הַמֶּלֶךְ בְּעָרֵי הַמִּבְצָר

יח

א בְּכָל־יְהוּדָה׃ וַיְהִי לִיהוֹשָׁפָט עֹשֶׁר וְכָבוֹד לָרֹב

them the Levites ... and with them ... the Kohanim. The purpose of the trek through Judah's cities was that the people could be taught the Torah. That is primarily the function of the *Kohanim* and the Levites (*Deuteronomy* 24:8). The officers mentioned in the previous verse were there in order to make sure that what was taught would be observed (*Mefaresh*).

9. וְעִמָּהֶם סֵפֶר תּוֹרַת ה׳ — *Having with them the Book of the Torah of HASHEM*. They brought a *Sefer Torah* with them in order that their teachings should not only encompass those commands of the Torah which appeal to the intellect, but also those which we know only because they are written in the Torah (*Malbim*).

10. וַיְהִי — *Thus* ... In the merit of the Torah which they studied they were able to live in peace with the surrounding nations (*Mefaresh*).

11. וְכֶסֶף מַשָּׂא — *And loads of silver*. This comes from נשא, *to carry*; thus, silver in such abundance that it had to be borne as a burden (*Mefaresh, Metzudos*).

12. בִּירָנִיּוֹת — *Castles*. בירה is usually a large building, a palace — see *I Chronicles* 29:1 (*Metzudos*). Here it means a castle fortified by towers (*Mefaresh*).

וְעָרֵי מִסְכְּנוֹת — *And storage cities*. The root is סכן, *to be of use* or *service*.

13. וּמְלָאכָה רַבָּה — *A great work force*. The translation follows *Metzudos*.

However, we also find מְלָאכָה used for *property* (cf. *Exodus* 22:7, 10 and, on that basis *Ibn Ezra* to *Genesis* 33:14). Accordingly, we could translate our phrase, *large holdings*.

14. וְאֵלֶּה פְקֻדָּתָם לְבֵית אֲבוֹתֵיהֶם — *The following are their numbers, taken according to their families*. These numbers seem to be for the soldiers stationed in Jerusalem, as in the previous verse. V. 19 elaborates further by identifying them as those who served the king — presumably in his capital city.

Ralbag suggests that it was important to

17 9-19 *Asael, Shemiramoth, Jonathan, Adoniahu, Toviahu and Tov*
Adoniah, the Levites; and with them Elishama and Yehoram, the
Kohanim. 9 *They taught in Judah, having with them the Book of*
the Torah of HASHEM. *They went about in all the cities of Judah,*
instructing in the midst of the people. 10 *Thus the fear of* HASHEM
was upon all the kingdoms of the land surrounding Judah, and
they did not make war against Yehoshaphat. 11 *And some of the*
Philistines brought Yehoshaphat a gift and loads of silver. Also
the Arabians brought him flocks; seven thousand seven hundred
rams and seven thousand seven hundred he-goats. 12 *Yeho-*
shaphat grew constantly until he became very great, and he built
castles and storage cities in Judah. 13 *He had a great work force in*
the cities of Judah and soldiers who were mighty warriors in
Jerusalem. 14 *The following are their numbers, taken according to*
their families: The tribe of Judah supplied officers over one
thousand: The general Adnah together with three hundred
thousand might men of valor. 15 *With him the general Ye-*
hochanan, together with two hundred and eighty thousand.
16 *With him the general Amasiah the son of Zichri who gave*
willingly to HASHEM, *together with two hundred thousand*
mighty men of valor. 17 *From Benjamin a mighty man of valor —*
Elyada, together with bow men with bucklers, two hundred
thousand. 18 *With him Yehozavad, together with one hundred*
and eighty thousand ready-equipped troops. 19 *These are the ones*
who served the king besides those whom the king placed in the
fortified cities throughout Judah.

18 1 *Yehoshaphat had an abundance of wealth and honor, and he*

give the numbers of the military in order to show how Judah was blessed by walking in God's ways. Several decades earlier, Aviah had been able to field an army of only four hundred thousand men (13:3), and now in Jerusalem alone there were over a million soldiers.

Judah is here divided into three families and *Malbim* thinks that these represent the three family units of Judah: Peretz, Zerach and Shailah.

16. הַמִּתְנַדֵּב לַה' — *Who gave willingly to* HASHEM. From נדב, *to offer up* or *give freely*. In the *hispael*, this implies *to give oneself*; thus, *to volunteer*. It is not made clear for what it is that Amasiah volunteered. It could, of course, be that his service in the army was shouldered voluntarily, but the term could refer to any freely rendered service. Thus *Nehemiah* 11:2 speaks of people who volunteered to live in Jerusalem when that was a hard thing to do.

Metzudos thinks that Amasiah was described as a מִתְנַדֵּב because it was his custom to give large free-will donations.

18. חֲלוּצֵי צָבָא — *Ready-equipped troops*. This is from חלץ, *to equip for war*; thus, warriors who are fully armed and equipped.

XVIII

◆§ The War at Ramoth Gilead

Yehoshaphat joins Ahab in a war against the Aramite occupiers of Ramoth Gilead. With a number of substantive changes which allow *Chronicles* to present the event from its particular

ב וַיִּתְחַתֵּן לְאַחְאָב׃ וַיֵּרֶד לְקֵץ שָׁנִים אֶל־אַחְאָב לְשֹׁמְרוֹן
וַיִּזְבַּח־לוֹ אַחְאָב צֹאן וּבָקָר לָרֹב וְלָעָם אֲשֶׁר עִמּוֹ
ג וַיְסִיתֵהוּ לַעֲלוֹת אֶל־רָמֹת גִּלְעָד׃ וַיֹּאמֶר אַחְאָב מֶלֶךְ־
יִשְׂרָאֵל אֶל־יְהוֹשָׁפָט מֶלֶךְ יְהוּדָה הֲתֵלֵךְ עִמִּי רָמֹת גִּלְעָד
וַיֹּאמֶר לוֹ כָּמוֹנִי כָמוֹךָ וּכְעַמְּךָ עַמִּי וְעִמְּךָ בַּמִּלְחָמָה׃
ד וַיֹּאמֶר יְהוֹשָׁפָט אֶל־מֶלֶךְ יִשְׂרָאֵל דְּרָשׁ־נָא כַיּוֹם אֶת־
ה דְּבַר יְהוָה׃ וַיִּקְבֹּץ מֶלֶךְ־יִשְׂרָאֵל אֶת־הַנְּבִאִים אַרְבַּע
מֵאוֹת אִישׁ וַיֹּאמֶר אֲלֵהֶם הֲנֵלֵךְ אֶל־רָמֹת גִּלְעָד
לַמִּלְחָמָה אִם־אֶחְדָּל וַיֹּאמְרוּ עֲלֵה וְיִתֵּן הָאֱלֹהִים בְּיַד
ו הַמֶּלֶךְ׃ וַיֹּאמֶר יְהוֹשָׁפָט הַאֵין פֹּה נָבִיא לַיהוָה עוֹד
ז וְנִדְרְשָׁה מֵאֹתוֹ׃ וַיֹּאמֶר מֶלֶךְ־יִשְׂרָאֵל ׀ אֶל־יְהוֹשָׁפָט עוֹד

perspective, the account parallels the one given in *I Kings*, ch. 22. See Section II to ch. 17, *Yehoshaphat in Kings and Chronicles*.

That *Kings* and *Chronicles* have widely divergent perspectives of the story of this war can be seen from the following: Each follows the account with a short section comprised of three verses. In *Kings*, these describe Ahab's death in graphic and bloody detail. For this description, *Chronicles* substitutes the prophecy of Yehu in which he castigates Yehoshaphat for joining forces with the wicked Ahab.

Clearly, *Kings* sees this war as the first step in the disintegration of Omri's dynasty (*I Kings* 21: 21-22) and the fulfillment of Elijah's prophecy against Ahab (v. 19 there).

By contrast, *Chronicles* focuses upon the the terrible error which Yehoshaphat had made in compromising his spiritual ideals in pursuit of an ill-conceived attempt to ingratiate himself with the depraved northern monarchy.[1]

1. וַיְהִי לִיהוֹשָׁפָט עֹשֶׁר וְכָבוֹד לָרֹב — *Yehoshaphat had an abundance of wealth and honor. Malbim* notes that this was already said at 17:5. He suggests that it is repeated here to point out that Yehoshaphat's wealth remained intact even after the huge building projects which were described in the previous chapter.

The verse has no parallel in *Kings*. This, because it is an introduction to the theme of the chapter which is unique to *Chronicles* — the sinful alliance with the wicked Ahab.

We understand this as follows:

Asa and, after him, Yehoshaphat were probably aware that it had been God's intention that the two kingdoms be reunited under Asa. This reunification had been anticipated with great longing. After the realization was born that the division was now to be permanent, both Asa and Yehoshaphat hoped to bridge the chasm as much as possible by entering into marriages with the royal house of the Northern Kingdom: Asa took Omri's daughter as a wife for Yehoshaphat and Yehoshaphat took Ahab's daughter for his son Yehoram [see Section II to ch. 17, *Yehoshaphat is Compared to David*, comm. to 21:5 and 7 and 22:1 where the tradition of the sages that Yehoshaphat was married ro Omri's daughter is disscussed.]

This association through marriage is explicated in our verse — its significance is limited to *Chronicles* because only in *Chronicles* do we have the indication that the kingdoms were to be reunited in Asa's reign (see comm. to 16:1).

Now, in the tradition of the Sages, Ahab was one of the wealthiest men the world had ever known (see *Berachos* 61b, *Tana d'Bai Eliyahu Rabbah* 9 and *Zutah* 24). Without a strong financial base Yehoshaphat might have felt

1. Although *Kings* makes no overt mention of Yehoshaphat's sin, there is a tacit assumption that the alliance was a mistake. At *II Kings* 1:17 we learn that Ahab's son Yehoram came to power in the second year of the rule of Yehoshaphat's son Yehoram. But this cannot be so, because as the chronology is given in *Kings*, Yehoshaphat's son Yehoram became king seven years *after* the ascension of Ahab's son Yehoram (see *Rashi* there for the computation). The solution offered by the Sages is that Yehoshaphat's last seven years are subsumed under his son's reign.

By joining Ahab, Yehoshaphat had sinned and forfeited his right to live. His life was saved, but his kingship was compromised. In the prophetic vision of *Kings*, even if not in a physical sense, the kingship had already passed to Yehoram.

18
2-7
allied himself in marriage to Ahab. 2 *After a lapse of years he*
went down to Ahab to Samaria, and Ahab slaughtered an
abundance of sheep and cattle for him and for the people who
were with him, thus persuading him to make war against
Ramoth Gilead. 3 *Ahab the king of Israel said to Yehoshaphat the*
king of Judah, 'Will you go with me to Ramoth Gilead?' And he
said to him, 'I am as you are, my people is as yours, involved with
you in the war.' 4 *Yehoshaphat said to the king of Israel,*
'Attempt to find out this day, what HASHEM says.' 5 *So the king of*
Israel gathered the prophets — four hundred men — and said to
them, 'Shall we go to Ramoth Gilead to war or shall I desist?'
They said to him, 'Wage war and God will give them into the
hand of the king.' 6 *Yehoshaphat said, 'Is there no other prophet*
of HASHEM here that we may enquire of him?' 7 *The king of Israel*

diffident about attempting to establish an alliance which was fraught with such potentially significant implications. Only once he felt secure in his own wealth and dignity did he feel free to take the steps which he hoped would improve the future relationship between the two kingdoms.

Thus we interpret the verse as implying criticism. Yehoshaphat's great wealth opened the door to a marital alliance with Ahab which, in turn, led to the disastrous military partnership described below.[1]

וַיִּתְחַתֵּן לְאַחְאָב — *And he allied himself in marriage to Ahab.* This phrase could refer to Yehoshaphat's own marriage to Ahab's sister, [see reference in comm. to v. 1 above] or to the marriage which he contracted for his own son Yehoram with Ahab's daughter.

2. וַיֵּרֶד לְקֵץ שָׁנִים — *After a lapse of years he went down.* Ahab, who died in this war, reigned for twenty-two years (*I Kings* 16:29). Yehoshaphat became king in the fourth year of Ahab's reign (22:41 there), thus the events described here occured in approximately the eighteenth year of Yehoshaphat's reign.

The implication is that Yehoshaphat went to visit Ahab because he was his kinsman through marriage. This, as we saw above, v. 1 serves as an introduction to the sinful alliance which was about to be formed.

וַיְסִיתֵהוּ לַעֲלוֹת אֶל־רָמֹת גִּלְעָד — *Thus persuading him to make war against Ramoth Gilead.* We have translated in accordance with *Chullin* 4b: It was the food — and by extension, the implied friendliness — which made Yehoshaphat amenable to persuasion.

3. כָּמוֹנִי כָמוֹךָ ... וְעִמְּךָ בַּמִּלְחָמָה — *I am as you are ... involved with you in the war.* See Section II, *The Alliance with Ahab*, for a discussion of how the two accounts treat Yehoshaphat's answer to Ahab.

4. אֶת־דְּבַר ה׳ — *What HASHEM says.* Yehoshaphat insists that Ahab call on true prophets — those who speak in the Name of HASHEM — and not those prophets of the Baal whom Ahab would surely have preferred (*Mefaresh*). He says *today* to imply that even though as a rule Ahab would not consult true prophets, he should do so *today* in consideration of Yehoshaphat's wishes (*Metzudos*).

5. אֶת־הַנְּבִאִים אַרְבַּע מֵאוֹת אִישׁ — *The prophets — four hundred men.* All these were true prophets as Yehoshaphat had requested. Their message was false only because they were misled by the *spirit* mentioned in v. 20 (*Mefaresh*). Yehoshaphat intuited that their message was false and therefore requested that another prophet be found. He did not doubt their integrity but suspected a problem since all four hundred couched their message in identical terms. This violated the tradition that no two prophets ever prophesy in exactly the same words (*Rashi* and *Mefaresh*).

Metzudos thinks that Ahab did not accede to Yehoshaphat's request. The four hundred were, indeed, prophets of the Baal. They used the phrase, *And God will give them over ...* only in order to deceive the king into thinking that they were true prophets.

6. הַאֵין פֹּה נָבִיא לַה׳ עוֹד — *Is there no other prophet of HASHEM here?* Has Jezebel killed every

1. Note, however, that *Shemos Rabbah* 31:3 gives Yehoshaphat as an example of one who was not spiritually harmed by his great wealth.

אִישׁ־אֶחָד לִדְרוֹשׁ אֶת־יהוה מֵאֹתוֹ וַאֲנִי שְׂנֵאתִיהוּ
כִּי־אֵינֶנּוּ מִתְנַבֵּא עָלַי לְטוֹבָה כִּי כָל־יָמָיו לְרָעָה הוּא
מִיכָיְהוּ בֶן־יִמְלָא וַיֹּאמֶר יְהוֹשָׁפָט אַל־יֹאמַר הַמֶּלֶךְ כֵּן׃
ח וַיִּקְרָא מֶלֶךְ יִשְׂרָאֵל אֶל־סָרִיס אֶחָד וַיֹּאמֶר מַהֵר °מיכהו
ט בֶן־יִמְלָא׃ וּמֶלֶךְ יִשְׂרָאֵל וִיהוֹשָׁפָט מֶלֶךְ־יְהוּדָה יוֹשְׁבִים
אִישׁ עַל־כִּסְאוֹ מְלֻבָּשִׁים בְּגָדִים וְיֹשְׁבִים בְּגֹרֶן פֶּתַח שַׁעַר
י שֹׁמְרוֹן וְכָל־הַנְּבִיאִים מִתְנַבְּאִים לִפְנֵיהֶם׃ וַיַּעַשׂ לוֹ
צִדְקִיָּהוּ בֶן־כְּנַעֲנָה קַרְנֵי בַרְזֶל וַיֹּאמֶר כֹּה־אָמַר יהוה
יא בְּאֵלֶּה תְּנַגַּח אֶת־אֲרָם עַד־כַּלּוֹתָם׃ וְכָל־הַנְּבִאִים נִבְּאִים
כֵּן לֵאמֹר עֲלֵה רָמֹת גִּלְעָד וְהַצְלַח וְנָתַן יהוה בְּיַד
יב הַמֶּלֶךְ׃ וְהַמַּלְאָךְ אֲשֶׁר־הָלַךְ ׀ לִקְרֹא לְמִיכָיְהוּ דִּבֶּר אֵלָיו
לֵאמֹר הִנֵּה דִּבְרֵי הַנְּבִאִים פֶּה־אֶחָד טוֹב אֶל־הַמֶּלֶךְ
יג וִיהִי־נָא דְבָרְךָ כְּאַחַד מֵהֶם וְדִבַּרְתָּ טוֹב׃ וַיֹּאמֶר מִיכָיְהוּ
יד חַי־יהוה כִּי אֶת־אֲשֶׁר־יֹאמַר אֱלֹהַי אֹתוֹ אֲדַבֵּר׃ וַיָּבֹא
אֶל־הַמֶּלֶךְ וַיֹּאמֶר הַמֶּלֶךְ אֵלָיו מִיכָה הֲנֵלֵךְ אֶל־רָמֹת
גִּלְעָד לַמִּלְחָמָה אִם־אֶחְדָּל וַיֹּאמֶר עֲלוּ וְהַצְלִיחוּ וְיִנָּתְנוּ
טו בְּיֶדְכֶם׃ וַיֹּאמֶר אֵלָיו הַמֶּלֶךְ עַד־כַּמֶּה פְעָמִים אֲנִי
מַשְׁבִּיעֶךָ אֲשֶׁר לֹא־תְדַבֵּר אֵלַי רַק־אֱמֶת בְּשֵׁם יהוה׃
טז וַיֹּאמֶר רָאִיתִי אֶת־כָּל־יִשְׂרָאֵל נְפוֹצִים עַל־הֶהָרִים כַּצֹּאן
אֲשֶׁר אֵין־לָהֶן רֹעֶה וַיֹּאמֶר יהוה לֹא־אֲדֹנִים לָאֵלֶּה
יז יָשׁוּבוּ אִישׁ־לְבֵיתוֹ בְּשָׁלוֹם׃ וַיֹּאמֶר מֶלֶךְ־יִשְׂרָאֵל אֶל־

°מִיכָיְהוּ ק׳

single one of God's prophets? (*Metzudos*)

7. כִּי כָל־יָמָיו לְרָעָה — *Only to my disadvantage, all his days*. According to tradition, it was Michaiahu who prophesied against Ahab at *I Kings* 20:42.

אַל־יֹאמַר הַמֶּלֶךְ כֵּן — *Let not the king say so*. As a prophet of God, he would surely not falsify his message. (*Metzudos*).

9. מְלֻבָּשִׁים בְּגָדִים — *Arrayed in robes*. They were dressed in their royal garments (*Mefaresh, Metzudos*).

בְּגֹרֶן פֶּתַח שַׁעַר שֹׁמְרוֹן — *On the threshing floor at the entrance of the gate of Samaria*. The threshing floors were located close to the city for protection (*Radak*). [See comm. to v. 30.]

Shemos Rabbah 5:12 suggests that the word is not to be taken literally. There is no reason why two kings would choose to meet on a threshing floor. Rather, they arranged themselves and their entourages along a circular pattern reminiscent of the shape of a threshing floor. This, so that their equality and amity might be apparent.

וְכָל־הַנְּבִיאִים מִתְנַבְּאִים לִפְנֵיהֶם — *All the prophets were prophesying before them*. Throughout the conversation between the two kings, the four hundred prophets had continued speaking their words of encouragement (*Radak*).

10. צִדְקִיָּהוּ בֶן־כְּנַעֲנָה — *Tzidkiahu son of Kenaanah*. He was one of the prophets of the Baal (*Metzudos*).

קַרְנֵי בַרְזֶל — *Iron horns*. In order to lend credence to his words, Tzidkiahu illustrated his message with a vivid, graphic image, (*Radak*).

כֹּה־אָמַר ה׳ — *Thus says* HASHEM. Tzidkiahu boasted of being privy to prophecy from HASHEM although he was a false prophet (*Radak*).

11. וְכָל־הַנְּבִאִים נִבְּאִים כֵּן — *All the prophets*

said to Yehoshaphat. 'There is another man through whom we
may search out HASHEM*'s wishes, but I have hated him, for he*
does not prophesy good for me but only to my disadvantage, all
his days. He is Michaiahu son of Yimla.'' Yehoshaphat said, 'Let
not the king say so.' 8 *The king of Israel called to an officer and*
said, 'Hasten to bring Michaiahu the son of Yimla.' 9 *The king of*
Israel and Yehoshaphat sat each on his throne arrayed in robes,
sitting on the threshing floor at the entrance of the gate of
Samaria. All the prophets were prophesying before them.
10 *Tzidkiahu son of Kenaanah made himself iron horns and said,*
'Thus says HASHEM*: With these shall you gore Aram until they*
are annihilated.' 11 *All the prophets were prophesying thus,*
saying, 'Make war against Ramoth Gilead and prosper. HASHEM
will deliver them into the hands of the king.' 12 *The messenger*
that went to call Michaiahu spoke to him, saying, 'See, the words
of the prophets are unanimously to the king's benefit. Let your
message be as theirs, and do speak positively.' 13 *Michaiahu said,*
' As Hashem lives, what my God says that I will say.' 14 *He came*
to the king and the king said to him, 'Michah, shall we go to war
against Ramoth Gilead or shall I desist?' He said, 'Wage war and
prosper; would that they be given into your hand.' 15 *The king*
said to him, 'I adjure you over and over that you speak to me only
the truth in the Name of HASHEM*.'* 16 *He said, ' I saw all Israel*
scattered upon the mountains like sheep which have no
shepherd. HASHEM *said: These have no one to take control; let*
each man return to his home in peace.' 17 *The king of Israel said*

were prophesying thus ... Targum adds: *'prophesied falsely*.

12. פֶּה־אֶחָד — *Unanimously.* Lit. *with one mouth*.

All of them are in full agreement, prophesying as the king would want them to. Therefore, do you also join with them and thereby avoid discord (*Metzudos*).

14. עֲלוּ וְהַצְלִיחוּ — *Make war and prosper*. Michaiahu does not give his message in the name of God (*Rashi*). Because of this, the king suspects that the next phrase, *would that they be given into your hand*, may not be a statement but a pious wish.

15. עַד־כַּמֶּה פְעָמִים אֲנִי מַשְׁבִּיעֶךָ — *I adjure you over and over*. *Metzudos* takes the phrase as a statement as we have rendered it rather than as a rhetorical question: *How many times must I adjure you?*

אֲשֶׁר לֹא־תְדַבֵּר אֵלַי רַק אֱמֶת בְּשֵׁם ה׳ — *That you speak to me only the truth in the Name of* HASHEM. Ahab seeks reassurance that Michaiahu had not spoken sarcastically or in the form of a pious wish, but as a Divinely inspired message. The king was unsure because Michayahu had not used God's Name (*Metzudos*).

The prophet's answer will confirm that Ahab's fears had been justified. Indeed, his words had been sarcastic. God had not promised that the campaign would prosper. On the contrary, it was doomed to failure and Ahab was to die.

16. רָאִיתִי — *I saw*. In prophetic vision (*Metzudos*).

לֹא־אֲדֹנִים לָאֵלֶּה — *These have no one to take control*. The prophet sees that Ahab is destined to be killed. Left to their own devices, the people will be as sheep who have lost their shepherd.

יָשׁוּבוּ אִישׁ־לְבֵיתוֹ בְּשָׁלוֹם — *Let each man return to his home in peace*. None but Ahab

יְהוֹשָׁפָט הֲלֹא אָמַרְתִּי אֵלֶיךָ לֹא־יִתְנַבֵּא עָלַי טוֹב כִּי
יח אִם־לְרָע: וַיֹּאמֶר לָכֵן שִׁמְעוּ דְבַר־יְהוָה רָאִיתִי
אֶת־יְהוָה יוֹשֵׁב עַל־כִּסְאוֹ וְכָל־צְבָא הַשָּׁמַיִם עֹמְדִים
יט עַל־יְמִינוֹ וּשְׂמֹאלוֹ: וַיֹּאמֶר יְהוָה מִי יְפַתֶּה אֶת־אַחְאָב
מֶלֶךְ־יִשְׂרָאֵל וְיַעַל וְיִפֹּל בְּרָמוֹת גִּלְעָד וַיֹּאמֶר זֶה אֹמֵר
כ כָּכָה וְזֶה אֹמֵר כָּכָה: וַיֵּצֵא הָרוּחַ וַיַּעֲמֹד לִפְנֵי יְהוָה וַיֹּאמֶר
כא אֲנִי אֲפַתֶּנּוּ וַיֹּאמֶר יְהוָה אֵלָיו בַּמָּה: וַיֹּאמֶר אֵצֵא וְהָיִיתִי
לְרוּחַ שֶׁקֶר בְּפִי כָּל־נְבִיאָיו וַיֹּאמֶר תְּפַתֶּה וְגַם־תּוּכָל צֵא
כב וַעֲשֵׂה־כֵן: וְעַתָּה הִנֵּה נָתַן יְהוָה רוּחַ שֶׁקֶר בְּפִי נְבִיאֶיךָ
כג אֵלֶּה וַיהוָה דִּבֶּר עָלֶיךָ רָעָה: וַיִּגַּשׁ
צִדְקִיָּהוּ בֶן־כְּנַעֲנָה וַיַּךְ אֶת־מִיכָיְהוּ עַל־הַלֶּחִי וַיֹּאמֶר אֵי
כד זֶה הַדֶּרֶךְ עָבַר רוּחַ־יְהוָה מֵאִתִּי לְדַבֵּר אֹתָךְ: וַיֹּאמֶר
מִיכָיְהוּ הִנְּךָ רֹאֶה בַּיּוֹם הַהוּא אֲשֶׁר תָּבוֹא חֶדֶר בְּחֶדֶר
כה לְהֵחָבֵא: וַיֹּאמֶר מֶלֶךְ יִשְׂרָאֵל קְחוּ אֶת־מִיכָיְהוּ וַהֲשִׁיבֻהוּ
כו אֶל־אָמוֹן שַׂר־הָעִיר וְאֶל־יוֹאָשׁ בֶּן־הַמֶּלֶךְ: וַאֲמַרְתֶּם כֹּה
אָמַר הַמֶּלֶךְ שִׂימוּ זֶה בֵּית הַכֶּלֶא וְהַאֲכִילֻהוּ לֶחֶם לַחַץ
כז וּמַיִם לַחַץ עַד שׁוּבִי בְשָׁלוֹם: וַיֹּאמֶר מִיכָיְהוּ אִם־שׁוֹב
תָּשׁוּב בְּשָׁלוֹם לֹא־דִבֶּר יְהוָה בִּי וַיֹּאמֶר שִׁמְעוּ עַמִּים

would fall in the battle (*Mefaresh*). See v. 30.

17. הֲלֹא אָמַרְתִּי אֵלֶיךָ — *Have I not told you.* It is as I have told you: These are his own ideas — born out of hatred of me — not a message from God (*Metzudos*).

18. לָכֵן — *Therefore.* Because you suspect that my words were not Divinely inspired, I will now describe my vision to you precisely. You will then know that, indeed, my message was an authentic prophecy (*Metzudos*).

עַל־יְמִינוֹ וּשְׂמֹאלוֹ — *On His right and on His left.* In the Heavenly court there are defenders and prosecutors. The defenders are ranged to the *right*, the accusers to the *left*, of God (*Rashi*).

19. וַיֹּאמֶר ה׳ — *HASHEM said.* The decision has been made. Ahab is guilty and must be led to his death at Ramoth Gilead.

מִי יְפַתֶּה אֶת־אַחְאָב — *Who will entice Ahab.* Which of Ahab's sins — metamorphosed into accusers before the Divine throne [רוחות] — will be the one to bring down the tyrant (*Malbim*).

וַיֹּאמֶר — *And he said* ... This verb has no subject. Who is speaking and what is being said?

Perhaps the meaning is as follows: Among all the *spirits*, each of whom was clamoring for attention, there was one persistent voice which was laying irresistible claim to be the one chosen. As yet he could not be identified among all the raucously, arguing candidates, but, as these quieted down — וַיֵּצֵא הָרוּחַ, *the spirit came forth* — that one whose claim had stood out from the very beginning.

20. וַיֵּצֵא הָרוּחַ — *The spirit came forth.* The Sages [*Sanhedrin* 89a] teach that this was the spirit of Navoth, the man whom Ahab had killed in order to take possession of his vineyard (*I Kings* ch. 21). It was this sin above all others which condemned Ahab (*Malbim*).

21. וְהָיִיתִי לְרוּחַ שֶׁקֶר בְּפִי כָּל־נְבִיאָיו — *I will* . . . *be a lying spirit in the mouths of all his prophets.* רוּחַ in our verse — in contrast to v. 20 — is simply a synonym for *speech* (*Metzudos*).

צֵא־וַעֲשֵׂה־כֵן — *Go forth and do so.* This is an apparently redundant urging. Its purpose is to encourage the spirit in its intentions (*Metzudos*).

The Sages have another interpretation for

to Yehoshaphat, 'Have I not told you that he would not prophesy
to my benefit, but only evil.' 18 *He said, 'Therefore, hear the word*
of HASHEM. *I saw* HASHEM *sitting upon His throne and all the*
heavenly hosts stood on His right and on His left. 19 HASHEM *said:*
Who will entice Ahab the king of Israel so that he shall make war
and fall at Ramoth Gilead. And he said. . .., this one said thus and
this one said thus. 20 *The spirit came forth and stood before*
HASHEM *and said: I will entice him.* HASHEM *said to him: How?*
21 *And he said: I will go forth and be a lying spirit in the mouths*
of all his prophets. He said: You shall entice him and also prevail,
go forth and do so. 22 *And now, behold,* HASHEM *has imbued the*
mouths of these, your prophets with a lying spirit. Indeed,
HASHEM *has spoken evil against you.'* 23 *Tzidkiahu son of*
Kenaanah approached, slapped Michaiahu on the cheek and
declared, 'How did the spirit of HASHEM *pass from me so that it*
would speak to you?' 24 *Michaiahu said, 'Behold, on that day you*
will see. You will flee into the innermost chambers in order to
conceal yourself.' 25 *The king of Israel said, 'Take Michaiahu and*
carry him back to Ammon the governor of the city, and to Yoash
the king's son. 26 *And say: Thus says the king: Place this one into*
jail and feed him scant bread and scant water until I return in
peace.' 27 *Michaiahu said, 'If you return in peace,* HASHEM *did not*
speak to me.' And he said, 'Hear you peoples, all of you.'

the word צֵא, *go forth*. It is a command to Navoth to leave the Divine Presence. He has offered to be a *lying spirit*. Even though his intentions were good, there is no room for falsehood in the vicinity of God.

22. וַה׳ דִּבֶּר עָלֶיךָ רָעָה — *Indeed,* HASHEM *has spoken evil against you*. The prophets who are giving you encouragement do so because there is a lying spirit within them. Theirs is not God's word. It is I who will tell you what God really said. What I shall report spells disaster for you.

23. מֵאִתִּי לְדַבֵּר אֹתָךְ ... — *. . . from me so that it would speak to you*. Tzidkiahu denies that Michaiahu can be telling the truth. The spirit of *HASHEM* had inspired him, and through him it had vested the other four hundred with the power of prophecy; there is no way that Michaiahu could be privy to a Divine message which had bypassed him (*Malbim*).

24. אֲשֶׁר תָּבוֹא חֶדֶר בְּחֶדֶר לְהֵחָבֵא — *You will flee into the innermost chambers in order to conceal yourself*. You will see the truth of my vision on the day of the battle. When Ahab is killed, as I have predicted, you will be seeking places to hide from the people lest they kill you for having lulled them into misplaced confidence (*Metzudos*).

25. וַהֲשִׁיבֻהוּ — *And carry him back*. The expression suggests that Michaiahu may have already been jailed on another occasion (*Mefaresh* and *Metzudos*).

26. שִׂימוּ זֶה — *Place this one*. This obviously disdainful expression is equivalent to *this worthless fellow*.

לֶחֶם לַחַץ — *Scant bread and scant water*. לַחַץ means *to squeeze* or *press* and, as a noun, *oppression*. Literally, then, the term means bread of oppression or, prison fare. He should be given only enough food to keep him alive (*Metzudos*).

27. לֹא־דִבֶּר ה׳ בִּי — HASHEM *did not speak to me*. If Ahab returns safely from the war you will be justified in assuming that what I said was of my own fabrication (*Metzudos*).

שִׁמְעוּ עַמִּים כֻּלָּם — *'Hear you peoples, all of you.'* Michaiahu addresses himself to members of all the various tribes — each of which can be called an עַם, *a people* (*Metzudos*). His

כח כֻּלָּם: וַיַּעַל מֶלֶךְ־יִשְׂרָאֵל וִיהוֹשָׁפָט מֶלֶךְ־יְהוּדָה
כט אֶל־רָמֹת גִּלְעָד: וַיֹּאמֶר מֶלֶךְ יִשְׂרָאֵל אֶל־יְהוֹשָׁפָט
הִתְחַפֵּשׂ וָבוֹא בַמִּלְחָמָה וְאַתָּה לְבַשׁ בְּגָדֶיךָ וַיִּתְחַפֵּשׂ
ל מֶלֶךְ יִשְׂרָאֵל וַיָּבֹאוּ בַּמִּלְחָמָה: וּמֶלֶךְ אֲרָם צִוָּה אֶת־שָׂרֵי
הָרֶכֶב אֲשֶׁר־לוֹ לֵאמֹר לֹא תִּלָּחֲמוּ אֶת־הַקָּטֹן אֶת־הַגָּדוֹל
לא כִּי אִם־אֶת־מֶלֶךְ יִשְׂרָאֵל לְבַדּוֹ: וַיְהִי כִּרְאוֹת שָׂרֵי הָרֶכֶב
אֶת־יְהוֹשָׁפָט וְהֵמָּה אָמְרוּ מֶלֶךְ־יִשְׂרָאֵל הוּא וַיָּסֹבּוּ עָלָיו
לְהִלָּחֵם וַיִּזְעַק יְהוֹשָׁפָט וַיהוָה עֲזָרוֹ וַיְסִיתֵם אֱלֹהִים
לב מִמֶּנּוּ: וַיְהִי כִּרְאוֹת שָׂרֵי הָרֶכֶב כִּי לֹא־הָיָה מֶלֶךְ יִשְׂרָאֵל
לג וַיָּשֻׁבוּ מֵאַחֲרָיו: וְאִישׁ מָשַׁךְ בַּקֶּשֶׁת לְתֻמּוֹ וַיַּךְ אֶת־מֶלֶךְ
°יָדְךָ ק׳ יִשְׂרָאֵל בֵּין הַדְּבָקִים וּבֵין הַשִּׁרְיָן וַיֹּאמֶר לָרַכָּב הֲפֹךְ °ידיך
לד וְהוֹצֵאתַנִי מִן־הַמַּחֲנֶה כִּי הָחֳלֵיתִי: וַתַּעַל הַמִּלְחָמָה בַּיּוֹם

purpose is to make them witnesses to his challenge (*Abarbanel*).

28. וַיַּעַל מֶלֶךְ־יִשְׂרָאֵל וִיהוֹשָׁפָט — *The king of Israel and Yehoshaphat ... went up.* The singular וַיַּעַל, instead of the plural וַיַּעֲלוּ, implies that the initiative lay with Ahab, and that Yehoshaphat only followed. Clearly, Yehoshaphat's enthusiasm had waned with Michaiahu's prophecy. Ahab, on the other hand, placed no credence in God's prophet and was as eager to allow himself to be deluded as before.

29. הִתְחַפֵּשׂ וָבוֹא בַמִּלְחָמָה — *One ought to disguise oneself to go to war.* Though Ahab did not believe Michaiahu, he bethought himself to take prudent precautions. If he was to be the intended victim, then it made sense to wear a disguise so that the forces of Aram would not realize that he was the king (*Abarbanel*).

Perhaps this is the explanation for the unexpected use of the infinitive [*to disguise oneself*] rather than a simple statement: I will disguise myself ... although for you it is not necessary. Ahab may have been embarrassed to say outright that he feared the words of the enemy whose standing as a Divine prophet he denied.

וְאַתָּה לְבַשׁ בְּגָדֶיךָ — *But you put on your robes.* You have nothing to fear since the prophecy was directed only at me (*Metzudos*). Furthermore, Aram's quarrel is with the Northern Kingdom, not with Judah. They wish you no harm (*Rashi*).

30. וּמֶלֶךְ אֲרָם צִוָּה — *The king of Aram had commanded* ... The Aramite king may have been informed by spies of Michaiahu's prediction that Ahab was to be killed in this war. From v. 9 we recall that the two kings had been sitting on the *threshing floor*, that is, in an open place accessible to all (*Mefaresh*).

31. וַיִּזְעַק יְהוֹשָׁפָט — *Yehoshaphat called out. Rashi* thinks that he called out to God in prayer and that God's help came in answer to that prayer (see fn. to v. 1).

Or, as *Mefaresh* and *Metzudos* see it, Yehoshaphat cried out to his soldiers for help. God saved him in spite of the fact that he had put his trust in man.

וַיְסִיתֵם אֱלֹהִים — *God moved them to depart from him. Malbim* thinks that סות, *to persuade* or *incite*, is always used when the persuader demonstrates that something is to be gained by following his wishes. God caused the Aramites to conclude that for political reasons it would be best not to antagonize Judah with whom they had amicable relations until now. When they realized that they were dealing with Yehoshaphat and not, as they had thought, with Ahab, they did not press their advantage.

32. וַיְהִי כִּרְאוֹת שָׂרֵי הָרֶכֶב — *When the captains of the chariots perceived ...*

Radak thinks that ראה here is not to be taken as *to see*, since it was not what they saw that convinced them that Yehoshaphat, not Ahab, was in front of them. It seems likely that they identified him by the sound of his voice or by the words which he used as he was crying out. Our translation reflects this view.

33. וְאִישׁ — *A man. Rashi* quotes the tradition of the Sages (*Yalkut Shimoni* 1:183; 2:103, 202) that this man was the Aramite general Naa-

[28] *The king of Israel and Yehoshaphat the king of Judah went up*
to Ramoth Gilead. [29] *The king of Israel said to Yehoshaphat, 'One*
ought to disguise oneself to go to war, but you put on your robes.'
The king of Israel disguised himself and thus they came to the war.
[30] *The king of Aram had commanded the captain of his chariots*
saying, 'Do not attack small or great, only the king of Israel.'
[31] *When the captain of the chariots saw Yehoshaphat and they*
thought him to be the king of Israel, they turned towards him to
attack. Yehoshaphat called out and HASHEM *helped him. God*
moved them to depart from him. [32] *When the captain of the chari-*
ots perceived that it was not the king of Israel, they turned back
from pursuing him. [33] *A man drew his bow with no specific intent*
and smote the king of Israel between the appendages and the
armor. He said to the charioteer, 'Turn your hand and take me out
from the front for I am ill.' [34] *The battle waxed great on that day,*

man who is known to us from *II Kings* ch. 5. The tradition seems based upon *II Kings* 5:1 where we learn that this Naaman had been instrumental in bringing about a major salvation for his people. The text does not specify what this salvation was. The Sages assume it to have been the killing of Ahab at Ramoth Gilead.

לְתֻמּוֹ — *With no specific intent.* He did not realize that the man at whom he was aiming was Ahab.

Ahab's disguise did not, in any way, help him. God had said that he would be killed at Ramoth Gilead, and he could not escape that fate.

Targum adds that he was killed in fulfillment of the prophecies of Elijah and Michaiahu. That of Elijah was made when Ahab seized Navoth's vineyard (*I Kings* ch. 21). As Ahab walks in his ill-gotten new property, Elijah confronts him and, in the course of a fierce and uncompromising denunciation, predicts that he would die (vs. 21-26). Earlier (v. 19), God had told Elijah to say that, after Ahab's death, his blood would be lapped up by dogs. *Kings* is careful to point out that this is precisely what happened (22:38).

When Michaiahu told Ahab that he would fall at Ramoth Gilead, this was not the first intimation of death which this prophet had conveyed to him. In an earlier confrontation between Israel and Aram (*I Kings* ch. 20), Israel had miraculously won a victory over a much larger Aramite army. Ben Haddad came to Ahab dressed in sackcloth and begged to have his life spared. Magnanimously, Ahab called him *brother* and treated him with dignity and respect. In God's eyes this was a fault. God sent a prophet — whom the Sages identify as Michaiahu — who informed Ahab that he would have to pay with his life for allowing Ben Haddad to go free. Ahab's death at the hands of Ben Haddad's army was the fulfillment of that prophecy.

בֵּין הַדְּבָקִים וּבֵין הַשִּׁרְיָן — *Between the appendages and the armor. Metzudos* explains that הַשִּׁרְיָן is an armor with perforations, which, unprotected, would render it vulnerable. Scale-like appendages are fixed to the armor in order to provide cover. An arrow managed to penetrate between the scales and the armor and enter through one of the holes.

The Sages believe this penetration to have been miraculous and cite it as an example of the *hard* giving way before the *soft*. (*Yalkut Shimoni* 1:183)

הֲפֹךְ יָדְךָ — *Turn your hand*. Do this in order to turn the chariot around (*Metzudos*).

מִן־הַמַּחֲנֶה — *From the front*. מַחֲנֶה from חנה, *to rest*, usually means a camp. However, by extension it is also used to describe an army — which is normally bivouacked in camps. Again, by extension, it connotes the *front* where the army is engaged in battle.

כִּי הָחֳלֵיתִי — *For I am ill. Metzudos* thinks that the word does not connote a wound but some ordinary sickness. Ahab feared that if he would admit that he was wounded, his driver would panic and the morale of the army would be undermined. For this reason he said only that he felt ill.

34. וַתַּעַל הַמִּלְחָמָה בַּיּוֹם הַהוּא — *The battle*

הַהוּא וּמֶלֶךְ יִשְׂרָאֵל הָיָה מַעֲמִיד בַּמֶּרְכָּבָה נֹכַח אֲרָם
א עַד־הָעָרֶב וַיָּמָת לְעֵת בּוֹא הַשָּׁמֶשׁ: וַיָּשָׁב
ב יְהוֹשָׁפָט מֶלֶךְ־יְהוּדָה אֶל־בֵּיתוֹ בְּשָׁלוֹם לִירוּשָׁלִָם: וַיֵּצֵא
אֶל־פָּנָיו יֵהוּא בֶן־חֲנָנִי הַחֹזֶה וַיֹּאמֶר אֶל־הַמֶּלֶךְ יְהוֹשָׁפָט
הֲלָרָשָׁע לַעְזֹר וּלְשֹׂנְאֵי יהוה תֶּאֱהָב וּבָזֹאת עָלֶיךָ קֶּצֶף
ג מִלִּפְנֵי יהוה: אֲבָל דְּבָרִים טוֹבִים נִמְצְאוּ עִמָּךְ כִּי־בִעַרְתָּ
הָאֲשֵׁרוֹת מִן־הָאָרֶץ וַהֲכִינוֹתָ לְבָבְךָ לִדְרֹשׁ הָאֱלֹהִים:
ד וַיֵּשֶׁב יְהוֹשָׁפָט בִּירוּשָׁלִָם וַיָּשָׁב וַיֵּצֵא בָעָם מִבְּאֵר שֶׁבַע

waxed great on that day. The fighting was fiercer than would normally have been the case. Wave upon wave of soldiers faced one another (*Metzudos*).

וּמֶלֶךְ יִשְׂרָאֵל הָיָה מַעֲמִיד — *But the king of Israel held himself up*. Ahab did not allow himself to sink down in his pain. He did not want his soldiers to realize that he had been wounded. They would surely have been panicked into fleeing (*Rashi*).

XIX

Yehoshaphat returns home. He is unaware of his error in associating with Ahab, and of his own miraculous escape from death. A prophet now apprises him of the enormity of his failing and makes him realize how very nearly he had been killed. The tendencies which had brought him so close to tragedy must be excised or controlled. His mistakes must not be repeated.

1. וַיָּשָׁב יְהוֹשָׁפָט ... אֶל־בֵּיתוֹ בְּשָׁלוֹם — *As Yehoshaphat ... returned home safely ...* Safely is probably the translation closest to the simple meaning of the verse. However, שָׁלוֹם has many connotations. Among them, the state of being at peace with oneself, untroubled by conscience (*Deuteronomy* 21:18). Yehoshaphat may well have felt sanguine about his spiritual state, unaware how seriously it had been compromised. It was because of this that the prophet accosted him.

We have translated, *As* ..., in order to reflect this connection.

אֶל־בֵּיתוֹ ... לִירוּשָׁלָם — *Home ... to Jerusalem*. If the meaning is simply, *to his home in Jerusalem*, the syntax would be awkward: we would have expected בִּירוּשָׁלַם, and בְּשָׁלוֹם should not have come between בֵּיתוֹ and לִירוּשָׁלַם.

It is more likely that the phrase וַיָּשָׁב ... אֶל־בֵּיתוֹ בְּשָׁלוֹם has the same connotation as the almost identical phrase in *Genesis* 28:21, וְשַׁבְתִּי בְשָׁלוֹם אֶל־בֵּית אָבִי. There, Jacob did not pray that he might return safely to his father's house in the physical sense, but rather that he might maintain the same spiritual perfection with which he had left it (see *Rashi* there). Thus, we understand our phrase as follows: Yehoshaphat returned to Jerusalem sanguine in his certainty that his religious standing had not been compromised.

2. הֲלָרָשָׁע לַעְזֹר וּלְשֹׂנְאֵי ה׳ תֶּאֱהָב — *Should you help the wicked and love those that hate* HASHEM? *Malbim* detects two criticisms. Helping the wicked is in itself forbidden. But simple help need not involve personal or emotional involvement. Yehoshaphat had not only given formal aid but had also regarded Ahab as a friend. This was particularly reprehensible.[1]

וּבָזֹאת עָלֶיךָ קֶּצֶף מִלִּפְנֵי ה׳ — *For this,* HASHEM*'s*

1. The thrust of our chapter certainly suggests that Yehoshaphat accepted Yehu's strictures and presumably repented upon his rash association with Ahab. It is therefore surprising that on at least two subsequent occasions he once more threw in his lot with Israel's wicked kings. At 20:35 ff. (*I Kings* 22:49 ff.) we find him on a joint maritime venture with Ahab's son Achaziah, and at *II Kings* he joins Ahab's other son, Yehoram, in a campaign against Moab.

In the absence of guidance from the commentators we may surmise that the prohibition against allying oneself with the wicked applies only when motivated by simple friendship, not when cooperation is sought out of political necessity or economic or military expedience.

Given this, it is possible that the first of Yehu's strictures would have had no force without the second. Had

19
1-4

but the king of Israel held himself up in the chariot, in the presence of the Arameans until the evening. He died at sunset.

As Yehoshaphat the king of Judah returned home safely to
Jerusalem. 2 *Yehu son of Chanani the seer came out to meet*
him and said to the king Yehoshaphat, 'Should you help the wicked and love those that hate HASHEM*? For this,* HASHEM*'s*
wrath was upon you. 3 *Nevertheless, you have accrued merits, for*
you have removed the asheirah-trees from the land and have set your heart to seek God.' 4 *Yehoshaphat now stayed in Jerusalem,*
but would occasionally go out among the people, from Be'er Sheva

wrath was upon you. You were almost killed in the ill-conceived war.

God's anger must have been great indeed. The Sages teach that Moses himself found it necessary to intercede with God and to beg that centuries later Yehoshaphat's life be spared. (*Sifri* to *Deuteronomy* 33:7 and *Rashi* there.) As it was, Yehoshaphat came very close to death. *Yerushalmi Berachos* 9:1 tells us that the enemy sword was already at his throat when God moved it away from him (18:31).

3. אֲבָל ... כִּי־בִעַרְתָּ הָאֲשֵׁרוֹת מִן־הָאָרֶץ וַהֲכִינוֹתָ לְבָבְךָ לִדְרֹשׁ הָאֱלֹהִים — *Nevertheless ... for you have removed the Asheirah trees from the land and have set your heart to seek God.* It is significant that it is the removal of idolatry, not Yehoshaphat's energetic propagation of Torah knowledge (17:7 ff.), which is to protect him from punishment.

The explanation lies in the context. By joining with Ahab, Yehoshaphat had exposed himself — and by extension his entire kingdom — to the pernicious influence of the idolatrous culture which was so pervasive in the north. It is the danger of such influence which underlies the prohibition against making common lot with the wicked. [See *Shaarey Teshuvah, Rabbeinu Yonah*, 3:51; 151;193.]

Yehoshaphat's vendetta against the icons showed that Judah would not succumb to these dangers. At 17:6 we saw with what ruthless efficiency he went after every last vestige of the cults which had proliferated under Aviah. It was this, more than the spreading of Torah knowledge, which would neutralize the effects of the tragic association with Ahab.

◈ Yehoshaphat Reforms the Judiciary

4-11. The rest of the chapter deals with Yehoshaphat's activities with respect to establishing courts in the provinces and, in a special sense, in Jerusalem.

Although the text does not explicate any connection between Yehu's chastisement and Yehoshaphat's decision to establish or at least refurbish the judiciary, we shall, based on a midrash cited by *Mefaresh*, assume such a connection. [See Section II, *Yehoshaphat and the Judiciary*.]

4. וַיֵּשֶׁב יְהוֹשָׁפָט בִּירוּשָׁלָ‍ִם — *Yehoshaphat now stayed in Jerusalem.* From this time on, he avoided going to visit Ahab's family (*Metzudos*).

וַיָּשָׁב וַיֵּצֵא בָעָם — *But would occasionally go out among the people.* The translation follows *Metzudos*. The verb ישב used to denote *repetition* can be found elsewhere in Scripture: cf. *Eichah* 3:3.

there been no emotional involvement, the actual alliance would not necessarily have been offensive. We can assume that the subsequent joint ventures were undertaken with appropriate motivation and without personal entanglements. That the joint venture described in 20:37 ended in disaster may have been because that which Yehoshaphat had considered to be a compelling reason was not deemed so by God.

We do not know why Yehoshaphat, knowing — as he must have — that an association with the wicked goes against the Torah's wishes, joined Ahab's project. It is possible that he allowed himself to believe that Ahab had repented his evil ways. Indeed, *I Kings* 21:27-28 indicates that after stealing Navoth's vineyard Ahab experienced an apparently sincere change of heart, and that the extreme penance to which he subjected himself was accepted by God.

Since here Yehoshaphat is criticized for associating with Ahab, we must assume that for all his sincere remorse there was no real change. Ahab probably regretted having been instrumental in Navoth's murder — all for possession of a paltry vineyard. But in essentials, he remained a destructive force with whom Yehoshaphat should have had no truck.

עַד־הַר אֶפְרָיִם וַיְשִׁיבֵם אֶל־יהוה אֱלֹהֵי אֲבוֹתֵיהֶם:
ה וַיַּעֲמֵד שֹׁפְטִים בָּאָרֶץ בְּכָל־עָרֵי יְהוּדָה הַבְּצֻרוֹת לְעִיר
ו וָעִיר: וַיֹּאמֶר אֶל־הַשֹּׁפְטִים רְאוּ מָה־אַתֶּם עֹשִׂים כִּי
לֹא לְאָדָם תִּשְׁפְּטוּ כִּי לַיהוה וְעִמָּכֶם בִּדְבַר מִשְׁפָּט:
ז וְעַתָּה יְהִי פַחַד־יהוה עֲלֵיכֶם שִׁמְרוּ וַעֲשׂוּ כִּי־אֵין
ח עִם־יהוה אֱלֹהֵינוּ עַוְלָה וּמַשֹּׂא פָנִים וּמִקַּח־שֹׁחַד: וְגַם
בִּירוּשָׁלַם הֶעֱמִיד יְהוֹשָׁפָט מִן־הַלְוִיִּם וְהַכֹּהֲנִים וּמֵרָאשֵׁי
הָאָבוֹת לְיִשְׂרָאֵל לְמִשְׁפַּט יהוה וְלָרִיב וַיָּשֻׁבוּ יְרוּשָׁלִָם:

וַיְשִׁיבֵם אֶל־ה׳ אֱלֹהֵי אֲבוֹתֵיהֶם — *Bringing them back to* HASHEM, *the God of their fathers.* Yehoshaphat set out to correct whatever false ideas and attitudes had grown up among the people and to teach those articles of faith which the Torah enjoins upon them. After he had put the people's spiritual house in order, he turned to correct societal ills by establishing the court system, as described in the next verses (*Malbim*).

The improved spiritual standing of the people may be directly tied to the establishment of the courts: The eleventh blessing in the *Amidah* reads: *Restore our judges as in earliest times ... and reign over us — You,* HASHEM, *alone — with kindness* ... The juxtaposition of these two thoughts must be understood as follows: God will only allow His Presence to rest [*reign over us*] in a society founded upon the absolute truth and justice of the Torah's laws [*restore our judges* ...]. [See *Hirsch* and *Munk* in their respective commentaries.] Thus our phrase may well lead into the next sentence. Yehoshaphat brought back the people to God — that is to His direct stewardship — through his judicial reforms.

5. וַיַּעֲמֵד שֹׁפְטִים ... לְעִיר וָעִיר — *He set up judges ... in each city.* This, in accordance with the Torah's requirement that judges be established in each city — see *Deuteronomy* 16:18. See further, Section II, *Yehoshaphat and the Judiciary*.

בְּכָל־עָרֵי יְהוּדָה הַבְּצֻרוֹת — *In all the fortified cities of Judah.* The fortified cities, which were relatively independent of central authority, required a stronger judicial presence, and are therefore mentioned specifically. Certainly courts were also established in the open cities (*Mefaresh*).

6. רְאוּ מָה־אַתֶּם עֹשִׂים — *Consider what you do!* The verb ראה is used not only to denote physical sight, but also for mental awareness, perception or consideration. See, for example, *Genesis* 27:27.

כִּי לֹא לְאָדָם תִּשְׁפְּטוּ כִּי לַה׳ — *You do not judge on behalf of man but on behalf of* HASHEM. There is no deceiving God. He will know if you discharge your duties dishonestly (*Metzudos*).

A more profound meaning may be implied: Each and every man, animated and defined by the spark of Divinity which lies within him, stands as a unique being — a compact universe [עוֹלָם קָטָן] (*Tanchuma, Pikudai* 3) before God. No other human, whether as a corporate body in the form of society or as an individual, has the right to stand in judgment over him. Within his own world he reigns supreme. Only God is superior to him and thus only God may presume to judge him. No human may sit in judgment over another, except as a direct agent of God. [See *Maharal, Nesivas Olam, Nesiv Gemilus Chasadim* 1 as explained and elaborated upon in *Rav Hutner's Pachad Yitzchak* to *Shavuos* 44.]

When Moses appointed judges, he adjured them: *Do not give anyone special consideration when rendering judgment. Listen alike to great and small. Do not stand in fear before any man, for judgment belongs to God* (*Deuteronomy* 1:16).

Ramban, based on our verse, explains: *It devolves upon God to execute justice among His creatures ... but He delegated the job to you. If you will be afraid and in fear trespass upon people's rights, then, [more than wronging man] you will have failed* HASHEM, *will have subverted the basis for your authority.*

The judge's mandate derives not from society which deputizes him to administer its laws [כִּי לֹא לְאָדָם תִּשְׁפְּטוּ], but directly from God [כִּי לַה׳].

For the dignity of the individual upon whom judgment is being passed, see further in Section II, *Yehoshaphat and the Judiciary*.

וְעִמָּכֶם בִּדְבַר מִשְׁפָּט — *And He is together with you in rendering judgment.* Imagine to

19
5-8

to the hill of Ephraim, bringing them back to HASHEM, the God of their fathers. 5 *He set up judges in the land in all the fortified cities of Judah, in each city.* 6 *He said to the judges, 'Consider what you do! You do not judge on behalf of man but on behalf of HASHEM, and He is together with you in rendering judgment.* 7 *Therefore, now let the fear of HASHEM be upon you; take heed and act, for there can be no iniquity, favoritism or taking of bribes with HASHEM our God.'* 8 *Also in Jerusalem Yehoshaphat made appointments from among the Levites, the Kohanim and the family heads of Israel. This for [the establishment of] Godly standards and for [the adjudication of] controversies. They returned to Jerusalem.*

yourselves that God were taking part in your deliberations. Or perhaps it is a promise: God will help you to arrive at the correct conclusion if, by taking your role seriously, you demonstrate that you stand in awe of Him (*Radak*).

Compare *Psalms* 82:1: *God stands in the assembly of the mighty; among the judges He will judge*.

7. וְעַתָּה — *Therefore, now*. Now that you know that you are going to act in God's behalf (*Metzudos*).

שִׁמְרוּ וַעֲשׂוּ — *Take heed and act*. *Targumim* render שמר as אִסְתַּמָּרוּ when the meaning is *take heed*, as for example, at *Genesis* 31:24. Thus: *Take heed that you act in accordance with the Torah and the laws* (*Metzudos*).

8-11. *Deuteronomy* 17:8-13 teaches that besides the courts which were to be established in every city, there was to be a central court in Jerusalem located within the Temple confines. [See *Rambam, Sanhedrin* 1:3.] This was not to be a court of appeal in the sense that we know such an institution today; that is a court of resort for litigants who think themselves wronged by a lower court. Its function, rather, was to guide the lower courts in matters in which these were not able to reach their own conclusion.

Both *Malbim* and *R' Dovid Tzvi Hoffman* assume that our passage deals with this central court. Just as Yehoshaphat made sure to comply with the Torah's dictate that courts be established in every city, so too did he make sure that this high court be in place.[1]

8. וְגַם בִּירוּשָׁלַםִ — *Also in Jerusalem* ... It might have been thought unnecessary to establish courts in Jerusalem since as the royal seat its judicial system could have been administered directly by the king. Nevertheless, Yehoshaphat established the court there (*Mefaresh*).

The *Mefaresh's* comment suggests that he does not take our passage as referring to the Great Sanhedrin. If it did, the expression וְגַם could be readily explained without his comment. The meaning would be that besides establishing the regular courts throughout the provinces, he *also* set up the high court in Jerusalem. See below that there are other indications that the *Mefaresh* disagrees with *Malbim* and *R' Dovid Tzvi Hoffman*.

מִן־הַלְוִיִּם וְהַכֹּהֲנִים וּמֵרָאשֵׁי הָאָבוֹת לְיִשְׂרָאֵל — *From among the Levites, the Kohanim and the family heads of Israel*. When *Deuteronomy* 17:9 speaks of the Great Sanhedrin it says, *And you shall come to the Kohanim the Levites and to the judge who shall be in those times*... This, *Rambam* (*Sanhedrin* 2:2) codifies as meaning that where possible the Sanhedrin should incorporate both *Kohanim* and Levites among its membership. Thus our verse accurately reflects the requirements for the establishment of the Great Sanhedrin.

From the fact that the Levites are mentioned first, *R' Dovid Tzvi Hoffman* deduces that the majority of the membership of Yehoshaphat's court came from their ranks. He points out that this would agree with *I Chronicles* 23:4 and 26:29 where David appoints the Levites as judges. Apparently theirs was the task of servicing the spiritual needs of the people. Thus also, the delegation which Yehoshaphat sent around the country to teach Torah (17:7-8) was comprised of only two *Kohanim* and five Israelites, but of ten Levites.

לְמִשְׁפַּט ה׳ וְלָרִיב — *This for the* [*establishment of*] *Godly standards and for* [*the adjudication of*] *controversies*. The translation takes the subject as the Great Sanhedrin. This Sanhedrin

1. For an exhaustive treatment and analysis of the standing of this institution in the centuries which preceded Yehoshaphat, see *R' Dovid Tzvi Hoffman, Deuteronomy*.

יט
ט־יא

ט וַיְצַו עֲלֵיהֶם לֵאמֹר כֹּה תַעֲשׂוּן בְּיִרְאַת יהוה בֶּאֱמוּנָה
י וּבְלֵבָב שָׁלֵם: וְכָל־רִיב אֲשֶׁר־יָבוֹא עֲלֵיכֶם מֵאֲחֵיכֶם ׀
הַיֹּשְׁבִים בְּעָרֵיהֶם בֵּין־דָּם ׀ לְדָם בֵּין־תּוֹרָה לְמִצְוָה
לְחֻקִּים וּלְמִשְׁפָּטִים וְהִזְהַרְתֶּם אֹתָם וְלֹא יֶאְשְׁמוּ לַיהוה
וְהָיָה־קֶצֶף עֲלֵיכֶם וְעַל־אֲחֵיכֶם כֹּה תַעֲשׂוּן וְלֹא תֶאְשָׁמוּ:
יא וְהִנֵּה אֲמַרְיָהוּ כֹהֵן הָרֹאשׁ עֲלֵיכֶם לְכֹל ׀ דְּבַר יהוה

had two essential functions: It was responsible for the total religious standing of the people, and it was the final decisor between conflicting opinions among judges of the lower courts (see comm. to v. 10).

For מִשְׁפַּט ה׳, we can ignore the renderings, *claim* or *right* (as in *Deuteronomy* 24:17), or *punishment* (as in *Ezekiel* 23:45). All these are inappropriate here.

The meaning here appears to parallel *Jeremiah* 8:7: There, the prophet bemoans Israel's sorry spiritual state by saying: *Even the stork in the heavens knows its seasons; the turtledove, the horse and the pelican adhere to their predetermined schedules, but My people do not know the* מִשְׁפַּט ה׳. From the context it is quite clear that the phrase denotes *appropriate behavior relative to* HASHEM.

רִיב is clearly a reference to the expression, דִּבְרֵי רִיבֹת בִּשְׁעָרֶיךָ, of *Deuteronomy* 17:8. This, as we shall see below, refers to disagreements among judges of the lower courts.

Mefaresh, as we saw above, does not appear to share the view that this passage refers to the Great Sanhedrin. He explains מִשְׁפַּט ה׳ as claims arising from monetary entanglements, while רִיב are actions in cases of murder or torts. Neither of these falls into the purview of the Great Sanhedrin.

וַיָּשֻׁבוּ יְרוּשָׁלָם — *They returned to Jerusalem.* Either, those who had been involved in the establishment of the provincial courts returned to their homes in Jerusalem after completing their work (*Radak* and *Metzudos*) or the people from the provinces who had been chosen to sit on the Great Sanhedrin left their homes to go back with Yehoshaphat to Jerusalem (*Malbim*).

9. כֹּה תַעֲשׂוּן — *Thus shall you act* ... Yehoshaphat exhorts the newly appointed judges (*Metzudos*).

בְּיִרְאַת ה׳ בֶּאֱמוּנָה וּבְלֵבָב שָׁלֵם — *In the fear of* HASHEM, *faithfully and with a whole heart.*

The translation follows *Metzudos*: three qualities are asked of the judges. This, in contrast to *trop*, which reads: *Thus should you act if you are to fulfill your duties in a God-fearing manner: Faithfully and with a whole heart.*

The judges sought out by Moses in the wilderness were to be, ... *capable people, God fearing, men of truth who detest profit* ... (*Exodus* 18:21). The parallel is striking:

Chronicles	*Exodus*
a. בְּיִרְאַת ה׳ — *In the fear of* HASHEM	a. יִרְאֵי אֱלֹהִים — *God fearing men*
b. בֶּאֱמוּנָה — *Faithfully*	b. אַנְשֵׁי אֱמֶת — *Men of truth*
c. וּבְלֵבָב שָׁלֵם — *And with a whole heart.*	c. שֹׂנְאֵי בָצַע — *Who detest profit.*

It is noteworthy that for בֶּאֱמוּנָה, *Targum* renders *faithfully and with truth*, but on three other occasions, when the term appears in a similar context (31:12 and 15 and 34:12), he uses only *faithfully*. Perhaps he means to hint at the אַנְשֵׁי אֱמֶת, *truth*, requirement of *Exodus* [b].

Malbim notes that *a whole heart* [c] implies a state in which no outside interest or inclination can sway a person's attitude. This can easily be seen as the equivalent of the quality of *detesting profit* recommended in *Exodus* [c].

10. מֵאֲחֵיכֶם הַיֹּשְׁבִים בְּעָרֵיהֶם — *From your brothers that dwell in their cities. R' Dovid Tzvi Hoffman* feels that this phrase confirms that we are dealing with the Great Sanhedrin and that *controversy* refers to disagreements among the judges of the lower, provincial courts. Only thus can we understand why the judges in Jerusalem would be called upon to render decisions for their *brothers who dwell in their cities*. Regular litigants would have had no reason to leave their cities in order to bring their grievances to Jerusalem. They could be expected to go to their own courts which had only now been established.

[9] *He commanded them saying, 'Thus shall you act. In the fear of* HASHEM, *faithfully and with a whole heart.* [10] *Any controversy that shall reach you from your brothers that dwell in their cities; be the issue a decision between blood and blood, or concerning Torah and command, statutes and laws. Admonish them so that they should not be deemed guilty by* HASHEM, *for this would expose you and your brothers to anger. Do this so that you may avoid guilt.* [11] *Now behold, Amariahu the chief Kohen is over you for all matters concerning* HASHEM; *and*

בֵּין־דָּם לְדָם — *Between blood and blood* ... There is sufficient similarity, between our phrase and the Torah's definition of the areas in which the Great Sanhedrin was to function, to confirm that we are dealing with the establishment of the Great Sanhedrin (*R' Dovid Tzvi Hoffman*).

Deuteronomy 17:8 envisions the Sanhedrin deciding cases in one of the three areas which we juxtapose here to the listing in *Chronicles*:

Chronicles	*Deuteronomy*
a. בֵּין־דָּם לְדָם — *Between blood and blood*	a. בֵּין־דָּם לְדָם — *Between blood and blood*
b. בֵּין־תּוֹרָה לְמִצְוָה — *or concerning Torah and command*	b. בֵּין־דִּין לְדִין — *between claim and claim*
c. לְחֻקִּים וּלְמִשְׁפָּטִים — *statutes and laws.*	c. וּבֵין נֶגַע לָנֶגַע — *between wound and wound.*

Since phrase [a] is precisely the same in both cases, it seems reasonable to assume that phrase [b] in *Deuteronomy* which deals with litigation between two parties is covered by מִשְׁפָּטִים in our phrase [c], and that [c] in *Deuteronomy* is an example of the statutes of *Chronicles*.[1]

Again, we see that we are dealing with the establishment of the Great Sanhedrin. תּוֹרָה, חֻקִּים and מִשְׁפָּטִים cannot be subjects for litigation. These come to court only when they are matters concerning which the judges of a lower court require guidance (*R' Dovid Tzvi Hoffman*).

וְהִזְהַרְתֶּם אֹתָם — *Admonish them*. When the lower courts come to you for guidance, you must admonish them to follow your ruling. Else, if they were to adhere to their earlier opinions, they would be guilty before God [וְלֹא יֶאְשְׁמוּ לַה'] (*Metzudos*).[2]

וְהָיָה־קֶצֶף עֲלֵיכֶם וְעַל־אֲחֵיכֶם — *For this would expose you and your brothers to anger*. If they persist in their former opinions because you failed to admonish them, you would be blamed for falling short in your duty, and they for disobeying your ruling (*Metzudos*).

כֹּה תַעֲשׂוּן וְלֹא תֶאְשָׁמוּ — *Do this so that you may avoid guilt*. If you admonish them and they fail to listen, you at least will have done your duty (*Metzudos*).

11. אֲמַרְיָהוּ כֹּהֵן הָרֹאשׁ — *Amariahu the chief Kohen*. See prefatory remarks to *I Chronicles*

1. *R' Dovid Tzvi Hoffman* demonstrates that, given that our passage deals with the establishment of the great Sanhedrin, it can shed light on the passage in *Deuteronomy*.

The verse there reads: ... כִּי יִפָּלֵא מִמְּךָ דָבָר לַמִּשְׁפָּט בֵּין־דָּם לְדָם, *When some judgment is hidden from you, between blood and blood* ... Some commentators (cf. *Ibn Ezra*) think that the three examples are in opposition to מִשְׁפָּט. Each is an example of the kind of מִשְׁפָּט concerning which there may be doubts: *Between blood and blood* refers to guilt in a capital case — should the accused be executed or not?; *between claim and claim* refers to monetary litigations; and *between wound and wound* refers to torts.

Thus, according to the simple meaning of the passage there is no reference to purely religious matters.

However, in the tradition of the Sages, *between blood and blood* is the question of whether a given show of menstrual blood is to be judged clean or unclean, and *between wound and wound* refers to the halachic standing of various leprous sores — that is, matters of religious but not judicial import (see *Rashi* there).

The passage in *Chronicles* which substitutes תּוֹרָה מִצְוָה חֻקִּים and מִשְׁפָּטִים for the examples given in *Deuteronomy*, clearly demonstrates that the expressions there are to be understood as the Sages did.

2. The Torah decrees the death penalty for a זָקֵן מַמְרֵא, *a rebellious sage;* that is, a judge from a lower court who refuses to accept the ruling of the Great Sanhedrin and continues to decide cases based on the opinion which had been rejected by them (see *Rambam, Hilchos Mamerim*).

כ
א־ב

וּזְבַדְיָהוּ בֶן־יִשְׁמָעֵאל הַנָּגִיד לְבֵית־יְהוּדָה לְכֹל דְּבַר־
הַמֶּלֶךְ וְשֹׁטְרִים הַלְוִיִּם לִפְנֵיכֶם חִזְקוּ וַעֲשׂוּ וִיהִי יְהוָה
עִם־הַטּוֹב׃
א וַיְהִי אַחֲרֵי־כֵן בָּאוּ בְנֵי־מוֹאָב וּבְנֵי עַמּוֹן וְעִמָּהֶם ׀
ב מֵהָעַמּוֹנִים עַל־יְהוֹשָׁפָט לַמִּלְחָמָה׃ וַיָּבֹאוּ וַיַּגִּידוּ

5:30-41 for a discussion of whether this Amariahu was a *Kohen Gadol* or the chief administrator of the *Kohanim*.

לְכֹל דְּבַר ה׳ . . . לְכֹל דְּבַר־הַמֶּלֶךְ — *For all matters concerning* HASHEM *... for all matters pertaining to the king. Rambam* speaks of two officials involved in the Great Sanhedrin: The wisest among them sits over them and he leads the session. He is the one whom the Sages refer to everywhere as *Nassi*, the prince. He is in the place of our teacher Moses. The wisest among the seventy is placed second to the leader, and sits at his right hand. He is known as *Av Beis Din*, the head of the court.

There is no indication that these two officials shared the division of responsibility reflected in our verse: that Amariahu was the one to whom all religious decisions were to be referred and Zevadiah was to be consulted in all matters which affected royalty (*Metzudos*). This division must be seen as a temporary disposition made by Yehoshaphat and conditioned by his times and needs.

וְשֹׁטְרִים הַלְוִיִּם לִפְנֵיכֶם — *The Levites are to be officials at your disposal.* They stood at the disposal of the court to enforce any decisions which were reached (*Metzudos*).

XX

◆§ God Wages War for Yehoshaphat

Yehoshaphat is now attacked by a confederation of nations. A chain of events is set in motion which portrays the bond between God and Israel in terms which are reminiscent of the closeness which marked this relationship at the time of the Exodus from Egypt. The passage of centuries, replete with numerous setbacks and disappointments, has not dimmed the luster of the love attending that betrothal. Israel's moment of danger still brings God's wrath to bear upon its enemies; Israel's victory is still regarded as vindication of God's mastery over the destiny of nations.

Although Moab is among the attackers, the war described here is not the same as the Moabite war of *II Kings* ch. 3. That one is an Israelite war in which the main protagonist is Ahab's son Yehoram. Yehoshaphat helps, but is not personally involved. Here, we have Yehoshaphat, on his own, repulsing an enemy who had already penetrated deeply into Judah. See Section II to ch. 17, *Yehoshaphat in Kings and Chronicles*, and Section II to this chapter, *Two Moabite Wars*.

1. וַיְהִי אַחֲרֵי־כֵן — *After this ...* We have discussed the motive which may have driven Moab to attack in Section II, *Two Moabite Wars*. Perhaps it was a desire to take vengeance against Yehoshaphat for the role which he had played in Yehoram's war.

But what if Yehoshaphat's war came first?

The phrase *After this* ... implies a connection with that which went before. But how could Yehoshaphat's judicial reforms have precipitated an attack upon his land?

When we consider some significant facts about this war, the following solution seems possible:

1. From the tone of Yehoshaphat's prayer (6-12), particularly from v. 11, it is evident that this was no minor border skirmish. Nothing less than the existence of Israel upon its land seems to have been at stake. Without God's intervention, they, for whom God had driven out Canaan's former inhabitants (v. 7), would themselves be exiled.

2. God's answer (v. 17), that it was His battle rather than theirs, clearly indicates what was involved. Through attacking Israel, the aggressors were challenging the very concept of a Divine Presence on earth.

There is an uncanny similarity between the wording of God's answer here, and that of Moses' exhortation to Israel on the banks of the Red Sea (*Exodus* 14:13). The miracle that

20
1-2

Zevadiahu the son of Ishmael, the prince of the House of Judah, for all matters pertaining to the king. The Levites are to be officials at your disposal. Now take courage and perform. May HASHEM *be with him who does that which is good.'*

1 *After this, the Moabites and the Amonites, joined by some of the Amonim, came to war against Yehoshaphat.* 2 *They came*

will grant victory to Yehoshaphat is, apparently, to create a moment in history akin to that at which the very seas split to allow Israel's Divinely ordained progress towards the land of its destiny. God's intervention is on a par with that first world-shattering testimonial to His love for His people.

We compare:

Chronicles	*Exodus*
a. לֹא לָכֶם לְהִלָּחֵם בָּזֹאת — *It is not your obligation to do battle in this matter*	a. וַיֹּאמֶר מֹשֶׁה אֶל־הָעָם אַל־תִּירָאוּ — *And Moses said to the people do not be afraid*
b. הִתְיַצְּבוּ עִמְדוּ וּרְאוּ — *stand ready be still and see*	b. הִתְיַצְּבוּ וּרְאוּ — *stand firm and see*
c. אֶת־יְשׁוּעַת ה׳ עִמָּכֶם — *and see how God will save you*	c. אֶת־יְשׁוּעַת ה׳ — *the salvation of* HASHEM
d. אַל־תִּירְאוּ וְאַל־תֵּחַתּוּ — *do not be afraid, nor be dismayed.*	d. אֲשֶׁר־יַעֲשֶׂה לָכֶם הַיּוֹם — *which He shall render you this day*
	e. ה׳ יִלָּחֵם לָכֶם — HASHEM *will make war for you*
	f. וְאַתֶּם תַּחֲרִשׁוּן — *and you shall be silent.*

3. The Sages identify the עֲמוֹנִים as Amalek [see below]. When Israel's arch enemy attacks, the stakes are clearly defined. Amalek is the implacable foe of the Divine. Neither God's Name nor His throne can be complete if Amalek is to have its way (See *Exodus* 17:14-16).

The explanation for all this must be sought in Yehoshaphat's special place in history — see comm. at 17:5. The seminal moment when his father Asa missed the opportunity of reuniting the two kingdoms placed Judah and its king at the center of Israel's destiny. Henceforth, their fortunes would be the hub of history's wheel.

Yehoshaphat's reform of the judiciary was his answer to the call of the moment. It was a first step in firming up the nation which would now, more than ever, have to be the repository of the Divine Presence among men. As God's nation assumes a new form and strikes out upon a new path, Amalek and its cohorts attack. In precisely the same way as the Exodus from Egypt goaded Amalek into a desperate attempt to nip the nascent infusion of sanctity into world history in the bud (*Exodus* 17:8 ff.), so too do they come now, in a vain response to Yehoshaphat's energetic shouldering of his destiny.

וְעִמָּהֶם מֵהָעַמּוֹנִים — *Joined by some of the Amonim.* The Amonite nation cannot be meant here. These were mentioned earlier as having joined in the attack.

Radak points out that throughout Scripture the true Amonites are always referred to as בְּנֵי עַמּוֹן, never as עֲמוֹנִים.[1] Hence these Ammonim are a different people who went under this name, only because they settled in Amonite territory.

Metzudos suggests that there may be an inversion of letters here, and that the מְעוּנִים of 26:7 are meant.

The Midrash teaches that the term refers to Amalekites who disguised themselves as Amonites and joined in the attack. We have a precedent for such a strategy on the part of Amalek in *Numbers* 21:1 where, in the tradi-

1. R' Y. Danziger has suggested that the reason for this may be that the name of the progenitor of this people was given as בֶּן עַמִּי (*Genesis* 19:38).

כ
ג־יא

לִיהוֹשָׁפָט לֵאמֹר בָּא עָלֶיךָ הָמוֹן רָב מֵעֵבֶר לַיָּם מֵאֲרָם
ג וְהִנָּם בְּחַצְצוֹן תָּמָר הִיא עֵין גֶּדִי: וַיִּרָא וַיִּתֵּן יְהוֹשָׁפָט
אֶת־פָּנָיו לִדְרוֹשׁ לַיהוָה וַיִּקְרָא־צוֹם עַל־כָּל־יְהוּדָה:
ד וַיִּקָּבְצוּ יְהוּדָה לְבַקֵּשׁ מֵיְהוָה גַּם מִכָּל־עָרֵי יְהוּדָה בָּאוּ
ה לְבַקֵּשׁ אֶת־יְהוָה: וַיַּעֲמֹד יְהוֹשָׁפָט בִּקְהַל יְהוּדָה וִירוּשָׁלִַם
ו בְּבֵית יְהוָה לִפְנֵי הֶחָצֵר הַחֲדָשָׁה: וַיֹּאמַר יְהוָה אֱלֹהֵי
אֲבֹתֵינוּ הֲלֹא אַתָּה־הוּא אֱלֹהִים בַּשָּׁמַיִם וְאַתָּה מוֹשֵׁל
בְּכֹל מַמְלְכוֹת הַגּוֹיִם וּבְיָדְךָ כֹּחַ וּגְבוּרָה וְאֵין עִמְּךָ
ז לְהִתְיַצֵּב: הֲלֹא | אַתָּה אֱלֹהֵינוּ הוֹרַשְׁתָּ אֶת־יֹשְׁבֵי הָאָרֶץ
הַזֹּאת מִלִּפְנֵי עַמְּךָ יִשְׂרָאֵל וַתִּתְּנָהּ לְזֶרַע אַבְרָהָם אֹהַבְךָ
ח לְעוֹלָם: וַיֵּשְׁבוּ־בָהּ וַיִּבְנוּ לְךָ | בָּהּ מִקְדָּשׁ לְשִׁמְךָ לֵאמֹר:
ט אִם־תָּבוֹא עָלֵינוּ רָעָה חֶרֶב שְׁפוֹט וְדֶבֶר וְרָעָב נַעַמְדָה
לִפְנֵי הַבַּיִת הַזֶּה וּלְפָנֶיךָ כִּי שִׁמְךָ בַּבַּיִת הַזֶּה וְנִזְעַק אֵלֶיךָ
י מִצָּרָתֵנוּ וְתִשְׁמַע וְתוֹשִׁיעַ: וְעַתָּה הִנֵּה בְנֵי־עַמּוֹן וּמוֹאָב
וְהַר־שֵׂעִיר אֲשֶׁר לֹא־נָתַתָּה לְיִשְׂרָאֵל לָבוֹא בָהֶם בְּבֹאָם
מֵאֶרֶץ מִצְרָיִם כִּי סָרוּ מֵעֲלֵיהֶם וְלֹא הִשְׁמִידוּם:
יא וְהִנֵּה־הֵם גֹּמְלִים עָלֵינוּ לָבוֹא לְגָרְשֵׁנוּ מִיְּרֻשָּׁתְךָ אֲשֶׁר

tion of the Sages, the attackers were Amalekites who, for reasons of their own, had disguised themselves as Canaanites.

Radak and *Metzudos* suggest that the Amalekites may have wanted to disguise themselves out of fear of reprisal. At that time, Edom - Amalek was still subject to Judah [see comm. to 21:8]. Prudence would demand a safeguard in the event that their attack prove unsuccessful.

2. מֵעֵבֶר לַיָּם — *From across the sea.* This is the Salt Sea (*Metzudos*). This, presumably, because Chatzetzon Tamar or Ein Gedi lies on the shore of the Dead Sea. See ArtScroll *Joshua* 15:62 for the exact location.

מֵאֲרָם — *From Aram.* On their way into Judah, the attacking armies passed Aram (*Metzudos*).

וְהִנָּם — *And behold, they are ...* There is a clear and present danger (*Metzudos*).

3. וַיִּתֵּן ... אֶת־פָּנָיו — *And set his face ...* An unusual expression which *Metzudos* feels denotes a sense of trust in God.

לִדְרוֹשׁ לַה׳ — *To seek out* HASHEM. See comm. to 15:2. The same significance which we saw in the choice of words there may be observed here too. At v. 25, we shall see that it was during this war that Egypt's treasure was once more restored to the Jewish people. [See Section II ch. 12, *Shishak's Campaign.*] It had been lost in Rechav'am's days because he had not sought out God with sufficient energy — [see at 12:14]. Yehoshaphat recovered it because he was willing to invest his entire being in the spiritual elevation of his people.

4. גַּם מִכָּל־עָרֵי יְהוּדָה — *Also from all the cities of Judah.* Not only the inhabitants of Jerusalem attended; all the cities of Judah were represented (*Mefaresh*).

5. בְּבֵית ה׳ — *In the House of* HASHEM. See v. 9.

הֶחָצֵר הַחֲדָשָׁה — *The new courtyard.* We know of no new courtyard in the Temple. *Metzudos* surmises that perhaps some repairs were made and in that sense the courtyard was renewed.

6. וְאֵין עִמְּךָ לְהִתְיַצֵּב — *So that none is able to withstand You.* An unusual form of the phrase which more often is used with ... לִפְנֵי, *before* ... cf. *Joshua* 1:5.

7. וַתִּתְּנָהּ — *And grant it* ... Even a mortal king would feel obliged to protect a gift which he had given to a loyal servant (*Mefaresh*).

לְזֶרַע אַבְרָהָם אֹהַבְךָ — *To the seed of Abraham who loved You.* We assume that Abraham

20
3-11

and told Yehoshaphat, saying, 'A great multitude has come
against you from across the sea, from Aram, and behold they are
in Chatzetzon Tamar which is Ein Gedi.' [3] *Yehoshaphat was*
afraid and set his face to seek out HASHEM, and proclaimed a fast
for all Judah. [4] *Judah gathered to entreat HASHEM; also from all*
the cities of Judah they came to entreat HASHEM. [5] *Yehoshaphat*
stood among the congregation of Judah and Jerusalem in the
House of HASHEM, in front of the new courtyard. [6] *He said,*
'HASHEM, God of our fathers, are You not God in the heavens and
You exercise dominion over all the kingdoms of the nations. In
Your hand is strength and might so that none is able to withstand
You. [7] *Did You, HASHEM our God, not drive out the inhabitants of*
this land, from before Your people, Israel, and grant it for all
eternity to the seed of Abraham who loved You? [8] *And they*
settled in it and have built You a sanctuary in it for Your Name,
saying: [9] *'If evil come upon us, the sword, judgment, pestilence or*
famine we will stand before this House and before You — for
Your Presence is within this House — and cry to You in our
affliction and You will hear and save. [10] *And now, behold the*
children of Amon, Moab and Mt. Seir whom You would not allow
Israel to invade when they came from the land of Egypt, but they
turned aside from them and did not destroy them. [11] *Now, behold*
they are requiting us by coming to drive us out from Your

rather than Jacob (see comm. to *I Chronicles* 16:13) is mentioned, because it was to him that the Land was promised at the Covenant between the Pieces (*Genesis* 17:8). See further at v. 10.

8-9. For the Temple as the focus for Israel's prayers, see Section II to ch. 6, *The Temple as a House of Prayer*.

9. שְׁפוֹט — *Judgment.* This will be so if a decision is made condemning us to some form of punishment (*Metzudos*).

וּלְפָנֶיךָ כִּי שִׁמְךָ בַּבַּיִת הַזֶּה — *And before You, for Your Presence is within this House.* When we stand before the Temple we will automatically be standing before You since the Temple is the locus of the Divine Presence (*Metzudos*).

10. וְהַר־שֵׂעִיר — *And Mount Seir.* This evidently refers to the *Amonim* mentioned in v. 1. That they are described as hailing from Mt. Seir would seem to confirm the tradition of the Sages that these were Amalekites - see comm. to v. 1. Mt. Seir is the home of Esau and his descendants.

אֲשֶׁר לֹא־נָתַתָּה לְיִשְׂרָאֵל לָבוֹא בָהֶם — *Whom You would not allow Israel to invade.* In *Deuteronomy*, ch. 2 we learn that the land occupied by each of the three nations — Edom, Moab and Amon — had been granted them by God as an eternal inheritance, and that the Israelites were in no way allowed to encroach upon it. Yehoshaphat mentions this point in order to underline the ingratitude and wickedness of these three nations. Israel had meticulously respected their rights and now, with no regard to this, they were repaying good with evil (*Mefaresh, Metzudos*).

If so, Yehoshaphat may well have argued Surely justice demanded that Israel, direct children of Abraham (v. 7), should not be driven from their inheritance.

11. וְהִנֵּה־הֵם גֹּמְלִים עָלֵינוּ — *Now, behold, they are requiting us.* The root גמל occurs in Scripture in two different senses. It can mean *to repay* or *recompense* with evil [see, for example *Psalms*, 7:5] and in such cases *Targum* renders it פרע, *to pay*. It is also used in the sense *to act badly toward someone* [see, for example, *Genesis* 50:15] and in such cases *Targum* retains the Hebrew, גמל.

Here, *Targum* renders פרע, and that is the

יב הוֹרַשְׁתָּנוּ: אֱלֹהֵינוּ הֲלֹא תִשְׁפָּט־בָּם כִּי אֵין בָּנוּ כֹּחַ לִפְנֵי
הֶהָמוֹן הָרָב הַזֶּה הַבָּא עָלֵינוּ וַאֲנַחְנוּ לֹא נֵדַע מַה־נַּעֲשֶׂה
יג כִּי עָלֶיךָ עֵינֵינוּ: וְכָל־יְהוּדָה עֹמְדִים לִפְנֵי יְהוָה גַּם־טַפָּם
יד נְשֵׁיהֶם וּבְנֵיהֶם: וְיַחֲזִיאֵל בֶּן־זְכַרְיָהוּ בֶּן־בְּנָיָה
בֶּן־יְעִיאֵל בֶּן־מַתַּנְיָה הַלֵּוִי מִן־בְּנֵי אָסָף הָיְתָה עָלָיו רוּחַ
טו יְהוָה בְּתוֹךְ הַקָּהָל: וַיֹּאמֶר הַקְשִׁיבוּ כָל־יְהוּדָה וְיֹשְׁבֵי
יְרוּשָׁלַםִ וְהַמֶּלֶךְ יְהוֹשָׁפָט כֹּה־אָמַר יְהוָה לָכֶם אַתֶּם
אַל־תִּירְאוּ וְאַל־תֵּחַתּוּ מִפְּנֵי הֶהָמוֹן הָרָב הַזֶּה כִּי לֹא
טז לָכֶם הַמִּלְחָמָה כִּי לֵאלֹהִים: מָחָר רְדוּ עֲלֵיהֶם הִנָּם עֹלִים
בְּמַעֲלֵה הַצִּיץ וּמְצָאתֶם אֹתָם בְּסוֹף הַנַּחַל פְּנֵי מִדְבַּר
יז יְרוּאֵל: לֹא לָכֶם לְהִלָּחֵם בָּזֹאת הִתְיַצְּבוּ עִמְדוּ וּרְאוּ
אֶת־יְשׁוּעַת יְהוָה עִמָּכֶם יְהוּדָה וִירוּשָׁלַםִ אַל־תִּירְאוּ
יח וְאַל־תֵּחַתּוּ מָחָר צְאוּ לִפְנֵיהֶם וַיהוָה עִמָּכֶם: וַיִּקֹּד
יְהוֹשָׁפָט אַפַּיִם אַרְצָה וְכָל־יְהוּדָה וְיֹשְׁבֵי יְרוּשָׁלַםִ נָפְלוּ

sense taken by the commentators. The three nations are taken to task for repaying good with evil (*Mefaresh, Metzudos*).

12. הֲלֹא תִשְׁפָּט־בָּם — *Will You not execute judgment upon them.* שפט can mean *to decide a controversy* or *discriminate between people*, or it can mean *to condemn* or *mete out a punishment*. In the first usage it goes together with בֵּין ... לְבֵין or with ... לְ ... בֵּין, and in the second usage it takes the accusative את. Its use with the prefix ב as in our phrase is unique and thus we can judge the meaning only from the context.

Targum renders with פרע, hence, *to punish*. For repaying good with evil, these nations deserve to be punished.

כִּי אֵין בָּנוּ כֹּחַ — *For we have no strength.* See fn. to 13:15 for *Eichah Rabbasi's* analysis of the attitudes of the four kings — David, Asa, Yehoshaphat and Chizkiahu — towards the wars which they were called upon to fight. In contrast to David who was willing to pursue and kill his enemies, and Asa who was at least willing to pursue them, Yehoshaphat has no *strength* to do either. He will pray but not get physically involved.

[It should be noted that this was not Yehoshaphat's practice in all the wars which he fought. Both in his alliance with Ahab and later with Ahab's son Yehoram he seems to have been perfectly willing to fight. His decision to remain absolutely passive must have derived from the particular nature of this war.]

וַאֲנַחְנוּ לֹא נֵדַע מַה־נַּעֲשֶׂה — *And we know not what we should do.* We do not know what steps we can take to save ourselves (*Metzudos*).

כִּי עָלֶיךָ עֵינֵינוּ — *For our eyes are upon You.* That You should help us and save us from their hands (*Mefaresh, Metzudos*).

13. גַּם־טַפָּם נְשֵׁיהֶם וּבְנֵיהֶם — *Even their little ones, wives and children.* טַף here is from טפף, *to take tripping, dancing steps* (*Radak, Shorashim*); thus, *little ones* who walk in a childish way. In *Ezekiel* 9:6 we have טַף in addition to בָּחוּר וּבְתוּלָה, which could well be the intent of בְּנֵיהֶם here and וּבְנֵיהֶם וּבְנוֹתֵיהֶם at 31:18. We conclude that טַפָּם are the younger and בְּנֵיהֶם, the older children.

14. בְּתוֹךְ הַקָּהָל — *In the midst of the congregation.* He stood among the people (*Metzudos*).

15. כִּי לֹא לָכֶם הַמִּלְחָמָה כִּי לֵאלֹהִים — *For the battle is not yours, but God's.* The phrase recalls *Exodus* 14:14 where, at the banks of the Red Sea, God told Israel that He would do battle for them — they were to remain silent.

In *Psalms* 83:3-4 we read: *For behold, Your foes are in an uproar and those who hate You have raised their head. Against Your nation they plot deviously, they take counsel against those whom You protect.* God has foes and those who hate Him. To fight Him they must unleash their wrath against the locus of His Divine Presence on earth — His people. Enemies of Israel are enemies of God, particu-

inheritance which You have granted us. [12] *O our God, will You*
not execute judgment upon them, for we have no strength before
this great multitude which comes against us and we know not
what we should do, for our eyes are upon You.' [13] *All Judah was*
standing before HASHEM, *even their little ones, wives and chil-*
dren. [14] *Then, upon Yachaziel son of Zechariahu, son of Benaiah,*
son of Yeiel, son of Mattaniah, the Levite of the sons of Asaph,
came the spirit of HASHEM *in the midst of the congregation.* [15] *He*
said, "Hearken, all Judah and inhabitants of Jerusalem and King
Yehoshaphat: Thus says HASHEM *to you: 'Fear not, nor be*
dismayed by reason of this great multitude, for the battle is not
yours, but God's. [16] *Go down against them tomorrow. Behold, they*
are coming up by the ascent to Hatzitz and you shall find them at
the end of the valley, before the wilderness of Yeru'el. [17] *It is not*
your obligation to do battle in this matter. Stand ready, be still
and see how God will save you, O Judah and Jerusalem. Do not be
afraid nor be dismayed. Tomorrow go out against them; HASHEM
is with you.' " [18] *Yehoshaphat bowed down with his face to the*
ground and all Judah and the dwellers in Jerusalem fell before

larly as in our case, enemies bent on wiping out the entire people. God recognizes Himself as the focus for this animosity and shoulders the responsibility for waging the battle. See comm. to v. 1.

16. הִנָּם עֹלִים בְּמַעֲלֵה הַצִּיץ — *Behold, they are coming up by the ascent to Hatzitz.* Even now they are climbing up the ascent so that by tomorrow they will be at the end of the valley near the desert of Yeru'el (*Metzudos*).

The name ציץ or הַצִּיץ does not occur elsewhere. *Targum* does not treat it as a proper noun but renders מסקנא דאודיקות. דק is the word with which the *Targumim* normally render words meaning *to look* or *gaze*. *Targum* evidently takes הַצִּיץ as deriving from the root צוץ, *to gaze* or *peek*, thus some kind of look-out point.

By telling the people precisely what to expect, the fear of the unknown would be mitigated (*Metzudos*).

17. לֹא לָכֶם לְהִלָּחֵם בָּזֹאת — *It is not your obligation to do battle in this matter.* See our analysis in comm. to v. 1.

הִתְיַצְּבוּ — *Stand ready. Hirsch* to *Exodus* 14:13 renders *stand ready*, and paraphrases ... *place yourselves expectantly there ... the one and only activity that such a critical moment demands of us is an internal one.* הִתְיַצֵּב — יצב, with the harsher, more emphasized צ sound — *to bring oneself to a state of calm, a mood of quietly standing and waiting.*

18. וַיִּקֹּד יְהוֹשָׁפָט אַפַּיִם אַרְצָה — *Yehoshaphat bowed down with his face to the ground.* What sentiment was Yehoshaphat expressing with His obeisance?

Of the fifteen times that יקד occurs in Scripture, most express gratitude [*Genesis* 24:26, 48; *Exodus* 12:27, 34:8, 41:31; *I Samuel* 28:14, *I Kings* 1:31; *I Chronicles* 29:20; *II Chronicles* 29:30]; some, awe [*Numbers* 22:4; *I Samuel* 24:9, *I Kings* 1:16, *Nehemiah* 8:6] and in one case the meaning is not clear [*Genesis* 43:28].

There is thus, at least, a presumption that Yehoshaphat was expressing thanks to God.

But is thanks in place before the promise is fulfilled?

V. 19 seems to answer in the affirmative. Even before the dawning of the next day, when they are to meet up with the enemy, the Levites are already singing songs of praise to God. On the next day the choristers continue with their song (v. 21) and it was to be those very songs of praise which precipitated the slaughter, spelling the final downfall of the three aggressors (v. 22).

Happy are the people for whom God's benign intercession is a foregone conclusion; happy are the people for whom the absolute certainty that their prayers — offered with earnest humility — will be answered, makes the technical question of the when and where

יט לִפְנֵי יהוה לְהִשְׁתַּחֲוֹת לַיהוָה: וַיָּקֻמוּ הַלְוִיִּם מִן־בְּנֵי
הַקְּהָתִים וּמִן־בְּנֵי הַקָּרְחִים לְהַלֵּל לַיהוה אֱלֹהֵי יִשְׂרָאֵל
כ בְּקוֹל גָּדוֹל לְמָעְלָה: וַיַּשְׁכִּימוּ בַבֹּקֶר וַיֵּצְאוּ לְמִדְבַּר תְּקוֹעַ
וּבְצֵאתָם עָמַד יְהוֹשָׁפָט וַיֹּאמֶר שְׁמָעוּנִי יְהוּדָה וְיֹשְׁבֵי
יְרוּשָׁלִַם הַאֲמִינוּ בַּיהוָה אֱלֹהֵיכֶם וְתֵאָמֵנוּ הַאֲמִינוּ
כא בִנְבִיאָיו וְהַצְלִיחוּ: וַיִּוָּעַץ אֶל־הָעָם וַיַּעֲמֵד מְשֹׁרְרִים
לַיהוָה וּמְהַלְלִים לְהַדְרַת־קֹדֶשׁ בְּצֵאת לִפְנֵי הֶחָלוּץ
כב וְאֹמְרִים הוֹדוּ לַיהוָה כִּי לְעוֹלָם חַסְדּוֹ: וּבְעֵת הֵחֵלּוּ
בְרִנָּה וּתְהִלָּה נָתַן יהוה ׀ מְאָרְבִים עַל־בְּנֵי עַמּוֹן מוֹאָב
כג וְהַר־שֵׂעִיר הַבָּאִים לִיהוּדָה וַיִּנָּגֵפוּ: וַיַּעַמְדוּ בְּנֵי עַמּוֹן
וּמוֹאָב עַל־יֹשְׁבֵי הַר־שֵׂעִיר לְהַחֲרִים וּלְהַשְׁמִיד וּכְכַלּוֹתָם

of no significance. Happy are they, whose song of jubilation need not wait for the salvation to become concrete.

Such absolute trust in God's goodness was woven into the very fiber of Israel's being from the earliest moment of their history. When Israel stood in fear for their very lives on the banks of the Sea of Reeds, they turned to Moses in consternation: Under such circumstances, what were they called upon to do? *Mechilta B'Shalach* 2 has Moses' answer: *Do you offer praise and exaltation, song, adoration and glory to Him Who will decide the outcome of this confrontation!* Immediately Israel began its song of jubilation (*R' Yitzchak Levi*, in an article discussing the reign of Yehoshaphat in *HaMaayan, Nissan* 5743).

19. מִן־בְּנֵי הַקְּהָתִים וּמִן־בְּנֵי הַקָּרְחִים — *Of the children of the Kehathites and the children of the Korachites*. Levi's son, Kehath, headed one of the three Levite branches. See *I Chronicles* 6:7.

20. לְמִדְבַּר תְּקוֹעַ — *To the wilderness of Tekoa.* Tekoa is a Judaean city which Rechav'am had built up (11:6). Previously (v. 16), the enemy had been located in the wilderness of Yeru'el. Perhaps our phrase describes a part of that wilderness which lay in the vicinity of the city of Tekoa.

הַאֲמִינוּ ... וְתֵאָמֵנוּ — *Believe ... and thus will you prove yourselves loyal.* We have rendered this difficult phrase according to *Radak*. אמן, *to confirm* or *support*, often describes loyalty or faithfulness when used in the *niphal*, passive tense, cf. *I Samuel* 2:35.

אמן can also mean *to be made firm*, *sure* or *lasting*, thus: Believe ... so that you will be firmly established (*Metzudos*).

אמן can also be used to describe the fulfillment of a promise — cf. *I Kings* 8:26. Thus: Believe ... so that the promises [made to you by God] will be fulfilled (*Malbim*).

הַאֲמִינוּ בִנְבִיאָיו — *Trust His prophets*. Make no attempt to defend yourselves or to attack the enemy. Trust the prophecy which placed this battle entirely in God's hands (*Malbim*).

21. וַיִּוָּעַץ — *He considered the people's needs carefully*. יעץ in the *niphal* normally means *to seek advice* or *to take counsel*; cf. 10:6. But usually it occurs, as it does there, together with the preposition אֶת, *with*. It is used with אֶל only here and in *II Kings* 6:5.

Now, if we assume the regular meaning and take אֶל to carry the same connotation as אֶת, we still do not know in what matter he took counsel with the people. The phrase seems to teach us nothing at all.

However, the *Kings'* passage clearly uses the word in the sense *to consider* carefully. This would be the meaning here, too. He thought out carefully how he might best inspire the people to the kind of faith which would be required of them if they were to be deserving of God's intervention. He concluded that the best way would be to inspire them with the songs of the choristers.

לְהַדְרַת־קֹדֶשׁ — *Majestic holiness*. See *I Chronicles* 16:29.

הֶחָלוּץ — *The army*. חלץ, *to equip for war*; thus, חָלוּץ, armed men who are ready and eager [see *Targum*, מזרזין] for war.

22. וּבְעֵת הֵחֵלּוּ בְרִנָּה וּתְהִלָּה — *When they*

HASHEM worshiping HASHEM. 19 *And the Levites of the children of*
the Kehathites and the children of the Korachites stood up to
praise HASHEM the God of Israel with an exceedingly loud voice.
20 *They rose early in the morning and went out to the wilderness*
of Tekoa. As they went out Yehoshaphat arose and said, 'Hear
me, O Judah and the dwellers of Jerusalem. Believe in HASHEM
your God and thus will you prove yourselves loyal; trust His pro-
phets and then will you succeed. 21 *He considered the people's*
needs carefully, and appointed choristers who sing to HASHEM,
those who sing ecstatic praises in awareness of majestic holiness,
as they step out at the head of the army, proclaiming: Praise HA-
SHEM, for His kindness endures forever. 22 *When they broke into*
song and jubilation, HASHEM placed an ambuscade against the
Amonites, Moab and Mount Seir who were coming against Ju-
dah, and they were smitten. 23 *The children of Amon and Moab*
rose up against the dwellers of Mount Seir utterly to annihilate

broke into song and jubilation. See fn. to 13:15 and comm. to v. 12, s.v. . . . כִּי.

Pesichta to *Eichah Rabbasi* 30 reads: . . . Yehoshaphat rose up and said, 'As for me I have strength neither to kill, nor to pursue. I shall sing songs of praise and, do You act!' God answered him, 'Thus will I do.' And so it is written: When they began to sing and to praise . . .

נָתַן ה׳ מְאָרְבִים — *HASHEM placed an ambuscade*. For מארב, see 13:13.

Who were these ambushers who were able to wreak such havoc among the invading army? They were not Jews, since Israel had been enjoined from engaging in any military activity. Were they other nations? How would these have penetrated deeply into Judah's territory in sufficient numbers to smite armies which were apparently sufficiently strong to have struck such fear into Yehoshaphat's heart? Even granting the element of surprise, it would seem that a huge force would be required to devastate three great armies. Where would such an army have come from?

Malbim paints the following scenario:

The three attacking nations were really enemies among themselves. They were only united in their hatred of Israel and in their desire to drive them from the land.

God's intervention took the form of making them forget their temporary amity, causing them to fight among themselves.

First, Moab formed an alliance with Edom and together they attacked Amon. Our verse is to be understood as follows: God placed an ambuscade against Amon. The ambuscade consisted of the Moabites and the Edomites.

[Although *Malbim* does not point to this, the *trop* of our verse seems to bear him out. There is a pause after בְּנֵי עַמּוֹן, which separates it from מוֹאָב וְהַר שֵׂעִיר, making the *Malbim's* interpretation possible. We have reflected this division in our translation.]

As a result of this ambuscade Amon was *smitten* [וַיִּנָּגֵפוּ], though not completely destroyed.

Moab then formed an alliance with what remained of the Amonites and the two nations turned against the Edomite army, utterly destroying it (v. 23).

Once this was accomplished, the Moabites and Amonites once more turned upon each other [עָזְרוּ אִישׁ־בְּרֵעֵהוּ לְמַשְׁחִית] until their ranks were so depleted that they ceased to exist as a coherent force.

The other commentators seem not to be troubled by the question which we have raised, and assume the ambuscade to have been directed upon all three attacking nations by unidentified forces. *Metzudos* is representative of this approach, and we shall continue the comm. based on his comments.

נָתַן ה׳ מְאָרְבִים — *HASHEM placed an ambuscade*. Unidentified forces were now instigated — through some form of Divine Providence to which we are not privy — to ambush the attacking army and to destroy it (*Metzudos*).

וַיִּנָּגֵפוּ — *And they were smitten*. They were badly hurt by the ambush and much weakened (*Metzudos*).

23. עַל־יֹשְׁבֵי הַר־שֵׂעִיר — *Against the dwellers of Mount Seir*. For reasons unspecified, Amon

כד בְּיוֹשְׁבֵי שֵׂעִיר עָזְרוּ אִישׁ בְּרֵעֵהוּ לְמַשְׁחִית׃ וִיהוּדָה בָּא
עַל־הַמִּצְפֶּה לַמִּדְבָּר וַיִּפְנוּ אֶל־הֶהָמוֹן וְהִנָּם פְּגָרִים
כה נֹפְלִים אַרְצָה וְאֵין פְּלֵיטָה׃ וַיָּבֹא יְהוֹשָׁפָט וְעַמּוֹ לָבֹז
אֶת־שְׁלָלָם וַיִּמְצְאוּ בָהֶם לָרֹב וּרְכוּשׁ וּפְגָרִים וּכְלֵי
חֲמֻדוֹת וַיְנַצְּלוּ לָהֶם לְאֵין מַשָּׂא וַיִּהְיוּ יָמִים שְׁלוֹשָׁה
כו בֹּזְזִים אֶת־הַשָּׁלָל כִּי רַב־הוּא׃ וּבַיּוֹם הָרְבִעִי נִקְהֲלוּ
לְעֵמֶק בְּרָכָה כִּי שָׁם בֵּרְכוּ אֶת־יהוה עַל־כֵּן קָרְאוּ
כז אֶת־שֵׁם הַמָּקוֹם הַהוּא עֵמֶק בְּרָכָה עַד־הַיּוֹם׃ וַיָּשֻׁבוּ
כָּל־אִישׁ יְהוּדָה וִירוּשָׁלִַם וִיהוֹשָׁפָט בְּרֹאשָׁם לָשׁוּב
כח אֶל־יְרוּשָׁלִַם בְּשִׂמְחָה כִּי־שִׂמְּחָם יהוה מֵאוֹיְבֵיהֶם׃ וַיָּבֹאוּ
יְרוּשָׁלִַם בִּנְבָלִים וּבְכִנֹּרוֹת וּבַחֲצֹצְרוֹת אֶל־בֵּית יהוה׃
כט וַיְהִי פַּחַד אֱלֹהִים עַל כָּל־מַמְלְכוֹת הָאֲרָצוֹת בְּשָׁמְעָם כִּי
ל נִלְחַם יהוה עִם אוֹיְבֵי יִשְׂרָאֵל׃ וַתִּשְׁקֹט מַלְכוּת יְהוֹשָׁפָט
לא וַיָּנַח לוֹ אֱלֹהָיו מִסָּבִיב׃ וַיִּמְלֹךְ יְהוֹשָׁפָט עַל־יְהוּדָה
בֶּן־שְׁלֹשִׁים וְחָמֵשׁ שָׁנָה בְּמָלְכוֹ וְעֶשְׂרִים וְחָמֵשׁ שָׁנָה
לב מָלַךְ בִּירוּשָׁלִַם וְשֵׁם אִמּוֹ עֲזוּבָה בַּת־שִׁלְחִי׃ וַיֵּלֶךְ בְּדֶרֶךְ
אָבִיו אָסָא וְלֹא־סָר מִמֶּנָּה לַעֲשׂוֹת הַיָּשָׁר בְּעֵינֵי יהוה׃

and Moab thought that the ambushers might have been Edomites. Accordingly, they now attacked their former ally (*Metzudos*).

עָזְרוּ אִישׁ בְּרֵעֵהוּ לְמַשְׁחִית — *Every man helped another to destroy*. The remaining soldiers formed constantly changing alliances with one another, in order to destroy a perceived enemy. There was constant internecine fighting among them until the armies were totally annihilated (*Metzudos*).

Ralbag thinks that the *help* mentioned here was, as it were, extended to Israel. The soldiers, by destroying each other, [אִישׁ בְּרֵעֵהוּ לְמַשְׁחִית] were really helping [עָזְרוּ] Israel.

24. עַל־הַמִּצְפֶּה לַמִּדְבָּר — *The watchtower to the desert*. צפה, to *look out* or *about*, *to watch*. Thus, מִצְפֶּה is a *watchtower*, a point from which to observe.

25. וַיָּבֹא יְהוֹשָׁפָט וְעַמּוֹ — *Yehoshaphat and his people came*. Egypt's treasure is about to return to Israel. See Section II to ch. 12, *Shishak's campaign*, and to ch. 17, *Yehoshaphat in Kings and Chronicles*.

וּפְגָרִים וּכְלֵי חֲמֻדוֹת — *And richly garbed dead bodies*. The translation follows *Malbim*.

וַיְנַצְּלוּ לָהֶם — *They collected*. נצל means *to empty out* (*Rashi* to *Exodus* 4:22). Lit: *They emptied out for themselves*.

26. לְעֵמֶק בְּרָכָה — *In Emek Berachah*. To the place which was given the name *Emek Berachah* because of the events described here (*Mefaresh*).

כִּי שָׁם בֵּרְכוּ אֶת־ה׳ — *Because it was there that they praised* HASHEM. *Radak* and *Ibn Janah* in their *Sefer HaShorashim* point out that ברך, which means *to bless* when God gives a בְּרָכָה to man, means *to praise* when man addresses a בְּרָכָה to God.

27. כִּי־שִׂמְּחָם ה׳ מֵאוֹיְבֵיהֶם — *Because* HASHEM *had granted them happiness in saving them from their enemies*. We have inserted the words, *in saving them*, into the text, in order to reflect *Metzudos'* understanding of the phrase.

29. כִּי נִלְחַם ה׳ עִם אוֹיְבֵי יִשְׂרָאֵל — *That* HASHEM *made war against Israel's foes*. See comm. to v. 15.

30. וַתִּשְׁקֹט מַלְכוּת יְהוֹשָׁפָט — *So the reign of Yehoshaphat was tranquil*. The first part of our verse tells that there was no internal strife (*Metzudos*); the second, that Yehoshaphat was also at peace with the neighboring nations.

and to destroy. When they had made an end of the dwellers of Seir, every man helped another to destroy. [24] *When Judah came to the watchtower to the desert, they looked upon the multitude and behold they were dead bodies fallen to the ground, and there were none that escaped.* [25] *Yehoshaphat and his people came to plunder their spoil and they found an abundance, riches, dead bodies with desirable clothes and they collected for themselves more then they could carry. They plundered the spoil for three days, it was so much.* [26] *On the fourth day they gathered in Emek Berachah because it was there that they praised* HASHEM, *therefore they called the name of that place Emek Berachah until this day.* [27] *Then all the men of Judah and Jerusalem set out to return joyously to Jerusalem with Yehoshaphat at their head, because* HASHEM *had granted them happiness in saving them from their enemies.* [28] *They came to Jerusalem with nebalim, harps and chatzotzros, to the House of* HASHEM. [29] *The fear of God came over all the kingdoms of the land when they heard that* HASHEM *made war against Israel's foes.* [30] *So the reign of Yehoshaphat was tranquil and* HASHEM *his God gave him rest from round about.* [31] *So Yehoshaphat ruled over Judah. He was thirty-five years old when he became king and ruled for twenty-five years in Jerusalem. His mother's name was Azuvah, the daughter of Shilchi.* [32] *He went in the path of his father, Asa, and did not turn aside from it to do that which was straight in the eyes of* HASHEM.

31-37. The general structure of this section is essentially the same as the passage in *I Kings* 22:41-51 which, as we saw in prefatory remarks to ch. 17, constitutes the entire space which *Kings* devotes to the description of Yehoshaphat's reign. It would appear as though, after *Chronicles* has completed its own account of Yehoshaphat's reign, presented as it is from its own unique perspective, it goes back to record also the assessment of the reign as it appears in the earlier book.[1] Nevertheless, as we shall see, changes are made to reflect the position of the passage in *Chronicles*.

32. וַיֵּלֶךְ בְּדֶרֶךְ אָבִיו אָסָא וְלֹא־סָר מִמֶּנָּה — *He went in the path of his father, Asa, and did not turn aside from it.* There are two apparently minor changes in this phrase from the form in which it appears in *Kings*. There, instead of וַיֵּלֶךְ בְּדֶרֶךְ, we have וַיֵּלֶךְ בְּכָל דֶּרֶךְ; and instead of מִמֶּנָּה, which treats דֶּרֶךְ as a feminine noun, we have מִמֶּנּוּ, in the masculine.

Perhaps the source of the difference lies in the way that Asa's reign was pictured in the two books. *Kings* records none of the strictures which appear in *Chronicles* and thus he is presented as an entirely righteous king. In contrast, the *Chronicles'* account contains serious reservations. We have offered explanation for these differing perspectives in comm. to ch. 16.

Thus, while in *Kings* the way of Asa is a perfect [masculine] one and every aspect of it

1. We have noted the constantly recurring formula: דִּבְרֵי . . . הָרִאשֹׁנִים וְהָאַחֲרוֹנִים, with which *Chronicles*, but never *Kings*, concludes many of the descriptions of the various reigns. In Section II to ch. 17, *Yehoshaphat Is Compared to David*, we suggested that since, as we have shown so often, the *Kings'* accounts tend to treat the events from the standpoint of the contemporary framework while *Chronicles* tends to go to the essence and place the occurrences into the perspective of eternity, it is possible that רִאשֹׁנִים refers to the perspective of the earlier books while אַחֲרוֹנִים has in mind the approach which *Chronicles* brings to the subject.

Given this, we can word the observation which we have made in the comm. thus: Besides giving us the דִּבְרֵי יְהוֹשָׁפָט הָאַחֲרוֹנִים, *Chronicles* also records the דִּבְרֵי יְהוֹשָׁפָט הָרִאשֹׁנִים. In this sense, Ezra would be paralleling the precedent of Yehu, son of Channani, as told in v. 34.

לג אַךְ הַבָּמוֹת לֹא־סָרוּ וְעוֹד הָעָם לֹא־הֵכִינוּ לְבָבָם לֵאלֹהֵי
לד אֲבֹתֵיהֶם: וְיֶתֶר דִּבְרֵי יְהוֹשָׁפָט הָרִאשֹׁנִים וְהָאַחֲרוֹנִים
הִנָּם כְּתוּבִים בְּדִבְרֵי יֵהוּא בֶן־חֲנָנִי אֲשֶׁר הֹעֲלָה עַל־סֵפֶר
לה מַלְכֵי יִשְׂרָאֵל: וְאַחֲרֵי־כֵן אֶתְחַבַּר יְהוֹשָׁפָט מֶלֶךְ־יְהוּדָה
לו עִם אֲחַזְיָה מֶלֶךְ־יִשְׂרָאֵל הוּא הִרְשִׁיעַ לַעֲשׂוֹת: וַיְחַבְּרֵהוּ

[כָּל] is worthy of emulation, this is not so in the *Chronicles'* perspective. The way of Asa lacks power and conviction [feminine], and the righteous Yehoshaphat follows it only in a general way.

33. אַךְ ... וְעוֹד הָעָם לֹא־הֵכִינוּ לְבָבָם — *However ... thus the people did not yet set their hearts ...* After the phrase, אַךְ הַבָּמוֹת לֹא־סָרוּ, the text in *Kings* goes on: עוֹד הָעָם מְזַבְּחִים וּמְקַטְּרִים בַּבָּמוֹת ; a standard formulation in *Kings* [1:22:44; 2:12:4; 2:14:4; 2:15:4 and 35] which never occurs in *Chronicles*. For an analysis of the *Chronicles'* approach see Section II, *Bamos in Kings and Chronicles*. See there, too, for our translation, ... *thus the people ....*

34. הָרִאשֹׁנִים וְהָאַחֲרוֹנִים — *The earlier and the later*. See fn. 31-37 above.

בְּדִבְרֵי יֵהוּא בֶן־חֲנָנִי — *In the words of Yehu son of Channani*. Yehu was the seer who castigated Yehoshaphat upon his return from the war in which he was allied with Ahab (19:2) (*Mefaresh*).

See comm. and fig. 1 at 12:15.

אֲשֶׁר הֹעֲלָה עַל־סֵפֶר מַלְכֵי יִשְׂרָאֵל — *Which were inserted in the Book of the Kings of Israel*. Yehoshaphat was king of Judah; we would not have expected his history to be written in the chronicles of the kings of Israel. Our verse tells us that they were inserted in the *Book of the Kings of Israel*. [העלה is in the *hophal*, the passive causative of עלה, *to go up*. Thus, *to be taken up*, *to be dealt with*, or *to be inserted*.] Perhaps the chronicles of the kings of Israel were considered an appropriate place to preserve these records because of the many contacts which Yehoshaphat had had with the kings of the North.

Malbim reads the verse as though it were written וַאֲשֶׁר. The details of Yehoshaphat's reign were preserved in two places: In the records which Yehu kept of the kings of Judah; and *also* in the records of the kings of Israel. There, those incidents in which Yehoshaphat's life touched upon the affairs of the Northern Kingdom are recorded.

◆§ Another Alliance

35. וְאַחֲרֵי־כֵן — *After that* ... In Section II, *Two Moabite Wars*, we discussed in which period of Yehoshaphat's reign the war with Moab took place. We saw that our verse has much to do with this. If *after that* means after the war described above, then obviously that war must have occurred during Achaziah's reign or earlier.

But, we saw that the simple reading of *Seder Olam* yields that the war took place towards the very end of Yehoshaphat's reign, long after the abortive maritime partnership with Achaziah. How, then, are we to understand the words *after that*?

We suggest the following solution:

The incident of the partnership in the matter of the ships is also told in *Kings*. However, the two accounts take up different aspects of the same story, and rather than the *Chronicles'* account being a repetition of the other, it appears to contain more; i.e., a filling in of details.

To demonstrate the relationship, we place the two next to one another (see comparison table next page).

By combining the two accounts, the following sequence emerges: Yehoshaphat makes a partnership with Achaziah to build the ships. A prophet castigates him for joining with the wicked king and predicts that the ships will break up, which they did. Achaziah then approaches Yehoshaphat with the idea that, at least, the sailors of the two nations should get together on some other ships, and Yehoshaphat turns down that suggestion.

However, as can be seen from the chart the two accounts augment one another but neither tells the whole story. The impression is strong that the *Chronicles'* account is supplying details which are missing from *Kings*.

The explanation may be as follows: In a fn. to 13:2, we made the suggestion that details of a reign which appear in *Kings* after the concluding sentence *The remaining matters of ... are written ...* are not a part of the prophetic account of the reign but are significant pieces of information which Jeremiah,

20
33-36

33 *However, the bamos were not eliminated, thus the people did not set their hearts to the God of their fathers.* 34 *The rest of Yehoshaphat's affairs, the earlier and the late are recorded in the words of Yehu son of Chanani which were inserted in the Book of the Kings of Israel.* 35 *After that Yehoshaphat, king of Judah, joined with Achaziah, king of Israel who acted wickedly.* 36 *He*

Chronicles	*Kings*
a. וְאַחֲרֵי־כֵן אֶתְחַבַּר יְהוֹשָׁפָט מֶלֶךְ־יְהוּדָה עִם אֲחַזְיָה מֶלֶךְ־יִשְׂרָאֵל הוּא הִרְשִׁיעַ לַעֲשׂוֹת — *After that Yehoshaphat king of Judah, joined Achaziah king of Israel, who acted wickedly.*	a.
b. וַיְחַבְּרֵהוּ עִמּוֹ לַעֲשׂוֹת אֳנִיּוֹת לָלֶכֶת תַּרְשִׁישׁ וַיַּעֲשׂוּ אֳנִיּוֹת בְּעֶצְיוֹן גָּבֶר — *He elicited his cooperation to manufacture ships to go to Tarshish. They made these ships at Etzion Gaver.*	b. יְהוֹשָׁפָט עָשָׂה אֳנִיּוֹת תַּרְשִׁישׁ לָלֶכֶת אוֹפִירָה לַזָּהָב — *Yehoshaphat manufactured Tarshish ships, so that he might go to Ophir for gold.*
c. וַיִּתְנַבֵּא אֱלִיעֶזֶר ... עַל־יְהוֹשָׁפָט ... כְּהִתְחַבֶּרְךָ עִם־אֲחַזְיָהוּ פָּרַץ ה׳ אֶת־מַעֲשֶׂיךָ — *Eliezer prophesied ... concerning Yehoshaphat ... When you joined with Achaziah, HASHEM frustrated your actions.*	c.
d. וַיִּשָּׁבְרוּ אֳנִיּוֹת וְלֹא עָצְרוּ לָלֶכֶת אֶל־תַּרְשִׁישׁ — *So the ships foundered and they were not able to go to Tarshish.*	d. וְלֹא הָלָךְ כִּי־נִשְׁבְּרוּ אֳנִיּוֹת בְּעֶצְיוֹן גָּבֶר — *But he did not go, for his ships foundered at Etzion Gaver.*
e.	e. אָז אָמַר אֲחַזְיָהוּ ... יֵלְכוּ עֲבָדַי עִם־עֲבָדֶיךָ בָּאֳנִיּוֹת וְלֹא אָבָה יְהוֹשָׁפָט — *Then Achaziah suggested ... 'Let my servants go with yours in ships.' But Yehoshaphat did not want.*

the writer of *Kings*, gleaned from available sources and considered important enough to add to his own prophetic description.

If so, it seems possible that in the sources available to Jeremiah not all the information was given, but that *Chronicles* had access to the missing details.

In that case, then the opening words *after that* ... may belong to the source from which *Chronicles* is quoting, and have no bearing at all on the war described in our chapter. It could, for example, go back to the description of Yehoshaphat's action against the prostitutes told in the section we are dealing with in *Kings* (v. 47), but not mentioned at all in *Chronicles*.

We may add that, as noted in prefatory remarks 31-37, this entire section does not seem to be an organic part of the *Chronicles* account, rather a paraphrase of the *Kings'* account. Hence, the words *after that* would not refer to the war described here, but must somehow — perhaps as we suggested — be accommodated within the given of the *Kings'* account.

Metzudos (v. 37) suggests that there may have been two separate occasions at which a partnership was formed.

אֶתְחַבַּר יְהוֹשָׁפָט — *Yehoshaphat ... joined*. The א in אֶתְחַבַּר is irregular and takes the place of the more usual ה (*Radak*).

אֶתְחַבַּר יְהוֹשָׁפָט ... עִם אֲחַזְיָה ... הוּא הִרְשִׁיעַ — *Yehoshaphat ... joined with Achaziah ... who acted wickedly*. The fact that Achaziah, the son of Ahab was a wicked king (*I Kings* 22:53) did not prevent Yehoshaphat from going into partnership with him (*Metzudos*). For a discussion see fn. to 19:2.

כ עִמּוֹ לַעֲשׂוֹת אֳנִיּוֹת לָלֶכֶת תַּרְשִׁישׁ וַיַּעֲשׂוּ אֳנִיּוֹת בְּעֶצְיוֹן
לז לז גָּבֶר: וַיִּתְנַבֵּא אֱלִיעֶזֶר בֶּן־דֹּדָוָהוּ מִמָּרֵשָׁה
עַל־יְהוֹשָׁפָט לֵאמֹר כְּהִתְחַבֶּרְךָ עִם־אֲחַזְיָהוּ פָּרַץ יהוה
אֶת־מַעֲשֶׂיךָ וַיִּשָּׁבְרוּ אֳנִיּוֹת וְלֹא עָצְרוּ לָלֶכֶת אֶל־
כא א תַּרְשִׁישׁ: וַיִּשְׁכַּב יְהוֹשָׁפָט עִם־אֲבֹתָיו וַיִּקָּבֵר עִם־אֲבֹתָיו
א־ד ב בְּעִיר דָּוִיד וַיִּמְלֹךְ יְהוֹרָם בְּנוֹ תַּחְתָּיו: וְלוֹ־אַחִים בְּנֵי
יְהוֹשָׁפָט עֲזַרְיָה וִיחִיאֵל וּזְכַרְיָהוּ וַעֲזַרְיָהוּ וּמִיכָאֵל
ג וּשְׁפַטְיָהוּ כָּל־אֵלֶּה בְּנֵי יְהוֹשָׁפָט מֶלֶךְ־יִשְׂרָאֵל: וַיִּתֵּן לָהֶם
| אֲבִיהֶם מַתָּנוֹת רַבּוֹת לְכֶסֶף וּלְזָהָב וּלְמִגְדָּנוֹת עִם־עָרֵי
מְצֻרוֹת בִּיהוּדָה וְאֶת־הַמַּמְלָכָה נָתַן לִיהוֹרָם כִּי־הוּא
ד הַבְּכוֹר: וַיָּקָם יְהוֹרָם עַל־מַמְלֶכֶת אָבִיו וַיִּתְחַזַּק

36. וַיְחַבְּרֵהוּ עִמּוֹ — *He elicited his cooperation.* The initiative for the joint venture apparently came from Yehoshaphat (*Metzudos*). Perhaps Yehoshaphat thought that since, under these circumstances, he was in control, this would not be considered *joining with the wicked*. In any event, he erred, as Eliezer told him in the next verse.

37. וְלֹא עָצְרוּ — *Were not able.* עצר means *to restrain* or *retain*. Together with כח, it is an idiom describing *ability* and occurs only in *Chronicles* and *Daniel*. Here, the word כח must be supplied by the reader (*Radak*).

XXI

With Yehoshaphat's death and his son Yehoram's ascension to the throne, a dark period descended over the kingdom of Judah. The high hopes raised during Yehoshaphat's benign rule were dashed. There would still be some wise and good rulers but, taken as a whole, the monarchy would move from impotence to outright wickedness, in an irreversible, depressing spiral. In the end, Solomon's Temple will lie in ruins, and the royal house of David will have become no more than a memory and a hope — not to be re-established until Messianic times.

1. וַיִּשְׁכַּב יְהוֹשָׁפָט עִם־אֲבֹתָיו — *Yehoshaphat lay with his fathers...* The information that a given king died, was buried in such and such a place and was succeeded by his son — given in this verse — is standard in the case of most kings. These three points are usually followed by three more: the age of the new king at the time that he ascended the throne, the duration of his reign and his mother's name. The first two of these three [but not the name of Yehoram's mother — see comm. there] are given in v. 5.

The almost universal structure of this formula which, for Yehoram, is followed in *II Kings* 8:16-17, makes it apparent that vs. 1 and 5 of our chapter are really one continuum and that vs. 2-4 contain information which is parenthetical. The import of this information — which is not given in the *Kings* account — will be discussed in comm. to those verses.

2-4. Yehoshaphat had a number of sons besides Yehoram. He showered these with gifts, but made his firstborn Yehoram heir to the throne. Subsequently, Yehoram murdered all his brothers — perhaps in order to consolidate his kingship by eliminating potential rivals; perhaps to silence their criticism of his evil ways (Commentators to v. 4, see below).

Why is this passage, not included in the *Kings'* account, significant in *Chronicles*? When did the events described here occur?

We shall attempt to solve the latter question in the comm. to the respective verses and come back to the first question after we have done so.

2. בְּנֵי יְהוֹשָׁפָט מֶלֶךְ־יִשְׂרָאֵל — *The sons of Yehoshaphat, king of Israel.*

Since *Israel* usually describes the Northern Kingdom as opposed to Judah, we would have expected Yehoshaphat to be described as king of *Judah*.

20 37 *elicited his cooperation to build ships that they might travel to Tarsis. They built the ships at Etzion Gaver.* [37] *Then Eliezer, son of Dodavahu from Mareishah prophesised against Yehoshaphat saying, 'As you joined with Achaziah,* HASHEM *has made your activities unsuccessful. So the ships foundered and were not able to travel to Tarsis.*

21 1-4 *Yehoshaphat lay with his fathers and was buried with his fathers in the City of David. Yehoram his son reigned in his stead.* [2] *He had brothers, the sons of Yehoshaphat, Azariah, Yechiel, Zechariahu, Azariahu, Michael and Shaphatiahu; all these were the sons of Yehoshaphat, king of Israel.* [3] *Their father gave them many gifts, silver, gold and peerless objects together with fortified cities in Judah. But the kingship he gave to Yehoram for he was the first-born.* [4] *Yehoram took control of his father's*

In addition to the explanation offered at 17:1, we may note that the use of the term *Israel* seems somewhat elastic — see, for example, 12:6, 23:2 and 28:19.

Nevertheless it seems strange that the unusual title *king of Israel* should be used here for no apparent reason.

If, as suggested in comm. to v. 1, vs. 2-4 are an artificial insertion between vs. 1 and 5 which, as part of a formula, belong together, we may surmise as follows: The source from which *Chronicles* drew the information concerning Yehoram's brothers [perhaps the *Chronicles of the Kings of Judah* which record the details of Yehoram's reign not recorded in *Kings*], may well have been using the term *Israel* consistently to describe the Southern Kingdom. This would be indicated by v. 4 where Yehoram kills not only his brothers but also the *princes of Israel* which by context would seem to refer to Judah. When *Chronicles*, for reasons of its own, imports this information into its own account of the reign, it leaves the original language intact.

3. **וּלְמִגְדָּנוֹת** — *And peerless objects.* The word describes that which is the very best in any given category, such as fruits, clothes or precious stones (*Radak, Sefer HaShorashim* and *Metzudos*).

וְאֶת־הַמַּמְלָכָה נָתַן לִיהוֹרָם — *But the kingship he gave to Yehoram* ... What does *giving the kingship* mean, and when did this take place?

V. 4 seems to indicate that this took place during Yehoshaphat's lifetime. We read *Yehoram took control of his father's kingship and strengthened himself*. Now the term וַיִּתְחַזֵּק is used frequently in *Chronicles* to describe a king establishing firmly his role as ruler. For example, at 1:1 we read: *Solomon, son of David, strengthened himself over his kingdom*. But it is *his* kingdom — not his father's. It is only in our verse that *his father's kingship* is used. The implication seems clear: Yehoram became king during his father's lifetime and it is *his father's kingship* which he took over. Yehoshaphat gave Yehoram the kingship at the same time that he gave the precious gifts to his other sons — during his own lifetime.

Whether upon his ascension to the throne in his father's lifetime Yehoram exercised full authority, or he ruled in conjunction with Yehoshaphat is a moot question. There are some commentators who believe that v. 5, which dates the beginning of Yehoram's reign, refers to his assumption of the kingship after his father's death. Apparently, his earlier appointment had been a limited one.

כִּי־הוּא הַבְּכוֹר — *For he was the first-born.*

Kesubos 103b teaches that the mere fact that Yehoram was the first born would not in itself have been sufficient to entitle him to the kingship. It is also required that he be a worthy successor to his father in both wisdom and fear of God. [See *Rambam, Melachim* 1:7. See also *Maharshah, P'nei Yehoshua* and *RaShash* there.] This is problematic inasmuch as Yehoram was manifestly not his father's equal in these matters — on the contrary, Yehoshaphat was among the most righteous

ה וַיַּהֲרֹג אֶת־כָּל־אֶחָיו בֶּחָרֶב וְגַם מִשָּׂרֵי יִשְׂרָאֵל׃ בֶּן־
שְׁלֹשִׁים וּשְׁתַּיִם שָׁנָה יְהוֹרָם בְּמָלְכוֹ וּשְׁמוֹנֶה שָׁנִים מָלַךְ
ו בִּירוּשָׁלָ͏ִם׃ וַיֵּלֶךְ בְּדֶרֶךְ ׀ מַלְכֵי יִשְׂרָאֵל כַּאֲשֶׁר עָשׂוּ בֵּית
אַחְאָב כִּי בַּת־אַחְאָב הָיְתָה לּוֹ אִשָּׁה וַיַּעַשׂ הָרַע בְּעֵינֵי
ז יהוה׃ וְלֹא־אָבָה יהוה לְהַשְׁחִית אֶת־בֵּית דָּוִיד לְמַעַן
הַבְּרִית אֲשֶׁר כָּרַת לְדָוִיד וְכַאֲשֶׁר אָמַר לָתֵת לוֹ נִיר

kings; Yehoram among the most wicked. *Tosafos Yeshanim* to *K'risus* ch. 1 suggests that Yehoram's wickedness developed only later. At the time of his appointment, he was still righteous. *Maharshah* adds that he only became wicked after his father's death.

This seems, indeed, to be borne out by *Seder Olam* ch. 17 according to which the assassination of the brothers took place only after Yehoshaphat's death [although there is no apparent indication of this in the text].

It is also possible that Yehoram may always have been as wicked as his later acts proved him to be. *Kesubos* does not mean that he actually was a worthy successor to his father but that he merely appeared to be so. Outwardly, he comported himself in an exemplary fashion. It was only after he came to power that his true nature became apparent. [See further in comm. to v. 15.]

4. וַיָּקָם יְהוֹרָם עַל־מַמְלֶכֶת אָבִיו — *Yehoram took control of his father's kingship*. See comm. to v. 3. The wording implies that Yehoram became king during his father's lifetime. This fact which is explicated here [מַמְלֶכֶת אָבִיו] is only hinted at in *Kings*. Perhaps it was deemed particularly significant in *Chronicles* where an issue is made of the fact that Yehoram too, because of the terrible illness which felled him, was unable to complete his reign, and lost his kingship to his son while he was yet alive — see comm. to 22:1. The operative principle would be מִדָּה כְּנֶגֶד מִדָּה, *the punishment tailored to the crime*. Because Yehoram had misused the opportunity granted him by Yehoshaphat's early abdication, he too lost his kingship earlier than he might otherwise have.

וַיַּהֲרֹג אֶת־כָּל־אֶחָיו — *He killed all his brothers*.

He may have killed them in order to quash any incipient rebellion (*Metzudos*) or because they protested against the evil ways upon which he was embarking (*Malbim*).

As noted above, *Kings* omits the entire incident. It appears to be significant only in the *Chronicles'* account, because it constitutes the first step in the systematic wiping out of the Davidic line of succession — later to be almost completed by Yehu's depredations (22:8) and the murders undertaken by Athaliah (v. 10 there) — which *Kings*, as will be explained in ch. 22, does not include.

5. בֶּן־שְׁלֹשִׁים וּשְׁתַּיִם שָׁנָה יְהוֹרָם בְּמָלְכוֹ — *Yehoram was thirty-two years old when he became king*. With this phrase, which is the second half of the standard formulation begun in v. 1, the thread of the narrative is picked up.

There is a noteworthy omission here. In the case of every other king, with the exception only of Achaz, the mother's name is given at this point in the standard formulation.

Why are we not told the name of Yehoram's mother?

In Section II to ch. 17, *Yehoshaphat Is Compared to David*, and in comm. to 18:1 we noted that, according to tradition, Yehoshaphat had married a daughter of the wicked Israelite king Omri. The link forged with the royal house of the Northern Kingdom by this marriage and by that of Yehoram to Ahab's daughter was to wreak untold havoc in the Davidic line — see at 22:2. Nevertheless, this marriage is not even hinted at in *Kings*, and in *Chronicles* we have only the merest of hints. Reference to this ill-fated marriage seems to have been purposely eliminated. In our passage, Yehoram's mother is not mentioned at all, and Yehoram's wickedness is laid to the door of his wife (*II Kings* 8:18 v. 6 here) and not to his mother.

The reason may be as follows: The woman whom Yehoshaphat married may well have been a God-fearing person of exemplary character. It is unlikely that the righteous Asa would have chosen any other for his great son Yehoshaphat. She may have exercised no pernicious influence at all and, on the contrary, to all outward appearances may have been a fitting wife and mother within the Davidic dynasty. The dreadful evil of this union which was to cause so much loss of life and to bring the entire dynasty to the brink of extinction lay not in the person of this woman but in her

kingship and strengthened himself. He killed all his brothers
by the sword and also some of the princes of Israel.
5 *Yehoram was thirty-two years old when he became king*
and ruled for eight years in Jerusalem. 6 *He went in the ways*
of the kings of Israel as the house of Ahab had done for
Ahab's daughter was his wife and he did evil in the eyes of
HASHEM. 7 *But HASHEM did not want to destroy the house of*
David because of the covenant which He had made with David
and as He had promised to grant him and his children kingship

lineage. That kings of the Davidic line could forget their unique standing to the extent of seeking alliance through marriage with the corrupt royalty of the Northern Kingdom was, in the profoundest sense, a betrayal of their destiny and carried within itself the seeds of the destruction of the entire line.

Thus, the significance of this marriage lies beneath the surface. It was in the nature of a vicious but unseen cancer which ate away at the moral fiber of the Davidic line. As such, its place is not in the open, explicated text. That is reserved for events which occurred in ways which anyone could see or apprehend (see fn. to *I Chronicles* 28:2.) Rather, the text contains oblique references which hint at a deep unperceived stratum of truth wherein the dynamics of the observable phenomena were grounded. In this way, the method by which Scripture conveys the truth reflects its reality. Until, as it were, the dam burst open in the unbridled evil of Yehoram and Achaziah — and later that of Athaliah — the stream of potential destruction ran beneath the ground, making its presence felt only in tiny ways — hints at what lay in the future.

If Scripture had mentioned Yehoram's mother, it would have had to identify her as Omri's daughter. Immediately, the question would arise as to why, in v. 6, Yehoram's evil ways are blamed on his wife and not on his mother. This, in turn, would have required that Scripture take a stand concerning her spiritual qualities.

The ambience of the entire section — as *Chronicles* wished to present it — was better served by eliminating any overt reference.

6. וַיַּעַשׂ הָרַע בְּעֵינֵי ה׳ — *And he did evil in the eyes of HASHEM*. The extent of the evil is explicated in v. 11 and can be gauged from v. 7 where we see that it was sufficiently great to raise the destruction of the Davidic line as a possibility. See below.

וְלֹא־אָבָה ה׳ לְהַשְׁחִית אֶת־בֵּית דָּוִיד — *But HASHEM did not want to destroy the house of David*. The implication is that, indeed, the house of David deserved destruction and that it was only God's covenant which prevented this.

But if Yehoram's sin was that *he went in the ways of the kings of Israel* . . . (v. 6), and these, at least for the moment, had not been destroyed, why was the *house of David* in greater danger?

The answer must surely lie in the more exalted mission of the Judean kings. As descendants of David and Solomon, it was they in whom Israel's Messianic destiny was grounded; it was they whose duty it was to nurture and guide their people to a national existence of sanctity and goodness, so that, by means of the Temple in their midst, they could be the locus of the Divine Presence on earth. If they did not rise to this mighty challenge, and allowed themselves to act like other kings whose destiny was not shaped by such a calling — then the entire justification of their being is eroded. They serve no more purpose and deserve to be destroyed.

Not so the kings of Israel. No such expectations existed for them and thus their failures were more bearable. Up to the time that their wickedness would *fill the measure* of Divine tolerance, they would be allowed to continue their empty and meaningless existence. See further in Section II, *God Will not Destroy the Davidic Line*.

נִיר — *Kingship*.

The base meaning of נִיר is *furrow*. From there, it is only a small step to *yoke*, since furrows are produced by the efforts of the oxen who are yoked to the plow. The yoke can easily be used as a metaphor for rulership (*Rashi*, *I Kings* 11:36).

Radak thinks that נִיר is to be understood as another form of נֵר, *a lamp*. The king, through the guidance which he gives his people, is much like a lamp which lights their path.

ח וּלְבָנָיו כָּל־הַיָּמִים: בְּיָמָיו פָּשַׁע אֱדוֹם מִתַּחַת יַד־יְהוּדָה
ט וַיַּמְלִיכוּ עֲלֵיהֶם מֶלֶךְ: וַיַּעֲבֹר יְהוֹרָם עִם־שָׂרָיו וְכָל־
הָרֶכֶב עִמּוֹ וַיְהִי קָם לַיְלָה וַיַּךְ אֶת־אֱדוֹם הַסּוֹבֵב אֵלָיו
י וְאֵת שָׂרֵי הָרֶכֶב: וַיִּפְשַׁע אֱדוֹם מִתַּחַת יַד־יְהוּדָה עַד
הַיּוֹם הַזֶּה אָז תִּפְשַׁע לִבְנָה בָּעֵת הַהִיא מִתַּחַת יָדוֹ כִּי
יא עָזַב אֶת־יהוה אֱלֹהֵי אֲבֹתָיו: גַּם־הוּא עָשָׂה בָמוֹת בְּהָרֵי
יב יְהוּדָה וַיֶּזֶן אֶת־יֹשְׁבֵי יְרוּשָׁלַםִ וַיַּדַּח אֶת־יְהוּדָה: וַיָּבֹא
אֵלָיו מִכְתָּב מֵאֵלִיָּהוּ הַנָּבִיא לֵאמֹר כֹּה ׀ אָמַר יהוה

8. בְּיָמָיו פָּשַׁע אֱדוֹם — *In his days Edom revolted.*

Even though God was not yet willing to destroy the house of David, the cracks in the edifice had begun to appear.

From the dawn of Jewish experience, when Rebecca had carried the twins in her womb and suffered from the mortal struggle in which they were engaged, history was to be defined in terms of the tension existing between the two poles of sanctity and depravity: between Jacob and Esau; between Israel and Edom.

Cesarea (Edom) and Jerusalem are to be the focuses of the two ideologies. If you hear that both are flourishing — do not believe it. When the one is in ascendancy the other must fall (see *Megillah* 6a). David had subjugated Edom and demonstrated unequivocally that God's presence rested in Israel. That era now comes to a close. It is the beginning of the end. [For an in-depth discussion see Section II to ch. 17, *Yehoshaphat in Kings and Chronicles*, and Section II to *I Chronicles*, *The Edomite war*, p. 449.]

פָּשַׁע — *Revolted.*

The translation follows *Targum* who renders with מרד, *to rebel*. For a similar usage, see above at 10:19.

9. וַיַּעֲבֹר יְהוֹרָם עִם־שָׂרָיו — *Yehoram crossed over with his officers. Kings* has *Yehoram crossed over to Tzair*. In our verse, the destination is not given.

Yehoram made a feeble attempt to crush the rebellion but, as the following verse indicates, he was not successful. His weakness manifested itself in two ways: He launched his attack at night, fearing to face the opposing army in daylight; and he engaged only those forces which were in his immediate vicinity [הַסּוֹבֵב אֵלָיו], and made no attempt to grapple with the main body of the Edomites (*Metzudos* and *Malbim*).

10. וַיִּפְשַׁע אֱדוֹם מִתַּחַת יַד־יְהוּדָה — *So Edom revolted from under the hand of Judah*. The *Mefaresh* wonders why this is repeated. It has already been told in v. 8. He suggests that *Chronicles* wanted to stress the association between the rebellion of Edom with that of Livnah. The insertion of v. 9 made it necessary to repeat the fact of Edom's rebellion.

It is also possible that v. 8 goes together with vs. 6 and 7, and is a description of the wickedness and futility of Yehoram's reign. It was he who brought Israel to such depths of degradation that Edom was able to extricate itself from Judah's control. Vs. 9 and 10 then tell the actual story of how this happened.

אָז תִּפְשַׁע לִבְנָה — *Then ... Livnah revolted.*

Rashi (*Kings*) wonders who these rebels were. He concludes that since Livnah was a city belonging to Judah, its inhabitants were presumably Israelites who were rebelling against their king. No motive is adduced. The explanation may be found in *Malbim's* understanding of the end of the verse. He takes the final phrase as supplying the motive. The people of Livnah were loyal to God and His Torah. They would not tolerate Yehoram's deviations.

When we consider the cosmic implications of the Edomite revolt, it seems incongruous, in the same context, to mention a small-scale rebellion of some of Yehoram's subjects. The one seems to detract from the significance of the other.

The *Mefaresh* offers a different interpretation: Livnah lay on the border with Edom and when the Edomites revolted, the people of Livnah joined forces with them and broke away from Yehoram's rule. The implication in terms of our perception of the significance of Edom's revolt would be as follows: Not only was Edom — symbol of Godlessness and evil — no longer subjugated by Israel, it even managed to make inroads into God's own people, eroding their sanctity, and encouraging them to break away from His rule. It was

for all days.
8 *In his days Edom revolted from beneath Judah's hand and appointed a king over themselves.*
9 *Yehoram crossed over with his officers and all the chariots with him; and he rose up by night and smote the Edomites that encompassed him and the officers of the chariots.*
10 *So Edom revolted from under the hand of Judah up to this day. Then, at that time Livneh was inspired to revolt from under his hand because he forsook HASHEM the God of his fathers.*
11 *Moreover he made bamos in the mountains of Judah and made the dwellers of Jerusalem be disloyal. Thus did he cause Judah to go astray.*
12 *A letter came to him from Elijah the prophet saying, 'Thus says HASHEM the God*

the beginning of that ascendancy which had been promised to Edom once Israel had toppled from its spiritual heights.

כִּי עָזַב אֶת־ה׳ — *Because he forsook HASHEM.*

See above for *Malbim's* explanation.

The *Mefaresh* sees the phrase as an explanation of the catastrophes which were overtaking Yehoram and his rule. He forsook *HASHEM*, the God of his fathers and so his kingship crumbled.

Kings reports the revolt of Edom and Livnah without explaining that they were caused by Yehoram's spiritual failings. Perhaps the connection between the sins which were committed and the catastrophes which ensued is self-understood in a prophetic book but not in *Chronicles*.[1]

תִּפְשַׁע לִבְנָה — *Livnah was inspired to revolt.*

The translation reflects the future tense of פשע.

11. גַּם — *Moreover*. If this verse is just a listing of some of the evil things that Yehoram did, we would have expected it to have a parallel in *Kings*. But a careful reading of v. 13 makes it clear that what is said here is the explanation of *He walked in the way of the kings of Israel* ... of v. 6. Vs. 7-10 are parenthetical. In that case, the function of our verse is to provide the background for Elijah's letter (vs. 12—15) which, for reasons discussed below, does not appear in *Kings*. Its absence from the *Kings* account is thus entirely consistent.

This verse places Yehoram into sharp contrast with Rechav'am. Rechav'am's reign had also witnessed a proliferation of idol worship (see *I Kings* 14:22 ff.), but that came about without his active instigation — see Section II to ch. 12, *Rechav'am Fails as King*. Yehoram, as did Israel's wicked kings, actually drove the people away from God.

בָּמוֹת — *Bamos*. Here, idolatrous altars are meant. (*Metzudos*). See at 14:2.

וַיֶּזֶן אֶת־יֹשְׁבֵי יְרוּשָׁלַם — *And made the dwellers of Jerusalem be disloyal*. זנה means *to commit harlotry; to be a harlot*. Idolatry is clearly a form of disloyalty to God, and the expression is appropriate (*Mefaresh*).

וַיַּדַּח אֶת־יְהוּדָה — *Thus did he cause Judah to go astray* . From נדח, *to thrust away*. Thus: He pushed Judah into being disloyal to God.

12-15. A letter arrives from the prophet Elijah. In it, Yehoram is apprised of the terrible fate which awaits him in punishment for his perfidy.

Our passage is fraught with mystery, for, both from Scriptural evidence and in the tradition of the Sages, Elijah had long since ceased to be among the living.[2]

There are a number of other difficulties as well: Why was Elijah, a prophet whose activities, as described in *Kings*, were centered exclusively in the Northern Kingdom under Ahab, the one to warn Yehoram? Why not any of the many prophets who must have been active in Judah? God had no need to go to the Northern Kingdom in order to find appropriate messengers to send to Asa (15:1)

1. *Chronicles* makes similar connections in the case of Saul's death (*I Chronicles* 10:13—14); and Shishak's campaign against Rechav'am (12:2), although *Kings* does not.

2. We recall that, as told in *II Kings* ch. 3, Yehoshaphat had joined Ahab's son Yehoram in a battle against Moab. On that occasion, Yehoshaphat had demanded that a prophet of God be consulted, and was told: ... *Elisha son of Shaphat is here who had served* [*lit. poured water upon the hands of*] *Elijah*. The implication is clear that already in Yehoshaphat's time Elijah had been succeeded by Elisha. The source of the Rabbinic tradition is in *Seder Olam*, ch. 7.

כא
יג־טז

אֱלֹהֵי דָּוִיד אָבִיךָ תַּחַת אֲשֶׁר לֹא־הָלַכְתָּ בְּדַרְכֵי יְהוֹשָׁפָט
יג אָבִיךָ וּבְדַרְכֵי אָסָא מֶלֶךְ־יְהוּדָה׃ וַתֵּלֶךְ בְּדֶרֶךְ מַלְכֵי
יִשְׂרָאֵל וַתַּזְנֶה אֶת־יְהוּדָה וְאֶת־יֹשְׁבֵי יְרוּשָׁלִַם כְּהַזְנוֹת
בֵּית אַחְאָב וְגַם אֶת־אַחֶיךָ בֵית־אָבִיךָ הַטּוֹבִים מִמְּךָ
יד הָרָגְתָּ׃ הִנֵּה יהוה נֹגֵף מַגֵּפָה גְדוֹלָה בְּעַמֶּךָ וּבְבָנֶיךָ
טו וּבְנָשֶׁיךָ וּבְכָל־רְכוּשֶׁךָ׃ וְאַתָּה בָּחֳלָיִם רַבִּים בְּמַחֲלֵה
טז מֵעֶיךָ עַד־יֵצְאוּ מֵעֶיךָ מִן־הַחֹלִי יָמִים עַל־יָמִים׃ וַיָּעַר

and to Yehoshaphat (20:14). Why could not the same have been done for Yehoram?

And if, indeed, Elijah was required for this prophecy, why a letter? Could Elijah not have come in person, as did the *man of God* who traveled from Judah to Bethel to bring his prophetic message to Yarov'am (*I Kings* 13:1), lending the prophecy the immediacy and impact of his overwhelming personality?

Radak and *Metzudos* explain that Elijah must have appeared to one of the prophets who functioned at the time, ordering him to write down the message and to convey it to Yehoram.

But why was all this necessary?

In comm. to 22:2 we shall see how, beginning with Yehoshaphat's marriage to Omri's daughter and the subsequent marriage of Yehoram to Ahab's daughter, the Davidic dynasty had forfeited its unique character and become subsumed, so to speak, under the house of Ahab. Certainly there would be no sharper and more direct way of bringing this truth home to them than to have Elijah, the constant nemesis of Ahab, be the bearer of the tidings of the destruction which threatened the Davidic line.

But, if that were the only purpose, it could have been accomplished with equal eloquence by sending Elisha, in his own right a prophet, to the Northern Kingdom. Why, then, was it necessary for Elijah to send a message from another world?

Surely this indicates beyond anything which we have seen till now the cosmic dimensions of Yehoram's wrongdoing. After Elijah's death or, more correctly, after his ascent to heaven, the dimensions of his significance in Israel's history changed. From being a prophet of the North charged with bringing God's word to Ahab, he became the symbol of Israel's eternity, harbinger of the Messiah. [See *Rambam, Melachim* 12:2.] It was he alone who would be able to bring home to Yehoram the unvarnished truth of what he had wrought — that through his perfidy and depravity the entire Messianic future of Israel was placed in jeopardy. Edom's revolt (see comm. to v. 8) was only the beginning of the disintegration of the Davidic kingship. The entire line was in danger of being physically destroyed — and with it any hope of the future so intimately tied to David's name.[1]

12. ה׳ אֱלֹהֵי דָּוִיד אָבִיךָ — *The God of your father David.*

The Judaic kings had forfeited their own identity and become subsumed under Ahab's house — see above. Elijah reminds Yehoram of his true spiritual heritage.

יְהוֹשָׁפָט אָבִיךָ . . . אָסָא מֶלֶךְ־יְהוּדָה — *Your father Yehoshaphat . . . Asa, king of Judah.* The fact that only Asa but not Yehoshaphat is given the title *king of Judah* may be part of the message. In v. 2 we saw Yehoshaphat described as *king of Israel* and, as quoted there from 17:1, that may have been because of his involvement with the royal house of Israel. The formulation of our verse may be a subtle hint that Yehoshaphat too was married to Omri's daughter and had, at least potentially, ceased to be a true *king of Judah*.

13. וְגַם אֶת־אַחֶיךָ בֵית־אָבִיךָ . . . הָרָגְתָּ — *And moreover, you killed your brothers of your father's family. . .*

It seems incongruous that a crime as heinous as fratricide should be mentioned almost as an afterthought. It is possible that Elijah's stricture is to be understood as follows: You failed both on a kingly and on a personal level.

However, when we consider the profound significance which attaches to the fact that this prophecy was sent through Elijah [see prefatory remarks 12-15], it seems unlikely that his rebukes would deal with personal failings. Murder is terrible, but it does not warrant a message from Elijah from beyond

1. That all this did not, in fact, happen, will become clear as we study Yoash's miraculous escape — see ch. 23.

of your father David: 'Because you did not go in the ways of
your father Yehoshaphat and in the ways of Asa, king of Judah,
13 *But you went in the way of the kings of Israel and made Judah*
and the dwellers of Jerusalem be disloyal, as the house of Ahab
cause disloyalty, and moreover, you killed your brothers of our
father's family, who were better than you. 14 *Behold,* HA-
SHEM *will strike mightily against your people and your children*
and your wives and all your substance. 15 *'And you shall have*
a great sickness — a disease of your bowels, until your bowels
fall out from the sickness days upon days'. 16 HASHEM *aroused*

the physical world.

Rather, this murderous act seems to be offered as a proof of the extent to which Yehoram had assumed the norms of the Northern Kingdom in which such violence could have been expected. 'You, Yehoram,' Elijah is saying, 'have shown yourself to be a true son of the house of Ahab. In assassinating your brothers you have placed yourself firmly into the context of that doomed dynasty. Moreover, you have become an unwitting accessory to the eradication of the Davidic line. As you killed your father's children, so will your children be killed. In throwing in your lot with Ahab, you have made yourself subject to the same fate as will overtake his house.'

14. הִנֵּה ה׳ נֹגֵף מַגֵּפָה גְדוֹלָה — *Behold,* HASHEM *will strike mightily.* נגף often describes a sickness in the form of a plague (*Numbers* 14:37, 17:13-15 and numerous other places), but can also be used for a military defeat (*I Samuel* 4:17; *II Samuel* 17:9, 18:7). From the description of the fulfillment of Elijah's prophecy given in vs. 16-19, it would appear that this latter interpretation is the meaning here.[1]

The annihilation of Yehoram's family which is forecast here seems to presage the slaughter of all his descendants — with the exception of the infant Yoash — at Yehu's (22:9) and Athaliah's (22:10) hands.

15. וְאַתָּה . . . — *And you . . .*

Yehoram himself is to die an agonizing death as punishment — or perhaps expiation — for his sins. But again we must ask why his fate as an individual should merit a prophecy from the great Elijah. And particularly, why was it important to record for posterity the precise nature of the sickness of which he was to die?

חוֹלִי מֵעַיִם, *the disease of the bowels*, plays an important role in Aggadic literature. Thus, *Shabbos* 11a sees it as the most terrible of all sicknesses: [Let man suffer] any disease — just not the sickness of the bowels; and *Shabbos* 118b teaches that most righteous people die of the sickness of the bowels. *Rashi* there sees a connection. The excruciating pain of this type of disorder will atone for the sins which these righteous people have committed and thus leave them free for a painless existence in *Olam HaBa*.

From this point of view the import of Elijah's prophecy would be simply that Yehoram's death will be particularly painful. The fact that the bowels would eventually fall out of the body would be simply one more horrific part of the gruesome death that awaited him.

Maharal perceives the sickness differently. The righteous die of it not because of the atoning force of the attendant agony but because of its cleansing power. The cleaning out of the body from the wastes contained in the digestive system presages the total purification of the soul when it leaves the body. When the righteous die, their souls will be unencumbered by the physical associations which compromise those of less exalted people.

If so, death by the sickness of the bowels would tend to define the sufferer as a צַדִּיק, *a righteous man*. Surely this was not the intent in the case of Yehoram.

Perhaps the sickness and death which Elijah is predicting for Yehoram are to be understood as symbolic. If a regular sickness of the bowels is considered as a cleansing process, then it follows that the bowels are viewed as a repository of filth. The falling out of the bowels would then symbolize the revelation of a depravity and shamefulness which had earlier been hidden.

In comm. to v. 3 we saw that when Yeho-

1. *Targum* may have understood the word as denoting a plague. He renders מוֹתָנָא, the term he uses for sickness (*I Chronicles* 21:22), rather than מַחְתָּא, which he uses for military defeat (*I Samuel* 4:17 and elsewhere).

יְהוָה עַל־יְהוֹרָם אֵת רוּחַ הַפְּלִשְׁתִּים וְהָעַרְבִים אֲשֶׁר
יז עַל־יַד כּוּשִׁים: וַיַּעֲלוּ בִיהוּדָה וַיִּבְקָעוּהָ וַיִּשְׁבּוּ אֵת
כָּל־הָרְכוּשׁ הַנִּמְצָא לְבֵית־הַמֶּלֶךְ וְגַם־בָּנָיו וְנָשָׁיו וְלֹא
יח נִשְׁאַר־לוֹ בֵּן כִּי אִם־יְהוֹאָחָז קְטֹן בָּנָיו: וְאַחֲרֵי כָּל־זֹאת
יט נְגָפוֹ יְהוָה ׀ בְּמֵעָיו לָחֳלִי לְאֵין מַרְפֵּא: וַיְהִי לְיָמִים ׀
מִיָּמִים וּכְעֵת צֵאת הַקֵּץ לְיָמִים שְׁנַיִם יָצְאוּ מֵעָיו
עִם־חָלְיוֹ וַיָּמָת בְּתַחֲלֻאִים רָעִים וְלֹא־עָשׂוּ לוֹ עַמּוֹ שְׂרֵפָה
כ כִּשְׂרֵפַת אֲבֹתָיו: בֶּן־שְׁלֹשִׁים וּשְׁתַּיִם הָיָה בְמָלְכוֹ וּשְׁמוֹנֶה
שָׁנִים מָלַךְ בִּירוּשָׁלָם וַיֵּלֶךְ בְּלֹא חֶמְדָּה וַיִּקְבְּרֻהוּ

shaphat had made Yehoram king, he had been deceived as to his true nature. The dreadful actions ascribed to Yehoram in our chapter demonstrate how sadly mistaken his father had been. Yehoram's depravity, which had once been concealed, became open for all to see. This may have been the symbolism intended.

But, if we take into consideration what we learned in comm. to v. 5, we understand the symbolism on a more profound level and, indeed, very much within the purview of Elijah's message. We noted there that the daughter of Omri whom Yehoshaphat, in the tradition of the Sages, married could well have been a good woman. Nevertheless, the very fact of an alliance with that wicked family began insidiously to erode the inner sanctity of the Davidic dynasty. Taken thus, the revealed bowels are a strikingly apt symbol. Yehoram himself is the *bowel* of the Davidic house which had become revealed. The illness which had been unobservable in its early stages was revealed in him in its true virulence.

16. וַיָּעַר ... אֵת רוּחַ ... — *[HASHEM] aroused [the Philistines'] greed.* From עור, *to rouse oneself* or *awaken*. In this context, רוּחַ is to be taken as *desire*. Hence, God stimulated Philistia's natural greed (*Metzudos*).

17. ויבקעוּהָ — *Breached its defenses.*

From בקע, *to cleave*. We have added the words *its defenses* to accord with *Metzudos'* interpretation of the phrase.

וְגַם־בָּנָיו — *Also his children.*

He was punished measure for measure. He had killed all his father's children, leaving only one — himself, so this is precisely what God meted out to him (*Ralbag*).

יְהוֹאָחָז — *Yehoachaz*. Ch. 22:1 speaks of Yehoram being succeeded by his son, אֲחַזְיָהוּ. The name is spelled the same, except that, the three letters denoting God's name [יהו] follow the name instead of preceding it (*Metzudos*).

יְהוֹאָחָז derives from אחז, *to hold*, thus, *HASHEM holds* or *supports*.

18. לָחֳלִי לְאֵין מַרְפֵּא — *With a disease from which he knew no respite*. He was not even able to find temporary relief (*Metzudos*).

19. וַיְהִי לְיָמִים מִיָּמִים — *It plagued him constantly*.

Lit. *It [was with him] from the beginning of the year till the end of the year*, without any respite at all (*Metzudos*).

וּכְעֵת צֵאת הַקֵּץ לְיָמִים שְׁנַיִם — *At the end of two years.*

Lit. *When the end came to two years.*

וְלֹא־עָשׂוּ לוֹ עַמּוֹ שְׂרֵפָה — *And his people did not burn a funeral pyre for him*. Even though a pyre would have been highly appropriate, in order to hide the odor of the putrefaction that must have set in as a result of his horrible sickness, God did not permit him to be so honored (*Mefaresh*).

For the custom to burn the king's personal utensils at the time of his funeral, see at 16:14.

The insertion of *his people* at this point is notable. The context does not really seem to require it. The people are not mentioned at the burning that was done for Asa — the only other king for whom such a ceremony is mentioned (16:14) — nor are they ever mentioned in connection with the burial of any of the other kings. It is always *they buried* — with the subject understood — as in our v. 20. Why, then, *his people*?

Perhaps we may solve this problem by reading our verse together with the next one, as follows:

V. 20 presents a problem in that its first part is a verbatim repetition of v. 5. The commentators offer no rationale for this apparent

the Philistine's greed, and that of the Arabs who bordered along-
side the Kushites. 17 *They came up against Judah, breached its*
defenses, and made off with all the fortune that lay in the king's
palace; also his children and wives so that no son remained to
him save only Yehoachaz, the youngest of his children. 18 *After*
all this, HASHEM *smote him in his bowels with a disease from*
which he knew no respite. 19 *It plagued him constantly, and, at*
the end of two years, his bowels fell out because of his sickness.
He died of horrible diseases, and his people did not burn a funer-
al pyre for him as they had burned for his fathers. 20 *He was*
thirty-two years old when he began to reign and he ruled eight
years in Jerusalem. He departed joyless and they buried him

redundancy. [See also at 27:1 and 8.]

This, may be explained if we can get a clear picture of the meaning of the phrase וַיֵּלֶךְ בְּלֹא חֶמְדָּה, which is unique and must be interpreted from context. The commentators (*Mefaresh* and *Metzudos*) take it as a description of Yehoram's tragic death after an empty, useless life. He left this world without ever having attained the things which would have made life pleasant or desirable.

There may be an alternative explanation: The root חמד is used in Scripture to describe the attraction a person might feel for someone of beautiful or impressive appearance [cf. *Isaiah* 53:2]. Now, normally, people could be expected to wish to gaze upon their king (*Isaiah* 33:17). But Yehoram filled all who looked at him with horror. Any attraction which his people might have felt for him, dissipated because of his loathsome appearance. He died without חֶמְדָּה.

Avos 5:25 defines the age of thirty as the time when man stands at the very height of his youthful vigor and energy. We can imagine the hope which the young thirty-two year old son of the beloved Yehoshaphat must have instilled in the people when his father made him king. He had eight long years in which those hopes could have been translated into a benign and beneficial rule. All this potential he squandered in a life of wickedness and dissipation, dying finally, still as a young man but unloved and unmourned. He was not even accorded the final dignity of being buried in the royal sepulchers.

Taken thus, the two verses go together: In spite of the promise of his ascendance to the throne [בֶּן שְׁלֹשִׁים וּשְׁתַּיִם הָיָה בְמָלְכוֹ] and the years of opportunity granted him [וּשְׁמוֹנֶה שָׁנָה מָלַךְ בִּירוּשָׁלָיִם], his people [עַמּוֹ], who under different circumstances would have been prostrate at the death of a young king, did not even bother to set a funeral pyre in his honor. This was because any sense of love or loyalty having long since been lost [וַיֵּלֶךְ בְּלֹא חֶמְדָּה], he was buried as a commoner and not as a king.

Our perception of the relationship between the two verses can also serve to explain another structural difficulty. From the account of Asa's death and the burning that was done in his honor (16:13—14), it is evident that this took place in conjunction with the burial. If so, we would have expected the description of Yehoram's burial (v. 20) to precede the information contained in v. 19. As we read the verses we find the two statements relate to one another as effect does to cause. No burning was performed (v. 19) because this ceremony is only appropriate for a royal burial. Such a burial, because of all that had occurred, was denied him (v. 20).

20. בֶּן־שְׁלֹשִׁים וּשְׁתַּיִם הָיָה בְמָלְכוֹ — *He was thirty-two years old when he became king.* This is apparently a repetition of v. 5. See comm. to previous verse for an explanation.

The report of Yehoram's death contains one other irregularity. In the case of every other king, with the exception only of Amon, there is a standard formula which concludes the account of the reign with the words *The rest of so and so's acts or matters are recorded in such and such a book*. This formula is missing here although we have it in *II Kings* 8:23. This may confirm the thesis which we will suggest in 22:1, that at the time of his death Yehoram was not considered king anymore — and that for this reason he was not given a royal burial — because in appointing Achaziah king the people had effectively deposed Yehoram. See below.

וַיֵּלֶךְ בְּלֹא חֶמְדָּה — *He departed joyless.*

See comm. to v. 19.

א בְּעִיר דָּוִיד וְלֹא בְּקִבְרוֹת הַמְּלָכִים׃ וַיַּמְלִיכוּ יוֹשְׁבֵי
יְרוּשָׁלִַם אֶת־אֲחַזְיָהוּ בְנוֹ הַקָּטֹן תַּחְתָּיו כִּי כָל־הָרִאשֹׁנִים
הָרַג הַגְּדוּד הַבָּא בָעַרְבִים לַמַּחֲנֶה וַיִּמְלֹךְ אֲחַזְיָהוּ
ב בֶּן־יְהוֹרָם מֶלֶךְ יְהוּדָה׃ בֶּן־אַרְבָּעִים וּשְׁתַּיִם שָׁנָה
אֲחַזְיָהוּ בְּמָלְכוֹ וְשָׁנָה אַחַת מָלַךְ בִּירוּשָׁלִָם וְשֵׁם אִמּוֹ
ג עֲתַלְיָהוּ בַּת־עָמְרִי׃ גַּם־הוּא הָלַךְ בְּדַרְכֵי בֵּית אַחְאָב כִּי

XXII

⊰ Achaziahuu Ascends the Throne

1. וַיַּמְלִיכוּ יוֹשְׁבֵי יְרוּשָׁלִַם אֶת־אֲחַזְיָהוּ — *Now the dwellers of Jerusalem proclaimed . . . Achaziahu king.* A comparison with the *Kings'* account yields that this proclamation took place while Yehoram was still alive — presumably, once his debilitating illness had begun in earnest.

And Yehoram lay with his fathers... and his son Achaziahu became king instead of him (*II Kings* 8:24). There is no mention of any extraordinary initiative taken by the inhabitants of Jerusalem, as there is in *Chronicles*.

Perhaps, then, *Kings*, where nothing had been mentioned of Yehoram's terrible illness, deals with the routine succession which, in the ordinary course of events, takes place after the previous king has died. But the illness which Yehoram suffered two years earlier, and which would almost surely have incapacitated him, plays an important part in the *Chronicles'* account. In that context it makes sense to note that the dwellers of Jerusalem took matters into their own hands and proclaimed Achaziahu king, even though his father was still alive.

This would explain why only the *dwellers of Jerusalem* were involved. At no other coronation are these mentioned as a separate group. The active participants are always either *the people of the land* (*II Kings* 21:24) or *all of Israel* (*I Kings* 16:16). We know of no good reason why, at a normal succession, only the people of Jerusalem would have been involved. If, however, we are dealing with an emergency coronation during the previous king's lifetime, then this is very understandable. Only the people of Jerusalem would have been sufficiently cognizant of the circumstances to have been in a position to take action [1].

הַבָּא בָעַרְבִים לַמַּחֲנֶה — *That had come to the camp from among the Arabs. Metzudos* demonstrates that the prefix ב may occasionally have the same meaning as מ, *from. Camp* refers to the Philistine army. Thus our phrase teaches that Achaziahu's brothers had been killed by the Arabs who were part of the Philistine army. See 21:16-17.

וַיִּמְלֹךְ אֲחַזְיָהוּ בֶּן־יְהוֹרָם מֶלֶךְ יְהוּדָה — *So Achaziahu son of Yehoram, king of Judah, became king.* The phrase seems redundant. It appears to add nothing to the statement made earlier that the dwellers of Jerusalem had made Achaziahu king. Nowhere does *Chronicles* use a similar phrase to describe an ascension to the throne.

There is another irregularity. Nowhere in *Kings* or *Chronicles* — except when needed for identification, as *In such and such a year of so and so king of Israel, so and so king of Judah became king* — is a king given the title *king of Judah or Israel* when his ascension to the throne is described.

The phrase seems to confirm the thesis propounded in comm. to the earlier part of this verse. We are dealing not with the regular orderly succession which occurred after Yehoram's death, but with the initiative which the inhabitants of Jerusalem took to crown Achaziahu king during Yehoram's lifetime. The phrase teaches that the project was

1. This thesis is confirmed by *Rashi* to *II Kings* 9:29 where we learn that Achaziahu assumed the kingship in the eleventh year of Ahab's son Yehoram. *Rashi* notes that 8:25 (there) had stated that Achaziahu had become king in Yehoram's twelfth year. To reconcile the two statements, *Rashi* suggests that Achaziahu's father Yehoram did, indeed, die in the twelfth year of the reign of Ahab's son Yehoram but that Achaziahu had already assumed the kingship one year earlier when his father became disabled because of his illness. [But see *Radak* there.]

in the City of David, but not in the graves of the kings.

Now the dwellers of Jerusalem proclaimed his youngest son
Achaziahu king in his stead, for the band that had come to the
camp from among the Arabs had killed all the earlier ones. So
Achaziahu son of Yehoram, king of Judah, became king. 2 *Achazia-*
hu had attained the forty-second year when he became king. He
ruled for one year in Jerusalem. His mother's name was Athaliahu
the daughter of Omri. 3 *He too went in the ways of Ahab's dynasty,*

successful. Achaziahu — even though his father was still alive — did, in fact, reign completely in his own right and was, in fact and in name, *king of Judah*. Yehoram's illness had effectively removed him from the kingship as evidenced by the complete lack of any royal honor at the time of his funeral — see comm. to the end of the previous chapter.[1]

2. בֶּן־אַרְבָּעִים וּשְׁתַּיִם שָׁנָה אֲחַזְיָהוּ בְּמָלְכוֹ — *Achaziahu had attained the forty-second year when he became king*. The more natural translation would have been: *Achaziahu was forty-two years old when he became king*. However, this statement is simply not true. Achaziahu could not have been forty-two when he succeeded his father, because Yehoram was only forty years old when he died. [He became king at thirty-two and reigned for eight years — 21:5 and 20.] Moreover, *II Kings* 8:26 states expressly that he was only twenty-two.

What, then, is the meaning of this statement?

Seder Olam Rabbah ch. 17 and *Tosefta, Sota* ch. 12 provide the answer. Forty-two years before Achaziahu had come to the throne, his great-grandfather, Asa, had taken Omri's daughter as a wife for his son Yehoshaphat. [See 17:3; 18:1; and 21:5 and 7.] In the eyes of Divine justice this travesty marked the Davidic line as a part of Omri's family. The doom and destruction which awaited Omri's line would now, engulf the royal family of Judah too (vs. 7-9). Our verse teaches that the year of Achaziahu's ascension to the throne coincided with the forty-second year since the promulgation of the decree which would result in the annihilation of the Davidic line. [For the computation, see *Rashi* to *II Kings* 9:29, and *Radak* to 8:26 there.] If, in 21:7 we saw how God, even at that late date, was not yet ready to will Judah's destruction, the time had now come when it could no longer be averted. See Section II, *The Forty-Two Years of 22:2*.

3-4. These two verses seem to be saying essentially the same thing — Achaziahu's counselors advised him badly, because of their association with the evil Ahab's dynasty. The differences are that in v. 3 the blame is cast upon Athaliahu, while in v. 4, people from among Ahab's dynasty are faulted. Furthermore, v. 4 speaks of the period *after the death of his father*.

Malbim thinks that the subject of v. 3 is Achaziahu's private life. As a youngster he grew up in the evil ways of the house of Ahab under the pernicious influence of his mother. V. 4 then goes on to say, that as king [*after his father's death*] he was similarly misled by his counselors, and ruled as the house of Ahab did — destructively.

If, as suggested above, Achaziahu had already assumed the kingship during Yehoram's lifetime, then both verses would be describing his bearing as king. While his father was still alive it was his mother who was his chief adviser. Once his father had died, that position was taken over by other counselors associated with the royal house of

1. This thesis can help explain the following: At *II Kings* 8:24 we read that Yehoram was buried, *with his fathers*, in the City of David. Our 21:20 reads *They buried him in the City of David, but not in the graves of the kings*.

We may surmise that there were family sepulchers in which all the sons of the king were buried together with their father, but that a special place, within the sepulcher, was reserved for the one son who had succeeded his father to the throne. Yehoram was buried *with his fathers*; that is, inside Yehoshaphat's sepulcher, but not at the site reserved for the son who had become king. At his death he had come to be regarded as a commoner.

ד אִמּוֹ הָיְתָה יוֹעַצְתּוֹ לְהַרְשִׁיעַ: וַיַּעַשׂ הָרַע בְּעֵינֵי יְהוָה
כְּבֵית אַחְאָב כִּי הֵמָּה הָיוּ־לוֹ יוֹעֲצִים אַחֲרֵי מוֹת אָבִיו
ה לְמַשְׁחִית לוֹ: גַּם בַּעֲצָתָם הָלַךְ וַיֵּלֶךְ אֶת־יְהוֹרָם
בֶּן־אַחְאָב מֶלֶךְ יִשְׂרָאֵל לַמִּלְחָמָה עַל־חֲזָאֵל מֶלֶךְ־אֲרָם
ו בְּרָמוֹת גִּלְעָד וַיַּכּוּ הָרַמִּים אֶת־יוֹרָם: וַיָּשָׁב לְהִתְרַפֵּא
בְיִזְרְעֶאל כִּי הַמַּכִּים אֲשֶׁר הִכֻּהוּ בָרָמָה בְּהִלָּחֲמוֹ
אֶת־חֲזָהאֵל מֶלֶךְ אֲרָם וַעֲזַרְיָהוּ בֶן־יְהוֹרָם מֶלֶךְ יְהוּדָה
יָרַד לִרְאוֹת אֶת־יְהוֹרָם בֶּן־אַחְאָב בְּיִזְרְעֶאל כִּי־חֹלֶה
ז הוּא: וּמֵאֱלֹהִים הָיְתָה תְּבוּסַת אֲחַזְיָהוּ לָבוֹא אֶל־יוֹרָם
וּבְבֹאוֹ יָצָא עִם־יְהוֹרָם אֶל־יֵהוּא בֶן־נִמְשִׁי אֲשֶׁר מְשָׁחוֹ
ח יְהוָה לְהַכְרִית אֶת־בֵּית אַחְאָב: וַיְהִי כְּהִשָּׁפֵט יֵהוּא

the Northern Kingdom. Athaliahu was shunted aside. We may surmise that Achaziahu recognized her ruthless ambition to be queen — saw in her a woman who would not shrink from murdering her own grandchildren in pursuit of her lust (v. 10) — and, given the chance, distanced her from the center of power.

In the *Kings'* account (*II Kings* 8:27) we read: *He went in the way of Ahab's dynasty, and did evil in the eyes of* HASHEM *as did Ahab's dynasty, for he was allied by marriage to the house of Ahab*. The destructive counsel which he received is not mentioned at all.

The thrust of this statement is not the same as the one in *Chronicles*. As we have noted on many occasions, *Kings* makes no mention at all of Yehoshaphat's marriage to Omri's daughter. It does not deal with the entire question of the catastrophic alliance between the two houses, except in this passage: Yehoram strayed because of his wife's influence. This is the extent of *Kings'* interest in the matter.

By contrast, in *Chronicles* the joining in marriage of the two royal lines drives the entire narrative. Its tragic consequences have been indicated in the previous verse as understood by the Sages [*had attained the forty-second year*]. The fact that Achaziahu was wicked does not need to be repeated. Instead, *Chronicles* traces the cause of Achaziahu's dissolution. It lies in the pernicious counsel which he received at the hands of his trusted advisers.

3. לְהַרְשִׁיעַ — *To act wickedly*.

רשע in the *hiphil*, causative, can also mean *to wreak havoc*, *to sow confusion* or *terror* (*I Samuel* 14:47, see commentators there). This may also be the meaning here. The leadership which Achaziahu provided, compromised by the imprint of idolatrous superstitions, proved to be destructive to the people.

4. לְמַשְׁחִית לו — *To his bane*. Their advice did not benefit him but, on the contrary, led to his downfall (*Metzudos*).

5. גַּם בַּעֲצָתָם . . . — *Moreover, at their advice*.

This war ultimately led to Achaziahu's death. *Chronicles*, but not *Kings*, makes the point that he was goaded into this ill-fated alliance by the Northern counselors. Within the *Chronicles'* perspective this is, indeed, germane. *Chronicles* wishes to teach that it was the involvement of Judah's kings with the royal house of the Northern Kingdom which so very nearly led to their total destruction. Here the outer contour of the events [the bad advice proffered by the Northern counselors] reflects the inner truth [that the alliance with the Northern Kingdom would spell the dissolution of the Davidic line].

וַיַּכּוּ הָרַמִּים אֶת־יוֹרָם — *Now, the Arameans wounded Yoram*.

The next verse shows that וַיַּכּוּ, which can also be used to describe a victory in battle, here refers to the individual wounds which Yehoram suffered.

The word אֲרַמִּים drops the א and becomes רַמִּים. Such deficient orthography is not unknown in Scriptural writing (*Radak*).

This story is told as background to Achaziahu's murder at Yehu's hands. The visit to Yehoram (v. 6), which put him in Yehu's power (v. 7), came about only because of the alliance described here.

6. כִּי הַמַּכִּים — *Of the wounds*. This is an

22
4-8

for his mother guided him to act wickedly. 4 *He acted wickedly*
in the eyes of HASHEM *as did Ahab's dynasty; for, to his bane, they*
were his counselors after the death of his father. 5 *Moreover, at their*
advice he joined Yehoram the son of Ahab king of Israel in making
war against Chazael king of Aram at Ramoth-Gilead. Now, the
Arameans wounded Yoram. 6 *He returned to be healed in Yezreel*
of the wounds which they had given him at Ramoth when he fought
with Chazael king of Aram. And Azariahu the son of Yehoram
king of Judah went down to see Yehoram the son of Ahab in Jezre-
el because he was sick. 7 *Now Achaziahu's debacle — that he*
came to Yoram — was brought about by God. Having come, he
went out with Yehoram against Yehu son of Nimshi, whom
HASHEM *had anointed to excise the family of Ahab.* 8 *While Yehu*

unusual usage for כִּי. *Kings* has מִן הַמַּכִּים.

הַמַּכִּים — *The wounds*. This is an unusual masculine form. The plural form of מַכֶּה is usually מַכּוֹת (*Radak*).

◈§ Achaziahu Is Drawn Toward His Death

וַעֲזַרְיָהוּ בֶּן־יְהוֹרָם . . . — *And Azariahu son of Yehoram*. Azariah is another name for Achaziahu (*Radak*, *Metzudos*).

Why call him by his other name just here, when throughout the narrative, Achaziahu is used? Moreover, *Kings* did not do the same. In the parallel verse (8:29) he is called Achaziahu as he is throughout the chapter.

We may surmise as follows: As we shall see below, the thrust of the *Chronicles'* narrative is to show how, step by step, Achaziahu is inexorably drawn towards the doom which Divine Providence had ordained forty-two years earlier for the Davidic line. The dynasty is to perish.

Perhaps Achaziahu was the official name which he carried as king, but Azariah, which is not used anywhere else, was a name by which he was known in private life. The impulse to visit his stricken ally and relative was a personal one, not taken as a kingly duty but out of friendly concern. Nevertheless, even this private action did not escape the long arm of providence. Invisible chains are dragging Achaziahu to the confrontation with Yehu, which will consummate the Divine decree, and spell his death.[1]

7. תְּבוּסַת אֲחַזְיָהוּ — *Achaziahu's debacle*.

The basic meaning of בוס seems to be *to tread down*. Indeed, *Targumim* occasionally render דוש, *to step upon*, even when the word is used to describe the destruction of an enemy. (See *Isaiah* 14:25, *Psalms* 108:14.) There is, however, a great degree of latitude to be found in the *Targumim*, so that at *Isaiah* 63:6 the word is given as קטל, *to kill*, and in *Psalms* 61:14 as כבש, *to press down*.

Our *Targum* renders תּוּסְקְפַת, which he also uses at 10:15 for נְסִבָּה, *that which is brought about* — (see comm. there); thus, perhaps *fate* or *destiny*.

לָבוֹא אֶל־יוֹרָם — *That he came to Yoram*.

Divine Providence dragged him willy-nilly to his fate. See comm. to v. 6.

וּבְבֹאוֹ יָצָא עִם־יְהוֹרָם אֶל־יֵהוּא בֶן־נִמְשִׁי אֲשֶׁר מְשָׁחוֹ ה׳ לְהַכְרִית אֶת־בֵּית אַחְאָב — *Having come, he went out with Yehoram against Yehu son of Nimshi, whom* HASHEM *had anointed to excise the family of Ahab. II Kings* 9:1 ff. tells in detail how Yehu, one of Ahab's officers, was anointed king over Israel by an anonymous prophet, in accordance with the command which God had given to Elijah (*I Kings* 19:16). He was to kill out the entire family of Ahab, as punishment for all the wickedness that they had perpetrated. The *Kings'* narrative then goes on to describe in detail the ruthless thoroughness with which Yehu carried out this mandate.

The *Kings'* narrative also mentions that, in the course of these events, Yehu had Achaziahu king of Judah killed when the latter was fleeing the field of battle (v. 27 there, see comm. to v. 9). There is no indication that this

1. This would explain why *Azariahu the son of Yehoram king of Judah* is used here. If our assumption is correct, then *king of Judah* describes Yehoram, not Achaziahu, who is appearing here in a private capacity. The sense of the verse would be that even though the visit was made by [the private] Azariahu, still, since he was the son of Judah's king he could not escape that fate which had been determined for the royal house.

עִם־בֵּית אַחְאָב וַיִּמְצָא אֶת־שָׂרֵי יְהוּדָה וּבְנֵי אֲחֵי אֲחַזְיָהוּ
ט מְשָׁרְתִים לַאֲחַזְיָהוּ וַיַּהַרְגֵם: וַיְבַקֵּשׁ אֶת־אֲחַזְיָהוּ וַיִּלְכְּדֻהוּ
וְהוּא מִתְחַבֵּא בְשֹׁמְרוֹן וַיְבִאֻהוּ אֶל־יֵהוּא וַיְמִתֻהוּ
וַיִּקְבְּרֻהוּ כִּי אָמְרוּ בֶּן־יְהוֹשָׁפָט הוּא אֲשֶׁר־דָּרַשׁ אֶת־
יְהוָה בְּכָל־לְבָבוֹ וְאֵין לְבֵית אֲחַזְיָהוּ לַעְצֹר כֹּחַ
י לְמַמְלָכָה: וַעֲתַלְיָהוּ אֵם אֲחַזְיָהוּ רָאֲתָה כִּי־מֵת בְּנָהּ

was done because Achaziahu was considered to be part of the house of Ahab. If we had only the *Kings'* account, we would have attributed Achaziahu's death to an over-zealousness which carried Yehu beyond his mandate.

However, as we saw in comm. to v. 2, the perspective with which *Chronicles* presents Achaziahu's story is based on the fact that, from the time of Yehoshaphat's marriage to Omri's daughter, the House of David had, in the eyes of God, become identified with Ahab's family. The destruction which was to overtake Omri's dynasty would engulf them too.

Our verse makes graphically clear how it was God's providence which drew Achaziahu along the path which was to lead to his death. Immediately when he came [וּבְבֹאוֹ], he went out towards the man who had been appointed by God to be his executioner. The next two verses continue to place Achaziahu's death into this context; see below.

8. וַיְהִי כְּהִשָּׁפֵט יֵהוּא עִם־בֵּית אַחְאָב — *While Yehu was executing judgment upon Ahab's family. Kings* gives a detailed account of the ruthlessly efficient way in which Yehu sought out and killed every last remnant of Ahab's family. *Chronicles* did not have to repeat this and merely hints at in our phrase.

וַיִּמְצָא ... וַיַּהַרְגֵם — *He found ... and slew them. II Kings* 10:13—14 reads: *Yehu chanced upon the relatives of Achaziahu king of Judah and said, 'Who are you?' They answered, 'We are Achaziahu's relatives and have come down to assist the children of the king and the children of the queen.' He said, 'Capture them alive!' So they captured them alive and slaughtered them ... forty-two men, not a single one remained of them.*

The commentators assume that the *Chronicles'* account builds on what was said in *Kings*, adding only some clarification: The *relatives* of *Kings* are nephews — his brothers had all been killed earlier at the hands of the Philistines and Arabs (21:17). These had come to Shomron to serve as adjutants to Achaziahu.

If, indeed, the two descriptions are of the same event then there is a problem of chronology. In the *Kings'* account the massacre occurs after Yehu entered Samaria (v. 12 there) which is apparently long after he had already killed Achaziahu (9:27—28, there). From our v. 9 it appears that Achaziahu was killed after the events described in our verse. See below, v. 9.

9. וַיְבַקֵּשׁ אֶת־אֲחַזְיָהוּ — *He hunted Achaziahu...*

This all evidently happened in Samaria [... *while he was hiding in Samaria*], and taken together with the fact that, as we saw above, the slaughter of his nephews also took place in Samaria, the passage is entirely logical and consistent. Yehu entered Samaria, chanced upon Achaziahu's nephews, through them discovered him and had him slain. See Section II, *Achaziahu's Death at Yehu's Hands*, for a discussion.

וַיִּקְבְּרֻהוּ — *And buried him*. The parallel verse in *Kings* (9:28) reads: *And his [Achaziahu's] servants carried him upon a chariot to Jerusalem and they buried him in his burial place with his fathers in the City of David*. To avoid the apparent contradiction, *Radak* and *Metzudos* interpret our phrase to mean not that Achaziahu was buried by Yehu's men but that Yehu granted permission to have him buried and this was done as described in the *Kings'* account.

In this interpretation, the statement at the end of the verse, that Achaziahu had no viable heir to succeed him, is not connected to the first part of the sentence, but introduces the next section: Athaliahu was able to murder the entire royal family because there was no suitable heir who could have stood up against her.

We suggest an alternative interpretation for two reasons: Firstly, it seems forced to render a verse in a way which divides so radically between the first and second parts. Secondly, it seems clear that the subject of *and they buried* is the same as the subject in the phrase *and they brought*. If it is a matter of granting permission for burial to take place, rather than the

was executing judgment upon Ahab's family, he found Judean
officials and Achaziahu's nephews attending Achaziahu,
and slew them. 9 *He hunted Achaziahu and they ferreted him*
out, while he was hiding in Samaria. They brought him to Yehu,
slew him and buried him. For they said, 'He is a son of Yehosha-
phat who sought out HASHEM *with all his heart.' There was no*
one in Achaziahu's family able to maintain the power to rule.
10 *Athaliahu the mother of Achaziahu saw that her son had died,*

physical act of interment, then surely that permission would have come from Yehu himself, not from his men. The wording should have been *He allowed him to come to burial*.

We suggest that the meaning of the phrase may be that, in fact, Achaziahu was buried in Samaria on Yehu's sufferance, for reasons explained below. Subsequently, his own servants may have exhumed him and carried him to Jerusalem and buried him in the family sepulcher, as related in *Kings*.

Our entire verse would then be understandable against the background of the *Chronicles'* perspective as we have learned to recognize it. This is as follows:

The Davidic line had become a part of Ahab's family. By Divine fiat it was Yehu's mandate to wipe them out together with Ahab's line. It was not just a question of killing individual people, but of denying kingship to David's descendants. There could have been no clearer statement for the denial of royal prerogatives than to leave Achaziahu unburied, to rot on the fields in precisely the same way that Yehu had ordered the body of Ahab's son Yehoram to be thrown out into the vineyard which Ahab had once forcibly taken from Naboth (*II Kings* 9:25). Nevertheless, this was not done. Even if Achaziahu no longer deserved the honor due to a king, he was still, after all, a grandson of the righteous Yehoshaphat. As a private individual he deserved to be buried respectfully. There was no danger that this burial would be interpreted as a royal prerogative, and thus defeat Yehu's purpose, since anyway there was no viable heir in Judah, and for all intents and purposes the lineage was at an end.[1]

בֶּן־יְהוֹשָׁפָט הוּא — *He is a son of Yehoshaphat.*
A grandson can also be called a son (*Metzudos*).

לַעְצֹר כֹּחַ לְמַמְלָכָה — *To maintain the power to rule.*

Radak and *Metzudos* take this phrase as an introduction to the next verse. Athaliahu was able to do as she wished, because she had to deal only with defenseless youngsters. *Ralbag* suggests that it may be meant to explain Yehu's confidence in feeling free to have Achaziahu killed. He was not afraid of any retaliation from the Judean royal family. See above for our suggestion for the interpretation of this phrase.

עצר, *to restrain*, is used in Scripture to denote kingship (*Radak* to *Judges* 18:7). A significant function of a king is to mold his people into a cohesive whole — to prevent them from scattering in all directions. (See *Rashi* to *I Samuel* 9:17.)

10. וַעֲתַלְיָהוּ ... רָאֲתָה כִּי־מֵת בְּנָהּ — *Athaliahu ... saw that her son had died.* The simple meaning is that Athaliahu committed her crime in reaction to her son's death. But see comm. to previous verse where we considered the possibility that what is recounted here took place before Achaziahu was killed by Yehu.

1. We say no *viable* heir because all of Achaziahu's sons were small children — witness the ease with which Athaliahu murdered them (v. 10) (Commentators).

When we consider that some time may have elapsed between Achaziahu's wounding and his death — he had first settled permanently in Megiddo and only at some time later come to Samaria — it is not impossible to say that by the time he was killed by Yehu, Athaliahu had already murdered all his children with the exception of Yoash who had been miraculously saved (v. 11), and of whom Yehu could not have known. In that case Yehu would have assumed that there were no heirs at all and that therefore Achaziahu was, in fact, the end of the line. See Section II, *Achaziahu's Death at Yehu's Hands*.

To assume this we would have to interpret v. 10 as saying that Athaliahu had already previously murdered all the royal lineage — an idea well able to be expressed by the syntax according to Scriptural usage. Furthermore, the phrase ... *saw that her son was dead* would not mean literally dead but wounded and impotent, and therefore *dead* for all practical purposes. This, too, is well within normal Scriptural usage — see *Berachos* 18b to *Deuteronomy* 17:6 and *Ezekiel* 21:30.

כב וַתָּקָם וַתְּדַבֵּר אֶת־כָּל־זֶרַע הַמַּמְלָכָה לְבֵית יְהוּדָה:
יא־יב יא וַתִּקַּח יְהוֹשַׁבְעַת בַּת־הַמֶּלֶךְ אֶת־יוֹאָשׁ בֶּן־אֲחַזְיָהוּ
וַתִּגְנֹב אֹתוֹ מִתּוֹךְ בְּנֵי־הַמֶּלֶךְ הַמּוּמָתִים וַתִּתֵּן אֹתוֹ
וְאֶת־מֵינִקְתּוֹ בַּחֲדַר הַמִּטּוֹת וַתַּסְתִּירֵהוּ יְהוֹשַׁבְעַת בַּת־
הַמֶּלֶךְ יְהוֹרָם אֵשֶׁת יְהוֹיָדָע הַכֹּהֵן כִּי הִיא הָיְתָה
יב אֲחוֹת אֲחַזְיָהוּ מִפְּנֵי עֲתַלְיָהוּ וְלֹא הֱמִיתָתְהוּ: וַיְהִי אִתָּם
כג בְּבֵית הָאֱלֹהִים מִתְחַבֵּא שֵׁשׁ שָׁנִים וַעֲתַלְיָה מֹלֶכֶת
א א עַל־הָאָרֶץ: וּבַשָּׁנָה הַשְּׁבִעִית הִתְחַזַּק יְהוֹיָדָע

וַתָּקָם — *And decided*. See comm. to *I Chronicles* 28:2 for *Gra's* interpretation of קום as used in Scripture.

וַתְּדַבֵּר אֶת־כָּל־זֶרַע הַמַּמְלָכָה — *To dispatch all the royal seed ... with a lingering death*. *Kings* has וַתְּאַבֵּד, from אבד, *to lose*. In the *piel* this becomes *to destroy*.

Commentators assume that דִּבֵּר is a verb formed from דֶּבֶר, *plague*; that is, that she killed the children by poison so that they died a slow and painful death, as does one who dies by the plague (*Metzudos* and *Malbim*).

Mefaresh also makes the point that the assassination was done by poisoning. He bases his explanation upon a peculiarity in the *Kings'* text. There, we are told that the baby Yoash was rescued from among the בְּנֵי הַמֶּלֶךְ הַמּוּמָתִים. This is the way the word is read, and it implies: *the king's children who had been murdered*. However, the word is written הַמְּמוֹתִים which, *Mefaresh* says, translates as *... who were being killed*. Both nuances are true. They had [already] been killed in the sense that a fatal poison, from which there could be no recovery, had been administered; but they were still being killed, in that theirs was a lingering death.

Why did *Chronicles* explicate that which *Kings* had only hinted at?

Perhaps the dying of these children was meant to be emblematic of the process of degeneration within the Davidic dynasty, set in motion by Yehoshaphat's marriage to Omri's daughter. As we have seen repeatedly, *Kings* makes no issue of this, and the killing of Achaziahu's children does not carry any significance beyond the horror of the act itself and its place in the process by which Yoash became king. By contrast, in *Chronicles* these murders are the final step in the process begun by the Philistines and the Arabs (21:17), and continued with ruthless efficiency by Yehu. In the drawn out death of these children, which but for the miraculous saving of Yoash would have effectively annihilated the line of Davidic succession, the whole sad process was symbolized.

11. וַתִּקַּח יְהוֹשַׁבְעַת ... אֶת־יוֹאָשׁ — *But Yehoshavath ... took Yoash ...* Throughout this chapter we have spoken of the Divine decree which ordained that the Davidic line was to be annihilated together with that of Omri. We traced the elements which joined together to contribute to the fulfillment of that decree, and in Athaliahu's final, murderous assault we should have fully expected it to have reached its realization.

Nevertheless, Yoash is saved, and while many lives are lost, the Davidic dynasty lives on. See Section II, *Eternal David*, for a discussion.

בַּחֲדַר הַמִּטּוֹת — *In the bedchamber*.

The bedchamber set aside for the use of the *Kohanim* in the Temple (*Mefaresh*).

Rashi to *Kings* brings the tradition of the Sages that *bedchamber* refers to the Holy of Holies in the Temple. Yehoshavath and her husband Yehoiada, who was *Kohen Gadol*, had access to that most sacred of places and concealed the young king, either in the cells surrounding it, or in the attic rooms over it (*Midrash Shocher Tov* 18). See Section II, *An Ecstasy of Love*, for a discussion.

12. וַיְהִי אִתָּם בְּבֵית הָאֱל־הִים — *So he was with them in God's House*.

We, who have never experienced the overwhelming sanctity of the Temple — not to speak of the Holy of Holies which even the *Kohen Gadol* was allowed to enter only on *Yom Kippur* — cannot conceive of the full implication of these words. There is nothing which could help us to grasp what a child who grew up for six years in such an environment must have been like. As we shall see at 24:17, Yoash did indeed appear to his contemporaries as something more than human.

22
11-12

and decided to dispatch all the royal seed of the house of Judah,
with a lingering death. 11 *But Yehoshavath, daughter of the king,*
took Yoash the son of Achaziahu and spirited him away from
among the murdered princes, and placed him and his nurse in the
bedchamber. Thus Yehoshavath the daughter of the king, the
wife of Yehoiada the Kohen — since she was Achaziahu's sister
— concealed him from Athaliahu, so that she did not kill him.
12 *So he was with them in God's House, concealed for six years,*
while Athaliahu ruled over the land.

23
1

Now, in the seventh year, Yehoiada found the fortitude

XXIII

◆ Yoash Is Crowned King

This chapter tells how Yehoiada arranged for Yoash to be crowned king, and of the deposal and killing of Athaliahu.

Within the context of *Chronicles'* perspective on the events of Yehoram's and Achaziahu's reigns, Yoash's story carries other implications than it does in *Kings*. In the latter there is no indication that the Davidic dynasty, as such, stood in danger. That Yoash was saved, and subsequently elevated to the kingship, has no significance beyond the narrow confines of the actual events. By contrast, in *Chronicles* we have — as detailed in the previous chapter — a virtual resurrection of the Davidic dynasty, with all that is implied in an event of such cosmic significance.

Such a perspective makes something more of Yehoiada than a man whose wife's initiative, coupled with his own wisdom and loyalty, enabled him to foil the murderous ambitions of Athaliahu. It moves him into the very center of Jewish history — makes him, indeed, one of its outstanding heroes — as the man responsible for preserving the essence of Jewish existence.

Aggadah takes note of Yehoiada's unique role, as follows.

At 24:15 we learn that Yehoiada was one hundred and thirty years old when he died. This brings his birth into Solomon's reign.[1]

Indeed, this is the tradition of the Sages in *Seder Olam* 18: At the very moment that disintegration [קָלְקָלָה or as *Yalkut* reads, קְלָלָה, *curse*] set in during Solomon's reign, Yehoiada, the one who was destined to correct it [הַמְּתַקֵּן], was born.

Clearly, Yehoiada is perceived as the savior of the Davidic dynasty.

In an earlier passage, *Seder Olam* 18 describes how Yoash had been hidden in the Holy of Holies, and asserts that David, with his prophetic eye, had this event in mind when, in *Psalms* 27:5, he said, *He will cache me in His shelter on the day of distress, will conceal me in the innermost chamber of His tent*. What then, *Seder Olam* asks, is the meaning of the next phrase: *He will lift me upon a rock*? It refers to Yehoiada, the man who can be described as a rock.

In Yehoiada, then, the Sages detected the firm, unyielding strength, the utter dependability and steadfast supportiveness of the rock. Israel's Messianic future could rest securely upon the shoulders of this man.

1. וּבַשָּׁנָה הַשְּׁבִעִית הִתְחַזַּק יְהוֹיָדָע — *Now, in the seventh year Yehoiada found the fortitude within himself . . .*

To facilitate comparison with the parallel verse in *Kings* (11:4), we quote it here with the translation according to *Radak* and *Metzudos*. We will then refer back to it, as indicated.

וּבַשָּׁנָה הַשְּׁבִיעִית שָׁלַח יְהוֹיָדָע וַיִּקַּח אֶת־שָׂרֵי הַמֵּאוֹת לַכָּרִי וְלָרָצִים וַיָּבֵא אֹתָם אֵלָיו בֵּית ה׳ וַיִּכְרֹת לָהֶם בְּרִית וַיַּשְׁבַּע אֹתָם בְּבֵית ה׳ וַיַּרְא אֹתָם אֶת־בֶּן־הַמֶּלֶךְ — *Now in the seventh year, Yehoiada sent to summon the captains of hundreds, the leaders and the runners, and brought them to him to* HASHEM*'s House, forged a covenant for them,*

1. Rechav'am reigned seventeen years; Aviyah, three years; Asa, forty-one years; Yehoshaphat, twenty-five years; Yehoram, eight years; Achaziahu, one year; Athaliahu, six years. Yehoiada certainly lived beyond the twenty-third year of Yoash's forty-year reign (*II Kings* 12:7 ff. and 24:14 here); a total of one hundred and twenty-four years.

וַיִּקַּח אֶת־שָׂרֵי הַמֵּאוֹת לַעֲזַרְיָהוּ בֶן־יְרֹחָם וּלְיִשְׁמָעֵאל
בֶּן־יְהוֹחָנָן וְלַעֲזַרְיָהוּ בֶן־עוֹבֵד וְאֶת־מַעֲשֵׂיָהוּ בֶן־עֲדָיָהוּ
ב וְאֶת־אֱלִישָׁפָט בֶּן־זִכְרִי עִמּוֹ בַבְּרִית׃ וַיָּסֹבּוּ בִּיהוּדָה
וַיִּקְבְּצוּ אֶת־הַלְוִיִּם מִכָּל־עָרֵי יְהוּדָה וְרָאשֵׁי הָאָבוֹת
ג לְיִשְׂרָאֵל וַיָּבֹאוּ אֶל־יְרוּשָׁלִָם׃ וַיִּכְרֹת כָּל־הַקָּהָל בְּרִית
בְּבֵית הָאֱלֹהִים עִם־הַמֶּלֶךְ וַיֹּאמֶר לָהֶם הִנֵּה בֶן־הַמֶּלֶךְ

administered an oath to them in HASHEM's House, and showed them the king's son. We note in the first place, that the *Kings'* account has no parallel for the phrase ... *found the fortitude within himself*. The phrase is used here in order to set the stage for a description of matters of great import, but has no place in that entirely low-key version of the events.

וַיִּקַּח אֶת־שָׂרֵי הַמֵּאוֹת . . . עִמּוֹ בַבְּרִית — *To join the captains of hundreds ... into a covenant with him*. A careful comparison between this and the *Kings'* verse quoted above shows that, in spite of a superficial similarity, they say entirely different things.

Let us postulate that the captains of hundreds mentioned in the two verses are the same. Our verse describes a covenant which Yehoiada made with them. [וַיִּקַּח goes together with עִמּוֹ בַבְּרִית at the end of the verse, and does not, as does the וַיִּקַּח of *Kings*, mean that he took the people.] The next verse then goes on to tell how these captains spread around the country, in order to round up the Levites and the family heads.

By contrast, while *Kings* also talks of captains of hundreds, it does not mention specific activities which they undertook. The covenant of which it speaks, parallels the one described in our v. 3, not the one mentioned in our verse.

Furthermore, we must wonder why, if the *Kings* account saw no need to identify the captains of hundreds by name, *Chronicles* would want to do so. One imagines that these names cannot have carried much meaning to the people in Ezra's time.

We note that the combination וַיִּקַּח . . . עִמּוֹ בַבְּרִית, is unique. The verb used to describe the forging of a covenant is almost always כרת as, indeed, it is used in v. 3.

We conclude that our phrase does not mean the forging of a covenant, in the sense that two parties with different interests enter into an agreement. Rather, Yehoiada seems to have been inviting these people to join him as partners in his conspiracy. Indeed, this seems borne out in v. 2, where their activity in collecting the Levites and family heads from throughout Judah seems to have been done on their own initiative. It is not Yehoiada who sent them but they, themselves, who spread out to do what was necessary.

As partners in the profoundly significant events in which they were privileged to play a role, they deserved to be mentioned by name, eternally to be remembered by an Israel forever in their debt.

In the *Kings'* account, in which the cosmic undertones are missing, there was no need either to spell out the specific role which these five people played nor to identify them by name. The general information that Yehoiada sent for various groups of people is sufficient. How this was done was of no interest within that perspective.

2. הַלְוִיִּם . . . וְרָאשֵׁי הָאָבוֹת לְיִשְׂרָאֵל — *The Levites ... as also the family heads of Israel.* These Levites are not mentioned in *Kings*, while *Chronicles* makes no mention of the runners which are mentioned there.

What role did the Levites have to play in the events which are about to unfold?

Since we find no specific duties for Levites in connection with either the establishment of the monarchy or with the crowning of an individual king, it appears that we must look for an answer in the unique circumstances which surrounded this particular coronation.

Jeremiah 33:20-23 reads as follows: *Thus says HASHEM, If My covenant with day and My covenant with night were to be broken, that day and night were no more to be in their correct time; then too would My covenant with David, My servant, be broken, that he should no more have a son ruling upon his throne, and [also My covenant] with the Levites, the Kohanim, My ministrants. Even as the hosts of heaven cannot be counted and the sand of the sea cannot be measured, so will I increase the seed of David, My servant and [of] the Levites, My ministrants.*

Monarchy and Levitic sanctity are bracketed together. The abrogation of the one is as unthinkable as the abrogation of the other. Together, and only together, do they give form and meaning to eternal Israel. This is the meaning of the triad, Israel, David and Levi,

23
2-3
within himself to join the captains of hundreds, Azariahu the son of Yerocham, Ishmael the son of Yehochanan, Azariahu, the son of Oved, Maaseiahu the son of Adaiahu, and Elishaphat the son of Zichri, into a covenant with him. 2 *They went about in Judah, mustering the Levites from all the cities of Judah, as also the family heads of Israel, and they came to Jerusalem.* 3 *Then, in God's House, the whole assembly made a covenant with the king. And he said to them, 'Behold the king's son shall reign,*

which plays such a significant role in the prophecies of Zechariah (*Zechariah* 4:4-7). See also 6:12-13 there.

It is fitting that at the crowning which had at its essence the guaranteed eternity of Israel's kingship, the Levites — the third leg of the triad — should also be represented.

In *Kings*, this point is not made because there, the preservation of the Davidic dynasty is not the issue. The concern is with the practical aspects of the coronation, and the protection of the new king. In that context the runners were significant while the Levites were not.

3. וַיִּכְרֹת כָּל־הַקָּהָל בְּרִית ... עִם־הַמֶּלֶךְ — *The whole assembly made a covenant with the king.* The *Kings* verse has וַיִּכְרֹת לָהֶם בְּרִית. *Rashi* explains that the intent of this covenant was to exact a promise from the people that they would assist in crowning Yoash king. *Mefaresh* assigns the same meaning to our phrase.

See Section II, *The King and the Son of the King*, for a different possibility.

4-7. These verses, which describe the dispositions which Yehoiada made for the protection of the king, seem to parallel vs. 5-8 in *II Kings*, ch. 11. However, a comparison between the two sections reveals a number of substantive differences.

Chronicles	Kings
a. זֶה הַדָּבָר אֲשֶׁר תַּעֲשׂוּ —*This you should do*	a. וַיְצַוֵּם לֵאמֹר — *He commanded them, saying*
b.	b. זֶה הַדָּבָר אֲשֶׁר תַּעֲשׂוּן — *This you shall do*
c. הַשְּׁלִשִׁית ... לַכֹּהֲנִים וְלַלְוִיִּם — *a third part ... both Kohanim and Levites*	c. הַשְּׁלִשִׁית מִכֶּם בָּאֵי הַשַּׁבָּת — *The third part of you, those that come on the Sabbath*
d. לְשֹׁעֲרֵי הַסִּפִּים — *... as sentries at the gates.*	d. וְשֹׁמְרֵי מִשְׁמֶרֶת בֵּית הַמֶּלֶךְ — *and stand watch at the king's palace.*
e. וְהַשְּׁלִשִׁית בְּבֵית הַמֶּלֶךְ — *A third is to be in the king's palace*	e. וְהַשְּׁלִשִׁית בְּשַׁעַר סוּר — *And a third part at the Sur Gate*
f. וְהַשְּׁלִשִׁית בְּשַׁעַר הַיְסוֹד — *and a third at the Yesod Gate*	f. וְהַשְּׁלִשִׁית בַּשַּׁעַר אַחַר הָרָצִים — *and a third part at the gate, behind the runners*
g.	g. וּשְׁמַרְתֶּם אֶת־מִשְׁמֶרֶת הַבַּיִת מַסָּח — *and you shall guard the house conscientiously.*
h. וְכָל־הָעָם בְּחַצְרוֹת בֵּית ה׳ — *All the people are to remain in the courts of the House of* HASHEM.	h.
i. וְאַל־יָבוֹא בֵית־ה׳ — *But let none come into the House of* HASHEM ...	i.
j.	j. וּשְׁתֵּי הַיָּדוֹת בָּכֶם — *Two segments from among you*
k.	k. כֹּל יֹצְאֵי הַשַּׁבָּת — *all who go out on the Sabbath,*
l.	l. וְשָׁמְרוּ אֶת־מִשְׁמֶרֶת בֵּית־ה׳ אֶל־הַמֶּלֶךְ — *shall stand guard over the House of* HASHEM *for the king.*
m. ... וְהִקִּיפוּ הַלְוִיִּם אֶת־הַמֶּלֶךְ סָבִיב ... — *The Levites shall encircle the king round about*	m. ... וְהִקַּפְתֶּם עַל־הַמֶּלֶךְ סָבִיב — *Now you shall encircle the king round about ...*

ד יִמְלֹךְ כַּאֲשֶׁר דִּבֶּר יהוה עַל־בְּנֵי דָוִיד׃ זֶה הַדָּבָר אֲשֶׁר
תַּעֲשׂוּ הַשְּׁלִשִׁית מִכֶּם בָּאֵי הַשַּׁבָּת לַכֹּהֲנִים וְלַלְוִיִּם
ה לְשֹׁעֲרֵי הַסִּפִּים׃ וְהַשְּׁלִשִׁית בְּבֵית הַמֶּלֶךְ וְהַשְּׁלִשִׁית
ו בְּשַׁעַר הַיְסוֹד וְכָל־הָעָם בְּחַצְרוֹת בֵּית יהוה׃ וְאַל־יָבוֹא
בֵית־יהוה כִּי אִם־הַכֹּהֲנִים וְהַמְשָׁרְתִים לַלְוִיִּם הֵמָּה
יָבֹאוּ כִּי־קֹדֶשׁ הֵמָּה וְכָל־הָעָם יִשְׁמְרוּ מִשְׁמֶרֶת יהוה׃
ז וְהִקִּיפוּ הַלְוִיִּם אֶת־הַמֶּלֶךְ סָבִיב אִישׁ וְכֵלָיו בְּיָדוֹ וְהַבָּא
ח אֶל־הַבַּיִת יוּמָת וִהְיוּ אֶת־הַמֶּלֶךְ בְּבֹאוֹ וּבְצֵאתוֹ׃ וַיַּעֲשׂוּ
הַלְוִיִּם וְכָל־יְהוּדָה כְּכֹל אֲשֶׁר־צִוָּה יְהוֹיָדָע הַכֹּהֵן וַיִּקְחוּ
אִישׁ אֶת־אֲנָשָׁיו בָּאֵי הַשַּׁבָּת עִם יוֹצְאֵי הַשַּׁבָּת כִּי לֹא
ט פָטַר יְהוֹיָדָע הַכֹּהֵן אֶת־הַמַּחְלְקוֹת׃ וַיִּתֵּן
יְהוֹיָדָע הַכֹּהֵן לְשָׂרֵי הַמֵּאוֹת אֶת־הַחֲנִיתִים וְאֶת־
הַמָּגִנּוֹת וְאֶת־הַשְּׁלָטִים אֲשֶׁר לַמֶּלֶךְ דָּוִיד אֲשֶׁר בֵּית

We follow *Metzudos* in his interpretation of the *Kings'* account. Yehoiada planned the coup to take place on *Shabbos*, so that two groups of *Kohanim* and Levites would be available to him. *Shabbos* is the day on which the *mishmaros* relieve one another, and therefore both the outgoing [k] and the incoming [c] groups would stand at his service. There were to be three separate groups of guards, each stationed at a different location. Since the entering *mishmar* was charged with the Temple duties, only half of them would be available for guard duty. These would man only one of the three stations, this to be located inside the palace [d].

The outgoing cadre had no current obligations, and could therefore fill two thirds of the required posts [k and l]. They would be stationed at the Sur Gate [e] and at the gate mentioned in [f].

Let us postulate that the *Chronicles'* account describes the same matters: The בֵּית הַמֶּלֶךְ of [e] in *Chronicles* would be identical with the location of the same name in [d] of *Kings*. The Yesod Gate of *Chronicles* [f] would be the same as the Sur Gate of *Kings* [e]. The סִפִּים of *Chronicles* [d] is to be identified with the שַׁעַר of *Kings* [f].

Indeed, this is how *Metzudos* interprets the passage.

But, if so, we are faced with an apparent contradiction. According to *Kings* [d], the בֵּית הַמֶּלֶךְ was to be manned by the incoming *mishmar*, but *Chronicles* [d] assigns the men of this group to the סִפִּים.

Metzudos notes the problem and because of it thinks that [d] in *Chronicles* is not to be read together with the first part of the verse. We are told that guards were to be stationed inside the king's palace, but we are not to assume that these were to be identified with the group mentioned in the first part of the verse.

Malbim offers a different solution: *Chronicles* had no need to repeat the dispositions which are already described in sufficient detail in *Kings*. The three groups here are not identical with the ones mentioned in *Kings*, but are all subdivisions of the first third mentioned there — the incoming *mishmar* which was to be in charge of the palace. The *Chronicles'* account explains, as the *Kings'* account does not, that this group were also divided into three, and that each of these sub-groupings was assigned to a different location in the palace.

For a different explanation see Section II, *Yehoiada's Two Speeches.*

4. בָּאֵי הַשַּׁבָּת לַכֹּהֲנִים וְלַלְוִיִּם — *That come in on the Sabbath, both Kohanim and Levites.* The Kohanite and Levite *mishmaros* served in the Temple on a weekly basis. Every *Shabbos*, after the *musaf* sacrifice had been brought, the current *mishmar* was relieved by the new one coming in. Thus, בָּאֵי הַשַּׁבָּת describes the incoming *mishmar*. The outgoing *mishmar* was also to play a role, as implied in v. 8 here and stated expressly in v. 7 of the *Kings'* account [k] (*Mefaresh* and *Metzudos*).

For a different explanation, see Section II, *Sentries at the Gates*.

5. בְּשַׁעַר הַיְסוֹד — *At the Yesod Gate*. It seems

in accordance with that which HASHEM had said concerning
David's descendants. 4 *This you should do; a third part of you*
that come in on the Sabbath, both Kohanim and Levites, shall
serve as sentries at the gates. 5 *A third is to be in the king's palace,*
and a third at the Yesod Gate. And all the people are to remain in
the courts of the House of HASHEM. 6 *But let none come into the*
House of HASHEM, except the Kohanim and they that minister
from among the Levites. They shall come in for they are holy but
the people shall be attentive to HASHEM's charge. 7 *The Levites*
shall encircle the king round about, each man with his implements
in his hand. Whoever enters the House shall be put to death. They
shall accompany the king when he comes in and when he goes
out.' 8 *The Levites and all Judah did all that Yehoiada the Kohen*
had commanded. Each man took his men, the ones that came in on
the Sabbath with the ones that went out on the Sabbath for Yehoi-
ada the Kohen had not dismissed the divisions. 9 *Yehoiada the*
Kohen gave the captains of the hundreds the spears, the bucklers,
and the shields that were King David's, which were in God's

likely that this is the same as the שַׁעַר סוּר of the *Kings'* account. The Sages say that both are names for the eastern entrance gate into the Temple. That gate was the beginning or *foundation* [יְסוֹד, *foundation*] of the special sanctity of the Temple, and it was from there that people who were ritually unclean were *turned away* [סוּר, to *turn away*].

וְכָל־הָעָם — *And all the people.*
See Section II, *The People.*

6. וְהַמְשָׁרְתִים לַלְוִיִּם — *And they that minister from among the Levites.* The translation follows *Metzudos. Radak* interprets as though the word had been written הַלְוִיִּם. It is to be understood in apposition, and the phrase is to be rendered: *The ministrants, the Levites.*

יִשְׁמְרוּ מִשְׁמֶרֶת ה׳ — *...shall be attentive to HASHEM's charge.*

Radak seems to read this expression as bearing on the guarding of the king. The Israelites are to perform their service in the courtyard; not in the buildings.

However, both *Mefaresh* and *Metzudos* interpret the phrase to mean that the people should conscientiously avoid those precincts which were forbidden to them.

7. וְהִקִּיפוּ הַלְוִיִּם אֶת־הַמֶּלֶךְ סָבִיב — *The Levites shall encircle the king round about.* As we suggested in Section II, *Yehoiada's Two Speeches*, this formulation, in contrast to the וְהִקַּפְתֶּם of the *Kings'* account, indicates that the Levites mentioned here are not the ones which were addressed until now. At this point, the *Chronicles'* account switches to a description how, and by whom, the king was to be guarded physically.

אִישׁ וְכֵלָיו בְּיָדוֹ — *Each man with his implements in his hand.* This refers to his weapons (*Mefaresh, Metzudos*).

וְהַבָּא אֶל־הַבַּיִת יוּמָת — *Whoever enters the House shall be put to death. House* refers to the Temple (*Targum*). Any unauthorized person was to be killed. Such a one might well be one of Athaliahu's loyal supporters, who might wish to harm the king (*Metzudos*).

8. ...וַיַּעֲשׂוּ הַלְוִיִּם וְכָל־יְהוּדָה ... וַיִּקְחוּ אִישׁ — *The Levites and all Judah did ... Each man took ...* The subject of וַיִּקְחוּ is not the same as that in the earlier phrase. Here the *captains of the hundreds*, mentioned further in the next verse, must be meant (*Metzudos*). This is explicated in the *Kings'* version.

Thus, our verse tells that both the groups with which the *Chronicles'* account has dealt, the assemblage summoned by Yehoiada to witness the great miracle that was about to happen, and the men charged with the physical protection of the king now moved into position.

... כִּי לֹא פָטַר יְהוֹיָדָע הַכֹּהֵן — *For Yehoiada the Kohen had not dismissed ...* He did not permit the outgoing *mishmar* to go home as they would normally have done. Thus, the available manpower for guarding the king would be doubled.

9. אֲשֶׁר לַמֶּלֶךְ דָּוִיד — *That were King David's.*

כג
י־יד

י הָאֱלֹהִים׃ וַיַּעֲמֵד אֶת־כָּל־הָעָם וְאִישׁ ׀ שִׁלְחוֹ בְיָדוֹ מִכֶּתֶף
הַבַּיִת הַיְמָנִית עַד־כֶּתֶף הַבַּיִת הַשְּׂמָאלִית לַמִּזְבֵּחַ וְלַבָּיִת
יא עַל־הַמֶּלֶךְ סָבִיב׃ וַיּוֹצִיאוּ אֶת־בֶּן־הַמֶּלֶךְ וַיִּתְּנוּ עָלָיו אֶת־
הַנֵּזֶר וְאֶת־הָעֵדוּת וַיַּמְלִיכוּ אֹתוֹ וַיִּמְשָׁחֻהוּ יְהוֹיָדָע וּבָנָיו
יב וַיֹּאמְרוּ יְחִי הַמֶּלֶךְ׃ וַתִּשְׁמַע עֲתַלְיָהוּ אֶת־קוֹל
הָעָם הָרָצִים וְהַמְהַלְלִים אֶת־הַמֶּלֶךְ וַתָּבוֹא אֶל־הָעָם בֵּית
יג יהוה׃ וַתֵּרֶא וְהִנֵּה הַמֶּלֶךְ עוֹמֵד עַל־עַמּוּדוֹ בַּמָּבוֹא
וְהַשָּׂרִים וְהַחֲצֹצְרוֹת עַל־הַמֶּלֶךְ וְכָל־עַם הָאָרֶץ שָׂמֵחַ
וְתוֹקֵעַ בַּחֲצֹצְרוֹת וְהַמְשׁוֹרְרִים בִּכְלֵי הַשִּׁיר וּמוֹדִיעִים
לְהַלֵּל וַתִּקְרַע עֲתַלְיָהוּ אֶת־בְּגָדֶיהָ וַתֹּאמֶר קֶשֶׁר
יד קָשֶׁר׃ וַיּוֹצֵא יְהוֹיָדָע הַכֹּהֵן אֶת־שָׂרֵי הַמֵּאוֹת ׀

This refers to that which David had made (*Metzudos*). There is no record elsewhere of David's having made shields. However, *I Kings* 10:17 and *II Chronicles* 9:16 both speak of shields which Solomon had made. *Malbim* suggests that these are the shields mentioned here, and that they are called David's because Solomon made them out of the gold that David had stored up.

10. וַיַּעֲמֵד אֶת־כָּל־הָעָם — *He positioned all the people.*

See Section II, *The People*.

שִׁלְחוֹ — *His sword*. The translation follows *Radak*.

מִכֶּתֶף הַבַּיִת הַיְמָנִית — *From the right shoulder of the House ...*

How were the people ranged? If it was in a straight north-south line from one side of the courtyard to the other, then סָבִיב, *round about*, at the end of the verse is difficult. Also, what do the words לַמִּזְבֵּחַ וְלַבָּיִת mean? [1]

The word כָּתֵף is never used to describe an abstract *side* of something. It is always the concrete walling that is on either side of an entrance [cf. *Exodus* 27:14 and 15]. This is in accordance with the basic meaning of *shoulder*. Accordingly, the phrase cannot mean that they were ranged from the right side to the left side of the Temple Court. If this would have been the case, the word כָּתֵף would have conveyed nothing. Rather, the people were ranged from the wall on the right side of the Temple entrance, all the way up to [עַד] which was on the left. This would be the best way to describe an arrangement wherein the people encircled the entire Temple Court. They started at the right shoulder, and reached all the way to the left. They were, indeed, stationed *around* the altar.

What does וְלַבָּיִת mean? *Targum* to *Kings* renders בֵּית כַּפּוּרֵי, the *Targum* of בֵּית הַכַּפֹּרֶת (*I Chronicles* 28:11) — the Holy of Holies. Apparently, then, two semi-circles of people started out from the southern shoulder of the Temple building. The one encircled the courtyard, the other went around the back of the building behind the Holy of Holies. Thus, the Temple area was completely surrounded. The sequence לַמִּזְבֵּחַ וְלַבָּיִת is appropriate, since the circle surrounding the courtyard — and therefore also the altar in which the king actually was to stand — was the more important of the two.

עַל־הַמֶּלֶךְ סָבִיב — *Round about the king.*

Yoash had not yet been brought out. The meaning of the phrase must be that they were ranged in such a way that they would be surrounding Yoash once he had been proclaimed king. See Section II, *The King and the Son of the King*.

11. וַיִּתְּנוּ עָלָיו אֶת־הַנֵּזֶר וְאֶת־הָעֵדוּת — *And placed upon him the crown and the trappings*. עָדָה is *to ornament oneself*, עֵדָה is *testimony*. *Radak* derives עדות from the former, and believes that reference here is to the kingly robes or insignia of royalty which were appropriate to the occasion.

If the word is to be taken as *testimony*, then

1. *Metzudos* inserts the words *in front*. They stood *in front* of the altar and the House. But if they stood in a straight line east of the altar, then [*in front of*] *the House* says nothing, and if they were west of the altar — between it and the Temple building — then they were not *in front* of the altar.

23
10-14

House [10] *He positioned all the people, each with his sword in his hand, from the right shoulder of the House till the left shoulder of the House — around altar and House — round about the king.* [11] *They brought out the son of the king and placed upon him the crown and the trappings and made him king. Yehoiada and his sons anointed him and they said, 'May the king live!'* [12] *Athaliahu heard the sound of the people running and extolling the king. So she came to the people into* HASHEM's *House.* [13] *She looked, and there was the king standing at his station by the entrance, officials and trumpets near the king; and all the people of the land rejoicing and sounding trumpets, and the choristers with instruments encouraging one another to extol. Athaliahu tore her clothes and called, 'A cabal, a cabal!'* [14] *Yehoiada the Kohen brought out the captains of the hundreds, the ones*

it would refer to the *Sefer Torah* which a king is required to have with him at all times (*Rashi* and *Metzudos*; see *Rambam, Hilchos Melachim* 3:1). This *Sefer Torah* was hung upon his arm like an amulet (*Metzudos*).

According to *Avodah Zarah* 44a, the words are to be read together — *the crown* [*which served as*] *a testimony*. According to the Sages' tradition, the crown which David had captured from Amon (*I Chronicles* 20:2) was shaped in a special way and was used to test the legitimacy of anyone who claimed the right to succeed to the Davidic throne. It would only fit people who were qualified for the kingship [see discussion in comm. there]. Here this crown was placed upon Yoash's head in order to dispel any doubts as to whether he was indeed a scion of the Davidic line.

וַיִּמְשָׁחֻהוּ — *And ... anointed him*. Normally, when a son succeeds his father, no anointing is required. It was done here only to establish Yoash as king against the pretensions of Athaliahu (*Horios* 11b).

יְחִי הַמֶּלֶךְ — *May the king live!*

Targum renders: May the king be successful.

12. אֶת־קוֹל הָעָם הָרָצִים — *The sound of the people running*. *Targum* (*Kings*) renders: *dancing*.

13. עַל־עַמּוּדוֹ — *At his station*. The place assigned to the king in the Temple Court (*Rashi* and *Metzudos*).

As *Rashi* and *Metzudos* render the word, there is no indication that it was an elevated platform. *Mefaresh*, adducing the usage of his own times — that at any official assembly the king would stand on a platform the better to be seen and heard — thinks that we are dealing with a platform of some sort. He equates it with the *kior* of 6:13 — see comm. there. This seems likely since throughout Scripture, עַמּוּד is a *pillar* or *column*.

בַּמָּבוֹא — *By the entrance*.

The royal station was positioned near the entrance to the Temple Court (*Metzudos*).

וְהַמְשׁוֹרְרִים בִּכְלֵי הַשִּׁיר — *And the choristers with instruments*. See comm. to *I Chronicles* 15:19.

וּמוֹדִיעִים לְהַלֵּל — *Encouraging one another to extol*.

From ידע, *to know*. The *hiphil* voice: *to make known*. Each showing the other how to praise (*Metzudos*). We have translated this unusual usage according to the context.

קֶשֶׁר קָשֶׁר — *A cabal, a cabal!* קֶשֶׁר is a *knot*, hence the connotation of people bound to each other in a plot.

14. ... וַיּוֹצֵא יְהוֹיָדָע הַכֹּהֵן — *Yehoiada the Kohen brought out* ... He brought the officers out from the Temple building (*Metzudos*). But there is no indication anywhere that prior to this moment they had been in the building. It seems much more likely that the officers would have been together with the men who were ranged around the Temple Court.

Perhaps the word is used in the sense of *to produce* or *to exhibit* (cf. *Psalms* 37:6; *Job* 12:22), that is, to make something evident, which had previously been obscured. When Athaliahu came into the Temple compound, her entire concentration had been on the boy-king standing at his royal station, and the jubilant populace rejoicing at the coronation. She did not focus at all on the fact that there were armed soldiers present and may indeed

פְּקוּדֵי הַחַיִל וַיֹּאמֶר אֲלֵהֶם הוֹצִיאוּהָ אֶל־מִבֵּית הַשְּׂדֵרוֹת
וְהַבָּא אַחֲרֶיהָ יוּמַת בֶּחָרֶב כִּי אָמַר הַכֹּהֵן לֹא תְמִיתוּהָ בֵּית
טו יְהוָה: וַיָּשִׂימוּ לָהּ יָדַיִם וַתָּבוֹא אֶל־מְבוֹא שַׁעַר־הַסּוּסִים
בֵּית הַמֶּלֶךְ וַיְמִיתוּהָ שָׁם:
טז וַיִּכְרֹת יְהוֹיָדָע בְּרִית בֵּינוֹ וּבֵין כָּל־הָעָם וּבֵין הַמֶּלֶךְ
יז לִהְיוֹת לְעָם לַיהוָה: וַיָּבֹאוּ כָל־הָעָם בֵּית־הַבַּעַל וַיִּתְּצֻהוּ
וְאֶת־מִזְבְּחֹתָיו וְאֶת־צְלָמָיו שִׁבֵּרוּ וְאֵת מַתָּן כֹּהֵן הַבַּעַל
יח הָרְגוּ לִפְנֵי הַמִּזְבְּחוֹת: וַיָּשֶׂם יְהוֹיָדָע פְּקֻדֹּת בֵּית יְהוָה
בְּיַד הַכֹּהֲנִים הַלְוִיִּם אֲשֶׁר חָלַק דָּוִיד עַל־בֵּית יְהוָה
לְהַעֲלוֹת עֹלוֹת יְהוָה כַּכָּתוּב בְּתוֹרַת מֹשֶׁה בְּשִׂמְחָה
יט וּבְשִׁיר עַל יְדֵי דָוִיד: וַיַּעֲמֵד הַשּׁוֹעֲרִים עַל־שַׁעֲרֵי בֵּית

have expected that her call *'A cabal, a cabal!'* would be answered by a loyal soldiery. To her shock, Yehoiada now produced the officers who were charged with executing her.

The *Kings'* account has ... וַיְצַו in place of וַיּוֹצֵא. See Section II, *The Officers' Involvement*.

אֶל־מִבֵּית הַשְּׂדֵרוֹת — *Between the ranks.*

In *Targum's* view, the שׂ, *sin*, replaces the ס, *samech*. He renders סְדָרֵי, *something set in order*; hence the soldiers' ranks (*Metzudos*). Athaliahu was to be taken out of the Temple in order that her dead body should not defile its hallowed precincts, but care was to be taken that she should at all times be surrounded by soldiers in order that she should not escape.

וְהַבָּא אַחֲרֶיהָ ... — *And whoever follows her.*

In order to help her (*Metzudos*).

יוּמַת — *Shall be put to death.* The passive voice is used. The involvement of the officers in the death of the intruder is of no significance when weighed against their task of killing Athaliahu. See further in Section II, *The Officers' Involvement*.

15. וַיָּשִׂמוּ לָהּ יָדַיִם — *They made way for her.*

They made room for her to pass through (*Metzudos*). יַד here implies *a place*, see *Deuteronomy* 23:13.

שַׁעַר־הַסּוּסִים — *The Susim Gate.*

סוּס is a *horse*. This was the gate by which horses entered the palace grounds (*Metzudos*).

16. בֵּינוֹ וּבֵין כָּל־הָעָם וּבֵין הַמֶּלֶךְ — *Between himself, all the people and the king.* See Section II, *The Covenants*, for an analysis of the covenant described here, in contrast to those described in *Kings*.

17. וַיָּבֹאוּ כָל־הָעָם בֵּית־הַבַּעַל וַיִּתְּצֻהוּ — *All the people went to the Baal's Temple, broke it down.* With Athaliahu's death, the link to the Northern Kingdom had been broken and the people who, even during the fifteen dark years since Yehoram's ascension to the throne, had remained loyal to God, now fell upon the most overt symbol of the moral degeneration which the union with the royal house of Israel had brought about.

In the next chapter, we shall have the opportunity to examine the degree to which Baal worship had proliferated in Judah and what its practical effect had been. *HaLevi* in *Tekufas HaMikra*, chs. 4 and 6 makes the point that it was both short lived and strictly localized — indulged in by the royal circle but not by the people as a whole.

His reasoning is as follows: The Baal was not introduced before Yehoram's reign — he was the first king concerning whom it is said that he *walked in the ways of the kings of Israel* (21:6) — and so it could not have lasted more than fifteen years. Our verse strongly implies that there was only one locale — close enough to the Temple, and therefore to the royal palace — to which the people could go in order to wreak destruction during the coronation ceremony. Their spontaneous act clearly shows that Baal worship had never met with their approbation.

18. וַיָּשֶׂם יְהוֹיָדָע פְּקֻדֹּת בֵּית ה׳ בְּיַד הַכֹּהֲנִים ... — *Yehoiada placed the administration of the House of* HASHEM *in the hands of the Kohanim* ... *Kings* has וַיָּשֶׂם הַכֹּהֵן פְּקֻדֹּת עַל בֵּית ה׳ and stops. The last part of our verse, and also the next one, have no parallel there.

Rashi on פְּקֻדֹּת [in *Kings*] writes that these were the Temple guards — those referred to in our v. 19.

appointed over the soldiery, and said to them, 'Take her out between the ranks and whoever follows her shall be put to death by the sword.' For the Kohen said, 'Do not kill her in the House of HASHEM.'
15 *So they made way for her; and she came to the entrance of the Susim Gate to the king's house; and they killed her there.*
16 *Yehoiada made a covenant between himself, all the people and the king, that they might be a people to* HASHEM.
17 *All the people went to the Baal's House, broke it down, smashed his altars and his images, and slew Mattan, the priest of the Baal, before the altar.*
18 *Yehoiada placed the administration of* HASHEM*'s House in the hands of the Kohanim, the Levites, whom David had appointed over* HASHEM*'s House, to bring burnt offerings to* HASHEM*, as is written in the Torah of* HASHEM*, with rejoicing and with song, by the hands of David.*
19 *He set the guards at the gates*

How, then, are we to understand our verse?

We note further that in the *Kings'* account הַכֹּהֵן is used, while here, Yehoiada is called by name.

We assume that the use of הַכֹּהֵן is appropriate when that which is being done is motivated not from personal but from ritual concern. Thus, in v. 14, the concern that Athaliahu die outside the sacred Temple precincts is ascribed to הַכֹּהֵן. Thus, also the reinstatement of the guarding roster [*Kings*] was the responsibility of Yehoiada the *Kohen Gadol*, not of Yehoiada the man.

By contrast, the *Chronicles'* account seems to describe an initiative which Yehoiada the man set in motion.

We suggest that our phrase must be understood in conjunction with 8:15. That verse clearly implies that the ultimate responsibility for the Temple administration, which had been installed in accordance with David's dispositions [v. 14 there], was to lie with the king.

Now, a careful reading of *I Chronicles* 23:27 ff. yields that this had not been David's intention. In a very detailed presentation of the dispositions which he had made for the Temple administration, no word is said about the king. It is the *Kohanim*, with Levite assistance, to whom the Temple administration is entrusted.

However, Solomon, for reasons which must have appeared compelling to him, transferred these prerogatives to the king. This arrangement may well have continued after Solomon's death —indeed, there is no text which suggests otherwise.

Our verse may mean that Yehoiada now stepped in and returned the responsibility to the *Kohanim*. Henceforth, the king would be excluded from any responsibility for the Temple administration.

Yehoiada may well have seen this moment as propitious for reverting to the original system. The royal rights had clearly been abused — with potentially tragic results — by Athaliahu.

It would make eminent sense to inaugurate this change now, at a time when the king was still a child and powerless to protest this abrogation of his prerogative.

But the timing may well have been influenced by another consideration — and this would be why the initiator, in *Chronicles*, is *Yehoiada*, not *the Kohen*. The eternal Davidic dynasty was about to be miraculously re-established — by Yehoiada, the man who from birth had been destined for that role [see prefatory remarks to this ch.]. Yehoiada may well have thought such a moment right for re-establishing the *Davidic* concept of the Temple administration. Here was a rebirth; an opportunity to regain the pristine purity which had been lost in the post-Davidic upheavals.

אֲשֶׁר חָלַק דָּוִיד עַל־בֵּית ה׳ — *Whom David had appointed over the House of* HASHEM. For the various divisions of tasks which David had assigned to the Levites, see *I Chronicles* 23:27 ff. See particularly vs. 30 and 31 for their responsibilities concerning the daily burnt offerings and their musical accompaniment. See also *I Chronicles* 24:4 and 5.

וּבְשִׁיר עַל יְדֵי דָוִיד — *And with song, by the hands of David*. These were songs which David had composed (*Metzudos*).

19. וַיַּעֲמֵד הַשּׁוֹעֲרִים — *He set the guards.*

These were not gatekeepers in the sense that this term applies to the regular guarding of the Temple. The Levite watchmen, who usually stood guard at various points in the Temple complex, played a ceremonial rather than a

כג
כ־כא

כ יְהוָה וְלֹא־יָבֹא טָמֵא לְכָל־דָּבָר׃ וַיִּקַּח אֶת־שָׂרֵי הַמֵּאוֹת
וְאֶת־הָאַדִּירִים וְאֶת־הַמּוֹשְׁלִים בָּעָם וְאֵת ׀ כָּל־עַם הָאָרֶץ
וַיּוֹרֶד אֶת־הַמֶּלֶךְ מִבֵּית יהוֹה וַיָּבֹאוּ בְּתוֹךְ־שַׁעַר הָעֶלְיוֹן
בֵּית הַמֶּלֶךְ וַיּוֹשִׁיבוּ אֶת־הַמֶּלֶךְ עַל כִּסֵּא הַמַּמְלָכָה׃
כא וַיִּשְׂמְחוּ כָל־עַם־הָאָרֶץ וְהָעִיר שָׁקָטָה וְאֶת־עֲתַלְיָהוּ
כד
א־ה
א הֵמִיתוּ בֶחָרֶב׃ בֶּן־שֶׁבַע שָׁנִים יֹאָשׁ בְּמָלְכוֹ וְאַרְבָּעִים
ב שָׁנָה מָלַךְ בִּירוּשָׁלִָם וְשֵׁם אִמּוֹ צִבְיָה מִבְּאֵר שָׁבַע׃ וַיַּעַשׂ
יוֹאָשׁ הַיָּשָׁר בְּעֵינֵי יְהוָה כָּל־יְמֵי יְהוֹיָדָע הַכֹּהֵן׃
ג־ד וַיִּשָּׂא־לוֹ יְהוֹיָדָע נָשִׁים שְׁתָּיִם וַיּוֹלֶד בָּנִים וּבָנוֹת׃ וַיְהִי
ה אַחֲרֵי־כֵן הָיָה עִם־לֵב יוֹאָשׁ לְחַדֵּשׁ אֶת־בֵּית יְהוָה׃ וַיִּקְבֹּץ

substantive role (*Rambam, Bais HaBechirah* 8:1). The guards which Yehoiada stationed now were probably a temporary precaution, made necessary by the unusual crowds and the tumultuous rejoicing which was about to take place.

20. וְאֶת־הָאַדִּירִים וְאֶת־הַמּוֹשְׁלִים בָּעָם — *The nobles and the governors of the people.* These expressions do not occur elsewhere, so we cannot know for certain what offices they describe. They do not appear to be the same as the כָּרִי and רָצִים mentioned in *Kings*. Those are military personnel, mustered in order to guard the king (v. 4 there).

See Section II, *The Nobles and the Governors*.

21. וְהָעִיר שָׁקָטָה וְאֶת־עֲתַלְיָהוּ הֵמִיתוּ — *And the city was tranquil, for they had slain Athaliahu* ... That Athaliahu was slain was already said at v. 15. Here it is mentioned only to explain why the city was quiet: With Athaliahu's death there was no one left to ferment discord.

XXIV

1. בֶּן־שֶׁבַע שָׁנִים יֹאָשׁ — *Yoash was seven years old*. Based on 22:12 and 23:1, we assume this to mean that Yoash was in his seventh year — not that he was seven years old.

2. כָּל־יְמֵי יְהוֹיָדָע הַכֹּהֵן — *All the days of Yehoiada the Kohen*. The description of the disintegration which set in after Yehoiada's death begins at v. 17. For further analysis, see Section II, *Different Perspectives on Yoash and the Monarchy*.

3. וַיִּשָּׂא־לוֹ יְהוֹיָדָע נָשִׁים שְׁתָּיִם — *Yehoiada took two wives.*

God showers the righteous with favors. In spite of his extremely old age, Yehoiada married and bore children (*Malbim*). [1]

As a *Kohen Gadol*, Yehoiada should not have been permitted to marry two wives. See *Rambam, Issurei Biah* 17:13 and *Maggid Mishneh* there.

Thus, all the classical commentators. *Joseph HaCohen, Kadmonios HaYehudim*, has the verse mean that Yehoiada took two wives for Yoash. The information is given to demonstrate Yehoiada's fatherly concern for the young king, and thus to underscore the heinousness of Yoash's ingratitude when he had Yehoiada's son Zechariah killed (v. 21).

4-14. This passage describes Yoash's plan to *renew* the House of *HASHEM* (v. 4). In its broad outlines, the passage seems identical to its parallel in *Kings* (ch. 12). This is, indeed, how most commentators read it. *Malbim*, however, points to significant textual variations, and because of them, feels that the two books are telling two different stories. *Kings* deals with certain technical innovations which Yoash made. He wished the *Kohanim* to take direct charge of the money which flowed into the Temple for necessary repairs, and to implement all that needed to be done, with dispatch. In *Chronicles*, talk is of an ambitious project to revamp the entire structure, and to restore it to

1. Even with *Malbim's* explanation, there seems little connection between Yehoiada's marriages and the story. We should understand *Malbim* at a deeper level. Yehoiada, by saving Yoash, and with him the Davidic dynasty, had re-established נֶצַח יִשְׂרָאֵל, *eternal Israel*. The future, which before had been in jeopardy, was once more assured. As a reward, God granted him children, a renewed hold upon his own future.

of HASHEM'*s House that none with any uncleanliness should
enter.* [20] *He took the captains of the hundreds, the nobles and the
governors of the people, together with the rest of the people, and
brought the king down from* HASHEM'*s House. They arrived at
the upper gate of the king's palace and placed the king on the
throne of the kingdom.* [21] *So all the people rejoiced and the city
was tranquil, for they had slain Athaliahu by the sword.*

*Yoash was seven years old when he began to rule and he
reigned for forty years in Jerusalem. His mother's name was
Tziviah from Be'er Sheva.* [2] *Yoash did that which was right in the
eyes of* HASHEM *all the days of Yehoiada the Kohen.* [3] *Yehoiada
took two wives and begot sons and daughters.* [4] *After this, Yoash
had the idea of rebuilding* HASHEM'*s House.* [5] *He gathered the*

its original beauty. For this project, huge additional sums would be required, and *Chronicles* tells the story of how all this was planned.

The differences between the two accounts do, indeed, seem to point to two separate projects. On the other hand, the general similarities are sufficiently pervasive to make unlikely the assumption that two completely different occurrences are being described.

Rather, it seems possible that Yoash's initiative encompassed both ideas. The Temple did require repairs, but there was also a persuasive motive for him to undertake a fundamental restoration. We have noted in the two previous chapters how Yoash was, as it were, a new *David* in a resurrected Davidic dynasty. It would be entirely in character that, just as the original David saw the culmination of a life of service to God in his involvement in the building of the Temple, so too would Yoash, educated as he was in his historic destiny by Yehoiada's tutelage, wish to make a restoration of the Temple to its pristine glory central to his accomplishments.

As we shall see below, this idea of Yoash's was not known to the people at large. It was *in Yoash's heart* (v. 4). If it was shared with anyone at all, it was only with Yehoiada (v. 6). Thus, the *Kings* account could well ignore it — particularly since it has no place in that book which never, in any way, deals with the *Davidic* aspect of Yoash's reign. By contrast, this theme is central to the *Chronicles'* account and therefore appears prominently in it — woven together with, and serving as background to, the story as it is told in *Kings*.

We shall let the *Chronicles'* version unfold through a careful analysis of the individual verses. At this point we mention only that the operative terms in identifying the two strands of the story are חִזֵּק and חִדֵּשׁ. חִזֵּק, *to repair* [see also *Ezekiel* 27:9 and 27], occurs also in the *Kings'* account [וְהֵם יְחַזְּקוּ אֶת־בֶּדֶק הַבָּיִת] and describes the activities centering upon the normal upkeep of the building and the Temple grounds. חִדֵּשׁ, on the other hand, occurs only in the *Chronicles'* account, and describes the renewal or restoration which was the unique concern of Yoash in his capacity as the *David* of his generation. That these terms have different connotations can be seen clearly from v. 12, ... לְחַזֵּק אֶת־בֵּית ה׳ ... לְחַדֵּשׁ בֵּית ה׳.

4. וַיְהִי אַחֲרֵי־כֵן — *After this*. Commentators do not explain this phrase, which has no parallel in *Kings*. After what incident did the following happen? Nothing seems to connect this verse with anything mentioned in the last three verses, particularly if v. 3 describes Yehoiada's and not Yoash's marriage.

The only possible meaning seems to be that it goes back to the coronation described in the previous chapter. After Yoash had been invested with the kingship, he determined to take the steps described here.

Thus, it occurs only in *Chronicles*. The thrust of the coronation narrative here had been Yoash's establishment as the new *David*. Recognizing his unique place in history, he now decided to emulate David, and to undertake a total refurbishing of the Temple. In *Kings*, where the subject is simply the making of necessary repairs, there is no connection to the coronation.

הָיָה עִם־לֵב יוֹאָשׁ — *Yoash had the idea.*

[Lit. *It was in Yoash's heart.*]

In prefatory remarks 4-14, we suggested

כד
ו־ז

אֶת־הַכֹּהֲנִים וְהַלְוִיִּם וַיֹּאמֶר לָהֶם צְאוּ לְעָרֵי יְהוּדָה וְקִבְצוּ
מִכָּל־יִשְׂרָאֵל כֶּסֶף לְחַזֵּק | אֶת־בֵּית אֱלֹהֵיכֶם מִדֵּי שָׁנָה
ו בְּשָׁנָה וְאַתֶּם תְּמַהֲרוּ לַדָּבָר וְלֹא מִהֲרוּ הַלְוִיִּם: וַיִּקְרָא
הַמֶּלֶךְ לִיהוֹיָדָע הָרֹאשׁ וַיֹּאמֶר לוֹ מַדּוּעַ לֹא־דָרַשְׁתָּ
עַל־הַלְוִיִּם לְהָבִיא מִיהוּדָה וּמִירוּשָׁלַםִ אֶת־מַשְׂאַת מֹשֶׁה
ז עֶבֶד־יהוֹה וְהַקָּהָל לְיִשְׂרָאֵל לְאֹהֶל הָעֵדוּת: כִּי עֲתַלְיָהוּ
הַמִּרְשַׁעַת בָּנֶיהָ פָרְצוּ אֶת־בֵּית הָאֱלֹהִים וְגַם כָּל־קָדְשֵׁי

that this phrase indicates that Yoash did not share his plan with the people — see the following verse in which he tells the *Kohanim* to gather money to *repair the House of your God* — not *to renew* it.[1]

5. . . . וַיִּקְבֹּץ אֶת־הַכֹּהֲנִים וְהַלְוִיִּם — *He gathered the Kohanim and the Levites* . . . For clarity we quote the parallel verse in *Kings* (v. 5). There is not sufficient similarity to allow for a phrase by phrase comparison:

Yoash said to the Kohanim, 'All hallowed moneys which are brought to HASHEM's House census money, or individual equivalency money, or any money which someone might wish to bring to the House of HASHEM, let the Kohanim take it . . .

Three different categories of moneys are mentioned.

Census money refers to the half-*shekalim* which every Jew was obliged to send annually to the Temple (*Exodus* 30:11 ff.). These half-*shekalim* were earmarked primarily for the purchase of communal sacrifices. However, they were also used for the upkeep of the Temple — see *Shekalim* 4:2.

Individual equivalency money is money donated to the Temple within the framework of the *equivalences* set down in *Leviticus*, ch. 27. This money was also used for the upkeep of the Temple. See *Arachin* 24a and *Rambam, Arachin* 1:10.

Finally, *any money*... are free-will gifts which were donated to the Temple treasury.

The *Kohanim* are exhorted to accept any such money from their acquaintances *who bring it to the House* and use it for needed repairs.

This verse differs substantively from ours, where the *Kohanim* and Levites are told to go forth into the Judean cities, and gather money for an annual refurbishing of the Temple. The three categories mentioned in *Kings* are not given.

Once more, as at 20:35 and 22:9, we take the two accounts together, and, from between them, glean a complete picture.

Taken together, the two passages yield as follows:

Yoash plans to rebuild the Temple (v. 4 in *Chronicles*). He does not wish to reveal his plan in its entirety, and clothes it in the form of an undertaking to perform necessary repairs — which in any case would be an indispensable part of the restoration. For the purpose of *Kings*, it is only this part of the plan which is significant, and for this reason *Kings* reports only the orders given to the *Kohanim* in that connection — detailing the various moneys which were halachically earmarked for such use (v. 5 in *Kings*).

At the same time, Yoash also orders the *Kohanim* to circulate and actively solicit contributions (v. 5C). His grand plan for a total rebuilding of the Temple would surely consume tremendous amounts of money. This is the subject of our verse.

For his project, Yoash has a specific form of donation in mind — it will be explicated in vs. 6 and 9 — but does not yet tell the *Kohanim* what it is.

לְחַזֵּק אֶת־בֵּית אֱלֹהֵיכֶם — *To repair the House of your God*. That לְחַזֵּק is not merely a synonymy for לְחַדֵּשׁ of the previous verse is evident from v. 12 where the two terms are mentioned to describe discrete activities. We must conclude that at this point, Yoash did not want his plans for a total restoration to be known — see above.

מִדֵּי שָׁנָה בְּשָׁנָה — *Annually*. This is not mentioned in *Kings*. We assume that it was meant to justify the unusual request to go out to collect the money in the cities. See above.

וְאַתֶּם תְּמַהֲרוּ לַדָּבָר — *You are charged to do this thing expeditiously*. It is evident that Yoash is particularly eager to get his project under way.

1. For confirmation that phrases such as ours indicate a secret resolve not shared with anyone else — see *Ramban* to *Genesis* 6:6 and 8:21.

Kohanim and the Levites and said to them: 'Go forth to the cities of Judah, and collect money from all Israel, to repair the House of your God, annually. You are charged to do this thing expeditiously.' But the Levites did not make haste.
6 *The king called for Yehoiada the chief and said to him: 'Why have you not required of the Levites to bring from Judah and Jerusalem the gift of Moses, servant of* HASHEM, *and of the congregation of Israel for the Tent of Meeting?'*
7 *For the evil-wreaking Athaliahu, her sons breached God's House and transferred to the Baalim all the*

The Levites who do not really understand his motivation are in no particular hurry to undertake their assignment. It seems reasonable to suppose that they felt that the moneys which would come in automatically, as described in *Kings*, would prove adequate for the repairs which needed to be made.

6. אֶת־מַשְׂאַת מֹשֶׁה עֶבֶד־ה' — *The gift of Moses, the servant of* HASHEM. *Mefaresh* writes that this refers to the *shekalim*, and that the unusual term מַשְׂאַת is used, because the obligation to render the annual half-*shekel* is introduced by the words כִּי תִשָּׂא אֶת־רֹאשׁ בְּנֵי־יִשְׂרָאֵל (*Exodus* 30:12).

Radak and *Metzudos* think that מַשְׂאַת refers to all the three categories of moneys described in the *Kings*, account. *Radak* in *Sefer HaSherashim* renders the term *gift* — that which is *lifted up* (נשא) by the giver to give to the recipient.

However, if this is so, why does the verse add the description *And of the congregation of Israel for the Tent of Meeting*? The *shekalim* had been given annually for centuries and were well known to the *Kohanim* and the people. Even if we assume that in the course of time they had come to be known as מַשְׂאַת מֹשֶׁה, there would be no need to add any other description. And that this description is of substantive significance can be seen from v. 9, where it is repeated in a slightly different form: *The gift of Moses, the servant of God, upon Israel in the wilderness.*

Moreover, as we noted from the passage in *Kings*, the *shekalim* and other gifts mentioned there were brought to the Temple. There would have been no need to gather them from the cities.

When Moses built the Tabernacle in the wilderness, various levies were imposed upon the people. Among them, a voluntary contribution in whatever amount they could afford (*Rashi* to *Exodus* 30:15).[1]

Yoash evidently wished to reactivate that self same levy for the purpose which he had in mind. That Moses in the wilderness had asked for similar cooperation appeared to him to be an appropriate precedent.

The *Kohanim* who were not privy to Yoash's plans — who, indeed, were unaware of the cosmic implications of his kingship which stimulated them — were lethargic about undertaking their assignment. They knew only of the need to *repair* the Temple (v. 5) and assumed correctly that the funds required for that would be forthcoming without any effort on their part. Enough money would be brought to the Temple by the people.

Yoash was not ready to share his plans with the *Kohanim*. He chides Yehoiada — who *was* aware of his intentions — for not having made clear to the *Kohanim* the special nature of the moneys which they were supposed to collect. This he could do without revealing the total truth of Yoash's intentions, as we shall see in the next verse.

7. כִּי עֲתַלְיָהוּ הַמִּרְשַׁעַת בָּנֶיהָ — *For the evil-wreaking Athaliahu, her sons... Targum* renders: *...and her sons.*

פָּרְצוּ אֶת־בֵּית הָאֱלֹהִים ... — *... breached the God's House*. The Temple, which had been built from strong materials, had stood for only some one hundred and fifty years. Had it not been for the willful damage perpetrated by Athaliahu and her sons, extensive damage would not normally have been expected (*Radak* and *Metzudos*).

But why is this explanation not given in *Kings*?

Again, the normal use of פרץ, *to breach*, in

1. *Ramban* there, based on our verse, thinks that this original voluntary donation for the building of the Tabernacle was later converted into an annual one — for its upkeep and repair.

In the comm., we assume that it was only a one-time levy. This, based upon the language, *gift of Moses*, and the description, ... *upon Israel in the wilderness.*

ח בֵּית־יהוה עָשׂוּ לַבְּעָלִים: וַיֹּאמֶר הַמֶּלֶךְ וַיַּעֲשׂוּ אֲרוֹן אֶחָד
ט וַיִּתְּנֻהוּ בְּשַׁעַר בֵּית־יהוה חוּצָה: וַיִּתְּנוּ־קוֹל בִּיהוּדָה
וּבִירוּשָׁלַםִ לְהָבִיא לַיהוה מַשְׂאַת מֹשֶׁה עֶבֶד־הָאֱלֹהִים
י עַל־יִשְׂרָאֵל בַּמִּדְבָּר: וַיִּשְׂמְחוּ כָל־הַשָּׂרִים וְכָל־הָעָם
יא וַיָּבִיאוּ וַיַּשְׁלִיכוּ לָאָרוֹן עַד־לְכַלֵּה: וַיְהִי בְּעֵת יָבִיא
אֶת־הָאָרוֹן אֶל־פְּקֻדַּת הַמֶּלֶךְ בְּיַד הַלְוִיִּם וְכִרְאוֹתָם
כִּי־רַב הַכֶּסֶף וּבָא סוֹפֵר הַמֶּלֶךְ וּפְקִיד כֹּהֵן הָרֹאשׁ וִיעָרוּ
אֶת־הָאָרוֹן וְיִשָּׂאֻהוּ וִישִׁיבֻהוּ אֶל־מְקֹמוֹ כֹּה עָשׂוּ לְיוֹם ׀
יב בְּיוֹם וַיַּאַסְפוּ־כֶסֶף לָרֹב: וַיִּתְּנֵהוּ הַמֶּלֶךְ וִיהוֹיָדָע אֶל־
עוֹשֵׂה מְלֶאכֶת עֲבוֹדַת בֵּית־יהוה וַיִּהְיוּ שֹׂכְרִים חֹצְבִים
וְחָרָשִׁים לְחַדֵּשׁ בֵּית יהוה וְגַם לְחָרָשֵׁי בַרְזֶל וּנְחֹשֶׁת
יג לְחַזֵּק אֶת־בֵּית יהוה: וַיַּעֲשׂוּ עֹשֵׂי הַמְּלָאכָה וַתַּעַל
אֲרוּכָה לַמְּלָאכָה בְּיָדָם וַיַּעֲמִידוּ אֶת־בֵּית הָאֱלֹהִים

Scripture describes the making of a single, perhaps major, breach. If such a breach existed and it was that which required repair, then the expression in *Kings . . .wherever some breakage might be found* (v. 6) would be inapt. That expression surely implies minor problems which need to be searched out if they are to be repaired.

It is not necessary to assume that the breach made by Athaliahu's sons left the walls broken down and in need of repair. They may well have broken down a wall — perhaps one which separated the palace from the House — and made it into a formal entrance. When Yoash talked of *repairs*, it would not have occurred to the *Kohanim* that he intended to change what, for all intents and purposes, had become a *fait accomplis*. Once they realized that this, too, was contemplated, they would understand the need for additional funds.

וְגַם . . . עָשׂוּ לַבְּעָלִים — *And transferred to the Baalim* . . . Had the House treasury not been plundered, no new funds would have been required (*Mefaresh*, *Radak*, *Metzudos*).

8. וַיִּתְּנֻהוּ בְּשַׁעַר בֵּית־ה׳ חוּצָה — *And set it in the gate of the* HASHEM*'s House on the outside*. Certainly, this is not the chest which is referred to in *Kings*. That one was made apparently on Yehoiada's own initiative, and placed on the right side of the altar. This one was made on the king's orders, and placed outside the courtyard. This seems to confirm that we are dealing with different moneys, collected for different purposes. The money earmarked for the repairs of the House was mainly Yehoiada's concern, and he arranged for its disposition. The money for the restoration of the House was kept apart from the other fund, and the king took a direct interest in it.

See also *Yerushalmi*, *Shekalim* 6:4, and *Korban HaEidah* there.

9-10. וַיִּתְּנוּ־קוֹל . . . וַיִּשְׂמְחוּ כָל־הַשָּׂרִים . . . — *They issued a proclamation . . . And all the princes . . . brought joyously*.

The people reacted enthusiastically to the proclamation, and realized that they were being called upon to emulate the generosity which their forefathers had displayed when the Tabernacle was being built.

10. וַיַּשְׁלִיכוּ לָאָרוֹן — *And cast into the chest*. In the *Kings'* account the *Kohanim* rather than the people, put the money into the chest. This was because that chest stood next to the altar — a location accessible only to the *Kohanim*.

עַד־לְכַלֵּה — *Until they had made an end*. They brought daily donations until every one of the people had brought his gift. None were missing (*Metzudos*).

11. אֶל־פְּקֻדַּת הַמֶּלֶךְ — *To the king's administrative office*.

For פְּקֻדָּה as *administration*, see *I Chronicles* 26:30.

כֹּה עָשׂוּ לְיוֹם בְּיוֹם — *Day by day*. The chest mentioned in *Kings* was apparently not emptied daily, but only when it was seen to be full (v. 11 there). Perhaps the restoration project required a more constant flow of money than did the repair work.

sacred objects of HASHEM's House. 8 *The king ordered that*
they make a chest, and set it in the gate of HASHEM's House
on the outside. 9 *They issued a proclamation throughout Ju-*
dah and Jerusalem, that the gift of Moses the servant
of HASHEM upon Israel in the wilderness be brought to HASHEM.
10 *And all the princes and all the people brought joyously,*
and cast into the chest until they had made an end. 11 *Now*
when the chest was brought to the king's administrative of-
fice, by the Levites, and when they saw that the money was
abundant, the king's scribe and the chief Kohen's officer would
come, empty the chest, and lift it up to return it to its place. This
they did day by day and gathered money in abundance. 12 *The*
king and Yehoiada gave it to the foremen charged with doing the
work of HASHEM's House so that they might hire masons and
carpenters to rebuild HASHEM's House and also those who
wrought in iron and copper so that they might repair HASHEM's
House 13 *The foremen fulfilled their duties, and the project*
flourished under their hands. They restored the House of God

Malbim has a novel approach to this seeming discrepancy which he also solves by postulating two separate chests — but in the following context:

V. 7 taught that Athaliahu and her sons emptied out the House treasury in order to use the money for Baal worship. The resources in the treasury consisted of the half-*shekalim* which every Jew sent annually to the House. Because the treasury was plundered and these *shekalim* were never used for their intended purpose, it now devolved upon all Israel to send not only their current half-*shekel* to the House but also to make up the loss to the House treasury and send *shekalim* for previous years.

When Yoash sent the *Kohanim* to travel around Judah in order to raise money for the restoration, he also charged them with collecting the *shekalim* for past years.

Thus, there were two categories of *shekalim* pouring into the House. Current *shekalim* [תַּקְלִין חַדְתִּין] and those from previous years [תַּקְלִין עַתִּיקִין]. The current *shekalim* are those dealt with in *Kings*. These were placed in the chest near the altar. *Chronicles* deals with those of previous years which were put in the chest near the entrance.

The halachic status of these two categories is not the same. From the current ones, the daily sacrifices were brought, and only what remained after that was earmarked for the House repairs. The *halachah* requires that the dividing of the money between the amounts required for the sacrifices and those which are to be used for other purposes, be done three times a year — this is the subject of the *Kings* passage.

By contrast, *shekalim* from past years are earmarked entirely for repair and upkeep [בֶּדֶק הַבַּיִת], and from these moneys the required amount was to be withdrawn daily. This is the meaning of the *Chronicles* passage.

12. **אֶל-עוֹשֵׂה מְלֶאכֶת עֲבוֹדַת בֵּית-ה׳ וַיִּהְיוּ שֹׂכְרִים** — *To the foremen charged with doing the work of HASHEM's House, so that they might hire...* The עוֹשֵׂה מְלֶאכֶת עֲבוֹדַת בֵּית-ה׳ are the managers — or in *Metzudos'* words, the *architects* — who in general were in charge of the work. The money was disbursed to them so that they would be able to hire the necessary labor. See further at 34:10.

לְחַדֵּשׁ ... לְחַזֵּק — *To rebuild ... repair*. This verse makes clear that two separate activities were involved. See prefatory remarks 4-14.

13. **וַתַּעַל אֲרוּכָה לַמְּלָאכָה בְּיָדָם** — *And the project flourished under their hands.* אֲרוּכָה is a metaphor borrowed from the field of health (*Radak* and *Metzudos*). It is a healing process, one that brings vigor and strength where earlier there had been sickness and debilitation. It is a graphic metaphor to describe the repairs made on a building whose beauty and firmness had fallen prey to the ravages of time.

כד
יד־כ

יד עַל־מַתְכֻּנְתּוֹ וַיְאַמְּצֻהוּ׃ וּכְכַלּוֹתָם הֵבִיאוּ לִפְנֵי הַמֶּלֶךְ
וִיהוֹיָדָע אֶת־שְׁאָר הַכֶּסֶף וַיַּעֲשֵׂהוּ כֵלִים לְבֵית־יהוה כְּלֵי
שָׁרֵת וְהַעֲלוֹת וְכַפּוֹת וּכְלֵי זָהָב וָכָסֶף וַיִּהְיוּ מַעֲלִים עֹלוֹת
טו בְּבֵית־יהוה תָּמִיד כֹּל יְמֵי יְהוֹיָדָע׃ וַיִּזְקַן יְהוֹיָדָע
וַיִּשְׂבַּע יָמִים וַיָּמֹת בֶּן־מֵאָה וּשְׁלֹשִׁים שָׁנָה בְּמוֹתוֹ׃
טז וַיִּקְבְּרֻהוּ בְעִיר־דָּוִיד עִם־הַמְּלָכִים כִּי־עָשָׂה טוֹבָה
בְּיִשְׂרָאֵל וְעִם־הָאֱלֹהִים וּבֵיתוֹ׃ וְאַחֲרֵי מוֹת
יז יְהוֹיָדָע בָּאוּ שָׂרֵי יְהוּדָה וַיִּשְׁתַּחֲווּ לַמֶּלֶךְ אָז שָׁמַע הַמֶּלֶךְ
יח אֲלֵיהֶם׃ וַיַּעַזְבוּ אֶת־בֵּית יהוה אֱלֹהֵי אֲבוֹתֵיהֶם וַיַּעַבְדוּ
אֶת־הָאֲשֵׁרִים וְאֶת־הָעֲצַבִּים וַיְהִי קֶצֶף עַל־יְהוּדָה
יט וִירוּשָׁלִַם בְּאַשְׁמָתָם זֹאת׃ וַיִּשְׁלַח בָּהֶם נְבִאִים לַהֲשִׁיבָם
כ אֶל־יהוה וַיָּעִידוּ בָם וְלֹא הֶאֱזִינוּ׃ וְרוּחַ אֱלֹהִים

עַל־מַתְכֻּנְתּוֹ — *To perfection*. *Mefaresh* and *Metzudos* render *on its base*, seeming to relate the word to כון, *to establish, set firm*.

But both *Radak* and *Ibn Janach* in their respective *Sefer HaShorashim* derive the word from תכן, to *measure*. Its meaning here is *balance* or *proportion*: *They created a beautifully proportioned, well-balanced building*. But in addition to the base-meaning, *Ibn Janach* seems to detect a nuance of *correctness* in the word [תִּקּוּן], and since *Targum*, too, renders עַל תִּקּוּנֵיהּ, that is the translation which we have chosen.

Without dealing with the derivation of the word, *Malbim* says that it describes the restoration of the building to its original beauty and majesty.

14. וּכְכַלּוֹתָם — *When they finished*. This was only once the work had ended. Prior to that, the moneys which had been donated could be used only for the repair work, not for the manufacture of House utensils (*Radak* based on *Kesubos* 106b).

וְהַעֲלוֹת — *Pestles*. The translation follows *Mefaresh* and *Metzudos*. Alternatives are: The boards on which meat is cut (*Mefaresh*); and *small ladles* (*Radak*).

וַיִּהְיוּ מַעֲלִים עֹלוֹת בְּבֵית־ה׳ תָּמִיד — *They brought up burnt offerings in the* HASHEM*'s House continually*. Reference is to the twice-daily תָּמִיד sacrifice, with which the daily House service opened and closed (*Metzudos*). But then the meaning of the verse is not clear: Did they then stop bringing the daily sacrifices when Yehoiada died? There is no indication of this anywhere. And why are we told this in this particular verse? It seems to have no connection with what went before.

The meaning of the sentence would be clear if we were to take תָּמִיד as the adverb *continually*. It was the practice in the House not to leave the altar empty but, when there were no obligatory sacrifices to be brought, to sacrifice burnt offerings which were paid for from the communal treasury. Our verse may be saying that the money that came into this chest was so abundant that even after all necessary sacred vessels had been made, there was still a sufficient amount left over to finance the bringing of these voluntary burnt offerings throughout Yehoiada's lifetime. There was enough money to bring these sacrifices *continually*.[1]

15. וַיִּזְקַן יְהוֹיָדָע — *Yehoiada became old*.
See prefatory remarks to ch. 23.

16. עִם־הַמְּלָכִים — *Among the kings*. Note that Yehoiada belonged to the royal family since he was a son-in-law of the king Yehoram (see 22:11).

בְּיִשְׂרָאֵל וְעִם־הָאֱלֹהִים וּבֵיתוֹ — *. . . of Israel, also of God and His House*. Yehoiada had helped Israel by re-establishing the Davidic dynasty (*Metzudos*), and by foiling Athaliahu's plans (*Malbim*). His beneficial acts for God and the House have been recounted in this and the previous chapter (*Metzudos* and *Malbim*).

Metzudos and *Malbim* follow *Targum* who understands בֵּיתוֹ as referring to the House.

1. The halachic legitimacy of this practice can be maintained on the basis of *Kesubos* 106b: Superfluous בֶּדֶק הַבַּיִת money could be utilized for the purchase of sacrificial animals at the discretion of the House treasurers.

to perfection, and made it durable. [14] *When they finished, they brought the rest of the money to the king and to Yehoiada. They converted it into utensils for* HASHEM'*s House — ministering vessels: Pestles, pans and implements made of gold and silver. They brought up burned offerings in* HASHEM'*s House continually, all the days of Yehoiada.* [15] *Yehoiada became old, satiated with age, and died: He was one hundred and thirty years old when he died.* [16] *They buried him in the City of David among the kings, for he had advanced the cause of Israel, also of God and His House.* [17] *After Yehoiada's death, the princes of Judah came and prostrated themselves before the king; then the king listened to them.* [18] *They forsook the House of* HASHEM *the God of their fathers and served the groves and the statues; and wrath came upon Judah and Jerusalem for this their sin.* [19] *He sent prophets to them to bring them back to* HASHEM. *They admonished them but they would not listen.* [20] *Then a spirit of God*

Within the context of our perception of Yoash as the resurrected *David* of his generation, it seems possible to interpret the phrase differently. In *I Chronicles* 17:14, God talks of the Davidic dynasty as *My House*. This may well be the meaning of *House* in our context, and the entire phrase ... *for he had advanced the cause of Israel, also of God and His House*, may have in mind the one overwhelming and central fact of Yehoiada's life. At the very forefront of Israel's heroes, it was he who assured that Israel's march toward its Messianic destiny would continue.

17-27. For a discussion of the deification of Yoash which took place after Yehoiada's death — see Section II, *Different Perspectives on Yoash and the Monarchy*.

17. וַיִּשְׁתַּחֲווּ לַמֶּלֶךְ אָז שָׁמַע הַמֶּלֶךְ אֲלֵיהֶם ... — ... *and prostrated themselves before the king; then the king listened to them.* They worshiped him as they would an idol — and he allowed himself to be deified (*Seder Olam Rabbah* 18, based on *midrashim*). Or, they swore fealty to him in the expectation that, in return, he would not interfere in their idolatrous excesses, and might even join them. Their ploy was successful — he *listened* to them (*Radak*).

The tradition that Yoash was viewed as something more than a mere mortal on the basis of his miraculous salvation in the Holy of Holies is firmly entrenched in aggadic literature.[1]

But *Radak's* interpretation certainly satisfies all considerations of context, grammar and syntax. Why is it not more clearly explicated in the text?

Perhaps, by treating the deification in this oblique manner, Scripture relegates it to the subsurface. It may not have been expressed in words, but rather implied in the obeisance [see *Maharal* quoted in fn. to *I Chronicles* 28:2 (p. 340)]. In Section II, *Different Perspectives upon Yoash and the Monarchy*, we will see that there was considerable ambiguity about this event, and that, for this reason, no mention of it is made in *Kings*. The treatment of the matter, which we have noted here, would tend to confirm this thesis.

18. וַיַּעַבְדוּ אֶת־הָאֲשֵׁרִים וְאֶת־הָעֲצַבִּים — *And served the groves and the statues. Malbim* thinks that these statues were not ordinary idols, but statues made in the likeness of the king, and that the groves of asheira-trees were planted in his name. This would contradict the thesis suggested in comm. to the previous verse that there was no unambiguous open worship of Yoash. The other commentators do not make *Malbim's* point.[2]

19. וַיָּעִידוּ בָם — *They admonished them.* The word derives from העיד, *to testify*. It is used to

1. For an analysis of what might motivate people to worship a human being, and of why he might acquiesce to be so worshiped, see *Ramban* to *Exodus* 20:3.

2. *Malbim* derives his interpretation from the end of our verse:. . .*for this their sin*. The apparently redundant *this* is understood as follows: Even though they did not serve any other idols — that is, that idolatry as such did not proliferate — still, *this* itself, that Yoash was deified, brought down God's wrath upon Judah and Jerusalem.

לָבְשָׁה אֶת־זְכַרְיָה בֶּן־יְהוֹיָדָע הַכֹּהֵן וַיַּעֲמֹד מֵעַל לָעָם
וַיֹּאמֶר לָהֶם כֹּה ׀ אָמַר הָאֱלֹהִים לָמָה אַתֶּם עֹבְרִים
אֶת־מִצְוֹת יהוה וְלֹא תַצְלִיחוּ כִּי־עֲזַבְתֶּם אֶת־יְהוָה וַיַּעֲזֹב
כא אֶתְכֶם׃ וַיִּקְשְׁרוּ עָלָיו וַיִּרְגְּמֻהוּ אֶבֶן בְּמִצְוַת הַמֶּלֶךְ בַּחֲצַר
כב בֵּית יְהוָה׃ וְלֹא־זָכַר יוֹאָשׁ הַמֶּלֶךְ הַחֶסֶד אֲשֶׁר עָשָׂה
יְהוֹיָדָע אָבִיו עִמּוֹ וַיַּהֲרֹג אֶת־בְּנוֹ וּכְמוֹתוֹ אָמַר יֵרֶא יְהוָה
כג וְיִדְרֹשׁ׃ וַיְהִי ׀ לִתְקוּפַת הַשָּׁנָה עָלָה עָלָיו חֵיל אֲרָם

describe an act of warning or admonition, because these are often performed in front of witnesses, so that they cannot later be denied (*Metzudos*).

20. וְרוּחַ אֱלֹהִים לָבְשָׁה — *Then a spirit of God took hold of* . . . Lit. *Then a spirit of God clothed* . . .

See comm. to *I Chronicles* 12:19. Here, *Targum* renders *a spirit of prophecy*, and *Malbim* too stresses that Zechariah was Divinely inspired.

וַיַּעֲמֹד מֵעַל לָעָם — *And he stood above the people*. The Sages detect a criticism here, and fault Zechariah for a lack of humility: Never forget your modesty, even if you are elevated to a position of power. This can be learned from Zechariah. He regarded himself as greater than all the people; son-in-law to the king; *Kohen*, prophet and judge. Under the impression of his exalted status, he spoke overbearingly (*Koheles Rabbah* 10:4). Zechariah probably chose an elevated place from which to address the people in order to make himself heard (*Mefaresh*). His message was surely one which, in its straightforward simplicity, had the ring of truth and could have elicited a positive response from the people. He failed to infuse it with the softness and modesty which could have made them responsive to his urging.

21. וַיִּקְשְׁרוּ עָלָיו וַיִּרְגְּמֻהוּ אֶבֶן בְּמִצְוַת הַמֶּלֶךְ — *They conspired against him and pelted him with stones by order of the king*. The phrase hides more than it reveals. קשר, *to knot* or *join together* [*in a conspiracy*], implies that we are not dealing here with a spontaneous killing, undertaken in the heat of rage at Zechariah's protest. Rather, the nobles, when they realized that Zechariah was intent upon thwarting their plans, laid a plot whereby they could cause his death. That the killing was done specifically *by order of the king* indicates a planned assassination. There is no indication or reason to suppose that the king was present in the Temple at the time of the protest.

But what does *by order of the king* mean? It seems inconceivable that Yoash should have been a party to an overt flouting of even a pretense of legality, and that *Kings* should make no mention of this. Even Jezebel — no respecter of the halachah — made sure that her premeditated murder of Navoth should have, at least, the outer trappings of a trial (*I Kings* 21:10). Would Yoash do less?

The halachah provides that a prerogative of the kingship is that the king is permitted to have someone who rebels against him or who even acts in a way which would tend to undermine his authority put to death (*Rambam, Melachim* 3:8). If Yoash perceived Zechariah as a danger to his rule, he could have invoked that royal privilege. However, two considerations stand in the way of such an interpretation. The authority to execute such a person is limited to having him killed by the sword (*Rambam* there) and here, Zechariah was stoned (*Malbim*). Also, it is completely inapplicable in a case in which the purported rebel is engaged in even a small *mitzvah* — as Zechariah certainly was. The king's authority ends when it clashes with God's will.

The *Aggadah* presents Zechariah's assassination as deriving from a personal confrontation with the king. *Midrash Shir HaShirim* (*Grunhut*) 3:2 has the following account: Yoash attempted to introduce a statue into the Temple building. Zechariah stood at the gates and said: 'You will have to kill me first.' So he killed him.

What was this *statue* which Yoash wanted to bring into the Temple? Was it an idol? Was it perhaps a statue of himself, to be erected not as an object of religious veneration but as a mark of respect for the king? Perhaps there was no physical statue at all — none, after all, is explicated in the text. Certainly, aggadic idiom could tolerate an interpretation such as: Yoash attempted to [do something which, in Zechariah's eyes, was as evil or as potentially destructive, as though he had wanted to]

24
21-23

took hold of Zechariah son of Yehoiada the Kohen and he stood above the people and said to them: 'Thus says God: "Why do you transgress the commands of HASHEM, *which cannot prosper? Because you have spurned* HASHEM, *He has also forsaken you.' "*
21 *They conspired against him and pelted him with stones by order of the king, in the court of* HASHEM*'s House.*
22 *Thus Yoash the king did not remember the kindness which Yehoiada, his father, had done to him, and killed his son. As he died, he said, 'May* HASHEM *witness and demand an account.'*
23 *At the turn of the year, the army of Aram came up against him.*

introduce a statue into the Temple building.

Given the sparseness of the information available to us, and the problems which are raised by what has been said, we may perhaps reconstruct the following sequence of events.

The nobles see Zechariah as implacably opposed to their idol worship. They determine to bring about his death in a way that will have a facade of legality. They persuade the king to take an action which, given the inflated sense of his own worth which had come about through their earlier flattery, would seem innocuous to him, but which they knew Zechariah could not permit. This would trap Zechariah into a confrontation with the king which, if Yoash was to maintain his authority, he could not permit and would, in defense of his position and prerogatives, have to order Zechariah's immediate execution. Once we postulate that Zechariah had to be killed on the spot, it is possible to conjecture that no sword was immediately available — a not unlikely circumstance within the Temple confines — and that under the circumstances he was killed by stoning.[1]

Our suggested reconstruction of the events makes possible our thesis, put forward in Section II to v. 2, *Different Perspectives upon Yoash and the Monarchy*, that Yoash was not openly involved in the idol worship practiced by the nobles.

בַּחֲצַר בֵּית ה׳ — *In the court of the* HASHEM*'s* House. Israel transgressed seven sins on that day: They killed a *Kohen*; prophet; and judge; shed innocent blood; *defiled the Temple court*; it was *Shabbos*; and also *Yom Kippur* (*Yerushalmi*, *Taanis* 4:5).

We may surmise that the stress on the fact that the murder took place within the Temple confines, thus defiling its sanctity, is significant because it provides a vivid contrast with the sensibilities of Zechariah's father Yehoiada. He had made sure that Athaliahu not be killed within the Temple so that it would not become defiled.

22. וְלֹא־זָכַר יוֹאָשׁ הַמֶּלֶךְ הַחֶסֶד . . . — *Thus Yoash the king did not remember the kindness . . .* The charge of ingratitude is leveled against Yoash. This seems to bear out our thesis from the previous verse. If the killing of Zechariah by the king's orders would have been a case of wanton murder, it hardly seems appropriate to fault him for what seems a less heinous crime. If, however, there was a veneer of legality, then it would be important to point to the underlying disintegration of personality. A modicum of appreciation for what Yehoiada had done for him would have stopped Yoash in his tracks.

יֵרֶא ה׳ וְיִדְרֹשׁ — *May* HASHEM *witness and demand an accounting.* I.e., I was killed because I defended God's honor. It is fitting that He should demand an accounting of my death (*Mefaresh*).

God did indeed seek an accounting. The *Aggadah* teaches that Zechariah's blood continued to seethe on the Temple grounds for two hundred and fifty-two years, until the destruction of the Temple. No attempt to cover it with earth and to hide the shameful deed was successful (*Koheles Rabbah* 3:16). When Nevuzaradan the Babylonian butcher-

1. For the purpose of our proposed thesis, we assume the limitation placed upon a king that he may kill only by the sword applies only where this is possible. If, for some reason, this cannot be done, any other method would be acceptable. This would place the king's prerogative to kill in the same category as death penalties which are imposed by the courts. In such cases, the halachah prescribes that the type of capital punishment specified by the Torah must be given but where that is impossible other methods of killing are acceptable (*Rambam*, *Sanhedrin* 14:8).

It is nowhere specified that in the case of the king's prerogative to kill, the halachah makes this accommodation. Therefore, we can only offer our suggestion as based upon a reasonable surmise.

וַיָּבֹאוּ אֶל־יְהוּדָה וִירוּשָׁלַם וַיַּשְׁחִיתוּ אֶת־כָּל־שָׂרֵי הָעָם
כד מֵעָם וְכָל־שְׁלָלָם שִׁלְּחוּ לְמֶלֶךְ דַּרְמָשֶׂק: כִּי בְמִצְעַר
אֲנָשִׁים בָּאוּ ׀ חֵיל אֲרָם וַיהוָה נָתַן בְּיָדָם חַיִל לָרֹב מְאֹד
כִּי עָזְבוּ אֶת־יְהוָה אֱלֹהֵי אֲבוֹתֵיהֶם וְאֶת־יוֹאָשׁ עָשׂוּ
כה שְׁפָטִים: וּבְלֶכְתָּם מִמֶּנּוּ כִּי־עָזְבוּ אֹתוֹ בְּמַחֲלְיִים רַבִּים

general came into the Temple and saw the seething blood, he demanded an explanation. When he heard the awful truth, he slaughtered myriads in an attempt to assuage the blood. When it continued to seethe, he asked Zechariah how much greater a vengeance he required. At that, the blood stopped boiling (*Gittin* 57b).

These and similar accounts occupy a prominent place in the aggadic literature surrounding the destruction of the Temple.They have also been immortalized in the *Kinos* of *Tishah B'Av*. For a discussion of why just this particular crime is treated as central to those seemingly unrelated tragedies, see ArtScroll *Ezekiel*, p. 363, ftn. to 21:28.

Within the context of our perception of Yoash's role in Jewish history, we may suggest the following: Yoash, as we have seen, was miraculously saved from death in order that through him the Davidic line should be perpetuated. The entire Messianic future of Israel was vested in him. He failed tragically in the high calling to which history had assigned him. The tangible symbol of that failing was Zechariah's blood, seething on the ground of the Temple court. It remained there to haunt each of the subsequent kings, until the destruction of the Temple. None of them managed to eradicate from themselves the profound failings which were symbolized by that blood; none managed to lift themselves to a level at which a new start could have been made. There were periods of hope — particularly during the benign reigns of Chizkiahu and Yosiah — but even these ended in disappointment. In the long view of history, the miraculous saving of Yoash and his subsequent crowning as king — events which were accompanied by so much hope — constituted a high point, which was then followed by the tragic descent into the darkness, culminating in destruction and exile.

23-24. *II Kings* 12:18-19 also has an account of an Aramean war towards the end of Yoash's life. The details are as follows: Chazael, king of Aram, campaigns successfully against the Philistine Gath, and then sets his sights upon Jerusalem. Yoash, by giving him vast sums of money taken from the royal and Temple treasuries, manages to buy him off. Jerusalem is spared.

There is little in common between that story and the one told in *Chronicles*. Do they describe two totally different occurrences, or are they complementary accounts of the same event?

Radak is explicit: There were two wars, and each of the two books describes one of them. *Rashi* is silent.

If, indeed, both accounts center upon one war, we would need to produce a complete picture of the events from within the two complementary accounts, and to understand why each of the two books takes a different perspective.

As point of departure we take *Metzudos'* interpretation of the phrase וַיַּשְׁחִיתוּ אֶת־כָּל־שָׂרֵי הָעָם מֵעָם . . . in v. 23. What does מֵעָם mean in this context? *Mefaresh* renders: *And destroyed all the nobles of the people* [*so that they should no longer be*] *a people*.

Radak understands the word as though it were written: *They destroyed all of the nobles of the people, and* [*also destroyed*] *some of the people*.

Metzudos has: *They destroyed all the nobles of the people* [*treating them differently*] *than the* [*rest*] *of the people* [*whom they spared*].

As *Metzudos* understands it, there were no casualties besides the nobles. This was to show that the campaign was a specific punishment for their having deified the king. Clearly, this was not the conscious motive of the Arameans. They did not realize that they were tools of Divine Providence, and must have had reasons of their own for focusing upon the nobles.

We cannot know what these motives were, but it seems clear that, if only the nobles were touched, this was not a full-fledged battle of two armies confronting one another. Rather, the Arameans must have come as a marauding band, intent upon a specific objective.

Thus, the picture which unfolds is as follows: Chazael, with his full army, plans to attack Jerusalem, but backs off after Yoash pays him an enormous tribute. He then

They reached Judah and Jerusalem and wiped out the aristoc-
racy from among the people. They sent all their spoils to the king
at Darmesek. 24 *For the forces of Aram came with a small*
company of men, and HASHEM *delivered a very great army into*
their hand, because they had forsaken HASHEM*, the God of their*
father. They executed judgments upon Yoash. 25 *When they*
departed from him — for they left him in grievous illness —

withdraws. This is the story as told in *Kings*. After that withdrawal a band of warriors, for reasons of their own which we today cannot fathom, go back independently in order to settle a score with the nobles. They take care not to hurt anyone else. This is the story which *Chronicles* tells. Clearly, this is a Divine punishment for the idolatrous practices of the nobles. *Kings*, which told nothing of these practices, has no interest in this episode. In the picture of the greater war, which had been successfully averted by the tribute which was paid, it was an insignificant excursion on the part of a small marauding group.

This suggested sequence of events has the merit that it also explains the statement in v. 23 that the attackers sent the spoils which they took to the king in Darmesek. If an ordinary war were being described, the disposition of the spoils by the victorious army would be of small interest. But if we are discussing an unauthorized excursion undertaken independently by a small group of soldiers, against the wishes of their commander who had chosen to withdraw, then this information is significant. The soldiers sent the spoils to the king as a justification of their unauthorized action. They had not done it to enrich themselves — that would have been inexcusable — and therefore donated the spoils to the royal treasury. Their true, conscious motive remains hidden, but for *Chronicles*, that is precisely the significant point. For practical purposes they were God's punishing arm extended against the nobles.

23. וַיְהִי לִתְקוּפַת הַשָּׁנָה — *At the turn of the year.* קוף or נקף means *to turn around*. תְּקוּפַת הַשָּׁנָה is the point at which the sun has, so to speak, turned around the earth and reached the precise point at which it stood at a given time. In our case, it was the anniversary of the day on which Zechariah was killed (*Metzudos*). *Targum* renders: *At the end of the year*.

חֵיל אֲרָם — *The army of Aram*. See prefatory remarks 23-24 where we surmised that this was a marauding band of soldiers, rather than a regular army.

...וַיַּשְׁחִיתוּ — *And wiped out...* שחת is rarely used to describe the killing of people, and then only when a huge and unexpected ravaging of a nation takes place. It seems an inappropriate term to use for the killing of *the aristocracy* [lit. *the nobles of the people*] of whom there cannot have been an overwhelming number. [Indeed, *Targum* softens the word to *killed*.] It suggests an absolute and utter obliteration. These nobles were an aberration, a malignant growth upon the body of the community of Israel, and had to be completely expunged.

מֵעָם — *From among the people*. For three possibilities of understanding this word, see prefatory remarks 23-24. We have followed *Metzudos*, and propose a translation that comes closest to the Hebrew idiom.

...וְכָל־שְׁלָלָם שִׁלְּחוּ — *They sent all their spoils* ... See prefatory remarks 23-24 for the significance of this phrase. It is possible that the use of the emphatic *piel*, instead of the expected *kal*, bears out our thesis. They *threw* the spoils from themselves; they wanted to distance themselves from any implication of mercenary intent.

24. כִּי — *For* ... The expression implies that the first part of the verse, in a sense, follows upon the second part, which explains the Aramean victory in terms of God's Providence. It was clear that the incident was to be regarded as Divine punishment since a small group of men were able to defeat an entire army (*Metzudos*).

וְאֶת־יוֹאָשׁ עָשׂוּ שְׁפָטִים — *They executed judgments upon Yoash*. From the position of this phrase in the verse, it is clear that we are to understand Yoash's fate as separate from that of the nobles. Moreover, the degree of his punishment was less than theirs. They were utterly obliterated; he was only punished. All this suggests the correctness of our thesis — that Yoash was not directly involved in the idol worship. His was a weakness that had succumbed to flattery — not an active evil.

In the tradition of the Sages, the punishment to which our verse alludes is homosexual

הִתְקַשְּׁרוּ עָלָיו עֲבָדָיו בִּדְמֵי בְּנֵי יְהוֹיָדָע הַכֹּהֵן וַיַּהַרְגֻהוּ
עַל־מִטָּתוֹ וַיָּמֹת וַיִּקְבְּרֻהוּ בְּעִיר דָּוִיד וְלֹא קְבָרֻהוּ
כו בְּקִבְרוֹת הַמְּלָכִים׃ וְאֵלֶּה הַמִּתְקַשְּׁרִים עָלָיו זָבָד בֶּן־
כז שִׁמְעָת הָעַמּוֹנִית וִיהוֹזָבָד בֶּן־שִׁמְרִית הַמּוֹאָבִית׃ וּבָנָיו
°יִרֶב ק׳ °וְרֹב הַמַּשָּׂא עָלָיו וִיסוֹד בֵּית הָאֱלֹהִים הִנָּם כְּתוּבִים
עַל־מִדְרַשׁ סֵפֶר הַמְּלָכִים וַיִּמְלֹךְ אֲמַצְיָהוּ בְנוֹ

assault. They subjected him to hardened criminals who had never in their lives known a woman. These men afflicted him sexually (*Mechilta, Beshalach* 5:1). According to *Midrash Torah, Va'Eira* 9, this was a fate to which each of the four humans who had been regarded as deities — Pharoah, Churam, Yoash and Nebuchadnezzar — were subjected.

Tifereth Zion explains: A human being who is considered imbued with Divine faculties is seen as the active conduit through which all matters, good or bad, benign or destructive, flow to the people or communities with whom he feels himself associated. Much as a man, through the conjugal act, quickens the potential life within the woman with vitality — so he too, in a much broader sense, is a source of life and sustenance, birth and death. There is no more graphic way to give the lie to this conceit than to condemn this *god* to the absolute passivity of being the victim of a homosexual assault, thereby denying him even that active, if limited role, which would be the normal prerogative of any man.

25. וּבְלֶכְתָּם מִמֶּנּוּ כִּי־עָזְבוּ אֹתוֹ . . . — *When they departed from him — for they left him...* When they let him go it was not out of mercy, but because they had done to him whatever they had set out to do (*Metzudos*).

בִּדְמֵי בְּנֵי יְהוֹיָדָע . . . — *For the blood of Yehoiada's ... sons ...* The plural, *sons*, is used, either because when Yoash had Zechariah killed, he also gave orders that Yehoiada's other children be put to death, or it may conform to the Biblical usage of occasionally using the plural form even when only one son is meant (see *Genesis* 46:23, *Numbers* 26:8, *Bava Basra* 143b) (*Radak, Metzudos*).

Ralbag suggests that the plural form indicates that Yoash was being punished not only for the death of Zechariah himself, but also for the children and descendants which he would have had, had he not been killed. This, in much the same way that the Sages teach that Cain was to be punished not only for Abel's death but also for all the children who might have been born to him [see *Rashi* to *Genesis* 4:11], and that not only Navoth's blood but also that of his as yet unborn children was blamed on Ahab [*II Kings* 9:26; see commentators there.]

Now, since potential descendants are obviously victims in every murder, it is clear that when an issue is made of them, as in the three cases mentioned, there must be a special reason for it. In our case, we can well understand this. As we have seen throughout the past few chapters, Yehoiada did more than save the individual Yoash from death at the hands of Athaliahu. The Davidic lineage and the Messianic future of Israel were at stake. In saving Yoash, Yehoiada guaranteed that millennia later there would be a Messiah in Israel. This magnified the heinousness of Yoash's crime. Yehoiada had given him eternity and he did not hesitate to kill Yehoiada's son, thus robbing him of his future.

Yoash's death is attributed to his guilt in having Zechariah killed. This once more bears out our thesis that Yoash had not been involved in the idol worship of the nobles. If he had been guilty of this also, it would surely have been mentioned.

עַל־מִטָּתוֹ — *On his bed*. This was also part of God's judgment against him. Zechariah had every right to consider himself safe. It could not have occurred to him that Yoash, who owed such a debt of gratitude to his father, would have him killed. Therefore, Yoash was killed on his bed — in a situation in which he was utterly unprepared for an assassination attempt.

וְלֹא קְבָרֻהוּ בְּקִבְרוֹת הַמְּלָכִים — *However, they did not bury him in the sepulchers of the kings*. Yehoram, too, had not been buried in the graves of the kings (21:20) but, as we showed in fn. to 22:1, this was because at the time of his death he was no longer the effective ruler.

In Yoash's case, the reason why this honor was denied him must have been because of the

his servants conspired against him in retaliation for the blood of Yehoiada the Kohen's sons. They slew him on his bed and he died, and they buried him in the City of David. However, they did not bury him in the sepulchers of the kings. [26] *These are the ones who conspired against him; Zavach son of Shimoth the Amonite, and Yehozavad son of Shimrith the Moabite.* [27] *And his sons, and the multitude of prophecies against him, and of how the House of God was firmly grounded is recorded in the Midrash of the Book of the Kings. Amatziahu his son reigned*

heinousness of his crime. We also find Achaz (28:27) and Menasseh (33:20) buried outside the royal sepulchers for the same reason.

Kings states that Yoash was buried *with his father*. See fn. to 22:1.

26. וְאֵלֶּה הַמִּתְקַשְּׁרִים עָלָיו . . . — *These are the ones who conspired against him*. The names of the assassins are also given in *Kings*, but without the information that they came from Amon and Moab respectively.

The Sages attach significance to the descent of these people. Amon and Moab are the prototypal ingrates in Scriptural thought. Abraham had given their progenitor, Lot, everything. Instead of helping Israel in their trek through the wilderness, they would not provide them with food, and Moab went so far as to hire Bilaam to curse the Israelites. It is not surprising that Yoash's assassins should be descended from such people. He too did not know the meaning of gratitude (v. 22). In *Kings*, which tells nothing of Zechariah's murder, the information is not significant.

There is another — structural — difference between the *Kings'* account and ours. After *Kings* ends its account of Hazael's campaign, it rounds off the description of Yoash's reign with the standard formula: *The rest of the matters concerning Yoash are recorded* ... — the equivalent of our v. 27. Only then does *Kings* tell of his assassination and the identity of the assassins. In *Chronicles*, this information is given before v. 27.

In fn. to 13:2, and at 20:35, we surmised that in *Kings*, information given after the formula does not bear the hallmark of prophetic interpretation, but rather is deemed important enough to record even though it is not part of the prophet's account. This can clearly explain the difference in structure. For reasons which were analyzed in Section II, *Different Perspectives upon Yoash and the Monarchy*, *Kings* does not deal at all with the tragedy of Yoash's later years. It does not record the killing of Zechariah and, therefore, lacks a logical and cohesive context within which to record the facts and details of Yoash's assassination. These are therefore relegated to the non-prophetic footnote of its account of the reign. In *Chronicles*, it is an essential part of the narrative.

27. וּבָנָיו יִרֶב הַמַּשָּׂא עָלָיו — *And his sons and the multitude of prophecies against him*. While in all other cases, translation follows the קְרִי (the way the word is read), rather than the כְּתִיב (the way it is written), we have here deviated from that rule. The כְּתִיב in our case is וְרָב, which is a noun meaning *multitude* or *abundance*. This fits smoothly into the syntax of the sentence, and lends itself readily to translation. Many prophecies were uttered in the days after Yehoiada's death (vs. 19-20) and these were recorded together with other pertinent material concerning Yoash's reign (*Radak*).

The קְרִי is יִרֶב, the third person future tense of רבה, which translates *shall multiply* (*Genesis* 1:23). What, in that case, does the phrase mean? *Radak* suggests that it is a case of the future tense being used in place of the past, and the phrase is to be rendered: *And the prophecies which abounded concerning him*.

Perhaps the future tense is used to hint at the following thought: Perhaps בָּנָיו should not be taken literally to mean *his sons*, but more broadly: [*The matter of*] *his descendants*. Our phrase would then mean: [*Concerning which*] *much prophecy* [*was yet to be said*]. Reference would be to the steady decline of the royal line which began from the time of Yoash's fall (comm. to v. 22). Much prophecy would yet be said in attempts to stem the tide which would culminate in the Temple's destruction.

וִיסוֹד בֵּית הָאֱלֹהִים — *Of how the House of God was firmly grounded*. The account of the improvements which Yoash had made to the Temple (*Metzudos*).

עַל־מִדְרַשׁ סֵפֶר הַמְּלָכִים — *In the Midrash of the Book of the Kings*. See comm. to 13:22 for the explanation of *Midrash* in this connection. See

כה
א־ד

א תַּחְתָּיו׃ בֶּן־עֶשְׂרִים וְחָמֵשׁ שָׁנָה מָלַךְ אֲמַצְיָהוּ
וְעֶשְׂרִים וָתֵשַׁע שָׁנָה מָלַךְ בִּירוּשָׁלָ͏ִם וְשֵׁם אִמּוֹ יְהוֹעַדָּן
ב מִירוּשָׁלָ͏ִם׃ וַיַּעַשׂ הַיָּשָׁר בְּעֵינֵי יהוה רַק לֹא בְּלֵבָב שָׁלֵם׃
ג וַיְהִי כַּאֲשֶׁר חָזְקָה הַמַּמְלָכָה עָלָיו וַיַּהֲרֹג אֶת־עֲבָדָיו
ד הַמַּכִּים אֶת־הַמֶּלֶךְ אָבִיו׃ וְאֶת־בְּנֵיהֶם לֹא הֵמִית כִּי

Section II, *Different Perspectives upon Yoash and the Monarchy*, for the significance of its use for the recording of the events of Yoash's reign.

XXV

◆§ Amatziahu Consolidates His Reign

The *Chronicles* account of Amatziahu's reign contains all the information given in *Kings* (ch. 14), but there is much that is told here that does not appear there. See the discussion in Section II to Ch. 24, *Different Perspectives upon Yoash and the Monarchy*.

There is almost no guidance in extant Midrashic sources, which would help us to gauge the significance of the events described here. Perhaps they will lend themselves to our understanding when we take note of the one, albeit oblique, piece of information which we can deduce from the Sages' teachings.

As we saw at 24:22, Zechariah's murder carried implications far beyond the wanton killing of an innocent individual. It placed a mark of failure upon the entire Davidic line that was to be descended from Yoash. The seething blood on the Temple floor was to haunt them until the destruction of the Temple. Amatziahu, then, was the first king whose reign began under the inauspicious sign of this blot of guilt and outrage. He could, of course, not know that it would prove to be indelible. We could reasonably expect that a king, beginning his reign as one who *did that which was right in the eyes of* HASHEM, would regard the eradication of this disgrace as the central task of his rule, and that whatever he undertook would be with this purpose in mind.

We shall try to understand the *Chronicles* account of Amatziahu's reign within this context.

1. בֶּן־עֶשְׂרִים וְחָמֵשׁ שָׁנָה מָלַךְ אֲמַצְיָהוּ — *Amatziahu took up the kingship at twenty-five years of age*. The wording is different than the usual formula which would have read: בֶּן־עֶשְׂרִים וְחָמֵשׁ שָׁנָה הָיָה בְמָלְכוֹ . . ., which is, in fact, used in the *Kings'* version.

Perhaps the more forceful and active מָלַךְ is used here in order to set the tone for Amatziahu's approach to the kingship. In the prefatory remarks we surmised that he would have been animated by an overwhelming desire to eradicate the blot of the seething blood on the Temple grounds. Accordingly, we would expect him to shoulder his responsibilities with a greater degree of zeal than would normally have been the case at the ascension of a new king.

2. רַק לֹא בְּלֵבָב שָׁלֵם — *Only not with a whole heart*.

This phrase requires definition in its own right and also, inasmuch as it replaces a different wording in *Kings*: . . .*but not like his father David; he did all as his father Yoash had done*.

At 15:17 we learn that the heart of Asa was . . . *whole all his days*. Since his reign was certainly not free from shortcomings, it is evident that a heart can be described as *whole* even though mistakes may have been made.

In what sense was Amatziahu worse than Asa, and why was the expression, which *Kings* deemed appropriate, changed in *Chronicles*?

The fact that in the very next verse *Kings* tells that, in spite of the fact that Amatziahu did that which was straight in the eyes of HASHEM, the *bamos* were not removed and that the people continued to use them for [Divine] sacrifice, suggests that the stricture of the previous verse — that Amatziahu had not lived up to David's standards — might refer to this shortcoming. He did not set a standard of such exalted sanctity as would have weaned the people away from this pernicious practice. This shortcoming would not have played a role in the *Chronicles'* account — see Section II to Ch.20, *Bamos in Kings and Chronicles*.

It may be that *Chronicles'* intention is to pick up the theme first indicated at 21:7. That verse pointed to an erosion of the inner core of sanctity, which had typified the Davidic line and upon which God's promise never to forsake His benevolence to David's family had been based. We noted there that it was that erosion which brought about the decree that

in his stead.

*Amatziahu took up the kingship at twenty five years of age,
and ruled for twenty-nine years in Jerusalem. His mother's
name was Yehoadan from Jerusalem.* [2] *He did that which was
straight in the eyes of* HASHEM, *only not with a whole heart.*
[3] *When the weight of his kingship prodded him, he killed those of
his servants who had slain the king, his father.* [4] *But he did not kill*

David's line was to be destroyed — a tragedy that would have come about, but for the fact that Yoash was miraculously saved. Yoash's backsliding after Yehoiada's death indicated that he would not be the one to rekindle the spark.

Our phrase assesses Amatziahu by the same standard. He did much that was good, and his reign in its totality can be described as benign. But his heart was not *whole*. He would not be the one who could arrest the downward spiral. Zechariah's blood would not be mollified during his reign.

3. וַיְהִי כַּאֲשֶׁר חָזְקָה הַמַּמְלָכָה עָלָיו — *When the weight of his kingship prodded him.* The parallel phrase in *Kings*, וַיְהִי כַּאֲשֶׁר חָזְקָה הַמַּמְלָכָה בְּיָדוֹ is clear. It means that the kingship was *secure* or *established, in* or *under his hand* or *control*. But what does ... חָזְקָה ... עָלָיו mean? If it is meant to convey the same idea, then at the very least, the phrasing is unusual. Moreover, it is difficult to conceive of a compelling reason to change the perfectly clear בְּיָדוֹ of *Kings*.

The combination חָזַק עָלָיו, occurs in Scripture in the sense, *to importune* or *urge* or *speak harshly and insistently* (cf. *Malachi* 3:13). Perhaps the sense of our phrase is similar. As we shall see in the next verse, Amatziahu may have been hesitant about killing his father's assassins. He was acutely aware of the heinous crime which Yoash had committed and was eager to make amends and to eradicate the mark of guilt. But, sensing himself to be in sure control of his kingdom, he felt himself pushed into an act of retribution which he might otherwise have wished to avoid. In this sense, his kingship *prodded* him to action.

וַיַּהֲרֹג אֶת־עֲבָדָיו... — *He killed those of his servants ...*

Kings has:. ..וַיַּךְ אֶת־עֲבָדָיו, *he smote his servants ....* There is a difference between the root הרג, *to kill*, which never means anything other than to put man or animal to death, and, נכה, *to smite*, which, while it is often used in the sense, *to kill someone*, also has many other connotations. It is used when God *strikes* someone with a sickness, or when a man *strikes* another upon the cheek, and in many other situations. It also carries the meaning of *to destroy* (*Radak, Sefer HaShorashim*).

Yoash's assassins could have been put to death under either of two possible halachic justifications. They could have been executed by the courts as common murderers, or by the king under the royal prerogative which we discussed at 24:21. In comm. to the next verse we shall surmise that, for reasons discussed there, Amatziahu chose to kill the assassins through the agency of the courts. Perhaps our verse indicates this by the use of הרג instead of נכה. The royal prerogative is unfettered by any of the limitations placed upon court-ordered executions. It lends itself more to the expression of נכה with its connotation of total destruction than to הרג, which is more appropriate to describe the formal execution for which the courts are empowered.

4. ... וְאֶת־בְּנֵיהֶם לֹא הֵמִית — *But he did not kill their sons ...* The second part of the verse explains that this accorded with the Torah's interdiction against killing sons for their father's transgressions.

But why would he otherwise have killed the children?

When a king kills in the exercise of his royal prerogative, he may do so without being hemmed by some of the limiting factors which inhibit court-ordered execution (*Rambam, Melachim* 3:8-10). In addition to the leniencies listed by *Rambam*, there is also the right to kill the children of the rebel. [This is apparent from the story of David and the Giveonites (*Yevamos* 79a) — *Maharitz Chayos* (*Toras HaNeviim* ch. 7).]

Amatziahu, then, had the option of killing the assassin's children in the exercise of his royal prerogative.

Why did he go to the courts rather than avail himself of this option?

It was a well-considered, deliberate decision.

כַּכָּתוּב בַּתּוֹרָה בְּסֵפֶר מֹשֶׁה אֲשֶׁר־צִוָּה יהוה לֵאמֹר
לֹא־יָמוּתוּ אָבוֹת עַל־בָּנִים וּבָנִים לֹא־יָמוּתוּ עַל־אָבוֹת כִּי
ה אִישׁ בְּחֶטְאוֹ יָמוּתוּ: וַיִּקְבֹּץ אֲמַצְיָהוּ אֶת־יְהוּדָה
וַיַּעֲמִידֵם לְבֵית־אָבוֹת לְשָׂרֵי הָאֲלָפִים וּלְשָׂרֵי הַמֵּאוֹת
לְכָל־יְהוּדָה וּבִנְיָמִן וַיִּפְקְדֵם לְמִבֶּן עֶשְׂרִים שָׁנָה וָמַעְלָה
וַיִּמְצָאֵם שְׁלֹשׁ־מֵאוֹת אֶלֶף בָּחוּר יוֹצֵא צָבָא אֹחֵז רֹמַח
ו וְצִנָּה: וַיִּשְׂכֹּר מִיִּשְׂרָאֵל מֵאָה אֶלֶף גִּבּוֹר חָיִל בְּמֵאָה
ז כִּכַּר־כָּסֶף: וְאִישׁ הָאֱלֹהִים בָּא אֵלָיו לֵאמֹר הַמֶּלֶךְ
אַל־יָבוֹא עִמְּךָ צְבָא יִשְׂרָאֵל כִּי אֵין יהוה עִם־יִשְׂרָאֵל כֹּל
ח בְּנֵי אֶפְרָיִם: כִּי אִם־בֹּא אַתָּה עֲשֵׂה חֲזַק לַמִּלְחָמָה
יַכְשִׁילְךָ הָאֱלֹהִים לִפְנֵי אוֹיֵב כִּי יֶשׁ־כֹּחַ בֵּאלֹהִים לַעְזוֹר
ט וּלְהַכְשִׁיל: וַיֹּאמֶר אֲמַצְיָהוּ לְאִישׁ הָאֱלֹהִים וּמַה־לַּעֲשׂוֹת

As we noted above, Amatziahu must have been acutely aware of the heinousness of his father's crime and would have been eager to establish a new and unblemished kingship. Under such circumstances an exercise of the royal prerogative might have been seen as tainted, and Amatziahu would have likely avoided it. He could punish the perpetrators of his father's death through the courts without the need to compromise himself by acting as king. For this he had to forgo the death of the sons which, once the matter was in the courts, was prohibited by the Torah.

כִּי כַכָּתוּב בַּתּוֹרָה בְּסֵפֶר מֹשֶׁה — *For [he acted] in accordance with that which is written in Moses' Torah*. The wording in *Kings* is: כַּכָּתוּב בְּסֵפֶר תּוֹרַת־מֹשֶׁה. Our translation requires the insertion of a word or words between כִּי and כַּכָּתוּב: *For [he acted] in accordance with that* or *For [he decided to act] in accordance with that which is written in the Torah*.

We suggest that *Chronicles* inserted the כִּי, because the wording in *Kings* leaves an unanswered question. The statement *He did not kill their sons ... that which is written in the Torah ...* is not compelling. That which is written in the Torah would not necessarily have stopped him from killing the sons, if he would have chosen to exercise the royal prerogative. Therefore, the כִּי is inserted to indicate a consideration. Amatziahu had a reason for killing the assassins in such a way that their execution would be governed by normal Torah law.[1]

. . . לֹא־יָמוּתוּ אָבוֹת — *Fathers shall not die*. This is a paraphrase of *Deuteronomy* 24:16. Our text seems to derive from this verse that children are not to be punished for the sins of their fathers. But this appears to be in disagreement with *Sanhedrin* 27b, which uses the verse to derive the disqualification of relatives as witnesses in a court of law.

Tosafos to *Kesubos* 29a (s.v.אלו) thinks that, although the entire verse is paraphrased here, only the last part ... *but each man shall be made to die for his own sin*, is meant to explain Amatziahu's actions. The earlier part of the verse has the meaning assigned to it by the Talmud.

Ramban (*Leviticus* 27:29) cites our verse as an example of a principle which he formulates and discusses at length in his glosses to *Sefer HaMitzvos, Shoresh* 2: Even when a Scriptural verse is interpreted homiletically in the Talmud, it does not, because of this, lose its simple meaning. The verse, then, speaks to us at two levels: As *d'rash* and as *p'shat*. At the *d'rash* level, it disqualifies relatives from bearing testimony; at the *p'shat* level, it bars the punishment of children for their parents' guilt.

◆§ The Edomite Campaign and Its Aftermath

5. שְׁלֹשׁ־מֵאוֹת אֶלֶף בָּחוּר יוֹצֵא צָבָא — *Three hundred thousand chosen men, able to go forth*

1. This may also explain the phrase כִּי כַכָּתוּב בַּתּוֹרָה, which the *trop* separates from בְּסֵפֶר מֹשֶׁה, in contrast to *Kings* where the phrase is: בְּסֵפֶר תּוֹרַת־מֹשֶׁה. The meaning may be that Amatziahu elected to have the assassins killed as murderers, which is a method mandated in the Torah. The royal prerogative does not stem from the Torah but is derived from a verse in *Joshua* 1:18: *Any man who will rebel against your utterance or will not listen to your words ... will be put to death*.

their sons, for [he acted] in accordance with that which is writ-
ten in Moses' Torah, as HASHEM commanded, saying: Fa-
thers shall not die for children, nor shall children die for fa-
thers. But each man shall die for his own sin.
5 *Amatziahu mus-*
tered Judah, organizing them into family units, under captains
of thousands, and captains of hundreds, appointed over Judah and
Benjamin. He counted them from twenty years old and up-
wards, and found them three hundred thousand chosen
men, able to go forth to war, holding spear and shield.
6 *He*
hired a hundred thousand warriors from Israel, for a hundred
talents of silver.
7 *The man of God came to him saying, 'O king, let*
not the army of Israel go with you, for HASHEM is not with Israel
— all the sons of Ephraim.'
8 *'For if you go alone, secure that you*
will do mightily in battle, God will cause you to fall before the
enemy. For God has the power either to support or to hinder.'
9 *But*
Amatziahu said to the man of God, 'And what is to be done with

to war. See Section II, *The Edomite Campaign*, for an analysis of the confrontation with Edom.

These numbers tell us of a numerical decline which paralleled the erosion of the spiritual heights which had been attained by the great kings of earlier generations. Asa had recruited three hundred thousand men from Judah alone; and these were joined by two hundred thousand from Benjamin (14:7). Yehoshaphat had mustered an army of 1,160,000 (17:14 ff.) (*Ralbag*).

6. וַיִּשְׂכֹּר מִיִּשְׂרָאֵל... — *He hired . . . from Israel*. The relatively small number of his own army (comm. v. 5) could well be a motive for this move, but see Section II, *The Edomite Campaign*, for another explanation.

7. וְאִישׁ הָאֱלֹהִים — *The man of God*. The Sages have a tradition that this was Amotz, a brother of Amatziahu, the father of the prophet Isaiah (*Radak*).

אַל־יָבוֹא עִמְּךָ צְבָא יִשְׂרָאֵל — *Let not the army of Israel go with you*. See Section II, *The Edomite Campaign*.

כִּי אֵין ה׳ עִם־יִשְׂרָאֵל — *For HASHEM is not with Israel*. Whatever spiritual lapses there had been in Judah, they could not be compared with the unrelieved downward spiral which the Northern Kingdom had undergone from the moment of its inception.

כֹּל בְּנֵי אֶפְרָיִם — *All the sons of Ephraim*. The whole of the Northern Kingdom was called Ephraim because their first king, Yarov'am, came from that tribe (*Metzudos*).

8. כִּי אִם־בֹּא אַתָּה — *For if you go alone*. The translation reflects *Malbim's* interpretation. The previous verse had stated that God would withhold His support, if the Israelites would be incorporated into Amatziahu's forces. Consequently, if Amatziahu chooses to ignore the words of the man of God, and wages the campaign with the joint army, then victory will not come by the hand of God. He will be going alone.

עֲשֵׂה חֲזַק לַמִּלְחָמָה — *Secure that you will do mightily in battle*. No amount of effort will affect the outcome. However mightily you fight, God will make you fall (*Malbim*).

Mefaresh takes the phrase as a challenge: See if you can fight mightily enough to win! You will find that nothing will help if God chooses that you should fail.

לַעְזוֹר וּלְהַכְשִׁיל... — *. . . either to support or to hinder*. God can help a small army win a battle against overwhelming odds, and can cause a mighty army to fall. You will not lose by sending the mercenaries away, and their presence will not swing the battle in your favor (*Mefaresh*).

9. וּמַה־לַּעֲשׂוֹת... — *And what is to be done . . .* If Amatziahu was willing to forgo the military advantage of an additional hundred thousand men because he realized that this was God's will, it is difficult to see what he thought would be the answer to the problem of the money. Did he believe that the man of God would change his mind to avoid the loss of the silver?

If the suggestion we made in Section II, *The*

כה
י־טז

לִמְאַת הַכִּכָּר אֲשֶׁר נָתַתִּי לִגְדוּד יִשְׂרָאֵל וַיֹּאמֶר אִישׁ
י הָאֱלֹהִים יֵשׁ לַיהוָה לָתֶת לְךָ הַרְבֵּה מִזֶּה׃ וַיַּבְדִּילֵם
אֲמַצְיָהוּ לְהַגְּדוּד אֲשֶׁר־בָּא אֵלָיו מֵאֶפְרַיִם לָלֶכֶת
לִמְקוֹמָם וַיִּחַר אַפָּם מְאֹד בִּיהוּדָה וַיָּשׁוּבוּ לִמְקוֹמָם
יא בָּחֳרִי־אָף׃ וַאֲמַצְיָהוּ הִתְחַזַּק וַיִּנְהַג אֶת־עַמּוֹ וַיֵּלֶךְ
יב גֵּיא הַמֶּלַח וַיַּךְ אֶת־בְּנֵי־שֵׂעִיר עֲשֶׂרֶת אֲלָפִים׃ וַעֲשֶׂרֶת
אֲלָפִים חַיִּים שָׁבוּ בְּנֵי יְהוּדָה וַיְבִיאוּם לְרֹאשׁ הַסָּלַע
יג וַיַּשְׁלִיכוּם מֵרֹאשׁ הַסֶּלַע וְכֻלָּם נִבְקָעוּ׃ וּבְנֵי הַגְּדוּד
אֲשֶׁר הֵשִׁיב אֲמַצְיָהוּ מִלֶּכֶת עִמּוֹ לַמִּלְחָמָה וַיִּפְשְׁטוּ בְּעָרֵי
יְהוּדָה מִשֹּׁמְרוֹן וְעַד־בֵּית חוֹרוֹן וַיַּכּוּ מֵהֶם שְׁלֹשֶׁת
יד אֲלָפִים וַיָּבֹזּוּ בִּזָּה רַבָּה׃ וַיְהִי אַחֲרֵי בוֹא אֲמַצְיָהוּ
מֵהַכּוֹת אֶת־אֲדוֹמִים וַיָּבֵא אֶת־אֱלֹהֵי בְּנֵי שֵׂעִיר וַיַּעֲמִידֵם
טו לוֹ לֵאלֹהִים וְלִפְנֵיהֶם יִשְׁתַּחֲוֶה וְלָהֶם יְקַטֵּר׃ וַיִּחַר־אַף
יְהוָה בַּאֲמַצְיָהוּ וַיִּשְׁלַח אֵלָיו נָבִיא וַיֹּאמֶר לוֹ לָמָּה
דָרַשְׁתָּ אֶת־אֱלֹהֵי הָעָם אֲשֶׁר לֹא־הִצִּילוּ אֶת־עַמָּם מִיָּדֶךָ׃
טז וַיְהִי ׀ בְּדַבְּרוֹ אֵלָיו וַיֹּאמֶר לוֹ הַלְיוֹעֵץ לַמֶּלֶךְ נְתַנּוּךָ

Edomite Campaign, concerning Amatziahu's motives in hiring the men from the Northern Kingdom is correct, then we may understand his question as follows: Since the money has already been spent, would it not be wiser to retain the services of the soldiers at least in the capacity of ordinary mercenaries? Granted that a joint army is out of question because God would not help but a different, less implicating partnership might still be possible.

יֵשׁ לַה׳ לָתֶת לְךָ הַרְבֵּה מִזֶּה — *Hashem is able to give you much more than this*. He will make up your loss from other sources (*Metzudos*).

10. וַיַּבְדִּילֵם אֲמַצְיָהוּ — *So Amatziahu detached* ... He separated them from the soldiers who had been drawn from Judah (*Metzudos*).

We must stand in awe of the trust in God which is demonstrated by Amatziahu's action. The man of God did not — at least as far as can be seen from the text — come as a prophet. He did not formulate his words as a message from God. It appears to be no more than advice, rendered on the basis of the deep insight into current affairs, which a man of his spiritual stature would have. Nevertheless, without demurring, Amatziahu is willing to do without a quarter of his projected army, and to lose this vast sum of money.

All the stranger, then, is the act of apostasy described in v. 14, which followed immediately upon the victory which the man of God had promised him if he would place his trust in God. See below.

11. וַיַּךְ אֶת־בְּנֵי־שֵׂעִיר — *He smote the Seirites. Eichah Rabbah* (*Pesichta* 14) describes the moment of Amatziahu's victory as a time when God *smiled upon Israel*. God apparently looked with particular favor upon Amatziahu's campaign. In Section II, *The Edomite Campaign*, we have suggested a possible motive for this aggressive war. Perhaps it would have met with even greater success if Amatziahu had not erred so terribly, as described in the next verse.

12. וַיְבִיאוּם לְרֹאשׁ הַסָּלַע — *And brought them to the top of the cliff*. See Section II, *The Edomite Campaign*, for a possible explanation for this strikingly cruel action.

The Sages castigate Amatziahu for doing this: When this happened, God said, 'I authorized the killing of gentiles with the sword only, and these have brought them to the top of the cliff, have thrown them down so that they burst open — I take no pleasure in this.' At that moment God said, 'What are these [Israelites] doing here [in the Holy Land]? Let them go into exile!'

The exile still lay well over two hundred

the hundred talents which I have given to the army of Israel?' So
the man of God said, 'HASHEM is able to give you much more than
this.' 10 *So Amatziahu detached the army which had come to him*
from Ephraim, so that they should return to their place. Therefore
they became very angry at Judah and returned home in fierce an-
ger. 11 *Amatziahu acted resolutely, and took along his people to the*
Valley of Salt. He smote the Seirites — ten thousand. 12 *And ten*
thousand children of Judah were captured alive, and brought them
to the top of the cliff and cast them down from the top of the
cliff, so that they all burst open. 13 *The men of the army whom*
Amatziahu sent back that they should not go with him to battle fell
upon the cities of Judah, from Samaria to Beis Choron, and smote
three thousand of them and took much spoil. 14 *Now it was after*
Amatziahu returned from smiting the Edomites, that he brought
the idols of the Seirites and set them up over himself as overlords,
paid obeisance to them and offered up to them. 15 *The anger of*
HASHEM was kindled against Amatziahu wherefore He sent a
prophet to him. He said to him, 'Why did you seek out the overlords
of this people, who did not save their people from your hands?' 16 *As*
he spoke to him, he said, 'Have they made you adviser to the king?

years in the future. Nevertheless, the Sages trace its beginnings to Amatziahu's ferocious killing of the captives. Apparently the Sages view the senseless cruelty involved as hitting at the very essence of Jewish being. A people for whom such an act was possible had no place in God's beloved country.

13. מִשֹּׁמְרוֹן וְעַד־בֵּית חוֹרוֹן — *From Samaria to Beis Choron. Mefaresh* deduces that they had already returned to the Northern Kingdom, and only then swept down south once more. For this reason it says *from Samaria* — which lay in the north — *to Beis Choron*. If they had engaged in the slaughter and pillaging on their way home the places would have been named in the other order.

◆§ Amatziahu Turns To Idol Worship

14. וַיְהִי אַחֲרֵי בוֹא אֲמַצְיָהוּ — *Now it was after Amatziahu returned* ... See Section II, *Amatziahu Serves Alien gods*, for an examination of Amatziahu's backsliding.

וַיַּעֲמִידֵם לוֹ לֵאלֹהִים — *And set them up over himself as overlords.* The translation reflects the point made by *HaLevi*, Section II, *Amatziahu Serves Alien gods*, that the idol worship which took place in Judah never in any sense implied the rejection of God as omnipotent Master of the universe, but was built on the assumption of the existence of intermediaries endowed with certain powers. The word אֱלֹהִים, which is also used in Scripture for *judge* (cf. *Exodus* 22:7), implies any powerful figure, and is not limited to a deity.

15. וַיִּחַר־אַף ה׳ בַּאֲמַצְיָהוּ — *The anger of HASHEM was kindled against Amatziahu.* Even if Amaziahu's was an honest mistake, it could not go unpunished. It touched upon the very essence of God's relationship with Israel. See Section II, *Amatziahu Serves Alien gods*.

אֲשֶׁר לֹא־הִצִּילוּ... — *Who did not save...* As we noted in Section II, *Amatziahu Serves Alien gods*, the prophet accuses Amatziahu not of wickedness but of folly. Would God entrust His beloved children to the stewardship of impotents who were unable to protect their own client nation? The awareness of the foolishness of what he had done should have shaken Amatziahu loose from his tragic mistake and galvanized him to repentance.

16. הַלְיוֹעֵץ לַמֶּלֶךְ נְתַנּוּךָ — *Have they made you adviser to the king?* The prophet had not given his message in God's Name. It sounded as though he was advising the king on his own initiative. As such, the king castigated him for his presumption (*Malbim*).

חֲדַל־לְךָ לָמָּה יַכּוּךָ וַיֶּחְדַּל הַנָּבִיא וַיֹּאמֶר יָדַעְתִּי כִּי־יָעַץ
אֱלֹהִים לְהַשְׁחִיתֶךָ כִּי־עָשִׂיתָ זֹּאת וְלֹא שָׁמַעְתָּ
יז לַעֲצָתִי: וַיִּוָּעַץ אֲמַצְיָהוּ מֶלֶךְ יְהוּדָה
וַיִּשְׁלַח אֶל־יוֹאָשׁ בֶּן־יְהוֹאָחָז בֶּן־יֵהוּא מֶלֶךְ יִשְׂרָאֵל
יח לֵאמֹר לְךָ נִתְרָאֶה פָנִים: וַיִּשְׁלַח יוֹאָשׁ מֶלֶךְ־יִשְׂרָאֵל
אֶל־אֲמַצְיָהוּ מֶלֶךְ־יְהוּדָה לֵאמֹר הַחוֹחַ אֲשֶׁר בַּלְּבָנוֹן
שָׁלַח אֶל־הָאֶרֶז אֲשֶׁר בַּלְּבָנוֹן לֵאמֹר תְּנָה־אֶת־בִּתְּךָ לִבְנִי
לְאִשָּׁה וַתַּעֲבֹר חַיַּת הַשָּׂדֶה אֲשֶׁר בַּלְּבָנוֹן וַתִּרְמֹס
יט אֶת־הַחוֹחַ: אָמַרְתָּ הִנֵּה הִכִּיתָ אֶת־אֱדוֹם וּנְשָׂאֲךָ לִבְּךָ
לְהַכְבִּיד עַתָּה שְׁבָה בְּבֵיתֶךָ לָמָּה תִתְגָּרֶה בְּרָעָה וְנָפַלְתָּ
כ אַתָּה וִיהוּדָה עִמָּךְ: וְלֹא־שָׁמַע אֲמַצְיָהוּ כִּי מֵהָאֱלֹהִים
כא הִיא לְמַעַן תִּתָּם בְּיָד כִּי דָרְשׁוּ אֵת אֱלֹהֵי אֱדוֹם: וַיַּעַל
יוֹאָשׁ מֶלֶךְ־יִשְׂרָאֵל וַיִּתְרָאוּ פָנִים הוּא וַאֲמַצְיָהוּ מֶלֶךְ־
כב יְהוּדָה בְּבֵית שֶׁמֶשׁ אֲשֶׁר לִיהוּדָה: וַיִּנָּגֶף יְהוּדָה לִפְנֵי
כג יִשְׂרָאֵל וַיָּנֻסוּ אִישׁ לְאֹהָלָיו: וְאֵת אֲמַצְיָהוּ מֶלֶךְ־יְהוּדָה

יָדַעְתִּי כִּי־יָעַץ אֱלֹהִים ... — *I know that God has determined...* The prophet answers that his information comes by Divine inspiration. He had not given advice on his own initiative (*Malbim*).

◆§ Confrontation with the Northern Kingdom

17. וַיִּוָּעַץ אֲמַצְיָהוּ — *Having considered the matter, Amatziahu ...* יעץ means *to advise* or *counsel*. In the *niphal*, passive voice, it could mean *to be advised by another* or *to find counsel within oneself*.

In the context of our suggestion for the motivation behind Amatziahu's message (Section II, *Amatziahu's Challenge to Yoash*), we understand the phrase as follows: Amatziahu had carefully thought out how he could clothe his desire for revenge in a respectable form. He concluded that he could issue an invitation for negotiating a reunion of the two kingdoms — an intimation of which ambition must have reached Yoash before this, when Amatziahu hired the mercenaries. Amatziahu reckoned that Yoash would spurn his offer and that he would then have the opportunity to wage the battle for which he was really spoiling.

The confidence evident in Yoash's answer (v. 18) indicates that Amatziahu miscalculated his military prowess badly. It was God who instigated his thoughts in order to punish him for the idol worship (*Malbim*).

לְךָ נִתְרָאֶה פָנִים — *'Come, let us meet face to face.' Targum* here and in *Kings* adds בִּקְרָבָא, *in battle*. Indeed, later in v. 21, the battle is described as וַיִּתְרָאוּ פָנִים. The commentators interpret that, even in their literal sense, the words convey a challenge to war. Amatziahu was saying that it was easy enough to have killed the three thousand unsuspecting citizens (v. 13). Let us see how you will fare in a face to face battle.

In Section II, *Amatziahu's Challenge to Yoash*, we have suggested that Amatziahu used an ambiguous expression in order to convey a dual message. Overtly, he was inviting Yoash to consider an amalgamation of the two kingdoms. In reality, he knew that Yoash would not agree, and that his invitation was, in fact, a declaration of war.

18. הַחוֹחַ אֲשֶׁר בַּלְּבָנוֹן — *The thistle that was in the Lebanon...* It is difficult to see how a marriage proposal is an appropriate parable for a declaration of war. Apparently with this problem in mind, *Targum* transfers the parable to the hiring of mercenaries. That act of hiring is the marriage proposal, and the subsequent destruction which the mercenaries wrought in Judah is the trampling of the wild beasts.

Radak (*Kings*) and *Metzudos* explain as follows: Even a suggestion of friendship would have been an insult to the cedar; certainly, then, a challenge to war is laughable.

Desist! Why should you be smitten?' So the prophet desisted
and said, 'I know that God has determined to destroy you because
you have done this and have not listened to my counsel.' 17 *Having*
considered the matter, Amatziahu, king of Judah, sent a message
to Yoash son of Yehoachaz, son of Yehu, king of Israel, saying,
'Come, let us meet face to face.' 18 *Yoash, king of Israel, sent a*
message to Amatziahu king of Judah, saying, 'The thistle that was
in the Lebanon sent to the cedar that was in the Lebanon, saying,
"Give your daughter to my son in marriage." Then the wild beasts
of the field that were in the Lebanon, passed by and trampled the
thistle. 19 *Because you tell yourself, how great it is that you have*
smitten Edom, you feel emboldened to seek greater glory. Why do
you not stay at home! Why stir up trouble, when you will surely
fall — you, together with Judah!' 20 *But Amatziahu would not*
hear: for it was so decreed by God in order that He might have
them overpowered. This, because they had sought out the Edom-
ean idols. 21 *So Yoash king of Israel made war. He and Amatziahu*
king of Judah faced off at Beth-Shemesh, which belongs to Ju-
dah. 22 *Judah was smitten by Israel; each man fled to his tents.*
23 *Yoash king of Israel seized Amatziahu king of Judah, the son*

If our perception of the events is correct, the problem need not arise. Overtly, Amatziahu was offering an amalgamation of the two kingdoms — precisely described in the passage as a proposal for marriage.

וַתַּעֲבֹר חַיַּת הַשָּׂדֶה — *Then the wild beasts of the field ... passed by.* The mighty cedar preserves its dignity. It will not carry out the destruction on its own. The animals are drafted to do the job (*Mefaresh*). Yoash's men will smash Amatziahu's army (*Metzudos*).

19. וּנְשָׂאֲךָ לִבְּךָ לְהַכְבִּיד — *You feel emboldened to seek greater glory.* We have translated in accordance with *Mefaresh* and *Metzudos* who take לְהַכְבִּיד to denote *honor* or *glory*. Amatziahu had tasted glory in his victory over Edom and now thirsts for more. In Section II, *Amatziahu's Challenge to Yoash*, we have discussed *Radak's* opinion that the word means *to wage further war*.

שְׁבָה בְּבֵיתֶךָ — *Why do you not stay at home.* Now that you have had a certain degree of success, stay at home so that the glory which you have earned should not be compromised (*Metzudos*).

לָמָּה תִתְגָּרֶה בְּרָעָה — *Why stir up trouble.* Why should you meddle with me, thereby bringing evil upon yourself (*Metzudos*).

20. לְמַעַן תִּתָּם בְּיָד — *In order that He might have them overpowered.* Lit. *In order that He might place them under their hand.*

Our verse refers back to v. 16 where the prophet had told Amatziahu that God had decided to destroy him (*Mefaresh*).

Amatziahu had wanted to amalgamate with the Northern Kingdom, in order that he might rule over the combined nation. He would be smashed by the very people whom he had wanted to absorb.

21. בְּבֵית שֶׁמֶשׁ אֲשֶׁר לִיהוּדָה — *At Beth-Shemesh, which belongs to Judah.* It is necessary to stress that the battle site was in Judah in order to explain why Amatziahu was taken to Jerusalem (v. 23). Had the armies met somewhere in the Northern Kingdom, it would have been more logical to take the captive king to Samaria (*Mefaresh*).

22. וַיִּנָּגֶף יְהוּדָה לִפְנֵי יִשְׂרָאֵל — *Judah was smitten by Israel.* The verse is identical to its parallel in *Kings*. In *Chronicles*, it takes on particular significance when we read it in context with v. 7 where the man of God told Amatziahu that *...HASHEM is not with Israel — all the sons of Ephraim.* Where previously Amatziahu had to send away the Israelite mercenaries in order to ensure the success of his campaign against the Edomites, he was now given over into their hands.

בֶּן־יוֹאָשׁ בֶּן־יְהוֹאָחָז תָּפַשׂ יוֹאָשׁ מֶלֶךְ־יִשְׂרָאֵל בְּבֵית
שָׁמֶשׁ וַיְבִיאֵהוּ יְרוּשָׁלַםִ וַיִּפְרֹץ בְּחוֹמַת יְרוּשָׁלַםִ מִשַּׁעַר
כד אֶפְרַיִם עַד־שַׁעַר הַפּוֹנֶה אַרְבַּע מֵאוֹת אַמָּה: וְכָל־הַזָּהָב
וְהַכֶּסֶף וְאֵת כָּל־הַכֵּלִים הַנִּמְצְאִים בְּבֵית־הָאֱלֹהִים עִם־
עֹבֵד אֱדוֹם וְאֶת־אוֹצְרוֹת בֵּית הַמֶּלֶךְ וְאֵת בְּנֵי הַתַּעֲרֻבוֹת
כה וַיָּשָׁב שֹׁמְרוֹן: וַיְחִי אֲמַצְיָהוּ בֶן־יוֹאָשׁ מֶלֶךְ יְהוּדָה
אַחֲרֵי מוֹת יוֹאָשׁ בֶּן־יְהוֹאָחָז מֶלֶךְ יִשְׂרָאֵל חֲמֵשׁ עֶשְׂרֵה
כו שָׁנָה: וְיֶתֶר דִּבְרֵי אֲמַצְיָהוּ הָרִאשֹׁנִים וְהָאַחֲרוֹנִים הֲלֹא
כז הִנָּם כְּתוּבִים עַל־סֵפֶר מַלְכֵי יְהוּדָה וְיִשְׂרָאֵל: וּמֵעֵת

23. אֲמַצְיָהוּ . . . בֶּן־יוֹאָשׁ בֶּן־יְהוֹאָחָז — *Amatziahu . . . son of Yoash, son of Yehoachaz . . . Ralbag* (*Kings*) suggests a reason why Amatziahu's ancestry is given up to Yehoachaz. He feels that the answer can explain the supercilious attitude which Yoash took towards Amatziahu throughout the entire confrontation.

Yoash's grandfather had been Yehu, whose God-given mission had been to wipe out the house of Ahab. Since the time that the two families had intermarried, the Judaic kings were considered to be part of that family. Yehu, true to his destiny, had killed Yehoachaz, Amatziahu's grandfather (22:9). The task was not yet completed. Yoash, scion of Yehu's house, now continues his grandfather's work by subjugating Amatziahu, the grandson of the hapless Yehoachaz.

וַיִּפְרֹץ בְּחוֹמַת יְרוּשָׁלַםִ — *He broke down the wall of Jerusalem. Abarbanel* explains that it was the custom of conquerors to breach the wall of a vanquished city, rather than to enter by the gate. In this way they made it clear that they entered from strength, and not upon the tolerance of the inhabitants of the city.

If our suggestion, that Amatziahu had proposed an amalgamation between the two states under Jerusalem's rulership, is correct, then a different explanation may be offered. The sanctity which gives Jerusalem its character is made viable through the walls which surround it. [Cf. קָלְטָתוּ מְחִיצוֹת, *The walls have contained it* (*Makkos* 20a), and see ArtScroll comm. to *Ezekiel* 48:30-35.] When Yoash contemptuously broke open Jerusalem's walls, he was, in effect, saying that there was nothing in Jerusalem worth preserving, no sanctity which could give it a claim upon his allegiance.

מִשַּׁעַר אֶפְרַיִם — *From the Ephraim Gate*. *Radak* suggests that this gate opened out to Ephraimite territory, and that when people from Ephraim came to the Temple they would enter by that gate.

שַׁעַר הַפּוֹנֶה — *The Turning Gate*. *Kings* has שַׁעַר הַפִּנָּה, *the corner gate*. *Metzudos* explains that a corner gate could be called *the turning gate*, because at a corner it is possible to turn in either of two directions.

24. וְכָל־הַזָּהָב וְהַכֶּסֶף — *And all the gold and the silver . . . Kings* has the more expected formulation וְלָקַח אֶת־כָּל הַזָּהָב וְהַכֶּסֶף, *And he took all the gold and the silver . . .* Our text misses the verb *And he took*, thus seeming to leave the verse without any inner logic. *Metzudos* thinks that וְלָקַח is understood from the context, and could thus be dispensed with. But he does not explain why it is not said explicitly as it is in *Kings*.

Rather than assume a missing word, it would seem that the text demands to be understood as though the תָּפַשׂ, *seized*, of the previous verse must be understood as referring, not only to Amatziahu, but also to the treasures with which our verse deals: He *seized* Amatziahu and also the treasures of Jerusalem.

The effect of this usage is to bracket the two together, and thereby to indicate that they were both premeditated. As the *Kings'* text stands it would be possible to assume that he took the treasures as an afterthought, when he became aware of them in Jerusalem. *Chronicles'* syntax makes clear that the taking of the gold and silver was part of the overall plan to humiliate Amatziahu and to point up his vanity in supposing that he might rule over an amalgamated state.

It would be appropriate to stress this in *Chronicles* more than in *Kings*. This, because as indicated by the use of לְהַכְבִּיד in v. 19, *Chronicles* showed that Yoash was well aware that Amatziahu was in reality spoiling for a battle rather than for the amalgamation of the two kingdoms [see Section II, *Amatziahu's*

*of Yoash, the son of Yehoachaz, at Beth-Shemesh, and brought
him to Jerusalem. He broke down the wall of Jerusalem from the
Ephraim Gate up to the Turning Gate, four hundred cubits.* 24 *And
all the gold and the silver, and all the vessels that were in God's
Temple, under Oved Edom, and the treasures of the king's palace,
and the hostage sons, and returned to Samaria.* 25 *Amatziahu, the
son of Yoash, king of Judah, lived after the death of Yoash, the
son of Yehoachaz, king of Israel, fifteen years.* 26 *What remains
of Amatziahu's affairs, the earlier and the latter, behold it is
recorded in the Book of the Kings of Judah and Israel.* 27 *Now*

Challenge to Yoash]. Under these circumstances it might well have been that it would not be important to Yoash to exact the fullest measure of humiliation. Nevertheless, he did so — in line with the disdainful tone of his parable and the breaching of Jerusalem's wall.

עִם־עֹבֵד אֱדוֹם — *Under Oved Edom*. Oved Edom was a Temple gatekeeper, appointed by David (*I Chronicles* 26:4—8, 15). This position of honor continued to be held by his family, and whoever held it carried the name of the original official (*Mefaresh, Radak*). Oved Edom is not mentioned in the *Kings'* account, and this is not surprising since *Kings'* had not previously described David's disposition concerning the Temple administration.

Targum and *Metzudos* offer a different interpretation. Oved Edom had been the man in whose care David placed the Ark after his abortive first attempt to bring it to Jerusalem (*I Chronicles* 13:13). While the Ark was in his possession, God blessed him with immense wealth. This he dedicated to the Sanctuary (*Targum*), but kept in his house (*Metzudos*). Yoash now took this treasure.

Again, this is not mentioned in *Kings*. The explanation may be that this was a symbolic treasure important for its historical significance more than for its actual value. On none of the previous occasions when Judah's kings had to buy off would-be attackers had this treasure been touched. Yoash may have wanted it as part of the calculated humiliation of Amatziahu, rather than for its value.

בְּנֵי הַתַּעֲרֻבוֹת — *The hostage sons*. ערב is *to pledge*. תַּעֲרֻבָה is something given as a surety. In our case, these refer to sons of officials who were part of the royal household, in order to ensure the loyalty of their fathers. Perhaps such hostage children were particularly important to Amatziahu whose memory of his father's assassination at the hands of his own servants must still have been fresh.

25. וַיְחִי אֲמַצְיָהוּ בֶן־יוֹאָשׁ . . . אַחֲרֵי מוֹת יוֹאָשׁ — *Amatziahu, the son of Yoash lived . . . after the death of Yoash* . . . This verse, which is paralleled in *Kings*, seems inappropriate here. In *Kings* where the stories of the kings of the Northern and Southern Kingdoms are constantly intertwined, and where, in fact, this verse is preceded by one telling of Yoash's death, the statement is apt. In *Chronicles*, however, there seems little reason to date Amatziahu's reign in terms of Yoash's death.

The explanation may be as follows:

In the tradition of the Sages, the first Temple stood for four hundred and ten years. However, when the number of years assigned to the kings whose rule spanned the Temple era are totaled, there are fifteen years too many. *Rashi's* solution is to subtract these fifteen years from the fifty-two years assigned to Uziah (26:3). He does this by postulating that Uziah assumed the kingship during Amatziahu's lifetime [based on 26:2, see there]. This came about because of Amatziahu's flight to Lachish (v. 27), which effectively removed him from exercising his kingship. *Rashi* postulates that Amatziahu's flight took place immediately after his defeat at Yoash's hands. Since he outlived Yoash by fifteen years we have the justification to assume that Yoash died shortly after his victory, and that, consequently, we are able to move fifteen of Uziah's fifty-two years to Amatziahu's reign. They can thus be eliminated from the total number of years assigned to the kings whose reigns spanned the Temple era.

Given this, our verse is an integral part of the information required for the accurate dating of the various reigns. *Chronicles* has every reason to record it.

26. הָרִאשֹׁנִים וְהָאַחֲרוֹנִים — *The earlier and the latter*. See at 9:29.

עַל־סֵפֶר מַלְכֵי יְהוּדָה וְיִשְׂרָאֵל — *The Book of the Kings of Judah and Israel*. This protocol appears to be the same as that in which the

כה אֲשֶׁר־סָר אֲמַצְיָהוּ מֵאַחֲרֵי יהוה וַיִּקְשְׁרוּ עָלָיו קֶשֶׁר
כח בִּירוּשָׁלַ͏ִם וַיָּנָס לָכִישָׁה וַיִּשְׁלְחוּ אַחֲרָיו לָכִישָׁה וַיְמִיתֻהוּ
כו כח שָׁם: וַיִּשָּׂאֻהוּ עַל־הַסּוּסִים וַיִּקְבְּרוּ אֹתוֹ עִם־אֲבֹתָיו בְּעִיר
א א יְהוּדָה: וַיִּקְחוּ כָּל־עַם יְהוּדָה אֶת־עֻזִּיָּהוּ וְהוּא בֶּן־שֵׁשׁ

reigns of Yotham (27:7), Achaz (28:26), Chizkiah (32:32), Yoshiah (35:26) and Yehoyakim (36:8) are recorded. In the case of Asa (16:11), the wording is different and implies that the story of his reign was recorded in two separate protocols: those of the kings of Judah and those of the kings of Israel.

If, indeed, there was a record common to the rulers of both kingdoms, it stands to reason that Amatziahu's reign should have been recorded there. The significant interaction between him and Yoash would have required a record that was focused on both kingdoms.

This cannot be the same book mentioned in connection with Yoshiah and Yehoyakim. Both these kings ruled after the Northern Kingdom had long ceased to exist. See further in comm. to 36:8.

27. וּמֵעֵת אֲשֶׁר־סָר אֲמַצְיָהוּ ... — *Now from the time that Amatziahu turned away* ... That time is evidently when he returned from the Edomite war and began serving the alien gods. This would imply that Amatziahu fled to Lachish immediately after the debacle of the war with Yoash. Our verse would then mean that he fled to Lachish, remained there for fifteen years (v. 25), and only then did the conspirators send after him to have him killed. This is *Rashi's* interpretation and by this means he is able to postulate that Uziahu reigned fifteen years during his father's lifetime — see comm. to v. 25.

Radak, however, believes that the word אַחֲרָיו, *after him*, implies that the conspirators followed him to Lachish immediately after his flight. It would not have been used if there had been a fifteen-year lapse between the two events. Rather, he suggests that the conspiracy did, indeed, begin at the time of Yoash's death, but that for close to fifteen years it was limited to harassment and general insubordination. During all that time there was no reason for Amatziah to flee. It was only in the later stages of the rebellion that matters deteriorated to the extent that Amatziah was no longer able to remain in Jerusalem. He fled to Lachish and, immediately after that, was killed.

וַיִּקְשְׁרוּ עָלָיו קֶשֶׁר — *They made a conspiracy against him*. *HaLevi*, in *Tekufas HaMikra* ch. 6, deduces the essential wholesomeness of the spiritual standing of the people during these turbulent times. The revolt seems to have been very broadly based — the mighty Amatziahu was unable to find protection in Jerusalem, and had to flee ignominously to Lachish. Even that attempt proved abortive, and his assassins needed only to *send after him* to have him killed in Lachish — a city in which apparently he had had reason to hope that he would be safe. All this because Amatziahu had *turned away from* HASHEM. The people refused to tolerate his deviation.

לָכִישָׁה — *To Lachish*. A city in Judah — see *Joshua* 15:39.

28. בְּעִיר יְהוּדָה — *In the city of Judah*. The expression is unique, and replaces ... *in Jerusalem ... in the City of David* from *Kings*.

Why would *Chronicles* have wanted to change such a simple and universally used expression into such an unusual one?

If our analysis of Amatziahu's ambitions is correct — that is, if he had indeed wanted to amalgamate the two states and rule over them from the capital city of Jerusalem — then the expression conveys a bitter irony. In the end he was, after all, buried in the *city of Judah*! The status of Jerusalem had not changed.

XXVI

◆§ Uziahu Begins a Strong and Productive Reign

With Uziahu's ascension to the throne a fundamental change in the destiny of the Jewish people begins. The writings of the four great prophets, Hosea, Isaiah, Amos and Michah, who were contemporary with him (*Pesachim* 87a), reveal a profound and corrosive spiritual malaise within the people. This caused God to begin that withdrawal of the Divine Presence from the Temple precincts, which centuries later, was to culminate in holocaust, destruction and exile.

The first intimations that all is not well are conveyed to Isaiah in a prophecy dated in the year of Uziahu's death (*Isaiah* 6:1). The Sages teach that this does not mean his actual passing, but

25
28 *from the time that Amatziahu turned away from* HASHEM, *they*
made a conspiracy against him in Jerusalem and so, he fled to
Lachish. But they sent after him to Lachish and slew him there.
28 *And they brought him upon horses and buried him with his*
fathers in the city of Judah.

26
1 *All the people of Judah took Uziahu who was sixteen years old*

refers to the portentous event of his leprosy, described in our v. 19. At that moment, a shattering earthquake smashed through the land (*Amos* 1:1). It agitated the Temple portals with the tremors which were ultimately destined to topple it (*R' S.R. Hirsch*).

Thus, Uziahu's reign is a watershed in Israel's history — the moment from which the long and tragic process of disintegration is to begin.

But for the moment, much that was evil and corrupt still lay beneath the surface (see *Doros HaRishonim, Tekufas HaMikra*, ch. 24). The pathos and sorrow of the myriad details which contributed to the debacle are, as yet, still the stuff of prophecy. They have no place in the books which record the details of a reign which in its outer contours was benign and — from certain perspectives — even constructive. *Kings* finds no significance in any of Uziahu's conquests and internal accomplishments, and gives only the sparsest details — mentioning the leprosy but not ascribing any cause [see Section II to ch. 24, *Different Perspectives upon Yoash and the Monarchy*]. *Chronicles* provides much more detail, but its focus is the king and not the people. By the time it was written, the prophecies had been tragically proved true. There was no need to spell out their dreadful message.

Nevertheless, it is unthinkable that such tragic erosions of the spiritual standing of the people were not somehow rooted in the king's failings, and we must expect these to penetrate the surface of even the most prosaic historical account of the reign.

A careful reading of our chapter will, indeed, yield hints of such failings. We shall understand this best when we contrast what we know of Uziahu, the king from whom the decline began in earnest, with Chizkiahu, who came within a hair's-breadth of not only arresting the downward plunge, but of actually leading his people to the fulfillment of its Messianic dreams.

Chs. 29 and 30 tell in detail how Chizkiahu inspired the people to a universal *teshuvah*, and how he encouraged them to re-establish their covenant with God. As we read these chapters, we gain the impression that all his efforts were centered upon the Temple service: The descriptions are all of ritual matters — the cleansing of the Temple from its defilements and a renewal of the sacrificial service in its most exalted form.

However, significantly, Midrashic literature abounds with allusions to the fact that Chizkiahu worked hard to lay down a solid and unshakeable substructure upon which this edifice of Divine service could rest securely — the study of Torah.

What did he do? He placed a sword by the door of the study hall and said: 'Whosoever does not engage in the study of the Torah shall be pierced by this sword.' They searched from Dan to Be'er Sheva and could not discover an ignorant person; from Givath to Antripas and could not find boy or girl, man or woman who was not well versed in [even] the [complicated] laws of ritual purity (*Sanhedrin* 94b).

Chizkiahu recognized that religious ecstasy plays an indispensable role in the spiritual experiences of the people, and finds appropriate and effective expression in the purity of self-dedication implicit in the sacrificial service of the Temple. It is to this that he summoned the people to effect their religious renewal. But by the very fact of its intensity, such ecstasy must be short lived. If there is to be durability and even permanence, then there must be a firm foundation. Chizkiahu understood that for this foundation nothing could replace total immersion in Torah study — total commitment to understanding and concomitant implementation of its laws.

If we are correct in our reading of the *Chronicles'* account of Uziahu's reign, we can detect hints and allusions to a lack of appreciation of this most basic of Torah tenets. In spite of an eagerness on his part to lead his life and to rule his people by Divine fiat (v. 5), he was not interested in the constant, unyielding and unforgiving demands of Torah study. Other priorities occupied his mind, and he allowed this most important of all of his responsibilities to lapse. Tragically, he was

ב עֶשְׂרֵה שָׁנָה וַיַּמְלִיכוּ אֹתוֹ תַּחַת אָבִיו אֲמַצְיָהוּ׃ הוּא בָּנָה
אֶת־אֵילוֹת וַיְשִׁיבֶהָ לִיהוּדָה אַחֲרֵי שְׁכַב־הַמֶּלֶךְ עִם־
אֲבֹתָיו׃
ג בֶּן־שֵׁשׁ עֶשְׂרֵה שָׁנָה עֻזִּיָּהוּ בְמָלְכוֹ וַחֲמִשִּׁים וּשְׁתַּיִם
°יְכָלְיָה ק׳ שָׁנָה מָלַךְ בִּירוּשָׁלִָם וְשֵׁם אִמּוֹ °יכיליה מִן־
ד יְרוּשָׁלִָם׃ וַיַּעַשׂ הַיָּשָׁר בְּעֵינֵי יְהוָה כְּכֹל אֲשֶׁר־
ה עָשָׂה אֲמַצְיָהוּ אָבִיו׃ וַיְהִי לִדְרֹשׁ אֱלֹהִים בִּימֵי זְכַרְיָהוּ

to learn that with an unstable foundation the edifice had to fall. That, ultimately, is the meaning of the earthquake that rattled the Temple portals!

It is noteworthy that *Chronicles* assumes as self-evident, that the people underwent a spiritual deterioration during Uziahu's reign. The description of Yotham's rule (27:2) states simply that the people *continued* to act corruptly. But nothing had been previously said concerning a regression on the part of the people. Apparently, then, it is assumed to derive unambiguously from the account of Uziahu's reign. Indeed, throughout the comm. to this chapter, we shall see nuances of style and content which point to failings of Uziahu as king — and specifically in the direction which we have indicated. Here we shall limit ourselves to the most explicit of these indications.

V. 10 tells of Uziahu's agricultural accomplishments and closes with the phrase . . .*for he loved husbandry* — a description never applied to anyone else in Scripture. As the Sages see it, it was the love of the earth which proved his undoing. We shall look at this more closely in comm. to that verse and limit ourselves here to quoting *Tanchuma* to *Noah*: *He was a king but exposed himself to [the lures of] the earth and did not pay attention to the [demands of the] Torah.*

The story of Uziahu which will unfold before us is that of a well-intentioned king, lulled into an unprobing acceptance of the apparently adequate surface adherence to Torah demands which was the norm among his people. He did not pick up that much of what was being done was by unthinking rote (*Isaiah* 29:13), and that under the pressure of subsurface tensions it was only a matter of time before the veneer would inevitably crack.

1. . . . וַיִּקְחוּ כָּל־עַם יְהוּדָה — *All the people of Judah took* . . . See comm. to 25:25 and 27 that in *Rashi's* view, this verse describes the installation of Uziahu as ruler in Amatziah's place fifteen years before the latter's death. This seems borne out by the next verse. See below.

2. הוּא בָּנָה אֶת־אֵילוֹת — *He built Eiloth, restoring it to Judah*. Eiloth, or Eilath, was an Edomite city. During Solomon's reign it appears to have been in Judah's control (8:17). It is likely that David took this city from the Edomites when, during his reign, they were subservient to Israel. When, during Yehoram's reign, Edom regained its independence (21:8), the city would have reverted to its original owners. It is likely that Amatziah would have used his successful campaign against Edom to regain the city. It may well have been damaged during the battles which made its recapture possible, and would not be considered *restored* to Judah until it was rebuilt. Amatziah, because of the troubles which followed the Edomite campaign, had not been able to effect the required repairs — and these were now undertaken by his son Uziahu. In this sense, Uziahu *restored* the city to Judah by building it (based on *Radak* and *Metzudos* to *Kings*).

This can explain a structural oddity. V. 3 tells of Uziahu's age at the time of his ascension to the throne and gives his mother's name. V. 4 goes on to make an assessment of his reign, which is then described in the subsequent verses. We would have expected that the information contained in vs. 3 and 4 should follow immediately upon v. 1, which tells of Uziahu's ascension to the throne. Only after this should his activities in connection with Eiloth be described, together with all the other building projects which he undertook.

The structure of our chapter obviously follows that of *Kings* where the problem is even more blatant. In *II Kings* ch. 14, vs. 21 and 22 parallel our vs. 1 and 2. Then, v. 23 moves away from Uziahu to a description of the reign of Yarov'am son of Yoash of the Northern Kingdom, which continues for the rest of the chapter. Only in ch. 15 is Uziahu's story once more picked up, beginning with a statement of his age at the ascension and of his

26
2-5

and made him king instead of his father, Amatziahu. [2] *He*
built Eiloth, restoring it to Judah after the king had lain with his
fathers.
[3] *Uziahu was sixteen years old when he became king and he*
reigned fifty-two years in Jerusalem. His mother's name was Ye-
choliah of Jerusalem. [4] *He did that which was right in the eyes of*
HASHEM, according to all that his father Amatziahu had done. [5] *It*
was his practice to inquire of God during the lifetime of Zechariahu,

mother's name (our v. 3), as is standard for the description of the reigns of all the kings.

That division, and the structure of our chapter which reflects it, can be readily explained on the basis of what we have seen. The building of Eiloth is viewed as belonging to Amatziahu's reign more then to Uziahu's. The latter was only completing what the former had begun. The description of his own activities begins later.

This could explain the use of the phrase . . . *after the king had lain with his fathers*. The activities belong to Amatziahu's reign even though he had already died. See below for alternative explanations.

אַחֲרֵי שְׁכַב־הַמֶּלֶךְ עִם־אֲבֹתָיו — *After the king had lain with his fathers*. It makes sense to stress that the building of Eiloth took place after Amatziahu's death, if only for practical purposes; Uziahu had already assumed the throne earlier. This would confirm *Rashi's* view of the succession. See comm. to v. 1.

Radak, who disagrees with *Rashi*, thinks that the verse teaches that Uziahu's fruitful activities began immediately after his father's death — that is, from the very beginning of his reign. As chaotic as the end of his father's last years had been — so orderly and successful was the son's rule from the very start.

3. בֶּן־שֵׁשׁ עֶשְׂרֵה שָׁנָה עֻזִּיָּהוּ בְמָלְכוֹ — *Uziahu was sixteen years old when he became king*. Our verse repeats what had already been said in v. 1. It is clearly taken from *Kings* where the repetition is necessary since the account of Uziahu's reign was interrupted by a passage dealing with the Northern Kingdom (see comm. to previous verse).

4. כְּכֹל אֲשֶׁר־עָשָׂה אֲמַצְיָהוּ אָבִיו — *According to all that his father Amatziahu had done.* Apparently this is also from the *Kings'* account — see comm. to v. 3 above. However, in the context of *Chronicles* it carries a quite different connotation than it does there. In *Kings* nothing is said of Amatziahu's idol worship and his reign is portrayed in uniformly positive terms. Thus, the assessment that Uziahu did as Amatziahu had done carries no undercurrent of criticism. In *Chronicles*, which explicated Amatziahu's failings, we have an implied criticism of Uziahu.

But *Mefaresh* and *Metzudos* both limit the comparison with Amatziahu to the latter's positive acts. Uziahu did *what was right* as Amatziahu had done — not those things in which his father erred.

5. וַיְהִי לִדְרֹשׁ אֱלֹהִים בִּימֵי זְכַרְיָהוּ — *It was his practice to inquire of God during the lifetime of Zechariahu*. Commentators assume Zechariahu to have been an otherwise unidentified prophet, who was active during Uziahu's reign. The king would consult this prophet for guidance in the exercise of his rulership.

In the context of the Sages' strictures that Uziahu was too involved in his agricultural pursuits and *did not pay attention to the [demands of the] Torah* (see prefatory remarks), our verse is most revealing. Uziahu has excellent intentions and seeks God's guidance in all his affairs — but chooses to do so through the medium of prophecy, not through a deep and careful study of the Torah. Prophecy is man's crowning glory, but is used correctly only in the context of a society based solidly and unshakably on the rock-strong foundation of Torah study. This is a truth that Chizkiahu understood and — as the Sages teach it — Uziahu apparently did not.

Uziahu's actions could not be faulted: *As long as he inquired of HASHEM, God made him prosper*, but in the long run, his lack of attention to his people's basic spiritual needs spelled disaster.

Mefaresh [apparently based on a non-extant *midrash*] explains that Zechariahu was another name for Uziahu himself. The sense of the verse is that during Uziahu's reign — blessed as the people were with a king who

הַמֵּבִין בִּרְאֹת הָאֱלֹהִים וּבִימֵי דָּרְשׁוֹ אֶת־יהוה הִצְלִיחוֹ
ו הָאֱלֹהִים: וַיֵּצֵא וַיִּלָּחֶם בַּפְּלִשְׁתִּים וַיִּפְרֹץ אֶת־חוֹמַת גַּת
וְאֵת חוֹמַת יַבְנֶה וְאֵת חוֹמַת אַשְׁדּוֹד וַיִּבְנֶה עָרִים
ז בְּאַשְׁדּוֹד וּבַפְּלִשְׁתִּים: וַיַּעְזְרֵהוּ הָאֱלֹהִים עַל־פְּלִשְׁתִּים
ח וְעַל־°הערביים הַיֹּשְׁבִים בְּגוּר־בָּעַל וְהַמְּעוּנִים: וַיִּתְּנוּ
הָעַמּוֹנִים מִנְחָה לְעֻזִּיָּהוּ וַיֵּלֶךְ שְׁמוֹ עַד־לְבוֹא מִצְרַיִם כִּי
ט הֶחֱזִיק עַד־לְמָעְלָה: וַיִּבֶן עֻזִּיָּהוּ מִגְדָּלִים בִּירוּשָׁלִַם
עַל־שַׁעַר הַפִּנָּה וְעַל־שַׁעַר הַגַּיְא וְעַל־הַמִּקְצוֹעַ וַיְחַזְּקֵם:
י וַיִּבֶן מִגְדָּלִים בַּמִּדְבָּר וַיַּחְצֹב בֹּרוֹת רַבִּים כִּי מִקְנֶה־רַב
הָיָה לוֹ וּבַשְּׁפֵלָה וּבַמִּישׁוֹר אִכָּרִים וְכֹרְמִים בֶּהָרִים
יא וּבַכַּרְמֶל כִּי־אֹהֵב אֲדָמָה הָיָה: וַיְהִי לְעֻזִּיָּהוּ

°הָעַרְבִים ק׳

interested himself in Divine revelation — it was customary to seek God's guidance by consulting prophets.

6-15. This passage details the ways in which God allowed Uziahu to prosper. Military exploits, building projects and agricultural activities are listed.

All these — but not a single word of concern for the spiritual betterment of the people. This is in sharp contrast to other righteous kings where military and building prowess are recorded — but where mention is also made of how they brought their people closer to God. This is the case with Asa (ch. 14), and also Yehoshaphat whose judicial reforms occupy such a central place in the description of his reign.

The treatment of Uziahu's reign — a statement that God made him prosper, followed by an account which centers exclusively on temporal successes — recalls *Chronicles'* treatment of Solomon (1:14 ff.), where the account of the dream at Giveon is immediately followed by a description of his wealth and well-stocked stables. We thought there that this was meant as a subtle form of criticism. In Solomon's mind, the acquisition of prolific wealth occupied too important a place. The same may be true of *Chronicles'* treatment of Uziahu. Subtly, the ground is laid for the subsequent mistakes which Uziahu is to make. His sense of priorities was wrong.

Given the tradition of the Sages that throughout this time the blood of the prophet Zechariahu was still seething on the Temple grounds, the tone of this description of Uziahu's reign is even more striking. Should his military, building and agricultural projects really have been the first priority of his reign?

6. וַיֵּצֵא וַיִּלָּחֶם ... וַיִּבְנֶה ... — *He went forth and fought ... He built ...* His campaign was so successful that not only was he able to breach the walls of the city, but could undertake building projects in the Philistine lands with impunity, as though master in his own house (*Malbim*).

בְּאַשְׁדּוֹד — *In Ashdod*. Ashdod itself is a city. The meaning must be that he built in the area of Ashdod.

7. וַיַּעְזְרֵהוּ הָאֱלֹהִים — *And God helped him*. In the *Kings'* account, Uziahu's name appears almost all the time as עֲזַרְיָהוּ. Perhaps there is some connection between that name and the use of this particular word here.

וְהַמְּעוּנִים — *And the Meunim*. See comm. to *I Chronicles* 4:41. *Metzudos*, based on the next verse, thinks that these people are identical with the עַמּוֹנִים.

8. וַיֵּלֶךְ שְׁמוֹ — *And his fame spread*. שֵׁם, which often means *name*, is also used to denote *fame* (*Metzudos*).

9. וַיִּבֶן ... בִּירוּשָׁלִַם — *He built ... in Jerusalem*. Jerusalem's walls needed to be shored up because of the damage done to them during Amatziahu's reign (*Mefaresh*).

שַׁעַר הַפִּנָּה — *The Corner Gate*. See comm. to 25:23.

שַׁעַר הַגַּיְא — *The Valley Gate*. See *Nehemiahu* 2:13 and 3:13.

הַמִּקְצוֹעַ — *The End Section*. *Metzudos* compares to *Exodus* 26:24. This corner is mentioned several times in *Nehemiahu* (cf. 3:19).

וַיְחַזְּקֵם — *And fortified them*. Our translation

the skillful interpreter of Divine visions. As long as he inquired of
HASHEM, God made him prosper. 6 *He went forth and fought the*
Philistines and breached the wall of Gath and the wall of Yavneh
and the wall of Ashdod. He built cities in Ashdod and among the
Philistines. 7 *And God helped him against the Philistines and*
against the Arabians that dwelt in Gur-baal and the Meunim.
8 *And the Amonites gave gifts to Uziahu and his fame spread even*
to the approaches to Egypt because be became very strong. 9 *He*
built towers in Jerusalem at the Corner Gate and the Valley Gate
and at the End Section, and fortified them. 10 *He built towers in the*
wilderness and hewed out many cisterns for he had much cattle;
and in the lowlands and in the plain; farmers and vintners in the
mountain and the fruitful hills, for he loved husbandry. 11 *Uziahu*

follows *Malbim*. *Metzudos* interprets as follows: He did not just build the towers and then leave them. He returned to them periodically to effect necessary repairs and to strengthen them.

10. וַיִּבֶן ... כִּי מִקְנֶה־רַב הָיָה לוֹ — *He built ... for he had much cattle*. The cisterns had to be dug so that the vast holdings in livestock could be watered.

כִּי־אֹהֵב אֲדָמָה הָיָה — *For he loved husbandry*. Uziahu's love of husbandry enabled him to make great strides in the agriculture of the country. But the Sages criticize him: Three men were strongly attracted to the earth, and no good came from them: Cain, Noah and Uziahu (*Bereishis Rabbah* 36:5). His eventual downfall — when he became a leper as a result of his attempt to involve himself in the Temple service — is blamed on his inordinate love of the earth. What caused all this to happen to him? He opened himself up to [the lures of] the earth and did not pay attention to the [demands of the] Torah (*Tanchuma, Noah* 13).[1]

R' Eli Munk in *The Call of the Torah* explains the deleterious effect which excessive involvement with husbandry can have on a person: Agriculture gives rise to a pride in material possessions and in the value they represent. On the one hand, agriculture is the basis of civilization; a great part of the inventions and arts have been evoked by it. Cooperation, the very cornerstone of life in society in the state, is a basic demand of agriculture, which thus sets the norms for social legislation. But, on the other hand, the agricultural worker comes closer and closer to the level of the clod he serves. He begins by bending his neck under the yoke of his desire for possessions; he ends by bending his spirit. He gets caught by this effort. As a result, one man subjugates and enslaves another. At the same time, the tiller of the soil comes to worship the forces of nature whose influence is seemingly critical for his success. The agricultural peoples were the first to lose the pure consciousness of God and humanity. They were the first to give themselves up to slavery and polytheism.

וּבַשְּׁפֵלָה וּבַמִּישׁוֹר — *And in the lowlands and in the plain*. Some of the cattle grazed in this location, some in that (*Metzudos*).

וּבַכַּרְמֶל — *And the fruitful hills*. כַּרְמֶל is both a proper noun — the name of a mountain (*I Kings* 18:19) and of a city (*Joshua* 15:55) — and a common noun used for a fertile tract of land. Our translation follows *Metzudos*.

1. In the context of the thoughts expressed in comm. to v. 5, we may perhaps interpret the Sages' stricture against Uziahu as a lover of husbandry differently.

Sanhedrin 94a speaks of *songs of jubilation* [זְמִירוֹת] which emanate from the earth [based on *Isaiahu* 24:16: *From the corners of the earth we hear songs ...*]. Perhaps the Talmud means that the constant resurging of life evident in every blade of grass, in each bud and flower which bursts forth from the earth, must find a responsive chord in the breast of the observer, must turn mind and heart upwards to the Creator. Uziahu loved the earth because it brought him into constant contact with God in much the same way that he sought that contact through his relationship with Zechariahu, the prophet mentioned in v. 5.

Again, then, we have the craving to be touched by the Divine — but without the unyielding and constant effort required in the study of the Torah.

חַיִל עֹשֵׂה מִלְחָמָה יוֹצְאֵי צָבָא לִגְדוּד בְּמִסְפַּר פְּקֻדָּתָם
בְּיַד °יעואל הַסּוֹפֵר וּמַעֲשֵׂיָהוּ הַשּׁוֹטֵר עַל יַד־חֲנַנְיָהוּ °וְעִיאֵל ק׳
יב מִשָּׂרֵי הַמֶּלֶךְ׃ °כֹּל מִסְפַּר רָאשֵׁי הָאָבוֹת לְגִבּוֹרֵי חָיִל
יג אַלְפַּיִם וְשֵׁשׁ מֵאוֹת׃ וְעַל־יָדָם °חֵיל צָבָא שְׁלֹשׁ מֵאוֹת אֶלֶף
וְשִׁבְעַת אֲלָפִים וַחֲמֵשׁ מֵאוֹת עוֹשֵׂי מִלְחָמָה בְּכֹחַ חָיִל
יד לַעְזֹר לַמֶּלֶךְ עַל־הָאוֹיֵב׃ וַיָּכֶן לָהֶם עֻזִּיָּהוּ לְכָל־הַצָּבָא
מָגִנִּים וּרְמָחִים וְכוֹבָעִים וְשִׁרְיֹנוֹת וּקְשָׁתוֹת וּלְאַבְנֵי
טו קְלָעִים׃ וַיַּעַשׂ | בִּירוּשָׁלַם חִשְּׁבֹנוֹת מַחֲשֶׁבֶת חוֹשֵׁב לִהְיוֹת
עַל־הַמִּגְדָּלִים וְעַל־הַפִּנּוֹת לִירוֹא בַּחִצִּים וּבָאֲבָנִים
גְּדֹלוֹת וַיֵּצֵא שְׁמוֹ עַד־לְמֵרָחוֹק כִּי־הִפְלִיא לְהֵעָזֵר עַד
טז כִּי־חָזָק׃ וּכְחֶזְקָתוֹ גָּבַהּ לִבּוֹ עַד־לְהַשְׁחִית וַיִּמְעַל בַּיהוָה
אֱלֹהָיו וַיָּבֹא אֶל־הֵיכַל יהוה לְהַקְטִיר עַל־מִזְבַּח הַקְּטֹרֶת׃
יז וַיָּבֹא אַחֲרָיו עֲזַרְיָהוּ הַכֹּהֵן וְעִמּוֹ כֹּהֲנִים | לַיהוָה שְׁמוֹנִים
יח בְּנֵי־חָיִל׃ וַיַּעַמְדוּ עַל־עֻזִּיָּהוּ הַמֶּלֶךְ וַיֹּאמְרוּ לוֹ לֹא־
לְךָ עֻזִּיָּהוּ לְהַקְטִיר לַיהוָה כִּי לַכֹּהֲנִים בְּנֵי־אַהֲרֹן
הַמְקֻדָּשִׁים לְהַקְטִיר צֵא מִן־הַמִּקְדָּשׁ כִּי מָעַלְתָּ וְלֹא־לְךָ
יט לְכָבוֹד מֵיְהוָה אֱלֹהִים׃ וַיִּזְעַף עֻזִּיָּהוּ וּבְיָדוֹ מִקְטֶרֶת
לְהַקְטִיר וּבְזַעְפּוֹ עִם־הַכֹּהֲנִים °וְהַצָּרַעַת זָרְחָה בְמִצְחוֹ

11. ... בְּמִסְפַּר פְּקֻדָּתָם — *Mustered by number ...* We have translated the passage in accordance with *Metzudos*. It is impossible for us to know the exact meaning of the technical terms used in contexts such as this.

12. רָאשֵׁי הָאָבוֹת לְגִבּוֹרֵי חָיִל — *Family heads in charge of the warriors*. The ל of לְגִבּוֹרֵי takes the place of שֶׁל, *of* (*Metzudos*).

13. וְעַל־יָדָם — *These commanded*. With our hands we exercise control. Hence, עַל יַד becomes a synonym for *command*.

בְּכֹחַ חָיִל — *As a mighty force*. A redundancy calculated to underline the great might of these soldiers (*Metzudos*).

14. וּלְאַבְנֵי קְלָעִים — *And catapults for the projectiles*. The ל indicates that Uziahu supplied those implements which were necessary to propel projectiles against the enemy (*Metzudos*).

15. חִשְּׁבֹנוֹת מַחֲשֶׁבֶת חוֹשֵׁב — *Devices ... engineered by expert designers*. חשב, *to think*, thus, the product of thought or inventiveness. Weapons were designed and produced with which it was possible to propel arrows and stones over long distances.

וְעַל־הַפִּנּוֹת — *And the battlements*. *Targum* renders *corners*. However, *Metzudos* citing *Zephaniahu* 1:16 thinks that this word, too, denotes a kind of tower.

כִּי־הִפְלִיא לְהֵעָזֵר — *For he took stupendous steps in order that he might be protected. Metzudos* understands this to refer to Uziahu's inventions; he developed marvelous machines whereby he would be helped in his military efforts.

◆§ Uziahu Attempts to Offer Up Incense in the Temple

16. גָּבַהּ לִבּוֹ עַד־לְהַשְׁחִית — *He became prideful to the point of ruin*. See Section II, *Uziahu and the Ketores*, for a discussion of Uziahu's attempt to offer up incense.

גַּבְהוּת הַלֵּב, the *upliftedness of the heart*, need not, of itself, be bad as we can see from Yehoshaphat (17:6). For this reason, לְהַשְׁחִית is added to point out that in Uziahu's case it was a ruinous pride (*Malbim*). The meaning of the phrase is that the pride was destructive to himself because it caused him to be wicked (*Metzudos*). *Ralbag* takes לְהַשְׁחִית transitively: He became prideful to the extent that he proceeded to *destroy*, or undermine the laws of the Torah, by attempting to bring the unauthorized incense.

had a force of fighting men that would go out in marauding bands, mustered by number by Ye'i'el the scribe and Maaseiahu the captain. This, through Chananiahu one of the king's generals.
12 *The grand total of family heads in charge of the warriors was two thousand six hundred.*
13 *These commanded a fighting army of three hundred and seven thousand five hundred, that went to battle as a mighty force to help the king against the enemy.*
14 *For them, for this whole army, Uziahu made shields and spears, helmets, coats of mail and bows and catapults for the projectiles.*
15 *He made devices in Jerusalem, engineered by expert designers, to be upon the towers and the battlements to cast arrows and great boulders. His fame spread far abroad for he took stupendous steps in order that he might be protected, so that he became strong.*
16 *When he became strong, he became prideful to the point of ruin, and trespassed against HASHEM his God. He entered the Sanctuary of HASHEM to burn incense upon the altar of incense.*
17 *Azariahu the Kohen followed him in, accompanied by eighty Kohanim of HASHEM, valiant men.*
18 *And they stood up against King Uziahu and said to him, 'It is not for you, Uziahu, to burn incense to HASHEM, but for the Kohanim, the sons of Aaron, who are consecrated to burn incense. Go out of the Sanctuary, for you have trespassed. This will bring you no honor from HASHEM God.*
19 *Then Uziahu was angry and the censer was in his hand to burn incense and while he was angry with the Kohanim, the leprosy broke forth upon his forehead*

Our verse is thus defining the cause of Uziahu's fall as being sinful pride. Because of this the Sages teach that one of the causes of leprosy is unjustified pride (*Tanchuma, Metzora* 3 and elsewhere). See further to v. 20.

וַיִּמְעַל בַּה' — *And trespassed against HASHEM* ... *Mefaresh* thinks that this expression indicates that the transgression was inadvertent. See Section II, *Uziahu and the Ketores*.

עַל־מִזְבַּח הַקְּטֹרֶת — *Upon the altar of incense.* The golden altar which stood in the Sanctuary, as opposed to the copper one which was located in the Temple courtyard.

17. עֲזַרְיָהוּ הַכֹּהֵן — *Azariahu the Kohen*. See *I Chronicles* 5:36 where a *Kohen*, Azariahu, is mentioned, and identified as ... *the one who ministered in the Temple which Solomon built in Jerusalem*. See comm. to *I Chronicles* 5:30-41 where we quote *Yalkut* to *Korah*, 654, that reference is to our Azariahu. He is described as having ministered in Solomon's Temple because of the bravery which he displayed in defying the king, thereby defending the sanctity of Solomon's Temple.

18. וְלֹא־לְךָ לְכָבוֹד מֵה' אֱלֹהִים — *This will bring you no honor from HASHEM God*. Far from the honor you think to receive from this act (*Metzudos*), you will, on the contrary, be punished and shamed (*Ralbag*).

19. וּבְיָדוֹ מְקַטֶּרֶת — *With the cense in his hand*. The implement used for bringing incense is usually called מַחְתָּה, *pan* (cf. *Leviticus* 16:12). However, once the incense is already upon it, it is called מְקַטֶּרֶת, *that which is used for bringing* קְטוֹרֶת (*Metzudos*).

Apparently, Uziahu was about to strike the *Kohanim* with the censer which was in his hand (*Mefaresh*).

וְהַצָּרַעַת זָרְחָה בְמִצְחוֹ — *The leprosy broke forth upon his forehead*. The use of the definite article, *the* leprosy, is discussed by *Aruch LaNer* to *Sanhedrin* 48b.

The leprosy appeared on Uziahu's forehead because it is there that the *Kohen Gadol* wears the plate [צִיץ] which proclaims him to be consecrated to God's service. Uziahu, inexcus-

כ לִפְנֵי הַכֹּהֲנִים בְּבֵית יהוה מֵעַל לְמִזְבַּח הַקְּטֹרֶת: וַיִּפֶן
אֵלָיו עֲזַרְיָהוּ כֹהֵן הָרֹאשׁ וְכָל־הַכֹּהֲנִים וְהִנֵּה־הוּא מְצֹרָע
בְּמִצְחוֹ וַיַּבְהִלוּהוּ מִשָּׁם וְגַם־הוּא נִדְחַף לָצֵאת כִּי נִגְּעוֹ
כא יהוה: וַיְהִי עֻזִּיָּהוּ הַמֶּלֶךְ מְצֹרָע | עַד־יוֹם מוֹתוֹ וַיֵּשֶׁב בֵּית
°הַחָפְשִׁית ק׳ °החפשות מְצֹרָע כִּי נִגְזַר מִבֵּית יהוה וְיוֹתָם בְּנוֹ עַל־בֵּית
כב הַמֶּלֶךְ שׁוֹפֵט אֶת־עַם הָאָרֶץ: וְיֶתֶר דִּבְרֵי עֻזִּיָּהוּ
הָרִאשֹׁנִים וְהָאַחֲרֹנִים כָּתַב יְשַׁעְיָהוּ בֶן־אָמוֹץ הַנָּבִיא:
כג וַיִּשְׁכַּב עֻזִּיָּהוּ עִם־אֲבֹתָיו וַיִּקְבְּרוּ אֹתוֹ עִם־אֲבֹתָיו בִּשְׂדֵה
הַקְּבוּרָה אֲשֶׁר לַמְּלָכִים כִּי אָמְרוּ מְצוֹרָע הוּא וַיִּמְלֹךְ

ably, aspired to that honor. The leprosy pointed unambiguously to the futility of that ambition (*Aruch LaNer*).

Malbim thinks that the leprosy appeared on the forehead in order to indicate the locus of Uziahu's fault. His was a scheming, ambitious mind. He refused to be satisfied with the abundance of blessings which were already his, and lusted after ever-greater attainments.

The expression זָרְחָה, from זרח, *to rise* [i.e., the sun], or *to come forth*, is appropriate for leprosy which, because it is whitish in color, seems to shine like the sun (*Metzudos*).

If our understanding of the Sages' perception of Uziahu's fault is correct, then the punishment of leprosy is singularly appropriate. Leprosy is perceived by the Sages as a living death (*Nedarim* 64b). The afflicted person functions like any other living human being, but slowly and subtly the extremities of his body begin to atrophy, die and subsequently fall off. Nothing could have more graphically described Uziahu's malaise. In all its outer manifestations, his reign was crowned by success. Within, the beginning of the end had begun to germinate.

לִפְנֵי הַכֹּהֲנִים בְּבֵית ה׳ מֵעַל לְמִזְבַּח הַקְּטֹרֶת — *Before the Kohanim, in the house of* HASHEM, *over the altar of the incense.* If, indeed, leprosy bespeaks the concept of death, then the gradation implied in this phrase is entirely appropriate.

Each of the three units mentioned represent, in the thought-world of the Torah, the idea of *life*. The *Kohen* must remain aloof from any connection with a dead body — *the sublimest manifestation* [*of God Whom he is to serve*] *is the elevating power of life, freeing, animating, raising man to free will and to eternal life, not the crushing power of death.* (*Hirsch* to *Leviticus* 21:5, on the prohibition of *Kohanim* against coming into contact with the dead body.) The House of *HASHEM*, of course, embodies this concept even more, and incense is the very elixir of life, as evidenced by *Numbers* 17:12.

All these harbingers of life were there; but death began creeping in.

מֵעַל לְמִזְבַּח הַקְּטֹרֶת — *Over the altar of the incense*. I.e., while standing over the altar of the incense (*Metzudos*).

20. וְגַם־הוּא נִדְחַף לָצֵאת כִּי נִגְּעוֹ ה׳ — *He also made haste to go out because* HASHEM *had smitten him*. He realized that the leprosy came to him as a punishment from God (*Metzudos*).

The spiritual strivings which found expression in his attempt to bring the incense were harshly rejected by God. To have value, such strivings must be firmly based upon the Torah's guidance. The earthquake which, in the tradition of the Sages, took place at that terrible moment accentuated this lesson.

21. עַד־יוֹם מוֹתוֹ — *Until the day of his death*. In the tradition of the Sages, Uziahu became a leper in the twenty-seventh year of his reign (*Seder Olam Rabbah* 19 and *Rashi* to *II Kings* 15:1). Thus, since the total reign lasted fifty-two years (v. 3), he was a leper for twenty-five years. See end of verse concerning Yotham's regency.

בֵּית הַחָפְשִׁית — *The house of release*. חפש means *to be free*, and thus, חָפְשִׁית should have the connotation of *freedom*. But what is a *house of release*?

Rashi (*II Kings* 15:5) quotes *Yerushalmi* that a house was set aside for Uziahu in the cemetery. The dead are *free* from all commandments (*Psalms* 88:6) and a house set among them could be called a house of release. The reason for locating the house in the cemetery would be based on the affinity between leprosy and death — see comm. to v. 19.

Radak and *Metzudos* think the name indi-

26
20-23

before the Kohanim in the House of HASHEM over the altar of the incense. [20] *Azariahu the Kohen Gadol and all the Kohanim turned to him and behold he was leprous on his forehead and they rushed him out from there; he also made haste to go out because HASHEM had smitten him.* [21] *So Uziahu the king was a leper until the day of his death. He dwelt in the house of release as a leper for he was interdicted from going to the House of HASHEM. Yotham his son had charge of the king's palace and judged the people of the land.* [22] *Isaiahu, the son of Amotz, the prophet wrote the rest of the matters of Uziahu, the earlier and the latter.* [23] *So Uziahu lay with his fathers. They buried him with his father in the king's burial field, for they said, 'He is a leper.'*

cates that Uziahu was freed from the burdens of kingship. His affliction made him unfit to rule, as indeed our verse teaches — Yotham became regent — and in that sense Uziahu now occupied a *house of release.*

Targum renders: *And he remained outside Jerusalem.* This accords with the halachah that a leper is forbidden to be in Jerusalem, which has the status of *Israelite camp* from which lepers are to be excluded (*Rambam, Tumas Tzora'as* 10:7).

But why *house of release?*

It is possible that this expression was coined to describe the dwelling of a leper whose condition had been definitely established [מְצוֹרָע מוּחְלָט]. The logic behind this would be as follows: When the indications of leprosy first appear, there is an initial period of quarantine during which the status of the afflicted person as an absolute מְצוֹרָע is not yet finalized [מְצוֹרָע מוּסְגָּר] (see *Leviticus* ch. 13). In describing this period, the Torah uses the term סגר, *to enclose,* which in *Rashi's* opinion (*Leviticus* 13:4) means that he is kept quarantined in a separate house pending the determination of his status according to criteria laid down by the halachah. It seems logical that the lodging to which he goes after he is finally proclaimed a מְצוֹרָע would be called the *house of release,* in contrast to the house which he occupied during the quarantine which was the *house of enclosure.*

כִּי נִגְזַר מִבֵּית ה׳ — *For he was interdicted from going to the House of HASHEM. Metzudos,* who had interpreted the previous phrase as describing Uziahu's freedom from the affairs of state, sees this phrase as developing this thought. Since, because of his ritual uncleanliness, Uziahu was disqualified from entering the Temple grounds, he decided to retire from active rule.

וְיוֹתָם בְּנוֹ עַל־בֵּית הַמֶּלֶךְ — *Yotham his son had charge of the king's palace.* 27:1 tells that Yotham was twenty-five years old when he became king. The Sages maintain that Uziahu was a leper for twenty-five years (see comm. above) and on this basis, have a tradition that when Yotham was conceived, Uziahu was already a finalized מְצוֹרָע. Thus it is clear that Yotham cannot have assumed the regency immediately when Uziahu became ill. Initially, there must have been a regency council; but when Yotham reached the age of competence, he assumed his father's duties (*Radak*).

22. כָּתַב יְשַׁעְיָהוּ בֶן־אָמוֹץ הַנָּבִיא — *Isaiahu, the son of Amotz, the prophet wrote* ... It is not likely that the Book of *Isaiahu* is meant, since this contains no overt references to the events of Uziahu's reign. More likely it is that Isaiah wrote another book which has been lost to us.

23. בִּשְׂדֵה הַקְּבוּרָה — *In the ... burial field.* He was buried *with* his fathers; that is, *near* them, in the field adjoining the royal sepulcher. He was not buried inside the actual sepulcher because of his leprosy (*Mefaresh, Metzudos*).

XXVII

Yotham's Reign

In both the *Kings'* and the *Chronicles'* accounts, Yotham is projected as an entirely righteous king. In the view of the *Mefaresh*, this justifies a cryptic statement made by R' Shimon bar Yochai in *Succah* 45b:

כז
א־ב

א יוֹתָם בְּנוֹ תַּחְתָּיו: בֶּן־עֶשְׂרִים וְחָמֵשׁ שָׁנָה יוֹתָם
בְּמָלְכוֹ וְשֵׁשׁ־עֶשְׂרֵה שָׁנָה מָלַךְ בִּירוּשָׁלָם וְשֵׁם אִמּוֹ
ב יְרוּשָׁה בַּת־צָדוֹק: וַיַּעַשׂ הַיָּשָׁר בְּעֵינֵי יהוה כְּכֹל
אֲשֶׁר־עָשָׂה עֻזִּיָּהוּ אָבִיו רַק לֹא־בָא אֶל־הֵיכַל יהוה

Chizkiahu said in R' Jeremiahu's name that R' Shimon bar Yochai had said: [In my merit (*Rashi*)] I can save the world from suffering, from the day that I was created until now. If my son Eliezer were with me then I could accomplish this, from the time that the world was created until now. And if Yotham the son of Uziahu were with us then we could accomplish this, from the time the world was created until its end.

[See *Yerushalmi, Berachos* 9:2; *Pesikta d'R' Kahana* 10 *Vayehi, BeShalach*, and *Bereishis Rabbah* 35 for alternative readings.]

Commentators have varying opinions about what made Yotham special. *Rashi* explains that it was extreme modesty, displayed during the years of his regency (see 26:21). He was effectively the ruler of the country but always acted in his father's name. *Aruch* (under פטר) believes that the three who are mentioned were unique among all the righteous of the world in that, in this world, they received none of the rewards stored up for them in the World to Come; and *Maharsha* thinks that the statement must be based upon a tradition that these three somehow suffered more than anyone else, and that through these sufferings they could bring about the required atonement.

Another explanation seems possible.

As we saw in comm. to 26:21, the tradition of the Sages is that Yotham was conceived at a time when Uziahu was already an absolute מְצוֹרָע. That is to say, he carried the stigma of that dreadful disease upon him. At 26:19 we recognized leprosy as a living death which symbolized the inner malaise, the inner rotting and disintegration which had begun to infest the nation during Uziahu's reign.

Conceived and born under such circumstances we might have expected Yotham to reflect that apparent hopelessness and to continue in the path of alienation which Uziahu had begun to tread.

That Yotham did not do this but, on the contrary, became totally righteous — in every aspect, as Uziahu had been before the debacle of the incense — demonstrated the inner health and resilience of the Davidic kingship, and provided an example that can well be projected upon the entire nation. If Yotham defied an apparent fate and rose above the circumstances that seemed to fetter him, then so too can Israel — weighed down though it is with sins and impurity — find its way once more to its inner essential goodness. Thus, Yotham joins R' Shimon bar Yochai in the defense of Israel.

Nevertheless, we must bear in mind the tradition of the Sages which we discussed at length in Section II to Ch. 24, *Different Perspectives Upon Yoash and the Monarchy*. There we saw that *Shemos Rabbah* 15:26 views Israel's monarchy as analogous to a waxing and waning moon. From the peak attained in Solomon's reign there was a steady decline which culminated, fifteen generations later, in total eclipse. We noted there that since the midrash, in describing the decline, lists each king by name, it appears that each of them, even those who as individuals were righteous, contributed to the general regression.

Thus, we would expect that Yotham too, in spite of his spiritual grandeur, would be projected as failing in the essential role of his kingship — the reversal of the catastrophic decline. And, indeed, as we shall see in comm. to v. 2, such a projection is made.

1. בֶּן־עֶשְׂרִים וְחָמֵשׁ שָׁנָה יוֹתָם בְּמָלְכוֹ — *Yotham was twenty-five years old when he began to reign.* See comm. to 26:21.

2. כְּכֹל אֲשֶׁר־עָשָׂה עֻזִּיָּהוּ אָבִיו — *In accordance with all that his father Uziahu had done.* This refers to Uziahu's righteous deeds, not to his transgressions — see below (*Mefaresh, Metzudos*).

רַק לֹא־בָא אֶל־הֵיכַל ה׳ — *However, he did not enter the Sanctuary of* HASHEM. *Metzudos* reads this as a continuation of the previous phrase. He followed in Uziahu's righteous ways, but did not follow him in those areas in which he had erred. Accordingly, he made no attempt to sacrifice incense in the Temple as his father had done.

Metzudos then interprets the final phrase *... and the people continued to act corruptly* as follows: Although Yotham was a righteous

Yotham his son reigned in his stead.

Yotham was twenty-five years old when he began to reign and he reigned for sixteen years in Jerusalem. His mother's name was Yerushah the daughter of Tzadok. 2 *He did what was right in the eyes of* HASHEM *in accordance with all that his father Uziahu had done. However, he did not enter the Sanctuary of* HASHEM

man, the people did not make him a model but continued along their evil ways. Thus, he treats the conjunctive *vav* [... וְעוֹד] as meaning *however*.

The syntax of the sentence would seem to run more smoothly if we take the *vav* as *and* or *thus*, and this is its meaning in *Radak's* view. He suggests that our verse means that Yotham refused to enter the Temple because of the catastrophe which had befallen his father there. Consequently, he brought all his sacrifices on private *bamos* outside the Temple precincts. As a result of this, the people, too, continued to act corruptly — that is, they continued to use the forbidden *bamos*.

This has the final part of the verse, ... *and the people continued to act corruptly*, referring to the illicit use of the *bamos*, and thus, paraphrasing the parallel verse in *Kings* (15:35) which reads *Only the bamos were not removed; the people continued to sacrifice and to burn on the bamos*. This is also *Malbim's* opinion. However, as we have analyzed in detail in Section II to 20:33, *Bamos in Kings and Chronicles*, *Chronicles* is never concerned with the continued proliferation of the *bamos* nor with the inability of the people to wean themselves away from their use.

We may suggest another interpretation for our phrase and the next.

In prefatory remarks to ch. 26, we suggested that the final part of the verse, ... *and the people continued to act corruptly* refers to the spiritual decline which is chronicled in such rich detail in Isaiahu's prophecies, and which had its genesis in Uziahu's neglect of serious Torah study. This continued during Yotham's reign until it culminated in the tragedies which occurred under Achaz.

If the final part of the verse has this meaning we can expect our phrase to be introductory to it.

We suggest that the phrase רַק לֹא־בָא אֶל־הֵיכַל ה׳ can be taken idiomatically in the same vein as מִי יַעֲלֶה בְהַר־ה׳, *Who can go up to the mountain of* HASHEM (*Psalms* 24:3), or, אַשְׁרֵי יוֹשְׁבֵי בֵיתֶךָ, *Happy are those that dwell in Your House* (*Psalms* 84:5).

We note further that הֵיכַל ה׳ may be taken as describing the spiritual state to which a person may aspire. *Jeremiahu* 7:4 castigates the people in the following terms: אַל־תִּבְטְחוּ לָכֶם אֶל־דִּבְרֵי הַשֶּׁקֶר לֵאמֹר הֵיכַל ה׳ הֵיכַל ה׳ הֵיכַל ה׳ הֵמָּה. The people are not to put their trust in a Temple of stone and wood [הֵיכַל ה׳ הֵיכַל ה׳]. Rather, it is their own spiritual state which is God's true dwelling place [הֵיכַל ה׳ הֵמָּה!] (*Malbim*; *Hirsch*).

Thus, our verse is to be understood as follows: Yotham did indeed follow in his father Uziahu's footsteps. He was righteous in all his dealings. However, he did not manage to reach the total spiritual state which would have enabled him to reverse the destructive trend which had set in during Uziahu's reign. The people continued to regress.

This verse, which replaces the one in *Kings* which deals with the *bamos*, is thus entirely consistent with *Chronicles'* approach throughout the book. It makes no mention of the *bamos*, but instead makes an assessment which puts Yotham's reign into perspective from its own point of view.

The choice of this particular idiom clearly mirrors 26:16 [... *he entered the Sanctuary of* HASHEM (וַיָּבֹא אֶל הֵיכַל ה׳)]. Its judgment of Yotham is tinged with irony: Indeed, Yotham walked entirely in Uziahu's righteous footsteps. but the final step which — albeit ill-advisedly — Uziahu had taken to elevate himself to the highest spiritual level of which he seemed capable, Yotham did not take. He made no attempt to reach his *Heichal*, his total commitment to spirituality. Had he done so, it might have halted the catastrophic decline to which Israel was succumbing.[1]

1. In such an idiomatic context, the root word בא would have a similar meaning to the one it carries in phrases like בָּא בַּיָּמִים (*Genesis* 24:1) or כִּי־תָבוֹא עַל־שְׂכָרִי (*Genesis* 30:33).

כז
ג־ט

ג וְעוֹד הָעָם מַשְׁחִיתִים: הוּא בָּנָה אֶת־שַׁעַר בֵּית־יְהוָה
ד הָעֶלְיוֹן וּבְחוֹמַת הָעֹפֶל בָּנָה לָרֹב: וְעָרִים בָּנָה בְּהַר
ה יְהוּדָה וּבֶחֳרָשִׁים בָּנָה בִּירָנִיּוֹת וּמִגְדָּלִים: וְהוּא נִלְחַם
עִם־מֶלֶךְ בְּנֵי־עַמּוֹן וַיֶּחֱזַק עֲלֵיהֶם וַיִּתְּנוּ־לוֹ בְנֵי־עַמּוֹן
בַּשָּׁנָה הַהִיא מֵאָה כִּכַּר־כֶּסֶף וַעֲשֶׂרֶת אֲלָפִים כֹּרִים חִטִּים
וּשְׂעוֹרִים עֲשֶׂרֶת אֲלָפִים זֹאת הֵשִׁיבוּ לוֹ בְּנֵי עַמּוֹן וּבַשָּׁנָה
ו הַשֵּׁנִית וְהַשְּׁלִשִׁית: וַיִּתְחַזֵּק יוֹתָם כִּי הֵכִין
ז דְּרָכָיו לִפְנֵי יְהוָה אֱלֹהָיו: וְיֶתֶר דִּבְרֵי יוֹתָם וְכָל־
מִלְחֲמֹתָיו וּדְרָכָיו הִנָּם כְּתוּבִים עַל־סֵפֶר מַלְכֵי יִשְׂרָאֵל
ח וִיהוּדָה: בֶּן־עֶשְׂרִים וְחָמֵשׁ שָׁנָה הָיָה בְמָלְכוֹ וְשֵׁשׁ־
ט עֶשְׂרֵה שָׁנָה מָלַךְ בִּירוּשָׁלָםִ: וַיִּשְׁכַּב יוֹתָם עִם־אֲבֹתָיו
וַיִּקְבְּרוּ אֹתוֹ בְּעִיר דָּוִיד וַיִּמְלֹךְ אָחָז בְּנוֹ תַּחְתָּיו:

3. הוּא בָּנָה אֶת־שַׁעַר בֵּית־ה׳ הָעֶלְיוֹן — *It was he who built up the upper gate of the House of* HASHEM. This gate was in existence long before Yotham's days (*Radak*). The meaning is either that he built a building over it, or that it had fallen down and he built it up once more (*Radak; Metzudos*).

וּבְחוֹמַת הָעֹפֶל — *And as for the citadel wall*. We have followed *Targum* who renders פַּלְטֵרִין usually *palace*, and *Radak* and *Metzudos* (to *Isaiahu* 32:14) who render *tower*. *Radak* here simply writes: *a high place*.

All these explanations take עֹפֶל as a common noun. However, it is now generally accepted that this is the name of a spur on the southern side of the Temple Mount. See maps in *Ir HaKodesh VeHaMikdash*.

Of the building exploits mentioned in this verse and the next, *Kings* mentions only Yotham's improvements of the upper gate. We may perhaps surmise that the other projects were considered insignificant at the time, and that only with the hindsight of history were their durability and importance recognized.

בָּנָה לָרֹב — *He developed it prodigiously*. He added towers to it (*Mefaresh*).

4. וְעָרִים בָּנָה בְּהַר יְהוּדָה — *Moreover, he built cities in the hills of Judah*. As in the case of Uziahu, a major issue is made of Yotham's building and military exploits (v. 5). However, our v. 6 puts these secular accomplishments into the framework of spiritual grandeur and thus they contribute towards a positive projection of Yotham's reign. This, in contrast to Uziahu where, as we noted at 26:6-15, no mention is made of any efforts to improve the spiritual standing of the people.

וּבֶחֳרָשִׁים — *And in the forests*. This word occurs rarely, and never in a context with an unambiguous meaning. Commentators assume it to mean *forest* which is certainly the meaning of the Aramaic, חוּרְשָׁא, which *Targum* always uses to translate the Hebrew, יַעַר.

Targum here renders: *In the strongly fortified cities*.

בִּירָנִיּוֹת — *Castles*. See at 17:12.

5. וְהוּא נִלְחַם עִם־מֶלֶךְ בְּנֵי־עַמּוֹן — *He fought against the king of the Amonites*. There is no other record of this war in Scripture. See ch. 20 for Yehoshaphat's war with the Amonites.

וּשְׂעוֹרִים עֲשֶׂרֶת אֲלָפִים — *And ten thousand of barley*. The word כּוֹר of the previous phrase must be read with this one too. There were ten thousand *cor* of barley.

Malbim explains this verse as follows: In 26:8 we learn that the Amonites paid tribute to Yotham's father Uziahu. If our verse tells us that Yotham fought against them, this implies that at one point they rebelled and refused to send their due. Yotham then forcefully subdued them once more and placed a levy upon them in that year to make up for the tribute that they had not paid during the time of their rebellion. The final phrase, . . . *so much did the Amonites render to him, in the second year and also in the third*, teaches that besides forcing them to make up for the lapsed tribute, he also exacted a fine from them for another two years.

6. כִּי הֵכִין דְּרָכָיו — *Because he went his way consistently*. See comm. to 12:1 and 14. In Section II ch. 12, *Rechav'am Fails as King*, we saw that *Metzudos* rendered the phrase כִּי לֹא הֵכִין לִבּוֹ: *He did not delve deeply in order to develop an intellectual appreciation to search out* HASHEM *and to know Him*. If we can

and the people continued to act corruptly. 3 *It was he who built up*
the upper gate of the House of HASHEM, and as for the citadel wall,
he developed it prodigiously. 4 *Moreover, he built cities in the hills*
of Judah, and in the forests he built castles and towers. 5 *He fought*
against the king of the Amonites and prevailed against them. That
year the Amonites gave him one hundred talents of silver, ten
thousand kor of wheat, and ten thousand of barley. So much did
the Amonites render to him in the second year and also in the
third. 6 *So Yotham became mighty because he went his way*
consistently before HASHEM his God. 7 *The rest of the matters of*
Yotham, all his wars and his ways, behold they are recorded in the
Book of the Kings of Israel and Judah. 8 *He was twenty-five years*
old when he began to reign and he reigned sixteen years in
Jerusalem. 9 *Yotham lay with his fathers and they buried him in*
the City of David. His son Achaz reigned in his stead.

interpret our phrase in the same way, then this assessment of Yotham's reign would be entirely appropriate. In contrast to Uziahu who, as we saw in the previous chapter, was prone to seeking out the short-lived ecstasy of extreme closeness to God, and who neglected the taxing, but in the long run, more rewarding study of the Torah, Yotham pursued just that intellectual path. He *went his way consistently before HASHEM*, walked firmly along the paths of the Torah. His was, therefore, a successful reign.

7. דִּבְרֵי יוֹתָם . . . וּדְרָכָיו — *The matters of Yotham . . . and his ways.* For *matters* and *ways* see comm. to 28:26.

סֵפֶר מַלְכֵי יִשְׂרָאֵל — *The Book of the Kings of Israel and Judah.* At 12:15 we have listed the names of the books in which, according to *Chronicles*, the records of the various kings were preserved. A glance at that list will show that the histories of the earlier kings — through Aviah — were invariably written by the prophets who were contemporary with them. The chronicles given for Asa (16:11), Yehoshaphat (20:34), Yoash (24:27), Amatziahu (25:26), and Uziahu (26:22) are discussed in the comm. to those respective verses.

From Yotham to the end, the records are uniformly kept in a book dealing with the kings of the two kingdoms, except that in the case of Yotham, Yoshiyahu (35:26) and Yehoyakim (36:8), Israel is mentioned before Judah, while in the case of Achaz (28:26) and Chizkiahu, Judah is mentioned before Israel. [For Menasseh who is an exception, see comm. to 33:18.]

Commentators do not discuss whether the difference in the order of the listings indicates that we are dealing with different books, or whether the sequence has no significance.

8. בֶּן־עֶשְׂרִים וְחָמֵשׁ שָׁנָה הָיָה בְמָלְכוֹ — *He was twenty-five years old when he began to reign.* This verse contains a precise repetition of the information given in v. 1, except that the name of Yotham's mother is not given.

Why was it necessary to repeat this information?

Malbim suggests that it is to avoid confusion with the period that Yotham was regent during his father's reign (26:21). Our verse wishes to make clear that the sixteen years of Yotham's rule are all counted from after Uziahu's death, and that the regency years are not included in the count. See Section II, *Yotham and the Campaign of Pekach and Retzin*, for another possible explanation.

9. וַיִּקְבְּרוּ אֹתוֹ בְּעִיר דָּוִיד — *And they buried him in the City of David. II Kings* 15:38 has בְּעִיר דָּוִד אָבִיו. Are we to attach any significance to the omission of the words *his father* in *Chronicles*?

Kings uses this formulation in four places: At *I Kings* 11:43 (Solomon); 15:24 (Asa); 22:51 (Yehoshaphat); and at *II Kings* 15:38 (Yotham). *Chronicles* uses it only in the case of Solomon but omits it in connection with the other three.

We cannot say that *Chronicles uses* אב as only an actual father, but not as an ancestor as witness, for example *II Chronicles* 28:11.

As can be seen in the comm. to the relevant chapters, the picture which *Chronicles* paints of Asa and Yehoshaphat is considerably more negative than that of *Kings*, while in the case of Solomon, many of the criticisms leveled in *Kings* are omitted in *Chronicles*. Perhaps, then, we may say that in the case of Solomon, *Chronicles had no reason to omit what even Kings* had said, but, in the other two cases, *his*

א בֶּן־עֶשְׂרִ֨ים שָׁנָ֤ה אָחָז֙ בְּמָלְכ֔וֹ וְשֵׁשׁ־עֶשְׂרֵ֣ה שָׁנָ֔ה מָלַ֖ךְ
בִּירוּשָׁלִָ֑ם וְלֹא־עָשָׂ֧ה הַיָּשָׁ֛ר בְּעֵינֵ֥י יְהוָ֖ה כְּדָוִ֥יד אָבִֽיו׃
ב וַיֵּ֕לֶךְ בְּדַרְכֵ֖י מַלְכֵ֣י יִשְׂרָאֵ֑ל וְגַ֧ם מַסֵּכ֛וֹת עָשָׂ֖ה לַבְּעָלִֽים׃
ג וְה֣וּא הִקְטִ֔יר בְּגֵ֖יא בֶן־הִנֹּ֑ם וַיַּבְעֵ֤ר אֶת־בָּנָיו֙ בָּאֵ֔שׁ

father was excised from the final assessment of the respective reigns, because, as these kings had been perceived from the *Chronicles* perspective, they had not lived up to David's example.

If we are correct in this thesis, then the omission of the words in connection with Yotham would also seem to imply a criticism. This would confirm what we surmised in the Introductory Remarks to this chapter and in comm to v. 1 — that in spite of the positive tone in which the reign is described, it fell short of its full potential. The downward spiral of the monarchy was not arrested.

XXVIII

◆§ Achaz's Reign

Both *Kings* and *Chronicles* give detailed accounts of Achaz's reign. The differences between the two accounts will be noted in the commentary.

1. וְלֹא־עָשָׂה הַיָּשָׁר . . . כְּדָוִיד אָבִיו — *He did not do that which was right . . . as his father David had done*. See Section II, *Achaz and Menasseh*.

2. וַיֵּלֶךְ בְּדַרְכֵי מַלְכֵי יִשְׂרָאֵל — *He went in the ways of the kings of Israel*. This describes a general spiritual malaise, rather than any specific sin.

An alternative might be to read the second part of the verse, ... *and also made molten images for the Baal*, as descriptive of the first — he acted as Israel's kings did in that he made molten images. However, this seems unlikely for the following reasons.

In *Kings*, the statement that Achaz went in the paths of Israel's kings is followed by ... *moreover, he passed his son through the fire according to the abominations of the nations whom* HASHEM *had driven out from before the Children of Israel* (our v. 3). Now, the verse itself makes clear that this form of child sacrifice was the practice of nations whom *HASHEM* had driven out, not of the kings of the Northern Kingdom.

Again, Baal service is not typical of the kings of Israel. As demonstrated by *HaLevi, Tekufas HaMikra* ch. 4, it does not appear before Ahab and terminates with the beginning of Yehu's reign — that is, it was pervasive for a maximum of thirty-six years.

וְגַם מַסֵּכוֹת עָשָׂה לַבְּעָלִים — *And also made molten images for the Baalim*. The introduction of the Baal [a fertility symbol shaped like a phallus [*Yerushalmi Avodah Zarah* 3:6] into Judah at this late stage is fraught with significance. Already since the days of Yehu, this cult had disappeared from the Northern Kingdom. Even during its heyday, it had been an aberration — its filth and depravity totally alien to the Jewish soul — imported by Ahab's Sidonite wife Jezebel. And now we have Achaz — scion of David's line — introducing this obscenity into Judah!

We talk of Achaz *introducing* Baal worship because prior to him, there is no evidence that this cult ever took root. The reference to the priest of the Baal at 23:17 comes during Yoash's reign — that is, after Athaliahu, daughter of Ahab's house, had introduced it — an aberration traceable to her non-Israelite antecedents. Significantly, the two previous references to Baalim — at 17:3 and 24:7 — are rendered by *Targum* as *idols* in general, not as a proper name. It is only in our verse that *Targum* begins to render *Baalim*.

Perhaps this is the meaning of *Ezekiel* 23:11 where the prophet compares Judah unfavorably with Israel, in regard to the idol worship that was practiced in the two kingdoms: *Now her sister Oholivah [Judah] observed, but she was even more corrupt in her lusting than she, and her promiscuity exceeded the harlotries of her sister [Israel]*. Israel's stumbling could be excused. It had succumbed to the foreign influence of Jezebel, an alien queen, and with her death the matter was closed. By contrast, Judah, without any outside pressures, opted for the Baal.

Kings makes no mention of these molten images; in fact, a case can be made that it makes no mention at all of any idol worship during Achaz' reign — see comm. to vs. 3 and **4.** Why would *Kings* not mention this significant erosion of Judah's spiritual standing?

We do not know the precise meaning of making *molten images for the Baal*. We think of the Baal as an idol which is worshiped by the normal forms of Divine or idolatrous service. In what way does erecting an image constitute service?

It is interesting that in all of Chizkiahu's

28
1-3

Achaz was twenty years when he became king and reigned sixteen years in Jerusalem. He did not do that which was right in the eyes of HASHEM *as his father David had done.* [2] *He went in the ways of the kings of Israel and also made molten images for the Baal.* [3] *He burned incense in the Ben Hinom Valley, and set his sons alight in the fire, in ac-*

reforms (see 30:14 and 31:1), no mention is made of the destruction of these molten images. Moreover, in the description of Menasseh's transgressions (33:3), we find him erecting *altars* to the Baalim, but not making any molten images.

It is possible that the images which Achaz erected were not used for actual worship — it is nowhere mentioned that he served the Baal. Perhaps there were only a few of them — and these were well hidden so that they escaped Chizkiahu's cleansing reforms.

If this was so, then Achaz's involvement with the Baal may not have been important enough for *Kings* to record. Its significance lay not in itself but in the fact that it laid the groundwork for future depravities. Thus, it is entirely appropriate that *Chronicles* which, as we develop in Section II, *Achaz and Menasseh*, pictures Achaz as the cause of all later problems, should record it even though *Kings* does not.

3. וְהוּא הִקְטִיר בְּגֵיא בֶן־הִנֹּם — *He burned incense in the Ben Hinom Valley.* קטר is *to go up in smoke* and in its *hiphil*, causative form, is normally used to describe the offering of the קְטֹרֶת, *incense*. This is how *Targum* renders it here.

This phrase does not appear in *Kings*, which says only that Achaz passed his son through fire. Perhaps, here too, the occurrences of the incense offerings were neither frequent nor public enough to have left a mark with which *Kings* would have been concerned.

A closer analysis yields that the burning of this incense may not have been an act of idol worship at all.

We turn first to the second part of our verse: . . . *and set his sons alight* . . ., which substitutes for the phrase: . . . *and also his son he passed through fire* . . . in *Kings*.

From *II Kings* 23:10, it is clear that the Ben Hinom Valley was the site for the Molech cult of which the Torah speaks in *Leviticus* 18:21. Commentators find it difficult to define precisely what was involved in this cult — see *Ramban* to *Leviticus* there — but the underlying principle seems to be the dictum of *Sanhedrin* 64a, that it was not a form of idol worship.

If it was not idol worship, what was it?

Meiri to *Sanhedrin* understands it to have been a ceremonial, marking entry into the priesthood of the fire cult. This ceremonial had the nature of a covenant. We know that the Covenant Between the Pieces (of Abraham) required that the contracting parties *pass through* agreed units. In this case, the candidates for the priesthood were *passed through* bands of fire [the *Kings'* version]. No actual idol worship is involved at this stage. The focus of fire worship is the *idea* [יְסוֹד]; fire, rather than a particular flame. Thus: If someone were to sacrifice or to burn incense to one of the priests or to a particular flame without having the *idea* of fire in mind — this would be meaningless.

We may thus assume that the burning of incense described in our verse was a part of this ceremony. It is viewed by *Chronicles* as a pernicious evil, not because it was an act of idol worship but because it contributed toward the legitimization of the fire cult. It helped create a spiritual climate which made the depredations of the later kings possible. As such, as we have seen above, it falls within the sphere of interest of *Chronicles*, but not of *Kings*.

וַיַּבְעֵר. . . — *And set . . .alight*. *Kings* has הֶעֱבִיר, *he passed through*. . ., an expression frequently used in connection with the Molech cult. See above for *Meiri's* explanation.

Ramban (*Leviticus* 18:21) explains that there was no requirement that the child should be actually burned. Rather, the victim was passed to and fro over or through the flames with a possibility that the fire could catch on. Thus, the *passing* could well involve a *burning*.

אֶת־בָּנָיו — *His sons*. *Kings* has *his son*, in the singular. In the tradition of the Sages (*Sanhedrin* 63b), reference is to Chizkiahu. *Rashi* there maintains that Achaz had no other sons.

Rashi seems to be contradicted by our verse which speaks of *sons*. In answer, *Margalios HaYam* points to *Bava Basra* 143b which holds that the plural *sons* may be used even when only one son is meant.

Note that we have the same change in connection with Menasheh. *II Kings* 21:6 has *his son* while our 33:6 has *his sons*.

We may perhaps surmise that the use of the plural in place of the singular lends a specific nuance. When the singular is used, then the focus is upon the individual son as a person. Achaz offended the person of his son by

כח
ד־ט

כְּתֹעֲבוֹת הַגּוֹיִם אֲשֶׁר הֹרִישׁ יהוה מִפְּנֵי בְּנֵי יִשְׂרָאֵל:
ד וַיְזַבֵּחַ וַיְקַטֵּר בַּבָּמוֹת וְעַל־הַגְּבָעוֹת וְתַחַת כָּל־עֵץ רַעֲנָן:
ה וַיִּתְּנֵהוּ יהוה אֱלֹהָיו בְּיַד מֶלֶךְ אֲרָם וַיַּכּוּ־בוֹ וַיִּשְׁבּוּ מִמֶּנּוּ
שִׁבְיָה גְדוֹלָה וַיָּבִיאוּ דַּרְמָשֶׂק וְגַם בְּיַד־מֶלֶךְ יִשְׂרָאֵל נִתָּן
ו וַיַּךְ־בּוֹ מַכָּה גְדוֹלָה: וַיַּהֲרֹג פֶּקַח בֶּן־רְמַלְיָהוּ בִּיהוּדָה
מֵאָה וְעֶשְׂרִים אֶלֶף בְּיוֹם אֶחָד הַכֹּל בְּנֵי־חָיִל בְּעָזְבָם
ז אֶת־יהוה אֱלֹהֵי אֲבוֹתָם: וַיַּהֲרֹג זִכְרִי ׀ גִּבּוֹר אֶפְרַיִם
אֶת־מַעֲשֵׂיָהוּ בֶּן־הַמֶּלֶךְ וְאֶת־עַזְרִיקָם נְגִיד הַבָּיִת וְאֶת־
ח אֶלְקָנָה מִשְׁנֵה הַמֶּלֶךְ: וַיִּשְׁבּוּ בְנֵי־יִשְׂרָאֵל מֵאֲחֵיהֶם
מָאתַיִם אֶלֶף נָשִׁים בָּנִים וּבָנוֹת וְגַם־שָׁלָל רָב בָּזְזוּ מֵהֶם
ט וַיָּבִיאוּ אֶת־הַשָּׁלָל לְשֹׁמְרוֹן: וְשָׁם הָיָה נָבִיא לַיהוה
עֹדֵד שְׁמוֹ וַיֵּצֵא לִפְנֵי הַצָּבָא הַבָּא לְשֹׁמְרוֹן וַיֹּאמֶר לָהֶם

passing him through the fire.

When the plural is used, it is the idea rather than the person which is meant. The heinousness of Achaz's act was not so much that he could do what he did to a fellow human as that he was willing to do violence to his entire future, as that future was expressed in the person of his only son. See further below.

וַיַּבְעֵר אֶת־בָּנָיו בָּאֵשׁ — *And set his sons alight in the fire*. In Section II, *Achaz and Menasseh*, we note that Achaz was possessed with the notion of driving the Divine Presence away from Israel. If this was, indeed, his wish, he could have chosen no better means than the committing of his son to the Molech cult.

Leviticus 20:3 describes one who gives his child to the Molech as *defiling My Sanctuary*. Why? The site for this gruesome ceremony was not God's Sanctuary, but the Ben Hinom Valley.

Rashi explains: *Sanctuary*, here, is not the Temple but the people of Israel. They are God's true dwelling place: He resides within their hearts, as surely as His Presence rests within the Temple.

This, however, is true only to the extent that we recognize and value it. Even eating an apple without acknowledging that it comes to us as God's gift, by making the appropriate blessing, drives the *Shechinah* away (*Berachos* 35b). Certainly then, one who takes the most precious of all gifts, his child, and actively hands him over to the Molech, is defiling the Sanctuary that is Israel (*Ramban*).

4. וַיְזַבֵּחַ וַיְקַטֵּר בַּבָּמוֹת — *He sacrificed and burned incense upon the bamos.* At 14:2, we learned that in general, *bamos* were used for Divine service. The practice was interdicted, but not idolatrous. There we surmised that perhaps in our verse, reference is to idolatrous *bamos*. Certainly, the end part of our verse, . . . *and in the hills and under every leafy tree*, recalls *Deuteronomy* 12:2 which deals with actual idol worship.

However, v. 25 seems to speak against this. There we learn that Achaz erected *bamos* for the purpose of *burning incense to other gods*. This would indicate that in our verse, where this is not explicated, the word has its more usual connotation.

In view of the fact that the commentators are silent on the issue, we must conclude that our verse could lend itself to either interpretation.

5. . . . מֶלֶךְ אֲרָם . . . מֶלֶךְ יִשְׂרָאֵל — . . . *The king of Aram . . . the king of Israel*. See Section II to ch. 27, *Yotham and the Campaign of Pekach and Retzin*, for a wide-ranging discussion.

Judah's humiliation at Pekach's hands must have been particularly painful. Memories must still have been alive of Amatziahu who, so that his army would not be tainted by participation of mercenaries from the Northern Kingdom, was willing to forgo one hundred silver talents (25:6—10). Now the shoe was on the other foot. One hundred and twenty thousand of Judah's soldiers fall to Israel!

6. . . . בְּעָזְבָם — *Because they had forsaken . . .* Achaz's sins were not limited to the royal household, as had been the case with the excesses of some of the earlier kings (see

cordance with the loathsome practice of the nations which
HASHEM had driven out from before the Children of Israel. [4] *He*
sacrificed and burned incense upon the bamos and in the hills
and under every leafy tree. [5] *So HASHEM his God delivered him*
into the hands of the king of Aram. They smote him and carried
off from him a great many captives whom they brought to
Darmasek. He was also delivered into the hand of the king of Is-
rael, who subjected him to a great defeat. [6] *In that Pekach son of*
Remaliahu slew one hundred and twenty thousand — all of them
valiant men — of Judah, in one day; because they had forsaken
HASHEM, the God of their fathers. [7] *And Zichri an Ephraimite*
warrior killed Maaseiahu the king's son and Azrikam the chief of
the household and Elkanah who was second to the king. [8] *The*
Israelites took two hundred thousand women, and boys and girls,
captive from their brothers, and also took away much spoils from
them. They brought the spoils to Samaria. [9] *Now a prophet of*
HASHEM was there, whose name was Oded. He came out to
meet the army that came to Samaria, and said to them,

comm. to 23:17), but had tainted large segments of the people.

7. מַעֲשֵׂיהוּ בֶּן־הַמֶּלֶךְ — *Maaseiahu the king's son.* This was Achaz's son (*Mefaresh*). The translation follows *Targum*. But *Rashi* to *Sanhedrin* 63b writes that Achaz had no son beside Chizkiahu.

Margalios HaYam notes that in the editions of *Chronicles* printed together with *Malbim*, the reading in the *Mefaresh* is different than in the other editions. In place of אָחָז, they have אִתּוֹ. Accordingly, *Mefaresh* takes the אֶת as meaning *with*, rather than as denoting the accusative. The meaning is that the Ephraimite warrior Zichri, aided by the king's [Pekach's] son Maaseiahu, killed Azrikam and Elkanah. Taken thus, there is no indication in our verse that Achaz had any son but Chizkiahu.

Margalios HaYam points out that only if this is, indeed, the correct reading in the *Mefaresh* does the comment which follows immediately upon this piece have any meaning.

8. בָּנִים וּבָנוֹת — *Boys and girls.* Minor children (*Metzudos*).

9-15. The account in the next few verses, of the noble bearing of the Israelite army, sounds a note of pathos as it is woven into the story which *Chronicles* has to tell. Throughout, this story has dealt only with the history of the Southern Kingdom. In what way is the account of the magnanimity which the Israelites displayed germane to Achaz's reign?

The event is of particular significance when we place it into its historical setting. Pekach was killed in the fourth year of Achaz (*Rashi* at *II Kings* 15:30). Accordingly, at the time of this war, his reign was drawing to its close. Pekach was the penultimate king of Israel; the Northern Kingdom was exiled during the reign of his successor, Hosea ben Eilah.

The exile of the Northern Kingdom took place in three waves: the first, during the year in which Hosea became king; the second, eight years later; and the last, at the end of his reign (*Rashi* to *II Kings* 17:1).

This event, then, took place no more than four years before the first wave of exile, and may have been considerably closer.

How does this picture of moral excellence agree with the unrelieved negative description of the Northern Kingdom given in *II Kings* 17:7-18?

From the contemporary perspective, which informs the historiography of *Kings*, there was nothing that could counteract the pervasive and deep-rooted evil of idol worship. Israel had sunk too low into the mire and filth of its cultic practices for any other merits to carry decisive weight. *Kings* has nothing good to say about the Northern Kingdom.

But if we read through the sad litany of transgressions listed there, we find that they are all concerned with the poisoning of relationships between Israel and God. Nothing

הִנֵּה בַּחֲמַת יְהוָה אֱלֹהֵי־אֲבוֹתֵיכֶם עַל־יְהוּדָה נְתָנָם
י בְּיֶדְכֶם וַתַּהַרְגוּ־בָם בְּזַעַף עַד לַשָּׁמַיִם הִגִּיעַ׃ וְעַתָּה
בְּנֵי־יְהוּדָה וִירוּשָׁלַםִ אַתֶּם אֹמְרִים לִכְבֹּשׁ לַעֲבָדִים
וְלִשְׁפָחוֹת לָכֶם הֲלֹא רַק־אַתֶּם עִמָּכֶם אֲשָׁמוֹת לַיהוָה
יא אֱלֹהֵיכֶם׃ וְעַתָּה שְׁמָעוּנִי וְהָשִׁיבוּ הַשִּׁבְיָה אֲשֶׁר שְׁבִיתֶם
יב מֵאֲחֵיכֶם כִּי חֲרוֹן אַף־יְהוָה עֲלֵיכֶם׃ וַיָּקֻמוּ
אֲנָשִׁים מֵרָאשֵׁי בְנֵי־אֶפְרַיִם עֲזַרְיָהוּ בֶן־יְהוֹחָנָן בֶּרֶכְיָהוּ
בֶן־מְשִׁלֵּמוֹת וִיחִזְקִיָּהוּ בֶּן־שַׁלֻּם וַעֲמָשָׂא בֶּן־חַדְלָי עַל־
יג הַבָּאִים מִן־הַצָּבָא׃ וַיֹּאמְרוּ לָהֶם לֹא־תָבִיאוּ אֶת־הַשִּׁבְיָה
הֵנָּה כִּי לְאַשְׁמַת יְהוָה עָלֵינוּ אַתֶּם אֹמְרִים לְהֹסִיף
עַל־חַטֹּאתֵינוּ וְעַל־אַשְׁמָתֵנוּ כִּי־רַבָּה אַשְׁמָה לָנוּ וַחֲרוֹן
יד אָף עַל־יִשְׂרָאֵל׃ וַיַּעֲזֹב הֶחָלוּץ אֶת־הַשִּׁבְיָה וְאֶת־
טו הַבִּזָּה לִפְנֵי הַשָּׂרִים וְכָל־הַקָּהָל׃ וַיָּקֻמוּ הָאֲנָשִׁים אֲשֶׁר־
נִקְּבוּ בְשֵׁמוֹת וַיַּחֲזִיקוּ בַשִּׁבְיָה וְכָל־מַעֲרֻמֵּיהֶם הִלְבִּישׁוּ
מִן־הַשָּׁלָל וַיַּלְבִּשׁוּם וַיַּנְעִלוּם וַיַּאֲכִלוּם וַיַּשְׁקוּם וַיְסֻכוּם
וַיְנַהֲלוּם בַּחֲמֹרִים לְכָל־כּוֹשֵׁל וַיְבִיאוּם יְרֵחוֹ עִיר־
טז הַתְּמָרִים אֵצֶל אֲחֵיהֶם וַיָּשׁוּבוּ שֹׁמְרוֹן׃ בָּעֵת
יז הַהִיא שָׁלַח הַמֶּלֶךְ אָחָז עַל־מַלְכֵי אַשּׁוּר לַעְזֹר לוֹ׃ וְעוֹד

is said of sins of a social nature. There is no reason to suppose that any but the highest ethical and moral standards prevailed.

In Ezra's time, the dangers of the idolatrous cults had begun to recede. Within such a context the essential goodness of the Ten Tribes must have taken on new significance. In a world freed from the pernicious influences of the past, their merits rather than their failings would be remembered.

That *Chronicles* includes this incident, bespeaks the longing of the Judean remnant to be rejoined to their lost brothers. In the context of Messianic eternity, Israel — all its twelve tribes — are one.

9. בַּחֲמַת ה׳ אֱלֹהֵי־אֲבוֹתֵיכֶם — *Because HASHEM the God of your fathers was angry.* It was not our merit which granted us victory but God's anger against Judah (*Metzudos*).

עַד לַשָּׁמַיִם הִגִּיעַ — *It has reached up to the very heavens.* A hyperbole. Surely Judah has been punished enough; more would be excessive (*Metzudos*).

10. רַק־אַתֶּם עִמָּכֶם אֲשָׁמוֹת — *You will only load yourselves with guilt* ... The translation follows *Metzudos*.

Targum takes אֲשָׁמוֹת as *guilt offerings*. Your victory should have given you pause to consider whether you yourselves are innocent of sin. It should have inspired you to bring guilt offerings for your own atonement.

Ralbag interprets: You have sins of your own on your conscience. This will only add to them.

11. כִּי חֲרוֹן אַף־ה׳ עֲלֵיכֶם — *For the fierce wrath of HASHEM is upon you.* The anger of HASHEM will come upon you, should you decide not to return the captives (*Metzudos*).

12. עַל־הַבָּאִים — *Over those that came.* To persuade them to return the captives.

מִן־הַצָּבָא — *From the battlefield.* צָבָא usually means *army*. However, it is sometimes used to denote a battlefield or warfare, in the sense that these ideas are associated with the army. Examples are *Joshua* 22:12 (but see *Radak* there) and *I Samuel* 28:1.

13. ... כִּי לְאַשְׁמַת ה׳ עָלֵינוּ — ... *would make us culpable before HASHEM.* The translation of this verse follows *Metzudos*.

14. וַיַּעֲזֹב הֶחָלוּץ — *So the military gave up the captives and the spoil.* See *Rambam*,

'Behold, because HASHEM the God of your fathers was angry
with Judah, He has delivered them into your hands and you
have wrought furious slaughter among them. It has reached up
to the very heavens. 10 *And now you propose to impress*
the Jerusalemite Judeans as slaves and bondwomen for
yourselves. You will only load yourselves with guilt before
HASHEM, your God. 11 *Now hear me and send back the cap-*
tives that you have taken captive from your brothers; for the
fierce wrath of HASHEM is upon you'. 12 *Then certain of the*
heads of the children of Ephraim, Azariahu the son of Yehocha-
nan, Berechiahu the son of Mesheleimoth, and Yechizkiahu the
son of Shallum and Amosa the son of Chadlai stood up over those
that came from the battlefield. 13 *They said to them, 'You shall*
not bring the captives here. Your plan would make us culpable
before HASHEM, only adding to our transgressions and guilt. It
would be a heinous crime for us, and bring fierce wrath against
Israel.' 14 *So the military gave up the captives and the spoil,*
leaving them to the princes and all the congregation. 15 *Then the*
men that had been mentioned by name rose up and took charge of
the captives, clothing their nakedness with the spoils, dressing
them, shodding them, and providing them with food and drink
and anointing them. They carried all the feeble among them upon
donkeys and brought them to Jericho, the city of palm trees to
their brothers. Then they returned to Samaria. 16 *At that time*
King Achaz sent to the Assyrian monarchy, for help. 17 *Moreover,*

Melachim 4:9, that the common soldiers are entitled to part of the spoils taken in war. Accordingly, the entire body of military men would have had to agree to this decision.

15. הָאֲנָשִׁים אֲשֶׁר־נִקְּבוּ בְשֵׁמוֹת — *The men that had been mentioned by name.* The ones that had been mentioned in v. 12 (*Metzudos*).

16. ... בָּעֵת הַהִיא — *At that time ...* This verse parallels *II Kings* 16:7. But in that account, Achaz solicited Assyria's help in order to frustrate the plot — hatched by rebellious elements in Jerusalem and abetted by Pekach of the Northern Kingdom and Retzin of Aram — to replace the Davidic line with an Ephraimite king. This episode is never mentioned in *Chronicles* — see Section II to ch. 27, *Yotham and the Campaign of Pekach and Retzin*.

Although the historical framework is missing from *Chronicles*, the story of the wooing of Assyria had to be told. It was to have the most profound effect upon the history of the period. It was Assyria which was shortly to carry the Ten Tribes into exile, and it was Assyria which, during Chizkiahu's days, would sweep inexorably into Judah, only to be stopped by direct Divine intervention at the very gates of Jerusalem (32:21). A careful reading of Isaiahu's prophecies regarding the period makes clear that these events had their genesis in Achaz's advances. They could not be ignored by *Chronicles*.

עַל־מַלְכֵי אַשּׁוּר — *To the Assyrian monarchy.* The translation allows for the plural, מַלְכֵי.

Why is the plural used? The parallel verse in *II Kings* 16:7 has, ... *to Tilgas Pilnesser king of Assur*, using the expected singular.

Chronicles may be making the point which we recognized above. Achaz's approach to Assyria was to bring about that country's involvement in the affairs of Israel for years to come. Other Assyrian kings, equally destructive to Israel's well-being, would follow the one whom Achaz petitioned.

יח אֲדוֹמִים בָּאוּ וַיַּכּוּ בִיהוּדָה וַיִּשְׁבּוּ־שֶׁבִי: וּפְלִשְׁתִּים פָּשְׁטוּ
בְּעָרֵי הַשְּׁפֵלָה וְהַנֶּגֶב לִיהוּדָה וַיִּלְכְּדוּ אֶת־בֵּית־שֶׁמֶשׁ
וְאֶת־אַיָּלוֹן וְאֶת־הַגְּדֵרוֹת וְאֶת־שׂוֹכוֹ וּבְנוֹתֶיהָ וְאֶת־
תִּמְנָה וּבְנוֹתֶיהָ וְאֶת־גִּמְזוֹ וְאֶת־בְּנֹתֶיהָ וַיֵּשְׁבוּ שָׁם:
יט כִּי־הִכְנִיעַ יהוה אֶת־יְהוּדָה בַּעֲבוּר אָחָז מֶלֶךְ־יִשְׂרָאֵל כִּי
כ הִפְרִיעַ בִּיהוּדָה וּמָעוֹל מַעַל בַּיהוָה: וַיָּבֹא עָלָיו תִּלְּגַת
כא פִּלְנְאֶסֶר מֶלֶךְ אַשּׁוּר וַיָּצַר לוֹ וְלֹא חֲזָקוֹ: כִּי־חָלַק אָחָז
אֶת־בֵּית יהוה וְאֶת־בֵּית הַמֶּלֶךְ וְהַשָּׂרִים וַיִּתֵּן לְמֶלֶךְ
כב אַשּׁוּר וְלֹא לְעֶזְרָה לוֹ: וּבְעֵת הָצֵר לוֹ וַיּוֹסֶף לִמְעוֹל
כג בַּיהוָה הוּא הַמֶּלֶךְ אָחָז: וַיִּזְבַּח לֵאלֹהֵי דַרְמֶשֶׂק הַמַּכִּים
בּוֹ וַיֹּאמֶר כִּי אֱלֹהֵי מַלְכֵי־אֲרָם הֵם מַעְזְרִים אוֹתָם לָהֶם
אֲזַבֵּחַ וְיַעְזְרוּנִי וְהֵם הָיוּ־לוֹ לְהַכְשִׁילוֹ וּלְכָל־יִשְׂרָאֵל:
כד וַיֶּאֱסֹף אָחָז אֶת־כְּלֵי בֵית־הָאֱלֹהִים וַיְקַצֵּץ אֶת־כְּלֵי

17. וְעוֹד אֲדוֹמִים בָּאוּ — *Moreover, the Edomites came.* Given the chance, the Edomites would have been eager to take vengeance for their terrible defeat at Amatziahu's hands — see 25:5-16.

וַיַּכּוּ בִיהוּדָה — *Killing Judeans.* The translation follows *Targum.*

18. בְּעָרֵי הַשְּׁפֵלָה וְהַנֶּגֶב — *The cities of the lowlands and of the south of Judah.* It is as though the word *cities* were written twice: *The cities of the lowlands and [the cities] of the south* (*Metzudos*).

19. כִּי הִפְרִיעַ בִּיהוּדָה — *For he had exposed Judah.* פרע means *to uncover* (*Metzudos*, and see *Rashi* to *Exodus* 33:25). Achaz's wickedness allowed the people to commit their sins in public, exposing them to the whole world in their depravity (*Metzudos*).

20. וַיָּבֹא עָלָיו תִּלְּגַת פִּלְנְאֶסֶר — *Tilgath Pilnesser ... came to his aid.* In *II Kings* 16:7 we learn that when Achaz was attacked by Retzin and Pekach, he sent a delegation to Tilgath (*sic*) in order to solicit his aid. We learn that the Assyrian king agreed to help, invaded Aram, sacked the capital Darmesek, and killed Retzin.

Our verse refers to those events. Tilgath Pilnesser came to his aid, in answer to his request (*Mefaresh*).

וַיָּצַר לוֹ וְלֹא חֲזָקוֹ — *But distressed him and thus was of no help to him.* In the long run, the relief from Aram proved to be no help. It gave Assyria a foothold in Judah's affairs, which ultimately proved more dangerous than the threat which it had helped avert (*Metzudos*).

Mefaresh believes that reference is to the huge fortune which Assyria squeezed out of the hapless Achaz, as described in the next verse.

21. ... כִּי־חָלַק אָחָז — *Even though Achaz divided up ...* The translation follows *Metzudos. Mefaresh* (see comm. to previous verse) would render *because.*

וְלֹא לְעֶזְרָה לוֹ — *It was of no help to him.* It did not help him as much as he had hoped. It is true that the threat from Aram was eliminated, but Assyria did nothing to help Achaz recover the cities which the Philistines had taken from him (v. 18) (*Mefaresh*).

22. ... וּבְעֵת הָצֵר לוֹ ... הוּא הַמֶּלֶךְ אָחָז — *Now in the time of his distress ... this selfsame King Achaz.* It might have been supposed that his troubles would turn him back to God (see comm. to next verse) but this was not to be. He remained the same King Achaz throughout.

We may surmise that the significance of this final phrase goes beyond the statement that he simply failed to take the message which was obviously being sent him through his troubles. Rather, it tells us that, throughout, he remained consistent to his perception of his role as king. As we develop in Section II,

*the Edomites came, killing Judeans and carrying away cap-
tives.* 18 *And the Philistines invaded the cities of the lowlands
and of the south of Judah and took Beth-shemash and Aiyalon
and Gederoth, and Soco with its suburbs and Timnah with
its suburbs and Gimzo with its suburbs, and settled there.*
19 *For* HASHEM *brought Judah low because of Achaz king of Ju-
dah, for he had exposed Judah, and had acted treacherous-
ly against* HASHEM. 20 *Tilgath Pilnesser the king of Assyria
came to his aid, but distressed him and thus was of no help
to him.* 21 *Even though Achaz divided up the House of* HASHEM
*and the house of the king and the princes, and gave to the king
of Assyria — it was of no help to him.* 22 *Now in the time of his
distress he acted even more treacherously against* HASHEM, *this
selfsame King Achaz.* 23 *He sacrificed to the gods of Darmesek
who smote him and said, 'Because the gods of the king of Aram
helped them, I will sacrifice to them that they may help me.' But
they were the ruin of him and of all Israel.* 24 *Achaz gathered the
vessels of God's House together, and cut up the vessels of*

Achaz and Menasseh, Achaz devoted his life to waging a vendetta against the Divine Presence in Israel. True to this dream, he could not now turn to God.

23. וַיִּזְבַּח לֵאלֹהֵי דַרְמֶשֶׂק — *He sacrificed to the gods of Darmesek*. In the *Kings'* account, nothing is mentioned of Achaz's idol worship. Instead, the following, in itself, inexplicable story is told. After Tilgath Pilnesser sacked Assyria, Achaz went to meet him at Darmesek. There he saw the altar which the Assyrians used in their idol worship, became enamored of its appearance, and immediately sent a description back to Jerusalem, with orders that the *Kohen Gadol*, Uriahu, erect its replica in the Temple. Solomon's altar was to be shunted to the side.

We discuss the implications of this story, and the reasons why it is not told in the *Chronicles'* account, in Section II, *The Alien Altar*.

הַמַּכִּים בּוֹ — *Who smote him*. This refers to the people — not the gods — of Darmesek (*Metzudos*).

וְהֵם הָיוּ־לוֹ לְהַכְשִׁילוֹ — *But they were the ruin of him* ... The more he served these idols, the more he was punished by God (*Metzudos*).

24. ... וַיֶּאֱסֹף אָחָז ... וַיְקַצֵּץ — *Achaz gathered ... and cut up...* There is a superficial likeness to the parallel verses in *Kings*, but a comparison of the two texts will show that they tell different stories (see chart next page).

In the *Kings'* text, we have a detailed account of the havoc which Achaz wreaked in the Temple. This is missing in *Chronicles*. On the other hand, *Chronicles* begins with the statement that Achaz gathered up the Temple vessels, and ends with the information that he closed the Temple gates. Neither of these two acts has a parallel in *Kings*. Thus, we are persuaded that, in spite of the superficial similarity resulting from the common term וַיְקַצֵּץ, the two accounts talk of different matters.

The *Kings'* account is simply a listing of the atrocities which Achaz perpetrated in the Temple.

Chronicles tells a different story. We address ourselves here to the gathering and cutting up of the sacred utensils. The closing off of the Temple gates will be discussed below.

Avodah Zara 54b interprets the words addressed to Chizkiahu at 29:19 as follows: Achaz had used the sacred vessels of the Temple for idol worship, and had thereby disqualified them from further use in the Temple. When Chizkiahu instituted his re-

בֵּית־הָאֱלֹהִים וַיִּסְגֹּר אֶת־דַּלְתוֹת בֵּית־יְהוָה וַיַּעַשׂ לוֹ
כה מִזְבְּחוֹת בְּכָל־פִּנָּה בִּירוּשָׁלִָם: וּבְכָל־עִיר וָעִיר לִיהוּדָה
עָשָׂה בָמוֹת לְקַטֵּר לֵאלֹהִים אֲחֵרִים וַיַּכְעֵס אֶת־יְהוָה
כו אֱלֹהֵי אֲבֹתָיו: וְיֶתֶר דְּבָרָיו וְכָל־דְּרָכָיו הָרִאשֹׁנִים
וְהָאַחֲרוֹנִים הִנָּם כְּתוּבִים עַל־סֵפֶר מַלְכֵי־יְהוּדָה
כז וְיִשְׂרָאֵל: וַיִּשְׁכַּב אָחָז עִם־אֲבֹתָיו וַיִּקְבְּרֻהוּ בָעִיר

II Chronicles: Chapter 28	*II Kings*: Chapter 16
a. 24. וַיֶּאֱסֹף אָחָז אֶת־כְּלֵי בֵית־הָאֱלֹהִים, *Achaz gathered the vessels of God's House together,*	a.
b. וַיְקַצֵּץ אֶת־כְּלֵי בֵית־הָאֱלֹהִים, *and cut up the vessels of God's House.*	b. 17. וַיְקַצֵּץ הַמֶּלֶךְ אָחָז אֶת־הַמִּסְגְּרוֹת הַמְּכֹנוֹת וַיָּסַר מֵעֲלֵיהֶם אֶת־הַכִּיֹּר וְאֶת־הַיָּם הוֹרִד מֵעַל הַבָּקָר הַנְּחֹשֶׁת אֲשֶׁר תַּחְתֶּיהָ וַיִּתֵּן אֹתוֹ עַל מַרְצֶפֶת אֲבָנִים וְאֶת־מוּסַךְ הַשַּׁבָּת ... וְאֶת־מְבוֹא הַמֶּלֶךְ ..., *King Achaz cut down the stands of the lavers and removed the laver from them and took down the basin from the copper cattle which were beneath it and set it upon a stone pavement. And the Sabbath shelter ... and the king's entrance ...*
c. ... וַיִּסְגֹּר אֶת־דַּלְתוֹת בֵּית־ה׳ וַיַּעַשׂ לוֹ מִזְבְּחוֹת *He closed the doors of* HASHEM*'s House and erected altars ...*	c.

forms, these defiled vessels had to be buried and new ones made in their place. The Talmud wonders how Achaz could have disqualified the vessels simply by using them for idol worship. This seems to contradict the established rule that no man can change the halachic standing of any object which he does not own [אֵין אָדָם אוֹסֵר דָּבָר שֶׁאֵינוֹ שֶׁלּוֹ]. Manifestly, Achaz did not own the Temple utensils. The solution offered is that Achaz must have performed some act which changed their physical state, and this would enable him to disqualify even something that he did not own.

We suspect that the Talmud has our verse in mind. Achaz *cut up* the Temple vessels in order to withdraw them from their sacred status and to dedicate them to the idol worship for which he intended them.

But if Achaz was absolutely wicked and cared nothing for the laws of the Torah, why would he first want to deprive the vessels of their sacred status? What prevented him from simply using them as they were?

This would seem to confirm the thesis which we developed in Section II, *The Alien Altar*. Achaz was intent upon withdrawing himself from a direct relationship to God, and to establish the new reality; henceforth, he was to be subject to intermediaries whom he would now have to placate. For this reason he had built a new throne in the Temple Court, and for this reason he had brought in the new altar. The disqualification of the sacred vessels was a part of the same pattern. These vessels had been used in the Divine service which had been appropriate before he had subordinated himself to the Assyrian king. He would withdraw them, and substitute others, more appropriate to the new realities.

If this interpretation is correct, we would have expected the cutting up of the vessels to be mentioned in *Kings*, rather than in *Chronicles* which does not even tell the story of the

*HASHEM's House. He closed the doors of HASHEM's House
and erected altars in every corner of Jerusalem.* [25] *And in ev-
ery city of Judah he made bamos to burn incense to other gods,
and angered HASHEM the God of his fathers.* [26] *The rest of his
matters and all his ways, the earlier and the latter, behold
they are recorded in the Book of the Kings of Judah and Israel.*
[27] *Achaz lay with his fathers and they buried him in the city,*

alien altar, for reasons discussed in Section II. We must assume that it was omitted from *Kings* for the same reasons that the closing off of the Temple gates was not mentioned there — see below.

וַיְקַצֵּץ אֶת־כְּלֵי בֵית־הָאֱלֹהִים — *And cut up the vessels of God's House.* He peeled off their golden overlay (*Metzudos*).

וַיִּסְגֹּר אֶת־דַּלְתוֹת בֵּית־ה׳ — *He closed the doors of HASHEM's House. Sanhedrin* 103b teaches that Achaz stopped the Divine service [בִּטֵּל אֶת הָעֲבוֹדָה]. We assume that this tradition is based on our verse. Confronted with closed doors, the people would turn away from the Holy Temple and go, instead, to the many altars which Achaz had put up *in all the corners of Jerusalem* (*Mefaresh* to 33:23).

It seems clear that some modest form of Divine service continued even after the closing of the Temple doors. The Talmud sees this depredation as only the beginning of a trend: Achaz stopped the Temple service ... Menasseh ... tore down the altar, Amon ... caused spider webs to cover the altar [from disuse]. To Amon's contribution, *Rashi* remarks: He eliminated the Temple service *completely.* The implication is that the earlier two kings had still tolerated some form of Divine service.

Kings does not record that Achaz closed the Temple gates. We may surmise that it happened at the very end of his reign and that it therefore made no significant mark on the daily lives of the people. Achaz was succeeded by Chizkiahu who immediately reversed all the evil that his father had perpetrated. The closing of the gates would be important only in that it laid the groundwork for further excesses on the part of Menasseh and Amon — Section II, *Achaz and Menasseh.* In any case, it must have happened some time after the events described in *Kings,* since Achaz would certainly not have made all the dispositions regarding the use of the new altar if his intention would have been to close down the Temple altogether.

25. בָּמוֹת לְקַטֵּר לֵאלֹהִים אֲחֵרִים — *Bamos to burn incense to other gods.* See comm. to v. 4.

וַיַּכְעֵס אֶת־ה׳ ... — *And angered HASHEM ... Chronicles* does not say this of any other king, including Menasseh. This would tend to confirm our thinking in Section II, *Achaz and Menasseh,* that from the *Chronicles'* perspective, Achaz — because he laid the groundwork for the wickedness of later generations — was the worst of the kings.

26. וְיֶתֶר דְּבָרָיו וְכָל־דְּרָכָיו ... — *The rest of his matters and all his ways.* The regular formula is that the דְּבָרִים of such and such a king are recorded in the various chronicles. *Chronicles* adds the word דֶּרֶךְ in the case of Aviah (13:22), Yotham (27:7) and here.

דֶּרֶךְ, from דָּרַךְ, *to step upon,* describes a person's way of life (see countless examples in *Proverbs* — an example is 21:2 there), while דָּבָר, a more general term, could be used for *events* (note: דִּבְרֵי הַיָּמִים). We may thus surmise that, where both are used, the latter describes the events of his reign while the former refers to the path which he, as a person, trod.

We may hazard the following suggestions based on our perception of the reigns of these three kings.

1. Aviah: In Section II to ch. 13, *Analysis of Aviah's Reign,* we analyzed the different approaches of *Kings* and *Chronicles* to Aviah. We concluded that, from the point of view of the monarchy, his reign was a total negative, and that therefore, *Kings* from its perspective, views him without any intrinsic worth, and as simply a link in the Davidic dynasty. *Chronicles,* by contrast, sees him as the person who spelled out for all generations the sole legitimacy of David's line as repository of Israel's future. As a man, if not as king, he blazed *a path* which *Chronicles* found important to record.

2. Yotham: In prefatory remarks to ch. 27, we found Yotham unique in Israel's history as

כט בִּירוּשָׁלַ֫ם כִּ֣י לֹ֣א הֱבִיאֻ֔הוּ לְקִבְרֵ֖י מַלְכֵ֣י יִשְׂרָאֵ֑ל וַיִּמְלֹ֛ךְ
א־ב א יְחִזְקִיָּ֥הוּ בְנ֖וֹ תַּחְתָּֽיו׃ יְחִזְקִיָּ֣הוּ מָלַ֗ךְ בֶּן־עֶשְׂרִ֤ים
וְחָמֵשׁ֙ שָׁנָ֔ה וְעֶשְׂרִ֤ים וָתֵ֙שַׁע֙ שָׁנָ֔ה מָלַ֖ךְ בִּירוּשָׁלָ֑͏ִם וְשֵׁ֣ם
ב אִמּ֔וֹ אֲבִיָּ֖ה בַּת־זְכַרְיָֽהוּ׃ וַיַּ֥עַשׂ הַיָּשָׁ֖ר בְּעֵינֵ֣י יהוָ֑ה כְּכֹ֥ל

the affirmer of eternity in the face of what appeared to be certain stagnation and death. His personal righteousness is such that he can, as it were, carry Israel upon his own shoulders up to the coming of the Messiah. He, too, was a *trail*blazer, his *path* through life, of eternal significance.

3. Achaz, too, laid down a new *path*. This one in the opposite direction. He proclaimed a world view which sees the driving of the Divine Presence from Israel as the focus of its aims. Others among Judah's kings would one day walk down that sorry road. He was the one who laid it.

27. בָּעִיר בִּירוּשָׁלַם כִּי לֹא הֱבִיאֻהוּ לְקִבְרֵי מַלְכֵי יִשְׂרָאֵל — *In the city, in Jerusalem, for they did not bring him into the sepulchers of the kings of Israel. II Kings* 16:20 has ... *and he was buried with his fathers in the City of David.*

Mikra UMassores suggests the following solution: The Mishnah in *Pesachim* (4:9) teaches that — in order to debase his father — Chizkiahu dragged his *bones* through the streets on a stretcher of ropes. Now *Tosafos Yom Tov* thinks that the expression *bones* indicates that this was not done at the original burial but that after the flesh had been worn away, the bones were exhumed and subjected to this indignity. But he is at a loss to explain why Chizkiahu would have exhumed his father's bones.

Mikra UMassores suggests the following rationale. According to *Sanhedrin* 96a, a miracle occurred on the day that Achaz died. The day was curtailed and lasted only two hours. This, so that there would be no time to bury the wicked Achaz with honor or to eulogize him. The halachah forbids a dead body to remain in Jerusalem overnight and so Achaz was hastily buried in a temporary grave in Jerusalem — away from the royal sepulchers. But even criminals who were executed for their crimes and buried in special graves are eventually moved in order to restore them to their family burial grounds (*Sanhedrin* 46a and *Rashi* there.) For this reason Chizkiahu would have decided at some point to exhume Achaz and restore him to the royal sepulchers. Thus, originally Achaz was buried *away* from his fathers (our verse) but later *with* them (*Kings*).

The term, *kings of Israel*, is unexpected since Achaz was king of Judah. *Metzudos* explains that the term *Israel* is also appropriate since David and Solomon, in whose reign the entire people had still been unified, were also buried there.

But why, just here, are we concerned with David and Solomon?

This would tend to confirm the thesis which we have suggested throughout the comm. to this chapter. The essence of Achaz's evil was his rejection of his Davidic ancestry; he was to be *servant and son* of the Assyrian Tiglath Pilnesser. It was particularly David and Solomon whose lineage he had spurned, and who would have been offended by his burial in the sepulcher of the kings.

XXIX

◆§ Chizkiahu's Reign

Chizkiahu's confrontation with the Assyrian forces, taking up no less than sixty-eight verses, is the high point of the *Kings'* account of his reign. *Chronicles* devotes just twenty-one verses to this confrontation. By contrast, it describes the cleansing of the Temple and the restoration of the sacrificial service in eighty-two verses. *Kings* makes no mention at all of these two matters.

Why is the Temple so important in the *Chronicles'* scheme, and why does *Kings* not share this perspective?

Sanhedrin 94a teaches that Chizkiahu was destined to become the Messiah.

Now when Isaiah talks of the Messiah's descent from the Davidic line he says: *A rod shall come out of Jesse's stem and a shoot will be produced from his roots* (*Isaiah* 11:1). The terms *stem* and *root* take us back to the very beginnings of the line and imply that the Messiah — although separated from David by many generations — will be considered to be the *David* of his generation. Thus, when Ezekiel sees into the Messianic future he looks forward to the time when God will ... *appoint over them a single shepherd ... My servant David ... and I, HASHEM, will be God to them and My servant David a prince among them* (*Ezekiel* 34:23-24).

29
1-2

in Jerusalem, for they did not bring him into the sepulchers of the kings of Israel. Chizkiahu his son reigned in his stead.

Chizkiahu began to reign when he was twenty five years old, and reigned for twenty-nine years in Jerusalem. His mother's name was Aviah the daughter of Zechariahu. 2 *He did that which was right in the eyes of HASHEM, according to all that*

Indeed, we find nuances in the *Chronicles'* account which indicate such a perception:

When Chizkiahu dies, he is buried not ... *in the City of David*, nor ... *in the sepulchers of the kings*, as the other kings of the Davidic line had been, but *in the choicest of the sepulchers of David's sons*, which, according to *Bava Kama* 16b, means that he was buried immediately next to David and Solomon. Again, the text (29:26) talks of ... *the instruments of David* being used in the music which was played in the Temple at Chizkiahu's behest. *Bamidbar Rabbah* 15:11 derives from this wording that these were instruments which only David himself had been allowed to play. How then could Chizkiahu have used them?

Surely, because he was the authentic *David* of his generation.

In Overview to *I Chronicles*, *David the King and David the Man* (p. xlii), we have seen that the main concern of *Chronicles* is the transcendent David whose life revolved about the building of the Temple. It is entirely logical for *Chronicles* to place Chizkiahu's activities in cleansing the Temple precincts and in re-establishing the sacrificial service into the center of its narrative. It is that, more than any of the other things which Chizkiahu did, which identifies him with the eternal *David*. *Kings*, from its perspective of presenting the here and now of history, sees no particular significance in the cleansing of the Temple, and places the confrontation with Syria at the center of its concerns.

See Section II, *Chizkiahu in Isaiah and Rabbinical Sources*, for a discussion of the picture of this great king, drawn in sources other than the Books of *Kings* and *Chronicles*.

1. יְחִזְקִיָּהוּ מָלַךְ — *Chizkiahu began to reign ...* The formulation is unique. The parallel verse in *Kings* has the normal form: *He was twenty-five years old when he became king ...*

Perhaps Chizkiahu's unique position among Judah's kings can explain the change. If the regular formula had been used, no special tone would have been set. The more festive formulation generates a sense of expectation: *Chizkiahu*, [for whom, as the potential Messiah, the world had been waiting,] *began to reign...*

2. וַיַּעַשׂ הַיָּשָׁר ... כְּכֹל אֲשֶׁר־עָשָׂה דָּוִיד אָבִיו — *He did that which was right ... according to all that David his father had done.* This formulation does not recur in *Chronicles*.[1]

Can we define the meaning more precisely?

A possible source for a correct understanding might be *I Kings* 11:38. There, in God's words to Solomon, we read: וְהָיָה אִם־תִּשְׁמַע אֶת־כָּל־אֲשֶׁר אֲצַוֶּךָ וְהָלַכְתָּ בִדְרָכַי וְעָשִׂיתָ הַיָּשָׁר בְּעֵינַי לִשְׁמוֹר חֻקּוֹתַי וּמִצְוֹתַי כַּאֲשֶׁר עָשָׂה דָּוִד עַבְדִּי. In this sentence, the phrase וְעָשִׂיתָ הַיָּשָׁר בְּעֵינַי is defined by לִשְׁמוֹר חֻקּוֹתַי וּמִצְוֹתַי. Doing *that which is right* in God's eyes, as David had done, is *keeping His statutes and commandments*.

Thus our verse might well mean: *He did that which was right in the eyes of HASHEM* [in that he kept His statutes and commandments] *according to all that David his father had done.*

But if this is the meaning which *Chronicles* attaches to the phrase, then it is difficult to see why, at 14:1, it leaves out the phrase, ... *like his father, David*, as we have pointed out in the fn.

Rather, it would appear as we suggested in comm. there that in *Chronicles'* usage, the phrase is not meant to be an assessment of the reign as a whole, but introduces that which follows immediately upon it. For that reason, ... *like his father, David* would have been inappropriate at 14:1, since the actions ascribed to Asa, immediately following upon

1.We have references to *walking before HASHEM as David your father had done* (7:17); *going in the ways of David and Solomon* (11:17); *going in the earlier ways of David his father* (17:3); and *going in the ways of David, his father* (34:2).

It is particularly striking that, in the one case in which *Kings* has the formulation *Asa did that which was right, like his father David* (*I Kings* 15:11), *Chronicles* (14:1) leaves out the words ... *like his father David*.

ג אֲשֶׁר־עָשָׂה דָּוִיד אָבִיו׃ הוּא בַשָּׁנָה הָרִאשׁוֹנָה לְמָלְכוֹ
בַּחֹדֶשׁ הָרִאשׁוֹן פָּתַח אֶת־דַּלְתוֹת בֵּית־יהוה וַיְחַזְּקֵם׃
ד וַיָּבֵא אֶת־הַכֹּהֲנִים וְאֶת־הַלְוִיִּם וַיַּאַסְפֵם לִרְחוֹב הַמִּזְרָח׃
ה וַיֹּאמֶר לָהֶם שְׁמָעוּנִי הַלְוִיִּם עַתָּה הִתְקַדְּשׁוּ וְקַדְּשׁוּ
אֶת־בֵּית יהוה אֱלֹהֵי אֲבֹתֵיכֶם וְהוֹצִיאוּ אֶת־הַנִּדָּה
ו מִן־הַקֹּדֶשׁ׃ כִּי־מָעֲלוּ אֲבֹתֵינוּ וְעָשׂוּ הָרַע בְּעֵינֵי יהוה־
אֱלֹהֵינוּ וַיַּעַזְבֻהוּ וַיַּסֵּבּוּ פְנֵיהֶם מִמִּשְׁכַּן יהוה וַיִּתְּנוּ־עֹרֶף׃
ז גַּם סָגְרוּ דַּלְתוֹת הָאוּלָם וַיְכַבּוּ אֶת־הַנֵּרוֹת וּקְטֹרֶת לֹא

this sentence, do not, in any way, parallel David's actions.

Here, by contrast, the phrase is entirely apt as we worked out in the prefatory remarks. We move immediately to Chizkiahu's activities on behalf of the Temple service. These are precisely those aspects of his reign which made him into the *David* of his generation.

3. הוּא בַשָּׁנָה הָרִאשׁוֹנָה ... פָּתַח ... — *He, in the first year ... opened ...* The syntax is highly unusual. We would have expected either: הוּא פָּתַח אֶת דַּלְתוֹת ... בַּשָּׁנָה ..., which would have paralleled the formulation in *Kings*: הוּא הֵסִיר אֶת־הַבָּמוֹת (*II Kings* 18:4); or בַּשָּׁנָה הָרִאשׁוֹנָה ... פָּתַח. Why should the dating of the events interrupt between subject and predicate?

If our understanding of the previous verse is correct, we may have an explanation. Burdened or exhilarated by the knowledge that he was to be the *David* of his generation, Chizkiahu threw himself into the task at hand with speed and determination. *He* — the chosen one — *in the first year* — that is, without any hesitation — shouldered his destiny.

הוּא בַשָּׁנָה הָרִאשׁוֹנָה לְמָלְכוֹ בַּחֹדֶשׁ הָרִאשׁוֹן — *He, in the first year of his reign, in the first month.* The events described in this chapter took place in *Nissan* of the first year of Chizkiahu's reign.

In the tradition of the Sages, the years of Jewish kings are always dated from the first of *Nissan*. If, for example, a king ascended the throne in *Adar*, then his second year would begin on the first of *Nissan*, even though he may have actually reigned only a single day.

Clearly, then, Chizkiahu must have become king in this same *Nissan*. Had he ascended the throne even one day earlier, *Nissan* would have fallen in his second, not his first, year.

But, in the tradition of the Sages, he was already king on the thirtieth day of the previous *Adar*. For it was on that day that, after the *Sanhedrin* had already proclaimed it to be the first of *Nissan*, he decided to override their decision, and to proclaim a leap year (*Sanhedrin* 12a).

The result of this decision was that the day would now be considered as the thirtieth of *Adar* instead of the first of *Nissan*, that the whole of the following month would be an *Adar Sheni*, and that *Nissan* would come a month later than it would have come, had the decision of the *Sanhedrin* stood.

In Chizkiahu's view, when that *Nissan* would have come, it would have begun the second year of his reign.

The Sages, as the Talmud reports the tradition, did not agree with Chizkiahu. Since *Nissan* had already been declared, or even if it had not yet been declared, since it was the day upon which it could have been declared, it was too late to add another month to the old year. They considered his declaration of a leap year void.

If we postulate that he became king on that disputed thirtieth of *Adar*, then, in their opinion, this would be the first of *Nissan* of his *first* year.

By giving the date as the first of *Nissan* of Chizkiahu's first year, the writer of *Chronicles* is declaring himself to be of the opinion of the Sages who disagreed with Chizkiahu. In Chizkiahu's own opinion, this day should have been called the thirtieth of *Adar* of his first year (*Margalios HaYam*).

This insight will be used extensively in the comm. to the next chapter.

פָּתַח אֶת־דַּלְתוֹת בֵּית־ה׳ — *Opened the portals of the House of* HASHEM. In v. 24 of the previous chapter we learned how Achaz, as part of his vendetta against the Divine Presence in Israel, had closed the gates of the Temple Court. Chizkiahu now reopened them (*Metzudos*).

וַיְחַזְּקֵם — *And repaired them*. V. 24 of the previous chapter talked of Achaz *cutting up* the Temple utensils. The gates would now

29
3-7

David his father had done. [3] He, in the first year of his reign, in the first month, opened the portals of the House of HASHEM and repaired them. [4] He brought the Kohanim and the Levites and gathered them together on the eastern plaza. [5] He said to them, 'Listen to me, O Levites! Now cleanse yourselves, and cleanse the House of HASHEM the God of your fathers, and take out the abomination from the Sanctuary. [6] For our fathers dealt falsely and did evil in the eyes of HASHEM our God, and forsook Him. They averted their faces from HASHEM's dwelling place, and turned their backs. [7] Also they closed the doors of the Entrance Hall thus extinguishing the lamps and preventing the in-

require repair (*Mefaresh*).

4. אֶת־הַכֹּהֲנִים וְאֶת־הַלְוִיִּם — *The Kohanim and the Levites*. From vs. 12-16 it is evident that the Levites were charged with cleansing the outer parts of the Temple, while the *Kohanim* attended to the Sanctuary.

לִרְחוֹב הַמִּזְרָח — *On the eastern plaza*. An area situated on the Temple mount (*Metzudos*).

5. הִתְקַדְּשׁוּ — *Cleanse yourselves*. What type of *cleansing* was required here? For the *Kohanim* to enter the Sanctuary (v. 16) they would have needed to wash hands and feet [קִדּוּשׁ יָדַיִם וְרַגְלַיִם] (*Kelim* 1:9). This, in addition to immersion in the mikveh, which would have been required of the Levites also, since no one — even if ritually clean — was permitted to enter the Temple courtyard without prior immersion (*Yoma* 30a and *Rashi* there).

But prior to this, they would have had to wait seven days, and be sprinkled with the ashes of the red heifer on the third and seventh day. This, because, during the time that Achaz had locked up the Temple, they would have been more lax about coming into contact with dead bodies, and the halachah requires that, unless one is absolutely certain that there was no such contact, the seven-day wait and the sprinkling be observed before entering the Temple precincts (*Rambam, Avos HaTumah* 13:3). This explains the seven-day wait mentioned in v. 17.

All these levels of *cleansing* would be included in the meaning of our term (*Mikra UMassores*).

וְהוֹצִיאוּ אֶת־הַנִּדָּה — *And take out the abomination*. נדה means *to move*; thus, נִדָּה, that which ought to be moved away (*Metzudos*), or, something disgusting or unclean (*Radak* in *Sefer HaShorashim*). In this case it refers to the idolatrous paraphernalia which Achaz had introduced into the Temple (*Radak*).

That idols should be described as something unclean is understandable. But the metaphor might just as well have been a dead body, which is also ritually unclean. נִדָּה with its association with the menstrual flow was chosen, in order to awaken a greater sense of aversion (*Mefaresh*).

6. כִּי־מָעֲלוּ אֲבֹתֵינוּ — *For our fathers dealt falsely*. The language of the exhortation implies that the people allowed themselves to be led astray by Achaz. The fault was not solely his.

וַיַּסֵּבּוּ פְנֵיהֶם מִמִּשְׁכַּן ה׳ — *They averted their faces from HASHEM's dwelling place*. They refused to see God's sanctuary as the focus of their prayers (*Metzudos*).

It is noteworthy that the Temple here is referred to as God's מִשְׁכָּן, His *habitation*, or the resting place of His שְׁכִינָה, *Divine Presence*. Nowhere else does *Chronicles* use this term; it is always, מִקְדָּשׁ, *Sanctuary* [see *I Chronicles* 22:19 and 28:10 and *II Chronicles* 20:8, 26:18, 29:21].

The term מִשְׁכָּן is particularly apt in the context of a description of Achaz's depredations. We saw throughout the previous chapter that the aim of his life was to drive the שְׁכִינָה away from Israel. The people who followed his lead turned their faces away from the Temple precisely because it was the dwelling place of the Divine Presence.

7. גַּם סָגְרוּ דַּלְתוֹת הָאוּלָם — *Also they closed the doors of the Entrance Hall*. The אולם is the Entrance Hall which leads into the Sanctuary in which the menorah and the golden altar stood. Once these doors were closed off, the *Kohanim* were unable to enter, the menorah remained unlit, the golden altar, bare of incense.

But we saw at 28:24 that Achaz closed off

ח הִקְטִירוּ וְעֹלָה לֹא־הֶעֱלוּ בַקֹּדֶשׁ לֵאלֹהֵי יִשְׂרָאֵל: וַיְהִי
°לְזַעֲוָה ק׳ קֶצֶף יהוה עַל־יְהוּדָה וִירוּשָׁלִָם וַיִּתְּנֵם °לזועה לְשַׁמָּה
ט וְלִשְׁרֵקָה כַּאֲשֶׁר אַתֶּם רֹאִים בְּעֵינֵיכֶם: וְהִנֵּה נָפְלוּ
אֲבוֹתֵינוּ בֶּחָרֶב וּבָנֵינוּ וּבְנוֹתֵינוּ וְנָשֵׁינוּ בַּשְּׁבִי עַל־
י זֹאת: עַתָּה עִם־לְבָבִי לִכְרוֹת בְּרִית לַיהוה אֱלֹהֵי יִשְׂרָאֵל
יא וְיָשֹׁב מִמֶּנּוּ חֲרוֹן אַפּוֹ: בָּנַי עַתָּה אַל־תִּשָּׁלוּ כִּי־בָכֶם בָּחַר

the entire Temple area. That itself would have made it impossible to light the menorah or to bring the incense. Why was it necessary to lock up the Entrance Hall to the Sanctuary building?

We may suggest the following: At 28:24 we noted that Achaz's depredations did not all take place at the same time. At the time when he had the new altar erected and ordered that the daily services be performed on it, he had obviously not yet closed off the Temple. Thus, it is also possible that, at an earlier stage, he closed up the Sanctuary [our verse] making it impossible to perform the lighting of the menorah and the burning of the incense, and only later decided to close the entire Temple.

For another possibility — that even after Achaz closed the Temple gates, some inconspicuous and modest form of Divine worship continued there — see comm to 28:24. This granted, it made sense for Achaz, if indeed he wanted to stop the lighting of the menorah and the offering up of incense, to make access to the Sanctuary impossible.

וְעֹלָה לֹא־הֶעֱלוּ בַקֹּדֶשׁ ... — *They did not bring up burnt offerings in the holy place*. This was not the result of the closing of the doors. The burnt offerings were brought on the copper altar which stood in the courtyard. Reference here is presumably to the daily sacrifices [תְּמִידִים] with which the daily service began and ended. At some time during his reign Achaz stopped the bringing of these burnt offerings.

8. וַיְהִי קֶצֶף ה׳ — *So HASHEM became angry ....* The implication is clear. God's anger and the resulting defeats upon the battlefield (v. 9) came about because of the abandonment of the sacrificial service. As if to stress this truth v. 9 adds the words על זאת, *because of this*.

But a careful reading of 28:1-8 seems to indicate that it was Achaz's blatant idol worship that underlay the military debacles.

Again, there are the terrible failings in every aspect of social and religious life, for which Isaiah so mercilessly castigates Judah. Certainly most of these had their roots in the evil influence of Achaz. Were these not enough to cause the military defeats?

Chizkiahu was the *David* of his generation. We saw in prefatory remarks to this chapter that David saw the building of the Temple, and the establishment and organization of its rituals, as central to his kingship.

Why?

In the view of the Sages, Israel's eternity — hallmark of David's Messianic destiny — is inextricably bound up with the concept of the sacrificial service in the Temple.

After having been promised that the Holy Land would be given him as an inheritance, Abraham asked God, *My Lord, HASHEM G-d, whereby shall I know that I am to inherit it?* (*Genesis* 15:8). To this, God replied that Abraham was to take certain animals and prepare them for the Covenant between the Parts.

Midrash Rabbah, Genesis 44:14, as understood by *Maharal* in *Gevuros HaShem*, explains as follows: Abraham had, of course, not doubted God's words. His need for a sign derived not from a need to have the gift confirmed, but from his puzzlement that it had been given for all eternity. What would guarantee, he wondered, that, generations later, his children might not sin and thus lose their rights to the Holy Land? God's answer was that the guarantee lay in the concept of the sacrificial services which the Torah provides for Abraham's children. The idea of an atoning sacrifice is based upon the assumption that sin cannot erode, nor indeed touch, an inner core of sanctity which lies at the essence of the Jewish soul. The Holy Land will never be completely lost because sin can never, ultimately, destroy the sanctity of the Jewish people.

Thus is Israel's eternity tied to the concept of the sacrifice.

Midrash Chaseiros ViYeseiros interprets our section in much the same vein. The Midrash starts out from the etymological assertion that the word for sacrifice, קָרְבָּן, is related to the

cense from being offered. They did not bring up burnt offerings in
the holy place, to the God of Israel. [8] *So* HASHEM *became angry with*
Judah and Jerusalem, and caused them to become an object of
horror, of appallment and of hissing as you can see with your eyes.
[9] *For behold our fathers have fallen by the sword, and our sons and*
our daughters and our wives are in captivity for this.
[10] *Now it is my intention to undertake a covenantal obligation to*
HASHEM, *God of Israel, that His fierce anger may be turned away*
from us. [11] *My sons, now be not apathetic, for* HASHEM *has chosen*

idea of קְרָב, *battle*. This, because ... *the sacrifice which Israel brings is its weapon of war*. Thus, the Midrash continues, Israel's successes in battle are contingent upon the bringing of sacrifices. Because of this, the closing of the Temple gates (v.7) resulted in military defeat (v. 9).

If the sacrifices are Israel's *weapon*, then this can only be for the reasons given by *Maharal*. They point to the indestructible core which defines Israel's roles vis-a-vis God and man.

It is true that, in an immediate sense, Israel was defeated in battle because of the idol worship described in ch. 28. But from a *Davidic* perspective that is not enough to explain the debacles. Chizkiahu delves beneath the surface, and finds a more deeply rooted and malignant malaise. By abandoning the Divine sacrificial service Achaz was attempting to undermine the entire relationship between God and Israel. It was this sub-surface reality which Chizkiahu addresses.

לְזַעֲוָה — *To become an object of horror*. The basic meaning is *a trembling*. Anyone who sees their fate trembles lest a similar one befall him (*Metzudos*).

לְשַׁמָּה וְלִשְׁרֵקָה — *Of appallment and of hissing*. שַׁמָּה from שמם, *to be desolate*; thus, to be without help in solving a problem, and therefore, remain surprised, or in the case of something shocking, *to be appalled*.

שרק, *to hiss*, describes the reaction of one who gloats over another's misfortune. Thus, in *Eichah* 2:15 and 16: *All who pass along the way . . . hiss . . . Could this be the city that was called Perfect in Beauty, Joy of all the Earth. All your enemies ... hiss ... They say: We have devoured her! Indeed, this is the day we have longed for; we have actually seen it!'*

These expressions are particularly apt here. Since Solomon had built the Temple, Israel had manifestly been different than all the neighboring nations. The Divine Presence among them had unmistakably marked them as a kingdom of *Kohanim* and a holy people. With what a mixture of appallment and gloating must Achaz's reign have been greeted. Here at last Israel's special status was shown to have been nothing but an outer shell. Achaz had succeeded in dragging his people down to the level of the savage and primitive people who surrounded them.

9. בַּשְּׁבִי — *In captivity* . . . Our loved ones are even now in captivity (*Metzudos*). See 28:17.

עַל־זֹאת — *For this*. According to *Midrash Tanchuma, Tetzaveh* 15, this refers to the elimination of the incense offering mentioned in v. 7. See Section II to ch. 28, *Achaz and Menasseh*, for a discussion.

10. לִכְרוֹת בְּרִית — *To undertake a covenantal obligation to* HASHEM. . . In Section II to ch. 23, *The King and the Son of the King*, we demonstrated that בְּרִית followed by the preposition ל signifies the undertaking of an obligation. In the absence of any other indication, we assume that, in this passage, it refers to the cleansing of the Temple described in the following verses.

This would explain Chizkiahu's charge to the Levites in the next verse. Apart from the general obligation to remove the contaminating uncleanliness from the Temple precincts, they were bound by a covenant to do so. There could be no negligence in the performance of such a duty.

The בְּרִית of our verse is thus analogous with the one in *Ezra* 10:3 which is also followed by the preposition . . .לְ. There, its purpose was to guarantee the removal of the foreign wives; here, it obligated the Levites to clean the Temple.

11. אַל־תִּשָּׁלוּ — *Be not apathetic*. Now, that we are bound by covenant. See comm. to verse above.

We have rendered *apathetic* in accordance with *Targum* who renders תִּתְרַשְּׁלוּן, which is generally used for רפה, *to relax one's efforts*.

יהוה לַעֲמֹד לְפָנָיו לְשָׁרְתוֹ וְלִהְיוֹת לוֹ מְשָׁרְתִים
יב וּמַקְטִרִים׃ וַיָּקֻמוּ הַלְוִיִּם מַחַת בֶּן־עֲמָשַׂי וְיוֹאֵל בֶּן־
עֲזַרְיָהוּ מִן־בְּנֵי הַקְּהָתִי וּמִן־בְּנֵי מְרָרִי קִישׁ בֶּן־עַבְדִּי
וַעֲזַרְיָהוּ בֶּן־יְהַלֶּלְאֵל וּמִן־הַגֵּרְשֻׁנִּי יוֹאָח בֶּן־זִמָּה וְעֵדֶן
יג בֶּן־יוֹאָח׃ וּמִן־בְּנֵי אֱלִיצָפָן שִׁמְרִי °ויעואל וּמִן־בְּנֵי אָסָף °וִיעִיאֵל ק׳
יד זְכַרְיָהוּ וּמַתַּנְיָהוּ׃ וּמִן־בְּנֵי הֵימָן °יחואל וְשִׁמְעִי °יְחִיאֵל ק׳
טו וּמִן־בְּנֵי יְדוּתוּן שְׁמַעְיָה וְעֻזִּיאֵל׃ וַיַּאַסְפוּ אֶת־אֲחֵיהֶם
וַיִּתְקַדְּשׁוּ וַיָּבֹאוּ כְמִצְוַת־הַמֶּלֶךְ בְּדִבְרֵי יהוה לְטַהֵר בֵּית
טז יהוה׃ וַיָּבֹאוּ הַכֹּהֲנִים לִפְנִימָה בֵית־יהוה לְטַהֵר וַיּוֹצִיאוּ
אֵת כָּל־הַטֻּמְאָה אֲשֶׁר מָצְאוּ בְּהֵיכַל יהוה לַחֲצַר בֵּית
יז יהוה וַיְקַבְּלוּ הַלְוִיִּם לְהוֹצִיא לְנַחַל־קִדְרוֹן חוּצָה׃ וַיָּחֵלּוּ
בְּאֶחָד לַחֹדֶשׁ הָרִאשׁוֹן לְקַדֵּשׁ וּבְיוֹם שְׁמוֹנָה לַחֹדֶשׁ בָּאוּ
לְאוּלָם יהוה וַיְקַדְּשׁוּ אֶת־בֵּית־יהוה לְיָמִים שְׁמוֹנָה

Ralbag suggests *to let go, turn away* or *to be lazy; Metzudos, to be careless* or *forgetful*.

לְשָׁרְתוֹ — *To serve Him*. To avoid the apparent redundancy of the next phrase, ... *and to be ministrants to Him*, we suggest that *to serve Him* refers to the cleansing of the Temple. It has fallen to your lot to be the ones privileged to restore the Temple to its purity and sanctity. Once that is done it will be you who are to be the ministrants and the ones who are to offer up.

Malbim avoids the redundancy by explaining that לְשָׁרְתוֹ describes the function of the Levites, while וְלִהְיוֹת לוֹ מְשָׁרְתִים of the latter part of the verse refers to the *Kohanim*.

12-14. Seven different groups of Levites are mentioned. V. 12 has two each from the three great Levite families, Gershon, Kehath and Merrari.

V. 13 mentions Elitzaphan as a family head — see comm. to *I Chronicles* 15:8.

In the last part of v. 13 and in v. 14 the descendants of the three chief choristers are mentioned. Asaph and Heiman are familiar from *I Chronicles* ch. 6 and other places. Eithan, the third chief chorister mentioned in *I Chronicles* ch. 6, was replaced by Yeduthun in *I Chronicles* 16:41 — see comm. there.

Perhaps the families of the choristers are mentioned separately here — although they themselves are also scions of the three great Levite families, Gershon, Kehath and Merrari — because vs. 25-27 make a special point of the musical accompaniment to the sacrifices brought by Chizkiahu.

15. וַיַּאַסְפוּ אֶת־אֲחֵיהֶם — *They gathered their brothers*. When v. 4 said that Chizkiahu brought the Levites to *the eastern plaza*, this apparently referred to those who were mentioned by name in v. 12-14. Now these gathered their families to aid in the gigantic task of cleansing the Temple.

וַיִּתְקַדְּשׁוּ — *And cleansed themselves*. At v. 5 Chizkiahu had told the *Kohanim* and the Levites to cleanse themselves. Here we are told that they did so.

כְמִצְוַת־הַמֶּלֶךְ בְּדִבְרֵי ה׳ — *By command of the king in the matters of* HASHEM. The translation follows *Metzudos* who renders as he does because to translate ... *by the words of* HASHEM would imply that there had been a prophecy to Chizkiahu and of this there is no mention anywhere.

However, *Ralbag* suggests that בְּדִבְרֵי ה׳ might refer, not to a prophecy to Chizkiahu, but to God's words in the Torah which require that all contaminating objects be removed from the Temple so that the Divine service could take place in accordance with the requirements laid down by the halachah.

Mikra UMassores takes the phrase in the same sense, but has it refer to the words of God in the תּוֹרָה שֶׁבְּעַל פֶּה, *the Oral Law*, which laid down the procedures described in the next verse.

This, as follows:

Two methods of ridding Sanctuary and courtyards of the defiling remnants of idol worship could have been used. The halachah is clear that, as long as *Kohanim* are available, no

you to stand before Him to serve Him; that you should be His
ministrants and burn offerings to Him.'
12 *Then the Levites arose,*
Machath the son of Amassai and Joel the son of Azariahu of the
sons of the Kehathites; and of the sons of Merrari, Kish the son of
Abdi and Azariahu the son of Yehallelel; and of the Gershonites,
Yoach the son of Zimmah and Eden the son of Yoach;
13 *And of the*
sons of Elitzaphan, Shimri and Ye'i'el; and of the sons of Assaph,
Zechariahu and Mattaniahu;
14 *And of the sons of Heiman, Yechiel*
and Shimie, and the sons of Yeduthun, Shemaiah and Uzziel.
15 *They gathered their brothers and cleansed themselves. They*
came by command of the king in the matter of HASHEM, in order
to cleanse the House of HASHEM.
16 *So the Kohanim went into the*
inner part of HASHEM's House so that they might cleanse it, and
brought out all the impurity that they found in HASHEM's House
into the Court of HASHEM's House. The Levites took it to carry it
out to the wadi of Kidron.
17 *They began the sanctifying on the first*
of the first month, and on the eighth day of the month, entered the
Hall of HASHEM. They cleansed HASHEM's House for eight days, and

Levite may enter the Sanctuary. Thus, there was no choice but that *Kohanim* had to enter the Sanctuary to clean it up.

Once this decision had been made, it left two possible ways of dealing with the idols in the Temple Courts. Since the *Kohanim* had anyway been defiled, it would have been possible to require that they themselves carry the abominations to the wadi of Kidron, and that the cleansing of the courtyards would also be left to them. This method would have cost much more time, but would have obviated the necessity of more people defiling themselves by coming into contact with the vestiges of idol worship.

On the other hand, if the speedy removal of the idols was of greater urgency, then more people would have had to become involved, thus generating more widespread defilement (see *Eruvin* 104b and 105a for detailed discussion). In any event, the latter course was chosen and this, in accordance with the oral law. Hence — בְּדִבְרֵי ה'.

16. וַיָּבֹאוּ הַכֹּהֲנִים לִפְנִימָה — *So the Kohanim went into the inner part* ... See comm. to the previous verse that, if available, only *Kohanim* — not Levites — are allowed to enter the Sanctuary building.

הַטֻּמְאָה — *The impurity*. Idols, the utensils used in their service, animals sacrificed to them and wine poured as libation before them, all convey ritual impurity (*tumah*) (*Rambam, Avos HaTumah* ch. 6).

וַיְקַבְּלוּ הַלְוִיִּם — *The Levites took it*. This, in accordance with the halachah that dispatch in removing the defilement must be maintained even at the cost of involving more people in the process — see *Eruvin* 104b and 105a and comm. to previous verse.

17. וַיָּחֵלּוּ . . . לְקַדֵּשׁ וּבְיוֹם שְׁמוֹנָה לַחֹדֶשׁ. . . . — *They began the sanctifying. . . and on the eighth day of the month* .... This seven-day sanctification process was required for the *Kohanim* and the Levites before they ever entered the Temple precincts — see discussion in comm. to v. 5.

Although the Temple precincts were anyway defiled by the idolatrous paraphernalia which were there, it is nevertheless preferable that these defilements be removed by people who are otherwise *tahor*, ritually clean (*Eruvin* 65a).

The seven-day period may also have been required because of previous contact with idols [thus, perhaps, *Rashi* to *Sanhedrin* 12a] if we postulate that such contact requires a seven-day cleansing period. However, there is some doubt whether this is the case — see *Gilyon HaShas* to *Yerushalmi, Pesachim* 9:1.

לַחֹדֶשׁ הָרִאשׁוֹן — *Of the first month*. See comm. to v. 3. Chizkiahu, who had proclaimed the leap year, would consider this month to be the second *Adar* of the previous year. The author of *Chronicles*, in sharing the view of the contemporary Sages, would consider it to be *Nissan*. See further in ch. 30.

לְיָמִים שְׁמוֹנָה — *For eight days*. The removal of

יח וּבְיוֹם שִׁשָּׁה עָשָׂר לַחֹדֶשׁ הָרִאשׁוֹן כִּלּוּ: וַיָּבוֹאוּ
פְנִימָה אֶל־חִזְקִיָּהוּ הַמֶּלֶךְ וַיֹּאמְרוּ טִהַרְנוּ אֶת־כָּל־בֵּית
יהוה אֶת־מִזְבַּח הָעוֹלָה וְאֶת־כָּל־כֵּלָיו וְאֶת־שֻׁלְחַן
יט הַמַּעֲרֶכֶת וְאֶת־כָּל־כֵּלָיו: וְאֵת כָּל־הַכֵּלִים אֲשֶׁר הִזְנִיחַ
הַמֶּלֶךְ אָחָז בְּמַלְכוּתוֹ בְּמַעֲלוֹ הֵכַנּוּ וְהִקְדָּשְׁנוּ וְהִנָּם לִפְנֵי
כ מִזְבַּח יהוה: וַיַּשְׁכֵּם יְחִזְקִיָּהוּ הַמֶּלֶךְ וַיֶּאֱסֹף אֵת
כא שָׂרֵי הָעִיר וַיַּעַל בֵּית יהוה: וַיָּבִיאוּ פָרִים־שִׁבְעָה וְאֵילִים

idolatrous objects would not have taken so long. The Sages teach that in addition to the movable objects, images had been engraved upon marble walls, and these had to be scraped away. This would take a long time (*Mefaresh*).

וּבְיוֹם שִׁשָּׁה עָשָׂר — *And ... on the sixteenth day*. Had Chizkiahu not proclaimed a leap year, this would have been the sixteenth day of *Nissan* — that is, the second day of Pesach. In that case the Pesach offering on the fourteenth would have had to be brought while the Temple was still defiled. Under such circumstances, Chizkiahu would surely have taken steps to insure that the cleansing process should be completed in fewer days. In this case, however, he had proclaimed the leap year — in his view this was *Adar* and no particular significance attached to the date.

18. וַיָּבוֹאוּ פְנִימָה אֶל־חִזְקִיָּהוּ הַמֶּלֶךְ — *Then they came to the inner chamber, to Chizkiahu the king*. *Mikra UMassores* suggests that פְּנִימָה is meant to stand in contrast to the *eastern plaza* of v.4. According to *Tamid* 5:6 this was an area where people who were ritually defiled [טָמֵא] would gather. Thus, it was an appropriate meeting place for the *Kohanim* and Levites as long as they had not yet cleansed themselves. Now, after their purification, they could enter the king's presence in his inner chamber — where Chizkiahu would surely have insisted upon ritual purity.[1]

טִהַרְנוּ אֶת־כָּל־בֵּית ה׳ — *We have cleansed all of* HASHEM*'s House*. *Mikra UMassores* suggests that this expression is analogous with ... *and they cleansed ... the gates and the walls* (*Nehemiah* 12:30). He thinks that the meaning there is that they scraped off the idolatrous images which had been engraved on these walls and gates. It is this time-consuming work which caused the cleansing of the Temple to require eight full days.

But *Rashi* there writes: That there should be nothing *tamei* in the city. Apparently, *cleaning gates and walls* means cleaning out the area which is contained by them. Here too, it would mean that all the idolatrous objects contained in the house were removed.

אֶת־מִזְבַּח הָעוֹלָה — *And the altar of the burnt offering*. It was not necessary to clean the outer altar of *tum'ah*. It was built onto the ground and was thus not susceptible to *tum'ah* (*Chagigah* 3:8). *Mikra UMassores* points out that, according to *Yoma* 59a, the word טהר used in connection with the altar could mean making its surface visible by removing the grime which encrusted it.

שֻׁלְחַן הַמַּעֲרֶכֶת — *The stacking table*. *Chagigah* 3:8 teaches that the table of the show-bread was susceptible to *tum'ah*. The *cleansing* of the table would thus have involved immersion in a *mikveh*.

19. אֲשֶׁר הִזְנִיחַ הַמֶּלֶךְ אָחָז ... — ... *which King Achaz ... caused to be abandoned*. *Targum* renders: ... [*whose sanctity King Achaz first*] *defiled and* [*which he then*] *made abominations in the service to idols*. *Metzudos*, too, sees a double implication: *He withdrew them from Divine service and served idols with them*.

But זנח in the *hiphil*, as *Chronicles* uses it, seems to be limited to *rejection* from a given state, without the implication that the rejected unit is then devoted to another purpose — see *I Chronicles* 28:9 and *II Chronicles* 11:14.

We may suggest an alternative when we consider the best way of rendering הֵכַנּוּ

1. Three verses earlier, the term פְּנִימָה was used to describe the inner sanctum of the Temple. It cannot be without significance that, here, it is used to describe the inner chamber of Chizkiahu's palace.

In the prefatory remarks to this chapter we recognized that Chizkiahu's activities surrounding the cleansing of the Temple were undertaken in his capacity as the *David* of his generation.

David, and his line, are the conduit through which the Divine Presence rests in Israel — see Section II to ch. 28, *Achaz and Menasseh*. The inner chamber of his palace is analogous with the inner sanctum of the Temple.

finished on the sixteenth day of the first month. [18] *Then they came to the inner chamber, to Chizkiahu the king, and they said, 'We have cleansed all of* HASHEM*'s House and the altar of the burnt offering and all its utensils, and the stacking table and all its utensils.* [19] *And all the utensils which King Achaz, during his treachery while he was king, caused to be abandoned, we have restored and sanctified. Behold, they are before the altar of* HASHEM. [20] *Chizkiahu the king rose early, called together the city fathers, and went up to the House of* HASHEM. [21] *They brought along seven bullocks, seven rams,*

וְהִקְדַּשְׁנוּ in the latter part of the sentence.

הֵכַנּוּ from כון, *to be firm, to establish*, should yield: *We have made usable.* Indeed, *Avodah Zarah* 52b suggests: *We made usable* — through immersion in the *mikveh*; *We have sanctified* — by application of the anointing oil.

But, as we noted in comm. to 28:24, the Talmud's conclusion is: הֵכַנּוּ — that they withdrew them [גנזום]; הִקְדַּשְׁנוּ — that they replaced them.

But how does כון imply *withdrawal? Targum* shows ambivalence by inserting a word not explicated in the text: We made them usable [תַּקֵּנְנָא], we withdrew them [טַמַּרְנָא], and replaced them [זַמֵּנְנָא חוֹרָנִין חִלּוּפֵהוֹן].

Perhaps, if we consider the phrase together with הִזְנִיחַ, we can have an understanding of how the Sages derived their teaching.

Let us postulate that הִזְנִיחַ means only that which it usually means — *to abandon*. This would then limit our verse to such utensils as had fallen into disuse during the time that the Temple had been closed, but which had not been used for idol worship.

In the context of such utensils, הֵכַנּוּ certainly means no more than *we have restored to use*.

But the very fact that the verse mentions only such utensils as were only *abandoned*, but not such as were used for actual idol worship, implies that if there were such, these would have been disqualified, and would have had to be replaced. Relative to such vessels, הֵכַנּוּ would have to mean *we have produced new ones* (thus, *Malbim*) and it is this that *Targum* seeks to convey by his ambivalent rendering.

בְּמַלְכוּתוֹ — *While he was king. Mikra UMassores* suggests that this phrase is meant to explain Achaz's actions. All that he had done had appeared to him to be a legitimate expression of his kingship. All the Judaic kings seemed to look upon the sacred vessels as their property, in the sense that they felt justified in disposing of them as they saw fit. It is only thus that we can understand how they repeatedly took the sacred treasures to bribe foreign kings or to buy their favors.

וְהִנָּם לִפְנֵי מִזְבַּח ה׳ — *Behold, they are before the altar of* HASHEM. They were there in readiness for the next day's *tamid* sacrifice. This offering would rededicate the altar to the Divine service; see below (*Mikra UMassores*).

20. שָׂרֵי הָעִיר — *The city fathers. Margalios HaYam* thinks that these were the Torah leaders of the generation. He adduces *Lamentations* 2:9, where the exile of Jerusalem's שָׂרִים results in a dearth of Torah. Indeed, we shall see in the course of the narrative (v. 30 and 30:2) how the opinions of these city fathers weighed when Torah decisions had to be made.

21. וַיָּבִיאוּ — *They brought along... Mikra UMassores* points out that presumably, the daily burnt offering [תָּמִיד] was sacrificed prior to the offerings listed here. The halachah is clear that no sacrifices are ever to be brought before the daily *tamid*.

Nevertheless, these offerings are mentioned first, because they constituted the main part of that day's Divine service. The *tamid* would have been brought independently of the king and the city fathers. The narrative backtracks to the *tamid* in v. 27.

וַיָּבִיאוּ פָרִים־שִׁבְעָה — *They brought along seven bullocks ... Mikra UMassores* suggests this ceremony was analogous with the dedication ceremonies described in *Numbers* ch. 7 for the Tabernacle in the wilderness. Achaz had temporarily shut down the Temple, and its sanctity had to be renewed.

On that occasion, each of the tribal princes had brought one bullock, one ram and one sheep as burnt offerings, and one goat as a sin offering. *Mikra UMassores* thinks that this

שִׁבְעָה וּכְבָשִׂים שִׁבְעָה וּצְפִירֵי עִזִּים שִׁבְעָה לְחַטָּאת
עַל־הַמַּמְלָכָה וְעַל־הַמִּקְדָּשׁ וְעַל־יְהוּדָה וַיֹּאמֶר לִבְנֵי
כב אַהֲרֹן הַכֹּהֲנִים לְהַעֲלוֹת עַל־מִזְבַּח יהוה: וַיִּשְׁחֲטוּ הַבָּקָר
וַיְקַבְּלוּ הַכֹּהֲנִים אֶת־הַדָּם וַיִּזְרְקוּ הַמִּזְבֵּחָה וַיִּשְׁחֲטוּ
הָאֵלִים וַיִּזְרְקוּ הַדָּם הַמִּזְבֵּחָה וַיִּשְׁחֲטוּ הַכְּבָשִׂים וַיִּזְרְקוּ
כג הַדָּם הַמִּזְבֵּחָה: וַיַּגִּישׁוּ אֶת־שְׂעִירֵי הַחַטָּאת לִפְנֵי הַמֶּלֶךְ
כד וְהַקָּהָל וַיִּסְמְכוּ יְדֵיהֶם עֲלֵיהֶם: וַיִּשְׁחָטוּם הַכֹּהֲנִים
וַיְחַטְּאוּ אֶת־דָּמָם הַמִּזְבֵּחָה לְכַפֵּר עַל־כָּל־יִשְׂרָאֵל כִּי
כה לְכָל־יִשְׂרָאֵל אָמַר הַמֶּלֶךְ הָעוֹלָה וְהַחַטָּאת: וַיַּעֲמֵד
אֶת־הַלְוִיִּם בֵּית יהוה בִּמְצִלְתַּיִם בִּנְבָלִים וּבְכִנֹּרוֹת
בְּמִצְוַת דָּוִיד וְגָד חֹזֵה־הַמֶּלֶךְ וְנָתָן הַנָּבִיא כִּי בְיַד־יהוה

was the case also in Chizkiahu's dedication. Five of the twelve tribes — the ones on the east bank of the Jordan and Yissachar and Zevulun — had already been exiled by the Assyrians, and therefore only seven tribes were left. The seven animals, which were brought from each kind enumerated in our verse, were brought in the name of the seven tribal chiefs who remained at that time.

Malbim, too, thinks that the number seven derives from the fact that there were seven tribes left after the first two Assyrian exiles. However, in his opinion, these were not dedication sacrifices, but were designed to atone for the idolatry practiced in the days of Achaz.

This, as follows:

Numbers 15:22 prescribes different sacrificial atonements for an individual who serves idols and for an entire community which does the same. In the latter case, every tribe had to bring a bullock as a burnt offering and a he-goat as a sin offering — see *Rambam, Shegagos* ch. 12.

These, then, are the first and fourth sacrifices described by our verse. The ram and sheep were voluntary gift offerings.

For both *Mikra UMassores* and *Malbim's* opinion — see further at vs. 22 and 23.

וּצְפִירֵי עִזִּים . . . לְחַטָּאת — *And . . . he-goats as a sin offering*. The Aramaic for שָׂעִיר is צָפִיר — see *Targum* to *Leviticus* 16:10.

In contrast to burnt offerings which may be brought voluntarily, a sin offering can be brought only when the halachah requires it. These sin offerings are a one-time exception [הוֹרָאַת שָׁעָה] (*Mefaresh*).

עַל־הַמַּמְלָכָה — *For the kingdom*. This was in order to elicit goodwill and to atone for them, so that the kingship should remain in their hands (*Metzudos*).

In Section II to ch. 28, *Achaz and Menasseh*, we learned that Achaz thought the nature of the Davidic kingship to have undergone a radical change. From having served as conduit for the Divine Presence to rest in Israel, it had become an abject plaything of blind and vindictive forces, which needed to be appeased through the cultic innovations which he cravenly instituted. In this light, it is particularly apt that the *kingdom* as such would require atonement. Chizkiahu, the new *David*, was reinstituting the pristine Davidic kingship!

וְעַל־הַמִּקְדָּשׁ — *And for the Temple*. That it should continue to stand in perpetuity (*Metzudos*).

וְעַל־יְהוּדָה — *And for Judah*. With five of the ten tribes of the Northern Kingdom already exiled, Chizkiahu must have realized that Israel's destiny was now inextricably tied to Judah. It would be this sadly truncated *remnant*, of which Isaiah speaks so often in his prophecies, which would lead the world to its Messianic destiny.

עַל־מִזְבַּח ה׳ — *On the altar of* HASHEM. It would not be on the altar which the hapless Uriah had built in the pattern of the one which Achaz had seen in Damesek.

22. וַיִּשְׁחֲטוּ הַבָּקָר — *They slaughtered the bullocks*. Normally sin offerings are brought before burnt offerings (*Zevachim* 89a). However, both dedication offerings [חַטָּאת נַחְשׁוֹן] (*Mikra UMassores*) and the communal atonement sacrifices for idol worship (*Malbim*) are *seven sheep and seven he-goats as a sin offering; for the kingdom and for the Temple and for Judah. He told the Aharonites, the Kohanim, to offer them on the altar of* HASHEM. [22] *They slaughtered the bullocks, and the Kohanim caught the blood and dashed it against the altar. They slaughtered the rams and dashed the blood against the altar. They slaughtered the sheep and dashed the blood against the altar.* [23] *They brought the he-goats for the sin offering to the king and the congregation, and they laid their hands upon them.* [24] *The Kohanim slaughtered them and smeared the blood on the altar to atone for all Israel; for the king had commanded that the burnt offering and the sin offering should be made for all Israel.* [25] *He established the Levites in* HASHEM*'s House with metzaltalyim, nevalim and kinoros, according to the command of David and Gad, the seer of the king and Nathan the prophet. For it was* HASHEM*'s*

halachic exceptions to this rule. [For dedication offerings, see *Zevachim* 9a and 90b and for the communal sin offerings, see *Rambam, T'midim UMusafim* 9:7.]

Malbim adds that since the bullock had to be brought before the goat, the two other burnt offerings were also brought first.

23. וַיִּסְמְכוּ יְדֵיהֶם עֲלֵיהֶם — *And they laid their hands upon them.* Again, dedication sacrifices and the communal atonement sacrifices for idol worship are exceptions to the rule that communal sin offerings do not require the laying-on of hands (see *Rambam, Ma'aseh HaKorbanos* 3:10) (*Malbim, Mikra UMassores*).

24. וַיְחַטְּאוּ — *And smeared* ... The translation is based on *Rashi* to *Exodus* 29:36. In contrast to the blood of all other sacrifices which had to be sprinkled or dashed against the altar (זרק — v. 22), that of sin offerings was smeared against it (*Rambam, Ma'aseh HaKorbanos* 5:7-9).

כִּי לְכָל־יִשְׂרָאֵל ... — *For all Israel* ... Although Chizkiahu, for practical purposes, ruled only over Judah, he felt himself responsible for all of Israel. This can be seen in ch. 30 where he invites everybody to join in the celebration of the Pesach.

25-26. It is clear that vs. 27-28 describe the bringing of the *tamid*, the sacrifice with which the daily sacrificial service was begun. This offering was accompanied by choral and instrumental music, שִׁיר (*Rambam, T'midim UMusafim* 6:8), and it is this *shir* which is described in those verses.

But what is the meaning of vs. 25-26? They cannot mean that the sacrifices which were described in v. 21-24 were also accompanied by *shir*, since *Arachin* 11b specifically rejects such an interpretation, maintaining that voluntary communal sacrifices do not require *shir*.

We shall attempt a solution in the comm. to v. 25.

25. וַיַּעֲמֵד — *He established*. For the use of the pronoun *he* instead of Chizkiahu's proper name, see comm. to v. 30.

בְּמִצְוַת דָּוִיד וְגָד ... וְנָתָן ... — *According to the command of David and Gad ... and Nathan*. *Targum* renders כְּתַפְקֶדְתָּא, that is, he interprets the word as though it were written with a כ, *kaph*, to be translated, *in accordance with*, instead of with a ב, *beis*, which should be translated *at* [*the command of*] ... *Metzudos*, too, interprets the verse thus. We have followed them in our translation.

But the fact remains that the word is written בְּמִצְוַת, with a *beis*. What can be meant by this expression? Certainly David himself had not commanded Chizkiahu to organize this *shir*.

Why are David's prophets, Gad and Nathan, mentioned here? The obligation to accompany certain sacrifices with *shir* is specified in the Torah [See *Arachin* 11a]. Why should David's prophets, or indeed, David himself, be involved?

Again, what is the meaning of the last phrase in our verse: *For it was* HASHEM*'s command, at the hand of His prophets?* *Metzudos* interprets: The requirement of *shir* was said by HASHEM through His prophets, even though it is not expressly stated in the Torah.

כט
כו־ל

הַמִּצְוָה בְּיַד־נְבִיאָיו׃
כו־כז וַיַּעַמְדוּ הַלְוִיִּם בִּכְלֵי דָוִיד וְהַכֹּהֲנִים בַּחֲצֹצְרוֹת׃ וַיֹּאמֶר
חִזְקִיָּהוּ לְהַעֲלוֹת הָעֹלָה לְהַמִּזְבֵּחַ וּבְעֵת הֵחֵל הָעוֹלָה
הֵחֵל שִׁיר־יהוה וְהַחֲצֹצְרוֹת וְעַל־יְדֵי כְּלֵי דָּוִיד מֶלֶךְ־
כח יִשְׂרָאֵל׃ וְכָל־הַקָּהָל מִשְׁתַּחֲוִים וְהַשִּׁיר מְשׁוֹרֵר
כט וְהַחֲצֹצְרוֹת °מחצצרים הַכֹּל עַד לִכְלוֹת הָעֹלָה׃ וּכְכַלּוֹת
לְהַעֲלוֹת כָּרְעוּ הַמֶּלֶךְ וְכָל־הַנִּמְצְאִים אִתּוֹ וַיִּשְׁתַּחֲווּ׃
ל וַיֹּאמֶר יְחִזְקִיָּהוּ הַמֶּלֶךְ וְהַשָּׂרִים לַלְוִיִּם לְהַלֵּל לַיהוה

°מַחְצְצְרִים ק׳

But, while it is true that the obligation to perform *shir* is not explicated in the Torah, *Arachin* 11a certainly derives it from Biblical sources. Of all the sources which are given, only one comes from the prophetic books and that is not the one which *Rambam* (*Klei Mikdash* 3:2) cites. Thus, it appears that the obligation to perform *shir* is derived from the *Torah*, as are countless other obligations. Their status as Torah-ordained obligations is never diminished by the fact that they are not explicated in the text. Why then, here, would there be an involvement of prophets? And why would the fact that *shir* is not explicated in the Torah be of interest here?

In comm. to *I Chronicles* 6:16-17 and 16:8-36 we found that David did, indeed, originate a *shir* for which there is apparently no source in the Torah. We found that during his reign, the Tabernacle, where all communal sacrifices were brought, stood at Giveon, but that the Holy Ark was first at Kiryath Yearim and then, after a short stay at the house of Oved Edom, was placed in a tent which David had erected for it in Jerusalem. In ch. 16 we learn of the *shir* service which David ordained, and which was to be performed at the location of the Ark in Jerusalem. We noted that, doubtless, the *shir* which the Torah requires during the offering up of the daily sacrifices was performed at Giveon. It follows that the *shir* at the Ark was an innovation. It is conceivable and, indeed, likely that David would not have created this entirely new form of service without the acquiescence of his prophetic advisers, and this may well be the meaning of our verse.

Chizkiahu, as the *David* of his generation, would have wanted to reactivate David's innovation. He felt himself *commanded* by David [בְּמִצְוַת]; that is, he felt prompted by the *David* within himself, to have these songs of jubilation sung, as his *alter ego* had done.

26. . . . וְהַכֹּהֲנִים . . . וַיַּעַמְדוּ הַלְוִיִּם . . . — *The Levites stood . . . and the Kohanim*. The theory propounded in the previous verse seems borne out by the sequence in which the ministrants are mentioned. At *I Chronicles* 16:6 we noted that, whereas in connection with David's disposition for the *shir* at the Ark, the Levites are mentioned before the *Kohanim* — at v. 39 there, when the disposition at Giveon is described, the *Kohanim* are mentioned first. This, since the main activity at Giveon was the bringing of sacrifices, to which the *Kohanim* were central. The sequence here follows the model of the *shir* before the Ark.

בִּכְלֵי דָוִיד — *With the instruments of David*. See prefatory remarks to this chapter for a discussion of this term.

וְהַכֹּהֲנִים בַּחֲצֹצְרוֹת — *And the Kohanim with trumpets*. See *I Chronicles* 16:6, and comm. there, that David's disposition for *shir* in front of the Ark included the blowing of trumpets by *Kohanim*.

27. . . . וַיֹּאמֶר חִזְקִיָּהוּ — *Chizkiahu directed* . . . *Arachin* 11b interprets the use of אמר, which is really too soft to imply an actual command, as indicating that, before Chizkiahu began the services, he — as any functionary appointed by a community would do — consulted whether or not to begin the bringing of the burnt offering.

[This tends to confirm *Mikra UMassores'* assumption that the sacrifice described here was brought before the ones described earlier — see comm. to v. 21. Certainly, Chizkiahu would have consulted before the ceremony started — not after he had already brought many sacrifices.]

In v. 20 we pointed out that the *city fathers* mentioned there were the Torah scholars who would be needed to direct the ceremonies. Presumably, it was with them that Chizkiahu consulted.

הָעוֹלָה — *The burnt offering*. The definite article implies that we are dealing with a known sacrifice — thus the *tamid*, with which the daily sacrificial service was to start.

In addition, this *tamid* was probably used to

command, at the hand of His prophets.
[26] The Levites stood with the instruments of David and
the Kohanim with the trumpets. [27] Chizkiahu directed that
the burnt offering be brought up on the altar. And when
the burnt offering began, the song of HASHEM *began on the*
trumpets and on the instruments of David, king of Israel. [28] All
the congregation prostrated themselves, and the singers sang
and the trumpeters sounded, constantly until they had made
an end of the burnt offering. [29] When they had made an end
of the bringing up, the king and all that were present with him
knelt down and prostrated themselves. [30] Chizkiahu the king and
the princes commanded the Levites to sing praises to HASHEM,

rededicate the altar [חֲנֻכַּת הַמִּזְבֵּחַ] which had fallen into disuse in Achaz's time and required a new dedication (*Mikra UMassores*). This, in accordance with the halachah (*Rambam, T'midim UMussafim* 1:12), that the morning *tamid* is the correct method whereby to dedicate the altar — see further at v. 31.

הֵחֵל שִׁיר־ה׳ — *The song of* HASHEM *began*. All obligatory communal burnt offerings were brought with musical accompaniment (*Rambam, Klei HaMikdash* 3:2).

וְהַחֲצֹצְרוֹת — *On the trumpets*. Trumpets were blown by *Kohanim* during the bringing of the *tamid* sacrifices. See *Tamid* 7:3 and *Rambam, T'midim UMusafim* 6:5.

The syntax of וְהַחֲצֹצְרוֹת וְעַל־יְדֵי כְּלֵי דָוִיד מֶלֶךְ־יִשְׂרָאֵל, is difficult. *Targum* translates as though the text read ... בַּחֲצֹצְרוֹת וְעַל יְדֵי , and it is this rendering which we follow in our translation.

28. מִשְׁתַּחֲוִים — *Prostrated themselves*. According to *Berachos* 34b, this term implies complete prostration with arms and legs spread out upon the ground.

וְהַשִּׁיר מְשׁוֹרֵר — *And the singers sang*. Taken literally, the phrase would have to be translated: *And the song sang*. *Radak* suggests that שִׁיר is, here, to be taken as *singer*, and this is how we have translated it. Thus, also *Targum*.

הַכֹּל — *Constantly*. *Metzudos* suggests this unusual translation. The choristers and trumpeters performed constantly, until the entire bringing of the sacrifice had been completed.

29. כָּרְעוּ — *Knelt down*. *Berachos* 34b defines כְּרִיעָה as genuflecting upon the knees. From there, it appears that the king is obliged to make more profound obeisance than the ordinary people. Besides prostrating himself, as indicated by the end of the verse, he also knelt. In this, he was apparently followed by his retinue (*Mikra UMassores*).

30. ... וַיֹּאמֶר יְחִזְקִיָּהוּ הַמֶּלֶךְ וְהַשָּׂרִים לַלְוִיִּם לְהַלֵּל — *Chizkiahu the king and the princes commanded the Levites to sing praises* ... The praises they are to sing are identified as *the words of David and Asaph the seer*.

We shall be able to identify this more closely if we first examine why a new command to the Levites was necessary. Vs. 27 and 28 have already reported the performance of the *shir* in connection with the bringing of the *tamid*, and have told us that this *shir* continued until that ceremony was completed. What new *shir* was now required?

Vs. 25 and 26 tell us that the Levite orchestra was set in place, but do not report that they began to perform. These musicians did not know what was planned for them. They had not played for the bringing of the *tamid*. Why were they there? Chizkiahu and the princes now tell them what they are to do.

In the comm.to v. 25, we suggested that this group of Levites was to perform the *shir* which David had ordained be sung in front of the Ark.

Indeed, *Mefaresh* identifies *the words of David and Asaph the seer* as referring to the psalms quoted in *I Chronicles* 16:8 ff., and which are introduced in v. 7 there: *On that day, on that occasion, David established [this] as pre-eminent in the praise of* HASHEM, *under the direction of Asaph and his brothers*. This would agree precisely with our thesis.

Our suggestion can help to solve a textual oddity. V. 25 reads: *He established the Levites* ..., using the pronoun *He* instead of the name Chizkiahu. This is the case, although many other subjects were dealt with since v. 20, where he had last been mentioned. We would have expected the use of his name instead of the pronoun, as it is used in v. 27 and in our verse.

If our suggestion that Chizkiahu, here, acted as the *David* of his generation is correct, we can understand

בְּדִבְרֵי דָּוִיד וְאָסָף הַחֹזֶה וַיְהַלְלוּ עַד־לְשִׂמְחָה וַיִּקְּדוּ
לא וַיִּשְׁתַּחֲווּ: וַיַּעַן יְחִזְקִיָּהוּ וַיֹּאמֶר עַתָּה מִלֵּאתֶם יֶדְכֶם
לַיהוָה גֹּשׁוּ וְהָבִיאוּ זְבָחִים וְתוֹדוֹת לְבֵית יְהוָה וַיָּבִיאוּ
לב הַקָּהָל זְבָחִים וְתוֹדוֹת וְכָל־נְדִיב לֵב עֹלוֹת: וַיְהִי מִסְפַּר
הָעֹלָה אֲשֶׁר הֵבִיאוּ הַקָּהָל בָּקָר שִׁבְעִים אֵילִים מֵאָה
לג כְּבָשִׂים מָאתָיִם לְעֹלָה לַיהוָה כָּל־אֵלֶּה: וְהַקֳּדָשִׁים בָּקָר
לד שֵׁשׁ מֵאוֹת וְצֹאן שְׁלֹשֶׁת אֲלָפִים: רַק הַכֹּהֲנִים הָיוּ לִמְעָט
וְלֹא יָכְלוּ לְהַפְשִׁיט אֶת־כָּל־הָעֹלוֹת וַיְחַזְּקוּם אֲחֵיהֶם
הַלְוִיִּם עַד־כְּלוֹת הַמְּלָאכָה וְעַד־יִתְקַדְּשׁוּ הַכֹּהֲנִים כִּי

the use of the pronoun and also the reason for including the *princes* in our verse. When the Levite orchestra was first told to hold themselves ready, they did not know for what purpose. Their orders came from an unknown source. In what capacity was the king making his disposition? Was it the Chizkiahu of the moment, or the Chizkiahu who as *David* bestrode the centuries? The uncertainty is expressed by the ambiguous *He*.

Now, however, Chizkiahu makes his purpose known, but, in his modesty, will not do so on his own but only in consultation with the princes.

וְאָסָף הַחֹזֶה — *And Asaph the seer*. See *I Chronicles* 25:1 for a description of the choristers as prophets.

וַיְהַלְלוּ עַד־לְשִׂמְחָה — *They rendered praise to the point of exultation*. A great feeling of joy grew out of the feeling of closeness to God which was generated by the singing of the praises (*Metzudos*).

If we are correct, that this was 'David's *shir*', there was special cause for exultation. With it, came the first intimation of Chizkiahu as the potential Messiah, and the knowledge that redemption was — so to speak — in their grasp.

וַיִּקְּדוּ — *They fell upon their faces*. Thus, *Berachos* 34b.

31. מִלֵּאתֶם יֶדְכֶם לַה' — *You have consecrated yourselves to HASHEM*. The expression מִלּוּי יָד is always used to denote consecration to a given appointment; cf. *Exodus* 32:29. Because, during Achaz's closing of the Temple the *Kohanim* had been unable to serve, they required a new installment ceremony. The halachah requires that a *Kohen* who is being newly installed to serve in the Temple must enter the Courtyard while the Levites are reciting the *shir* (*Rambam, Klei Mikdash* 5:15). Since the *shir* was performed while the *tamid* was being brought (vs. 27-28), all *Kohanim* who were present were now once more consecrated to the service.

וְכָל־נְדִיב לֵב עֹלוֹת — *And as many as were of a willing heart, burnt offerings*. The sacrifices mentioned earlier are peace offerings, and they, as well as the thanks offerings, were eaten, in part, by the people who brought them. By contrast, the burnt offerings were consumed completely by the altar — the owners received nothing. Consequently, a greater *willingness of heart* was required for bringing the burnt offering (*Radak*).

32. וַיְהִי מִסְפַּר הָעֹלָה — *And the number of the burnt offerings ... was ...* When we compare the numbers in our verse with those of the next, we can readily see that bringing the burnt offerings required a greater willingness of heart. Far fewer of these offerings were brought.

לְעֹלָה לַה' כָּל־אֵלֶּה — *All these were a burnt offering to HASHEM*. Actually, the number of the sacrifices counted in this verse and the next is relatively small. Even if we do not compare this occasion with Solomon's consecration (5:6 and 7:5), since obviously Judah in Chizkiahu's time was much poorer than all of Israel in its heyday, they are still considerably smaller than those which are given from other occasions. See, for example 15:11, for the sacrifices brought from the spoils of war in the time of Asa, and 35:8 ff. for the number of animals required for the Pesach offering in Josiah's days. [See also at 30:24.]

Perhaps the explanation lies in the timing. This consecration took place a scant two weeks after Chizkiahu assumed the throne. Under Achaz, the Divine service had atrophied and people had lost the habit of bringing sacrifices to God. Indeed, we see that, even the *Kohanim* — usually the most zealous in this respect [כֹּהֲנִים זְרִיזִים הֵם] — were tardy in readying themselves for the Divine service (v. 34). Under these circumstances, the smaller number of sacrifices was still very large.

in the words of David and Asaph the seer. They rendered praise to the point of exultation; they fell upon their faces and prostrated themselves. 31 *Then Chizkiahu made a proclamation, saying, 'Now that you have consecrated yourselves to* HASHEM, *approach and bring sacrifices and thanks offerings to* HASHEM'*s House.' So the congregation brought sacrifices and thanks offerings, and as many as were of a willing heart, burnt offerings.* 32 *And the number of the burnt offerings which the congregation brought was seventy bullocks, a hundred rams and two hundred lambs; all these were a burnt offering to* HASHEM. 33 *The consecrated animals numbered six hundred bullocks and three thousand sheep* 34 *But the Kohanim were too few so that they could not flay all the burnt offerings, so their brothers the Levites supported them till the work was ended and until the Kohanim had sanctified themselves; for*

We may suggest another reason why the bringing of sacrifices was somewhat muted in Chizkiahu's time when compared to other occasions.

It is clear that Achaz's closing down of the Temple was not merely negative in its results. It was not only a cessation of Divine service but resulted in an active enhancement of the superstitious cults which were part and parcel of idol worship. People did not only stop sacrificing to God but they engaged in the pernicious practices of idolatry so that, doubtlessly, their entire concept of the sacrificial service became distorted. From the sanctifying, elevating experience of a symbolic sacrifice of self to the benign purifying and refining service of God, animal sacrifice turned into the black and filthy rites designed to placate blind natural forces, which wished to shackle helpless and impotent humanity to their brute power.

It would have been no easy task to wean the masses away from such a distorted view of service. As we saw in Section II, *Chizkiahu in Isaiah and Rabbinical Sources*, Chizkiahu saw as his most important priority, the propagation and teaching of Torah — a re-educating of the people to the spiritual values which they had forsaken. Thus, from an educational standpoint, it was essential to keep the sacrificial service within such bounds as would not overwhelm the easily impressionable multitudes with an overpowering physical presence, thereby dimming the inner spiritual light which was so desperately needed to illuminate the dark superstitions which had engulfed the people.

33. וְהַקֳּדָשִׁים — *The consecrated animals*. This term describes the peace and thanksgiving offerings which were brought on this occasion (*Metzudos*).

Why are these sacrifices described by the general term קֳדָשִׁים, while the burnt offerings of the previous verse are identified by name?

Perhaps, the very fact that the greater part of these sacrifices was eaten by the owners brought about a custom to refer to them as *consecrated animals*. In practical terms, there was little to distinguish them from ordinary animals. When we consider that from ordinary animals, the foreleg, the jaw and the maw had to be given to the *Kohen* (*Deuteronomy* 17:3), a case can be made that in the case of these sacrifices from which only the chest and the hind-leg had to be given (*Leviticus* 7:31-32), the owner actually received a greater part of the animal. Thus it was only their *sanctity* which gave them the character of sacrifice and this was reflected in their name.

34. רַק הַכֹּהֲנִים הָיוּ לִמְעָט — *But the Kohanim were too few*. Considering the relatively few burnt offerings which were brought, it is surprising that the *Kohanim* should have been overwhelmed by the amount of work.

Margalios HaYam suggests that many *Kohanim* may have become disqualified from Divine service by participating in idolatry during Achaz's reign. Such disqualification derives from *Ezekiel* 44:10. This source yields that such *Kohanim* lose their status as *Kohanim* and are regarded simply as Levites [see *Meshech Chochmah* to *Leviticus* 1:5]. Thus, the Levites who helped with the skinning may really have been *Kohanim* who could no longer participate in the actual service. That they had cleansed themselves with greater zeal than the true *Kohanim* could be explained as a gesture of penitence when they realized — through their reduced state — just how serious their sin had been. See further below.

וְעַד־יִתְקַדְּשׁוּ הַכֹּהֲנִים — *And until the Kohanim had sanctified themselves*. Even after these dedication ceremonies, the Levites continued

כט לה הַלְוִיִּם יִשְׁרֵי לֵבָב לְהִתְקַדֵּשׁ מֵהַכֹּהֲנִים: וְגַם־עֹלָה לָרֹב
לה־לו בְּחֶלְבֵי הַשְּׁלָמִים וּבַנְּסָכִים לָעֹלָה וַתִּכּוֹן עֲבוֹדַת בֵּית־
לו יהוָה: וַיִּשְׂמַח יְחִזְקִיָּהוּ וְכָל־הָעָם עַל הַהֵכִין הָאֱלֹהִים
ל א לָעָם כִּי בְּפִתְאֹם הָיָה הַדָּבָר: וַיִּשְׁלַח
א יְחִזְקִיָּהוּ עַל־כָּל־יִשְׂרָאֵל וִיהוּדָה וְגַם־אִגְּרוֹת כָּתַב עַל־

to assist the *Kohanim* until such a time as the entire pool of available *Kohanim* had cleansed themselves (*Metzudos*). See further at 30:15.

כִּי הַלְוִיִּם יִשְׁרֵי לֵבָב לְהִתְקַדֵּשׁ מֵהַכֹּהֲנִים — *For the Levites were more upright in heart to sanctify themselves than the Kohanim. Mefaresh* at 30:15 explains that the *Kohanim* could simply not bring themselves to believe that Chizkiahu's intentions were pure. They felt that, with a father as wicked as Achaz, it was unlikely that the young king — so early in his reign — would be serious in his reforms. The Levites, on the other hand, those *Kohanim* who had been disqualified because of their idol worship — see above — would have been eager to qualify for some form of service.

If the Levites mentioned in our verse are actual Levites — and not disqualified *Kohanim* — it is also possible to find a rationale. It seems likely that the *Kohanim* had been more closely enmeshed in Achaz's excesses than had the Levites. It was, after all, Uriah, a *Kohen*, who had agreed to Achaz's preposterous suggestion that an altar, modeled upon the Damasken monstrosity, be erected. *Mikra UMassores* points out that it is highly unlikely that such a major reform could have been undertaken without consultation and acquiescence on the part of the other *Kohanim*. Perhaps, then, as a group, the *Kohanim* had sunk lower than the Levites and were proportionately less eager to recant.

35. וְגַם־עֹלָה לָרֹב . . . — *Also, [there was] an abundance of the burnt offerings . . . Malbim* explains that this verse continues to explain why the *Kohanim* needed help. The burnt offerings had to be taken up limb by limb to the altar — something which only *Kohanim* were qualified to do. This could involve as many as twenty-four *Kohanim* for each sacrifice — see *Rambam, Maasei HaKarbonos* 6:10 ff.

The fats of the peace offerings, which were the only parts of those sacrifices which were burned on the altar, had also to be taken there by *Kohanim*; as also the libations of wine which accompanied the burnt offerings.

The sequence in which the *fats of the peace offerings* interrupt between the two services dealing with the burnt offerings can be explained logically. Both the limbs of the burnt offering and the fats of the peace offering were burned on the altar and therefore belong together. The libation which was poured but not burned is then listed separately.

It is not clear why only the libations for the burnt offerings should be mentioned. In fact, peace offerings, too, are accompanied by libations (*Numbers* ch.15). *Ralbag* suggests that עֹלָה in the phrase dealing with the libation, is not to be translated as *burnt offering*, but as anything that is *brought up* upon the altar — including the peace offerings.

וַתִּכּוֹן עֲבוֹדַת בֵּית־ה׳ — *Thus the service of the House of HASHEM was set in order*. Perhaps this expression is used to echo 8:16 where it describes the completion of Solomon's building of the Temple. Such an identity of expression is appropriate since Chizkiahu was, as it were, renewing the Temple and making a fresh beginning.

36. עַל הַהֵכִין הָאֱלֹהִים לָעָם — *For that which God had prepared for the people*. Two explanations are possible: *Targum* and *Mefaresh* interpret in the sense of setting the heart of the people straight. God had helped them to repent the sins that had been committed during Achaz's reign.

Metzudos has it refer to the Temple. Chizkiahu rejoiced at the wondrous way in which the Temple was so quickly set into perfect order.

כִּי בְּפִתְאֹם הָיָה הַדָּבָר — *For the thing was done suddenly*. The meaning is the same according to both interpretations to the earlier phrase. It was God's special providence which enabled the people to reorient themselves to God's service in such a short time, and also that the Temple could be rededicated so soon.

XXX

◆§ Chizkiahu Celebrates the Pesach

Chizkiahu's first concern upon becoming king was the celebration of the upcoming Pesach. The centrality of this issue can be gauged by the profuse detail lavished upon it in this chapter.

29 *the Levites were more upright in heart to sanctify themselves*
35-36 *than the Kohanim.* 35 *Also, [there was] an abundance of the burnt*
offerings in addition to the fats of the peace offerings and the
libations for the burned offerings. Thus the service of the House
of HASHEM *was set in order.* 36 *Chizkiahu and all the people*
rejoiced for that which God had prepared for the people; for the
thing was done suddenly.

30
1 *Chizkiahu sent to all Israel and Judah, and also he wrote letters*

We must try to understand why just this particular ritual was of such overwhelming significance in the *Chronicles'* account.

R' Yitzchok Isaac Prag in *Tzitz HaSadeh 10* demonstrates that the function of the *Pesach* offering is different than that of any of the other sacrifices. These latter are brought for רֵיחַ נִיחוֹחַ, so that God would, as it were, be pleased with their fragrance . This concept is never mentioned in the context of the *Pesach*. More than for God, this sacrifice is for man. Its purpose is to wean the celebrant away from idol worship.[1]

Given this unique function of the *Pesach*, it is natural that at a time when there was a massive rejection of the idolatrous cults and a rededication to the service of God, there should be a particularly meaningful celebration of the Pesach. Thus it was with Yoshiahu (see ch. 35) and, so too, was Chizkiahu inspired to educate the people towards just this service (*R' Gedaliah Schorr* in *Ohr Gedalyahu*).

1. וַיִּשְׁלַח יְחִזְקִיָּהוּ — *Chizkiahu sent* ... This took place after the deliberations described in the next verse (*Radak*). Once the decision had been taken to make a leap year (see below), and that Pesach would be in the *second* month, Chizkiahu was ready to launch his project for a universal celebration of the Pesach.

עַל־כָּל־יִשְׂרָאֵל וִיהוּדָה — *To all Israel and Judah*. V. 5 tells us that Chizkiahu's announcements were made from *Be'er Sheva up to Dan*, which is the expression favored by Scripture to describe the entire area of the Jewish state under Solomon (*I Kings* 5:5). This would imply that all the tribes were contacted although, in the course of the narrative, only Ephraim and Menasheh (vs. 1, 10, [11] and 18); Zevulun (vs. 10, 11 and 18); Asher (v. 11) and Issachar (v. 18) are mentioned.

We can account for all the tribes as follows: By the time that Chizkiahu became king, Assyria had already carried off two groups of exiles. In the tradition of the Sages, these comprised Reuven, Gad and half of Menasseh on the western bank of the Jordan, and Naphtali and Zevulun. [See *Isaiah* 8:23 and *Rashi* there, and comm. to *I Chronicles* 5:25—26.] Given this background, we have, in fact, accounted for all the tribes as follows: Reuven had already been exiled; Simeon had his cities dispersed within Judah's territory and is therefore included in Judah; Issachar is mentioned; Zevulun is mentioned — we must assume that although the tribe as a whole was already exiled, there were nevertheless pockets of people left who responded to Chizkiahu's message; Dan is mentioned in the phrase ... *from Be'er Sheva till Dan*; Naphtali, was already exiled; Gad was already exiled; Asher

1. Briefly, *R' Prag* cites the following indications to the correctness of his thesis:

1. *Mechilta* to *Exodus* 12:21 interprets the difficult מִשְׁכוּ in the phrase מִשְׁכוּ וּקְחוּ לָכֶם צֹאן, *Draw* [or *drag, pull along*] *and take for yourselves sheep* [for the *Pesach* offering], as indicating: *Draw* [or *remove*] [yourselves from idol worship and then] *take for yourselves sheep* ...

2. *Mechilta* to *Exodus* 12:48 and *Sifri* to *Numbers* 9:14 both speak of a possibility [which is, however, halachically rejected] that any gentile who becomes a Jew [גֵּר] would immediately, as part of the process of the proselytization, have to bring a *Pesach* offering. Since, manifestly, the proselyte has nothing to do with the historical events associated with the *Pesach*, and since, moreover, those historical associations would be appropriate only on the fourteenth of Nissan when every one else brings the *Pesach*, it is clear that this possibility could only have been a function of that aspect of the *Pesach* which defines it as an induction into God's service.

3. To *R' Prag's* arguments we may add that, in spite of the fact that any sacrificial rite is an act of *service*, only the *Pesach* offering is called by that name in the Torah (*Exodus* 12:25 and 26 and 13:5). *Maharal* takes this to indicate that the *Pesach* offering was that act of *service* which changed Israel from Pharaoh's slaves into the servants of God. This concept is entirely within the framework of *R' Prag's* ideas.

אֶפְרַיִם וּמְנַשֶּׁה לָבוֹא לְבֵית־יְהוָה בִּירוּשָׁלָ͏ִם לַעֲשׂוֹת פֶּסַח
ב לַיהוָה אֱלֹהֵי יִשְׂרָאֵל: וַיִּוָּעַץ הַמֶּלֶךְ וְשָׂרָיו וְכָל־הַקָּהָל
ג בִּירוּשָׁלָ͏ִם לַעֲשׂוֹת הַפֶּסַח בַּחֹדֶשׁ הַשֵּׁנִי: כִּי לֹא יָכְלוּ
לַעֲשֹׂתוֹ בָּעֵת הַהִיא כִּי הַכֹּהֲנִים לֹא־הִתְקַדְּשׁוּ לְמַדַּי

is mentioned; Ephraim and Menasheh are mentioned; and Benjamin is included in Judah.

Thus, we have Chizkiahu contacting the entire Jewish people. This is entirely in character with the Messianic role to which he was destined.

That he was able to contact the tribes of the Northern Kingdom with the presumption that they would, if they wished, be able to participate in the ceremony, confirms the tradition of the Sages that Hosea ben Eilah, the last of the kings of the Northern Kingdom, eliminated the sentries which had been set up to make sure that there would be no traffic between the north and the south. Egress, then, was possible to all who sought it (*Taanis* 30b) (*Da'as Soferim*).

וְגַם־אִגְּרוֹת כָּתַב עַל־אֶפְרַיִם וּמְנַשֶּׁה — *And also he wrote letters to Ephraim and Menasheh. Da'as Soferim* suggests that these letters may have contained Chizkiahu's assurances that coming to celebrate the Pesach was a purely religious act and had no political implications. Chizkiahu had no wish to interfere with Hosea ben Eilah's kingship.

This may help us to deal with an apparent contradiction between our verse, which implies that letters were sent only to Ephraim and Menasseh and that the message to the rest of Israel was oral, and v. 6 which tells that the messengers bore letters to all of *Israel and Judah*.

The answer may be that, indeed, the invitation to join in the *Pesach* celebration was made by letter to all the tribes — and that is the subject of v. 6. But letters disclaiming any political intent were necessary only to Ephraim and Menasheh. This, because Shomron, the capital city of the Northern Kingdom was situated between Ephraim and Menasheh (*Tevuas HaAretz*), and the problem of a possible misunderstanding would have been most sensitive there.

וַיִּוָּעַץ הַמֶּלֶךְ וְשָׂרָיו וְכָל־הַקָּהָל . . . — *The king, his princes and the whole congregation . . . decided upon consideration. . .* This verse serves as the basis for the tradition of the Sages that Chizkiahu instituted a leap year against the opinion of the Torah authorities of his generation.[1]

Radak questions this tradition on two counts: He finds no evidence in the text that the decision was taken on the last day of *Adar*, nor that the Torah authorities disagreed with the decision. On the contrary, our verse tells us that Chizkiahu sought counsel with the princes — presumably the Sages of the times.

[*Radak* addresses himself only to the issue of the tardy enactment [#2 in fn.] and does not consider the incorrect motivation [#1 in fn.]. This is entirely consistent with the passage in *Sanhedrin*. It is *Rambam's* innovation to consider the mistaken

1. The complexities involved in this controversy are discussed in detail in *Sanhedrin* 12a and b, and have given rise to a considerable amount of literature which attempts to grapple with a wide range of problems. [For a bibliography, see *Margalios HaYam* to *Sanhedrin* 12a.]

Within the framework of our comm. we cannot possibly deal with all the opinions. We will base the comm. upon *Rambam* (*Bi'as Mikdash* 4:17-18), and interpret the verses as does *Margalios HaYam*.

In the eyes of his opponents, Chizkiahu erred in two areas:

1. The halachah permits the *Pesach* to be brought in the eventuality of the majority of the community being ritually unclean (*tamei*), and such a situation is consequently not one which would justify the institution of a leap year. When Chizkiahu became king, the greater part of the community was *tameh* (see below) and Chizkiahu should consequently not have instituted a leap year.

2. The decision to institute a leap year must be made at the latest, during the *Adar* of the year which is to have the extra month added. Once *Nissan* has begun, it is too late. According to the tradition of the Sages, it need not actually be *Nissan* for the opportunity to have been missed. Already the thirtieth day of *Adar* — since it could become *Nissan* if the new moon is sighted — is too late. Chizkiahu made his decision on the thirtieth of *Adar*.

We will further assume that, in the eyes of Chizkiahu's opponents, a leap year declared under these conditions is void, and further, that *Chronicles* dates the events as though no leap year had been instituted. This, because the author of *Chronicles* accepted the opinion of those Sages who disagreed with Chizkiahu. See comm. to 29:3 and 17.

These assumptions are not universally accepted but will make the interpretation of the verses in this chapter simpler.

to Ephraim and Menasheh, to come to HASHEM's House in Jerusalem, to celebrate Pesach to HASHEM the God of Israel.
2 The king, his princes and all the congregation in Jerusalem, decided upon consideration, to celebrate Pesach in the second
month. 3 For they could not celebrate it at that time, for the Kohanim had not sanctify themselves in sufficient numbers,

motivation as part of the issue.]

Margalios HaYam answers both objections:

1. Had the decision been taken at a legitimate time, the leap year would have been valid. If so, the *first month* of 29:3 would have fallen in Chizkiahu's second year. But the text there defines it as *the first month of the first year*. Necessarily, then, we must conclude that the Sages — including the writer of *Chronicles* — held the institution to be void because of tardiness, and considered the month, which Chizkiahu would have called the second *Adar* of his first year, as the first *Nissan* of his first year.

2. V. 4 states expressly that the matter was good in the eyes of the king and of the congregation — but omits the princes who were mentioned in our verse. The implication is clear — the princes, in fact, did not find it *good*, but held the leap year which Chizkiahu had instituted to be void.

לַעֲשׂוֹת הַפֶּסַח בַּחֹדֶשׁ הַשֵּׁנִי — *To celebrate the Pesach in the second month. Chronicles is consistent in its use of the term second month. In Chizkiahu's opinion it would, of course, be Nissan* or the first month — see above (*Margalios HaYam*).

Rambam believes that Chizkiahu's motivation for introducing an extra *Adar* was to allow time for the people to achieve a state of ritual cleanliness. In the case at hand, this was not sufficient justification for lengthening the year.

Chizkiahu's reason for taking this unnecessary — and interdicted step — may have been as follows:

As we noted above, this was no ordinary *Pesach*. It was to be a rededication, in the wake of the apostasy of Achaz's reign, of our entire people to God's service. In addition, it functioned also as part of the cleansing of the defiled Temple. As such, Chizkiahu may well have felt that even though the strict application of the halachah would permit the sacrifice to be made amid communal defilement — this was no way to make a new beginning (*Margalios HaYam*). This, in much the same way that there was an insistence that the oil with which the Hasmoneans rekindled the *menorah* should be undefiled, although halachically this would not have been necessary. (See ArtScroll *Chanukah*, p. 93.)

There is some disagreement as to the source of the *tum'ah* of the people. *Rashi* to *Sanhedrin* 12a explains that the people had been defiled through contact with idols during Achaz's reign, and Chizkiahu feared that there would be no time for them to cleanse themselves in the two weeks left between the last day of *Adar* and the fourteenth of *Nissan*. [But v. 3 implies that the problem of defilement was limited to the *Kohanim*.]

Tosafos brings *Yerushalmi, Pesachim* 9:1, that the skull of Arnon the Yevusite (see *I Chronicles* ch. 21) was discovered under the altar and thus defiled all those who passed over it. [See Section II, *The Skull of Arnon*, for a discussion.] Accordingly, only the *Kohanim* who had access to the altar area would have been defiled (*Noda BiYehudah II Orach Chayim* 86).

When a majority of the *Kohanim* are ritually defiled, the *Pesach* may be brought without their first becoming cleansed (*Pesachim* 79a). There was, therefore, no halachic reason for a leap year to be instituted.

3. בָּעֵת הַהִיא — *At that time.*

That is, at the correct time, in the upcoming month of Nissan (*Metzudos*).

[The use of בָּעֵת הַהִיא to describe the correct time would seem to confirm the tradition of the Sages that the decision was taken on the thirtieth day of *Adar*; that is, on a day which could already have been part of *Nissan*. If the decision had been taken at some earlier point, the expression *at that time* would have been inappropriate.]

כִּי הַכֹּהֲנִים לֹא־הִתְקַדְּשׁוּ לְמַדַּי — *For the Kohanim had not sanctified themselves in sufficient numbers*. The unique לְמַדַּי is taken by the commentators to be a contraction of לְמַן דַּי (*Radak, Metzudos*). The celebration of the Pesach would require a great number of *Kohanim*, and although many had cleansed themselves, many had not. There would not be a sufficient number to serve the needs of the community (*Ralbag*).

ד וְהָעָם לֹא־נֶאֶסְפוּ לִירוּשָׁלָם׃ וַיִּישַׁר הַדָּבָר בְּעֵינֵי הַמֶּלֶךְ
ה וּבְעֵינֵי כָּל־הַקָּהָל׃ וַיַּעֲמִידוּ דָבָר לְהַעֲבִיר קוֹל בְּכָל־
יִשְׂרָאֵל מִבְּאֵר־שֶׁבַע וְעַד־דָּן לָבוֹא לַעֲשׂוֹת פֶּסַח לַיהוָה
ו אֱלֹהֵי־יִשְׂרָאֵל בִּירוּשָׁלָם כִּי לֹא לָרֹב עָשׂוּ כַּכָּתוּב׃ וַיֵּלְכוּ
הָרָצִים בָּאִגְּרוֹת מִיַּד הַמֶּלֶךְ וְשָׂרָיו בְּכָל־יִשְׂרָאֵל וִיהוּדָה
וּכְמִצְוַת הַמֶּלֶךְ לֵאמֹר בְּנֵי יִשְׂרָאֵל שׁוּבוּ אֶל־יהוה אֱלֹהֵי
אַבְרָהָם יִצְחָק וְיִשְׂרָאֵל וְיָשֹׁב אֶל־הַפְּלֵיטָה הַנִּשְׁאֶרֶת
ז לָכֶם מִכַּף מַלְכֵי אַשּׁוּר׃ וְאַל־תִּהְיוּ כַּאֲבוֹתֵיכֶם וְכַאֲחֵיכֶם
אֲשֶׁר מָעֲלוּ בַּיהוָה אֱלֹהֵי אֲבוֹתֵיהֶם וַיִּתְּנֵם לְשַׁמָּה כַּאֲשֶׁר
ח אַתֶּם רֹאִים׃ עַתָּה אַל־תַּקְשׁוּ עָרְפְּכֶם כַּאֲבוֹתֵיכֶם תְּנוּ־יָד
לַיהוה וּבֹאוּ לְמִקְדָּשׁוֹ אֲשֶׁר הִקְדִּישׁ לְעוֹלָם וְעִבְדוּ
ט אֶת־יהוָה אֱלֹהֵיכֶם וְיָשֹׁב מִכֶּם חֲרוֹן אַפּוֹ׃ כִּי בְשׁוּבְכֶם
עַל־יהוה אֲחֵיכֶם וּבְנֵיכֶם לְרַחֲמִים לִפְנֵי שׁוֹבֵיהֶם וְלָשׁוּב

וְהָעָם לֹא־נֶאֶסְפוּ לִירוּשָׁלָם — *Nor had the people congregated in Jerusalem*. The organization of the *Pesach* celebration, with the vast number of people involved, would necessitate an early start. The fact that the people were not yet there made it impossible to anticipate a smooth celebration.

Mikra UMassores points out that here, too, Chizkiahu erred. According to *Sanhedrin* 11a, the inability of a large section of the community to be in Jerusalem in time for the *Pesach* is justification for instituting a leap year only if they have already left their homes and are on the way. Otherwise — as in our case — no leap year is declared.

4. וַיִּישַׁר הַדָּבָר . . . — *The arrangement appeared appropriate . . .*

Having sought counsel with one another (v. 2), they now concluded that the decision should be made (*Metzudos*).

בְּעֵינֵי הַמֶּלֶךְ וּבְעֵינֵי כָּל־הַקָּהָל — *In the eyes of the king and in the eyes of the whole congregation*.

We noted above that the שָׂרִים of v. 2 are missing here. Evidently, they did not concur with the decision, and this is the source of the Sages' tradition that the Torah authorities did not agree with Chizkiahu's institution of the leap year (*Margalios HaYam*).

5. מִבְּאֵר־שֶׁבַע וְעַד־דָּן — *From Be'er Sheva to Dan*. See comm. to v. 1.

כִּי לֹא לָרֹב עָשׂוּ כַּכָּתוּב — *For it had been a long time since they had celebrated in accordance with the written specifications.* Much encouragement was needed since, for many years, the celebration of the *Pesach* had fallen into disuse (*Metzudos*).

6. בָּאִגְּרוֹת — *With letters*. See comm. to v. 1.

שׁוּבוּ אֶל־ה׳ . . . — *Return to* HASHEM . . . The call to repentance expressed in this and the following verses is unique in the annals of the monarchy of the first Temple. We do not find a similar proclamation even in the times of Yoshiahu, who was faced with much the same conditions as was Chizkiahu.

In the Overview *David the King and David the Man* (*I Chronicles* p. xlv, *The Essential David*), we recognized that David's Messianic destiny was inextricably tied to his role as the one who *established the yoke of teshuvah* (*Avodah Zarah* 5a). We defined the nature of this yoke as describing the inevitability of an ultimate return to God — an inevitability which permeates and animates world history.

As the *David* of his times, it is entirely to be expected that Chizkiahu would see a call to *teshuvah* as absolutely central to his role.

In this context, it is particularly apt that his message is directed to the *Children of Israel*, and that HASHEM is described as *God of Abraham, Isaac and Israel*. This stresses the shared past — with its implied shared destiny — and bypasses the temporary divisions of the present. Chizkiahu, as it were, towers above the divisions caused by politics and diverse loyalties and addresses the soul of his fragmented people.

הַפְּלֵיטָה הַנִּשְׁאֶרֶת לָכֶם — *The remnant that is left to you.*

At 29:21 we noted that five tribes of the Northern Kingdom had already been carried into exile. *The remnant that is left to you* would

nor had the people congregated in Jerusalem. 4 *The arrange-*
ment appeared appropriate in the eyes of the king and in the eyes
of the whole congregation. 5 *So they decided to announce*
throughout Israel, from Be'er Sheva to Dan, that people should
come and celebrate Pesach in Jerusalem, for HASHEM, *the God*
of Israel. For it had been a long time since they had celebrated in
accordance with the written specifications. 6 *So the runners, with*
letters by the hand of the king and his princes, went through all
Israel and Judah. By the king's orders they announced, 'Child-
ren of Israel, return to HASHEM *the God of Abraham, Isaac and*
Israel, so that He will return to the remnant that is left to you, out
of the hand of the kings of Assyria. 7 *Now be not like your fathers*
and like your brothers who acted treacherously against HASHEM
the God of their fathers so that he made them an appallment as
you see. 8 *Now be not stiff necked as your fathers were. Stretch*
out your hand to HASHEM *and come to His Sanctuary which He*
has sanctified forever, and serve HASHEM *your God so that His*
fierce anger may turn away from you. 9 *For if you turn back to*
HASHEM, *your brothers and your sons shall find compassion*
before them that led them captive and shall come back into this

therefore appear to be the remaining tribes of the Northern Kingdom. The fact that this message was sent also to Judah is another indication of the universality of Chizkiahu's approach. The exiled tribes had been lost to the Southern Kingdom as much as to their brothers to the north.

What is meant by the thought that God . . . *will return to the remnant* . . .? Perhaps Chizkiahu was hinting at the possibility that a wholehearted repentance might prevent the rest of the tribes of the Northern Kingdom from being carried into exile. In any case, this hope foundered. It was not long before the rest of the Israelite tribes fell to Assyria.

מִכַּף מַלְכֵי אַשּׁוּר — *Out of the hand of the kings of Assyria*. Who had already taken some of the tribes into exile (*Metzudos*).

7. כַּאֲבוֹתֵיכֶם וְכַאֲחֵיכֶם — *Like your fathers and like your brothers*. In v. 9 only brothers, not fathers, are mentioned. From the context there, which talks about their brothers' captors, it seems reasonable to conclude that *brothers* are their contemporaries — the tribes already taken into exile. *Fathers* are the earlier generations which were invariably punished whenever they dealt falsely with God (*Mefaresh*).

לְשַׁמָּה — *An appallment*. See at 28:8.

8. כַּאֲבוֹתֵיכֶם — *As your fathers were*. In the context of an exhortation to return to the Temple worship, it seems likely that *fathers* here refers to Yarov'am's generation. The people of those times had spurned the Temple in favor of the statues which he erected in Beth El and Dan. See further at v. 10.

תְּנוּ־יָד — *Stretch out your hand*. Translation follows *Targum*. *Metzudos* understands the term in the sense of shaking the hand as one would do in undertaking some kind of formal obligation.

אֲשֶׁר הִקְדִּישׁ לְעוֹלָם — *Which He has sanctified forever*. That Yarov'am's generation had rejected the Temple, in no way lessened its sanctity. They had erred, but God continued to dwell in Jerusalem. It was now up to them to rectify their mistake.

וְעִבְדוּ אֶת־ה׳ אֱלֹהֵיכֶם — *And serve* HASHEM *your God*. There is particular significance to the term *and serve* in the context of the celebration of the *Pesach*. See prefatory remarks to this chapter for the unique aspect of *service* which inheres in the *Pesach* offering.

9. אֲחֵיכֶם וּבְנֵיכֶם — *Your brothers and your sons*. For *brothers* see comm. to v. 7. The use of *sons* here apparently assumes that the tribes of the Northern Kingdom intermarried with one another, and that the people of the remaining tribes would therefore have children and grandchildren among the exiles.

לְרַחֲמִים — *Shall find compassion*. This com-

ל
י־טו

לָאָרֶץ הַזֹּאת כִּי־חַנּוּן וְרַחוּם יְהוָה אֱלֹהֵיכֶם וְלֹא־יָסִיר
י פָּנִים מִכֶּם אִם־תָּשׁוּבוּ אֵלָיו׃ וַיִּהְיוּ
הָרָצִים עֹבְרִים מֵעִיר ׀ לָעִיר בְּאֶרֶץ־אֶפְרַיִם וּמְנַשֶּׁה
יא וְעַד־זְבֻלוּן וַיִּהְיוּ מַשְׂחִיקִים עֲלֵיהֶם וּמַלְעִגִים בָּם׃ אַךְ
אֲנָשִׁים מֵאָשֵׁר וּמְנַשֶּׁה וּמִזְּבֻלוּן נִכְנְעוּ וַיָּבֹאוּ לִירוּשָׁלִָם׃
יב גַּם בִּיהוּדָה הָיְתָה יַד הָאֱלֹהִים לָתֵת לָהֶם לֵב אֶחָד
יג לַעֲשׂוֹת מִצְוַת הַמֶּלֶךְ וְהַשָּׂרִים בִּדְבַר יְהוָה׃ וַיֵּאָסְפוּ
יְרוּשָׁלִַם עַם־רָב לַעֲשׂוֹת אֶת־חַג הַמַּצּוֹת בַּחֹדֶשׁ הַשֵּׁנִי
יד קָהָל לָרֹב מְאֹד׃ וַיָּקֻמוּ וַיָּסִירוּ אֶת־הַמִּזְבְּחוֹת אֲשֶׁר
בִּירוּשָׁלִָם וְאֵת כָּל־הַמְקַטְּרוֹת הֵסִירוּ וַיַּשְׁלִיכוּ לְנַחַל
טו קִדְרוֹן׃ וַיִּשְׁחֲטוּ הַפֶּסַח בְּאַרְבָּעָה עָשָׂר לַחֹדֶשׁ הַשֵּׁנִי

passion will express itself in that the captors would allow the exiles to return to their land (*Metzudos*).

If we take our verse together with v. 6, where we saw the hope expressed that the remaining tribes would not be carried away, we can recognize the scope of Chizkiahu's hopes. This *Pesach* celebration was to be no less than a reversal of the entire downward trend which had plagued Israel since the glory days of Solomon's reign. A truly Messianic perspective of his historic role!

10. וַיִּהְיוּ מַשְׂחִיקִים עֲלֵיהֶם וּמַלְעִגִים בָּם — *But they laughed at them and mocked them*. Chizkiahu's hopes of reversing the tide of exile were dashed. The majority of the people derided his message and only individuals [אֲנָשִׁים (v. 11)] allowed themselves to be persuaded. The fate of the remainder of the Ten Tribes was sealed. They, too, were to be led into captivity (*Malbim*).

Why did the Israelites reject the message of repentance which Chizkiahu had sent them with so much hope?

A careful reading of v. 8 and v. 11 can yield an answer. In v. 8, Chizkiahu exhorted the people not to be *stiff necked*, and v. 11 describes the people who did come as *humbling themselves*.

We recall from 10:16 that in establishing the break-away Northern Kingdom, the people had rejected the kingdom of Heaven, the kingship of the Davidic line, and the Holy Temple. To answer Chizkiahu's call would have meant to negate the history and tradition of many generations. Of such humbleness the majority did not find themselves capable.

11. אֲנָשִׁים — *Diverse men*. Few from among the many (*Malbim*).

וַיָּבֹאוּ לִירוּשָׁלִָם — *And came to Jerusalem*. The addition of the words *to Jerusalem* tells the story of the inner battle which these heroes must have fought. Their sacred cities had been Beth El and Dan, and it was there that they had turned for their spiritual sustenance. The trek to Jerusalem spelled a repudiation of their entire past.

12. ... גַּם בִּיהוּדָה — *Also ... upon Judah* ... Even the people of Judah had been weaned away from God's service during Achaz's reign. The fact that now they agreed with unanimous enthusiasm, to participate in the *Pesach* celebration, could be considered the result of Divine intervention (*Malbim*).

בִּדְבַר ה׳ — *In accordance with the word of* HASHEM. *Metzudos* translates: *In the matter [of the Pesach] which is God's command*. However, we have followed *Targum* who renders the prefix ב as though it were a כ, in precisely the same way as at 29:25 — see comm. there. This, for the following reasons:

As *Metzudos* renders the phrase, it seems to add nothing to what has already been said. We know the subject of the command of the king and the princes from the entire narrative and, in addition, there seems to be little reason to stress that the obligation to bring the *Pesach* offering is God's command. That is, of course, assumed throughout.

If the word is to be understood as כִּדְבַר ה׳, then it would parallel 35:6 where the same expression is used in connection with Yoshiahu's *Pesach*, and would, indeed, be in tune

land. For HASHEM your God is gracious and merciful and will not
turn His face away from you if you return to Him.' 10 So the run-
ners passed from city to city through the country of Ephraim and
Menasheh up to Zevulun. But they laughed at them and mocked
them. 11 Nevertheless, diverse men from Asher, Menasheh and
Zevulun humbled themselves and came to Jerusalem. 12 Also the
hand of God was upon Judah to inbue them with one heart to
obey the command of the king and the princes in accordance with
the word of HASHEM. 13 There assembled in Jerusalem a great
multitude to celebrate the Feast of Matzos in the second month; a
very great congregation. 14 They bestirred themselves to remove
the altars which were in Jerusalem, and all the altars for incense
they removed, and cast into the wadi of Kidron. 15 They slaugh-
tered the Pesach on the fourteenth day of the second month.

with the rest of *Chronicles* in which, as we noted at fn. to *I Chronicles* 6:34, there is always a tendency to stress that the sacrificial services were performed in accordance with the Torah's dictates.

What, then, would be the reason for the text to write בִּדְבַר ה׳ when כִּדְבַר ה׳ is meant?

The reason could be very much akin to our suggestion at 29:25. Overtly, all that was visible was a conscientious adherence to the Torah's requirement for bringing the *Pesach* offering — כִּדְבַר ה׳ — but inwardly Chizkiahu felt himself driven by Divine fiat — בִּדְבַר ה׳ his Messianic destiny challenged him to summon his people to the religious rededication implicit in the Pesach celebration.

13. לַעֲשׂוֹת אֶת־חַג הַמַּצּוֹת — *To celebrate the Feast of Matzos.* In the Torah the fourteenth of *Nissan* is called פֶּסַח, and the name חַג הַמַּצּוֹת is used for the seven-day festival starting on the fifteenth. There is a marked contrast between the language which describes Chizkiahu's plans and that which reports the people's compliance. Chizkiahu was concerned with the celebration of the *Pesach* — the sacrificing of the *Pesach* offering (vs. 1, 2, 5, 8), but the people seem to stress the *Feast of Matzos* (our verse and v. 21).

This could be consistent with the ideas presented in the prefatory remarks to this chapter. Chizkiahu, aware of his Messianic destiny, had the idea of a fundamental rededicating of his people to God's worship. This, as we saw there, would be implicit in the bringing of the *Pesach* offering.

The people, on the other hand, were not ready for such a total recommitment to their obligation. They came to celebrate the *Feast of Matzos*, with all its overtones of Divine love and concern, but could not bring themselves to treat the *Pesach* with the right respect (see v. 21).

לַעֲשׂוֹת אֶת־חַג הַמַּצּוֹת בַּחֹדֶשׁ הַשֵּׁנִי — *To celebrate the Feast of Matzos in the second month.* Without the assumption which we have made throughout the comm. — that the chronology which *Chronicles* uses is based on the opinion of the Torah authorities who disagreed with Chizkiahu's institution of the leap year — this phrase would be an inner contradiction. There is no such thing as a *Feast of Matzos* in the *second month*. When an individual was not able — for halachically defined reasons — to bring the *Pesach* in *Nissan*, the Torah provides for a substitute celebration in the second month [פֶּסַח שֵׁנִי], but the celebration of that Pesach lasts only one day.

Here, according to Chizkiahu's thinking, the celebration of the Pesach described in our verse took place in *Nissan* — the first month. *Chronicles* refers to it as the *second month* because that is how the Sages viewed it (*Margalios HaYam*).

14. ... וַיָּקֻמוּ — *They bestirred themselves ...* See comm. to *I Chronicles* 28:2 that the root קום is often used to denote a change of direction or attitude. From having been deeply involved in the idol worship which had been instituted by Achaz, the people now changed, and joined Chizkiahu in eradicating its every vestige.

15. לַחֹדֶשׁ הַשֵּׁנִי — *Of the second month.* See comm. to v. 13.

וְהַכֹּהֲנִים וְהַלְוִיִּם נִכְלְמוּ וַיִּתְקַדְּשׁוּ וַיָּבִיאוּ עֹלוֹת בֵּית
טז יהוה: וַיַּעַמְדוּ עַל־עָמְדָם כְּמִשְׁפָּטָם כְּתוֹרַת מֹשֶׁה
אִישׁ־הָאֱלֹהִים הַכֹּהֲנִים זֹרְקִים אֶת־הַדָּם מִיַּד הַלְוִיִּם:
יז כִּי־רַבַּת בַּקָּהָל אֲשֶׁר לֹא־הִתְקַדָּשׁוּ וְהַלְוִיִּם עַל־שְׁחִיטַת
יח הַפְּסָחִים לְכֹל לֹא טָהוֹר לְהַקְדִּישׁ לַיהוה: כִּי מַרְבִּית
הָעָם רַבַּת מֵאֶפְרַיִם וּמְנַשֶּׁה יִשָּׂשכָר וּזְבֻלוּן לֹא הִטֶּהָרוּ
כִּי־אָכְלוּ אֶת־הַפֶּסַח בְּלֹא כַכָּתוּב כִּי הִתְפַּלֵּל יְחִזְקִיָּהוּ
יט עֲלֵיהֶם לֵאמֹר יהוה הַטּוֹב יְכַפֵּר בְּעַד: כָּל־לְבָבוֹ

וְהַכֹּהֲנִים וְהַלְוִיִּם נִכְלְמוּ — *The Kohanim and the Levites were ashamed.* They had been tardy in cleansing themselves (v. 3), not believing that Chizkiahu would so quickly undo all that his father had instituted (*Mefaresh*). They were therefore responsible for the disputed institution of the leap year. For this reason they felt ashamed (*Metzudos, Malbim*).

We may surmise that the *Kohanim* and Levites themselves belonged among the Sages who opposed Chizkiahu's proclamation of the leap year. Thus, in bringing the *Pesach* offering in a month that they themselves considered the second month — and therefore disqualified from the celebration of *Pesach* — they were being untrue to their own convictions; surely this was reason enough to feel ashamed.

This could explain why they now brought *burnt offerings* to the Temple. *Metzudos* points out that these were brought in order to elicit forgiveness for their tardiness. *Vayikra Rabbah* 7:3 teaches that a burnt offering atones for *thoughts of the heart*, a concept which may well include an act of hypocrisy.

וַיִּתְקַדְּשׁוּ — *And sanctified themselves.* The phrase must apparently be understood in the sense that they had already cleansed themselves prior to the bringing of the *Pesach* described in the earlier part of the verse.

16. וַיַּעַמְדוּ עַל־עָמְדָם כְּמִשְׁפָּטָם — *They stood in their place in accordance with their rank.* The translation follows *Metzudos* who has it refer to the Levites — not to the *Kohanim*. Some explanation is necessary.

The slaughtering of a sacrifice does not require a *Kohen*, but the receiving of the blood [קַבָּלָה], the carrying of it to the altar [הולָכָה], and the sprinkling [זְרִיקָה] may not be done by anyone who is not a *Kohen*. Consequently, the end of our verse. *The Kohanim sprinkling the blood from the hands of the Levites*, must be understood to mean that the *Kohanim* undertook the act of sprinkling from its very beginning — from the *receiving* onwards, from the hands of the Levites — that is, from the Levites who had slaughtered the sacrifice (*Malbim*).

Our phrase, then, is the introduction to the latter part of the sentence. The Levites did not go beyond that which the Torah of Moses permitted them. It was the *Kohanim* who sprinkled [received] the blood and not they.

מִיַּד הַלְוִיִּם — *From the hands of the Levites.* The explanation offered above is particularly apt, if the *Levites* of our verse are those *Kohanim* who had become disqualified from the Divine service because of their idol worship (see comm. to 29:34). If that is the case, then it is particularly noteworthy that they accepted the limitations placed upon them by the halachah, and made no attempt to regain their former standing.

17. ... כִּי ... וְהַלְוִיִּם — *For ... therefore the Levites ...* This verse is an explanation of the previous one. Normally, since the slaughter of the sacrifice does not need to be done by a *Kohen*, the owners themselves would have slaughtered their own sacrifices (*Metzudos*) or, at the very least, would have been present in the Temple courtyard so as to be personally involved in the preparation for this all-important ceremony (*Da'as Soferim*). This was not possible here since many of the people were still *tamei* and could therefore not enter the Temple precincts. Because of this, the Levites took over the entire function of the owners.

However, the Levites could only do this in regard to the slaughtering of the offering; the eating at night had to be done by the owners themselves (*Radak*). Thus, it transpired, that this *Pesach* offering was eaten by large numbers of people who were *tamei* — something normally forbidden by the Torah and punishable by *kares* (*Radak*).

How could Chizkiahu have allowed this to happen?

The Kohanim and the Levites were ashamed and sanctified themselves and brought burnt offerings to HASHEM's House
16 *They stood in their place in accordance with their rank, in compliance with the Torah of Moses, man of God; the Kohanim sprinkling the blood from the hands of the Levites.*
17 *For there were many in the congregation that had not cleansed themselves, therefore the Levites had charge of slaughtering the Pesach offerings, for everyone that was not ritually clean so that he might himself deal with that which is sacred to HASHEM.*
18 *For a multitude of the people — many from Ephraim and Menasseh, Issachar and Zevulun — had not sanctified themselves, so that they ate the Pesach otherwise than is written. But Chizkiahu prayed for them, saying, 'May the good HASHEM pardon'*
19 *'each*

Here we have diverging opinions which will affect the interpretation of the following few verses.

Radak and *Metzudos* believe that, indeed, the eating of the *Pesach* by these ritually unclean people was forbidden, and this is the meaning of the phrase *they ate the Pesach otherwise than is written*, in the following verse. Chizkiahu allowed this to happen as a הוֹרָאַת שָׁעָה, *a one-time ruling* (*Metzudos*), because he recognized the sincerity of the people (v. 19) and did not want them to be disqualified from this profoundly evocative service of God. He prayed to God that under these exceptional circumstances He should forgive the people this transgression (v. 18), and God accepted his prayer (v. 20).

Rambam (*Bias Mikdash* 4:17-18) disagrees. He believes that the expressions of רַבַּת בַּקָּהָל our verse, and מַרְבִּית הָעָם of v. 18 imply that not just a great number of individuals but the majority of the community were *tamei*. Under these circumstances, the Torah permits the bringing of the *Pesach* in a state of *tumah* (see comm. to v. 2) and thus no sin was committed. For this reason, he interprets the phrase ... *they ate the Pesach otherwise than is written* of the next verse, differently than do *Radak* and *Metzudos*, and this influences the interpretation of vs. 19 and 20 also — see there.

[It transpires that in *Rambam's* view, Chizkiahu's institution of the leap year did not have the desired effect. His purpose had been to avoid the necessity of bringing the *Pesach* while the community was *tamei* (see comm. to v. 2) and, in the end, most people had still not taken advantage of the extra month's grace to cleanse themselves.]

לְהַקְדִּישׁ לַה׳ — *So that he might himself deal with that which is sacred to HASHEM.* Translation follows *Metzudos*.

18. כִּי מַרְבִּית הָעָם ... — *For a multitude of the people* ... The tribes listed are all from the Northern Kingdom. *Da'as Soferim* suggests that these were less attuned to the laws of ritual cleanliness than were the people of Judah, since those laws had fallen into disuse throughout the long years that access to Jerusalem was denied the people of the Ten Tribes.

כִּי־אָכְלוּ אֶת־הַפֶּסַח בְּלֹא כַכָּתוּב — *So that they ate the Pesach otherwise than is written*. We have translated כִּי, *so that*, in accordance with *Radak* and *Metzudos*: The transgression consisted of eating the *Pesach* in a state of *tumah*.

However, as noted in comm. to v. 17, *Rambam* disagrees and thinks that the uncleanliness — since it encompassed the greater part of the community — presented no problem. In his view, the transgression lay in Chizkiahu's proclamation of the leap year. Both his motive — the ritual uncleanliness of the people and his timing — the last day of *Adar* were inappropriate and unjustified in halachic terms. In the context of the verse he would probably here render כִּי as *although*. Although the *Pesach* was eaten in halachically unacceptable conditions, in that it should have been done a month earlier, the majority of the people were still *tamei* — thus negating the entire purpose.

כִּי הִתְפַּלֵּל יְחִזְקִיָּהוּ — *But Chizkiahu prayed for them* ... The context demands the unusual translation *but* for כִּי

Chizkiahu prayed that God forgive the peoples' transgression of eating the *Pesach* while ritually unclean (*Radak* and *Metzudos*); or that God forgive his own transgression of instituting a halachically unjustified leap year (*Rambam*).

ה׳ הַטּוֹב יְכַפֵּר בְּעַד — *May the good HASHEM*

הֵכִ֔ין לִדְר֛וֹשׁ הָאֱלֹהִ֖ים ׀ יהוָ֣ה אֱלֹהֵ֣י אֲבוֹתָ֑יו וְלֹ֖א כְּטָהֳרַ֥ת
כ הַקֹּֽדֶשׁ׃ וַיִּשְׁמַ֤ע יהוה֙ אֶל־יְחִזְקִיָּ֔הוּ
כא וַיִּרְפָּ֖א אֶת־הָעָֽם׃ וַיַּעֲשׂ֣וּ בְנֵֽי־יִ֠שְׂרָאֵל
הַֽנִּמְצְאִ֨ים בִּירוּשָׁלִַ֜ם אֶת־חַ֧ג הַמַּצּ֛וֹת שִׁבְעַ֥ת יָמִ֖ים
בְּשִׂמְחָ֣ה גְדוֹלָ֑ה וּֽמְהַלְלִ֣ים לַ֠יהוָֹה י֣וֹם ׀ בְּי֗וֹם הַלְוִיִּ֛ם
כב וְהַכֹּהֲנִ֖ים בִּכְלֵי־עֹ֥ז לַיהוָֹֽה׃ וַיְדַבֵּ֣ר יְחִזְקִיָּ֗הוּ עַל־לֵב֙
כָּל־הַלְוִיִּ֔ם הַמַּשְׂכִּילִ֥ים שֵֽׂכֶל־ט֖וֹב לַיהוָ֑ה וַיֹּאכְל֤וּ אֶת־
הַמּוֹעֵד֙ שִׁבְעַ֣ת הַיָּמִ֔ים מְזַבְּחִים֙ זִבְחֵ֣י שְׁלָמִ֔ים וּמִ֨תְוַדִּ֔ים

pardon. The sentence appears truncated and calls for a direct object: May the good HASHEM pardon — the transgression. Since it is self-understood, the text relies on the reader to supply the ending (*Metzudos*).

Metzudos thinks that the next verse, *He set his whole heart to seek out God*, is a new thought and describes Chizkiahu's spiritual standing.

Mefaresh cites *Thirty-Two Midos of R' Yose HaGellili* 11, which views vs. 18 and 19 as an example of a single thought being [apparently arbitrarily — but see below] divided into two sentences. Thus, we must read as follows: *May the good HASHEM pardon each one who set his heart* ... This is also *Radak's* view and eliminates the problem of the truncated verse. Of course, this reading is only possible if we agree with *Radak* and *Metzudos* that we are dealing with the transgression of eating the *Pesach* while ritually unclean. This sin was committed by numerous people and Chizkiahu now prayed that God look at their intentions which were beyond reproach, rather than at their actions which were flawed. *Rambam*, in whose view only Chizkiahu transgressed, will have to share *Metzudos'* interpretation.

Da'as Soferim suggests an explanation for the apparently arbitrary splitting of one thought into two verses. He thinks that this was done to bring home the lesson that normally, good intentions will not excuse a sinful act. The verse stops with the incompleted ...בְּעַד, in order to indicate that, strictly speaking, there is no reason why God should show mercy.

19. כָּל־לְבָבוֹ הֵכִין — *Each one who set his heart*. We have translated in accordance with the tradition of the Sages (*Thirty-Two Midos*), as held also by *Radak*, that our verse is a continuation of the previous one, and that it supplies the object for that otherwise truncated verse — see above.

Metzudos — and as explained above, *Rambam* — would take our verse as a new thought and have it refer to Chizkiahu, rendering: *He set his whole heart* ...

וְלֹא כְּטָהֳרַת הַקֹּדֶשׁ — *Though not in accordance with the purity appropriate to the sacred*. The people had only good intentions, even though their actions in eating the *Pesach* while they were ritually impure did not accord with the usage appropriate to the sacred (*Radak*). Or, Chizkiahu sought out God with all his heart, even though not all his actions attained full purity — as witness his unjustified proclamation of the leap year (*Rambam*).

20. וַיִּרְפָּא אֶת־הָעָם — *And healed the people*. He healed them in that He forgave their transgression (*Metzudos*), or that He accepted their sacrifice (*Rambam*).

21. בְּנֵי־יִשְׂרָאֵל — *The Children of Israel*. At 28:8 this term had been used to describe the tribes of the Northern Kingdom in contrast to their brothers in the south who were called *Judeans* (v. 10). Here, the term evidently is meant to include everybody who was in Jerusalem to celebrate the *Pesach*, and is, perhaps, used to underline that very fact. In the context of Chizkiahu's Messianic destiny he had managed — at least temporarily — to create a new, unified *Children of Israel*.

חַג הַמַּצּוֹת — *The Feast of Matzos*. See comm. to v. 13.

בִּכְלֵי־עֹז לַה׳ — *With instruments of praise to HASHEM*. The translation follows *Targum* who renders: בְּזֵינֵי תּוּשְׁבַּחְתָּא. He apparently thinks that the term עֹז in contexts such as *Psalms* 29:1 or 59:17 is a synonym for *praise*.

Alternatives are: *trumpets* [apparently because of the *strength* required to blow into them] (*Mefaresh*); *instruments by which a person might involve his entire energy in the service of God* (*Radak*); or *instruments of first quality* (*Metzudos*).

one who set his heart to search out You, HASHEM, the God of his fathers; though not in accordance with the purity appropriate to the sacred.' 20 *HASHEM listened to Chizkiahu and healed the people.* 21 *The Children of Israel that were present in Jerusalem celebrated the Feast of Matzos seven days with great joy; the Levites and the Kohanim praising HASHEM daily with instruments of praise to HASHEM.* 22 *Chizkiahu spoke persuasively to all the Levites who have a profound insight into matters of HASHEM. So they ate the festival sacrifices seven days, sacrificing peace offerings and expressing their gratitude through thanks offerings*

22. וַיְדַבֵּר יְחִזְקִיָּהוּ עַל־לֵב כָּל־הַלְוִיִּם — *Chizkiahu spoke persuasively to all the Levites.* In order to bring love of God into their hearts, he used language to which they would be receptive (*Metzudos*).

הַמַּשְׂכִּילִים שֵׂכֶל־טוֹב לַה׳ — *Who have a profound insight into matters of HASHEM.* The translation combines *Radak* (*Sefer HaShorashim*) with *Metzudos*. *Radak* relates שכל to *observation* [הַשְׁגָּחָה] and *analysis* [עִיּוּן], while *Metzudos* interprets לַה׳ as: ... *in the matter of the service of HASHEM.*

Both *Mefaresh* and *Ralbag* take the phrase in reference to the Levitical hymns of the previous verse. *Shir*, songs of jubilation to God, must derive from a profound and stirring appreciation of God's hand in history. The Levites, entrusted with the duty of engaging in the *shir*, needed to possess the intellectual ability to do it, and the Divine service, justice.

וַיֹּאכְלוּ אֶת־הַמּוֹעֵד — *So they ate the festival sacrifices* ... Thus, all the commentators. *Metzudos* points out that the term *sacrifices* is implied and that we have here a מִקְרָא קָצֵר a truncated verse.

But why was it truncated? Why should the word זֶבַח have been left out?

We may surmise as follows: The word *eating* can also describe the act of learning — see *Chullin* 6a to *Proverbs* 23:1. The analogy is simple — one, who eats, absorbs the food into his body and thus enables it to sustain him. In a spiritual sense, this is precisely what someone who learns is doing. He absorbs the knowledge and thus enables it to sustain and animate him.

The omission of the word זֶבַח allows for a dual interpretation of the phrase. Certainly they ate the sacrifices which were brought, but this alone would have been a purely physical act. In addition, though, they *absorbed* the festival itself. They allowed their consumption of the sacrifices to penetrate deeply into their consciousness, exposing themselves to the subsurface, essential messages of the Pesach festival. It is perhaps for this reason that Chizkiahu had talked to the Levites *who had a profound insight*. It was they who had the capability of relating to the feast in this most ideal manner.

וּמִתְוַדִּים — *And expressing their gratitude through thanks offerings.* Translation follows *Targum*, *Mefaresh* and *Metzudos*. The latter two write that תודות, *thanks offerings*, were brought in order to express gratitude to God for miracles performed for them.

[Both *Mefaresh* and *Metzudos* use the word נֵס, *miracle*, but do not make clear what *miracle* might be meant. Perhaps gratitude was being expressed for the newly found spirit of repentance, and the movement toward reunification between the two kingdoms, which had been awakened through Chizkiahu's initiative.]

But it is difficult to accept the view that actual thanks offerings were brought. These had to be accompanied by loaves of bread which were *chametz* (see *Rambam*, *Maaseh HaKorbonos* 9:17) and could thus not have been brought on Pesach (*Malbim*).

It would be possible to render מִתְוַדִּים as *thanking*, and still not be forced into an assumption that actual *thanks offerings* were brought. Perhaps the verse simply means that the bringing of the שְׁלָמִים, *peace offerings*, was accompanied by a feeling of gratitude to HASHEM. This could help to explain the unique use of the reflexive מִתְוַדִּים instead of the regular מוֹדִים to express *thanks*. The reflexive voice would carry the nuance of inwardness, a deeply felt indebtedness, as opposed to the overt expression of thanks implied in the bringing of sacrifices.

Ralbag takes the word in its more normal usage — *to confess*. They confessed their past transgressions, in conjunction with the bringing of the festival sacrifices. Surely, this too, would not have been done in a formal sense. The festival sacrifices are not sin offerings,)

כג לַיהוָה אֱלֹהֵי אֲבוֹתֵיהֶם: וַיִּוָּעֲצוּ כָּל־הַקָּהָל
לַעֲשׂוֹת שִׁבְעַת יָמִים אֲחֵרִים וַיַּעֲשׂוּ שִׁבְעַת־יָמִים שִׂמְחָה:
כד כִּי חִזְקִיָּהוּ מֶלֶךְ־יְהוּדָה הֵרִים לַקָּהָל אֶלֶף פָּרִים וְשִׁבְעַת
אֲלָפִים צֹאן וְהַשָּׂרִים הֵרִימוּ לַקָּהָל פָּרִים אֶלֶף וְצֹאן
כה עֲשֶׂרֶת אֲלָפִים וַיִּתְקַדְּשׁוּ כֹהֲנִים לָרֹב: וַיִּשְׂמְחוּ | כָּל־קְהַל
יְהוּדָה וְהַכֹּהֲנִים וְהַלְוִיִּם וְכָל־הַקָּהָל הַבָּאִים מִיִּשְׂרָאֵל
כו וְהַגֵּרִים הַבָּאִים מֵאֶרֶץ יִשְׂרָאֵל וְהַיּוֹשְׁבִים בִּיהוּדָה: וַתְּהִי
שִׂמְחָה־גְדוֹלָה בִּירוּשָׁלִָם כִּי מִימֵי שְׁלֹמֹה בֶן־דָּוִיד מֶלֶךְ
כז יִשְׂרָאֵל לֹא כָזֹאת בִּירוּשָׁלִָם: וַיָּקֻמוּ הַכֹּהֲנִים הַלְוִיִּם

and no confession is made as they are brought. Rather, we are dealing with a spontaneous outpouring of repentance in conjunction with the joy of the festival.

23. שִׁבְעַת יָמִים אֲחֵרִים — *Another seven days.* The first seven days were devoted to the observance of the Pesach festival. The rule that אֵין מְעָרְבִין שִׂמְחָה בְּשִׂמְחָה, *we do not allow one occasion for joy to intrude upon another*, made it imperative to set aside another week for the celebration of the Temple inauguration.

See 7:8-10 for an analogy from Solomon's days. There, too, beside the joyous days of Succos, seven special days were set aside for inaugural celebration.

24. ...כִּי — *For* ... Because Chizkiahu and the princes had donated animals from their own flocks, there was ample meat for the extended celebrations (*Metzudos*).

הֵרִים לַקָּהָל אֶלֶף פָּרִים — *Had set aside a thousand bullocks for the people.* At 29:32 we noted the relatively small number of sacrifices which were brought at the beginning of Chizkiahu's reign. We thought there that Chizkiahu purposely kept the sacrificial service small so that the people, attuned as they were to the distortions of the idolatrous cults, should not be overwhelmed by sheer numbers, which would tend to overshadow the spirituality of the Divine sacrificial service. Evidently, after the successful celebration of the *Pesach* with all that this implied, this was no longer perceived as a danger. Sacrifices could once more be brought in suitable numbers.

וַיִּתְקַדְּשׁוּ כֹהֲנִים לָרֹב — *The Kohanim had sanctified themselves in great numbers.* There were sufficient *Kohanim* who had cleansed themselves from their ritual impurity (*tum'ah*), so that this awesome number of sacrifices could readily be brought (*Metzudos*).

This, in contrast to the earlier weeks of Chizkiahu's reign when sufficient *Kohanim* had not been available (v. 3).

25. וְהַגֵּרִים הַבָּאִים מֵאֶרֶץ יִשְׂרָאֵל — *So too with the alien residents that came from the land of Israel.* Who are these aliens and why are they mentioned as a separate entity here?

[See *I Chronicles* 22:2 and at 2:17 for an analysis of the expression גֵּרִים אֲשֶׁר בְּאֶרֶץ יִשְׂרָאֵל used there. See also below on הַבָּאִים מֵאֶרֶץ יִשְׂרָאֵל.]

Significantly, these *alien residents* are mentioned here, in connection with the celebration of the second seven days (v. 23), while the joy of the Pesach celebration (v. 21) is ascribed to ... *the Children of Israel that were present in Jerusalem*. Indeed, a contrasting of our verse with v. 21 underlines the profound differences between the two descriptions. There, only one group - *Children of Israel* — is mentioned, while in our verse we have no fewer than five different categories.

We assume the difference to be grounded in the varying natures of the two celebrations. The sacrificing of the *Pesach* offering and the celebration of the Festival of Matzos have a common message for all the people: It is a reaffirmation of Israel's closeness [the *passing-over* symbolized by the *Pesach* offering]; and a rededication to God's service [... *they are My servants whom I took out from the land of Egypt*]. Even גֵּרִים, *proselytes*, who do not share the historical heritage, have an equal part in its symbolism (*Exodus* 12:48).

Not so the reopening and the rededication of the Temple. The joy of that occasion was different for the people of Judah, who had

30
23-27

to HASHEM the G-d of their fathers. 23 Then all the assembled
people decided, after due consideration, to celebrate another
seven days. So, joyously, they celebrated another seven days. 24
For Chizkiahu king of Judah had set aside a thousand bullocks
and seven thousand sheep for the people; and the princes had set
aside a thousand bullocks and ten thousand sheep for the people.
The Kohanim had sanctified themselves in great numbers. 25 All
of Judah's population, the Kohanim and the Levites rejoiced
together with all the people that came from Israel. So too, the
alien residents that came from the land of Israel, and those who
lived in Judah. 26 So there was great joy in Jerusalem for since the
time of Solomon the son of David king of Israel there was not the
like in Jerusalem. 27 The Kohanim the Levites arose and blessed

tasted at close proximity the ugliness and shame of Achaz's depredations, than it was for the people of Israel to whom, for centuries it had been no more than a dream. The *Kohanim* and the Levites who were most directly involved in the Divine service surely had their very own feelings of gratitude and gladness.

But what of the גֵּרִים? Who are they and in what way were their expressions of joy unique? For an understanding, we should first analyze the concept: ... *that came from the Land of Israel*.

Within the context of our verse, the expression is readily understandable. It substitutes a geographic term: *the Land of Israel*, for one which denotes family descent: ... *from Israel*, in the earlier part of the verse. The people mentioned earlier were part of the families of Judah and Israel. The *alien residents* could only be described as coming from the land.

But inasmuch as our expression is identical with that used in *I Chronicles* 22:2 and at 2:17, it appears likely that the meaning should be the same in all three cases.

The expression argues for *Radak's* view (2:16) that these aliens were the remnants of the seven Canaanite nations. Having rejected idol worship, they did not fall under the category of those who were interdicted from living in the land — see *Exodus* 23:23. They were גֵּרֵי תוֹשָׁב, *non-Jews whose halachic status places them above the category of idol worshipers and grants them the right of residence in Israel*. For such גֵּרֵי תוֹשָׁב, the expression ... *who came from the Land of Israel*, is entirely apt.

But, in what sense are these *alien residents*, who are not even Jews, involved in the rededication of the Temple?

It seems likely that here, once more, we meet up with Chizkiahu's Messianic destiny. The intensity of the religious revival which he was able to instigate set in motion a centrifugal force which began to draw even the outer fringes of society into the purifying fire of its ecstasy. These *aliens*, drawn inexorably inward, were to be the first trickle of the mighty stream which would one day flow from all the nations to the *mountain of the House of HASHEM* (*Isaiah* 2:2).

26. ... כִּי מִימֵי שְׁלֹמֹה — *For since the time of Solomon* ... There was a particular element of joy in Chizkiahu's celebration because there is a special sweetness in a closeness which comes after a protracted distancing. Never before, in the history of the first commonwealth, had the Temple been shut down as it had been during Achaz's reign (*Mefaresh*).

Other reasons this celebration was special were because it lasted a full fourteen days (*Ralbag*); or because it was a dedication of the Temple akin to Solomon's inaugural celebration (*Metzudos*); or because it was the first time since [after] Solomon's reign that the Northern and Southern Kingdoms were combined. In the intervening centuries, only Judah had celebrated (*Malbim*).

27. הַכֹּהֲנִים הַלְוִיִּם — *The Kohanim and the Levites*. Throughout our chapter, *Kohanim* and Levites have been mentioned together as discrete groups within the community, and *Ralbag* surmises that here, too, we must assume the conjunctive *vav* and understand the phrase as though it were written הַכֹּהֲנִים וְהַלְוִיִּם. This blessing was not the daily *Birkas Kohanim* — if it were, there would have been no need to mention it specifically. Rather, it was a special blessing in which the Levites joined the *Kohanim* — see further below.

וַיְבָרְכוּ אֶת־הָעָם וַיִּשָּׁמַע בְּקוֹלָם וַתָּבוֹא תְפִלָּתָם לִמְעוֹן לא
קָדְשׁוֹ לַשָּׁמָיִם: א וּכְכַלּוֹת כָּל־זֹאת יָצְאוּ כָל־יִשְׂרָאֵל א
הַנִּמְצְאִים לְעָרֵי יְהוּדָה וַיְשַׁבְּרוּ הַמַּצֵּבוֹת וַיְגַדְּעוּ
הָאֲשֵׁרִים וַיְנַתְּצוּ אֶת־הַבָּמוֹת וְאֶת־הַמִּזְבְּחוֹת מִכָּל־יְהוּדָה

וַיְבָרְכוּ אֶת־הָעָם — *And blessed the people*. We are not told what this blessing was, nor whether it was to be analogous to Aharon's blessing of the people at the inauguration of the Tabernacle (*Leviticus* 9:22). There, too, we are simply told that Aharon blessed the people but no indication of the content is given.

Yerushalmi, Taanis 4:1 calls Aharon's blessing, a בְּרָכָה סְתוּמָה, an *unspecified blessing*, but maintains that, in reality, Aharon used the regular formula for *Birkas Kohanim* given at *Numbers* 6:22 ff.

[Solomon's blessing of the people at the inauguration of the Temple is also not specified in *Chronicles*, but the text is given in *Kings* — see comm. to 6:3.]

In *Leviticus* 9:23 we learn that after Aharon had blessed the people, Moses and Aharon came out of the Tabernacle and once more blessed the people together. According to *Toras Kohanim* (*Rashi* there), this was a prayer that their efforts in inaugurating the Tabernacle should elicit God's goodwill, and that He should permit His *Shechinah* to dwell upon their handiwork. It seems likely that something akin to this was also the subject of the blessing here — see further below.

Mefaresh believes that the blessing was that their brethren who had been led into the Assyrian exile should be returned to them in accordance with the hope expressed by Chizkiahu (v. 9). He maintains that the next phrase ... *and He listened to their voice*, indicates that the prayer was answered, and that at least some of the captives returned.

וַיִּשָּׁמַע בְּקוֹלָם — *And He listened to their voice*. The translation follows *Metzudos*.

If this is, indeed, the meaning of the phrase, the syntax is difficult for two reasons: Firstly, *He listened* would have to be rendered with the *kal*, active voice — וַיִּשְׁמַע. In וַיִּשָּׁמַע, which is the *nifal*, passive voice, the subject seems to be the *voice* rather than the one who heard it. But then the ב in בְּקוֹלָם is out of place. The phrase וַיִּשָּׁמַע קוֹלָם would have been correct, and would have to be translated: *And their voice was heard*. [Indeed, this is *Targum's* translation — apparently ignoring the prefix ב.]

Again, even if the *kal* had been used, the phrase would have been difficult. In the last few verses, God had not been mentioned at all, and the use of the pronoun seems inapt. We would have expected: *And [HASHEM] listened to their voices*.

A literal translation, taking into account both the use of the *nifal* and the prefix ב, would have to be as follows:

Both in Scriptural Hebrew (*Psalms* 18:45) and in later usage (*Sanhedrin* 82b), we find the *nifal* of שמע used to express *obedience*. [That is, to be made to listen; *to obey*.] Thus, the phrase would have to be rendered: *And He obeyed their voice*. Such a concept would obviously seem inappropriate when used in connection with God, and this could well explain the use of the pronoun. In spite of the ambiguity which this causes — or possibly because of it — its use is appropriate here, in order to avoid the blatant use of the concept to *obey* in connection with God's Name.

But what can this concept possibly mean? In what sense does God obey?

The concept of God being, as it were, *obedient* to the wishes of the righteous, is not foreign to Aggadic thought: thus the well-known dictum: צַדִּיק גּוֹזֵר וְהַקָּבָּ״ה מְקַיֵּם, *the righteous man decrees and God fulfills* (based on *Shabbos* 59b), and this may be the underlying thought here.

We may be guided in our conjecture by the use of מְעוֹן קָדְשׁוֹ, *His holy habitation*, as a synonym for *heaven* in our verse. We find God, as it were, being forced to answer Israel's prayer on another occasion at which מָעוֹן and שָׁמַיִם occur together.

In *Deuteronomy* 26:15 we learn that, as part of the declaration which each Jew is required to make when he completes his tithing obligation each third year, he says: *Look down from Your holy habitation in heaven and bless Your people, Israel ...*, to which *Rashi* (based on *Sifri* and *Mishnah* in *Maaser Sheni*) remarks: *We have done that which you have decreed upon us — do You now do that which it is incumbent upon You to do, as You promised: If you will walk in My statutes ... I will bring your rain at the correct time*. *Malbim* there points out that the language which the Torah uses conveys the idea of a demand rather than of a request.

There are, then, things that Israel can do

31
the people and He listened to their voice and their prayer came up to His holy habitation to the heaven.

1
When all this was finished, all Israel that were present went out to the cities of Judah. They smashed the pillars, hewed down the groves, and broke down the bamos and the altars from

which justify a *demand* of God, that He react in a positive manner.

The attribute of God, that He allows Himself to be, as it were, commanded by the righteous, may well be associated with that part of heaven known as מָעוֹן (see *Kli Yakar* to *Deuteronomy* there). According to *Chagigah* 12b, מָעוֹן is that part of heaven in which God silences daily the hymns of glory sung to Him by the heavenly choir, so that He might devote Himself to the well-being of Israel. Thus, מָעוֹן projects God in His unlimited love for His people, before whom even the angels must be silent. Surely, this contrasting of the angels with Israel has its source in the fact that the jubilation of the angels is not the outgrowth of free choice but an expression of their essence. Israel, by its free-will subjugation to God's demands can, in turn, demand God's attention, and He is, as it were, forced to turn away from the angels' praises and to devote Himself to Israel's needs.

Our verse, then, is telling us that the people's rededication was of such sincerity and magnitude that God felt Himself, as it were, forced to accede to the blessing of the *Kohanim*, that His Divine Presence might rest among them.

XXXI

◆§ The Aftermath of the Celebration

1. **וּכְכַלּוֹת כָּל-זֹאת** — *When all this was finished*. Certainly the meaning of the phrase is that the people's zeal — described in our verse — derived from the joyous celebrations of which we have just learned.

It seems possible that there is an additional meaning. The previous verse had stated that: *... their prayer came up to His holy habitation*. But how would the author of *Chronicles* know this? Perhaps, the fact that the entire populace [כָּל יִשְׂרָאֵל הַנִּמְצְאִים] found it in themselves to eradicate every last vestige of idol worship with such exemplary enthusiasm, showed a spiritual uplifting which could only have resulted from an outpouring of God's spirit upon them.

יָצְאוּ כָל-יִשְׂרָאֵל... וַיְשַׁבְּרוּ — *All Israel went out ... smashed* ... The description recalls 23:17, where we learn how the spiritually uplifting experience of Yoash's coronation spurred the people to the zealous destruction of the Baal Temple.

There is, however, a major difference. At 23:17 the *Chronicles* account is almost exactly the same as that in *Kings*, while here there seems to be a substantive change. The *Kings* account ascribes the destruction of all the idolatrous facilities to Chizkiahu himself [*He removed...smashed...cut off...*(2:18:4)] while here, the same activity is carried out by *all Israel*.

Obviously, then, the intention is to convey the truth that when *Kings* talks of Chizkiahu himself destroying, the meaning is that he did this by inspiring the people to take action. The difference between the two accounts lies in the emphasis. *Kings* is interested in the occurrence for what it tells about Chizkiahu — *Chronicles*, in the interaction between king and people.

When we compare the account here with those describing Asa's and Yehoshaphat's elimination of idol worship (14:1-4; 17:6), we find differences from both in this matter. The two earlier accounts described the king as the prime mover in the eradication while ours talks of the people. But from the *Kings* account, it is evident that the story could have been told in precisely the same way as the other two — that Chizkiahu *did* all this. The change in emphasis is clearly significant.

Perhaps it is within the spirit of a Messianic framework, that the king [=Messiah] recedes into the background and the people come to the fore. According to *Devarim Rabba* 5:11, Israel will one day wish to reject the entire concept of human kingship. It had brought nothing but misery. They will cry: *We do not want a king! We want our first King, ... for God is our Judge ... our Lawgiver ... our King ...(Isaiah* 33:22). And God will answer them: *Truly that is what I shall do, as it is written* (*Zechariah* 14:9), *And God will be King over*

לא
ב־ג

וּבִנְיָמִן וּבְאֶפְרַיִם וּמְנַשֶּׁה עַד־לְכַלֵּה וַיָּשׁוּבוּ כָּל־בְּנֵי
ב יִשְׂרָאֵל אִישׁ לַאֲחֻזָּתוֹ לְעָרֵיהֶם: וַיַּעֲמֵד יְחִזְקִיָּהוּ אֶת־
מַחְלְקוֹת הַכֹּהֲנִים וְהַלְוִיִּם עַל־מַחְלְקוֹתָם אִישׁ | כְּפִי
עֲבֹדָתוֹ לַכֹּהֲנִים וְלַלְוִיִּם לְעֹלָה וְלִשְׁלָמִים לְשָׁרֵת
ג וּלְהֹדוֹת וּלְהַלֵּל בְּשַׁעֲרֵי מַחֲנוֹת יהוה: וּמְנָת
הַמֶּלֶךְ מִן־רְכוּשׁוֹ לָעֹלוֹת לְעֹלוֹת הַבֹּקֶר וְהָעֶרֶב וְהָעֹלוֹת
לַשַּׁבָּתוֹת וְלֶחֳדָשִׁים וְלַמֹּעֲדִים כַּכָּתוּב בְּתוֹרַת יהוה:

the whole land. [For detailed discussion see ArtScroll *Ezekiel*, prefatory remarks to ch. 34.]

Clearly, then, the Messianic king does not stand in contradiction to God's direct stewardship over the people. He stands not as himself but as conduit for God's kingship over His people. When the history of the Messianic era will be written, it will be the story of God and His people — not of their king — and in the *Chronicles* account it is not Chizkiahu as instigator of the reforms who is central to the story, but the people who carried them out.[1]

2. וַיַּעֲמֵד יְחִזְקִיָּהוּ אֶת־מַחְלְקוֹת הַכֹּהֲנִים וְהַלְוִיִּם — *Chizkiahu ordered the cadres of Kohanim and Levites* ... Once more we find Chizkiahu as the *David* of his generation. The establishment of the *mishmaros* of the Levites and the *Kohanim* had occupied an important place in David's preparations for the Temple [*I Chronicles*, chs. 23 and 24], and now *Chronicles* stresses that Chizkiahu, too, involved himself in these arrangements.[2]

הַכֹּהֲנִים וְהַלְוִיִּם — *Of the Kohanim and the Levites* .... The next phrase defines the function of each of these groups: ... *for burnt offerings and for peace offerings*, are the areas of responsibility of the *Kohanim*, while ... *to minister and to give thanks and to praise*, is the task of the Levites (*Metzudos*).

בְּשַׁעֲרֵי מַחֲנוֹת ה׳ — *In the gates of the camps of* HASHEM. *Mefaresh* and *Malbim* read as though the words: ... *and stood guard at* ... were inserted: The Levites did two things: They sang *shirah* [לְהוֹדוֹת וּלְהַלֵּל], and also stood guard at the gates.

Metzudos takes מַחֲנוֹת ה׳ as a synonym for *Temple*: The Levites sang *shirah* in the Temple. But why should the Temple be called *camps of* HASHEM, and why just in the context of Chizkiahu's disposition?

We suggest that this expression, too, reflects Chizkiahu's Messianic destiny.

We quote *Isaiah* 29:1—3: הוֹי אֲרִיאֵל אֲרִיאֵל קִרְיַת חָנָה דָוִד ... וַהֲצִיקוֹתִי לַאֲרִיאֵל ... וְחָנִיתִי כַדּוּר עָלָיִךְ ..., *Woe Ariel, Ariel! The city in which David camped ... thus I will press in upon Ariel ... and encircle it as with a camp...*

The prophet is castigating Jerusalem for its sins and threatening to bring besieging armies against it. He calls Jerusalem: *Ariel, Ariel the city in which David camped*.

Now *Ariel* is Ezekiel's expression for the altar (*Ezekiel* 43:15), and this is *Ibn Ezra's* understanding of the term here: Jerusalem is called *Ariel* because it is the city in which the altar stood.

But why describe Jerusalem in terms of the altar, and why as the city in which David *camped*?

Literally, אֲרִיאֵל means *lion of God*, and is the name given to the roof of the altar on which the fire consuming the sacrifices was located. As *Hirsch* understands the term (*Exodus* 27:8), it is so called because ... *with lion's power as* אֵשׁ אוֹכְלָה, *a consuming fire*, [*it*] *awaited the offerings of self-sacrifice* with

1. Our explanation may help clarify why the *Chronicles* account omits mention of the fact that Chizkiahu destroyed the copper snake which Moses had made — see *II Kings* 18:4.

The Sages view this incident as an indication of Chizkiahu's personal greatness (*Chullin* 6b). It was significant in the *Kings* account in which the king stands at the center. It is irrelevant within the ambience which *Chronicles* seeks to evoke.

2. There is a subtle difference between the wording used here, and in similar phrases found at 8:14 and 35:2, in connection with Solomon and Yoshiahu, respectively.

At 8:14 Solomon establishes אֶת מַחְלְקוֹת הַכֹּהֲנִים עַל עֲבֹדָתָם; that is, he simply makes sure that the already existing cadres of *Kohanim* are assigned to their specific areas of responsibility. At 35:2, Yoshiahu orders הַכֹּהֲנִים עַל מִשְׁמְרוֹתָם, the individual *Kohanim* to their divisions.

It is only here that the מַחְלְקוֹת הַכֹּהֲנִים are ordered to their מַחְלְקוֹת. The phrase is obscure, but apparently connotes a rearrangement of the *mishmar* system, as we have understood it in the comm.

31
2-3

all Judah and Benjamin, and in Ephraim and Menasheh, utterly. Then all the Israelites returned, every man to his possession, to their own cities. 2 *Chizkiahu ordered the cadres of the Kohanim and the Levites to their divisions, each man, Kohen and Levite, to his duty. These, for burnt offerings and for peace offerings, to minister, to give thanks and to praise, in the gates of the camps of* HASHEM. 3 *And that which the king donated from his possessions for burnt offerings — the burnt offerings of the morning and the evening and the burnt offerings for the Sabbaths, the new moons and the festivals as it is written in the Torah of* HASHEM.

which Israel dedicated itself to God. Thus, Ariel signifies the conquering force of spirituality which seeks to draw everything into the orbit of its sanctity.

Certainly this objective — that nothing remain impervious to, and withdrawn from, the benign aura of Divine proximity — is associated with the Messianic idea. At that time, all mankind will come to recognize the truth and flock to Jerusalem and Zion to be taught of God's word through the Torah (*Isaiah* ch. 2).

In the course of the study of *Chronicles*, we have come to recognize in David, the mighty fighter of God's wars which, while they expressed themselves in their outer form as battles against the surrounding heathens were, in reality, the means by which evil was to be eradicated from the world. This eradication of all that is inimical to sanctity, paved the way for Solomon, the man of peace, who would build the Temple and provide the dwelling place for God among man. [See *I Chronicles*, prefatory remarks to ch. 17.]

Thus, in a very real way, Jerusalem was the city of David's *encampment*. It was like an army camp from which the world was to be conquered and drawn into the purifying fire of the *lion of God* — the sanctifying altar which stood in the Temple Court.

Isaiah's vision thus falls into place with absolute precision. Jerusalem the *warring* city — where the *lion of God* crouched ready to consume, and where David *camped*, ready to do battle — would now have enemy forces ranged against it. God Himself [וְחָנִיתִי] would create His own *camp of war*, in order to destroy it.

In Chizkiahu's burning zeal to purify the land and to pull both his own and the Northern Kingdom back into the orbit of sanctity, the source of which was the Temple which he had now rededicated with so much care and love — that Temple itself became a מַחֲנֶה, an *encampment*, in which the seeds of a peaceful Messianic world-conquest were sown.

3. וּמְנָת הַמֶּלֶךְ — *And that which the king donated* .... The translation follows *Metzudos*. *Targum* renders with the more conventional *portion*.

The sense of our verse is that Chizkiahu donated from his own property, the money required for the communal sacrifices listed. [See *Menachos* 65a and *Rambam, Shekalim* 4:1, that these must come from communal funds. The king would first have had to donate the money to the Temple treasury.]

He did this in order to lighten the burden of the people (*Ralbag*).

Malbim offers a novel explanation which places this verse squarely within the context of *Chronicles'* presentation of Chizkiahu's story — as the *David* of his generation, the potential Messiah.

He understands מְנָת הַמֶּלֶךְ not as the donation given by the king, but as one received by him (as מְנָת הַכֹּהֲנִים in the next verse). The sense is, that Chizkiahu paid for the communal sacrifices from that portion of his possessions which had come to him from the people's gifts. These had been made to him not as an individual but as a public figure, and thus had the nature of communal funds. *Malbim* makes the point that this function of the king is foretold in *Ezekiel's* prophecies concerning the Messianic king. [See ArtScroll *Ezekiel* to 45:17, and particularly in fn. to 45:8.]

Thus, we have Chizkiahu as the only Biblical king concerning whom we find a usage which is otherwise only associated with the Messiah.

כַּכָּתוּב בְּתוֹרַת ה׳ — *As it is written in the Torah of* HASHEM. This phrase surely does not refer to the fact that the money for the sacrifices came from Chizkiahu. Such a practice is nowhere specified in the Torah. Rather, its subject is the latter part of the verse: The

לא
ד־י

ד וַיֹּאמֶר לָעָם לְיוֹשְׁבֵי יְרוּשָׁלַ͏ִם לָתֵת מְנָת הַכֹּהֲנִים וְהַלְוִיִּם
ה לְמַעַן יֶחֶזְקוּ בְּתוֹרַת יהוה: וְכִפְרֹץ הַדָּבָר הִרְבּוּ בְנֵי־
יִשְׂרָאֵל רֵאשִׁית דָּגָן תִּירוֹשׁ וְיִצְהָר וּדְבַשׁ וְכֹל תְּבוּאַת
ו שָׂדֶה וּמַעְשַׂר הַכֹּל לָרֹב הֵבִיאוּ: וּבְנֵי יִשְׂרָאֵל וִיהוּדָה
הַיּוֹשְׁבִים בְּעָרֵי יְהוּדָה גַּם־הֵם מַעְשַׂר בָּקָר וָצֹאן וּמַעְשַׂר
קָדָשִׁים הַמְקֻדָּשִׁים לַיהוה אֱלֹהֵיהֶם הֵבִיאוּ וַיִּתְּנוּ עֲרֵמוֹת
ז עֲרֵמוֹת: בַּחֹדֶשׁ הַשְּׁלִשִׁי הֵחֵלּוּ הָעֲרֵמוֹת לִיסּוֹד
ח וּבַחֹדֶשׁ הַשְּׁבִיעִי כִּלּוּ: וַיָּבֹאוּ יְחִזְקִיָּהוּ
וְהַשָּׂרִים וַיִּרְאוּ אֶת־הָעֲרֵמוֹת וַיְבָרְכוּ אֶת־יהוה וְאֵת עַמּוֹ
ט יִשְׂרָאֵל: וַיִּדְרֹשׁ יְחִזְקִיָּהוּ עַל־הַכֹּהֲנִים
י וְהַלְוִיִּם עַל־הָעֲרֵמוֹת: וַיֹּאמֶר אֵלָיו עֲזַרְיָהוּ הַכֹּהֵן הָרֹאשׁ

sacrifices enumerated were brought in accordance with the Torah law.

4. לָתֵת מְנָת הַכֹּהֲנִים וְהַלְוִיִּם — *To give that which was due to the Kohanim and the Levites.* He exhorted the populace to be conscientious in giving the *terumah* and the tithes which were the due of the *Kohanim* and the Levites (*Metzudos*).

לְמַעַן יֶחֶזְקוּ בְּתוֹרַת ה׳ — *So that they might devote themselves to the Torah of* HASHEM. [Lit., *hold firm.*]

Freed from the need to earn their own living, they will be able to devote themselves to their spiritual duties (*Metzudos*).

Sanhedrin 90b derives from our verse that *terumah* may not be given to a *Kohen* who does not study the Torah. Its sole purpose is that the *Kohanim* might devote themselves to spiritual matters. *Mikra UMassores* suggests that this itself may have been an institution which Chizkiahu promulgated as part of his general effort to revitalize Torah learning in Israel (see prefatory remarks to ch. 29). Certainly, faced with the possibility of losing their *terumah*, the *Kohanim* would have made great efforts to encourage Torah learning among the people.

5. וְכִפְרֹץ הַדָּבָר — *When the matter was firmly established.* We follow *Metzudos* who suggests that פרץ can mean *to be strong.*

The sense of the phrase is that the people in their enthusiasm went far beyond the requirements of the halachah and brought gifts which were not required by the Torah — see further below. In this sense, *Radak* takes פרץ more closely to its usual meaning, *to break out* or *burst forth.* The tithing *burst forth* beyond the halachic boundaries and included gifts not required by the halachah.

הִרְבּוּ ... רֵאשִׁית דָּגָן תִּירוֹשׁ וְיִצְהָר וּדְבַשׁ ... — *Gave in abundance ... the first fruits of grain, wine, oil and honey.* The term *first fruits* can refer to either *terumah* or *bikkurim*. In the case of *grain, wine and oil* the former may be meant; in the case of *honey* [meaning *dates* from which honey is made], reference must be to *bikkurim* since *terumah* is not given from dates (*Radak*).

Mikra UMassores suggests two ways in which the people were more generous than they need have been: firstly, the Torah does not specify an exact amount to be given either for *terumah* or for *bikkurim*. The people gave *in abundance*, that is that they gave a great deal more than the minimum required. Secondly, the obligation is to give the fruit to the *Kohen* — the Israelite is not obliged to turn grapes into wine, olives into oil or dates into honey. In the event, the people took the extra trouble to give the *Kohanim* a finished product.

וְכֹל תְּבוּאַת שָׂדֶה — *And of all the produce of the field.* They gave *terumah* even from such species as are exempt from the Torah law (*Nedarim* 55a).

וּמַעְשַׂר הַכֹּל לָרֹב הֵבִיאוּ — *And the tithe of all things they brought in abundance.* The species which the Torah exempts from *terumah* and *bikkurim* need also not be tithed. In their enthusiasm, the people here too went beyond the requirements of the halachah and tithed these exempt species (*Mikra UMassores*).

6. *Mikra UMassores* continues to interpret this passage so that it yields the fact that the people

*4 He ordered the people, those who lived in Jerusalem, to give that
which was due to the Kohanim and the Levites, so that they might
devote themselves to the Torah of HASHEM. 5 When the matter was
firmly established, the Israelites gave in abundance the first fruits
of grain, wine, oil and honey, and of all the produce of the field and
the tithe of all things, brought in abundance. 6 And the Israelites
and the Judaeans who dwelt in the cities of Judah, they also
brought in the tithe of oxen and sheep, and the tithe of hallowed
things which were hallowed to HASHEM their God, they brought
and laid them in piles. 7 In the third month they began to lay the
foundation for the piles, and finished them in the seventh month.
8 Chizkiahu and the princes came, saw the piles, and blessed
HASHEM and His people Israel. 9 Chizkiahu questioned the Kohan-
im and the Levites concerning the piles. 10 Azariahu the head*

went over and above the call of duty in their gifts to the *Kohanim*:

... הַיּוֹשְׁבִים בְּעָרֵי יְהוּדָה ... מַעְשַׂר בָּקָר וָצֹאן — ... *who dwelt in the cities of Judah ... the tithe of oxen and sheep*. The law concerning the tithes separated from oxen and sheep [מַעְשַׂר בְּהֵמָה] is as follows: The owners retain their rights to the animal but, rather than slaughter it in the ordinary way, they bring it as a sacrifice, offering up the required portions upon the altar. The rest of the animal is eaten by the owners, governed, however, by the restrictions which apply to the eating of sacrificial meat. Among these is the requirement that the meat be eaten in Jerusalem.

The people who lived in the provinces would thus have had to remain in Jerusalem for several days until they had eaten up all the meat from their tithes. Rather than spend all this time, they gave the meat to the *Kohanim* and Levites who lived in Jerusalem. This arrangement allowed the owners to return to their homes, while at the same time freeing the recipients from the worries of providing their own food.

וּמַעְשַׂר קָדָשִׁים — *And the tithe of hallowed things* ... Produce belonging to the Temple treasury was exempt from the obligation of tithing. Thus, a farmer who deeded his harvest to the Temple had no obligation to tithe. In their enthusiasm, the people tithed even such produce (*Radak, Metzudos*).[1]

הֵבִיאוּ — *They brought* ... The law requires *Kohanim* and Levites to collect their gifts from the farms, and does not oblige the owner to bring them anywhere. The people, in order to free the *Kohanim* for their Torah studies, went beyond their halachic obligations and brought the gifts to Jerusalem.

עֲרֵמוֹת עֲרֵמוֹת — *Piles* ... From ערם, *to pile up* — see *Exodus* 15:8.

7. לְיסּוֹד — ... *to lay the foundations*. The expression is borrowed from its more common usage in connection with laying the foundation of a building (*Metzudos*). The people began to heap up the piles in the third month.

8. וַיְבָרְכוּ אֶת־ה׳ — *And blessed* HASHEM... They blessed God for having inspired the people to be so generous in their giving (*Mefaresh* and *Metzudos*).

9. וַיִּדְרֹשׁ יְחִזְקִיָּהוּ — *Chizkiahu questioned...* Chizkiahu was shocked at the enormous quantities which he found. He suspected that perhaps the *Kohanim* had not taken any of the produce for themselves, and that everything that had been donated was stacked up in these piles. He demanded an explanation (*Mefaresh* and *Metzudos*).

10. עֲזַרְיָהוּ הַכֹּהֵן הָרֹאשׁ — *Azariahu, the head Kohen*. *Malbim* points out that the title *head Kohen* is not identical to כֹּהֵן גָּדוֹל, *High Priest*. It is the title of some other functionary (see detailed discussion at *I Chronicles* 5:30-41). See further in comm. to v. 13.

1. We must assume that these commentators mean that tithes were given for the hallowed produce from other produce which had not been hallowed. Clearly, the owners would have had no authority to seperate tithes once the property had passed from them to the Temple treasury.

לא
יא־טו

לְבֵית צָדוֹק וַיֹּאמֶר מֵהָחֵל הַתְּרוּמָה לָבִיא בֵית־יהוה
אָכוֹל וְשָׂבוֹעַ וְהוֹתֵר עַד־לָרוֹב כִּי יהוה בֵּרַךְ אֶת־עַמּוֹ
יא וְהַנּוֹתָר אֶת־הֶהָמוֹן הַזֶּה׃ וַיֹּאמֶר יְחִזְקִיָּהוּ
יב לְהָכִין לְשָׁכוֹת בְּבֵית יהוה וַיָּכִינוּ׃ וַיָּבִיאוּ אֶת־הַתְּרוּמָה
°כָּנַנְיָהוּ ק׳ וְהַמַּעֲשֵׂר וְהַקֳּדָשִׁים בֶּאֱמוּנָה וַעֲלֵיהֶם נָגִיד °כוננ‍יהו הַלֵּוִי
יג וְשִׁמְעִי אָחִיהוּ מִשְׁנֶה׃ וִיחִיאֵל וַעֲזַזְיָהוּ וְנַחַת וַעֲשָׂהאֵל
וִירִימוֹת וְיוֹזָבָד וֶאֱלִיאֵל וְיִסְמַכְיָהוּ וּמַחַת וּבְנָיָהוּ פְּקִידִים
°כָּנַנְיָהוּ ק׳ מִיַּד °כוננ‍יהו וְשִׁמְעִי אָחִיו בְּמִפְקַד יְחִזְקִיָּהוּ הַמֶּלֶךְ
יד וַעֲזַרְיָהוּ נְגִיד בֵּית־הָאֱלֹהִים׃ וְקוֹרֵא בֶן־יִמְנָה הַלֵּוִי
הַשּׁוֹעֵר לַמִּזְרָחָה עַל נִדְבוֹת הָאֱלֹהִים לָתֵת תְּרוּמַת יהוה
טו וְקָדְשֵׁי הַקֳּדָשִׁים׃ וְעַל־יָדוֹ עֵדֶן וּמִנְיָמִן וְיֵשׁוּעַ וּשְׁמַעְיָהוּ
אֲמַרְיָהוּ וּשְׁכַנְיָהוּ בְּעָרֵי הַכֹּהֲנִים בֶּאֱמוּנָה לָתֵת לַאֲחֵיהֶם

מֵהָחֵל הַתְּרוּמָה לָבִיא — *From the time that the terumah was brought* ... We have been using the gifts from the very first moment that they were brought here. If you wonder why, after four whole months there is still so much left — it is because God has blessed His people with abundant harvests (*Mefaresh*).

אָכוֹל וְשָׂבוֹעַ וְהוֹתֵר — *We have eaten, been satisfied and have left over.* We never ate sparingly, and, nevertheless, there is so much left (*Mefaresh*).

וְהַנּוֹתָר אֶת־הֶהָמוֹן הַזֶּה — *What is left is this great store.* The huge piles which you see are what is left after we have already eaten our fill (*Metzudos*). In *Radak's* view, הָמוֹן refers to the crowds of *Kohanim* who thronged about the Temple grounds: These piles are designated for distribution among this multitude of people.

11. לְשָׁכוֹת — *Storage chambers.* These were storage areas in which to place the *terumah* (*Mefaresh*).

12. וְהַקֳּדָשִׁים — *And the hallowed things.* *Terumah* and tithes have already been mentioned. What, then, can *hallowed things* mean?

Metzudos suggests that these are *terumah* which was given from such species as are halachically exempt. Such a gift would not carry the formal name *terumah*.

Ralbag thinks that it could refer to מַעֲשֵׂר שֵׁנִי, the *second tithe*. After one tithe had been separated from the produce for the benefit of the Levites, another (*second*) tithe had to be taken. This was to be eaten by the owner himself, but had to be consumed in Jerusalem with certain restrictions, deriving from its sacred character. The people may well have sent in their *second tithe*, and just as this was done with the animal tithes — see comm. to v. 6 — assigned it to the *Kohanim* and Levites who lived in Jerusalem.

13. וַעֲזַרְיָהוּ נְגִיד בֵּית־הָאֱלֹהִים — *Azariahu was the governor of the House of God.* See comm. to v. 10. See also comm. to נְגִיד בֵּית הָאֱלֹהִים at *I Chronicles* 9:11.

14-19. Both in the language which is used, and in the dispositions which are described in this section, there is much that is obscure. Certainly we must expect such difficulties when dealing with institutions and procedural affairs which are separated from our experience by so many centuries.

Most commentators assume our section to be a continuation of the previous one, and that the dispositions described here concern the distribution of the gifts which had been stored in the *piles* mentioned before [thus: *Mefaresh, Radak, Metzudos, Malbim* and *Mikra UMassores*]. Each of these commentators suggests different meanings for the various phrases and none of the possibilities provide a smoothly flowing text.

We shall explain the passage as does *Ralbag*: It concerns other arrangements which Chizkiahu made for the efficient running of the Temple services — in much the same way as David, in his time, had devoted much time and energy to these and similar procedural matters.

14. ... וְקוֹרֵא בֶן־יִמְנָה הַלֵּוִי — *Also Kore son of Yimnah the Levite* ... V. 13 had identified the people concerned with the administration of the *piles*. We now learn of other appointments made by Chizkiahu dealing with other aspects

Kohen from the house of Tzadok answered him and said, 'From the
time that the terumah was brought into HASHEM*'s House we have*
eaten, been satisfied, and have left over, for HASHEM *has blessed*
His people. What is left is this great store.' 11 *So Chizkiahu ordered*
that storage chambers be set aside in HASHEM*'s House and so they*
were set aside. 12 *They brought in the terumah and the tithe and*
the hallowed things faithfully; and over them Chananiahu the
Levite was comptroller, and Shimei, his brother, was his deputy.
13 *And Yechiel and Azaziahu and Nachath and Asael and Yeri-*
moth and Yozabad and Eliel and Yismachiahu and Machath and
Benaiahu were officials under the hand of Chananiahu and Shimei
his brother by the appointment of Chizkiahu the king. Azariahu
was the Governor of the House of G-d. 14 *Also Kore the son of Yim-*
nah the Levite, the gate-keeper to the east, was in charge of the free
will offerings made to God, to distribute the offerings made to HA-
SHEM*, and of the most holy things.* 15 *And under him were Eden and*
Minyamin and Yeshua and Shemaiahu, Amariahu and Shechani-
ahu in the Kohanite cities, in positions of trust. They were to dist-

of the running of the Temple. In this concern he is once again functioning as the *David* of his generation.

עַל נִדְבוֹת הָאֱלֹהִים — *Was in charge of the free will offerings made to God.* Such gifts as people would make towards the upkeep of the Temple [בֶּדֶק הַבָּיִת] were in Kore's charge.

לָתֵת תְּרוּמַת ה׳ וְקָדְשֵׁי הַקֳּדָשִׁים — *To distribute the offerings made to* HASHEM*, and of the most holy things. The most holy things* refers to the portion which the *Kohanim* receive from those sacrifices which the halachah classifies as *most holy*, such as the sin offering or the guilt offering.

But commentators are silent concerning the meaning of *terumah* in this context. Normally, the portion given the *Kohanim* from produce would be given directly by the farmer and would not have to be apportioned by a Temple official. Of course, reference could be to the *terumah* which had been stored in the *piles* described in the earlier part of this chapter.

We may also surmise that the term refers to the portion due the *Kohanim* from those sacrifices which have a lesser degree of sanctity [קָדָשִׁים קַלִּים]. This, in contrast to the קָדְשֵׁי הַקֳּדָשִׁים of the earlier phrase. The rationale for describing the portion given the *Kohen* from these sacrifices as תְּרוּמָה would be *Leviticus* 7:32, which refers to the shank bone which the *Kohen* receives from the peace offering [שְׁלָמִים as representative of קָדָשִׁים קַלִּים] as a תְּרוּמָה to the *Kohen*. The expression תְּרוּמַת ה׳, which our verse uses to describe these gifts, would be appropriate in the light of v. 34 there, which makes clear that these gifts are not the *Kohen*'s in his own right, but are first *taken* by God, for Himself, and then passed on to His ministrant.

15. וְעַל־יָדוֹ עֵדֶן ... בְּעָרֵי הַכֹּהֲנִים — *And under him were Eden ... in the Kohanite cities. Ralbag* does not explain עַל יָדוֹ. Our translation, which places these men secondary to Kore in the hierarchy of the officialdom, accords with *Malbim* and *Metzudos*.

Kore functioned in the Temple, while the men identified in this verse were stationed in the Kohanite cities. For their function — see below.

Ralbag wonders why such power over the Kohanite distributions, should be given to the Levites. The Torah designates these as servants of, or assistants to, the *Kohanim*. Kore and the officials under him, appear to hold positions of authority. He answers that, in fact, the Levite control over the distribution of the Kohanite gifts, was of great service to the *Kohanim*. Their primary concern was to be the study of Torah. To free them from petty administrative duties was to allow them to concentrate on that most important task and privilege.

בֶּאֱמוּנָה — *In positions of trust. Ralbag* renders *to give faithfully*; that is, he reads, בֶּאֱמוּנָה together with לָתֵת. Our translation follows the

טז בְּמַחְלְקוֹת כַּגָּדוֹל כַּקָּטָן: מִלְּבַד הִתְיַחְשָׂם לִזְכָרִים מִבֶּן
שָׁלוֹשׁ שָׁנִים וּלְמַעְלָה לְכָל־הַבָּא לְבֵית־יהוה לִדְבַר־יוֹם
יז בְּיוֹמוֹ לַעֲבוֹדָתָם בְּמִשְׁמְרוֹתָם כְּמַחְלְקוֹתֵיהֶם: וְאֵת
הִתְיַחֵשׂ הַכֹּהֲנִים לְבֵית אֲבוֹתֵיהֶם וְהַלְוִיִּם מִבֶּן עֶשְׂרִים
יח שָׁנָה וּלְמָעְלָה בְּמִשְׁמְרוֹתֵיהֶם בְּמַחְלְקוֹתֵיהֶם: וּלְהִתְיַחֵשׂ
בְּכָל־טַפָּם נְשֵׁיהֶם וּבְנֵיהֶם וּבְנוֹתֵיהֶם לְכָל־קָהָל כִּי
יט בֶאֱמוּנָתָם יִתְקַדְּשׁוּ־קֹדֶשׁ: וְלִבְנֵי אַהֲרֹן הַכֹּהֲנִים בִּשְׂדֵי
מִגְרַשׁ עָרֵיהֶם בְּכָל־עִיר וָעִיר אֲנָשִׁים אֲשֶׁר נִקְּבוּ בְּשֵׁמוֹת

trop, which separates the two words. We render with *Mikra UMassores* who maintains that in Scriptural usage, אֱמוּנָה denotes any office of trust to which a person is appointed.

לָתֵת לַאֲחֵיהֶם בְּמַחְלְקוֹת — *They were to distribute correctly apportioned parts to their brothers*. The translation follows *Ralbag*, who associates this phrase with the word בֶּאֱמוּנָה of the previous one. The division was to be done faithfully, that is, fairly, with equal portions given to all — great and small.

כַּגָּדוֹל כַּקָּטָן — *To the great as to the small*. Perhaps this is a standard idiom whenever a division is to be described: See *I Chronicles* 25:8 and 26:13.

The text does not make clear what it is that these men were supposed to distribute. It cannot mean the sacrificial portions mentioned in v. 14, since these had to be eaten either within the Temple confines or, at the very least, in Jerusalem. The distributions described here took place in the Kohanite cities. We must assume that reference is to the various gifts which had been stored in the *piles* of v. 6. See further at v. 19.

16. ...מִלְּבַד — *Besides* .... The duties about to be described here are entirely separate from the function of distributing the various Kohanite portions.

הִתְיַחְשָׂם — *Assigning* ... *to their families*. To understand *Ralbag's* rendering of this complex verse, some background information is necessary: From *I Chronicles* chs. 23-25, it will be recalled that both *Kohanim* and Levites were divided into twenty-four *mishmaros*, that is, *divisions* or *watches*, which rotated for duty in the Temple. We learned further that each *mishmar* was then divided into seven בָּתֵּי אָבוֹת, *family groups*, each of whom served on one day of the week.

It is these family groups which are the subject of the dispositions described in our verse. It is they who *come to the House of HASHEM on a particular day*.

It was the duty of the men who were stationed in the various Kohanite cities to determine to which family group each *Kohen* belonged so that he would be sure to report for the Temple service at the correct time.

לִזְכָרִים מִבֶּן שָׁלוֹשׁ שָׁנִים וּלְמַעְלָה — *Males, three years and older*. It was the practice of *Kohanim* who came to do service in the Temple, to bring their young sons along so that they might be trained for the day when they would be of age to serve (*Malbim* and *Mikra UMassores*). Under three years of age they could not be brought into the Temple (*Radak*).

לְכָל־הַבָּא לְבֵית־ה׳ לִדְבַר־יוֹם בְּיוֹמוֹ — *This, for all who came to HASHEM's House on a particular day*. See above under הִתְיַחְשָׂם.

בְּמִשְׁמְרוֹתָם כְּמַחְלְקוֹתֵיהֶם — *In their watches as they were divided*. As the *mishmaros* were divided into בָּתֵּי אָבוֹת, the *family units*. Thus, מַחְלוֹקֶת here is not used as a synonym for מִשְׁמָר as it is in *I Chronicles* 23:6 and 24:1, but describes the fact that each מִשְׁמָר was the subject to another division — that of the family unit.

17. וְאֵת הִתְיַחֵשׂ הַכֹּהֲנִים לְבֵית אֲבוֹתֵיהֶם — *Also determining the paternal groupings to which the Kohanim belonged*. Besides determining the narrow בֵּית אָב of each *Kohen*, it was also necessary to know precisely to which מִשְׁמָר he belonged.

וְהַלְוִיִּם מִבֶּן עֶשְׂרִים שָׁנָה וּלְמַעְלָה בְּמִשְׁמְרוֹתֵיהֶם בְּמַחְלְקוֹתֵיהֶם — *And assigning those Levites, twenty years and older, to their watches according to their divisions.*. The Levites, too, were divided into *mishmaros* and *batei avos* (*I Chronicles* ch. 23), and it was the duty of the men listed in v. 15 to know precisely which Levite belonged to which *mishmar* and *bais av*, so that he could make himself available for

*ribute correctly apportioned parts to their brothers; to the great
as to the small.* 16 *Besides assigning males, three years and older,
to their families. This, for all who came to* HASHEM*'s House on a
particular day, to serve in their watches as they were divided.*
17 *Also determining the paternal groupings to which the Kohan-
im belonged, and assigning those Levites, twenty years and
older, to their watches, according to their divisions.* 18 *And to
establish the family lines of all their little ones, their wives
their sons and their daughters of each grouping; for by the
faithful service of these, they would set themselves apart in
sanctity.* 19 *For the descendants of Aaron, Kohanim in the open
fields around their cities, there were men identified by name,*

service on the required day.

Why were the Levites not counted from three years upwards? Would they, too, not have brought their youngsters to the Temple in order to expose them to the duties which they would one day be called upon to perform?

In the absence of guidance from the commentators, we suggest the following:

I Chronicles 23:27 gives great prominence to an edict that David had made in the latter part of his life — that the Levites were to be counted from age twenty, as opposed to the original practice which was to count them only from thirty (see v. 3 there and comm. in both places). Chizkiahu, the *David* of his generation, would have wanted to adhere precisely to David's ruling. Thus, we have two possibilities: Either the three-year-olds were, in fact, not counted. Chizkiahu's wish to do precisely what David had said, outweighed the practical considerations; or they were, indeed, counted but the text makes no issue of it in order to underline Chizkiahu's inner affinity to David.

18. וּלְהִתְיַחֵשׂ בְּכָל־טַפָּם — *And to establish the family lines of all their little ones ...* For טַף as *little one*, see comm. to 20:13.

Even the little ones needed to be identified so that when they grew up, they would know to which *mishmar* they belonged.

נְשֵׁיהֶם וּבְנֵיהֶם וּבְנוֹתֵיהֶם לְכָל־קָהָל — *Their wives, their sons and their daughters of each grouping.* קָהָל here, is used as it was in Talmudic times — to denote a particular grouping, such as *Kohanim* or Levites [see *Kiddushin* 73a] (*Mikra UMassores*).

The *mishmaros* were organized according to patrilinial descent. Why, then, was it necessary to trace the family lines of wives and daughters? Perhaps it was necessary to determine whether there was any illegitimacy connected with their birth, which would effect their children, and deny them the status of qualified *Kohanim* or Levites. Alternatively, the genealogical records of the women may have been needed to determine if they could receive the Kohanite gifts from the produce. According to *Yevamos* 99b women could not collect *terumah* directly from the threshing floor, but could have it sent to their homes. This would be true only for women who had no halachic illegitimacy attached to them (*Mikra UMassores*).

כִּי בֶאֱמוּנָתָם יִתְקַדְּשׁוּ־קֹדֶשׁ — *For by the faithful service of these, they would set themselves apart in sanctity.* Were it not for the careful and accurate listing of each *Kohen* and Levite in the correct *mishmar* and *beis av*, it could well be that the day on which they were to serve would arrive and they, not having realized that it was time for their duty, would be *tamei*. The faithful and committed concern of the officials would avoid this dilemma. The *Kohanim* and Levites will have sanctified themselves in good time.

19. וְלִבְנֵי אַהֲרֹן הַכֹּהֲנִים בִּשְׂדֵי מִגְרַשׁ עָרֵיהֶם — *For the descendants of Aaron, Kohanim in the open fields around their cities.* These were *Kohanim* who did not take part in the Temple service (*Malbim*), but, instead busied themselves in the fields around their cities (*Metzudos*).

אֲנָשִׁים אֲשֶׁר נִקְּבוּ בְּשֵׁמוֹת — *There were men, identified by name.* V 15 had mentioned the officials who had charge of the distributions in the Kohanite cities. However, these officials did not deal with the individual recipients. Rather, in each city there were leading citizens, identified by name, to whom the main officials delegated the actual task of distribution.

לא כ־כא

לָתֵת מָנוֹת לְכָל־זָכָר בַּכֹּהֲנִים וּלְכָל־הִתְיַחֵשׂ בַּלְוִיִּם׃
כ וַיַּעַשׂ כָּזֹאת יְחִזְקִיָּהוּ בְּכָל־יְהוּדָה וַיַּעַשׂ הַטּוֹב וְהַיָּשָׁר
כא וְהָאֱמֶת לִפְנֵי יהוה אֱלֹהָיו׃ וּבְכָל־מַעֲשֶׂה אֲשֶׁר־הֵחֵל ׀
בַּעֲבוֹדַת בֵּית־הָאֱלֹהִים וּבַתּוֹרָה וּבַמִּצְוָה לִדְרֹשׁ לֵאלֹהָיו
בְּכָל־לְבָבוֹ עָשָׂה וְהִצְלִיחַ׃

לב א

א אַחֲרֵי הַדְּבָרִים וְהָאֱמֶת הָאֵלֶּה בָּא סַנְחֵרִיב מֶלֶךְ־אַשּׁוּר

לְכָל־זָכָר בַּכֹּהֲנִים וּלְכָל־הִתְיַחֵשׂ בַּלְוִיִּם — *To all the males among the Kohanim, and to the Levites listed in the genealogical tables*. The *Kohanim* did not need to bring documentary proof of their familial purity; the fact that they served actively in the Temple, was sufficient proof of their standing [אֵין בּוֹדְקִין מִן הַמִּזְבֵּחַ וּלְמַעְלָה]. The Levites had to supply documentary evidence (*Malbim*).

20. וַיַּעַשׂ כָּזֹאת יְחִזְקִיָּהוּ בְּכָל־יְהוּדָה — *Moreover, Chizkiahu did thus in all of Judah*. Just as Chizkiahu made sure that those matters which were of particular concern in the Kohanite cities were attended to, so also, did he do throughout Judah what was necessary and important in the lives of the people. He was an exemplary king, who was concerned with the best possible governance for the people (*Ralbag*).

הַטּוֹב וְהַיָּשָׁר וְהָאֱמֶת — *That which was good, right and true*. *Malbim* suggests: *Good* — in his relations to God; *right* — in his relations to man; and *true* — in his beliefs.

Malbim's understanding of the terms may help to explain the following: At the beginning of Chizkiahu's reign (29:2), we are told that he did that which was יָשָׁר in the eyes of HASHEM, but neither טוֹב, nor אֱמֶת are mentioned. According to *Malbim's* rendering, we may say as follows: An assessment of a reign would be made solely on the basis of the king's relationship to his subjects. His personal standing would have no place in such a context. Neither טוֹב nor אֱמֶת, would be appropriate there.

When we consider the three categories of meritorious acts mentioned in the next verse — the Temple service, Torah and *mitzvos*, it seems possible that *good*, *right* and *truth* might refer to them. The structure would be as follows:

הַטּוֹב: We have an indication of how the Sages interpreted this term in connection with Chizkiahu. In *II Kings* 20:3, Chizkiahu entreats God to cure him from his illness in the merit of the טוֹב which he had done. *Berachos* 10b explains what he meant: He had always been meticulous in beginning his prayers immediately upon mentioning the redemption from Egypt in connection with the recitation of the *Shema* [סְמִיכוּת גְאוּלָה לִתְפִלָּה]. *Rabbeinu Yonah* explains: By juxtaposing the two thoughts: Redemption and prayer — which is an act of serving God — he demonstrated his understanding of the significance of the redemption from Egypt. It was not meant to make Israel *free*, but to change them from being slaves to Pharaoh to being servants of God. From thanking God for that redemption, he moves immediately to an act of service, i.e., prayer.

Within this thought-world, we can readily appreciate that טוֹב may well refer to the *service of the House of God*, in the next verse.

וְהַיָּשָׁר: *Psalms* 19:9 talks of God's commands being, יְשָׁרִים. *Radak* interprets this to mean that they appeal to the intellect because of their innate fairness and propriety: הַיָּשָׁר may well refer to the מִצְוָה of the next verse.

וְהָאֱמֶת: *Rashi* (*Sanhedrin* 94b) interprets וְהָאֱמֶת of 32:1 as referring to the widespread study of Torah during Chizkiahu's reign. Thus, the term could readily refer to the *Torah* of v. 21.

21. לִדְרֹשׁ לֵאלֹהָיו — *Seeking out his God*. *Metzudos* reads this together with the previous word, וּבַמִּצְוָה, ... *in that he commanded to search out his God*. However, the *trop* separates the two, and yields the interpretation which we assumed in comm. to the previous verse — that Chizkiahu wholeheartedly undertook to encourage three things: The Temple service; Torah; and mitzvos. Our phrase then adds that he did all these things with pure intentions, that is, in order thereby to *search out his God*.

בְּכָל־לְבָבוֹ — *He involved his whole heart*. Again, we follow the *trop* which separates this phrase from the final וְהִצְלִיחַ, thereby joining it to the earlier part of the verse which must be understood: *In all the things which he undertook ... he involved his whole heart*, and thus, his efforts were crowned with *success*.

וְהִצְלִיחַ — *And prospered*. This assessment of

31
20-21 *in every city, to distribute portions to all the males among the*
Kohanim, and to the Levites listed in the genealogical tables.
20 Moreover Chizkiahu did thus in all of Judah and he did that
which was good, right and true before HASHEM, his God. 21 And
in all the things which he undertook, whether it concerned the
service in the House of God, Torah or the commandments,
seeking out his God, he involved his whole heart — and
prospered.

32
1 *After these matters, these conscientiously undertaken efforts,*

Chizkiahu's success in all his endeavors recalls a similar one made of David: *And David was successful* [מַשְׂכִּיל] *in all his ways and HASHEM was with him.* (*I Samuel* 18:15). God smiled upon Chizkiahu's efforts as He had once done for David. The stage was set to bring Chizkiahu's Messianic potential to its anticipated climax. See next chapter.

XXXII

☙ Sancheriv at Jerusalem

The story of the confrontation between Sancheriv and Chizkiahu has already been told in *II Kings* ch.18 — and in much greater detail. *Kings* devotes a full sixty-eight verses to the description of this seminal event, while *Chronicles* has just twenty-one. Through sharper focus on a number of salient details, *Chronicles* brings its own perspective to bear. Moreover, by adding certain facts which are not recorded in *Kings*, it creates an ambience of its own.

אַחֲרֵי הַדְּבָרִים וְהָאֱמֶת הָאֵלֶּה בָּא סַנְחֵרִיב — *After these matters, these conscientiously undertaken efforts, Sancheriv came*. The dissonance between the two parts of the sentence is glaring. The implication is that the invasion of Sancheriv is somehow related to the events described previously. In the thought-world of Scripture, it is inconceivable that Chizkiahu's noble bearing should be repaid by the terrors of the Assyrian invasion.

Radak and *Metzudos* explain that despite Chizkiahu's personal righteousness, there was still much that was wrong with the people. Their spiritual attainments fell pitifully short of Chizkiahu's expectations. Their shortcomings, not Chizkiahu's righteousness, brought Sancheriv to war against Jerusalem. Evidently, these commentators understand ... אַחֲרֵי as *in spite of* ...

But the sins of the people are never mentioned.

Sanhedrin 94b gives the following background to this story: God had made an oath that He would cause Assyria to attack Jerusalem. God knew that if he would tell Chizkiahu of His plans, he would beg off, willingly doing without the anticipated victory in order not to be first exposed to the fearful tensions which would surely precede it. Therefore, without first consulting Chizkiahu, God swore that the confrontation would occur. God had determined that Assyria was to be destroyed.

But the Talmud stops there. It is not made clear why the destruction of Assyria was a matter of such urgency.

Surely, the meaning is as follows: Chizkiahu is to be the Messiah, Sancheriv is to play the role of Gog, King of Magog. His destruction is to pave the way to Israel's ultimate vindication.

Our verse takes on new meaning: Far from the two halves standing in contradiction to one another, they set the tone for the *Chronicles* perspective of the narrative. Chizkiahu's righteousness made him the man of destiny — the potential Messiah — against whom the forces of Sancheriv were to be thrown. They were to go to their inevitable destruction in accordance with God's plan — in Aggadic idiom, His oath, — for the final denouement of history's secrets.[1]

1. See ArtScroll *Ezekiel*, chs. 38 and 39, for an in-depth analysis of the significance of this epic battle.The reason why God's intention did not come to fruition need not concern us here. We will deal with it at the end of this chapter.

לב
ב־ז

וַיָּבֹא בִיהוּדָה וַיִּחַן עַל־הֶעָרִים הַבְּצֻרוֹת וַיֹּאמֶר לְבִקְעָם
ב אֵלָיו: וַיַּרְא יְחִזְקִיָּהוּ כִּי־בָא סַנְחֵרִיב וּפָנָיו לַמִּלְחָמָה עַל־
ג יְרוּשָׁלָםִ: וַיִּוָּעַץ עִם־שָׂרָיו וְגִבֹּרָיו לִסְתּוֹם אֶת־מֵימֵי
ד הָעֲיָנוֹת אֲשֶׁר מִחוּץ לָעִיר וַיַּעְזְרֻהוּ: וַיִּקָּבְצוּ עַם־רָב
וַיִּסְתְּמוּ אֶת־כָּל־הַמַּעְיָנוֹת וְאֶת־הַנַּחַל הַשּׁוֹטֵף בְּתוֹךְ־
הָאָרֶץ לֵאמֹר לָמָּה יָבוֹאוּ מַלְכֵי אַשּׁוּר וּמָצְאוּ מַיִם רַבִּים:
ה וַיִּתְחַזַּק וַיִּבֶן אֶת־כָּל־הַחוֹמָה הַפְּרוּצָה וַיַּעַל עַל־
הַמִּגְדָּלוֹת וְלַחוּצָה הַחוֹמָה אַחֶרֶת וַיְחַזֵּק אֶת־הַמִּלּוֹא עִיר
ו דָּוִיד וַיַּעַשׂ שֶׁלַח לָרֹב וּמָגִנִּים: וַיִּתֵּן שָׂרֵי מִלְחָמוֹת
עַל־הָעָם וַיִּקְבְּצֵם אֵלָיו אֶל־רְחוֹב שַׁעַר הָעִיר וַיְדַבֵּר עַל־
ז לְבָבָם לֵאמֹר: חִזְקוּ וְאִמְצוּ אַל־תִּירְאוּ וְאַל־תֵּחַתּוּ מִפְּנֵי
מֶלֶךְ אַשּׁוּר וּמִלִּפְנֵי כָּל־הֶהָמוֹן אֲשֶׁר־עִמּוֹ כִּי־עִמָּנוּ רַב

וַיָּבֹא בִיהוּדָה — *Invaded Judah*. According to *II Kings* 18:13, this occurred in the fourteenth year of Chizkiahu's reign, ten years after Assyria had taken the people of the Northern Kingdom into captivity (vs. 9 ff., there).

וַיִּחַן עַל־הֶעָרִים הַבְּצֻרוֹת — *And set up camps against the fortified cities*. The account in *Kings* begins with the capture of those cities. Apparently the provisions, recounted here but not in *Kings*, which Chizkiahu made for the defense of Jerusalem (vs. 2-8) took place while the fortified cities were still under siege (*Malbim*).

Metzudos, however, thinks that וַיִּחַן need not be limited to the intention alone, but can also incorporate the accomplishment. Thus: He intended to take the cities, and, in fact, took them. As such, the description here is the same as in *Kings*.

וַיֹּאמֶר לְבִקְעָם אֵלָיו — *He planned to breach them so that he might take them*. בקע means to *break open* or *into*.

2. ...כִּי־בָא סַנְחֵרִיב וּפָנָיו לַמִּלְחָמָה עַל־יְרוּשָׁלָםִ — ...*That Sancheriv had come and that he was turned to war against Jerusalem*. The *trop*, which makes a stop at *Sancheriv*, clearly indicates two separate thoughts. Chizkiahu became aware that Sancheriv had invaded; and that he intended to attack Jerusalem.

But what is the meaning of the first observation? Why is there a significance to Assyria's coming if not the danger which this posed to Jerusalem?

The answer may lie in a closer analysis of the *Chronicles'* account.

The narrative seems to lack inner logic. In vs. 3-9, we see Chizkiahu preparing for battle with foresight and prudence. He denies water to the potential besiegers, builds fortifications, lays in arms, and exhorts his troops to be valiant in the face of overpowering physical advantage. All seems set for a tenaciously fought defense of Jerusalem.

Sancheriv's messenger arrives and delivers his taunting message. Suddenly, Chizkiahu appears to be totally impotent; he can do no more than turn to God in prayer. He said, 'I cannot kill nor pursue nor even say *shirah*. I will sleep on my bed and You do what is necessary' [*Eichah Rabbah (Pesichta* 30) and see fn. to 13:15].

How does this agree with the earlier passage in which we find Chizkiahu making preparations for war?

A basic question which must be asked is whether Chizkiahu was aware of Isaiah's prophecies concerning Sancheriv's destruction at the gates of Jerusalem. We have already noted that much of the first twelve chapters of *Isaiah* is devoted to the Assyrian downfall, and there are many references to the fact that it is to happen miraculously — see, for example, 9:1-4. Moreover, the juxtaposition of the passage in 10:24-34, which deals explicitly with Assyria, to the Messianic visions of ch. 11, makes clear the tradition of the Sages that it would have been possible for Chizkiahu himself to become the Messiah.

It seems inconceivable that Chizkiahu should have been unaware of these prophecies and their implications.

In the absence of guidance from the commentators, we suggest that Chizkiahu may, indeed, have known of Assyria's impending downfall, and the Messianic destiny that

Sancheriv, king of Assyria came, invaded Judah and set up camps against the fortified cities. He planned to breach them so that he might take them. 2 *Chizkiahu saw that Sancheriv had come and that he was turned to war against Jerusalem.* 3 *After consultation with his princes and his warriors, he decided to stop up the waters of the wells which were outside the city. And they helped him.* 4 *So a great many people came together and stopped up all the wells, and the river which rushes through the land. They said, 'Why should the kings of Assyria come and find much water?'* 5 *He fortified himself and completely built up the wall which had been breached, raising it above the towers, and another wall outside. He reinforced the plaza of the City of David and manufactured an abundance of weapons and shields.* 6 *He set military commanders over the people and gathered them together to him to the boulevard at the city's gate, and addressed them persuasively, saying,* 7 *'Be strong and of good courage! Be not afraid nor dismayed by the Assyrian king and by the multitude that is with him, for we have something greater than*

hinged upon it. However, he could not have known that the moment was now, nor that he was the chosen man. He saw an ordinary war developing — Sancheriv was besieging the fortified cities of Judah as he would the cities of any other country which he coveted — there was nothing to alert him to the apocalyptic undertones of what was developing. An ordinary war called for ordinary preparations, and of these he knew himself capable. It was only after he heard the tenor of Sancheriv's message (see comm. below) that he realized the enormity of the events through which he was living, and the challenge which was being offered him. It was then that he felt unworthy of a personal involvement. Let God Himself destroy His enemies, and thereby bring history to its climax. He would be passive and not, by his own efforts, stand in the way of the Divine revelation.

All this may serve as the basis for our understanding of the first phrase in this verse: Chizkiahu saw that Sancheriv had come — he saw Assyria invading and the stage being set for the fulfillment of Isaiah's visions. He chose not to read the signs, but instead, took steps which may have been appropriate in an ordinary war, but were misplaced in a Messianic confrontation — see below.

3. עִם־שָׂרָיו — *With his princes.* Presumably the Sages — see comm. to 30:2. See Section II, *The Diversion of the Waters,* for a discussion of the degree to which the Sages supported Chizkiahu's actions.

לִסְתּוֹם — *To stop up.* So that the enemy would be denied a supply of water (*Metzudos*).

וַיַּעְזְרֻהוּ — *And they helped him.* To close up the wells (*Metzudos*).

4. וְאֶת־הַנַּחַל ... — *And the river ....* This is the Gichon (*Radak* and *Malbim*). See Section II, *The Diversion of the Waters.*

בְּתוֹךְ־הָאָרֶץ — *Through the land.* Outside Jerusalem (*Metzudos*).

5. הַחוֹמָה הַפְּרוּצָה — *The wall which had been breached.* At 25:23 we learned how Yoash of the Northern Kingdom had made a breach of four hundred cubits in Jerusalem's wall (*Malbim*).

וַיַּעַל עַל־הַמִּגְדָּלוֹת — *Raising it above the towers.* The translation follows *Metzudos.*

וְלַחוּצָה הַחוֹמָה אַחֶרֶת — *And another wall outside.* In front of the main wall he built another one (*Metzudos*).

אֶת־הַמִּלּוֹא — *The plaza.* See *I Chronicles* 11:8.

שֶׁלַח — *Weapons.* See comm. to 23:10.

6. וַיְדַבֵּר עַל־לְבָבָם לֵאמֹר — *And addressed them persuasively. Targum* adds: *And spoke words of comfort to them.*

7. כִּי־עִמָּנוּ רַב מֵעִמּוֹ — *For we have something greater than he has.* This will be explained in the next verse.

Metzudos renders רַב as *greater and*

ח מֵעִמּוֹ: עִמּוֹ זְרוֹעַ בָּשָׂר וְעִמָּנוּ יהוה אֱלֹהֵינוּ לְעָזְרֵנוּ
וּלְהִלָּחֵם מִלְחֲמֹתֵנוּ וַיִּסָּמְכוּ הָעָם עַל־דִּבְרֵי יְחִזְקִיָּהוּ
ט מֶלֶךְ־יְהוּדָה: אַחַר זֶה שָׁלַח סַנְחֵרִיב
מֶלֶךְ־אַשּׁוּר עֲבָדָיו יְרוּשָׁלַיְמָה וְהוּא עַל־לָכִישׁ וְכָל־
מֶמְשַׁלְתּוֹ עִמּוֹ עַל־יְחִזְקִיָּהוּ מֶלֶךְ יְהוּדָה וְעַל־כָּל־יְהוּדָה
י אֲשֶׁר בִּירוּשָׁלַםִ לֵאמֹר: כֹּה אָמַר סַנְחֵרִיב מֶלֶךְ אַשּׁוּר
יא עַל־מָה אַתֶּם בֹּטְחִים וְיֹשְׁבִים בְּמָצוֹר בִּירוּשָׁלָםִ: הֲלֹא
יְחִזְקִיָּהוּ מַסִּית אֶתְכֶם לָתֵת אֶתְכֶם לָמוּת בְּרָעָב וּבְצָמָא

stronger, while *Targum* has *many more*.

8. וּלְהִלָּחֵם מִלְחֲמֹתֵנוּ — *And to fight our battles*. In Chizkiahu's eyes this is *our battle*. God will extend His help, but is not identified as the target against which Sancheriv is pitting his forces. This is in sharp contrast to what we saw was Scripture's assessment of the Moabite war against Yehoshaphat (20:15), and bears out our suggestion in comm. to v. 2 here, that Chizkiahu was not, at this point, aware of the implication of this war.

9-23. The *Chronicles'* account of the confrontation with the Assyrians is not merely a shortened version of what was said in *Kings* and *Isaiah*. Besides the omissions which are, indeed, many, there are also verses and complete sections which are unique to *Chronicles*.

An analysis of *Chronicles'* intention in presenting the story in its own peculiar way requires a rigorous comparison with the earlier account so that the differences may be placed in sharp relief.

We offer first a short synopsis of the Assyrian arguments as they are presented in *II Kings* ch.18:

1. 19-21: The futility of placing trust in Pharaoh and an Egyptian alliance.

2. 22: God's displeasure with Chizkiahu for removing the altars and the *bamos*.

3. 23-24: Israel's forces are ridiculously puny and impotent when compared to the mighty forces ranged against them.

4. 25: It is God's own plan that Assyria is to capture Jerusalem.

5. 28-29: Chizkiahu is not able to save Israel from the Assyrians.

6. 30-32: Assyria's intentions are benign. The people will not lose much by capitulating.

7. 33-35: The gods of other nations were not able to help their people against the Assyrians. So, too, would the God of the Jews prove impotent against them.

Of these seven points the *Chronicles'* account has equivalents for only 2 and 7.

There are also three significant additions in the *Chronicles'* account: (1) V. 16 which, in *Chronicles'* own words, defines the gist of the Assyrian statement as being made: . . . *against* HASHEM *God, and against His servant Chizkiahu*. (2) Twice, in vs. 17 and 19, outrage is expressed at the equating of God with the deities of the other nations; and (3) V. 23 tells of the reaction of the neighboring peoples to the destruction of the Assyrian army — something not mentioned in the *Kings'* account.

The thrust, then, of *Chronicles* is self-evident. It is not the intention to tell the story of what happened — that is done in detail in the earlier books — but to project the essential nature of the confrontation in its true dimensions. This was no ordinary war — for which the preparations made by Chizkiahu and described at the beginning of the chapter would have been prudent and appropriate. It is a war directed against the God of Israel, precisely as David in his psalm dealing with the Gogian war had described it: *Against* HASHEM *and against His anointed* (*Psalms* 2:2) — *against* HASHEM *God, and against Chizkiahu his servant* (our v. 16).

In this context, our v. 19 is particularly significant. The account of the Assyrian challenge ends at v. 18. V. 20 documents Chizkiahu's reaction. What, then, is the function of v. 19?

The *Mefaresh* writes: *The author expresses outrage at Sancheriv's churlishness, for taunting the living God*. We would say that *Chronicles* makes a special point of underlining the thrust of his message: Sancheriv's is no ordinary war; it is not Jerusalem (v. 2) which is the focus of his ambition, but the very essence of Israel's special status. He wishes to denigrate God to the level of a tribal deity [God is offended by Chizkiahu's limiting of Divine

he has. [8] *He has an army of flesh, but we have HASHEM our God to help us and to fight our battles.' The people trusted the words of Chizkiahu king of Judah.* [9] *After this, Sancheriv king of Assyria sent his servants to Jerusalem — while he was at Lachish and together with all his forces — to Chizkiahu king of Judah and to all of Judah in Jerusalem, saying,* [10] *Thus says Sancheriv king of Assyria: 'Upon what are you placing your trust that you continue to dwell in Jerusalem?* [11] *Clearly Chizkiahu is urging you on, only to condemn you to die by famine and by thirst,*

service to a single altar (v. 12)], and the same impotence is ascribed to Him as Sancheriv believes to have perceived in the gods of all the other peoples whom he has conquered. It is the call of Gogian defiance foretold in the *Psalms*: *Let us cut their cords and cast off their ropes* (2:3). Let us free ourselves from the moral restraints which the acknowledgement of one omnipotent God would place upon us!

In such a context, Assyria's destruction becomes a fulfillment of David's vision: *He who sits in heaven will laugh, the Lord will mock them* ... (*Psalms* 2:4), and our v. 23, which describes the beginning of a movement of the nations toward a recognition of Israel's uniqueness, is the foretaste of that state in which the Psalmist calls to the people of the world, *And now O kings be wise ... Serve HASHEM in awe ... yearn for purity ...* (2:10-12).

We believe it likely that it is the *Chronicles'* account of the confrontation which led the Sages to detect, in this clash, the potential of the Gogian war.

9\. ... אַחַר זֶה — *After this ... . II Kings* 18:13ff. tells how, in the fourteenth year of Chizkiahu's reign, Sancheriv captured the fortified cities of Judah, and how, in answer to Chizkiahu's plea for mercy and his offer to shoulder any tribute that might be imposed, he demanded huge payments of silver and gold. To fulfill his obligation, Chizkiahu emptied out both the House treasury and his own royal vaults and, in addition, peeled the gold veneer off the Sanctuary gates. After all this was done, Sancheriv sent his messengers from Lachish and these delivered the speech of which the precis is given here.

Malbim explains that Chizkiahu's original offer to pay tribute was made in order to buy time for the military preparations described in the *Chronicles'* account, and it was when Sancheriv realized this duplicity that he sent the message from Lachish.

This, then, would be the meaning of our phrase: After Sancheriv saw that Chizkiahu had every intention of waging war, he sent his servants to convince him of the futility of such defiance.

עֲבָדָיו ... וְהוּא עַל־לָכִישׁ — *His servants ... while he was at Lachish. II Kings* 18:17 reads: *The kings of Assyria sent Tartan and Ravsaris and Ravshakeh from Lachish to King Chizkiahu, with a great army — against Jerusalem ...*

עַל־יְחִזְקִיָּהוּ ... — *to Chizkiahu* ... This connects with ... *sent his servants to Jerusalem*, at the beginning of the verse: Sancheriv sent ... to Chizkiahu ... (*Metzudos*).

10. ... עַל־מָה אַתֶּם בֹּטְחִים — *Upon what are you placing your trust* ... If there were some hope of ultimate victory, it would make sense to suffer the rigors of a prolonged siege. Since you are bound to capitulate in the end, it is foolish to draw out the agony (*Metzudos*).

V. 11 makes clear that מָה stands for their trust that God will help them. [This is explicated in *II Kings* 18:22.] Our verse begins the argument that they cannot hope for help from God because of the thought developed in v. 12.

11. הֲלֹא יְחִזְקִיָּהוּ מַסִּית אֶתְכֶם — *Clearly Chizkiahu is urging you on.*

In v. 9 we saw that Sancheriv's message was addressed to both Chizkiahu and the people of Judah. The אַתֶּם of v.10 could well have included both. But our verse is manifestly directed only to the people. This dissonance may be the result of the fact that the thought expressed in this verse is apparently taken over from a different section of the *Kings'* narrative. There, nothing is said of the people starving until a later point: Chizkiahu's representatives had begged Ravshakeh to use Aramaic instead of Hebrew so that the listening crowds on the wall should not understand what was being said. To this Ravshokeh rejoined belligerently (v. 27) that, on the

לב
יב־יח

יב לֵאמֹר יְהוָה אֱלֹהֵינוּ יַצִּילֵנוּ מִכַּף מֶלֶךְ אַשּׁוּר: הֲלֹא־
הוּא יְחִזְקִיָּהוּ הֵסִיר אֶת־בָּמֹתָיו וְאֶת־מִזְבְּחֹתָיו וַיֹּאמֶר
לִיהוּדָה וְלִירוּשָׁלַםִ לֵאמֹר לִפְנֵי מִזְבֵּחַ אֶחָד תִּשְׁתַּחֲווּ
יג וְעָלָיו תַּקְטִירוּ: הֲלֹא תֵדְעוּ מֶה עָשִׂיתִי אֲנִי וַאֲבוֹתַי
לְכֹל עַמֵּי הָאֲרָצוֹת הֲיָכוֹל יָכְלוּ אֱלֹהֵי גּוֹיֵ הָאֲרָצוֹת
יד לְהַצִּיל אֶת־אַרְצָם מִיָּדִי: מִי בְּכָל־אֱלֹהֵי הַגּוֹיִם הָאֵלֶּה
אֲשֶׁר הֶחֱרִימוּ אֲבוֹתַי אֲשֶׁר יָכוֹל לְהַצִּיל אֶת־עַמּוֹ
טו מִיָּדִי כִּי יוּכַל אֱלֹהֵיכֶם לְהַצִּיל אֶתְכֶם מִיָּדִי: וְעַתָּה
אַל־יַשִּׁיא אֶתְכֶם חִזְקִיָּהוּ וְאַל־יַסִּית אֶתְכֶם כָּזֹאת
וְאַל־תַּאֲמִינוּ לוֹ כִּי־לֹא יוּכַל כָּל־אֱלוֹהַּ כָּל־גּוֹי וּמַמְלָכָה
לְהַצִּיל עַמּוֹ מִיָּדִי וּמִיַּד אֲבוֹתָי אַף כִּי אֱלֹהֵיכֶם לֹא־
טז יַצִּילוּ אֶתְכֶם מִיָּדִי: וְעוֹד דִּבְּרוּ עֲבָדָיו עַל־יְהוָה הָאֱלֹהִים
יז וְעַל יְחִזְקִיָּהוּ עַבְדּוֹ: וּסְפָרִים כָּתַב לְחָרֵף לַיהוָה אֱלֹהֵי
יִשְׂרָאֵל וְלֵאמֹר עָלָיו לֵאמֹר כֵּאלֹהֵי גּוֹיֵ הָאֲרָצוֹת
אֲשֶׁר לֹא־הִצִּילוּ עַמָּם מִיָּדִי כֵּן לֹא־יַצִּיל אֱלֹהֵי יְחִזְקִיָּהוּ
יח עַמּוֹ מִיָּדִי: וַיִּקְרְאוּ בְקוֹל־גָּדוֹל יְהוּדִית עַל־עַם יְרוּשָׁלַםִ

contrary, he would make a point of speaking Hebrew because he was specifically addressing himself to the people who, through the rigors of famine, would bear the brunt of the siege. *Chronicles* transfers this speech to Ravshokeh's original statement, and thus we have the incongruity of a passage directed only to the people in the middle of a speech initially directed (and then continued in v. 13) also to Chizkiahu.

The thrust of Ravshakeh's argument is that the people should not allow Chizkiahu to manipulate them into a belligerent stance. It is they who would starve during a protracted siege. The king would eat well, in an abundantly stocked palace. Ravshakeh could not have known Chizkiahu's practice of sustaining himself on a diet of a few vegetables a day (*Sanhedrin* 94b).

12. הֲלֹא־הוּא יְחִזְקִיָּהוּ — *Is it not this same Chizkiahu* . . . The heathen Ravshakeh cannot grasp the sublime purity of the concept that one central place of worship is more pleasing to God than the multiplicity of the private *bamos* which Chizkiahu had removed.

Towards the end of the period of the First House, such ideas penetrated even the ranks of Israel's own people. Thus, the generation of the destruction argued: *Abraham was one and inherited the land, but we are many, the land is given to us for an inheritance* (*Ezekiel* 33:24). *Tosefta* to *Sotah* (6:5) explains their logic: If Abraham, who served only one God inherited the land, we who serve many gods would surely inherit the land. If Abraham who sacrificed only one son inherited the land, we who sacrifice our sons and daughters should surely inherit the land.

For a discussion, see *ArtScroll Ezekiel*, p. 163, fn. to 8:12.

13-15. In this passage Ravshakeh reveals the perception of God for which he is castigated in v. 19. He sees God as another tribal deity who will prove as impotent against Assyria as the gods of all the other nations have been.

13. אֲנִי וַאֲבוֹתַי — *I and my fathers*. Two other Assyrian kings are mentioned as conquerors of the Northern Kingdom: Pul (*II Kings* 15:19) and Tiglath Pilesser (v. 29 there) (*Mefaresh*).

14. אֲשֶׁר יָכוֹל לְהַצִּיל אֶת־עַמּוֹ מִיָּדִי . . . לְהַצִּיל אֶתְכֶם — *That could save his people from my hand . . . to save you*. V. 13 had spoken of the inability of the tribal gods to save their *land* [אֶת־אַרְצָם] from Assyria's hand; here the issue is the *people* [אֶת־עַמּוֹ].

The expression seems to carry significance beyond the fact that it avoids redundancy from the previous verse: In the parallel passage in *Kings*, there are two sections, the contents of which are similar to this one. The first (18:32-35) seems to be addressed to the people

*saying, "HASHEM our God will save us from the hand of the king
of Assyria."* 12 *Is it not this same Chizkiahu who eliminated His
bamos and His altars, exhorting Judah and Jerusalem, saying:
"You shall worship before but one altar and upon it you shall sacri-
fice."* 13 *Do you not know what I and my fathers have done to all
the people of the lands? Were the gods of the people of the lands
in any way able to save their lands from my hands?* 14 *Who was
there among the gods of those nations which my fathers utterly de-
stroyed, that could save his people from my hand, that your God
should be able to save you from my hand?* 15 *So now let not Chizkia-
hu dupe you nor persuade you, thus. Do do not believe him! No god,
of any nation or kingdom, will be able to save his people from my
hand and from the hand of my fathers. Certainly your God will not
be able to save you from my hand.'* 16 *And his servants spoke still
more against HASHEM God and against Chizkiahu, His servant.* 17
*He also wrote letters to taunt HASHEM, God of Israel, and to speak
against Him saying: As the gods of the nations of the lands which
did not save their people from my hand, so, too, the God of Chizkia-
hu shall not save His people from my hand.* 18 *And they called out
with a loud voice in the Jew's language to the people of Jerusalem*

and not to Chizkiahu, and there the stress is constantly on the *land* as it is in our v. 13.[1]

The second, addressed to Chizkiahu (19:10—13), talks neither of the land nor of the people, but of the kings and their ability to rule over their nations [*Where is the king of Chamath* ...(v. 13)].

Thus, the use of *people* in our verse is significant. It is not duplicated in any of the other passages.

Perhaps, by changing to the concept of *people*, *Chronicles* wishes to create a subtle change of emphasis. Ravshakeh recognizes that Israel is very different from the other nations. Whereas the identity of these is tied to their land, and the destruction of their land inevitably presages their own disintegration as a viable entity, this is not the case with Israel. Particularly, if we are correct in our assumption that we are dealing here in terms of eternal Israel and its Messianic destiny, is it true that history has richly illustrated how independent the people are of territorial ties. Therefore, Israel would not be threatened by the certain destruction of their land. If Ravshakeh is to intimidate them, then he must do so by predicting the annihilation of the people, and not of the land.

15. כְּזֹאת — *Thus*. By claiming that it is reasonable to rely on God's support (*Metzudos*).

אַף כִּי אֱלֹהֵיכֶם — *Certainly your God*. Whom you have offended by removing the *bamos* and the altars (*Metzudos*).

16. עַל־ה׳ הָאֱלֹהִים וְעַל יְחִזְקִיָּהוּ עַבְדּוֹ — *Against HASHEM God and against Chizkiahu His servant*. See prefatory remarks 9-23. The *Kings* account has no equivalent to this verse. In much the same way as do vs. 17 and 19, this sentence appears to express *Chronicles'* outrage at the heinousness of Ravshakeh's blasphemy.

17. . . . וּסְפָרִים כָּתַב — *He also wrote letters* ... These letters are mentioned at *II Kings* 19:14.

18. וַיִּקְרְאוּ בְקוֹל־גָּדוֹל יְהוּדִית — *And they called out with a loud voice in the Jew's language*. The background is *II Kings* 18:26 ff., where Chizkiahu's servants ask Ravshakeh to talk in Aramaic so that the listening crowds would not understand. Ravshakeh defies them (v. 27) and points out that this, precisely, is his intention: He wants the people to hear the message, as our verse goes on to explain.

1. This is true with the exception of the end of v. 32 which reads: ... *and do not listen to Chizkiahu in that he persuades you, saying, HASHEM will save us*. Perhaps this would indicate that the terms are really interchangeable.

אֲשֶׁר עַל־הַחוֹמָה לְיָרְאָם וּלְבַהֲלָם לְמַעַן יִלְכְּדוּ אֶת־
יט הָעִיר׃ וַיְדַבְּרוּ אֶל־אֱלֹהֵי יְרוּשָׁלָםִ כְּעַל אֱלֹהֵי עַמֵּי הָאָרֶץ
כ מַעֲשֵׂה יְדֵי הָאָדָם׃ וַיִּתְפַּלֵּל יְחִזְקִיָּהוּ הַמֶּלֶךְ וִישַׁעְיָהוּ
כא בֶן־אָמוֹץ הַנָּבִיא עַל־זֹאת וַיִּזְעֲקוּ הַשָּׁמָיִם׃ וַיִּשְׁלַח
יהוה מַלְאָךְ וַיַּכְחֵד כָּל־גִּבּוֹר חַיִל וְנָגִיד וְשָׂר בְּמַחֲנֵה מֶלֶךְ
אַשּׁוּר וַיָּשָׁב בְּבֹשֶׁת פָּנִים לְאַרְצוֹ וַיָּבֹא בֵּית אֱלֹהָיו
כב °ומיציאו מֵעָיו שָׁם הִפִּילֻהוּ בֶחָרֶב׃ וַיּוֹשַׁע יהוה אֶת־
יְחִזְקִיָּהוּ וְאֵת ׀ יֹשְׁבֵי יְרוּשָׁלַםִ מִיַּד סַנְחֵרִיב מֶלֶךְ־אַשּׁוּר
כג וּמִיַּד־כֹּל וַיְנַהֲלֵם מִסָּבִיב׃ וְרַבִּים מְבִיאִים מִנְחָה לַיהוה

°וּמִיצִיאֵי ק׳

19. ... וַיְדַבְּרוּ ... — *So they spoke* ... The narrative could well have continued with our v. 20, and we would not have missed this sentence. By inserting it, *Chronicles* takes us, as it were, behind the scenes to observe its own thinking in reproducing an episode which had been adequately dealt with in *Isaiah* and *Kings*. In expressing its own outrage at the philosophical stance underlying Ravshakeh's taunts, it teaches us what the underlying essence of the episode is: Jerusalem is only a peripheral pawn in a much larger game. God Himself, as Master of the world, is the target of Sancheriv's attack.

20. ... וַיִּתְפַּלֵּל יְחִזְקִיָּהוּ ... וִישַׁעְיָהוּ ... — *Chizkiahu ... and Isaiah ... prayed* .... The singular וַיִּתְפַּלֵּל implies that the initiative to pray came from Chizkiahu. Isaiah joined in once Chizkiahu had begun.

This may be the reason that in the *Kings'* account Isaiah is not shown as praying at all. There are two prophecies (19:6 ff. and 21 ff.) dealing with Sancheriv's eventual downfall and promising that God would protect Jerusalem, but no prayer.

Perhaps, in the *Kings'* account in which the danger to Jerusalem is central, the prophet's prayer is not significant. The responsibility for the safety of the city lies, in the final analysis, with the king. But in *Chronicles*, where the essence of the confrontation is spelled out, and God Himself is, as it were, under attack, silence on the prophet's part would have been incongruous.

21. ... וַיִּשְׁלַח ה׳ מַלְאָךְ ... — HASHEM *sent an angel* ... The account of the destruction is somewhat more detailed in *Kings*: *That same night the angel went forth and smote one hundred and eighty-five thousand in the Assyrian camp. They arose in the morning and behold, there were dead bodies* (v. 35).

וַיָּשָׁב בְּבֹשֶׁת פָּנִים לְאַרְצוֹ — *Then, embarrassed, he returned to his own land*. In both the *Kings'* and the *Isaiah* accounts, the story of Sancheriv's return to his country and his eventual assassination at the hands of his own sons is told in a verse by itself, and not together with the account of the destruction of the Assyrian army.

See Section II, *A Missed Opportunity*, for a discussion of this difference.

... וּמִיצִיאֵי מֵעָיו — *His own offspring* .... Both *Kings* and *Isaiah* identify the sons by name, tell of their flight to the land of Ararat and note that Sancheriv was succeeded by Eisarchadon.

Chronicles does none of this and two possible explanations suggest themselves: Perhaps, by the time *Chronicles* was written, the details of the Assyrian empire — long since superceded by Babylon and Media-Persia — were no longer of any significance.

It is also possible that the elimination of non-essential details is part of the pattern of sparseness begun in the first part of the verse. In contrast to the earlier books, no statistics are given concerning the number of slain Assyrians. It is as though *Chronicles* purposely gives only a grudging account in order to underline the sorrow at the failed opportunity. (See Secion II, *A Missed Opportunity*.) Really, in the long view of history, these events which could so easily have been vastly significant do not count for very much.

22. וּמִיַּד־כֹּל — *And from the hands of all.* What is this phrase meant to convey? Commentators do not explain. It is, of course, possible that the meaning is, that just as God saved Chizkiahu and the people of Jerusalem from the Assyrian danger, so too, did He help them on all other occasions when enemies threatened. However, nowhere else do we find any attacks upon Chizkiahu and, on the contrary, the next few verses indicate that

32
19-23

that were on the wall to terrify and to confuse them so that they should be able to capture the city. [19] *So they spoke of the God of Jerusalem as of the gods of the people of the earth which are the work of men's hands.* [20] *Chizkiahu the king and Isaiah son of Amotz, the prophet, prayed because of this, and cried to heaven.* [21] *HASHEM sent an angel who destroyed every warrior, commander and officer in the king of Assyria's army. Then, embarrassed, he returned to his own land, and came to his idol's temple. His own offspring felled him, there, by the sword.* [22] *Thus did HASHEM save Chizkiahu and the dwellers of Jerusalem from the hands of Sancheriv king of Assyria and from the hands of all, and settle them securely in the surrounding area.* [23] *And many brought gifts*

subsequent to the miraculous destruction of Assyria, all the neighboring nations respected Chizkiahu deeply and would not have wanted to wage war against him.

Does it mean, then, that other nations were involved in Assyria's attack? Again, we find no mention of this.

Rather, it would seem that we have here confirmation for the tradition of the Sages that Sancheriv's war could have been the Gogian war.

We examine the ideas contained in this tradition.

Sanhedrin 95b teaches that the number of soldiers in Sancheriv's army was identical with that of the forces of the four kings with whom Abraham waged war (*Genesis* ch.14), and with that which will, at some date in the future, come with Gog king of Magog, for the final confrontation between Israel and the nations.

The symbolic significance of the numbers is explained by *Maharal*, but need not concern us here. The bringing together of the three apparently unconnected wars should, however, be analyzed.

Maharal sees these three wars as attempts on the part of the gentile world to annihilate the Jewish people. This attempt would logically be undertaken under three circumstances: The first opportunity would be the moment when the Jewish people appeared on the stage of history. Immediately, this would call forth a counter-reaction on the part of the nations — and that is the story of the four kings.

Again, in the final moments before the ultimate redemption and vindication of Israel, in the moment in which the Messiah finally appears, there would be one last desperate attempt to reverse the tides of history — and that is the Gogian war foretold by the prophets.

The other logical moment would be when Israel is weakest and in its most vulnerable position. The nadir of Israel's existence was that instant in which four-fifths of its body was suddenly lopped off — when the Ten Tribes were carried into exile, to be lost until the Messianic redemption. And this is the story of Sancheriv's attack.

We must understand *Maharal's* thesis against the background of the midrash's assertion that the numerical value of **גוג ומָגוג** is seventy, and that this symbolizes the fact that the Gogian war will be waged in the name of all the seventy nations of the world.

God's salvation of Israel from the hands of the Assyrians was, in fact, *from the hand of all*, in the sense that Assyria here represented all seventy nations of the world.

וַיְנַהֲלֵם מִסָּבִיב — *And settle them securely in the surrounding area.* נהל usually means *to lead*. Accordingly, *Metzudos* suggests: *He lead all the people from roundabout, gently* [נהל implies a *gentle* leading, as in *Psalms* 23:2]. But what is the meaning of this phrase in our context? Who are the people from roundabout, and why is their fate of interest to us?

We have followed *Targum* who renders: וְאַשְׁרִינוּן לְרוּחְצָן חֲזוֹר חֲזוֹר. שרה in the *Targumim* is used to render words like שכן, *to dwell*. The meaning of the phrase could be that, after the destruction of the Assyrian army, the people of Jerusalem were able to dwell securely even outside the city walls, and had nothing to fear from the Assyrian forces who presumably were still occupying the cities of Judah which had been previously captured.[1]

1. *Targum's* rendering of נהל is in line with other *Targumim* which treat the word much less rigidly than do the classical commentators. Thus, for example, we have *Exodus* 15:13: נֵהַלְתָּ בְעָזְּךָ אֶל נְוֵה קָדְשֶׁךָ: understood by

לִירוּשָׁלִַם וּמִגְדָּנוֹת לִיחִזְקִיָּהוּ מֶלֶךְ יְהוּדָה וַיִּנַּשֵּׂא לְעֵינֵי
כָל־הַגּוֹיִם מֵאַחֲרֵי־כֵן׃
כד בַּיָּמִים הָהֵם חָלָה יְחִזְקִיָּהוּ עַד־לָמוּת וַיִּתְפַּלֵּל אֶל־
כה יהוה וַיֹּאמֶר לוֹ וּמוֹפֵת נָתַן לוֹ׃ וְלֹא־כִגְמֻל עָלָיו הֵשִׁיב
יְחִזְקִיָּהוּ כִּי גָבַהּ לִבּוֹ וַיְהִי עָלָיו קֶצֶף וְעַל־יְהוּדָה
כו וִירוּשָׁלִָם׃ וַיִּכָּנַע יְחִזְקִיָּהוּ בְּגֹבַהּ לִבּוֹ הוּא וְיוֹשְׁבֵי יְרוּשָׁלִָם
כז וְלֹא־בָא עֲלֵיהֶם קֶצֶף יהוה בִּימֵי יְחִזְקִיָּהוּ׃ וַיְהִי לִיחִזְקִיָּהוּ
עֹשֶׁר וְכָבוֹד הַרְבֵּה מְאֹד וְאוֹצָרוֹת עָשָׂה־לוֹ לְכֶסֶף וּלְזָהָב

23. וְרַבִּים מְבִיאִים מִנְחָה לַה׳ . . . וּמִגְדָּנוֹת לִיחִזְקִיָּהוּ — *And many brought gifts to HASHEM . . . and precious things to Chizkiahu* . . . The end of the verse . . . *from then on, he was highly regarded by all the nations*... indicates that the bearers of the *gifts* and *precious things* were the gentile nations. Given this, it appears that this verse is also one of those which project the Messianic overtones of the confrontation between Israel and the Assyrians.

In *Genesis* 49:10 we have Jacob's vision of the Davidic kingship: *The scepter shall not depart from Judah nor a scholar from among his descendants until Shiloh arrives, and his will be an assemblage of nations.*

The general consensus of Rabbinic interpretation is that *Shiloh* is a reference to the Messianic king. [For details see ArtScroll *Genesis* p. 2152.] *Rashi* quotes a midrash that שִׁילֹה is a composite of שַׁי לוֹ, *a gift for him* — a reference to the fact that all the peoples of the world will bring gifts to the Messiah.

This assumption is based on *Psalms* 76:12 where we read: . . . *they will present gifts to the awesome ones*. Significantly, there are two interpretations to that psalm. *Radak* has it refer to the time after victory will have been won in the Gogian war, while in *Metzudos'* view it alludes to our passage. Rabbinic tradition, which has been the basis for our understanding of the *Chronicles'* account of Chizkiahu, teaches that the two are really one — or could have been had Chizkiahu risen to the challenge. See ArtScroll *Tehillim*, p. 954.

Our verse is manifestly that part of the Chizkian saga which might have been the beginnings of the Messianic gift-bearing, and which, in the end, became at least the foreshadowing of that great historic moment.[1]

וּמִגְדָּנוֹת — *And precious things*. מֶגֶד denotes something that is luxurious and sweet (*Rashi*, *Deuteronomy* 33:13).

וַיִּנַּשֵּׂא — *He was highly regarded* . . . *Radak* reads this word as though it were written, וַיִּתְנַשֵּׂא, *and he exalted himself*. He detects here the first inklings of the pride for which Chizkiahu is castigated in v. 25.

⤳ Chizkiahu's Sinful Pride

24. בַּיָּמִים הָהֵם — *In those days*. Three days before the destruction of Sancheriv's army (*Metzudos*).

See Section II, *Chizkiahu's Illness*, for a

Targum as סְבַרְהִי, which is the *Targumim's* favored rendering for נשא, *to bear*. Thus, *You with Your strength bore them to Your holy dwelling place. Rashi* (there) remarks that *Targum* is inexact, and does not follow the Hebrew which, in *Rashi's* opinion, should have been translated: *You led* . . .

Now, the Aramaic סבר, *to bear*, is also used when describing the idea: *Being supported by the land* [see, for example, *Targum* to *Genesis* 13:6], and from that meaning the concept *to dwell* is not far removed. Thus, for example, *Targum Yonassan* to the *Exodus* verse quoted above renders: *You caused them to inherit the House Mount*.

It is noteworthy that *Targum* to *Isaiah* 49:10 renders: וְעַל־מַבּוּעֵי מַיִם יְנַהֲלֵם with יַשְׁרִינוּן, precisely as *Targum* to our verse takes the word; but *Targum* to *Psalms* 23:2 renders the almost identical phrase: עַל־מֵי מְנֻחוֹת יְנַהֲלֵנִי with דַּבְּרָנִי from דבר, *to lead*.

1. *Isaiah* 18:7 also depicts this Messianic gift-bearing and writes: *At that time a gift will be borne to HASHEM of hosts, a people* . . . [a description of Israel follows]. What do these words seek to convey? In what way are the people of Israel, themselves, the gift which the nations will, one day, bring?

The possibility, of course, exists that the word, *by*, is assumed: A gift will be brought *by* Israel.

However, the commentators interpret differently. They think that the gift which the nations will bring is — the people of Israel. When the Messiah comes, the nations will bring back the Ten Tribes whom they had dragged into exile. (See *Metzudos*.)

This is now foreshadowed by our verse.

to HASHEM to Jerusalem and precious things to Chizkiahu, king of Judah. From then on, he was highly regarded by all the nations. 24 *In those days Chizkiahu became deathly ill. He prayed to HASHEM; He spoke to him; and vouchsafed him a sign.* 25 *But Chizkiahu, because his heart was proud, did not reciprocate in kind. Therefore there was wrath upon him and upon Judah and Jerusalem.* 26 *Chizkiahu humbled himself from the pride of his heart, he and the dwellers of Jerusalem, so that the wrath of HASHEM did not come upon them during Chizkiahu's lifetime.* 27 *Chizkiahu had exceedingly much wealth and honor and made himself treasure houses for silver and gold and*

discussion of *Chronicles'* treatment of the story of Chizkiahu's sickness and its aftermath.

חָלָה יְחִזְקִיָּהוּ עַד־לָמוּת — *Chizkiahu became deathly ill.* Chizkiahu had seen in prophetic spirit, that if he were to have a son, this son would be wicked. Because of this, he decided not to marry. As a punishment, God made him deathly ill. Isaiah chided him that he had no business to allow such considerations to influence his actions. He was to do what God had commanded and leave the future in God's hands (*Berachos* 10a).

וַיִּתְפַּלֵּל אֶל־ה׳ — *He prayed to HASHEM.* The text of Chizkiahu's prayer is given in *II Kings* 20:2-3. As discussed in Section II, *Chizkiahu's Illness*, the Sages criticize him for basing his entreaty upon his own merits.

וַיֹּאמֶר לוֹ — *He spoke to him. Metzudos* points out that the phrase is incomplete. It is left to the reader to supply the obvious — that God told him that his prayer was accepted. See Section II, *Chizkiahu's Illness*.

The text of God's answer is given in *II Kings* 20:4-7.

וּמוֹפֵת נָתַן לוֹ — *And vouchsafed him a sign. II Kings* 20:10-11 tells of Chizkiahu's choice of the sign. He asked that the sun regress ten degrees from the place it had already reached. See Section II, *Chizkiahu's Illness*, for the implication of the choice of this particular sign.

25. וְלֹא־כִגְמֻל ... הֵשִׁיב יְחִזְקִיָּהוּ — *But Chizkiahu did not reciprocate in kind.* Reference is to the exaggerated respect which Chizkiahu paid to the Babylonian ambassadors (*II Kings* 20:12-13; see below).

כִּי גָבַהּ לִבּוֹ — *Because his heart was proud.* See Section II, *Chizkiahu's Illness*.

וַיְהִי עָלָיו קֶצֶף — *Therefore, there was wrath upon him.* In *II Kings* 20:5-7, Isaiah castigates Chizkiahu, and prophesies that one day his descendants would be chamberlains in the Babylonian court.

Sanhedrin 104a pictures the exaggerated respect which Chizkiahu showed his guests. He had them eat at his own table and, moreover, his own wife attended their needs. Such fawning is deemed inappropriate, and would be punished by the Babylonian exile. *Maharal* explains: By going far beyond his formal obligations, Chizkiahu demonstrated an intrinsic subservience to the Babylonians. This was later to express itself in actual servitude.

The simple meaning of the passage in *II Kings* is that God's anger came about because of the pride Chizkiahu displayed by opening up his treasure houses for their inspection — particularly, as expanded by the tradition of the Sages, that he opened up the Ark in order to show them the tablets which helped him to victory in war — see Section II, *Chizkiahu's Illness*.

26. וְלֹא־בָא עֲלֵיהֶם ... בִּימֵי יְחִזְקִיָּהוּ — *... did not come upon them during Chizkiahu's lifetime.* Another 110 years were to pass before the destruction.

27-30. By placing these verses at the end of the description of Chizkiahu's reign, *Chronicles* clearly intends to contribute substantively to our impression of the life and works of this great king. The passage has no parallel in either *Kings* or *Isaiah*.

It seems legitimate to ask why *Chronicles* chose just this picture with which to close its account. In the historical consciousness of the Jewish people, Chizkiahu is remembered for quite different accomplishments.

We recall him as the man who thrust a sword into the entrance of the Beis HaMidrash indicating that *Whoever does not occupy himself with the study of Torah shall be pierced by the sword.* During his reign it was that *... they searched from Dan to Be'er Sheva*

וּלְאֶ֣בֶן יְקָרָ֔ה וְלִבְשָׂמִים֙ וּלְמָ֣גִנִּ֔ים וּלְכֹ֖ל כְּלֵ֥י חֶמְדָּֽה׃
כח וּמִ֨סְכְּנ֔וֹת לִתְבוּאַ֥ת דָּגָ֖ן וְתִיר֣וֹשׁ וְיִצְהָ֑ר וְאֻרָוֺת֙ לְכָל־
כט בְּהֵמָ֣ה וּבְהֵמָ֔ה וַעֲדָרִ֖ים לָאֲוֵרֽוֹת׃ וְעָרִים֙ עָ֣שָׂה ל֔וֹ
וּמִקְנֵה־צֹ֥אן וּבָקָ֖ר לָרֹ֑ב כִּ֥י נָֽתַן־לוֹ֙ אֱלֹהִ֔ים רְכ֖וּשׁ רַ֥ב
ל מְאֹֽד׃ וְה֣וּא יְחִזְקִיָּ֗הוּ סָתַם֙ אֶת־מוֹצָ֞א מֵימֵ֤י גִיחוֹן֙ הָֽעֶלְי֔וֹן
°וַיַּשְּׁרֵ֥ם ק׳ °ויישרם לְמַֽטָּה־מַּעְרָ֖בָה לְעִ֣יר דָּוִ֑יד וַיַּצְלַ֥ח יְחִזְקִיָּ֖הוּ
לא בְּכָל־מַעֲשֵֽׂהוּ׃ וְכֵ֗ן בִּמְלִיצֵ֣י ׀ שָׂרֵ֣י בָבֶ֗ל הַֽמְשַׁלְּחִ֤ים עָלָיו֙
לִדְר֗שׁ הַמּוֹפֵת֙ אֲשֶׁ֣ר הָיָ֣ה בָאָ֔רֶץ עֲזָב֖וֹ הָאֱלֹהִ֑ים לְנַ֨סּוֹת֔וֹ
לב לָדַ֖עַת כָּל־בִּלְבָבֽוֹ׃ וְיֶ֛תֶר דִּבְרֵ֥י יְחִזְקִיָּ֖הוּ וַחֲסָדָ֑יו הִנָּ֣ם

and could not find an ignorant person; from Givath to Antripath and could not find boy or girl, man or woman, who was not versed in the laws of tumah and taharah (*Sanhedrin* 94b).

Would we not have expected that this legacy would be the one which *Chronicles* would wish us to remember?

At 1:14-17 we posed a similar question with regard to *Chronicles'* treatment of Solomon's wealth. There, too, we wondered why *Chronicles* makes no mention of Solomon's wisdom but only of the profligate spending which marked his reign. We concluded that *Chronicles'* silence is based upon the judgment of history. Solomon's wisdom in the end proved to be no blessing. It was to be a contributing factor toward some of the great tragedies which were to follow. *Chronicles* makes this point by omitting mention of it in the account of his reign.

Perhaps, here we have a similar truth. In the long run, Chizkiahu had proved to be a disappointment to God. *Bereishis Rabbah* 19 brackets him together with Adam, Cain and Balaam as the four men in history who did not live up to God's expectations. It is particularly noteworthy that *II Kings* 18:5 ... *after him there was none like him among all the kings of Judah, nor those that were before him*, is not duplicated in *Chronicles*. It seems possible that this assessment was true from the point of view of *Kings*, which takes the reign as a self-contained unit and compares it to any other single reign. But *Chronicles* has a different perspective. During the dreadful half century of Menasheh's and Amon's rule, much of the Torah which Chizkiahu had taught had been forgotten; his mark upon the people dimmed. In the great challenge that God had posed for him and which in one stroke could have changed history, he had failed. By omitting mention of his spiritual achievements, *Chronicles* may be making the point which the Sages made in *Bereishis Rabbah*: The great hope attached to Chizkiahu's reign ended in disillusion.

27. וּלְכֹל כְּלֵי חֶמְדָּה — *And for all kinds of desirable objects*. He made storage house for these, too (*Mefaresh*).

28. . . . וְאֻרָוֺת — *And mangers* . . . See comm. to 9:25.

וַעֲדָרִים לָאֲוֵרוֹת — *And appropriate dispositions for the mangers*. To render עֲדָרִים in the usual way as *flocks*, as does *Metzudos*, leaves us with a difficulty. Why *flocks for mangers* when the previous phrase has already said that there were mangers for all the animals?

Radak adduces *I Chronicles* 12:34 and 39 where we have the root עדר used as a synonym for ערך, *to arrange* or *organize*. The sense here would be that each manger was arranged for the most efficient functioning.

29. . . . כִּי נָתַן־לוֹ אֱלֹהִים — *For God gave him* . . . . We assume this phrase to refer back to the entire description of Chizkiahu's wealth. It all came to him from God — presumably as a reward for the meritorious life which he lived.

30. . . . וְהוּא יְחִזְקִיָּהוּ — *He was Chizkiahu who* . . . *Bereishis Rabbah* 37:3 interprets the apparently redundant וְהוּא to indicate that he remained the same righteous Chizkiahu throughout his career. This point would have to be made in view of the fact that Chizkiahu was censured by the Sages for having stopped up the Gichon waters (*Berachos* 10b). The Midrash teaches that his actions were due to an oversight, and did not impinge upon his essential goodness (*Tiferes Zion*).

. . . סָתַם — *Stopped up* . . . See Section II, *The Diversion of the Waters*, for a discussion. There we suggest that the incident mentioned

32
28-32

precious stones and spices and shields, and for all kinds of desirable objects. [28] *Storage houses for the crops of grain, wine and oil, and mangers for all kinds of animals, and appropriate dispositions for the mangers.* [29] *He made himself cities and had great flocks of sheep and cattle, for God gave him abundant possessions.* [30] *He was Chizkiahu who stopped up the upper source of the Gichon waters and directed them downwards to the west of the City of David — and Chizkiahu prospered in all his works.* [31] *And so too in the matter of the ambassadors sent to him by the princes of Babylon, to find out about the wonder that had happened in the land, God forsook him in order to test him; to know all that was in his heart.* [32] *Now the rest of the matters of Chizkiahu and his pieties are*

in our verse may not have been the one criticized by the Sages. This seems to be supported by *Avos d'R' Nosson*, which claims that in doing that which our verse describes, he acted in accordance with God's wishes.

However, two considerations militate against this: Firstly, the וְהוּא at the beginning of our verse seems to indicate that the diversion of the waters was wrong. It was for only this reason that it was necessary to note that this did not impinge upon his essential goodness. So too, the וְכֵן of the next verse. By introducing the incident of the ambassadors — in which Chizkiahu faltered — with the words *And so too*, the point is surely made that the earlier action was also reprehensible (*Ralbag*).

וַיַּצְלַח יְחִזְקִיָּהוּ בְּכָל־מַעֲשֵׂהוּ — *And Chizkiahu prospered in all his works*. In Section II, *The Diversion of the Waters*, we quoted *Avos d'R' Nosson* 2:4 that this phrase indicates that he acted in accordance with God's wishes [הִסְכִּימָה דַעְתּוֹ לְדַעַת הַמָּקוֹם]. See there for discussion.

31. וְכֵן . . . — *And so too* . . . Besides being wrong in the matter of the Gichon, he also erred in his reception of the Babylonian ambassadors (*Ralbag*).

בִּמְלִיצֵי שָׂרֵי בָּבֶל הַמְשַׁלְּחִים עָלָיו . . . — *The ambassadors sent to him by the princes of Babylon*. מֵלִיץ, which in *Genesis* 42:23 means *an interpreter*, is used here as *an ambassador* or *messenger*. This, because such a person conveys the words of the sender to the person to whom they are addressed, in much the same way that an interpreter makes communication possible (*Metzudos*).

הַמּוֹפֵת אֲשֶׁר הָיָה בָאָרֶץ — *The wonder that had happened in the land*. The Sages (*Pesikta* quoted in *Rashi* to *Kings*) teach that the Babylonian king had heard about the miracle of the regression of the sun. *Ralbag* thinks that reference is to the miraculous wiping out of the Assyrian forces.

עֲזָבוֹ הָאֱלֹהִים — *God forsook him*. In contrast to other occasions when God sent Chizkiahu guidance through the prophets, God left him to his own devices so that the occasion might serve as a test (*Ralbag*).

In any event, Chizkiahu erred. He should not have shown the ambassadors the treasure houses — and certainly should not have opened the Ark for them (*Mefaresh*).

32. וַחֲסָדָיו — *And his pieties*. See comm. to 6:42 for the use of חֶסֶד as *piety*.

It is particularly significant that *Chronicles* substitutes חֲסָדָיו for גְּבוּרוֹתָיו, which is the term used in the *Kings* account. What reason could there be for rejecting the other term?

It is not possible to know precisely how *Chronicles* uses the term גְּבוּרָה, but it seems evident that its connotation is different than it was for Jeremiah in *Kings*: In *Kings* the term is used frequently to describe the reigns of various kings. Most of these are from the Northern Kingdom, and therefore have no parallel in *Chronicles*. However, two, Asa and Yehoshaphat, are from Judah, and it is noteworthy that in both cases, *Chronicles* omits the term when describing those kings — see 16:11 ff. and 21:34 ff. Thus, with only one exception, *Chronicles* never uses the term גְּבוּרָה to describe a reign. That exception is David, concerning whom it is used at *I Chronicles* 29:30.

Thus, if the term would have been retained here, it would have unambiguously bracketed

לב כְּתוּבִים בַּחֲזוֹן יְשַׁעְיָהוּ בֶן־אָמוֹץ הַנָּבִיא עַל־סֵפֶר מַלְכֵי
לג לג יְהוּדָה וְיִשְׂרָאֵל׃ וַיִּשְׁכַּב יְחִזְקִיָּהוּ עִם־אֲבֹתָיו וַיִּקְבְּרֻהוּ
בְּמַעֲלֵה קִבְרֵי בְנֵי־דָוִיד וְכָבוֹד עָשׂוּ־לוֹ בְמוֹתוֹ כָּל־יְהוּדָה
לג א וְיֹשְׁבֵי יְרוּשָׁלִָם וַיִּמְלֹךְ מְנַשֶּׁה בְנוֹ תַּחְתָּיו׃ בֶּן־
א שְׁתֵּים עֶשְׂרֵה שָׁנָה מְנַשֶּׁה בְמָלְכוֹ וַחֲמִשִּׁים וְחָמֵשׁ שָׁנָה

Chizkiahu with David — as *Chronicles* has done throughout the Chizkiahu chapters.

But at this point this would have been entirely inappropriate inasmuch as we have seen the censure of the Sages, that Chizkiahu failed in his Davidic role, reflected in the last few verses of the *Chronicles* account.

Thus, it is possible to suggest that חֲסָדָיו was substituted in order to underline that in the final assessment of his reign, Chizkiahu could no longer be seen as the *David* of his generation.

בַּחֲזוֹן ... עַל־סֵפֶר מַלְכֵי יְהוּדָה וְיִשְׂרָאֵל — *In the vision . . . and in the Book of the Kings of Judah and Israel.* In accordance with *Targum* and *Metzudos,* we have inserted *and*, as though the text would have read . . . וְעַל סֵפֶר. The sense of the verse is that, in addition to the records which were kept in the royal chronicles, the details of Chizkiahu's reign are recorded in the Book of *Isaiah*.

33. בְּמַעֲלֵה קִבְרֵי בְנֵי־דָוִיד — *In the finest of the sepulchers of the descendants of David.* We have translated in accordance with *Radak* and *Metzudos*, who base their rendering on *Bava Kama* 16b, which derives from our verse that Chizkiahu was buried in the immediate vicinity of the graves of David and Solomon. (See prefatory remarks to ch. 29.)

Targum, however, renders מַסּוֹקִית, the term favored by the *Targumim* for *ascent*. See, for example, *Targum* to *Isaiah* 15:5. Thus, he seems to take our phrase to mean *on the slope of*.

וְכָבוֹד עָשׂוּ־לוֹ בְמוֹתוֹ. . . — . . . *did him honor at his death. Bava Kama* 16b and 17a records two opinions as to what this honor was. According to one interpretation, a temporary house of study [יְשִׁיבָה] was established near his grave. This was in recognition of the enormous contribution which he had made towards Torah study (*Tosafos*).

The other interpretation is that a *Sefer Torah* was placed on his coffin and people declared: *He fulfilled that which this [Sefer Torah] demands!*

Thus was Chizkiahu's personal integrity and extreme righteousness honored, even though, on the grand scale, he had failed to turn the tides of history.

XXXIII

◆§ Menasheh's Depredations

A comparison between this chapter and ch. 21 in *II Kings*, which is its parallel, reveals differences in the accounts of Menasheh's reign, which seem more profound and more far-reaching than those which were noted in connection with any of the other kings. Whereas *Kings* pictures a life of unrelieved wickedness, laying the impending destruction of Jerusalem and the House squarely at Menasheh's door, *Chronicles* not only makes no mention at all of any responsibility for the destruction, but pictures a sincerely penitent man who made herculean efforts to eradicate the evils which, earlier in his reign, he had initiated.

A careful analysis of the aggadic material concerning Menasheh may help us understand the differing perspectives of the two books.

We begin by noting that the Mishnah records a major disagreement concerning the quality of Menasheh's *teshuvah* as described in *Chronicles*. The anonymous opinion, recorded in *Sanhedrin* 90a, is that Menasheh is to be counted among the kings who have no portion in the World to Come — his penitence has no real standing. R' Yehudah, on the other hand, holds that the penitence was effective, and that it regained for him his portion in the afterlife.

The commentary will be based upon the anonymous tradition.

The Mishnah (*Sanhedrin* 90a), speaks of three kings who lost their portion in the world to come: Yarov'am, Ahab and Menasheh. In accordance with the Rabbinic view that names spell

32 *recorded in the vision of Isaiah son of Amotz the prophet and in*
33 *the Book of the Kings of Judah and Israel.* [35] *Chizkiahu lay with*
his fathers and they buried him in the finest of the sepulchers of
the descendants of David. And all of Judah and the dwellers of
Jerusalem did him honor at his death. And Menasheh his son
reigned in his stead.

33
1 M*enasheh was twelve years old when he began to reign, and*

out the essential nature of those who bear them, the Talmud offers aggadic interpretations for the names of each of these three kings.[1]

Now, in the case of Menasheh, we find two opinions as to how his name [=his intrinsic evil] is to be understood. *Sanhedrin* 102b offers these possibilities: 1. מְנַשֶּׁה conveys the idea שֶׁנָּשָׁה יָהּ, *The one who forgot God*; or 2. שֶׁהִנְשִׁי אֶת יִשְׂרָאֵל לַאֲבִיהֶם שֶׁבַּשָּׁמַיִם, *The one who caused Israel to forget their Father in heaven*.

We read these two opinions as disagreeing about the nature of the intrinsic evil that lay within Menasheh: Did it center in his own personality [1], or did it express itself only in the misguided leadership which he gave to the people [2]? The first opinion holds that Menasheh, as a person, was incorrigibly evil — but his influence upon his people was not innately pernicious. The second opinion holds that the essential evil expressed itself in his kingship — it did not touch upon his personality.

We shall, for the purpose of the comm., assume the first of the two opinions. It appears to be yielded by the Mishnah, *Sanhedrin* 90a, as follows:

As noted above, the anonymous opinion reported in that Mishnah is that Menasheh had forfeited his portion in the World to Come. R' Yehudah argues, on the basis of our v. 13: ... *And he prayed to Him ... and He heard his supplication and brought him back to Jerusalem, to his kingship* — a clear indication that Menasheh's penitence was accepted by God. The anonymous *Tanna* retorts: *To his kingship* did He bring him back, but not to life in the World to Come.

The meaning, as we read it, is that on a personal level, Menasheh was indeed lost, and his *teshuvah* had no standing at all. It was only as king — a calling in which he had failed terribly — that his penitence was effective. He had lost his kingship because he had grievously misled his people. Upon repenting and realizing his errors, that kingship was restored to him. This, however, did not effect his personal standing. He was, and remained, incorrigibly wicked — banned eternally from the World to Come.

Given this interpretation of the Mishnah, we may say that the story told in *Kings* is the personal saga of Menasheh — and in that story his penitence had no effect and is therefore not recorded. By contrast, *Chronicles* tells the story of Menasheh's kingship. In that context, the repentance was effective — and an important part of the story.

This thesis will be developed further in the comm. Here, we note only one further confirmation for the correctness of our analysis. Our v. 3 tells of the *bamos* which Menasheh built, of the altars which he erected for the Baal, and of the *asheirah*-trees which he had made — precisely as does v. 3 of the *Kings* account. However, the *Kings'* account adds: ... *as Ahab the king of Israel had done*, but *Chronicles* omits this phrase. Now, *Sanhedrin* 102b teaches that it is precisely this phrase which teaches that Menasheh had forfeited his portion in the World to Come: ... *as Ahab king of Israel had done. Menasheh is to be compared to Ahab; as Ahab has no portion in the World to Come so, too, Menasheh has no portion*. Inasmuch as the basis for this teaching is missing from the *Chronicles'* account, we may surmise that within the context of *Chronicles'* interest, it is, indeed, not true. His person, but not his kingship, was comparable to Ahab. As a man he was as incorrigible as Ahab had been, but not as a king. His kingship could be, and in fact was, reconstituted.

1. בֶּן־שְׁתֵּים עֶשְׂרֵה שָׁנָה מְנַשֶּׁה בְמָלְכוֹ — *Menasheh was twelve years old when he began to reign.* Chizkiahu became king at twenty-five and ruled for twenty-nine years — that is, he died

1. Since their evil nature was part of their essential being, their names carried connotations of the evil that inhered in them.

ב מָלַךְ בִּירוּשָׁלָֽם׃ וַיַּעַשׂ הָרַע בְּעֵינֵי יְהֹוָה כְּתֽוֹעֲבוֹת הַגּוֹיִם
ג אֲשֶׁר הוֹרִישׁ יְהוָה מִפְּנֵי בְּנֵי יִשְׂרָאֵֽל׃ וַיָּשָׁב וַיִּבֶן
אֶת־הַבָּמוֹת אֲשֶׁר נִתַּץ יְחִזְקִיָּהוּ אָבִיו וַיָּקֶם מִזְבְּחוֹת
לַבְּעָלִים וַיַּעַשׂ אֲשֵׁרוֹת וַיִּשְׁתַּחוּ לְכָל־צְבָא הַשָּׁמַיִם וַיַּעֲבֹד
ד אֹתָֽם׃ וּבָנָה מִזְבְּחוֹת בְּבֵית יְהֹוָה אֲשֶׁר אָמַר יְהוָה
ה בִּירוּשָׁלַ͏ִם יִֽהְיֶה־שְּׁמִי לְעוֹלָֽם׃ וַיִּבֶן מִזְבְּחוֹת לְכָל־צְבָא

at fifty-nine. If his heir was then only twelve years old, he must have fathered him relatively late in life. We recall the tradition of the Sages that Chizkiahu had planned not to marry, so that he might avoid bearing a wicked son. It was only after he became deathly ill and was castigated by Isaiah for allowing his fears to interfere with his duties, that he married [see at 32:24].

As in the case of the other kings, the *Kings* account, in the parallel verse, gives the name of Menasheh's mother. In its accounts of earlier kings, *Chronicles*, too, had followed this practice. Here, and in the records of the subsequent kings, the mothers' names are omitted, even though *Kings* records them.

In the case of Menasheh, the omission of the mother's name may tend to confirm the thesis suggested in prefatory remarks to this chapter. We are concerned here with Menasheh the king — not with Menasheh the man. The mother's influence is felt more specifically in the personal standing of the child.

וַחֲמִשִּׁים וְחָמֵשׁ שָׁנָה מָלַךְ בִּירוּשָׁלַםִ — *And he reigned fifty-five years in Jerusalem.* Menasheh ruled longer than any other king and, when we combine the years of his reign with the two years of his son, Amon, then we have fifty-seven years of unrelieved wickedness in Jerusalem. This could explain the apparently total ignorance of Torah in Yoshiahu's time [see 34:18 ff.].

But the Sages (*Sanhedrin* 103a) have the tradition that Menasheh's wickedness spanned only twenty-two years and that he was penitent for thirty-three years. This would make the ignorance in Yoshiahu's time difficult to understand. *Radak* (*II Kings* 22:8) raises this question and because of it prefers to assume that Menasheh's repentance, as told in *Chronicles*, took place at the end of his life — too late to leave its mark on the populace.

2. וַיַּעַשׂ הָרַע . . . כְּתוֹעֲבוֹת הַגּוֹיִם — *He did evil . . . just like to the abominations of the nations.* Neither in *Kings* nor in *Chronicles* is the reign of any other king described in these terms. [The phrase occurs once more, to describe Achaz's practice of passing his son through fire (28:3), but it is not given as an assessment of the total reign.]

In the *Kings'* account where, as we have seen, the destruction is laid at Menasheh's door, such an assessment is apt. It stands to reason that when the state of depravity of the previous occupants of the land had been reached, this should be followed by destruction and exile.[1]

But *Chronicles* never blames Menasheh for the subsequent exile and destruction — for reasons discussed in prefatory remarks to ch. 28. Why, then, this devastating assessment?

We must conclude that *Chronicles* uses the phrase in order to hint at the truth laid down in *Kings*, even though the *Chronicles'* portrayal of the period provides no justification for this judgment.

3. הַבָּמוֹת אֲשֶׁר נִתַּץ יְחִזְקִיָּהוּ — *The bamos which Chizkiahu, his father, had broken down.* At 31:1 we saw that *Chronicles* stresses the fact that it was the people — not the king himself — who had broken down the *bamos* and destroyed the various idolatrous cult objects. Why, here, is the action ascribed to the king?

However, it must be noted that the *piel* voice [נִתַּץ] is occasionally used to denote the causative. [לָמַד, *to learn*, לִמֵּד, *to teach*; that is, *to cause to learn*.] Thus, it is possible that our verse should be understood to mean: . . . *the bamos which Chizkiahu . . . caused to be broken down.*

וַיָּקֶם מִזְבְּחוֹת לַבְּעָלִים — *He established altars for the Baalim.* At 28:2 we discussed the introduction of Baal worship into Judah under

1. Indeed, in the detailed explanation which is given in *Kings* for the exile of the ten northern tribes [*II Kings* 17:7 ff.], it is stated that the destruction came about when the Jews reached the level of depravity which had caused the Canaanite nations to be expelled from the land. This is followed by a litany of sins which is remarkably similar to that given for Menasheh here and in *Kings*. [Compare: v. 3 to vs. 9 and 16 there; v. 5 to v. 16 there; v. 6 to v. 17 there.]

he reigned fifty-five years in Jerusalem [2] *He did evil in* HASHEM*'s sight, just like the abominations of the nations which* HASHEM *had driven out from before the Israelites.* [3] *He built up once more the bamos which Chizkiahu, his father, had broken down. He established altars for the Baalim, made asheirah-trees, and prostrated himself before all the heavenly hosts, and served them.* [4] *He built altars in* HASHEM*'s House, about which* HASHEM *had said, 'In Jerusalem shall My Name be forever.'* [5] *He built altars to all the host*

Achaz, after it had long been eliminated in the Northern Kingdom. We surmised that the molten images which Achaz erected may not have been in the public domain, and would have been an expression of only the very beginning of that cult. If this is so, then Menasheh's raising up of altars to the Baalim would be taking Achaz's innovations a step further. This would then be an illustration of the thesis developed in Section II to ch. 28, *Achaz and Menasheh* — that, in *Chronicles'* view, Achaz's depredations are the seed from which the later excesses under Menasheh developed.

וַיַּעַשׂ אֲשֵׁרוֹת — *Made asheirah-trees.* The parallel verse in *Kings* has: *And made Asheirah-trees as Ahab, king of Israel, had done.* See prefatory remarks to this chapter for the significance of the comparison to Ahab, and why no such resemblance is indicated in *Chronicles.*

There are other implications to the fact that *Kings* notes an affinity to Ahab, but *Chronicles* does not.

In the same passage of the Talmud which discusses the implications of Menasheh's name [see prefatory remarks], there is also an aggadic analysis of the name Ahab: אַחְאָב is interpreted as a fusing of two words: אָח, *brother*, and אָב, *father*. Ahab was a *brother* to heaven, and a *father* for idol worship.

Maharal offers the following interpretation for the concept *brother to heaven*. In his view it indicates an assumption of equality which precludes any and every form of subordination. Ahab was utterly and irredeemably outside the sway of any Godly influence. In connection with the judgment of Scripture that Ahab was more wicked than any of the Israelite kings that had preceded him, R' Yochanan teaches: Ahab wrote upon the gates of Shomron: *Ahab denies Israel's God; therefore, he has no portion in Israel's God*! *Maharal* understands this provocative insolence as a function of Ahab's status as *brother to heaven*. His alienation was total.

Maharal notes that, for all his wickedness, Menasheh did not sink to the same depths as Ahab had reached. In the context of our discussion, and bearing in mind that *Kings* compares Menasheh to Ahab, but *Chronicles* does not, we may formulate what we have learned as follows: In his personal life — the subject of the *Kings'* account — Menasheh was totally wicked in the same sense as Ahab was, and, indeed, he forfeited his portion in the World to Come. However, whereas Ahab's corruption extended to his function as king [Ahab wrote on the gates of Shomron . . .], Menasheh, as ruler, had not totally compromised himself. In this capacity there was room for hope and, indeed, *Chronicles* reports Menasheh's far-reaching and effective *teshuvah*. See further at v. 7.

4. וּבָנָה מִזְבְּחוֹת — *He built altars.* For the purpose of idol worship (*Mefaresh*).

אֲשֶׁר אָמַר ה׳ — *About which* HASHEM *had said* . . . This expresses *Chronicles'* sense of outrage at Menasheh's perfidy. Vs. 6 and 7 are to be understood in the same vein (*Mefaresh*).

בִּירוּשָׁלַם . . . — *In Jerusalem* . . . It is noteworthy that the altars which Menasheh built are seen as offending only God's presence *in Jerusalem*, while the image which he erected, as described in v. 7, offends that presence both as manifest in *this house*, and in *Jerusalem*. See Section II, *Jerusalem and the Altar*, for an analysis.

בִּירוּשָׁלַם יִהְיֶה־שְׁמִי לְעוֹלָם — *In Jerusalem shall My Name be forever.* For the difference in wording between this verse and its parallel in *Kings*, see Section II, *Menasheh and the Divine Presence in the House.*

5. וַיִּבֶן מִזְבְּחוֹת לְכָל־צְבָא הַשָּׁמָיִם — *He built altars to all the host of heaven.* In v. 3 we already have Menasheh prostrating himself before the heavenly hosts. No mention is made there of building altars nor of any idol worship taking place within the House precincts. Perhaps we have here a progression

ו הַשָּׁמָיִם בִּשְׁתֵּי חַצְרוֹת בֵּית־יהוה: וְהוּא הֶעֱבִיר אֶת־
בָּנָיו בָּאֵשׁ בְּגֵי בֶן־הִנֹּם וְעוֹנֵן וְנִחֵשׁ וְכִשֵּׁף וְעָשָׂה אוֹב
וְיִדְּעוֹנִי הִרְבָּה לַעֲשׂוֹת הָרַע בְּעֵינֵי יהוה לְהַכְעִיסוֹ: וַיָּשֶׂם
ז אֶת־פֶּסֶל הַסֶּמֶל אֲשֶׁר עָשָׂה בְּבֵית הָאֱלֹהִים אֲשֶׁר אָמַר
אֱלֹהִים אֶל־דָּוִיד וְאֶל־שְׁלֹמֹה בְנוֹ בַּבַּיִת הַזֶּה וּבִירוּשָׁלַםִ
אֲשֶׁר בָּחַרְתִּי מִכֹּל שִׁבְטֵי יִשְׂרָאֵל אָשִׂים אֶת־שְׁמִי
ח לְעֵילוֹם: וְלֹא אֹסִיף לְהָסִיר אֶת־רֶגֶל יִשְׂרָאֵל מֵעַל

of evil, as we find later in the case of the image. See v. 7.

בִּשְׁתֵּי חַצְרוֹת בֵּית־ה׳ — *In the two courtyards of the House of* HASHEM. The courtyard of the *Kohanim* and that of the Israelites (*Metzudos*, see discussion at 4:9).

6. ... וְהוּא הֶעֱבִיר אֶת־בָּנָיו בָּאֵשׁ — *He also made his children pass through the fire* ... For a full discussion of this practice, and also of the use of the plural, בָּנָיו, instead of the singular, בְּנוֹ, which is found in *Kings*, see comm. to 28:3.

...וְעוֹנֵן — *Divined auspicious times* .... The various occult rites listed here are all forbidden, and typify the very antithesis of a Jewish life as envisaged by the Torah — see *Deuteronomy* 18:14 and comm. to *I Chronicles* 10:13.

Most of the terms are explained in *Sanhedrin* 65b and quoted by *Rashi* in various parts of the Torah commentary.

עוֹנֵן: One who attaches particular significance to times: Today is a good day to go out; tomorrow a good day to buy, and so on.

מְנַחֵשׁ: One who reads omens: His bread fell from his mouth; his staff from his hand, and so on.

מְכַשֵּׁף: A sorcerer. See *Exodus* 22:17.

אוֹב: One who attempts to communicate with the dead. These rites often involve a human skull.

יִדְּעוֹנִי: An oracle. He foretells the future through the agency of a bone inserted in his mouth.

לְהַכְעִיסוֹ — *To provoke Him*. The prefix ל, *lamed*, can, in this context, have two possible meanings: It can connote a direct intention; that is, he committed much evil with the purpose of angering God. It is also used in Scripture to describe an anticipated result rather than a direct intention. [Cf. *I Samuel* 20:30: ... *for you chose Jesse's son to your own shame* [... לְבָשְׁתְּךָ] *and the shame of your mother's nakedness*. Jonathan's friendship with David was not intended to produce shame, but Saul anticipates that this would inevitably result from it.] Thus, our verse might mean that Menasheh did much evil; thus, inevitably causing God to be angry.

We assume the former interpretation on the basis of 34:25 where the idol worship practiced in the years preceding Yoshiahu's reign are described as לְמַעַן הַכְעִיסֵנִי, an expression certainly denoting a direct intention.

The Sages seem also to have a tradition that Menasheh's sins were committed with the intention of angering God. In *Sanhedrin* 103b they speak of the image which Menasheh erected [see next verse] as having been given four faces so that ... *the Divine Presence might see and be provoked* [by it]. Later, on that same page, the Sages place in Amon's mouth the expression, *The earlier* [kings] *had no idea how to provoke* [God. I will demonstrate how to do it]. Clearly, an assumption is made that there was intent to provoke God.

7. פֶּסֶל הַסֶּמֶל אֲשֶׁר עָשָׂה — *The graven image which he had made*. פֶּסֶל, from פסל, *to hew into shape*, describes a graven object; סֶמֶל is explained by *Rashi* (*Deuteronomy* 4:16) as a shape [צוּרָה].

Sanhedrin 103b notes that in v. 19 there is a reference to פְּסִילִים, in the plural, while in our verse the singular, פֶּסֶל, is used. The Sages maintain that both references are to the same image. Originally, Menasheh gave it only one face. Subsequently, he created four faces for it — one turned to each direction — so that from whichever side the *Shechinah* entered, God would be confronted by one of the faces, and be provoked by it.

בְּבֵית הָאֱלֹהִים — *In God's House*. In an extremely significant passage in *Sanhedrin* 103b, the Sages detect a progression of evil between Menasheh and Amon. Menasheh placed the image in the Holy Sanctuary — the outer part of the House building — but did not bring it into the Holy of Holies. Amon brought it into the Holy of Holies.

What are we to learn from the fact that

33
6-8

of heaven, in the two courtyards of HASHEM's *House.* [6] *He also made his children pass through the fire in the Valley of Ben Hinom, divined auspicious times, read omens, practiced sorcery, established communication with the dead and a system of oracles. He did more and more evil in* HASHEM's *sight, to provoke Him.* [7] *He placed the graven image which he had made, in God's House, concerning which God had said to David and to his son Solomon, 'In this House and in Jerusalem, which I have chosen from all the tribes of Israel, I will place My name forever.* [8] *'And I will no more remove Israel's presence from upon*

Menasheh stopped short of the final desecration of which Amon proved himself capable? *Sanhedrin* 103b makes very clear in its discussion of Amon's perfidy, that the purpose of the image was, as it were, to drive God out of His own House. The image was meant to *replace* Him. Apparently, then, Menasheh, who did not go so far, intended to drive God out of the outer House precincts, but was willing to have Him remain ensconced within the Holy of Holies.

We believe to have confirmed here that thesis which we suggested in prefatory remarks to this chapter. Our analysis of text and aggadic tradition yielded that the depths of Menasheh's depredations were reached only in respect to his personal standing. As scion of the Davidic line and bearer of Israel's future he was not irretrievably lost. As our v. 13 makes clear, his penitence did bring him back *to his kingship*, even though, according to the anonymous opinion recorded in the Mishnah, he himself lost his portion in the World to Come.

Now our analysis at 22:11 has yielded the particular affinity between the Davidic royal line and the Holy of Holies. We noted that when Solomon was to be excluded from the World to Come, it was a fire that issued from the Holy of Holies which convinced the Sages that his essential sanctity had remained inviolate. Again, it was in the Holy of Holies that Yoash, last scion of the royal line with whose death David's house would have come to an end, was saved from the crazed sword of Athaliah.

In comm. there, we suggested reasons for this particular affinity.

In stopping short of bringing the image into the Holy of Holies, Menasheh was indicating that his was not a vendetta against the Davidic line.

In general terms it may be stated that, in the view of the Sages, the focus of Menasheh's vendetta was the sacrificial service. In *Sanhedrin* 103b we have the tradition that Menasheh destroyed the altar [see v. 16], and further, *Zevachim* 61b teaches that the heavenly fire which descended upon the altar when Solomon inaugurated the House remained there throughout the ages, until it was removed by Menasheh.

We may note that in this matter of the altar, Menasheh was taking further a process that had been set in motion by Achaz. He had debased Solomon's altar by shunting it aside in favor of a different model [Section II to ch. 28, *The Alien Altar*]. The process of denigrating the institution of Divine sacrifice, as it had been practiced through the ages, was now picked up by Menasheh. He broke down the altar completely.

In Section II to ch. 28, *Achaz and Menasheh*, we analyzed the root-branch relationship between the reigns of these two kings. This progression in the matter of the altar serves as one vivid example of this progression.

בַּבַּיִת הַזֶּה וּבִירוּשָׁלַם ... — *In this House and in Jerusalem* ... See Sec. II, *Jerusalem and the Altar*.

לְעֵילוֹם — *Forever*. The word appears to be associated with the idea of concealment [עלם, *to be concealed*]. This is suggested by *Radak* in *Sefer HaShorashim* [under עלם] where he discusses the meaning of the word עוֹלָם for *world*. He suggests that it derives from the deep mystery in which the world is shrouded. The world *conceals* more than it reveals. As noted in Sec. II, *Menasheh and the Divine Presence in the House*, this meaning of the word seems particularly appropriate in our context.

Radak offers also an alternative interpretation: עוֹלָם may be related to עֶלֶם, *youth*, and is used to describe the world in its eternal freshness and vigor. Perhaps he understands its use in our context thus: God's presence in His House and city is strong and unchangeable. It will not allow itself to be compromised by Menasheh's puny efforts.

8. ... וְלֹא אוֹסִיף לְהָסִיר — *And I will no more*

הָאֲדָמָה אֲשֶׁר הֶעֱמַדְתִּי לַאֲבוֹתֵיכֶם רַק ׀ אִם־יִשְׁמְרוּ
לַעֲשׂוֹת אֵת כָּל־אֲשֶׁר צִוִּיתִים לְכָל־הַתּוֹרָה וְהַחֻקִּים
ט וְהַמִּשְׁפָּטִים בְּיַד־מֹשֶׁה׃ וַיֶּתַע מְנַשֶּׁה אֶת־יְהוּדָה וְיֹשְׁבֵי
יְרוּשָׁלִָם לַעֲשׂוֹת רָע מִן־הַגּוֹיִם אֲשֶׁר הִשְׁמִיד יהוה מִפְּנֵי
י בְּנֵי יִשְׂרָאֵל׃ וַיְדַבֵּר יהוה אֶל־מְנַשֶּׁה וְאֶל־עַמּוֹ
יא וְלֹא הִקְשִׁיבוּ׃ וַיָּבֵא יהוה עֲלֵיהֶם אֶת־שָׂרֵי הַצָּבָא אֲשֶׁר

remove ... All this is part of God's promise to David and Solomon begun in the previous verse. It continues to express *Chronicles'* outrage at Menasheh's perfidy: God had promised so much and, notwithstanding this, Menasheh had erected the image (*Mefaresh*).

9. וַיֶּתַע מְנַשֶּׁה ... — *Thus, Menasheh made ... err*. In the *Kings'* version the parallel verse begins with the words *But they did not listen*, and then continues exactly as does our verse.

Chronicles omits that phrase, but not entirely. In v. 10 we are told that God *spoke* to Menasheh and his people, but וְלֹא הִקְשִׁיבוּ, *they did not pay heed*. This phrase in v. 10 has no parallel in the *Kings* version, and it appears that *Chronicles*, for reasons which we should analyze, moved the phrase from its place in the *Kings'* account and replaced it in a different context.

An analysis of the two accounts yields as follows:

First, *Kings*.

In that account, vs. 3-6 tell some of the evil things which Menasheh had done. In v. 7 this list is continued with the story of the image, and the enormity of this sin is underlined with a quote of what God had told David and Solomon concerning the sanctity of the House. This quote continues through the end of verse 8. The listing of Menasheh's crimes is picked up once more, but only in v. 16. Vs. 9-15, beginning with the words *But they did not listen*, constitute an interjection which interrupts the list in order to record outrage at the fact that the Jews did not pay heed to God's warnings.

This passage lays the impending destruction squarely at Menasheh's door, and sees its historical genesis in the fact that the warning which God had addressed to David and Solomon had not been heeded with sufficient seriousness.

Chronicles, on the other hand, makes no judgment concerning the degree to which the warning of the previous verse had borne fruit. We recall from Section II to ch. 28, *Achaz and Menasheh*, that in *Chronicles* it is Achaz, not Menasheh, who is seen as the source of the ultimate destruction. In the context of this perspective, the recording of the *Kings'* passage would have been inappropriate. The previous verse, thus, does not serve as a springboard for a historical judgment of the people, but simply to express outrage at the heinousness of Menasheh's crime. Our verse is simply a continuation of Menasheh's story which is told — without interruption — till the end.

What of the statement in v. 10 that the people did not pay heed?

It could simply be one more facet of the tragic story which is being told, or it could be something more.

In v. 8, *Chronicles* had bemoaned Menasheh's insensitivity to the mystic bond that exists between the people and the land of Israel. How could Menasheh have erected the image when he knew the reality of God's presence in the land and was aware of Israel's historic destiny! In v. 10, this thought is taken a step further. The land and the concept of prophecy are inextricably bound together (*Kuzari* 2:14). If an entire people can remain closed to God's entreaty that they repent, if the message sent through His prophets with so much love can be ignored, then indeed it is a sign that they have lost touch with their inner core of sanctity. In the long run, they would have to be removed from the land which nurtures prophecy, so that their presence would no longer spell out a denial of that gift.

רָע מִן־הַגּוֹיִם ... — *Evil beyond that which the nations ... had done*. See comm. to v. 2. Since in our verse we find Menasheh inciting the people to a level of evil which went beyond that which the heathen nations had done, we must assume that v. 2 which talks of evil at the same level as that of the nations [but not beyond] is not meant to describe the degree of heinousness of the transgressions, but rather is only an introduction to the list of sins that follows. He did in accordance with the evil of the nations in that he rebuilt the *bamos* (v. 3) and so on. Our verse, on the other hand, deals with the degree of blame attached to these

the land which I gave to your fathers, provided only that they carefully observe all that I commanded them, all the teachings, the statutes and the laws, at the hand of Moses.' [9] *Thus, Menasheh made Judah and the inhabitants of Jerusalem err, practicing evil beyond that which the nations, which* HASHEM *destroyed from before Israel, had done.* [10] *Then* HASHEM *spoke to Menasheh and his people, but they did not pay heed.* [11] *So* HASHEM *brought the captains of*

usages and judges them more severely than the abominations of the unschooled heathens who may not have known better.

10. וַיְדַבֵּר ה׳ אֶל־מְנַשֶּׁה וְאֶל־עַמּוֹ — *Then* HASHEM *spoke to Menasheh and his people.* Although we are not told explicitly what this message was, we can surmise from the context that these prophets called upon Menasheh and the people to repent.

Kings has . . . וַיְדַבֵּר ה׳ בְּיַד עֲבָדָיו הַנְּבִיאִים, *Then* HASHEM *spoke through His servants, the prophets . . .*, and then goes on to spell out the message of destruction which they conveyed. *Chronicles* does not have this passage.

Thus, the two books describe two completely different prophetic activities, and this explains the two significant differences in the wording which they employ.

In *Chronicles*, God Himself talks — that this was done by way of prophecy (*Metzudos*) is not explicated, while *Kings* states explicitly that God sent prophets. The difference may lie in the nature of the message. God, Who is wholly good, is not directly associated with a message of destruction; consequently *Kings* states explicitly that these warnings were delivered by prophets. But God cares passionately that Israel should repent, and this is reflected in the *Chronicles'* wording.

Again, *Chronicles* tells us to whom the message was addressed — *Menasheh and his people*, while *Kings* does not do so. Thus, the impression is projected that in *Kings* the message is a timeless one: The prophets do not specifically address their own generation. Their warnings that wickedness brings destruction in its wake, the teaching that the ultimate destruction must be laid at Menasheh's door, is universal. By contrast, the call to repentance referred to in *Chronicles* was clearly addressed to contemporary ears.

אֶל־מְנַשֶּׁה וְאֶל־עַמּוֹ — *To Menasheh and his people*. In prefatory remarks to this chapter we concluded that, as opposed to the *Kings'* narrative which tells of Menasheh's personal story, *Chronicles* deals with his kingship. This may be reflected in our phrase: The exhortation to repent is addressed to Menasheh as he is defined in his relationship to the people.

◆§ Menasheh's Exile and Repentance

11-13. The prefatory remarks to this chapter examine why the story of Menasheh's *teshuvah* is not told in *Kings*. Here, we should inquire why the account of his exile, which occupies a prominent role in the *Chronicles* account, is also not given there.

A closer analysis of the structure of the *Kings'* account may yield a solution.

Vs. 3-9 are essentially parallel to the verses in *Chronicles* and detail the various wickednesses which Menasheh perpetrated. Vs. 10 then tells of the prophets whom God sent to predict the destruction which was to come about as a result of Menasheh's sins. Vs. 11-15 then give a verbatim account of the message which these prophets delivered.

V. 16 then reads: *And moreover, Menasheh shed much innocent blood . . .* The opening word וְגַם, *and moreover*, indicates that this is a continuation of the list begun in vs. 3-9. It is clearly not part of the prophecy quoted in vs. 11-15.

[For an analysis of the tradition of the Sages, that this verse refers to the killing of the prophet Isaiah at Menasheh's instigation, see Section II, *Menasheh and Isaiah*.]

We conclude that the prophetic section is a self-contained passage which has been interposed into a list which really belongs together.

Why was this done? Could the list not have been completed first and the prophecy left to the end?

The interruption gives eloquent expression to the writer's passionate outrage at the sheer horror of Menasheh's perfidy. A structured format which follows a logical sequence is appropriate for a situation in which the emotions are not deeply touched. Here, the overwhelming pathos of the realization that what might have been was not to be, that the hope which had shone so brightly in the heyday of David and Solomon's glory was to be dashed, demanded immediate expression; it could not await the ordering of an appropriate

לְמֶ֣לֶךְ אַשּׁ֔וּר וַיִּלְכְּד֥וּ אֶת־מְנַשֶּׁ֖ה בַּֽחֹחִ֑ים וַיַּֽאַסְרֻ֙הוּ֙
יב בַּֽנְחֻשְׁתַּ֔יִם וַיּֽוֹלִיכֻ֖הוּ בָּבֶֽלָה׃ וּכְהָצֵ֣ר ל֔וֹ חִלָּ֕ה אֶת־פְּנֵ֖י
יג יְהֹוָ֣ה אֱלֹהָ֑יו וַיִּכָּנַ֣ע מְאֹ֔ד מִלִּפְנֵ֖י אֱלֹהֵ֥י אֲבֹתָֽיו׃ וַיִּתְפַּלֵּ֣ל
אֵלָ֗יו וַיֵּעָ֤תֶר לוֹ֙ וַיִּשְׁמַ֣ע תְּחִנָּת֔וֹ וַיְשִׁיבֵ֥הוּ יְרוּשָׁלַ֖ם
יד לְמַלְכוּת֑וֹ וַיֵּ֣דַע מְנַשֶּׁ֔ה כִּ֥י יְהֹוָ֖ה ה֥וּא הָֽאֱלֹהִֽים׃ וְאַֽחֲרֵי־כֵ֞ן

opportunity.

It is perhaps this same sense of outrage which caused the omission of any mention of Menasheh's capture and subsequent release. Under the overwhelming impression of the tragedy which Menasheh's actions were to bring about, everything else fades into insignificance. In a different context and under different circumstances, there may be much to be learned from Menasheh's experiences, but for now the prophet's eyes are, as it were, riveted to the burning House. Nothing else can demand his attention.

When we consider that Jeremiah, who in the tradition of the Sages was the author of *Kings*, functioned a scant fifty years after Menasheh's death, at a time when the saga of that tragic king must still have been altogether clear in the people's memory, we can imagine the impact which the omission of these salient facts of the reign must have made. More eloquently than any words it would have brought home the stark tragedy of that blighted life.

11. וַיִּלְכְּדוּ אֶת־מְנַשֶּׁה בַּחֹחִים — *They caught Menasheh with hooks.* The combination of לכד with חוֹחַ is unique and difficult to understand. לכד, when used to denote the capture of men, is used either alone [e.g. וְנִלְכְּדוּ גִּבּוֹרֶיהָ (*Jeremiah* 51:56)] or with an indication of *into* what the person was trapped [e.g. פַּח, *trap* (*Isaiah* 24:18); רֶשֶׁת, *net* (*Psalms* 9:16), or שַׁחַת, *pit* (*Eichah* 4:20)].

But חוֹחִים are not traps *into* which a captured person or animal is driven but *hooks* which are clamped into the cheek or nostril in order to drag the prisoner along unwillingly.

It is also noteworthy that although אָסַר בַּנְחֻשְׁתַּיִם occurs on several other occasions [Samson in *Judges* 16:21; Tzidkiahu in *II Kings* 25:7, *Jeremiah* 39:7 and 52:11, and Yehoiakim in 36:6], it is never accompanied by לָכַד בְּחוֹחַ, although in at least two of the three examples [Samson and Tzidkiahu] the captors showed extreme cruelty to their hapless prisoner.

All this inclines us towards the assumption that we have here an idiomatic expression. The חַח, *hook*, is usually placed in the cheek or nostril of an animal so as to drag it along by force. Consequently, its metaphorical use in Scripture signals an inexorable dragging towards a given fate, without reference to the victim's wishes. Thus is it used, at *Ezekiel* 29:4, in connection with Pharaoh and at 38:4 concerning Gog, king of Magog.

Thus, here too, perhaps the phrase, instead of being translated *caught ... with hooks*, might better be rendered *was captured without any possibility of resistance*. This would be a particularly felicitous expression to describe Menasheh's capture. In his struggle with his terrible craving for idol worship [see Section II, *Menasheh and the Divine Presence in the House*], he felt himself willy-nilly dragged towards a cult which he knew to be pernicious and which he wanted, with every fiber of his being, to avoid. He was to learn now what real coercion felt like. He would realize that that other force was much weaker. Had he been motivated enough, he could surely have withstood it.

בַּנְחֻשְׁתַּיִם — *With fetters.* The word derives from נְחוֹשֶׁת, *copper*, doubtless the material from which these fetters were made.

12. וּכְהָצֵר לוֹ — *When he was distressed. Yerushalmi, Sanhedrin* 10:9 has the tradition that he was placed in a copper cauldron and a fire lit beneath it. In his agony he called upon all the idols which he had so assiduously served, but none answered him. See further below.

חִלָּה אֶת־פְּנֵי ה׳ אֱלֹהָיו — *He entreated HASHEM his God.* We continue *Yerushalmi's* account: When he saw that none of the idols helped at all, he said: 'I recall that my father used to teach me the Scriptural verse: *When you are in distress and all these things have happened to you, you will finally return to HASHEM your God ... He will not abandon you nor destroy you.* I will call to Him. If He answers, good; if not, He will have shown Himself to be no different [than the idols].'

וַיִּכָּנַע מְאֹד — *And humbled himself greatly.* Here we have the account of Menasheh's penitence. In prefatory remarks to this chap-

33
12-14

the Assyrian king against them. They caught Menasheh with
hooks, and bound him with fetters [12] *When he was distressed, he*
entreated HASHEM *his God, and humbled himself greatly before the*
God of his fathers. [13] *So he prayed to Him and He granted his plea,*
and heard his entreaty. He brought him back to Jerusalem, to his
kingship, so that Menasheh knew that HASHEM *is God.* [14] *After that*

ter, we have suggested an explanation for the fact, that no mention of it is made in the *Kings* account.

There is another possible explanation: When a person sins and by his sin causes others to transgress, then he cannot hope for God's forgiveness as long as those whom he influenced are still carrying on the evil ways which he implanted in them. Certainly, no person who has caused others to sin can enjoy bliss in Eden as long as those whom he had influenced are suffering because of him.

Indeed, Menasheh repented, but God would not accept his penitence as long as the effects of his evildoings were still current. *Kings* was written by Jeremiah at a time when idol worship was still rampant. There were many who, because of Menasheh's pernicious teachings, were serving idols — and suffering for it. Thus, for Jeremiah, Menasheh's penitence did not exist. However, by the time that *Chronicles* was written by Ezra in the era of the Second House, idol worship had long become a thing of the past, and Menasheh's evil influence had no more practical effect. It was only then that his penitence became acceptable to God (*Emunas Chachamim* by *R' Avi Ad Sar Shalom* (circa. 1730), quoted by *R' Y. Koperman* (*HaMaayan*, *Tammuz* 5744).

13. וַיִּתְפַּלֵּל אֵלָיו וַיֵּעָתֶר לוֹ — *So he prayed to Him and He granted his plea.* We continue with *Yerushalmi's* account: The ministering angels *stopped up all the openings* so that Menasheh's prayer should not come up before the Holy One, Blessed Is He. They said: 'Would You accept penitence from a man who put up an image in the Sanctuary?' He answered: 'If I do not accept his penitence then I am shutting the door before all other penitents.'

וַיֵּעָתֶר לוֹ — *And He granted his plea.* עתר, *to entreat*. In the *nifal* voice, *to allow oneself to be entreated* or *to grant the plea.*

Sanhedrin 103a teaches that there was something very special about the acceptance of Menasheh's penitence. God, as it were, opened up a subterranean passage in heaven through which the penitence — which could not enter by normal paths — could reach Him. *Maharal* explains that, in contrast to other sinners who, once they repent, can expect their sins to be forgiven by right [מִצַּד הַדִּין], Menasheh had sunk so low that he had forfeited any expectation that, by right, his penitence be accepted. God allowed it to *come* to Him only because of an outpouring of absolute goodness [מִצַּד הַחֶסֶד הַגָּמוּר].

There are variant readings in *Sanhedrin* as to the precise manner in which the idea of the subterranean passage is derived from our verse. Certainly, it seems connected with the fact that the letters ע and ח are interchangeable and that consequently it would be possible to read וַיֵּחָתֵר, *he dug*, instead of וַיֵּעָתֶר. (See *Dikdukei Soferim* there.) *Maharal* explains that the Talmud's justification derives from the unexpected sequence of the words in our sentence: וַיִּשְׁמַע, *and heard*, should have preceded וַיֵּעָתֶר, *and granted his plea*. וַיֵּעָתֶר was placed first, implying something that had to be done before God *heard*. Hence the idea of the tunnel which was required to bring the penitence before God.

וַיְשִׁיבֵהוּ יְרוּשָׁלַםִ לְמַלְכוּתוֹ — *He brought him back to Jerusalem, to his kingship.* We have seen, in prefatory remarks to this chapter, that those who list Menasheh among the kings who forfeited their portion in the World to Come find their source in this phrase. Menasheh's penitence had only limited results: He was indeed returned *to his kingship*, but not to his previous standing as a man of Israel who is destined after death to enter a celestial Eden.

כִּי ה׳ הוּא הָאֱלֹהִים — *That* HASHEM *is God*. In *Genesis* 2:5 where God is referred to as HASHEM ELOKIM, *Rashi* explains: HASHEM is His Name. *Elokim* implies that He is Judge and Master of all.

In the context of what we have come to learn of Menasheh's superstitions — particularly the areas in which he felt threatened by Isaiah's prophecies [see Sec. II, *Menasheh and Isaiah*] — this formulation is particularly apt. Menasheh had always known the truth of the existence of God [HASHEM] but had not been

בָּנָ֣ה חוֹמָ֣ה חִ֠יצוֹנָ֠ה ׀ לְעִיר־דָּוִ֨יד מַעְרָ֤בָה לְגִיחוֹן֙ בַּנַּ֔חַל
וְלָבוֹא֙ בְּשַׁ֣עַר הַדָּגִ֔ים וְסָבַ֣ב לָעֹ֔פֶל וַיַּגְבִּיהֶ֖הָ מְאֹ֑ד וַיָּ֧שֶׂם
טו שָֽׂרֵי־חַ֛יִל בְּכָל־הֶעָרִ֥ים הַבְּצֻר֖וֹת בִּיהוּדָֽה׃ וַ֠יָּסַר אֶת־
אֱלֹהֵ֨י הַנֵּכָ֤ר וְאֶת־הַסֶּ֙מֶל֙ מִבֵּ֣ית יְהוָ֔ה וְכָל־הַֽמִּזְבְּח֗וֹת אֲשֶׁ֥ר
טז בָּנָ֛ה בְּהַ֥ר בֵּית־יְהוָ֖ה וּבִירוּשָׁלִָ֑ם וַיַּשְׁלֵ֖ךְ ח֥וּצָה לָעִֽיר׃ °ויכן֙
°וַיִּ֙בֶן֙ ק׳
אֶת־מִזְבַּ֣ח יְהוָ֔ה וַיִּזְבַּ֣ח עָלָ֔יו זִבְחֵ֥י שְׁלָמִ֖ים וְתוֹדָ֑ה וַיֹּ֙אמֶר֙
יז לִֽיהוּדָ֔ה לַֽעֲב֔וֹד אֶת־יְהוָ֖ה אֱלֹהֵ֥י יִשְׂרָאֵֽל׃ אֲבָל֙ ע֣וֹד הָעָ֔ם
יח זֹבְחִ֖ים בַּבָּמ֑וֹת רַ֖ק לַיהוָ֥ה אֱלֹהֵיהֶֽם׃ וְיֶ֨תֶר דִּבְרֵ֤י מְנַשֶּׁה֙
וּתְפִלָּת֣וֹ אֶל־אֱלֹהָ֔יו וְדִבְרֵי֙ הַחֹזִ֔ים הַֽמְדַבְּרִ֣ים אֵלָ֔יו בְּשֵׁ֖ם

able to conceive of His immanence — His interest and involvement in the affairs of man. He had known HASHEM but not Elokim. Now, when God saw his agony and freed him from his captors he realized that HASHEM is also Elokim.

14. וְאַחֲרֵי־כֵן בָּנָה חוֹמָה חִיצוֹנָה — *After that he built an outer wall ...* V. 15 tells us how Menasheh removed all the vestiges of idol worship which he had introduced upon the House Mount and in Jerusalem. The fact that *Chronicles* first of all chose to tell of the fortifications which Menasheh built for Jerusalem seems to draw attention to a distorted sense of priorities. Despite Menasheh's repentance he still, upon his return, turned first to the temporal needs of the people, and only then to the renewal of their spirit. Indeed, this seems to confirm the opinion of the Sages quoted above, that his penitence left much undone — he returned to his kingdom but did not create a fundamental change within himself.

Nonetheless, we cannot be certain that this is the intent of the positioning of this verse. This, because a careful comparison between the *Chronicles'* and *Kings'* accounts reveals an apparent difference in attitude towards the fortification efforts of the various kings who engaged in these activities.

Chronicles tells of fortifications being built by: Rechav'am (11:5-12); Asa (14:6); Yehoshaphat (17:12); Uzziah (26:6 and 9); Yotham (27:3—4); Chizkiah (32:5); and Menasheh.

It seems particularly significant that each one of these were righteous kings [Rechovoam's activities take place in the earlier years of his reign when, according to the *Chronicles'* account, he still walked in the ways of David and Solomon (11:17)], and this could imply that the act of fortification was viewed with approbation. Now, not a single one of these instances is given in *Kings*.

The total consistency with which *Chronicles* reports these activities approvingly while *Kings* leaves them out, seems to indicate a difference in perspective.

Perhaps the prophetic eye [*Kings*] sees little merit in the prudent fortification of a city. Wars are won or lost by direct Divine intervention. In a prophetic era the Torah's promise that righteousness is rewarded by victory in battle, while defeat follows upon sin, becomes a palpable reality. A king might be better occupied in raising the spiritual level of his people than in strengthening the walls of his city. *Kings* sees no special merit in such activities. *Chronicles*, however, was written in times in which the Divine stewardship of human affairs was more covert and thus, from its perspective, these activities are laudable. The fact that such works are reported of only the righteous kings seems to indicate that the wicked kings tended not to engage in such prudent measures. In their lust for idol worship they ignored the needs of their subjects and engaged in their cultic abominations in the hope of eliciting favor and protection from the particular idol to which caprice or superstitious terror inclined them.

When we consider that Menasheh's building activities are recorded only after his penitence, this may indicate the correctness of our thesis. While he was still an idol worshiper he relied on those false deities for help and ignored his people. Only after he turned to God did he take his kingly obligations seriously.

In such a context there may be no implied criticism in the fact that the building activities are recorded before the elimination of the idols. Perhaps Menasheh felt that it was necessary to assure the safety of the city before the spiritual reforms were undertaken.

מַעְרָבָה לְגִיחוֹן בַּנַּחַל — *West of Gichon, in the valley*. The wall ran west of the Gichon stream which lay in the valley to the east of the holy city (*Metzudos*).

וְלָבוֹא בְשַׁעַר הַדָּגִים — *Going within the Dagim Gate*. The phrase describes the direction in

he built an outer wall for the City of David, west of Gichon, in the
valley, going within the Dagim Gate, and he encompassed the
Ophel. He raised it up to a very great height. He stationed army
officers in all the fortified cities of Judah.
15 *He took away the*
strange gods and the image out of HASHEM'*s House, and all the al-*
tars he built in the mountain of HASHEM'*s House and in Jerusalem,*
and cast them out of the city.
16 *He built up the altar of* HASHEM
and offered up upon it peace-offerings and thanksgiving offerings.
He told Judah to serve HASHEM, *God of Israel.*
17 *But the people cont-*
inued to sacrifice on the bamos, though exclusively to HASHEM *their*
God.
18 *Now the rest of that which concerns Menasheh, his prayer*
to his God, and the messages of the seers who spoke to him in the

which the wall was built (*Metzudos*). . . . בּוֹא בְּ means *to enter* (cf. *Genesis* 19:8).

וְסָבַב לָעֹפֶל — *And he encompassed the Ophel.* For *Ophel* see on 27:3.

15. וְאֶת־הַסֶּמֶל — *And the image.* Reference is to the פֶּסֶל הַסֶּמֶל of v. 7.

וַיַּשְׁלֵךְ חוּצָה לָעִיר — *And cast them out of the city.* From v. 22 where we learn that Amon served the very images which Menasheh had served, it appears that Menasheh did not destroy the idols, but simply threw them outside the city. Amon recovered them from there.

16. וַיִּבֶן אֶת־מִזְבַּח ה׳ — *He built up the altar of* HASHEM. We read [*k'ri*] וַיִּבֶן, although the text reads [*k'siv*] ויכן. The vocalization appearing in the text is invariably that of the *k'ri*; the *k'siv* would have to be vocalized וַיָּכֶן [as in *I Chronicles* 15:1, 22:5 and at 17:5 and 26:14], *He prepared* [if we are to follow the meaning of the majority of the instances quoted above], or *He established* [if the meaning at 17:5 is followed]. See Sect. II, *Menasheh and the Sacrificial Service*, for an analysis of these two versions.

וְתוֹדָה — *And thanksgiving offerings.* One of the four people who, according to *Berachos* 59b, have to offer thanks to God, is one who has been freed from captivity. It is eminently appropriate that Menasheh, upon his release, would want to bring a thanksgiving offering. *Mefaresh* explains that he offered thanks to God for returning him to Jerusalem and his kingship.

וַיֹּאמֶר לִיהוּדָה . . . — *He told Judah*. . . It is impossible to miss the contrast between this tepid exhortation and Chizkiah's impassioned plea (29:5-11). *Chronicles* appears to want to make clear the inadequacy of Menasheh's penitence.

17. אֲבָל עוֹד הָעָם זֹבְחִים . . . — *But the people continued to sacrifice* . . . The proliferation of illicit *bamos* devoted to Divine service plagued other kings who were more righteous than Menasheh. See 15:17 for the situation in Asa's reign and 20:33 for Yehoshaphat. It seems likely that *Chronicles* here means to point out the inadequacy of Menasheh's penitence. One would expect a true penitent who had seen the error of his ways to make a particular effort to eradicate every vestige of sin. In this sense Menasheh's shortcoming, in the matter of the *bamos*, was more damning than that of the other kings.

18. וּתְפִלָּתוֹ . . . וְדִבְרֵי הַחֹזִים . . . — *His prayer* . . . *and the messages of the seers* . . . These events were recorded in the *Records of the Kings of Israel*. V. 19 speaks of a different chronicle — that one written by the prophets. It is likely that each of these records brings its own perspective to bear upon the events of Menasheh's reign.

Now it seems likely that the records of our verse take the *Kings'* view. Menasheh's prayer remains unanswered, and his wickedness is seen as, ultimately, causing the destruction of the House. In this context it is likely that the *words of the seers* are those recorded in *II Kings* 21:11 ff.

It certainly seems likely that these prophecies were addressed to Menasheh before his repentance. If so, the sequence in this verse is problematic. Why should the unanswered prayer, which was offered up later as part of Menasheh's penitence, be mentioned before the prophecies which had been said earlier?

However, if our perception of this verse is correct, then the order of the listing is entirely logical. The prophecies may have been made earlier, but, because Menasheh's penitence had been so hollow and ineffectual, because his prayer had, to a large extent, remained unanswered, they were unaffected. Their dire predictions were as fresh and real after the *teshuvah* as they had been before.

לג
יט־כד

יט יְהוָה אֱלֹהֵי יִשְׂרָאֵל הִנָּם עַל־דִּבְרֵי מַלְכֵי יִשְׂרָאֵל: וּתְפִלָּתוֹ
וְהֵעָתֶר־לוֹ וְכָל־חַטָּאתוֹ וּמַעְלוֹ וְהַמְּקֹמוֹת אֲשֶׁר בָּנָה בָהֶם
בָּמוֹת וְהֶעֱמִיד הָאֲשֵׁרִים וְהַפְּסִלִים לִפְנֵי הִכָּנְעוֹ הִנָּם
כ כְּתוּבִים עַל דִּבְרֵי חוֹזָי: וַיִּשְׁכַּב מְנַשֶּׁה עִם־אֲבֹתָיו וַיִּקְבְּרֻהוּ
בֵּיתוֹ וַיִּמְלֹךְ אָמוֹן בְּנוֹ תַּחְתָּיו:
כא בֶּן־עֶשְׂרִים וּשְׁתַּיִם שָׁנָה אָמוֹן בְּמָלְכוֹ וּשְׁתַּיִם שָׁנִים מָלַךְ
כב בִּירוּשָׁלִָם: וַיַּעַשׂ הָרַע בְּעֵינֵי יהוה כַּאֲשֶׁר עָשָׂה מְנַשֶּׁה
אָבִיו וּלְכָל־הַפְּסִילִים אֲשֶׁר עָשָׂה מְנַשֶּׁה אָבִיו זִבַּח אָמוֹן
כג וַיַּעַבְדֵם: וְלֹא נִכְנַע מִלִּפְנֵי יהוה כְּהִכָּנַע מְנַשֶּׁה אָבִיו כִּי
כד הוּא אָמוֹן הִרְבָּה אַשְׁמָה: וַיִּקְשְׁרוּ עָלָיו עֲבָדָיו וַיְמִיתֻהוּ

עַל־דִּבְרֵי מַלְכֵי יִשְׂרָאֵל — *In the Records of the Kings of Israel*. At 28:27 we learned that the *kings of Israel* are David and Solomon — so called because in their days the kingdoms had not yet been split. The ineffectiveness of Menasheh's prayer, in the sense that it did not prevent the destruction of the House, would belong into the records of the Davidic and Solomonic sagas. The House which they had established with so much forethought, love and energy was to be destroyed because of the folly of this man.

19. וְהֵעָתֶר־לוֹ — *And how his plea was granted*. The chronicles referred to in this verse, in contrast to those mentioned earlier, take the *Chronicles'* perspective of Menasheh's reign. In this view his penitence was real, and his prayers were answered. See prefatory remarks to this chapter.

Mefaresh comments: [God] returned him to his kingship.

וְכָל־חַטָּאתוֹ ... — *And all his sins*. Since our verse tells about Menasheh's prayer being answered, this phrase apparently carries the connotation: in spite of all his sins. His former wickedness did not prevent his prayers from being accepted.

וְהַפְּסִלִים — *And the graven images*. We have seen above that the Sages interpret the use of the plural form here, when the singular had been used in vs. 7 and 15, to indicate that the image was changed from having one face to having four — one facing each direction — so that ... *the Shechinah should see and be angered*, from whichever way It would approach.

We deem it significant that this truth comes to us only from the prophetic record [דִּבְרֵי חוֹזָי] and is once more stressed in the story of Amon's reign (v. 22), but is not told either in v. 7 which tells how Menasheh erected the image, nor in v. 15 where he removed it.

In Section II, *Menasheh and Isaiah*, we recognized the dreadful inner struggles and turmoil to which Menasheh was subjected. On the one hand he wanted desperately to perceive God as a remote and unresponsive deity. Only this perception would leave room and justification for the idolatrous cults to which he felt himself so inexorably drawn. On the other hand, he knew the truth, wanted terribly not to capitulate to the fatal attractions of the idols, and would have rejoiced if he had somehow been prevented from following his predilections (Section II, *Menasheh and the Divine Presence in the House*).

Thus, Menasheh both loved God and hated Him. Loved Him enough to hate himself for needing to betray Him, but hated Him for being the source of the inner unrest and turmoil by which he was plagued.

But Menasheh did not allow that hatred to rise to the surface of his consciousness. He did not kill Isaiah outright but created the subterfuge of a trumped-up charge of contradicting the Torah of Moses. Consciously, Menasheh saw himself not as the betrayer of God but as the defender of His Torah.

What then made him change the *image* into *images*? Why replace the one face with four?

We cannot know what conscious thoughts occupied Menasheh's mind when he took that heinous step. He had left the Holy of Holies inviolate and must have viewed himself as one to whom the honor of God was dear. He would certainly not have admitted to himself that he was waging a vendetta against Him, would indeed have denied that here was an inner fury, lashing out impotently against the God Who would allow his conscience no rest. It is really of no concern to us to know how he justified his action to himself. Whatever it was, it was not the truth. That was left to the prophetic eye of

33
19-24

name of HASHEM, God of Israel, they are written in the Records of
the Kings of Israel.
19 *And his prayer, and how his plea was granted,*
and all his sins and betrayals, the places upon which he built bamos and erected asheirah-trees, and the graven images, before he humbled himself; they are all recorded in the records of the seers.
20 *Menasheh lay with his fathers, and they buried him in his palace.*
Amon, his son, reigned in his stead.
21 *Amon was twenty-two years old when he began to reign, and he reigned two years in Jerusalem.*
22 *He did that which was evil in the eyes of HASHEM as Menasseh, his father, had done. As for all the graven images which Menasheh, his father, had made, Amon sacrificed to them and served them.*
23 *But he did not humble himself before HASHEM, as Menasheh, his father, had humbled himself, because he is the Amon who did ever more evil.*
24 *His servants conspired against him, and assassinated*

the *seers* to uncover. They saw the פֶּסֶל as פְּסָלִים. They mercilessly dissected Menasheh's most innermost drives and motivations, and found the true meaning of his actions.

But that which Menasheh had so carefully hidden from himself he was not able to hide from his son. Amon labored under no illusions. He understood his father well, and took that first step to its logical conclusion. If, indeed, the פֶּסֶל is a פְּסָלִים then it belongs not in the Sanctuary, but in the Holy of Holies.

חוזָי — *The seers.* The form is irregular and would normally be חוזים. *Radak* adduces other examples from Scripture where this form occurs. *Metzudos* takes the word as a proper noun — the name of a prophet who recorded the details of Menasheh's reign.

20. בֵּיתוֹ — *In his palace. Kings* has ... *in the garden of his palace.* But they wouldn't bury him in the royal sepulcher. His wickedness precluded him from that honor.

21. בֶּן־עֶשְׂרִים וּשְׁתַּיִם שָׁנָה — ... *twenty-two years old.* Menasheh was a penitent for the final thirty-three years of his life. Accordingly, Amon was born to an ostensibly righteous father. The fact that the next verse tells that ... *he did ... evil ... as Menashe his father had done*, seems to confirm the perception that Menasheh's penitence had not penetrated beneath the surface. Menasheh had changed into a reasonably good king but had remained an essentially evil person.

In the *Kings'* account this verse closes with the name of Amon's mother, as is the usage in its accounts of most of the kings. In Section II, *Amon the Renegade — Yoshiahu the Man of Destiny*, we recognize that *Chronicles* purposely left out from its account of Amon all those statements which would identify him as a legitimate link in the chain of the Davidic kingship. Our explanation there may well account for the omission of the mother's name here.

22. וּלְכָל־הַפְּסִילִים — *As for all the graven images.* See comm. to v. 19.

23. וְלֹא נִכְנַע מִלִּפְנֵי ה׳ . . . כִּי . . . — *But he did not humble himself before HASHEM ... because ...* The meaning may be as follows: Menasheh had been able to humble himself *before HASHEM*, because his religious philosophy allowed for a Supreme Being — albeit remote from the world and relegated to the mysterious and inaccessible Holy of Holies.

But *because* Amon *did ever more evil*, and moved the image into the Holy of Holies, absolutely denying God a presence among men — he had no God before Whom he could humble himself. For Amon there was no hope.

הוּא אָמוֹן הִרְבָּה אַשְׁמָה — *He is the Amon who did ever more evil.* R' Yochanan and R' Elazar disagree concerning the implications of this phrase. The one believes that Amon burned the Torah; the other that he violated his mother (*Sanhedrin* 103b). See Section II, *Amon Plunges to New Depths of Evil*, for a discussion.

24-25. Amon is assassinated by a group of plotters from among his servants who, in turn, are then killed by the *people of the land*. These latter then proclaim Yoshiahu as king. Neither of the two groups are identified further nor are any motives assigned. See below and Section II, *Amon the Renegade — Yoshiahu the Man of Destiny*, for an analysis.

24. וַיִּקְשְׁרוּ עָלָיו עֲבָדָיו — *His servants conspired against him.*

כה בְּבֵיתוֹ: וַיַּכּוּ עַם־הָאָרֶץ אֵת כָּל־הַקֹּשְׁרִים עַל־הַמֶּלֶךְ
אָמוֹן וַיַּמְלִיכוּ עַם־הָאָרֶץ אֶת־יֹאשִׁיָּהוּ בְנוֹ תַּחְתָּיו:
א בֶּן־שְׁמוֹנֶה שָׁנִים יֹאשִׁיָּהוּ בְמָלְכוֹ וּשְׁלֹשִׁים וְאַחַת שָׁנָה
ב מָלַךְ בִּירוּשָׁלִָם: וַיַּעַשׂ הַיָּשָׁר בְּעֵינֵי יהוה וַיֵּלֶךְ בְּדַרְכֵי
דָּוִיד אָבִיו וְלֹא־סָר יָמִין וּשְׂמֹאול:
ג וּבִשְׁמוֹנֶה שָׁנִים לְמָלְכוֹ וְהוּא עוֹדֶנּוּ נַעַר הֵחֵל לִדְרוֹשׁ
לֵאלֹהֵי דָּוִיד אָבִיו וּבִשְׁתֵּים עֶשְׂרֵה שָׁנָה הֵחֵל לְטַהֵר
אֶת־יְהוּדָה וִירוּשָׁלִַם מִן־הַבָּמוֹת וְהָאֲשֵׁרִים וְהַפְּסִלִים

See Section II, *Amon the Renegade — Yoshiahu the Man of Destiny*, for our perception of this conspiracy.

HaLevi (*Tekufas HaMikra* ch. 29) interprets as follows. The *servants* were a small group of people, loyal to God, who decided to assassinate Amon in order to stop him from leading the people to ultimate destruction. They did not want the child Yoshiahu to succeed his father, because they suspected that so young a boy would surely not be able to change course from the ways which his grandfather and father had established. They intended to find some other — more reliable — descendent of the Davidic line and to install him as king.

25. עַם־הָאָרֶץ — *The people of the land*. These, in *HaLevi's* view, were the bulk of the people, whose loyalty to the Torah had been eroded during the long, dark years of Menasheh's and Amon's reigns. They wanted to preserve the licentious way of life that had become the norm in Judah, and knew no better way to do this than to make Yoshiahu king. Surely this young and malleable child could be relied upon to accept their guidance and continue upon the path laid down by his father.

The story of the frustration of these plans is told in the next chapter.

XXXIV

The nadir of the Davidic kingship had been reached with Amon's depredations. He had, as it were, driven God out of the House, making a mockery of all of that for which Israel had stood through the ages. With the idolatrous image firmly ensconced in the Holy of Holies, there was really nothing left of that special essence of sanctity which had made Israel beloved by God.

It was time that the Davidic concept be revitalized and resurrected.

Unique among all the kings of Judah, Yoshiahu had, centuries earlier, already become destined to play a pivotal role in that restoration. To trace this remarkable king's first appearance upon the stage of history, we must go back to the days when the Northern Kingdom first split from Judah. As Yarov'am was about to sacrifice upon the renegade altar which he had erected at Bethel, a prophet appeared to him. The message he bore vaulted over hundreds of years and looked ahead to the time when a *Yoshiahu* would arise to wreak terrible havoc among the idol worshipers: *O altar, altar! Thus said HASHEM: A son shall be born to the house of David, Yoshiahu by name, and he shall slaughter upon you the priests of the bamos who bring offerings upon you. And human bones shall he burn upon you!* (*I Kings* 13:1-2)

History knows of only six people whose names had been assigned to them before they were born (*Pirkei d'R'Eliezer* 32). There were only six people who were marked for such greatness that providence had mapped out the life path along which they would be called upon to tread. [See Overview to *I Chronicles*, *Names and their Significance in Scripture* (p. xxxiv).]

One of them was Yoshiahu.

What secrets are contained in his name? *Pirkei d'R'Eliezer* teaches that it implies: יָאֵי שַׁי הוּא לְפָנֶיךָ, *He is a most appropriate gift to be offered up to You!* We understand this to mean that through him as king, in whom the entire people were personified, the nation was once more to be offered up to God. He would touch and bring to life the inner core of sanctity which is the lifeblood of the true Israel. Yoshiahu would have it in him to carry his people toward their Messianic future. See Section II to ch. 33, *Amon the Renegade — Yoshiahu the Man of Destiny*.

33
25
him in his palace. [25] The people of the land slew all who had
conspired against King Amon, and the people of the land crowned
Yoshiahu, his son, king in his stead.

34
1-3
*Yoshiahu was eight years old when he became king and ruled
thirty-one years in Jerusalem. [2] He did that which was right
in the eyes of HASHEM and walked in the ways of his father David.
He did not stray right or left. [3] Now in the eighth year of his reign
while he was yet young, he began to seek out the God of his father
David; and in the twelfth year he began to cleanse Judah and Jerus-
alem from the bamos and the asheirah-trees and the graven images*

Yoshiahu Eliminates Idol Worship

1. This verse is a verbatim quote from the *Kings'* version (ch. 22) except that there, as is normally the case where a king is first introduced, the mother's name is given. Here it is omitted. The explanation may be based upon the insights which we learned in the prefatory remarks to this chapter: In *Chronicles'* long-range view of history, Yoshiahu towers above his chronological position in David's family. He is God's anointed one, destined to fill the role of the *Yoshiahu* whose coming was foretold centuries earlier. He belongs to eternal Israel — his parentage is irrelevant.

בֶּן־שְׁמוֹנֶה שָׁנִים — *Eight years old.* The fact that the successor to the throne was a young child could have caused different reactions among the people. See comm. to 33:24 and 25, and Section II, to ch. 33 *Amon the Renegade — Yoshiahu the Man of Destiny.*

2. וַיַּעַשׂ הַיָּשָׁר בְּעֵינֵי ה׳ — *He did that which was right in the eyes of HASHEM.* This verse is virtually identical with its parallel in the *Kings'* account. Both tell of Yoshiahu's righteousness and that he was a true carrier of the Davidic tradition. But see Sec. II, *Yoshiahu's Reign in the Eyes of Kings and Chronicles,* for a discussion of some substantive differences in nuance.

וַיֵּלֶךְ בְּדַרְכֵי דָּוִיד אָבִיו — *And walked in the ways of his father David. Chronicles* does not use this phrase in describing any other king.

Perhaps, the phrase is meant to imply something more than simple approval: This youngster was a true scion of David's family. There was every indication that he, indeed, was the *Yoshiahu,* the son who would be born *to the house of David,* whose birth had been predicted many years earlier when the prophet came to Yarov'am.

3. וּבִשְׁמוֹנֶה שָׁנִים לְמָלְכוֹ — *Now in the eighth year of his reign.*

Yoshiahu *began to seek out the God of his father David,* when he was sixteen years old. What of the first eight years of his reign — three of which came after he had already attained majority?

Halevi believes that during this period he did, indeed, act under the sway of those *people of the land,* who had made him king in the hope that he could be brought up to adhere to the wicked ways of Menasheh and Amon. See comm. to 33:24. This appears borne out by *II Kings* 23:25 which teaches that no other king had ever *turned back to God* as Yoshiahu had done. The implication is that Yoshiahu had begun his reign on the wrong footing.

Metzudos reads our verse quite differently: *When he was eight years old, that is, at the beginning of his reign ....* Given this interpretation, there is no indication that Yoshiahu was ever wicked. Indeed, *Shabbos* 56b maintains that whoever thinks that Yoshiahu sinned is mistaken. The verse in *Kings* which implies that he was the penitent *par excellence* is to be understood as follows: In his earlier years, while he was still a youngster, he had made mistakes in the administration of justice. He had made incorrect decisions, awarding money to litigants who were in the wrong. In his later years he repaid these moneys to the parties whom he had wronged, out of his own pocket.

הֵחֵל לִדְרוֹשׁ לֵאלֹהֵי דָּוִיד אָבִיו — *He began to seek out the God of his father David.* He sought out *the God of his father, David,* not, *the God of [Israel's] fathers,* as at 14:3.

As in the previous verse, the stress is upon the fact that Yoshiahu is a scion of the Davidic line. He is the *Yoshiahu* of the centuries-old prophecy — the man of destiny who is to revitalize the concept of מַלְכוּת בֵּית דָּוִד, the kingship in which Israel's future is vested.

הֵחֵל לְטַהֵר אֶת־יְהוּדָה וִירוּשָׁלַם — *He began to cleanse Judah and Jerusalem.* In the *Kings*

לד
ד־ח

ד וְהַמַּסֵּכוֹת: וַיְנַתְּצוּ לְפָנָיו אֵת מִזְבְּחוֹת הַבְּעָלִים וְהַחַמָּנִים
אֲשֶׁר־לְמַעְלָה מֵעֲלֵיהֶם גִּדֵּעַ וְהָאֲשֵׁרִים וְהַפְּסִלִים
וְהַמַּסֵּכוֹת שִׁבַּר וְהֵדַק וַיִּזְרֹק עַל־פְּנֵי הַקְּבָרִים הַזֹּבְחִים
ה לָהֶם: וְעַצְמוֹת כֹּהֲנִים שָׂרַף עַל־°מזבחותים וַיְטַהֵר
ו אֶת־יְהוּדָה וְאֶת יְרוּשָׁלִָם: וּבְעָרֵי מְנַשֶּׁה וְאֶפְרַיִם וְשִׁמְעוֹן
ז וְעַד־נַפְתָּלִי °בחר בתיהם סָבִיב: וַיְנַתֵּץ אֶת־הַמִּזְבְּחוֹת
וְאֶת־הָאֲשֵׁרִים וְהַפְּסִלִים כִּתַּת לְהֵדַק וְכָל־הַחַמָּנִים גִּדַּע
ח בְּכָל־אֶרֶץ יִשְׂרָאֵל וַיָּשָׁב לִירוּשָׁלִָם: וּבִשְׁנַת

°מִזְבְּחוֹתָם ק׳

°בְּחַרְבֹתֵיהֶם ק׳

account, Yoshiahu first orders the removal of the idolatrous utensils from the House itself. Judah and Jerusalem are mentioned only in the next verse (*II Kings* 23:4 ff.).

The description in *Chronicles* makes no mention at all of anything being removed from the House. This is particularly striking since, as we saw in our analysis of Amon in the previous chapter, it was the installation of the image in the Holy of Holies which marked the low-point of his perfidies. Would we not have expected that Yoshiahu's great reformation should begin with the cleansing and rededication of the House itself, and that such a cleansing should receive prominent mention in the account of his reforms?

To answer this question correctly, we must recall the totally different structure of the two books in their treatment of the reigns of Menasheh, Amon and Yoshiahu.

The difference lies in the fact that, as we saw in the analysis of Menasheh's reign, *Kings* makes no mention at all of his penitence. Given this, we recognize that a simple reading of the *Kings'* account would yield that all the abominations which had proliferated in the House and land during the period of Menasheh's wickedness were still in place when Amon came to power. Nothing specific is then added concerning that king's wickedness; we learn only that he continued in his father's path. Again, taking only the surface meaning of the *Kings'* account, the impression is still that when Yoshiahu became king the situation was precisely as it had been during the worst of Menasheh's excesses. And it was the idolatrous paraphernalia which had proliferated under Menasheh that Yoshiahu set out to remove.

But *Chronicles* had allowed us a glimpse behind the scenes, and thus we know that whatever had been installed by Menasheh had already been removed by him himself as a result of his *teshuvah*. Hence, as far as the text of *Chronicles* is concerned, the cleansing which Yoshiahu undertook could have had as its object only such things as were brought back or innovatively installed by Amon.

But a reading of the Amon account yields that, in fact, none of the excesses which the Sages attribute to him are explicated in the text. We read only that he served the idols whom his father Menasheh had served and that *he did ever more evil* (33:23).

Thus, in the context of *Chronicles*, mention of the cleansing of the House would have been out of place.

The question thus becomes a different one. Why are we not told explicitly about the many evils which Amon perpetrated? Why, above all, do we not learn from the text about the erection of the image in the Holy of Holies?

Perhaps it is for the same reason that so much else is left out concerning Amon and his reign. As we explored in Section II to ch. 33, *Amon the Renegade — Yoshiahu the Man of Destiny*, *Chronicles* goes out of its way to delegitimize this catastrophic reign. Any account, however sparse, would have dignified Amon's as a reign worthy of note. The utter disdain in which history holds this renegade, whose every action was designed only to deny Davidic destiny, is best expressed by silence.

4. . . . וַיְנַתְּצוּ לְפָנָיו — *And they broke down . . . in his presence*. It is striking that the breaking down of the Baal altars is not done by the king himself but by others, *in his presence*, while all the other acts of cleansing in our passage are associated with the king himself [. . . גִּדַּע, שִׁבַּר and so on].

At 31:1 we noted that it lies in the nature of a Messianic context to allow the king to recede into the background and, where both he as initiator and the people as executors are involved, to stress the action of the people.

Further, at 33:3 we noted in a similar context that the *piel* voice occasionally denoted the causative and that נִתֵּץ there, and, consequently גִּדַּע, שִׁבַּר and similar ex-

34
4-8

and the molten images. [4] *And they broke down the altars of the*
Baalim in his presence, and the sun images that were on high above
them he smashed, and the asheirah-trees and the graven images
and the molten images he broke into pieces, and made dust of them,
and strewed it upon the graves of those that had sacrificed upon
them. [5] *As for the bones of the priests, he burned them upon their*
altars, thus purging Judah and Jerusalem. [6] *And in the cities of*
Ephraim, Menasheh and Shimeon all the way up to Naphtali, they
wielded their wrecker's tools round about. [7] *He broke down the alt-*
ars and beat the asheirah-trees and the graven images into powder,
and cut down all the sun images throughout the land of Israel, and
returned to Jerusalem. [8] *Now, so that land and temple might be*

pressions in our passage, could well mean that these actions were not undertaken by Yoshiahu himself but rather performed by the people at his instigation. Accordingly, גִּדַּע and שִׁבַּר may have the same meaning as וַיְנַתְּצוּ לְפָנָיו; that is, that the king initiated but the people executed.

We may thus, perhaps, conclude that the phrase וַיְנַתְּצוּ לְפָנָיו has the purpose of teaching that the subsequent *piel* expressions are all to be taken as the causative, and that the meaning is that all the actions were undertaken by the people. The reason for stressing this would be based on a similar consideration as obtained in the case of Chizkiahu at 31:1: The glory of the ideal Jewish king lies not in his own greatness but in being able to call the people to the implementation of great deeds.

וַיְנַתְּצוּ לְפָנָיו אֵת מִזְבְּחוֹת הַבְּעָלִים — *And they broke down the altars of the Baalim in his presence.* Reference would not be to the altars of the *Baal* which Menasheh had put up (33:3). These would surely have been removed during the long years of Menasheh's penitence. Perhaps, although there is no mention of this in the text, Amon rebuilt these abominations.

וְהַחַמָּנִים אֲשֶׁר־לְמַעְלָה מֵעֲלֵיהֶם — *And the sun images that were on high above them....* חַמָּנִים is from חַמָּה, *sun.* Menasheh had introduced the worship of heavenly bodies (33:3) and these sun images were placed above the *Baal* altars (*Mefaresh*).

וַיִּזְרֹק עַל־פְּנֵי הַקְּבָרִים — *And strewed it upon the graves.* He scattered the powder upon the graves of the people who had served the idols. He did this in order to shame them (*Metzudos*), as if to say, *See what you served during your lives!* (*Radak, Kings*).

Kings (23:6) reports this usage only in connection with the *asheirah*-tree which had stood in the House.

הַקְּבָרִים הַזֹּבְחִים — *The graves of those that had sacrificed ... Radak* points out that the phrase is to be understood as though it read: הַקְּבָרִים [קִבְרֵי] הַזֹּבְחִים.

5. וְעַצְמוֹת כֹּהֲנִים שָׂרַף עַל־מִזְבְּחוֹתָם — *As for the bones of the priests, he burned them upon their altars.* See prefatory remarks to this chapter. Yoshiahu here is playing out the role predicted for him by the *man of God* quoted at *I Kings* 13:2.

6. וְשִׁמְעוֹן וְעַד־נַפְתָּלִי — *And Shimeon all the way up to Naphtali.* Although the ten tribes had already been exiled by Assyria, small pockets of them still occupied the areas of the former Northern Kingdom (*Metzudos*).

בְּחַרְבֹתֵיהֶם — *They wielded their wrecker's tools.* They destroyed the idolatrous altars in the Israelite cities with tools made for that purpose (*Metzudos*).

Radak renders the word as *desolate places.* It describes the area left desolate after the idolatrous altars had been destroyed.

7. ... וַיְנַתֵּץ — *He broke down ...* This verse describes the purging of the areas described in the previous verse, while v. 4 had spoken of a similar cleansing of Judah and Jerusalem. It is thus that אֶרֶץ יִשְׂרָאֵל in the latter part of the verse is to be understood — the land of the Northern Kingdom.

◆§ The House Repairs

8-13. By means of subtle changes in emphasis and nuance, *Chronicles* tells this story from a different perspective than that used in *Kings.* There it is told as an event, of interest in its own right; here, it is presented as framework for the finding of the *Sefer Torah* and the spiritual revival which this event precipitated.

שְׁמוֹנֶה עֶשְׂרֵה לְמָלְכוֹ לְטַהֵר הָאָרֶץ וְהַבָּיִת שָׁלַח אֶת־שָׁפָן
בֶּן־אֲצַלְיָהוּ וְאֶת־מַעֲשֵׂיָהוּ שַׂר־הָעִיר וְאֵת יוֹאָח בֶּן־יוֹאָחָז
ט הַמַּזְכִּיר לְחַזֵּק אֶת־בֵּית יהוה אֱלֹהָיו׃ וַיָּבֹאוּ אֶל־חִלְקִיָּהוּ
הַכֹּהֵן הַגָּדוֹל וַיִּתְּנוּ אֶת־הַכֶּסֶף הַמּוּבָא בֵית־אֱלֹהִים אֲשֶׁר

8. וּבִשְׁנַת שְׁמוֹנֶה עֶשְׂרֵה לְמָלְכוֹ — *Now, in the eighteenth year of his reign ...* The formula is precisely that used twice in v. 3, and thus it inevitably focuses our attention to a theme of spiritual development: *In the eighth year ... and in the twelfth year ... and in the eighteenth year ...* In *Kings* where the stages of v. 3 are not given, this nuance is entirely missing.

There is another significant diversion from the *Kings'* narrative. In our verse we have שָׁלַח, *he sent*, without the subject being further identified because it is a continuation of what went before. In *Kings* we have שָׁלַח הַמֶּלֶךְ, *the king sent*, since it is this phrase which begins the story. The result is that in *Kings* the impression is given that the House repairs were a kingly initiative undertaken as part of the royal prerogative, while in *Chronicles* it is viewed as a part of Yoshiahu's personal development.

HaLevi in *Tekufas HaMikra*, ch. 17, makes the point that from the days of Yoash's reforms and onwards, the responsibility for the upkeep of the House moved from the hands of the *Kohanim* into the purview of the king — see, for example, at 24:11 where we find the king's scribe, together with the representative of the *Kohen Gadol*, overseeing the disbursement of the moneys collected for House repairs. Thus, it is altogether proper that the initiative for the repairs should have lain with the king.

Nevertheless, while a given action may be prompted by a formal obligation, this in no way precludes a personal attitude and motivation, quite apart from any official position.

In the course of the comm. we will demonstrate that, because of Yoshiahu's historic role as the one who is to teach Israel to exist and to function without a House in its midst and without a scion of the Davidic line at its head, [See Section II, *Yoshiahu's Reign in the Eyes of Kings and Chronicles.*] *Chronicles* prefers to stress those aspects of the event which derive from Yoshiahu's personality rather than those which are a function of his kingship.

לְטַהֵר הָאָרֶץ וְהַבָּיִת — *So that land and House might be cleansed*. The translation follows *Radak*. The *kings of Judah* had been responsible for the ravages to which the House had been exposed (v. 11). The sorry state in which Yoshiahu found the House was an indication of the bankruptcy of those catastrophic reigns. The cleansing process was needed, not only for the House itself, but also for the *land*. The state of the monarchy, the way it looked upon itself, its sense of purpose and duty, all this lay in disrepair as much as the courtyards and buildings upon which they should have lavished their concern and care.

This approach to the story creates an appropriate backdrop to the finding of the *Sefer Torah* which, as we shall see below, was to be the harbinger of the devastating message that Yoshiahu's reforms had been too little and had come too late, and that both House and monarchy were doomed.

שָׁלַח ... לְחַזֵּק אֶת־בֵּית ה׳ אֱלֹהָיו — *He sent ... to repair the House of* HASHEM*, his God*. These men are charged with the duty of repairing the House. That they approach Chilkiahu (v. 9) appears to be of their own initiative.

This contrasts with the *Kings'* account in which the king sends Shaphan the scribe, saying, *Go up to Chilkiah the Kohen Gadol ....* No authorization is given to Shaphan to act on his own.

The difference may stem from the divergence in approach which we noted above and of which we will see further evidence in other textual discrepancies between the two accounts. In *Kings* the subject is Yoshiahu's formal action as king. The initiative does indeed lie with him, but the correct channel through which to implement the plan is the *Kohen Gadol*. It is to him that the emissaries are directed. The story took place precisely as described in *Kings*.

In *Chronicles* the thrust is on Yoshiahu's personal motivation. Essentially he is the repairer of the House. He, as a person, feels it incumbent upon himself to undo the damage which the *kings of Judah* (v. 11) had perpetrated. His personal emissaries are central to the story. That they acted through the *Kohen Gadol* is coincidental.

אֶת־שָׁפָן ... וְאֶת־מַעֲשֵׂיָהוּ ... וְאֵת יוֹאָח — *Shaphan ... and Maaseiahu ... and Yoach ....* In *Kings*, only Shaphan is mentioned. The explanation may be as above. The formal responsibilities were to be enacted through the scribe [see also at 24:11]. From the formal standpoint it is insignificant that others may have accompa-

*cleansed, he, in the eighteenth year of his reign, sent Shaphan the
son of Atzaliahu and Maaseiah the governor of the city and Yoach
the son of Yoachaz the recorder, to repair the House of HASHEM, his
God.* 9 *They came to Chilkiahu the Kohen Gadol and delivered the
money that was brought into the House of God, which the Levite*

nied Shaphan.

Here, where Yoshiahu's personal involvement is stressed, all those emissaries whom he considered important to the task are mentioned by name. That here the delegation is not viewed in formal terms may perhaps be deduced from the fact that Shaphan is here, in contrast to *Kings*, not given his title of *scribe*.

We do not know what the position ascribed to Maaseiahu as שַׂר הָעִיר precisely entails. The only other place where it occurs is at 18:25 and there it involved a responsibility for jailing one whom the king had condemned to imprisonment. There seems at least a possibility that this Maaseiahu is identical with the Assaiah of v. 20 who is described as עֶבֶד הַמֶּלֶךְ, *servant of the king*. This may well describe a private confidant. Perhaps, then, his inclusion in the delegation would also create the ambience of a personal rather than an official involvement.

הַמַּזְכִּיר — *The recorder*. See *I Chronicles* 18:15.

9. וַיָּבֹאוּ אֶל־חִלְקִיָּהוּ — *They came to Chilkiahu* . . . See comm. to previous verse.

וַיִּתְּנוּ אֶת־הַכֶּסֶף הַמּוּבָא בֵית־אֱלֹהִים — *And delivered the money that was brought into the House of God*. The king's delegation *delivered* certain moneys. Our verse does not say to whom. One possibility would seem to be that they gave it to Chilkiahu: *They came to Chilkiahu and gave* [him] *the money* . . .

Another possibility is that the . . . וַיִּתְּנוּ of the next verse picks up our phrase. That is, that since the object of וַיִּתְּנוּ is a very long and complex one, the predicate is repeated in the next verse in order to take up the narrative without losing the thread.

If, indeed, it is the delegates themselves who handed the money to the overseers (v. 10), what is the significance of the introductory phrase of our verse: *They came to Chilkiahu the Kohen Gadol*?

The answer may be found in v. 14 where we read that the *Sefer Torah* was found when . . .*they brought out the money which had been donated to HASHEM's House*. This certainly implies that the money mentioned in our verse was stored in some secret recess within the House complex. We shall discuss this further below, but in the meantime the following picture emerges: There was money kept within the House complex, access to which required the help of the *Kohen Gadol*. For this reason the delegation went first to Chilkiahu. However, once the money was recovered, its disbursement lay entirely in the hands of the king or his delegates, and it was they who gave the money to the overseers.

The *Kings'* version paints a different picture: As we saw above, the message there is directly to Chilkiahu. They are to tell him to . . . *use up the money that was brought into HASHEM's House* . . . Thus, it is not they who are to disburse any money. They are to tell Chilkiahu to do that which is incumbent upon him.

The solution must be as follows: From the expression used in both *Kings* and *Chronicles*, אֲשֶׁר אָסְפוּ . . . שֹׁמְרֵי הַסַּף, *which the gatekeepers had gathered*, it is clear that the subject is not moneys that were brought to the House in the normal course of events but which were collected specifically for the purpose of undertaking House repairs. This recalls a similar collection initiated by Yoash and planned to take place annually (24:5). [See further there, at vs. 6, 8 and 14.]

As can be seen from a comparison between the *Kings'* version of the Yoash initiative and that of *Chronicles* (comm. 24:5), the collection which he initiated fell very much into his own purview, and was entirely separate from the administration of the regular House income.

We may thus surmise as follows: The immediate responsibility for work to be done on the House fell to the *Kohen Gadol* — witness that the overseers were Levites (vs. 12 and 13); that is, House functionaries. But in relation to the king's personally collected funds, the *Kohen Gadol* was only an executor acting for the king. Thus, money given to him and passed on to the workers can be said to have been *given* to the workers by the king or his personal representatives.

The *Kings'* version, which is interested only in the formal event, states simply that Chilkiahu was told to do that which he was charged with doing — which was to pass money which he had received to the appropriate people.

Chronicles which, as we saw above, has an interest in projecting the king's involvement, chooses to describe the same event in its essential properties — the king or his representatives are the real *givers*. This, in order to

לד **י־יג**

אָסְפוּ־הַלְוִיִּם שֹׁמְרֵי הַסַּף מִיַּד מְנַשֶּׁה וְאֶפְרַיִם וּמִכֹּל
°וַיָּשֻׁבוּ ק׳ שְׁאֵרִית יִשְׂרָאֵל וּמִכָּל־יְהוּדָה וּבִנְיָמִן °וישבי יְרוּשָׁלָםִ׃
י וַיִּתְּנוּ עַל־יַד עֹשֵׂה הַמְּלָאכָה הַמֻּפְקָדִים בְּבֵית יְהוָה וַיִּתְּנוּ
אֹתוֹ עוֹשֵׂי הַמְּלָאכָה אֲשֶׁר עֹשִׂים בְּבֵית יְהוָה לִבְדּוֹק
יא וּלְחַזֵּק הַבָּיִת׃ וַיִּתְּנוּ לֶחָרָשִׁים וְלַבֹּנִים לִקְנוֹת אַבְנֵי מַחְצֵב
וְעֵצִים לַמְחַבְּרוֹת וּלְקָרוֹת אֶת־הַבָּתִּים אֲשֶׁר הִשְׁחִיתוּ
יב מַלְכֵי יְהוּדָה׃ וְהָאֲנָשִׁים עֹשִׂים בֶּאֱמוּנָה בַּמְּלָאכָה
וַעֲלֵיהֶם ׀ מֻפְקָדִים יַחַת וְעֹבַדְיָהוּ הַלְוִיִּם מִן־בְּנֵי מְרָרִי
וּזְכַרְיָה וּמְשֻׁלָּם מִן־בְּנֵי הַקְּהָתִים לְנַצֵּחַ וְהַלְוִיִּם כָּל־מֵבִין
יג בִּכְלֵי־שִׁיר׃ וְעַל הַסַּבָּלִים וּמְנַצְּחִים לְכֹל עֹשֵׂה מְלָאכָה

underline that perspective which, in its view, is significant.

שֹׁמְרֵי הַסַּף — *The gatekeepers*. The term is discussed and analyzed in fn. to *I Chronicles* 9:19.

מְנַשֶּׁה וְאֶפְרַיִם — *Menasheh and Ephraim*. As we saw at v. 6, Yoshiahu's kingship extended into areas of the former Northern Kingdom.

Kings does not stress this. The explanation may be as follows: Surely there would have been only pockets of population in the northern territories; the bulk of the subjects over whom Yoshiahu ruled was certainly concentrated in Judah and Benjamin. When *Kings* uses the expression [אֲשֶׁר אָסְפוּ שֹׁמְרֵי הַסַּף מֵאֵת הָעָם], it surely means the known and clearly defined *people*, that is, the nation of Judah. The interest of the *Kings'* narrative does not extend beyond this.

If, nevertheless, the men who gathered the funds went further north, this may well have been done on the personal initiative of the king and not because it would have been normal procedure. He may have wanted to involve all the people — even those who need not have participated — in the sense which we recognized at 31:1 and in comm. to v. 4 above. In Yoshiahu's perceived role as the one to whose lot it fell to educate the people to an exiled existence, [see Section II, *Yoshiahu's Reign in the Eyes of Kings and Chronicles*] it would make sense to involve the people, as people, independently of the formal requirements. For *Chronicles* this is an extremely significant part of the story.

וַיָּשֻׁבוּ יְרוּשָׁלָםִ — *And they returned to Jerusalem*. *Kings* does not record the return to Jerusalem. This omission would be entirely reasonable if only Maaseiahu and Yoach left to go back to Jerusalem. These two are never mentioned in the *Kings'* account, and what they did would have been of no interest. From v. 14 it does, indeed, appear that Shaphan remained at the House site.

But certainly the plain meaning of the verse seems to imply that all three returned. The events described in v. 14 could well have taken place at another time.

An alternative would be to take our phrase as being chronologically out of place. It means simply that, after all that needed to be done had been done, the three emissaries returned to Jerusalem. The account then goes back to a description of the events that took place before their return. Such a usage would fall within normal Scriptural style.

But why mention their return to Jerusalem and why, if it is significant, does *Kings* not make an issue of it?

It is particularly significant that it is only the *k'ri*, the reading of the word, which yields *and they returned* ... The *k'siv*, the way the word is written, yields וְיוֹשְׁבֵי יְרוּשָׁלָיִם, *and* [*from*] *those that lived in Jerusalem*. The phrase goes with what was said before: The moneys were collected from Menasheh and Ephraim; all the remainder of Israel; all of Judah and Benjamin; and from *those that lived in Jerusalem*.

Now, mention of *those that lived in Jerusalem* as a separate entity within Judah is well established [see 20:15, 18, 20; 32:25; 33:9; in our chapter, v. 30; and 35:18] and thus, would be entirely logical in our context, too. Why, then, does the *k'ri* change it to וַיָּשֻׁבוּ?

The return to Jerusalem is significant in the sense that it places the delegation in a clearly defined position vis-a-vis the restoration project. They are not House functionaries; they act as agents of the king and their place is by his side and not in the House. This is important to note in the *Chronicles'* perspec-

gate-keepers had gathered from Menasseh and Ephraim and from
all the rest of Israel and from all Judah and Benjamin, and they
returned to Jerusalem. [10] *They gave it to the foremen who were*
placed in charge of HASHEM*'s House. The foremen handed it to the*
workers who labored in HASHEM*'s House so that they could survey*
and repair the House. [11] *They gave it to the artisans and to the*
builders so that these might buy hewn stones, and lumber for
couplings and to lay the beams for the houses which the kings of
Judah had allowed to decay. [12] *The men worked faithfully.*
Appointed over them, to urge them on, were the Levites, Yachath
and Obadiahu of the Merrari family, and Zachariah and Meshul-
lam of the Kehathite family. Also Levites, all of whom were skilled
musicians. [13] *Such were also appointed over the porters. There*
were, also, overseers over all the foremen for all categories of work.

tive which puts Yoshiahu's personal involvement into the center of the narrative, but not in *Kings*.

The *k'ri-k'siv* system yields the following: Their return to Jerusalem had no significance to the casual observer: They went back after their duties had been performed, in the ordinary course of events. One could only see the expected collection of funds from all segments of society — including *those that lived in Jerusalem* and nothing more. It is only *Chronicles*, by having it read וַיָּשֻׁבוּ, which draws our attention to the inner significance of an outwardly ordinary act.

10. עֹשֵׂה הַמְּלָאכָה — *The foremen* [lit. *They who produce the work*]. The actual laborers are enumerated in v. 11. The עֹשֵׂה הַמְּלָאכָה are the *overseers* who are in overall charge of the project (*Metzudos*).

The root עשה means not only *to make* or *do* something directly, but also to generate something indirectly. Thus, it is used of plants *producing* or *yielding* flour (*Hosea* 8:7) and of setting into motion events, which eventually yield results — see *Ecclesiastes* 3:14, *God has* [עָשָׂה] *acted so that* [man] *should stand in awe before Him*.

Thus, we are not surprised to find עשה used to describe not those men who actually do the work but rather, those who see to it that it is produced in the end.

לִבְדּוֹק וּלְחַזֵּק הַבָּיִת — *So that they could survey and repair the House*. In *II Kings* 22:5 repairs are called בֶּדֶק הַבָּיִת. בֶּדֶק is from בדק, *to search*, since the breakages in the building are not always immediately visible and are found only by checking (*Metzudos*).

11. לֶחָרָשִׁים — *To the artisans*. חָרָשׁ is an artisan (see *Rashi*, *Exodus* 28:11). He works in stone (*Exodus* 28:11); iron (*Isaiah* 44:12); wood (*Isaiah* 44:13) and the like.

לַמְחַבְּרוֹת — *For couplings*. From חבר, *to join*. See comm. to *I Chronicles* 22:3.

וּלְקָרוֹת אֶת־הַבָּתִּים — *And to lay the beams for the houses*. קוֹרָה is a *beam*. The verbal form is rare. See *Psalms* 104:3; *Nehemiah* 2:8 and 3:3 and 6.

אֲשֶׁר הִשְׁחִיתוּ מַלְכֵי יְהוּדָה — *Which the kings of Judah had allowed to decay*. Certainly Menasheh and Amon are meant.

12. וְהָאֲנָשִׁים עֹשִׂים בֶּאֱמוּנָה — *The men worked faithfully*. *Kings* reads: *But no accounting was made with them concerning the money that had been given into their hands, for they acted faithfully* (*II Kings* 22:7). Here, too, this may well be the meaning. The workers were not required to give an accounting of how they spent the money which had been given to them. They were trusted to spend it wisely and for the purposes for which it was meant. See Section II, *The Faithful Workers*, for another explanation.

לְנַצֵּחַ — *To urge them on*. Thus, *Metzudos*.

13. וְעַל הַסַּבָּלִים — *Such were also appointed over the porters*. Foremen were also appointed to be in charge of the men who carried the building materials (*Metzudos*).

וּמְנַצְּחִים לְכֹל עֹשֵׂה מְלָאכָה — *Overseers over all the foremen*. In v. 10 we recognized that the עֹשֵׂה מְלָאכָה are not the actual laborers, but foremen. These מְנַצְּחִים would then seem to be a higher echelon of administrator.

לַעֲבוֹדָה וַעֲבוֹדָה וּמֵהַלְוִיִּם סוֹפְרִים וְשֹׁטְרִים וְשׁוֹעֲרִים:
יד וּבְהוֹצִיאָם אֶת־הַכֶּסֶף הַמּוּבָא בֵּית יהוה מָצָא חִלְקִיָּהוּ
טו הַכֹּהֵן אֶת־סֵפֶר תּוֹרַת־יהוה בְּיַד־מֹשֶׁה: וַיַּעַן חִלְקִיָּהוּ
וַיֹּאמֶר אֶל־שָׁפָן הַסּוֹפֵר סֵפֶר הַתּוֹרָה מָצָאתִי בְּבֵית יהוה
טז וַיִּתֵּן חִלְקִיָּהוּ אֶת־הַסֵּפֶר אֶל־שָׁפָן: וַיָּבֵא שָׁפָן אֶת־הַסֵּפֶר
אֶל־הַמֶּלֶךְ וַיָּשֶׁב עוֹד אֶת־הַמֶּלֶךְ דָּבָר לֵאמֹר כֹּל
יז אֲשֶׁר־נִתַּן בְּיַד־עֲבָדֶיךָ הֵם עֹשִׂים: וַיַּתִּיכוּ אֶת־הַכֶּסֶף
הַנִּמְצָא בְּבֵית־יהוה וַיִּתְּנוּהוּ עַל־יַד הַמֻּפְקָדִים וְעַל־יַד
יח עוֹשֵׂי הַמְּלָאכָה: וַיַּגֵּד שָׁפָן הַסּוֹפֵר לַמֶּלֶךְ לֵאמֹר סֵפֶר נָתַן
יט לִי חִלְקִיָּהוּ הַכֹּהֵן וַיִּקְרָא־בוֹ שָׁפָן לִפְנֵי הַמֶּלֶךְ: וַיְהִי

לַעֲבוֹדָה וַעֲבוֹדָה — *For all categories of work.* The translation follows *Metzudos.*

סוֹפְרִים וְשֹׁטְרִים וְשׁוֹעֲרִים — *Scribes, officers and gatekeepers.* The *scribes* were charged with keeping a record of moneys earmarked for the House repairs; the *officers* were the officials who enforced the levies for this purpose and the *gatekeepers* kept a check on the men who came to work (*Metzudos*).

For שֹׁטְרִים in this context — see comm. to *I Chronicles* 23:4.

14. וּבְהוֹצִיאָם אֶת־הַכֶּסֶף — *As they brought out the money.* When יצא in the *hiphil* is used in the sense, *to bring out an inanimate object*, it most frequently is followed by either ... מ, *from*, to indicate the place from which it was brought out (*Exodus* 12:39), or, ...ל, *to*, to inform where it was brought (here 29:16). Here we have neither: The focus is not on the fact that the money was taken from here to there, but that it had, so to speak, to be dredged up from the deepest recesses of the House vaults so that people had to go where they had rarely gone before — which made the discovery of the *Sefer Torah* possible.

מָצָא חִלְקִיָּהוּ הַכֹּהֵן — *Chilkiahu the Kohen found.* The finding of the *Sefer Torah* is a seminal point in Yoshiahu's reign. In Section II, *The Finding of the Sefer Torah*, we discuss in detail the various possible approaches to this momentous occasion.

Kings does not describe the finding directly. The event itself was ordinary enough and did not warrant mention. It was only with hindsight that the providence inherent in the finding became clear.

סֵפֶר תּוֹרַת־ה׳ בְּיַד־מֹשֶׁה — *The Book which records HASHEM's Torah at the hand of Moses. Kings* uses סֵפֶר הַתּוֹרָה, that is, with the definite article. Some commentators feel that this usage, and the *Chronicles'* description ... *at the hand of Moses*, indicate that this was the *Sefer Torah* which Moses himself had written.

A rigorous examination of these expressions shows that they do not necessarily yield such a conclusion.

In the first place, סֵפֶר הַתּוֹרָה can have two meanings: *Rashi* to *Deuteronomy* 29:20 points to two different Scriptural usages: סֵפֶר הַתּוֹרָה הַזֶּה, and סֵפֶר הַתּוֹרָה הַזֹּאת. In the first example, הַזֶּה modifies סֵפֶר הַתּוֹרָה; that is, *this Book which contains the Torah — Sefer* is masculine; and, in the second case הַזֹּאת modifies הַתּוֹרָה; that is, *the Book which contains this Torah* — Torah is feminine.

Thus when סֵפֶר הַתּוֹרָה is used, we cannot know whether it is to be rendered *the Sefer Torah*, which might point to a particular, specially significant Torah scroll, or whether the meaning is *the Book containing the Torah*, which would carry no special connotation. In our case it could be argued that this would seem to be the meaning of the *Kings'* phrase. This, because in *Chronicles* that is certainly the connotation of סֵפֶר תּוֹרַת־ה׳ בְּיַד־מֹשֶׁה.

In the second place, even if we translate *the Sefer Torah*, this still does not mean that a particular scroll is meant; witness *Deuteronomy* 29:20 which uses סֵפֶר הַתּוֹרָה הַזֶּה, but certainly does not refer to any particular scroll.

If we again turn to the *Chronicles'* phrase: סֵפֶר תּוֹרַת־ה׳ בְּיַד־מֹשֶׁה, this also need not imply that the scroll was the one written by Moses. We find, for example, *I Chronicles* 11:3 using כִּדְבַר ה׳ בְּיַד־שְׁמוּאֵל, describing an oral prophecy where the phrase בְּיַד שְׁמוּאֵל certainly does not indicate that it was written by hand. We find similar usages at *II Chronicles* 10:15, 29:25, 33:8 and 35:6.

Thus, we conclude that neither of the phrases proves persuasively that a particular *Sefer Torah* was meant.

Scribes, officers and gatekeepers came from among the Levites.
14 *As they brought out the money which had been donated to* HA-
SHEM'*s House, Chilkiahu the Kohen found the Book which records*
HASHEM'*s Torah at the hand of Moses.* 15 *Chilkiahu made a state-*
ment, telling Shaphan the scribe, 'I have found the Book of the
Torah in HASHEM'*s House.' Chilkiahu gave the Book to Shaphan.*
16 *Shafan brought the Book to the king. In addition, he reported*
back to the king saying, 'All that your servants were commis-
sioned to do, they are doing.' 17 *They have melted down the silver*
which was to be found in HASHEM'*s House, and they have given*
it to those that were appointed over them, and to the overseers. 18
Shaphan the scribe told the king, saying, 'Chilkiahu the Kohen
handed me a Book.' Then Shaphan read in it to the king. 19 *When*

15. וַיַּעַן חִלְקִיָּהוּ וַיֹּאמֶר ... — *Chilkiahu made a statement, telling ....* וַיַּעַן invariably connotes a festive declaration (cf. *I Chronicles* 12:18 and 29:31 above), and seems inappropriate here. Indeed, *Kings* does not have it.

We must conclude that this is part of *Chronicles'* hindsight. In retrospect, what appeared at the time to be no more than an ordinary conversation turned out to be a watershed event in Israel's history.

סֵפֶר הַתּוֹרָה — *A Book of the Torah*. There are two ways in which this phrase might be rendered (comm. v. 14). Our translation matches the expression of the previous verse, סֵפֶר תּוֹרַת ה׳ בְּיַד מֹשֶׁה.

וַיִּתֵּן חִלְקִיָּהוּ ... — *Chilkiahu gave ... Kings* records that Shaphan read the Book. In *Chronicles* this is not told. We assume that Shaphan glanced through the *Sefer Torah* to see whether something would strike him and convey to him a message that could be construed as פְּסוֹק לִי פְּסוּקָךְ [see Section II, *The Finding of the Sefer Torah*]. He found nothing — providence had the king, not him, in mind. The impact of the Book's message of doom was reserved for Yoshiahu.

This would tend to confirm the thesis presented in Section II, *Amon the Renegade - Yoshiahu the Man of Destiny*, to ch. 33. Yoshiahu, more than being his people's mentor for the present, was destined to guide them through the wilderness of exile. The significance of the message contained in the Torah was not for the here and now — and Shaphan who was a man of the present saw nothing significant. Yoshiahu, whose soul was larger than the immediate moment, caught the impact of the Torah's message.

16. וַיָּבֵא שָׁפָן ... — *Shaphan brought ...* Again, we have *Chronicles'* hindsight. Consciously, Shaphan only *came* to the king (*Kings*). Events showed that he was meant to *bring* the *Sefer Torah* to the king.

וַיָּשֶׁב עוֹד ... דָּבָר ... — *In addition, he reported back ...* This expression seems to put the report to the king about the conscientious performance of the work into a secondary position — a nuance understandably missing in *Kings* where we have וַיָּבֹא instead of וַיָּבֵא. The implication here is that, in addition to bringing the *Sefer Torah* — his main purpose in coming — he also gave a progress report concerning the work that was being done.

17. וַיַּתִּיכוּ אֶת־הַכֶּסֶף — *They have melted down the silver*. The silver was melted down in order to make coins which could then be spent (*Metzudos*).

18. סֵפֶר נָתַן לִי חִלְקִיָּהוּ הַכֹּהֵן — *Chilkiahu the Kohen handed me a Book*. No special issue is made of either the fact that a Book was found under unusual circumstances, or that it was in any way special.

וַיִּקְרָא־בוֹ שָׁפָן — *Then Shaphan read in it*. *Kings* has וַיִּקְרָאֵהוּ, *and [Shaphan] read it*. The *Kings'* version talks of reading the whole Book, the *Chronicles'* version of reading *in it*; that is, part of it.

The change seems to confirm the thesis suggested in Section II, *The Finding of the Sefer Torah*. We need not assume that the Book was rolled to any particular place. Shaphan, in fact, read much more than the relevant part. The king's attention was caught by the verses dealing with the exile. The *Kings'* account deals with the events as they happened; *Chronicles* is concerned with the significant parts of the events.

כ כִּשְׁמֹעַ הַמֶּלֶךְ אֵת דִּבְרֵי הַתּוֹרָה וַיִּקְרַע אֶת־בְּגָדָיו: וַיְצַו
הַמֶּלֶךְ אֶת־חִלְקִיָּהוּ וְאֶת־אֲחִיקָם בֶּן־שָׁפָן וְאֶת־עַבְדּוֹן
בֶּן־מִיכָה וְאֵת | שָׁפָן הַסּוֹפֵר וְאֵת עֲשָׂיָה עֶבֶד־הַמֶּלֶךְ
כא לֵאמֹר: לְכוּ דִרְשׁוּ אֶת־יְהוָה בַּעֲדִי וּבְעַד הַנִּשְׁאָר
בְּיִשְׂרָאֵל וּבִיהוּדָה עַל־דִּבְרֵי הַסֵּפֶר אֲשֶׁר נִמְצָא כִּי־
גְדוֹלָה חֲמַת־יְהוָה אֲשֶׁר נִתְּכָה בָנוּ עַל אֲשֶׁר לֹא־שָׁמְרוּ
אֲבוֹתֵינוּ אֶת־דְּבַר יְהוָה לַעֲשׂוֹת כְּכָל־הַכָּתוּב עַל־הַסֵּפֶר
כב הַזֶּה: וַיֵּלֶךְ חִלְקִיָּהוּ וַאֲשֶׁר הַמֶּלֶךְ אֶל־חֻלְדָּה
תָּקְהַת ק׳ הַנְּבִיאָה אֵשֶׁת | שַׁלֻּם בֶּן־תוקהת בֶּן־חַסְרָה שׁוֹמֵר
הַבְּגָדִים וְהִיא יוֹשֶׁבֶת בִּירוּשָׁלַםִ בַּמִּשְׁנֶה וַיְדַבְּרוּ אֵלֶיהָ

19. אֵת דִּבְרֵי הַתּוֹרָה — *... the words of the Torah. Deuteronomy* 28:36 predicts that the time would come when a king who was elevated to the kingship by the people, without Divine fiat, would be dragged into captivity. This is what Yoshiahu read in the *Sefer Torah*. He immediately assumed that it was he whose fate was being described. He had ascended to the kingship by the will of the people (*Mefaresh*).

וַיִּקְרַע אֶת־בְּגָדָיו — *He tore his clothes*. The tearing of clothes seems to have been a practice which expressed a variety of emotions: Thus, Reuven rends his garments out of chagrin at Joseph's disappearance from the pit (*Genesis* 37:29), while Jacob tears his as a sign of mourning (v. 34, there). Israel's king Yoram tore his clothes out of fear of the seemingly impossible demands which the Aramite king was making of him (*II Kings* 5:7); and Ezra rent his in shock at the degree of intermarriage which had taken place among the returners to Judah (*Ezra* 9:3).

We cannot know for certain what emotion caused Yoshiahu to rend his clothes. V. 27 implies that it was to symbolize a humbling of self before God. Perhaps, too, it was part of an act of penitence for the sins of omission and commission hinted at in v. 21.

20. עֶבֶד־הַמֶּלֶךְ — *The king's servant*. All the king's subjects can be described as his servants. Asaiah's title clearly derived from the fact that he was Yoshiahu's body servant. His inclusion in the delegation indicates that Yoshiahu, the man — not only the king — was intimately involved in the proceedings.

21. וּבְעַד הַנִּשְׁאָר בְּיִשְׂרָאֵל וּבִיהוּדָה — *Concerning the remnant of Israel and Judah*. The parallel verse in *Kings* has: וּבְעַד הָעָם וּבְעַד כָּל יְהוּדָה. *Israel* is not mentioned, and there is nothing about the concept of *remnant*.

This brings us to the issue of Yoshiahu's relationship to the northern territories — a matter in which there appears to be some difference between the *Kings'* and *Chronicles'* accounts.

At one point *Kings* does mention — albeit in a less detailed manner than *Chronicles* — that Yoshiahu had some interests in the northern territories. Thus, in his cleansing of the land he removed ... *all the houses of the bamos which were in the cities of Samaria* (*II Kings* 23:19). [Our v. 6 has a much more detailed description — see there.] However *Kings* does not have the evocative בְּכָל־אֶרֶץ יִשְׂרָאֵל of our v. 7, nor the מִכָּל־הָאֲרָצוֹת אֲשֶׁר לִבְנֵי יִשְׂרָאֵל of v. 33.

Again, at 35:18 in the description of the participants at the *Pesach* celebration, *Chronicles* lists יִשְׂרָאֵל separately from *Kohanim, Levites and all of Judah* — a reference not found in the *Kings'* description.

The reference to the *remnant* in our verse is also worthy of note. The simple meaning of the phrase has it apply both to *Israel* and to *Judah*. Why would the people of Judah be described as a *remnant* — none of their compatriots had been exiled?

Perhaps here, once again, we meet Yoshiahu as the מְשִׁיחַ ה׳. It is true that, at the time of his reign, Judah still existed as a separate political entity, but, with the dissolution of the Northern Kingdom by way of the Assyrian exile, the division of God's גּוֹי אֶחָד, *one people*, into two separate national units became meaningless. The division into two kingdoms had been an aberration in terms of Israel's Divine destiny and peoplehood, and in the terms of Yoshiahu's Messianic destiny, unfettered by the time-bound realities of the here and now, the people of Judah were no less a *remnant* than their brothers who lived in what was formerly the Northern Kingdom.

34
20-22

the king heard the words of the Torah, he tore his clothes. [20] *The king commanded Chilkiahu and Achikam the son of Shaphan and Avdon the son of Michah and Shaphan the scribe and Asiah the king's servant, saying.* [21] *'Go find out* HASHEM*'s intentions — implied in the matter of the Book which was discovered — concerning me and the remnant of Israel and Judah. For the wrath of* HASHEM *which has been poured out against us is great because our fathers did not keep the word of* HASHEM *in accordance with all that is written in this Book.'* [22] *Chilkiahu and those whom the king had sent went to Chuldah the prophetess, the wife of Shallum the son of Tokhath the son of Chasrah, keeper of wardrobe. She sat in Jerusalem, in the study-house. They spoke to her to that*

In the *Kings'* perspective, the fact that Yoshiahu's reforms touched also upon cities of the North is mentioned as part of the factual description of what transpired; no special issue is made of that fact. *Chronicles*, on the other hand, finds unbounded significance in the truth that Yoshiahu's activities centered equally on both Judah and the territories of the former Northern Kingdom, and gives appropriate play to this fact.

עַל אֲשֶׁר לֹא־שָׁמְרוּ אֲבוֹתֵינוּ אֶת־דְּבַר ה׳ — *Because our fathers did not keep the word of* HASHEM. The change from the *Kings'* version appears substantive. There the text reads: *Because our fathers did not listen to the words of this Book, to do in accordance with all that was written concerning us*. Thus *this Book* is central. It contains a message to which earlier generations did not listen. Here the Book is described only as a vehicle by the means of which *the word of* HASHEM is conveyed. [The change from שָׁמְעוּ to שָׁמְרוּ is readily understood in this context. The former is appropriate to the specific wording of the Book. The latter, to the ideas expressed in a Divine message which, in its essence, is not tied to a particular text.]

The change in wording can be readily explained on the basis of the differences which we remarked earlier. *Kings* gives a description of the actual events which occurred. In these, the Book is central. It was the text contained in the Book which was read. At the essential level with which *Chronicles* deals, God's message is not bound to the confines of the text in the Book: It is there; it is read; but is not really tied to it.

22. וַיֵּלֶךְ חִלְקִיָּהוּ וַאֲשֶׁר הַמֶּלֶךְ — *Chilkiahu and those whom the king had sent went ... Kings* lists the names of all the people who had been delegated, but still uses the singular וַיֵּלֶךְ, thereby evidently indicating that Chilkiahu was the really important messenger and that the others merely accompanied him. This could explain why *Chronicles* lists only him. Nevertheless, it is noteworthy that *Chronicles* thought fit to make this change, and, moreover, to further shorten the phrase by the conspicuous omission of the verb שָׁלַח, which leaves the phrase without any literal meaning. The verb must be supplied in order that the phrase convey anything.

Perhaps *Chronicles* is using a literary device to have us contrast the cavalier way in which it treats the delegation, to the detailed description — apparently without real significance — of Chuldah, her husband and the location at which she functioned. The royal delegation becomes insignificant when compared to the source of the Divine word in Israel.

We may surmise as follows: We shall note at v. 23, that Chuldah's prophecy seems to be directed to Yoshiahu at two levels: As *the man who sent you to me* (v. 23), and as *the king of Judah* (v. 26). We shall see that *the man* is the Yoshiahu who is unbounded by time and place, and who is to look beyond the immediate problems to the future of his people, while *the king of Judah* is the Yoshiahu of the present. By downplaying the royal delegation, certainly a function of the *king of Judah*, *Chronicles*, in accordance with its unique perspective, brings home to us that its main interest is the message which is addressed to Yoshiahu the man.

אֶל־חֻלְדָּה הַנְּבִיאָה — *To Chuldah the prophetess*. The Sages (*Megillah* 14b) teach that he sent to Chuldah rather than to Jeremiah because, as a woman, she might be more prone to mercy.

There appears to be an assumption that the personality of the prophet influences the content of the message — an assumption that appears strange if we picture a prophet as simply a conduit through whom God sends messages to His people. However, this is not necessarily the case.

כג כָּזֹאת: וַתֹּאמֶר לָהֶם כֹּה־אָמַר יהוה אֱלֹהֵי יִשְׂרָאֵל אִמְרוּ
לָאִישׁ אֲשֶׁר־שָׁלַח אֶתְכֶם אֵלָי:
כד כֹּה אָמַר יהוה הִנְנִי מֵבִיא רָעָה עַל־הַמָּקוֹם הַזֶּה וְעַל־
יוֹשְׁבָיו אֵת כָּל־הָאָלוֹת הַכְּתוּבוֹת עַל־הַסֵּפֶר אֲשֶׁר קָרְאוּ
כה לִפְנֵי מֶלֶךְ יְהוּדָה: תַּחַת | אֲשֶׁר עֲזָבוּנִי °ויקטירו לֵאלֹהִים

°וַיְקַטְּרוּ ק׳

It appears that in many instances only the general message, but not the specific words, is given by God to the prophet and it is left to him to interpret his vision, and to pass it on to the people. This concept is discussed at length in Wolf's *Neviei HaEmes*, ch. 7 sub-section 4 who, in turn, quotes *Maharil Diskin* and *Rav Eliezer Shach's Avi Ezri* to *Yesodei HaTorah* 7:6.

The main source for this assertion is *Rashi* to *Jeremiah* 23:33. There, we are told that the people occasionally asked Jeremiah, מַה־מַּשָּׂא ה׳, *What prophecy [lit. burden] is HASHEM sending you?* God expresses outrage at this question and predicts punishment and suffering for those who ask it. In v. 36 we are then taught that: כִּי הַמַּשָּׂא יִהְיֶה לְאִישׁ דְּבָרוֹ, *... for the prophecy is given to a man of His word*. *Rashi* offers a number of explanations for this cryptic passage. One of them, as follows: The people asked for the מַשָּׂא, the *exact words* which God had used in addressing the prophet. They believed that — inasmuch as a prophet is free to interpret the message he receives according to his own understanding — Jeremiah had given God's words a meaning which was much more stringent than had been intended. They felt that they would be able to detect different nuances which would imply that the destruction which Jeremiah was predicting would not come about. To this the answer came, that God entrusted His message only to such a man as could be relied upon to interpret God's words in precisely the way that He had intended.

Thus we have *Rashi* assuming that the prophet has a degree of leeway in interpreting the words told him by God. He does not [at least not in every case] have to pass them on verbatim.

Thus it is possible that Yoshiahu thought that Chuldah — as a woman — would read her prophecy in a more merciful way than Jeremiah would have done.

Another explanation offered there is that Yoshiahu sent to Chuldah rather than to Jeremiah because the latter had left the country at the time in order to bring back the exiles of the ten lost tribes.

The tradition that Yoshiahu brought back most or some of the ten lost tribes is discussed at length in ArtScroll *Ezekiel* 37:15-22 (p. 572).

Rashi to *Sanhedrin* 110b writes that not many returned at that time, but *Tiferes Yisrael* (there) demonstrates that probably most of them did return then.

Tosefos to *Gittin* 36a concludes from this tradition that during the period of the Second House there were representatives of all twelve tribes in Israel.

שׁוֹמֵר הַבְּגָדִים — *Keeper of the wardrobe*. The royal clothes (*Metzudos* and *Mefaresh*), or the Kohanite vestments (*Mefaresh*).

בַּמִּשְׁנֶה — *In the study-house*. With *Rashi* in *Kings*, we follow *Targum* in his rendering of מִשְׁנֶה [from, שנה, *to learn*].

Rashi also points out that according to *Midos* 1:3, there were two gates on the southern side of the Second Temple called the gates of Chuldah — presumably because that is where she functioned. מִשְׁנֶה might then have the meaning: *the double gate*.

Alternatively, *Metzudos* and *Rashi* suggest that the word may be rendered, *secondary*. Huldah sat between the main city wall and another outer wall. This area is *secondary* to the city.

23. אִמְרוּ לָאִישׁ אֲשֶׁר־שָׁלַח אֶתְכֶם אֵלָי — *Say to the man who sent you to me*. The phrase, strange even in itself, contrasts starkly with v. 26: *And to the king of Judah who sent you to search out HASHEM....* Is Chuldah addressing a *man* or a *king*?

The answer may lie in the theme which we worked out in Section II *Yoshiahu's Reign in the Eyes of Kings and Chronicles*. The Yoshiahu of *Kings* is the historical monarch whose benign rule took place within a given time frame and a particular historical reality. The Yoshiahu of *Chronicles* is the man of destiny; the scion of the Davidic line who is to revitalize Israel and to imbue it with the inner strength it would need for its trek through exile.

The former is the *king of Judah*, the latter is the *man* whose great soul elevates him beyond the confines of time and space, and makes him the man of destiny — the anointed of HASHEM.

Chuldah's message contained two elements: The inevitability of the destruction, and the fact that Yoshiahu himself would not experience it. The first was said to Yoshiahu the man — it was this information given to him which appraised him of his historical destiny. The temporary respite (vs. 26-28) is told to the *king of Judah*. It concerned the here and now, and was thus information required by a king in order to discharge the duties of his kingship adequately.

effect. [23] *She said to them: Thus says* HASHEM, *God of Israel: Say to the man who sent you to me.* [24] *Thus says* HASHEM: *I will bring evil upon this place and upon its inhabitants; all the curses that are written in the book which they read before the king of Judah.* [25] *Because they have forsaken Me, and offered up to other gods*

24. כֹּה אָמַר ה׳ — *Thus says* HASHEM . . . We assume that this does not mean that God sent this prophecy to Chuldah, but that this is her interpretation of that which Yoshiahu had read in the *Sefer Torah: Thus says* HASHEM [by having caused the book to be found, and having the relevant passages catch your eye].

We assume this to be the meaning of the verse because only then can we understand the king's energetic reaction to the prophecy. According to *Jeremiah* 25:3 Jeremiah had begun his prophetic activity in the thirteenth year of Yoshiahu's reign and from that time had called upon the people of Judah to repent on their evil ways as the only hope of averting the impending tragedy of the destruction. Thus, at least for five years (v. 8) Yoshiahu must have heard essentially the same message which Chuldah now told him. Why then was this prophecy special?

The answer must be that the fact that it was not simply an oral prophecy but was based on the finding of the Book gave it a special solemnity.

We understand this in terms of *Ramban's* teaching (*Genesis* 12:6) that there is a fundamental difference between a prophecy that is limited to an oral announcement by the prophet and one that is accompanied by a symbolic act which gives expression to the prophecy in tangible form. The former need not necessarily come about; changed circumstances can bring a change in what is to be. The latter, however, once made tangible by the symbolic act becomes irreversible.

Perhaps, then, the finding of the book with its implied message of doom created a degree of certainty concerning the destruction which was missing in Jeremiah's purely oral prophecies.

We use the expression, *degree of certainty*, advisedly. Even given the significance of the finding of the book, the decree was certainly still reversible through sincere penitence.

This can be seen not only from Yoshiahu's reactions as described in both the *Kings* and our accounts, but it is expressly stated in a number of Jeremiah's prophecies, some of which were said as late as Zedekiah's reign. See *Jeremiah* 25:1 ff; 36:1-7; 22:3-4.

See also *Seder Olam Rabba* end of ch. 24 where we learn that the Divine decree that Israel was to be exiled from its land was signed [that is, finalized] in the fourth year of Yehoyakim's reign.

כָּל־הָאָלוֹת — *All the curses* .... *Kings* has, אֵת כָּל דִּבְרֵי הַסֵּפֶר. The two books are consistent with their treatment in v.18 — see above. In *Kings* the whole book is read — hence, כָּל דִּבְרֵי הַסֵּפֶר; in *Chronicles* only the relevant parts are dealt with — hence, אֵת כָּל־הָאָלוֹת.

אֲשֶׁר קָרְאוּ לִפְנֵי מֶלֶךְ יְהוּדָה — . . . *Which they read before the king of Judah*. *Kings* has, אֲשֶׁר קָרָא מֶלֶךְ יְהוּדָה, *Which the king of Judah read*. *Radak* points out that Yoshiahu did not read the book himself (*II Kings*, 22:10) and that, thus, the *Chronicles'* version is, as it were, an explanation of the more ambiguous *Kings* phrasing. He further brings the teaching of the Sages (*Succah* 38b), based on the *Kings* wording, that שׁוֹמֵעַ כְּעוֹנֶה, one who hears a given passage is considered, halachically, as having articulated that which he has heard.

לִפְנֵי מֶלֶךְ יְהוּדָה — *Before the king of Judah*. The contrast to the אִישׁ of v. 23 is striking. It seems to confirm the thesis which we suggested above: The reading was done before the king; Shaphan knew Yoshiahu only in that capacity. Chuldah addressed the message to the transcendent *man* who towered above the time-bound kingship.

25. תַּחַת אֲשֶׁר עֲזָבוּנִי וַיְקַטְּרוּ . . . — *Because they have forsaken Me, and offered up* . . . What idol worship is meant here? We saw in Section II *Yoshiahu's Reign in the Eyes of Kings and Chronicles* that, according to both accounts, Yoshiahu had begun to cleanse Judah of all vestiges of idolatry, long before the *Sefer Torah* was found. Why, then, should Chuldah castigate Israel for idol worship which was even then being eradicated?

In fact, unbeknown to Yoshiahu, idol worship was still rampant in the land.

Taanis 22b teaches that Yoshiahu had misread his own people. *Eichah Rabbah* (*Bober*) 1:18 describes their deviousness: What did the scoffers of that generation do? They drew the images of their idols on two panels of a swinging door, so that when the door was open, only half the picture could be seen. The inspectors whom Yoshiahu delegated to check that there were no idols in any of the homes were handily deceived. They never saw the whole idol. It was only after they had left, and the doors had closed behind them, that the idol

אֲחֵרִים לְמַעַן הַכְעִיסֵנִי בְּכֹל מַעֲשֵׂי יְדֵיהֶם וְתִתַּךְ חֲמָתִי
כו בַּמָּקוֹם הַזֶּה וְלֹא תִכְבֶּה׃ וְאֶל־מֶלֶךְ יְהוּדָה הַשֹּׁלֵחַ אֶתְכֶם
לִדְרוֹשׁ בַּיהוָה כֹּה תֹאמְרוּ אֵלָיו כֹּה־אָמַר יהוה
כז אֱלֹהֵי יִשְׂרָאֵל הַדְּבָרִים אֲשֶׁר שָׁמָעְתָּ׃ יַעַן רַךְ־לְבָבְךָ
וַתִּכָּנַע ׀ מִלִּפְנֵי אֱלֹהִים בְּשָׁמְעֲךָ אֶת־דְּבָרָיו עַל־הַמָּקוֹם
הַזֶּה וְעַל־יֹשְׁבָיו וַתִּכָּנַע לְפָנַי וַתִּקְרַע אֶת־בְּגָדֶיךָ וַתֵּבְךְּ
כח לְפָנָי וְגַם־אֲנִי שָׁמַעְתִּי נְאֻם־יְהוָה׃ הִנְנִי אֹסִפְךָ אֶל־אֲבֹתֶיךָ
וְנֶאֱסַפְתָּ אֶל־קִבְרוֹתֶיךָ בְּשָׁלוֹם וְלֹא־תִרְאֶינָה עֵינֶיךָ בְּכֹל
הָרָעָה אֲשֶׁר אֲנִי מֵבִיא עַל־הַמָּקוֹם הַזֶּה וְעַל־יֹשְׁבָיו
כט וַיָּשִׁיבוּ אֶת־הַמֶּלֶךְ דָּבָר׃ וַיִּשְׁלַח הַמֶּלֶךְ וַיֶּאֱסֹף
ל אֶת־כָּל־זִקְנֵי יְהוּדָה וִירוּשָׁלִָם׃ וַיַּעַל הַמֶּלֶךְ בֵּית־יְהוָה
וְכָל־אִישׁ יְהוּדָה וְיֹשְׁבֵי יְרוּשָׁלִַם וְהַכֹּהֲנִים וְהַלְוִיִּם
וְכָל־הָעָם מִגָּדוֹל וְעַד־קָטָן וַיִּקְרָא בְאָזְנֵיהֶם אֶת־כָּל־דִּבְרֵי
לא סֵפֶר הַבְּרִית הַנִּמְצָא בֵּית יְהוָה׃ וַיַּעֲמֹד הַמֶּלֶךְ עַל־עָמְדוֹ
וַיִּכְרֹת אֶת־הַבְּרִית לִפְנֵי יְהוָה לָלֶכֶת אַחֲרֵי יְהוָה וְלִשְׁמוֹר

was once more visible.

Menasheh and Amon had apparently done their work too well. Even the great Yoshiahu's reforming zeal could not wean the people away from the thought-mode and practices of half a century.

וְתִתַּךְ חֲמָתִי ... וְלֹא תִכְבֶּה — *My anger is poured out ... and it shall not be extinguished*. *Kings* has ... וְנִצְּתָה חֲמָתִי. In this, the two books are consistent with their respective usages in v.21 where *Chronicles* has חֲמַת־ה׳ אֲשֶׁר נִתְּכָה בָנוּ, in place of אֲשֶׁר הִיא נִצְּתָה בָנוּ of *Kings*.

In this connection we note that the *Chronicles'* usage of נתך = anger is much more within the linguistic tradition than the *Kings'* version of נצת = anger. The *Chronicles'* usage occurs frequently in Scripture (cf. *Jeremiah* 42:18, 44:6 among many); the *Kings* usage is unique to Yoshiahu's and Chuldah's respective speeches.

נצת shares the connotation of *burning* (*Jeremiah* 17:27 among many); and *desolation* (*Jeremiah* 9:11 among many) (see *Radak*, *Shorashim*). The relationship would seem to be that flames leave desolation in their wake. נתך which essentially means, *to pour out*, describes the movement of the fire rather than its destructive force.

In this sense, נצת seems to be the stronger term and we can understand why *Chronicles* seeks to mitigate the implication. From the *Kings'* perspective, which reports the story as it happened, it would make sense to make the warning as strong as possible. Total destruction is threatened. *Chronicles*, written with the returnees from the Babylonian exile in mind, would have wanted to establish a sense of kinship to the Jerusalem of the past. It had not been totally destroyed.

Whether this suggestion has validity or there was another reason, *Chronicles* must have had a potent reason for changing to נתך. The ending of the verse, וְלֹא תִכְבֶּה, seems inappropriate for נתך which is never used to describe the burning of fire as is נצת. By substituting נתך, *Chronicles* left the sentence with a lack of inner logic.

26. וְאֶל־מֶלֶךְ יְהוּדָה ... — *As for the king of Judah* ... See comm. to v. 23.

27. עַל הַמָּקוֹם הַזֶּה וְעַל־יֹשְׁבָיו — *Concerning this place and its inhabitants*. *Kings* adds, לִהְיוֹת לְשַׁמָּה וְלִקְלָלָה, *that it become desolation and curse*. That *Chronicles* omits this phrase may bear out the thesis suggested above — there is a wish to mitigate the full implications of the threat.

וַתִּקְרַע אֶת־בְּגָדֶיךָ — *Rent your garments*. See comm. to v. 19.

וְגַם ... — *Also* ... The term may imply reciprocity. Just as you summoned great effort to make your penitence meaningful so too will I do more than would normally be expected.

28. אֶל קִבְרוֹתֶיךָ — *Your sepulcher*. Your father's graves (*Radak*). *Radak* is evidently troubled by the plural form. To avoid this problem we have rendered, *sepulcher*. These were normally built to accommodate several graves.

בְּשָׁלוֹם וְלֹא־תִרְאֶינָה עֵינֶיךָ ... — ... *In peace. Your eyes will not see* ... Yoshiahu died a vio-

that they might provoke Me with all their actions. Therefore My
anger is poured out upon this place and it shall not be
extinguished. 26 *As for the king of Judah who sent you to inquire*
from HASHEM, *thus shall you say to him: 'Thus says* HASHEM *the*
God of Israel: Concerning the words that you have heard.
27 *'Because your heart was receptive and, when you heard His*
words concerning this place and its inhabitants, you humbled
yourself before God. Moreover you felt crushed before Me,
rent your garments and wept before Me. I also have heard.'
says HASHEM. 28 *'Behold, I will bring you together with your*
fathers and you shall be gathered to your sepulcher in peace. Your
eyes will not see all the evil which I shall bring upon this place
and its inhabitants.' Then, they brought back word to the king. 29
The king sent out to convene all the elders of Judah and
Jerusalem. 30 *The king, together with all the men of Judah, the*
inhabitants of Jerusalem, the Kohanim, the Levites and all the
people, great and small, went up to HASHEM*'s House. He read to*
them the entire contents of the Book of the Covenant which had
been found in HASHEM*'s House.* 31 *The king stood in his place and*
concluded the covenant before HASHEM, *to follow* HASHEM, *to keep*

lent death in battle. *Peace* refers to the fact that he did not have to witness the destruction of land and people. (*Mefaresh, Radak, Metzudos*)

וַיָּשִׁיבוּ אֶת־הַמֶּלֶךְ דָּבָר — *Then, they brought back word to the king.* The messengers whom the king had sent (v. 20) reported Chuldah's prophecy to him.

29. וַיִּשְׁלַח הַמֶּלֶךְ וַיֶּאֱסֹף — *The king sent out to convene ...*. *Kings* has **וַיִּשְׁלַח הַמֶּלֶךְ וַיַּאַסְפוּ אֵלָיו**. The people seem to come of their own volition, while here, it is the king who brings them. Perhaps the change reflects the insight which we saw in comm. to v. 25 — the people of Yoshiahu's generation were only outwardly penitent. In secret they retained their attachment to idolatry. Thus they appeared to come voluntarily and enthusiastically to take part in the making of the covenant (*Kings*), but in reality it was imposed upon them from above (*Chronicles*).

30. וַיַּעַל ... בֵּית ה' — *...went up to* HASHEM*'s* House. The covenant is to be made *in the presence of* HASHEM (v. 31). This can be done best in the House.

31. וַיַּעֲמֹד הַמֶּלֶךְ עַל־עָמְדוֹ — *The king stood in his place.* A special location set aside for the king's use. [**עָמְדוֹ** from **עמד**, *to stand*]. *Kings* has **עַל הָעַמּוּד**, *by the pillar.*

וַיִּכְרֹת אֶת־הַבְּרִית לִפְנֵי ה' — *And concluded the covenant before* HASHEM. A covenant is normally made between two contracting parties. This is usually made clear by talking of a **בְּרִית** ... **עִם**, or a ... **בְּרִית בֵּין ... וּבֵין**.

Here, there is no indication who the contracting parties might be.

The options are: 1. Yoshiahu with God. 2. Yoshiahu and the people with God. 3. Yoshiahu with the people.

1. The next phrase, ... with all *his* heart and with all *his* soul, might argue for the exclusion of the people from the covenant. Only Yoshiahu seems to be bound. However, see below, that *Kings* does not have the modifying *his*, in these phrases.

2. The statement in the next verse *the inhabitants of Jerusalem acted in accordance with the covenant ...*, seems to indicate that the people were included in the covenant. But this need not be so. We recall that the previous verse had described the Torah as the *Book of the Covenant*, and the end of our verse, too, speaks of, *the requirements of the covenant that were written in this book*. Thus, when we learn that the people of Jerusalem acted in accordance with the *covenant*, there is no indication whether this is the one that Yoshiahu now concluded, perhaps in their behalf, or whether it is simply another way of saying that they abided by the laws of the Torah.

3. There is no hint that God undertook, as it were, any obligation under this covenant. This might argue for the assumption that the contracting parties were king and people.

For a discussion of the idea of, **בְּרִית**, see at 23:3,

לד
לב-לג

אֶת־מִצְוֹתָיו וְעֵדְוֹתָיו וְחֻקָּיו בְּכָל־לְבָבוֹ וּבְכָל־נַפְשׁוֹ
לַעֲשׂוֹת אֶת־דִּבְרֵי הַבְּרִית הַכְּתוּבִים עַל־הַסֵּפֶר הַזֶּה:
לב וַיַּעֲמֵד אֵת כָּל־הַנִּמְצָא בִירוּשָׁלַםִ וּבִנְיָמִן וַיַּעֲשׂוּ יֹשְׁבֵי
לג יְרוּשָׁלַםִ כִּבְרִית אֱלֹהִים אֱלֹהֵי אֲבוֹתֵיהֶם: וַיָּסַר יֹאשִׁיָּהוּ
אֶת־כָּל־הַתֹּעֵבוֹת מִכָּל־הָאֲרָצוֹת אֲשֶׁר לִבְנֵי יִשְׂרָאֵל
וַיַּעֲבֵד אֵת כָּל־הַנִּמְצָא בְּיִשְׂרָאֵל לַעֲבוֹד אֶת־יְהֹוָה
אֱלֹהֵיהֶם כָּל־יָמָיו לֹא סָרוּ מֵאַחֲרֵי יְהֹוָה אֱלֹהֵי
א אֲבוֹתֵיהֶם: וַיַּעַשׂ יֹאשִׁיָּהוּ בִירוּשָׁלַםִ פֶּסַח
לַיהֹוָה וַיִּשְׁחֲטוּ הַפֶּסַח בְּאַרְבָּעָה עָשָׂר לַחֹדֶשׁ הָרִאשׁוֹן:

לה
א

and see also v.16, there.

בְּכָל־לְבָבוֹ וּבְכָל־נַפְשׁוֹ — *With all his heart and with all his soul. His* heart and *his* soul. Apparently it is Yoshiahu, and not the people, who is party to the covenant. *Kings* has בְּכָל לֵב וּבְכָל נֶפֶשׁ, which, at least, leaves room for the possibility that the people, also, were involved.

Perhaps, the change in wording reflects the same truth which we saw above in comm. to v.29, and will see again in v.32, below. Formally, the people, together with Yoshiahu, were parties to the covenant. But, with the hindsight of history, *Chronicles* recognizes the bitter truth that there was no real inner change in them. The idols, painted upon the folding doors, were a sad reality. The people's commitment was a sham.

דִּבְרֵי הַבְּרִית — *The requirements of the covenant* .... דִּבְרֵי הַבְּרִית is a combination, used frequently throughout Scripture. In the Torah it is used specifically to describe the Ten Commandments (*Exodus* 34:28), and the covenant at Arvos Moab (*Deuteronomy* 29:8). This latter is the *Tochachah* which, according to the commentators, had attracted the attention of the king when the *Sefer Torah* was found.

32. וַיַּעֲמֵד — *He impressed ... [into the covenant]. Kings* has וַיַּעֲמוֹד כָּל הָעָם בַּבְּרִית, in the active, rather than the causative voice. *Targum*, there, renders, *The people accepted* .... In support of *Targum's* rendering, *Radak* adduces, הֲיַעֲמֹד לִבֵּךְ, *Can your courage endure Ezekiel* (22:14) where עמד conveys the idea of something *strong, firm* and *enduring*. Hence, a serious and committed acceptance.

Chronicles does not have the people accepting the covenant of their own volition, but has the king *impressing* them into its demands.

With the wisdom of hindsight, *Chronicles* apparently saw that the people's commitment had not been real. In the secret recesses of their hearts they could not tear themselves loose from the fatal attraction of their idolatrous habits. See comm. to 29 and 31.

וּבִנְיָמִן — ... *And Benjamin*. The phrase is obscure. *Benjamin*, presumably the tribal territory, should be bracketed with *Judah*, not with *Jerusalem*. Moreover, since it is clear from v.6 that Yoshiahu's influence extended into huge areas of the Northern Kingdom, we would have expected that the people who lived in all those territories, not only those from Benjamin, would also have been included in Yoshiahu's efforts in behalf of the covenant.

וַיַּעֲשׂוּ יֹשְׁבֵי יְרוּשָׁלַםִ ... — *So that the inhabitants of Jerusalem acted in accordance* ... Once more, we have an impression of only limited success: Yoshiahu had involved many different groups in the covenant, but only the *inhabitants of Jerusalem* complied with its provisions.

כִּבְרִית אֱלֹהִים — *In accordance with the covenant of God* .... The Torah (*Metzudos*).

33. וַיָּסַר יֹאשִׁיָּהוּ — *Yoshiahu removed* ... The cleansing of the land from the vestiges of idol worship was already described in vs. 3-7. See Section II *Yoshiahu's Reign in the Eyes of Kings and Chronicles* for an analysis of the sequence of events.

וַיַּעֲבֵד ... — *Thus impressing* ... The *hiphil* of עבד, *to work*, carries the connotation of force [cf. *Exodus* 1:13]. We once more have the indication that the people were not really willing to shoulder their obligations under the covenant.

The sense of the phrase is that, in the absence of all the cultic objects which Yoshiahu had removed, the people were forced to serve God. Had they still been available, the

34
32-33 *His commandments, His testimonial laws and His statutes, with all his heart and with all his soul, to act in accordance with the requirements of the covenant that were written in this book.* [32] *He impressed all those who were present in Jerusalem and Benjamin [into the covenant], so that the inhabitants of Jerusalem acted in accordance with the covenant of God, the God of their fathers.* [33] *Yoshiahu removed all the abominations from the entire land-mass that belonged to the Children of Israel, thus impressing all who were in Israel to serve HASHEM their God. All his days they did not turn away from behind HASHEM, the God of their fathers.*

35
1 *Yoshiahu celebrated a Pesach dedicated to HASHEM in Jerusalem: They slaughtered the Pesach [lamb] on the fourteenth*

people might well have made use of them.

כָּל־הַנִּמְצָא בְּיִשְׂרָאֵל — *All who were in Israel.* There seems to be a clear contrast to כָּל־הַנִּמְצָא בִּירוּשָׁלַם וּבִנְיָמִן of the previous verse. Yoshiahu impressed into the service of God, even those people who had not willingly shouldered the covenant.

XXXV

1. וַיַּעַשׂ יֹאשִׁיָּהוּ בִּירוּשָׁלַם פֶּסַח לַה׳ — *Yoshiahu celebrated a Pesach dedicated to HASHEM in Jerusalem.* The contrast to the *Kings'* version is sharp: There the text reads (23:21): *The king commanded all the people, saying: 'Celebrate a Pesach dedicated to HASHEM, your God, as is written in this book of the covenant'.*

In *Chronicles* the king is central. It is *he* who celebrates the *Pesach,* while in *Kings* he tells the people to do so. Moreover, missing in *Chronicles* is the *Kings'* phrase: *... as is written in this book of the covenant,* which traces the king's initiative to the fact that the Torah, which had just been found, commands us to bring the *Pesach.*

In addition, it may be significant that *Chronicles* mentions Jerusalem while *Kings* does not.

The explanation may lie with the thesis concerning Yoshiahu's *Pesach* which we suggested in Section II to ch. 34, *Yoshiahu's Reign in the Eyes of Kings and Chronicles.* The significance of Yoshiahu's *Pesach* went beyond the fulfillment of one of the Torah's commands. It represented the readying of the people for a new mode of Divine service — one which would not require the Holy House and which could accompany them through the dark years of exile which lay ahead. We saw there that this theme is central to the *Chronicles'* account, but plays no role in the *Kings'* version.

Accordingly we may suggest as follows:

In *Kings,* the celebration of the *Pesach* is portrayed as simply the fulfillment of one of the Torah's commands. Hence the phrase that it was done in accordance with that which was written in the *Sefer Torah*; note also, the fact that the stress is on the people. It was they who were to bring the *Pesach* offerings. From the standpoint of the halachah, the king has no standing as far as the celebration of the *Pesach* is concerned. There is no particular reason why the fact that the celebration took place in Jerusalem should be underscored. It is self-understood that the *Pesach* was brought in Jerusalem.

In the *Chronicles'* standpoint Yoshiahu sees this *Pesach* celebration as an opportunity to set the people upon the path that he had been destined to lead them. He is the initiator, and in his hands it becomes an educational tool. The fact that it is a fulfillment of the Torah's command recedes into the background against the significance for the future. There is a special poignancy that this celebration took place in Jerusalem — it was, after all, to lend them spiritual strength for the trek through exile when Jerusalem would only be a sweet memory.

בְּאַרְבָּעָה עָשָׂר לַחֹדֶשׁ הָרִאשׁוֹן — *On the fourteenth day of the first month.* The day upon which the Torah specifies that the *Pesach* is to

לה ב וַיַּעֲמֵד הַכֹּהֲנִים עַל־מִשְׁמְרוֹתָם וַיְחַזְּקֵם לַעֲבוֹדַת בֵּית
ב־ד °הַמְּבִינִים ק׳ ג יְהוָה: וַיֹּאמֶר לַלְוִיִּם °המבונים לְכָל־יִשְׂרָאֵל הַקְּדוֹשִׁים
לַיהוָה תְּנוּ אֶת־אֲרוֹן־הַקֹּדֶשׁ בַּבַּיִת אֲשֶׁר בָּנָה שְׁלֹמֹה
בֶן־דָּוִיד מֶלֶךְ יִשְׂרָאֵל אֵין־לָכֶם מַשָּׂא בַּכָּתֵף עַתָּה עִבְדוּ
°וְהָכִינוּ ק׳ ד אֶת־יְהוָה אֱלֹהֵיכֶם וְאֵת עַמּוֹ יִשְׂרָאֵל: °והכונו לְבֵית־

be brought. See *Exodus* 12:6 and *Leviticus* 23:5.

2. וַיַּעֲמֵד הַכֹּהֲנִים עַל־מִשְׁמְרוֹתָם — *He organized the Kohanim into their mishmaros.* The system whereby only specific *mishmaros* served at any *given* time was waived during the *Yom Tov* celebrations (*Rambam, Klei HaMikdash* 4:4). Clearly, the organization described in this verse is not to be understood as being a part of the *Pesach* celebration.

We understand this verse to be parenthetical. V. 1 tells that Yoshiahu celebrated the *Pesach*: V. 2 then says that prior to this he had firmed up the organizational arrangements of the House service. In addition, he had made appropriate dispositions for the Ark (v. 3). Only at v. 4 is the story of the *Pesach* picked up once more from v. 1.

וַיְחַזְּקֵם לַעֲבוֹדַת בֵּית ה׳ — *Imbuing them with enthusiasm for the service of* HASHEM*'s House.* See comm. above. The connotation is of a general invigorating of the House functionaries, rather than for the specific purpose of bringing the *Pesach* offering.

3. וַיֹּאמֶר לַלְוִיִּם — *He said to the Levites ... Metzudos* thinks that these are *Kohanim* and are called Levites only in the sense that they were descended from the tribe of Levi. See comm. to *I Chronicles* 15:2.

הַמְּבִינִים לְכָל־יִשְׂרָאֵל — *Educators for all Israel.* Only the most worthy among the Levites — those who were the teachers of the people and were looked up to by them, whose actions would therefore be beyond question — were deemed suitable to be involved in the momentous decision to remove the Ark from the Holy of Holies (*Mikra U'Massores*).

תְּנוּ אֶת־אֲרוֹן הַקֹּדֶשׁ בַּבַּיִת — *Place the Holy Ark in the vault ...* Commentators note that the verse could be understood on the assumption that during Menasheh's or Amon's reign, the Ark was removed from its place in the Holy of Holies, and that Yoshiahu was now having it replaced there. However, *Radak* wonders why he would have waited so long to do so. Surely this is something that could have been done much earlier in the reign.

The tradition of the Sages (*Yoma* 52b and elsewhere) is that Yoshiahu was here ordering that the Ark be removed from the Holy of Holies and hidden in a subterranean chamber which Solomon had built in anticipation that one day it might be necessary to save the Ark from an impending destruction.

According to the interpretation of the Sages the text is problematic. Why, if the Ark is being removed from the Holy of Holies in order to be hidden, should the words imply that it was being taken *to* the House which Solomon had built?

Perhaps we are to understand the verse as follows: The Sages teach that Nebuchadnezzar could never have burned down the House if it had not yet had its inner sanctity eroded by Israel's sins. By the time of the conquest only an outer shell remained: Nothing was left of the initial glory of Solomon's House (*Shir HaShirim Rabbah* 3:3).

If we postulate that this inner erosion began in Menasheh's reign, continued during that of Amon, and remained unchanged in spite of Yoshiahu's effort, and that it was for that reason that Chuldah was able to predict that land and people were doomed, then it is possible that the interpretation of the Sages is, indeed, the simple meaning of the verse. The House itself was no longer *the House which Solomon had built*, and in its essential nature had long since disappeared. Only subterranean chambers of which no one knew and which had consequently not been defiled could truly be called by that name.

Given this explanation we are perhaps in a position to understand the perplexing spelling המבונים in this verse. It is a case of *k'ri/k'siv* — the word is read הַמְּבִינִים, but written הַמְּבוּנִים. What does הַמְּבוּנִים mean? The word does not recur in Scripture. In later Talmudic Hebrew we do find the word formed from בנה, *to build*, meaning *to be built up* or *established*, but this would have little meaning in our context. If the word would be a highly irregular form derived from בון, *to understand*, it would seem to connote *those imbued with understanding* — the passive form of the *k'ri* which means *to pass on understanding to others*.

The removal and secreting of the Ark was no small matter. The Ark had been the seat of the

day of the first month. 2 *He organized the Kohanim into their*
mishmaros, imbuing them with enthusiasm for the service of
HASHEM's House. 3 *He said to the Levites — educators for*
all Israel, hallowed to HASHEM, 'Place the holy Ark in the
vault which Solomon, son of David king of Israel built. No
longer will you carry upon your shoulders. Now, serve
HASHEM, your God, and His people Israel. 4 *'Now group your*

Divine Presence in Israel, it had made the Sinaitic revelation a tangible presence among the people (see *Ramban*, introduction to *Terumah*), and had served as the focus for all their prayers — see comm. to 6:32-33 and also to v. 11 there. Its removal meant that a precious link between God and His people was to be broken and the הֶסְתֵּר פָּנִים, *the hiding of God's face*, which in our thinking is the most tragic aspect of the *galuth* experience, was about to begin.

This awesome undertaking was to be entrusted only to such *Kohanim* [Levites] who were imbued with a special kind of understanding — who realized that the glorious edifice that towered above them in the House Mount was really nothing more than an empty shell, and that the true House of Solomon was now in the subterranean chambers which have not and would not be defiled.

אֵין־לָכֶם מַשָּׂא בַּכָּתֵף — *No longer will you carry upon your shoulders*. Once you have carried the Ark upon your shoulders to its place of hiding, you will no longer have any duties of carrying the Ark: Thus you will be free to serve Israel in different ways (*Metzudos*).

This is essentially the approach of all the classical commentators: The task of bearing the Ark upon your shoulders is past; turn now to your different duties.

But it is difficult to see why this point should be made. There had been no occasion for four hundred years — since the building of the House — for the Ark or any other of the holy vessels to be carried on the shoulder.

Mikra U'Massores thinks that this phrase was an instruction for carrying the Ark on the way to its hiding place. He deduces from *Chullin* 24a that once the House had been built, even if for some contingency it became necessary to carry the Ark, the Torah command that the Ark had to be transported *on the shoulders* (*Numbers* 7:9) did not apply. Thus, *place the Ark in the vault ... but do not carry it there on your shoulders*.

But why would Scripture want to record such a time-bound instruction? Even if we postulate that after centuries of disuse it was not commonly known, it is nevertheless a technicality which seems to have no place in the narrative.

The following explanation seems possible: The significance of Yoshiahu's *Pesach* — as, in our perception, *Chronicles* sees it — was that it came to prepare the people for a new phase of their relationship to God. A bitter exile stretched before them and they needed to be prepared for fundamental changes. The removal of the Ark became a highly significant part of their education. They would have to learn to survive spiritually without it. Our phrase may mean as follows: There was a time when Israel wandered through a desert and you, the Levites, accompanied them, proudly bearing the Ark — symbol of G- d's presence among them — on your shoulders. Israel is about to embark once more upon a trek throughout the desert — one infinitely more terrible and frightening then the other — the *wilderness of the nations* (*Ezekiel* 20:35; and see ArtScroll edition there). But in this wilderness you will not accompany them with the Ark upon your shoulders. It will remain, hidden in its vault, until the ultimate redemption.

עַתָּה עִבְדוּ אֶת־ה׳ ... וְאֵת ... יִשְׂרָאֵל — *Now, serve HASHEM ... and ... Israel*. Serve God with music [שִׁיר] and his people Israel by slaughtering and skinning their *Pesach* offerings (*Mefaresh*).

In the context of our interpretation of the previous phrase we could suggest: Now that the Ark has been secreted and the new phase in the relationship between God and Israel has begun, shoulder the responsibilities which this changed situation places upon you as teachers of the people [הַמְּבִינִים לְכָל יִשְׂרָאֵל]. Put yourself at the service of both God and Israel by instructing the people in their new role.

4-5. We shall interpret these two difficult verses in accordance with *Mikra U'Massores*:

We have already noted in comm. to v. 2 that the division of *Kohanim* into *mishmaros* was waived on *Yom Tov*. Any *Kohen* who wished was allowed to take part in the sacrificial service. However, this was true only of the priestly *mishmaros*. The Levite *mishmaros* and the Israelite *maamodos* were unchanged on *Yom Tov*.

As we saw in v. 2, it was Yoshiahu's wish to

אֲבֹתֵיכֶם כְּמַחְלְקוֹתֵיכֶם בִּכְתָב דָּוִיד מֶלֶךְ יִשְׂרָאֵל
ה וּבְמִכְתַּב שְׁלֹמֹה בְנוֹ: וְעִמְדוּ בַקֹּדֶשׁ לִפְלֻגּוֹת בֵּית הָאָבוֹת
ו לַאֲחֵיכֶם בְּנֵי הָעָם וַחֲלֻקַּת בֵּית־אָב לַלְוִיִּם: וְשַׁחֲטוּ הַפָּסַח
וְהִתְקַדְּשׁוּ וְהָכִינוּ לַאֲחֵיכֶם לַעֲשׂוֹת כִּדְבַר־יהוה בְּיַד־
ז מֹשֶׁה: וַיָּרֶם יֹאשִׁיָּהוּ לִבְנֵי הָעָם צֹאן כְּבָשִׂים וּבְנֵי־

strengthen the institution of the priestly *mishmaros*. In order to accomplish this, he made arrangements for all priestly *mishmaros*, although functioning equally, to group together and position themselves in the courtyard in such a way that the particular *mishmar* which, in the normal course of events, would be on duty now, would be close to the current Levite *mishmar* and Israelite *maamad* so that its identity would be obvious to all.

These arrangements are the subject of our two verses.

4. וְהָכִינוּ לְבֵית־אֲבֹתֵיכֶם כְּמַחְלְקוֹתֵיכֶם — *Now group your family units in your divisions. Metzudos* renders as though the phrase read: . . . וְהָכִינוּ עַצְמְכֶם.

We assume that the *Kohanim* are being addressed — see *Metzudos'* interpretation of לְוִיִּם in v. 3 — and that, as *Mikra U'Massores* explains, these are being told that, while the *Pesach* was being brought, they should group themselves according to their *mishmaros* although these had no formal halachic standing on this *Yom Tov* day.

בִּכְתָב דָּוִיד מֶלֶךְ יִשְׂרָאֵל וּבְמִכְתַּב שְׁלֹמֹה בְנוֹ — *This, in accordance with David king of Israel's written instructions and the written proclamation of his son, Solomon . . . Mikra U'Massores* surmises that David's *written instructions* is referring to the *Megillas Binyan Bais HaMikdash* alluded to at *I Chronicles* 28:19. This written directive also dealt with dispositions for the establishment of the *mishmaros* (v. 13 there).

He further assumes that Solomon would have issued detailed proclamations concerning these divisions once the House had been finally built, and what had till then been theory was put into practice. He thinks that מִכְתַּב is a *written proclamation* as, perhaps, in *Isaiah* 38:5, our 21:12 and *Ezra* 1:1.

5. בַקֹּדֶשׁ . . . — *Within the hallowed precincts* . . . The House courtyard (*Metzudos*) where the *Pesach* sacrifices were brought.

לִפְלֻגּוֹת בֵּית הָאָבוֹת לַאֲחֵיכֶם בְּנֵי הָעָם — *Near your brothers, the people's, family divisions. Metzudos* interprets the phrase to mean that each Israelite family unit [בֵּית אָב] was to group itself together for the purpose of bringing the *Pesach*. If so, these *family divisions* are not the Israelite *maamodos*. Of these there would, at any given moment, have been only one group.

Our translation follows *Mikra U'Massores* (comm. v. 4). The sense of the phrase is that the priestly *mishmar* which would have been on duty on that day had the *mishmar* divisions not been waived for the purpose of bringing the *Pesach*, was to station itself in the vicinity of the Israelite *maamad*.

וַחֲלֻקַּת בֵּית־אָב לַלְוִיִּם — *And near the family divisions of the Levites*. All the family units of the Levites should also group themselves together (*Metzudos*). See above for *Mikra U'Massores'* perception.

6. וְשַׁחֲטוּ הַפָּסַח — *Then slaughter the Pesach*. The slaughtering of sacrifices can be done by any Jew. Therefore, this phrase should be understood as meaning: See to it that the *Pesach* be slaughtered by whomever this will be done. *Mikra U'Massores* thinks this is underscored by v. 11 where *They slaughtered . . .* has no subject explicated, while the sprinkling is done by *Kohanim* and the skinning by Levites.

Metzudos, however, in v. 11 writes that the slaughtering was done by the Levites.

וְהִתְקַדְּשׁוּ — *Purify yourselves*. The translation follows *Metzudos*. That וְהִתְקַדְּשׁוּ follows וְשַׁחֲטוּ seems to bear out our contention that the former was not addressed to the *Kohanim* directly. While the people were slaughtering their offerings, the *Kohanim* were to purify themselves for the duties which they would have to perform.

If הִתְקַדְּשׁוּ does, indeed, mean *to purify* or *cleanse oneself*, then the usage would be the same as in ch. 30 vs. 15 and 24 in connection with Chizkiahu's *Pesach*.

However, we note that the term can also mean *prepare yourselves* (cf. *Numbers* 11:18), and this may well be meant here. The vast amount of sacrifices which were to be brought would surely have required a special effort. This rendering can help in understanding the next part of the verse — see below.

family units in your divisions. This, in accordance with David king of Israel's written instructions and the written proclamation of his son, Solomon. 5 *'And, within the hallowed precincts, position yourselves near your brothers, the people's, family divisions, and near the family divisions of the Levites.'* 6 *'Then slaughter the Pesach; purify yourselves and prepare your brothers; to act in accordance with the word of HASHEM at the hand of Moses.'* 7 *Yoshiahu donated small-stock, lambs and*

וְהָכִינוּ לַאֲחֵיכֶם — *And prepare your brothers*. If the *Kohanim* are being addressed, then it would be simplest to assume that the *brothers* are the Levites who were to be readied for their tasks. This would be the flaying of the offerings (v. 13). But, if so, ... *in accordance with the word of HASHEM at the hand of Moses* must be read as a separate thought. Nowhere in the Torah is there a requirement that the Levites are to skin the sacrifices. They did so here only because of the exigencies of the moment — the vast number of sacrifices to be brought.

Indeed, the *trop* indicates that the two phrases are to be taken separately and the sentence is to be rendered thus: *Make yourselves ready and, too, prepare your brothers* [so that all of you together can] *act in accordance with the word of HASHEM at the hand of Moses*.

7-9. In this section we learn how Yoshiahu and his officers or princes supplied the people with animals for the *Pesach* celebration. We find three groupings for these donations: Yoshiahu himself gave animals to the people as a whole; a group of officers identified in v. 5 gave to the *Kohanim*; and the officers of the Levites supplied the Levites (v. 9).

Two groups of animals are mentioned: lambs and kids for the *Pesach* offering; and cattle. The text does not explicate what these cattle were to be used for. Certainly, as the Torah specifies, and as v. 7 makes clear, only sheep and goats are acceptable for the *Pesach*.

Metzudos and *Ramban* to *Deuteronomy* 16:2 write that the cattle were for the שַׁלְמֵי חֲגִיגָה, *the peace offerings*, which were brought in conjunction with the *Pesach* (*Rambam, Korban Pesach* 10:12). These שַׁלְמֵי חֲגִיגָה are the קֳדָשִׁים mentioned in v. 13. We assume that the cattle were also used for the עוֹלָה, *the burnt offering*, mentioned in v. 12.

The proportion of cattle to sheep seems to have been 1 to 10: Yoshiahu gave 30,000 lambs and kids and 3,000 cattle (v. 7); the Levite princes 5,000 lambs and kids and 500 cattle; the princes who supplied the *Kohanim*, 2,600 lambs and kids and 300 cattle. Given the closeness to the expected 260, we assume that the system may have called for a rounding off to the nearest hundred.

That there was a proportion of only one to ten between the שַׁלְמֵי חֲגִיגָה and the *Pesach* offerings can be readily explained. The former were not obligatory, and no greater need was perceived.

Why did Yoshiahu and his princes donate the animals to the people? Chizkiahu in his time also gave vast amounts of animals to the people for sacrifices (see 30:24), but these were for the purpose of celebrating the additional seven days of rejoicing which were added on after *Pesach*. The actual *Pesach* offerings were apparently supplied by the people themselves.

We may surmise as follows: *Daas Soferim* to v. 7 wonders about the exact meaning of מֵרְכוּשׁ הַמֶּלֶךְ. Does it mean Yoshiahu's private property or the royal coffers — the wealth belonging to the monarchy?

If the latter, thus it is possible that Yoshiahu wished to make a statement about the monarchy. The *Pesach*, as we have seen, is the offering which implies a rededication to God's service — a tearing away of oneself from idolatrous practices. These terrible practices had disastrously found currency among the people because of the depredation of the kings — Menasheh and Amon. By making the royal treasury the source of the *Pesach* offerings, Yoshiahu was inaugurating a change in the attitude of the monarchy. From being the instigator to defection from God, it would become the means of serving Him. [See ArtScroll *Ezekiel*, fn. to 45:20 (p. 717) for a discussion of the opinion that in the Messianic era all communal sacrifices will be paid for by the royal treasury. The idea expressed by that seems much the same as the one we have worked out here.]

7. לִבְנֵי הָעָם — ... *to the people*. The term בְּנֵי הָעָם is used only in our chapter, at vs. 5, 7, 12 and 13, and nowhere else in Scripture. There must surely be a specific connotation to the combination — one which is appropriate only in the context of Yoshiahu's *Pesach* celebration.

לה
ח־יב

עִזִּים הַכֹּל לַפְּסָחִים לְכָל־הַנִּמְצָא לְמִסְפַּר שְׁלֹשִׁים אֶלֶף
ח וּבָקָר שְׁלֹשֶׁת אֲלָפִים אֵלֶּה מֵרְכוּשׁ הַמֶּלֶךְ: וְשָׂרָיו
לִנְדָבָה לָעָם לַכֹּהֲנִים וְלַלְוִיִּם הֵרִימוּ חִלְקִיָּה וּזְכַרְיָהוּ
וִיחִיאֵל נְגִידֵי בֵּית הָאֱלֹהִים לַכֹּהֲנִים נָתְנוּ לַפְּסָחִים
ט אַלְפַּיִם וְשֵׁשׁ מֵאוֹת וּבָקָר שְׁלֹשׁ מֵאוֹת: °וכוננידהו
וּשְׁמַעְיָהוּ וּנְתַנְאֵל אֶחָיו וַחֲשַׁבְיָהוּ וִיעִיאֵל וְיוֹזָבָד שָׂרֵי
הַלְוִיִּם הֵרִימוּ לַלְוִיִּם לַפְּסָחִים חֲמֵשֶׁת אֲלָפִים וּבָקָר חֲמֵשׁ
י מֵאוֹת: וַתִּכּוֹן הָעֲבוֹדָה וַיַּעַמְדוּ הַכֹּהֲנִים עַל־עָמְדָם
יא וְהַלְוִיִּם עַל־מַחְלְקוֹתָם כְּמִצְוַת הַמֶּלֶךְ: וַיִּשְׁחֲטוּ הַפָּסַח
יב וַיִּזְרְקוּ הַכֹּהֲנִים מִיָּדָם וְהַלְוִיִּם מַפְשִׁיטִים: וַיָּסִירוּ הָעֹלָה

°וְכָנַנְיָהוּ ק׳

At 23:3 we discussed the meaning of בֵּן הַמֶּלֶךְ as used in that passage. We found that מֶלֶךְ, in that context, refers to David, the quintessential *king* of Israel for all times, and that בֵּן מֶלֶךְ implies the righteous among his descendants, who succeeded him to his throne. In much the same way, we suggest that עָם in our passage, stands for the eternal people of Israel, while בְּנֵי הָעָם are the particular people who were alive in Yoshiahu's time. Their significance lies not in themselves as individuals, but, rather, as representatives of their people. Yoshiahu, in fulfillment of his task as educator to the generations of the exile, had to relate to generations as yet unborn. Those who were physically present at his *Pesach* celebration were no more than representatives of an eternal nation.

צֹאן — *Small-stock*. A term used for both sheep and goats.

כְּבָשִׂים וּבְנֵי־עִזִּים — *Lambs and young goats*. The Torah specifies that the animals for the *Pesach* offering must be in their first year. See *Exodus* 12:5.

הַכֹּל לַפְּסָחִים — *All for the Pesach offerings*. The cattle mentioned later were for different sacrifices.

לְמִסְפַּר שְׁלֹשִׁים אֶלֶף — *Thirty thousand by number*. מִסְפָּר, *number*, with the prefix ל usually indicates a congruence between the numbers of two units. Thus, in *Judges* 21:23, וַיִּשְׂאוּ נָשִׁים לְמִסְפָּרָם, *they married women according to their numbers*, implies a congruence between the number of men and women. Each man married one woman — see *Metzudos* there.

Taken thus, the 30,000 of our phrase refers to the people — not the flock. The sentence means that Yoshiahu donated a *Pesach* sacrifice for each of the thirty thousand people who were present in Jerusalem.

If so, there is a subtle difference between the *Pesach* offerings and the 3,000 cattle. There, the number of animals is given. Moreover, the same difference exists also between Yoshiahu's gift and that of the princes in vs. 8 and 9. There, too, the number of animals is given, even for the *Pesach* offerings.

The implication would be that Yoshiahu, in the zeal of his educational goals, was concerned with each individual Jew. Each was unique and he made sure that each would have what he needed in order to achieve the rededication implied in the *Pesach* offering. The princes, on the other hand, simply dealt with numbers. A certain amount of animals was required — and this they donated.

8. לָעָם לַכֹּהֲנִים וְלַלְוִיִּם — *To the people, that is, to the Kohanim and the Levites*. The use of עָם in this verse stands in marked contrast to בְּנֵי הָעָם in the previous verse. Our interpretation there makes the change readily understandable. Yoshiahu was dealing with eternal Israel of which the people in the House were only representatives. The princes saw only the *Kohanim* and Levites of their generation in front of them.

9. וְכָנַנְיָהוּ וּשְׁמַעְיָהוּ ... — *And Chananiahu and Shemariahu* ... See 31:12, where men of these names are given as נְגִידִים in the times of Chizkiahu. *Da'as Soferim* points out that this is one more example of the trend, noted often before, that the Levite names tended to repeat themselves in different generations. [See *I Chronicles* ftn to 9:10, and comm. to v. 21 there.]

אֶחָיו — *His brothers*. Apparently this refers to Chananiahu. Shemariahu and Nethanel were his brothers.

young goats, to the people, all for the Pesach offerings. For those present, thirty thousand by number, together with three thousand heads of cattle. All these came from the king's coffers. [8] *And his officials donated gifts to the people, that is, to the Kohanim and the Levites. Chilkaiah, Zechariahu and Yechiel, highest authorities in God's House, gave two thousand six hundred to the Kohanim for the Pesach offering, and three hundred heads of cattle.* [9] *And Chananiahu and Shemariahu and Nethanel, his brothers, and Chashaniahu, and Ye'i'el and Yozavad the chiefs of the Levites gave five thousand to the Levites for the Pesach offerings, and five hundred heads of cattle.* [10] *So the service was set in order. The Kohanim stood at their stand and the Levites according to their mishmaros, as the king had commanded.* [11] *They slaughtered the Pesach offering. The Kohanim immediately poured, and the Levites flayed.* [12] *They set aside that which was to be offered up*

10. וַתִּכּוֹן הָעֲבוֹדָה — *So the service was set in order ....* See comm. to 29:35 where we noted the similarity between this same expression describing Chizkiahu's reestablishment of the House order and the one used when Solomon completed the inauguration. By using the same expression here, *Chronicles* is placing Yoshiahu within the tradition of the House builders: Solomon, Chizkiahu and now, Yoshiahu.

There may, however, be another insight hidden within this phrase. A careful reading of our chapter shows an uncharacteristic and unique repetition of the root כון, *to set in order* or *to prepare*. Thus, in v. 4 the *Kohanim* are to organize themselves [הָכִינוּ] in appropriate positions; in v. 6 they are to ready [הָכִינוּ] their brothers; in our verse the service was set in order [וַתִּכּוֹן]; in v. 14 the Levites prepared [twice הֵכִינוּ] the *Pesach* offerings for the *Kohanim*; in v. 16 the service is once more set in order [וַתִּכּוֹן]; and in v. 20 the verse looks back and sees how Yoshiahu had set the house in order [הֵכִין].

The use of the same root for a number of different meanings within the same context is striking, and, moreover, nowhere in Scripture do we find a similar, almost artificial, concentration of use for this root.

Perhaps the constant repetition of the root, meaning essentially *to prepare*, is designed to reflect the essence of Yoshiahu's kingship as we have understood it. Its entire thrust was to prepare the people for the impending exile.

עַל־עָמְדָם — ... *at their stand*. The same expression in *Daniel* 8:17 and 18 is interpreted by *Radak* (*Shorashim*) as the place at which a person stands. *Targum* renders דוּכָן, the platform from which the *Kohanim* delivered their blessing.

Metzudos renders: At their places, each *mishmar* separately.

כְּמִצְוַת הַמֶּלֶךְ — *As the king had commanded*. Who had said that each *mishmar* was to stand separately (vs. 4 and 5) (*Metzudos*).

11. וַיִּשְׁחֲטוּ הַפָּסַח — *They slaughtered the Pesach offering*. *Metzudos* writes that it was the Levites who slaughtered the sacrifices. See comm. to v. 6 above. We assume that *Metzudos'* opinion is based on 30:16.

וַיִּזְרְקוּ הַכֹּהֲנִים מִיָּדָם — *The Kohanim immediately poured*. מִיָּדָם here connotes *immediately*. As soon as the animal had been slaughtered, the *Kohanim* caught the blood, carried it to the altar, and poured it out at the base (*Mikra U'Massores*).

וְהַלְוִיִּם מַפְשִׁיטִים — *And the Levites flayed*. At 29:34 we also found the Levites skinning the sacrifices when the *Kohanim* were unable to do so because of the press of the huge number of animals involved.

12. וַיָּסִירוּ הָעֹלָה — *They set aside that which was to be offered up*. *Metzudos* believes that עֹלָה, which usually means *a burnt offering*, is here used to describe those parts of the *Pesach* offering which were to be burnt on the altar. These were set aside so that the rest of the *Pesach* — those parts which were meant to be eaten — could then be given to the various family groups [לְמִפְלַגּוֹת לְבֵית־אָבוֹת]. The parts that had been set aside were taken for the

לְתִתָּם לְמִפְלַגּוֹת לְבֵית־אָבוֹת לִבְנֵי הָעָם לְהַקְרִיב
יג לַיהוָה כַּכָּתוּב בְּסֵפֶר מֹשֶׁה וְכֵן לַבָּקָר: וַיְבַשְּׁלוּ הַפֶּסַח
בָּאֵשׁ כַּמִּשְׁפָּט וְהַקֳּדָשִׁים בִּשְּׁלוּ בַּסִּירוֹת וּבַדְּוָדִים
יד וּבַצֵּלָחוֹת וַיָּרִיצוּ לְכָל־בְּנֵי הָעָם: וְאַחַר הֵכִינוּ לָהֶם
וְלַכֹּהֲנִים כִּי הַכֹּהֲנִים בְּנֵי אַהֲרֹן בְּהַעֲלוֹת הָעוֹלָה
וְהַחֲלָבִים עַד־לָיְלָה וְהַלְוִיִּם הֵכִינוּ לָהֶם וְלַכֹּהֲנִים בְּנֵי
טו אַהֲרֹן: וְהַמְשֹׁרְרִים בְּנֵי־אָסָף עַל־מַעֲמָדָם כְּמִצְוַת דָּוִיד
וְאָסָף וְהֵימָן וִידֻתוּן חוֹזֵה הַמֶּלֶךְ וְהַשֹּׁעֲרִים לְשַׁעַר וָשָׁעַר

purpose of bringing them up to HASHEM [לְהַקְרִיב לַה׳] upon the altar. Thus:

a) וַיָּסִירוּ הָעֹלָה — the parts for the altar.
b) . . . לְתִתָּם — the parts to be eaten.
c) . . . לְהַקְרִיב — the parts for the altar.

In this system, the syntax is not simple.

Mikra U'Massores thinks that עולה here is to be understood in its more usual meaning. It is to be taken as *burnt offering* and, specifically, the עוֹלַת קַיִץ לַמִּזְבֵּחַ, the sacrifices which were brought during lax periods so that the altar should not stand idle.

The background for understanding our verse is as follows: We noted at v. 4 that the normal division into *mishmaros* was waived during *Yom Tov* periods and that all *Kohanim* had equal rights to serve at that time. However, this held true only for those sacrifices which were specifically associated with the *Yom Tov*. Sacrifices which had to be brought on those days, but not because of the *Yom Tov*, were handled by the *mishmar* whose turn it was at that time.

The meaning of our verse is thus as follows: From among all the animals which had been designated to be brought that day — most of which were, of course, for the *Pesach* offerings — the animals which were to be used for קַיִץ לַמִּזְבֵּחַ were removed by the Levites who were in charge of the House organization. These were given over to the current *mishmar* [לְמִפְלַגּוֹת לְבֵית־אָבוֹת לִבְנֵי הָעָם] to sacrifice. [בְּנֵי הָעָם, in this context, are the אַנְשֵׁי מַעֲמָד, the group of Israelites who functioned together with the current *mishmar*.]

כַּכָּתוּב בְּסֵפֶר משֶׁה — *In accordance with that which was written in the book of Moses*. As *Metzudos* understands the earlier part of this verse, this phrase modifies לְהַקְרִיב לַה׳. They burned those parts of the sacrifice which required burning upon the altar, in accordance with the Torah's directives.

According to *Mikra U'Massores* it explains why the burnt offerings were given over to the *mishmar* whose turn it was to do the service at that time. This accords with the Torah's directive (*Deuteronomy* 18:6-8) that only *Yom Tov* offerings were to be shared equally among all the *Kohanim*. All others would be serviced by the functioning *mishmar*.

וְכֵן לַבָּקָר — *And so too, for the cattle*. In prefatory remarks 7-9, we learned of the שַׁלְמֵי חֲגִיגָה which were brought together with the *Pesach* offering. The *cattle* are those animals which were used for those sacrifices. The sense of the phrase is as follows: Just as the Levites made sure that those parts of the *Pesach* which were to be brought upon the altar were set aside from those parts which were to be eaten by the owners, so too, did they service the שַׁלְמֵי חֲגִיגָה in this manner (*Metzudos*).

Mikra U'Massores reads this phrase together with the next sentence which tells how the Levites involved themselves with roasting the *Pesach* offerings: Just as the Levites helped roast the *Pesach* for people who did not have the time to attend to this themselves, so too, did they help with cooking the שַׁלְמֵי חֲגִיגָה.

13. וַיְבַשְּׁלוּ הַפֶּסַח בָּאֵשׁ כַּמִּשְׁפָּט — *They roasted the Pesach offering in fire in accordance with the law. Exodus* 12:8 teaches that the *Pesach* offering is to be roasted in fire, and v. 9 there expressly forbids cooking. Thus, although we never find בשל to mean *roasting* in any other context, we must assign this meaning here (*Radak*). *Mikra U'Massores* suggests that the word כַּמִּשְׁפָּט is here to avoid any ambiguity that might arise from the use of בשל for roasting. The latter term was used for roasting at the time that *Chronicles* was written.

HaKesav VeHaKabbalah (*Exodus* 23:19), on the basis of the fact that בשל is used also for *ripening* (cf. *Genesis* 40:10), suggests that the base meaning of the word is *to make something edible*. Thus it can be used equally well for roasting as for cooking.

וְהַקֳּדָשִׁים בִּשְּׁלוּ — *They cooked the holy sacrifices* . . . The שַׁלְמֵי חֲגִיגָה did not have to be

*so that that which was to be distributed might be given to the
people's family groups. This, so that sacrifice might be made to
HASHEM in accordance with that which was written in the book
of Moses. And so too, for the cattle.* [13] *They roasted the Pesach
offering in fire in accordance with the law. They cooked the holy
sacrifices in siros, devadim and tzeilachos, and rushed them to
the people.* [14] *After this, they made arrangements for themselves
and for the Kohanim. For the Kohanim, sons of Aaron, were
involved with sacrificing the parts to be burned and the fats,
right up to the night. So the Levites made arrangements for
themselves and for the Kohanim, sons of Aaron.* [15] *So too, the
choristers, the Asaphites, remained at their posts in accordance
with the command of David and Asaph and Heiman and
Yeduthun, seer to the king. Thus, the gatekeepers at each gate*

roasted, so these were cooked in water using the utensils listed below.

בַּסִּירוֹת וּבַדְּוָדִים וּבְצֵלָחוֹת — *In siros, devadim and tzeilochos.* סִיר is mentioned in *Exodus* 16:3 as a receptacle in which meat is kept and eaten. דְּוָד or דּוּד does not occur in the Torah, but is found occasionally in Scripture. In at least some of these places it must be understood as *basket* (*Radak, Shorashim*), so we may surmise that it is a receptacle for meat — perhaps shaped or perforated like a basket. צַלַּחַת also occurs in Scripture: In *II Kings* 21:13 it is mentioned as a utensil which is wiped clean. This would suggest a plate which is wiped clean of its food. But *Metzudos* there seems to take it as a kind of pot which is cleansed of its contents prior to storing it. *Rashi* to *Proverbs* 19:23 seems to assume that it is a pot in which food is cooked on the fire. Since we find צְלוֹחִית as a *bottle* (*Radak, Shorashim*) it is perhaps bottle shaped.

We have left the terms untranslated since we cannot know their precise meaning.

וַיָּרִיצוּ לְכָל־בְּנֵי הָעָם — *And rushed them.* This translation is from רוּץ, *to run*. The phrase could either be an explanation for the fact that the Levites, rather than the owners, took care of the cooking. It was done in order to expedite the procedures.

Or, it could be connected to the next sentence. The Levites hastened to provide the people with their needs so that there would be time to prepare the *Pesach* offerings for those *Kohanim* and Levites who did not have the time to do it on their own.

14. וְאַחַר — *After this*. I.e., after they had finished roasting the *Pesach* offerings and cooking the שַׁלְמֵי חֲגִיגָה for the people.

הֵכִינוּ לָהֶם וְלַכֹּהֲנִים — *They made arrangements for themselves and for the Kohanim.* The *Kohanim* were busy with their tasks. Without the help of the Levites, they would not have had the time to set up their own *Pesach* celebration.

The Levite choristers and gatekeepers were also too busy to prepare their own *Pesach* offerings. The other Levites did it for them.

15. וְהַמְשֹׁרְרִים בְּנֵי־אָסָף . . . וְאָסָף וְהֵימָן וִידִתוּן — *So too, the choristers, the Asaphites ... and Asaph and Heiman and Yeduthun.* Songs composed by David and his three chief choristers were performed by the Asaphites (*Metzudos*).[1]

חוֹזֵה הַמֶּלֶךְ — *Seer to the king.* Apparently this refers to Yeduthun. Asaph had been described as a *seer* at 29:30, and Heiman is given that title at *I Chronicles* 25:5. See comm. to that verse and to v. 1 there.

1. It is not clear why only the Asaphites performed at Yoshiahu's *Pesach* celebrations. Normally all three families would participate in the *shirah* — see *I Chronicles*, ch. 6, vs. 18, 24 and 29.

Moreover, why were the songs composed by David and all his chief composers? It was the custom to recite the *Hallel* while the *Pesach* offerings were brought (*Pesachim* 5:7). Were the psalms which we associate with *Hallel* composed by all four?

We may surmise that the music described in this verse was special. Perhaps on this occasion of rededication, Yoshiahu found it appropriate to inspire the participants with music and psalms, beyond that which was normally done. The special power of music would be harnessed to elicit true repentance from the people. See Section II to ch. 34, *The Faithful Workers*.

אֵין לָהֶם לָסוּר מֵעַל עֲבֹדָתָם כִּי־אֲחֵיהֶם הַלְוִיִּם הֵכִינוּ
טז לָהֶם׃ וַתִּכּוֹן כָּל־עֲבוֹדַת יְהוָה בַּיּוֹם הַהוּא לַעֲשׂוֹת
הַפֶּסַח וְהַעֲלוֹת עֹלוֹת עַל מִזְבַּח יְהוָה כְּמִצְוַת הַמֶּלֶךְ
יז יֹאשִׁיָּהוּ׃ וַיַּעֲשׂוּ בְנֵי־יִשְׂרָאֵל הַנִּמְצְאִים אֶת־הַפֶּסַח בָּעֵת
יח הַהִיא וְאֶת־חַג הַמַּצּוֹת שִׁבְעַת יָמִים׃ וְלֹא־נַעֲשָׂה פֶסַח
כָּמֹהוּ בְּיִשְׂרָאֵל מִימֵי שְׁמוּאֵל הַנָּבִיא וְכָל־מַלְכֵי יִשְׂרָאֵל
׀ לֹא־עָשׂוּ כַּפֶּסַח אֲשֶׁר־עָשָׂה יֹאשִׁיָּהוּ וְהַכֹּהֲנִים וְהַלְוִיִּם
יט וְכָל־יְהוּדָה וְיִשְׂרָאֵל הַנִּמְצָא וְיוֹשְׁבֵי יְרוּשָׁלָםִ׃ בִּשְׁמוֹנֶה
כ עֶשְׂרֵה שָׁנָה לְמַלְכוּת יֹאשִׁיָּהוּ נַעֲשָׂה הַפֶּסַח הַזֶּה׃ אַחֲרֵי
כָל־זֹאת אֲשֶׁר הֵכִין יֹאשִׁיָּהוּ אֶת־הַבַּיִת עָלָה נְכוֹ
מֶלֶךְ־מִצְרַיִם לְהִלָּחֵם בְּכַרְכְּמִישׁ עַל־פְּרָת וַיֵּצֵא לִקְרָאתוֹ

16. כְּמִצְוַת הַמֶּלֶךְ יֹאשִׁיָּהוּ — *Just as King Yoshiahu had ordered.* Once more the central role which Yoshiahu played is stressed. See comm. to v. 1.

17. הַנִּמְצְאִים — *Who were present. Targum* renders: *Who were loyal.*

Targum's rationale may have been that, in contrast to 30:21 where in a similar context we have הַנִּמְצְאִים בִּירוּשָׁלַםִ, we have here only the הַנִּמְצְאִים without the location being given. An analysis of the usage of הַנִּמְצְאִים in Scripture yields that in most cases either a location or another description [e.g. *with him*] is given. The exceptions are our verses, 5:11 and 31:1.

אֶת־הַפֶּסַח . . . וְאֶת־חַג הַמַּצּוֹת — *The Pesach . . . and the Feast of Matzos . . . Pesach* would seem to refer to the bringing of the *Pesach* offering on the 14th of Nissan, and the *Feast of Matzos* would be the seven-day Passover celebration, beginning on the next day — see *Exodus* 23:15. However, *Metzudos* understands חַג הַמַּצּוֹת as referring to the various sacrifices which had to be brought in conjunction with the festival.

18. וְלֹא־נַעֲשָׂה פֶּסַח כָּמֹהוּ — *No Pesach like it had been celebrated* . . . See Section II, *A Unique Pesach*, for an analysis of the special character of Yoshiahu's *Pesach* celebration.

. . . אֲשֶׁר־עָשָׂה יֹאשִׁיָּהוּ — *That celebrated by Yoshiahu.* Six different participants are listed: Yoshiahu; the *Kohanim*; the Levites; all of Judah; the Israelites who were there — apparently dwellers in what was formerly the Northern Kingdom; and the inhabitants of Jerusalem.

Two points should be noted: The six categories are not mentioned in the *Kings'* version; and moreover, in our v. 17 we read only of *the Israelites who were present* celebrating the *Pesach* with, apparently, no need to specify the various groupings.

This may tend to confirm the thesis suggested above. If, indeed, the essential significance of this *Pesach* celebration was to ready the people for their impending exile existence, then it would be logical to break them down into components, each of which was related to the present state of affairs in a different way. King, *Kohen*, Levite, Judahite, Israelite and Jerusalemite each had a different perspective on life, and would need to be instructed separately to cope with the challenges of the future. In v. 17 this breakdown was not required and it was sufficient to say that the *Israelites who were present* celebrated the *Pesach*.

אֲשֶׁר־עָשָׂה יֹאשִׁיָּהוּ — *That celebrated by Yoshiahu.* The singular form is unexpected. It could imply that which we have seen a number of times in this passage — that in *Chronicles'* perspective the entire initiative for the celebration of the *Pesach* is seen to come from Yoshiahu.

וְיִשְׂרָאֵל הַנִּמְצָא — *The Israelites who were present.* The plural of v. 17 would seem more appropriate. The singular form of our verse can be explained by the fact that the group, rather than the individual, is meant — see comm. to earlier part of this verse.

19. בִּשְׁמוֹנֶה עֶשְׂרֵה שָׁנָה — *In the eighteenth year* . . . See Section II, *The Final Years*, for analysis of this verse.

20. . . . אַחֲרֵי כָּל־זֹאת — *After all this. Bereishis Rabbah* 44:6 teaches that while אַחַר is used to describe events which came about

did not have to leave their duties: their brothers the Levites made
the arrangements for them. 16 *So the entire order of the Divine*
service was well organized on that day, from performing the
Pesach service to bringing up burnt offerings on the altar of
HASHEM — just as king Yoshiahu had ordered. 17 *The Israelites who*
were present celebrated the Pesach at that time, and the Feast of
Matzos seven days. 18 *Since the days of Samuel the prophet, no*
Pesach like it had been celebrated in Israel. None of Israel's kings
celebrated anything like that celebrated by Yoshiahu, the Kohan-
im, the Levites, all of Judah, the Israelites who were present, and
the inhabitants of Jerusalem. 19 *This Pesach was celebrated in the*
eighteenth year of Yoshiahu's reign. 20 *After all this that Yoshiahu*
had set the House in order, Necho, king of Egypt, came to make war
against Charkemish by the Euphrates, and Yoshiahu went out

after a short time lapse, אַחֲרֵי is used when a longer period of time interrupted between the points described. Nevertheless, the phrase is striking when we consider that we are dealing with a period of thirteen years — from the eighteenth (v. 19) till the thirty-first year (v. 1). See Section II, *The Chronicles' View of Yoshiahu's Failures*.

אֲשֶׁר הֵכִין יֹאשִׁיָּהוּ אֶת־הַבַּיִת — *That Yoshiahu had set the House in order*. It is clear that the description of Yoshiahu's tragic death raises a theological question. The description of his reign has been entirely positive. There have been no qualifications to the litany of righteous acts which he has performed. Why, then, was he killed? The terrible way in which he died seems to fly in the face of the principles of reward and punishment which are the hallmark of Divine justice as it is depicted in the Scriptural books.

We suggest that perhaps our phrase is meant critically, and may be *Chronicles'* answer to this theological problem:

It is instructive to compare the description of Chizkiahu's *Pesach* as told in ch. 30, with that of Yoshiahu, described in our chapter. It is clear that the emphasis is entirely different.

In the celebration of Chizkiahu's *Pesach*, the people are central: Chizkiahu sets the celebration in motion with a fiery exhortation to penitence (30:6-9). Then we learn of his prayer that God might forgive all those who were truly sincere in His service (18-20). Then, v. 21 stresses the great joy with which the celebration took place — specifically mentioning the people [בְּנֵי יִשְׂרָאֵל] (v. 21). V. 23 then describes how the people, in the ecstasy of the moment [וַיִּוָּעֲצוּ כָּל הַקָּהָל], decided to add another seven days of rejoicing.

All reference to such a participation of the people is missing in the description of Yoshiahu's *Pesach*. Whatever is said centers around the technicalities of the House arrangements. If there was an intention that the people be inspired to rededicate themselves to God's service in a meaningful way, then at least to the extent that *Chronicles* reports the event, that intention was frustrated.

All this is, we believe, hinted at in our phrase. *After all this, that Yoshiahu had set the House in order!* Yoshiahu should have dealt with the people — instead, he focused upon the House. The House which was destined to be destroyed was well organized — but the people who would henceforth be the carriers of the Divine Presence on earth were ignored.

Together with the juxtaposition to the previous verse, which we discussed in Section II, *The Chronicles View of Yoshiahu's Failures*, Yoshiahu's shortcomings are revealed. His last significant activity was the *Pesach* celebration rather than the education of the people in the intervening years — and that celebration fell short of its full potential.

נְכוֹ מֶלֶךְ־מִצְרַיִם — *Necho, king of Egypt*. In *Kings*, the Egyptian king is referred to as פַּרְעֹה נְכֹה. From this, *Radak* concludes that נְכֹה is not a proper name, but an adjective meaning, *lame*. He points out that *Targum*, here, renders: *Pharaoh, the lame*.

בְּכַרְכְּמִישׁ עַל־פְּרָת — *Against Charkemish by the Euphrates*.

The way from Egypt to Charkemish passes through the Land of Israel. It was Necho's intention to pass through but not to attack the Israelites (*Mefaresh*).

כא יֹאשִׁיָּהוּ׃ וַיִּשְׁלַח אֵלָיו מַלְאָכִים ׀ לֵאמֹר ׀ מַה־לִּי וָלָךְ
מֶלֶךְ יְהוּדָה לֹא־עָלֶיךָ אַתָּה הַיּוֹם כִּי אֶל־בֵּית מִלְחַמְתִּי
וֵאלֹהִים אָמַר לְבַהֲלֵנִי חֲדַל־לְךָ מֵאֱלֹהִים אֲשֶׁר־עִמִּי
כב וְאַל־יַשְׁחִיתֶךָ׃ וְלֹא־הֵסֵב יֹאשִׁיָּהוּ פָּנָיו מִמֶּנּוּ כִּי לְהִלָּחֶם־
בּוֹ הִתְחַפֵּשׂ וְלֹא שָׁמַע אֶל־דִּבְרֵי נְכוֹ מִפִּי אֱלֹהִים וַיָּבֹא
כג לְהִלָּחֵם בְּבִקְעַת מְגִדּוֹ׃ וַיֹּרוּ הַיֹּרִים לַמֶּלֶךְ יֹאשִׁיָּהוּ
וַיֹּאמֶר הַמֶּלֶךְ לַעֲבָדָיו הַעֲבִירוּנִי כִּי הָחֳלֵיתִי מְאֹד׃
כד וַיַּעֲבִירֻהוּ עֲבָדָיו מִן־הַמֶּרְכָּבָה וַיַּרְכִּיבֻהוּ עַל רֶכֶב
הַמִּשְׁנֶה אֲשֶׁר־לוֹ וַיּוֹלִיכֻהוּ יְרוּשָׁלַ͏ִם וַיָּמָת וַיִּקָּבֵר
בְּקִבְרוֹת אֲבֹתָיו וְכָל־יְהוּדָה וִירוּשָׁלַ͏ִם מִתְאַבְּלִים עַל־
כה יֹאשִׁיָּהוּ׃ וַיְקוֹנֵן יִרְמְיָהוּ עַל־יֹאשִׁיָּהוּ וַיֹּאמְרוּ
כָל־הַשָּׁרִים ׀ וְהַשָּׁרוֹת בְּקִינוֹתֵיהֶם עַל־יֹאשִׁיָּהוּ עַד־הַיּוֹם
וַיִּתְּנוּם לְחֹק עַל־יִשְׂרָאֵל וְהִנָּם כְּתוּבִים עַל־הַקִּינוֹת׃

וַיֵּצֵא לִקְרָאתוֹ יֹאשִׁיָּהוּ — *And Yoshiahu went out against him*. See Section II, *The Chronicles' View of Yoshiahu's Failures*, for an explanation of why Yoshiahu decided to attack Pharaoh in spite of the fact that the latter had no aggressive intentions.

21. וַיִּשְׁלַח אֵלָיו — *He sent him* ... Necho assures Yoshiahu that he has no intention to attack him, and that his only wish is to traverse the country in order to get to Charkemish faster.

וֵאלֹהִים אָמַר לְבַהֲלֵנִי — *God has ordered that I hasten*. Necho sees himself as having been ordered by God to make war on the Assyrian king (*Radak* and *Metzudos*). He has been told to *hasten* and therefore Yoshiahu need not fear that he will stop to fight the Israelites (*Malbim*).

His Divine orders may have come to him through Jeremiah (*Radak* and *Metzudos*) or, as *Mefaresh* suggests and as is assumed in the *kinnah* of *Kalir* [אֵיכָה אֱלִי קוֹנְנוּ מֵאֵילָיו] and in various midrashim (*Eichah Rabbasi* to *Eichah* 1:17), he thought that Isaiah's prophecy from *Isaiah* 19:2, וְסִכְסַכְתִּי מִצְרַיִם בְּמִצְרַיִם, *and I will entangle Egypt with Egypt*, summoned him to this battle.

Taanis 22b, on the other hand, interprets Necho's words as referring to Egypt's national deity. The very fact that Necho invoked his idol convinced Yoshiahu that he could be victorious against him. *Targum* follows this opinion and interprets the three expressions, אֱלֹהִים in this and the next verse, as referring to the Egyptian deity.

חֲדַל־לְךָ מֵאֱלֹהִים אֲשֶׁר־עִמִּי — *Do not interfere with God, Who is with me* .... If God is meant, Necho is exhorting Yoshiahu not to meddle with the Divine plan. If reference is to his idol, he is threatening in the context of his own beliefs.

22. כִּי לְהִלָּחֶם־בּוֹ הִתְחַפֵּשׂ — *But camouflaged himself so as to be able to fight against him.* Translation follows *Ralbag*. From 18:29 we see that it was customary for the king to disguise himself when he went out to war, so that the enemy soldiers would not be able to pick him out from among the other soldiers.

Metzudos thinks that the meaning here is not to disguise himself but to get dressed in armor ready for battle.

Malbim has the phrase referring to Necho. Yoshiahu thought that Necho was only pretending to hurry through the land. In reality, he was in no hurry at all and would — if left alone — make war against the Israelites.

דִּבְרֵי נְכוֹ מִפִּי אֱלֹהִים — *Necho's Divinely inspired words*. The simplest way to understand this phrase is surely that אֱלֹהִים refers to God and that the phrase is critical of Yoshiahu. He should have listened to the Divine message.

As we have seen above, *Taanis* 22b takes אֱלֹהִים, in v. 21, as an idol. The Talmud gives no explanation of our phrase which obviously poses a problem: Why is it necessary to tell us that Yoshiahu did not listen to Necho's idolatrous illusions?

In view of the fact that the Talmud maintains that Necho's mention of his idol

against him. 21 *He sent him messengers, saying: 'What have I to*
do with you, king of Judah! I come not against you this day but
against those with whom I am to wage war. God has ordered that
I hasten. Do not interfere with God, Who is with me, so that He will
not destroy you.' 22 *But Yoshiahu would not turn away, but*
camouflaged himself so as to be able to fight against him. He did
not listen to Necho's Divinely inspired words. He went out to fight
in the Valley of Meggido. 23 *The archers shot at King Yoshiahu. The*
king said to his servants, 'Move me! For I am gravely ill'. 24 *So his*
servants moved him from the chariot and put him in his secondary
conveyance. They brought him to Jerusalem and he died. He
was buried in the sepulchers of his fathers. All of Judah and
Jerusalem mourned over Yoshiahu. 25 *Then Jeremiah lamented*
over Yoshiahu. All male and female singers would mention
Yoshiahu in their elegies up to this very day. They created a firmly
established custom in Israel. It is recorded in the Lamentations.

persuaded Yoshiahu to fight against him, we could render our phrase ... [because] *it came from the mouth of an idol*. He did not listen to Necho because he had invoked his deity, and thus forfeited, in Yoshiahu's eyes, any hope of victory.

See Section II, *Yoshiahu's Death*, for an analysis of the differing approaches of *Kings* and *Chronicles* to Yoshiahu's death.

23. הַעֲבִירוּנִי — *Move me!* Move me from the war chariot into a second one (v. 24). It was probably more roomy and comfortable for a wounded man.

24. וַיִּקָּבֵר בְּקִבְרוֹת אֲבֹתָיו — *He was buried in the sepulchers of his fathers*. The *Kings'* account (23:30) has: וַיִּקְבְּרֻהוּ בִּקְבֻרָתוֹ, *And they buried him in his grave*. *Radak* thinks that he had probably prepared a grave for himself among the royal sepulchers.

25. וַיְקוֹנֵן יִרְמְיָהוּ — *Then Jeremiah lamented* .... According to the tradition of the Sages, the fourth chapter of *Eichah* [אֵיכָה יוּעַם זָהָב] is the elegy which Jeremiah sang over Yoshiahu.

Why was the lament over Yoshiahu included in *Megillas Eichah* which mourns the destruction of Jerusalem and the Holy House? Why, if Jeremiah mourned Yoshiahu's death so bitterly, does he not mention this in *Kings* which, according to *Bava Basra* 15a, he authored?

The mourning which took place was not just the understandable sorrow over the death of a righteous king. There had been other good kings whose passing had not evoked the same kind of reaction. Rather, it is the untimely death of the man whose role it was to forge a nation which could carry the Divine Presence through centuries of exile which provoked this outpouring of grief.

And so, his death is part of the destruction and exile threnody. When Israel on *Tisha B'Av* weeps and mourns its glorious past and bemoans the tragedy of its exile existence, the awareness of what Yoshiahu might yet have done intensifies that sorrow. Jeremiah's elegy belongs in *Eichah* and will remain with Israel [לְחֹק], until the final redemption.

וַיֹּאמְרוּ כָל־הַשָּׁרִים וְהַשָּׁרוֹת . . . יֹאשִׁיָּהוּ — *All male and female singers would mention Yoshiahu*. The sense is, that whenever dirges will be sung for some sorrowful occasion, the tragedy of Yoshiahu will also be mentioned, and that too will be mourned (*Metzudos*).

וַיִּתְּנוּם לְחֹק עַל־יִשְׂרָאֵל — *They created a firmly established custom in Israel*. חֹק is not only a *law* or *statute*, but also any custom that is consistently and predictably adhered to. See, for example, *Leviticus* 20:23.

In our own time we include a *kinnah*, mourning Yoshiahu's untimely death, in the order of *kinnos* which we say on *Tishah B'Av*.

The Sages (*Yalkut Shimoni II*, 201) read our phrase to mean that it was made a custom or a law to sing elegies and dirges for the death of all of Israel's great men.

עַל הַקִּינוֹת — *In the Lamentations*. In the Book of *Eichah* (*Metzudos*). We have pointed out above that, in the tradition of the Sages, ch. 4

כו־כז וְיֶ֛תֶר דִּבְרֵ֥י יֹאשִׁיָּ֖הוּ וַחֲסָדָ֑יו כַּכָּת֖וּב בְּתוֹרַ֥ת יְהוָֽה׃ וּדְבָרָ֕יו
הָרִאשֹׁנִ֖ים וְהָאַחֲרֹנִ֑ים הִנָּ֣ם כְּתוּבִ֔ים עַל־סֵ֥פֶר מַלְכֵֽי־
א יִשְׂרָאֵ֖ל וִיהוּדָֽה׃ וַיִּקְחוּ֙ עַם־הָאָ֔רֶץ אֶת־
יְהוֹאָחָ֖ז בֶּן־יֹאשִׁיָּ֑הוּ וַיַּמְלִיכֻ֥הוּ תַֽחַת־אָבִ֖יו בִּירוּשָׁלִָֽם׃
ב בֶּן־שָׁל֧וֹשׁ וְעֶשְׂרִ֛ים שָׁנָ֖ה יוֹאָחָ֣ז בְּמָלְכ֑וֹ וּשְׁלֹשָׁ֣ה חֳדָשִׁ֔ים
ג מָלַ֖ךְ בִּירוּשָׁלִָֽם׃ וַיְסִירֵ֥הוּ מֶֽלֶךְ־מִצְרַ֖יִם בִּירוּשָׁלִָ֑ם וַֽיַּעֲנֹשׁ֙
ד אֶת־הָאָ֔רֶץ מֵאָ֥ה כִכַּר־כֶּ֖סֶף וְכִכַּ֥ר זָהָֽב׃ וַיַּמְלֵ֨ךְ מֶֽלֶךְ־
מִצְרַ֜יִם אֶת־אֶלְיָקִ֣ים אָחִ֗יו עַל־יְהוּדָה֙ וִיר֣וּשָׁלִַ֔ם וַיַּסֵּ֥ב
אֶת־שְׁמ֖וֹ יְהוֹיָקִ֑ים וְאֶת־יוֹאָחָ֣ז אָחִ֗יו לָקַ֥ח נְכ֖וֹ וַיְבִיאֵ֥הוּ

of *Eichah* is the dirge with which Jeremiah mourned Yoshiahu.

26. וַחֲסָדָיו — *And his pieties.* See comm. to 6:42 and 32:32.

27. וּדְבָרָיו הָרִאשֹׁנִים וְהָאַחֲרֹנִים — *And his earlier and latter matters.* See comm. to 17:3 for our perception of this phrase. We thought that רִאשֹׁנִים refers to the perspectives which the earlier books bring to bear on a given topic, while אַחֲרֹנִים are the specific *Chronicles'* view. In the case of Yoshiahu where we have traced such differences consistently, the phrasing is particularly apt.

XXXVI

The last hope for Judah's regeneration has gone. Now there will be only a dreadful decline. It will culminate, a short twenty-two years later, in destruction and exile.

Four kings reigned during this period: two of them for only three months each; two for eleven years each. Each of the four reigns, a tragic story of impotence and degradation; each, a travesty of the מַלְכוּת בֵּית דָּוִד, the glorious *Davidic kingship*, of which these four were the last protagonists.

These four reigns seem to be shortchanged both in the *Kings'* and *Chronicles'* accounts. Details are sparse and much that could have been said — as is apparent from a careful reading of *Jeremiah* and *Ezekiel* — is left out. But, with all its spartan economy, *Kings* seems loquacious when compared to *Chronicles*. The *Kings'* account has forty-nine verses against *Chronicles* which has only twenty-one for all four kings. [The breakdown according to the four kings is: Yehoachaz 2/3; Yehoyakim 5/10; Yehoyachin 3/11; Tzidkiahu 11/25.]

It appears that, in prophetic vision, these four kings are considered as one group — all belonging to the house of Yoshiahu. Ezekiel (ch. 19) is told to *take up a lamentation for the princes of Israel*, and in both the metaphors which he uses, a pride of lions and a fruitful vine, there is reference to a *mother*. [מָה אִמְּךָ לְבִיאָה, *Alas, your mother was a lioness*, and אִמְּךָ כַגֶּפֶן בְּדָמְךָ, *As one whose mother was a vine, are you likened*.] Most commentators assume that the *mother* is Yoshiahu, and that the *princes of Israel* are one or more of the four kings dealt with in our chapter.[1]

The implication is surely that these kings — more than being individuals who are to be considered in their own right are seen simply as the residue of the Yoshiahuan kingship. In effect, Yoshiahu was the last king of the Davidic line — the one under whose protective wing the exile was to have been lived out.

We may suggest that this is the explanation for *Chronicles'* cursory treatment of the reigns. Particularly for *Chronicles*, the story of the Davidic line ends with Yoshiahu. He, in the long view of history is seen as the true precursor of the Messiah. His disappointing progeny are an aberration to whom only scant attention need be paid.

---

1. The grouping of the four kings under the rubric of Yoshiahu's family seems borne out by the final words of that chapter: קִינָה הִיא וַתְּהִי לְקִינָה, *It is a lamentation and became a lamentation*, which certainly finds an echo in our 35:25, וַיְקוֹנֵן יִרְמְיָהוּ עַל־יֹאשִׁיָּהוּ . . . וְהִנָּם כְּתוּבִים עַל־הַקִּינוֹת, *Then Jeremiah lamented for Yoshiahu . . . and they are written in the Lamentations*.

35
26-27

[26] *Now all the rest of the matters of Yoshiahu and his pieties performed in accordance with that which is written in* HASHEM*'s Torah ...* [27] *And his earlier and latter matters are written in the Book of the Kings of Israel and Judah.*

36
1-4

The people of the land took Yehoachaz, the son of Yoshiahu, and made him king in place of his father in Jerusalem. [2] *Yehoachaz was twenty-three years old when he began to reign and he reigned three months in Jerusalem.* [3] *Then the king of Egypt deposed him in Jerusalem and fined the land a hundred talents of silver and a talent of gold.* [4] *So the king of Egypt made his brother Elyakim king over Judah and Jerusalem and changed his name to Yehoyakim. As for his brother Yehoachaz, Necho took him and*

1. ... וַיִּקְחוּ עַם־הָאָרֶץ ... — *The people of the land took* ... Yehoachaz was not the oldest of Yoshiahu's sons. He was twenty-three at the time of his father's death (v. 2), and Yehoyakim who succeeded him only three months later (v. 2) was twenty-five. Thus it was that it required a special initiative on the part of the *people of the land* to make the younger man king (*commentators*).

See Section II, *Yehoachaz' Kingship*, for an analysis of why the people decided to make the younger son king, and of the status of his kingship in the general history of the Jewish people.

וַיַּמְלִיכֻהוּ תַחַת־אָבִיו — *And made him king in place of his father*. The *Kings* account (23:31) mentions that the people anointed Yehoachaz king. It also gives the name of Yehoachaz's mother, though *Chronicles* does not. In line with *Chronicles'* view that Yehoachaz's kingship had no legal standing [see Section II, *Yehoachaz' Kingship*], any details which would tend to indicate a normal succession to the throne are omitted.

The next verse in *Kings* then states that Yehoachaz did evil in the eyes of HASHEM. Again this is left out in *Chronicles*. We may surmise that any assessment of the reign — even a negative one — would have tended to legitimize it.

3. וַיְסִירֵהוּ מֶלֶךְ־מִצְרַיִם בִּירוּשָׁלָם — *Then the king of Egypt deposed him in Jerusalem*. The expression *in Jerusalem* is difficult. This, in view of the *Kings'* account. There we have: *Pharaoh Necho shackled him* [וַיַּאַסְרֵהוּ from אסר, *to tie*, rather than וַיְסִירֵהוּ from סור, *to remove*] *in Rivlah in the land of Chamoth, from ruling in Jerusalem*.

Apparently, then, Pharaoh's actions took place in Rivlah, not in Jerusalem.

Malbim's solution is as follows: Necho *removed* Yehoachaz from the kingship *in Jerusalem* as stated in our verse. Then he took him to Rivlah and *shackled* him there in order that he should not be able to return and reassert his kingship, and that is the *Kings'* account. Thus, the two narratives augment one another. However, *Malbim* offers no explanation why the one aspect should have been told in *Kings* and the other in *Chronicles*.

See Section II, *Pharaoh Necho Deposes Yehoachaz*, for another possibility.

... וַיַּעֲנֹשׁ אֶת־הָאָרֶץ — *And fined the land*. He levied an annual tax (*Ralbag*). See Section II, *Yehoachaz' Kingship*, for *Radak's* suggestion that Yehoachaz may have attempted to avenge his father's death at Pharaoh's hands. This would explain the fine. It was levied to punish the people for their aggression.

4. אֶלְיָקִים אָחִיו — ... *his brother Elyakim*. In *Kings*, Elyakim is introduced as son of Yoshiahu rather than as brother of Yehoachaz. See Section II, *Yehoyakim: Son of Yoshiahu or Brother of Yehoachaz*, for a discussion.

וַיַּסֵּב אֶת־שְׁמוֹ יְהוֹיָקִים — *And changed his name to Yehoyakim*. Rulers frequently change the names of officials whom they appoint. Thus did Pharaoh change Joseph's name, and Moses change that of Joshua ... all this to stress the appointee's dependence on the monarch (*Mefaresh*).

Radak to *Kings* expresses the same thought and adds that the name Yehoyakim [יָהוּ - יָקִים, *God establishes*] is meant to imply that although the people had spurned him, the older brother, and appointed Yehoachaz in his stead, God had not forsaken him and was now establishing him in his kingship.

לו
ה־ט

ה מִצְרָֽיְמָה׃ בֶּן־עֶשְׂרִים וְחָמֵשׁ שָׁנָה֙ יְהוֹיָקִים
בְּמָלְכוֹ וְאַחַת עֶשְׂרֵה֙ שָׁנָה מָלַךְ בִּירוּשָׁלָ͏ִם וַיַּעַשׂ הָרַע
ו בְּעֵינֵי יְהוָה אֱלֹהָֽיו׃ עָלָיו עָלָה נְבוּכַדְנֶאצַּר מֶלֶךְ בָּבֶל
ז וַיַּאַסְרֵהוּ בַּֽנְחֻשְׁתַּיִם לְהֹלִיכוֹ בָּבֶֽלָה׃ וּמִכְּלֵי֙ בֵּית יְהוָה
ח הֵבִיא נְבוּכַדְנֶאצַּר לְבָבֶל וַיִּתְּנֵם בְּהֵיכָלוֹ בְּבָבֶֽל׃ וְיֶתֶר
דִּבְרֵי יְהוֹיָקִים וְתֹעֲבֹתָיו אֲשֶׁר־עָשָׂה֙ וְהַנִּמְצָא עָלָיו הִנָּם
כְּתוּבִים עַל־סֵפֶר מַלְכֵי יִשְׂרָאֵל וִיהוּדָה וַיִּמְלֹךְ יְהוֹיָכִין
ט בְּנוֹ תַּחְתָּֽיו׃ בֶּן־שְׁמוֹנֶה שָׁנִים֙ יְהוֹיָכִין בְּמָלְכוֹ

וַיְבִיאֵהוּ מִצְרָיְמָה — *And brought him to Egypt. Kings* has *and he died there*. It seems likely that *Chronicles* omits this as part of the system which we have noted above — that Yehoachaz's reign is to be delegitimized. The implication is that once he has left the arena of our concern, once he has been taken to Egypt, his fate is no longer of any interest to us.

5. ... מָלַךְ בִּירוּשָׁלַםִ וַיַּעַשׂ הָרַע ... — *He reigned in Jerusalem. He did that which was evil ... Chronicles* omits the name of Yehoyakim's mother which is given in *Kings*. See comm. to v.1.

וַיַּעַשׂ הָרַע ... — *He did that which was evil* ... The *Kings'* account has *He did evil in the eyes of HASHEM, in all matters just as his father had done*. The explanation of why this phrase is omitted in *Chronicles* may be as follows:

From *Sanhedrin* 103b it appears that, in the tradition of the Sages, Yehoyakim was by far the most wicked among the kings.

When Yehoyakim ascended the throne, he said, 'The earlier kings did not even know how to anger God [they were amateurs at wickedness, I can elicit much greater fury than they]. Do we need Him for anything other than the light [of the sun]? We have Parvaim gold for our use [which shines brightly]. Let Him keep His light [for Himself. We do not need it].' [The people] said to him, 'Is gold and silver not His, as it is written, *Silver and gold is Mine, says HASHEM of Hosts*?' So he answered them, 'He has already given it to us, as it is written, *As for the heavens, the heavens belong to HASHEM, but the earth He has given to the sons of man*.'

Evidently, the evil evinced in the hurling of this challenge against God is seen as a greater rebellion than that of any of the preceding kings [... the earlier kings did not even know ...] and this could be the reason why *Chronicles* left out the phrase *according to all that his father had done*. This would have implied that Yehoyakim's evil deeds fell into a similar category as those of his father when, in fact, they were much worse.

See Section II, *Yehoyakim Is Uniquely Evil*, for a discussion of why *Kings* has this phrase and what this has to say concerning the disparate approach of the two books to Yehoyakim's reign.

6. עָלָיו עָלָה נְבוּכַדְנֶאצַּר מֶלֶךְ בָּבֶל — *Against him, Nebuchadnezzar king of Babylon came up*. The *Kings'* account has: *In his days, Nebuchadnezzar king of Babylon came up, Yehoyakim became his servant for three years, and then rebelled against him*. Then the passage goes on to tell how the armies of a number of other countries were sent by God against Judah. No more mention is made of Babylon, and the account of the reign ends with the statement: *Yehoyakim lay with his fathers and Yehoyachin his son reigned in his stead*.

The difference between the two accounts is striking. See Section II, *Yehoyakim — The Most Tragic of Israel's Kings*, for a wide-ranging analysis.

לְהֹלִיכוֹ בָּבֶלָה — *To bring him to Babylon*. The intention was to take him to Babylon, but this was never realized since he died on the way as Jeremiah had predicted (*Metzudos*).

See above, and see comm. to next verse for *Radak's* opinion.

7. וּמִכְּלֵי בֵּית ה' — *Some of the vessels of HASHEM's House. Mefaresh* equates ... מִכְּלֵי with ... מִקְצָת כְּלֵי which is the expression used in *Daniel* 1:2.

The passage in *Daniel* reads as follows: *In the third year of the reign of Yehoyakim, king of Judah, Nebuchadnezzar, king of Babylon came to Jerusalem and besieged it. The Lord gave Yehoyakim, king of Judah, into his hand with some of the vessels of God's House. He brought them to the land of Shinear* ...

The implication of that wording is clear:

brought him to Egypt. 5 *Yehoyakim was twenty-five years*
old when he began to reign and he reigned eleven years
in Jerusalem. He did that which was evil in the eyes of HASHEM
his God. 6 *Against him, Nebuchadnezzar king of Babylon came*
up and bound him with shackles to bring him to Babylon.
7 *Nebuchadnezzar brought some of the vessels of* HASHEM'*s*
House to Babylon and placed them in his palace in Babylon.
8 *Now the rest of the matters of Yehoyakim and the abomin-*
ations which he committed and that which was discovered
concerning him, behold they are written in the Records of the
Kings of Israel and Judah. Yehoyachin, his son reigned in his
stead. 9 *Yehoyachin was eight years old when he began to reign*

Both Yehoyakim and the vessels were, in fact, brought to Babylon.

Since our passage seems to refer to that incident, *Radak* infers that in our v. 6 the meaning must also be that Yehoyakim was actually taken to Babylon. The *lamed* in לְהֹלִיכוֹ must be taken as substituting for a *vav*, as though the word were written וְהֹלִיכוֹ. *Radak* concludes that our vs. 6 and 7 refer to incidents which happened in the earlier part of Yehoyakim's reign at which time he was actually taken to Babylon. His fate in the eleventh and final year of his reign, when he died and his corpse was thrown out in accordance with Jeremiah's prophecy, is not recorded in *Chronicles*.

8. וְתוֹעֲבֹתָיו אֲשֶׁר־עָשָׂה — *And the abominations which he committed.* A litany of sins is recorded in *Jeremiah* 22:13-14. *Radak* maintains that the *Records of the Kings of Israel and Judah* mentioned at the end of the verse, is, in fact, the Book of *Jeremiah*.

Mefaresh explains that the word *abomination* hints at the fact that he cohabited with his mother. According to *Sanhedrin* 103b this sin was committed by Amon but no mention of it is made in connection with Yehoyakim. However, *Vayikra Rabbah* 19:6 reports: He wore *kilaim*, extended his foreskin [so that he appeared to be uncircumcised], cohabited with his mother, his daughter-in-law and his father's wife. He killed husbands, afflicted their wives and confiscated their money for the treasury.

וְהַנִּמְצָא עָלָיו — *And that which was discovered concerning him.* These were abominations which he committed in secret and which came to light much later (*Metzudos*).

We have discussed in Section II, *Yehoyakim Is Uniquely Evil*, the Aggadic tradition that the phrase means *that which was found upon him*, and that the meaning is a tattoo [thus, also *Mefaresh*] because he had tattooed either the Divine Name or an idolatrous name upon his male organ.

וַיִּמְלֹךְ יְהוֹיָכִין בְּנוֹ תַּחְתָּיו — *Yehoyachin, his son, reigned in his stead.* We have pointed out in Section II, *Yehoyakim - The Most Tragic of Israel's Kings*, that this statement is unique in that the information concerning the succession is not preceded by the statement that the reigning king had died. See there for the implications.

9. בֶּן־שְׁמוֹנֶה שָׁנִים יְהוֹיָכִין בְּמָלְכוֹ — *Yehoyachin was eight years old when he began to reign ...* See Section II, *The Chronicles' View of Yehoyachin's Reign*, for an extensive discussion of the method by which *Chronicles* treats this hapless king.

II Kings 24:8 gives Yehoyachin's age when he ascended the throne as eighteen.

Seder Olam's (ch. 25) solution is that, in fact, Yehoyachin was eighteen when he became king, as stated in the *Kings'* account. The count of *eight years* in *Chronicles* does not give his age, but dates the ascension by the years of Nebuchadnezzar's reign. (Compare *II Kings* 24:12, ... *and the king of Babylon took him in the eighth year of his [Nebuchadnezzar's] reign*).

The commentators have a different suggestion: Knowing the uncertainties of the succession in those turbulent times, Yehoyakim had appointed his son Yehoyachin as his successor as soon as he, Yehoyakim, ascended the throne. At that time Yehoyachin was a child of eight. Thus both statements can be accommodated. Yehoyachin was eight when he was appointed as successor to his father, and he was eighteen when he assumed the throne.

Both explanations tend to confirm the thesis

לו
י־יד

וּשְׁלֹשָׁה חֳדָשִׁים וַעֲשֶׂרֶת יָמִים מָלַךְ בִּירוּשָׁלָ͏ִם וַיַּעַשׂ
י הָרַע בְּעֵינֵי יְהוָה: וְלִתְשׁוּבַת הַשָּׁנָה שָׁלַח הַמֶּלֶךְ
נְבוּכַדְנֶאצַּר וַיְבִאֵהוּ בָבֶלָה עִם־כְּלֵי חֶמְדַּת בֵּית־יְהוָה
יא וַיַּמְלֵךְ אֶת־צִדְקִיָּהוּ אָחִיו עַל־יְהוּדָה וִירוּשָׁלָ͏ִם: בֶּן־
עֶשְׂרִים וְאַחַת שָׁנָה צִדְקִיָּהוּ בְמָלְכוֹ וְאַחַת עֶשְׂרֵה שָׁנָה
יב מָלַךְ בִּירוּשָׁלָ͏ִם: וַיַּעַשׂ הָרַע בְּעֵינֵי יְהוָה אֱלֹהָיו לֹא
יג נִכְנַע מִלִּפְנֵי יִרְמְיָהוּ הַנָּבִיא מִפִּי יְהוָה: וְגַם בַּמֶּלֶךְ
נְבוּכַדְנֶאצַּר מָרָד אֲשֶׁר הִשְׁבִּיעוֹ בֵּאלֹהִים וַיֶּקֶשׁ אֶת־
עָרְפּוֹ וַיְאַמֵּץ אֶת־לְבָבוֹ מִשּׁוּב אֶל־יְהוָה אֱלֹהֵי יִשְׂרָאֵל:
יד גַּם כָּל־שָׂרֵי הַכֹּהֲנִים וְהָעָם הִרְבּוּ °למעול־מַעַל כְּכֹל

°לִמְעָל־ק׳

which we suggested above. *Chronicles* is not interested in Yehoyachin's reign in its own right. It is viewed as only an extension of Yehoyakim's reign. In *Seder Olam*'s view this point is made by dating his reign by Nebuchadnezzar's rather than his own years, which are insignificant. Again, according to the commentators his appointment during his father's lifetime is more significant than the actual start of his own reign — he is, after all, only an adjunct of his father's reign.

וּשְׁלֹשָׁה חֳדָשִׁים וַעֲשֶׂרֶת יָמִים . . . — *And ... three months and ten days. Kings* has only the rounded three months; the ten days are not mentioned. Certainly, that is what we would expect; nowhere else in the historical records are extra days mentioned. Times are always rounded off to the nearest year or, as in the case of Yehoachaz, to the nearest month.

In the context of our understanding of *Chronicles'* handling of Yehoyachin's reign, the explanation may be as follows: If this were an accounting of Yehoyachin's reign as an independent king, indeed, there would be no logic in giving the days — as in all other cases the duration would have been rounded off. As part of Yehoyakim's tragedy — that though he was succeeded by his son, that reign was short-lived and soon his line was aborted and his brother became king, the usage adds dramatic impact. Even if we stretch the reign out to its fullest — even if we count the days, there were only three months and ten days left for Yehoyakim-Yehoyachin: After that — oblivion.

10. וְלִתְשׁוּבַת הַשָּׁנָה — *At the turn of the year.* This was at the exact point of the year at which the Babylonian forces had come up against Yehoyakim (*Metzudos*). [Apparently, the final defeat of Yehoyakim took nine months. The Babylonians had come on a given date, nine months later Yehoyakim was taken and died, and three months later Yehoyachin was taken captive.]

Thus, consistent with the path which we have traced, the events of Yehoyachin's reign are tied to Yehoyakim — a connecting link that is missing in *Kings*. This date had a threatening portent for Yehoyakim. It was the beginning of the end for his own reign and also for that of his son, whose reign was really only an extension of his own.

שָׁלַח הַמֶּלֶךְ נְבוּכַדְנֶאצַּר — *King Nebuchadnezzar sent ... Mefaresh* and *Metzudos* point out that in the *Kings'* account we learn that Yehoyachin went of his own volition [with *his mother, his servants, his princes and his chamberlains*] to put himself into Nebuchadnezzar's hands.

Chronicles, with only a cursory interest in this reign, omits this detail.

עִם־כְּלֵי חֶמְדַּת בֵּית־ה׳ — *Together with the most desirable vessels of* HASHEM*'s House.* The phrase goes with the earlier one, *and he brought him to Babylon*, thus making the point that the holy vessels were also taken to Babylon. See Section II, *The Exile of the Sacred Vessels*, for a discussion of the significance of the exile of the holy vessels.

כְּלֵי חֶמְדַּת בֵּית־ה׳ — *The most desirable vessels of the House of* HASHEM. The translation follows *Metzudos*.

וַיַּמְלֵךְ אֶת־צִדְקִיָּהוּ אָחִיו. . . — *He made his brother, Tzidkiahu king ... His brother* refers to Yehoyakim (*Mefaresh* and *Metzudos*). See Section II, *The Chronicles View of Yehoyachin's Reign*, for a discussion of the implications of this interpretation.

From *I Chronicles* 3:16 we learn that Yehoyachin had a son, Tzidkiahu. However, it is

*and he reigned three months and ten days in Jerusalem. He did
that which was evil in the eyes of* HASHEM. [10] *At the turn of the
year King Nebuchadnezzar sent for him to be brought to Babylon,
together with the most desirable vessels of* HASHEM'*s House. He
made his brother, Tzidkiahu, king over Judah and Jerusalem.*
[11] *Tzidkiahu was twenty-one years old when he began to reign.
He reigned eleven years in Jerusalem.* [12] *He did that which was
evil in the eyes of* HASHEM. *He did not humble himself before*
HASHEM'*s message by Jeremiah the prophet.* [13] *Moreover, he
rebelled against King Nebuchadnezzar who had made him swear
by God, but he stiffened his neck and hardened his heart rather
than repent before* HASHEM, *God of Israel.* [14] *Also all the Kohanite
officials and the people were exceedingly disloyal, acting in*

clear that in the tradition of the Sages (*Horios* 11b and *Kereisos* 5b), the Tzidkiahu who succeeded him to the throne was not his son, but his uncle of that name. That seems borne out by *II Kings* 24:17 where Tzidkiahu is called a דּוֹד, *an uncle* of Yehoyachin.

Given that Tzidkiahu was an uncle of Yehoyachin, it would seem possible to translate אָחִיו in our verse in the wider sense of *relative* as it is frequently used throughout Scripture — see specially *Genesis* 14:16 and 29:12 and *Leviticus* 10:4, where it is used to describe a nephew. With this meaning it could refer to Yehoyachin himself and we can avoid the textual awkwardness of having it go back on Yehoyakim.

11. בֶּן־עֶשְׂרִים וְאַחַת שָׁנָה — *Twenty-one years old*. See Section II, *Chronicles' View of Tzidkiahu's Reign*, for a wide-ranging analysis of Tzidkiahu's reign and the disparate approaches of *Kings* and *Chronicles*.

Tzidkiahu was the youngest of Yoshiahu's sons and could well have been only ten at his father's death. This would make him twenty-one at the time of his succession (*Radak*).

12. ... וַיַּעַשׂ הָרַע ... לֹא נִכְנַע — *He did that which was evil ... He did not humble himself* ... The extent of his evil was that he did not humble himself before Jeremiah but he was not guilty of abominations which Yehoyakim had committed or of that which had been *found upon him* (v. 8) (*Mefaresh*).

The *Mefaresh's* assertion, that with the exception of his not subjugating himself to Jeremiah's pronouncements (see below), Tzidkiahu was a righteous person, is in agreement with the tradition of the Sages. Tzidkiahu was a totally righteous person, a צַדִּיק גָּמוּר, in whose merit God did not destroy the world as He would have done because of the extreme wickedness of that generation (*Sanhedrin* 103a).

Jeremiah had repeatedly called upon Tzidkiahu to subjugate himself to Nebuchadnezzar's demands and to content himself with ruling over a minor vassal state. [See particulary *Jeremiah* ch. 27; the theme is repeated in many other places.] As discussed in Section II, *Chronicles' View of Tzidkiahu's Reign*, Tzidkiahu, under pressure of the aristocracy, could not bring himself to take this step. This refusal to bow to Jeremiah's demands is the subject of our verse.

13. וְגַם בַּמֶּלֶךְ נְבוּכַדְנֶאצַּר מָרָד — *Moreover, he rebelled against King Nebuchadnezzar*. The story of the oath of loyalty which Tzidkiahu had made to Nebuchadnezzar, and of his subsequent disloyalty, is told in *Ezekiel* ch. 17. See Artscroll *Ezekiel* there for a detailed discussion.

מִשּׁוּב אֶל־ה׳ אֱלֹהֵי יִשְׂרָאֵל — *Rather than repent before* HASHEM, *God of Israel*. The path of rebellion against Nebuchadnezzar led away from God, Whose wish, at this point, was that Israel should lose its independence so that it might once more be free to turn inward to its own spiritual concerns. See ArtScroll *Ezekiel* Overview VII, p.xlv, *A Lowly Kingdom*.

14. גַּם כָּל־שָׂרֵי הַכֹּהֲנִים — *Also all the Kohanite officials*. This is the only place where *Kohanite officials* are mentioned: In *Jeremiah* the offending aristocracy is referred to either as שָׂרִים, without further description, or as שָׂרֵי יְהוּדָה (cf. 26:10).

We may perhaps surmise that, in this verse too, *Chronicles* had the *lowly kingdom*, which should have come about, in mind. Possibly, in such a subordinate vassal state, leadership —

תֹּעֲבוֹת הַגּוֹיִם וַיְטַמְּאוּ אֶת־בֵּית יהוה אֲשֶׁר הִקְדִּישׁ
טו בִּירוּשָׁלָם: וַיִּשְׁלַח יהוה אֱלֹהֵי אֲבוֹתֵיהֶם עֲלֵיהֶם בְּיַד־
מַלְאָכָיו הַשְׁכֵּם וְשָׁלוֹחַ כִּי־חָמַל עַל־עַמּוֹ וְעַל־מְעוֹנוֹ:
טז וַיִּהְיוּ מַלְעִבִים בְּמַלְאֲכֵי הָאֱלֹהִים וּבוֹזִים דְּבָרָיו
וּמִתַּעְתְּעִים בִּנְבִאָיו עַד עֲלוֹת חֲמַת־יהוה בְּעַמּוֹ עַד־
יז לְאֵין מַרְפֵּא: וַיַּעַל עֲלֵיהֶם אֶת־מֶלֶךְ °כשדיים וַיַּהֲרֹג
בַּחוּרֵיהֶם בַּחֶרֶב בְּבֵית מִקְדָּשָׁם וְלֹא חָמַל עַל־בָּחוּר
יח וּבְתוּלָה זָקֵן וְיָשֵׁשׁ הַכֹּל נָתַן בְּיָדוֹ: וְכֹל כְּלֵי בֵּית
הָאֱלֹהִים הַגְּדֹלִים וְהַקְּטַנִּים וְאֹצְרוֹת בֵּית יהוה וְאֹצְרוֹת
יט הַמֶּלֶךְ וְשָׂרָיו הַכֹּל הֵבִיא בָבֶל: וַיִּשְׂרְפוּ אֶת־בֵּית
הָאֱלֹהִים וַיְנַתְּצוּ אֵת חוֹמַת יְרוּשָׁלָם וְכָל־אַרְמְנוֹתֶיהָ
כ שָׂרְפוּ בָאֵשׁ וְכָל־כְּלֵי מַחֲמַדֶּיהָ לְהַשְׁחִית: וַיֶּגֶל הַשְּׁאֵרִית

°כַּשְׂדִּים ק׳

which would have been mainly concentrated on spiritual matters — would have been vested in the *Kohanim*, much as it was during the period of the Second House. *Chronicles* bemoans that these potential leaders of the people, too, had failed.

The *Mefaresh* points out that the *Kohanim* are singled out for blame since it was their duty to instruct the people — and in this they failed.

וַיְטַמְּאוּ אֶת־בֵּית ה׳ — *They defiled* HASHEM's *House*. See *Ezekiel* ch. 8 for a graphic description of the defilement of the House which took place under Tzidkiahu.

אֲשֶׁר הִקְדִּישׁ בִּירוּשָׁלָם — *Which He had sanctified in Jerusalem*. The House had been sanctified so that the Divine Presence might rest there forever (*Mefaresh*). Instead, it had become a hotbed of the most crass and debasing idolatrous practices.

15. אֱלֹהֵי אֲבוֹתֵיהֶם ... כִּי־חָמַל ... — *The God of their fathers ... because He took pity*... The use of *God of their fathers* here is surely highly significant. That God constantly sent prophets to call the people to repentance was an act of mercy on His part [כִּי חָמַל ...] which drew on the merits of the Patriarchs. The present generation did not deserve it.

For a discussion of the question as to whether in the generation of the destruction, זְכוּת אָבוֹת, the *merit of the Patriarchs*, was still operative, see *Shabbos* 55a and ArtScroll *Ezekiel* comm. to 9:4 and fn. there.

בְּיַד־מַלְאָכָיו — *Through His messengers*. God's prophets are meant, as can be seen in the next verse where מַלְאֲכֵי הָאֱלֹהִים is used as a synonym for נְבִיאָיו.

We may legitimately ask why, in this context, *Chronicles* uses מַלְאָךְ instead of נָבִיא.

We may suggest that the purpose is to differentiate the true prophets, those whom God had *sent*, from the false prophets who were lulling the people into a false sense of security. In ch. 23 Jeremiah devotes an entire prophecy to these spurious prophets and makes the point: *I did not send these prophets but they ran. I spoke not to them but they prophesied* (v. 21).

וְעַל־מְעוֹנוֹ — *And on His habitation*. מָעוֹן never appears in *Chronicles* for House. At 30:27 it was used as a synonym for heaven, which is common usage, as for example at *Deuteronomy* 26:15. Throughout Scripture, מָעוֹן indicating House appears only in poetic passages as in *Psalms* 76:3. This verse and the next two seem also to have poetic rhythm. It is as though, in the face of the overwhelming tragedy of the destruction, *Chronicles* is lifted beyond the ordinariness of a prose account, to the pulsating throbs of a dirge.

In 30:27 we noted that מָעוֹן is that part of heaven in which God daily silences the hymns of glory sung to Him by the heavenly choir so that he might devote Himself to the well-being of Israel. Perhaps the term is used here for its evocative power. So much love had been poured out in His House. Ought it not to be saved?!

16. וַיִּהְיוּ מַלְעִבִים בְּמַלְאֲכֵי הָאֱלֹהִים — *But they mocked the messengers of God*. This is the only time in Scripture that לעב is used. *Metzudos* and *Radak* cite *Targum* to *Genesis* 27:12 where it is used to render מְתַעְתֵּעַ, which

accordance with all the abominations of the nations. They de-filed HASHEM's House which He had sanctified in Jerusalem.
15 *Then HASHEM the God of their fathers addressed them through His messengers, each and every day, always trying, because He took pity on His people and on His habitation.*
16 *But they mocked the messengers of God, despised His words and scoffed at His prophets, to a point that the anger of HASHEM rose against His people, without any possibility of abatement.*
17 *So He brought up against them the king of the Chaldeans who, in their Sanctuary, slew their young men with the sword. He had no compassion on young man or maiden, the old and the very ancient; He gave them all into his hand.*
18 *And all the utensils of God's House, great and small, and the treasures of HASHEM's House, and the treasures of the king and his princes — he brought all to Babylon.*
19 *They burned God's House and broke down the wall of Jerusalem. They burned all her palaces in fire, and consigned all her cherished possessions to destruction.*
20 *Those that were left*

they also interpret as *one who mocks* — see below. In fact, the word appears quite frequently in *Targumim* to render expressions like לעג, קלס, עלל, and הלל. *Eliyahu Bachur* in his *Meturgaman* makes the point that the two roots לעב and לעג are closely related.

וּמִתַּעְתְּעִים בִּנְבִאָיו — *And scoffed at His prophets*. *Targum Yonasan* to *Genesis* 27:12, כִּמְתַעְתֵּעַ, renders מְגַחֵךְ, *one who laughs* or *scoffs*. Thus, *Metzudos* here in his second rendering. Earlier, he suggests that the word derives from תעה, *to go astray*. The people claimed that the prophets of God erred in their interpretation of events. This is also the opinion of *Ibn Ezra* in *Genesis* there.[1]

17. וַיַּעַל עֲלֵיהֶם — *So He brought up against them*. The subject is HASHEM of the previous verse.

וַיַּהֲרֹג ... בְּבֵית מִקְדָּשָׁם ... — *Who, in their Sanctuary, slew* ... Israel had defiled the Holy House (v. 14); now they were to pay the price inside those very precincts (*Mefaresh*). *Mefaresh* could have added that in *Ezekiel's* prophetic vision of the massacre which was to be wreaked upon the Jews of Jerusalem, this precise point is made: *So He said to them: 'Defile the House and fill the courtyards with the slain men ...'* (*Ezekiel* 9:7).

Ch. 9 in *Ezekiel*, in which the prophet is shown a massacre of Jerusalem, seems to be a foreshadowing of the events described here (*Mefaresh*).

וְיָשֵׁשׁ — *And the very ancient*. A יָשֵׁשׁ is older than a זָקֵן (*Radak, Shorashim*). Both *Radak* and *Metzudos* suggest that the word is related to יֵשׁ, *being* or *existence*, in the sense that this person's *being* has stretched over a long period of time.

18. וְכֹל כְּלֵי בֵּית הָאֱלֹהִים — *And all the utensils of God's House* ... Earlier, in v. 7 in connection with Yehoyakim's exile, and in v. 10 in connection with Yehoyachin's exile, only some of the vessels had been taken. Now, with the destruction of the House, all that was left was taken into exile.

See Section II, *The Exile of the Sacred Vessels*.

19. לְהַשְׁחִית — *To destruction*. The contrast to the previous verse is striking. The House utensils were taken captive to Babylon; Jerusalem's cherished artifacts were consigned to the flames. If the motive for taking the House vessels would have been greed, then surely everything would have been taken. Apparently, then, it was not the value of the sacred vessels which caught the Babylonian eye, but the role which they played in Jewish life. See Section II, *The Exile of the Sacred Vessels*.

1. According to one interpretation of *Rashi* at *Jeremiah* 23:36, we do indeed find that the prophets were challenged to defend their interpretation of God's words. As *Rashi* reads that passage, the false prophets challenged the true prophets to tell them the exact words in which a prophecy had come to them, so that they could offer their own interpretation as an alternative to the way the true prophet had understood it.

מִן־הַחֶרֶב אֶל־בָּבֶל וַיִּהְיוּ־לוֹ וּלְבָנָיו לַעֲבָדִים עַד־מְלֹךְ
כא מַלְכוּת פָּרָס: לְמַלֹּאות דְּבַר־יהוה בְּפִי יִרְמְיָהוּ עַד־
רָצְתָה הָאָרֶץ אֶת־שַׁבְּתוֹתֶיהָ כָּל־יְמֵי הָשַּׁמָּה שָׁבָתָה
כב לְמַלֹּאות שִׁבְעִים שָׁנָה: וּבִשְׁנַת אַחַת לְכוֹרֶשׁ
מֶלֶךְ פָּרַס לִכְלוֹת דְּבַר־יהוה בְּפִי יִרְמְיָהוּ הֵעִיר יהוה
אֶת־רוּחַ כּוֹרֶשׁ מֶלֶךְ־פָּרַס וַיַּעֲבֶר־קוֹל בְּכָל־מַלְכוּתוֹ

20. הַשְּׁאֵרִית מִן־הַחֶרֶב — *Those that were left from the sword.* See fn. to Section II, *The Chronicles' View of Yehoyachin's Reign*, for a discussion of this phrase.

עַד־מְלֹךְ מַלְכוּת פָּרָס — *Until the rise of the Persian empire.* See ArtScroll *Daniel* p. 334 for a chronology of the period. Nebuchadnezzar destroyed the House in the nineteenth year of his reign, corresponding to the year 3338 from Creation. He was succeeded by his son, Evil Merodach, in the year 3364. He, in turn, was succeeded by Belshazzar in the year 3387. Two years later Belshazzar was assassinated in the year 3389, bringing the Babylonian Empire to an end after precisely seventy years.

In the next year, the Persian Cyrus proclaimed the right of the Jews to return to *Eretz Yisrael.*

21. לְמַלֹּאות דְּבַר־ה׳ בְּפִי יִרְמְיָהוּ — *To fulfill the word of* HASHEM *by the mouth of Jeremiah.* Jeremiah had prophesied that God would *remember* His people after seventy years of Babylonian rule (*Jeremiah* 28:10).

Our verse makes clear that these seventy years were to be in fulfillment of the Torah's assertion that the exile would come as atonement and appeasement to the land, for the transgression of the *shemittah* laws, which require abstention from any agricultural endeavors during the seventh year — and which were ignored during much of the First Commonwealth (*Leviticus* 26:34).

See *Rashi* to *Leviticus*, there, for the computations which yield that precisely seventy *shemittah* and *yovel* years were desecrated.

22-23. The final two verses of *Chronicles* are almost identical with the first two verses and part of the third verse of the Book of *Ezra*.

That *Chronicles* ends with the same verses as *Ezra* begins, indicates that the two are really one book, dealing with Israel's genealogy and its redemption from Babylon (*Ramban*, in *Sefer HaGeulah*). See prefatory remarks to *I Chronicles* ch. 9 for a wide-ranging discussion of the relationship between the two books.

We feel that the quoting of these two verses is crucial to the correct understanding of the Book of *Chronicles* and to the history which it records. By bracketing its account between the genealogical lists which begin with Adam — the beginning of human history, and ending with a look to the future redemption, the history — receives the hallmark of eternity. In contrast to *Samuel* and *Kings* which recorded the historical events from the perspective of the here and now, *Chronicles*, as we have seen throughout the comm., views them from the perspective of Israel's Messianic future — the ultimate revival of the Davidic dynasty.

The comm. to these final two verses is, with the exception of the final piece, taken from the ArtScroll edition of *Ezra* by *R' Yosef Rabinowitz*.

◆§ The Proclamation

22. אַחַת — *The first.* This does not mean his first year as king of Persia, for Cyrus had long been the Persian monarch, but the first year of his rule over the Babylonian empire after the death of his father-in-law, Darius the Mede (*Ibn Ezra*).

[In *Isaiah* 45:1-5 the prophet declares that God empowered Cyrus to conquer Babylon in order to deliver the Jewish people from Babylonian exile (see *Rashi* there). Thus, the passage may be understood in terms of Cyrus' elevation to the role of redeemer. *The first year of Cyrus* refers to the first year that Cyrus, through his conquest of Babylon, assumed his role as the instrument of redemption.]

לְכוֹרֶשׁ — *Of Cyrus* [*Koresh*]. Cyrus, king of Persia, accompanied his father-in-law, Darius, king of Media, in the conquest of the Babylonian empire. Darius replaced Belshazzar, last of the Babylonian kings (*Daniel* 5:30, 6:1), and ruled for one year. He died in battle, and was immediately succeeded by his son-in-law, Cyrus [1] (*Rashi* from *Yossipon, Daniel* 6:29) in the year 3390.

1. The historical tradition that Cyrus, king of Persia, was the son-in-law of Darius, king of Media, is quoted by *Ibn Ezra* (*Daniel* 6:1) as well. See ArtScroll *Daniel* 6:1.

from the sword, he exiled to Babylon, where they became slaves to him and to his sons until the rise of the Persian empire. 21 *To fulfill the word of* HASHEM *by the mouth of Jeremiah until the land had been appeased of the sabbaths, for as long as she was desolate she rested to a full seventy years.* 22 *And in the first year of Cyrus king of Persia, upon the conclusion of* HASHEM*'s word by the mouth of Jeremiah,* HASHEM *aroused the good will of Cyrus, king of Persia; and he issued a proclamation throughout his kingdom*

Cyrus' dominion included the Land of Israel, with its amalgam of gentile nationals [see 4:9, 10]. He permitted the return of the Jewish exiles from Babylon, where they had been banished when the Babylonians destroyed the House over half a century earlier [see prologue]. His reign lasted three years (*Rashi, Megillah* 11b from *Seder Olam*). He was followed by Ahasuerus, the husband of Queen Esther, who was succeeded by their son Darius (*Rashi*). [See table following page.]

The name *Cyrus* — in Hebrew, כֹּרֶשׁ, *Koresh* — has the same letters as כשר, *kosher*. *Rashi* (4:7) comments that the name *Koresh* therefore indicates that Cyrus was a virtuous (*kosher*) king. *Ibn Ezra* adds that his name was given in recognition of his virtuous behavior towards the Jewish people.

Rashi here quotes the *Talmud*: [He was named] *Koresh* because he was a virtuous [*kosher*] king ... what was his true name? Darius (*Rosh Hashanah* 3b).

These Talmudic remarks concern Darius, son of Esther and Ahasuerus. Darius reigned some fourteen years after Cyrus, and presided over the completion of the House [see *Rashi*, *Haggai* 1:1]. His name does not appear in the Book of *Ezra* until 4:24. He is referred to in Scripture as Darius, and it is only through Rabbinic tradition (*Rosh Hashanah* 3b) that we are informed that he was surnamed *Koresh* because of his virtue. Yet, *Rashi* invokes the Talmudic statement concerning Darius, in relation to the Cyrus mentioned here. Evidently, *Rashi* feels that the Talmudic explanation of Darius' surname *Koresh* may be applied as well to his virtuous predecessor, King Cyrus [*Koresh*].

לִכְלוֹת דְּבַר־ה׳ בְּפִי יִרְמְיָהוּ — *Upon the conclusion of* HASHEM*'s word by the mouth of Jeremiah.* This occurred at the conclusion of the seventy-year period about which Jeremiah prophesied: *After seventy years of Babylon are completed: I shall remember you... to restore you to this place* (*Jeremiah* 29:10) (*Rashi*).

See *Rambam* in *Moreh* [Guide] II:45 for a different understanding of this verse.

[The prophecy was not literally *by the mouth of Jeremiah*, but was transmitted in a letter dispatched by the prophet to the Babylonian exiles (*Jeremiah* 29:11).]

Rashi to *Megillah* 12a (based on *Seder Olam* and *Megillah* 11b, 12a) interprets *seventy years of Babylon* to mean seventy years of Jewish subjugation to Babylon, and computes these years from the year 3320 [see table] — the second year of the reign of Nebuchadnezzar, founder of the Babylonian empire, when his conquest of the Jewish kingdom took place. Nebuchadnezzar's rule over the Jews lasted over forty-three years. His son and successor, Evil Merodach, completed the forty-fourth year and reigned for twenty-two years afterward. He was followed by Belshazzar, last of the Babylonians, whose rule lasted three years. His kingdom was conquered by Darius the Mede, who reigned for one year, completing the passage of seventy years from the Babylonian conquest of the Jewish people. [Although Darius was not of Babylonian descent, his rule is included in the seventy years. Evidently, *seventy years of Babylon* refers to the passage of seventy years from the Babylonian conquest, but does not necessarily mean seventy years under the sovereignty of Babylonian kings.] Cyrus, who followed Darius, immediately granted permission for the House's reconstruction.

However, *R' Yeshayah (Ri) MiTrani* begins the computation of the *seventy years of Babylon* with the *first year* of Nebuchadnezzar's rule. His reign lasted over forty-four years. His successor, Evil Merodach, completed the forty-fifth year, and continued on the throne for another twenty-one years, and part of a twenty-second year. He was followed by Belshazzar, who completed the twenty-second year and ruled for two years thereafter. Darius succeeded him for one year, completing the passage of a total of seventy years from the establishment of the Babylonian Empire (see chart following page).

הֵעִיר ה׳ אֶת־רוּחַ כּוֹרֶשׁ — HASHEM *aroused the good will of Cyrus*. *Ralbag* suggests that Cyrus was inspired by a dream in which it was revealed that God had given him all the kingdoms of earth, and now commanded him to build the House in Jerusalem.

Malbim cites *Josephus*, who relates that when Cyrus learned of the miraculous downfall of Belshazzar [see *Daniel* 5][1], he vowed to rebuild the Sanctuary.

1. The Babylonian monarch Belshazzar and his forces had defeated the invading armies led by Darius the Mede and Cyrus (*Rashi, Daniel* 5:1). At the victory celebration, Belshazzar and his entourage drank from the

לו כג וְגַם־בְּמִכְתָּב לֵאמֹר: כֹּה־אָמַר כּוֹרֶשׁ ׀ מֶלֶךְ פָּרַס
כג כָּל־מַמְלְכוֹת הָאָרֶץ נָתַן לִי יהוה אֱלֹהֵי הַשָּׁמַיִם
וְהוּא־פָקַד עָלַי לִבְנוֹת־לוֹ בַיִת בִּירוּשָׁלַםִ אֲשֶׁר בִּיהוּדָה
מִי־בָכֶם מִכָּל־עַמּוֹ יהוה אֱלֹהָיו עִמּוֹ וְיָעַל׃

The Seventy Years of Babylon

	King	Rule over Jews	B.C.E.	No. Years
ACCORDING TO RASHI	Nebuchadnezzar	3320-3363 (midyear)	440-397 (midyear)	43½
	Evil Merodach	3363 (midyear)-3386	397 (midyear)-374	22½
	Belshazzar	3386-3389	374-371	3
	Darius	3389-3390	371-370	1
ACCORDING TO RI MITRANI	Nebuchadnezzar	3319-3363 (midyear)	441-397 (midyear)	44½
	Evil Merodach	3363 (mid.)-3385 (mid.)	397 (mid.)-375 (mid.)	22
	Belshazzar	3385-3388	375 (mid.)-372	2½
	Darius	3388-3389	372-371	1

Another explanation given by *Malbim* is that Cyrus was inspired by the words of *Isaiah* (44:28): *My shepherd Cyrus shall fulfill My every wish, and shall proclaim, 'Let Jerusalem be rebuilt and the Sanctuary be founded.'*

וַיַּעֲבֶר־קוֹל בְּכָל־מַלְכוּתוֹ וְגַם־בְּמִכְתָּב — *And he issued a proclamation throughout his kingdom ... and in writing as well.* The proclamation was announced orally and distributed in written form, with the royal seal (*Ibn Ezra*).

Malbim comments that the proclamation was committed to writing to insure its implementation. According to Persian law, a written decree of the king could not be rescinded, as stated in *Esther* 8:8: *For an edict which is written in the king's name, and sealed with the royal signet, may not be revoked.*[1]

Malbim also notes that this documentation of Cyrus's proclamation proved to be of great significance in the eventual restoration of the House. After the first wave of Jewish exiles returned to the Holy Land and laid the House's foundation (chs. 2, 3), Cyrus accepted the slander of the enemies of Judah and Benjamin, and ordered the construction halted (ch. 4). Eighteen years later, Darius sanctioned the resumption of the House construction based upon the discovery in the royal archives of a copy of Cyrus's original proclamation (6:12). Thus it was only through the documentation of Cyrus's decree that Darius was later able to justify his sanctioning of the resumption of the House's construction.

23. כֹּה־אָמַר כּוֹרֶשׁ מֶלֶךְ פָּרַס — *So says Cyrus king of Persia.* The Sages teach that the Persian king's sponsorship of the return to Jerusalem was evidence of Jewish unworthiness in the eyes of God. A more deserving generation would have merited a return to the Land free from alien domination. The Sages state in *Berachos* 41a: *Ezra's generation was destined for a redemption as miraculous as that of Joshua's days [when the greatly*

sacred House vessels which Nebuchadnezzar had taken during the sack of the House in Jerusalem. A hand then appeared miraculously, and spelled out a mysterious message, which Daniel interpreted as the prediction of Belshazzar's downfall. Later the same night, Belshazzar was murdered [by one of his own attendants (*R' Saadiah Gaon*)].

1. This comment is apparently contradicted by subsequent events (ch. 4), when the enemies of Judah and Benjamin persuaded the king to withdraw his sanction for the House's reconstruction. *Malbim*, however, reconciles the apparent contradiction, explaining that the enemies convinced the king, through a slanderous misrepresentation of the activities in Jerusalem, that the Jews had grossly overstepped the terms of the edict. The decree had specified that they were granted permission only to rebuild the House. Instead, the enemies alleged, they were actually rebuilding and fortifying the entire city with its surrounding walls, indicating that they planned a rebellion. The king accepted the slander and halted the work in Jerusalem because he assumed that the construction taking place was unauthorized by his edict. Thus, the enemies were successful in circumventing the objective of the proclamation without actually repealing it.

36
23

— and in writing as well — saying. [23] *So says Cyrus king of Persia: All the kingdoms of the earth has* HASHEM, *God of heaven, delivered to me and He has commanded me to build Him a House in Jerusalem which is in Judah. Anyone among you of His entire people, may* HASHEM *his God be with him, let him go up!*

outnumbered Jewish army conquered Eretz Yisrael in a series of miraculous victories; see *Joshua*], *but their misdeeds prevailed. Rashi* (there) explains that this unworthiness made the return to Zion contingent upon Cyrus' permission, and caused those who returned to suffer the domination of Cyrus's successors, Ahasuerus [of the Book of *Esther*] and Darius [Ahasuerus' son who completed the construction of the House; see ch. 6].

כָּל־מַמְלְכוֹת הָאָרֶץ נָתַן לִי ה׳ — *All the kingdoms of the earth has* HASHEM *... delivered to me.* God has placed all the kingdoms under my rule (*Rashi*), and I am, therefore, obliged to fulfill His command (*Metzudos*).

Cyrus did not actually rule over all mankind. He exaggerated deliberately to enhance his prestige (*Megillah* 11b).

אֱלֹהֵי הַשָּׁמַיִם — *God of heaven. Ibn Ezra* and *Malbim* note that Cyrus refrained from describing HASHEM as God of heaven *and earth* because of his erroneous belief that HASHEM does not intervene in earthly affairs, but relegates the dominion over earth to man. This is indicated, as well, by the statement *All the kingdoms of the earth has* HASHEM *delivered to me*, i.e., Cyrus thought that the power to influence the destiny of the kingdoms of earth was related to himself in particular (*Ibn Ezra*; *Malbim*). [Where Jerusalem was concerned, however, Cyrus did acknowledge that Divine guidance was in effect. See comm. to v. 3.]

וְהוּא־פָקַד עָלַי — *And He has commanded me.* The command was not given directly, but through the prophet Isaiah (44:28): [HASHEM] *Who says of Cyrus, 'My shepherd shall fulfill My every wish, and shall proclaim, "Let Jerusalem be rebuilt and the Sanctuary be founded,"* ' and (45:1), *So says* HASHEM *His illustrious Cyrus: 'I have strengthened his right arm'* (*Rashi*).

לִבְנוֹת־לוֹ בַיִת בִּירוּשָׁלַםִ — *To build Him a House in Jerusalem.* According to R' Yochanan (*Yoma* 9b), the *Shechinah*, Divine Presence, did not reside in the Second House as it had in the First, because the Second House was built through the efforts of Persian kings Cyrus, and later Darius, whereas the First was constructed by King Solomon.

This opinion is based on the Biblical passage describing the blessing bestowed by Noah upon his two sons — Shem, the ancestor of the Jewish people, and Japheth, forefather of the Persians: *May God extend Japheth, but He will dwell in the tents of Shem* (*Genesis* 9:27). R' Yochanan interprets: Although God shall extend Japheth, He shall dwell only in the tents of Shem (*Yoma* 9b, 10a).

[The interpretation may be understood as follows: Japheth's creative impulse will, with God's inspiration, extend to the sacred area generally reserved for Shem. I.e., Japheth's Persian progeny will construct a sanctuary. Nevertheless, He shall dwell only in the tents of Shem — Japheth's sanctuary will not be God's dwelling place, for the *Shechinah* shall reside only in the House erected by King Solomon and the Jewish descendants of Shem (see *Rashi, Genesis* 9:27).]

The prophetic ordination of Cyrus as the restorer of the House does not conflict with the Rabbis' assertion that the *Shechinah* would not reside in a House built by a Persian. Although the Second House would not achieve the very highest level of sanctity, it would serve as the focal point of the Jewish attachment to God. When He saw that the Jews were deserving of such a sanctuary, God made it known, through His prophet, that they would be given the House and that Cyrus would be the instrument for the fulfillment of Providential design.

Reish Lakish disagrees, attributing the loss of the *Shechinah* to the fact that the entire nation did not return from Babylon (*Yoma* 9b), as it is written: *The entire congregation* [*of returnees*] *... forty-two thousand three hundred sixty*. This was a small minority of the community of exiles.

מִי־בָכֶם מִכָּל־עַמּוֹ — *Anyone among you of His entire people.* Cyrus's proclamation was worded to address all of Cyrus's subjects, including the non-Jews, inviting the Jews among them to go up to Jerusalem to build the House (*Rashi*). Although only the Jews were qualified to perform the work of construction, Cyrus obligated the gentiles to share in the building of the House. They were to help send the Jews to Jerusalem (*Malbim*).

[This obligation is spelled out further in verse 4 where the gentiles were instructed to provide financial support for the Jewish immigrants.]

ה׳ אֱלֹהָיו עִמּוֹ — *May* HASHEM *his God be with*

him. The translation follows *Rashi*, who understands this phrase as a blessing invoking Divine assistance, interjected by Cyrus into the invitation to the Jews to emigrate.

Ibn Ezra disagrees with *Rashi*, rendering יְהִי אֱלֹהָיו עִמּוֹ, *with whom his God was* [*Ibn Ezra* understands יְהִי, *May He* (future tense), as הָיָה, *was* (past tense)]; i.e., whom God had blessed with the wealth with which to go up to Jerusalem. The entire sentence thus reads: *Any among you of His people with whom his God has been* [whom God endowed with wealth enough to go up] — *let him go up to Jerusalem*.

In *Ibn Ezra's* view then, Cyrus began the proclamation by urging emigration for those Jews wealthy enough to afford the trip. The closing statement of the proclamation (v. 4) provides that those Jews who could not afford to emigrate were to receive the necessary funds from their gentile neighbors.

וְיָעַל — *Let him go up*. It is noteworthy that the quote from *Ezra* ends in the middle of a verse. There the sentence continues: . . . *to Jerusalem which is in Judah, and build the House of* HASHEM, *God of Israel — He is the God — which is in Jerusalem*.

This seems to confirm all that we have surmised about *Chronicles'* view of history. *Let him go up* is not to be limited to a specific historic event — the return to Zion from the Babylonian exile — but is to look to the future. Jewish history — when the Messiah comes — will end with just these words: *Let him go up*!

תם ונשלם שבח לאל בורא עולם

Section Two
Analyses and Expositions

Chapter One

◆§ Solomon and Moses

We may surmise another reason for Solomon's decision to go to Giveon rather than sacrificing at a private *bamah* in Jerusalem.

We note that in the latter part of our verse the Tabernacle is described as having been made by Moses, the servant of *HASHEM*. Why would this description, which is absent from a similar context at *I Chronicles* 21:29, where David is the subject, be used here?

Moreover, in the parallel passage in *I Kings*, Solomon's pilgrimage to Giveon is explained simply because ... *that was the great bamah*, and no mention is made of the fact that the Tabernacle had been made by Moses.

The appellation *servant of HASHEM* is the noblest to which man can aspire since it describes that state in which a person is permeated by the awareness of his absolute dependence upon God. Not everyone deserves to be described by such an exalted title. In fact, the Sages teach that Solomon described himself as God's servant (*I Kings* 3:9) but that God denied him this description. He called David *My servant* (*I Kings* 11:13 and *II Kings* 19:34), but not Solomon.

Now Solomon's craving to merit the description *servant of HASHEM* may be understood in terms of *Rosh HaShanah* 21b which teaches that Koheles (Solomon) wished to be just like Moses [in the attainment of wisdom]. (See *Pachad Yitzchak, Shaar Chodesh HaAviv* 68 who quotes and explains the point made by the Kabbalists that the letters of Solomon's name שְׁלֹמֹה can be rearranged to read לְמֹשֶׁה, *towards Moses*.) Solomon's ambition — which in the event remained unrealized — was to attain Moses' level of perfection — to be a *servant of HASHEM* just as Moses had been.

Perhaps it was this very craving which turned his very first steps as king towards Giveon — home of the Tabernacle which Moses the servant of *HASHEM* had built. In the case of David this played no role — and therefore it is not mentioned at *I Chronicles* 21:29, as we noted above — but it was central to Solomon's thinking and motivation.

Thus, in the *Kings'* account the central theme is Solomon's desire to sacrifice. The pilgrimage to Giveon was coincidental to that motivation. The altar which Solomon required happened to be in Giveon. In the *Chronicles'* account the pilgrimage itself is central. Solomon wished to go to Giveon because it was there that he could come into contact with the Tabernacle which Moses the servant of *HASHEM* had made. The sacrifices which he brought there are relative to this motivation, an afterthought.

A comparison of the two texts indicates that our analysis is correct (see chart opposite page).

The relationship between the two accounts would thus be much the same as the one we recognized in ch. 17 concerning the two accounts of David's suggestion that he build the Temple. (See pref. remarks to that chapter and Section II there.) We saw there that the *Samuel's* account dealt with the overt motivation while *Chronicles* delved into an inner layer of consciousness. Here too, the *Kings'* account seems to teach that aspect of the pilgrimage which everyone was able to grasp. *Chronicles* is concerned with the inner drives which motivated Solomon where the people's eyes could not follow.

II Chronicles Ch. 1	I Kings Ch. 3
a. 3. וַיֵּלְכוּ שְׁלֹמֹה וְכָל־הַקָּהָל עִמּוֹ לַבָּמָה אֲשֶׁר בְּגִבְעוֹן, *Then Solomon together with the whole congregation went to the bamah at Giveon*	a. 4. וַיֵּלֶךְ הַמֶּלֶךְ גִּבְעֹנָה, *Now the king went to Giveon*
b.	b. לִזְבֹּחַ שָׁם, *to sacrifice there,*
c. כִּי־שָׁם הָיָה אֹהֶל מוֹעֵד . . . אֲשֶׁר עָשָׂה מֹשֶׁה עֶבֶד־ה׳, *because the Tent of Meeting which Moses the servant of* HASHEM *had made in the desert was there.*	c. כִּי־הִיא הַבָּמָה הַגְּדוֹלָה, *for this was the great bamah;*
d. 6. וַיַּעַל שְׁלֹמֹה שָׁם עַל־מִזְבַּח הַנְּחֹשֶׁת לִפְנֵי ה׳ אֲשֶׁר לְאֹהֶל מוֹעֵד וַיַּעַל עָלָיו עֹלוֹת אָלֶף, *Solomon made an offering there upon the copper altar — before* HASHEM, *for it was part of the Tent of Meeting; he made an offering upon it of a thousand burnt offerings.*	d. אֶלֶף עֹלוֹת יַעֲלֶה שְׁלֹמֹה עַל הַמִּזְבֵּחַ הַהוּא, *one thousand burnt offerings would Solomon offer up upon that altar.*

◆§ The Vision at Giveon

We are struck by a significant difference between the two accounts. *Kings* talks of the location — *At Giveon* ... while *Chronicles* stresses the timing — *That night* ...

We begin our analysis by contrasting Solomon's request as it is recorded in *Kings* with the way it is presented in *Chronicles* (see chart, following page).

We note three apparently major differences. 1. *Chronicles* makes no mention of Solomon's perception of himself as an untried youngster (b). 2. Whereas in *Kings*, Solomon asks for a *listening heart, in order to judge this people, to comprehend the difference between good and evil*; in *Chronicles*, he asks for *wisdom and knowledge that I may go out before this people and come in*. 3. The phrase *going out and coming in* seems to occupy a different place in the two narratives.

The exact meaning of the idiom *to go out and come in* is difficult to pin down, but it surely seems to denote a general stewardship of the people rather than a specific function such as judging them. (See *Numbers* 27:17 and *Deuteronomy* 31:2.) From *Ramban* (*Numbers* there) it appears to refer to Torah leadership (*Sotah* 13b), while *Ibn Ezra* interprets it to denote generalship and execution of wars (thus also *Mefaresh* here). It certainly does not describe the specific act of judging the people.

Based on this understanding, the argument in *Kings* is as follows. My extreme youth makes the general stewardship of the people an overwhelming task (b), the more so because they are so very many (c). The specific task of judging the people [which is only one of many duties] is particularly hard when one realizes that the people are not only numerous (c) but difficult (e).

כָּבֵד in (e) can be understood as 'a numerous' people (see for example Genesis 50:9) or a 'heavy' or *difficult* people, which is the more frequent usage of כבד. It seems likely that Solomon in his mind's ear heard the echo of Moses' complaint (*Numbers* 11:14), 'I cannot bear these people myself ... for they are too כָּבֵד for me.' The context there seems to demand that this word be understood as *difficult*. We assume this meaning here, too.

Therefore, that I may judge them well, grant me a *listening ear* so that I may not only

II Chronicles Ch. 1	*I Kings Ch. 3*
a. 9. עַתָּה ה׳ אֱלֹהִים יֵאָמֵן דְּבָרְךָ עִם דָּוִיד אָבִי, *Now O HASHEM, God, may Your words with my father David be fulfilled*	a. 7. וְעַתָּה ה׳ אֱלֹהָי אַתָּה הִמְלַכְתָּ אֶת־עַבְדְּךָ תַּחַת דָּוִד אָבִי, ... *Now HASHEM my God, You have made Your servant king, in the place of David, my father,*
b.	b. וְאָנֹכִי נַעַר קָטֹן לֹא אֵדַע צֵאת וָבֹא, *and I am a young lad, unable to know how to go out or how to come in.*
c. כִּי אַתָּה הִמְלַכְתַּנִי עַל־עַם רַב כַּעֲפַר הָאָרֶץ, *[I ask this] for You have made me king over a people as numerous as the dust of the earth.*	c. 8. וְעַבְדְּךָ בְּתוֹךְ עַמְּךָ אֲשֶׁר בָּחָרְתָּ עַם־רָב אֲשֶׁר לֹא־יִמָּנֶה וְלֹא יִסָּפֵר מֵרֹב, *And Your servant is among Your people which You have chosen, a numerous people which cannot be counted or given number because they are so many.*
d. 10. עַתָּה חָכְמָה וּמַדָּע תֶּן־לִי וְאֵצְאָה לִפְנֵי הָעָם־הַזֶּה וְאָבוֹאָה, *Now grant me wisdom and knowledge, that I may go out before this people, and come in*	d. 9. וְנָתַתָּ לְעַבְדְּךָ לֵב שֹׁמֵעַ לִשְׁפֹּט אֶת־עַמְּךָ לְהָבִין בֵּין־טוֹב לְרָע, *So grant Your servant a listening heart, in order to judge this people, to comprehend the difference between good and evil,*
e. כִּי־מִי יִשְׁפֹּט אֶת־עַמְּךָ הַזֶּה הַגָּדוֹל, *for who could [otherwise] provide leadership for this people of Yours that is so great?*	e. כִּי מִי יוּכַל לִשְׁפֹּט אֶת־עַמְּךָ הַכָּבֵד הַזֶּה, *for who can judge this difficult people?*

hear that which they say but also that which they mean — that I may distinguish between good and evil and thus be able to judge them well (d).

Thus, Solomon's request centers upon help in the specific task of judging the people. From the structure of the narrative in *Kings*, it is clear that this is the thrust of the story since the incident at Giveon is immediately followed by the story of Solomon's insightful decision in the matter of the dispute of the two mothers concerning the infant who had died (*I Kings* 2:16 ff.). [Note also the introduction to the story .... *Then* two women came. The event grew out of the preceding one.] This decision richly illustrates the *listening heart* which Solomon had been granted.

In our reading of this passage in *Kings*, there is really no mention at all of profound wisdom which would express itself in a deep understanding of matters outside the confines of the immediate needs of administering justice. We are thus left without a clear understanding of verses like *I Kings* 5.10-14 which describe Solomon's wisdom in the most general terms, and of incidents like the visit of the queen of Sheba who came to test Solomon with her riddles — matters which seem to be little influenced by the specific insightfulness into the human character which was the subject of Solomon's request.

Moreover, we note that the statement in I *Kings* 5:9 ff., concerning the abundance of wisdom which God gave to Solomon, comes entirely independent of the dream at Giveon.

Perhaps this general wisdom with which Solomon was blessed is the subject of his request as recorded in *Chronicles*. Here, there is no mention of the *listening heart* so necessary to really delve into the minds of litigating parties. Rather, Solomon craves wisdom and knowledge to enable him to . . . *go out before this people and come in*; it is the entire stewardship of his nation which occupies his mind. As noted in the comm. and reflected in our translation, the Hebrew שפט carries connotations beyond the concept of *judging*.

As we have already indicated in Section II, *Solomon and Moses*, to v. 3, the two narratives must be seen as two different perspectives of what happened. *Kings* deals with the overt, conscious and perceived event; *Chronicles* with the inner drives which have their place in the deep recesses of Solomon's being.

At the overt level Solomon's motivation was a simple one. He felt himself young and inexperienced, weighed down by the burden of a load that seemed too great. He utilizes the offer that he may ask for anything, to beg for help in the administration of justice.

But there was another, more profound level at which Solomon spoke. It was not the technical problem of his youth that occupied his mind, not the specific and defined issue of whether or not he would judge this or that case correctly. Rather, it was his place in the history of his people — the craving to be like Moses, the definition of his entire kingship, which drove him to seek not wealth, but wisdom at God's hands. Solomon king of Israel was hidden inside Solomon the child.

In consideration of the insights which we gained in Section II, *Solomon and Moses*, to v. 3, we are now in a position to understand why *Kings* stresses the location of the vision while *Chronicles* deals with the time.

In *Kings*, the location of God's appearance was significant. Giveon had held no special importance for Solomon — he went there only because it was there that the altar which he needed was located. God's love of Solomon was such that he appeared to him in Giveon although Solomon's presence there was only coincidental.

In the *Chronicles'* narrative, Solomon went to Giveon because it was there he wanted to be. He wanted to find God at the Tabernacle which Moses servant of Hashem had made. It is natural that if he was to be granted the vision at all, it would be at Giveon. There was no need to stress this. It was, however, significant that the vision came immediately. On the very day that he had gone there in answer to his inner craving to be *like Moses*, with no delay at all, God appeared to him.

Chapter Two

◆§ Solomon and Churam

The *Kings'* narrative has three exchanges of messengers. In v. 15 we learn that Churam sent his servants to Solomon . . . *for he had heard that they had anointed him king in succession of his father, for Churam had always loved David.* Seemingly in reaction to this gesture of friendship, Solomon sends Churam a message soliciting his help in building the Temple. He prefaces his request with a short historical survey detailing God's refusal to let David build the Temple and His promise that David's son would have this privilege (vs. 17—19). Then follows a brief request for help in the form of permission to cut cedar from the Lebanon; an offer to have Solomon's servants cooperate with Churam's workers; and an offer to pay for Churam's work force (v. 20).

Chronicles does not mention Churam's initial gesture at all. It opens with Solomon's message to Churam, which seems quite different from the one described in *Kings*. The historical background is missing altogether. Instead, Solomon reminds Churam of the cedars which Churam had sent to help David build a palace for himself (v. 2). He then tells Churam of his intention to build a Temple [without any reference to the fact that David had even wanted to do this, or that he was acting as David's son] and accompanies this with a detailed description of the sacrificial services for which this Temple was to be used (v. 3). Vs. 4 and 5 tell of the need to have a great and imposing building and Solomon's recognition of his own inadequacy for such a gigantic project on his own. V. 6 asks for an artisan skilled in work with precious metals, while vs. 7—9, in asking for cedar and other wood from Churam's forests, essentially parallel v. 20 in *Kings*.

To aid us in appreciating the contrast between the two passages we offer the following chart:

II Chronicles Ch. 2	*Kings*
A.	A. Churam's messengers
B. Solomon's messengers	B. Solomon's messengers
C.	C. Historical background
D. Reminder of help given David	D.
E. Statement of Temple's purpose and Solomon's inadequacy	E.
F. Temple's projected size	F.
G. Request for skilled artisans	G.
H. Request for cedars . . .	H. Request for cedars . . .

Rashi, the *Mefaresh*, *Radak* and *Metzudos* content themselves with explaining the respective passages and do not address themselves at all to the differences between the two narratives.

Abarbanel is most concerned with the omission in *Chronicles* of Churam's original delegation. He explains this by assuming that this original gesture had no bearing on the building of the Temple, which is *Chronicles'* main concern, but was simply a matter of courtesy from an old established monarch to a young son of an esteemed friend. For *Chronicles* this had no importance. He sees Solomon's request and Churam's response in *Chronicles* as essentially the same as in *Kings* and makes no attempt to analyze the passages closely. This seems to be also *Ralbag's* understanding. He notes simply that *Kings* describes this exchange much more briefly than does *Chronicles*, thereby indicating that he views the two accounts as essentially the same.

We assume that the apparent discrepancies can be explained on the basis of different perspectives which the two books have of the same incident. We suggest that these two perspectives are consistent with those which we traced in detail in comm. and Section II to *I Chronicles* ch. 17 which describes David's initial urge to build the Temple.

We found there that *Kings*, in line with the objective of that book as we understood it, told the story from the point of view of the monarchy. David as king thought that the time had come for him to fulfill his kingly obligations to build the Temple. By contrast, *Chronicles* had dealt with David the man and the question of his inner spiritual readiness to be the one to bring the Divine Presence to rest permanently in Israel.

These same two complementary perspectives continue to orient the two accounts with which we are dealing here. Solomon was functioning at two levels: as heir to his father's throne and as the man of peace who, in his person, was to be the vindication of his father's inner struggles. Both these roles were active in Solomon's relationship with Churam. The one is described in *Kings*, the other in our chapter.

V. 1 in *Chronicles*, gives information which, as in *Kings*, is also given at the end of the chapter, sets the tone as follows:

We recall that Solomon's delegation to Churam had, in *Kings*, been preceded by a delegation from Churam to Solomon. The entire thrust of the narrative in *Kings* implies that *Solomon's* delegation came as a *response* to Churam's initiative. When Solomon, as a young boy, became king, Churam as an old friend of his father David immediately sent his congratulations coupled with an offer to help in any way he could — perhaps by sending cedars for a royal palace as he had done for David. Solomon takes up the offer and asks for assistance in building the Temple.

Once Churam had acceded to Solomon's request for help and Solomon had been assured of sufficient material for the execution of his plans, Solomon drafts the requisite number of workers for the project. The account of the draft appears, quite properly, at the end of the narrative.

Chronicles goes out of its way to place the initiative entirely with Solomon. V. 18 of the previous chapter (which has no parallel in *Kings*) had already spoken of Solomon's intention to build a Temple. Our verse describes the steps which he took to guarantee a sufficient work force for this gigantic project. Only then does Solomon send a message to Churam.

An entirely different ambience is thus provided. While in *Kings*, Solomon is awakened to the chance of fulfilling the mandate which his father had given him to build the Temple through Churam's initiative, in *Chronicles* he acts on his own. Moreover, he is determined to draw Churam into his plans.

From the point of view of the legal obligations of the monarchy, Solomon was indeed justified in waiting for Churam's advances. He needed Churam's help and was in no position to request it until Churam had shown himself willing to continue the friendship he had shared with David. Immediately, when Churam made the requisite gesture, Solomon reacts with a request couched in exactly those terms which were appropriate under the circumstances.

What would be *Chronicles'* perspective? The legalities of Solomon's kingly duties are dealt with in *Kings* and are not *Chronicles'* concern. How does the relationship with Churam fit into the story of the inner David and Solomon? Surely this heathen king could not know, nor should he, of David's inner struggle and of the final victory which was his and which was expressed by his son — the man of peace — beloved by God.

We must stop to ask ourselves a question: Was it a good thing that God's and Israel's Temple should be built with Churam's help? Would it not have been better if all the required resources could have been found among the Jews themselves?

As *Sforno* (*Exodus* 38:21) understands it, it was, indeed, most undesirable. Of all the sanctuaries erected by Israel, only Moses' Tabernacle never fell into non-Jewish hands — and that, because only Israel had been involved in its construction. Solomon's Temple, built with Tyre's help; the Second Temple, in which gentiles were also involved, Herod's edifice — all fell to conquerors. There is an inherent weakness in a Temple which must depend on the goodwill of the heathen.

Why then did Solomon draw Churam into his plans? Could he not have made do with the vast quantities of material which David had readied for him?

The answer seems clear. As we saw in Section II to *I Chronicles* ch. 17, p. 436, *Analysis . . .*, Solomon's was the peace which David had wrested from his lifelong struggle with an evil impulse which was only finally vanquished at the end of his life. Israel was at peace with its neighbors because there was peace and harmony within Israel's heart.

Was not the time ripe then for the next step in Israel's path towards the Messianic era? Perhaps Israel's neighbors could be changed from a passive non-enmity towards Israel into an active participation in bringing the Divine Presence to rest among man. And who among the nations would be more fitting than the great Churam representing as he does in Rabbinic thought the Edomite culture which is in eternal strife with Israel's sanctity? (See Section II to *I Chronicles* ch. 14, p. 424, *Ascendancy over Tyre*.) Had Churam not shown his readiness to bow before David's overpowering stature when he sent him the cedars to build his palace? Perhaps, if he could be coaxed into a partnership in building the Temple, this would be the beginning of the realization of the Messianic idea. This idea of attracting the best among the nations and finding their place within Israel's sanctity was surely the driving force behind Solomon's many unions with women from other nations. (See *R' Tzaddok HaKohen* in *Machshevos Charutz* 82b, 90b.) Would not this same ambition have driven Solomon to want to incorporate Churam into his plans for building the Temple?

These thoughts, then, motivated Solomon when he approached Churam, and it is this perspective — a natural outgrowth from the one adopted in ch. 17 concerning David's longings — which *Chronicles* takes. From this perspective, Churam's initial approach was irrelevant to Solomon's thinking. It has no place in the *Chronicles'* account.

And so, *Chronicles* moves the statement concerning the number of available workers to the beginning of the narrative. From Solomon's standpoint everything is ready. He does not need Churam. It is Churam who needs to be needed.

◆§ Churam's Reply

Vs. 10—15 record Churam's answer to Solomon. There are substantive differences between this passage and its parallel in *Kings* which we examine in the comparison table on the following page:

We begin our analysis by noting that our main concern must be with vs. 10-11 in *Chronicles* as they relate to v. 21 in *Kings*. This, because vs. 12-15 in *Chronicles* are no more than a point-by-point response to Solomon's requests in exactly the same way as are vs. 22-23 in *Kings*. Such differences as exist within that section can be readily traced to the different ways in which the requests had been formulated.

Taking, then, the earlier parts of the message as the field of our analysis we note the following points:

1. V. 21 in *Kings* is not part of the message to Solomon. It tells of Churam's thoughts when he received Solomon's delegation. The message begins at v. 22 and is limited to a factual response to Solomon's requests. By contrast, vs. 10-11 in *Chronicles* are a part of the message.

2. The message contained in the *Chronicles'* account in vs. 10— 11 seems to be divided into two. V. 10 seems to be a written message [בִּכְתָב] and, since it is couched in the second person and is thus less formal, seems more in the nature of a private communication accompanying the formal answer to Solomon's requests which begins in v. 11 [וַיֹּאמֶר חוּרָם] with a stylized opening leading up to Churam's reaction to Solomon's requests.

3. A glance at the chart will show that if any comparisons are to be made they must be between the *Kings'* passage and v. 11. V. 10 has no parallel in *Kings*.

The thrust of the two texts is entirely different. In *Kings*, Churam appraises the situation in Israel and is struck by the difficulty of ruling over such a vast people. He had been worried that his good friend David might be succeeded by an inept son who would allow his father's kingdom to drift without wise guidance. Solomon's message reassures him. David's legacy seems to be in good hands.

These are the thoughts of one king about another.

V. 10 in *Chronicles* sets a quite different tone. Churam is happy not because the Davidic dynasty seems secure but because the people have a monarch who can lead them to their destiny. God must love His people very much to give them a king so able to fill their needs.

This assessment of the monarchy, not as an end in itself — that is, from the point of view of the king — but as a means towards an end greater than itself is now reflected in v. 11.

Whereas in *Kings*, Churam simply blesses *HASHEM* — a formulation which tells us nothing about Churam's understanding of this God [Pharaoh had said, *Who is HASHEM that I should listen to His voice?* (*Exodus* 5:2)], *Chronicles* has a quite different formulation. God is Creator of heaven and earth — that is, He is the universal God, but He is still *God of Israel*. Within the universal scheme Israel has a particular function. God is blessed for giving David a wise son, not because thereby David's narrow interest is served, but because that wisdom will enable Solomon to lead Israel to its particular destiny — as host to the Divine Presence [בַּיִת לַה'].

Chronicles	Kings
a. 10. וַיֹּאמֶר חוּרָם מֶלֶךְ־צֹר בִּכְתָב וַיִּשְׁלַח אֶל־שְׁלֹמֹה בְּאַהֲבַת ה׳ אֶת־עַמּוֹ נְתָנְךָ עֲלֵיהֶם מֶלֶךְ, *Churam king of Tyre said in a written reply — and this he sent to Solomon — 'Because* HASHEM *loves this people he has made you king over them.*	a. 21. וַיְהִי כִּשְׁמֹעַ חִירָם אֶת־דִּבְרֵי שְׁלֹמֹה וַיִּשְׂמַח מְאֹד, *When Churam heard Solomon's words, he was very happy.*
b. 11. וַיֹּאמֶר חוּרָם בָּרוּךְ ה׳ אֱלֹהֵי יִשְׂרָאֵל אֲשֶׁר עָשָׂה אֶת־הַשָּׁמַיִם וְאֶת־הָאָרֶץ אֲשֶׁר נָתַן לְדָוִיד הַמֶּלֶךְ בֵּן חָכָם יוֹדֵעַ שֶׂכֶל וּבִינָה אֲשֶׁר יִבְנֶה־בַּיִת לַה׳ וּבַיִת לְמַלְכוּתוֹ, *Churam said, 'Praised be* HASHEM, *God of Israel, Who has made heaven and earth and has given David a wise son endowed with wisdom and understanding who will build a Temple for* HASHEM *and a palace for the exercise of his kingship.*	b. וַיֹּאמֶר בָּרוּךְ ה׳ הַיּוֹם אֲשֶׁר נָתַן לְדָוִד בֵּן חָכָם עַל־הָעָם הָרָב הַזֶּה, *and said, "Praised be God, today Who has given David a wise son over this great people.*
c. 12. וְעַתָּה שָׁלַחְתִּי אִישׁ־חָכָם יוֹדֵעַ בִּינָה לְחוּרָם אָבִי, *Now I have sent an artisan, one from my father Churam, endowed with good judgment.*	c. 22. וַיִּשְׁלַח חִירָם אֶל־שְׁלֹמֹה לֵאמֹר שָׁמַעְתִּי אֵת אֲשֶׁר־שָׁלַחְתָּ אֵלָי אֲנִי אֶעֱשֶׂה אֶת־כָּל־חֶפְצְךָ בַּעֲצֵי אֲרָזִים, *Churam sent to Solomon, saying, "I have heard that which you have sent me, I will do all that you desire with cedar wood . . .*
d. 13. בֶּן־אִשָּׁה מִן־בְּנוֹת דָּן וְאָבִיו אִישׁ־צֹרִי יוֹדֵעַ לַעֲשׂוֹת בַּזָּהָב־וּבַכֶּסֶף בַּנְּחֹשֶׁת בַּבַּרְזֶל בָּאֲבָנִים וּבָעֵצִים בָּאַרְגָּמָן בַּתְּכֵלֶת וּבַבּוּץ וּבַכַּרְמִיל וּלְפַתֵּחַ כָּל־פִּתּוּחַ וְלַחְשֹׁב כָּל־מַחֲשָׁבֶת אֲשֶׁר יִנָּתֶן־לוֹ עִם חֲכָמֶיךָ וְחַכְמֵי אֲדֹנִי דָּוִיד אָבִיךָ, *A son of a woman from among the daughters of Dan . . . he is skilled in crafting from, gold, silver, copper, iron, stone, and wood, and from purple, sky-blue wool, linen and crimson materials. Also, he can engrave any patterns and do any weaving that that he may be asked to do, together with your artisans and the artisans of your father, David.*	d. 23. עֲבָדַי יֹרִדוּ מִן־הַלְּבָנוֹן יָמָּה וַאֲנִי אֲשִׂימֵם דֹּבְרוֹת בַּיָּם עַד־הַמָּקוֹם אֲשֶׁר־תִּשְׁלַח אֵלַי וְנִפַּצְתִּים שָׁם וְאַתָּה תִשָּׂא וְאַתָּה תַּעֲשֶׂה אֶת־חֶפְצִי לָתֵת לֶחֶם בֵּיתִי, *My servants will bring it to the sea from the Lebanon and I will place it on rafts in the sea to the place which you will indicate to me and will cause them to be broken up there and you will carry and you will do my wish to supply my household needs.*
e. 14. וְעַתָּה הַחִטִּים וְהַשְּׂעֹרִים הַשֶּׁמֶן וְהַיַּיִן אֲשֶׁר־אָמַר אֲדֹנִי יִשְׁלַח לַעֲבָדָיו, *And now, the wheat and the barley . . .*	e.
f. 15. וַאֲנַחְנוּ נִכְרֹת עֵצִים מִן־הַלְּבָנוֹן כְּכָל צָרְכֶּךָ וּנְבִיאֵם לְךָ רַפְסֹדוֹת עַל־יָם יָפוֹ וְאַתָּה תַּעֲלֶה אֹתָם יְרוּשָׁלָםִ, *And we will cut all the lumber you need from the Lebanon and ship it by floats on the sea of Jaffa and you take it up to Jerusalem.*	f.

The two modes of response reflect accurately the differences which we had found in the forms of the requests — see above, *Solomon and Churam*. In *Kings*, one monarch had made a request of another monarch for help in a project he had in mind. Churam, as king, displays no interest in the project [note that throughout, the Temple is not mentioned and even in v. 23 Solomon is simply told to take the logs — the destination is of no interest — while *Chronicles* in v. 15 talks of taking the lumber to Jerusalem]; he simply accedes to the request. His satisfaction that his old friend's son seemed likely to be a good ruler over a difficult people was a matter for his own reflection. There was no reason to include it in his message.

In *Chronicles*, Churam the man had been addressed. He understands this, and therefore sends a private message together with his formal reply. Even this formal reply contains Churam's appreciation of Solomon as the man who would lead Israel to its destiny and by inference, Churam's enthusiastic offer of help can be construed as a preparedness to throw in his lot with that destiny.

[For an assessment of Churam's spiritual grandeur and his dismal end, see ArtScroll *Yechezkel*, pref. remarks to ch. 28, p. 461.]

Chapter Four

⁂ The Copper Altar

It is not easy to determine what dispositions Solomon made concerning the outer altar. The Scriptural record itself is not clear, and the tradition which the Sages had concerning this altar requires that a number of verses be reinterpreted.

The Scriptural evidence indicates that there was, indeed, a copper altar in Solomon's Temple. There are references at *I Kings* 8:64; *II Kings* 16:14; *Ezekiel* 9:2; here and at 7:7. These two latter instances state clearly that this altar was made by Solomon. The others do not explicate this and consequently, could be referring to the copper altar which had been built by Betzalel in Moses' time. It is to be presumed that this ancient relic would have been brought from Giveon once Solomon had built his Temple.

If it was, indeed, Moses' copper altar which served as the outer altar in Solomon's Temple, this would explain the total omission of any mention in *Kings* of the building of a copper altar by Solomon. There, detailed accounts are given of all the vessels which Solomon made, but there is absolutely no mention of an outer altar. This, and the omission of the altar from David's instructions to Solomon (see *I Chronicles* 28:11 ff.) could be simply explained if, in fact, no altar had to be built since the one remaining from Moses was used.

There is one point which would still require an explanation: Why, in the account of how, after the completion of the Temple building, Solomon brought up the remains of the Tabernacle from Giveon (*I Kings* 8:1-5, *II Chronicles* 5:2-5) is no mention made of this altar? Does this not indicate that Moses' altar was never brought to the Temple?

However, for this, *Halevi* (*Tekufas HaMikra* Ch. 47) offers a simple answer: The altar must have been brought up to the new Temple site long before the other vessels. For, while all the other vessels needed simply to be put down in their assigned places, the altar required intricate installation so that the drainage system for the libations would work perfectly. Certainly, by the time the rest of the Tabernacle's contents were transferred, the altar would already have been in place.

We should conclude from all this that indeed the outer altar in the Temple was the one which had been passed down, through the centuries, from the Tabernacle in the wilderness.

But what of this verse and also of 7:7 which clearly assume that Solomon did build a copper altar? See further in Section II, *The Heavenly Fire*, to ch. 7.

Perhaps the answer may lie in the dimensions which are given here for the altar which Solomon built. The length and width are both given as twenty cubits. Now, as made clear in the comm., these measurements refer only to that part of the altar roof upon which the sacrifices were burnt. The actual altar was much larger.

But, why is only this area defined? Why, if *Chronicles* is going to mention this altar, should only partial dimensions be given?

If, indeed, the altar which was to be used in Solomon's Temple was that which Moses had made, then this can be readily explained. The one which Solomon made was not meant to be used as the permanent altar. Solomon made it only in order to cope with the huge amount of animals which were to be sacrificed in connection with the dedication ceremonies. These would obviously overwhelm Moses' altar, which had an area of only one square cubit available for burning the sacrifices. The dimensions of this temporary altar were of no significance and with the exception of the huge twenty-by-twenty burning area — which was the justification for its being built — are therefore not given.

In the event, even this altar proved inadequate and Solomon had to sanctify the floor of the Temple courtyard so that it could be used to burn those sacrifices which could not be handled on even the expanded altar (7:7).

The Scriptural record now yields the following: There were two altars in the Temple court: the small one, still remaining from Moses' days, and the larger one which Solomon built. Moses' altar had already gone through some five hundred years of exposure to the searing flames which burned constantly upon it, and we can safely assume that it would no longer have been suitable for extended use (*HaLevi, Tekufas HaMikva* ch. 47). It is therefore likely that the intention was to use it in tandem with the new altar — a situation which would be analogous with the usage in Shiloh — see *Zevachim* 61b. In the course of time, it was retired completely [נִגְנַז] and its place was taken by Solomon's altar. This would explain why Solomon's altar is mentioned in *Chronicles* but not in *Kings*. It had not initially been intended for permanent use and therefore had no place in the account of Solomon's building — nor in David's charge to Solomon. However, in the course of time it became the permanent altar, and so *Chronicles* found it important to record that Solomon had had it made. This could well be the picture that is yielded by the Scriptural passages.

The Sages, however, had a different tradition. In the first place, they assume that Solomon's altar was not made of copper but of stone (*Zevachim* 61b and *Shabbos* 55a), and this necessitates that all Scriptural references to a copper altar must be reinterpreted to mean: The [stone] altar [which replaced] the copper [altar which Moses had made]. Again, they assume that Moses' altar was withdrawn from the very beginning (See *Yalkut Shimoni Exodus* 303). This teaches us that on the day that this one [Solomon's altar] was built, this one [Moses' altar] was withdrawn. These assumptions are the basis for a wide-ranging discussion of the relevant Scriptural passages recorded in *Zevachim* 59a to 60a.

Chapter Six

◆§ The Temple as a Dwelling for God

V. 18 poses a rhetorical question. Clearly, there is an assumption that there is a self-evident answer. In *Radak's* view, it is that the Temple is no more than the locus towards which Israel's prayers are to be directed. Nevertheless, it is clear that in some sense there is a Divine Presence in the Temple. We should make some attempt to understand this.

Let us first assert unequivocally that in the eyes of the Sages, God indeed resides within the Temple confines. Midrashic literature is replete with references to such a quasi constriction of the Divine into man-made space. Perhaps the most poignant of these is *Shemos Rabbah* 33:1 which compares God's desire for a Temple to that of a loving father who has given his daughter in marriage. Distraught at the thought of parting from the object of his adoration, but aware that she must join her husband, he begs his son-in-law to set aside a small room for him, so that he can always remain in close proximity to his child.

At 34:4 (there) God compares Himself to a shepherd, a keeper of a vineyard and a father. The shepherd cannot part from his flock, the keeper's place is in the vineyard and no father is fulfilled away from his children. Therefore, there must be a Temple — a place in which His Presence might rest.

In another midrash, God tells of constricting His Presence [שְׁכִינָה] into a cubit-by-cubit space.

The inaugural prayer itself had made that clear enough. The Temple is to be a *habitation* for God, a *home*, in which God might dwell for all eternity (v. 2).

And yet, Solomon himself seems ambivalent. Not only does he question whether such a thing is at all possible (v.18), but, he seems to affirm that very impossibility by asking God to accept Israel's prayers . . . *from the place of Your dwelling — the heaven*. It is then in the heaven, not in the Temple, that God is said to dwell, and Solomon repeats this many times throughout the prayer.

What had become of the *habitation*, the *home* of v. 2?

Inescapably, we must conclude that both the heavens and the Temple are God's dwelling place.

But, how is this possible?

The problem does not begin with Solomon's Temple. The Sages appear to have touched upon it in connection with the Tabernacle in the wilderness. *Bamidbar Rabbah*, quoted by *Ramban*, on *Exodus* 25:1 teaches that the Divine Voice which communicated with Moses in the Tabernacle *came down* in a *fiery flame* from heaven, entered the Holy of Holies between the *cheruvim* and was there apprehended by Moses.

Again, we note the duality. God's Presence is *in* the Holy of Holies — it is from there that He speaks to Moses — but the Heavenly Voice descends from heaven.

In the course of his discussions *Ramban* analyzes Solomon's inaugural prayer, and notes the constant reference to God's listening from heaven. He explains that *listening from heaven* is descriptive of God's attribute of mercy. This assertion is made in the context of a kabbalistic exposition to which we are not privy. But while we cannot understand its full implication, it may help us toward a solution of the problem with which we are grappling here.

After the sin of the golden calf, God made clear that He does not wish to dwell among the people any more. God's close proximity makes sin utterly intolerable. A sinner must immediately pay the price of his backsliding (*Exodus* 33:5). Because of this, the nature of

God's presence among Israel underwent a radical change.

Sforno believes that the institution of Tabernacle and Temple became necessary only after the sin of the golden calf. Prior to that God had said ... *wherever I allow My Name to be mentioned, I will come and bless you* (*Exodus* 20:21). Each man would have been his own *Kohen*, each house a Tabernacle. God's presence would have been an almost palpable fact in the everyday lives of the people. He would have been *there* among them in absolute closeness.

All this underwent a radical change. No more could God's presence among the multitudes be considered as given. God had, so to speak, withdrawn Himself to the heavens. He would still maintain a presence among them but it would not be absolute.

God would indeed leave this heavenly abode to dwell among His beloved children but it would be a *leaving*. He belongs — in heaven. Indeed, He is Shepherd, Keeper of the vineyard and Father, and, in those capacities, would want to be with His charges. But, even as such relationships, close and loving as they may be, do not exhaust the entire personality — one retains an existence separate from his activities — so too the Tabernacle can never replace the heavens as God's abode. It can only be auxiliary to them. God's voice would indeed come to Moses from between the *cheruvim* in the Holy of Holies, but it would first have to descend from the heavens.

◆§ The Temple as a House of Prayer

Vs. 32-33 make clear that the Temple is also to serve as a center of prayer for any non-Jew who, having heard of God, might wish to turn to Him.

The passage recalls a similar one in *Isaiah* 56:7, where the Temple is described as a ... *house of prayer for all the nations* (See *Ibn Ezra* and *Radak* there).

The passage in *Isaiah* and the lesson which the Sages derive from it may help us to better understand the attitude which both David and Solomon had toward the Temple.

A striking aspect of Solomon's inaugural prayer is the exclusive attention which he pays to the Temple as a house of prayer. This function is never mentioned in the Torah, and even in the rest of Scripture is limited to Solomon's prayer and the passage in *Isaiah*. Solomon could so easily have mentioned the other functions which the Temple fills, such as being the place at which sacrifices are to be brought and where the three pilgrim festivals are to be celebrated. He mentions nothing of all this — only begs God to listen to the prayers addressed to Him by way of the Temple.

It is also noteworthy that from *I Chronicles* ch. 17 onward, when David first conceived of the idea of building a Temple, the stress has constantly been on providing a permanent place for the Ark. Never are the other Temple functions mentioned.

We may begin our analysis by noting that it appears from *Berachos* 30a that, when we speak of the Temple as the focus of our prayers, we actually mean the Ark. The Gemara teaches that, when praying outside the Land of Israel, one is to turn toward Israel; when in Israel he should turn to Jerusalem, and in Jerusalem toward the Temple. Within the Temple he is to turn to the Holy of Holies. If he should be in the Holy of Holies he is to turn towards the *Kapores*, the cover of the Ark.

Thus, it is specifically the Ark which is the ultimate focus of Israel's prayers — we assume because it is the locus of the *Shechinah*, the Divine Presence.[1]

---

1. This insight can help us to understand what seems to be an entirely cryptic *aggadah* in *Shabbos* 30a.

When the gates of the Sanctuary proved recalcitrant, and refused to open up to allow Solomon

Now *Megillah* 18a makes clear that there is a very special affinity between David and prayer: The Gemara discusses the order of the blessings in the *Amidah*. The blessing in which we ask that God accept our prayer follows directly upon the one in which we ask that the Davidic messiah might soon come. Once David is mentioned, the Gemara teaches, our thoughts turn immediately toward prayer. In *Psalms* 109:4 where David sings: *As for me — I am prayer*, David describes himself not as one who prays but sees his entire nature suffused with prayer — his very being is prayer incarnate.

We have now recognized David's affinity to prayer, and that in the Temple, it is the Ark which is its particular focus. We can now understand why in David's dreams it was the Temple as home of the Ark which was central. Surely the Temple has many other functions but for David, its all-consuming significance was as house of prayer — and therefore as home of the Ark.

Solomon began his inaugural prayer with a review of David's desire to build the Temple and of God's refusal to allow him to do so. That refusal was tempered by the promise that it would be built by his son. From this perspective it is entirely appropriate that in his prayer, Solomon should stress the particular aspect of the Temple which, from David's viewpoint, was the most significant.

When we view the Temple as a place where sacrifices are to be offered to God, or as the center of the pilgrim festival celebrations, it has a uniquely Jewish character. As a house of prayer its attraction is universal.

[See further at 7:1.]

◆§ The Temple or the People?

God is to answer the people's prayers in two ways. He is to champion their cause, and He is to forgive their sins. Thus, the connotation in *Chronicles*. In *Kings* there is a radically different treatment (see table opposite page).

In the *Chronicles* version,. . .*and forgive Your people* is a continuation from, *champion their cause*. By contrast, the *Kings* version ends the previous thought with the words *and champion their cause*. *You shall forgive Your people* begins a new verse which introduces a section which is missing in *Chronicles*.

Clearly, the *Chronicles* version is not a shortened form of *Kings* but has a different thrust entirely.

The ending line of the prayer makes this very clear: In *Kings*, Solomon moves away from the narrow issue of the Temple and begs that Israel's prayers be heard whenever [and by implication, from wherever] they call to God, whereas in *Chronicles*, the concern is still for the prayers *of this place*.

---

to bring in the Ark, he invoked *twenty-four pleadings*, all to no avail. The gates opened only when he mentioned the merit of his father David.

Rashi there explains that these *twenty-four pleadings* are the twenty-four times that either the word *prayer* or *entreaty* is mentioned in Solomon's inaugural prayer.

But how are these to be considered *pleadings*? These are not prayers which Solomon offered up but, rather, descriptions of the prayers which others might one day recite there. Why should mention of these prayers have been expected to persuade the gates to open and to admit the Ark?

With what we have learned the answer is simple. The focus of all the prayers described by the twenty-four terms which Solomon used was to be the Ark. Would we not then have supposed that the desperate need that the Ark should be there to act as the point to which those prayers were to be addressed would have persuaded the obdurate gates to open?

Nevertheless, they opened only when David's merits were mentioned.

II Chronicles Ch.6	I Kings Ch. 8
a. 39. וְשָׁמַעְתָּ ... אֶת־תְּפִלָּתָם וְאֶת־תְּחִנֹּתֵיהֶם, *Now, do You listen ... to their prayers and their entreaties.*	a. 49. וְשָׁמַעְתָּ ... אֶת־תְּפִלָּתָם וְאֶת־תְּחִנָּתָם, *Now do you ... listen to their prayers and their entreaties*
b. וְעָשִׂיתָ מִשְׁפָּטָם, *Champion their cause,*	b. וְעָשִׂיתָ מִשְׁפָּטָם, *and champion their cause.*
c. וְסָלַחְתָּ לְעַמְּךָ אֲשֶׁר חָטְאוּ־לָךְ, *and forgive Your people that which they sinned against You.*	c. 50. ... וְסָלַחְתָּ לְעַמְּךָ אֲשֶׁר חָטְאוּ־לָךְ ... וּנְתַתָּם לְרַחֲמִים לִפְנֵי שֹׁבֵיהֶם וְרִחֲמוּם, *You shall forgive Your people for that which they have sinned against You ... granting them mercy in the eyes of their captors.*
d.	d. 51. כִּי־עַמְּךָ וְנַחֲלָתְךָ הֵם אֲשֶׁר הוֹצֵאתָ ... מִמִּצְרַיִם, *For they are Your people whom You took out from the land of Egypt ...*
e. 40. ... עַתָּה אֱלֹהַי יִהְיוּ־נָא עֵינֶיךָ פְּתֻחוֹת, *Now, my God may Your eyes be open ...*	e. 52. לִהְיוֹת עֵינֶיךָ פְתֻחֹת אֶל־תְּחִנַּת עַבְדְּךָ וְאֶל־תְּחִנַּת עַמְּךָ יִשְׂרָאֵל, *That Your eyes may be open to Your servant's entreaty and the entreaty of Your people Israel,*
f. לִתְפִלַּת הַמָּקוֹם הַזֶּה, *to the prayers of this place.*	f. לִשְׁמֹעַ אֲלֵיהֶם בְּכֹל קָרְאָם אֵלֶיךָ, *that You listen to them from wherever they might call to You.*
g.	g. 53. ... כִּי־אַתָּה הִבְדַּלְתָּם לְךָ, *For You have set them aside for Yourself ...*

Kings clearly moves the focus from Temple to people. With the Exodus, God established a very special relationship with Israel (v. 51). That itself is sufficient reason for God to be attentive to their pleading.

It is entirely logical that the inaugural prayer should end on such a note. From countless verses in Scripture and Midrashic teachings it is clear that God's real dwelling place is not in any building but in the hearts of His people. Solomon underlines this truth by recalling the early love between God and Israel, and then drawing the necessary conclusion: wherever and whenever they will turn to God, He will be there lovingly to accept their prayer.

But all this is missing from the *Chronicles'* version.[1]

---

1. There are at least two more instances in which we can recognize this difference in perspective.

In comm. to v. 3 we noted that the text of Solomon's blessing is not given in *Chronicles*. In *Kings* it occupies an important position following immediately upon the completion of the inaugural prayer (vs. 55-61). This blessing makes no mention of the Temple at all and deals solely with Israel's relationship to God, as His chosen people. Its inclusion in the *Kings'* account subtly shifts the emphasis from the Temple to the people while its exclusion from *Chronicles* leaves the Temple central to the account.

The same shift in emphasis is evident in God's answer to the inaugural prayer. In *Kings*, God simply says, *I have heard your prayers and entreaties which you have poured out before Me. I*

The two books are consistent with the different perspectives which they had brought to bear upon David's request that he be permitted to build the Temple.

The *Samuel-Kings'* treatment had consistently been concerned with the objective obligations incumbent upon the monarchy. As kings, David, and subsequently Solomon, were obliged to fulfill the command to build the Temple. Central as this obligation is among the kingly duties, it does not exhaust them. In the final analysis, the king is ruler over the people, and it is the nurturing of the people toward their true role — to be the real bearers of the Divine Presence — that is his central goal. The building of the Temple is only a stepping stone towards the fulfillment of the greater destiny.

Not so in *Chronicles* where David the man is central. There the tension centers around the question of whether David would, in his own person and subsequently through his progeny, be able to lead Israel towards their destiny. As we have seen a number of times, David's vindication came with the entry of the Ark into the Holy of Holies. The Temple, built by Solomon, confirms David as God's chosen one and as such it is central to the account.

---

have sanctified this Temple which you have built, inasmuch as My Presence will be there eternally, and that My eyes and heart shall be there for all days (*I Kings* 9:3). This statement is general, and does not enter into the specifics of Solomon's prayer that the Temple should serve as a conduit when Israel, at the times of its troubles, turns to God.

By contrast, *Chronicles* (7:12-16) stresses that God will listen to the prayers of *this place* (v. 15).

Chapter Seven

⌁§ The Heavenly Fire

Why is the story of the heavenly fire omitted in *Kings*?

Zevachim 61b teaches: The fire that descended from heaven [upon the copper altar] for Moses remained until the days of Solomon. The fire which came down for Solomon remained until Menasheh removed it.

Clearly, a new fire descended from heaven upon Solomon's altar.

This new fire would indeed have been required if Solomon had built a new altar to replace the one which Moses had made. But, if the old altar continued in use, no new fire would have been needed.

We have discussed this issue in detail in Section II to ch. 4, *The Copper Altar*. We noted there that the simple meaning of the texts appears to yield a different picture from the one preserved in the tradition of the Sages.

Certain it is that there is no record in *Kings* of Solomon having made a new altar. Accordingly, *Kings* is consistent in not mentioning the new fire.

The same picture emerges from another passage.

In v. 7 we learn that Solomon sanctified the Temple floor for the purpose of burning sacrifices upon it — this was because the altar could not cope with the multitude of offerings which were brought on that day.

We contrast the text in *Chronicles* with the parallel verse in *Kings*.

II Chronicles Ch. 7	*I Kings* Ch. 8
a. 7. כִּי־מִזְבַּח הַנְּחֹשֶׁת אֲשֶׁר־עָשָׂה שְׁלֹמֹה, *This, because the copper altar which Solomon had made*	a. 64. כִּי־מִזְבַּח הַנְּחֹשֶׁת אֲשֶׁר לִפְנֵי ה׳, *For the copper altar which was before God*
b. לֹא יָכוֹל לְהָכִיל אֶת־הָעֹלָה וְאֶת־הַמִּנְחָה, *was unable to accommodate the burnt offering, the meal offering . . .*	b. קָטֹן מֵהָכִיל אֶת הָעֹלָה וְאֶת הַמִּנְחָה, *was too small to accommodate the burnt offering . . .*

Both phrases seem to be consistent with our thesis. *Kings* which has not mentioned an altar built by Solomon talks of an *altar which is before* HASHEM which could well refer to Moses' altar, while *Chronicles* talks of the altar which Solomon built.

In the second phrase, *Kings* reports that the altar was *too small*. This would indeed be true if Moses' altar is meant. The one-by-one-cubit space available for burning the sacrifices would have been hopelessly inadequate for the needs of the inauguration. By contrast, the twenty-by-twenty-cubit space of Solomon's altar should have provided ample room. In the event, even that was overwhelmed by the sheer multitude of the sacrifices.

⌁§ The Inauguration and Succos

Vs. 8-10 describe how Solomon and the people celebrated Succos in the year of the inauguration. There are significant differences between this, and the *Kings* account (see comparison table following page).

II Chronicles Ch. 7	I Kings Ch. 8
a. 8. וַיַּעַשׂ שְׁלֹמֹה אֶת־הֶחָג בָּעֵת הַהִיא, *Solomon celebrated the festival at that time*	a. 65. וַיַּעַשׂ שְׁלֹמֹה בָעֵת הַהִיא אֶת הֶחָג, *Solomon celebrated the festival at that time*
b.	b. . . . וְכָל־יִשְׂרָאֵל עִמּוֹ, *and all Israel with him . . .*
c. שִׁבְעַת יָמִים, *for seven days*	c. שִׁבְעַת יָמִים, *seven days*
d.	d. וְשִׁבְעַת יָמִים, *and seven days*
e.	e. אַרְבָּעָה עָשָׂר יוֹם, *fourteen days.*
f. . . . וְכָל־יִשְׂרָאֵל עִמּוֹ, *and all Israel was with him*	f.
g. 9. וַיַּעֲשׂוּ בַּיּוֹם הַשְּׁמִינִי, *On the eighth day they made*	g. 66. בַּיּוֹם הַשְּׁמִינִי, *On the eighth day*
h. עֲצָרֶת, *Atzeres*	h.
i. כִּי חֲנֻכַּת הַמִּזְבֵּחַ עָשׂוּ שִׁבְעַת יָמִים וְהֶחָג שִׁבְעַת יָמִים, *for they celebrated the inauguration of the altar for seven days and the festival — for seven days.*	i.
j. 10. וּבְיוֹם עֶשְׂרִים וּשְׁלֹשָׁה לַחֹדֶשׁ הַשְּׁבִיעִי, *On the twenty-third day of the seventh month*	j.
k. שִׁלַּח אֶת־הָעָם, *he sent the people*	k. שִׁלַּח אֶת־הָעָם, *he sent the people off.*
l.	l. וַיְבָרְכוּ אֶת־הַמֶּלֶךְ, *They blessed the king*
m. לְאָהֳלֵיהֶם, *to their tents*	m. וַיֵּלְכוּ לְאָהֳלֵיהֶם, *and went to their tents*
n. שְׂמֵחִים וְטוֹבֵי לֵב, *happy and of good heart . . .*	n. שְׂמֵחִים וְטוֹבֵי לֵב, *happy and of good heart . . .*

This is an instance in which *Chronicles* elucidates the *Kings'* account. The interpretation of the *Kings'* passage must be substantively changed in the light of that which *Chronicles* teaches.

If we were to take the *Kings'* account on its own, the following picture would emerge: Solomon, and all Israel with him (b), celebrated the festival [of Succos] at that time (a) for seven days (c). Subsequently, [that is, beginning on *Shemini Atzeres*] they celebrated — the inauguration festivities — for another seven days (d), for a total of fourteen days (e).

On the eighth day (presumably, the eighth day from the beginning of inauguration festivities) (g) Solomon sent the people home (k). After having blessed the king (l) they left for their tents (unencumbered by any limitations placed by *Yom Tov*, since this was more than a week after *Shemini Atzeres*) (m), happy and of good heart (n).

This timetable has the inauguration festivities taking place after Succos. Yom Kippur was in no way compromised, and the people left for home on the very day [the *eighth day*] on which Solomon sent them.

This sequence of events does not accord with the tradition of the Sages (*Moed Katan* 9a), according to which the inauguration ceremonies preceded Succos, such that, necessarily, the people did not fast on Yom Kippur of that year.

This tradition is surely based upon the *Chronicles* account, according to which Solomon sent the people home on the twenty-third day of the seventh month — that is, on the day after *Shemini Atzeres*. Clearly then, the inauguration ceremonies were celebrated before Succos.

This forces us to reinterpret the *Kings'* account as follows:

Solomon and all the people with him (b) celebrated the inauguration festival (a) for seven days [including Yom Kippur] (c). Then for another seven days (d), for a total of fourteen days (e), they celebrated Succos. On the eighth day [that is, on *Shemini Atzeres*] (g), he sent the people home [that is, he gave them permission to leave — they would not have been allowed to travel on Yom Tov] (k). They blessed the king [which cannot be precisely timed. This may have taken place on *Shemini Atzeres* when he first sent them, or, it could have been when they returned once more on the twenty-third] (l), and went home [on the twenty-third day, as in *Chronicles*] (m), happy and of good heart (n).

See further in the comm. to the individual verses.

◆§ Solomon's House

Chronicles has, at 1:18 and 2:11, mentioned Solomon's intention to build himself a palace . In contrast to *Kings*, which notes the building of that palace at 7:1, *Chronicles* makes no mention of it. Clearly, our verse is taken from the *Kings'* account. But, it appears to be anachronistic. Since *Chronicles* does not describe the building of this palace, why does it report its completion?

There are significant differences between this passage and its parallel in *Kings* (see table on following page).

There are two major differences:

Kings has no parallel to the (d) phrase. From this it follows that the two accounts are to be translated as we have done. In *Chronicles* there are three distinct ideas: 1. Solomon finished the two building projects; 2. In both he accomplished all that he had set out to do; and 3. God appeared to him. In *Kings*, all three thoughts are connected. God appeared to Solomon after he had finished his two building projects and had fulfilled certain cravings which animated him.

In addition, *Chronicles* has no parallel to the comparison with the vision at Giveon (f).

The latter may be explained by the differing attitudes which *Kings* and *Chronicles* have toward that event. At 1:14-17 we saw that *Chronicles*, as indeed Solomon himself, in the tradition of the Sages, looks upon that event negatively. Solomon felt that he had misused the wisdom which he had been granted on that occasion. In the *Kings* perspective, these abuses still lay in the future, and the assessment of the vision is positive.

Clearly, the positive comparison which *Kings* makes here (f) would not be appropriate in the *Chronicles'* view.

The difference in structure between the two passages can now also be explained.

The Sages (*Zohar*, *Shemos* 4a) interpret *the king's house* in the *Kings* narrative as

II Chronicles Ch.7	*I Kings Ch. 9*
a. 11. וַיְכַל שְׁלֹמֹה, *And Solomon finished*	a. 1. וַיְהִי כְּכַלּוֹת שְׁלֹמֹה לִבְנוֹת, *It was when Solomon finished building*
b. אֶת־בֵּית ה׳ וְאֶת־בֵּית הַמֶּלֶךְ, *HASHEM's House and the king's house.*	b. אֶת־בֵּית־ה׳ וְאֶת בֵּית הַמֶּלֶךְ, *HASHEM's House and the king's house*
c. וְאֵת כָּל־הַבָּא עַל־לֵב שְׁלֹמֹה לַעֲשׂוֹת, *and all that had occurred to Solomon to bring about*	c. וְאֵת כָּל־חֵשֶׁק שְׁלֹמֹה אֲשֶׁר חָפֵץ לַעֲשׂוֹת, *and all Solomon's cravings which he desired to bring about,*
d. בְּבֵית ה׳ וּבְבֵיתוֹ הִצְלִיחַ, *in HASHEM's House and in his house, he brought to a successful conclusion.*	d.
e. 12. וַיֵּרָא ה׳ אֶל־שְׁלֹמֹה, *HASHEM appeared to Solomon*	e. 2. וַיֵּרָא ה׳ אֶל־שְׁלֹמֹה שֵׁנִית, *HASHEM appeared to Solomon a second time*
f. בַּלָּיְלָה, *in the night*	f. כַּאֲשֶׁר נִרְאָה אֵלָיו בְּגִבְעוֹן, *as He had appeared to him at Giveon*
g. וַיֹּאמֶר לוֹ, *and said to him ...*	g. ... וַיֹּאמֶר, *And said ...*

referring to the Holy of Holies. The *king* is not Solomon, but God.

This interpretation cannot hold true in the *Chronicles* account. There, the (d) phrase follows onto (c) in which Solomon had been mentioned. *His house* can only refer to Solomon's palace.

If, indeed, the *king's house* in *Kings* is the Holy of Holies, we can readily understand what is meant by the cryptic reference in the (c) phrase to the cravings which had animated him. To what does this refer?

At 5:10, comm. and fn., we noted the significance which *Chronicles* attaches to the fact that the shards of the broken tablets were contained in the ark which Solomon triumphantly brought into the Holy of Holies. In the light of what we learned in Section II, *Solomon and Moses*, to ch. 1, this significance carries an added dimension. Solomon's life — the craving of his heart — was to be like Moses'. That craving found its tangible focus in the shards which lay in the Holy of Holies. They were Moses' tablets. They were the perpetual hint and beckoning challenge of what might have been and what could yet come about.

In the *Kings'* perspective, looking, as it were, from the time frame of Giveon, when Solomon had not yet abused his wisdom, Solomon's "house" could well be identical with the chamber of the King — the Holy of Holies. It was there that his life found meaning, and that his true self found expression.

And so, while the simple meaning of the phrase surely has the king's palace in mind, the Sages found a hint for a quite different dwelling place: this one of the spirit, housing Solomon's most precious aspirations.

None of this holds true in the *Chronicles'* perspective. Solomon had not lived up to the potential which lay in the Giveon vision. His dwelling place was truly in his palace. That, and no more, is the meaning of *the king's house* in the *Chronicles'* version.

And so, there is no talk of *cravings*. There are only ideas which Solomon had concerning the structure of the two buildings — and these he managed to implement.

Chapter Eight

◆§ Solomon and Pharaoh's Daughter

Solomon's marriage to the Egyptian princess has not been mentioned in *Chronicles*. We learn of it at *I Kings* 3:1, which reads: *Solomon joined in marriage with Pharaoh, the king of Egypt. He married Pharaoh's daughter and brought her to the City of David, pending the building of his palace and HASHEM's House and the walls of Jerusalem.*

The implication of that wording is, that from the very beginning, her stay in the City of David was meant to be only temporary.

The simple meaning of our verse ... *for he said* ... appears to indicate a change of mind. Once the Ark had been brought into the City of David, Solomon found it inappropriate that his wife remain there. Thus, we have an apparent contradiction between the two accounts.

It will be instructive to compare our verse with its parallel in *Kings*:

II Chronicles Ch. 8	*I Kings* Ch. 9
a.	a. 24. אַךְ, *However,*
b. 11. ... וְאֶת־בַּת־פַּרְעֹה הֶעֱלָה שְׁלֹמֹה, *Solomon brought up Pharaoh's daughter*	b. בַּת־פַּרְעֹה עָלְתָה מֵעִיר דָּוִד, *Pharaoh's daughter came up from the City of David*
c. לַבַּיִת אֲשֶׁר בָּנָה־לָהּ, *to the house which he had built for her,*	c. אֶל־בֵּיתָהּ אֲשֶׁר בָּנָה־לָהּ, *to her house, which he had built for her*
d. ... כִּי אָמַר לֹא־תֵשֵׁב אִשָּׁה, *for he said, 'No woman shall dwell ...*	d.
e. אֲשֶׁר־בָּאָה אֲלֵיהֶם אֲרוֹן ה׳, *inasmuch as the Ark of HASHEM had been brought there*	e.
f.	f. אָז בָּנָה אֶת־הַמִּלּוֹא, *at that time he built up the plaza.*

The major differences appear to be as follows:

1. The introduction, *However* ... (a) is missing in *Chronicles*.

2. In *Chronicles* Solomon takes the initiative [b]. In *Kings* the decision appears to be hers.

3. In *Kings* she moves to *her house* (c). In *Chronicles* it is simply *the house*.

4. The reasons which motivated Solomon (d) and (e) are not given in *Kings*.

5. *Chronicles* makes no mention of the plaza (f).

The tone of the *Kings'* narrative is set by the introductory *However* ... It is one of criticism of Solomon for building up the plaza. All the other projects which he had undertaken had constituted a legitimate exercise of his kingship. They served to aggrandize and strengthen the country. But for building up the plaza there was no excuse. This area had originally been set aside for the use of the people. They benefited not at all from the buildings which he erected there. These were simply conveniences for housing the retinue of the Egyptian princess (*Rashi*).

This wanton disregard of the people's sensibilities precipitated Yarov'am's rebellion, and eventually, albeit indirectly, led to to the establishment of the Northern Kingdom (*Sanhedrin* 101b).

We may thus say that the entire passage in *Kings* has precisely this purpose: to set the stage for the dramatic events which were to flow from it. In this context, the cause of the move is not relevant. It is the move itself, not that Solomon instigated it, that is important. Moreover, the requisitioning of the plaza is central to the story.

In *Chronicles*, neither Yarov'am's rebellion nor the split in the kingdoms is mentioned. The telling of the story must have a different purpose.

When did Solomon make the decision to move the princess out of the City of David? What made him decide to do so?

Judging from the place which the story occupies in the narrative, we would assume that it happened some time after the Temple had been completed. But the considerations which motivated Solomon (d and e) should have made even a temporary residence in the sacred precincts intolerable.

We may perhaps surmise as follows: In comm. to 7:17-22 we discussed Solomon's motivation in marrying Pharaoh's daughter. We learned that he perceived this bond as the first step toward the Messianic destiny, which is to bring all the nations of the world into the orbit of Israel's sanctity. We saw there that Solomon had miscalculated and that, far from ushering in the Messianic era, the marriage sowed the seeds of tragedy.

At what point did Solomon awaken to the fact that his dreams were not to be realized? We may surmise that as time passed and the expected spiritual results of his actions did not materialize, he would have come to recognize that he had erred. Perhaps this was the point at which he came face to face with the inappropriateness of the presence of Pharaoh's daughter in the City of David. Until that point, she had been a symbol of all that was holy in Israel's destiny. Far from being an anachronism, her proximity to Israel's most sacred shrine underlined the glorious future which her position as Solomon's wife presaged. But with the dawn of recognition of the error, came the awareness that, after all, she was only a wife. As such she had no place within the city. Accordingly, Solomon takes the initiative to move her out of the area in which her presence had become a travesty. In the *Kings'* account Solomon's change of heart has no place and the move is not associated with him.

We are now in a position to deal with the apparent contradiction which we noted before. Both the *Kings'* narrative — which implies that her installation in the City of David was from the very beginning only a temporary measure — and the implication of the *Chronicles'* account — that it was a new consideration — may exist side by side.

Solomon always intended to build a separate palace for his wife. Her rank demanded such a home. This is reflected in the *Kings'* account. She moves into *her house* (c). It had always been destined for her.

But *Chronicles* introduces a new consideration. It suddenly became important to build a house for Pharaoh's daughter not because her station demanded it but because her presence in David's city had suddenly become intolerable. He built *a house* for her.

Chapter Nine

◈§ The Queen of Sheba

It is not easy to understand why this story should have been told.

In Solomon's forty-year reign there must have been myriad events which found no place in the scriptural account. Why should a gentile queen's, seemingly puerile, wish to test the great Solomon's wisdom be deemed significant? In particular the type of riddles which, in the tradition of the Sages, were asked seem entirely irrelevant to the immortal builder of the Temple, the Beloved of G-d.[1] [See comm. to v.1.]

The inclusion of this story in *Chronicles* is particularly problematic. At 1:14-17 we noted that, while *Kings* goes to great lengths to describe Solomon's wisdom, *Chronicles* nowhere makes any issue of it. Again, *Chronicles* has no parallel to *I Kings* ch. 5 where a detailed description of Solomon's household is given. These are the two elements of Solomon's kingship which so attracted the Queen of Sheba. In *Chronicles*, then, the logical underpinnings for the story are missing.

There are very few Talmudic or Midrashic sources to help us in our analysis; the one Talmudic statement which we have, seems at first sight to confuse rather than to elucidate.

R' Shmuel bar Nachmeini taught in R'Yonasan's name: Whoever thinks that מַלְכַּת שְׁבָא was a woman is mistaken. The word [מַלְכַּת which most frequently denotes the construct form of מַלְכָּה, *queen*] is to be understood as מַלְכוּתָא, *rulership*, or, *a royal retinue*.

The simple meaning of this teaching seems to be that, in fact, the ruler of Sheba was a king. He came with his royal retinue.

But what lesson can an interpretation which, patently, contradicts the simple meaning of the text, have for us? No ethical or moral principle seems at stake. Why make this point?

Maharal may help us understand. The connotation of the unusual feminine form, מַלְכַּת, to describe a rulership, is to show that it was somehow *lacking* [מַלְכוּת חֲסֵרָה], that is, it was weak and dependent. He does not explain in what way it was weak nor why this knowledge is significant to us.

Maharal's insight enables us to interpret the Gemara's teaching in such a way that it does not contradict the simple meaning of the verse. Solomon's visitor was, of course, a woman — the Queen of Sheba as the text implies. R' Shmuel merely says that whoever thinks that the rulership of this country just happened to be in the hands of a woman is mistaken. It reflects a general *lacking*, a weakness or dependence in the nature of Sheba's government. The ruler was a woman because Sheba was a weak nation.

Why is this significant?

Earlier in *Bava Basra* (there) the Sages discuss at which point in history the story of Job took place. Many opinions are offered. One, on the basis of *Job* 1:15, *And Sheba attacked...*, claims that the story happened in the days of the Queen of Sheba, that is in the period which we are discussing here.

Maharal (there) explains that the various opinions center around the issue of the role which Satan plays in the Job saga. Each seeks out a period during which Satan, in his role of spoiler, was particularly strong.

---

1. She asked: What goes out for seven, comes in for nine, two pour out and one drinks?

The answer: A woman's menstrual flow goes out for seven days; the fetus lives inside her for nine months, her two breasts provide nourishment and the baby drinks (*Midrash Mishlei*).

Maharal does not explain why our period would be one of particular influence for the Satan. He says only that the weakness of the Sheba rulership was an invitation to him to exercise his wiles.

The following explanation is possible:

Weakness craves strength and fulfillment, even as a wife would seek these through her relationship to her husband. A heathen people, longing for enlightenment to dispel the frustration and stupor of their empty existence, might well have its most graphic expression in the metaphor of womanhood.

The Queen of Sheba, hearing of Solomon's *fame in HASHEM's Name* (the *Kings'* version), decided to come to Jerusalem, there to find that to which in the depth of her soul she aspired. She was the prototype of all the gentile nations who will one day come to Zion in their multitudes, to quench their spiritual thirst. The first step of mankind's regeneration would, with her coming, have been taken. Small wonder that such a moment in history would have evoked a response from Satan.

The Sages teach that Solomon had relations with the Queen of Sheba and that from that union Nevuchadnezzar the ultimate destroyer of Solomon's Temple was descended. In whatever way we understand this tradition, it surely means, at the very least, that somehow the visit turned to catastrophe and became the cause of Israel's exile among the nations. Far from fulfilling its potential of being the beginning of the era when Israel would be perceived as mankind's teacher and source of inspiration, it became the very opposite.

◆§ Solomon's Wealth

In *Kings* too, following the account of the Queen of Sheba's visit, there is a listing of Solomon's wealth. *Malbim* suggests that the purpose of that passage is to record how God fulfilled the promise of wealth which He had made to Solomon at Giveon.

This may well be so in *Kings*. Clearly, the story of the sagacity of Solomon's decision in the case of the two women (*I Kings* 3:16 ff.), and the lyric description of his wisdom (*I Kings* 5:9-14) have this same purpose in regard to the promise of wisdom and understanding which God had made. Moreover, the positioning of the description of the wealth at the very end of the Solomon saga plays a significant role in evaluating its significance. Just as at the vision at Giveon it was not the main focus of Solomon's desires, so too, in actual fact, it was of only secondary importance. We learn of it at the end of Solomon's story as, almost, an afterthought.

However, for two reasons this cannot explain the fact that this information is included in *Chronicles*. Firstly, *Chronicles* seems unconcerned with showing that God had fulfilled the promise to grant Solomon wisdom — it is never mentioned except as it plays a role in the visit of the Queen of Sheba. Secondly, there has already been a description of Solomon's wealth earlier, at 1:15. The promise had clearly been fulfilled; why mention it once more?

What is the attitude of the Sages toward Solomon's wealth? Do they view it as a gift of God, underlining the exalted nature of Solomon's kingship, or do they condemn it as unseemly profligacy?

Of the three prohibitions which the Torah places upon the king — that he not have too many wives or horses, nor too much wealth (*Deuteronomy* 17:16-17) — Solomon clearly transgressed the first two (*Sanhedrin* 21b.) *Yerushalmi* and many midrashim make clear that he also transgressed the third.

This is the opinion recorded by *Rambam*, (*Sefer HaMitzvos* Negative Commands 365), although some Rishonim (see *Ran* and *Yad Ramah* to *Sanhedrin*, there) disagree.

We would expect the tone of the narrative to reflect one of these two opinions. If the accumulation of wealth involved no transgression, the tone should be one of approval, since it was a manifestation of God's care in fulfilling His promise. If, however, Solomon erred, the text ought to convey disapproval.

What is the ambience of the account?

In the thought world of Scripture it is invariably G-d who grants wealth — never man who achieves it independently of Divine favor. So does Hannah sing in her jubilant hymn of praise (*I Samuel* 2:7) and so does Solomon himself assume as a matter of course in his own prayer to God. (*Proverbs* 30:8). Certainly, if the wealth is bestowed in fulfillment of God's promise, this should be mentioned.

At Giveon it had been stated unequivocally that both Solomon's wisdom and his wealth were to come to him from G-d (1:12). In the case of the wisdom this is invariably stated (v. 23 here and *I Kings* 5:9 ff and v. 26 there) but never, in either book, is this point made concerning the wealth. It flows to Solomon through his own initiatives, or is brought by the many visitors who come to bask in the light of his benign rule.

By omission, rather than by commission, a gulf seems to be established between God's good will and Solomon's acquisition of wealth.

It can be argued that this omission is more striking by far in *Chronicles* than in *Kings*.

It can be shown that *Chronicles* much more than *Kings* makes a point of stressing how everything ultimately derives from G-d's providence. We adduce the following examples, [1] from the first chapter and [2] from the twenty-fourth.

II Chronicles Ch. 1; Ch. 24	*I Kings Ch.2; II Kings Ch. 12*
[1] a. 1:1. וַיִּתְחַזֵּק שְׁלֹמֹה בֶן־דָּוִיד עַל־מַלְכוּתוֹ, *Solomon the son of David then strengthened his hold over his kingdom.*	[1] a. 2:12. וּשְׁלֹמֹה יָשַׁב עַל־כִּסֵּא דָּוִד אָבִיו וַתִּכֹּן מַלְכֻתוֹ מְאֹד, *Solomon sat on the throne of David his father. His kingship was firmly established.*
b. וַה׳ אֱלֹהָיו עִמּוֹ וַיְגַדְּלֵהוּ לְמָעְלָה, *HASHEM, his God, was with him, and made him exceedingly great.*	b. 2:46. וְהַמַּמְלָכָה נָכוֹנָה בְּיַד־שְׁלֹמֹה, *The kingship was firmly established in Solomon's hands.*
[2] a. 24:24. כִּי בְמִצְעַר אֲנָשִׁים בָּאוּ חֵיל אֲרָם, *For Aram came with few people,*	[2] a. 12:18. אָז יַעֲלֶה חֲזָאֵל מֶלֶךְ אֲרָם, *Then Hazael the king of Aram came up* . . .
b.	b. וַיָּשֶׂם חֲזָאֵל פָּנָיו לַעֲלוֹת עַל־יְרוּשָׁלָם, *and Hazael set his face to go up against Jerusalem.*
c. וַה׳ נָתַן בְּיָדָם חַיִל לָרֹב מְאֹד, *but HASHEM gave a great army into their hands.*	c.
d. . . . כִּי עָזְבוּ אֶת־ה׳, *for they had forsaken HASHEM.*	d.

There are many more examples that could be brought. It is probable that this difference in approach between the two books lies in their respective positions in the canon. *Kings* belongs to the books of Prophets and was apparently written with prophetic vision, while *Chronicles* which is part of the Hagiographa was written by Divine inspiration but without prophetic insight. In a prophetic context God's constant and direct involvement in the affairs of man is assumed and does not need to be stressed. *Chronicles* with a lesser perception of the essence as opposed to the form of events does not assume God's involvement and therefore must explicate it.

Be that as it may, it becomes obvious that the omission of God's name in the *Kings'* description of Solomon's wealth is less striking than its omission in *Chronicles*. In *Kings* it might be supposed that in common with all the other matters with which the book deals, there is a tacit assumption that all derives from God. That assumption is apparently not present in *Chronicles*.

By having disapproval implied rather than having it stated explicitly, we are taught as follows:

The amassing of the wealth need not in itself be sinful. Only *too much* money is interdicted — and that is a flexible concept. The *Kings'* account is at the worst neutral, leaving a final assessment to the judgment of history. In *Chronicles* the same account has a more negative slant. In line with other aspects of Solomon's reign, his great wealth turned out to be no blessing.

◆§ Solomon Does Not Lose His Portion in the World to Come

Vs. 29-31, which wrap up Solomon's reign, parallel *I Kings* 11:41-43.

Between the foregoing and these verses, *Kings* has a long passage detailing: Solomon's love for foreign women; his weakness in allowing them free reign in the pursuit of their idol worship; God's anger and admonition to Solomon; the various enemies who, in consequence of Solomon's lapses were to plague the later part of his reign; Yarov'am's defiance of the king; and finally Yarov'am's meeting with Achiah the Shilonite in which the prophet promises him kingship over the ten tribes of Israel who are destined to break away from Solomon's descendants.

Why should these events, which were to have such a profound effect on Jewish history, be omitted from *Chronicles*?

Abarbanel thinks that it is *Chronicles'* purpose to present Solomon's reign in the best possible light. Such matters as tend to discredit him are omitted.

Our detailed analysis of the difference between the *Chronicles'* and *Kings'* accounts of Solomon's reign, as they appear the past nine chapters, has yielded that, on the contrary, *Chronicles* has, through countless nuances, tended to present the reign in the negative light in which it appears in the eyes of history.

If this is so, we would need to find a different solution to these striking omissions.

The mishnah in the tenth chapter of *Sanhedrin* tells of three kings and four commoners who forfeited their portion in the World to Come.

Yerushalmi (10:2), tells that when the Sages judged those three kings, they wanted to include Solomon among them. They felt that on the basis of what we are told concerning the idol worship practiced during his reign — at the very least with his implied acquiescence — he would surely deserve a fate similar to theirs. As they were about to include him, David came and prostrated himself before them, begging them not to pass this judgment upon his beloved son.[1]

1. *Bavli* in *Sanhedrin* 104b, also records the tradition that the Sages wanted to include Solomon among the kings who lost their portion in the World to Come, but differs from the account

What is the meaning of this *aggadah*?

In the thought-world of the Sages, the *World to Come* is not a location, nor is it a time frame. It is within every man. It is the deepest essence of his being, the spark of the Divine which defines him as an image of God, and which in normal circumstances remains inviolate and therefore indestructible in the face of sin. It is the locus of the ultimate mystery of life, where transience touches immortality. It is axiomatic in Rabbinic thought that sin may sully but never destroy that essential inner core of immortality; excepting only in the dreadful state which the Sages give the name of *losing one's portion in the World to Come*. There is a degree of sin so terrible in its all consuming evil, that even the sanctity of that spark of eternity falls prey before it. Its corrosive, destructive energy eats away, and eventually destroys, even that innermost spark of humanity.

When the Sages judged that Solomon should rightfully be counted among those who had lost their portion in the World to Come, this meant that they had determined that his innermost being had been irreparably contaminated by whatever sins of omission or commission had been transgressed. The basis for immortality had effectively been eroded.

David prostrated himself before them. Surely this can only mean that the Sages suddenly bethought themselves, who the inner Solomon really was. Was Solomon not merely an extension of the saintly David whose every breath of life was animated by that pure soul which his unrelenting struggles had finally yielded? Was he not at the very moment of his birth called *Beloved of God* (*II Samuel* 12:25), just because his being was the fruit of a life already fully and richly lived, and would not, anymore, have to be tested in the crucible of life? David lived on in his beloved son as he will one day live on in the Messiah, ultimate scion of the eternal royal line which had its genesis in him. This line passes inexorably and specifically through Solomon.

Solomon's sins, heinous as they may have been, could never touch that eternally pure soul, so closely identified with David. They are aberrations, grievous and destructive, breeding untold tragedy and catastrophe, but they do not touch eternity. The Davidic essence of Solomon's being remains inviolate — he does not lose his portion in the World to Come.

We have seen repeatedly that the *Chronicles'* perspective of the Solomonic saga is to view Solomon as extension of and vindication for, his father David. This is in contrast to the *Kings'* approach which is meant as a factual recording of the historical events of the reign. Thus, in the *Chronicles'* narrative there is no room for an accounting of short-comings which the Sages see as aberrations. These do not touch upon the Davidic essence of Solomon's being.

---

preserved in *Yerushalmi* in significant details. *Shelah* (Vol 2, p. 74 Jerusalem 1960) in *Maseches Pesachim* examines the two traditions and demonstrates that there is no essential disagreement between them. For our thesis, the *Yerushalmi* version is the relevant one.

Chapter Ten

◆§ Yarov'am's Return

Did Yarov'am return from Egypt on his own initiative, or was he summoned? See comm. to v. 2.

Yarov'am is one of the truly tragic figures of Jewish history. The Sages (*Sanhedrin* 102a) describe his greatness and purity in almost lyric terms. Surely God would not have chosen him as king over the Ten Tribes if he would not have been head and shoulders above all his contemporaries in Torah knowledge and sanctity.

And yet — he alone among all sinners in Israel — became the prototype of ultimate evil: Yarov'am son of Nevat, who sinned — and caused others to sin.

The Sages ascribe his downfall to simple pride. Once elevated to the kingship, he became obsessed. He could not countenance the possibility of the people's loyalty reverting to the Davidic line — and did not hesitate to ruin them so that he might protect himself.

Such spiritual erosion does not come overnight. Surely, when Yarov'am was still in Egypt and heard about Solomon's death and the impending coronation, he would not have rushed back in order to ferment rebellion. He would surely still have viewed himself as a modest and saintly person for whom such precipitate action would have been unseemly. He waited to be summoned.

This is what happened, and this is how *Kings* reports the events.

Chronicles, with the long view of history, sees Yarov'am as the cause of the untold misery which his unbending self-interest brought about. The one-time saint has been lost in the sinner who evolved. The spark of egotism must have been there from the very beginning. Overtly, Yarov'am waited to be called; in reality he was eager to go, and can thus be said to have gone on his own initiative.

◆§ The Confrontation

What are the rights and wrongs in this confrontation between king and subjects?

Clearly, not everything in this matter is black and white. *Kings* and *Chronicles* present substantively different pictures of Rechav'am's reign in general, and of the confrontation in particular.

We note four major differences:

1. *Chronicles* at 11:17 reports that in the first three years of Rechav'am's reign, the people were led in the ways of David and Solomon. Only after that did Rechav'am, and all the people with him, forsake the Torah of HASHEM (12:1).

Kings says nothing at all of this initial, positive period. Its assessment of Rechav'am's reign is unrelievedly negative: *And Judah did evil in the eyes of* HASHEM *and they brought forth His anger more than their fathers had done . . .* (14:22 ff.).

Since *Kings* has nothing good to say about the reign, we must conclude that Rechav'am's handling of the confrontation is also condemned. But *Chronicles*, which sees the first three years as positive, may well have a different attitude towards that event.

2. *Kings* makes no mention of the vast building programs which Rechav'am initiated (11:5-12). In the absence of this information, his response to the people that he intended to intensify the burden which his father had imposed upon them remains simply a

belligerent threat, unexplained and therefore unjustified by any real sense of purpose. *Chronicles*, which acquaints us with Yarov'am's ambitious projects, softens the impact of the apparently bellicose answer. Yarov'am had a real need to impose additional levies upon his people.

3. The advice of the elder statesmen is reported quite differently in *Chronicles* than in *Kings*, for which see Section II, *The Response of the Elders*. The *Chronicles* treatment is much more sympathetic to Rechav'am.

4. In the people's outraged response, their rejection of God is stated much more clearly than in *Kings* (see fn. to comm. at v. 16). Their outright blasphemy puts Rechav'am into a much better light.

What kind of a man was Rechav'am? Surely, as v. 15 makes clear, he made a terrible error in choosing the response which he did. But was his intention evil? Is there room in the Torah's view of the monarchy for his perception of the form his kingship was to take?

What was driving the people in their rebellion? Clearly, they were spoiling for a fight, seeking a confrontation with Rechav'am (comm. to v. 1).

But it was not a personal quarrel. R' Shimon bar Yochai taught that they were determined to jettison three values: God, the Davidic line and the House [see v. 16]. R' Shimon ben Menassiah taught that Israel would not flourish until they once more assert their loyalty to these three values (*Rashi* to *Hosea* 3:5. A slightly different reading can be found in *Yalkut Shimoni* to *I Samuel*, ch. 8).

Let us then postulate that Rechav'am sensed this spirit of rebellion in his subjects. Let us say that he recognized a rejection not against himself but against the God Whose rule he, as scion of the Davidic line, embodied on earth. What would his duties be as king?

Where — besides from his immediate advisors — could Rechav'am have looked for guidance in this sensitive situation? Perhaps he could have learned from his grandfather, David.

At *I Chronicles* 28:2, David had addressed the people as, . . . *my brothers and my subjects*. *Sotah* 40a wonders at the two seemingly contradictory expressions. Are they his *brothers* or his *subjects*? R' Elazar's solution: If you listen to me [that is, you are loyal to God — *Rashi*], then you are my brothers, but, if not, then you are my subjects.

Rechav'am, then, had precedent for a strict, unyielding position vis-a-vis his subjects. God Himself, when describing Joshua's leadership functions, had said, 'Let him take a rod in his hand and beat them over the head' (*Sanhedrin* 8a).

Clearly, it is possible to defend Rechav'am's stance. He was misguided, but not motivated by any evil impulse.

It appears that *Chronicles* takes this more positive view, while *Kings* stresses the negative aspects.

The different approaches may be influenced by the perspectives which the two books bring to bear on Shishak's campaign. In ch. 12 it will become clear that *Chronicles* views his conquest in terms of the starkest significance, while the *Kings'* view is more narrow.

Given this, it became imperative for *Chronicles* to make clear that this debacle was to be laid at Rechav'am's rather than at Solomon's door. Had Rechav'am's reign been portrayed as entirely negative, as it appears in *Kings*, then an impression would have been created that, from the turning point in Solomon's reign when he began to fall short of his destiny, a steady decline was initiated which, in the end, resulted in Shishak's conquest. The great Solomon would thus have been faulted not only in the division of the kingdom but also in this terrible defeat.

Chronicles avoids this erroneous impression by showing that Solomon left a great and good king to succeed him. His subsequent change of heart was not of Solomon's making. Indeed, as developed in ch. 12, the Sages make a point of explaining Shishak's success in terms of Rechav'am's own backsliding.

In *I Kings*, ch. 12, none of this was necessary. Accordingly, Rechav'am's handling of the confrontation is portrayed as negative. In actual fact, it had been a tragic misjudgment.

◆§ The Response of the Elders

Chronicles and *Kings* differ substantively in their accounts of the response made by the elders:

II Chronicles Ch. 10	*I Kings Ch. 12*
a. 7. אִם־, *If*	a. 7. אִם־הַיּוֹם, *If today*
b. תִּהְיֶה לְטוֹב לְהָעָם הַזֶּה, *you will be of benefit to this people*	b. תִּהְיֶה־עֶבֶד לָעָם הַזֶּה, *you will be a servant to this people*
c. וּרְצִיתָם, *and find satisfaction in them*	c. וַעֲבַדְתָּם, *and serve them*
d.	d. וַעֲנִיתָם, *and answer them*
e. וְדִבַּרְתָּ אֲלֵהֶם דְּבָרִים טוֹבִים, *and speak good words to them,*	e. וְדִבַּרְתָּ אֲלֵיהֶם דְּבָרִים טוֹבִים, *and speak good words to them*
f. . . . וְהָיוּ לְךָ עֲבָדִים, *then they shall be servants to you . . .*	f. . . . וְהָיוּ לְךָ עֲבָדִים, *then they will be servants to you . . .*

The Kings' version has the immediate answer in mind. This is clear from the wording of (a) *if today*, and from (d) *. . . and answer them.*

The elders are guiding Rechav'am in formulating an appropriate response. He cannot hope to subjugate the people unless he is first accepted by them as king. Once crowned he can do as he wishes. He must, first and foremost, make himself palatable to the people. This he can do only if — for the moment — he is willing to demean himself and permit himself to be controlled by his own subjects. Hence, the servant-theme in (b) and (c).[1]

The elders are, in a sense, conspiring with Rechav'am with the aim of constricting the people's freedom. In this context, when the king rejects the counsel of the elders, the argument does not revolve around a theory of kingship but around the practical utility of a ploy which they have suggested.

Chronicles, by eliminating those phrases which imply immediacy (a and d), sets a different tone.

The suggestion, that Rechav'am should relate to his subjects as a servant to a master, is a fundamental tenet in the Torah's view of the monarchy. *Rambam* (*Melachim* 2:6) views it as the very essence of kingship. Every decision which is made, every move that is undertaken must be exclusively for the good of the people.

This is how *Chronicles* understands the elders' suggestion that Rechav'am make himself servant to the people. The word *servant* is not used. This could be misinter-

1. The expression עֶבֶד can have the connotation of groveling and demeaning oneself before a more powerful force, as in *Proverbs* 22:7.

preted and understood in the sense that the *Kings* account takes it. Instead, *Chronicles* goes to the essence: Kingship must be for the people's benefit (b). It can be exercised best in a positive atmosphere (c) not made tense by constant demands.

The elders are not directly answering Rechav'am's question. They are not telling him how to formulate his answer (a and d). This they leave to him. Once his concept of kingship is as it should be he will be able to work out for himself how best to respond to the people's challenge.

A close reading of the text, then, tends to confirm *Targum's* interpretation which is the basis of our translation; see comm.

Taken thus, Rechav'am's rejection of the elders' advice constitutes a fundamental disagreement with the elders' position. His perception of his royal duties — at least in the present context — is different than theirs. See *The Confrontation*.

In *The Confrontation*, we listed the difference in approach which the two books take to the advice of the elders as one of the indications that the *Chronicles'* approach is more sympathetic to Rechav'am than is that of *Kings*. Our present analysis provides the background. In *Kings*, Rechav'am and the elders are pictured as together plotting how to deceive the people. In *Chronicles*, the issue is a debate concerning the nature of the monarchy.

Chapter Twelve

◆§ Rechav'am's Regression

There appear to be three significant differences between the *Kings'* and *Chronicles'* accounts of Rechav'am's regression:

1. *Kings* gives a detailed listing of the sins which were committed, while *Chronicles* satisfies itself with a general statement that evil was done.

2. In *Kings*, the blame is laid upon *Judah* the people, while in *Chronicles* it is the king who does evil — the people just follow along.

3. There is a striking imbalance between the two accounts in the relative space devoted to the national backsliding on the one hand and the subsequent campaign of Shishak on the other. In *Kings*, the description of Judah's evil ways takes three full verses and Shishak's campaign is described in two. By contrast, *Chronicles* deals with the regression in one short phrase but lavishes eight verses on the Egyptian campaign.

The omission in *Kings* of any mention that Rechav'am himself did evil is particularly significant when we consider that, among all the kings who ruled in Judah, Rechav'am is the only one upon whom *Kings* passes no judgment at all. That is, there is no parallel to our v. 14, in which *Chronicles* makes its assessment of his reign: *He did evil in the eyes of* HASHEM ... (see chart below).

	is equivalent to:	in the matter of:	judgment
–	*I Kings* 15:3	Aviah	N
II Chronicles 14:1	*I Kings* 15:11	Asa	P
II Chronicles 20:32	*I Kings* 22:43	Yehoshaphat	P
II Chronicles 21:16	*II Kings* 8:18	Yehoram	N
II Chronicles 22:4	*II Kings* 8:27	Achaziahu	N
II Chronicles 24:2	*II Kings* 12:2	Yehoash	P
II Chronicles 25:2	*II Kings* 14:3	Amatziahu	P
II Chronicles 26:4	*II Kings* 15:3	Uziahu	P
II Chronicles 27:2	*II Kings* 15:34	Yotham	P
II Chronicles 28:2	*II Kings* 16:2	Achaz	N
II Chronicles 29:2	*II Kings* 18:3	Chizkiahu	P
II Chronicles 33:2	*II Kings* 21:2	Menasheh	N
II Chronicles 33:22	*II Kings* 21:19	Amon	N
II Chronicles 34:2	*II Kings* 22:2	Yoshiahu	P
–	*II Kings* 23:32	Yehoachaz	N
II Chronicles 36:5	*II Kings* 23:37	Yehoyakim	N
II Chronicles 36:10	*II Kings* 24:9	Yehoyachin	N
II Chronicles 36:12	*II Kings* 24:18	Tzidkiahu	N

Note: We give only one verse although the actual assessment may spread over a number of verses. In each case we indicate whether the judgment is positive (P) or negative (N).

From the chart it is clear that such an omission is extremely rare. Normally, both books make assessments and invariably these are in essential agreement with one another. The two exceptions, Aviah and Yehoachaz, will be discussed when we get to those kings.

Rechav'am's sin was, that he *forsook the Torah of HASHEM*. Now this phrase can have a wide range of meaning. It can describe the apostasy of idol worship — as in *Deuteronomy* 31:16, and it can describe someone who does not cherish the wisdom of the Torah as he should — as in *Proverbs* 4:2 and 6.

What is the precise shade of meaning in our phrase?

The answer lies in v. 14. There we are told that Rechav'am, *did evil, for he did not set his heart to search out HASHEM*. *Metzudos* explains: He made no attempt to think deeply into his religious convictions [see comm. there].

No positive evil there. Simply a lack of deeply committed Torah leadership. The people were allowed to lapse into the evil of idol worship because of a lethargic and uncaring leadership. The king himself did not succumb to any sin — hence no negative assessment is made in *Kings*. *Judah* — the people — were the sinners.

Chronicles, however, views the king's spiritual lethargy as significant. Accordingly, it records an assessment: *He did evil in the eyes of HASHEM*.[1]

Why is the king's backsliding of concern to *Chronicles*?

The answer may lie in the disproportionate amount of space which *Chronicles* accords to Shishak's conquest. Clearly, this is viewed as the significant event of Rechav'am's reign. As background to that tragedy, Rechav'am's backsliding is important.

Thus: *Kings*, which downplays the Egyptian campaign (see below), has no interest in Rechav'am's personal shortcomings. As part of the history of the two kingdoms — which *Kings* records —Judah's idol worship is of significance, and becomes the focus of the narrative.

By contrast, Shishak's campaign is central to *Chronicles'* concern. It is viewed as the direct result of Rechav'am's lethargy. The people's sins play no role in this story.

It is impossible to overestimate the importance which the Sages attach to Shishak's campaign against Rechav'am. To understand it better we quote *Pesachim* 119a.

The discussion centers on *all the silver and gold in the world*, which Joseph had accumulated for Egypt while he was vizier to Pharaoh. It was this treasure which the Jews took along when they left Egypt — in fulfillment of God's promise to Abraham, that they would leave Egypt *with great treasure* (*Genesis* 15:14). They kept it until Shishak came and recaptured it from Rechav'am.

It seems evident that the Sages see Rechav'am's defeat at Shishak's hand as a seminal point in Jewish history. The significance of the booty which he took, went far beyond its monetary worth. A certain something which had been established at the dawn of Israel's peoplehood was forfeited. The *great treasure* returned to Egypt. [Compare *Pesachim* 87b.]

---

1. Our perception may help us understand the cryptic Aggadic teaching of the Sages (*Sanhedrin* 48b) that Rechav'am was a זָב *a man considered tamei because of a discharge* [from his male organ]. This discharge is not a seminal emission but is the result of a weakness in the semen-producing glands which cannot contain the semen and thus allows it to flow or dribble out without the normal forceful ejaculation which usually expels it. (*Rambam, Peirush HaMishnayos to Zavim*).

This would be an ideal metaphor to describe Rechav'am's impotence as king. Uncleanliness was spread all around him, not because of a positive evil which he injected into society but because of an internal weakness which allowed the impurity to issue forth.

We can understand the implications better if we trace the further movement of this treasure. As the Talmud describes it, it went through many more changes of hand; From Shishak to the Kushite king Serach; from him to Judah's Asa; from him [by way of Hadrimon] to the Amonites; from them to Judah's Yehoshaphat, where it remained until Assyria's Senchariv took it from the hapless Achaz, only to have it retaken by Judah's righteous Chizkiahu. Once more it remained with the Jews until Babylon conquered it from Tzidkiah at the final destruction of the Temple. From Babylon it then moved to Persia; from there to Greece; from there to Rome — where it lies up to this very day.

What can be the meaning of this Aggadic teaching?

We recognize the last four holders — they are the Four Kingdoms of Daniel's dream [see ArtScroll *Daniel* p. 102 ff.] who in the world view of the Sages were the dominant nations after the destruction of the Temple and who together span history until the end of days.

We may thus conclude that, in Aggadic idiom, Egypt's treasure is power. Needless to say, by its very nature that power is neutral. It can subdue and crush mankind beneath the feet of some dictatorial despot, but it can also be used to exercise benign control of all that the physical world has to offer.

This is the true significance of God's promise to Abraham. Israel's redemption could have left them a holy people divorced entirely from the concerns — and therefore the attractions — of this world. They might have lived in constant uplifting communion with God but remained strangers to the human condition. God's promise to Abraham guaranteed otherwise. Indeed, God wished His people to be a *kingdom of priests and a holy nation* but in the Torah's scheme of things that very priesthood and that very holiness demands involvement in the here and now. *Kohen* means not only *priest* but also *prince* [see *Rashi* there]. Israel would acquire the means of coming to grips with all the lures of a very real world.

And so Israel left Egypt ready to tackle nationhood in their own land. Their challenge was to convert that nationhood — in its outer trappings so similar to that of the surrounding peoples — into one which would distinguish them as bearers of the Divine Presence on earth. Grounded in such an existence, their influence and dominion would spread — as it did in Solomon's time — to the ends of the inhabited world.

The dangers of such a destiny were legion. Power can so easily corrupt, and the pull to assimilationist tendencies at the national level was strong. Notwithstanding these difficulties, adherence to Torah and its challenges would have made everything possible. Torah is like the emollient which a father places upon his son's wound (see *Kiddushin* 30b). There is no pleasure which the boy would have to deny himself as long as he kept the emollient on the wound. If he took it off, the wound would fester and sickness would ensue.

For many centuries the treasure lay ready, awaiting the moment at which Israel could assume the mantle of leadership. Solomon's reign accomplished this in full. There was no reason why Rechav'am should not have been able to continue and expand upon the foundations laid by his father.

But Rechav'am *forsook the Torah of* H*ASHEM*. He, as it were, removed the emollient from the wound. It festered and putrid poisons oozed out to contaminate and defile the kingdom. Rechav'am would never lead the people to become the *priestly* and *holy nation* of mankind. He forfeited the right to the treasure and Shishak reclaimed it. The money of Egypt *returned to its rightful place*.

The ebb and flow of Israel's spiritual growth and decline continued to create conditions which caused the treasure once more to return to Jewish hands. Asa, Yehoshaphat and Chizkiahu were all kings who had it in them to elevate Israel to the ideal heights which it had enjoyed in Solomon's days — but the influence they had on their times was short lived. Again and again the potential was frittered away and the treasure lost. With the destruction of the Temple it disappeared into the mists of history, not to return until the Messiah brings it — and us — back.

This, then, is the full import of Shishak's campaign against Jerusalem. It intimated — for the very first time since the euphoria of the Exodus — that after all, Israel would not rise to the challenge of its great calling. The tragedy of Rechav'am was that, without being positively evil, he was nevertheless instrumental in the collapse. He summoned no greatness. He was blind to destiny. The essence of kingship — Israel's kingship — eluded him.

And so, it was not idol worship, but the impotence of a weak and myopic king which determined that Israel was no longer to be trusted with the power that lay concealed in Egypt's treasure.

This is a story which *Chronicles* but not *Kings* wishes to record. Both the war in which Asa captured the treasure back from the Kushites and that in which Yehoshaphat took it from the Amonites are recorded in *Chronicles* but not in *Kings*. The entire perspective revealed in *Pesachim* seems to be one which is germane to the *Chronicles* presentation of the long view of the historical events, but not to that of *Kings*.

Chapter Thirteen

◈ Analysis of Aviah's Reign

The *Chronicles'* description of Aviah's reign is unabashedly positive. Not only is there no condemnatory judgment as there is at *I Kings* 15:3 [see chart above, p. 366], but an unmistakable ambience of approval imbues the description of the reign.

This is in stark contrast to *Kings*: *And he walked in all the sins of his father which he had committed before him and his heart was not complete with* HASHEM *his God as the heart of his father David [had been]* (15:3).

This goes far beyond the differences which we encounter on every page of *Chronicles*. Those are matters of emphasis — a detail missing in one account appears in the other, a changed expression, a fresh perspective uncovered. Here we are faced with an open contradiction: Was Aviah wicked or righteous?

The omission in *Kings* of any mention of the major war between Aviah and Yarov'am is also striking. We would have expected that a battle, which claimed the lives of half a million men of the Northern Kingdom alone, would have warranted mention.

We begin by attempting to establish the degree of Aviah's wickedness as given in *Kings*.

The relevant verse reads: *And he walked in all the sins of his father which he had committed before him and his heart was not complete with* HASHEM *his God as the heart of his father David [had been].*

Clearly, *the sins of his father* do not connote positive evil. If that were the case there would be little point in concluding the criticism by stating that Aviah had fallen short of David's perfection.

What then are those sins?

In Section II to ch. 12, *Rechav'am's Regression*, we saw that in the *Kings* version, no sins are ever attributed to Rechav'am himself. It is the people, not he, who did evil. We established there that Rechav'am was guilty of only excessive, and inexcusable, passivity — such as left the people without leadership or inspiration. The resulting slide into idolatry is laid at his door.[1]

Thus, Aviah too is accused of no more than that he continued in his father's ways and took no steps to inhibit the moral decline of the people.[2]

We now turn to vs. 4-5 in the *Kings'* account of Aviah's reign: *For, on account of David's merit,* HASHEM *his God gave him a remnant in Jerusalem, to establish his son after him and to strengthen Jerusalem. For David did that which was straight in the eyes of* HASHEM *and did not turn away from all that He commanded him all the days*

---

1. An analogy for such usage can be found at *I Kings* 15:12 where we are told that Asa removed the abominations which *his father had instituted*. But *I Kings* 14:24 ascribes these abominations to *Judah*, not to the king himself.

2. In confirmation, we note that even in *Kings*, there is no statement that Aviah *did evil in the eyes of* HASHEM — a formula used for every one of the kings of Judah who are assessed negatively. [See *II*:8:16 for Yehoram; *II*:8:27 for Achaziah; *II*:16:2 for Achaz, where the formula is not used but the heinous deeds which he committed are spelled out; *II*:21:2 for Menasheh; *II*:21:20 for Amon; *II*:23:32 for Yehoachaz; *II*:23:37 for Yehoyakim; *II*:24:9 for Yehoyachin; and *II*:24:19 for Tzidkiahu.]

of his life, excepting only in the matter of Uriah the Hittite.

The implication is clear. Aviah has no claim to the kingship in his own right. He is viewed simply as a means of perpetuating the Davidic line.[1]

We conclude that in the view of *Kings* which deals with the prophetic perceptions of the monarchy, Aviah's reign was a negative. He is defined as no more than a link in the chain of the Davidic dynasty but has no standing of his own among Israel's kings. The events of his reign — be they even as momentous as the war described in *Chronicles* — have no place in the history of the monarchy. Both by what he writes and by what he leaves out, Jeremiah makes it clear that Aviah does not exist — in his own right — in the roster of Judah's kings.

But *Chronicles* has something other than recording the history of the monarchy in mind. The focus is upon the Davidic dynasty as it stretches out to the Messianic future. While King Aviah was a failure in that he could not or would not put a stop to the erosion of the national morality, his was, nevertheless, an important chapter in Israel's odyssey. The war which he waged and his ringing affirmation of the exclusive legitimacy of the Davidic line are significant milestones in the Messianic saga. In this context, the negative assessment of Aviah's rule made by *Kings* is not germane, and *Chronicles* therefore does not record it.

◆§ Aviah's Speech

On the surface, the sentiments expressed in this speech seem above reproach. There is clearly an earnest desire for rapprochement with his brothers to the north, coupled with an unwavering identification with all the principles which, ideally, would animate David's line of succession on its path toward the Messianic future.

Indeed, a careful reading yields that the elements which make up this speech are precisely contoured to react to the three key fundamentals of Judaism which the northern secessionists had sought to jettison: God, the Davidic line, and the House service [see Section II to ch. 10, *The Confrontation*].

All this accords with the observation made above — that *Chronicles* presents Aviah in a positive light.

However, a closer analysis reveals that all is not well. As noted in comm. to vs. 7, 8, 17 and 19, the Sages tend toward a negative assessment. That they did so indicates that

---

1. Among the kings concerning whom a negative assessment is made, a statement similar to this is made only in the case of Yehoram (II:8:19).

The essential differences are more significant than the surface similarity.

They are:

1. The Yehoram account is spread over nine verses of which this statement takes up only one. Significant events of his reign are given reasonable play.

By contrast, except for the subsidiary statement that there was war between Aviah and Yarov'am, nothing at all is said about the events of Aviah's reign, and vs. 4-5, which deny him personal legitimacy, take up a full quarter of the sparse eight verses which are devoted to him.

2. The wording in the Yehoram account is: *Now* H*ASHEM did not want to destroy Judah*.... Thus, it is an explanation for the fact that God did not destroy the land. It is not directed to the specific fact of Yehoram's kingship. Here the verse reads: ... *For in the merit of David,* H*ASHEM his God gave him a remnant in Jerusalem*..., i.e., the explanation is directed to Aviah's kingship.

We conclude that the conclusions which we draw from this wording concerning Aviah would not be applicable to Yehoram.

they found reason to cast doubt upon Aviah's sincerity.

Was Aviah's analysis of the establishment of the Northern Kingdom correct? He seems to deny it any and all legitimacy. Vs. 6 and 7 make clear that in his view, Yarov'am was no more than a rebellious slave, and that the people who supported him were without substance and acted without justification.

In fact, of course, this is not the perspective projected in *Kings* 11:29 ff. There we see God unambiguously promising the kingship of Israel to Yarov'am. There is a proviso only, that it would not be *for all days*. In the tradition of the Sages, reconciliation and reunification should have occurred at the end of thirty-six years (*Seder Olam Rabbah* chs. 15 and 16). Up to that time the Northern Kingdom had absolute legitimacy. Only this persuaded Rechav'am to cancel his initial military response to the insurgency (11:2-4).

Aviah may not have known of a specific thirty-six-year time span and may well have anticipated an earlier reunification; withal, this would not justify his falsification of the events.

There is, then, a large degree of ambiguity in the words and actions of this king. See further in comm. to v. 22.

Chapter Sixteen

◆§ Asa's Illness

Sotah 10a teaches that Asa became ill as a punishment for impressing *talmidei chachamim* into the labor force, which was drafted with the purpose of removing the fortifications erected by Basha. *None was spared* (*I Kings* 15:22).

This verse does not occur in *Chronicles*. Accordingly, we are left without a rationale for Asa's sickness (which affected his feet). It is of course possible that the *Chronicles'* account relies on what was said in *Kings*, but in view of the fact that *Chronicles* treats the sickness much more fully than does *Kings* this seems unlikely.

Rather, we may assume that from the *Chronicles'* perspective, there was another cause for the sickness.

What is the place of feet in Aggadic thought?

R' Tzadok of Lublin (*Yisrael Kedoshim*) thinks as follows:

The Sages in *Sanhedrin* 91a wanted to find a parable to explain the concept that body and soul together constitute one entity, and that on the day of judgment God would treat each person as a unison of the two. They tell the story of the king who, not willing to trust the fruit of his orchard to ordinary watchmen who might be tempted to steal them, appointed two men — one blind and the other lame — as sentries. The lame man would be able to see the fruit but would have no means by which to reach them; the blind man could walk but would not know where to go. The sentries frustrated the king's plan. The blind man took the lame one upon his shoulders and directed by him, carried him to the fruit.

Thus, we have the soul compared to eyes. It has wisdom and insight but it is lame. It can only attain its goals by way of the body's physical properties. The body is comparable to legs; it can move around but knows not where to go unless directed by the soul.

Asa had recovered the *treasure of Egypt* in his victory over the Kushite forces. This was in recognition of the unbounded trust in God's providence which he had demonstrated on that occasion. He was now challenged by the unbridled worldly power which was implicit in this treasure. Would he control it and use it to lead Israel toward its Messianic destiny — or would he permit it to shackle him to its glittering, worldly promise?

The *treasure of Egypt* had become Asa's feet. These could be his willing servants to carry him whither the eyes of his spiritual grandeur might direct, or they could overpower him and drag him willy-nilly, on a blind rush to nothingness.

Once in possession of the treasure, Asa's perspectives underwent a tragic change. Suddenly, his fate seemed to rest with Ben Haddad rather than with God. If disaster is to be averted, he reasoned, the heathen general must be bribed.

Asa had become sick — terribly sick — as regards his sense of priorities initially, and consequently, in his legs.

It is not for nothing that v. 12 teaches that the sickness, which began in the lower extremities, eventually spread upward.

In the sense in which we have understood the symbolism of Asa's sickness, this would mean that Asa's failing did not stop with the mishandling of his worldly powers. Eventually, his spiritual standing too became compromised.

Chapter Seventeen

◆§ Yehoshaphat in *Kings* and *Chronicles*

As background to our discussion of Yehoshaphat's reign and the treatment which it receives in *Kings* and *Chronicles*, we note that it spanned a period covered by three of Israel's kings: Ahab, Achaziahu and Yehoram. The interaction between Yehoshaphat and each one of these three Israelite kings helped shape his reign in significant ways.

Our analysis will deal with two topics: 1. The wars in which Yehoshaphat fought. 2. The reforms in Torah study and in the judiciary, which he wrought.

Yehoshaphat's Wars

Yehoshaphat fought three major wars. He was allied with Ahab when that king attempted to dislodge the Arameans from their occupation of Ramoth Gilead (*I Kings* 22:2-40 and *II Chronicles* 18:2-34). This war is described in *Kings* but not as part of Yehoshaphat's story. It is presented in the context of Ahab's reign and Yehoshaphat appears in only a supporting role. By contrast, *Chronicles* reports the entire war in great detail within the context of Yehoshaphat's reign.

The next war resulted from an attack by the combined forces of Moab and Amon upon Judah. In this war, none of Israel's kings was involved. It is reported in great detail in *Chronicles* 20:1-30 but is not mentioned at all in *Kings*.

The third war came about when the king of Moab rebelled against Israel's sovereignty during the reign of Ahab's son Yehoram. Yehoram asked Yehoshaphat for help and Yehoshaphat agreed to join him in battle. This war is described in detail in *Kings* (II 3:4-27), but again as part of Israel's history, not within the description of Yehoshaphat's rule. It is not mentioned in the *Chronicles'* account.

Yehoshaphat's Reforms

We may gain a better understanding of the reasons behind these disparate ways of treating the wars when we consider the second grouping — the apparently far-reaching reforms which Yehoshaphat instituted in the field of Torah learning (ch. 17) and in the judicial system (ch. 19). These are reported with detailed approbation in *Chronicles* but are ignored in the *Kings'* account.

Why would *Kings* not report these very real accomplishments?

Perhaps, in the *Kings'* purview, they are overshadowed by a catastrophe of vast proportions which, unwittingly, Yehoshaphat set into motion.

In the short description which *Kings* devotes to Yehoshaphat's reign there is a verse which is not repeated in the parallel passage in *Chronicles* [21:31-37]: *There was no king in Edom; a governor was [in place of a] king.*

What is the significance of this piece of information? Why does *Kings* find it necessary to make this point, and why does *Chronicles* make no mention of it?

We have discussed the significance of the governors which King David established in Edom in Section II to ch. 18 of *I Chronicles*, *The Edomite War*, p. 449. In the constant struggle for ascendancy between Israel and Edom — the struggle which is the stuff of which history is made — these governors, established by Israel over its rival, were tangible evidence that, by virtue of its moral and ethical superiority, it had risen to the top.

In such a context, the information given at *II Kings* 8:22 and *II Chronicles* 21:10 — that during the reign of Yehoshaphat's son Yehoram, Edom gained its independence, rejecting the governors which Israel had imposed upon it — takes on profound significance. It points to a fundamental reordering of the historical balance. No longer could Israel view itself in fulfillment of its great calling. For long, dark centuries it would walk its path to eternity under the threatening shadow of Edom's sinister might. With only a brief respite during the period of the Second House, the awesome power of evil inherent in Edomite supremacy would hold sway over the fate of humanity.

The blow fell during Yehoram's reign — he was a wicked king whose actions precipitated the debacle. But the ultimate fault lay with Yehoshaphat. For it was he who had allied himself in marriage with the evil Ahab's house (18:1) by taking one of the Israelite princesses as a wife for Yehoram. It was her pernicious influence which led her husband astray.

This is the significance of the *Kings'* verse which we quoted above. In Yehoshaphat's days there was *no king in Edom, a governor . . .* ruled instead. Yehoshaphat was the last king of whom this could be said. In his son Yehoram's days, Edom rose free and unfettered to throw off Israel's dominion.

This was stark tragedy. In the balance sheet which *Kings* drew up of Yehoshaphat's reign, it was the one lastingly significant point. The improvements in Torah learning, the establishment of a strong judiciary all these gains were dissipated in the tumultuous years which followed Yehoshaphat's benign reign. They left no imprint upon Jewish history. But his reign would always be remembered as the last one in which no kings — only governors — ruled in Edom; the last during which Israel still maintained the standing which had defined its destiny.

To make this point in a sharp, unambiguous manner, *Kings* leaves out any mention of Yehoshaphat's accomplishments. Worthy as these were, *Kings* preferred to ignore them. Their mention would have detracted from the centrality of the one, all- important phrase. In his days — but not after him — there was as yet no king in Edom.

Chronicles, on the other hand, is less interested in defining the reigns of the particular kings than it is in depicting their personalties as scions of the Davidic line and as progenitors to the Messiah. In such a context, Yehoshaphat did indeed measure up to the most exacting standards, and each and every one of his accomplishments in raising the spiritual level of his people merits mention.

Having defined the differing perspectives of the two books, we can now attempt to understand their treatment of the various wars.

The battle for Ramoth Gilead in which Yehoshaphat joined Ahab and the one against Moab where he fought at the side of Ahab's son Yehoram were not Judah's wars but Israel's. In the *Kings'* perspective which deals with the history of the monarchy, their description belongs in the sections dealing with the Israelite kings. In that context, Yehoshaphat's part is entirely subsidiary to that of the kings who were the principals. *Kings* is entirely logical in omitting any mention of them when describing Yehoshaphat's reign.

On the other hand, *Chronicles* too is consistent with its own perspective — that of presenting the portrait of Yehoshaphat the man. The alliance which he made with Ahab was of profound significance in that it constituted a grave misjudgment on his part. He had joined forces with a thoroughly wicked man and thus compromised his own religious standing. For this he was roundly castigated by the prophet (19:2 ff.). From the fact that the description of the judicial reforms follows immediately upon this, it appears that they were influenced by these occurrences. We have a sequence of sin, penitence and positive reaction which contribute to a rounding out of the picture of Yehoshaphat's person.

By contrast, the alliance with Ahab's son Yehoram had no discernible effect upon Yehoshaphat. The question as to why, after accepting the prophet's strictures of his alliance with the wicked Ahab, he nevertheless accepted Yehoram's invitation is a valid one but should be treated in comm. to *Kings*. Be that as it may, the incident left no mark and, as such, does not concern *Chronicles*.

The war against Moab and Amon which is reported in *Chronicles* but not in *Kings* is also part of a pattern. It was in this war that Yehoshaphat recaptured the *treasure of Egypt* which Asa had squandered in bribing Ben Haddad. We have already seen that all the wars in which this *treasure of Egypt* is an issue are given in *Chronicles* but not in *Kings*.

◈§ Yehoshaphat Is Compared to David

The assessment of a given reign in terms of how it measured up against that of David occurs frequently in *Kings*; less so in *Chronicles*.[1]

But *Kings* makes no such assessment for Yehoshaphat. What is its meaning and significance in the *Chronicles'* account?

Again, there seems no logical progression from the first to the last parts of the sentence. Clearly, the comparison to David puts Yehoshaphat in a category of unusual piety. Should it then be necessary to say that he did not serve the Baal?

There is a tradition preserved in *Seder Olam* ch. 17 and *Tosefta* to *Sotah* ch. 12 that Yehoshaphat was married to a daughter of the wicked Omri, who had been king in Israel before Ahab.[2]

The basis for this tradition lies entirely in *Chronicles*. Neither of the verses upon which it is based [see fn.] occurs in *Kings*.

We may surmise that *Kings* ignores this union entirely because, in contrast to the disastrous effects which such a union had on his son Yehoram [see 21:6], Yehoshaphat remained untouched by it. Since it did not affect his reign in any way, it was not considered germane.

The creeping rapprochement between the two kingdoms, of which the two marriages are symptomatic, is an issue with which, as we shall see in later chapters, *Chronicles* comes to grips. Nevertheless, Yehoshaphat's union is not explicated in order that an otherwise blameless record should not be overtly besmirched.

Against this background, we may offer the following explanation of our verse: The phrase which states that Yehoshaphat walked in David's path has a different meaning than in all the other cases in which such a comparison is made. Usually, it is a statement which affirms the righteousness of a given monarch. Here, it is meant to stand in contrast to 21:6 where Yehoram's tragedy is tied to the fact that his

---

1. In *Kings*, the comparisons are made for: Solomon (*I* 11:6,33); Aviah (*I* 15:2); Asa (I 15:11); Amatziahu (*II* 14:3); Achaz (*II* 16:2); Chizkiahu (*II* 18:3); Yoshiahu (*II* 22:2).

In *Chronicles*, in addition to our case we have only Achaz (*II* 28:1); Chizkiahu (*II* 29:2), and Yoshiahu (*II* 34:2).

2. This tradition stems from the problematic dating for Achaziahu's ascension to the throne at 22:1. The reasoning of the Sages will be discussed there and at 18:1.

wife came from the Israelite court. The sense is that, in spite of the fact that Yehoshaphat was married to an alien wife, he still maintained the standards of the Davidic royal house.

In such a context, it is entirely appropriate to stress that Yehoshaphat did not allow himself to be dragged into Baal worship.

Kings has no parallel to this verse because, for it, this marriage did not exist.

We are now ready to attempt a closer definition of the phrase בְּדַרְכֵי דָּוִיד אָבִיו הָרִאשֹׁנִים, *in the earlier paths of his father David*.

Chronicles often sums up the reigns of the various kings by noting that their *earlier and later* [רִאשֹׁנִים וְאַחֲרוֹנִים] matters are recorded in such and such a source. This formula is used also in the case of David (*I Chronicles* 29:29). It seems likely that the meaning of רִאשֹׁנִים in our verse would be determined by its meaning in that oft-recurring phrase. We have sought to understand its meaning precisely in comm. to 29:29 — see there.

We may postulate that when *Chronicles* writes that the דְּבָרִים רִאשֹׁנִים וְאַחֲרֹנִים of a given king are recorded in such and such a place, the meaning is that both the perspectives of the *earlier and later books* have been preserved.

Above in *Yehoshaphat in Kings and Chronicles* we learned that Yehoshaphat was no exception. In his case too, *Kings* dealt with his reign while *Chronicles* was interested in his person.

When our verse uses בְּדַרְכֵי דָּוִיד אָבִיו הָרִאשֹׁנִים the meaning is as follows: It is true that the interest of *Chronicles* will focus on Yehoshaphat the man. Nevertheless, it should be noted that even from the perspective of the *earlier* books — the exercise of his kingship — he behaved in an exemplary manner, not allowing his alien wife to influence him negatively.

Chapter Eighteen

◌ The Alliance With Ahab

Yehoshaphat's response to Ahab's request is not identical in the two accounts. The difference may well be explained by the difference in perspective which we observed in the prefatory remarks to this chapter.

II Chronicles Ch. 18	*I Kings* Ch. 22
a. 3. וַיֹּאמֶר לוֹ — *And he said to him,*	a. 4. ...וַיֹּאמֶר יְהוֹשָׁפָט — *And Yehoshaphat said . . .*
b. כָּמוֹנִי כָמוֹךָ — *'I am as you are,*	b. כָּמוֹנִי כָמוֹךָ — *'I am as you are,*
c. וּכְעַמְּךָ עַמִּי — *my people is as yours,*	c. כְּעַמִּי כְעַמֶּךָ — *your people is like mine,*
d. וְעִמְּךָ בַּמִּלְחָמָה — *involved with you in the war.'*	d. כְּסוּסַי כְּסוּסֶיךָ — *your horses are like mine.'*

We note that in (c) the wording is reversed and that in (d) *Chronicles* substitutes an entirely different phrase.

The combination of two comparative *Kaphs* [...כּ ... כּ] (*Kings* c.) can indicate various levels of similarity. The two units being compared may remain entirely distinct from one another and the comparison limited to certain specified similarities. An example is at *Leviticus* 7:7. There the text reads: *The sin offering and the guilt offering are the same* [כַּחַטָּאת כָּאָשָׁם], *one law governs them; they belong to the Kohen who offers them up*. In this case, the two offerings belong in discrete categories: One is a חַטָּאת, the other an אָשָׁם. They share only this common feature — that the flesh can be eaten by the *Kohen* who had charge of offering them up.

Quite different is the degree of comparison implied in the term כָּכֶם כַּגֵּר at *Numbers* 15:15. The context makes abundantly clear that the Torah is granting absolute equality to the proselyte: *You [single and indivisible] congregation! One law shall apply to you and the stranger who dwells. It shall be an eternal statute that you and the stranger* [כָּכֶם כַּגֵּר] *shall stand equally before HASHEM. One single teaching and one single law shall govern you and the stranger who lives with you.*

What level of identification is meant here?

A careful reading of the text in both *Kings* and *Chronicles* indicates a progression in the degree of Yehoshaphat's involvement in the war. Yehoshaphat's original suggestion that the word of *HASHEM* be consulted is couched in the second person: *I beg you to attempt to find out this day what HASHEM says* (v. 4 here, v. 5 in *Kings*). But after Ahab consults the false prophets and Yehoshaphat is forced to insist that a true prophet be consulted, he seems already sufficiently involved to put his request in the first person, *Is there not another prophet of HASHEM that we may find out from him?*

This progression seems to be accurately reflected in *Kings* but not in *Chronicles* (see table, following page).

Chronicles	Kings
a. 5. וַיֹּאמֶר אֲלֵהֶם ... — ... *and said to them,*	a. 6. וַיֹּאמֶר — *And said ...*
b. הֲנֵלֵךְ אֶל־רָמֹת גִּלְעָד לַמִּלְחָמָה — *'Shall we go to Ramoth Gilead to war*	b. הַאֵלֵךְ עַל־רָמֹת גִּלְעָד לַמִּלְחָמָה — *'Shall I go to Ramoth Gilead to war*
c. אִם־אֶחְדָּל — *or shall I desist?'*	c. אִם־אֶחְדָּל — *or shall I desist?'*
d. 14. וַיֹּאמֶר ... אֵלָיו — *and ... said to him,*	d. 15. וַיֹּאמֶר — *And said ...*
e. מִיכָה הֲנֵלֵךְ אֶל־רָמֹת גִּלְעָד — *'Michah, shall we go to war in Ramoth Gilead*	e. הֲנֵלֵךְ אֶל־רָמֹת גִּלְעָד לַמִּלְחָמָה — *Shall we go to Ramoth Gilead to war*
f. אִם־אֶחְדָּל — *or shall I desist?'*	f. אִם־נֶחְדָּל — *or shall we desist.*

The *Kings'* version is consistent. On the first occasion, when Yehoshaphat had still excluded himself from direct interest by addressing Ahab in the second person, Ahab arrogates all decisions to himself. It is he who will decide either to go forward or to desist. After Yehoshaphat indicated his closer involvement, the decisions are vested in both of them: *We* will either go or stay.

In *Chronicles*, this consistency is missing. Both in the earlier verse and the later one the decision to go is to include both; the decision to stay is Ahab's alone.

We suspect that the use of the plural in the earlier verse in *Chronicles* derives from a difference in connotation in the ... כ ... כ comparison. The *Chronicles'* version betrays a much closer involvement than does the one in *Kings*.

By using the same formula for all the three units — *I am like you; my people are like your people; my horses are like your horses* — the *Kings'* text makes clear that only an external similarity is meant. The horses are not involved. The meaning must be something like: 'My horses are as ready as yours'; or, 'you control my forces as you do yours.' In that context, the two earlier phrases carry the same value: 'I am as willing to go as you are; my people will obey you as do your own,' or similar meanings. A distancing is maintained; 'I, my people and my horses are a distinct unit. We share a given purpose with you.'

By substituting *involved with you in the war* for the phrase dealing with the horses, *Chronicles* creates a different ambience for the entire passage. The word עִמְּךָ, *with you,* has an immense number of shades in meaning — among them one denoting a common lot or absolute identity. See for example *I Chronicles* 24:5. This impression is reinforced in the different wordings of the (b) section. It is not כְּעַמִּי כְּעַמֶּךָ, where *my people* and *your people* remain discrete entities joined only by some external commonality but וּכְעַמְּךָ עַמִּי, *my people is as yours*: Dispose of them as you would of your own!

It may well be that the actual words used by Ahab were those quoted in *Kings*. At this point it was still his and not Yehoshaphat's campaign. But now Yehoshaphat's inner ear already picked up what in his inner soul he knew to be true. He was committed to throw in his lot with the wicked Ahab. The meal which they had shared had done its job. He knew that if the decision would be to desist it would be Ahab's decision — not his, for he wished to go — but that if they were to go ahead, he and Ahab would be as one.

With an exquisite ear for nuance, *Chronicles* reinforces this inner truth by not changing the form even after Yehoshaphat had already verbalized his unambiguous involvement. He wanted to go: If the decision would be to give up the plans, then it would be Ahab, not he, who reached that decision.

Chronicles further reinforces its perception by another subtle change in nuance. We present the answers given, first by the other prophets and then by Michaiahu, the true prophet of *HASHEM*.

Chronicles	*Kings*
a. 5. וַיֹּאמְרוּ עֲלֵה וְיִתֵּן הָאֱלֹהִים בְּיַד הַמֶּלֶךְ — *They said, 'Wage war* [עֲלֵה singular] *and God will give them into the hand of the king.'*	a. 6. וַיֹּאמְרוּ עֲלֵה וְיִתֵּן אֲד־נָי בְּיַד הַמֶּלֶךְ — *They said, 'Wage war* [עֲלֵה, singular] *and HASHEM will give them into the hand of the king.'*
b. 14. וַיֹּאמֶר עֲלוּ וְהַצְלִיחוּ וְיִנָּתְנוּ בְּיֶדְכֶם — *He said, 'Wage war* [עֲלוּ plural] *and prosper; would that they be given into your hand.'*	b. 15. וַיֹּאמֶר אֵלָיו עֲלֵה וְהַצְלַח וְנָתַן ה׳ בְּיַד הַמֶּלֶךְ — *He said to him, 'Wage war* [עֲלֵה, singular] *and prosper. HASHEM has given them into the hand of the king.'*

In the *Kings'* version, even Michaiahu, to whom Ahab had addressed his query in the plural, uses the singular in his answer. Politeness requires that even if the king is willing to have Yehoshaphat share in the honor of making decisions in the campaign, this should not be reflected in the answer which the prophet gives. Ahab is his master and it is to him that the prophecy is addressed.

In *Chronicles* there is a change. The other prophets know nothing of the inner tensions which set Yehoshaphat's heart into turmoil. There is no inner meaning to their outward answer. Even though the question had been couched in the plural, the answer is directed to Ahab alone. But Yehoshaphat knows that the prophet of *HASHEM* is privy to his most private thoughts. He hears himself included in the bitter irony of his answer.

Chapter Nineteen

◆§ Yehoshaphat and the Judiciary

Yehoshaphat made two apparently innovative moves: He appointed provincial judges and established a central court in Jerusalem.

Clearly, some arrangement must have been in place before he undertook these reforms. It is patently obvious that no nation could have existed for five centuries without some workable, locally based system for enforcing the law of the land and for adjudicating among the people.[1]

---

1. For a picture of how justice was administered prior to Yehoshaphat's reforms, we must go to the Scriptural sources. There are hints in *Judges*, *Samuel* and *Kings*, but a very clear picture does not emerge.

Judges: From the death of Joshua up to the establishment of the monarchy, Israel's leaders were known as שׁוֹפְטִים, from שפט, which is generally rendered *to judge*, but can also mean *to govern* [see comm. at 1:10]. Accordingly, we have no proof that these leaders were judges in the sense that they sat on courts and administered justice. [See *R' A. Shoshanah*, *Derech Binah* to *Judges*, *Introduction*, p. 7.]

Tosafos to *Bava Kama* 15a, s.v. אֲשֶׁר takes *Judges* 4:4: *And she [Devorah] judged Israel at that time* to mean that Devorah was a judge in the formal sense of the word. But even if that was the case, there is certainly no indication that there was a court-system established throughout the land. On the contrary, the language of the verse implies that judicial activity centered about her person or, at the most, her court.

Rashi to *Judges* 11:37 quotes a Midrashic source in which Jephthah's daughter suggests applying to a Sanhedrin in order to have her father's vow annulled. This cannot be taken as proof that a permanent Sanhedrin was functioning. It is conceivable that one could have been convened for the express purpose of annulling a vow.

We may conclude that for this period there is no specific allusion to the court system envisioned by the Torah.

Samuel: *I Samuel* 7:15 talks of Samuel traveling around the country in order to administer justice. While this does not prove that there were no courts — Samuel may well have had to oversee their functioning — it does not confirm the existence of such courts. The simple meaning of the text would tend to a picture of a justice system centered upon Samuel's person and administered on the occasion of his annual visits.

This seems confirmed by *Shabbos* 55b and 56a where the bearing of Samuel's sons is contrasted unfavorably with that of their father. Whereas Samuel had traveled around the land in order to bring justice to the people, his sons, so that they might increase the income of their court administrators and personnel, stayed in their hometown and had the people come to them. The implication is that people from all the cities came to be judged by Samuel's sons.

Kings: *And it was that every man who had a quarrel and came to the king for judgment, Avshalom would call to him and ask him, 'From which city are you?' and he would answer, 'Your servant comes from one of the tribes of Israel.'* (*II Samuel* 15:2). Thus, the description of the administration of justice in David's times. Clearly, there were no local authorities to whom to turn. Litigation had to be brought to Jerusalem.

Solomon too appears to have seen the administration of justice as his personal fiefdom. Thus, at *I Kings* 3:9 he begs God for *a listening heart*, the better to understand the litigants who come before him. For possession of the living infant, the quarreling mothers did not turn to a court, but came to the king himself.

All the sources combine to create the impression that there was no court system in place until one was established by Yehoshaphat.

However, we note that in ch. 16 of *Doros HaRishonim*, *Tekufas HaMikra*, *HaLevi* analyzes

Whatever that arrangement may have been, it seems not to have been systemized, and to the extent that it did exist it appears to have drawn its authority from a central figure — Judge or King.

But the establishment of local courts in every city is mandated by the Torah (*Deuteronomy* 16:18; *Rambam, Sanhedrin* ch. 1). Is it possible that over a period of some five hundred years, such a basic societal and halachic requirement was simply ignored?

R' Dovid Tzvi Hoffman, Leviticus [Introduction to *Shoftim*], is willing to postulate just that. During centuries in which idol worship often flourished, and prostitution proliferated (*I Kings* 14:12 and 22:47), it should come as no surprise if other basic Torah standards fell by the wayside.

This may have come about as follows:

In a wide ranging discussion of the judicial system as envisioned by the Torah, *Derashos HaRan* (*D'rush* 11) recognizes two discrete systems: One is that which is to be administered by the courts, the other by the king.

The courts are required to apply Torah law with undeviating consistency. They do not, in their own right, have the flexibility to make exceptions for real-life situations in which these laws may, occasionally, be too rigid to meet the practical needs of a functioning people.

For such contingencies, the Torah provides a corrective — a system of justice, grounded in the king. He has the authority on a case-by-case basis — never permanently — to abrogate Torah law [in civil and some criminal cases] as he sees fit.

Ideally, these two systems function side by side, and in their interplay with one another produce the ideal Torah society. It is, however, conceivable that the one system — that grounded in the royal prerogative — could function independently for an indefinite period. There would be nothing inherently illegitimate in such a usage.

Perhaps, with such a system available, the establishment of the courts was, indeed,

---

the sources which bear upon the existence of a judiciary in early Scriptural times.

He makes the following points:

1. *Deuteronomy* uses two terms which are germane to this issue [cf. 22:15 and 25:7 there]: שַׁעַר, literally *gate*, as the description of the location at which the court sat, and זְקֵנִים, literally *elders*, as the name by which judges were known.

Thus, when we read in *II Samuel* 15:2 that, in his attempt to win the hearts of litigants who came to Jerusalem for judgment, Avshalom stood, עַל יַד דֶּרֶךְ הַשַּׁעַר, we now realize that the true meaning of שַׁעַר in this phrase is not *gate*, but the *court* over which David normally presided.

Similarly, we now know the precise meaning when we read that Boaz, as he laid the foundations for his marriage to Ruth, went to the שַׁעַר and dealt with the זִקְנֵי הָעִיר.

Even when the term does not occur in the context of litigation, we can now assign more precise meanings: *I Kings* 8:1 tells how Solomon gathered the זִקְנֵי יִשְׂרָאֵל, the רָאשֵׁי הַמַּטּוֹת, and the נְשִׂיאֵי הָעֵדָה. Clearly, the זִקְנֵי הָעֵדָה are the judges.

We may conclude that terms such as זְקֵנִים ,זִקְנֵי הָעֵדָה or זִקְנֵי יִשְׂרָאֵל, which are scattered throughout Scripture, would be understood best if we would assume that the Sanhedrin or other courts are meant.

2. When Jezebel engineered Navoth's death, she did not simply order her servants to kill him. She realized that such a wanton crime would never be countenanced by the people. Instead, by producing false witnesses, she conspired to have him killed by judicial process. A careful reading of the passage (*I Kings* ch. 21) shows that the procedure followed agrees in every detail with the requirements laid down by the Torah for the resolution of such cases.

HaLevi's analysis certainly yields that courts existed in Israel from the earliest times. It does not demonstrate that the system was that which is envisioned by the Torah. He does not address the question of Yehoshaphat's reforms.

not seen as urgent. The period of the Judges did not lend itself to the kind of central control required for the inauguration of a judicial system on a national scale. The leadership of the Judges was not of a dynastic nature — by definition they could not pass their office on to their children. They probably saw their task cast in a temporary mold, the filling of immediate needs rather than the establishment of institutions which would outlast them.

Once a centralized system of justice had, over the centuries, become ingrained, we may assume that changing it into a localized court system would require great energy and determination. The reigns of Saul and David, ridden as they were by constant internal and external strife, would not have lent themselves to such a far-reaching restructuring of society.

Once the monarchy had begun on the basis of the old system, it is quite possible that in the comparatively short period before Yehoshaphat's time, nothing occurred which made it imperative to change. And thus, as *R' Dovid Tzvi Hoffman* suggests, the same *laissez faire* which allowed the prostitutes to proliferate also prevented the energetic pursuit of the fulfillment of the Torah goal of a localized system of justice.

Until Yehoshaphat came along!

What galvanized Yehoshaphat into action in a matter which his predecessors had allowed to slide?

The Asheirah and the Unworthy Judge: *Mefaresh*, apparently based on a Midrashic source which has been lost to us, suggests that it was Yehu's reference to Yehoshaphat's elimination of the *Asheiros* which gave him the idea to devote himself to the establishment of the courts. He remembered the juxtaposition of the two in *Deuteronomy* ch. 16 where the obligation to appoint judges (vs. 16-70) is followed immediately by the prohibition to plant an *Asheirah*, or indeed any tree, in the vicinity of God's altar.

From this association the Sages derive the teaching that one who appoints a judge who is not worthy of that office is equivalent to one who plants an idolatrous grove (*Sanhedrin* 7b).

What is the connection?

The practice of idolatry did not only severely damage the relationship between man and God. It exerted a deeply pernicious influence upon the social structure of the community, denying the individual the dignity which derives from a personal, and therefore unique, standing before God. We need only think of the horribly degrading service demanded by the ubiquitous Baal which involved excreting before him, or the human sacrifice which the Molech craved, to recognize the absolute erosion of personal worth implicit in these cults.

The Torah's system of justice stands in absolute contrast to this. By locating the Sanhedrin, the highest body within the judicial hierarchy, in the Temple, it teaches unambiguously that each man's due derives directly from his standing before God. It is a justice system which is based not on current judicial philosophy, but on the immutable correctness of God's view of man and human relationships. It is the absolute truth. It governs all relationships between individuals, each of whom through the Divine spark within him touches uniqueness and infinity — and partakes, in the final analysis, of Godliness.

A judge, unworthy of administering such a system; too obtuse to recognize the worth of the individual who stands before him, is the equivalent of the *Asheirah*. Given free reign he will reduce the individual to a cog in a blindly revolving wheel of fate.

In this sense, the justice system of the courts is infinitely superior to that grounded in the royal prerogative. The latter may, indeed, be needed as a corrective for those cases which, due to circumstances, may require a different remedy than that laid down by the Torah. But its very utility expresses its inadequacy. It is the product of human thought. It lacks the absolute and inevitable correctness of the Torah law which lies within the purview of the courts.

This is the realization to which Yehoshaphat was brought. If, indeed, his life was saved because he had uprooted the *Asheiros*; if God had spared him because he had struck such a significant blow for the dignity of the individual before God, then this was a sign to him that he was called upon to correct the abuses of the past. He would use his kingly powers to actualize the Torah's ideal society by instituting the court system.

Chapter Twenty

◆§ The Moabite Wars

Given that there were two Moabite wars in which Yehoshaphat was involved, it becomes necessary to examine the sequence in which they took place.

[For the sake of clarity we shall refer to the one as Yehoram's war and to the other as Yehoshaphat's war.]

There are at least two good reasons for supposing that Yehoshaphat's war was the latter of the two. In the first place, this would have provided Moab with a motive for attacking Judah. Moab would have had every reason for wishing to take vengeance for the ignominious defeat which it had suffered at Yehoram's hands — a defeat in which Yehoshaphat had played a significant role.

Again, the ambience of the *Chronicles'* account seems to require that it be seen as the high point in Yehoshaphat's experiences of the Divine. The very heavens do battle for him. He is absolutely passive; the enemy armies slaughter one another. All that is left for him to do is to collect the spoils and return to Jerusalem in an ecstasy of gratitude to God. After such an experience, the campaign described in *Kings* — although it too saw its share of miracles — seems anticlimactic. Yehoshaphat had already experienced God's providence at closer quarters.

Standing against this chronology is our v. 35 describing an alliance between Yehoshaphat and Ahab's son Achaziah [whose reign antedated that of his brother Yehoram], which apparently took place after Yehoshaphat's war. Necessarily, Yehoshaphat's war would have taken place long before that of Yehoram.

However, our hypothesis seems borne out by our reading of *Seder Olam Rabbah* 17. The text as it appears in the printed versions and as quoted by *Radak* to *II Kings* 8:16 reads as follows: *In the fifth year of Yehoram son of Ahab king of Israel and Yehoshaphat king of Judah. . . .* [This teaches that] as they returned from the war after having destroyed Amon, Moab and the Seirites, they crowned Yehoram son of Yehoshaphat king over Judah.

Now the fifth year of Yehoram (king of Israel), whose reign had been preceded by that of his brother, Achaziah, must have fallen very shortly before Yehoshaphat's death, since Yehoshaphat outlived Ahab by only seven years. Since *Seder Olam* is referring to Yehoshaphat's war — *. . . having killed Amon, Moab and the Seirites*, who were involved in Yehoshaphat's but not in Yehoram's war — this places that war towards the end of Yehoshaphat's life, certainly not during the reign of Achaziah.

But, as printed, *Seder Olam* is difficult: *As they returned* implies that Yehoram was involved in the war under consideration; but of this there is no record. An alliance between the two kings is recorded only in *Kings* in connection with Yehoram's war and not in *Chronicles* in connection with Yehoshaphat's war.

To explain *Seder Olam* we have two options:

R' Yaakov Emden in his glosses suggests that although there is no record that Yehoram joined in Yehoshaphat's war, the Sages may nevertheless have had a tradition that, in fact, he was involved.

There is also the possibility that the correct reading in *Seder Olam* is, *After they destroyed Moab* and not, *After they destroyed Amon, Moab and the Seirites*. This appears to have been the reading which was before *Rashi* who paraphrases *Seder Olam* (*Kings*, there): . . . *when they returned from the war which they fought against Moab. Thus did we learn in Seder Olam* (*Dov Ber Rathner*). Thus, reference is to Yehoram's war, not to Yehoshaphat's; this latter one may well have taken place much earlier, while Achaziah was still king.

In summation we may say that, according to *Seder Olam* as printed and explained by *R' Yaakov Emden*, Yehoshaphat's war took place towards the end of his reign, long after Achaziah had ceased to be king — just as we surmised above. If this is so, we would have to accommodate v. 35 from which it would appear otherwise — see comm. there.

According to *Rashi's* reading, it seems likely that Yehoshaphat's war took place during Achaziah's reign as indicated by our v. 35. As noted above, this would leave us without an obvious motive for Moab's attack. See comm.

As for the argument that Yehoram's war seems like a regression from the much greater spiritual impact of Yehoshaphat's war — we will have to differentiate between Judah and the Northern Kingdom. As noted in the comm., the high level of the supernatural, which was manifest during Yehoshaphat's war, derived from the very special place which God's providence had reserved for the small kingdom of Judah. In that war, God indeed allowed the full outpouring of His love to become evident. The other battle was not really Judah's or Yehoshaphat's. Here, the interests of the Northern Kingdom were involved. Yehoshaphat's role was limited to that of an ally. It lies in the nature of that event that God's hand should have been less evident.

◆§ Bamos in *Kings* and *Chronicles*

The following is a possible solution for the change in wording noted in comm. to v. 33.

We begin by analyzing the full sentence as it occurs four times in *Kings*: (a)רַק הַבָּמוֹת לֹא־סָרוּ (b) עוֹד הָעָם מְזַבְּחִים וּמְקַטְּרִים בַּבָּמוֹת . What does the (a) part of the sentence say, and how does the (b) part relate to it?

סור in the *kal*, the simple voice, means *to turn aside*, *to remove*, and occasionally, in the passive sense, *to be removed* (see, for example, *Exodus* 25:15). Thus the first part of the sentence, if rendered literally, would mean: *The bamos* did not go away, or *the bamos* were not removed.

But since this phrase always follows upon the statement that such and such a king followed a righteous path except in the matter of the *bamos*, we would have expected the use of the *piel*, the active voice. Thus for example in our case, v. 32 which reads *He went in the path of his father Asa* . . . should be followed by the statement . . . *but he did not remove the bamos*. The passive *the bamos did not go away*, or *were not removed* is syntactically awkward.

The passive form is particularly striking in the passage in *I Kings* (15:11-14) which describes Asa's activities: וַיַּעַשׂ אָסָא הַיָּשָׁר בְּעֵינֵי ה׳ . . . וַיָּסַר אֶת־כָּל־הַגִּלֻּלִים אֲשֶׁר עָשׂוּ אֲבֹתָיו וְגַם אֶת מַעֲכָה אִמּוֹ וַיְסִרֶהָ מִגְּבִירָה . . . וְהַבָּמוֹת לֹא סָרוּ. In the case of the abominations and Maachah, סור appears in the active voice, with Asa as the subject: Asa *removed* (וַיָּסַר) *the abominations* . . . and *demoted* Maachah *from her position of power*. We would have expected this to be followed by the statement: *But he did not remove* (לֹא הֵסִיר) *the bamos*. Instead, we have the passive *were not removed* (לֹא־סָרוּ).

The explanation may be as follows: We recall that these *bamos* were not used for idol worship but in the service of God. This, however, was forbidden once the Temple had been built. (See 14:2 and 15:17.) Now while the Torah explicitly commands us to destroy all idolatrous altars, no such obligation exists in the case of the *bamos* which were in no way connected to idol worship. While their use was certainly forbidden, they could simply have been left standing and — it might be expected — they would gradually disappear because of disuse and consequent neglect. Even kings who were completely righteous had no reason to actively remove the *bamos*. They were justified in hoping that these would, of themselves, disintegrate. That this did not, in fact, happen is because the people — contrary to expectations — refused to be weaned away from them and continued to use them.

This, then, is the meaning of the verse in *Kings*. The (b) part is to be understood as an explanation of the (a) part. The *bamos* did not disappear, as might have been expected, *because* the people continued using them.

Chronicles' interest is an entirely different one. Here we are concerned, not with the reason why the *bamos* did not disappear but with the result of the fact that they remained a fact of life in Judah. [Note the וְעוֹד instead of the עוֹד of *Kings*. The word introduces a new idea: *As a result* the people did not set their heart . . .]

For *Chronicles'* purpose it was important to establish that all was not well with the people of Judah. This is because of *Chronicles'* presentation of the reign of Yehoshaphat's son, Yehoram. Where *II Kings* (8:18) is satisfied with a general statement that he walked in the paths of the kings of the Northern Kingdom and did evil in the eyes of God, *Chronicles* goes into much greater detail. In particular, *Chronicles* quotes a letter written to Yehoram by the prophet Elijah in which he is accused of having made *Judah and the inhabitants of Jerusalem go astray just like the house of Ahab made* [*Israel*] *go astray* (21:13).

Now when we consider that the combined reign of the two righteous kings Asa and Yehoshaphat spanned a period of sixty-six years, it seems highly improbable that the scant eight years of Yehoram's reign would have been sufficient to bring about a measurable deterioration in the religious stance of the people. If nevertheless this did occur, it requires an explanation. Ezra teaches that the problem lay with the *bamos* which still proliferated throughout the land. These acted as a drain upon the religious commitment of the people. With their relationship to God undermined by this weak spot they fell prey to the forces which Yehoram's apostasy set in motion.

The sentence is to be translated: *However, the bamos did not disappear* [or, *were not removed*] *and thus the people did not set their heart to the God of their fathers.*

Chapter Twenty-One

⌘ God Will Not Destroy the Davidic Line

At 22:2 and 7 we will learn that many years earlier, when Yehoshaphat married Omri's daughter, God had already decreed that the Davidic line was to be destroyed. This invests our verse with a special poignancy. God is, as it were, fighting the unavoidable. The disastrous alliance with Omri's house must, perforce, bring destruction in its wake. But God will not have it so. Somehow, the continuity of the Davidic line must be preserved.

This context, which is unique to *Chronicles* since *Kings* has no parallel to either 22:2 or 7, helps to explain the difference between the *Kings* and *Chronicles* versions of our verse:

II Chronicles Ch. 21	*II Kings Ch. 8*
a. 7. וְלֹא־אָבָה ה׳, *But* HASHEM *did not want*	a. 19. וְלֹא־אָבָה ה׳, *But* HASHEM *did not want*
b. לְהַשְׁחִית אֶת־בֵּית דָּוִיד, *to destroy the House of David*	b. לְהַשְׁחִית אֶת־יְהוּדָה, *to destroy Judah*
c. לְמַעַן הַבְּרִית אֲשֶׁר כָּרַת לְדָוִיד, *because of the covenant which He had made with David*	c. לְמַעַן דָּוִד עַבְדּוֹ, *because of David His servant*
d. וְכַאֲשֶׁר, *and as He had*	d. כַּאֲשֶׁר, *As He had*
e. . . . אָמַר לָתֵת לוֹ, *promised to grant him . . .*	e. . . . אָמַר־לוֹ לָתֵת, *promised to grant him . . .*

We note that in (b) *Chronicles* substitutes, בֵּית דָּוִיד for יְהוּדָה and that in (c) it makes reference to a covenant with David, which *Kings* does not mention. Also, as a result of this difference, *Chronicles* adds a conjunction in (d), because it introduces a new thought (e).

Malbim takes note of the change in (b) and sees it as *Chronicles'* explanation of the expression used in *Kings*: יְהוּדָה is to be understood as *king of Judah* — namely, *the House of David*.

We understand this as follows:

To refer to the king by the name of his country is to underline the strong ties between the two — indeed, to submerge the king's identity into that of his people. God had great love for David and great love for His people Israel. In the moment when destruction faces them and they are to be engulfed by their own betrayal, the two loves fuse and God perceives the boundless pity of the loss of this unison of king and people who could —if they had wished — have aspired to such great heights. *Chronicles* has a different tale to tell:[1]

Beginning with Yehoshaphat's reign, *Chronicles* has been occupied with the catastrophic blurring of the lines which divide the royal house of Judah from the northern

---

1. The same usage is repeated when, centuries later the actual destruction came. See *II Kings* 24:2. *And* HASHEM *sent the bands of the Chaldeans . . . against* **him**; *sent them against* **Judah** *to destroy* **him**.

rulers. We have noted how *Chronicles*, as opposed to *Kings*, makes this issue central to its concerns — see prefatory remarks to ch. 18; Section II to ch. 18, *The Alliance with Ahab*; 19:2 and 3. There is also the hint at 18:1 concerning the marital alliance which is not mentioned in *Kings*, and then we have the all-important verses at 22:2 and 7. These latter verses indicate — as we shall see there — that by overstepping the bounds which should have separated the two royal houses, the Judean kings acted traitorously to the destiny vested in the Davidic dynasty, and eroded the very justification for their existence.

In this wider context, it is understandable why *Chronicles* refines its account and sees the *House of David*, rather than *Judah*, as the focus of God's wrath.

Once we have focused on the *House of David* and placed it in contrast to *Judah*, which projects, as we have seen, the unison of king and nation, we can define the *covenant which He had made with David* (c), as distinct from the promise common to *Kings* and *Chronicles* (d) and (e), in the sense that his dynasty was to retain the kingship forever.

At *I Chronicles* 17:13, we recognized two strands which ran through God's promises to David. There was the guarantee that the kingship was to be vested in his family eternally — and this was the focus of the *Samuel*'s account. Then there was too the promise that God's Divine spirit, that which He had taken away from the ill-fated Saul, would never depart from David or his descendants. This was *Chronicles'* interest.

This latter promise may well be the *covenant which He had made with David*, (c), of which *Kings* — as *Samuel* before it — makes no mention, but which is absolutely central to the *Chronicles'* account.

God, then, did not want to destroy David's *house* for He had promised that His Divine spirit would never depart from its scions.

But did that spirit not depart? Could Yehoram, and Achaziah after him, have acted as they did if God's Divine spirit had still imbued them? Particularly do we see the tragic absence of that spirit in Yoash whose reign under Yehoiada's tutelage had begun in such an auspicious vein (ch. 23 — 24:16) and who, after his mentor's death, so tragically fell to the lowest depths of depravity (24:17 ff.). Surely such terrible failings point to the absence of just that inner spirit which, had it been present, would surely have sustained the impetus of those earlier years.

The answer lies in the wording which God had used: וְחַסְדִּי לֹא־אָסִיר מֵעִמּוֹ, *I will not deprive him of My benevolence* (*I Chronicles* 17:13). God will never actively deprive David's descendants of His Divine spirit. But if they reject their Davidic ancestry, if by intermarrying with Omri's family, they become, as it were, *the House of Ahab* (see 22:3), then, of itself, it will depart from them. The *House of Ahab* is not the *House of David*.

As Yehoram began his ill-fated reign, the final culmination of all these tragedies still lay in the future but only because God was not yet ready, as it were, to confirm that David's *House* had become traitorous to all that for which he had stood. He did not wish to destroy them.

Margalios HaYam to *Sanhedrin* 98b cites the following tradition concerning the interpretation of our verse:

As our verse indicates, Yehoram was wicked enough to have deserved that the eradication of the Davidic line, which came about in his son Achaziah's reign, should already come in his time. But, while Achaziahu had the infant son Yoash whose potential righteousness made it possible for God to spare his life, thus guaranteeing the perpetuation of the Davidic dynasty, Yehoram had only wicked children. Had the destruction come in his time, it would have been total. God did not wish this and therefore delayed it to a more propitious time.

Chapter Twenty-Two

◈§ The Forty-Two Years of 22:2.

Given that the forty-two years of v. 2 are not to be understood as Achaziahu's age but as the time lapse since God had decreed that the royal line of Judah was to be wiped out, there are two issues which should claim our attention: 1. How do the words of the text yield the teaching of the Sages? 2. Can the teaching of the Sages be viewed as פְּשַׁט, *the simple meaning of the text?*

1. In Rabbinic usage, the concept of being part of a given time frame is expressed by identifying the man or thing with which we are concerned as being a בֶּן of that particular time frame. Thus, the *Mishnah* in *Bechoros* 9:5 describes animals born during the month of Elul as אֱלוּלִין and *Yerushalmi*, *Rosh Hashanah* 1:1 expresses that as בְּנֵי אֱלוּל, *animals associated with* [*the time frame of*] *Elul*. In the same sense, it has been suggested that, once the tradition of the Sages becomes a given, our phrase could mean that Achaziahu belonged to that stage in time associated with the forty-second year of the decree.

2. We have seen from countless examples that a close reading of the *Chronicles'* texts frequently yields insights expressed by the Sages.

Before we analyze our own case we should point to 16:1 where we have a similar situation. A date is given which, because of internal chronological considerations, cannot mean what it appears to say. Because of this, the Sages ascribe a different meaning. At 16:13 we found that a seemingly unconnected verse can be understood only on the basis of the Sages' interpretation.

Thus we see that in *Chronicles* we may expect a verse such as ours to have a different meaning than the surface impression might suggest, and, provided only that it does no violence to the syntactical or linguistic continuity and meaning of the passage, it may be considered — within the context of *Chronicles* — to be the פְּשַׁט, *the simple meaning of the text.*

What is the internal evidence?

The formulation in *Chronicles* is almost identical with that in *Kings*. Nevertheless, a careful analysis will yield differences in nuance.

II Chronicles Ch. 22	*II Kings* Ch. 8
a. 2. בֶּן־אַרְבָּעִים וּשְׁתַּיִם שָׁנָה אֲחַזְיָהוּ בְמָלְכוֹ, [*Literally,*] *Achaziahu was forty-two years old when he became king*	a. 26. בֶּן־עֶשְׂרִים וּשְׁתַּיִם שָׁנָה אֲחַזְיָהוּ בְמָלְכוֹ, *Achaziahu was twenty-two years old when he became king*
b. וְשָׁנָה אַחַת מָלַךְ בִּירוּשָׁלָם, *he reigned one year in Jerusalem,*	b. וְשָׁנָה אַחַת מָלַךְ בִּירוּשָׁלָם, *he reigned one year in Jerusalem,*
c. וְשֵׁם אִמּוֹ, *and his mother's name...*	c. וְשֵׁם אִמּוֹ, *and his mother's name...*

A superficial reading of our verse makes it appear precisely parallel to the one in *Kings*, thus apparently obviating the possibility of assigning a different interpretation.

However, in spite of the surface similarity, we must conclude that the *Chronicles'* passage has a different meaning than the one in *Kings*. Analysis of v. 1 has yielded that Achaziahu assumed the throne — in fact as well as in name — some two years before his father's death. Thus the term בְּמָלְכוֹ in v. 2 would have to refer to that time. However, in the *Kings* account, where nothing was mentioned of Yehoram's illness, בְּמָלְכוֹ would have the more usual meaning — *when he became king* [after his father's death]. Now, clearly, the one year which Achaziahu is said to have reigned in Jerusalem is to be counted from Yehoram's death — as the *Kings'* account makes clear. But, if so, then in the *Chronicles'* account there is no cohesion between the first and second parts of the sentence. The one year which Achaziahu reigned in Jerusalem is not counted from the time described by בְּמָלְכוֹ in the first part.

Thus, since even taking the words of the verse in their more usual connotation would leave us with syntactical problems, the Sages found the license to interpret the phrase in accordance with their tradition (*had attained the forty-second year*; see comm.).

◈§ Achaziahu's Death at Yehu's Hands

See comm. for the apparently straightforward account of Achaziahu's death at Yehu's hands.

A problem arises when we consider the *Kings'* account of the same occurrence. It appears to be radically different. At *II Kings* 9:27 ff., after the description of how Ahab's son Yehoram had been killed in flight by Yehu, we read: *Achaziah king of Judah saw and fled by way of the garden pavilion. Yehu pursued him and said, 'Smite this one also upon the chariot' ... so he fled to Megiddo and died there.*

The implication is that, as he was fleeing from Yehu at Jezreel, Achaziah was wounded, and subsequently made his way to Megiddo where he died of his wounds. There is no mention of his hiding, or indeed ever having been in Samaria; certainly nothing is said of his having been brought before Yehu and killed by him.

At 20:35 ff. we had an instance of *Chronicles* filling in details of an incident which had been described in *Kings*. We found that we were able to create a chart whereby the two narratives augmented one another and, together, told a more complete story than either did separately. This is the approach which the commentators take to our problem. Our task is, therefore, twofold. We must examine how the two narratives can be synchronized in such a way that they produce a coherent account, and we will have to try to understand why *Kings* concentrated on the particular aspects which are told there, and why *Chronicles* found the other ones to be significant.

The following solutions for the synchronization of the two accounts are suggested by the commentators:

Rashi: *Rashi* takes account of the tradition of the Sages (*Sanhedrin* 102b) that the phrase in our verse ...*while he was hiding in Samaria* ... hints at a shocking act of spiritual depravity: While living in Samaria, Achaziahu occupied himself by systematically excising God's name from a Torah scroll, and replacing it with names of idols. Interpreted thus, *Rashi* feels that the phrase can be taken parenthetically and not as part of the narrative. It is introduced only with the purpose of pointing out the extent of Achaziahu's perversion.

The sequence of events was as follows:

[Information deriving from *Kings* is marked (K); from *Chronicles* (C).]

[Yehu] searched for Achaziah and found him (C) as he was fleeing by way of the garden pavilion (K) [Achaziahu was extremely wicked in that he used to excise God's name from the Torah, for which purpose he had to go to Samaria and hide from the people of Judah who would not have tolerated such perfidy] (C). They brought him to

Yehu (C) who told them to kill him on the chariot (K), which they did (C).[1]

Radak and *Abarbanel*: Both these commentators think that the events described in *Chronicles* came about after those described in *Kings*. The sequence is as follows: As Achaziahu was fleeing from the scene of Yehoram's death, Yehu ordered his men to shoot him. They did so, wounding him grievously. He did, however, manage to avoid capture and fled to Megiddo (K). Some time after this, he moved to Samaria, continuing to hide there, until he was flushed out by Yehu's search parties who brought him to Yehu and ordered him killed (C).

The problem in this sequence is the statement וַיָּמָת שָׁם, *and he died there*, in the *Kings'* narrative. This implies that Achaziahu died in Megiddo and not in Samaria. The two commentators deal with this, each in his own way. *Radak* suggests that וַיָּמָת can be understood not literally as dying but, as it is occasionally used in Scripture, as becoming paralyzed. After he became paralyzed in Megiddo, he was transferred to Samaria where he subsequently died.

Abarbanel's solution is to take שָׁם, *there*, not in a geographical sense — for he did not die in Megiddo but in Samaria — but as describing the context. He died in the context of his escape to Megiddo. The details, including the fact that at some later point he went to Samaria, are given in *Chronicles*.

Malbim: From the battlefield (K) Achaziahu fled to Samaria (C). After Yehu entered Samaria and killed out Achaziahu's entire entourage (v. 8), the latter fled to Megiddo (K). There, Yehu's men searched for him and upon finding him, brought him to Yehu who had him killed (C).

Of the four possibilities, the approach of *Radak* and *Abarbanel* seems simplest since, in contrast to those of *Rashi* and *Malbim*, it does not require the constant interplay between the two accounts. But both of the interpretations offered for וַיָּמָת שָׁם seem forced. The writer of *Kings* would not have relied on *Chronicles* to clarify his meaning. The terms, as they stand, would certainly have been misleading.

We suggest another possibility for interpreting the phrase which, moreover, has the advantage of helping us understand the second point which we raised above — why each of the two Books finds the particular parts of the story which they recounted to be significant.

The point can be made that Scripture sometimes talks of someone dying in a given place, not in order to give information concerning the actual act of dying, but rather to stress that he remained in that place until the time of his death.

Let us examine *Jeremiah* 22:11-12: *For thus says* HASHEM *to Shalum son of Yoshiahu king of Judah... who went out from this place. He shall no more return there. But in the*

---

1. *Maharal* (*Chiddushei Aggados, Sanhedrin*) points out a weakness in *Rashi's* thesis. If the phrase is simply a description of the depths to which Achaziahu had sunk, it has no direct bearing on the narrative at this point, and should not have been mentioned here.

Maharal believes that the Sages' tradition is, indeed, an integral part of the story. It provides a vivid picture of the desperation which agitated the final hours of this pathetic king. Holed up in a bunker in Samaria, knowing that Yehu was hunting him, knowing that he would soon be discovered, he jettisons the last vestiges of his proud Davidic heritage. Gripped by terror, he allows his vile superstitions to guide his trembling hands. He will make a final desperate attempt to appease the malevolent forces which seem inexorably to be closing in on him. He will excise God's name from the *Sefer Torah*. Perhaps this will curry favor with the forces of darkness.

This is the level to which the House of David had sunk!

Maharal clearly rejects *Rashi's* interpretation of the relationship between the two passages, and will have to follow one of the other commentators.

place to which they exiled him he shall die and this land he shall never see again.

It is obvious that the significance is not that the act of dying will take place in Babylon but, as the text itself makes clear, that Shalum is to stay in Babylon until the day of his death and will nevermore return to his native land.[1]

Here, too, we assume the same meaning. The verse means simply that he remained in Megiddo for the rest of his life and never returned again to take up his kingship in Judah. The purpose of the verse is not to pinpoint the precise location of his actual death — in the event it actually took place in Samaria, as described in *Chronicles*. Needless to say, it is possible to have one's main domicile in Megiddo and nevertheless to appear in Samaria at a given time. The point is that he never returned to Judah, his kingship having effectively ceased.

We are now ready to examine the different perspectives reflected in the two Books.

We have already noted that throughout, *Chronicles* focuses on the fact that Achaziahu's death was significant beyond his individual tragedy, and carried the much broader implication of the Divinely ordained destruction of the House of David. This point is never explicitly made in *Kings*.

From the *Kings'* perspective, the details given are entirely adequate. When Yehu ordered his bowmen to shoot the fleeing king, this did not carry the implication of a Divinely ordained eradication — it was done in the heat of the moment. Achaziahu was wounded severely enough to have abandoned any hope of returning to Judah and resuming his throne. He went to Megiddo and died *there*; that is, he lived out his life as an invalid in the Northern Kingdom, leaving behind a vacuum in Judah which was tragically filled by Athaliah. The details of how he actually died are, in this context, unimportant.

Chronicles, on the other hand, is interested in the fact that Achaziahu met his end at the hands of Yehu as part of the latter's mandate to eradicate the house of Ahab, of which the family of Judah's kings had so sadly become a part. The juxtaposition of v. 9 to v. 8 shows clearly that when Yehu *hunted* Achaziahu, it was specifically so that the destruction of Judah's royal house, begun in the events described in v. 8, would be as complete as possible. In such a context, the details of Achaziahu's death are pertinent.

◈ Eternal David

Are we to understand that, despite a Divine decree to the contrary, the destruction of the Davidic line did not come about? [2].

---

1. For other apparent examples of this usage, see *Judges* 1:7, *II Kings* 23:34, and *Ezekiel* 12:13.

We suspect that this is the true meaning of the famous passage in *Ruth* in which Ruth pledges her undying loyalty to her mother-in-law, Naomi, and to her God and people: . . .*For wherever you go I will go; where you lodge I will lodge; your people are my people, and your God is my God. Where you die I will die and there I will be buried.*

What did Ruth mean when she said that *where you die I will die*? Naomi was an elderly woman and Ruth probably a young girl. She must have anticipated that she would outlive her mother-in-law by many years. Why would the place in which she was eventually to die be significant?

Presumably, she meant that she would remain forever in the country in which Naomi would die, and would never feel the need to move back to her own country, Moab.

2. *Sanhedrin* 95a and b deals with the issue, but from a different perspective — that is, from within a different aggadic tradition — than we have used in our approach to this chapter. There, the assumption is that the decree that David's line should be destroyed derived from the fact that

We believe that we stand here at the mystical conjunction of the Jewish people and their kingly house: Israel and David; David and Israel live in and with each other. Both together constitute the essence — hence, meaning and focus — of God's world.

Thus says HASHEM, *'If ever My covenant with day and night were to cease; if ever I were to abrogate the laws governing heaven and earth; then would I cast away the seed of Jacob and My servant David, in that I would not appoint a ruler from among his descendants over the seed of Abraham, Isaac and Jacob'* (*Jeremiah* 33:25—26).

Every month, in the blessing and prayer on the New Moon, we make a straightforward declarative statement: *David king of Israel lives and endures*. In its simple assertiveness, this declaration is unique. *Whenever, in other connections, the Jew invokes the memory of one of the great personalities of the past, it is in the form of a hope or wish: he prays for the coming of the Redeemer, or that his forerunner the prophet Elijah be speedily sent. Only of David the king is it asserted that he actually is alive, lives and endures.*

... the personality of the greatest king of Israel lives on ... The life of King David and the life of Israel's nation are fused into one. As long as Israel lives, King David lives in its midst; and as the Jewish commonwealth is immortal, its ruler is also immortal (*Biberfeld, David King of Israel*).

The Messianic ideal animates creation from its very inception:

The four expressions in *Genesis* 1:2, תֹהוּ, בֹהוּ, חֹשֶׁךְ and תְהוֹם, all descriptive of a world in chaos, are said to describe the bleak emptiness, the dark and frightening abyss of the Godless rule of Babylon, Media, Greece and Rome respectively. The physical world writhing in an agony of becoming, presages the world of man struggling painfully towards redemption. Even as these four states of disorder were, in the beginning of time, imbued with meaning by the רוּחַ אֱלֹהִים, *the Divine Presence*, which hovered over them, so shall the travails of man lead ultimately to redemption at the hands of the Messiah, for: *the spirit of God hovered*, that is the spirit of the Messiah as it is written (*Isaiah* 11:2): *And the spirit of* HASHEM [רוּחַ ה'] *shall rest upon him* (*Bereishis Rabbah* 2).

Isaiah makes very clear who this Messiah, upon whom the spirit of *HASHEM* will rest, is to be. His exalted vision — beacon of hope for a world in agony — of a future of peace and harmony in which wolves and lambs will no longer live in perpetual strife is unambiguously tied to David. He is the *twig growing out of Jesse's branch* (v. 1 there) upon whom the future rests.

God had, indeed, decreed that the Davidic line be eradicated. But even God's decrees can be countermanded by overriding considerations. [See *Ramban* to *Genesis* 12:6 and *Derashos HaRan* 2.] Thus, for example, we have God *going back* on the evil which he had spoken concerning Israel (*Exodus* 32:14, and see *Ibn Ezra* there, but see also *Targum*), or as *Ezekiel*, ch. 20, teaches, God intended to destroy Israel in Egypt but overrode that decree so that His Name would not be desecrated (see ArtScroll comm. there).

Here too, the fact that Yoash was eventually saved does not alter the truth that the

---

he, albeit inadvertently, had been the cause of the destruction of the priestly city of Nov (*I Samuel*, ch. 21). On that basis, the Talmud maintains that just as at Nov there had been one lone survivor — Evyasar the son of the *Kohen Gadol*, Achimelech — so too, here, Yoash was permitted to escape.

Within this context, there had never been a decree that the destruction should be complete.

We, however, have gone with *Seder Olam's* contention (see comm. to v. 2) that the decree derived from the alliance made with Omri's family. There seems no reason why that decree should not have been all-encompassing as implied in the language that the Sages use — that David's line should be destroyed.

Davidic line had deserved destruction. They had erred grievously and, but for salvation which sprang from the profound mystery of the bond between God and Israel [see below on חֲדַר הַמִּטּוֹת], would have gone under. God willed otherwise and Yoash was saved.[1]

Mefaresh quotes a midrash which asserts that David had this in mind when he wrote *Psalm* 12, where the superscription is, *For the conductor; on the Sheminis ... Sheminis* is an eight-stringed instrument and that is certainly the simple meaning of the phrase. But aggadically it can be rendered as *the eighth*. David was uttering the prayer contained in that psalm, *Save, HASHEM, for the devout is no more, for truthful men have vanished from mankind*, for the descendant who was eighth in line from him [David, Solomon, Rechav'am, Aviah, Asa, Yehoshaphat, Yehoram, Achaziahu, Yoash]. He was praying to God to save Yoash from death.

We believe the meaning of this midrash to be similar to the *Yerushalmi*'s which we quoted in Section II to ch. 9, *Solomon Does Not Lose His Portion in the World to Come*, according to which David prostrated himself before the Sages who wanted to list Solomon among the kings who had forfeited their portion in *Olam HaBa*. We thought there, that the inner meaning of this teaching is that the Sages came to realize that essentially Solomon was an extension of his saintly father and that, therefore, he must have an inner core of sanctity within him which could never be eroded. Similarly, here, the Sages may well mean that it was the *David* within Yoash who was uttering this prayer. He was, after all, scion of David's house. There was that within him which could not be destroyed.

◆§ An Ecstasy of Love

What can be the meaning of this aggadic teaching? Why is the Holy of Holies called *bedchamber*, and why just in this context?

Certainly, *bedchamber* evokes a peerless imagery of adoration. The two short words compress the entire word-picture which *Shir HaShirim* paints of the passionate closeness between God and Israel.

It is in the Holy of Holies, locus of the Divine Presence in Israel, that this relationship finds its most graphic expression.

---

1. A case can be made that the text of *Chronicles* reflects the truth that there was, indeed, a decree in which Yoash, too, had been included. In a sense he had already been *destroyed* but was granted an entirely new lease on life.

(1). The phrase ...[*she*] *spirited him away from among the murdered princes* implies that all were already dead. In comm. to v. 10, we saw how *Kings*, by writing a word in one way and having it read in another, deals with this anomaly.

The *Chronicles'* version has no such ameliorating written version. We are left with the jarring statement that he was taken from among the *dead*. In this way, the impact of the miraculous in his salvation remains intact.

(2). The name יוֹאָשׁ belongs to that group of names which are formed from a combination of God's Name and some quality with which the bearer of the name was perceived to be imbued. Its basic form is יְהוֹאָשׁ, with אָשׁ deriving from, אשש, *to lay a foundation*; thus, *God is strength* or *support*.

In common with all such names, the ה is occasionally dropped.

Now, in the *Kings'* account, as is to be expected, the name occurs in both its forms, and this is entirely regular. But in *Chronicles* there is not a single instance in which the ה is retained, and moreover, in 24:1 the name is even spelled without the ו — יאָשׁ — a form which cannot derive from God's Name.

We suspect that the author of *Chronicles* may have wished to hint at another possible derivation of the name — from יאשׁ, *to despair*. Yoash is that king of whose life one would have had to despair, had it not been for God's miraculous intervention.

But why draw attention to this aspect of the Holy of Holies just here?[1]

It seems that when the Holy of Holies becomes the instrument for the preservation of the Davidic dynasty, then it is just that aspect of its sanctity — that it is *bedchamber*, locus of love between God and Israel — which is material.

Yerushalmi (*Sanhedrin* 10:2) tells us that when the Sages wanted, because of certain shortcomings, to count Solomon among those kings who had forfeited their portion in the World to Come, a fire issued from the Holy of Holies and threatened to engulf them. (See above, for another version of this story.)

Once more, the Holy of Holies is involved in preserving the Davidic line.

In Section II to ch. 6, *The House as a House of Prayer*, we recognized that, from the standpoint of David the man of prayer [וַאֲנִי תְפִלָּה], the Holy of Holies has particular significance. It is there that the Ark is lodged, and it is to the Ark — locus of the Divine Presence in Israel — that we turn when we pray.

This is because prayer is a meeting, a פְּגִיעָה, an *encounter* with God (*Berachos* 26b). Prayer does the apparently impossible. It bridges the gulf between finite and infinite, between man and God. The unison achieved at the peak of prayerful ecstasy is the closest possible of all encounters — and its focus is the Ark in the Holy of Holies.

Israel and David are one. [See *An Overview / David the King and David the Man*, vol. 1, p. xlii.] If Israel is to persevere, then it can do so only because there is hope and destiny, in the Messianic future — tied inextricably to David. That Israel will endure, and that therefore the House of David can and will never be destroyed, has its source in that mystic union with God, which reaches its ultimate expression in the *bedchamber* which is the Holy of Holies.

---

1. The expression *bedchamber* is also used in the *Kings'* account of these events but, as *Malbim* points out, the simple translation of the verse there precludes understanding it in precisely the way in which it is used here.

The verse there reads: . . .*and she spirited him away from among the princes who were* [*being*] *killed; him and his nurse, in the bedchamber, and they hid him from Athaliahu, so that he was not killed*. The *bedchamber* mentioned there is apparently the place where the suffering children lay, not the hiding place for Yoash.

It is clear that the Holy of Holies is given the appellation *bedchamber* only in *Chronicles* but not in *Kings*. This is consistent with the explanation which we offer here. To the extent that this expression is germane to the salvation of the Davidic line, it does not belong in the *Kings'* account, since that never deals with that aspect of the story.

Chapter Twenty-Three

◆§ The King and the Son of the King

What was the purpose of the covenant described here?

Mefaresh believes that, just as the one described in *Kings* was designed to elicit the people's cooperation in proclaiming Yoash king, so here, too, Yehoiada wished to pledge the people to collude in his plan.

But the language is very different in the two accounts: In the first place, in *Kings* (*II* Ch. 11) Yehoiada is active, [וַ]..יִּכְרֹת לָהֶם, while here the covenant is made by the people [וַיִּכְרֹת כָּל־הַקָּהָל ...]. Furthermore, in *Kings* the preposition ל is used — לָהֶם, while here we have עִם. If, for a moment, we postulate that ל has the same meaning as עִם, *with*, then it would transpire that in *Kings* the contracting parties are Yehoiada and the people, while here the text states explicitly that the contracting parties are the congregation and the king. The implication is surely that different covenants are meant.

The fact is that a careful reading of the texts yields that when the preposition ל is used, and where, therefore, the literal translation would be: So and so made a בְּרִית *to* so and so, the meaning is that the subject makes a certain commitment to the other party; for example, to be loyal (*Exodus* 23:32), offer protection (*Joshua* 9:6), and so on. Unless the usage in *Kings* is extremely irregular, the meaning of the phrase would be that Yehoiada made a commitment to the people. In that context, one would suppose that he promised them that they would come to no harm by joining in his plot — they would be adequately protected from any counter-action which Athaliahu might undertake. Having done his part, he then elicited an oath from them [וַיַּשְׁבַּע אֹתָם ...] that they, too, would do their utmost.

What is the meaning of our phrase? The implication of the preposition עִם is surely that there are two contracting parties before us. But here the young prince had not yet been produced and, moreover, from the next phrase where Yehoiada tells them, *Behold, the king's son shall reign . . .*, there is a strong indication that before that point, they were not even aware why they had been summoned; they did not, in fact, know that anyone had been saved from Athaliahu's slaughter.

Besides this, there is a textual oddity. If we examine the *Kings'* account closely, we see an absolute consistency in the use of the phrases בֶּן הַמֶּלֶךְ and הַמֶּלֶךְ, in describing Yoash. בֶּן־הַמֶּלֶךְ is used, as expected, when talking of Yoash before the coronation. [v. 4: . . .*and he showed them the son of the king*; v. 12: *He brought out the son of the king. . .*]. Vs. 5—8 in which הַמֶּלֶךְ is used exclusively, even though the coronation had not yet taken place, deal with the situation after the crowning. Yehoiada is exhorting the people and issuing orders how the king [as he would be at that point] was to be guarded from any possible harm. From v. 12 and onwards, in which the coronation is described, only הַמֶּלֶךְ is used.

We would expect the same treatment in *Chronicles*, and, indeed, the same consistency is evident. [Even v. 10 must be describing what is to be later, since the prince is only produced in v. 11.] The exception is our phrase. The covenant is being made now — that is, before the coronation — and nevertheless, הַמֶּלֶךְ is used.[1]

---

1. It appears from *Metzudos* that he avoids both problems by reading the phrase as follows: *The whole assembly made a covenant [that they would be helpful] to the king.*

However, while this avoids the problems which we have raised, it does so only at the cost of

Again, even if we could assume that הַמֶּלֶךְ in our phrase refers to Yoash, it seems awkward to refer to him as בֶּן־הַמֶּלֶךְ in the very same verse. We should surely be justified in assuming that when הַמֶּלֶךְ is used in the first part of a sentence and בֶּן־הַמֶּלֶךְ in the next, the one refers to the father and the other to the son. But Yoash was the son of Achaziahu and that tragic figure was obviously not a contracting party in the earlier part of the verse.

If we analyze Yehoiada's words as given in the latter part of the verse, they also seem to lack inner logic. Yehoiada said, *Behold, the king's son shall reign in accordance with that which* HASHEM *had said concerning David's descendants*. What is it that God had said? Certainly not that each king would be succeeded by his own son; of the last kings of Judah, Yehoachaz was succeeded by his brother and Yehoyachin by his uncle.

We suggest that the covenant in our verse was not made with an individual king, but with David the quintessential king of Israel: the *son of the king* is not Yoash per se but a worthy descendant and carrier of the Davidic destiny.[1]

In the long eye of history there is the *king*, and that is David: *David king of Israel lives and endures*! Then, there are the righteous among his descendants, those who carry on the Davidic tradition, and these are the *son of the king*. Through them as a conduit, the Messiah, *David* of eternity (see *Ezekiel* 34:23, *Hosea* 3:5 among many examples) will arise. He will sprout from a seed which, while for centuries it had lain dormant, never even for a moment lost its potency to generate rebirth (*Zechariah* 6:12).

We cannot know, for Scripture does not tell us, all the things which Yehoyada said to the assembled Levites and elders who were about to witness the miraculous rebirth of the Davidic line. How could people, before whose unbelieving eyes a child was suddenly to be produced out of the Holy of Holies, from within the awesome mystery of the union of God and Israel, be adequately prepared? Would they all perhaps have joined in reciting some of David's Psalms in which he sings of the promise of eternity which lay within his loins? Certainly under the impact of that exalted moment, the vision of הַמֶּלֶךְ and בֶּן־הַמֶּלֶךְ would have animated their inner eye.

And so, before Yehoyada produced Yoash, the individual whom destiny had called to be the בֶּן־הַמֶּלֶךְ of that generation, the people renewed their pledge of fealty to the king. And not *to* the king [לַמֶּלֶךְ] but *with* the king [עִם הַמֶּלֶךְ]. David may not have been with them in body, but he was, nevertheless, a tangible presence in their midst.

◆§ Yehoyada's Two Speeches

A careful analysis of the accounts in *Kings* and *Chronicles* yields as follows (see table in Section I, above, p. 167):

In spite of a surface similarity between the two records of Yehoyada's words, it is clear that there were, in fact, two speeches — each addressed to a different group.

---

taking a phrase which occurs numerous times in Scripture — וַיִּכְרֹת . . . בְּרִית . . . עִם. . ., and assigning a meaning which it never has elsewhere.

2. This is clearly how the Sages understand the terms *king* and *son of the king* in *Psalms* 72:1. There, Solomon had sung: *O God! Grant an understanding of Your justice to* the king, *and of Your righteousness to* the son of the king.

The Sages (*Vayikra Rabbah* 30:3) remark on the fact that, in this verse, David refers to himself [through Solomon's mouth] as *king*, while elsewhere he describes himself as a destitute beggar (*Psalms* 102:1). Clearly, David viewed himself differently at different times. When he thought of those of his descendants who would be righteous — the *son of the king* — then he reveled in his standing as, *king*. When, in his mind's eye, he saw those of his progeny who would be wicked, he viewed himself as a pauper.

V. 5 in *Kings*: *He commanded them* ... clearly goes back to the *captains of the hundreds, the leaders and the runners* of v. 4. These had earlier been brought into the Temple (v. 4), so that they could guard the young king once he had been produced [see v. 9].

Having shown the king to the soldiery (v. 4), Yehoyada now explained how he wished them to deploy themselves. He informed them that the outgoing and incoming *mishmaros* were to be co-opted into the guard detail (v. 5 ff.).

In *Chronicles*, the speech was clearly addressed to a different group. The fact that the (a) phrase from *Kings* has no parallel in *Chronicles* shows clearly that v. 4 in *Chronicles* continues straight from vs. 2 and 3, and that it addressed the Levites, the heads of the families, and the entire assembly, which had been mentioned in those two verses. None of these were soldiers. There is no mention here of the captains of the hundreds. Obviously, too, the *Levites from all the cities of Judah* (v. 2), were not the incoming and outgoing *mishmaros*.

It is clear, then, that Yehoyada here was not addressing the people who, in the first place, would have to guard the king. These are mentioned in v. 7. There, the *Chronicles* wording, *The Levites shall encircle* ... marks it as different from the *Kings'* version, *Now you shall encircle* ... In *Kings*, the soldiery was being addressed; in *Chronicles*, the people.

The deployment which Yehoyada was organizing here was not, then, meant for guarding the king. This can be demonstrated from the fact that neither of the two *Kings* verses which actually mention guard duty (d) and (g) have a parallel in *Chronicles*. In addition, we note that, while *Chronicles* assigns a role for *all the people* (h), *Kings* makes clear that the guard duty was limited to the three groups of Levites.

Rather, we assume that Yehoyada was assigning positions for the people who were to be present to witness the momentous occasion which would once more establish the eternity of the Davidic line.

◆§ **Sentries at the Gate**

In *Yehoiada's Two Speeches*, we saw that in the *Chronicles* account, the people rather than the soldiery were being addressed. The question of how the king is to be physically guarded is not taken up until v. 7. Who, then, was being deployed at this point, and why? How should we understand the term בָּאֵי הַשַּׁבָּת, when the audience to which it was addressed consisted of the *Levites of all the cities of Judah*, and the *family heads of Israel* (v. 4), rather than the House *mishmaros*?

A careful reading yields two points worthy of note: Firstly, that the equivalent passage in *Kings* (c) does not have לַכֹּהֲנִים וְלַלְוִיִּם. The term בָּאֵי הַשַּׁבָּת in *Kings* is assumed to be self-explanatory. Secondly, we should examine the task to which the group in our verse was assigned: They are to be *sentries at the gates*. What precisely is this function?

The guard duty normally assigned to the Levites as part of their regular obligations was ceremonial rather than substantive: Thus, *Rambam*, *Beis HaBechirah* 8:1: The Levites stood guard, not as a means of protection from enemies or robbers, but in order to lend respect and grandeur to the House. A palace with sentries deployed has more standing than one which is not guarded.

We may assume, then, that the task assigned in our verse was ceremonial — an important part of the crowning ceremony. It is fitting that guards should attend the entrances to the location at which a king is being crowned.

To whom should this ceremonial guard duty have been assigned? The incoming *mishmar* was already fully accounted for. In addition to the Temple tasks which they would have to fulfill, they were also made responsible for the physical protection of the king (v. 7). Someone else would have to be found.

The ceremonial guard was to be selected from among the group which Yehoyada was addressing in the *Chronicles'* account. But of the two segments, the *Levites from all the cities of Judah* and the *family heads of Israel*, only the former were qualified to stand guard in the Temple. [See *Midos* 1:1.]

This is the sense of our verse. A third part of the audience, consisting wholly of the *Kohanim* and Levites among them, was to become a part of an expanded incoming *mishmar* [בָּאֵי הַשַּׁבָּת], so that they could fulfill the ceremonial role which was required.

◆§ The People

Who were these people who have not been mentioned before, and what was their role in the events which are about to unfold?

We begin by comparing our v. 10 with v. 11 in the *Kings'* account:

II Chronicles Ch. 23	*II Kings Ch. 11*
a. 10. וַיַּעֲמֵד, *He positioned*	a. 11. וַיַּעַמְדוּ, *And stood*
b. אֶת־כָּל־הָעָם, *all the people*	b. הָרָצִים, *the runners*
c. וְאִישׁ שִׁלְחוֹ בְיָדוֹ, *each with his sword in his hand*	c. אִישׁ וְכֵלָיו בְּיָדוֹ, *each with his implements in his hand*
d. . . . מִכֶּתֶף הַבַּיִת, *from the [right] shoulder of the House . . .*	d. מִכֶּתֶף הַבַּיִת, *from the [right] shoulder of the House*

The two verses are almost completely identical and this would yield that כָּל־הָעָם in the (b) phrase in *Chronicles* corresponds to הָרָצִים in the *Kings'* version.

There are, however, a number of considerations which speak against this identification:

In the *Chronicles'* account, the people are told by Yehoyada where they are to stand. They act upon Yehoyada's orders, as borne out by our verse, which says expressly that it was he who positioned them in the specific areas in which he wanted them. In the *Kings'* account, the runners assume their positions on their own [וַיַּעַמְדוּ הָרָצִים]. Yehoyada tells them nothing at all.

Again, we must ask ourselves why our v. 6 has no parallel in the *Kings'* account. If it was necessary to exhort the Israelites not to enter the sacred precincts of the Temple structure, why is this not done in *Kings*?

The solution which suggests itself is as follows: The *runners* of the *Kings* account were a disciplined soldiery under the command of their own officers. These latter would know best how to deploy their men, and these, in turn, would stand where they were ordered. There was no need to tell them not to enter the Temple building.

In *Chronicles*, as we have suggested above [*Yehoyada's Two Speeches*], we are dealing with an assembly of people who came to observe the coronation, but were in no sense a disciplined soldiery. These people, whom nobody controlled, had to be exhorted not to encroach into areas which the halachah placed out of bounds for them. Although their immediate function was not a military one, Yehoyada nevertheless saw an opportunity to use them and [in v. 10] packed the courtyard with them for the purpose of reinforcing the line of the runners.

This may also explain why in the *Kings'* account (v. 11) the runners had אִישׁ וְכֵלָיו בְּיָדוֹ, *each with his implements in his hand*, while our v. 10 specifies שִׁלְחוֹ, which means *his sword*. The *implements* of a professional soldiery are obviously weapons, while we would not have known what *implements* are in the hands of a people who were not soldiers. It was necessary to stress that these were swords.

◆§ The Officers Involvement

V. 14 substitutes וַיּוֹצֵא for the וַיְצַו of *Kings*. Why the change?

There are some other substantive changes in the *Chronicles'* text, and these may hold the answer.

II Chronicles Ch. 23	*II Kings Ch. 11*
a. 14. וְהַבָּא אַחֲרֶיהָ, *Whoever follows her*	a. 15. וְהַבָּא אַחֲרֶיהָ, *Whoever follows her,*
b. יוּמַת בֶּחָרֶב, *shall be put to death by the sword.*	b. הָמֵת בֶּחָרֶב, *kill by the sword.*
c. כִּי אָמַר הַכֹּהֵן, *For the Kohen said,*	c. כִּי אָמַר הַכֹּהֵן, *For the Kohen said,*
d. לֹא תְמִיתוּהָ בֵּית ה׳, *'Do not kill her in the House of HASHEM.'*	d. אַל־תּוּמַת בֵּית ה׳, *'Let her not be killed in the House of HASHEM.'*
e. 15. . . . וַיָּשִׂימוּ לָהּ יָדַיִם, *So they made way for her . . .*	e. 16. . . . וַיָּשִׂמוּ לָהּ יָדַיִם, *So they made way for her*
f. וַיְמִיתוּהָ שָׁם, *and killed her there.*	f. וַתּוּמַת שָׁם, *and she was killed there.*

The two accounts reverse the use of the active and passive voices in respect to the killing of Athaliahu and of the people who might wish to come to her aid. In the *Kings'* account, Athaliahu is *to be killed* and the officers are given no active role in her death (d) and (f). They are active only in killing any would-be helper (b).

In *Chronicles*, the reverse is true. It is they who are to kill Athaliah (d) but the person who may come to her aid is to *be killed* (b).

The difference in nuance may be influenced by the use of the term . . . וַיְצַו, *and he ordered*. Once ordered, the officers have no choice in the matter — they are, in fact, passive tools in the hands of their commander. They become active only in the case of the intruder concerning whose intentions they must use their own judgment and initiative. By eliminating the statement that orders were issued, *Chronicles* leaves room for the killing of Athaliahu to be ascribed to the officers.

In comm. to v. 1, we suggested that *Chronicles*, as opposed to *Kings*, identifies the officials by name because of the cosmic significance which *Chronicles* ascribes to their action. It could well be that for the same reason, *Chronicles* wished to have the action itself associated with them, instead of having them be simply tools in the hands of their commander.

◆§ The Covenant

The difference between the covenant described here and the ones described in *Kings* is striking.

We compare the two accounts (see table on following page):

II Chronicles Ch. 23	*II Kings* Ch. 11
a. 16. וַיִּכְרֹת יְהוֹיָדָע, *Yehoyada made*	a. 17. וַיִּכְרֹת יְהוֹיָדָע, *Yehoyada made*
b. בְּרִית, *a covenant*	b. אֶת־הַבְּרִית, *the covenant*
c. בֵּינוֹ, *between himself,*	c. בֵּין ה׳, *between HASHEM*
d. וּבֵין כָּל־הָעָם, *and the people*	d. וּבֵין הַמֶּלֶךְ, *and the king*
e. וּבֵין הַמֶּלֶךְ, *and the king*	e. וּבֵין הָעָם, *and the people*
f. לִהְיוֹת לְעָם לַה׳, *that they might be a people to HASHEM*	f. לִהְיוֹת לְעָם לַה׳, *that they might be a people to HASHEM,*
g.	g. וּבֵין הַמֶּלֶךְ וּבֵין הָעָם, *and between the king and the people.*

The most immediately striking point is that (g) in *Kings* has no parallel in *Chronicles*. Where *Kings* speaks of two separate covenants — the one between God, the king and the people ((c), (d) and (e)) the other between only the king and the people (g) — *Chronicles* records only the former one ((c), (d) and (e)).

That one, judging from the identical wording of the (f) phrases, seems to be the same in both versions.

However, this assumption too we must query. This because of the striking change in the (c) phrase. Where the third party in the *Kings* version is God; in the *Chronicles* version it is Yehoyada himself.

Of possible significance also is that in the (b) phrase, *Kings* speaks of הַבְּרִית, *the known or expected covenant*, while *Chronicles* does not have the definite article. It speaks of *a covenant*.

The two books are consistent with the divergent positions they have taken towards Yoash's crowning.

Both covenants described in *Kings* are the expected ones [הַבְּרִית] at a coronation. King and people, first of all, dedicate themselves to God's service [the king is first because he is the initiator and guide of the people], and then undertake obligations towards one another, inherent in their respective positions. *Kings*, which sees here only the contours of an ordinary coronation — although, of course, in extraordinary circumstances — confines itself to describing these covenants.

These covenants are not significant from the *Chronicles'* perspective. Important is the rededication of the people to their eternal destiny under the impact of the realization that the Davidic line had, after all, not been destroyed. The covenant to which Yehoyada summons them has as its purpose that they should, with renewed energy and vigor, reconstitute themselves into the mold in which God had cast their historic nationhood.

In the covenant described here, Zechariah's vision of the golden candelabrum with the olive trees on either side — of the people of Israel drawing inspiration from its king and its *Kohen*, from its David and its Aaron (see *Zechariah* 4:1-14 and midrashim there) — comes alive. Here too, Israel is in the center; Yehoyada — the *Aaron* of his generation (see *I Chronicles* 12:28) — stands for the *Kehunah*, and the boy-king Yoash for the reborn Davidic kingship.

The Nobles and the Governors

We have noted that the *nobles and governors* of the *Chronicles'* account are not the same as the *leaders and runners* of *Kings*.

We compare the two passages:

II Chronicles Ch. 23	II Kings Ch. 11
a. 20. . . . וַיּוֹרֶד אֶת־הַמֶּלֶךְ, *And brought the king down . . .*	a. 19. . . . וַיֹּרִידוּ אֶת־הַמֶּלֶךְ, *They brought down the king . . .*
b. . . . וַיָּבֹאוּ, *They arrived . . .*	b. וַיָּבוֹאוּ, *They arrived*
c. וַיּוֹשִׁיבוּ אֶת־הַמֶּלֶךְ, *and placed the king*	c. וַיֵּשֶׁב, *and he sat*
d. עַל כִּסֵּא הַמַּמְלָכָה, *on the throne of the kingdom.*	d. עַל־כִּסֵּא הַמְּלָכִים, *on the royal throne.*

In *Chronicles*, Yehoyada is the subject of the (a) phrase; in *Kings*, it is the people. In the (c) phrase, *Chronicles* has the people placing the king upon his throne, while in *Kings* he ascends the throne by himself.

The difference between the soldiery and the nobility explains these changes simply. The soldiers had been charged to be with the king, *when he comes in and when he goes out* (v. 7). Thus, *they took the king down* in *Kings*. On the other hand, they, as bodyguards, had no role in the actual ascension to the throne — from their perspective he *sat on the throne*, i.e., without their help.

The nobles are passive during the walk from the Temple to the palace. Yehoyada, who was the instigator of the whole affair, is the one who takes the king down. Once, however, the palace has been reached it is the nobility and the people who, as a group, proclaim Yoash king over themselves and *place* the king upon the throne.

The two books are consistent with the differing perspectives which they have, throughout, brought to bear upon this story. In *Kings*, the crowning is not different than any other such ceremony, and the active involvement of the people is not significant. In *Chronicles*, it is the people who identify themselves once more with the destiny which inheres in the rulership of the Davidic dynasty.

This will also explain the changes in the (d) phrase. In *Kings*, the significant point is that Yoash became king [כִּסֵּא הַמְּלָכִים]; in *Chronicles*, that the Davidic kingship [כִּסֵּא הַמַּמְלָכָה] was maintained.

Chapter Twenty-Four

◈§ Different Perspectives Upon Yoash and the Monarchy

The following is the parallel verse in *Kings* (*II* Ch. 12 to our v. 2: וַיַּעַשׂ יְהוֹאָשׁ הַיָּשָׁר בְּעֵינֵי ה׳ כָּל־יָמָיו אֲשֶׁר הוֹרָהוּ יְהוֹיָדָע הַכֹּהֵן.

Rashi, in an attempt to have that verse agree with ours, brackets the phrase כָּל־יָמָיו אֲשֶׁר הוֹרָהוּ יְהוֹיָדָע together and writes that Yoash was only righteous during Yehoyada's lifetime. But after Yehoyada died, the nobles began to deify the king. They said, 'Anyone who enters the Holy of Holies, for even a moment, must die. You were hidden there for six years. You are no mortal!' The king allowed himself to be persuaded.

But neither *Targum* nor the cantillation seems to agree with this. *Targum* renders: *Yoash did that which was right in the eyes of* HASHEM *all his days, as Yehoyada the Kohen had taught him*, clearly dividing the phrase into two, making the break at כָּל־יָמָיו. This accords with the cantillation, which marks these words with an *ethnachta*, a stop sign. The first part of the sentence, then, says that Yoash did that which was right in the eyes of *HASHEM all his days*. The next part must be understood, either as *Targum* does: ... *as* Yehoyada had taught him, or ... *because* Yehoyada had taught him, or ... *in accordance* with that which Yehoyada had taught him.

But in that case, the verse in *Kings* contradicts not only the verse in *Chronicles* which says that Yoash did what was right only during Yehoyada's lifetime, but it seems also to ignore the events which are recorded in our v. 17 and onwards.

The internal, textual evidence in *Kings* seems to confirm *Targum's* interpretation, and to contradict *Rashi's*. It seems clear that there is no reference to any overt wrongdoing on Yoash's part. The introductory verse to Amatziahu's reign (*II Kings* 14:3) reads: *He did that which was right in the eyes of* HASHEM, *only not like David, his father; he did everything as his father Yoash had done*. Clearly, the assessment is positive. He fell short of David's prodigious accomplishments, but his reign was generally benign. This, in *Kings*, is said with the phrase: *He did in everything as his father Yoash had done*. Yoash's reign, then, is presented as satisfactory. This is a far cry, indeed, from the description in *Chronicles*.

An analysis of this problem will lead us into a deeper appreciation of the respective functions of the two books, *Kings* and *Chronicles*. However, before we enter into that discussion, our more immediate concern is to deal with the apparent contradiction between the verse in *Kings*, which implies that there was no real wrongdoing on Yoash's part, and the story as told in *Chronicles*.

Superficially we may do this as follows: A careful reading of our chapter from v. 17 onwards does not, in fact, yield that Yoash, in any way, joined the idolatrous orgies described there. V. 17 says only that he *listened to them* when the nobles made obeisance to him. This may have been simply flattery, a sycophantic toadying designed to win his, at least tacit, acquiescence to their plans. Vs. 18-20 then constantly talk of *them*, that is, the nobles, serving idols, being reprimanded by prophets and being addressed by Zechariah. Even v. 21, which says that *they* assassinated Zechariah *by order of the king*, need not reflect a complete reversal of the king's righteousness. As we shall see in comm. to v. 20, Zechariah had indeed acted in an unseemly manner, and

Yoash may well have judged him to be in contempt of the monarchy, and liable to the death penalty.

Indeed, the text seems to confirm that Yoash was not involved in the rampant idol worship of the nobles. V. 23 tells how the armies of Aram came upon Judah and mentions specifically that the nobles were destroyed, apparently in punishment for their idol worship. No mention is made of Yoash. His death (v. 25) is ascribed solely to the killing of Zechariah.

Taken in this way, the passage does, indeed, say much about Yoash's personal shortcoming — *He listened to them* — but does not say anything about the way he ruled the people. In all his outward dealings he may have been an exemplary king, indeed, doing what was *right in the eyes of HASHEM*.

This could well be the attitude taken by the *Kings'* account. As we have seen countless times, *Kings* looks at the history of the period from the point of view of the monarchy, rather than assessing the person of the monarchs.

Indeed, it seems clear that there was a degree of ambiguity in all these events. At 24:27 we find that Yoash's ... *sons, the multitude of prophecies against him and the re-establishing of the House of God* [but, note well, not his idol worship!] *are recorded in the midrash of the Book of Kings*. At 13:22 we demonstrated that a book described as *midrash* would be one which deals in ambiguities, revealing nuances not immediately apparent to the casual observer of contemporary events. Thus, it seems likely that this was the case in Yoash's reign. There was the observable king continuing in a benign and positive rule over his people until the end, and then there were the dark undercurrents which needed to be explored and defined if the total picture was to emerge.

While our analysis of the text may well serve to eliminate the apparent contradictions, it does not explain why the *Kings'* account should totally ignore events of the magnitude of those described here.

We suggest that a pattern may be detected in the contrasting ways in which *Kings* and *Chronicles* respectively, deal with Yoash and with Amatziahu and Uziahu, the two kings who followed him. This discovery will lead to a more precise appreciation of the respective functions of the two books.

The lives of each of these three men ended in tragedy. Yoash and Amatziahu were assassinated and Uziahu was stricken by leprosy. All this is recorded in the *Kings'* accounts of the reigns — but in a way in which this prophetic book seems to be untrue to its own standards.

We believe it to be axiomatic that at least part of the purpose of the historical accounts within the framework of Scripture is to teach and to demonstrate the functioning of Divine Providence. Things happen because God wills that they happen, and God wills that the Torah's teaching — that good deeds generate good rewards and that evil will be punished — should be actuated in the lives of individuals and of nations. Examples abound in *Kings*, in which the dynamics of the great events of the period are described in precisely these terms.

Given this, the stark juxtaposition of apparently exemplary lives and rules with tragic events cries out for an answer — which in *Kings* is not forthcoming but which is the very essence of the *Chronicles'* account.

Yoash: In the case of Yoash we have two particularly striking instances: Ch. 12, in *Kings*, is devoted to Yoash's efforts to make repairs for the Temple, and lavishes great detail upon the description of this apparently worthy activity. This, up to v. 17. Without a break, v. 18 then continues: *Then Chazael king of Aram rose up... and* [*Chazael*] *set his face to go up against Jerusalem*. Nothing is said to explain why Yoash's concern for the glory of God's House should be rewarded by war.

V. 19 then describes how Yoash bought off Chazael with the treasures of the Temple and the palace. This is taught in a neutral manner. No criticism is stated or implied. Vs. 21 and 22 then tell of Yoash's assassination.

Amatziahu: Concerning Amatziahu we are told that, while not measuring up to the standards set by David, he nevertheless did that which was right in God's eyes — as Yoash had done (*II Kings*: 14:3). Then comes a successful campaign against Edom (v. 7), with no hint of anything untoward. Later, we have him challenging the Northern Kingdom's Yoash to a war in which he is defeated (vs. 8-14). At v. 19 we learn of a plot, fermented against him in Jerusalem, which forced him to flee to Lachish where he was subsequently murdered. All this without any explanation.

Uzziahu: The description of Uzziahu's reign occupies only three verses (*II Kings* 15:3-5). They tell: 1. That he did that which was right in the eyes of *HASHEM*; 2. That the *bamos* were not removed during his reign; and 3. That he was afflicted with leprosy until the day of his death. No explanation is given.

In every one of these instances, *Chronicles* gives extensive background which sets forth precisely why these things happened.

Why is *Kings* silent? And more! Why, by juxtaposing tragic fates to good deeds, does *Kings* unambiguously point to a question, if it does not intend to give an answer?

The explanation must lie in the essential difference of approach to the issues, between the prophetic (*Kings*) and the Hagiographic (*Chronicles*) books. In Overview (*The Uniqueness of Chronicles, The Difference between the Prophets and the Writings*, Vol.1, p. xvii) we have discussed the dictum of the Sages, that matters pertaining to the קֵץ, *the Messianic destiny of mankind*, have their place in the Hagiographia, rather than in the books of the Prophets. Here, we may take this basic truth for granted and go on to analyze how the matters contained in the *Chronicles* account of these three kings, but omitted in *Kings*, pertain to that Messianic destiny.

The thrust of our argument will be based on the assumption that, as we saw in the case of Yoash, the rules of these kings were benign but that their failings were personal ones. We are therefore advancing the thesis that in a non-Messianic context, these three men were indeed good kings who did *what was right in the eyes of HASHEM*, and therefore, as far as the overt interest of *Kings* is concerned, this assessment is correct. The book may hint at some deeper sub-surface failings, but since these belong to a level of truth to which prophecy has no access, it must leave them to an oral tradition which, no doubt, was a part of the national heritage. It was left to *Chronicles* — history of our Messianic destiny — to commit these truths to writing.

Let us then examine how the personal failings of Judah's kings play a role in the Messianic drama.

We will be led to the conclusion that the institution of the monarchy, as it was established by Samuel, must disintegrate as a necessary precondition to the Messianic kingship.

We begin by quoting *Shemos Rabbah* 15:26: [Israel's monarchy is compared to the moon.] Just as the moon's cycle lasts for thirty days, so too, will the monarchy last through thirty generations. The moon begins to wax on the first day of the month and becomes full on the fifteenth. From then till the thirtieth day, its light diminishes. Thus, too, Israel. There were fifteen generations from Abraham to Solomon, at which point the full moon was attained. From then on, the kings, too, began to diminish [in stature]: . . .

When Tzidkiahu came, concerning whom it says: *He blinded Tzidkiah's eyes* (*II Kings* 25:7), the light of the moon gave out. . .

Thus we see that the period of the monarchy is projected as a sustained downward spiral. In the course of its exposition, the *midrash* mentions every one of the kings by name. It is clear that each one among them — even the most righteous — played a role in this debacle.

What is the significance of this downward spiral in terms of the Messianic idea?

The Torah (*Deuteronomy* 17:14) envisions a time when the people would demand the establishment of a monarchist form of government: *Let us appoint a king over ourselves*. To this *Devarim Rabbah* 5:11 remarks:

God said, 'Do you really want a king? See, I will give you kings, and you shall find out that they are a catastrophe for you: Saul causes you to fall on Mount Gilboa . . . David brings about a plague . . . Ahab precipitates a drought . . . Tzidkiahu destroys the House.'

When Israel saw the results of their monarchy they all called out, 'We do not want a king! We want our erstwhile king, *for HASHEM is our King — He will be our salvation!'*

God said to them, 'I swear that this is what I will do.' [As it is written] *Then HASHEM will be King over the whole world.*

Clearly, the Messianic kingship is to rise up from out of the ruins of a failed monarchial system. It will succeed, where the earlier experiment had failed, because God, not man, will be the true ruler.

That God's kingship would express itself through the person of the Davidic-Messianic king, becomes clear from a careful reading of *Ezekiel* ch. 34. There, using the metaphor of the selfish, self-serving shepherd for the kings of Israel, God promises that, in the Messianic future, He would Himself . . .*tend My sheep and lay them down* . . .*the lost, I will seek out and the banished, I will retrieve*. . . (34:15-16). But then at v. 23 the prophecy continues . . . *And I will appoint over them a single shepherd and he shall tend you, My servant David*. . .

The original monarchy, from its very inception, had not been what God had wished. *For they have not rejected you; but they have rejected Me from ruling over them*, God said to Samuel (*I Samuel* 8:4). Hosea had said, *I have given you a king in My anger and have taken him away in My fury* (*Hosea* 13:11). But it was yet to serve a purpose. The very disintegration of the monarchy which, in its totality, had interposed itself between God and His people, would ready the soil for the true, Messianic kingship. Its impotence would underscore all that had been misconceived in its establishment, and point the way to the ideal national structure which will be represented by the Messiah, and which will reflect the ideal society which God had in mind for man.

Thus, in the reigns of the three kings whom we have examined here, we have surface and sub-surface dynamics. Within the context of contemporary history, their rules were benign and each left a positive mark upon land and people. This is the perspective with which *Kings* deals. Under the surface they lose progressively greater touch with the Davidic ideal of kingship, which is well on the way to complete erosion. This is the story which *Chronicles* tells because it is the story of the laying of the foundations for the Messianic kingdom.

Chapter Twenty-Five

◈ The Edomite Campaign

The campaign against Edom, together with the various events which preceded it and followed in its wake, occupy twelve verses in *Chronicles*. *Kings* devotes just one verse to the incident. It reports that Amatziahu smote Edom, killing ten thousand in the process, and that on this occasion he captured a rock, gave it a name, and that it carried this name up to the time *Kings* was written.

Clearly, *Chronicles* views this campaign as a major event in Amatziahu's reign. What is its significance?

Besides the central fact that Amatziahu apparently waged an aggressive war against Edom with no explanation offered either in *Kings* or in *Chronicles* for what may have motivated it, there are two subsidiary aspects of the campaign which require analysis. Firstly, there is the abortive plan to hire 100,000 mercenaries from the Northern Kingdom; and then, the seemingly barbarous killing of the ten thousand captives by hurling them from a cliff (v. 12).

After Amatziahu had hired the mercenaries for the vast sum of one hundred talents of silver, a man of God comes to him advising him to send them back. Amatziahu accepts the advice although he must have feared the reaction which this would cause (v. 13). He is prepared, not only to trust God for help in a war for which he now felt himself undermanned, but also to forego the enormous financial investment which he had made.

The man of God had suggested that the mercenaries be sent packing because ... *HASHEM is not with Israel, all the sons of Ephraim*. But if these were ordinary mercenaries paid to carry arms, with no personal involvement in the fight, why would this matter? They did not come as representatives of Israel — could for practical purposes have been from any heathen country — were indeed no more than hirelings to Amatziahu and subsidiary to him and his orders. How did God's dissatisfaction with the Northern Kingdom impinge on their usefulness as soldiers in a Judean army?

The facts of the story require a different assessment of Amatziahu's purpose in hiring these people and of their standing within his army.

We begin by trying to understand Amatziahu's purpose in the challenge which he sent to the northern Yoash, as told in v. 17. The text reads: *Come let us meet face to face*. But what does this mean? *Targum* adds the words *for the purpose of fighting a battle*. Within the context of the *Chronicles'* account we could suppose that it was a declaration of a war of vengeance, for the three thousand Judeans who had been wantonly murdered by the disenchanted mercenaries (v. 13). But this cannot be because *Kings* tells nothing of these mercenaries and still records the challenge. What place could it possibly have in that account?

In the ninth book of the *Antiquities*, *Josephus* describes Amatziahu's reign. He has this to say about the message which Amatziahu sent to Yoash: In his pride he wrote to Yoash the king of Israel and commanded him to humble himself before him, he and all his people as they had once been subservient to David and Solomon his forefathers. If he should refuse to cooperate he is informed that the matter of the rulership would be decided on the battlefield.

Now Josephus' traditions cannot be accepted uncritically, but it is well established that in matters not concerning contemporary politics and his standing with the Romans, his writings are by and large reliable. He would have had no reason to falsify records of Amatziahu's intentions in this matter and we may tentatively assume that Josephus may have been in possession of records which assign this motive to Amatziahu.

From this assumption it is not a far step to suspect that Amatziahu's purpose in hiring one hundred thousand soldiers from the Northern Kingdom was to lay the groundwork for an eventual alliance which he would dominate. The campaign against Edom was to be a joint Judean and Israelite one.

Certainly, such a motive would explain the stricture which the man of God leveled against Amatziahu. God would not be with an army under the joint sponsorship of the two kingdoms. He was *with* Judah but not with Israel.

What could have been the purpose of this campaign? Why would Amatziahu have wanted that the Northern Kingdom should be represented?

When we consider what we learned at 21:8 concerning the cosmic significance of Edom's revolt during Yehoram's reign, we may have a solution.

We have postulated that in the wake of the Judean Yoash's terrible crime, Amatziahu would have been eager to re-establish a purified Davidic dynasty. What better way to do this than to attempt to undo the most graphic symbol of the decline of that dynasty — the independence of Edom! Such a motive would lift this campaign from the ranks of an ordinary war to one of major historical import and explain well why, if his ambitions were to unite the two kingdoms, he would want the army to be a joint one. Moreover, it would explain the assumption of the man of God that God would, in fact, help Amatziahu once the mercenaries were gone (v. 8). It was indeed to be a battle worthy of God's intercession.

If we are correct in our assumption this may help us to understand the cruel fate of the ten thousand prisoners taken alive. In the first place, if it was Amatziahu's intention to re-annex Edom into a vassal state, he may have found it necessary to demonstrate his determination in the kind of unambiguous terms which a brutish and obscene nation like Edom could understand. For this there was precedent in David's actions against Moab. See *I Chronicles*, Section II, *The Destruction of Amon* (p. 456).

Secondly, the conquest of the Edomites may, in Amatziahu's mind, have had additional significance: It may have carried the overtones of the wiping out of Amalek which the Torah commands (*Deuteronomy* 25:17) and which, in the first place, is incumbent upon the king (see *Rambam, Melachim* 1:2).[1]

Possibly, in his eagerness to establish a pure and unsullied Davidic kingship he allowed himself to be goaded into an excessive and, in the event, unjustified, zeal in eradicating the irredeemable evil that is typified by Amalek.

If our analysis of the events is correct, this would, indeed, explain why these details belong in the *Chronicles'* account but not in *Kings*. They are a function of Amatziahu's attitude towards his kingship which, in turn, came about because of his father Yoash's tragic spiritual decline. For reasons discussed in the previous chapter, this decline is recorded in *Chronicles* but not in *Kings*.

---

1. It seems significant that Josephus, in his description of the events, switches from *Edom* to *Amalek*. When he describes the war he identifies the enemy as Edom. Later, in Yoash's answer to Amatziahu he has him say ... *you have no justification to boast because of your success against the Amalekites* ...

◆§ Amatziahu Serves Alien Gods

The idol worship appears to have begun only after — perhaps long after — Amatziahu returned home from the battle. Clearly, the decision to do this dreadful thing was well considered.

What made Amatziahu take such a shocking step? He had shown his boundless trust in God by going into battle with inadequate forces and had willingly forfeited vast sums of money for no other reason than that he had been so advised by a man of God. He had, with Divine help, won a stunning victory. Why, after all this, would he be moved to apostasy?

Two considerations make it clear that, indeed, no apostasy was involved here. In the first place, both *Chronicles* and *Kings* describe Amatziahu as a righteous king, albeit with some caveats. *Kings* does not even mention the episode of the idol worship. Had Amatziahu, out of wickedness and rebellion, thrown off the yoke of heaven, none of this would have been possible.

The prophet's strictures in v. 15 also make this clear. He does not castigate Amatziahu for wickedness but for folly: Why worship idols whose impotence had only now been demonstrated? This would be a sensible approach to someone who had made an honest mistake — not to someone who had, out of wickedness, jettisoned the Torah.

Where, then, had Amatziahu erred?

HaLevi in *Doros HaRishonim, Tekufas HaMikra*, ch. 7 explains Amatziahu's idol worship within the framework of his wide-ranging analysis of Israel's spiritual state during the years of the first Temple. He demonstrates that idol worship never implied a denial of God or of His omnipotence. Rather, it was based on an assumption that God chose to relate to this world through intermediaries and that these intermediaries, although in no way independent of God, were nevertheless empowered to grant or withhold favors. Accordingly, it was important to appease them or elicit their goodwill by means of certain forms of sacrificial service.

Thus, there was no inherent contradiction between Amatziahu, on the one hand believing in and serving God, and on the other hand subscribing to a cult which would make it logical for him to want to appease Edom's gods after he had defeated their worshipers so decisively. [Thus, also *Sforno* to *Exodus* 23:24.] Perhaps too, we may surmise that he had pangs of conscience about the cruel fate he had meted out to the captives, and feared a reprisal at the hands of the offended heavenly powers.

But, would Jeremiah in *Kings* or Ezra in *Chronicles* describe a king who erred in such a fundamental tenet of Jewish belief as doing *that which was right* in God's eyes? If, indeed, this was what Amatziahu believed, then he was reverting to mistakes made at the very dawn of human experience [see *Rambam, Avodah Zarah* ch. 1] — the very ideas against which Abraham had done battle and which are refuted in every line of the Torah and in every moment of Jewish experience. If some of Israel's kings were too weak to withstand the onslaught of heathen ideologies which held sway at that time, then those kings are described as wicked and as deviating from the paths of the Torah. No essential strictures seem to attach to Amatziahu.

Above, in *The Edomite Campaign*, we suggested that Amatziahu, eager to restore his people's sadly tarnished spiritual standing, was interested in re-establishing Israel's dominance over Edom. The Israel-Edom relationship, the litmus test of Israel's spiritual pre-eminence, had been dislocated during Yehoram's reign. The decline reached its nadir with the wanton murder of Zechariah. Amatziahu was determined to reverse the trend.

If this, indeed, was Amatziahu's purpose — it had failed. He had won a battle, but had failed in his primary objective. Nowhere is it stated that Israel regained its ascendancy over Edom. On the contrary, the Sages teach that from Yehoram's time onwards, Edom maintained its independence.

Amatziahu may well have seen this frustration of his plans as God's rejection of his efforts to return the Davidic dynasty to its earlier purity. Further, he may have, as a result of his insensitive and cruel treatment of the prisoners, felt a profound alienation from the Divine spirit within him. God had utterly rejected this senseless savagery as a viable response to the situation and had judged it as sowing the first seeds of the eventual exile. Amatziahu must have felt within himself that he had failed.

Given this sense of failure, his turning to the idols may be explained as follows:

In a phrase difficult to understand, *Deuteronomy* 4:19 says: *When you raise your eyes to the sky and see the sun, moon, stars and other heavenly bodies, do not bow down to them nor worship them. It was to all the [other] nations under the heavens that God assigned them. But as for you, God himself took you and brought you out from the iron crucible that was Egypt, so that you could be His special nation, as you are today.*

What does the Torah mean when it says — in the context of the prohibition against idol worship — that God had *assigned* the heavenly bodies to *the other nations*? Does this legitimize the worship of these heavenly bodies by anyone who is not a Jew? Among the various interpretations offered by the commentators, *Ramban* comes closest to a view which, if it does not legitimize such service, at least provides logical underpinnings for it.

He writes: The other nations have a ... specific angelic overlord assigned to them, as it is written in *Daniel*; ... because of this, they tend to deify them and to serve them. You are different: *But as for you, God Himself took....* You are God's own portion — not subject to any intermediary. *He took you out from the iron crucible* ... in opposition to the overlords [of Egypt] who, had God not helped you, would have prevented your escape ... He did this so that you should become His inheritance, be a particular treasure for His great Name.

The non-Israelite, then, has a justification for paying obeisance to his overlord. His access to God is, indeed, through this intermediary. That the Torah forbids him this indulgence does not alter the essential logic of his approach.

Israel, on the other hand, is blessed with direct access to God. For them such service is unthinkable.

But is it? Had not God in a certain sense rejected them? Perhaps now that they no longer dominated Edom — was it not fitting that Edom should dominate them? Certainly God's answer to Rebecca (*Genesis* 25:23) would so indicate. And if indeed, they were now to fall under Edom's sway, would that not mean that God would relinquish His direct stewardship over them, and place them under the hegemony of the Edomite overlords? Would God regard as His very own, a people in whose Temple the now unrequited blood of *Kohen* and prophet seethed?

These thoughts and others like them may have animated Amatziahu after he returned from the battle upon which he had pinned so much hope. He had, so to speak, given God his all in terms of unbounded trust and willingness to forfeit wealth and military security.

That *all* had apparently not been enough. Edom had, indeed, been defeated in battle, but had retained its independence. Zechariah's blood continued to seethe with unabated fury in the Temple grounds, resisting all attempts to assuage it. Amatziahu drew what to him seemed the logical conclusion: God's special relationship with Israel is over. It is time to appease their new Edomite overlords.

If our understanding of the events is correct, then this backsliding of Amatziahu is an integral part of the *Chronicles* narrative and has no place in *Kings* which, as we have seen throughout the past few chapters, contains none of the elements which form the underpinnings of the story.

◆§ Amatziahu's Challenge to Yoash

The story of Amatziahu's challenge to Israel's king, Yoash, is told also in *Kings*. Neither of the books adduces a motive.

In *Kings*, the account is introduced by the word אָז: *Then, Amatziahu sent messengers* ... This wording implies that the action was undertaken as a result of a specific cause (*Malbim*). *Radak* and also *Metzudos* and *Malbim* identify this cause as a desire for vengeance for the unwarranted slaughter which the Israelite forces had undertaken when, furious at having been rejected, they returned to their country (v. 13 in *Chronicles*).

Metzudos sees this implied in Amatziahu's words: *Let us come face to face*. His meaning was: It was easy enough for your men to accomplish their murderous purposes against an unsuspecting citizenry. Let us see how they will fare in a face to face confrontation with a regular army. *Malbim* adds that, as indicated in our v. 16, God wanted to punish Amatziahu for his idol worship and therefore placed the idea of the challenge in his mind.

This approach to the matter sees the challenge motivated by events described in *Chronicles* but not even hinted at in *Kings*. But this would leave the *Kings'* account without any inner logic. Surely the fact that the challenge is described in *Kings* requires that a motive, independent of the events recounted in *Chronicles*, be found.

The motives ascribed by the commentators may of course also be true, and a combination of the two may help to explain the two major textual changes between the two accounts.

We have dealt with the first of these changes — the use of וַיִּוָּעַץ to introduce the description instead of the אָז of *Kings*, in comm. to v. 17. Here we address ourselves to the second one.

In Yoash's answer to Amatziahu's challenge, we find a change in wording.

II Chronicles Ch. 25	*II Kings* Ch. 10
a. 19. אָמַרְתָּ הִנֵּה הִכִּיתָ אֶת־אֱדוֹם, *Because you tell yourself, how great it is that you have smitten Edom*	a. 10. הַכֵּה הִכִּיתָ אֶת־אֱדוֹם, *Surely you have smitten Edom*
b. וּנְשָׂאֲךָ לִבְּךָ לְהַכְבִּיד, *you feel embold-ened to seek greater glory.*	b. וּנְשָׂאֲךָ לִבֶּךָ, *and so you feel embold-ened.*
c. עַתָּה שְׁבָה בְּבֵיתֶךָ, *Why do you not stay at home!*	c. הִכָּבֵד וְשֵׁב בְּבֵיתֶךָ, *Retain your dignity, and stay at home.*

The הִכָּבֵד, *retain your dignity*, of (c) in *Kings* becomes, לְהַכְבִּיד, *to seek greater glory*, that is, to wage further war (*Radak*), in the (b) section in *Chronicles*. As such, *Chronicles* does ascribe a motive of sorts. Flushed by his victory over Edom, Amatziahu is hungry for more military conquests. This quasi-motive, then, is missing in *Kings*.

Above, in *The Edomite Campaign*, we noted a tradition preserved in *Josephus' Antiquities*, that it was Amatziahu's purpose to reunite the two kingdoms and, in the tradition of David and Solomon, to establish himself as ruler of the renewed nation. We thought that it was with this ambition in mind that he originally hired the mercenaries from the Northern Kingdom.

This motive could well have explained the challenge as described in *Kings*. At the peak of his military prowess Amatziahu judged the moment ripe for the fulfillment of his ambition. None of the events described in *Chronicles* but missing in *Kings*, would be needed to justify this motive.

In *Chronicles*, however, we are aware of a circumstance which could well have dampened Amatziahu's ambition. He had somehow come face to face with the realization that the apparent success against Edom had been an empty one, and that his hopes for re-establishing a new and revitalized Davidic dynasty were not to be realized. It was this realization which, as we saw above, catapulted him into a self-denigration which resulted in his idol worship. In such a state of mind it seems unlikely that he would have felt capable or even desirous of realizing such a dream.

But, in the context of *Chronicles*, another, more sinister consideration became operative: A need to avenge the unwarranted attack upon his people and land which the soldiers of the Northern Kingdom had launched.

And so, his challenge, couched in the neutral wording: *Let us meet face to face*, which overtly could well be construed as an invitation to enter upon negotiations designed to unite the two kingdoms, became in reality a declaration of war. In his heart, he knew that Yoash would not agree to his plan and that certainly his challenge would result in a military confrontation. This, in truth, is what he really wanted: Yoash understood this and, in the *Chronicles'* perspective, hinted at that realization in his answer: I recognize that your true intention is to wage additional war. Do not do so for it will end in disaster for you.

Chapter Twenty-Six

⁂ Uziahu and the Ketores

The story of Uziahu's abortive attempt to bring up incense before God occurs in *Chronicles* but not in *Kings*. There, indeed, the fact that he was struck by leprosy is mentioned — but only in order to explain Yotham's regency during his father's lifetime. In prefatory remarks to this chapter we have discussed how this event helped reveal the first fissures in the apparently solid and durable institution of state and monarchy. As yet too minute to warrant recording in the historical accounts of the otherwise placid and constructive reign, these fissures were all too real in terms of their long-range effects. If *Kings*, in its concentration on the description of the reign on its own terms, was able to ignore the causes of Uziahu's leprosy, *Chronicles*, with its eye to eternity, needed to deal with them.

How are we to understand this terrible aberration on the part of a king whom both *Kings* and *Chronicles* describe as having done that which was straight in the eyes of God?

We begin by quoting *Tanchuma Noach* 13: Concerning Uziahu it says: *For he loved husbandry*. He was a king, but abandoned himself to the earth and did not concern himself with the Torah. One day he came to the *Bais Midrash* and asked the people there what they were studying. They answered him [that they were studying the verse concerning the Temple service in which it says:] *Any stranger who approaches shall die* (*Numbers* 1:51). Uziahu said to them, 'The most Holy is a King and I too am a king. It is fitting that a king minister to the King, and bring up incense before Him.'

It is unthinkable that Uziahu should have wanted to defy an explicit prohibition of the Torah. A *stranger* is forbidden to approach the Divine service and, as a stranger, Uziahu would surely not have presumed to do so. Rather, we must understand his assertion *I too am a king* as meaning that as king he felt that the appellation *stranger* did not describe him. He was no *stranger* to God and could safely approach His hallowed service.

In Section II to ch.19, *Yehoshaphat and the Judiciary*, we had occasion to discuss *Rashi's* assertion that the Torah grants a king the prerogative — on a case by case basis; never permanently — to abrogate its laws and to act in a way which he deems appropriate in a given situation.

Surely this is the prerogative which Uziahu sought to invoke on this occasion. In an ecstasy of rapture brought about by his perception of himself as a model king — the ideal metaphor for God's kingship over the universe — he craved an expression for that feeling of identity which would permit him to be transported to the absolute peak of intimacy of which a human being is capable in his relation with the Divine.

For this expression he could not have chosen better than the burning of the קְטֹרֶת, *the incense*. We are not privy to the depths of religious feeling which this *most beloved of all sacrifices* (*Bamidbar Rabbah* 18:7) evoked in the people who were privileged to experience its potency, but we do know that it exercised a fatal attraction to those who willy-nilly craved close proximity to God.

Nadav and Avihu, Aaron's sons, who had lived out their lives in absolute purity and blamelessness (*Vayikra Rabbah* 20:8), and whom God brought closer to Himself than any other human being (*Pesikta Rabbasi* 46:14), died when they brought unauthorized incense in the height of religious ecstasy generated by God's Divine Presence coming to rest in Israel (*Leviticus* 10:1 ff.). Millennia after that tragedy, Israel still remembers them by fasting on the anniversary of their death (*Orach Chayim* 580:2). How, then, are we to understand their sin if not as a momentary inability to control the terrible longing for proximity with God, which refused to allow itself to be quenched, and which drove them to go that one step beyond the limits which the discipline of Torah had placed upon them?

When Korach rebelled against Moses' authority he was abetted by two hundred and fifty ... *men of rank in the community, representatives at the assembly and famous* (*Numbers* 16:2). In order to demonstrate the legitimacy of Aaron's appointment as *Kohen Gadol*, Moses asked all of them to submit to a test. The next day all two hundred and fifty of them would, together with Aaron, bring an incense-offering. God, by accepting the one and refusing the others, would indicate who was His chosen. All died when a fire came down from God and consumed them (*Numbers* 16:1-34). Later, God describes these two hundred and fifty as having *sinned with their soul* (17:1). *HaAmek Davar* explains: It was because of the cravings of their soul that they sinned. They knew full well that the incense of only one of them would be accepted — knew that all the others would die, and still they did it! It was worth their while to sacrifice their lives for that sublime moment in which, by means of the קְטֹרֶת offering, their souls would connect with God.

It is against this background that we must judge Uziahu's actions. In his moment of ecstasy he felt himself — knew himself — to be the ideal ministrant to God on earth: *It is fitting that a king minister to the King*; he felt an unquenchable longing for God welling up inside him, and intuited that only through the קְטֹרֶת could this craving be quieted.

Tanchuma tells us the details of this story in the context of its criticism of Uziahu that he ... *abandoned himself to the earth and did not concern himself with the Torah*. This is in accordance with everything which we have learned in connection with this king. The same man who sought Divine fiat through direct prophetic contact instead of through the less direct but more constant and thus more demanding study of the Torah (v. 5), allowed himself to be carried away by a moment's rapture, to invoke his authority to temporarily abrogate the Torah laws in order to seek the fleeting moment of total unison with the Divine.

Here, indeed, were the ingredients for the earthquake which shook the Temple portals; the first step in the actual departure of the Divine Presence from the Temple.

Chapter Twenty-Seven

◆§ Yotham and the Campaign of Pekach and Retzin

We may suggest another possibility which will explain the apparent redundancy of v. 8.

V. 36 in *II Kings* ch. 15 is precisely the same as our v. 7, except that it substitutes *The Chronicles of the Kings of Judah* for our *Book of the Kings of Israel and Judah.* V. 38 there is essentially the same as our v. 9.

Thus, in both accounts we have one verse interspersed between the statement that the other details of the reign were recorded in the appropriate book, and the statement that Yotham died and was buried. But the information given in these respective, intervening verses is completely different in the two accounts. V. 37 there reads: *In those days* H*ASHEM* *began to send against Judah Retzin the king of Aram and Pekach son of Remaliahu*, while our verse, as we have seen, is a repetition of v. 1.

We suggest that *Chronicles* inserted a verse which is essentially redundant, in order to highlight the omission of the information given in *Kings*. Had there simply not been an intervening verse, we might have supposed that the information given in *Kings* was left out in the same way that the two accounts occasionally add or omit certain details without any particular significance. The truth, however, is that in this instance, *Chronicles* had a specific and fundamental reason for leaving out what *Kings* had said — and this is conveyed by substituting a verse which can add nothing to what was already known. Clearly, it has no purpose other than to draw attention to the fact that something was left out.

Let us analyze the meaning of the verse in *Kings*.

The campaign of Retzin and Pekach against Judah is mentioned in both *Kings* and *Chronicles*, and in addition, is the subject of prophetic vision in chs. 7 and 8 of *Isaiah*. In all these sources these events involve Achaz the son of Yotham. Nowhere, except in the *Kings'* verse which we are now considering, is any connection made to Yotham.

Because of this, *Radak*, *Metzudos* and *Ralbag* all maintain that *In those days* ... means after Yotham's death — not during his reign.

But, if so, why should the campaign be mentioned as part of the description of Yotham's reign?

Because of this problem, *Rashi* and *Abarbanel* maintain that what is said in *Kings* did, in fact, take place during Yotham's reign. However, this was not the full-fledged war — this was to develop later in Achaz's days — but only preliminary skirmishes (*Abarbanel*).

Let us analyze the significance of this campaign.

We are struck by the fact that the description differs radically from *Kings* to *Chronicles*.

II Kings 16:5 writes: *Then, Retzin the king of Aram and Pekach, son of Remaliahu the king of Israel went up to make war against Jerusalem, but they were unable to wage war*.

The implication is clear. The campaign ended in a debacle for the two kings. The preparation which they had made for war came to naught.

The picture is quite different in *Chronicles*. At 28:5 and 6 *Chronicles* clearly describes major victories won by both kings, with Pekach killing an incredible one hundred and twenty thousand men of Judah in a single day.

Malbim points out that *Isaiah* 7:2 would seem to indicate that there were indeed two separate stages in the campaign. Initially, the two kings invaded Judah independently of each other and won the victories described in *Chronicles*. After that they decided to join forces and to march on Jerusalem. In this plan they were thwarted, and it is this aborted march on Jerusalem which is the subject of the *Kings* account.

From the *Kings* account we have no way of knowing what motivated the two kings in their wish to take Jerusalem. However, what is left unexplicated there, is spelled out in detail in Isaiah's prophecy: *Inasmuch as Aram has plotted evil against you, Ephraim and the son of Remaliah, saying 'Let us go up against Judah, besiege it and breach it and let us crown a king within it — Ben Toval'* (*Isaiah* 7:5-6).

The intention, then, was to eradicate the royal line of David and to establish Ben Toval, an Ephraimite, as king — see commentators there.

This vendetta against the Davidic line did not originate from outside the land. Achaz's subjects themselves seem to have fomented a rebellion, and to have sought help from the invading forces: *Inasmuch as this people has rejected the Shiloach waters which flow slowly and find* [*instead*] *joy in Retzin and* [*in*] *the son of Remaliah* (*Isaiah* 8:6).

The *Shiloach waters* are a metaphor for the Davidic line (*Sanhedrin* 94b) and thus, the verse clearly states that the people themselves had rejected the Davidic leadership and found joy in the anticipation of Retzin and Pekach's victory. This would result in crowning the Ephraimite Ben Toval as king.

God was determined to thwart this incipient rebellion and the campaign aborted, as told in the *Kings* account.

It is to these events that the cryptic verse which *Kings* inserts into the description of Yotham's reign refers.

But why should it be told as part of Yotham's story, when it belongs so much more naturally to the reign of his son Achaz?

This can mean nothing else but that even during Yotham's apparently benign reign, fissures began to appear in the apparently solidly based Davidic kingship.

But if it is true that Yotham's shortcomings were, in part, responsible for precipitating the rebellion, it is also true that his righteousness had much to do with guaranteeing that it would fail, and that the Davidic line would remain unscathed.

II Kings 15:30 tells of Pekach's death in the following words: *Hosea son of Eilah plotted against Pekach son of Remaliahu and smote him so that he died, and ruled in his place in the twentieth year of Yotham son of Uziah*.

The dating is problematic since Yotham reigned for only sixteen years and the correct wording would have been *the fourth year of Achaz*.

One of the two answers offered by *Seder Olam* is that already during Yotham's reign God had decreed that Pekach should die. For this reason the text chose to date the death by the [theoretical] years of Yotham, rather than by the actual years of Achaz.

Pekach's campaign was foredoomed. Long before the wars broke out in earnest — during Achaz's reign — Yotham's piety had already guaranteed that the attackers would not succeed.[1]

---

1. Although this passage sees Yotham as Pekach's nemesis, he is contrasted, in a different passage, to Yotham's grandson, Chizkiahu.

In a cryptic Aggadic passage in *Sanhedrin* 94b we learn: R' Yochanan taught: *The curse of*

Thus, from its very beginnings, the movement to displace the Davidic line carried within itself the seeds of its own abortion. There was never any real threat. *Chronicles* was justified in ignoring the entire incident.

The perspective of *Chronicles* demanded that this incipient rebellion be ignored — and not only ignored but shown for what it was — an aberration which from its very beginning was doomed to failure. For this reason it substituted a redundant verse to demonstrate, unambiguously, that the incident has no place in the Messianic history of the Jewish people.

HASHEM lies in the house of the wicked, but the dwelling of the righteous shall be blessed (*Proverbs* 3:33). The first part of this verse describes Pekach, who was such a glutton that he would eat forty *se'ah* of pigeons for dessert. The second describes Chizkiahu whose entire meal would consist of a liter of vegetables.

Maharal sees this passage as a contrast between two modes of kingship. Chizkiahu is the protagonist of the Davidic line which is not driven by unbridled ambition, and does not demand to swallow up everything in its path. Pekach is the aggressive despot with an unsatiable appetite for power.

Chapter Twenty-Eight

◆§ Achaz and Menasheh

There are significant differences between the *Kings'* and *Chronicles'* accounts of Achaz's reign: The *Chronicles'* account is much more negative than that of *Kings*.

In *Chronicles'* view, Achaz occupies a very special place in the history of the monarchy.

This can best be appreciated by first contrasting the *Chronicles* description of the reign of his grandson Menasheh with that given in *Kings*.

The *Kings'* account is unreservedly negative, not only in its treatment of Menasheh as a person, but also as it projects his role in the destruction of the Temple. Although that tragedy still lay far in the future, it was his evil influence which so undermined the spiritual standing of the people that they no longer deserved to welcome the Divine Presence in their midst. This is clearly spelled out at *II Kings* 21:10-16; 23:26 and 24:3.

Now, none of these passages appear in *Chronicles*, and nowhere in the book is it hinted that Menasheh is in any way to blame for the destruction. Menasheh is, in fact, portrayed sympathetically, since he is said to have undergone a sincere penitence during the later years of his reign. This penitence is not mentioned at all in *Kings*.

For Achaz, the reverse is true. The devastating account of the degree to which idol worship proliferated during his reign, which appears in our vs. 24-26, does not appear in *Kings*. The account, as a whole, is less condemnatory.

Why are these two reigns treated so differently in the two books?

Proverbs 24:30-31 reads: *I passed by a field owned by a lazy man; and by a vineyard [owned] by a man who lacked heart. Behold, thorns had grown all over it; its face was covered by thistles; its stone wall was crumbling.* Each of these five phrases refers to one of the wicked kings beginning with Achaz: It is he who is described as the *lazy man*; Menasheh is the one who *lacked heart*; the *thorns* are Amon; the *thistles*, Yehoyakim; and finally, the *crumbling wall*, symbolic of the destroyed Temple, describes Tzidkiahu (*Sanhedrin* 103a).

Maharal explains that this interpretation is meant to convey that the root of the decline lay with Achaz. Just as the owner's laziness resulted in all the other abuses of the vineyard, so Achaz laid the ground for all the subsequent backsliding.

This, in *Maharal*'s view, is reflected in *Sanhedrin* 103b, in three areas: the vendetta against Torah learning (see below); the elimination of the Temple service (see v. 24); and the legitimization of forbidden and incestuous marriages (see comm. to v. 3). Achaz began a trend towards evil which was then carried further by each of the wicked kings who followed him.

Thus, we may say that Achaz relates to Menasheh as does the seed to the tree; the potential to the actualization. The relative significance of these two may well differ, depending on the perspective of the historian. The degree of wickedness was, in fact, greater with Menasheh; the excesses of his reign made the destruction of the Temple inevitable. But these were only an outgrowth of Achaz's depredations; his shortcomings set the downward spiral in motion.

Kings deals with the tangible events of the history of the period. In this context Menasheh was the greater catastrophe. His wickedness precipitated the destruction. But for *Chronicles*, in whose long term perspective the inner dynamics are more significant, it is Achaz upon whom the focus lies. *Chronicles* omits mention of the fact that the destruction came about because of Menasheh's evil, since this would have drawn attention away from the seminal role which Achaz played.

In the tradition of the Sages, Achaz is depicted as waging a consistent vendetta against the שְׁכִינָה, the *Divine Presence*, in Israel. *Yerushalmi, Sanhedrin* 10:2 tells how he prevented children from learning Torah by dismantling the entire educational system in Israel. He argued: If we eradicate Torah from the youngsters, they will know nothing when they grow up. Where ignorance of Torah pervades, there can be no prophecy or Divine inspiration. God will no longer permit His Divine Presence to rest in Israel.

Again, in *Isaiah* 7:11-12 we find the prophet offering Achaz a heavenly sign that he has nothing to fear from the two attacking kings, Pekach and Retzin. Achaz rejects this Divine favor with the words: *I shall not request a sign. I shall not test HASHEM*. The Sages (*Tanchuma, ed. Buber* to *VaYeitze* i 14) interpret: I know full well that God can reassure me with such a sign, but I do not wish that the Name of Heaven should be hallowed through me.

Certainly Achaz's efforts to abolish the Temple service indicate a wish to banish the Divine Presence from Israel, as does also his sanctioning of forbidden marriages. This, since the Sages teach that God wishes to dwell only among a people with an unimpeachably pure family life (*Kiddushin* 70b).

Perhaps most noteworthy is *Midrash Tanchuma* to *Tetzaveh* 15. The midrash there is concerned with the significance of the קְטוֹרֶת, the *incense-offering*. The midrash refers to 29:7 where Chizkiahu lists a number of terrible things that Achaz had done: He had closed up the doors of the Sanctuary; extinguished the lights of the *Menorah*; abolished the daily incense, and the daily burnt-offering. V. 9 there then goes on: *Now, behold our fathers have fallen by the sword; our sons, daughters and wives gone to captivity*, עַל־זֹאת, *because of this*. The singular זֹאת indicates that the captivity is to be traced to only one sin. But several had been mentioned. The midrash concludes that one among all the sins listed was more heinous than the others and, in effect, was the sole cause of the catastrophe. This sin the midrash identifies as the abolishment of the קְטוֹרֶת.

Now, the bringing up of incense is absolutely the highest expression of man's ability to form a union with the Divine. [See Section II to Ch. 26, *Uziahu and the Ketores*.] It is significant that just this offering was the special focus of Achaz's hatred. Achaz wanted no breath of sanctity to touch human life.

How are we to understand the sudden appearance, on the stage of Jewish history, of a king such as Achaz?

The answer lies in an appreciation of the Talmud's identification of Achaz as the *lazy man* of the *Proverbs'* passage. On the surface this seems surprising. All Achaz's shortcomings seem to have been positive ones. Nowhere does the text explicate that he was remiss about doing something that he should have done.

But there is perhaps a hint. V. 1 states that . . .*he did not do that which was right in the eyes of HASHEM as his father David had done*. When we consider the terrible sins ascribed to Achaz in the following verses, this seems to be an understatement. There is a vast chasm between not living up to David's example, and acting as Achaz did.

We suggest the following solution, which will also help us to place Achaz into his historical context.

The Sages in *Toras Kohanim* (quoted by *Rashi* to *Leviticus* 26:16) delineate seven stages through which we can expect a person who does not invest energy and effort into

Torah study to pass. They are: not learning; not doing; looking down upon others who do practice; hating the sages; preventing others from learning and doing; denying the commands; and finally, denying God.

Surely this sequence is not arbitrary. Without an energetic commitment to Torah study, the performance of *mitzvos* lacks the firm foundation and understanding which would make it meaningful. The rest follows by itself. He who finds the *mitzvah*-obligations to be threatening and irksome, must assuage his conscience by denying the validity of the source from which his discomfiture derives.

What is true for the individual may be true also on the communal level.

Uziahu did not learn enough Torah. He favored the ecstasy of the moment over the long effort which עֲמֵלוּת בַּתּוֹרָה, *the energetic involvement in Torah study*, demands. [See Section II to ch. 26, *Uziahu and the Ketores*.] This neglect took its toll. The spiritual level of the people gradually eroded — we saw them continuing their backsliding in Yotham's reign. [See prefatory remarks to ch. 26.] Inevitably, it produced the more advanced stage of decay in Achaz. Each of the steps delineated in *Toras Kohanim* was taken. Schools and study halls were closed and a vendetta declared against Torah, and those who studied it. Crazed by a hatred which only the frustrated and the alienated can feel, he deluded himself that the *Shechinah* could be banned from Israel.

All this came about through the neglect of Torah studies. In stark contrast to his father David, Achaz felt no longing for the sweet pleasures enjoyed by those who feel close to God. Instead, stunted and filthied by the evil which he had invited into himself, Achaz and his people plummeted downwards to the depths of degradation.

Debased and dispirited, the people were in no shape to resist Menasheh's depredations. His poisoned vines were lodged in fertile soil, tilled and nourished by Achaz's evil.

It is from this perspective that *Chronicles* records Achaz's reign.

◆§ The Alien Altar

The story of the alien altar which Achaz introduced into the Temple seems to defy all logic.

What could possibly have been his motive for this heinous insult to Solomon's altar, Israel's most sacred possession, and, given the sheer horror of this crime, why does *Chronicles* ignore it?

We suggest that the story is to be understood within the context of the rebellion against the Davidic line which coalesced around the attack of Pekach and Retzin. *Chronicles* makes no mention of the alien altar for the same reason that it says nothing of that rebellion — see above, *Yotham and the Campaign of Pekach and Retzin*.

Yerushalmi, Sanhedrin 10:2 teaches that one of Achaz's crimes was that *he established a throne* [כִּסֵּא] in the Temple Court. Since Achaz, as scion of the Davidic line, was permitted to sit in the Temple Court [see *I Chronicles* 17:16 for a discussion], it is difficult to see why this should be considered a sin.[1]

A close reading of the events described in *II Kings* ch. 16 may yield an explanation. When it became clear that Pekach and Retzin constituted a terrible danger to his reign, Achaz sent messengers to the Assyrian Tiglas Pilnesser soliciting his help. His words

---

1. This is unless the expression of the *Yerushalmi . . . he built a throne* is meant to convey that he made a permanent structure, ignoring the rule that no additions were allowed upon the original design for the House given to David — see *I Chronicles* 28:9.

were, *I am your servant and your son! Go up now and save me ...* (v. 7) What is the precise implication of the idea expressed in the terms ... *your servant and your son*?

We have seen that Pekach and Retzin had a more sinister purpose than a simple invasion of the land. Their goal was the eradication of the Davidic line. In such a conflict Achaz does not figure as an individual, but as protagonist of that dynasty. This is made abundantly clear in *Isaiah* 7:2 where, on the occasion upon which Achaz was informed of the impending attack, he is referred to, not by name but, by his role as scion of the Davidic line — *It was told to the House of David...*

Seen from this perspective, it is not Achaz the man who describes himself as *servant and son* of the Assyrian king, but Achaz as *the House of David*. The implication is clear. In return for the protection of Tiglas Pilnesser, Achaz is willing to subordinate the entire kingship of Israel to him. Henceforth, the Davidic line will not only be servants of Assyria — that is, bound to them for loyalty and service — but will be *son* to them — derive their entire legitimacy from their goodwill.

This may well be the meaning of the throne which Achaz established in the Temple Court. At *I Chronicles* 17:16 we learned that only Davidic kings were allowed to sit in this Court, all others must always be standing. Surely the inner meaning of this dispensation for the Davidic kings is this: Everyone else could enter only as a ministrant — and had to indicate this by standing — constantly poised for service. The scions of the Davidic line came as manifestations of the Divine kingship on earth. They came not as ministrants but as the conduit through which God dwelt among His people.

But in Achaz's view this had now changed. No more was the *House of David* under God's direct and unimpeded stewardship. Henceforth, it was subordinate to the Assyrian hegemony and would have to approach God by way of that intermediary. Achaz established a *throne* which would appropriately reflect his new relationship with God. The throne that his ancestors had used did not reflect the new reality.

We may understand the matter of the altar in the same way. We note that Achaz discovered the new altar when he was in Damasek to greet Tiglas Pilnesser after the latter's victory over the two kings. Now, it was the custom of Israel's kings during the period of the first Temple to sacrifice daily upon the altar in the Temple [see *HaLevi, Tekufas HaMikra* ch. 55] — no doubt symbolically to testify to the subordination of their kingship to God's. There was no more graphic way in which Achaz could have demonstrated that the relationship had now been altered radically than by arranging for the erection of an altar in the Aramean mode. Aram was now entirely subjugated to Assyria and thus, by using the mode of their altar, Achaz was saying that his Divine service would henceforth be performed as a vassal king heading a vassal state, subordinate to Assyria.

This would explain the sequence of events described in *Kings*. When Achaz returned from Damasek he immediately brought *his burnt-offering, his meal-offering, his libations and the blood of his offerings* upon the new altar. Only then did he command Uriahu that from now on, all communal and private offerings were to be brought upon that altar, with the earlier one remaining for only occasional use. The implication is that Achaz's main concern was for the sacrifices which he brought as king. The other new arrangements were made only as an afterthought.

Chapter Twenty-Nine

◆§ Chizkiahu in *Isaiah* and Rabbinical Sources

There are four sources which provide insight into the life of Chizkiahu: *Isaiah, Kings* and *Chronicles*, and the tradition of the Sages as preserved in the Talmud and midrashim. Each appears to concentrate upon a different aspect of this multi-faceted king, relegating the qualities considered in the other texts to a subsidiary role.

We deal with the *Kings'* and *Chronicles'* accounts in the comm. Here we will consider the other two.

Isaiah: Except for chs. 36-39, where Chizkiahu's confrontation with the Assyrian forces is described, his name does not occur in the book [except at 1:1 to identify the period during which Isaiah was active]. Nevertheless, his presence is felt ubiquitously throughout the early prophetic chapters, appearing constantly as the idealized king in whom the future of the *remnant* [שְׁאָר] — the indestructible core of the Jewish people who in Isaiah's vision carry in themselves Israel's future — is vested. [1]

The language of those of Isaiah's prophecies which the Sages identify as dealing with Chizkiahu, is couched in unmistakably Messianic terms. For understanding, we turn to *Ramban* in *Sefer HaGeulah*.

Ramban is puzzled by the fact that many of the prophecies which manifestly deal with Chizkiahu, are interpreted by the Sages as describing the Messiah — that is, as pointing to events which still lie in the future. He words his solution as follows:

"... Therefore, the following appears to me. The Sages view all the prophecies which contain messages of abundant comfort as having been given to the prophet with an eye to the future of Israel and David's descendant ... with the built-in proviso that they could refer to Chizkiahu. For if Israel and Chizkiahu had fully repented, then God would have caused their confrontation with Sancheriv, under whose banner most of the nations of the world were gathered, to be the final judgment and would have destroyed these before those [thus making Chizkiahu the Messiah]. But when the time came and their merits were not sufficient and, moreover, the guilt of the nations was not yet completely full, and justice required that they be given more time, the option of [making] Chizkiahu [the Messiah] became void, and all the comforting prophecies remained destined for some future Messianic king who would be descended from him, and only some of them were fulfilled now, in accordance with what they deserved."

Thus, we may say that in Isaiah's visions, Chizkiahu is the king of the future whose reign, weighted with potential, could — had he but risen to the challenge — have been a great watershed in the history of his people. He is the man of destiny, the man who could have been the Messiah.

We shall see aspects of that vision reflected in the *Chronicles'* account.

Talmud and Midrash: In these sources, Chizkiahu is depicted as the ideal scion of the Davidic line, as that is described in Section II to *I Chronicles*, ch.17 (p. 436), *Analysis* ...

Here we find him searching out God on his own initiative in spite of all that his father Achaz had done to drive the Divine Presence out of Israel (*Bamidbar Rabbah* 14:7); exercising iron control over his human frailties and thus maintaining stupendous

1. For full treatment of the שְׁאָר concept, and the role which Chizkiahu plays within it, see Hirsch's masterful analysis in *The Collected Writings of Rabbi Samson Raphael Hirsch*, Vol. 4.

heights of personal purity and sanctity (*Zohar* 1:228b); and creating an ideal atmosphere for his prayers, by placing them within the context of thanking God for having taken Israel out of Egypt [סְמִיכוּת גְּאֻלָּה לִתְפִילָּה] (*Berachos* 10b).

We see him concerned about the spiritual standing of the people: Destroying the copper snake which had been revered since Moses' times, when he saw that its presence had begun to exert a pernicious influence upon the pure monotheism of the masses; taking steps to ensure that, in their sickness, people would turn to God rather than put their faith in the medical arts [גָּנַז סֵפֶר רְפוּאוֹת]; and repressing all normal feelings of filial loyalty by dragging his father's body through the streets, rather than arranging a respectable funeral — in order to demonstrate the depth of degradation which must be the lot of one whose life's ambition is to wean Israel away from its God (*Berachos* 10b).

But by far, his major concern was the re-establishment of Torah in Israel after Achaz's depredations — see prefatory remarks to ch. 26. At a level far removed from the people as a whole, he initiated the final drafting of the Scriptural Books: *Isaiah, Proverbs, Shir HaShirim* and *Koheles* (*Bava Basra* 15a), in the case of *Proverbs* having to salvage remnants of Solomon's wisdom from the ruin and destruction that Achaz had wrought (*Gra* to *Proverbs* 25:1). But most tangibly felt were his reforms in the educational system. These were to leave no life untouched: He thrust a sword into the doors of the study hall and said, 'Whoever does not immerse himself in Torah study shall be pierced by this sword.' They searched from Dan to Beer Sheva and were unable to find an illiterate Jew, and from Givath to Antripath and could not find boy or girl, man or woman who were not conversant with [even] the laws of *tumah* and *taharah* (*Sanhedrin* 94b).

A more rounded picture will emerge when the information gleaned from these two sources is combined with what we shall learn in the comm.

Chapter Thirty

⸎ The Skull of Arnon

That Arnon's skull should have been lying under the holy altar, defiling everything there up to Chizkiahu's reign, is obviously impossible to accept. Moreover, this skull appears on two other occasions. *Yalkut, Shir HaShirim* 3, implies that such a skull, apparently from one of Arnon's ancestors, was there already when David first bought the threshing floor, and from *Yerushalmi, Sotah* 5:2 it appears that it was there once more, when the returnees from Babylon erected the new Temple in the days of Haggai the prophet.

Teshuvos Chasam Sofer, Yoreh Deah 340, suggests that Arnon's family graves were situated near the Temple area. Under normal conditions, there were strong walls separating the two. However, during periods when the upkeep of the Temple was neglected — such as during Achaz's reign, and certainly during the decades during which the Temple lay in ruins, the dividing walls broke down and parts of the skeletons may well have rolled over into the sacred areas.

However, *Minchas Elazar* 4:76, citing sources that all graves were moved out of Jerusalem with the exception of the royal sepulchers and the grave of Chuldah the prophetess, considers even this solution inadequate. He feels that it is unthinkable that a Yevusite cemetery would have been tolerated in such close proximity to the Temple. Rather, he suggests that this *skull* was not an actual part of a skeleton but was an icon preserved by Arnon's family, who would use every opportunity to smuggle this revered relic into the sacred Temple precincts.

We suggest another alternative.

The expression *the skull of Arnon the Yevusite* — particularly since it appears three different times in three different contexts — suggests an Aggadic connotation. *Maharal* to *Avos* 2:7 thinks that in such contexts, גֻּלְגּוֹלֶת, *the skull*, does not mean a part of the body at all, but rather describes a *personality*, inasmuch as the essence of a person lies in the brain which is encased in the skull.

Within such a context, the expression would not mean that an actual skull was found, but that Arnon's heathen and defiling personality was still leaving an impression upon the place.

The sense would be that the sacred Temple precincts needed constantly to be wrested from a pernicious heathen presence.[1]

This would appear to be the sense of *Zohar* II:214 which talks of a רוּחַ הַטּוּמְאָה, an *aura of tumah*, which lay over the area before David acquired it, and describes how Arnon wielded control over the place and the mighty efforts — much blood and much death — which were required to dislodge him from it.

---

1. This is particularly apparent in the *Shir HaShirim* source. There the Sages make their statement in connection with 3:4 . . . *I grasped Him, determined that never again would I lose hold of Him*. The midrash remarks: *This refers to David when he snatched the threshing floor from Arnon the Yevusite and found the skull of Arnon beneath the altar. He refused to allow this to cause the disqualification of the location for Israel's sacrifices*. The implication is that, without great determination, David would have felt discouraged and have given up on the plan. But an actual skull could have been easily removed and would not have been any obstacle.

The picture which emerges is that of a constant tension between defilement and sanctity in this most holy place on earth. When the constant effort to maintain high spiritual standards is relaxed, then *the skull of Arnon* reappears — his pernicious presence makes itself felt.

Once again we have Chizkiahu in the role of *David*, wresting the location of sanctity from the grasp of *tumah*.

Thus, we conclude that *Yerushalmi Pesachim* means as follows: There *was* some degree of actual *tumah* in the Temple precincts which defiled the *Kohanim*. This became possible only because the *skull of Arnon* had reappeared and the Divine aura no longer rested upon the Temple area, protecting it from any encroachment of uncleanliness.

Chapter 32

⇜§ The Diversion of the Waters

Upon the advice of his princes and warriors, Chizkiahu decided to deny Sancheriv the convenience of a ready drinking supply, by stopping up the wells which lay outside the city walls. The comm., based on 30:2, assumes that Chizkiahu's *princes* are the Torah Sages.

Berachos 10b and *Pesachim* 56a list six things of significance which Chizkiahu undertook — three with the agreement of the Sages and three over their objections. One to which the Sages did not agree, was that he *stopped up the waters of the Gichon* [*river*]. That he did this is not explicated here, but at v. 30 below. *Radak*, there, is troubled on two counts: V. 3 tells of his seeking the advice of the princes [Sages] and of their supporting him. How, then, can it be said that he did what he did over their objections? Moreover, *Avos d'R' Nosson* (2:4) states explicitly that in diverting the Gichon waters, he did what God would have wanted him to do [הִסְכִּימָה דַעְתּוֹ לְדַעַת הַמָּקוֹם], and proves it from the final phrase there: *And Chizkiahu was successful in all his actions*.

Maharsha (to *Berachos*) suggests a partial solution: Gichon is not mentioned in the earlier passage in which Chizkiahu sought and received the Sages' support. This was limited to the stopping up of the wells. The interference with the flow of the Gichon was undertaken solely upon his own initiative. This would explain why, in the strictures of the Talmud, only Gichon, and not the other waters, is mentioned.

However, if we examine the passage at 27-30 which is the context in which the diversion of the Gichon is mentioned, we find the tone to be entirely positive — it is a list of all of Chizkiahu's successes — and there is no hint of any form of stricture. How, then, does the Talmud assume that this was done against the will of the Sages?

We can, however, find a source for *Maharsha's* thinking within our own passage. If we compare v. 3 to v. 4, we find that in v. 3 only the wells are mentioned, while v. 4 mentions also *the river that rushes through the land*. This *river Radak* and *Malbim* identify as the Gichon. Given this, the context itself seems to indicate that he went beyond the agreement with the Sages and, moreover, the fact that the Gichon is not identified by name, may hint at the displeasure of the Sages at this action.[1]

Maharsha's suggestion does, indeed, serve to eliminate the problems which *Radak* raises, but leaves a basic question unanswered: Why should the Sages have agreed to the stopping up of the wells but not to that of Gichon? *Rashi* (*Pesachim* there) explains the objection of the Sages: He should have trusted in God Who had said: *And I shall protect this city to save it*.[2]

---

1. If we are correct in this assumption, then v. 30 would have no bearing on this issue at all. In our passage the various waterways are *stopped up*, while there, the diversion of the waters to the City of David is central. It may well be that the *stopping up* of the waters was done against the wishes of the Sages, but that the diversion was well conceived and, in fact, was, as *Avos d'R' Nosson* points out, what God would have wanted him to do.

2. It is difficult to understand *Rashi*. The verse he quotes comes from *II Kings* 19:34. There, immediately prior to the destruction of the Assyrian army, God promises to protect the city from destruction. All this took place long after Chizkiahu stopped up the waterways. This he had done

But *Rashi's* reasoning would be valid for the wells as well as for the Gichon. Why should the Sages have agreed to the stopping of all the waterways, and have objected only to interference with Gichon?

In the absence of any guidance from the commentators, we suggest as follows:

There seems to have been a very special relationship between the Gichon river and the royal line of David.

The halachah prescribes that, when a king from the House of David is to be anointed, it must be done at a flowing stream (*Horios* 12a). The source adduced is *I Kings* 1:33 where David orders that Solomon is to be crowned king, with the words: '*. . . and take him down to Gichon, and anoint him there.*' The Talmud explains the symbolism: So that their rule shall continue to flow [just as a well flows continuously]. Thus the eternity of the Davidic dynasty seems, in some way, to be bound up with the flow of the Gichon. This connection is further accentuated by Isaiah when he compares the Davidic kings to *the waters of the Shiloach* [=Gichon — see *Rashi* there] *which flows slowly* [*Isaiah* 8:6].

Because of these symbolic implications, no Davidic king would have chosen to stop up the Gichon, unless he was truly desperate. The strategic aim of denying water to the Assyrian forces could have been achieved by stopping up the wells. This was a reasonable and prudent course of action, to which the Sages agreed. If Chizkiahu had trusted God as completely as he should have done, he would not have found this additional step important.

☙ A Missed Opportunity

In comm. we noted that, whereas in *Kings* and *Isaiah*, the account of the destruction of Sancheriv's army and that of his return home and subsequent assassination are told in two separate verses — here they are combined into one.

Is there any significance to this apparently substantive change?

First, a brief synopsis of how *Kings* and *Isaiah* tell this story.

1. Ravshakeh's speech [*II Kings* 18:19-35].

2. Chizkiahu's request to Isaiah, asking his intercession [19:2-5].

3. Isaiah replies that Chizkiahu has nothing to fear from the Assyrians: '*. . . Behold I will incite him: He shall hear a rumor, return to his land, and I shall make him fall by the sword in his land*' [19:6-7].

Rashi explains that the two halves of the message are not connected. Sancheriv will hear a rumor that the Ethiopian king, Tirhakah, plans to make war against him. He will leave the Land of Israel in order to take up that challenge. This is the first half of Isaiah's response.

The second half of the message, that Sancheriv would return to his land only to be assassinated there, would become fulfilled much later. First he would return to Israel from the Ethiopian campaign loaded down with the captured treasures which he will have taken there. This is God's plan for enriching Chizkiahu. Chizkiahu will appropriate these spoils after the Assyrian army will have been annihilated. Only after all this would the broken Sancheriv return home.

---

as the Assyrians were besieging the fortified cities, long before they ever came to Jerusalem. Perhaps we must assume that *Rashi* does not mean that Chizkiahu should have relied upon the promise contained in this particular verse, but refers to the entire gamut of Isaiah's prophecies which stress again and again that Assyria would not be permitted to conquer Jerusalem.

4. Before he leaves for the Ethiopian campaign, Sancheriv sends another message to Chizkiahu, threatening to return when he is free once more [19:9-13].

5. Chizkiahu goes to the Temple and pours out his heart in prayer to God [19:14-19].

6. God responds by way of a prophecy from Isaiah: That message concludes with the promise that Jerusalem will be protected [19:20-34].

7. V. 35 then tells of the destruction of the Assyrian camp, and vs. 36-37 of Sancheriv's return to Ninveh and his death there.

The narrative seems structurally problematic.

Why did Chizkiahu not go to the Temple and entreat God for help [5], and why did Isaiah not deliver his detailed prophecy [6], after Ravshakeh's first speech [1]? The second message [4] seems to have added nothing to the first, other than the threat of the expected return of the Assyrian army. Both Chizkiahu's prayer [5] and Isaiah's answer [6] would have been equally appropriate after the first speech [1].

Malbim raises a question: Why, from Sancheriv's point of view, was it logical to send the second message? Surely he would have been better served if Chizkiahu had, indeed, been lulled into a sense of security by Assyria's departure, and relaxed his defenses. This would have given Sancheriv the advantage of surprise upon his return. By warning Chizkiahu, he was giving him a chance to improve his fortifications, forge new alliances, and, in general, make Sancheriv's hoped-for victory much more difficult. *Malbim* answers that Sancheriv had hopes that, in face of the threat that the respite was only to be a temporary one, Chizkiahu would prove willing to accept Assyrian terms, and capitulate.

In the context of our analysis, we suggest that another answer may be possible.

We have already noted in comm. to v. 2 that Chizkiahu may not have immediately realized the full import of the Assyrian threat. From the preparations he made for battle — in contrast to his later passivity — it is apparent that he thought that he was facing an ordinary war. We suggest that Ravshakeh's original speech did not dispel this impression. There was nothing about it which would not have been appropriate in a more ordinary confrontation. It was only after Sancheriv — against all military logic — sent the second message, that Chizkiahu realized that more was at stake. Had Sancheriv only wanted to conquer Jerusalem, no further words were called for. By hurling his second challenge he made it obvious that he was challenging God Himself.

After the first message Chizkiahu did not yet feel called upon to make special prayers in the Temple. He requested help from the prophet, as he would have done in any normal time of danger. The extraordinary intercessions on the part of both king and prophet came later, when the full dimensions of the confrontation became obvious.

If our analysis is correct, then the prophecy concerning Sancheriv's return to his land and subsequent assassination is placed in a much narrower perspective than the prophecy concerning Assyria's destruction. It is in the nature of a punishment for an unprovoked attack but has none of the cosmic Gogian implications of the ultimate holocaust.

We are now ready to appreciate the significance of having the two events bracketed into one verse in the *Chronicles'* account, in sharp contrast to *Kings* and *Isaiah* where they are given in separate verses.

We suggest that, subtly, with the hindsight of history, *Chronicles* is underlining Chizkiahu's failure, as the Sages perceive it. Whether or not the destruction of the Assyrian forces would be the Gogian holocaust or just one more miracle in the long line of Divine salvation with which Jewish history is replete lay in Chizkiahu's hands. His failure to say *shirah* relegated the destruction to the realm of the ordinary. While *Isaiah* and *Kings*, which describe the events from a contemporary standpoint consciously separate the two, *Chronicles*, by combining them in one sentence and thereby obviating any implied scaling of significance, records the disappointment of history: The moment had passed. The opportunity for Chizkiahu to reach the pinnacle had been lost. Other Gogs would arise. Redemption had been pushed into the mists of an unknown future.

◆§ Chizkiahu's Illness

The story of Chizkiahu's illness, its attendant details and its aftermath occupies nineteen verses in the *Kings'* account. To this we can add twelve verses from *Isaiah* (38:9-20), where we hear the paeans of thanks which he sang upon his recovery.

Chronicles devotes just three verses to the entire incident.

Mefaresh and *Metzudos* both remark that *Chronicles* was able to be brief because the story had already been told in the earlier books.

But, why tell the story at all, if it is known from earlier sources?

The purpose becomes clear from v. 25. We are guided to the essence, rather than to the outer contours of the story. We are not told of the pomp and ceremony with which Chizkiahu received the Babylonian ambassadors; we do not follow them into the king's treasure houses nor into the Holy of Holies where they are shown the Holy Ark, nor do we hear Isaiah's shattering words of doom. *Chronicles'* interest — lying beneath these surface events — is directed to Chizkiahu's pride which lay at the root of the debacle, and to the fact that this brought about a deep and rending change in the relationship between God and people.

Chronicles accomplishes its purpose, conveys the relative insignificance of the actual happenings when compared to their essential implications, by the short, almost staccato, treatment of four major events: the illness, the prayer, the promise and the sign — all of which are compressed into a single verse. The . . . וַיֹּאמֶר לוֹ of v. 24 is particularly striking: We are not even told what it is that God said to Chizkiahu. Let the sensitive reader supply the obvious (*Metzudos*); the details are of no concern to us. Rather, we are directed to consider the vastly significant meaning of these cataclysmic events.

To appreciate *Chronicles'* castigation of Chizkiahu in v. 25, we must pass some of the events in review.

Some three days before the destruction of the Assyrian forces [thus *Rashi*], Chizkiahu becomes deathly ill. He entreats God to remember the exemplary life which he has led. Isaiah is sent to him with the message that he is to be cured. Chizkiahu asks for a sign that he will live, and this, too, is granted: The sun moves back ten degrees, measurably lengthening the duration of the day. The Babylonian king hears of this miracle (*Rashi*), and sends ambassadors to Chizkiahu. These are received cordially and with exaggerated respect. Isaiah prophesies that one day Chizkiahu's descendants will serve as chamberlains in the Babylonian court.

Malbim notes that it is inconceivable that a sign of such public nature would be given for the sake of an individual's peace of mind. Rather, he assumes, the purpose of the sign was to assure Chizkiahu that Assyria would be miraculously annihilated. The very fact that Chizkiahu assumed that the sign was meant to apprise him personally of the course which his illness would take, and that he projected it as such to the Babylonian ambassadors, evoked censure for unjustified pride (v. 25).

But Chizkiahu's words are, *What is the sign that* HASHEM *will heal me and that I will go up to* H*ASHEM's House on the third day?* The implication is surely that the sign was to be directed to Chizkiahu himself.

Rather, in the context of what we have learned in this chapter we may suggest as follows: All this happened long after Sancheriv's second message. Chizkiahu must already have had an intimation that the upcoming confrontation with Assyria would be — at least potentially — the Gogian war, and that he had it within himself to become the Messiah. His sudden sickness would then have had connotations beyond his individual concerns; his death would have meant the end of the Messianic potential of that era.

The choice of the particular sign — that the sun should regress — seems highly significant. Nowhere is nature more immutable than in the constant and unvarying circular motions of the heavenly constellations. Small wonder that it was always the sun which was the focus of man's desire to exchange his subservience to God for the blandishments of a worship that saw physicality as the predominant reality (see *Pachad Yitzchak* to *Rosh Hashanah* 27). Sun-worship is the declaration that physical existence is eternal, without beginning and without end — excluding any possibility of a Divine Providence.

If Chizkiahu can be master over the sun, then, indeed, his is the spiritual grandeur which can represent God's kingship over the world. The sign of the regression of the sun was God's statement that the Messianic idea was alive and vested in Chizkiahu.

But as we saw in comm. to 31:1, the very essence of the Messianic kingship is his absolute recession from any personal identity, and his total fusion with his task of being no more than a conduit for the Divine stewardship of Israel. A king who has, as it were, an existence of his own, outside of the fact that he is scion of the Davidic line, is automatically disqualified from the Messianic role. This was Chizkiahu's mistake when he couched his prayer in terms of his own meritorious life, and this was the lesson which he was taught when God answered him that the help that He would send would be only for His and David's sake.

But in the end, Chizkiahu did not learn the lesson. *When Chizkiahu saw the Babylonian's ambassadors he became exceedingly proud in his heart and showed them all the treasure houses — he even opened the Ark for them and showed them the Tablets and said to them, 'With these we fight our battles and are victorious'* (*Yalkut, Bereishis*, 77).

The ambassadors had come to learn of Chizkiahu's glory. There is no doubt that, in showing them the Tablets and telling them how it was that these guaranteed victory in battle, he was placing himself into the picture: These are part of my glory, it is I in whom they find expression, and through whom their help is activated. *Yalkut* makes this clear: 'How could you,' asks God, 'have had the temerity to show them the Tablets, *the work of My hands*? How can you perceive an active and significant role for yourself? Have I not taught you that if you are to be Messiah, you must recede totally into your function? How can you, as an individual, glory in God's salvation?'

This is the catastrophic pride of which v. 25 speaks, and this event became a watershed in Jewish history. From the profound love borne of the anticipation of the Messianic experience, a fierce anger was generated against a people which could dissipate such an opportunity. The golden moment itself turned into a devastating indictment. How malignant must be the malaise which produces such a lethargy of heart and mind. So much hope frustrated, such obduracy where greatness had beckoned!

Nothing will help now but that the cancer of self-aggrandizement be excised in the bitter school of a Babylonian exile. But *Chronicles* does not explicate this. For *Chronicles*, the sorrow does not lie in the anticipated tragedy, but in the underlying anger of God.

Chapter Thirty-Three

⸎ Jerusalem and the Altar

We suggest that the idolatrous *altars* are viewed as a desecration of the true *altar* which, as we will demonstrate, is associated more with Jerusalem than with the Temple. The image, on the other hand, militated against God's Divine Presence which is a function of the Temple.

At 4:1 we quoted *Rambam* (*Bais HaBechirah* 2), who explains the extreme importance that was attached to the precise location at which the altar stood: Adam, Cain and Abel, Noach and Abraham had all sacrificed there, and it was hallowed as the spot from which Adam had been created. Thus, although halachically the altar is a part of the Temple, its unique attribute as the ideal location for sacrifice predated the Temple and is, to that extent, independent of it.[1] [See also *Rambam, Beis HaBechirah* 6:4 and *Kessef Mishneh* there. It transpires that even after the destruction of the Temple the altar can still fulfill its halachic function.[2]]

But, while the altar's halachic status is not dependent upon the Temple, it is, clearly, a function of Jerusalem. The very name, יְרוּשָׁלַיִם, is formed from words which carry associations from the sacrificial service. *Bereishis Rabbah* 56:16 teaches that the word is a combination of the terms used by Abraham on the one hand and Noach's son Shem [the Malki Tzedek of *Genesis* 14:18] on the other. After Abraham was willing to bring the supreme sacrifice of offering up his son, he gave the place at which the test had taken place a name: ה׳ יִרְאֶה, *HASHEM will see*. *Targum* renders: *Before God will all the generations perform their service* and *Rashi* explains that this refers to the sacrificial service. The

---

1. The quasi-independent status of the altar is expressed at *I Chronicles* 22:1 where, as a result of the heavenly fire which had descended upon his altar at Arnan's threshing floor (I:21:26)David realized that he had discovered the site of the Holy Temple. He said: *This is the House of HASHEM, God, and this is the altar for burnt offerings of Israel*, apparently dividing his discovery into two separate categories.

This is confirmed by *Meshech Chochmah (Sidrah R'ei)* who addresses the change in expression between *I Chronicles* 21:26 and v. 28, there. The earlier verse tells that David built an altar and *offered up* [וַיַּעַל] burnt-offerings and peace offerings. V.28 then tells that, when David realized that God had answered him by having the heavenly fire descend and consume his sacrifice, he proceeded to *slaughter* offerings [וַיִּזְבַּח] there.

The sense of these verses is to be understood as follows: Originally, before David was aware of the fact that this was to be the site of the permanent altar, he performed the entire sacrificial service — including those portions which would normally require a Kohen — in accordance with the established rule that on a private *bamah* Israelites are as qualified as Kohanim. However, as soon as he became aware that this was to be the eternal altar, he disqualified himself from any involvement other than the slaughtering of the sacrifice which can, even in the Temple, be done by anyone. He saw to it that the rest of the service was performed by Kohanim.

Thus we see that in the view of *Meshech Chochmah*, the altar assumed its formal and halachic status independently of the building of the Temple.

2. For the halachic connection between the altar and the Temple, see *Rambam, Bais HaBechirah* 1:6 and in *Sefer HaMitzvos, Positive Commands* 20. There he explains that the Torah's command to build an altar is not to be counted formally as part of the six hundred and thirteen commandments, since, together with the other utensils to be used in the Temple, it is subsumed under the general command to built a Temple.

syllable יְרוּ in יְרוּשָׁלַיִם, takes the place of יִרְאֶה [ה׳], the *vav*, with a numerical value of six, substituting for the *aleph* [one] and the *hei* [five].

Malki Tzedek is described as מֶלֶךְ שָׁלֵם, *king of Salem*, at the moment at which he came out to meet the conquering Abraham (*Genesis* 14:18). He is also the *Kohen of Almighty God*. He brings out *bread and wine* to offer the exhausted soldiers (*Rashi* there), and in so doing hints at the meal offerings and libations which Abraham's sons would one day offer up [in Salem] (*Bereishis Rabbah* 43:6, quoted in *Rashi*). The שָׁלֵם, with which his kingship is described, supplies the second half of the name יְרוּשָׁלַיִם.

Thus, we may say that the altar derives its sanctity less from the Temple than from the holy city of Jerusalem. It is the God Whose Name rests in that city Who is offended by the erection of the alien altars.

◆§ Menasheh and the Divine Presence in the Temple

To examine the differences between this phrase and its parallel in *Kings*, we contrast the two texts:

II Chronicles Ch. 33	*II Kings* Ch. 21
4. בִּירוּשָׁלַםִ יִהְיֶה־שְׁמִי לְעוֹלָם, *In Jerusalem shall My Name be forever.*	4. בִּירוּשָׁלַםִ אָשִׂים אֶת־שְׁמִי, *In Jerusalem I shall place My Name.*

We note the change from אָשִׂים, *I shall place*, to יִהְיֶה, *[My Name] shall be*, and the fact that *Kings* omits לְעוֹלָם, *forever*.

In this choice of terms, the two books follow a consistent pattern: We contrast God's response to Solomon's inaugural prayer as given in the two sources:

II Chronicles Ch. 7	*I Kings* 9
a. 16. וְהִקְדַּשְׁתִּי אֶת־הַבַּיִת הַזֶּה ..., *And now ... I have sanctified this House*	a. 3. הִקְדַּשְׁתִּי אֶת־הַבַּיִת הַזֶּה אֲשֶׁר בָּנִתָה, *I have sanctified this House which you have built*
b. לִהְיוֹת־שְׁמִי שָׁם עַד־עוֹלָם, *That My Name be there, forever*	b. לָשׂוּם־שְׁמִי שָׁם עַד־עוֹלָם, *To place My Name there, forever*

Once more we note the change from שום to היה.

To aid in understanding the different language, we should examine also the treatment accorded by the two books to Menasheh's erection of the image in the Temple (v.7):

II Chronicles Ch. 33	*II Kings* Ch. 21
a. 7. בְּבֵית הָאֱלֹהִים אֲשֶׁר אָמַר אֱלֹהִים אֶל־דָּוִיד ..., *In God's House, concerning which God had said to David ...*	a. 7. ...בַּבַּיִת אֲשֶׁר אָמַר ה׳ אֶל דָּוִד, *In the House concerning which* HASHEM *said to David...*
b. בַּבַּיִת הַזֶּה וּבִירוּשָׁלַםִ אֲשֶׁר בָּחַרְתִּי מִכֹּל שִׁבְטֵי יִשְׂרָאֵל, *In this House and in Jerusalem which I have chosen from among all the tribes of Israel*	b. בַּבַּיִת הַזֶּה וּבִירוּשָׁלַיִם אֲשֶׁר בָּחַרְתִּי מִכֹּל שִׁבְטֵי יִשְׂרָאֵל, *In this House and in Jerusalem which I have chosen from among all the tribes of Israel,*
c. אָשִׂים אֶת־שְׁמִי לְעֵילוֹם , *I shall place My Name for all eternity.*	c. אָשִׂים אֶת־שְׁמִי לְעוֹלָם, *I shall place My Name for all eternity.*

Here we have *Chronicles* using שום, as does *Kings*, but substituting the unique form of לְעֵילוֹם for the commonly used לְעוֹלָם.

We offer the following explanations.

היה [*My Name shall be . . .*] describes a Presence, but makes no reference to its source. It is intimated that the *Shechinah* resides in the Temple, but God is not perceived as directly *placing* that aura there. God *Himself* is too hidden to be apprehended. שום, [*I shall place My Name . . .*] on the other hand, involves God, as it were, directly.

When we speak of God's Presence *being* at the Temple site לְעוֹלָם, we surely mean that, even during such times as the Sanctuary lies in ruins, God's Presence remains ensconced within the sacred confines of the Temple Mount [See *Rambam*, *Bais HaBechirah* 6:16, and see discussion at 7:20].

Accordingly, the term *forever* is much more appropriate when היה is used than it is with שום. When the Temple lies in ruins, it is easier to apprehend a more nebulous aura than it is to be aware of a direct Divine Presence.

Now, at 7:20 we learned from *Meshech Chochmah*, that the uncertain vision of *Ruach HaKodesh*, with which *Chronicles* was written, has a lesser appreciation of the reality of the Divine Presence than has the prophetic assurance of the earlier books.

Accordingly, we understand well why *Chronicles* tends more to the use of, היה. It does not pretend to the more developed perception implied by שום. On the other hand, this muted perception can be said to exist *forever*, more readily than the other.[1]

We can now examine the use of the various terms, in the context of Menasheh's sins.

In a poignant vignette *Sanhedrin* 102b tells of a conversation which, in a dream, the *amora*, Rav Ashi, had with Menasheh. Aware that Menasheh had been a great Torah scholar, Rav Ashi taxes him with his idol worship. How could a man of his stature have erred so badly?

Menasheh answers that Rav Ashi, who lived in a period in which idol worship had long lost its attraction, could have no inkling of the fatal fascination which it exerted at the time. Had Rav Ashi lived then, he would have lifted up his clothes so that they should not impede him in his headlong rush to savor those same idols, the worship of which he now decried.

What is the meaning of the idea of lifting up the clothes in order to better run to the service of the idols?

Maharal explains: There are people of an exalted spiritual stature who, nevertheless, can occasionally — for a variety of reasons — be subject to an uncontrollable urge to sin. Again, there are those of a lowly nature to whom sin is a way of life. The difference between the two can be seen when an obstacle gets in the way, and an intended transgression cannot be committed. The great man will be happy — he does not want to sin, but fell victim to an unnatural desire which, temporarily, beat down his defenses. If something prevents him from acting in a way entirely out of character for his spiritual standing, he will rejoice. The second man, on the other hand, will be annoyed at the obstacle. He wishes to live with his passions and resents a frustration of his intentions.

Menasheh tells Rav Ashi that this is the difference between the two of them. Menasheh was a man of exalted spiritual standing. Nothing would have pleased him more than that his clothes would have tripped him up on the way to the idol worship. Essentially the concept was abhorrent to him. Had Rav Ashi lived then, he — by

---

1. At *I Kings* 9, שום is combined with לְעוֹלָם, because there God expresses, as it were, a hope. Ideally, even the larger perception would last beyond the physical reality of stones and mortar.

contrast — would have relished the opportunity to commit the idolatrous abominations. He would have raised his clothes to make sure that nothing would stop him.

We have, then, a picture of Menasheh, as a man knowing full well that his ways were terribly wrong, but unable to control his burning passion for the comfort he derived from the idols whose indulgence he craved.

In the context of our discussion we would describe his situation in the following terms: Menasheh craved spiritual support, but, through a life of wickedness, could not find it in the reality of God's Presence in the Temple. He intuited the reality of God's Presence — that the *Shechinah* can be felt in the precincts of the Holy Temple even when God seems furthest away [יִהְיֶה־שְּׁמִי לְעוֹלָם . . ., the *Chronicles'* version]. In his depravity, however, he had lost touch with the awareness of God's *direct* stewardship, the knowledge or feeling that not only an aura of Godliness, but an actual Presence of God [אָשִׂים אֶת־שְׁמִי, the *Kings'* version] animates the Temple. This truth eluded him. And so, in his desperation for direct contact with something higher and more powerful than he, he turned to idol worship. He felt himself drawn inexorably into its beguiling embrace, knowing all the while that more and more he was losing contact with the true source of life — and suffering in that realization.

Between them, the *Chronicles'* and *Kings'* versions provide the background against which we need to understand Menasheh's idol worship

Not so in the case of the פֶּסֶל, the *image*, which is described in v. 7. There is no record of Menasheh's serving this image or sacrificing to it, and thus it cannot be construed as being an understandable, if illicit, outlet for his need to subjugate himself to some power which he could, at least, grasp and understand. It was erected to make a statement: God has no place here; the image is to replace Him! Admittedly, Menasheh did not, as Amon would later do, wish to drive God out of the Temple. As we shall learn at v.7, he erected it in the Sanctuary, not in the Holy of Holies. But he did want to relegate Him to the Holy of Holies: There was a place in his religious philosophy for an inscrutable mysterious and inaccessible Being — but he was determined that that Being not intrude upon his affairs. As Amon would one day wish to drive God out of the Temple entirely (*Sanhedrin* 103b), so Menasheh would attempt to banish Him from those parts of the Temple in which human contact with the Divine is symbolized.

There was rebellion here, a pitting of man against God or, at least against an immanent God — One Who could properly be regarded as God of Israel. Menasheh, here, was fighting a Presence which he understood — but was determined to shunt aside.

In this context, *Chronicles* too uses אָשִׂים — it gives the story its entire focus — but compensates by substituting לְעֵילוֹם, with its connotation of *something hidden* [see comm.], for לְעוֹלָם. It is not for *Chronicles* — imbued with *Ruach HaKodesh* but denied prophecy — to state unequivocally that the, אָשִׂים state is indeed also one of, לְעוֹלָם.

◆§ Menasheh and Isaiah

The Sages are troubled by the seeming hyperbole of the description of Menasheh's bloodshed. Is it really possible that there could have been enough victims to fill Jerusalem with blood from gate to gate? They therefore read the verse to mean something quite different: Menasheh put the venerable prophet Isaiah to death and since *the soul of a righteous man is as significant as an entire world*, this murder is described as filling Jerusalem with blood (*Sanhedrin* 103b).

Reference to Isaiah's death at Menasheh's hands appears throughout aggadic literature and should be briefly analyzed.

Menasheh evidently did not launch a vendetta against prophecy or prophets as such. Nowhere is there a hint that he, in any way, wished to harm Joel, Nahum or Chabakkuk who were also contemporary with him.

Why, then, kill Isaiah?

Significantly, the Sages have a tradition that this was no random killing. Menasheh brought Isaiah to judgment because of what the king claimed to be heretical passages in some of his prophecies. Isaiah could readily have defended himself against these charges, but preferred to allow Menasheh to delude himself into thinking that he was no wanton murderer (*Yevamos* 49b).

This means that Menasheh felt threatened by certain passages in Isaiah's prophecy.

A brief analysis of the points raised by Menasheh may indicate the direction which his thinking took, and yield a clearer understanding of the ambivalence which seems to have plagued this complex and tragic man.

As the Talmud tells it, three points troubled Menasheh:(a) The Torah teaches man's inability to perceive God and live (*Exodus* 33:20), while Isaiah plainly claims to have *seen* God (*Isaiah* 6:1); (b) the Torah describes God as being accessible to man's prayer at any time (*Deuteronomy* 4:7), while Isaiah exhorts Israel to seek out God ... *when He is accessible* (*Isaiah* 55:6); (c) the Torah talks of man being born with a fixed number of years (*Exodus* 23:26), while Isaiah added fifteen years to Chizkiahu's life (*II Kings* 20:6).

Needless to say, there are answers to each of these problems, and these the Talmud supplies: For (a): The Torah excludes the possibility of perceiving God, only with the clarity of vision which Moses had attained. *Sight* of God, at a lesser degree of clarity — that attained by Isaiah — is not precluded. For (b): The Torah's assertion that God is accessible at all times, holds true for a communal approach to Him. When Isaiah talks of particularly auspicious times, this refers to an individual. For (c): The relevant passage in the Torah is to be interpreted differently. There is never an implication of a predetermined number of days.

What troubled Menasheh?

It seems that he felt willing to deal with a remote God, invisible to any eye but that of Moses, Whose interest lies only with the community of Israel, but for Whom the individual, cast into the world upon a predetermined road, does not exist.

Such a view of world and man has room for the idol worship which Menasheh craved. The natural forces, before whom he cringed, would mediate for him with a Creator for Whom he, as a person, had no relevance.

Isaiah made such a world view impossible. He spoke of an immanent, caring God; One Who allows Himself to be apprehended in a meaningful manner, Who cares for every individual and accepts his prayers; Whose relationship with that individual is not severed at birth, but continues throughout life ever ready to play a caring, nurturing role.

Isaiah had to be killed. The threatening truths which he had revealed must be delegitimized. Menasheh does not hesitate to bring the venerable prophet before a bar of justice which, at least for Menasheh's peace of mind, could be construed as legitimate. He has him condemned to death in the vain hope that his hateful teachings would disappear with him.

◆§ Menasheh and the Sacrificial Service

What are we to make of the two versions, the *k'ri* and the *k'siv*, of v. 16?

The existence of a *k'siv* version forces us to examine the *k'ri* with particular care. Why read something other than is written? Apparently וַיִּבֶן has significance beyond its simple meaning.

This impression is reinforced by the remarkable fact that nothing had been said previously of the tearing down of the altar which would have explained the necessity of rebuilding it. The reforms listed in v. 15 are a natural outgrowth of what had been said before. We had learned of the image and the idolatrous altars, and expect to hear that, in the zeal of his penitence, Menasheh got rid of those. But why tell us that he built up an altar of the destruction of which we know nothing at all?

Our verse is apparently the source of a cryptic tradition preserved by the Sages (*Sanhedrin* 103a): Achaz discontinued the Divine Service [בִּטֵּל אֶת הָעֲבוֹדָה]; Menasheh destroyed the altar [הָרַס אֶת הַמִּזְבֵּחַ]; Amon allowed cobwebs to gather upon the altar [הֶעֱלָה שְׁמָמִית עַל גַּבֵּי הַמִּזְבֵּחַ]. Evidently the Sages gathered that Menasheh destroyed the altar from the fact that, as our verse teaches, it was necessary for him to build it up once more.

But, there is a structural problem in this tradition. Since, evidently in line with the Talmud's account of other depredations practiced by these three kings, this progression is meant to describe an escalation of evil from Achaz through Menasheh to Amon, we would expect Amon's perfidy to be greater than that of Menasheh. But why is allowing the altar to be covered by cobwebs from disuse, worse than destroying the entire altar (*Margalios HaYam*)?

There is another tradition preserved by the Sages which may help shed light on the difficulties which we have raised: The fire which descended from heaven in Solomon's days did not leave [the altar] until Menasheh removed it (*Zevachim* 61b). The source for this tradition is adduced by *Rashi* (*II Kings* 16:14) to the fact that Menasheh is said to have destroyed the altar — hence evidently removing the fire. Again, there is no source, beside our verse which tells that he rebuilt it, which teaches that Menasheh had destroyed the altar.

We suggest that the term הָרַס, used in *Sanhedrin* to say that Menasheh destroyed the altar, does not refer to a literal destruction but to the eradication of the heavenly fire.[1]

The removal of the fire would certainly confound the purpose of the altar, and be counted an act of destruction.

We permit ourselves this metaphorical interpretation because of two considerations: Firstly, it allows for a logical progression, through Menasheh, from Achaz's perfidy to that of Amon: and, secondly, because we feel this to be implied by the *k'ri-k'siv* of our verse. The re*building* of the altar [*k'ri*] was not an actual building — it was only a re-*establishing* [*k'siv*] of its character. By causing the heavenly fire to depart, Menasheh did not destroy the altar physically, but denuded it of its essence. It is called a *rebuilding* only in an essential but not in a physical sense.

We shall now examine the progressive evil of the three kings:

As we have seen, Achaz בִּטֵּל אֶת הָעֲבוֹדָה, *discontinued the Divine Service*. The term הָעֲבוֹדָה, with its use of the definite article, seems to describe a specific, known, service. Had we had a phrase such as בִּטֵּל עֲבוֹדַת הַמִּזְבֵּחַ, the implication would have been that no sacrifices at all were brought. As it is, we can well interpret the phrase as referring to the public Temple service, such as the sacrificing of the תְּמִידִים, *the daily burnt-offerings,* and the מוּסָפִים, *the additional* sacrifices brought on special days. Individuals may well

---

1. The use of הרס in a non-physical sense is well established: Thus, for example, הָרַס עֵצָה, *to confound a plan* (*Midrash Tehillim* 9 to v. 7).

have continued to sacrifice.[1]

What then was Menasheh's contribution to the downward spiral?

The answer may well lie in what we must conclude to have been Menasheh's attitude to the Divine Service. At v. 7 we saw him introducing the image into the Sanctuary — but not, as Amon was later to do — into the Holy of Holies. Thus, God was not, as it were, driven out of His Temple — just forced to share it with another deity — see comm. there.[2]

Maharal (*Gevuros* 69) explains the Torah view of the sacrificial service. It is to testify to God's uniqueness. By offering up a sacrifice we testify that, really, nothing at all has any right to exist outside the orbit of His sanctity. In truth, all that we are, all that we have, should be subjected to the consuming flame of His holiness. Since this is impossible, we symbolize this truth by means of the sacrifices which we bring.

Once a duality had been established within the Temple, the sacrificial service became bereft of all Jewish meaning. It is entirely possible — and may indeed well have been the case — that even during the worst times of Menasheh's wickedness, the altar was still used to bring sacrifices to God. But these sacrifices were not what the Torah had had in mind. They degraded Divine Service to the level of a superstition — acts of appeasement such as were common in all the debased idolatrous cults. As such they were utterly foreign to the pure and lofty Torah ideals which assume a unique, all-powerful and all-giving God, Who permits His people to approach Him by means of the sacrificial service, but Who remains untouched by it.

When such a state had been reached the heavenly fire departed from the altar. How could it remain to testify to the empty lie which the sacrificial service had become? The altar was effectively — if not physically — destroyed.

But, if the altar was still in use during Menasheh's reign, this stopped with Amon's ascent to power. As we shall see below, Amon moved the image from the outer chamber in which Menasheh had erected it, into the Holy of Holies. He, as *Sanhedrin* 103b teaches and as we shall see below, actually *drove* God out of His Temple. There was no more the Divine Presence and no more purpose for even the outer trappings of the sacrificial service on the Divine altar. It fell into total disuse, and thus, Amon brought *cobwebs up upon the altar*.

◆§ Amon Plunges to New Depths of Evil

How are we to understand the heinous crimes which Amon is said to have committed? What are the implications, the meaning, of burning the Torah? Of violating one's mother?

We have already noted that the Sages, at *Sanhedrin* 103a, see a progression of evil from Achaz to Menasheh to Amon. This progression is delineated in three areas: Their

---

1. *He closed the doors of the House of* HASHEM (28:24) may mean that he closed the main gates through which the crowds would have thronged. There is no indication that individuals were unable to gain access.

2. In *Pesichta* to *Eichah Rabbah*, the matriarch Rachel is depicted as pouring out her prayers to God to have mercy upon His exiled children. She argues that if she, in her frail humanness, had been willing to bring a צָרָה, a *co-wife* into, her own house — which she did when she revealed the secret signs, which Jacob had given her, to Leah so that the latter would not be discovered and shamed — then God in His infinite grandeur should find it in Himself to forgive the bringing of a צָרָה [apparently Menasheh's image] into His house.

Clearly, it was Menasheh's purpose to establish a dual presence within the Temple confines.

respective relationships to the sacrificial service, to the Torah and to forbidden marriages are traced.

☐ **Achaz**

1. Eliminates the Temple service.
2. Seals the Torah.
3. Permits forbidden marriages.

☐ **Menasheh**

1. Destroys the altar.
2. Clips out the Divine Names.
3. Violates his sister.

☐ **Amon**

1. Brings cobwebs upon the altar.
2. Burns the Torah.
3. Violates his mother.

We have discussed the progression concerning the sacrificial service above, *Menasheh and the Sacrificial Service*.

In connection with the other two categories our concern should be with Menasheh and Amon. Achaz's approach in both cases was general in nature. He *sealed* the Torah by disrupting the educational system (Section II to ch.28 *Achaz and Menasheh*), and *permitted* incestuous marriages — that is, he saw no evil in such unions (*Rashi*, to *Sanhedrin*).

But what is the significance of *clipping out the Divine Names* in relation to burning the Torah, and what is the progression between violating one's sister and one's mother?

We believe that all are of one piece with the ideas expressed in the matter of the sacrificial service as explained above.

In the case of their vendetta against the Torah, it is simple enough to trace a parallel. Menasheh removed the Divine fire from the altar thereby *destroying* it, and clipped the Divine Names out of the Torah — thereby secularizing it. We have seen that Menasheh did not object to a God relegated to the Holy of Holies — he wanted another deity, a צָרָה, to co-exist with Him. The Torah which, in every sentence, documents God's intense involvement in the affairs of man, needed to be changed. [We postulate that Menasheh *clipped* selectively. It seems likely that he would have retained a Torah which would picture a remote God — one fittingly ensconced in the Holy of Holies. Witness his court case against Isaiah for allegedly contradicting the Torah where, in Menasheh's view, it depicted a God Whose existence his religious philosophy could accommodate.]

Amon, who *allowed cobwebs to form on the altar* because he had driven God out of the Temple completely, had no use for any Torah and therefore, burned it.

The matter of the forbidden marriages is more complex but can, we feel, be explained in the same manner.

We will first examine Amon's violation of his mother. As *Sanhedrin* 103b teaches, she asked him, 'Can you have any pleasure from the source from which you issued?' Upon this, he answered, 'I [am not doing this for pleasure, I] have no purpose other than to anger [God with my action].

Why can there be no pleasure from *the source from which you issued* and why was this form of depredation an ideal way to anger God?

The Torah uses the same expression, בעל, both for the conjugal act (*Genesis* 20:3) and for expressing mastery over land or other property (*Isaiah* 62:4), freely interchanging the two concepts (cf. *Isaiah* 62:5). It is clear, then, that it views the mastery which the man exercises over his conjugal partner (see *Isaiah* 54:5 and *Sanhedrin* 22b) as crucial to the act. That sense of mastery must, in normal circumstances, be totally absent where the partner is one's mother. There is no more graphic illustration of one's essential dependence than *the source from which you issued*. Such an act would be deprived of a crucial factor in generating pleasure.

It would, however, be an appropriate act for one who refuses to make peace with the reality of his dependence upon another and craves a means of self-assertion that would, in a warped sense, provide him with the ultimate victory: He overpowers the very source of his existence, thus, forcibly denying the truth which he is not willing to acknowledge.

Thus, the violation of his mother becomes the precise parallel of the act of driving God out of the Temple. Amon *angers* God by asserting mastery over that which, by its very nature rejects such mastery. He asserts his total independence of God in the most graphic manner possible. It is the ultimate act of פְּרִיקַת עוֹל, *the throwing off of the yoke of heaven*.

Not so Menasheh. Just as he stopped short of bringing the image into the Holy of Holies, so too did he not violate his mother.

His transgression was to violate his sister. What does the Torah tell us about the fraternal relationship?

It is one of mutual responsibility.

When the Torah speaks of a brother having forbidden conjugal relations with his sister, it labels the act with the word, חֶסֶד (*Leviticus* 20:17). *Ramban* explains that the term describes the offending brother. His obligation towards his sister is one of brotherly caring. It is his duty to assume responsibility that she settle into a suitable marriage. His act is a gross violation of his duties.

But, these responsibilities seem to be reciprocal. *Open to me, my sister,* cries the dew-covered and rain-drenched lover of *Shir HaShirim* 5:2. A brother has the right to expect his sister to open her doors to him when he stands in need.

It is, perhaps in this sense that *Shemos Rabbah* 52:4 tells of an ecstasy of love in which God calls Israel not only His daughter but also His sister — and bases it upon the very verse of *Shir HaShirim,* which we have quoted. God offers us His protective love but expects that in return we open our world to Him. As the lover in *Shir HaShirim* so He too wishes to enter Israel's abode — wishes to dwell among men.

And Menasheh banished Him! Relegated Him, as it were, to the Holy of Holies, to a mysterium beyond the ken of man.

Menasheh displayed his total disdain for the responsibilities generated by the fraternal relationship by violating his sister.

◆§ Amon the Renegade — Yoshiahu the Man of Destiny

Our passage is notable for the omission of seemingly significant material from the *Kings'* account, and also for a change in language. We present the two accounts together (see table opposite page).

Vs. 25 and 26 from the *Kings'* account thus have no parallel in *Chronicles*. This omission is striking, not only because of the contrast it forms with *Kings*, but also because the formula appears with almost every other king, and its absence here calls for an explanation.

We begin by noting that although the *Kings'* account has the formula, there, too, there is an irregularity. In almost every case where the וְיֶתֶר formula is used, it precedes the

II Chronicles Ch. 33	*II Kings Ch. 21*
a. 24. וַיִּקְשְׁרוּ עָלָיו עֲבָדָיו, *His servants conspired against him*	a. 23. וַיִּקְשְׁרוּ עַבְדֵי־אָמוֹן עָלָיו, *Now the servants of Amon conspired against him*
b. וַיְמִיתֻהוּ בְּבֵיתוֹ, *and killed him in his house.*	b. וַיָּמִיתוּ אֶת־הַמֶּלֶךְ בְּבֵיתוֹ, *and killed the king in his house.*
c. 25. וַיַּכּוּ עַם־הָאָרֶץ, *But the people of the land slew*	c. 24. וַיַּךְ עַם־הָאָרֶץ, *The people of the land smote . . .*
d. . . . וַיַּמְלִיכוּ, *and made . . . king.*	d. וַיַּמְלִיכוּ עַם־הָאָרֶץ, *and the people of the land crowned . . .*
e.	e. 25. וְיֶתֶר דִּבְרֵי אָמוֹן אֲשֶׁר עָשָׂה, *The rest of the matters of Amon which he did*
f.	f. הֲלֹא־הֵם כְּתוּבִים, *are recorded . . .*
g.	g. 26. וַיִּקְבֹּר אֹתוֹ בִּקְבֻרָתוֹ בְּגַן־עֻזָּא, *He [they] buried him in his grave in the garden of Uzza*
h.	h. וַיִּמְלֹךְ יֹאשִׁיָּהוּ בְנוֹ תַּחְתָּיו, *and Yoshiahu his son reigned in his stead.*

statement that the king died. Here we have the statement that Amon died in v. 23 and the וְיֶתֶר formula does not appear till v. 25.

This latter appears to be common usage when the king in question dies a violent death, or where an equivalently tragic end is recounted. Thus the same order is used in the stories of Yoash (24:25-27) [assassination]; Yoshiahu (35:24-27) [death in battle]; and Yehoyakim (36:6-8) [exile]. [See comm. to 24:26]

The solution, then, is self-evident. The וְיֶתֶר formula is used when there is nothing more of significance to tell about the reign. That the king died is not in and of itself important and therefore follows after וְיֶתֶר. However, in a case in which the way that death occurred is itself part of the story of the king, it is entirely logical that it should precede the formula.

We have now demonstrated that vs. 23 and 24 of *Kings* are not meant to tell the fact of the death but to tell the circumstances. The information which normally follows the וְיֶתֶר formula is supplied in v. 26, which does not need to report the fact of the death and so limits itself to the details of the burial. Seen thus, v. 26 is the parallel of every other verse which tells about the death of a given king and therefore, *. . . and his son Yoshiahu reigned after him* is not redundant, although we already learned in v. 24 that he had been proclaimed king. It is the normal formula followed in describing every succession.

If, then, our analysis of the *Kings* passage is correct, then we can formulate the *Chronicles'* omission as follows: *Chronicles* tells those parts of the story which are significant in the Amon saga but omits those verses which in the *Kings'* account serve the function of placing the Amon saga, his death and Yoshiahu's succesion in a category similar to that of all the other Judaean kings.

Chronicles, then, in contrast to *Kings* (h), does not view Yoshiahu's as an orderly succession to the throne, but sees him as becoming king only as a result of the popular proclamation of the *people of the land* (d).

What is the difference in implication between the plural . . . וַיַּמְלִיכוּ (d), and the singular וַיִּקְבֹּר (g) of the *Kings'* account, and why does *Chronicles* (d) choose to use the plural?

We should examine the popular proclamation of the עַם־הָאָרֶץ more closely.

It seems highly significant that it is the very same עַם הָאָרֶץ who killed the plotters (b) who also crowned Yoshiahu king (c). Indeed, it is significant that the crowning of Yoshiahu seems somehow more connected with the killing of the plotters (c, d) than with the assassination of Amon [a,b]. Surely the succession to the throne is a function of the death of the king rather than of the punishing of his assassins?

The conclusion is inescapable: The servants who assassinated Amon had not intended that Yoshiahu should succeed him. It was only by eliminating them that the עַם־הָאָרֶץ assured that Amon's own son should become king.

Who then were these servants who killed Amon (a)? What was their motive for committing regicide and whom had they wished to install as king in place of the slain Amon?

Who were the עַם־הָאָרֶץ? What was their quarrel with the servants? How does Yoshiahu's succession tie in with this quarrel?

We may be helped in determining the answers to some of these questions by noting a textual oddity in *Kings*. Within v. 24, the עַם־הָאָרֶץ are first treated in the singular (c), and then in the plural (d). Then at (g), where the subject can only be these same עַם־הָאָרֶץ, the singular is once more used.

V. 25 in *Chronicles* treats the עַם הָאָרֶץ consistently in the plural — . . . וַיַּמְלִיכוּ . . . וַיַּכּוּ (c, d).

We postulate that the use of the singular when describing a group of people points to a unanimity and singleness of purpose — they acted as one man (see *Rashi*, *Exodus* 19:2); the plural, on the other hand, indicates a multiplicity of ideas and motivations. We may thus conclude that, in the *Kings'* view, there was unanimity among the עַם־הָאָרֶץ that the assassins should be punished (c) and that Amon should be buried (g), but that in the matter of Yoshiahu's succession there was, at the very least, a diversity of motivation.

The unanimity concerning the punishing of the assassins and the burial of Amon point to the likelihood that loyalty to the kingly house was at issue. We may hypothesize that the servants of Amon were of his ilk — vicious, unscrupulous — and that the attempt to kill the king derived from some court intrigue of which we cannot, nor do we need to, know the cause. Whatever the issues, these servants were willing to institute an entirely new kingly line and it was this that drew the wrath of the עַם־הָאָרֶץ upon them. These would not countenance the replacement of the Davidic line of kingship, and whatever their own view of Amon as king — and we shall see that there may well have been some ambivalence — they recognized the legitimacy of his kingship and determined to punish his assassins and to accord him a fitting burial.

While in their loyalty they were all like-minded, they could well have differed in their motives for choosing Yoshiahu as king. As we shall see in the following chapter, there was much religious ambivalence in that generation. There were those who readily acceded to Yoshiahu's reforms — and were presumably always religiously inclined — and there were those who even after Yoshiahu's efforts at re-educating his people, continued to frustrate his intentions and refused to be weaned away from idol worship.

Thus we can readily believe that two entirely different motives may have animated the עַם־הָאָרֶץ when they determined that Yoshiahu should be the successor to the throne. Some may have assumed that a child of his tender years would surely continue in the ways of his father's house and permit the continued licentiousness which they craved, while others may have intuited that which was eventually to come about — that in Yoshiahu they would find the great reformer who would be able to turn back the nation from the destructive course upon which it was bent.

This, then, is the *Kings'* account. The עַם־הָאָרֶץ proclaimed Yoshiahu king as soon as they had killed the assassins (c, d) and this guaranteed the orderly transfer of kingship from father to son (h) precisely as in all the other successions described in the book.

What of the *Chronicles'* account?

We postulate that here as in so many other instances, *Chronicles'* perspective is that which views the event not within the context of the here and now, but from its place in the story of Israel's eternity. What, in the long range, is Amon's place in history and what Yoshiahu's?

Looking first at Yoshiahu, it is obvious that the Sages see him as occupying a seminal position in the story of the monarchy in particular, and in Israel's Messianic destiny in general.

At 35:25 we learn how bitterly the prophet Jeremiah bemoaned Yoshiahu's untimely death at the Pharaoh's hands and the elegy which he composed on that occasion. In the tradition of the Sages, that elegy is the fourth chapter in *Megillas Eichah*. Two verses in particular should claim our attention. We quote vs. 20 and 21.

> רוּחַ אַפֵּינוּ מְשִׁיחַ ה׳ נִלְכַּד בִּשְׁחִיתוֹתָם אֲשֶׁר אָמַרְנוּ בְּצִלּוֹ נִחְיֶה בַגּוֹיִם. שִׂישִׂי וְשִׂמְחִי בַּת אֱדוֹם . . . גַּם־עָלַיִךְ תַּעֲבָר־כּוֹס תִּשְׁכְּרִי וְתִתְעָרִי
>
> *The breath of our nostrils, HASHEM's anointed, was caught in their traps; He, under whose protection we had thought we would live among the nations.*
>
> *Rejoice and exult, O daughter of Edom . . ., to you too, will the cup pass; you will be drunk and will vomit.*

Yoshiahu, then, is God's anointed one — His מָשִׁיחַ — but nowhere do we find him being physically anointed. Clearly, the meaning is that he is a man of Divine destiny (see *Isaiah* 45:1) — he who is *the breath of Israel's nostrils* — the very essence of its national hope and destiny, its very survival and breath of life.

But why is *Edom* mentioned in v. 21? Edom, the implacable enemy of Israel which destroyed the second Temple, but whose place on the world stage of history lay centuries in the future at the time of Yoshiahu's death?

Midrash Chaseiros ViYeseiros (p. 294) notes that of three times that וַיְקוֹנֵן, *and he bemoaned*, is used in Scripture, two are defective [the word is spelled without the *vav* — וַיְקֹנֵן] and only the one which tells of Jeremiah's elegy over Yoshiahu is written full. The explanation given is that in the other cases the mourning was not complete — שֶׁהָיָה אַחֲרֵיהֶן יְשׁוּעָה, the tragedies led to ultimate salvation. But not in the case of Yoshiahu: *This teaches us that from the moment that Yoshiahu was killed, Israel's final strength was broken* [נִגְדְעָה קַרְנָן שֶׁל שׂוֹנְאֵי יִשְׂרָאֵל]. *Then did Jeremiah sing his elegy, 'The breath of our nostrils, HASHEM's anointed.*

Yoshiahu, then, was the man in whom Israel's destiny was vested. He was the one last hope that, ... *under his protection* [בְּצִלּוֹ, *in his shade*] ...*we would live among the nations*. He was, in short, a true scion of the Davidic line who could have carried his people through to their Messianic destiny. With his failure and death, the long and tragic exile-experience of Israel was guaranteed. *Edom rejoiced and exulted*.

Why did God's providence bring Yoshiahu upon the stage of history at this particular moment?

The answer must lie in a correct appreciation of Amon's depredations. As we saw in comm. to v.7, Menasheh had stopped short of introducing the image into the Holy of Holies thereby affirming the continuing validity and viability of the concept of the Davidic kingship. Amon, by bringing it into the Holy of Holies, demonstrated his disdain for that concept. In determining to drive God completely from His Temple, Amon denied not only Him, but also himself as a link in the chain of eternity that spans the generations between David and the Messiah. Amon banished Israel's very soul, and left an empty and meaningless shell.

This is the sub-surface meaning of the servants' intention of replacing the Davidic line with another king. Their overt action of rebellion — motivated by whatever insignificant considerations they may have had in mind — was only the outer manifestation of the inner erosion of the viability of מַלְכוּת בֵּית דָּוִד. Amon had repudiated his Davidic nature — he would be replaced by a non-Davidic king.

In this context the action of the עַם־הָאָרֶץ is lifted from the narrower confines of loyalty to an individual king, to the deeper and broader historical landmark of the people of Israel opting for their essence — a reaffirmation of their Messianic future, a determination to make their way through history with David at their head. Thus did Yoshiahu become the man of destiny — מְשִׁיחַ ה׳, the focus of Israel's hope and trust in its future, בְּצִלּוֹ נִחְיֶה בַגּוֹיִם.

At this level of consciousness we can well understand why *Chronicles* uses the plural form וַיַּכּוּ where *Kings* had used וַיַּךְ. Even if at the superficial level of loyalty to an individual king it is possible to assume a degree of single-mindedness to justify the use of the singular, surely at the much more profound and essential level of affinity to Messianism there must be as many levels and nuances as there are people.

We are now ready to understand why *Chronicles* left out the . . . וְיֶתֶר formula.

Chronicles tells the story of the מַלְכוּת בֵּית דָּוִד. A king who repudiates that very concept is an aberration and is not given the formal status of king in its scheme. The story of Amon's death, the assassination and the reaction of the עַם־הָאָרֶץ, the people who opted for their historical destiny, is indeed germane to the story which *Chronicles* has to tell. But, the formula which would have placed this renegade king into the regular line of succession has no place in this story.

Chapter Thirty-Four

◆§ Yoshiahu's Reign in the Eyes of *Kings* and *Chronicles*

We have noted that our v. 2 is virtually identical with its parallel in *Kings*. Nevertheless, a careful analysis of how the two books treat the story of Yoshiahu yields an entirely different focus of interest. Accordingly, we assume that each book had its own understanding of the phrase *He did that which was right ...*

What do the two books say of Yoshiahu's kingly activities?

Let us look at the two accounts:

II Chronicles Ch. 34	*II Kings* Ch. 22
1. 34:2: Yoshiahu is a righteous king.	1. 22:2: Yoshiahu is a righteous king.
2. 3(a): At age sixteen he begins to search out God.	2.
3. 3(b)-7: Cleansing the land from idol worship.	3.
4. 8-28: Temple repairs; the *Sefer Torah*; Chuldah's prophecy.	4. 4-20: Temple repairs; the *Sefer Torah*; Chuldah's prophecy.
5. 29-32: The covenant.	5. 23:1-3: The covenant.
6. 33: Abominations are removed and people forced to serve God.	6. 4-20: Cleansing land and Temple from idol worship.
7. 35:1-2: Preparations for the *Pesach*.	7. 21-23: The *Pesach*.
8. 3: The Ark is hidden.	8.
9. 4-19: The Pesach.	9.
10.	10. 24: Magic rites are eliminated.
11.	11. 25-28: In spite of Yoshiahu's righteousness the destruction will come.
12. 20-27: Yoshiahu's death and Jeremiah's and the people's mourning.	12. 29-30: Yoshiahu's death at the hands of Pharaoh.

Three major events take up the lion's share of the two accounts: the finding of the *Sefer Torah* and its attendant details; the cleansing of the land from all vestiges of idol worship; and the *Pesach*.

Of these, the first [4] is treated in essentially the same way in both accounts, the other two are not.

We note the following differences: The cleansing of the land in *Kings* is described in 17 verses [6] after the story of the *Sefer Torah* [4] and the covenant [5], while in *Chronicles* it takes up only 4 1/2 verses [3], and this before the story of the *Sefer Torah* [4].

In the story of the *Pesach* the proportions are reversed. In the *Kings'* description it takes up just three verses [7], while in *Chronicles* there is a total of eighteen verses when we combine numbers [7] and [9]. In addition, the *Chronicles'* account interrupts the story of the *Pesach* with the information that Yoshiahu had the Ark concealed [8].

From the relative and respective length with which the two subjects are treated, we would seem to be justified in concluding that in the *Kings'* account the cleansing of the land is the more important event, while in the *Chronicles'* account the *Pesach* is more significant.

But why would this be so?

What of the positioning? Why does the cleansing of the land precede the finding of the *Sefer Torah* in *Chronicles*, but follow it in *Kings*?

Malbim's solution is that Yoshiahu began the cleansing process earlier in the reign, but completed it after the finding of the *Sefer Torah*. Thus, both accounts are true. It is possible to locate the process before the incident of the *Sefer Torah* because that is when it began [*Chronicles*], and it is equally legitimate to tell of it later, because that is when it ended [*Kings*]. But *Malbim* does not explain why the one book chose the one system and the other treated the events differently.

The impression is that the two books wish to project different results from the finding of the *Sefer Torah* and the subsequent establishment of the covenant. In the *Kings* perspective the *Pesach* was just one *mitzvah* among the many which Yoshiahu and the people no doubt kept: The important result of the religious initiative was the final cleansing of the land from the idols which had previously defiled it. It is told after the finding of the *Sefer Torah*, because it is projected as the most important outcome from that event.

Chronicles, on the other hand, for reasons which we shall see below, sees the *Pesach* as the significant result of the covenant. For this reason it relegates the account of the cleansing of the land to an earlier part of the narrative (as *Malbim* above), thereby leaving the full impact of the covenant for the bringing of the *Pesach*.

What is the significance of this?

In prefatory remarks to ch. 30, we recognized the function of the *Pesach* offering: It stands for a dedication or rededication to God's service — a repudiation of idol worship in all its forms. We noted there that it was for that reason that particularly Chizkiahu, who ruled after Achaz, and Yoshiahu who followed upon Menasheh and Amon, saw the *Pesach* as so central to their reigns: They were called upon to eradicate the mistakes of the past and to set the people once more upon the road to God's service.

But while Yoshiahu had much in common with Chizkiahu, there was a factor which placed him into a radically different historical context. Menasheh's catastrophic reign had left its indelible mark upon the people and the die had been cast that the Temple would be destroyed and the people exiled from the land. If Yoshiahu had ever harbored a hope that he would be able to stem the tide and reverse the inexorable path, he learned otherwise when the *Sefer Torah* was found, and when Chuldah confirmed the inevitable.

Suddenly history had placed a new and unexpected burden upon the shoulders of Yoshiahu, the man of destiny. If indeed, as Chuldah was to tell him, he personally was to escape the final horrors of the disintegrating commonwealth, if he was not to witness the exile — then why had its inevitability been revealed to him? Why had he been shown the dreadful passage in the *Sefer Torah*?

Surely there was only one answer: He was the one whom God had chosen to ready the people for the trauma of exile. He was to teach them how to serve God and dedicate oneself to Him when the Temple, the tangible manifestation of the reality of His Presence, would only be a memory.

The rededication implicit in Yoshiahu's *Pesach* celebration must be understood as being preparatory to the exile experience. The hiding of the Holy Ark is an integral part of this process.

Why?

Because in a real sense, with the removal of the Ark, the Temple became downgraded to the level of a *bamah*. [For details, see comm. to 1:3]. For practical purposes, once the Ark was no longer there, the Temple had lost much of its original meaning. The act of removing it defines the dynamics and thrust of Yoshiahu's *Pesach* celebration.[1]

We now have a perspective upon the celebration of Yoshiahu's *Pesach* as contrasted with that of Chizkiahu. Both, indeed, were rededications, but where Chizkiahu's was a re-establishment of the correct stance of an Israel serving its God within the optimum conditions of independent life in its own country and centered in its own Temple, Yoshiahu's was to ready the people for an exile state.

It is clear that in the long view of history, this educational task which Yoshiahu filled was infinitely more significant than the cleansing of the land from the vestiges of idol worship which, after all, was only a temporary respite. Immediately after Yoshiahu's death, it began to proliferate once more.

We can now understand the difference in treatment between the two books. In the short-range perspective of *Kings* the cleansing of the land projected Yoshiahu as the great reformer, while the bringing of the *Pesach* had no special significance beyond itself. Hence, the long and detailed description of the cleansing and its central position as the main result of the finding of the *Sefer Torah*. In *Chronicles* it is told earlier — and in much sparser detail — in order to allow the infinitely more important bringing of the *Pesach* — in terms of eternity, the crown of Yoshiahu's accomplishments — to occupy the more central role.

We are also now in a position to understand why *Kings* leaves out the information contained in numbers [2] and [3], and moves straight to the account of the finding of the *Sefer Torah*. The fact that Yoshiahu's religious development took place in stages is of no particular relevance to the cleansing of the land. The events of his eighth and twelfth year were no more than stages that lead to the final cleansing and as such were subsidiary to it — insignificant in the total picture.

However, from the point of view of *Chronicles*, the way stations upon Yoshiahu's religious odyssey are vitally important. That a child brought up under the influence of a Menasheh and an Amon could — in his tender years — find his way back to God is solid proof of the undying spark of sanctity within the Jewish soul which, given the chance, will assert itself under the most adverse conditions. It is this seed of sanctity which would guarantee Israel's survival in exile, and which would be receptive to the teachings which Yoshiahu was to bequeath to his people.

Thus we see that *Kings* and *Chronicles* bring very different perspectives to bear upon the events of Yoshiahu's reign and that therefore, although they both make the same

---

1. See *Tiferes Yisrael* (*Boaz* 4) to *Megillah* 1:10 for an explanation of the fact that the Second Temple had the halachic character of Temple rather than of *bamah*, although there was no Holy Ark. *Tiferes Yisrael* believes that this is so because once the location had been sanctified it could never lose its halachic status. Nevertheless, it is clear that this is only a *halachic* definition. The absence of the Ark certainly downgraded the degree of the Divine Presence — see comm. to 33:4.

general statement that Yoshiahu did that which was straight in the eyes of HASHEM, they had different aspects of his activities in mind.

☙ The Faithful Workers

In comm. to v. 12 we noted that our verse apparently parallels the one in *Kings*. There are, however, a number of considerations which make it possible that the phrase in *Chronicles* has a different meaning.

Firstly, *Kings* 12:16 makes precisely the same statement concerning the workers who, many years earlier, had made the repairs initiated by Yoash. *Chronicles* has no parallel for that verse. Evidently, then, within the context of the *Chronicles'* view of events, the honesty of the workmen is not significant. Why, then, does he make an issue of it here?

Secondly, *Chronicles* makes the statement that the work was done בֶּאֱמוּנָה, in the context of a detailed description of the Levite overseers. If, indeed, the workers were closely watched, their meticulous honesty seems less worthy of mention.

Again, the question must be asked why *Chronicles* records the Levite involvement in such detail (vs. 12 and 13), where *Kings* had not found it necessary even to mention it.

Perhaps a careful reading of text and content of vs. 12 and 13 can yield some answers.

The use of נצח, twice within two verses to describe the function of overseeing the work, is striking. The expression, in this sense, occurs only rarely in *Chronicles* [*I Chronicles* 2:1 and 17, and 23:4].

Again, we must examine the function of the Levites *who were skillful musicians*. What role did they play in the Temple repairs? *Metzudos* explains that they played music while the repair work was being done. But why was this necessary? It could, of course, be that the music was played simply to ease the monotony of the work but if this were the case, it seems strange that *Chronicles* would find it important enough to record. Also, we do not find other building projects accompanied by music. Thus, no mention is made of any music during the building of the Jerusalem wall which is described in detail in *Nehemiah* ch. 2. Only at the inauguration of the wall (ch. 12 there) did the Levites play.

We recall that *Gra* at *I Chronicles* 23:4 explains the use of the root נצח to describe the making of music, because it is through the deeply felt beauty of music that the soul can be touched and the יֵצֶר הָרַע, *the evil inclination*, conquered. [נצח, *to conquer* or *overpower*.]

Yoshiahu's Temple repairs were no simple matter. After the catastrophic years of Menasheh's and Amon's rule, nothing less than a total re-orientation towards the Temple and its significance for Israel was required. As we saw in the previous chapter, Amon had *driven* God out of His Temple and utterly denuded it of any spiritual content. It fell to Yoshiahu to bring the *Shechinah*, the Divine Presence, back among the people.

But for God to allow His *Shechinah* to rest upon the fruits of man's labor would surely require that it be performed in total dedication to the sacred goal of becoming hosts to the Divine. Any personal ambition, any hopes for financial gain or self-aggrandizement would certainly disqualify the building from being a suitable home for God's Presence on earth.

Accordingly, the work had to be done בֶּאֱמוּנָה. It had to be a totally religious act and this, our text tells us, the workers accomplished. The fact that they were overseen by the Levites gave the work its spiritual dimension. The music which they made would surely have contributed to the elimination of any external motivations, and made possible a labor of spiritual purity such as would be required for the great task at hand.

⌘ The Finding of the Sefer Torah

While bringing out the money for the Temple repairs, Chilkiahu discovers a *Sefer Torah*. It is brought to the king who reads it and is so perturbed by its contents, that he sends a delegation to Chuldah the prophetess in order that the import of what he has seen might be interpreted to him.

These are the bare outlines of this story which has perplexed the commentators in a number of its details. The underlying difficulty is the implication that the king was surprised by what he read in the *Sefer Torah*. Could this righteous king have been ignorant of the contents of the Torah?

Commentators grapple with two other issues: Was there something special about the particular *Sefer Torah* that was discovered, and how and why was the king convinced that it contained a significant message for him?

The commentators fall into two essential categories: There are those who hold that for one reason or another the Torah had really been forgotten and Yoshiahu did, indeed, only become aware of its contents on this occasion [A]. There are those who believe that Yoshiahu was well aware of the contents of the Torah but was galvanized into his actions, either because of the specialness of the particular *Sefer Torah* which was found, and/or through the way and form in which its message was conveyed to him [B].

We base the comm. on what we perceive to be *Rashi's* opinion. Here we offer some of the other approaches.

A listing such as the one which follows would normally begin with *Rashi*. However, since *Rashi's* remarks are very terse and can best be understood against the background of *Radak's* more copious analysis, we shall quote *Radak* first.

Radak [A]: The *Sefer Torah* was not *found* in the sense that it was discovered unexpectedly. It was the *Sefer Torah* which was kept at the side of the Holy Ark (*Deuteronomy* 31:26 and *Bava Basra* 14a and b) and it is from there that it was taken. *Radak* sees no special significance in the fact that it was this particular *Sefer Torah* which was brought to Yoshiahu and thus does not belong in the [B] category.

He reasons that during the fifty-two years of Menasheh's reign, the Torah must have been totally forgotten and that, therefore, its contents came as a surprise to Yoshiahu who had been a child when Menasheh died and who had been reared by Amon who was even more wicked than Menasheh had been.

He is troubled by the fact that, as we saw in ch. 33, Menasheh repented his wickedness. Would he then not have made certain that Torah would once more be studied? To say that Menasheh repented toward the end of his life and that, therefore, he had no time to re-instate the Torah, conflicts with the tradition of the Sages that he was penitent for a full thirty-three years. *Radak* remains puzzled.

Rashi [A] [B]: *Rashi's* remarks are so short that we cannot obtain a clear picture without taking several of them together. When Chilkiah tells Shaphan that he *found* a *Sefer Torah* (*II Kings* 22:8), *Rashi* comments: [It was] hidden beneath a ledge where they concealed it when Achaz burned the Torah.[1]

---

1. From this *Rashi* we cannot deduce anything regarding the existence of other Torah scrolls. No doubt these proliferated during Chizkiahu's reign (*Radak*) and may well have existed in abundance even during Menasheh's, Amon's and certainly Yoshiahu's reigns. This particular copy had been hidden and was now discovered.

To v. 13 (there) which shows Yoshiahu sent a delegation to Chuldah, *Rashi* remarks: He saw that *HASHEM will take you and your king whom you have installed over you . . .* (*Deuteronomy* 28:36).[1]

In *Shabbos* 56b the Talmud interprets *II Kings* 23:25 to mean that Yoshiahu reimbursed all litigants who had lost cases that had come before him in judgment up to the eighteenth year of his reign. *Rashi* comments: [This was the year] in which Chilkiahu found the *Sefer* Torah. When Yoshiahu thought deeply and carefully into its laws, he realized that he may have made mistakes in his judgments.[2]

We see, then, that *Rashi* combines both [A] and [B] in his understanding of the incident: A *Sefer Torah* which had been hidden up to that point was discovered [A], and contained a message of doom [B]. We will discuss *Rashi* further, below.

Abarbanel, Metzudos, Malbim [B]: Based on v. 14: סֵפֶר תּוֹרַת־ה׳ בְּיַד־מֹשֶׁה, these commentators assume that the *Sefer Torah* which was found was the one which had been written personally by Moses and placed at the side of the Holy Ark (*Deuteronomy* 31:24). It had been hidden to protect it from the depredations of the earlier kings and its rediscovery was a matter of great moment. In addition it was rolled to the passage in *Deuteronomy* which threatens exile for transgressing the laws of the Torah. Yoshiahu interpreted the entire event as a warning, and took the steps which are described in the story.

Sforno, Mikra U'Massores [B]: *Sforno* (to *Deuteronomy* 31:9) believes that the *Torah* mentioned in that verse does not refer to the complete *Sefer Torah*, but to a scroll which contained only those sections of the Torah which were to be read by the king in his seven-yearly reading of the Torah. [See *Sotah* 7:8 for a description of the ceremony at the *mitzvah of Hakhel*, and for a listing of the sections of the Torah which were read on that occasion. The *Tochachah*, the section describing exile as a result of sin, figures prominently among them.]

In addition to these sections this scroll also contained the record of the *bris*, the *covenant* which Joshua concluded with the people (*Joshua* 24:25-26). V. 26 reads, *And Joshua wrote these matters in the Book of this Torah of God . . .*

Sforno evidently is influenced in his interpretation by our v. 30 where the *Sefer Torah* is referred to as סֵפֶר הַבְּרִית. The scroll which contained the *Hakhel* readings ends with the words: *. . . besides the covenant* [הַבְּרִית] *which he established with them in Chorev*. This, together with the record of Joshua's בְּרִית, could well give rise to the description . . . *to act in accordance with the* בְּרִית *written in this Book* (v. 31).[3]

---

1. The implication is that Yoshiahu was perturbed by the message in the *Sefer Torah* rather than by the fact that it was discovered. *Rashi* does not make the point [as others do, see below] that the *Sefer Torah* was rolled to that passage.

There is no extant midrash that Yoshiahu saw this verse in the *Sefer Torah* which Chilkiahu found. The Talmud (*Yoma* 52b and elsewhere) tells that Yoshiahu undertook to bury or hide the Ark (see 35:3) because he had *seen* this verse — but the Talmud nowhere indicates that it was in the *Sefer Torah* which Chilkiahu found that he saw it.

Rashi has not yet stated explicitly that Yoshiahu had been unaware that the Torah contained this verse.

2. The implication is clearly that up to that point the Torah had not been known to him — but see further below.

3. It can be argued further that since Joshua saw fit to record his בְּרִית in this particular scroll, he regarded it as a סֵפֶר הַבְּרִית. Apparently he saw the concept of בְּרִית as central to the *Hakhel* readings.

Mikra U'Massores adds that the midrashic tradition that the first words that caught Yoshiahu's eyes were the ones which predicted the exile helps to further explain the impact which the finding of the *Sefer Torah* made. He compares the providential noticing of this verse to the idea of פְּסוֹק לִי פְּסוּקָךְ which we find frequently in the Talmud (*Hagigah* 15a, b and elsewhere). The Sages would occasionally view as providentially inspired a Scriptural verse quoted to them by a child who was asked at random what he had learned that day in school. The contents of that verse would guide them in their actions. Here, too, Yoshiahu felt that his eyes would not have fallen upon that particular verse, if God had not wanted him to notice it and to draw conclusions from it.[1]

HaLevi, Doros HaRishonim [B]: *HaLevi* views the incident within the larger framework of the period. As we saw in comm. to vs. 24 and 25 of the previous chapter, *HaLevi* believes that the עַם הָאָרֶץ who crowned Yoshiahu king were the bulk of the people who had fallen under the evil influences of Menasheh and Amon, and who thought that by making the young and apparently malleable child, Yoshiahu, king, they could perpetuate the licentious way of life which they valued.

Indeed, for the first few years of his reign Yoshiahu was totally under their sway, and it was only little by little that he managed to assert his own deeply religious tendencies. This gradual thrust towards independence began tentatively in the eighth year of his reign (v. 8), and attained a new stage in the twelfth (there), until finally, in the eighteenth year — at age twenty-six — he felt strong enough to undertake the major purification of the Temple. This act — in paralleling the same activity undertaken by Yoash who had felt called upon to eradicate the pernicious defiling resulting from Athaliah's evil reign — placed him among the great reformers among Judah's kings.

This reforming zeal gained an important impetus with the finding of the *Sefer Torah*. During Menasheh's depredations the *Sefer Torah*, which had always been lying at the side of the Holy Ark, had been lost. It was intended that, as part of the entire cleansing process, a new *Sefer Torah* would be written to replace the old one. To everyone's surprise the *Sefer Torah*, which had been thought to be lost, was rediscovered in the course of the Temple repairs. This was regarded as a symbol of God's approbation for the reforming activities.

In addition, there is the tradition of the Sages that the *Sefer Torah* was rolled to the *Tochachah*, and these factors combined to bring about the events which are here described.

Tzvi Kaplan [in *Sefer Hazikaron* for *HaLevi*] [A]: The author of this essay reviews the various solutions to the problems, much as we have done here, and points out that the *p'shuto shel mikra* does not contain any hints of either a special copy of the *Sefer Torah* nor of its being rolled to a specific place. He feels that the unadorned text yields as follows:

The Sages teach that Amon either destroyed (*Seder Olam*) or burned a Torah (*Sanhedrin* 103b). This is to be taken literally and means that after the two years of Amon's reign there were, in fact, no *Sifrei Torah* in the entire land. Yoshiahu was six when his father ascended the throne and, while it is true that his grandfather Menasheh had, by that time, already become a penitent, Amon was surely not affected by this and

1. We note that *Mikra U'Massores* does not mention or stress the fact that the *Sefer Torah* was rolled to that spot — only that these words first caught his eye. See further below in our exposition of what we believe to be *Rashi's* approach.

reared his own son in total ignorance of the Torah.

Thus, it is entirely possible that Yoshiahu — with all his cravings for a religious life — had, in fact, never throughout his life seen a *Sefer Torah*. His knowledge of the Torah's demands came to him orally from the elders of the generation who still remembered the Torah from earlier years, but who were unwilling to rely on their own memory in writing a new text and who, in accordance with the dictum that the written Torah may not be quoted verbatim orally, would have taught him the general requirements but not acquainted him with the actual text.

There was, however, one *Sefer Torah* which had escaped Amon's holocaust. From the time of Achaz's depredations, this *Sefer Torah* had been *hidden beneath a ledge* [the midrash, while not extant, was apparently known to *Rashi* — see above]. The existence of the *Sefer Torah* was not generally known and may well have escaped even Chilkiahu's attention. Thus, it lay hidden through the decades awaiting providential discovery when God would will that it be found.

Now, in the wake of Yoshiahu's Temple purification, it was indeed discovered, thus granting that righteous king his first glimpse of the sacred texts of which till now he had only heard. The discovery was seen as an omen and Yoshiahu took the steps described in our narrative.

There are serious considerations which raise questions concerning most of the assumptions made by the various commentators. These force us to make another attempt to analyze the text, and see whether it could yield other insights.

Some of the considerations are as follows: The assumption [A] that, for whatever reason, the Torah was not known or that *Sifrei Torah* were unavailable must be questioned. Both *HaLevi* and *Mikra U'Massores* devote entire tracts to proving how thoroughly the laws of the Torah were woven into the lives of the people throughout the period of the First Temple. Whatever the depredations of individual kings, it is inconceivable that knowledge of the Torah could have been stamped out. To say that it was, or that not a single *Sefer Torah* had been hidden throughout the land, would make the wicked Judaic kings seem worse than any of the tyrants who over the centuries, attempted to wean Israel away from the Torah. In addition, *Mikra U'Massores* makes the point that a king as righteous as Yoshiahu would surely not have rested until he was able to fulfill the *mitzvah* of *Hakhel*, which required that every seven years the king read specific passages from the Torah to the people.

We cannot escape the likelihood that, in fact, Torah was well known throughout the land and *Sifrei Torah* probably proliferated. These are assumptions upon which *HaLevi* and *Mikra U'Massores* base their interpretations and we cannot but share them.

But we must also question the assumption that the *Sefer Torah* which was found was in some way special, or that it was rolled to a specific place. Besides the fact that we would have expected such details to be explicated in the text, the ambience of the entire narrative seems to militate against this.

An examination of the text demonstrates this:

1. In the *Kings'* account there is not even a statement, parallel to our v. 14, that the *Sefer Torah* was found. The story begins with Chilkiahu telling Shaphan that he found a *Sefer Torah*. If, indeed, there was something out of the ordinary in the discovery — such as that it was a national treasure, the *Sefer Torah* that Moses himself had written — it would seem that the narrative would have required that this be stressed.

2. There is no indication in the text that Chilkiahu intended Shaphan to bring the *Sefer Torah* to the king. We are told simply that he gave it to Shaphan. This is

particularly striking in the *Kings* account for the following reason: In *Chronicles*, v. 16 begins, וַיָּבֵא שָׁפָן, *Shaphan brought . . .*, which, at least, implies that Shaphan brought the *Sefer Torah* to the king — apparently because he attached some significance to it. In the parallel verse in *Kings* we have וַיָּבֹא שָׁפָן, *Shaphan came* — with no indication that he even brought the *Sefer Torah* along with him until he mentions it in the course of his report to the king.

3. In both the *Kings'* and the *Chronicles'* account, Shaphan makes no special issue out of the *Sefer Torah*. He gives the king an account of the work that is being done in the Temple, and only then mentions the *Sefer Torah*. It stands to reason that, if there would have been something particularly significant about the *Sefer Torah*, he would have told it to the king first. A report that the *Sefer Torah* written by Moses had been discovered would surely warrant mention before the fact that the repairs were going well.

4. Even when Shaphan begins to tell the king about the *Sefer Torah*, he makes no mention of the fact that it was *found*; only, *Chilkiahu handed me a Book*. The fact that the *Sefer Torah* was found seems not, in any way, to have contributed to its significance.

If, then, the Torah was well known among the people and certainly to the righteous king who for the past ten years of his life had conscientiously sought out God, and if, moreover, there was nothing special about the *Sefer* which was found, how are we to understand the story?

We suggest the following interpretation which may well be accommodated by *Rashi's* terse remarks as we quoted them above.

We believe it to be significant that in the *Kings'* account (v. 8) we are told that when Chilkiahu gave the *Sefer Torah* to Shaphan, the latter read it. No mention of this is made in the *Chronicles'* account.

The underlying principle of our interpretation will be the concept of פְּסוֹק לִי פְּסוּקָךְ as we recognized it in the section above dealing with the interpretation of *Mikra U'Massores*.

The simple unadorned text yields as follows: As the money was being taken out of the Temple vaults, a *Sefer Torah* which had been hidden there since the days of Achaz was discovered. Chilkiahu thought that the unexpected uncovering of this *Sefer Torah* might be considered to be some sort of an omen and handed it to Shaphan to see what he would think. The event in and of itself was unexceptional and Chilkiahu had no particular plan that the king should be told about it.

Shaphan — as told in *Kings* — opened the *Sefer Torah* and read the familiar text hoping to be struck by some special passage which he would then consider in the nature of the providential פְּסוֹק לִי פְּסוּקָךְ, but found nothing which seemed to him striking.

He then went to the king in order to give him a report concerning the progress of the Temple purification, taking the *Sefer Torah* along but without any particular intention of showing it to the king — וַיָּבֹא, and not וַיָּבֵא. Only later, in the course of the conversation, did it occur to him to mention to the king the fact that Chilkiahu had given him the *Sefer Torah*.

The king reads the Book in much the same way as Shaphan had done — he is sure that some message must be implied. His eyes fall on the section of the *Tochachah* [the בְּרִית of vs. 30 and 31], and he draws the conclusions which are described in the passage.

At the same time, since the passage which caught his eye was only part of the entire Torah which had been brought to his attention, he felt called upon to re-study and re-evaluate the entire Torah. While doing this, he discovered mistakes which he had made in judgments during the years in which he had been less meticulous in his analysis of the

Torah requirements. These mistakes he now rectified. This could well be *Rashi's* meaning in *Shabbos* 56b when he says that as a result of finding the *Sefer Torah*, Yoshiahu *thought deeply and carefully* into it.

Thus, the *Kings'* account, which, as always, addresses the events as they happened — and this is a precise description.

In the comm. to the individual verses it becomes clear that while *Chronicles* tells essentially the same story, there are, nevertheless, differences in nuance which reflect its interest in the essence rather than in the outer contours of the events.

Chapter Thirty-Five

◆§ A Unique *Pesach*

What was special about Yoshiahu's *Pesach* celebration?

To gain a correct perspective, we compare our v. 18 with its parallel in *Kings*.

II Chronicles 35:18	*II Kings 23:22*
a. וְלֹא־, *No*	a. כִּי לֹא, *For no*
b. נַעֲשָׂה פֶסַח כָּמֹהוּ בְּיִשְׂרָאֵל, *Pesach like it had been celebrated in Israel*	b. נַעֲשָׂה כַּפֶּסַח הַזֶּה, *Pesach like this had been celebrated*
c. מִימֵי שְׁמוּאֵל הַנָּבִיא, *since the days of Samuel the prophet*	c. . . . מִימֵי הַשֹּׁפְטִים, *since the days of the Judges . . .*
d. וְכָל־מַלְכֵי יִשְׂרָאֵל, *[and] none of Israel's kings . . .*	d. וְכֹל יְמֵי מַלְכֵי יִשְׂרָאֵל וּמַלְכֵי יְהוּדָה, *and all the days of the kings of Israel and Judah.*

To understand the differences between the two versions, we should first point out that the *Kings'* verse follows immediately upon a sentence which reads: *The king commanded all the people, saying, 'Celebrate a Pesach offering to HASHEM your God, as is written in this book of the covenant.'* No description of the ceremonies is given. Thus the phrase *For no Pesach like this had been celebrated* ... has no point of reference. Clearly, something is missing. *Radak* notes that this sentence can only be the ending of a lengthy description, perhaps the one contained in the *Chronicles'* account, which the *Kings'* account omits. He draws an analogy to *Joshua* 2:24, where it is also obvious that only the final sentence of a much longer description is given.

But if the omitted description is, indeed, the one recorded in *Chronicles*, then the wording in *Kings*, ... כִּי לֹא, *For no* ..., is unexpected. The וְלֹא of *Chronicles* seems much more appropriate.

Again, the change in [c] seems significant. The change from שֹׁפְטִים to שְׁמוּאֵל הַנָּבִיא is substantive. *Radak's* [and *Metzudos'* to *Kings*] statement that Samuel, too, was one of the שֹׁפְטִים does not explain why the one book chose the one mode of expression while the other did not. Moreover, there seems to be a distinct difference in connotation. מִימֵי הַשֹּׁפְטִים deals with a historical period; מִימֵי שְׁמוּאֵל הַנָּבִיא implies something special about Samuel, the man.

Furthermore, what is the difference in (d) between the *Kings'* version, מַלְכֵי יִשְׂרָאֵל וּמַלְכֵי יְהוּדָה, and the wording in *Chronicles*, וְכָל־מַלְכֵי יִשְׂרָאֵל, with the מַלְכֵי יְהוּדָה omitted?

We must first analyze the special quality of Yoshiahu's *Pesach* which, as the texts made clear, had not been equaled for so many centuries. What was the unique element which marked this celebration as different from all the others?

We begin by examining what some of the commentators have to say on the relevant verses.

Rashi [to מִימֵי הַשֹּׁפְטִים]: *Chronicles has 'From Samuel's days.' For Samuel, too, brought about a general repentance when he gathered the people to Mitzpah*. Thus, he understands the verse as follows: No leader, between Samuel and Yoshiahu, had used the opportunity of the *Pesach* celebration to bring about a spiritual regeneration of the people.

Rashi also suggests a different interpretation: The stress is on the fact that Yoshiahu's *Pesach* was brought in Jerusalem, with representation from all Israel. This had not occurred since Samuel's days, since the people of the Northern Kingdom were unable to journey to Jerusalem for the celebrations, and were constrained to bring their offerings at Dan and Bethel. *Mefaresh* quotes *Rashi* but objects to the explanation. Surely during David's and Solomon's reigns — long after Samuel — the *Pesach* was universally celebrated in Jerusalem!

Mefaresh: Yoshiahu's *Pesach* was unique in that he, the king, supplied all the animals to the populace. But *Mefaresh* does not explain why this was particularly significant, nor why just the period of the monarchy is excluded. We do not find the Judges supplying the animals for the *Pesach* sacrifices any more than did the Kings.

Radak: Yoshiahu's *Pesach* was unique in that all Israel were united, as with one heart. Even Chizkiahu's *Pesach* had not been the same since there were many, at that time, who did not participate. But *Radak* does not make clear how this could be meant when in neither of the two books any issue is made of this togetherness. *Kings* tells us nothing at all, and *Chronicles* limits itself to a description of the technicalities of the Temple service. Nothing is said of the attitude of the people. Also, we do not find a similar unity in the period of the Judges.

Metzudos: Yoshiahu's *Pesach* was unique in its extreme purity and the perfection of the celebration. Here, too, we are puzzled since no issue is made of this purity in the description and there seems no reason to suppose that the *Pesach* celebrations of the period of the Judges was any more exalted than during the period of the monarchy.

Abarbanel: The uniqueness of Yoshiahu's *Pesach* derived from a high degree of purity, coupled with the elimination of idol worship and of the *bamos*. These latter had been a scourge even during the heyday of David's and Solomon's reigns. True, Chizkiahu had also celebrated an exemplary *Pesach*, but, at that time, there were many who derided him, and many who were unclean. Only this, Yoshiahu's *Pesach*, was free from all such taints.

But *Abarbanel's* thesis contains two elements which raise questions. It is true that in the *Kings'* account, there is a clear connection between the cleansing of the land from idol worship, and the *Pesach* celebration. The one leads into the other. But this is not the case in *Chronicles*. There, the description of the cleansing of the land is given before the account of the finding of the *Sefer Torah*. There is no implied connection between that and the *Pesach* celebration. Moreover, Abarbanel's assertion, that the penitence of the people in Yoshiahu's time was untainted, is in contradiction to the tradition of the Sages that, on the contrary, the scoffers of his time continued their worship unabated.

What, then, was the unique quality of Yoshiahu's *Pesach*?

We suspect that *Kings* and *Chronicles* had two different qualities in mind, and that these two qualities would be expressed respectively as not having been equaled since the time of the Judges (*Kings*) and the time of Samuel (*Chronicles*).

What is the hallmark of the historical period which we know as the days of the Judges — a hallmark which is instantly recognized by the reader as being absolutely essential to that period and which therefore need not be explicated? The book itself seems to give the answer: בַּיָּמִים הָהֵם אֵין מֶלֶךְ בְּיִשְׂרָאֵל אִישׁ הַיָּשָׁר בְּעֵינָיו יַעֲשֶׂה, *In those days there was no king in Israel. Each man did that which was right in his own eyes* (*Judges*

17:6, 21:25). It was a time of religious anarchy during which there were constant fluctuations between the people sinking to great depths of idol worship and depravity, being exposed to the predation of their enemies, and, because of their suffering, turning back to God. He would then send a Judge who would save them, only to have them slide back into their old ways after varying periods of tranquility, at which point the cycle would begin once more.

Thus we may describe the period of the Judges as one during which, periodically, the people as a whole were galvanized into a sincere and potent *teshuvah*, although, as events constantly showed, not a lasting one — that is, not one which touched their souls deeply enough to make a permanent change. [See *Meiri*, *Chibur HaTeshuvah*, *Maamar* 1, ch. 2, p. 52 for an analysis.]

During the days of the monarchy these spiritual fluctuations ceased. After the strong kingships of David and Solomon, the basic tenets of Torah and the negation of the idolatrous cults became firmly established among the people and — leaving aside the renegade breakaway Northern Kingdom — the nation as a whole always remained true to its standards. As *HaLevi* demonstrates frequently in his *Tekufas HaMikra*, the occasional lapses into idol worship were never widespread, and tended to center around the court and the aristocracy.

If we now turn to the *Kings'* passage, it seems clear from the internal evidence that the thrust of its perception of Yoshiahu's *Pesach* celebration is the *teshuvah* element in it. A close reading of 23:21-25 yields this conclusion.[1]

We can now return to the (a), (c), and (d) elements of the *Kings* passage. The (a) part is the conclusion of a passage describing the sincere repentance of the entire people. We can surmise that the sentence immediately preceding it would have said how the people cried and confessed their shortcomings, to which the ... כִּי לֹא נַעֲשָׂה, *for no ... had been celebrated*, would be a logical conclusion. The (b) and (c) phrases would then state that no such universal *teshuvah* had occurred since the days of the Judges — with the implication that during that period there would surely have been similar religious revivals as we discussed above — whether or not in conjunction with *Pesach*

---

1. We offer a short analysis:

V. 21: The king commands the people to bring the *Pesach*: *As is written in this book of the covenant*. *Analysis*: The finding of the *Sefer Torah* galvanizes the king into action. Observance had been lax and the finding of the Torah is perceived as an indication that greater and more serious adherence to the law is expected.

Vs. 22-23: The verses summarize the fact that the *Pesach* was celebrated. As we saw above, *Radak* believes that v. 22, כִּי לֹא נַעֲשָׂה כַּפֶּסַח הַזֶּה, *For no Pesach like this had been celebrated*, indicates that a descriptive passage was left out. In the context of the whole passage — see further below — we suspect that the omitted passage would have been a description of the people's repentance (similar to the repentance accompanying Chizkiahu's *Pesach* at 30:22). This could perhaps explain why the description was, in fact, left out. V. 26, there, teaches that in spite of everything, HASHEM's anger did not subside and that Jerusalem was still doomed. A detailed description of the people's penitence might have created too flagrant a dichotomy.

V. 24: This verse states in brief that Yoshiahu cleansed the land of all vestiges of the idolatrous cults ... *in order to uphold the words of the Torah which were written on the Book which Chilkiahu had found* ... The cleansing of the land was described in great detail in earlier verses. Its repetition here can only mean that the celebration of the *Pesach* was to be put in the context of the general religious regeneration which took place as a result of the finding of the *Sefer Torah*.

V. 25: This has no parallel in *Chronicles* and tells us that no king before or after Yoshiahu was ever as sincere and perfect a penitent as he had been. Manifestly, this sentence places the entire passage in the context of a *teshuvah* revival as we have argued.

celebrations. The (d) phrase describes the period of the monarchy in contrast to that of the Judges.

None of the nuances which indicate the *teshuvah* element are present in the *Chronicles'* account; it is therefore impossible to assume that this is the uniqueness of Yoshiahu's *Pesach* from the *Chronicles'* perspective. We must seek that uniqueness in the particular shadings of the account as it is told in *Chronicles*. These shadings — as we have seen throughout — indicate that this *Pesach* was to be a dedication of the people to God's service in the form that the service was to take once there would be no more Temple and they would be scattered in exile; Thus, a dedication to a new mode of relating to their Divine task. Such a change in the nature of the Jewish people had not occurred in Israel since the days when Samuel had instructed them how to comport themselves under the monarchy — an institution which had not existed before and which was to make demands of its own, to which the nation had to be educated.

In this context the (d) phrase, וְכָל מַלְכֵי יִשְׂרָאֵל, *and none of Israel's kings*, is extremely apt. *Metzudos* explains that this refers to David and Solomon who are called *kings of Israel*, because, in their days, the entire nation had been united and the Northern Kingdom had not yet come into being. It seems clear, in the context of *Chronicles*, that this phrase is meant to be read in contrast to 30:26, where the joy of Chizkiahu's festival was said to be the greatest since the days of *Solomon son of David, king of Israel*, which implies that during the times of David and Solomon there were comparable joyous occasions. Our verse makes the point that even in those blessed reigns, there was nothing like Yoshiahu's *Pesach*. The point being made may well be the one we suggested: Not since before the monarchy had there been the need to orient the entire nation towards a new and untried set of circumstances. Yoshiahu was to be for the exile what Samuel had been for the monarchy.

◆§ The Final Years

To gain a correct perspective of the relationship between vs. 18 and 19, we compare them to their parallels in *Kings* (see table opposite page).

As an introduction to our analysis we note that the *parshah* division in *Chronicles* brackets v. 19 with the story of Yoshiahu's death at the hands of Pharaoh, marking it as an introduction to that section rather than as a conclusion to the foregoing one. We shall examine this below, but first we will demonstrate that this is not the position which it occupies in *Kings*.

This is, of course, clear from the structure of the *Kings'* narrative where vs. 24-28 interrupt between our verse and v. 29 in which the story of Yoshiahu's death begins. Moreover, the introductory words to the sentence, . . . כִּי אִם (b), show clearly that it is a continuation from v. 22, . . . כִּי לֹא נַעֲשָׂה (a). The function of the verse seems to serve to round off the narrative, to glance back with satisfaction that the celebration of the *Pesach* was performed in such an exemplary manner. This would also explain the phrase לַה׳ בִּירוּשָׁלָם, which is not paralleled in the *Chronicles'* account [but introduces it in v.1 — see comm. there]. This was indeed a most wonderful *Pesach* celebration — dedicated to HASHEM in the best manner possible and in the sanctity of Jerusalem!

In *Chronicles*, as we have seen, the verse evidently introduces the next section. What does it lend to that narrative?

We suggest that the value of its contribution lies in its juxtaposition to the follow-

II Chronicles 35:18-26	*II Kings 23:22-29*
a. 18. . . . וְלֹא־נַעֲשָׂה פֶסַח כָּמֹהוּ, *No Pesach like it had been celebrated . . .*	a. 22. . . . כִּי לֹא נַעֲשָׂה כַּפֶּסַח הַזֶּה, *For no Pesach like it had been celebrated*
b.	b. כִּי אִם־, *except*
c. 19. בִּשְׁמוֹנֶה עֶשְׂרֵה שָׁנָה . . . נַעֲשָׂה הַפֶּסַח הַזֶּה, *This Pesach was celebrated in the eighteenth year . . .*	c. 23. בִּשְׁמֹנֶה עֶשְׂרֵה שָׁנָה . . . נַעֲשָׂה הַפֶּסַח הַזֶּה, *this Pesach was celebrated in the eighteenth year*
d.	d. לַה׳ בִּירוּשָׁלָם, *to* HASHEM *in Jerusalem.*
e	e. 24. וְגַם אֶת־הָאֹבוֹת, *Also the Ovos*
f.	f. 25. . . . וְכָמֹהוּ לֹא־הָיָה, *There was none like him . . .*
g.	g. 26. . . . אַךְ לֹא־שָׁב, *But [God's anger] did not recede . . .*
h.	h. 27. . . . וַיֹּאמֶר ה׳ גַּם אֶת־יְהוּדָה אָסִיר, HASHEM *said, 'Judah, too, will I remove . . .'*
i.	i. 28. וְיֶתֶר דִּבְרֵי יֹאשִׁיָּהוּ, *The remainder of Yoshiahu's matters . . .*
j. 20. . . . אַחֲרֵי כָל־זֹאת . . . עָלָה נְכוֹ, *After all this . . . Necho . . . came*	j. 29. בְּיָמָיו עָלָה פַרְעֹה נְכֹה, *In his days, Pharaoh Necho came up . . .*
k. 21-25. . . . וַיִּשְׁלַח, *He sent . . .*	k.
l. 26. . . . וְיֶתֶר דִּבְרֵי יֹאשִׁיָּהוּ, *Now the rest of the matters of Yoshiahu . . .*	l.

ing verse: *After all this . . .* (j). At 34:1 we learn that Yoshiahu ruled for thirty-one years. This means that for the thirteen intervening years there is total silence. *Chronicles* finds nothing worth reporting from the celebration of the *Pesach* until Yoshiahu's death.[1]

We shall see below that, in the final analysis, Yoshiahu failed as the educator of his generation. He deceived himself concerning their spiritual standing and allowed himself to be lulled into the acceptance of the easy and comfortable assumption that all was well, that the people had truly been weaned away from their idolatrous predilections when, in fact, these pernicious ideas still held sway firmly among them. It may well be that *Chronicles'* way of sharing disapproval of Yoshiahu's passivity, during a period which might well have been used to inspire the people to true penitence, is to stress — by telling us the year of the *Pesach* celebration and then passing straight on to the thirty-first year — the emptiness of the intervening years.

1. [It is quite possible that vs. 24 and 25 in the *Kings'* account — that Yoshiahu eliminated the various idolatrous cults and that he was a penitent on the grand scale — are descriptions of the kinds of activities which occupied the intervening years. If so, *Chronicles'* silence on this score is even more significant.]

◆§ The *Chronicles'* View of Yoshiahu's Failures

The account of Yoshiahu's death is substantively different in *Kings* than it is in *Chronicles*. In contrast to the detailed description in *Chronicles*, *Kings* encapsulates the entire incident into two verses: *In his days Pharaoh Necho went up against the king of Assyria to the Euphrates. King Yoshiahu went to meet him. As he saw him in Megiddo he killed him. His servants carried him dead from Megiddo ...*

Moreover, the account in *Kings* follows v. 28 there: *And the rest of Yoshiahu's matters and all that he did are written in the Chronicles of the Kings of Judah*. See fn. to 13:2, and comm. to 24:26, where we analyze the phenomenon of information given after the ... וְיֶתֶר formula. We found that, as a general rule, we expect a natural death, which has no special significance as part of the narrative, to come after the formula, but a violent death which has something to tell us about the king, to be told before. In our case, this is the expected system and is used in *Chronicles*.

Why not in *Kings*?

Before we analyze the teaching of the texts in *Kings* and *Chronicles* we note the tradition of the Sages concerning the shortcomings which underlay the tragedy of Yoshiahu's untimely death.

Taanis 22b teaches: Why was Yoshiahu punished? Because he should have consulted Jeremiah and did not do so. The background to this is given in *Eichah Rabbasi* (to *Eichah* 1:18). When Pharaoh decided to pass through Judah on the way to his war with the Assyrian king, Yoshiahu decided, against Jeremiah's advice, to oppose him. Yoshiahu thought that the verse in *Leviticus* 22:6, which promises that when Israel walks in God's statutes no army would pass through its lands, meant that even an army which had no aggressive intentions towards Israel would not traverse the land. He felt that Israel at this point acted in perfect conformity to God's wishes and consequently felt justified in attempting to repulse Pharaoh. He did not realize that his people were still idol worshipers. He had sent inspectors around the land to make sure that there were no idols in any of the houses, but these had been duped by the people. Idolatrous images had been painted on the doors in such a way that when the doors were open these could not be identified but when they were closed, the image was complete. Jeremiah was aware of the failings of the people and vainly tried to stop the king. Yoshiahu did not listen and was overtaken by tragedy.

We have, then, two elements in the Sages' perception of Yoshiahu's shortcomings: He allowed himself to be deceived about the people's spiritual state; and failed to accept guidance from Jeremiah.

Given Yoshiahu's historic task of educating the people to the service of God in exile conditions, both these failings are catastrophic. Without the central Temple upon which to focus the spiritual strivings of the people, concern must necessarily shift to the individual household which, for better or worse, becomes the shrine of each man's Divine service. And, in the absence of guidance from the *Kohen Gadol's Urim* and *Tummim*, the spiritual leader, be he prophet or rabbi, must be central to the religious and temporal decisions which the people are called upon to make. We shall see that the *Chronicles* text hints at both these failings and thus makes clear the causes for Yoshiahu's — and Israel's — tragedy.

As we have seen numerous times, *Kings* does not deal with Yoshiahu's historic role as educator of the people for the exile experience. Within the short-term view of its description of Yoshiahu's reign within the context of the here and now, Yoshiahu's death remains a mystery. We have already noted above (comm. to v. 18) that it may be for this very reason that *Kings* curtails the description of the *Pesach* and does not report the details of the *teshuvah* that accompanied it. Because of this the whole matter is reduced to its barest outline and relegated to the position after the וְיֶתֶר formula: Prophecy is silent on the tragedy of Yoshiahu's death. It is only in the *Chronicles* perspective of Israel's eternity, that Yoshiahu's true role becomes clear.

In the comm. to the text we will try to pick up the nuances of the *Chronicles* perception of what happened, and why.

☙ Yoshiahu's Death

There are substantive differences between the detailed account of Yoshiahu's death as told in *Chronicles*, and the short, unadorned picture drawn in *Kings*. After v. 29 there tells of Necho's campaign against the Assyrian king, the verse goes on as follows: ... *King Yoshiahu went out to meet him and upon seeing him, he killed him at Megiddo. His servants carried him dead from Megiddo, brought him to Jerusalem and buried him in his sepulcher...* This is all that *Kings* has to say about the confrontation, and it seems to differ from the *Chronicles* account in two important details. Necho kills Yoshiahu *upon seeing him*, which seems to preclude the entire discussion reported in *Chronicles*. Also, the *Kings* account seems to make clear that Yoshiahu died at Megiddo and that he was carried to Jerusalem when he was already dead, while our v. 24 indicates clearly that he died in Jerusalem.

A careful analysis of the language of the two accounts yields a simple solution to the first problem:

Chronicles	*Kings* 23
a. 20. ...וַיֵּצֵא לִקְרָאתוֹ יֹאשִׁיָּהוּ, *And Yoshiahu went out against him*	a. 29. ... וַיֵּלֶךְ הַמֶּלֶךְ יֹאשִׁיָּהוּ לִקְרָאתוֹ וַיְמִיתֵהוּ *King Yoshiahu went out to meet him, and he killed him.*
b. 21.... וַיִּשְׁלַח אֵלָיו, *He sent him ...*	b.
c. 22-24.... וַיָּמָת ... וַיָּבֹא לְהִלָּחֵם ..., *He went out to fight ... and he died ...*	c.

Chronicles has ... וַיֵּצֵא, *He went out*. The focus is on leaving Jerusalem. There is no implication that Yoshiahu had yet reached the battlefield. Indeed, v. 21 has ... וַיִּשְׁלַח, *He sent ...*, meaning that Necho communicated his words through a messenger, but had not yet seen him in person. After Yoshiahu had rejected the message, v. 22 relates that וַיָּבוֹא, *he came*, which is the point at which Yoshiahu reached the battlefield. At that point, indeed, the first moment at which Necho actually saw him, Yoshiahu was killed. This is precisely what the *Kings* account yields. It uses ... וַיֵּלֶךְ. The focus is not on leaving Jerusalem but on *going towards* Megiddo. The וַיֵּלֶךְ ... לִקְרָאתוֹ is the parallel of the ... וַיָּבֹא of v. 22 in *Chronicles*, and it is therefore accurate to say that Necho killed him [through his archers] *upon seeing him.*

The *Kings* account thus dovetails completely with *Chronicles* save only that it leaves out Necho's message and Yoshiahu's rejection. This, of course, requires an explanation. We shall see that this omission can well be explained by the two different perspectives which the two books bring to bear on the subject, but this can best be done by first addressing ourselves to the second question which we raised: Did Yoshiahu die at Megiddo as is implied in *Kings*, or in Jerusalem as appears from *Chronicles*?

We suggest the following solution: V. 24 reads: ...וַיּוֹלִיכֻהוּ יְרוּשָׁלַיִם וַיָּמָת. There is an irregularity in the syntax. A phrase such as this would normally close with שָׁם, *there*. Thus: He came [or was brought] to such and such a place, וַיָּמָת שָׁם, *and died there*. [See *Numbers* 20:1 and 28; 33:34]. Here, the שָׁם is missing. This raises the question whether the phrase means that Yoshiahu actually died in Jerusalem, or whether, perhaps something else is meant.

In view of the clear implication from *Kings* that Yoshiahu was killed at Megiddo, we suggest that וַיָּמָת here does not mean that he actually died in Jerusalem. Rather, it was there that the fact of his death first fully impacted upon the people. In the course of the mourning (v. 24) and the eulogizing (v. 25), it suddenly became clear just what a tragic loss had befallen them.[1]

We can formulate our conclusion by saying that *Kings* is concerned with the actual death, while *Chronicles* is more interested in its implications.

It is for this reason, too, that only *Chronicles* records the conversation between Yoshiahu and Necho.

Kings views the reign and the man from the point of view of here and now. Yoshiahu was a great and good king whose death was a tragedy which is not to be understood in the context of Divine justice, as *Kings* views it. The shortcomings evident in the confrontation between the two kings; Yoshiahu's unawareness of the true spiritual state of the people and his disobedience to the prophet's advice, are not enough to explain the catastrophe. *Kings*, as it were, poses the question by reporting the death after the וַיֶּתֶר formula, and leaves it at that. [See above, *The Chronicles View of Yoshiahu's Failures*].

In *Chronicles'* long-term perspective, these shortcomings are, as we saw above, catastrophic and, moreover, serve to negate Yoshiahu's destiny as educator of his people. The confrontation with Necho, in all its details and nuances, is highly significant and is, accordingly, presented in full. Yoshiahu's death is no ordinary one. High hopes are dashed to the ground. No more can it be said: *In his protection we can live among the nations*. The moment of the realization of the full dimensions of the tragedy can be described as the point of Yoshiahu's *death* more accurately than the instant of the physical demise.

---

1. The use of מות to describe not physical death, but the realization of the implication of that death, is analogous to *Deuteronomy* 10:6 where Aaron is described as dying at Moseirah, in flagrant contradiction to the well known fact that he actually died at Hor HaHar. *Rashi's* solution is that the actual death took place at Hor HaHar but that the full impact was only felt at Moseirah.

Chapter Thirty-Six

☙ Yehoachaz's Kingship

Why did the people make Yehoachaz king and what was the standing of his kingship?

Based on a suggestion of *Radak* we may surmise as follows:

Both *Kings* and *Chronicles* state briefly that Pharaoh deposed Yehoachaz. But how did Pharaoh become involved in Judah's internal affairs — he had told Yoshiahu expressly that he had no designs upon Judah?

Radak suggests that Yehoachaz may have sought to attack Pharaoh in order to avenge Yoshiahu's death. This, *Radak* claims, seems borne out by Ezekiel's vision (*Ezekiel* 19:2-4). There, as we saw in the comm., the Yoshiahuan family is compared to a pride of lions and, the part which apparently refers to Yehoachaz reads as follows: . . . *amidst young lions she reared her cubs. And she reared up one of her cubs; he became a young lion and he learned to tear prey, man did he devour. So against him were gathered nations, in their pit he was caught and they brought him with hooks to the land of Egypt.*

The description of the brash aggressive behavior attributed to this young lion could well describe a meditated — or even an actual — attack against Egypt, in retaliation for what they had done to Yoshiahu.

We may thus surmise that the people intuited that of Yoshiahu's three sons, Yehoachaz would be the one most likely to initiate such a war of vengeance — and turned to him for that reason.[1]

Now, as can be seen from his rebellious bearing towards Babylon, Yehoyakim was no passive, spineless puppet. We are justified in assuming that he had pro-Egyptian leanings. This would disqualify him in the eyes of the people who were bent on a punitive campaign against Pharaoh Necho, but made him an eminently suitable candidate in Pharaoh's eyes.

Given the motive, we can now examine the status of the kingship.

Horios 11b asks how the younger brother could have been made king in view of the halachah that older sons invariably take precedence. The answer given is that, in this case, Yehoyakim did not have the spiritual stature to fill his father's shoes. [אֵינוֹ מְמַלֵּא מְקוֹם אֲבוֹתָיו].

What, then, does this say about Yehoachaz? Was he a מְמַלֵּא מְקוֹם אֲבוֹתָיו? Did he approximate Yoshiahu's spiritual grandeur? The Talmud's text does not necessarily yield this: It says only that Yehoyakim had not attained the required stature. The meaning could be that under these circumstances the regular laws of succession are inapplicable and the way is open to appoint anyone.

No *midrashim* are extant which would tell us whether Yehoachaz was a good or an evil person. Even the statement in the *Kings'* account (v. 32), that, . . . *he did evil in the eyes of* HASHEM *according to all that his fathers had done*, is not conclusive. It could

---

1. Indeed, Yehoyakim, the older son, seems to have had no stomach for fighting against Egypt. As soon as he was installed into the kingship by Pharaoh, he was absolutely compliant in paying the tribute which the Egyptian king had demanded (*Kings* v.35).

refer to the execution of his kingship rather than to his standing as a man — as is the case with Tzidkiahu (comm. to v.10).

There seems no reason to assume that Yehoachaz's succession was anything but halachically valid. Now *Rambam* teaches that, . . . *whoever is not God fearing, even if he is wise, he is not to be appointed to any position in Israel* (*Melachim* 1:7). Accordingly, we tend toward the conclusion that Yehoachaz was, in fact, a righteous person, fit for the kingship.

However, we cannot ignore the possibility that Yehoachaz's kingship lacked legal standing. From *Rashi* to *Kereisos* 5b it appears that when the succession is in dispute [as it was here because of the elder brother Yehoyakim's pretensions], the orderly transfer of power through inheritance is lifted, and a new appointment to kingship may be necessary. This would require the participation of the Sanhedrin and a prophet (*Rambam, Melachim* 1:3) in precisely the same way as does the original establishment of the kingly line (See *Mishpat HaMeluchah* to *Rambam*, there.) The עַם הָאָרֶץ who made Yehoachaz king, would surely have lacked the required halachic standing.

That Yehoachaz had, in fact, no legal standing as king seems clear from the *Kings* account of how Pharaoh made Yehoyakim king. In v. 34 we read: *Pharaoh Necho made Elyakim, son of Yoshiahu, king in place of his father, Yoshiahu* . . . . It is clear, there, that Yehoyakim is to succeed, not his brother Yehoachaz who actually preceded him on the throne, but his father, Yoshiahu. For Pharaoh, at least, Yehoachaz is non-existent; Yoshiahu's throne is not filled until Yehoyakim ascends it.

It is, perhaps, for this reason that both *Kings* and *Chronicles* are so sparing in their respective accounts of the reign. It is difficult to understand why, if *Radak's* thesis, that Yehoachaz had set out to avenge his father's death, is correct, this should not have been recorded in the historical accounts of his reign — particularly since Ezekiel, as we saw above, seems to see the event as central. But, if indeed, the kingship had no legal standing, this might well explain the omission.

◆§ Pharaoh Necho Deposes Yehoachaz

There are major differences between the *Kings* and *Chronicles* accounts.

The *Kings'* acount itself contains, as it were, two different stories. This by means of a *k'ri-k'siv*, a situation in which the word involved is read differently than it is written.

The relationship between the written and the articulated form may be expressed in one of two ways: The *kri* tends to describe the more overt, tangible aspect, while the *k'siv* deals with the essence. See, for example, *I Chronicles* 11:22.

Another type of relationship seems possible. The *k'ri* relates to the *k'siv* as commentary or interpretation relate to text. The *k'siv* could be defined as תּוֹרָה שֶׁבִּכְתָב, the *written Torah*, while the *k'ri* would be the תּוֹרָה שֶׁבְּעַל פֶּה, the oral, amplifying Torah which provides multi-dimensional body to the written word.

For an analysis of the *k'ri-k'siv* contained in the *Kings'* account, it is best to place the two versions next to each other (see figure 1 following page):

וַיַּאַסְרֵהוּ derives from the root, אסר, *to tie up* and cannot smoothly be used together with the מִמְּלֹךְ of the *k'ri*. One cannot say: He shackled him . . . from being king. Accordingly — and so it appears from both *Radak* and *Metzudos*, — the *k'ri* must assume the meaning וַיְסִירֵהוּ, *He deposed him*, as we have indicated in the chart.

Given our thesis that the *k'ri* is to be regarded as an interpretation of the *k'siv*, we can say as follows: The event that is recorded in the text is the overt action that took place

II Kings 23:33	
K'ri	*K'siv*
a. וַיַּ[א]סִ[י]רֵהוּ, *[Then the king of Egypt] deposed him*	a. וַיַּאַסְרֵהוּ, *Then the king of Egypt] shackled him*
b. . . . פַּרְעֹה, *Pharaoh . . .*	b. פַּרְעֹה נְכֹה בְרִבְלָה בְּאֶרֶץ חֲמָת, *Pharaoh Necho in Rivlah in the land of Hamas*
c. מִמְּלֹךְ, *from ruling*	c. בִּמְלֹךְ, *as he began to reign*
d. בִּירוּשָׁלָיִם, *In Jerusalem*	d. בִּירוּשָׁלָם, *in Jerusalem*
e. . . . וַיִּתֶּן, *and fined . . .*	e. וַיִּתֶּן עֹנֶשׁ עַל הָאָרֶץ, *and fined the land*

figure 1

at Rivlah. The new king, almost immediately upon ascending the throne, is captured by Necho, ignominiously shackled, and dragged off to Egypt. To this seemingly simple event, the *k'ri* adds a new dimension. The binding of the king has a depth to it — it is tantamount to an elimination of his kingship — it is not only וַיַּאַסְרֵהוּ, but וַיְסִירֵהוּ. It does, indeed, take place in Rivlah, but, at a more profound level, the stage is Jerusalem. Pharaoh, the king of Egypt, has exerted his influence in Judah's capital, and decided that the new king is not, and never has been, a king.

This amplification, which, in *Kings* is relegated to the *k'ri*, becomes the actual text in *Chronicles*. The *binding* of Yehoachaz, the subject of the text in *Kings*, is of no interest here. Only the wider implication warrants mention.

If we now place the *k'ri* in *Kings* next to the text in *Chronicles*, we have as follows:

II Chronicles 36:3	II Kings 23:33
a. וַיְסִירֵהוּ, *[The king of Egypt] deposed him*	a. וַיַּ[א]סִ[י]רֵהוּ, *[Pharaoh Necho] shackled [or deposed] him*
b. מֶלֶךְ מִצְרַיִם, *The king of Egypt*	b. פַּרְעֹה נְכֹה בְרִבְלָה בְּאֶרֶץ חֲמָת, *Pharaoh Necho in Rivlah in the land of Hamas*
c.	c. מִמְּלֹךְ, *from ruling*
d. בִּירוּשָׁלַםִ, *in Jerusalem*	d. בִּירוּשָׁלַםִ, *in Jerusalem*
e. . . . וַיַּעֲנֹשׁ, *and fined . . .*	e. וַיִּתֶּן, *and fined . . .*

figure 2

Rivlah disappears completely in the *Chronicles'* narrative. It is not Pharaoh Necho, the man, bent on avenging an attack on his person, but the *king of Egypt*, the ruler of a foreign country who acts, *in Jerusalem*, as in his own land. He alone decides who is to rule over the Jews. The total impotence of the non-king Yehoachaz is thus asserted.

◆§ Yehoyakim: Son of Yoshiahu or Brother of Yehoachaz?

We note that *Kings* identifies Elyakim as Yoshiahu's son, while *Chronicles* introduces him as Yehoachaz's brother. (Elyakim *is* Yehoyakim 36:3.)

The intent of the *Kings'* passage seems clear: Necho wishes to establish a line of succession which is to his liking. He therefore chooses a son of the deceased king and crowns him in place of his father.

Why does *Chronicles* not use the same system? Why choose to make an issue of the fact that Elyakim was Yehoachaz's brother? That this relationship is significant can be seen, also, from the second half of the verse. In contrast to *Kings* which states simply that Necho took Yehoachaz to Egypt, *Chronicles* speaks of *Yehoachaz, his brother*.

Above, in *Yehoachaz's Kingship*, we concluded that, in *Chronicles'* eyes, Yehoachaz's reign had no formal legitimacy. What of Yehoyakim? Is he to be counted among Israel's kings?

We may be able to conclude from *Jeremiah* 36:30 that, in the perspective of eternal Israel, Yehoyakim does not figure in the royal line:

Therefore, thus says HASHEM, concerning Yehoyakim, king of Judah, 'No descendant of his shall sit on the throne of David .... The message seems clear enough: No son of Yehoyakim is to sit upon Israel's throne. But, *Radak*, asks, that is simply not so. Yehoyakim was succeded by his son Yehoyachin.

Radak suggests that, since Yehoyachin reigned for only three months before he was exiled, he did not, in fact, *sit on the throne of David* in any significant way.

But, *Radak's* answer cannot stand without further elucidation. For we know that after Yehoyachin's penitence in Babylon (see below) he was granted a child, Zerubavel, from whom, as we learn at *I Chronicles* 3:17 ff, the Messianic king is to be descended. How, then can it be true to say that none of Yehoyakim's descendants will ever sit on David's throne?

We can only conclude that Yehoyachin, after his penitence, is no more considered to be a son of Yehoyakim. Having, as it were, recreated himself through *teshuvah*, he carries in himself the quality of belonging to the house of David, but not as a son of his father.

Chronicles may have intended this nuance by identifying Yehoyakim as *brother of Yehoachaz*, rather than as *son of Yoshiahu*. In the long perspective with which it deals, Yehoyakim joins Yehoachaz in the line of non-kings whose very being was an aberration in the Davidic line.

◆§ Yehoyakim Is Uniquely Evil

Chronicles omits *Kings'* assessment that Yehoyakim did evil, *according to all that his fathers had done*, for reasons discussed in the comm.

Why, then, does *Kings* have the phrase?

The answer may lie in the specific nature of Yehoyakim's evil, as it is perceived in the tradition of the Sages.

There is a marked difference between the description of Yehoyakim's reign and that of the other evil kings. Always, there is a description of how the evil influence of the king affected the people — idols spread throughout the land and there was a general erosion of religious standards. Nothing of the kind is said either in *Kings* or *Chronicles* concerning Yehoyakim. There is the statement that he did evil — but almost total silence about what form that evil took.

The wickedness ascribed in the Talmud, the challenge hurled at God to withdraw His light, does not even have a source in Scripture. Apparently there was such a tradition among the Sages, but it is nowhere explicated. There is another evil of which Yehoyakim is accused: It is based on a phrase in *Chronicles* which has no counterpart in *Kings*. Our

v. 8 tells that the record of Yehoyakim's depredations and, *that which was discovered concerning him*, is recorded in the Chronicles of the kings of Israel and Judah. What is meant by the phrase, *that which was discovered concerning him?*

Sanhedrin 103b records two opinions: One, that it refers to the name of an idol which he had tattooed upon his male organ; the other, that it refers to the Divine Name of God which he had tattooed upon his male organ. Clearly, this evil is a private one. It is a mark which he placed upon himself — the people remained unaffected.

In what, precisely, did Yehoyakim sin? What lies at the bottom of his assertion that mankind has no more need of the sun because it possesses the glitter of the Paravine gold? Why is this sin worse than those committed by the earlier kings? And what was the point of tattooing his male organ with, either an idolatrous or the Divine Name?

Significantly we do not find Yehoyakim accused of idol worship. This depredation, which played such a central role in the description of the reigns of the wicked kings who preceded him, does not appear in connection with this king. And it may be precisely this which marks him as different.

The idol worshiper has an affinity for the spiritual. He realizes that the physical world does not exhaust existence. His error lies in the source from which he draws his spirituality. Instead of the pure waters of Divine Service, he quenches his thirst in the murky filth of the idolatrous cults.

But, Yehoyakim wanted none of this. The focal point of all idolatry had always been the sun; this because of its centrality in the solar system from which the astrological calculation which governed the lives of the idolaters drew their legitimacy. But Yehoyakim rejected the very sun. *Let Him take His light away!* The clarity, understanding and vision which was thought to come from the light of the sun — that is, from contact with the spiritual — could now come from the Paravine gold. God had given the earth to man. There was no more need for any contact with a world of spirituality. All power could now flow from the Paravine gold in Yehoyakim's treasure houses. The break with the spiritual was complete.

And this, surely, is the meaning of the names tattooed on his male organ. He would know no deity, whether idols or even God Himself, other than his own physical life force. For him there was nothing, at all, outside the world of the body.

Sanhedrin 82a tells, how, centuries later, one of the great Talmudic sages found a skull lying out in the open, which he identified as that of Yehoyakim. He attempted to bury it, but it would never stay in the ground. Always it was cast out onto the open field. In the end the skull was burned.

Maharal explains that the idea of burial is associated with coming to rest [מְנוּחָה], and this resting was to be denied Yehoyakim.

The meaning of the fact that the earth denied him the resting of burial is best understood in terms of our thesis. The earth rejected him because he had denied it that which grants it legitimacy. Through insisting that there was no bridge between the mundane and the spiritual he had made the earth into just a clod of earth. Such pure physicality can never grant rest and repose. The physical world has validity only as ante-chamber and conduit to the World to Come.

We have now seen that Yehoyakim's wickedness does, indeed, fall into an entirely different category than that of the earlier kings. Theirs was an open, public espousal of the cult of idol worship; his, a more private and personal denial of any spiritual meaning to human existence.

We may now understand why none of this is explicated in Scripture and even the hint

— וְהַנִּמְצָא עָלָיו — is to be found in only *Chronicles*, not in *Kings*. Yehoyakim's wickedness was a private affair, eroding only his own soul — his generation, as the Sages teach (*Sanhedrin* 103a), was righteous. Such a private spiritual aridity does not fall within the interest of *Kings*. In *Chronicles* it is hinted because in the perspective of the Messianic destiny it is significant since it condemns Yehoyakim to total oblivion.

Because *Chronicles* is sensitive to this unique dimension of Yehoyakim's evil, it omits the phrase that his wickedness was in line with that of his father. No comparison to the evil of any other king would have been appropriate.

◆§ Yehoyakim — The Most Tragic of Israel's Kings

In the comm. we noted substantive differences between the *Kings* and *Chronicles* accounts of Yehoyakim's relationships with Nebuchadnezzar.

There are three other passages in Scripture which throw light upon the degree and dating of Nebuchadnezzar's involvement in Yehoyakim's reign and upon Yehoyakim's death.

One is in *Daniel* 1:1 where we read: *In the third year of Yehoyakim's reign, Nebuchadnezzar the king of Babylon came upon Jerusalem and besieged it. God placed Yehoyakim, king of Judah in his hands together with some of the vessels of the House of God ...*

The second is in *Jeremiah* 22:18 where we read: *Therefore, thus says* HASHEM *concerning Yehoyakim son of Yoshiahu, king of Judah. 'No elegies will be made over him: "Woe for our master, woe for his glory." Like a donkey will he be buried, dragged out and discarded beyond the gates of Jerusalem.'*

Finally, there is *Ezekiel* 19:9 where in a passage apparently referring to Yehoyakim we read: *Then they put him in a neck stock with hooks and brought him to the king of Babylon that they might bring him into fortresses ....*

There are varying opinions among the commentators as to how all these facts can be reconciled. [For details see ArtScroll, *Daniel*, fn. to 1:1, and ArtScroll *Ezekiel*, fn. to 17:4 and comm. to 19:9.] As *Radak* and *Ibn Ezra* see it, Yehoyakim was taken captive by Nebuchadnezzar in the early years of his reign (*Kings*, *Daniel* and *Ezekiel*), was then returned to Jerusalem, where, after an initial period during which he remained loyal to the Babylonians (*Kings*), he rebelled (*Kings*). In reaction to this insurgence Nebuchadnezzar came once more against Jerusalem and took Yehoyakim captive with the intention of taking him once more to Babylon (*Chronicles*). This plan was never realized because before he could reach that destination, he died on the way and was thrown by the roadside and not brought to burial (*Jeremiah*).

Given this accommodation of the various sources, we must now ask why the information was divided between *Kings* and *Chronicles* as it was. *Kings* deals only with the earlier parts of the reign. It is silent about the ending of the rebellion, tells nothing of Nebuchadnezzar's second coming, and, in fact, describes Yehoyakim's death in completely conventional terms: *Yehoyakim lay with his fathers and Yehoyachin, his son, reigned in his stead*. This statement in no way even hints at his ignominious end.

Chronicles, on the other hand, mentions only Nebuchadnezzar's second coming.

Again, even in *Chronicles* we are left with an unsatisfying account of Yehoyakim's end. Indeed, there is a hint that he died before he reached his intended destination, but the actual fulfillment of Jeremiah's prophecy is not explicated. On the contrary, the text seems to go out of its way to hide the details of his death. This we see from v. 8. There, after a description of Yehoyakim's various evil deeds we have the terse statement: *And Yehoyachin, his son reigned in his stead*. Yehoyakim's death is not mentioned. In this, the treatment of this king is unique. In every other case in *Chronicles*, the succession of the new king is given in conjunction with the death of the old. [Usually: *And . . . lay with his fathers and . . . reigned in his stead*.] Only here is a succession reported without any mention of what happened to the previous king. This unusual formulation unambiguously draws attention to the fact that the account of Yehoyakim's death — which had been prophetically ordained — is omitted.

Thus we may say that in *Kings*, Yehoyakim's death is camouflaged by the standard formula: *Yehoyakim lay with his fathers . . .*, and in *Chronicles*, an unusual circumstance is hinted at but not explicated.

There is another, apparently overt attempt, to conceal something of Yehoyakim's wickedness. The first *mishnah* in the tenth chapter of *Sanhedrin* lists three kings who, because of their wickedness, were denied a portion in the World to Come: Yarov'am, Ahab and Menasheh. The Talmud (103b) asks why Yehoyakim is not listed and gives no answer. The implication is clear that, in fact, he has no portion in the World to Come, but nevertheless is not listed. This, for no reason that the Talmud can fathom.

If then we can fathom no reason why Yehoyakim would be left out from the list, then the omission can be explained only in terms of an intentional concealment. Why would the Sages of the Mishnah wish to conceal Yehoyakim's wickedness?

It is possible to suggest that a special poignancy attaches to the tragedy of this king. And this, because of a unique position which he occupies in the Davidic dynasty and saga.

In *Jeremiah* 22:13 we find a castigating prophecy addressed to Yehoyakim (see *Rashi* and *Radak*, there). In vs. 15,16 we read: . . . *Your father, after all, ate and drank but did justice and charity — and thus it was good for him. He judged the poor and the destitute and it was good. This, after all, is knowledge of Me. The words of* HASHEM.

In his explanation, *Radak* writes that Yehoyakim was constantly fasting — thinking that such mortification of the flesh would atone for his many sins. The prophet is teaching him that this is not the way to God. Yehoyakim's father ate and drank as much as he wanted but had a successful reign because he was a just and righteous king. It is not necessary to fast but to be good.

But who is the *father* mentioned in this verse? The commentators assume it to be Yoshiahu. However, *Radak* quotes *Targum* that David is meant. Yehoyakim, because he was a descendant of David, thought that he could be like him.

The phrase to which *Targum* makes his point, opens the sentence which we quoted above: . . . הֲתִמְלֹךְ כִּי אַתָּה מְתַחֲרֶה בָאָרֶז אָבִיךָ הֲלֹא־אָכַל. The phrase is difficult to translate, largely because the *hispael* of חרה, *to burn* [מְתַחֲרֶה], is unclear. Again, what does הֲתִמְלֹךְ, *Will you reign*, imply?

The commentators deal with this phrase in varying ways:

Rashi: *Do you really think that you will reign for many days because you strive eagerly* [מְתַחֲרֶה, apparently taken in the sense *to become heated*, because of extreme effort — but this is not *Rashi's* usual interpretation — see below.] *to impose your rule, strictly to underline the fact that you are king*? [*Rashi* does not make clear how he understands בָּאָרֶז — see below for the other commentators.]

Radak: *Do you believe that the pleasure that you take* [מְתַחֲרֶה has the meaning, מִתְעָרֵב] *from your cedar structures* [the previous verse describes the buildings covered with cedar wood which Yehoyakim built upon the backs of the people] *will keep you king for many years*?

[*Metzudos* and *Mahari Kra* have essentially the same explanation except that *Mahari Kra* renders מִתַּחֲרֶה as, מִתְנָאֶה [or, perhaps, מִתְגָּאֶה.]

Maharit: Do you think that you will reign as long as your father Yoshiahu, who could be compared to a cedar tree in his greatness?

To understand *Targum's* rendering we first examine the usual meaning of מְתַחֲרֶה in the *hispael*. *Rashi* to *Proverbs* 24:19 and *Megillah* 6b renders, לִהְיוֹת כְּמוֹתָם or אֲחִיזַת מַעֲשָׂיו, that is, *to emulate*. Thus, in this case, *to emulate the cedar*.

We saw that *Targum* suggests that *the cedar* is David. This would reflect aggadic tradition, such as that in *Pirkei d'R' Eliezer* 19: Just like the cedar in the Lebanon has multitudinous roots below in the ground, so that even if all the winds in the world came to blow they could not uproot it from its place, so too, the son of David [the Messianic scion of the Davidic line who embodies *David* within himself]. His merit and deeds before God are so many that even if all the wicked of the earth were to come against him, they could not move him from his place.

Thus, we find Yehoyakim wishing to emulate David in the sense of acquiring the same degree of permanence and firmness with which the latter was blessed. He too wanted a dynasty that would last forever.

In what sense are we to take this, and what, precisely, does it imply? We saw above that the commentators read the phrase as though the words, *forever* or *for a long time*, were written: Do you really wish that your reign will last for long?

But, in *Targum* this implied insertion finds no echo. In what sense does he understand הֲתִמְלֹךְ?

We may conjecture as follows:

In *Shemos Rabbah* 15:25 the Sages teach that just as the cycle of the moon is thirty days, so too, the kingship in Israel lasts thirty generation. Beginning from Abraham it reached its fullest, most glorious, point in the fifteenth generation — Solomon [Abraham, Isaac, Jacob, Judah, Peretz, Chetzron, Ram, Aminadav, Nachshon, Salmon, Boaz, Oved Yishai, David, Solomon] and then waned until it finally became extinguished when Tzidkiahu's eyes were finally blinded.

The commentators have much difficulty with this midrash in as much as Tzidkiahu was not the fifteenth but the nineteenth of the kings after Solomon. [Rechv'am, Aviah, Asa, Yehoshaphat, Yehoram, Achaziah, Yehoash, Amatziahu, Uziah, Yosam, Achaz, Chizkiahu, Menasheh, Amon, Yoshiahu, Yehoachaz, Yehoyakim, Yehoyachin, Tzidkiahu]. Many suggest that, in fact, as implied in Chuldah's prophecy, the dynasty should have reached its end with Yoshiahu. He was indeed the fifteenth from Rechav'am. Because of his righteousness the end was deferred to the reign of his son Tzidkiahu, the sixteenth in line. Yehoachaz, Yehoyakim and Yehoyachin are not counted since Tzidkiahu himself was Yoshiahu's son and thus they were in no way involved in his succession.

Given these truths, we may guess at Yehoyakim's own perception of his kingship. We have seen above that Yehoachaz's kingship had no standing; Pharaoh had made Yehoyakim king, *in place of his father Yoshiahu*. That being so, he saw himself as direc follower of Yoshiahu in whose reign the thirty-generation kingship of the Davidic line had presumably ended. He perceived himself as a new *David* destined to restore the decadent line which had ended with his father. Perhaps, he even saw himself as the potential Messiah — the ultimate renewer of the Davidic line.

If, then, we assume *Radak's* interpretation that Yehoyakim was constantly fasting, hoping that by mortifying his flesh he could atone for all the evil which he was doing, then, a tragic figure indeed, rises before our eyes. A man, with a destiny as large as all eternity; a *David* who would re-establish the Davidic line after its decadence [יְהוֹ־יָקִים], who drowns in an abyss of absolute evil — desperately clinging to the hope that somehow, in some way, he would be able to redeem himself.

Perhaps, we have now solved the mystery of the secrecy, which both in Scripture and in Rabbinic tradition surrounds this tragic figure. Perhaps, a merciful veil of oblivion is to be drawn over this most tragic of Judah's kings.

◈§ The *Chronicles'* View of Yehoyachin's Reign

Chronicles' treatment of Yehoyachin's reign is perhaps more puzzling than that of any of the other kings. No mention at all is made of the event which, barring only the destruction of the Temple, is probably the most far reaching in the history of the Jewish people — the great exile of Israel's elite to Babylon.

We shall first quote the passage from *Kings*, briefly discuss its significance, and then address its omission from the *Chronicles'* account.

At that time the servants of Nebuchadnezzar, king of Babylon came up against Jerusalem, and the city was besieged. Nebuchadnezzar, king of Babylon came upon the city ... And he exiled all of Jerusalem, all the officers and all the warriors — ten thousand exiles and all the carpenters and locksmiths. Only the poor of the land remained. And he exiled Yehoyachin to Babylon ...

This was an exile of the upper echelons of the people. In the tradition of the Sages the *locksmiths* and *carpenters* are the Torah authorities, and it was they who laid the groundwork for the community in Babylon which was to be the backbone of Judaism for many centuries to come. Their presence in Babylon guaranteed that when, eleven years later, the bulk of the people would arrive, they would find an established Torah infrastructure ready to absorb and to support them (*Gittin* 88a). It was they among whom Torah was nurtured, the basis of the Mishnah [through Hillel the Babylonian] established, the Talmud ultimately evolved and thus, the eternity of Israel guaranteed.

How can we explain the fact that *Chronicles* omits any mention of this seminal event? [1]

The explanation may be as follows: There is a substantive difference between the way *Kings* and *Chronicles* describe Tzidkiahu's ascension to the throne: *Kings* has: *And the king of Babylon made Mataniah his [Yehoyachin's] uncle, king in his stead ...,* while *Chronicles* has: *... and he made Tzidkiahu, his [Yehoyakim's] brother, king. ...*

The fact that *Chronicles* refers back to Yehoyakim even though a description of Yehoyachin's reign intervenes, seems to indicate that the latter's reign is viewed as simply a continuation of the former's. It is as though the text read something like this: Yehoyakim's depredations are recorded in the Chronicles of the Kings of Israel and Judah; he was briefly succeeded by his son who was almost immediately taken captive to Babylon, at which point his brother became king. Thus, Yehoyachin's reign as an

---

1. There is clearly an intent to excise any mention of the exile.

Both *Kings* (2:25:11) and *Jeremiah* (39:9 and 52:15), when they speak of the final holocaust in Tzidkiahu's days, mention: *... the rest of the people who had remained in the city*. Reference is clearly to those who remained after the first wave of exiles had left with Yehoyachin. In the parallel verse, *Chronicles* (v. 20) has: *... He exiled those that were left from the sword*. Not, *those that were left in the city* (after the first exile), but, *those that were left from the sword* [that is, from the slaughter which took place in the wake of Nebuchadnezzar's attack in Tzidkiahu's own days]. Any hint of an earlier exile is thus effectively avoided.

independent unit is effectively ignored, and consequently even the vastly significant events of the exile are not told.

Why would *Chronicles* deny Yehoyachin's reign validity in its own right, and how does it view that reign within the context of the Yehoyakim saga?

The figure of Yehoyachin as projected in Scripture is one of deep mystery. We are told that, . . . *he did evil in the eyes of HASHEM according to all that his father had done* (*Kings* 24:9); or, . . . *he did evil in the eyes of HASHEM* (*Chronicles*, here). Surely this indicates that he was a wicked king — but not, apparently, worse than any of the other kings whose reigns had been described in the same terms. Indeed, we find precisely the same descriptions for Tzidkiahu, although in the tradition of the Sages, Tzidkiahu was a perfectly righteous man. We may say, then, that, as far as the description in *Kings* and *Chronicles* is concerned, Yehoyachin was wicked — but not in any special way. Neither book contains even a hint of the things that he did wrong.

Nevertheless, in *Jeremiah* (22:24 ff.) we find the most terrible imprecations uttered against this king, without any indication of why he would deserve a fate so much more terrible than that of any of the other wicked kings who preceded him:

By My life, the words of HASHEM, that even if Kaniahu [Yehoyachin], the son of Yehoyakim, king of Judah, were a signet ring upon My right hand — from there I would tear you off.

After the prophet goes on to describe how Yehoyachin would be carried into exile and would never return to the land for which he longed so much, he continues: *O land, land, land, listen to the words of HASHEM. Thus says HASHEM, 'Inscribe this man as childless, a man who will see no success in his life. For none of his seed shall sit upon David's throne nor ever rule over Judah.'*

It is clear that such curses would not have been warranted if there would not have been some particularly pernicious evil in this man. But, even in the tradition of the Sages, there is no record of any wrong that he did. When the Talmud (*Sanhedrin* 103a and b) goes into great length about various abominations committed by the other evil kings — even such for which there are no hints in the Scriptural texts and which must have been passed down by word of mouth — nothing at all is said about Yehoyachin. We have no record at all of his wickedness.

The explanation may lie in the fact of Yehoyachin's penitence — see comm. to *I Chronicles* 3:17.

We must differentiate between the Yehoyachin before repentance and the one after.

Great is *Teshuvah* for it brings man close to the *Shechinah* . . .. Yesterday this man was hated by God, disgusting, distanced and an abomination. Today he is loved, held dear, close and befriended. So too do we find that the same expressions which God uses to distance the sinners, He uses to bring the penitents . . . close . . . Concerning Yechaniah [Yehoyachin] in his wickedness it says, *Inscribe this man to be childless, a man who will see no success in his days. If Yechaniah . . . were a signet ring on My right hand. . ..* But, once he repented in his exile, it says concerning his son Zerubavel, *'On that day . . . I will take you Zerubavel, son of Shaltiel, and place you like a signet ring. . .*(*Rambam, Teshuvah* 7:6)

Teshuvah, then, is a rebirth, a new coming into being. The Yehoyachin who is to bear Zerubavel and through him become the progenitor to the Messianic king has no connection, as it were, to the old Yehoyachin, the subject of Jeremiah's imprecations. That one is part of the doomed dynasty of Yehoyakim, is only a footnote to that tragic reign. The events of his reign, the depth of evil to which he sank, are of no import —

they are excised forever from the Torah record. The Yehoyachin to be remembered is the hero of repentance, father of Zerubavel, progenitor of the Messiah.

◆§ The Exile of the Sacred Vessels

In the comm. we note that *Chronicles* makes an issue of the fact that the sacred Temple vessels were also exiled to Babylon.

The *Kings'* account makes no mention of this: The parallel verse (*II* 24:13) reads: *And he took out from there all the treasures of HASHEM's House, and the treasures of the king's palace, and broke down [וַיְקַצֵּץ] all the golden vessels which Solomon, king of Israel had made in HASHEM's House.* The vessels are smashed — but no mention is made that they were taken captive to Babylon.

A careful reading yields that in both the cases of Yehoyakim and of Tzidkiahu the same discrepancy between the two books exists. Our v.7, describing Yehoyakim's downfal, talks of Nebuchadnezzar bringing some of the holy vessels from HASHEM's Temple to Babylon and depositing them in his palace. This is not mentioned in the *Kings'* account.

In the case of Tzidkiahu the wording of the relevant passages is as follows: Our v. 18 reads: *And all the vessels of the House of God, great and small, . . . all he brought to Babylon*. The *Kings'* account (*II Kings* ch. 25) is as follows: V.13 describes how the great copper vessels were broken down and the copper was transported to Babylon. V.14 then tells that the Babylonians *took* the smaller copper vessels. No mention is made of what they did with them. It is not stressed that they brought them to Babylon. V.15 then says that pans and tossing basins, of both gold and silver, were taken by the *chief butcher*. But, once more, no mention is made of the fact that they were taken to Babylon.

Thus, we see that a theme that seems significant to *Chronicles* is entirely ignored in *Kings*.

There can be no doubt about the deep significance of the exile of the vessels. Jeremiah (*Jeremiah* 27:16 ff.) devotes an entire prophecy to the exiled vessels [and this, at a time when Yehoyakim's exile was already languishing in Babylon and we would have supposed that the people, rather than the sacred vessels, would be uppermost in the minds of those left in Jerusalem] which ends with the words: *To Babylon they shall be brought and there they shall remain until the day that I shall consider them, the words of HASHEM, and I shall bring them up and return them to this place*.

Thus, in the prophetic eyes of Jeremiah, the exiled vessels play an important role in the story of Judah's decline.

What is that significance, and why is any mention of it omitted from *Kings*?

An idea of the significance of the exiled vessels may be gleaned from *Ramban* to *Megillah* 11b. He notes an apparent discrepancy between *Ezra* 1:7 where we learn that the vessels were sent by Cyrus, to be brought back to Jerusalem, together with the first wave of returnees, and the tradition of the Sages that at Ahasuerus's banquet he made use of the sacred vessels. According to the *Ezra* source they were no longer in Babylon.

Ramban's solution:

As for the matter of the vessels used by Ahasuerus, this happened because in the first exile [Yehoyakim] Nebuchadnezzar took only some of the vessels . . . and it was these that Cyrus sent back with the first wave, because for them, seventy years had elapsed. But the rest of the vessels remained in the Temple till the destruction . . . and for them seventy years had not yet elapsed and so they remained in Babylon until the Temple was rebuilt. The fate of the vessels was identical with the fate of the Temple and the people. The first lot was returned seventy years after the first exile — and those that remained in the Temple till the destruction were returned only later when the rebuilding of the Temple began ...

But what could be the meaning of this? How are we to understand that the vessels, too, just like the people, went through two waves of exile — and were returned in two waves so that they too might have undergone precisely seventy years away from Jerusalem?

Sforno (to *Exodus* 30:1) defines the function of the sacred vessels as being to facilitate the coming to rest of the Divine Presence in the Temple. Thus, we may say, that it is through them and by their use, that Israel fulfills its destiny of being carriers of the Divine upon earth. When Israel is in exile and the *Shechinah,* as we are taught in countless places, has accompanied them there, then the vessels cannot remain in the land. They have no function to fulfill and, on the contrary, their presence in the land would constitute a cruel mockery of the exiled people.

Also more: If we perceive Israel's destiny as bringing the *Shechinah* to rest in the world and see the sacred vessels as the means by which they accomplish this — then we understand well why some of the sacred vessels would accompany each wave of exiles on their road. As the tie between people and land loosens, as each portion of the people leaves, a portion of sacred vessels leaves with them; their fate is intertwined. The nature and essence of the people is defined by the vessels and each step in the erosion of the people's presence in the land is paralleled by an erosion of the completeness of the vessels' presence in the land.

We may go even further: The location of the vessels effectively defines the nature of the people's presence in the land. *Kesubos* 110b had wanted to derive from *Jeremiah* 27:22, *To Babylon they shall be brought and there they shall remain until I shall consider them... and bring them up ...,* that it is forbidden, of one's own volition, to go up from Babylon to the Land of Israel. We are to remain there until God brings us back. The Talmud refutes this proof and maintains that it is permitted for people to return to the land. The verse that prohibits return refers to the vessels. It transpires, then, that though the people are allowed to return, the vessels are not. This can only mean, that as long as the vessels are in Babylon, the return of the people is insignificant in the larger context. Their return will not signal the resumption of their Divine destiny until the vessels, too, will return.

Thus we learn of the profound significance of the exile of the sacred vessels, in the long-range perspective of Jewish history. *Chronicles*, with its historical perspective centering upon the eternity of Israel, with its historical eye fixed upon essence rather than form, sees this exile of the vessels as crucial to the understanding of Israel's story. In the *Kings* account, no such significance is percieved.

◆§ *Chronicles'* View of Tzidkiahu's Reign

The story which *Chronicles* tells of Judah's last king, is very different from the one recorded in *Kings*. Where *Kings* gives a detailed account of the siege and fall of the city, the flight and capture of the king and the ultimate exile of the people together with the plundering of the Temple, *Chronicles* concentrates almost completely upon the causes of the tragedy and gives only cursory mention to the details of the destruction.

We must analyze the reasons for this difference in emphasis. To do so, we must examine Tzidkiahu's role in history. The tradition, which the Sages have preserved, seems at odds with that which Scripture writes about him.

In the tradition of the Sages, Tzidkiahu was a צַדִּיק גָּמוּר, an *entirely righteous person*, sufficiently good to have saved his entire generation from destruction. He is described as wicked, only in the sense that he failed to prevent the people from acting as wickedly as they did.

Why do the Sages insist upon viewing this king differently than the Scriptural record seems to present?

The problem is even greater when we consider *Ezekiel* 21:30 where — as *Rashi* interprets — Tzidkiahu is described as a *corpse of wickedness* [חָלָל רָשָׁע]. According to *Berachos* 18b, this verse yields that, *the wicked are considered dead even during their lifetime*. Would this be an apt description of Tzidkiahu if he was, indeed, totally righteous?

In ArtScroll, *Ezekiel*, there, and Overview VII and VIII, pp. xlv, xlix, and Appendix I, the point is made that Tzidkiahu was an individual of the highest moral and ethical caliber, who was nonetheless a tragic failure as king. Here, we should consider the matter further.

We begin our analysis by noting that our v.12 seems, to some degree, to mitigate Tzidkiahu's apparent wickedness: a) וַיַּעַשׂ הָרַע בְּעֵינֵי ה׳ אֱלֹהָיו b) לֹא נִכְנַע מִלִּפְנֵי יִרְמְיָהוּ הַנָּבִיא. The (b) section seems to delimit the statement in (a). The evil which Tzidkiahu did, was only that he did not humble himself before Jeremiah the prophet. This refers to Jeremiah's exhortation that Tzidkiahu subjugate himself to Nebuchadnezzar's rule and agree to convert Judah into a *lowly kingdom* — a vassal state in the Babylonian empire.

But, this understanding of our verse cannot stand on its own: How can we reconcile it with the statement in *Kings*, that Tzidkiahu's evil was of a kind with that of the totally wicked Yehoyakim?

We may surmise that the tradition of the Sages derives from a taking together of a number of passages in Scripture which do, indeed, seem to yield the picture preserved in the midrashic literature.

The religious standing of the state over which Tzidkiahu ruled was deplorable. Abetted by legions of false prophets who encouraged them [see ArtScroll, *Ezekiel*, Overview IX, p.lvi, *The False Prophets*], the people had sunk to the lowest forms of depravities. Some of these are graphically depicted in ch.8 of *Ezekiel* and discussed in the ArtScroll comm. there.

What was Tzidkiahu's role in this disintegration of the religious fiber of people who, only twenty-two years earlier, had undergone such a zealous *teshuvah* experience under Yoshiahu?

In *Ezekiel* 17:12-14 we read as follows: . . . *the king of Babylon came to Jerusalem and took its king and its princes and brought them to him to Babylon. Then he took from the seed of royalty (Tzidkiahu) and made a covenant with him and brought him into an oath and took away the mighty of the Land. That he shall be a* מַמְלָכָה שְׁפָלָה, *a lowly kingdom, that he might not be lifted up. That he should keep his covenant in order that it might endure*. [See ArtScroll, *Ezekiel*, Overview VII, p.xlv, *A Lowly Kingdom*.]

Jeremiah makes abundantly clear that Tzidkiahu himself could have been the ruler of this *lowly kingdom*:

So said HASHEM, *Lord of Hosts, God of Israel: If you go out to the ministers of the king of Babylon, you will save your own life, this city will not be consumed by fire, and you and your family will live . . .* (*Jeremiah* 38:17).

And again:

Thus, says HASHEM, *Go down to the house of the king of Judah [Tzidkiahu] and speak there these words. And you shall say: 'Hear the words of* HASHEM, *king of Judah who occupies the throne of David ... Thus says* HASHEM: *Practice justice and charity ... For if you do this thing, then kings occupying David's throne will enter these gates...'* (*Jeremiah* 22:1—4).

But, how could this be? With all the evil that was rampant in the country under Tzidkiahu's rule, how could God have wanted his kingship to continue?

This can be only if Tzidkiahu was entirely innocent of any involvement in the people's depravities, was himself a righteous person.

In truth, a careful reading of our *Chronicles'* passage will yield the same conclusion — when we compare it to the descriptions in *Chronicles* of other wicked kings.

V. 14 ascribes the evils which obtained at the time, to the *Kohanite officials and the people*, without indicating in any way that Tzidkiahu was involved. We contrast this to 21:11 where, concerning Yehoram, we read: *Moreover, he made high places in the mountains of Judah and made the dwellers of Jerusalem go astray and drew Judah away*. The blame of the people's backsliding is clearly placed on the king.

Again, in connection with Achaz we read: *And in every city in Judah he made high places to burn incense to other gods ....* (28:25). We assume that he himself did not worship in every city of Judah, but rather that he inaugurated idol worship for the people. Nevertheless it is *he* who made the high places.

So, too, with Menasheh. The description in ch.33 surely depicts an erosion of the religious standing of the entire people. Nevertheless, Menasheh himself is described as the perpetrator.

Thus, Scriptural evidence confirms that Tzidkiahu himself did not engage in any of the depravities, that if indeed he was *wicked*, it was only in the sense that he failed to use his royal powers to inhibit the excesses practiced by the people.

From this realization it is only a short step to the assumption that he was indeed a *Tzaddik* — of such a stature that he was able — as is recorded in the *Sanhedrin* passage paraphrased above — to save his entire generation from destruction. We have already seen in the quote from *Jeremiah*, above, that the prophet stresses that as king of Judah, he *occupies the throne of David* — he is a true scion of that illustrious line. Earlier, at 21:12 Jeremiah had made the point even more graphically. He called Tzidkiahu, בֵּית דָּוִד, *House of David*, apparently to underline that Tzidkiahu indeed incorporated within himself all the kingly qualities of David's house.

Thus, we have the basis for the tradition of the Sages. But what are we to make of the assessment in *Kings* that he did evil in accordance with the ways of Yehoyakim? And what of the verse in *Ezekiel* which describes him as a *corpse of wickedness*?

We must conclude that the differentiation between Tzidkiahu the man and Tzidkiahu, the king, which we made above, is an artificial one. The king is charged with the duty of exalting the true law [of HASHEM] and to fill the world with righteousness [לְהָרִים דַּת הָאֱמֶת וּלְמַלְאוֹת הָעוֹלָם צֶדֶק] (*Rambam*, *Melachim* 4:10). If he fails to do this, even though he is not actively evil, he is as wicked as one who actually practices evil. The king, upon whom the entire spiritual standing of his people rests, may never passively stand by. And thus, Tzidkiahu, by his quiet acquiescence, *does* the same amount of evil as Yehoyakim. His passivity guarantees the perpetration of the latter's depravities. And this, as the Sages interpret it, is the meaning of the verse in *Kings*.

A careful reading of the passage may, indeed, yield that the Scriptural text itself indicates that the comparison to Yehoyakim is not meant to be understood in precisely the same way as other such comparisons throughout the book of *Kings*.

Nowhere else in *Kings*, when a negative assessment is made, is the person who serves as an example identified by name only.

1. אֲבִיָּם: וַיֵּלֶךְ בְּכָל־חַטֹּאות אָבִיו — (1:15:3)
2. יְהוֹרָם: וַיֵּלֶךְ בְּדֶרֶךְ מַלְכֵי יִשְׂרָאֵל — (2:8:18)
3. אֲחַזְיָהוּ: וַיֵּלֶךְ בְּדֶרֶךְ בֵּית אַחְאָב — (2:8:27)
4. אָחָז: וַיֵּלֶךְ בְּדֶרֶךְ מַלְכֵי יִשְׂרָאֵל — (2:16:3)
5. מְנַשֶּׁה: וַיַּעַשׂ . . . כְּתוֹעֲבֹת הַגּוֹיִם — (2:21:2)
6. אָמוֹן: וַיַּעַשׂ . . . כַּאֲשֶׁר עָשָׂה מְנַשֶּׁה אָבִיו — (2:21:20)
7. יְהוֹאָחָז: וַיַּעַשׂ . . . כְּכֹל אֲשֶׁר־עָשׂוּ אֲבֹתָיו — (2:23:32)
8. יְהוֹיָקִים: וַיַּעַשׂ כְּכֹל אֲשֶׁר־עָשׂוּ אֲבֹתָיו — (2:23:37)
9. יְהוֹיָכִין: וַיַּעַשׂ . . . כְּכֹל אֲשֶׁר־עָשָׂה אָבִיו — (2:24:9)

As can be seen from the list, only once is a name mentioned at all — Amon [6] is compared to Menasheh — but, there too, *his father*, is added.

Never once, as in our case, is the comparison simply person to person.

We assume that the formula, *his father(s)*, is preferred to an identification by name, because the evil actions undertaken by the son are perceived as inherited traits. The meaning of the phrase seems to be that so and so was his father's son in that he continued in his ways.

If we now examine the text concerning Yehoachaz [7] and Yehoyakim [8], the two brothers of Tzidkiahu, we find them described as following the ways of their *fathers*. Commentators assume that reference is to Menasheh and Amon. The meaning seems clear: The text is telling us that Yehoachaz and Yehoyakim were not really *sons* of Yoshiahu, their biological father. They inherited their nature from their grand and great-grandfathers.

Now, in the case of Tzidkiahu we would have expected the same usage. As we have seen above, Jeremiah had prophesied that Yehoyakim was not to have any descendants who would follow him on the throne (36:30). Tzidkiahu, then, must be viewed as inheriting his throne from his father Yoshiahu rather than from his brother, Yehoyakim. Why then not say of Tzidkiahu what had been said of his two brothers — that he did evil as his *fathers* [Menasheh and Amon] had done?

Clearly, then, the phrase has a meaning, all of its own: Tzidkiahu, through his passivity *did* evil as much as Yehoyakim, through his activity, had done. Both, equally, brought ruin upon their people.

Tzidkiahu is, then, a *corpse of wickedness*. His unpardonable passivity makes this totally righteous man, totally wicked!

In what sense, then, was he righteous?

We may surmise that it is in the context of the *lowly kingdom*, envisioned by Ezekiel and described by Jeremiah, that Tzidkiahu's righteousness becomes relevant.

Tzidkiahu's impotence as king stemmed entirely from his unwillingness or inability to curb the national fervor of his corrupt aristocracy. The princes, who would prove to be his nemesis, would not tolerate the military and political realities, would not accept God's decree that the heyday of Judaen power was over. They refused to make peace with the idea that henceforth they could hope to continue their national existence only as a small vassal state within the huge Babylonian empire (*Jeremiah* 25:15 ff.).

To trace and fully understand the three-poled struggle, between king, prophet and aristocracy — a struggle which pulled and tore at the fabric of the nation during the eleven final and tragic years of independence — would require a careful study of much of the book of *Jeremiah*. Within the context of our analysis, it must suffice to consider the terrible pathos which infused the final confrontation between Jeremiah and the king, as the death throes had already begun, as darkness was about to fall.

Tzidkiahu had arranged a secret meeting with the prophet. In a final, impassioned, prophecy, Jeremiah apprises him of his options. It is still not too late: *Jeremiah said to Tzidkiahu: 'Thus says* H*ASHEM, God of Hosts, God of Israel: "If you will really go out to the officers of the Babylonian king, then you may remain alive, and this city will not be consumed by fire — you and your family will live."'*

The king wanted desperately to obey — but finds an excuse: How can he surrender? The Babylonian will hand him over to the Jews who had already defected to them, and these would then abuse him (v. 19).

Once more, the prophet reassures him. All will be well. Tzidkiahu will be safe with his captors. But, if he refuses to surrender, then the end will be terrible indeed.

Tzidkiahu's tragedy is encapsulated in his reaction to this prophecy. Instead of allowing himself to be galvanized into action at this eleventh hour, he has only one request to make: *Let no man know of this matter ... Should the aristocrats hear that I talked to you and come and ask you: 'Tell us now of what you talked to the king...'* (v. 24)

Nothing, as much as this final craven fear that the princes might hear of his conversation with Jeremiah, could point more dramatically to the terrible paralysis that had overtaken the king. The cosmic implication of the prophecy were entirely lost to him — he knew only the terror of discovery.

But all this derived only from the situation as it was. Had Tzidkiahu risen to the occasion, had he taken the final, admittedly difficult, step of surrender, then in one moment the internal pressures which he found so hard to withstand would have been dissipated. The princes would have become irrelevant and Tzidkiahu would have been freed to become the ideal leader and model for his people. With political independence a thing of the past, there would have been only the spiritual welfare of his subjects to concern him. As a צַדִּיק גָּמוּר he would have made an exemplary king.

Israel's tragedy, then, is that neither king nor people were willing to listen to Jeremiah. On that single, point, whether or not God's word would be the guide of their actions, the fate of the world hung. Jeremiah was ignored and the night of exile — still not ended — fell.

The divergent approaches of *Kings* and *Chronicles* to the story of Tzidkiahu can now be readily understood. Tzidkiahu, through his unwarranted and craven passivity, was indeed a חָלָל רָשָׁע, a *corpse of wickedness*. Such was the sad truth, and this is the perspective of *Kings* which records the overt story of the destruction. What might have been is of no concern to *Kings*, the tragic story of holocaust and exile holds center-stage.

Chronicles, which, throughout, has addressed essence rather than form, portrays the picture in terms of what might have been done to perpetuate the Davidic dynasty which is the focus of its concerns. Here the dreadful obduracy of king and people — their refusal to allow themselves to be guided by God's prophets — is of central importance. Here, there is no wickedness in the general meaning of the word — in the context of the מַמְלָכָה שְׁפָלָה, Tzidkiahu would have been a צַדִּיק גָּמוּר! The evil is only that he would not allow himself to be guided by Jeremiah, squandered the opportunity which had been granted him to be the progenitor of a new Davidic line which, although under drastically altered circumstance, could have averted the destruction and kept the state alive until Nebuchadnezzar's ascendance would have run its course.